INTERNAL SECURITY AND SUBVERSION: PRINCIPAL STATE LAWS AND CASES

A Da Capo Press Reprint Series

CIVIL LIBERTIES IN AMERICAN HISTORY

GENERAL EDITOR: LEONARD W. LEVY

Claremont Graduate School

U.S. Senate
Committee on the Judiciary
89th Congress
1st Session

INTERNAL SECURITY AND SUBVERSION: PRINCIPAL STATE LAWS AND CASES

Prepared by the American Law Division
Legislative Reference Service
Library of Congress

DA CAPO PRESS • NEW YORK • 1971

99210

A Da Capo Press Reprint Edition

This Da Capo Press edition of
Internal Security and Subversion
is an unabridged republication of
the edition published in
Washington, D.C., in 1965.

Library of Congress Catalog Card Number 75-152125

SBN 306-70121-9

Published by Da Capo Press, Inc.
A Subsidiary of Plenum Publishing Corporation
227 West 17th Street, New York, N.Y. 10011
All Rights Reserved

Manufactured in the United States of America

INTERNAL SECURITY
AND SUBVERSION:
PRINCIPAL STATE LAWS
AND CASES

INTERNAL SECURITY AND SUBVERSION
Principal State Laws and Cases

A STUDY

PREPARED FOR THE

SUBCOMMITTEE TO INVESTIGATE THE ADMINISTRATION OF THE INTERNAL SECURITY ACT AND OTHER INTERNAL SECURITY LAWS

OF THE

COMMITTEE ON THE JUDICIARY
UNITED STATES SENATE

BY

THE AMERICAN LAW DIVISION
LEGISLATIVE REFERENCE SERVICE
LIBRARY OF CONGRESS

Printed for the use of the Committee on the Judiciary

U.S. GOVERNMENT PRINTING OFFICE

41-738   WASHINGTON : 1965

RESOLUTION

Resolved by the Internal Security Subcommittee of the Senate Committee on the Judiciary, That the study, "Internal Security and Subversion—Principal State Laws and Cases," prepared by the American Law Division, Legislative Reference Service, Library of Congress, be printed and made public.

> JAMES O. EASTLAND, *Chairman.*
> THOMAS J. DODD, *Vice Chairman.*
> JOHN L. McCLELLAN.
> SAM J. ERVIN, Jr.
> BIRCH BAYH.
> GEORGE A. SMATHERS.
> ROMAN L. HRUSKA.
> EVERETT McKINLEY DIRKSEN.
> HUGH SCOTT.

Dated October 19, 1965.

INTRODUCTION

The Internal Security Subcommittee is proud to publish this study of "Internal Security and Subversion—Principal State Laws and Cases." This is the first time that a compilation of State laws and cases on this subject has been made, and I believe it will prove to be a reference work of great and lasting value.

The subcommittee appreciates the cooperation and diligence of the Legislative Reference Service of the Library of Congress, and we are especially grateful to Mr. Raymond J. Celada of the American Law Division, who supervised the compilation and prepared the document.

JAMES O. EASTLAND, *Chairman.*

LETTER OF TRANSMITTAL

LIBRARY OF CONGRESS,
LEGISLATIVE REFERENCE SERVICE,
May 28, 1965.

Hon. JAMES O. EASTLAND,
Chairman, Committee on the Judiciary,
U.S. Senate, Washington, D.C.

DEAR MR. CHAIRMAN: Pursuant to your request, we have completed and I am pleased to transmit herewith a study entitled "Internal Security and Subversion: Principal State Laws and Cases," prepared by Mr. Raymond J. Celada of the American Law Division, Legislative Reference Service.

The study reflects legislation in force in 1964 and judicial decisions reported through that year. As suggested, we have added a category relating to admission to the practice of law. Since the latter is largely regulated by boards of bar examiners having wide discretion in the determination of character and fitness, the study includes relevant information furnished us by the various State organizations of this kind.

The information contained in the study falls into eight general categories: Criminal advocacy, registration, outlawing subversive organizations, loyalty of public officers and employees and teachers, admission and exclusion from the bar, the denial of incidental benefits to subversive persons or subversive organizations, and finally a miscellaneous section. Some of these categories are subdivided into narrower and more specific headings. The section dealing with unlawful advocacy, for example, is divided into sedition, anarchy, criminal syndicalism, communism, etc. Likewise, the section dealing with loyalty of State officers and employees is arranged on the basis of the nature of the office or employment, i.e., elective or nonelective, and civil defense.

Certain statutory provisions of doubtful significance today have been omitted from the study. These include so-called red flag statutes, statutes dealing with incitement to violence during periods of hostilities, and sabotage.

Appendix A consists of 36 tables summarizing much of the material covered in the main body of the study.

Appendix B contains the texts of landmark Supreme Court decisions in the general area of security and subversion.

The study is designed as a convenient reference guide for the use of Members of Congress and others in this vital area of continuing national interest. We earnestly hope it will adequately serve this purpose.

Sincerely yours,

HUGH L. ELSBREE,
Director, Legislative Reference Service,
Library of Congress.

CONTENTS

(The references are to page numbers)

CONTENTS

APPENDIX A—TABLES

APPENDIX B—TEXT OF SELECTED SUPREME COURT DECISIONS ON STATE SECURITY MATTERS

TABLE OF CASES

PRINCIPAL STATE LAWS AND CASES DEALING WITH INTERNAL SECURITY AND SUBVERSION

ALABAMA

Unlawful Advocacy

1. ANARCHY

Code of Alabama, Title 14, § 19. *Criminal anarchy defined.*— Criminal anarchy is the doctrine that organized government should be overthrown by force or violence, or by assassination of the executive head or the executive officials of government, or by any unlawful means. The advocating of such doctrine either by word of mouth or writing is a felony.

Id. § 20. *Unlawful acts and penalty.*—Every person who:

By the word of mouth or writing shall advocate, advise, or teach the duty, necessity or propriety of overthrowing or overturning organized government by force or violence, or by assassination of the executive head or any of the executive officials of government, or by any unlawful means; or

Shall print, publish, edit, issue or knowingly circulate, sell, distribute or publicly display any book, paper, document, or written or printed matter in any form containing or advocating, advising or teaching the doctrine that organized government should be overthrown by force, violence or any unlawful means; or

Shall openly, willfully and deliberately justify by word of mouth or writing the assassination or unlawful killing or assaulting of any executive or other officer of the United States or of any State or of any civilized nation having an organized government because of his official character, or any other crime, with intent to teach, spread or advocate the propriety of the doctrines of criminal anarchy; or

Shall organize or help to organize or become a member of or voluntarily assemble with any society, group or assembly of persons formed to teach or advocate such doctrine,

Shall be punished by imprisonment in the State penitentiary for not more than ten years, or by a fine of not more than five thousand dollars, or by both.

Id. § 21. *Assemblage to advocate anarchy.*—Whenever two or more persons assemble for the purpose of advocating or teaching the doctrines of criminal anarchy, as defined in section 19 of this title, such an assembly is unlawful, and every person voluntarily participating therein by his presence, aid or instigation, shall be punished by imprisonment in the State penitentiary for not more than ten years, or by a fine of not more than five thousand dollars, or both.

1

Id. § 22. *Permitting premises to be used to advocate anarchy.*—
Every owner, agent, superintendent, janitor, caretaker, or occupant
of any place, building or room, who shall willfully and knowingly
permit therein any assemblage of persons prohibited by section 21 of
this title, or who, after notification that the premises are so used, shall
permit such use to be continued, shall be guilty of a misdemeanor.

2. SEDITION

Code of Alabama, Title 14, § 22(1). *Subversive conspiracy or advocacy.*—That any person conspiring, consorting, or colluding with, or
inducing, aiding, abetting, counseling, persuading or advising, by word
of mouth, writing, advertising, precept or otherwise, any person or persons, to subvert, overturn, destroy or change the form of Government,
either State or Federal, establish by law in this State and in the United
States, by force or violence, or other than by orderly process of law
and as a result of the free expression in lawful manner of the will of
the majority, shall upon conviction be deprived of his citizenship in
this State and in addition may be fined not more than one thousand
dollars or imprisoned in the penitentiary for not more than two years,
one or both, at the discretion of the court trying the case.

Id. § 22(2). *Subversive organizations outlawed.*—Any political,
social or other organization having as a doctrine, purpose or objective
the accomplishment or the aiding or abetting in the accomplishment
of, the acts forbidden in section 22(1) hereof is hereby declared an
illegal and outlaw organization, shall be denied all rights as a political
party, may be dissolved and enjoined from carrying on its said illegal
objective, and shall not be permitted to meet or function in the State
of Alabama; and any such organization so meeting or functioning,
and each person aiding, abetting or participating in such meeting or
functioning shall, upon conviction, be punished as provided for violation of section 22(1).

REGISTRATION

Code of Alabama, Title 14, § 97(1). *"Communist" defined.*—A
"Communist" is a person who:

(A) is a member of the Communist Party, notwithstanding the
fact that he may not pay dues to, or hold a card in, said party; or

(B) knowingly contributes funds or any character of property
to the Communist Party; or

(C) commits or advocates the commission of any act reasonably
calculated to further the overthrow of the Government of the United
States of America, the government of the State of Alabama, or the
government of any political subdivision of either of them, by force
or violence; or

(D) commits or advocates the commission of any act reasonably
calculated to further the overthrow of the Government of the United
States, the government of the State of Alabama, or the government
of any political subdivision of either of them, by unlawful or unconstitutional means, and the substitution of a Communist government
or a government intended to be substantially directed, dominated
or controlled by the Union of Soviet Socialist Republics or its
satellites.

Id. § 97 (2). *"Communist Party" defined.*—The "Communist Party" is any organization in the United States which (a) is substantially directed, dominated or controlled by the Union of Soviet Socialist Republics or its satellites, and which (b) in any manner advocates, or acts to further, the world Communist movement.

Id. § 97 (3). *"Communist front organization" defined.*—A "Communist front organization" is any organization, the members of which are not all Communists, but which is substantially directed, dominated or controlled by Communists or by the Communist Party.

Id. § 97 (4a) (Supp. 1963). *Communists and officers of Communist Party and Communist front organizations required to register.*—1. Each person remaining in this State for as long as one day who is a Communist, Nazi, or Muslim or is knowingly a member of a Communist front organization, shall register with the department of public safety on or before the fifth consecutive day that such person remains in this State, and at such intervals thereafter as may be directed by in the department of public safety.

2. Such registration shall be under oath and shall set forth the name (including any assumed name used or in use), address, business occupation, purposes of presence in the State of Alabama, sources of income, place of birth, places of former residence, and features of identification, including fingerprints, of the registrant; organizations of which registrant is a member; names of persons known by registrant to be Communists, Nazis, or Muslims or members of any Communist front organization as the case may be; and any other information requested by the department of public safety which is relevant to the purposes of this section.

3. Each and every officer of the Communist Party and each and every officer of Communist front organizations, knowing said organizations to be Communist front organizations, and each and every member of Nazi or Muslim organizations, knowing said organizations to be Nazi or Muslim organizations, shall register or cause to be registered said party or organizations with the department of public safety, if said party or organizations have any members who reside, permanently or for a period of more than thirty days, in the State of Alabama. Such registration shall be under oath and shall include the name of the organization, the location of its principal office and of its offices and meeting places in the State of Alabama; the names, real and assumed, of its officers; the names, real and assumed, of its members in the State of Alabama and of any person who has attended its meetings in the State of Alabama; a financial statement reflecting receipts and disbursements and by whom and to whom paid; and any other information requested by the department of public safety which is relevant to the purposes of this statute. Such registrations shall be made within thirty days after the effective date of this section, and thereafter at such intervals as are directed by the department of public safety.

4. Failure to register as herein required, or the making of any registration which contains any false statement or any omission, shall constitute a felony and shall be punishable by a fine of not less than $1,000 or more than $10,000, or by imprisonment in the penitentiary for not less than two or more than ten years, or by both.

5. The registration records shall be open to inspection by all law enforcement officers of the United States, of this State or of any other State or Territory of the United States. Such records may also, in the discretion of the department of public safety, be open for inspection by the general public.

Id. § 97(8). *Enforcement.*—The attorney general of the State of Alabama, all circuit, deputy and county solicitors, the department of public safety, and all law enforcement officers of this State shall each be charged with the duty of enforcing the provisions of this chapter.

Annotation:

Knox v. *State*, 3 Ala. App. 482, 87 So. 2d 671 (1956). Defendant was convicted under an indictment charging that he was a Communist, that he knowingly contributed funds or property to the Communist Party, and that he failed to register with the department of pubic safety after remaining in the State for five consecutive days. The incriminating evidence against the defendant—inadvertently found by the police who were searching the apartment building for a stolen radio—consisted of some books, pamphlets and tracts communistic in nature. Defendant had informed police that these materials had been left by a stranger. On appeal, the court reversed the conviction and held that the possession of communisitc literature did not tend to establish to the required degree that the defendant was a Communist and knowingly contributed funds or property to the Communist Party.

EXCLUSION FROM THE ELECTIVE PROCESS

Code of Alabama, Title 17, § 31. *Applicants for registration required to take oath.*—The board of registrars shall have power to examine, under oath or affirmation, all applicants for registration, and to take testimony touching the qualifications of such applicants. In order to aid the registrars to judicially determine if applicants to register have the qualifications to register to vote, each applicant shall be furnished by the board a written questionnaire, which shall be uniform in all cases with no discrimination as between applicants, the form and contents of which questionnaire shall be prescribed by the Supreme Court of Alabama and be filed by such court with the secretary of state of the State of Alabama. The questionnaire shall be so worded that the answers thereto will place before the registrars information necessary or proper to aid them to pass upon the qualifications of each applicant. The questionnaire shall be answered in writing by the applicant, in the presence of the board without assistance. There shall be incorporated in such answer an oath to support and defend the Constitution of the United States and the constitution of the State of Alabama and a statement in such oath by the applicant disavowing belief in or affiliation at any time with any group or party which advocated the overthrow of the Government of the United States or the State of Alabama by unlawful means. The answers and oaths shall be duly signed and sworn to by the applicant before a member of the board. Such questionnaire and the written answers of the applicant thereto shall be filed with the records of the board of registrars. If solely because of physical handicaps the applicant is unable to read or write, then he shall be exempt from the above stated requirements which he is unable to meet because of such physical handicap, and in such cases a member of the board shall read to the applicant the questionnaire and oaths herein provided for and the applicant's answers thereto shall be written down by such board member; and the applicant shall be registered as a voter if he meets all other requirements herein set out. Each member of the board is authorized to administer the oaths to be taken by the applicant and witnesses.

Annotation:

Rep. Atty. Gen., Oct.–Dec., 1939, p. 197. A witness who testifies in behalf of an applicant for registration is required to take the prescribed oath.

Code of Alabama, Title 17, § 345. *Persons to be candidates must be qualified to hold office.*—The name of no candidate shall be printed upon any official ballot used at any primary election unless such person is legally qualified to hold the office for which he is a candidate, and unless he is eligible to vote in the primary election in which he seeks to be a candidate and possesses the political qualifications prescribed by the governing body of his political party.

Code of Alabama, Title 14, § 97(6). *Communists barred from ballot.*—The name of any Communist or of any nominee of the Communist Party shall not be printed upon any ballot used in any primary or general election in this State or in any political subdivision thereof.

Code of Alabama, Title 14, § 22(2). *Subversive organizations outlawed.*—Any political, social or other organization having as a doctrine, purpose or objective the accomplishment, or the aiding or abetting in the accomplishment of, the acts forbidden in section 22(1) hereof is hereby declared an illegal and outlaw organization, shall be denied all rights as a political party, may be dissolved and enjoined from carrying on its said illegal objective, and shall not be permitted to meet or function in the State of Alabama; and any such organization so meeting or functioning, and each person aiding, abetting or participating in such meeting or functioning shall, upon conviction, be punished as provided for violation of section 22(1).

NOTE: For § 22(1), see Sedition under Unlawful Advocacy, *supra.*

LOYALTY OF STATE OFFICERS AND EMPLOYEES

1. ELECTIVE AND NONELECTIVE PERSONNEL

Alabama Constitution, Art. XV, § 279. *Oath.*—All members of the legislature, and all officers, executive and judicial, before they enter upon the execution of the duties of their respective offices, shall take the following oath or affirmation:

"I, _____, solemnly swear (or affirm, as the case may be) that I will support the Constitution of the United States, and the constitution of the State of Alabama, so long as I continue a citizen thereof; and that I will faithfully and honestly discharge the duties of the office upon which I am about to enter, to the best of my ability. So help me God."

2. NONELECTIVE PERSONNEL

Code of Alabama, Title 14, § 97(1). *"Communist" defined.*—A "Communist" is a person who:

(A) is a member of the Communist Party, notwithstanding the fact that he may not pay dues to, or hold a card in, said party; and

(B) knowingly contributes funds or any character of property to the Communist Party; or

(C) commits or advocates the commission of any act reasonably calculated to further the overthrow of the Government of the United States of America, the government of the State of Alabama, or the government of any political subdivisions of either of them, by force or violence; or

(D) Commits or advocates the commission of any act reasonably calculated to further the overthrow of the Government of the United States, the government of the State of Alabama, or the government of any political subdivision of either of them, by unlawful or unconstitutional means, and the substitution of a Communist government or a government intended to be substantially directed, dominated or controlled by the Union of Soviet Socialist Republics or its satellites.

Id. § 97(2). *"Communist Party" defined.*—The "Communist Party" is any organization in the United States which (a) is substantially directed, dominated or controlled by the Union of Soviet Socialist Republics or its satellites, and which (b) in any manner advocates, or acts to further, the world Communist movement.

Id. § 97(3). *"Communist front organization" defined.*—A "Communist front organization" is any organization, the members of which are not all Communists, but which is substantially directed, dominated or controlled by Communists or by the Communist Party.

Id. § 97(7). *Communists and members of Communist front organizations ineligible for public employment.*—No person may hold any nonelective position, job or office for the State of Alabama, or any political subdivision thereof, where the remuneration of said position, job or office is paid in whole or in part by public moneys or funds of the State of Alabama, or of any political subdivision thereof, where reasonable grounds exist, on all of the evidence, for the employer or other superior of such person to believe that such person is a Communist or a knowing member of a Communist front organization.

3. CIVIL DEFENSE PERSONNEL

Code of Alabama, Title 37A, § 19(85). *Loyalty oath required.*—No person shall be employed or associated in any capacity in any civil defense organization established under this chapter who advocates a change by force or violence in the constitutional form of the Government of the United States or in this State or the overthrow of any Government of the United States by force or violence, or who has been convicted of, or is under indictment or information, charging any subversive act against the United States. Each person who is appointed to serve in an organization for civil defense shall, before entering upon his duties, take an oath, in writing, before a person authorized to administer oaths, or the State civil defense director or his duly authorized representative, which oath shall be substantially as follows:

"I, _____, do solemnly swear (or affirm) that I will support and defend the Constitution of the United States and the constitution of the State of Alabama, against all enemies, foreign and domestic; that I will bear true faith and allegiance to the same; that I take this obligation freely, without any mental reservation or purpose of evasion; and that I will well and faithfully discharge the duties upon which I am about to enter.

"And I do further swear (or affirm) that I do not advocate, nor am I a member of any political party or organization that advocates, the overthrow of the Government of the United States or of this State by force or violence; and that during such time as I am a member of the (name of civil defense organization) I will not advocate nor become a member of any political party or organization that advocates the overthrow of the Government of the United States or of this State by force or violence."

TEACHERS' LOYALTY

Code of Alabama, Title 14, § 97(7). *Communists and members of Communist front organizations ineligible for employment.*—No person may hold any nonelective position, job or office of the State of Alabama, or any political subdivision thereof, where the remuneration of said position, job or office is paid in whole or in part by public moneys or funds of the State of Alabama, or of any political subdivision thereof, where reasonable grounds exist, on all of the evidence, for the employer or other superior of such person to believe that such person is a Communist or a knowing member of a Communist front organization.

EXCLUSION FROM THE BAR

Rules of the Alabama State Bar provide that every person who intends to apply for the State Bar Examination shall first register as a law student with the Board of Commissioners. Question 9 on the application for registration inquires as to the registrant's loyalty. It asks:

(9) (a) Do you believe in the form of, and are you loyal to, the Government of the United States?

(b) Are you a member of the Communist Party or affiliated with such party, or have you ever been?

(c) Do you believe in, are you a member of, or do you support, any organization that believes in or teaches the overthrow of the United States Government by force or by illegal or unconstitutional methods? Or have you ever believed in, belonged to or supported any such organization?

Question 15 on the Application for the Bar Examination also inquires as to the applicant's loyalty to the Government of the United States, as to his present or past membership or affiliation with the Communist Party, and his belief in membership of or support of any organization that believes in or teaches the overthrow of the United States Government by force or by illegal or unconstitutional methods. The text of question 15 follows:

(15) (a) Do you believe in the form of, and are you loyal to, the Government of the United States?

(b) Are you a member of the Communist Party or affiliated with such party, or have you ever been?

(c) Do you believe in, are you a member of, or do you support, any organization that believes in or teaches the overthrow of the United States Government by force or by illegal or unconstitutional methods? Or have you ever believed in, belonged to or supported any such organization?

Correspondence received from the Board of Commissioners of the Alabama State Bar states that the forms containing the above questions "have been in use for many years" but, thus far, they had "never had an application for registration or for the bar examination indicating that the applicant was, ever had been a member of or affiliated with the Communist Party or any other organization inquired about." Notwithstanding this lack of precedent, every indication points to the fact that in the event of "opposite answers" the "applicant would be denied" admission.

Exclusion From Incidental Benefits

TEXTBOOKS

Code of Alabama, Title 52, § 433(6a). *Textbooks to include statement relative to Communist beliefs of author and author of any book cited therein.*—Neither the State Textbook Committee nor the State Board of Education or any other public body or official shall consider for adoption or approval, or adopt or approve for use in the public schools or trade schools or institutions of higher learning of this State any textbook or other written instructional material (not including periodical newspapers and magazines nor legal opinions by courts of record) which does not contain a statement by the publisher or author thereof indicating clearly and with particularity that the author of the book or other writing and the author of any book or writings citing therein as parallel or additional reading is or is not a known advocate of communism or Marxist socialism, is or is not a member or ex-member of the Communist Party, and is or is not a member or ex-member of a Communist-front organization (as designated by the United States Congress, or any committee thereof, or the Attorney General of the United States).

Id. §433(6b). *Enforcement.*—The use of any book or other writing which is prohibited by section 433(6a) may be enjoined upon the application of any resident taxpayer.

MISCELLANEOUS

Code of Alabama, Title 52, § 545(1) (Supp. 1963). *Course on communism.*—The legislature of the State of Alabama hereby finds it to be a fact that (a) the political ideology commonly known and referred to as communism is in conflict with and contrary to the principles of constitutional Government of the United States of America as epitomized in its national Constitution, (b) the successful exploitation and manipulation of youth and student groups throughout the world today are a major challenge which free world forces must meet and defeat, and (c) the best method of meeting this challenge is to have the youth of the State and Nation thoroughly and completely informed as to the evils, dangers and fallacies of communism by giving them a thorough understanding of the entire Communist movement, including its history, doctrines, objectives and techniques.

In all public high schools of this State adequate instruction shall be given each year in the history, doctrines, objectives and techniques of communism and shall be for the primary purpose of instilling in the minds of the students a greater appreciation of democratic processes, freedom under law, and the will to preserve that freedom.

The direction of study shall be one of orientation in contrasting the Government of the United States of America with the Soviet Government and shall emphasize the free-enterprise-competitive economy of the United States of America as the one which produces higher wages, higher standards of living, greater personal freedom and liberty than any other system of economics on earth. It shall lay particular emphasis upon the dangers of communism, the ways to fight communism, the evils of communism, the fallacies of communism, and the false doctrines of communism.

The State Textbook Committee and the State Board of Education shall take such action as may be necessary and appropriate to prescribe suitable textbook and instructional material as provided by State law, using as one of its guides the official reports of the House Committee on Un-American Activities and the Senate Internal Security Subcommittee of the United States Congress.

No teacher or textual material assigned to this instruction shall present communism as preferable to the system of constitutional government and free-enterprise-competitive economy indigenous to the United States of America.

The course of study hereinabove provided for shall be taught in all of the public high schools of the State no later than the school year commencing in September 1964, or as soon thereafter as the city or county superintendent of education deems it feasible.

ALASKA

Unlawful Advocacy

CRIMINAL SYNDICALISM

Alaska Stat. § 11.50.010. *Criminal syndicalism defined.*—Criminal syndicalism is the doctrine which advocates crime, sabotage, violence, or other unlawful methods of terrorism as a means of accomplishing industrial or political reform or which advocates the overthrow, by force or violence, of the government of this State. The advocacy of this doctrine, whether by word of mouth or writing, is a felony punishable as provided in § 20 of this chapter.

Id. § 11.50.020. *Unlawful acts and penalty.*—A person is guilty of a felony and is punishable by imprisonment in the penitentiary for not more than 10 years, or by a fine of not more than $5,000, or by both, who

(1) by word of mouth or writing, advocates or teaches the duty, necessity or propriety of crime, sabotage, violence or other unlawful methods of terrorism as a means of accomplishing industrial or political reform;

(2) prints, publishes, edits, issues or knowingly circulates, sells, distributes, or publicly displays a book, paper, document or other written matter containing or advocating, advising or teaching the doctrine that industrial or political reform should be brought about by crime, sabotage, violence or other unlawful methods of terrorism;

(3) openly, willfully and deliberately justifies, by word of mouth or writing, the commission or the attempt to commit crime, sabotage, violence or other unlawful methods of terrorism with intent to exemplify; spread or advocate the propriety of the doctrine of criminal syndicalism; or

(4) knowingly and willfully organizes or helps to organize, or becomes a member of or voluntarily assembles with a society, group or assemblage of persons formed to teach or advocate the doctrine of criminal syndicalism.

Id. § 11.50.030. *Assemblage to advocate criminal syndicalism.*—An assemblage of two or more persons for the purpose of advocating or teaching the doctrine of criminal syndicalism as defined in §§ 10 and 20 of this chapter is unlawful and a person willfully, knowingly and voluntarily participating in the assemblage by his presence, aid or instigation is guilty of a felony, and is punishable by imprisonment in the penitentiary for not more than 10 years, or by a fine of not more than $5,000, or by both.

Id. § 11.50.040. *Permitting premises to be used to advocate criminal syndicalism.*—The owner, agent, superintendent, janitor, caretaker or occupant of a place, building or room, who willfully and knowingly permits an assemblage in it of persons prohibited by § 30 of this

11

chapter, or who, after notification by a peace officer that the premises are so used, permits the use to be continued, is guilty of a misdemeanor, and is punishable by imprisonment in jail for not more than one year, or by a fine of not more than $500, or by both.

LOYALTY OF STATE OFFICERS AND EMPLOYEES

1. ELECTIVE AND NONELECTIVE PERSONNEL

Alaska Constitution, Art. XII, § 4. *Persons advocating forceful overthrow of government or members of party advocating forceful overthrow of government not qualified for public office.*—No person who advocates, or who aids or belongs to any party or organization or association which advocates, the overthrow by force or violence of the Government of the United States or of the State shall be qualified to hold any public office of trust or profit under this constitution.

Id. § 5. *Oath of office.*—All public officers, before entering upon the duties of their offices, shall take and subscribe to the following oath or affirmation: "I do solemnly swear (or affirm) that I will support and defend the Constitution of the United States and the constitution of the State of Alaska, and that I will faithfully discharge my duties as _____ to the best of my ability." The legislature may prescribe further oaths or affirmations.

2. NONELECTIVE PERSONNEL

Alaska Stat. § 39.05.130. *Oath required.*—A public officer or employee of the State, before entering upon the duties of his office, shall take and sign the following oath or affirmation:

"I do solemnly swear (or affirm) that I will support and defend the Constitution of the United States and the constitution of the State of Alaska, and that I will faithfully discharge my duties as _____ to the best of my ability."

3. CIVIL DEFENSE PERSONNEL

Alaska, Stat. § 26.20.160. *Loyalty oath required.*—(a) No person shall be employed or associated in any capacity in a civil defense organization established under this chapter who advocates a change by force or violence in the constitutional form of the Government of the United States or in this State or the overthrow of any government in the United States by force or violence, or who has been convicted of or is under indictment or information charging a subversive act against the United States.

(b) Each person who is appointed to serve in an organization for civil defense shall, before entering upon his duties, take the following oath in writing, before a person authorized to administer oaths in this State:

"I _____, do solemnly swear that I will support and defend the Constitution of the United States and the constitution of the State of Alaska, against all enemies, foreign and domestic; that I will bear true faith and allegiance to the same; that I take this obligation freely, without any mental reservation or purpose of evasion; and that I will well and faithfully discharge the duties upon which I am about to enter.

"And I do further swear that I do not advocate, nor am I, nor have I ever been, a member of any political party or organization that advocates, the overthrow of the Government of the United States or of this State by force or violence; and that during such time as I am a member of any organizaion for civil defense within the State of Alaska, I will not advocate nor become a member of any political party or organization that advocates the overthrow of the Government of the United States or of this State by force or violence."

EXCLUSION FROM THE BAR

Correspondence received from the Alaska Bar Association discloses the absence of any statutory or case law and rules or regulations that deal specifically with admission to the Bar of applicants having been or being accused of communism or other forms of subversion. Rather, "the sum total of devices used to inquire into an applicant's background, loyalty and character, coupled with the fact that applicants to the Bar are being investigated by the National Conference of Bar Examiners would seem to amount to adequate safeguard within constitutional compasses against the admission of undesirable or unqualified elements, including herein those who may be inclined to disloyal and subversion in the communistic and any other subversive sense."

MISCELLANEOUS

Alaska Stat. § 24.45.020. *Lobbyists required to take non-Communist oath.*—(a) Every lobbyist registering under the provisions of § 10 of this chapter shall take the non-Communist oath required of State employees and a copy of this non-Communist oath shall be filed with the department of administration, with the name of the lobbyist's party affiliation, if any.

(b) It is unlawful for a member of a Communist, Fascist or subversive organization, as classified and listed by the Attorney General of the United States, to promote, advocate or oppose the passage or defeat by the legislature of a bill, resolution or legislative measure.

NOTE.—The following statement appears as a reviser's note to the foregoing section:

"State employees are no longer required to take a non-Communist oath. (See AS 39.05.130 for the oath State employees now take.) Therefore a question arises under subsection (a) as to what oath lobbyists take, if any."

ARIZONA

Unlawful Advocacy

SEDITION

Arizona Rev. Stat. § 13–707 (Supp. 1963). *Unlawful acts and penalty.*—A. A person who knowingly or willfully commits, or aids in the commission of any act to overthrow by force or violence the government of this State, or of any of its political subdivisions, is guilty of sedition against the State of Arizona.

B. A person who knowingly or willfully advocates the overthrow by force or violence of the government of this State, or of any of its political subdivisions, is guilty of sedition against the State of Arizona.

C. A person who knowingly or willfully becomes or remains a member of the Communist Party of the United States, or its successors, or any of its subordinate organizations, or any other organization having for one of its purposes the overthrow by force or violence of the government of the State of Arizona, or any of its political subdivisions, and said person had knowledge of said unlawful purpose of said Communist Party of the United States or of said subordinate or other organization, is guilty of sedition against the State.

D. Any person who violates any provisions of this article is guilty of a felony, and upon conviction thereof shall be punished by a fine of not more than twenty thousand dollars, or imprisonment in the State prison for not more than twenty years, or both.

Outlawing the Communist Party

Arizona Rev. Stat. § 16–205 (Supp. 1963). *Legislative findings and statement of policy.*—A. Upon evidence and proof which has been presented before this legislature, other State legislatures, the Congress of the United States and in the courts of the United States and in the courts of the several States; and although recognizing that the Federal Constitution vests the conduct of foreign relations in the Federal Government and the Federal Constitution guarantees to the several States a republican form of government and protection against foreign invasion and domestic violence, this State has the duty of self-preservation and the taking of necessary measures to cooperate with the Federal Government in the preservation of the peace and safety of the State of Arizona and in order to carry out Article 2, section 21, of the Arizona constitution relating to free and equal elections and Article 7, section 12, of the Arizona constitution relating to the enactment of laws to secure the purity of elections; and in order to guard against the abuse of the elective franchise by the Communist Party of the United States which from time to time has qualified as a purported legitimate political party in the State of Arizona; and in order to secure to the citizens of this State their inalienable personal rights and liberty of conscience secured by the provisions of the constitution of Arizona and in order to protect the peace and safety of the State of Arizona from the overthrow of its constitutional government by force or violence, and of its political subdivisions, the legislature of the State of Arizona finds and declares that, unlike other political parties which have evolved their policy and programs through public means, by the reconciliation of a wide variety of individual views, and submit those policies and programs to the electorate at large for approval or disapproval, the policies and programs of the Communist Party are prescribed for it by the foreign leaders of the world Communist movement.

B. The Communist Party members have no part in determining its goals, and are not permitted to voice dissent to party objectives. Unlike members of political parties, members of the Communist Party are recruited for indoctrination with respect to its objectives and methods, and are organized, instructed, and disciplined to carry into action slavishly the assignments given them by their hierarchical chieftains. Unlike legitimate political parties, the Communist Party acknowledges no constitutional or statutory limitations upon its conduct or upon that of its members. The Communist Party is relatively small numerically, and gives scant indication of capacity ever to attain its ends by lawful political means. The peril inherent in its operation arises not from its numbers, but from its failure to acknowledge any limitation as to the nature of its activities, and its dedication to the proposition that the present constitutional Government of the United States, the governments of the several States, and the government of the State of Arizona and its political subdivisions ultimately must be brought to ruin by any available means, including resort to force and violence.

C. The establishment of a totalitarian dictatorship in any country results in the suppression of all opposition to the party in power, the subordination of the rights of individuals to the State, the denial of fundamental rights and liberties which are characteristic of a representative form of government, such as freedom of speech, of the press, of assembly, and of religious worship, and said totalitarian dictatorship ruthlessly suppresses academic freedom and inquiry into any human knowledge except the official doctrines of the dictatorship. This results in the maintenance of control over the people through fear, terrorism, and brutality.

D. It is the public policy of this State to protect the safety of the constitutional government of the State of Arizona by constitutional means and at the same time protect the rights of the members of our free society to speak, to assemble, and to inquire, including the principle of academic freedom which by fostering healthy self-criticism is especially vital in the progress of man's moral values and in man's exploration of the secrets of the atom on this planet and in outer space. To protect the safety of this State and the right of free citizens in a free society to inquire and to understand totalitarianism, it is essential that the schools, colleges, and universities teach objectively and critically the governmental and social forms of past and present totalitarian slave states, including the foreign languages spoken therein.

The rights set forth in this subsection do not include the right to embrace communism or to attempt to persuade others to embrace communism.

E. The direction and control of the world Communist movement is vested in and exercised by the Communist dictatorship of a foreign country.

F. The Communist dictatorship of such foreign country, in exercising such direction and control and in furthering the purposes of the world Communist movement, establishes or causes the establishment of, and utilizes, in various countries, action organizations which are not free and independent organizations, but are sections of a worldwide Communist organization and are controlled, directed, and subject to the discipline of the Communist dictatorship of such foreign country.

G. The Communist action organizations so established and utilized in various countries, acting under such control, direction, and discipline, endeavor to carry out the objectives of the world Communist movement by bringing about the overthrow of existing governments by any available means, including force or violence if necessary, and setting up Communist totalitarian dictatorships which will be subservient to the most powerful existing Communist totalitarian dictatorship. Although such organizations usually designate themselves as political parties, they are in fact constituent elements of the worldwide Communist movement and promote the objectives of such movement by conspiratorial and coercive tactics, instead of through the democratic processes of a free elective system or through the freedom-preserving means employed by a legitimate political party which operates as an agency by which people govern themselves.

H. In the United States and in this State those individuals who knowingly and willfully participate in the world Communist movement, when they so participate, in effect repudiate their allegiance to the United States and this State, and in effect transfer their allegiance to the foreign country in which is vested the direction and control of the world Communist movement.

I. The Communist movement in the several States is an organization numbering thousands of adherents, rigidly and ruthlessly disciplined. Awaiting and seeking to advance at a moment when the several States may be so far extended by foreign engagements, so far divided in counsel, or so far in industrial or financial straits, that overthrow of the Government of the United States and of the several States by force or violence may seem possible of achievement, it seeks converts far and wide by an extensive system of schooling and indoctrination. Such preparations by Communist organization in other countries, including the recent events in the neighboring country of Cuba, have aided in supplanting existing governments. The Communist organization in the United States and in the several States, pursuing its stated objectives, the recent successes of Communist methods in other countries, and the nature and control of the world Communist movement itself, present a clear and present danger to the security of the Government of the United States, the governments of the several States, and the government of the State of Arizona, including its political subdivisions, that make it necessary that the State of Arizona enact appropriate legislation, recognizing the existence of such worldwide Communist conspiracy, and designed to prevent it from accomplishing its purposes in this State and its political subdivisions. Therefore, the Communist Party should not be permitted to avail itself of the privileges, rights, and immunities conferred by law upon legitimate political parties.

Id. § 16–206 (Supp. 1963). *Communist Party of the United States not entitled to any privileges, rights, or immunities attendant upon any legal bodies.*—The Communist Party of the United States, or any successors of such party regardless of the assumed name, the object of which is to overthrow by force or violence of the Government of the United States, or the government of the State of Arizona, or its political subdivisions shall not be entitled to be recognized or certified as a political party under the laws of the State of Arizona and shall not be entitled to any of the privileges, rights, or immunities attendant upon legal political bodies recognized under the laws of the State of Arizona, or any political subdivision thereof; whatever rights, privileges, or immunities shall have heretofore been granted to said Communist Party of the United States as defined in this section, or to any of its subsidiary organizations, by reason of the laws of the State of Arizona, or of any political subdivision thereof, are hereby terminated and shall be void.

NOTE.—Membership in the Communist Party with knowledge of its subversive purpose is deemed to be sedition. Arizona Rev. Stat. 13–707 (Supp. 1963). See Unlawful Advocacy, Sedition, *supra.*

EXCLUSION FROM THE ELECTIVE PROCESS

Arizona Rev. Stat. § 16–206 (Supp. 1963). *Communist Party of the United States is not entitled to recognition or certification as a political party.*—The Communist Party of the United States, or any successors of such party regardless of the assumed name, the object of which is to overthrow by force or violence the Government of the United States, or the government of the State of Arizona, or its political subdivisions shall not be entitled to be recognized or certified as a political party under the laws of the State of Arizona and shall not be entitled to any of the privileges, rights, or immunities attendant upon legal political bodies recognized under the laws of the State of Arizona, or any political subdivision thereof; whatever rights, privileges, or immunities shall have heretofore been granted to said Communist Party of the United States as defined in this section, or to any of its subsidiary organizations, by reason of the laws of the State of Arizona, or of any political subdivision thereof, are hereby terminated and shall be void.

LOYALTY OF STATE OFFICERS AND EMPLOYEES

I. ELECTIVE AND NONELECTIVE PERSONNEL

Arizona Rev. Stat. § 13–707 (Supp. 1963). *Seditious acts and penalty.*—A. A person who knowingly or willfully commits, or aids in the commission of any act to overthrow by force or violence the government of this State, or of any of its political subdivisions, is guilty of sedition against the State of Arizona.

B. A person who knowingly or willfully advocates the overthrow by force or violence of the government of this State, or of any of its political subdivisions, is guilty of sedition against the State of Arizona.

C. A person who knowingly or willfully becomes or remains a member of the Communist Party of the United States, or its successors, or any of its subordinate organizations, or any other organization having for one of its purposes the overthrow by force or violence of the government of the State of Arizona, or any of its political subdivisions, and said person had knowledge of said unlawful purpose of said Communist Party of the United States or of said subordinate or other organization, is guilty of sedition against the State.

D. Any person who violates any provisions of this article is guilty of a felony, and upon conviction thereof shall be punished by a fine of not more than twenty thousand dollars, or imprisonment in the State prison for not more than 20 years, or both.

Id. § 13–707.01 (Supp. 1963). *Persons convicted of sedition barred from State office or employment.*—Any person who is convicted of violating any provision of this article shall automatically be disqualified and barred from holding any office, elective or appointive, or any position of trust, profit, or employment with this State, or any political subdivision of this State, or any county, city, town, municipal corporation, school district, public educational institution, or any board, commission, or agency of any of the foregoing.

Arizona Rev. Stat. § 38–231 (Supp. 1963). *Officers and employees required to take loyalty oath.* A. In order to insure the statewide application of this section on a uniform basis, each board, commission, agency, and independent office of the State, and of any of its political subdivisions, and of any county, city, town, municipal corporation, school district, and public educational institution, shall immediately upon the effective date of this act completely reproduce § 38–231 as set forth herein, to the end that the form of written oath or affirmation required herein shall contain all of the provisions of said section for use by all officers and employees of all boards, commissions, agencies, and independent offices.

B. For the purposes of this section, the term officer or employee means any person elected, appointed, or employed, either on a part-time or full-time basis, by the State, or any of its political subdivisions or any county, city, town, municipal corporation, school district, public educational institution, or any board, commission or agency of any of the foregoing.

C. Any officer or employee elected, appointed, or employed prior to the effective date of this act shall not later than ninety days after the effective date of this act take and subscribe the form of oath or affirmation set forth in this section.

D. Any officer or employee within the meaning of this section who fails to take and subscribe the oath or affirmation provided by this section within the time limits prescribed by this section shall not be entitled to any compensation unless and until such officer or employee does so take and subscribe to the form of oath or affirmation set forth in this section.

E. Any officer or employee as defined in this section having taken the form of oath or affirmation prescribed by this section, and knowingly or willfully at the time of subscribing the oath or affirmation, or at any time thereafter during his term of office or employment, does commit or aid in the commission of any act to overthrow by force or violence the government of this State or of any of its political subdivisions, or advocates the overthrow by force or violence of the government of this State or of any of its political subdivisions, or during such term of office or employment knowingly or willfully becomes or remains a member of the Communist Party of the United States or its successors or any of its subordinate organizations or any other organization having for one of its purposes the overthrow by force or violence of the government of the State of Arizona or any of its political subdivisions, and said officer or employee as defined in this section prior to becoming or remaining a member of such organization or organizations had knowledge of said unlawful purpose of said organization or organizations, shall be guilty of a felony and upon conviction thereof shall be subject to all the penalties for perjury; in addition, upon conviction under this section, the officer or employee shall be deemed discharged from said office or employment and shall not be entitled to any additional compensation or any other emoluments or benefits which may have been incident or appurtenant to said office or employment.

F. Any of the persons referred to in Article XVIII, section 10 of the Arizona constitution as amended, related to the employment of aliens, shall be exempted from any compliance with the provisions of this section.

G. In addition to any other form of oath or affirmation specifically provided by law for an officer or employee, before any officer or employee enters upon the duties of his office or employment, he shall take and subscribe the following oath or affirmation:

State of Arizona, County of _____ I, _____
(type or print name)

do solemnly swear (or affirm) that I will support the Constitution of the United States and the constitution and laws of the State of Arizona; that I will bear true faith and allegiance to the same, and defend them against all enemies, foreign and domestic, and that I will faithfully and impartially discharge the duties of the office of _____ (name of office) _____ according to the best of my ability, so help me God (or so I do affirm).

(signature of officer or employee)

Id. § 38–233 (Supp. 1963). *Filing and recording of loyalty oaths.*— A. The official oaths of State elective officers shall be filed of record in the office of the Secretary of State. The official oaths of all other State officers and employees shall be filed of record in the office of the employing State board, commission or agency.

B. The official oaths of notaries public and of elective county and elective precinct officers shall be filed of record in the office of the county recorder, except the oath of the recorder, which shall be filed with the clerk of the board of supervisors. The official oaths of all other county and precinct officers and employees shall be filed of record in the office of the employing county or precinct board, commission or agency.

C. The official oaths of all city, town or municipal corporation officers or employees shall be filed of record in the respective office of the employing board, commission or agency of the cities, towns and municipal corporations.

D. The official oaths of all officers and employees of all school districts shall be filed of record in the office of the superintendent of public instruction.

E. The official oaths of all officers and employees of each public educational institution except school districts shall be filed of record in the respective offices of said public educational institutions.

F. The official oath or affirmation required to be filed of record shall be maintained as a permanent official record.

2. CIVIL DEFENSE PERSONNEL

Arizona Rev. Stat. § 26–356. *Loyalty oath required.*—A. A person who advocates or has advocated a change by force or violence in the constitutional form of Government of the United States or of this State, or the overthrow by force and violence of any government in the United States, or who has been convicted of or is under indictment or information charged with any subversive act against the United States, shall not be employed or associated in any capacity in a civil defense organization established under this chapter.

B. Each person appointed to serve in a civil defense organization shall, before entering upon his duties, take an oath in writing before a person authorized to administer oaths in this State substantially as follows:

I, _____, do solemnly swear (or affirm) that I will support and defend the Constitution of the United States and the constitution of the State of Arizona against all enemies, foreign and domestic, that I will bear true faith and allegiance to the same; that I take this obligation freely without mental reservation or purpose of evasion; that I will well and faithfully discharge the duties upon which I am about to enter. I further do swear (or affirm) that I do not advocate, nor am I a member of any political party or organization that advocates the overthrow of the Government of the United States or of this State, or of any government in the United States, by force or violence, and that during such time as I am a member of the (name of civil defense organization), I will not advocate nor become a member of any political party or organization that advocates the overthrow of the Government of the United States or of this State, or of any government in the United States, by force or violence.

TEACHERS' LOYALTY

Arizona Rev. Stat. § 15–231. *Public school teachers and administrative officers required to take loyalty oath.*—Every teacher and administrative officer in public schools shall, upon receiving a certificate to teach and before delivery of the certificate, or at the time of signing a contract of employment as a teacher or administrative officer in public schools for a period of service at a particular school, take and subscribe to the oath prescribed for public officers pursuant to § 38–231, before the State superintendent of public instruction, county superintendent of schools, justice of the peace, notary public, or any other person qualified to administer oaths in accordance with §§ 33–501 through 33–516. The person taking the oath shall file a copy of the acknowledged oath in the office of the State superintendent of public instruction.

Arizona Rev. Stat. § 38–231 (supp. 1963). *Form of oath.*—A. In order to insure the statewide application of this section on a uniform basis, each board, commission, agency, and independent office of the

State, and of any of its political subdivisions, and of any county, city, town, municipal corporation, school district, and public educational institution, shall immediately upon the effective date of this act completely reproduce § 38–231 as set forth herein, to the end that the form of written oath or affirmation required herein shall contain all of the provisions of said section for use by all officers and employees of all boards, commission, agencies and independent offices.

B. For the purposes of this section, the term officer or employee means any person elected, appointed, or employed, either on a part-time or full-time basis, by the State, or any of its political subdivisions or any county, city, town, municipal corporation, school district, public educational institution, or any board, commission or agency of any of the foregoing.

C. Any officer or employee elected, appointed, or employed prior to the effective date of this act shall not later than ninety days after the effective date of this act take and subscribe the form of oath or affirmation set forth in this section.

D. Any officer or employee within the meaning of this section who fails to take and subscribe the oath or affirmation provided by this section within the time limits prescribed by this section shall not be entitled to any compensation unless and until such officer or employee does so take and subscribe to the form of oath or affirmation set forth in this section.

E. Any officer or employee as defined in this section having taken the form of oath or affirmation prescribed by this section, and knowingly or willfully at the time of subscribing the oath or affirmation, or at any time thereafter during his term of office or employment, does commit or aid in the commission of any act to overthrow by force or violence the government of this State or of any of its political subdivisions, or advocates the overthrow by force or violence of the government of this State or of any of its political subdivisions, or during such term of office or employment knowingly and willfully becomes or remains a member of the Communist Party of the United States or its successors or any of its subordinate organizations or any other organization having for one of its purposes the overthrow by force or violence of the government of the State of Arizona or any of its political subdivisions, and said officer or employee as defined in this section prior to becoming or remaining a member of such organization or organizations had knowledge of said unlawful purpose of said organization or organizations, shall be guilty of a felony and upon conviction thereof shall be subject to all the penalties for perjury; in addition, upon conviction under this section, the officer or employee shall be deemed discharged from said office or employment and shall not be entitled to any additional compensation or any other emoluments or benefits which may have been incident or appurtenant to said office or employment.

F. Any of the persons referred to in Article XVIII, section 10 of the Arizona constitution as amended, related to the employment of aliens, shall be exempted from any compliance with the provisions of this section.

G. In addition to any other form of oath or affirmation specifically provided by law for an officer or employee, before any officer or employee enters upon the duties of his office or employment, he shall take and subscribe the following oath or affirmation:

State of Arizona, County of _____ I, _____ do sol-
(type or print name)
emnly swear (or affirm) that I will support the Constitution of the United States and the constitution and laws of the State of Arizona; that I will bear true faith and allegiance to the same, and defend them against all enemies, foreign and domestic, and that I will faithfully and impartially discharge the duties of the office of _____ (name of office) _____ according to the best of my ability, so help me God (or so I do affirm).

_____
(signature of officer or employee)

Id. § 38–233 (Supp. 1963). *Filing and recording of loyalty oath.*—A. The official oaths of State elective officers shall be filed of record in the office of the secretary of state. The official oaths of all other State officers and employees shall be filed of record in the office of the employing State board, commission or agency.

B. The official oaths of notaries public and of elective county and elective precinct officers shall be filed of record in the office of the county recorder, except the oath of the recorder, which shall be filed with the clerk of the board of supervisors. The official oaths of all other county and precinct officers and employees shall be filed of record in the office of the employing county or precinct board, commission or agency.

C. The official oaths of all city, town or municipal corporation officers or employees shall be filed of record in the respective office of the employing board, commission or agency of the cities, towns and municipal corporations.

D. The official oaths of all officers and employees of all school districts shall be filed of record in the office of the superintendent of public instruction.

E. The official oaths of all officers and employees of each public educational institution except school districts shall be filed of record in the respective offices of said public educational institutions.

F. The official oath or affirmation required to be filed of record shall be maintained as a permanent official record.

_____

Annotation:

Elfbrandt v. *Russell*, 94 Arizona 1, 381 P. 2d 554 (1963). Appellant, schoolteacher, and others similarly situated, requested a declaration that the Arizona Officers and Employees Loyalty Oath deprived her of her rights under the State and Federal Constitutions. The Court acknowledged that the loyalty oath requirement diminished the individual's freedom of association and hence the unfettered communication of ideas, but held that the statute satisfied constitutional restraints since the conduct sacrificed to governmental interests only minimally and incidentally conflicted with the First Amendment and that the gravity of the evil sought to be reached, discounted by its improbability, justified the invasion. In the course of its opinion the Court stated: (1) that since the Arizona Declaration of Rights, Art. 2, § 7, Constitution of Arizona, permitted public officers and employees to either swear or affirm in a manner most consistent with and binding upon the conscience of the person, the compulsive subscription did not impinge on religious or conscientious scruples; (2) that qualifications for public officers and employees may be fixed by the legislature where not otherwise prescribed by the Constitution; (3) that the power to prescribe qualifications of public officers and employees was essential to the independence of the States and to their peace and tranquillity and should be free from external interference unless conflicting with the Constitution of the United States; (4) that for good and sufficient reasons, positions of public importance may be denied to groups of persons identified by their particular interests; (5) that the legislature in order to preserve the integrity of the public service and safeguard it from disloyalty may enact statutes designed to reasonably attain those ends; (6) that loyalty may be a prescribed qualification for the holding of public employment; (7) that an oath was an expression of devotion to the government, an express engagement of that which every citizen owes to his government; (8) that when confronted with the problem of the State's interest in security, sanctions may be supplied to coerce and deter its enemies from seeking or holding public office and employment; (9) that the State may demand an oath of a person seeking public office that he is not engaged in the commission of any act to overthrow by force or violence the government of the State or any of its political subdivisions; (10) that the oath requirement did not suffer from indiscriminate classification of innocence with the knowing activity as was found in *Wieman* v. *Updegraff*, 344 U.S. 183, 73 S. Ct. 215, 97 L. Ed. 216 (1952); (11) that the oath requirement did not suffer from vagueness and indefiniteness in placing an accused on trial for an offense, the nature of which he is given no warning, for punishment was restricted to specified acts knowingly and willfully committed; (12) that the oath requirement did not violate any right protected by the Fifth and Sixth Amendments to the Constitution of the United States for neither are there penalties imposed for past activities nor was appellant required to divulge her past activities or associations; (13) that the Act was not a Bill of Attainder imposing punishment without conviction in the course of judicial proceedings; (14) that the oath requirement did not deny substantive due process since it clearly warned of the consequences of refusal; (15) that the legislature was not unaware of the decisions of the Supreme Court of the United States and therefore used the word "advocate" as meaning concrete action for the forceful overthrow of the government rather than principles divorced from action; (16) that the language of § 38–231, subd. E had no relationship to beliefs; prohibited any membership in any organization having for *one* of its purposes the overthrow by force and violence of the government of the State of Arizona or any of its political subdivisions including passive and nominal memberships; (17) that the critical act forbidden was the knowing or willful joining or remaining a member of an organization with knowledge of the illegal purposes; the membership contemplated by the statute must be determined not by conduct from which an inference may be drawn but by objective acts of joining and acceptance as members; (18) that while § 38–233 required that the oath be filed of record, it did not contemplate that the filing be rejected by the public officer in charge of the board or agency with which the filing is required, and, hence, there was no denial of procedural due process.

EXCLUSION FROM THE BAR

Correspondence received from the Committee on Examinations and Admissions, State Bar of Arizona, states that "there are no * * * regulations or official opinions which specifically relate to Communists or subversives applying for admission" to the Bar other than question 27 contained in the application. That question reads as follows:

27. Are you now or have you ever been a member of the Communist Party or any organization that advocates the overthrow of the United States Government by force or violence?

Although "there has never been any case in which either a Communist or a subversive has applied for admission to the State Bar, at least where the file reflected such affiliation," there seems to be little doubt that, "if such did appear, the Committee would refuse to recommend such an applicant for admission to practice."

ARKANSAS

Unlawful Advocacy

1. ANARCHY

Arkansas Stat. § 41–4107. *Unlawful acts and penalty.*—It shall be unlawful for any person or persons, to write, indict, dictate, speak, utter, publish or declare or be interested in writing, indicting, dictating, speaking, uttering, publishing or declaring any word, sentence, speech or article of whatsoever nature or kind, with the intent to encourage, advise, aid, assist or abet in the infliction of any personal injury upon any person or the taking of human life, or destruction or injury to either public or private property, without due process of law, or in any manner to disseminate knowledge or propaganda which tends to destroy or overthrow the present form of government of either the State of Arkansas, or the United States of America, by any violence or unlawful means whatsoever, or whoever shall employ any such means aforesaid, which are calculated to cause such results aforesaid, shall be guilty of a misdemeanor, and, upon conviction, shall be punished by a fine of not less than ten dollars [$10], nor more than one thousand dollars [$1,000], and may be imprisoned in the county jail not exceeding six [6] months, or both, at the discretion of the court.

2. SUBVERSIVE ACTIVITIES

Arkansas Stat. § 41–4111. *Subversive activities defined.*—(a) It shall be unlawful for any person, (1) to knowingly or willfully advocate, abet, advise, or teach the duty, necessity, desirability, or propriety of overthrowing or destroying any government in the United States by force or violence, or by the assassination of any officer of any such government; (2) with the intent to cause the overthrow or destruction of any government in the United States, to print, publish, edit, issue, circulate, sell, distribute, or publicly display any written or printed matter advocating, advising, or teaching the duty, necessity, desirability, or propriety of overthrowing or destroying any government in the United States by force or violence; (3) to organize or help to organize any society, group, or assembly of persons who teach, advocate, or encourage the overthrow or destruction of any government in the United States by force or violence; or to be or become a member of, or affiliate with, any such society, group, or assembly of persons, knowing the purposes thereof. (b) For the purposes of this section, the term "government in the United States" means the Government of the United States, or the government of this State.

Id. § 41–4112. *Attempts and conspiracies prohibited.*—It shall be unlawful for any person to attempt to commit, or to conspire to commit, any of the acts prohibited by the provisions of this act [§§ 41–4111—41–4113].

Id. § 41–4113. *Penalty.*—(a) Any person who violates any of the provisions of this act shall be deemed guilty of a felony and, upon conviction thereof, be fined not more than ten thousand dollars [$10,000.00] or imprisoned for not more than ten [10] years, or both such fine and imprisonment. (b) No person convicted of violating any of the provisions of this act [§§ 41–4111—41–4113] shall, during the five years next following his conviction, be eligible for employment by the State of Arkansas, or by any department or agency thereof. (c) No person who is a member of a Nazi, Fascist or Communist society, or any organization affiliated with such societies, shall be eligible for employment by the State of Arkansas, or by any department, agency, institution, or municipality thereof.

REGISTRATION

Arkansas Stat. § 41–4125 (Supp. 1963). *Members of the Communist Party and related organizations required to register.*—From and after the passage of this Act [§§ 41–4125—41–4127], any member of one of the following organizations is required to register with the Director of the Arkansas State Police:

(1) The Communist Party of the United States.

(2) The Communist Political Association.

(3) The Communist Party of any State of the United States, of any foreign state, or of any political or geographical subdivision of any foreign state.

(4) Any section, subsidiary, branch, affiliate, or subdivision of any such association or party.

(5) The direct predecessor or successors of any association or party, regardless of what name such group or organization may have used, may now bear, or may hereafter adopt.

(6) Any organization which advocates or teaches the overthrow by force or violence or other unconstitutional means of the Government of the United States or the State of Arkansas.

(7) An individual who is not a member of one of the above organizations, but who writes, publishes, or causes to be written or published or who circulates, orally or otherwise any information advocating, or teaching the overthrow by force or violence or other unconstitutional means of the Government of the United States or the State of Arkansas.

Id. § 41–4126 (Supp. 1963). *Registration file open to public.*—The director of State police will maintain such registration in a file which shall be open to the public at all times.

Id. § 41–4127 (Supp. 1963). *Penalty.*—Any person falling within the classes enumerated in this Act [§§ 41–4125—41–4127] who shall fail to so register within [90] days after the effective date of this Act shall be punished, upon conviction, by a fine of not less than $50.00 nor more than $1,000.00, or by not less than six [6] months nor more than two [2] years in the State penitentiary or both.

OUTLAWING THE COMMUNIST PARTY

Arkansas Stat. § 41–4128 (Supp. 1963). *"Communist Party" defined.*—For the purposes of this Act [§§ 41–4128—41–4131], "Communist Party" shall mean:

(a) The Communist Party of the United States.

(b) The Communist Political Association.

(c) The Communist Party of any State of the United States, of any foreign state, or any political or geographical subdivision of any foreign state.

(d) Any section, subsidiary, branch, affiliate, or subdivision of any such association or party.

(e) Any organization which advocates or teaches the overthrowal by force or violence or other unconstitutional means of the Government of the United States or the State of Arkansas.

Id. § 41–4129 (Supp. 1963). *Legislative findings regarding the Communist Party.*—The General Assembly of the State of Arkansas hereby finds and determines that the Communist Party advocates, teaches and encourages the overthrowal of the Government of the United States and of the State of Arkansas by force and violence, the same being contrary to the Constitution of the United States and of the State of Arkansas, and, that the existence of the Communist Party, and membership in such party, is an immediate and constant threat to the peace, safety and security of the State of Arkansas and of the people thereof.

Id. § 41–4130 (Supp. 1963). *Communist Party barred from operating in the State.*—It shall be unlawful for the Communist Party to operate in the State of Arkansas, and it shall be unlawful for any person in the State of Arkansas to knowingly be a member of or belong to, the Communist Party. Membership in the Communist Party shall be prima facie evidence that a person advocates, teaches and encourages the forceful and violent overthrowal of the government of the State of Arkansas.

Id. § 41–4131 (Supp. 1963). *Penalty.*—Any person violating the provisions of this Act [§§ 41–4128—41–4131] shall, upon conviction thereof, be imprisoned for a period of not less than one [1] year nor more than twenty-one [21] years, or shall be fined in an amount of not less than one thousand dollars ($1,000.00) nor more than five thousand dollars ($5,000.00), or be both so fined and imprisoned.

EXCLUSION FROM THE ELECTIVE PROCESS

Arkansas Stat. § 3–1604. *Communist Party and related organizations barred from ballot.*—No political party (2) [a] which is directly or indirectly affiliated by any means whatsoever with the Communist Party of the United States, the Communist international, or any other foreign agency, political party, organization or government; or (b) which either directly or indirectly advocates, teaches, justifies, aids or abets the overthrow by force or violence, or by any unlawful means, of the Government of the United States or this State; or (c) which directly or indirectly carries on, advocates, teaches, justifies, aids, or abets a program of sabotage, force and violence, sedition or treason against the Government of the United States or this State, shall be recognized, or qualified to participate, or permitted to have the names of its candidates printed on the ballot, in any election in this State.

No newly organized political party shall be recognized or qualified to participate or permitted to have the names of its candidates printed on the ballot in any election in this State until it has filed an affidavit, by the officers of the party in this State under oath that (a) it is not directly or indirectly affiliated by any means whatsoever with the Communist Party of the United States, the third Communist international, or any other foreign agency, political party, organization or government; or (b) that it does not either directly or indirectly advocate, teach, justify, aid or abet the overthrow by force or violence, or by any unlawful means of the Government of the United States or this State; or (c) it does not directly or indirectly carry on, advocate, teach, justify, aid or abet a program of sabotage, force and violence, sedition or treason against the Government of the United States or this State. The affidavit herein provided for shall be filed with the secretary of state and he shall make such investigation as he may deem necessary to determine the character and nature of the political doctrines of such proposed new party, and if he finds that such proposed new party advocates doctrines or has affiliations which are in violation of the provisions of this act [§§ 3-1604, 3-1605], he shall not permit such party to participate in the election.

Id. § 3-1605. *Penalty.*—Any person who shall violate any provision of this act, [§ 3-1604] shall be guity of a misdemeanor, and upon conviction shall be fined in any sum not less than $100.00 nor more that $1,000.00, and in addition thereto may be imprisoned for not more than six [6] months.

NOTE.—Communist Party barred from operating in State; see Outlawing the Communist Party, *supra.*

Annotation:

Field v. *Hall*, 201 Ark. 77, 143 S.W. 2d 567 (1940). Appellants, nominees of the Communist Party, filed a petition in mandamus against the secretary of state to compel him to accept their certificates of nomination and to print the same on the ballot. The Supreme Court of Arkansas affirming the judgment of the lower court, held that the statute barring from the ballot any political party which advocated overthrow of the government by force and violence imposed discretionary authority on the secretary of state to determine whether a political party which had certified nominations of candidates for office advocated subversion. In the course of its decision the court stated: (1) that discretionary authority conferred upon the secretary of state to determine whether a political party which has certified nominations of candidates for office to him advocated the overthrow of the government by force or violence was subject to control by the courts if exercised arbitrarily and without information to justify his act; (2) that since the statute did not provide for a trial the secretary's refusal to grant appellants a trial was not, as a matter of law, arbitrary or an abuse of discretion; (3) that there was substantial evidence in the record tending to show that the Communist Party in Arkansas which had adopted the constitution of the Communist Party of the United States of America, advocated the enforcement of its doctrines by overthrowing other established governments in order to do so; (4) that the State legislature had authority to establish conditions precedent to the existence and operation of political parties.

Loyalty of State Officers and Employees

1. ELECTIVE AND NONELECTIVE PERSONNEL

Arkansas Constitution, Art. XIX, § 20. *Oath.*—Senators and Representatives and all judicial and executive State and County officers, and all other officers, both civil and military, before entering on the duties of their respective offices, shall take and subscribe to the following oath or affirmation: "I, _____, do solemnly swear (or affirm) that I will support the Constitution of the United States, and the constitution of the State of Arkansas, and that I will faithfully discharge the duties of the office of _____, upon which I am now about to enter."

2. NONELECTIVE PERSONNEL

Arkansas Stat. § 3-1404. *Advocating overthrow of the government unlawful.*—It shall be unlawful for any person employed in any capacity in any department of the State of Arkansas to have membership in any political party or organization which advocates the overthrow of our constitutional form of government.

Id. § 3-1405. *Penalty.*—Any person violating any of the provisions of this act [§§ 3-1403—3-1405], or concerned in the violation thereof, shall, upon conviction, be deemed guilty of a misdemeanor and subject to be fined in any sum of not less than $50.00 nor more than $250.00 for each and every such offense, and shall be removed from office or employment upon the proclamation by the Governor and thereafter rendered ineligible to hold any office or employment in any of the departments of the State of Arkansas.

Arkansas Stat. § 41-4111. *Subversive activities defined.*—(a) It shall be unlawful for any person; (1) to knowingly or willfully advocate, abet, advise, or teach the duty, necessity, desirablity, or propriety of overthrowing or destroying any government in the United States by force or violence, or by the assassination of any officer of any such government; (2) with the intent to cause the overthrow or destruction of any government in the United States, to print, publish, edit, issue, circulate, sell, distribute, or publicly display any written or printed matter advocating, advising, or teaching the duty, necessity, desirability, or propriety of overthrowing or destroying any government in the United States by force or violence; (3) to organize or help to organize any society, group, or assembly of persons who teach, advocate, or encourage the overthrow or destruction of any government in the United States by force or violence; or to be or become a member of, or affiliate with, any such society, group, or assembly of persons, knowing the purposes thereof. (b) For the purposes of this section, the term "government in the United States" means the Government of the United States, or the government of this State.

Id. § 41-4113. *Persons convicted of subversive activities and members of Communist societies ineligible for public employment.*—(a) Any person who violates any of the provisions of this act shall be deemed guilty of a felony and, upon conviction thereof, be fined not more than ten thousand dollars [$10,000.00] or imprisoned for not more than ten [10] years, or both such fine and imprisonment. (b) No person convicted of violating any of the provisions of this act

[§§ 41–4111—41–4113] shall, during the five years next following his conviction, be eligible for employment by the State of Arkansas, or by any department or agency thereof. (c) No person who is a member of a Nazi, Fascist or Communist society, or any organization affiliated with such societies, shall be eligible for employment by the State of Arkansas, or by any department, agency, institution, or municipality thereof.

3. CIVIL DEFENSE PERSONNEL

Arkansas Stat. § 11–1931. *Loyalty oath required.*—(a) No person shall be employed or associated in any capacity in any civil defense organization established under this Act [§§ 11–1916—11–1933] who advocates or has advocated a change by force or violence in the constitutional form of the Government of the United States or in this State or the overthrow of any government in the United States by force or violence, or who has been convicted of or is under indictment or information charging any subversive act against the United States. Each person who is appointed to serve in an organization for civil defense shall, before entering upon his duties, take an oath, in writing, before a person authorized to administer oaths in this State, which oath shall be substantially as follows:

"I, _____, do solemnly swear (or affirm) that I will support and defend the Constitution of the United States and the constitution of the State of Arkansas, against all enemies, foreign and domestic; that I will bear true faith and allegiance to the same; that I take this obligation freely, without any mental reservation or purpose of evasion; and that I will well and faithfully discharge the duties upon which I am about to enter.

"And I do further swear (or affirm) that I do not advocate, nor am I a member of any political party or organization that advocates the overthrow of the Government of the United States or of this State by force or violence; and that during such time as I am a member of the _____, I will not advocate nor become a member of any political party or organization that advocates the overthrow of the Government of the United States or of this State by force or violence."

TEACHERS' LOYALTY

Arkansas Stat. § 3–1404. *Advocating overthrow of government unlawful.*—It shall be unlawful for any person employed in any capacity in any department of the State of Arkansas to have membership in any political party or organization which advocates the overthrow of our constitutional form of government.

Annotation:

Shelton v. *Tucker*, 364 U.S. 479, 81 S. Ct. 247, 5 L. Ed. 2d 231 (1960). In this case the Court held invalid an Arkansas statute requiring every teacher in the State's public schools to file an affidavit listing without limitation every organization to which he belonged or regularly contributed during the past five years. The Court held that the "unlimited and indiscriminate sweep of the statute" brought it under the prohibitions of the Fourteenth Amendment. It noted that teachers in Arkansas are hired from year to year and have no tenure. As a consequence, when petitioners refused to file the affidavit their contracts were not renewed. The Court pointed out that compelling a teacher to disclose his every associational tie impaired his freedom of association. Furthermore, since there was nothing in the statute making the information thus acquired confidential, it might be made available to the public, which would provide an opportunity to pressure teachers who belonged to unpopular or minority organizations. Conceding the State's right to know about certain associational ties of its teachers, it declared that "that purpose cannot be pursued by means that broadly stifle fundamental personal liberties when the end can be more narrowly achieved." The statutory requirement's "comprehensive interference with associational freedom goes beyond what might be justified in the exercise of the State's legitimate inquiry into the fitness and competency of its teachers."

EXCLUSION FROM THE BAR

Correspondence received from the State Board of Law Examiners, Little Rock, discloses the absence of any regulations pertaining to admission to the bar of persons who are or have been Communists and states "this problem has never come up."

CALIFORNIA

Unlawful Advocacy

CRIMINAL SYNDICALISM

West's Anno. Penal Code § 11400. *Criminal syndicalism defined.*—
"Criminal syndicalism" as used in this article means any doctrine or
precept advocating, teaching or aiding and abetting the commission of
crime, sabotage (which word is hereby defined as meaning willful and
malicious physical damage or injury to physical property), or unlawful acts of force and violence or unlawful methods of terrorism as a
means of accomplishing a change in industrial ownership or control,
or effecting any political change.

Id. § 11401. *Unlawful acts and penalty.*—Any person who:

1. By spoken or written words or personal conduct advocates,
teaches or aids and abets criminal syndicalism or the duty, necessity
or propriety of committing crime, sabotage, violence or any unlawful
method of terrorism as a means of accomplishing a change in industrial ownership or control, or effecting any political change; or

2. Willfully and deliberately by spoken or written words justifies
or attempts to justify criminal syndicalism or the commission or attempt to commit crime, sabotage, violence or unlawful methods of terrorism with intent to approve, advocate or further the doctrine of
criminal syndicalism; or

3. Prints, publishes, edits, issues or circulates or publicly displays
any book, paper, pamphlet, document, poster or written or printed
matter in any other form, containing or carrying written or printed
advocacy, teaching, or aid and abetment of, or advising, criminal syndicalism; or

4. Organizes or assists in organizing, or is or knowingly becomes a
member of, any organization, society, group or assemblage of persons
organized or assembled to advocate, teach or aid and abet criminal syndicalism; or

5. Willfully by personal act or conduct, practices or commits any
act advised, advocated, taught or aided and abetted by the doctrine or
precept of criminal syndicalism, with intent to accomplish a change in
industrial ownership or control, or effecting any political change;

Is guilty of a felony and punishable by imprisonment in the State
prison not less than one nor more than 14 years.

Annotations:

Whitney v. *California*, 274 U.S. 357, 47 S. Ct. 641, 71 L. Ed. 1095
(1927). Petitioner, a member and organizer of the Communist Labor
Party, was convicted of the crime of criminal syndicalism. The California Criminal Syndicalism Act defined criminal syndicalism as
"any doctrine or precept advocating, teaching, or aiding and abetting
the commission of crime, sabotage (which word is hereby defined as
meaning willful and malicious physical damage or injury to physical

property), or unlawful acts of force and violence or unlawful methods of terrorism as a means of accomplishing a change in industrial ownership or control, or effecting any political change," and declared guilty of a felony any person who "organizes or assists in organizing, or is or knowingly becomes a member of any organization, society, group or assemblage of persons organized or assembled to advocate, teach or aid and abet criminal syndicalism." The Supreme Court affirmed the conviction and held that the Syndicalism Act did not violate the due process and equal protection clauses of the 14th amendment. It declared: (1) that the Act was not repugnant to the due process clause by reason of vagueness and uncertainty of definition; (2) that the Act, plainly met the essential requirement of due process that a penal statute be "sufficiently explicit to inform those who are subject to it, what conduct on their part will render them liable to its penalties," and be couched in terms that are not "so vague that men of common intelligence must necessarily guess at its meaning and differ as to its application"; (3) that the Act was not repugnant to the equal protection clause as class legislation since it affected all alike; (4) that the Act as applied in this case was not repugnant to due process as a restraint on free speech, assembly and association.

People v. *Chambers*, 22 C.A. 2d 687, 72 P. 2d 746 (1937). Appellants were indicted for violation of the criminal syndicalism statutes. Specifically, they were charged with organizing, joining, and managing various associations with the purpose of advocating, teaching, aiding, and abetting criminal syndicalism as a means of accomplishing a change in the industrial ownership and control of property and to effect political changes and conspiracy to commit that offense. The court reversed the convictions and discharged appellants from custody on grounds that the verdict was inconsistent with another verdict rendered in this case by the same jury at the same time acquitting the appellants of the same charges under a second indictment. In the course of its opinion, the court held, *inter alia:* (1) that the California Syndicalism Act did not violate the Fourteenth Amendment to the United States Constitution; and (2) that it was no defense to a charge of criminal syndicalism against those who actually organize associations for that purpose, and who teach, advocate, aid, encourage, and abet the confiscation of property and the destruction of government by intimidation, force, and violence, that they failed to actually incite revolution.

Black v. *Cutler Laboratories*, 43 C. 2d 778, 278 P. 2d 905 (1955), certiorari granted 350 U.S. 816, 76 S. Ct. 51, 100 L. Ed. 730, certiorari dismissed 351 U.S. 292, 76 S. Ct. 824, 100 L. Ed. 1188, rehearing denied 352 U.S. 859, 77 S. Ct. 21, 1 L. Ed. 2d 69. Appellant, a pharmaceutical corporation, appealed from a judgment entered upon the granting of an order confirming the award of an arbitration board. By the award, it was held that appellant had discharged one of its employees in violation of a collective bargaining agreement, and that the employee was entitled to reinstatement and to back pay. On appeal appellant argued, among other things, that an arbitration award which directed that a member of the Communist Party who was dedicated to that party's program of "sabotage, force, violence and the like" be reinstated to employment in a plant which produced antibiotics used by both the military and civilians was against public policy, as expressed in both Federal and State laws, and was therefore illegal and void. The court sustained appellant's contention and reversed the judgment. In the course of its opinion, the court declared that membership in the Communist Party with full implication of dedication to sabotage, force, violence and the like, which party membership was believed to entail, constituted a violation of the California Criminal Syndicalism Act.

REGISTRATION

West's Anno. Corp. Code § 35000. *Short title.*—This title may be cited as the Subversive Organization Registration Law.

Id. § 35001. *Jurisdiction and declaration of purpose.*—This title is enacted in the exercise of the police power of this State for the protection of the public peace and safety by requiring the registration of subversive organizations which are conceived and exist for the purpose of undermining and eventually destroying the democratic form of government in this State and in the United States.

Id. § 35002. *Subversive organization defined.*—As used in this title, "subversive organization" means every corporation, association, society, camp, group, bund, political party, assembly, and every body or organization composed of two or more persons or members, which comes within either or both of the following descriptions:

(a) Which directly or indirectly advocates, advises, teaches, or practices, the duty, necessity, or propriety of controlling, conducting, seizing, or overthrowing the Government of the United States, of this State, or of any political subdivision thereof by force or violence.

(b) Which is subject to foreign control as defined in section 35003.

Id. § 35003. *"Subject to foreign control" defined.*—An organization is "subject to foreign control" if it comes within either of the following descriptions:

(a) It solicits or accepts financial contributions, loans, or support of any kind directly or indirectly from, or is affiliated directly or indirectly with, a foreign government or a political subdivision thereof, an agent, agency, or instrumentality of a foreign government or political subdivision thereof, a political party in a foreign country, or an international political organization.

(b) Its policies, or any of them, are determined by or at the suggestion of, or in collaboration with, a foreign government or political subdivision thereof, an agent, agency, or instrumentality of a foreign government or a political subdivision thereof, a political party in a foreign country, or an international political organization.

Id. § 35004. *Exclusions from scope of "subversive organization".*— "Subversive organization" does not include any labor union or religious, fraternal, or patriotic organization, society, or association whose objectives and aims do not contemplate the overthrow of the Government of the United States, of this State, or of any political subdivision thereof by force or violence.

Id. § 35005. *Effect and scope of law.*—This title imposes additional requirements upon corporations, associations, or organizations which are subversive organizations. Neither the fact that such a corporation, association, or organization was organized pursuant to law nor that its affairs and activities are in any respect regulated by law exempts it from complying with this title.

Id. § 35006. *Rules and regulations.*—The secretary of state may adopt and promulgate such rules and regulations as may be necessary to carry out the provisions of this title, and may alter, amend, or repeal such rules and regulations.

Id. § 35007. *Separability provision.*—If any provision of this title, or the application thereof to any person, corporation, association, organization, or circumstances, is for any reason held invalid, ineffective, or unconstitutional by a court of competent jurisdiction, the remainder of this title, or the application of such provision to other persons, corporations, associations, organizations, or circumstances, shall not be affected thereby, and the legislature hereby declares the severability of the several sections and provisions of this title, and that it would have enacted this title without the invalid provisions or the invalid applications, as the case may be, had such invalidity been apparent.

Id. § 35100. *Registration procedure and required information.*— Every subversive organization in existence on September 13, 1941, shall within 30 days after that date, and every subversive organization thereafter organized shall within 10 days after its organization, file with the secretary of state, on such forms and in such detail as he may prescribe, the following information and documents:

(a) A complete and detailed statement subscribed, under oath, by all of its officers, showing all of the following:

(1) Its name and post office address.

(2) The names and addresses of all its branches, chapters, and affiliates.

(3) The names, nationalities, and resident addresses of its officers and members, and the qualifications required for membership in it.

(4) The nature and extent of its existing and proposed aims, purposes, and activities.

(5) The times and places of its meetings.

(6) The description and location of the real property and the kind, quantity, and quality of the personal property owned by it, its assets and liabilities, the methods for the financing of its activities, and the names and addresses of all persons, organizations, and other sources who or which have contributed money, property, literature, or other things of value to the organization or any of its branches, chapters, or affiliates for any of its purposes.

(7) Such other information as the secretary of state may from time to time require.

(b) A true copy, certified by all of its officers, of all of the following:

(1) Its charter, articles of association, or constitution, and its bylaws, rules, and regulations.

(2) Its oath, affirmation, or pledge of membership, if any.

(3) Each agreement, resolution, and other instrument or document relating to its organization, powers, and purposes and the powers and duties of its officers and members.

(4) Each book, pamphlet, leaflet, or other printed, written, or illustrated matter directly or indirectly issued or distributed by it or in its behalf, or to or by its members with its knowledge, consent, or approval.

(5) Such other documents as the secretary of state may from time to time require.

(c) A description of the uniforms, badges, insignia, or other means of identification prescribed by it, and worn or carried by its officers or members, or any of such officers or members.

(d) In case it is subject to foreign control, a statement of the manner in which it is so subject.

Id. § 35101. *Changes in charter, etc., required to be reported.*— Every subversive organization shall within 10 days after any revision or amendment of, or other change with respect to, its charter, articles of association, constitution, bylaws, rules, regulations, oath, affirmation, or pledge of membership, or any part thereof, file with the secretary of state a true copy certified by all of its officers of the revised, amended, or changed charter, articles of association, constitution, bylaws, rules, regulations, oath, affirmation, or pledge of membership, or part thereof.

Id. § 35102. *Changes in officers, aims, purposes, etc., required to be reported.*—Every subversive organization shall within 10 days after a change has been made in its officers, or in its aims, purposes, activities, property holdings, or methods and sources of financing its activities, file with the secretary of state a statement subscribed under oath by all of its officers showing the change.

Id. § 35103. *Periodic membership reports required.*—Every subversive organization shall at least once in each period of six months file with the secretary of state a statement subscribed under oath by all of its officers showing the names and residence addresses of all persons who have been admitted to membership during that period or, if no members have been admitted during that period, a statement to that effect similarly subscribed.

Id. § 35104. *Report of political activities required.*—Every subversive organization shall within 10 days after the adoption thereof file with the secretary of state, on such form and in such detail as he may prescribe, each resolution adopted, or the minutes of any meeting held by it, authorizing or providing for concerted action by its officers, members, or a part of its membership, to promote or prevent the passage of any act of legislation by any local, State, or Federal legislative body, or to support or defeat any candidate for public office.

Id. § 35105. *Reports, etc., open to public.*—All statements or documents filed with the secretary of state under this title are public records and shall be open to public examination and inspection at all reasonable hours.

Id. § 35200. *Mail privileges restricted.*—A subversive organization shall not send, deliver, mail, or transmit, or suffer or permit to be sent, delivered, mailed, or transmitted, to any person in this State who is not a member of the organization any anonymous letter, document, leaflet, or other written or printed matter. All letters, documents, leaflets, or other written or printed matter issued by a subversive organization which are intended to come to the attention of a person who is not a member of the organization shall bear the name of the organization and the names and residences of its officers.

Id. § 35300. *Penalty for violation by organization.*—Any subversive organization which violates any provision of this title is guilty of a felony punishable by fine of not less than one thousand dollars ($1,000) nor more than ten thousand dollars ($10,000). Any such violation constitutes a separate and distinct offense for each day, or part thereof, during which it is continued.

Id. § 35301. *Penalty for violations by officers, etc.*—Any officer or member of the board of directors, board of trustees, executive committee, or other similar governing body of a subversive organization who violates any provision of this title, or permits or acquiesces in the violation of any provision of this title by the organization is guilty of a felony punishable by fine of not less than five hundred dollars ($500) nor more than five thousand dollars ($5,000), or by imprisonment in a State prison for not less than six months nor more than five years, or by both.

Id. § 35302. *Penalty for violations by members, etc.*—Any person who becomes or remains a member of any subversive organization, or attends a meeting thereof, with knowledge that the organization has failed to comply with any provision of this title, is guilty of a misdemeanor punishable by fine of not less than ten dollars ($10) nor more than one thousand dollars ($1,000), or by imprisonment in the county jail for not less than 10 days nor more than one year, or by both.

Annotation:

People v. *Noble*, 68 C.A. 2d 853, 158 P. 2d 225 (1945). Appellants, members of an association known as the "Friends of Progress"—a pro-Nazi group—were convicted of violating the Subversive Organization Registration Act. The Act required, *inter alia*, the registration of every group of two or more persons that either advocated the forceful overthrow of the government or was "subject to foreign control." The district court reversed on grounds that the evidence was insufficient to sustain the conviction of the offense charged in the indictment. Although this finding obviated the necessity of passing upon the constitutionality of the Act, the court stated: "We are frank to state that we are in grave doubt as to the constitutionality of the California Subversive Registration Act * * *."

EXCLUSION FROM THE ELECTIVE PROCESS

West's Anno. Elec. Code. § 6431. *Party advocating forceful overthrow of government ineligible to participate in primary election.*—No party shall be recognized or qualified to participate in any primary election which either directly or indirectly carries on, advocates, teaches, justifies, aids, or abets the overthrow by any unlawful means of, or which directly or indirectly carries on, advocates, teaches, justifies, aids, or abets a program of sabotage, force and violence, sedition or treason against, the Government of the United States or of this State.

Annotation:

Communist Party of the United States v. *Peek*, 20 C. 2d 536, 127 P. 2d 889 (1942). Plaintiffs, the Communist Party of the United States and three members thereof brought this action seeking, *inter alia*, a judgment declaring unconstitutional the statutory provision that no party which used or adopted as any part of its party designation the word Communist or any derivative thereof should qualify to participate in any primary election. The act also prohibited qualification of any party affiliated in any way with the Communist Party as well as any party for which less than 2,500 voters had declared their intention of affiliating "25 days prior to the last preceding election." Finally, the act authorized the secretary of state, with the advice and consent of the attorney general, to determine which parties were qualified to participate in any primary election. The superior court of Los Angeles sustained general demurrers to the various causes alleged by defendants and dismissed the action. The Supreme Court of California acknowledged that the lower court did not abuse its discretion in refusing to grant declaratory relief, principally because a speedy and adequate remedy was provided in the elections code. Similarly, the court sustained the dismissal of the writ to mandate defendants to qualify the Communist Party to participate in the primary election on grounds that that action was improper to compel future acts. The court reversed, however, the dismissal of plaintiffs challenge to the constitutionality of the mentioned sections which were grounded on relief authorized by the elections code, with respect to the statutory provision providing that no party may qualify to participate in a primary election which employed the designation "Communist," the court declared it to be invalid as unreasonable. "Assuming for the moment * * * that the legislature has power to deny the use of the primary election machinery to particular groups of dangerous citizens, it does not follow that it may do so by a statute which merely operates to deny to such groups the use of a particular name." It reasoned that the name adopted by a political party was frequently without any value in ascertaining the political beliefs of its adherents, and if the beliefs were dangerous, the danger would not be removed by a change in the name of the party. The court refused to take judicial notice of the subversive character of the Communist Party on grounds that this was contrary to precedent and belied by plaintiffs denials. The implications arising out of the legislative findings with respect to the party did not affect a different result since (1) it was not the function of the legislature to determine whether a statute declaring a general policy had been violated in a particular case, that being a judicial function, and (2) that a statute which purported to determine that a particular person or group violated a general law was contrary to the constitutional prohibition against special legislation. For identical reasons the court held invalid that part of the act forbidding foreign affiliation. On the other hand, a portion of the same section excluding political parties advocating the forceful overthrow of the government, was held to be within the legislature's power to prescribe tests and conditions for participation in primary elections. With respect to the third provision in issue—the requirement that "25 days prior to the last preceding primary election," not less than 2,500 voters should have declared their intention to affiliate with the party seeking to qualify—the court held it to be an unreasonable exercise of the legislature's power to establish tests and conditions for participation in primary elections. "* * * it is clear that no party, however substantial it might be, could participate in a primary election in this State unless it had 2,500 registered voters at a date 2 years prior to the time when it sought to assert its right. In the case of a newly organized party the test imposes an absolute bar to participation in a primary election held after its organization because the right to participate is measured by events which transpired before it was in existence. Such a test cannot possibly avoid impairing constitutional rights of suffrage by barring from the ballot political parties which represent substantial numbers of citizens." Plaintiffs' challenge to the provision conferring discretion to determine party doctrines was also sustained on grounds that before the constitutional right to vote may be taken away from a citizen, he must be given an opportunity to be heard in his own behalf. "* * * where the party system is made an integral part of the elective machinery any attempt to bar a particular party from the ballot results in an infringement of the individual voter's right of suffrage."

Loyalty of State Officers and Employees

1. ELECTIVE AND NONELECTIVE PERSONNEL

California Constitution, Art. 20, § 3. *Oath.*—Members of the legislature, and all public officers and employees, executive, legislative, and judicial, except such inferior officers and employees as may be by law exempted, shall, before they enter upon the duties of their respective officers, take and subscribe the following oath or affirmation:

"I, _____, do solemnly swear (or affirm) that I will support and defend the Constitution of the United States and the constitution of the State of California against all enemies, foreign and domestic; that I will bear true faith and allegiance to the Constitution of the United States and the constitution of the State of California; that I take this obligation freely, without any mental reservation or purpose of evasion; and that I will well and faithfully discharge the duties upon which I am about to enter.

"And I do further swear (or affirm) that I do not advocate, nor am I a member of any party or organization, political or otherwise, that now advocates the overthrow of the Government of the United States or of the State of California by force or violence or other unlawful means; that within the five years immediately preceding the taking of this oath (or affirmation) I have not been a member of any party or organization, political or otherwise, that advocated the overthrow of the Government of the United States or of the State of California by force or violence or other unlawful means except as follows:

(If no affiliations, write in the words "No Exceptions")

and that during such time as I hold the office of_____
(name of office)

I will not advocate nor become a member of any party or organization, political or otherwise, that advocates the overthrow of the Government of the United States or of the State of California by force or violence or other unlawful means."

And no other oath, declaration, or test, shall be required as a qualification for any public office or employment.

"Public officer and employee" includes every officer and employee of the State, including the University of California, every county, city,

city and county, district, and authority, including any department, division, bureau, board, commission, agency, or instrumentality of any of the foregoing.

Id. § 19. *Persons advocating forceful overthrow of government barred from public office and employment in the event of hostilities.*— Notwithstanding any other provision of this constitution, no person or organization which advocates the overthrow of the Government of the United States or the State by force or violence or other unlawful means or who advocates the support of a foreign government against the United States in the event of hostilities shall:

(a) Hold any office or employment under this State, including but not limited to the University of California, or with any county, city or county, city, district, political subdivision, authority, board, bureau, commission or other public agency of this State; or

(b) Receive any exemption from any tax imposed by this State or any county, city or county, city, district, political subdivision, authority, board, bureau, commission or other public agency of this State.

The legislature shall enact such laws as may be necessary to enforce the provisions of this section.

2. NONELECTIVE PERSONNEL

West's Anno. Gov't Code. § 1027. *Declaration of legislative findings.*—The legislature of the State of California finds that:

(a) There exists a world-wide revolutionary movement to establish a totalitarian dictatorship based upon force and violence rather than upon law.

(b) This world-wide revolutionary movement is predicated upon and it is designed and intended to carry into execution the basic precepts of communism as expounded by Marx, Lenin, and Stalin.

(c) Pursuant to the objectives of the world communism movement, in numerous foreign countries the legally constituted governments have been overthrown and totalitarian dictatorships established therein against the will of the people, and the establishment of similar dictatorships in other countries is imminently threatening. The successful establishment of totalitarian dictatorships has consistently been aided, accompanied, or accomplished by repeated acts of treachery, deceit, teaching of false doctrines, teaching untruth, together with organized confusion, insubordination, and disloyalty, fostered, directed, instigated, or employed by Communist organizations and their members in such countries.

(d) Within the boundaries of the State of California there are active disciplined Communist organizations presently functioning for the primary purpose of advancing the objectives of the world communism movement, which organizations promulgate, advocate, and adhere to the precepts and the principles and doctrines of the world communism movement. These Communist organizations are characterized by identification of their programs, policies, and objectives with those of the world communism movement, and they regularly and consistently cooperate with and endeavor to carry into execution programs, policies and objectives substantially identical to programs, policies, and objectives of such world communism movement.

(e) One of the objectives of the world communism movement is to place its members in State and local government positions and in

State supported educational institutions. If this objective is successful, propaganda can be disseminated by the members of these organizations among pupils and students by those members who would have the opportunity to teach them and to whom, as teachers, they would look for guidance, authority, and leadership. The members of such groups would use their positions to advocate and teach their doctrines and teach the prescribed Communist Party line group dogma or doctrine without regard to truth or free inquiry. This type of propaganda is sufficiently subtle to escape detection.

There is a clear and present danger, which the legislature of the State of California finds is great and imminent, that in order to advance the program, policies and objectives of the world communism movement, Communist organizations in the State of California and their members will engage in concerted effort to hamper, restrict, interfere with, impede, or nullify the efforts of the State and the public agencies of the State to comply with and enforce the laws of the State of California and their members will infiltrate and seek employment by the State and its public agencies.

Id. § 1028. *Advocating forceful overthrow of government cause for dismissal.*—It shall be sufficient cause for the dismissal of any public employee when such public employee advocates or is knowingly a member of the Communist Party or of an organization which during the time of his membership he knows advocates overthrow of the Government of the United States or of any State by force or violence.

Id. § 1028.1 (Supp. 1963). *Public employees required to testify.*—It shall be the duty of any public employee who may be subpenaed or ordered by the governing body of the State or local agency by which such employee is employed, to appear before such governing body, or a committee or subcommittee thereof, or by a duly authorized committee of the Congress of the United States or of the legislature of this State, or any subcommittee of any such committee, to appear before such committee or subcommittee, and to answer under oath a question or questions propounded by such governing body, committee or subcommittee, or a member or counsel thereof, relating to:

(a) Present personal advocacy by the employee of the forceful or violent overthrow of the Government of the United States or of any State.

(b) Present knowing membership in any organization now advocating the forceful or violent overthrow of the Government of the United States or of any State.

(c) Past knowing membership at any time since October 3, 1945, in any organization which, to the knowledge of such employee, during the time of the employee's membership advocated the forceful or violent overthrow of the Government of the United States or of any State.

(d) Questions as to present knowing membership of such employee in the Communist Party or as to past knowing membership in the Communist Party at any time since October 3, 1945.

(e) Present personal advocacy by the employee of the support of a foreign government against the United States in the event of hostilities between said foreign government and the United States.

Any employee who fails or refuses to appear or to answer under oath on any ground whatsoever any such questions so propounded shall be guilty of insubordination and guilty of violating this section and shall be suspended and dismissed from his employment in the manner provided by law.

Id. § 1369. *Penalty.*—Every person having taken and subscribed to the oath or affirmation required by this chapter, who while holding office, advocates or becomes a member of any party or organization, political or otherwise, that advocates the overthrow of the Government of the United States by force or violence or other unlawful means, is guilty of a felony, and is punishable by imprisonment in the State prison not less than one or more than fourteen years.

Annotations:

Garner v. *Los Angeles Board*, 341 U.S. 716, 71 S. Ct. 909, 95 L. Ed. 1317, (1951), rehearing denied 342 U.S. 843, 72 S. Ct. 21, 96 L. Ed. 637. In 1941, the California Legislature amended the Charter of the city of Los Angeles so as to provide, generally, that no person shall hold or retain or be eligible for any public office or employment in the service of the city (1) who advises, advocates or teaches the overthrow by force or violence of the State or Federal Government or belongs to an organization which does so, or (2) who, within the five years prior to the effective date, had so advised, advocated or taught or had belonged to an organization which did so. In 1948, the city passed an ordinance requiring each of its officers and employees to take an oath that he had not within the five years preceding the effective date of the ordinance, did not now, and would not while in the service of the city, advise, advocate, or teach the overthrow by force, violence or other unlawful means, of the State or Federal Government or belong to an organization which had that purpose or had had such purpose during the past five years. The ordinance also required every employee to execute an affidavit "stating whether or not he is or ever was a member of the Communist Party * * *." Petitioners, civil service employees of the city of Los Angeles, were discharged for refusing to comply with the oath and affidavit requirements and brought this action for reinstatement and unpaid salaries. On appeal petitioners argued that the ordinance violated the proscription against bills of attainder and ex post facto laws as well as depriving them of freedom of speech and assembly and of the right of petition. The Supreme Court affirmed the decision ordering petitioners' dismissal. With respect to the affidavit requirement the court held that a municipal employer was not disabled because it was an agency of the State from inquiring of its employees as to matters that might prove relevant to their fitness and suitability for the public service. Similarly, the oath requirement insofar as it operated from the date of the adoption, was a reasonable regulation to protect the municipal service by establishing an employment qualification to the State and the Federal Government. As with the National Government, a State has the power to reasonably restrict the political activity of its employees in order to protect the integrity and competency of the civil service. Since the activity covered by the oath had been proscribed for a period prior to that embraced thereby, the ordinance was not ex post facto. Nor was the ordinance a bill of attainder since no punishment was imposed by a general regulation which simply set forth standards of qualifications and eligibility for public employment. Assuming that the oath requirement would be construed to apply only to knowing membership in the proscribed organizations, the Court concluded by denying any merit to petitioners' due process contentions.

Nelson v. *Los Angeles*, 362 U.S. 1, 80 S. Ct. 527, 4 L. Ed. 2d 494 (1960). Petitioners, employees of the County of Los Angeles, were subpenaed to appear before a subcommittee of the House Un-American Activities Committee, but refused to answer various questions concerning subversion. Previously each petitioner had been ordered by the county board of supervisors to answer any questions asked by the subcommittee relating to his subversive activity and a State statute compelled public employees to give testimony relating to such activity on pain of discharge "in the manner provided by law." Thereafter, petitioners were discharged on the ground of insubordination and violation of the mentioned statute. One petitioner, a permanent employee, was given a hearing which resulted in confirmation of his discharge. The second petitioner, a temporary employee, was denied a hearing on the ground that his status did not entitle him to such under the civil service rules. The supreme court, the justices dividing equally, affirmed the first petitioner's dismissal without comment. It also affirmed second petitioner's dismissal holding that since his discharge was based solely on insubordination and violation of the statute and not on his invocation of the fifth amendment, there was no violation of due process.

Hirschman v. *Los Angeles County*, 39 C. 2d 698, 249 P. 2d 287 (1952), rehearing denied 39 C. 2d 698, 250 P. 2d 145. Plaintiffs, permanent civil service employees of Los Angeles County, were discharged for refusing to execute the oath and affidavits prescribed by orders of the county board of supervisors. Under the orders county employees were required to swear that they were not, and since a specified date, had not been members of any therein named organization advocating the overthrow of the government by force and violence. The county civil service commission, after a hearing, sustained the discharges and plaintiffs instituted this action to compel their reinstatement and payment of back wages. The court affirmed a judgment denying the requested relief. Noting that properly construed the provisions required scienter, the court held "that public employees may properly be required to furnish information regarding their memberships in organizations which to their knowledge, have advocated the overthrow of the government by force and violence."

Wirin v. *Ostly*, 191 C.A. 2d 710, 13 Cal. Rptr. 31 (1961), certiorari denied 368 U.S. 952, 82 S. Ct. 393, 7 L. Ed. 2d 385. In this case the court held the requirement that a candidate for the office of notary public take the oath prescribed in Article XX, section 3 of the constitution did not unconstitutionally abridge freedom of speech, freedom of conscience, freedom of religion, freedom of thought, the right of privacy of opinion without due process, in violation of the First and Fourteenth Amendments.

---

3. CIVIL DEFENSE PERSONNEL

West's Anno Gov't Code § 3100. *Declaration of legislative policy.*—It is hereby declared that the defense of the civil population during the present state of world affairs is of paramount state importance requiring the undivided attention and best efforts of our citizens. In furtherance of such defense and in the exercise of police power of the State in protection of its citizens, all public employees are hereby declared to be civil defense workers subject to such civilian defense activities as may be assigned to them by their superiors or by law.

Id. § 3100. *"Civil defense worker" and "public employees" defined.*—For the purpose of this chapter the term "civil defense worker" includes all public employees and all volunteers in any civilian defense organization accredited by the State Disaster Council. The term "public employees" includes all persons employed by the State or any county, city, city and county, State agency or public district, excluding aliens legally employed.

Id. § 3102. *Oath required to be executed before entering upon duties of employment.*—All civil defense workers shall, before they enter upon the duties of their employment, take and subscribe to the oath or affirmation required by this chapter. In the case of intermittent, temporary, emergency or successive employments, then in the discretion of the employing agency, an oath taken and subscribed as required by this chapter shall be effective for the purposes of this chapter for all successive periods of employment which commerce within one calendar year from the date of such subscription.

Id. § 3103. *Form of oath.*—The oath or affirmation required by this chapter is the oath or affirmation set forth in section 3 of Article XX of the constitution of California.

NOTE.—For text of oath, see Loyalty oath, Elective and Nonelective personnel, *supra.*

Id. § 3104. *Administration of oath.*—The oath or affirmation may be taken before any officer authorized to administer oaths; provided, that the oath or affirmation of any civil defense worker of the State may be taken before his appointing power or before any person authorized in writing by his appointing power. Such authorization shall be filed with the State Personnel Board, and any person so authorized by his appointing power may administer the oath required by this chapter.

No fee shall be charged by any person before whom the oath or affirmation is taken and subscribed.

Id. § 3105 (Supp. 1963). *Filing of oath.*—The oath or affirmation of any civil defense worker of the State shall be filed with the State personnel board within 30 days of the date on which it is taken and subscribed.

The oath or affirmation of any civil defense worker of any county shall be filed in the office of the county clerk of the county except that where election precinct officers take and subscribe to such oath or affirmation which is an integral part of a claim for compensation, such oath and claim for compensation may be filed in either the office of the county auditor or in the office of the clerk of the board of supervisors of the county.

The oath or affirmation of any civil defense worker of any city shall be filed in the office of the city clerk of the city.

The oath or affirmation of any civil defense worker of any other agency or district shall be filed with such officer or employee of the agency or district as may be designated by such agency or district.

Id. § 3106. *Repeated oath taking not required.*—Compliance with this chapter shall, as to State employees, be deemed full compliance with Chapter 4, Part 1, Division 5, Title 2 of this code, requiring taking of oaths by State employees.

Id. § 3107 (Supp. 1963). *Receipt of compensation conditioned upon execution of oath.*—No compensation nor reimbursement for expenses incurred shall be paid to any civil defense worker by any public agency unless such civil defense worker has taken and subscribed to the oath or affirmation required by this chapter. It shall be the duty of the person certifying to public payrolls to ascertain and certify that such civil defense worker has taken such oath or affirmation. Whenever there is more than one officer certifying to public payrolls the governing body of a city or county or school district may designate and make it the duty of a certain officer or officers to ascertain and certify that such civil defense worker has taken such oath or affirmation. The governing body of a city or county or school district may designate and make it the duty of a local civil defense and disaster officer to ascertain and certify that each volunteer civil defense worker has taken such oath or affirmation.

Nothing in this chapter, however, shall prevent the correction of any technical error or deficiency in an oath taken pursuant to this chapter; provided, such correction is made before the civil defense worker is actually paid or reimbursed.

Id. § 3108. *Penalty for perjury.*—Every person who, while taking and subscribing to the oath or affirmation required by this chapter, states as true any material matter which he knows to be false, is guilty of perjury, and is punishable by imprisonment in the State prison not less than one nor more than 14 years.

Id. § 3109. *Penalty for violation of oath.*—Every person having taken and subscribed to the oath or affirmation required by this chapter, who, while in the employ of, or service with, the State or any county, city, city and county, State agency, public district, or civilian defense organization advocates or becomes a member of any party or organization, political or otherwise, that advocates the overthrow of the Government of the United States by force or violence or other unlawful means, is guilty of a felony, and is punishable by imprisonment in the State prison not less than one or more than 14 years.

TEACHERS' LOYALTY

West's Anno. Educ. Code § 8455. *Communist indoctrination prohibited.*—No teacher giving instruction in any school, or on any property belonging to any agencies included in the public school system, shall advocate or teach communism with the intent to indoctrinate any pupil with, or inculcate a preference in the mind of any pupil for communism.

The legislature in prohibiting the advocacy or teaching of communism with the intent to indoctrinate any pupil with or inculcate a preference in the mind of any pupil for, such doctrine does not intend to prevent the teaching of the facts of the above subject but intends to prevent the advocacy of, and inculcation and indoctrination into communism as is hereinafter defined, for the purpose of undermining the patriotism for, and the belief in, the Government of the United States and of this State in the minds of the pupils in the public school system.

For the purposes of this section, communism is a political theory that the presently existing form of Government of the United States or of this State should be changed, by force, violence, or other unconstitutional means, to a totalitarian dictatorship which is based on the principles of communism as expounded by Marx, Lenin, and Stalin.

Id. § 13121. *Teaching certificate conditioned upon execution of oath.*—Except as provided in this code, no certification document shall be granted to any person unless and until he has subscribed to the following oath or affirmation: "I solemnly swear (or affirm) that I will support the Constitution of the United States of America, the constitution of the State of California, and the laws of the United States and the State of California, and will by precept and example, promote respect for the flag and the statutes of the United States and of the State of California, reverence for law and order, and undivided allegiance to the Government of the United States of America." The oath or affirmation shall be subscribed before any person authorized to administer oaths or before any member of the governing board of a school district or of any county board of education and filed with the State board of education. Any certificated person who is a citizen or subject of any country other than the United States, and who is employed in any capacity in any of the public schools of the State shall, before entering upon the discharge of his duties, subscribe to an oath to support the institutions and policies of the United States during the period of his sojourn within the State. Upon the violation of any of the terms of the oath or affirmation, the State board of education shall suspend or revoke the credential which has been issued.

NOTE.—Following §§ 12951–12958 comprise comprehensive act dealing with Communism and the Public Schools.

West's Anno. Educ. Code § 12951. *Declaration of legislative findings.*—The legislature of the State of California finds that:

(a) There exists a worldwide revolutionary movement to establish a totalitarian dictatorship based upon force and power rather than upon law.

(b) This worldwide revolutionary movement is predicated upon and it is designed and intended to carry into execution the basic precepts of communism as expounded by Marx, Lenin, and Stalin.

(c) Pursuant to the objectives of the world communism movement, in numerous foreign countries the legally constituted governments have been overthrown and totalitarian dictatorships established therein against the will of the people, and the establishment of similar dictatorships in other countries is imminently threatening. The successful establishment of totalitarian dictatorships has consistently been aided, accompanied, or accomplished by repeated acts of treachery, deceit, teaching of false doctrines, teaching untruth, together with organized confusion, insubordination, and disloyalty, fostered, directed, instigated, or employed by Communist organizations and their members in such countries.

(d) Within the boundaries of the State of California there are active disciplined Communist organizations presently functioning for the primary purpose of advancing the objectives of the world communism movement, which organizations promulgate, advocate, and adhere to the precepts and the principles and doctrines of the world communism movement. These Communist organizations are characterized by identification of their programs, policies, and objectives with those of the world communism movement, and they regularly and consistently cooperate with and endeavor to carry into execution programs, policies, and objectives substantially identical to programs, policies, and objectives of such world communism movement.

(e) One of the objectives of the world communism movement is to place its members in local government positions and in the public school system. If this objective is successful, propaganda can be disseminated by the members of these organizations among public school pupils by those members who would have the opportunity to teach them and to whom, as teachers, they would look for guidance, authority, and leadership. The members of such groups would use their positions to advocate and teach their doctrines and teach the prescribed Communist Party line group dogma or doctrine without regard to truth or free inquiry. This type of propaganda is sufficiently subtle to escape detection in the classroom.

There is a clear and present danger, which the legislature of the State of California finds is great and imminent, that in order to advance the program, policies, and objectives of the world communism movement, Communist organizations in the State of California and their members will engage in concerted effort to hamper, restrict, interfere with, impede, or nullify the efforts of the governing boards of school districts to comply with and enforce section 8455 of the Education Code of the State of California which prohibits the advocacy or teaching of communism with the intent to indoctrinate any pupil with or inculcate a preference in the mind of any pupil for communism for the purpose of undermining the patriotism for and the belief in the Government of the United States and of the State of California in the minds of the pupils of the public school system.

The legislature specifically finds that the requirement that all persons (certificated or noncertificated) now employed by the school districts of this State, or hereafter making application for employment by any of such districts, shall declare under oath that they are not knowingly members of the Communist Party, is a reasonable measure to meet the clear and present danger hereinabove found.

The legislature further specifically finds that an indirect or evasive answer to a question relating to any of the matters specified in Section 12955 or 12956, or an answer which neither affirms nor denies shall, for the purposes of this act and chapter, be considered as a failure and refusal to answer, regardless of the ground or explanation given for any such answer.

Id. § 12952. *Employment of Party members prohibited.*—No person who is knowingly a member of the Communist Party shall after September 9, 1953, be employed by, or, except as provided in Section 12953, retained in the employment of, any school district. Prior to the first day of service as an employee of any school district, the applicant shall state under oath whether or not he is knowingly a member of the Communist Party. If the applicant states that he is knowingly a member of the Communist Party, he shall not become an employee of any school district.

Id. § 12953. *Former Party members required to file statement of disaffiliation.*—Any employee of any school district who on September

9, 1953, is or since October 3, 1945, was knowingly a member of the Communist Party, and who has not previously filed the statement required by this section, shall within ninety (90) days of the effective date of the amendment of this section made at the 1955 regular session of the legislature, file with the governing board of the school district employing him a verified statement that he is no longer a member of the Communist Party and that such membership has been terminated in good faith. Any such employee who fails to file such a statement within the time specified shall be guilty of insubordination and guilty of violating this section and shall be suspended and dismissed from his employment in the manner provided by law.

Id. § 12954. *Party membership deemed insubordination; cause for dismissal.*—Any employee of any school district who after September 9, 1953, knowingly becomes a member of the Communist Party shall be guilty of insubordination and guilty of violating this section and shall be suspended and dismissed from his employment in the manner provided by law.

Id. § 12955. *School district employees required to testify.*—It shall be the duty of any employee of any school district who may be subpenaed by a United States Congressional Un-American Activities Committee or a subcommittee thereof or a California Legislative Un-American Activities Committee or a subcommittee thereof or any other committee or subcommittee of the United States Congress or the California Legislature or of either house of either thereof to appear before said committee or subcommittee and specifically to answer under oath a question or questions propounded by any member or counsel of the committee or subcommittee relating to:

(a) Present personal advocacy by the employee of the forceful or violent overthrow of the Government of the United States or of any State or political subdivision.

(b) Present knowing membership in any organization which, to the knowledge of such employee, advocates the forceful or violent overthrow of the Government of the United States or of any State or political subdivision.

(c) Past knowing membership at any time since October 3, 1945, in any organization which, to the knowledge of such employee, during the time of the employee's membership advocated the forceful or violent overthrow of the Government of the United States or of any State or political subdivision.

(d) Past knowing membership of such employee in the Communist Party at any time since October 3, 1945.

(e) Present knowing membership of such employee in the Communist Party.

(f) Present personal advocacy by the employee of the support of a foreign government against the United States in the event of hostilities.

Any employee who fails or refuses to answer under oath on any ground whatsoever any such question propounded by any member or counsel of any such committee or subcommittee shall be guilty of insubordination and guilty of violating this section and shall be suspended and dismissed from his employment in the manner provided by law.

Id. § 12956. *School district employees required to answer questions propounded by governing school body.*—It shall be the duty of any employee of any school district who is ordered to appear before the governing board of the employing school district to appear and specifically to answer under oath a question or questions propounded by a member or counsel of the governing board or by the superintendent of schools relating to any of the matters specified in section 12955.

Any employee who fails or refuses to appear or to answer under oath on any ground whatsoever any such question propounded by a member or counsel of the governing board or by the superintendent of schools shall be guilty of insubordination and guilty of violating this section and shall be suspended and dismissed from his employment in the manner provided by law.

Id. § 12957. *Membership in the Communist Party cause for dismissal.*—It shall be sufficient cause for the suspension and dismissal, in the manner provided by law, of any employee of a school district when such employee is knowingly a member of the Communist Party.

Id. § 12958. *Penalty.*—Any certificated employee of a school district who violates any of the provisions of sections 12952 to 12957, inclusive, of this code shall be guilty of unprofessional conduct and shall be suspended and dismissed in the manner provided by law.

West's Anno. Educ. Code § 13403 (k). *Membership in the Communist Party cause for dismissal of permanent employee.*—No permanent employee shall be dismissed except for one or more of following causes:

(k) Knowing membership by the employee in the Communist Party.

Id. § 13408. *Procedure.*—Upon the filing of written charges, duly signed and verified by the person filing them with the governing board of a school district, or upon a written statement of charges formulated by the governing board, charging a permanent employee of the district with immoral conduct, conviction of a felony or of any crime involving moral turpitude, with incompetency due to mental disability, with violation of section 8455 of this code, with knowing membership by the employee in the Communist Party or with violation of any provision in sections 12952 to 12958, inclusive, of this code, the governing board may, if it deems such action necessary, immediately suspend the employee from his duties and give notice to him of his suspension, and that 30 days after service of the notice, he will be dismissed, unless he demands a hearing.

If the permanent employee is suspended upon charges of knowing membership by the employee in the Communist Party or for any violation of section 8455, 12952, 12953, 12954, 12957, or 12958 of this code, he may within 10 days after service upon him of notice of such suspension file with the governing board a verified denial, in writing, of the charges. In such event the permanent employee who demands a hearing within the 30-day period shall continue to be paid his regular salary during the period of suspension and until the entry of the superior court judgment, if and during such time as he furnishes to the school district a suitable bond, or other security acceptable to the governing board, as a guarantee that the employee will repay to the school district the amount of salary so paid to him during the period of suspension in case the superior court judgment is that he may be dismissed. If the judgment determines that the employee may not be dismissed, the school district shall reimburse the employee for the cost of the bond.

West's Anno. Educ. Code § 24306 (Supp. 1963). *Causes for dismissal, demotion, or suspension.*—A permanent or probationary academic or nonacademic employee may be dismissed, demoted, or suspended for the following causes:

(a) Immoral conduct.
(b) Unprofessional conduct.
(c) Dishonesty.
(d) Incompetency.
(e) Physical or mental unfitness for position occupied.
(f) Failure or refusal to perform the normal and reasonable duties of the position.
(g) Conviction of a felony or conviction of any misdemeanor involving moral turpitude.
(h) Fraud in securing appointment.
(i) Drunkenness on duty.
(j) Addiction to the use of narcotics or habit-forming drugs.

Id. § 24307. *Inclusions within "unprofessional conduct.*—"Unprofessional conduct" as used in section 24306 includes, but is not limited to:

(a) Membership in, or active support of, a "Communist front," a "Communist action" organization, or a Communist organization, as those terms are now defined in the act of the Congress of the United States designated as "Internal Security Act of 1950."

(b) Persistent active participation in public meetings conducted or sponsored by an organization mentioned in subdivision (a) of this section.

(c) Willful advocacy of the overthrow of the Government of the United States or of the State, by force, violence, or other unlawful means, either on or off the campus.

(d) Willful advocacy of communism, either on or off the campus, for the purpose of undermining the patriotism of pupils, or with the intent to indoctrinate any pupil with communism or inculcate a preference for communism in the mind of any pupil.

Annotations:

Laguna Beach Unified School District v. *Lewis*, 146 C.A. 2d 463, 304 P. 2d 59 (1957). Respondent school district instituted this action against dismissed schoolteacher for a judicial determination as to whether the charges for which she was dismissed were true, and if true, whether they constituted grounds for dismissal. Appellant was charged with unprofessional conduct: (1) in that she distributed a pamphlet entitled "Time to Resist" outside a classroom, (2) in that she falsely denied before the governing board of the school district that she distributed the pamphlet, and (3) that she refused to answer questions of a congressional investigating committee. The court sustained the denial of appellant's motion to dismiss the complaint. Distribution of a pro-Communist pamphlet was held to be contrary to the oath to support the Constitution and an act of unprofessional conduct. The court further held that if the charge of giving false testimony were true, appellant's conduct could be classified as dishonest, hostile to the welfare of the general public, and contrary to good morals and she could be dismissed. In view of the State law requiring employees to give testimony regarding subversion, defendant had no right to refuse to answer at least with respect to her activities subsequent to the law's enactment.

Board of Education v. *Mass,* 47 C. 2d 494, 304 P. 2d 1015 (1957). Defendant schoolteacher declined to answer questions before a congressional committee, basing his refusal on the ground of privilege against self-incrimination under the Fifth Amendment. State law provided that any school employee who failed or refused on any ground whatsoever to answer questions put to him by a legislative committee relating to specified matters, including past or present knowing membership in the Communist Party, was guilty of insubordination and should be dismissed in the manner provided by law. Although defendant offered to answer any questions under oath at a meeting of the school board, he was dismissed on grounds that State law allowed no discretion in the matter. The Supreme Court of California reversed on the ground that the intervening decision in *Slochower* v. *Board of Higher Education,* 350 U.S. 551, 76 S. Ct. 637 100 L. Ed. 692 (1956), required that before an employee may be found guilty of insubordination or dismissed for refusing to answer under the claim of self-incrimination, there must be a full hearing and a determination that his reasons for invoking the privilege are not sufficient.

Steinmetz v. *California State Board of Education,* 44 C. 2d 816, 285 P. 2d 617 (1955), certiorari denied 351 U.S. 915, 76 S. Ct. 708, 100 L. Ed. 1448. Petitioner was dismissed from his position as an associate professor at San Diego State College because of his refusal, at a hearing before the State board of education, to answer two questions as to whether he was or had been a member of the Communist Party. The State board acted pursuant to a statute providing that it was the duty of any public employee, when ordered, to appear before the governing body of the State or local agency by which he was employed and to answer under oath questions relating to membership in the Communist Party among other things. The law further provided that "any employee who fails or refuses to appear or to answer under oath on any ground whatsoever any such questions so propounded shall be guilty of insubordination and guilty of violating this section and shall be suspended and dismissed from his employment in the manner provided by law." The court refused petitioner's request to compel his reinstatement and held that the statute under which he was dismissed was not rendered invalid by the fact that it required an employee to answer questions as to his membership in the Communist Party without regard to his knowledge of the nature of the party. A statute which compels disclosure of information concerning a public employee's membership in a proscribed organization, must be distinguished from those which provide for discharge or disqualification because of membership or refusal to take an oath denying membership. Under the latter type of statute, knowledge of the character of the organization has been held essential, *Wieman* v. *Updegraff,* 344 U.S. 183, 73 S. Ct. 215, 97 L. Ed. 216 (1952), and the legislation has been sustained only when it expressly or impliedly required such knowledge, *Adler* v. *Board of Education,* 342 U.S. 485, 72 S. Ct. 380, 96 L. Ed. 517 (1952). On the other hand, where the statutes provide merely for the disclosure of information, a requirement that the employee have knowledge of the nature of the organization is not necessary. *Garner*

v. *Board of Public Works*, 341 U.S. 716, 71 S. Ct. 709, 95 L. Ed. 1317 (1951). The Court concluded by emphasizing that petitioner was not dismissed because of membership in any organization but because of his refusal to answer questions as to his fitness for public employment.

Pockman v. *Leonard*, 39 C. 2d 676, 249 P. 2d 267 (1952). Petitioner, an associate professor, instituted this action to compel respondents to certify his name and to pay him salary which was withheld because of his failure to execute the oath required by the Levering Act. That Act provided that public employees are "civil defense workers subject to such civilian defense activities as may be assigned to them by law", and defined public employees as all persons employed by the State or any county, city, city and county, State agency or public district, excluding aliens. All civil defense workers were required to take the prescribed oath within the first 30 days of employment. It further provided that no compensation should be paid to any civil defense worker by any public agency unless he had subscribed to the oath, and that it was the duty of the person certifying to public payrolls to ascertain and certify that the oath had been taken by such workers. The court allowed petitioner compensation for services rendered up to thirty days following the effective date of the statute. The petitioner having failed to take the oath, however, was not entitled to compensation for any subsequent period. In sustaining the validity of the statute as applied to petitioner, the court declared that a governmental body had the right to direct that its employees shall not belong to organizations which they know advocate overthrow of the government, and that they may be required to make sworn statements as a condition to or obtaining employment.

Board of Education v. *Wilkinson*, 125 C.A. 2d 100, 270 P. 2d 82 (1954). This case involved a proceeding on a complaint by the board of education against a teacher, charging that there was cause for her dismissal. Defendant, a permanent high school teacher, refused to answer questions propounded by a congressional investigating committee regarding past and present membership in the Communist Party contrary to a rule of the board of education. The court affirmed her dismissal holding, *inter alia*, that when defendant refused to answer the questions she was guilty of unprofessional conduct and subject to dismissal. "A teacher's employment in the public schools is a privilege, not a right. A condition implicit in that privilege is loyalty to the government under which the school system functions. It is the duty of every teacher to answer proper questions in relation to his fitness to teach our youth when put to him by a lawfully constituted body authorized to propound such questions."

37 Ops. Atty. Gen. 112. The State board of education may not deny or revoke teaching credentials on the sole ground that the individual invoked the Fifth Amendment privilege in a Federal proceeding.

Orange Coast Junior College District v. *St. John*, 146 C.A. 2d 455, 303 P. 2d 1056 (1957). In this case—a proceeding by a school district to dismiss a teacher on charges of violating provisions of the Education Code dealing with the oath of applicants for employment and the duty to testify—the court held that the board of trustees of a school district could require a teacher, as a condition of continued employment, to state under oath that he was not knowingly a member of the Communist Party.

Exclusion From the Bar

West's Anno. Bus. & Prof. Code § 6064.1. *Persons advocating forceful overthrow of government ineligible for admission.*—No person who advocates the overthrow of the Government of the United States or of this State by force, violence, or other unconstitutional means, shall be certified to the Supreme Court for admission and a license to practice law.

Id. § 6160.1. *Advocating forceful overthrow of government cause for disbarment.*—Advocating the overthrow of the Government of the United States or of this State by force, violence, or other unconstitutional means, constitutes a cause for disbarment or suspension.

Question 20 of the Application for Admission to Practice Law, inquiries as to membership, past or present, in the Communist Party or other subversive organizations. It provides:

20. Are you now or have you ever been (*a*) a member of or affiliated with the Communist Party, or (*b*) a member of or affiliated with any political party or other organization which according to your knowledge at the time of your membership or affiliation advocated the overthrow of the Government of the United States or of this State by force, violence, or other unconstutitional means, or (*c*) an advocate of the overthrow of the Government of the United States or of this State by force, violence, or other unconstitutional means? Unless your answer is "No," please explain fully on an attached sheet all circumstances surrounding such membership, affiliation, or advocacy and the termination thereof, if it has been terminated.

Paragraph 27 informs the applicant of the statutory prohibition against the admission to practice of persons who advocate overthrow of the State Bar of California states that the committee has not barred execution of the application is deemed to indicate compliance with the requirement. It provides:

27. Section 6064.1 of the Business and Professions Code provides: No person who advocates the overthrow of the Government of the United States or of this State by force, violence, or other unconstitutional means, shall be certified to the supreme court for admission and a license to practice law.

It will be understood that the applicant, by executing and filing this application, certifies that he meets the requirement of this section.

Identical provisions are contained on the Form for Registration as a law student (Question 6 and paragraph 20).

Correspondence received from the Committee of Bar Examiners of the State Bar of California states that the committee has not barred any applicant to the practice of law for past membership in the Communist Party where such membership has been disclosed and after investigation the committee has been convinced that the applicant is qualified and that such membership has been finally terminated.

Annotations:

Konigsberg v. *State Bar*, 353 U.S. 252, 77 S. Ct. 772, 1 L. Ed. 2d 810 (1957), rehearing denied 354 U.S. 927, 77 S. Ct. 1374, 1 L. Ed. 2d 1441. The State Committee of Bar Examiners refused to certify petitioner to practice law on grounds that he had failed to prove (1) that he was of good moral character and (2) that he did not advocate the overthrow of the Government of the United States by unconstitutional means. On appeal to the California Supreme Court, petitioner argued that he had satisfactorily proved that he met all the requirements for admission to the bar, and that the Committee's action deprived him of rights secured by the Fourteenth Amendment. The State supreme court denied the petition for review. The Supreme Court of the United States reversed and held that the refusal to admit petitioner to the bar because he failed to demonstrate that he was a person of good moral character and because he failed to show that he did not advocate the overthrow of the Government was not supported by evidence in the record and constituted a denial of due process and equal protection of the laws. "Obviously," the Court declared, "the State could not draw unfavorable inferences as to his truthfulness, candor, or his moral character in general if his refusal to answer was based on a belief that the United States Constitution prohibited the type of inquiries the committee was making." Furthermore, the mere fact of past membership in the Communist Party, if true, without anything more, was not an adequate basis for concluding that petitioner was disloyal or a person of bad character.

Konigsberg v. *State Bar*, 336 U.S. 36, 81 S. Ct. 997, 6 L. Ed. 2d 105 (1961), rehearing denied 368 U.S. 869, 82 S. St. 21, 7 L. Ed. 2d 69. On remand from the Supreme Court, *supra*, petitioner moved in the State supreme court for immediate admission to the bar. The court vacated its previous order denying review and referred the matter to the Bar Committee for further consideration. At the ensuing committee hearings, petitioner introduced further evidence as to his good moral character, reiterated his disbelief in violent overthrow, and stated that he had never knowingly been a member of any organization which advocated such action. He persisted, however, in his refusal to answer any questions relating to his membership in the Communist Party. The committee again declined to certify him, this time on the ground that his refusal to answer had obstructed a full investigation into his qualifications. The California Supreme Court refused to review and denied petitioner's motion for direct admission to practice. The Supreme Court affirmed declaring that the Fourteenth Amendment did not prohibit a State from denying admission to a bar applicant who refused to answer questions having a substantial relevance to his qualifications.

Exclusion From Incidental Benefits

1. TAX EXEMPTIONS

California Constitution, Art. 20, § 19. *Person or organizations advocating forceful overthrow of government ineligible for tax exemption.*—Sec. 19. Notwithstanding any other provision of this constitution, no person or organization which advocates the overthrow of the Government of the United States or the State by force or violence or other unlawful means or who advocates the support of a foreign government against the United States in the event of hostilities shall:

(a) Hold any office or employment under this State, including but not limited to the University of California, or with any county, city or county, city, district, political subdivision, authority, board, bureau, commission or other public agency or this State; or

(b) Receive any exemption from any tax imposed by this State or any county, city or county, city, district, political subdivision, authority, board, bureau, commission, or other public agency of this State.

The legislature shall enact such laws as may be necessary to enforce the provisions of this section.

West's Anno. Tax & Rev. Code § 32. *Loyalty declaration required.*—Any statement, return, or other document in which is claimed any exemption, other than the householder's exemption, from any property tax imposed by this State or any country, city or county, city, district, political subdivision, authority, board, bureau, commission, or other public agency of this State shall contain a declaration that the person or organization making the statement, return, or other document does not advocate the overthrow of the Government of the United States or of the State of California by force or violence or other unlawful means nor advocate the support of a foreign government against the United States in event of hostilities. If any such statement, return, or other document does not contain such declaration, the person or organization making such statement, return, or other document shall not receive any exemption from the tax to which the statement, return, or other document pertains. Any person or organization who makes such declaration knowing it to be false is guilty of a felony. This section shall be construed so as to effectuate the purpose of section 19 of Article XX of the Constitution.

Annotations:

Speiser v. *Randall*, 357 U.S. 513, 78 S. Ct. 1332, 2 L. Ed. 2d 1460 (1958). Appellants, veterans of World War II, were denied the veterans' property-tax exemption for refusal to execute an oath that they did not advocate the overthrow of the Federal or State Government by unlawful means or advocate the support of a foreign government against the United States in the event of hostilities. The filing of such an oath was required as a prequisite to qualification for the tax exemption. The statute containing the oath requirement effectuated a provision of the State constitution denying tax exemptions to any person advocating subversion. The State supreme court sustained the accessors actions against the appellants on grounds that the constitutional amendment denied, the tax exemptions only to claimants who engaged in speech which might be criminally punished consistently with the First Amendment's guarantees of free speech. The Supreme Court reversed and held that the enforcement of the statute, by placing the burden of proof and persuasion on the taxpayers, denied them freedom of speech without procedural safeguards required by the due process clause of the Fourteenth Amendment. "* * * we hold that when the constitutional right to speak is sought to be deterred by a State's general taxing program due process demands that the speech be unincumbered until the State comes forward with sufficient proof to justify its inhibition" underlying the Court's ruling was the idea that "a discriminatory denial of a tax exemption for engaging in speech is a limitation on free speech."

First Unit. Church v. *Los Angeles*, 357 U.S. 545, 78 S. Ct. 1350, 1 L. Ed. 2d 1484 (1958). This case, a companion to *Speiser, supra*, was reversed on similar grounds, i.e., the enforcement of the tax-exemption denial placed the burden of proof and persuasion on the taxpayer in violation of due process. Having thus disposed of the case, the Court refused to pass upon appellants' additional contention that the provisions were invaled under the Fourteenth Amendment as abridgments of religious freedom and as violations of the principle of separation of church and state.

Id. § 23705 (Supp. 1963). *Incorporated organizations; loyalty declaration required.*—Any incorporated organization which claims any exemption prescribed by this article shall file annually with the Franchise Tax Board, on or before May 15th, a declaration that it does not advocate the overthrow of the Government of the United States or of the State of California by force or violence or other unlawful means nor advocate the support of a foreign government against the United States in event of hostilities. If any such organization incorporates, qualifies to do intrastate business, commences activities within this State, revives or is restored to good standing in any year after May 15th, it shall make and file such declaration before it is allowed any exemption prescribed by this article. Any incorporated organization which makes such declaration knowing it to be false is guilty of a felony. This section shall be construed so as to effectuate the purpose of section 19 of Article XX of the Constitution.

No exemption under this article shall be allowed to any incorporated organization for any year in which it fails to file on or before May 15th the annual declaration required by this section.

Annotation:

Op. Leg. Counsel, 1959 Assembly Journal 1205. The requirement of a loyalty declaration by an incorporated organization which claims an exemption from taxation is unconstitutional. Citing as authority, *Speiser* v. *Randall*, 357 U.S. 513, 78 S. Ct. 1332, 2 L. Ed. 2d 1460 (1958).

---

2. SCHOOL PROPERTY

West's Anno. Educ. Code § 16551 (Supp. 1963). *Utilization of school property for non-school purpose authorized.*—The governing board of any school district may grant the use of school buildings or grounds for public, literary, scientific, recreational, educational, or public agency meetings, or for the discussion of matters of general or public interest upon such terms and conditions as the board deems proper, and subject to the limitations, requirements, and restrictions set forth in this chapter (commencing at section 16551).

Id. § 16564. *Use of school property to further program of forceful overthrow of government forbidden.*—Any use, by any individual, society, group, or organization for the commission of any act intended to further any program or movement the purpose of which is to accomplish the overthrow of the Government of the United States or of the State by force, violence, or other unlawful means shall not be permitted or suffered.

Any individual, society, group, or organization which commits any act intended to further any program or movement the purpose of which is to accomplish the overthrow of the government by force, violence or other unlawful means while using school property pursuant to the provisions of this chapter (commencing at section 16551), is guilty of a misdemeanor.

Id. § 16565. *Statement of information required.*—No governing board of a school district shall grant the use of any school property to any person or organization for any use in violation of section 16564.

For the purpose of determination by such governing board whether or not any individual, society, group or organization applying for the use of such school property intends to violate section 16564, the governing board shall require the making and delivery to such governing board, by such applicant of a written statement of information in the following form:

STATEMENT OF INFORMATION

The undersigned states that, to the best of his knowledge, the school property for use of which application is hereby made will not be used for the commission of any act intended to further any program or movement the purpose of which is to accomplish the overthrow of the Government of the United States by force, violence, or other unlawful means;

That _____, the organization on whose behalf he is making application for use of school property, does not, to the best of his knowledge, advocate the overthrow of the Government of the United States or of the State of California by force, violence, or other unlawful means, and that, to the best of his knowledge, it is not a Communist-action organization or Communist-front organization required by law to be registered with the Attorney General of the United States. This statement is made under the penalties of perjury.

(Signature)

The school board may require the furnishing of such additional information as it deems necessary to make the determination that the use of school property for which application is made would not violate section 16564 of the Education Code.

Any person applying for the use of school property on behalf of any society, group, or organization shall be a member of such applicant group and, unless he is an officer of such group, must present written authorization from such applicant group to make such application.

The governing board of any school district may, in its discretion, consider any statement of information or written authorization made pursuant to the requirements of this section as being continuing in effect for the purposes of this section for the period of one year from the date of such statement of information or written authorization.

Id. § 16566. *Penalty.*—Written statements of information as required by section 16565 need not be under oath, but shall contain a written declaration that they are made under the penalties of perjury, and any person so signing such statements who willfully states therein as true any material matter which he knows to be false, is subject to the penalties prescribed for perjury in the Penal Code of this State.

Annotation:

American Civil Liberties Union of Southern California v. *Board of Education of City of Los Angeles,* 55 C. 2d 167, 359 P. 2d 45 (1961), certiorari denied 368 U.S. 819, 82 S. Ct. 34, 7 L. Ed. 2d 25. Petitioners instituted this action to compel the board of education to grant their application for the use of a school auditorium in which to hold a series of monthly meetings. Their application was denied by the board because the petitioners refused to furnish the "Statement of Information" required by statute. The statute in question provided that no school district should grant use of school property to groups seeking to overthrow the government and requiring the applicant to sign a statement that school property will not be used for the accomplishment of such purpose. The court ordered the mandate to issue and held the statute to be unconstitutional on the ground that the test oath abridged both the State and Federal constitutional guarantees of free speech and assembly. It concluded that the statute required an unconstitutional disclosure and attempted to create an unconstitutional power of prior restraint upon the rights of free speech and assembly.

_____

3. PROFESSIONAL CERTIFICATE

West's Anno. Bus. & Prof. Code § 9028(d). *Advocating forceful overthrow of the government cause for revocation of social worker's certificates.*—The board may suspend or revoke the certificate of any registrant if:

*   *   *   *   *   *   *

(d) He advocates the overthrow of the government by force and violence or other unlawful means.

COLORADO

ANARCHY AND SEDITION

Colorado Rev. Stat. 1953, § 40–23–7. *Anarchy and sedition defined.*—Every person who, in this State either orally or by writing, printing, exhibiting, or circulating written or printed words or pictures, or otherwise, shall advocate, teach, incite, propose, aid, abet, encourage, or advise resistance by physical force to, or the destruction or overthrow by physical force of, constituted government in general, or of the Government or laws of the United States or of this State shall be deemed guilty of anarchy and sedition and shall be guilty of a felony.

Id. § 40–23–8. *Destruction of life and property for anarchistic and seditious purposes.*—Every person who in this State, either orally or by writing, printing, exhibiting, or circulating written or printed words or pictures, shall advocate, teach, incite, propose, aid, abet, encourage, or advise the unlawful injury or destruction of private or public property by the use of physical force or violence or physical injury, or the unlawful injury by the use of physical force or violence of any person, or the unlawful taking of human life, either as a general principle or in particular instances, as a means of affecting governmental, industrial, social, or economic conditions, shall be deemed guilty of anarchy and sedition and shall be guilty of a felony.

Id. § 40–23–9. *Anarchistic and seditious associations unlawful.*—Any association, organization, society, or corporation one of whose purposes or professed purposes is to bring about any governmental, social, industrial or economic change in this State or in the United States, by the use of physical force, violence or physical injury, or which teaches, advocates, advises or defends the use of physical force, violence or physical injury to person or property, or threats of such injury, to accomplish such change, or which shall by any such means prosecute or pursue such purpose or professed purpose, is hereby declared to be anarchistic and seditious in character and to be an unlawful association.

Id. § 40–23–10. *Membership in unlawful associations declared to be a felony.*—Any person who, in this State shall act or profess to act as an officer of any such unlawful association, or shall speak, write or publish as a representative or professed representative of any such unlawful association, or, knowing the purpose, teachings and doctrine of such association, shall become or continue to be a member thereof, or contribute dues, money or other things of value to it or to any one for it, shall be guilty of a felony.

Id. § 40–23–11. *Publication or circulation of anarchistic and seditious literature.*—Any person, corporation, association, organization, or society who or which, in this State, knowingly prints, publishes, edits, issues, circulates, sells or offers for sale, or distributes, or has in his possession for the purpose of distribution, any book, pamphlet, picture, paper, circular, card, letter, writing, print, publication or document of any kind, in which is taught, advocated or advised the use of physical force, violence or physical injury to person or property, or threats of such injury, as a means of accomplishing any governmental, social, industrial or economic change in his State or in the United States, shall be deemed guilty of anarchy and sedition and shall be guilty of a felony.

Id. § 40–23–12. *Conspiracy to commit anarchy and sedition.*—Any two or more persons who, in this State, shall conspire, confederate or agree to commit any act or thing declared by sections 40–23–7 to 40–23–15 to be unlawful, shall be deemed guilty of a felony, and any persons who in this State, shall do any act in furtherance or pursuance of such a conspiracy formed either in this State or elsewhere, shall be deemed guilty of a felony.

Id. § 40–23–13, as amended, sess. Laws 1962, c. 51, p. 153. *Penalty.*—Any person who shall be guilty of any of these offenses defined in sections 40–23–7 to 40–23–12, upon conviction, shall be punished by imprisonment in the State penitentiary not exceeding twenty years, or by fine not exceeding ten thousand dollars or by both such fine and imprisonment; and any corporation, organization, association, or society committing any of the offenses hereinbefore defined, shall, upon conviction, be fined in a sum not exceeding ten thousand dollars and in addition the officers thereof shall be punished by imprisonment in the State penitentiary for a term not exceeding less than one year nor more than twenty years, or by fine not exceeding ten thousand dollars or by both such fine and imprisonment.

Id. § 40–23–14. *Penalty for violation resulting in death.*—Any person who, by his own act committed in violation of any of the provisions of sections 40–23–7 to 40–23–15, or who by inciting another to commit an act in violation of any of the provisions of sections 40–23–7 to 40–23–15, shall cause the death of any person, shall be deemed guilty of murder in the first degree and be punished accordingly.

Id. § 40–23–15. *"Person" defined.*—Wherever the word "person" is found in sections 40–23–7 to 40–23–15 the same shall include one or more persons, and shall likewise include any association, partnership, corporation, organization or society.

LOYALTY OF STATE OFFICERS AND EMPLOYEES

1. ELECTIVE AND NONELECTIVE PERSONNEL

Colorado Constitution, Art. XII, § 8. *Oath.*—Every civil officer, except members of the general assembly and such inferior officers as may be by law exempted, shall, before he enters upon the duties of his office, take and subscribe an oath or affirmation to support the Constitution of the United States and the State of Colorado, and to faithfully perform the duties of the office upon which he shall be about to enter.

2. CIVIL DEFENSE PERSONNEL

Colorado Rev. Stat. 1953, § 24–1–15. *Loyalty oath required.*—No person shall be employed or associated in any capacity in any civil defense organization established under this article who advocates or has advocated a change by force or violence in the constitutional form of the Government of the United States or in this State or the overthrow of any government in the United States by force or violence, or who has been convicted of or is under indictment or information charging any subversive act against the United States. Each person who is appointed to serve in an organization for civil defense, before entering upon his duties, shall take an oath, in writing, before a person authorized to administer oaths in this State, which oath shall be substantially as follows:

"I, _____, do solemnly swear (or affirm) that I will support and defend the Constitution of the United States and the constitution of the State of Colorado, against all enemies, foreign and domestic; that I will bear true faith and allegiance to the same; that I take this obligation freely, without any mental reservation or purpose of evasion; and that I will well and faithfully discharge the duties upon which I am about to enter.

"And I do further swear (or affirm) that I do not advocate, nor am I a member of any political party or organization that advocates the overthrow of the Government of the United States or of this State by force or violence; and that during such time as I am a member of the (name of civil defense organization), I will not advocate nor become a member of any political party or organization that advocates the overthrow of the Government of the United States or of this State by force or violence."

TEACHERS' LOYALTY

Colorado Rev. Stat. 1953, § 123–17–14 (Supp. 1961). *Public school teachers required to take oath to support Federal and State Constitutions.*—(1) Any person now holding a certificate to teach in any public school in the State of Colorado or who shall hereafter be issued a certificate to teach in such public schools within the State of Colorado shall subscribe to the following oath or affirmation: *Provided,* That any such person employed to teach in a temporary capacity who is a citizen of a nation other than the United States shall not be required to take such oath:

"I solemnly swear or affirm that I will support the Constiution of the State of Colorado and of the United States of America and the laws of the State of Colorado and of the United States, and will teach, by precept or example, respect for the flags of the United States and of the State of Colorado, respect for law and order and undivided allegiance to the government of one country, the United States of America."

(2) The said oath or affirmation shall be executed in triplicate and one copy filed in the office of the State commissioner of education, one copy retained by the applicant making such oath or affirmation, and one copy shall be filed with the officer or board in charge of any such public school.

Id. § 123–17–15 (Supp. 1961). *Private school teachers required to take oath to support Federal and State Constitutions.*—Every teacher employed to teach in any private or parochial school or in any academy, college, or university or other institution of learning in the State of Colorado, before entering upon, or continuing, the discharge of his or her duties, shall be required to take the same oath or affirmation of allegiance as that prescribed for public school teachers in section 123–17–14: *Provided*, That any such person employed to teach in a temporary capacity who is a citizen of a nation other than the United States shall not be required to take such oath. Such oath or affirmation shall be executed in triplicate and one copy filed in the office of the State commissioner of education, one copy retained by the person making such oath or affirmation, and one copy filed with the officer or board in charge of such private or parochial school, academy, college, or university or other institution of learning in which such person is employed, or is to be employed, within the State of Colorado.

Id. § 123–17–16. *Penalty.*—Any person who, being in charge of any public, private or parochial school or any academy, college, university or other institution of learning within the State of Colorado, who shall allow or permit any teacher to enter upon the discharge of his duties or give instruction therein, unless such teacher shall have taken and subscribed to the oath or affirmation of allegiance provided for, shall be guilty of a misdemeanor and upon conviction thereof shall be punished by a fine of not more than one hundred dollars or six months' imprisonment, or both.

Exclusion From the Bar

Rules governing admission to the Bar of the State of Colorado require that applicants for admission on motion shall state under oath that they "[believe] in the form of government of the United States and [have] never been disloyal thereto". (Rule 204; question 2 on the application form.) The Rules impose an identical requirement with respect to all other applicants. (Rule 204; question 2 on the application form.)

Rule 220 sets forth the oath of admission, which oath reads in relevant part:

I Do Solemnly Swear by the Ever-Living God that:

I will support the Constitution of the United States and the constitution of the State of Colorado;

Correspondence received from the Colorado State Board of Law Examiners states "the Supreme Court of Colorado has never outlined any general or specific policy concerning" the admission to practice of "Communists, subversives, etc."

CONNECTICUT

UNLAWFUL ADVOCACY

SEDITION

Connecticut Gen. Stat. Anno. § 53–5. *Unlawful acts and penalty.*—Any person who speaks, or writes, prints and publicly exhibits or distributes, or who publicly exhibits, posts, or advertises any disloyal, scurrilous, or abusive matter concerning the form of government of the United States, its military forces, flag, or uniforms, or any matter which is intended to bring them into contempt or which creates or fosters opposition to organized government, shall be fined not more than five hundred dollars or imprisoned not more than five years or both.

Id. § 53–6. *Assemblage to advocate sedition.*—Any person who, in public or before any assemblage of ten or more persons, advocates in any language any measure, doctrine, proposal or propaganda intended to injuriously affect the Government of the United States or the State of Connecticut shall be fined not more than one thousand dollars or imprisoned not more than three years or both.

Annotation:

State v. *Sinchuk*, 96 Connecticut 605, 115A. 33 (1921). Defendant was accused of sedition in that "with force and arms [he] did publicly exhibit or advertise certain disloyal, scurrillous, or abusive matter concerning the form of government of the United States and its flag and certain matter which was intended to bring them into contempt, or which creates or fosters opposition to organized government * * *." Defendant demurred, in part, on grounds that the statute was unconstitutional. The Supreme Court of Errors of Connecticut held the statute constitutional over objections that it fixed no ascertainable guilt and violated various provisions of the State and Federal Constitutions.

LOYALTY OF STATE OFFICERS AND EMPLOYEES

1. ELECTIVE AND NONELECTIVE PERSONNEL

Connecticut Constitution, Art. X, § 1. *Oath.*—Members of the General Assembly, and all officers, executive and judicial, shall, before they enter on the duties of their respective offices, take the following oath or affirmation, to wit:

You do solemnly swear (or affirm, as the case may be) that you will support the Constitution of the United States, and the constitution of the State of Connecticut, so long as you continue a citizen thereof; and that you will faithfully discharge, according to law, the duties of the office of _____ to the best of your abilities. So help you God.

67

2. CIVIL DEFENSE PERSONNEL

Connecticut Gen. Stat. Anno. § 28–12. *Loyalty oath required.*—No person shall be employed or associated in any capacity in any civil defense organization established under this chapter who advocates a change by force or violence in the constitutional form of the Government of the United States or of this State or the overthrow of any government in the United States by force or violence, or who has been convicted of or is under indictment or information charging any subversive act against the United States. Each person who is appointed to serve in an organization for civil defense shall, before entering upon his duties, take an oath verbally before a local civil defense officer or officers empowered by the director to enlist volunteers, which oath shall be substantially as follows: "I, _____, do solemnly swear (or affirm) that I will support and defend the Constitution of the United States and the constitution of the State of Connecticut, against all enemies, foreign and domestic; that I will bear true faith and allegiance to the same; that I take this obligation freely, without any mental reservation or purpose of evasion; and that I will well and faithfully discharge the duties upon which I am about to enter. And I do further swear (or affirm) that I do not advocate, nor am I a member of an affiliate of any organization, group or combination of persons that advocates the overthrow of the Government of the United States or of this State by force or violence or which is totalitarian, Fascist, Communist, or subversive, or which has adopted or shows a policy of advocating or approving the commission of acts of force or violence to deny other persons their rights under the Constitution of the United States, or which seeks to alter the form of Government of the United States by unconstitutional means; and that during such time as I am a member of the (name of the civil defense organization) I will not advocate nor become a member or an affiliate of any such organization or group, or combination of persons. And I do further swear (or affirm) that I am not a Communist or Fascist."

Exclusion From the Bar

Connecticut does not appear to have any rule or regulation which pertains to the admission of persons who are or have been Communists or subversives. Similarly, the various forms employed by the State do not contain any questions directly on the subject.

DELAWARE

SEDITION

11 Delaware Code § 862. *Unlawful acts and penalty.*— (a) As used in this section, "sedition" means—

(1) Any utterance or conduct, either individually or in connection or combination with another or others, which proximately causes any violence or demonstration of violence against this State or the United States, or clearly advocates a change by means of violence in the form of the State or Federal Government;

(2) The distribution, through sale, gift or otherwise, of any printed or written matter in any form which proximately causes any violence or demonstration of violence against this State or the United States, or clearly advocates a change by means of violence in the form of the State or the Federal Government; or

(3) Organizing or helping to organize, or knowingly becoming or remaining a member of an assembly, society, or group having as its purpose or one of its purposes violence, or a demonstration of violence, against this State or the United States, or the advocacy of a change, through violence, in the form of the State or the Federal Government.

(b) Whoever commits any act of sedition is guilty of a felony and shall be fined not less than $100 nor more than $10,000 or imprisoned not more than 20 years, or both.

(c) No person shall be convicted of sedition unless on the testimony of two witnesses to the same utterance, conduct or act or on confession in open court.

REGISTRATION

20 Delaware Code § 3501 (Supp. 1962). *"Communist Party", "Communist front organization", and "Communist" defined.*—The "Communist Party," for the purpose of this chapter, is any organization which is substantially directed, dominated or controlled by the Union of Soviet Socialist Republics or by any of its satellites, or which in any manner advocates, or acts to further, the world Communist movement.

A "Communist front organization," for the purpose of this chapter, is any organization which is listed as such by the Attorney General of the United States.

A "Communist" is a person who: (1) Is a member of the Communist Party, notwithstanding the fact that he may not pay dues to, or hold a card in, said party; or

(2) Knowingly contributes funds or any character of property to the Communist Party; or

(3) Commits or advocates the commission of any act reasonably calculated to further the overthrow of the Government of the United

States of America, the Government of the State of Delaware, or the government of any political subdivision of either of them, by force or violence; or

(4) Commits or advocates the commission of any act reasonably calculated to further the overthrow of the Government of the United States, the government of the State of Delaware, or the government of any political subdivision of either of them, by unlawful or unconstitutional means, and the substitution of a Communist government or a government intended to be substantially directed, dominated or controlled by the Union of Soviet Socialist Republics or its satellites.

Id. § 3502 (Supp. 1962). *Communists, members of Communist front organizations and officers of the Communist Party required to register.*— (a) Each person entering this State who is a Communist or is a member of a Communist front organization, shall register immediately with the State police of the State of Delaware. Each person who is a resident of the State of Delaware and who is a Communist or is a member of a Communist front organization, shall register with the State police of the State of Delaware within 30 days after June 12, 1953, and thereafter between the first and fifteenth day of January in each and every year.

(b) Such registration shall be under oath and shall set forth the name (including any assumed names used or in use), address, business, occupation, purpose of presence in the State of Delaware, sources of income, place of birth, places of former residence, and features of identification, including fingerprints, of the registrant; organizations of which registrant is a member and any other information requested by the State police which is relevant to the purposes of this chapter.

(c) Each and every officer in the Communist Party residing in the State of Delaware and each and every officer of Communist front organizations residing in the State of Delaware shall register or cause to be registered said party organization with the State police. Such registration shall be under oath and shall include the name of the organization, the location of its principal office and of its offices and meeting places in the State of Delaware; the names, real and assumed of its officers; a financial statement reflecting receipts and disbursements and by whom paid and to whom paid; and any other information requested by the State police which is relevant to the purpose of this chapter.

Such registration shall be made within 30 days after June 12, 1953, and thereafter between the first and fifteenth days of January in each and every year.

(d) Failure to register as herein required, or the making of any registration which contains any material false statement or omission, shall constitute a felony and shall be punishable by a fine of not less than $1,000, or more than $10,000, or by imprisonment of not less than two or more than ten years, or by both.

Id. § 3503 (Supp. 1962). *Enforcement.*—The attorney general of the State of Delaware, and all law enforcement officers of this State, shall each be charged with the duty of enforcing the provisions of this chapter.

EXCLUSION FROM THE ELECTIVE PROCESS

15 Delaware Code § 4104. *Political party advocating subversion, sedition, or treason barred from ballot.*

* * * * * * *

"Political party" means an organization of bona fide citizens and voters of any county in this State, which shall, by means of a convention, primary election or otherwise, nominate candidates for public office to be filled by the people at any general or special election within this State. No political party shall be recognized and given a place on the ballot which advocates the overthrow by force or violence, or which advocates or carries on a program of sedition or of treason by radio, speech or press, of our local, State or National Government. No newly organized political party shall be permitted on the ballot until it has filed an affidavit by its officers, under oath, that it does not advocate the overthrow of local, State or National Government by force or violence, and that it is not affiliated in any way with any political party or organization, or subdivisions of organizations, which does advocate such a policy by radio, speech or press. No organization shall be regarded as a political party that does not represent at least 500 bona fide citizens and voters of the county in which it exists. If the clerk of the peace has any doubt as to the sufficiency of the number of bona fide voters represented by any organization in any county, he may demand a certificate containing the signatures and addresses of 250 voters belonging to such an organization.

"Principal political parties," or words equivalent thereto or so designating political parties designate the Democratic Party and the Republican Party.

LOYALTY OF STATE OFFICERS AND EMPLOYEES

1. ELECTIVE AND NONELECTIVE PERSONNEL

Delaware Constitution, Art. XIV. *Oath.*—Members of the General Assembly and all public officers executive and judicial, except such inferior officers as shall be by law exempted, shall, before they enter upon the duties of their respective offices, take and subscribe the following oath or affirmation:

"I do solemnly swear (or affirm) that I will support the Constitution of the United States, and the constitution of the State of Delaware, and that I will faithfully discharge the duties of the office of _____ according to the best of my ability"; and all such officers, except as aforesaid, who shall have been chosen at any election, shall, before they enter upon the duties of their respective offices, take, and subscribe the oath or affirmation above prescribed, together with the following addition thereto, as part thereof:

"And I do further solemnly swear (or affirm) that I have not directly or indirectly paid, offered or promised to pay, contributed, or offered or promised to contribute, any money or other valuable thing as a consideration or reward for the giving or withholding a vote at the election at which I was elected to said office."

No other oath, declaration or test shall be required as a qualification for any office of public trust.

2. NONELECTIVE PERSONNEL

29 Delaware Code § 5102. *Oath to support the Constitution.*— Every officer and employee of the State of Delaware or any political subdivision thereof shall take an oath to support and defend the Constitution of the United States and the constitution of the State of Delaware before commencing his duties as such officer or employee.

3. CIVIL DEFENSE PERSONNEL

20. Delaware Code § 3118. *Loyalty oath required.*—No person shall be employed or associated in any capacity in any civil defense organization established under this chapter who advocates a change by force or violence in the constitutional form of the Government of the United States or in this State or the overthrow of any government in the United States by force or violence, or who has been convicted of or is under indictment or information charging any subversive act against the United States.

Each person who is appointed to serve in an organization for civil defense shall, before entering upon his duties, take an oath, in writing, before a person authorized to administer oaths in this State, which oath shall be substantially as follows:

"I, --------------------, do solemnly swear (or affirm) that I will support and defend the Constitution of the United States and the constitution of the State of Delaware, against all enemies, foreign and domestic; that I will bear true faith and allegiance to the same; that I take this obligation freely, without any mental reservation or purpose of evasion; and that I will well and faithfully discharge the duties about which I am about to enter.

"And I do further swear (or affirm) that I do not advocate, nor am I a member of any political party or organization that advocates, the overthrow of the Government of the United States or of this State by force or violence; and that during such time as I am a member of the department of civil defense I will not advocate nor become a member of any political party or organization that advocates the overthrow of the Government of the United States or of this State by force or violence."

Id. § 3119. *Penalty.*—Whoever violates any provision of this chapter or any rule, order, or regulation made pursuant to this chapter shall be fined not more than $1,000 or imprisoned not more than 120 days, or both.

TEACHERS' LOYALTY

29 Delaware Code § 5102. *Oath to support the Constitution.*—Every officer and employee of the State of Delaware or any political subdivision thereof shall take an oath to support and defend the Constitution of the United States and the constitution of the State of Delaware before commencing his duties as such officer or employee.

14 Delaware Code § 1204 (Supp. 1962). *Teacher's certificate subject to revocation for disloyalty.*—A professional status certificate may be revoked upon dismissal for immorality, misconduct in office, incompetency, willful neglect of duty or disloyalty, provided full and fair hearing and appeal shall have been allowed as elsewhere set forth in this title.

A teacher shall not forfeit his professional status certificate and his rights appertaining if he be transferred against his will to an educational position for which he is not certified.

EXCLUSION FROM THE BAR

Question 16 on the application for registration as a student of law inquires whether the registrant can conscientionsly take the oath of admission. It reads as follows:

16. Every attorney admitted to practice in Delaware is required to subscribe to the following oath:

I, _____, do solemnly swear (or affirm) that I will support the Constitution of the United States and the constitution of the State of Delaware; that I will behave myself in the office of an attorney within the courts according to the best of my learning and ability and with all good fidelity as well to the court as to the client; that I will use no falsehood, nor delay any person's cause through lucre or malice.

(a) Do you know of any reason why you could not conscientiously subscribe to the foregoing oath?—Yes or No.

(b) If the answer is in the affirmative, furnish details on an attached sheet.

Correspondence received from the Board of Bar Examiners of the State of Delaware explains that the board has "never dealt with an application involving a known Communist and [has] no general practice or policy concerning such applications. Each case is determined on its own merits."

FLORIDA

Unlawful Advocacy

1. ANARCHY

Florida State. Anno. § 876.01. *Criminal anarchy, criminal communism, etc., defined.*—Criminal anarchy, criminal communism, criminal nazi-ism, or criminal fascism are doctrines that existing form of constitutional government should be overthrown by force or violence or by any other unlawful means, or by assassination of officials of the government of the United States or of the several States. The advocacy of such doctrines either by word of mouth or writing or the promotion of such doctrines independently or in collaboration with or under the guidance of officials of a foreign state or an international revolutionary party or group is a felony.

Id. § 876.02. *Unlawful acts and penalty.*—Any person who—

(1) By word of mouth or writing advocates, advises, or teaches the duty, necessity, or propriety of overthrowing or overturning existing forms of constitutional government by force or violence; of disobeying or sabotaging or hindering the carrying out of the laws, orders, or decrees of duly constituted civil, naval, or military authorities; or by the assassination of officials of the Government of the United States or of the State of Florida, or by any unlawful means or under the guidance of or in collaboration with officials, agents, or representatives of a foreign state or an international revolutionary party or group; or

(2) Prints, publishes, edits, issues, or knowingly circulates, sells, distributes, or publicly displays any book, paper, document, or written or printed matter in any form, containing or advocating, advising or teaching the doctrine that constitutional government should be overthrown by force, violence, or any unlawful means; or

(3) Openly, willfully and deliberately urges, advocates, or justifies by word of mouth or writing the assassination or unlawful killing or assaulting any official of the Government of the United States or of the State of Florida because of his official character, or any other crime, with intent to teach, spread, or advocate the propriety of the doctrines of criminal anarchy, criminal communism, criminal nazi-ism, or criminal fascism; or

(4) Organizes or helps to organize or becomes a member of any society, group, or assembly of persons formed to teach or advocate such doctrines; or

(5) Becomes a member of, associated with or promotes the interest of any criminal anarchistic, communistic, nazi-istic, or fascistic organization, or helps to organize or becomes a member of or affiliated with any subsidiary organization or associated group of persons who advocates, teaches, or advises the principles of criminal anarchy, criminal communism, criminal nazi-ism, or criminal fascism;

75

Shall be guilty of a felony and upon conviction thereof be subject to imprisonment for not more than ten years or a fine of not more than ten thousand dollars, or both.

Id. § 876.03 *Assemblage to advocate criminal anarchy and criminal communism, etc.*—Whenever two or more persons assemble for the purpose of promoting, advocating, or teaching the doctrine of criminal anarchy, criminal communism, criminal nazi-ism, or criminal fascism, as defined in § 876.01 of this law, such an assembly or organization is unlawful, and every person voluntarily participating therein by his presence, aid, or instigation shall be guilty of a felony and upon conviction thereof shall be subject to imprisonment for not more than ten years or a fine of not more than ten thousand dollars, or both.

Id. § 876.04, as amended, Sess. Laws 1955, ch. 29615, § 33. *Permitting premises to be used to advocate criminal anarchy, criminal communism, etc.*—No owner, agent, superintendent, janitor, caretaker, or occupant of any place, building or room, shall willfully and knowingly permit therein any assemblage of persons prohibited by § 876.03 and if such person after notification that the premises are so used, permits such use to be continued, he shall be guilty of a misdemeanor and upon conviction thereof subject to imprisonment for not more than one year or fine of not more than one thousand dollars, or both.

2. SEDITION

Florida Stat. Anno. § 779.05. *Inciting insurrection or sedition; penalty.*—If any person shall incite an insurrection or sedition amongst any portion or class of the population of this State, or shall attempt by writing, speaking, or by any other means to incite such insurrection or sedition, the person so offending shall be punished by imprisonment in the State prison not exceeding twenty years.

3. SUBVERSIVE ACTIVITIES

Florida Stat. Anno. § 876.22 (Supp. 1963). *"Organizations," "Subversive organization," "Foreign government," and "Subversive person" defined.*—As used in §§ 876.23–876.31:

(1) "Organizations" means an organization, corporation, company, partnership, association, trust, foundation, fund, club, society, committee, political party, or any group of persons, whether or not incorporated, permanently, or temporarily associated together for joint action or advancement or views on any subject or subjects.

(2) "Subversive organization" means any organization which engages in or advocates, abets, advises, or teaches, or a purpose of which is to engage in or advocate, abet, advise, or teach activities intended to overthrow, destroy, or to assist in the overthrow, destruction of, the constitutional form of the Government of the United States, the constitution or government of the State, or of any political subdivision of either of them, by revolution, force, violence, or other unlawful means.

(3) "Foreign subversive organization" means any organization, directed, dominated or controlled directly or indirectly by a foreign government which engages in or advocates, abets, advises, or teaches, or a purpose of which is to engage in or to advocate, abet, advise, or teach, activities intended to overthrow, destroy, or to assist in the overthrow,

destruction of the constitutional form of the Government of the United States, or of the State, or of any political subdivision of either of them, and to establish in place thereof any form of government the direction and control of which is to be vested in, or exercised by or under, the domination or control of any foreign government, organization, or individual.

(4) "Foreign government" means the government of any country, nation, or group of nations other than the Government of the United States of America or of one of the States thereof.

(5) "Subversive person" means any person who commits, attempts to commit, or aids in the commission, or advocates, abets, advises, or teaches by any means any person to commit, attempt to commit, or aid in the commission of any act intended to overthrow, destroy, or to assist in the overthrow, destruction of the constitutional form of the Government of the United States, or of the State, or any political subdivision of either of them, by revolution, force, violence, or other unlawful means; or who is a member of a subversive organization or a foreign subversive organization.

Id. § 876.23 (Supp. 1963). *Unlawful acts and penalty.*—(1) It shall be a felony for any person knowingly and willfully to:

(a) Commit, attempt to commit, or aid in the commission of any act intended to overthrow, destroy, to assist the overthrow, destruction of, the constitutional form of the Government of the United States, or of the State, or any political subdivision of either of them, by revolution, force, violence, or other unlawful means; or

(b) Advocate, abet, advise, or teach by any means any person to commmit, attempt to commit, or assist in the commission of any such act under such circumstances as to constitute a clear and present danger to the security of the United States, or of the State, or of any political subdivision of either of them; or

(c) Conspire with one or more persons to commit any such act; or

(d) Assist in the formation or participate in the management or to contribute to the support of any subversive organization or foreign subversive organization knowing said organization to be a subversive organization or a foreign subversive organization; or

(e) Destroy any books, records, or files, or secretes any funds in this State of a subversive organization or a foreign subversive organization, knowing said organization to be such.

(2) Any person who violates any of the provisions of this section shall be fined not more than twenty thousand dollars, or imprisoned in the penitentiary for not less than one year nor more than twenty years, or both.

Id. § 876.24 (Supp. 1963). *Membership in subversive organization unlawful.*—It shall be a felony for any person after the effective date of this law to become, or after July 1, 1953, to remain a member of a subversive organization or a foreign subversive organization knowing said organization to be a subversive organization or foreign subversive organization. Any person convicted of violating this section shall be fined not more than five thousand dollars, or imprisoned in the penitentiary for not less than one year nor more than five years, or both.

Id. § 876.25 (Supp. 1963). *Additional penalty.*—Any person convicted by a court of competent jurisdiction of violating any of the provisions of §§ 876.23, 876.24, in addition to all other penalties therein provided, shall from the date of such conviction be barred from:

(1) Holding any office, elective or appointive, or any other position of profit or trust in or employment by the government of the State or of any agency thereof or of any county, municipal corporation or other political subdivision of said State;

(2) Filing or offering for election to any public office in the State; or

(3) Voting in any election held in this State.

Id. § 876.26 (Supp. 1963). *Subversive organizations outlawed.*— It shall be unlawful for any subversive organization or foreign subversive organization to exist or function in the State and any organization which by a court of competent jurisdiction is found to have violated the provisions of this section shall be dissolved, and if it be a corporation organized and existing under the laws of the State a finding by a court of competent jurisdiction that it has violated the provisions of this section shall constitute legal cause for forfeiture of its charter and its charter shall be forfeited, and all funds, books, records, and files of every kind and all other property of any organization found to have violated the provisions of this section shall be seized by and for the State, the funds to be deposited in the State treasury and the books, records, files and other property to be turned over to the attorney general of Florida.

Id. § 876.27 (Supp. 1963). *Enforcement.*—The attorney general of the State, all prosecuting attorneys, the secretary of state, and all law enforcement officers of this State shall each be charged with the duty of enforcing the provisions of §§ 876.22–876.31.

Id. § 876.28 (Supp. 1963). *Grand jury investigation.*—The judge of any court exercising general criminal jurisdiction when in his discretion it appears appropriate, or when informed by the attorney general that there is information or evidence of the character described in § 876.27 to be considered by the grand jury, shall charge the grand jury to inquire into violations of §§ 876.22–876.31 for the purpose of proper action, and further to inquire generally into the purposes, processes and activities and any other matters affecting communism or any related or other subversive organizations, associations, groups, or persons.

NOTE.—Sections 876.22 to 876.30 are cited the Subversive Activities Law.

Annotation:

Gibson v. *Florida Legislative Investigating Committees*, 108 So. 2d 729 (1958), certiorari denied, 360 U.S. 919, 79 S. Ct. 1443, 3 L. Ed. 2d 1535. This case involved a legislative committee's petition for an order compelling answer to questions addressed to witnesses in the course of an inquiry as to whether members of the Communist Party or fellow travelers had penetrated and infiltrated the NAACP to an extent requiring State action. During the course of its opinion the Supreme Court of Florida held that Congress had preempted the field of controlling seditions against the Government of the United States but that the State of Florida had the power to control or prevent sedition against the State. On this point the court said:

"We do not accord to the opinion of the highest court in the land in *Commonwealth of Pennsylvania* v. *Nelson, supra,* the broad comprehensive sweep that is contended for it by the appellants and even conceded by the briefs of the appellee committee. Admittedly, that decision has been the subject of much comment and some adverse criticism. See Report of Committee on Federal-State Relationships, Conference of Chief Justices, August 23, 1958. In support of the decision see remarks of Chief Justice Charles Alvin Jones of Pennsylvania filed with the Conference on the same date.

"The supreme courts of some States have taken the position that the *Nelson* decision determined that by the passage of the Smith Act, Congress has preempted every aspect of the field of controlling seditious conduct, even when directed against a particular State. Cf. *Albertson* v. *Millard*, 345 Mich. 519, 77 N.W.2d 104; *Braden* v. *Commonwealth*, *Ky.*, 291 S.W.2d 843. Illustrative of a more limited interpretation of the Nelson opinion is *Commonwealth* v. *Gilbert*, 343 Mass. 71, 134 N.E.2d 13. There, the Supreme Judicial Court of Massachusetts held that because of the *Nelson* case an indictment charging advocacy of the violent overthrow of the government of Massachusetts would have to be quashed on the theory that Congress had preempted the field. The Massachusetts court, however, expressly stated that in its view there could be some kinds of sedition directed so exclusively against the State as to fall outside the scope of *Commonwealth of Pennsylvania* v. *Nelson*, *supra*.

"In *State* v. *Diez*, Fla. 1957, 97 So. 2d 105, we ourselves have previously taken note of the *Nelson* decision. As against the identical contention now submitted by these appellants, we upheld Section 876.22, Florida Statutes, FSA., requiring a so-called Loyalty Oath as a condition to public employment in this State. We there pointed out and we here repeat for emphasis that in the *Nelson* case the State of Pennsylvania had indicted Nelson for advocacy of the violent overthrow of the Government of the United States contrary to the Pennsylvania statute. See *Commonwealth* v. *Nelson*, 377 Pa. 58, 104 A.2d 133. Nowhere in the charges against Nelson were there any allegations of seditious conduct against the State. The decision of the court must necessarily be read in the light of the factual situation which produces it. In the *Nelson* case the Supreme Court of the United States was confronted solely and entirely with the charge of seditious conduct against the United States in violation of a State statute. It is inconceivable to us that the decision could or should be given controlling effect in situations which were not even remotely before the Supreme Court of the United States when its decision was rendered. We certainly respect the authoritative effect of the *Nelson* decision to the extent that it holds that Congress has preempted the field of controlling sedition against the Government of the United States. Under all recognized bases for interpreting and construing judicial decisions, we do not feel compelled to accord to the *Nelson* opinion a more comprehensive or far-reaching effect.

"We adopt this view simply because we are not persuaded by *Nelson* or any other decision with the virility of the States to cope with purely internal problems can be reduced to a condition of impotency by any astute process of judicial sterilization."

State v. *Kelly*, 76 So. 2d 798 (1954). This case involved habeas corpus proceedings to obtain the release from custody of various persons for refusing to answer questions before the grand jury with reference to contacts and associations with the Communist Party and subversive organizations. Each defendant refused to answer on the ground his answers might tend to incriminate him. All invoked the protection of the Fifth Amendment. The court ordered the petitioners discharged stating that since the questions asked them before the grand jury were such that the answers might constitute a link in the chain of evidence leading to their conviction for criminal communism and since they invoked the constitutional privilege against self-incrimination, their commitment for contempt for refusing to answer such questions was without legal authority. The court reasoned that since the Florida law (§ 876.01 to 876.04) was patterned after the Smith Act, 18 U.S.C. 2385—"both having been designed for the same purpose"—interpretation of the former should follow the latter. As a result, it felt compelled to follow *Blau* v. *United States*, 340 U.S. 159, 71 S. Ct. 223, 95 L. Ed. 170 (1950).

State v. *Diez*, 977 So. 2d 105 (1957). Defendant was charged with perjury in that having been required by law to take an oath, and being under oath, he swore that he did not and would not lend his aid to the Communist Party. In point of fact, he had given aid to the Party. The Supreme Court of Florida sustained the lower court's decision to grant defendant's motion to quash the information holding that they were defective for failing to specify that defendant had "willfully" given to aid to the Communist Party. One of the grounds supporting the motion to quash not accepted by the court was "that by Federal law the field of sedition legislation had been preempted by the Federal Government" and therefore, the State statutes relied on were invalid. After a review of *Pennsylvania* v. *Nelson*, 350 U.S. 497, 76 S. Ct. 477, 483, 100 L. Ed. 640 (1956) the court concluded by saying:

"Up to this point we have treated of the question whether or not the statutes requiring loyalty oaths have become ineffectual because of the opinion of the Supreme Court of the United States in *Commonwealth of Pennsylvania* v. *Nelson*, * * * We think they have not."

Exclusion From the Elective Process

Florida State Anno. § 97.021(6) (a). *General purpose of a legitimate "political party."*

*   *   *   *   *   *   *

Any group of citizens may organize as a "political party" if the general purpose of the organization is for election to office of qualified persons, and the determination of public issues under the accepted democratic processes of the United States.

*   *   *   *   *   *   *

Id. § 99.021(1) (i). *Candidates for public office required to take loyalty oath.*—Every candidate for nomination to any office is required to take and subscribe to an oath or affirmation in writing, in which he shall state:

*   *   *   *   *   *   *

(i) That he has taken the oath as required by §§ 876.05–876.10.

Id. § 876.05 *Form of oath.*—All persons who now or hereafter are employed by or who now or hereafter are on the payroll of the State, or any of its departments and agencies, subdivisions, counties, cities, school boards and districts of the free public school system of the State or counties, or institutions of higher learning and all candidates for public office, are hereby required to take an oath before any person duly authorized to take acknowledgments of instruments for public record in the State in the following form:

"I, _____, a citizen of the State of Florida and of the United States of America, and being employed by or an officer of _____ and a recipient of public funds as such employee or officer, do hereby solemnly swear or affirm that I will support the Constitution of the United States and of the State of Florida; that I am not a member of the Communist Party; that I have not and will not lend my aid, support, advice, counsel or influence to the Communist Party; that I do not believe in the overthrow of the Government of the United States or of the State of Florida by force or violence; that I am not a member of any organization or party which believes in or teaches, directly or indirectly, the overthrow of the Government of the United States or of Florida by force or violence."

And said oath shall be filed with the records of the governing official or employing governmental agency prior to the approval of any voucher for the payment of salary, expenses, or other compensation.

Id. § 876.10 (Supp. 1963). *Penalty.*—If any person required by the provisions of §§ 876.05–876.10 to execute the oath herein required executes such oath, and it is subsequently proven that at the time of the execution of said oath said individual was guilty of making a false statement in said oath, he shall be guilty of perjury, and shall be prosecuted and punished for the crime of perjury in the event of conviction.

Id. § 876.23 (Supp. 1963). *Subversive activities and penalty.*— (1) It shall be a felony for any person knowingly and willfully to:

(a) Commit, attempt to commit, or aid in the commission of any act intended to overthrow, destroy, to assist the overthrow, destruction of, the constitutional form of the Government of the United States, or of the State, or any political subdivision of either of them, by revolution, force, violence, or other unlawful means; or

(b) Advocate, abet, advise, or teach by any means any person to commit, attempt to commit, or assist in the commission of any such act under such circumstances as to constitute a clear and present danger to the security of the United States, or of the State, or of any political subdivision of either of them; or

(c) Conspire with one or more persons to commit any such act; or

(d) Assist in the formation or participate in the management or to contribute to the support of any subversive organization or foreign subversive organization knowing said organization to be a subversive organization or a foreign subversive organization; or

(e) Destroy any books, records, or files, or secretes any funds in this State of a subversive organization or a foreign subversive organization, knowing said organization to be such.

(2) Any person who violates any of the provisions of this section shall be fined not more than twenty thousand dollars, or imprisoned in the penitentiary for not less than one year nor more than twenty years, or both.

Id. § 876.24 (Supp. 1963). *Membership in subversive organization unlawful.*—It shall be a felony for any person after the effective date of this law to become, or after July 1, 1953, to remain a member of a subversive organization or a foreign subversive organization knowing said organization to be a subversive organization or foreign subversive organization. Any person convicted of violating this section shall be fined not more than five thousand dollars, or imprisoned in the penitentiary for not less than one year nor more than five years, or both.

Id. § 876.25 (Supp. 1963). *Persons convicted of subversive activities disenfranchised and barred from public office.*—Any person convicted by a court of competent jurisdiction of violating any of the provisions of §§ 876.23, 876.24, in addition to all other penalties therein provided, shall from the date of such conviction be barred from:

(1) Holding any office, elective or appointed, or any other position of profit or trust in or employment by the government of the State or of any agency thereof or of any county, municipal corporation or other political subdivision of said state;

(2) Filing or offering for election to any public office in the State; or

(3) Voting in any election held in this State.

Id. § 876.30 (Supp. 1963). *Persons convicted as subversive person ineligible to be candidate.*—No person shall become a candidate nor shall be certified by any political party as a candidate for election to any public office created by the constitution or laws of this State if he has ever been tried and convicted as a subversive person as defined in § 876.22.

NOTE.—For definition of subversive person, see Subversive Activities under Unlawful Advocacy, *supra.*

Annotation:

1952 Op. Atty. Gen. 120. The clerk of the circuit court should preserve the candidate's oath and the loyalty oaths required to be executed by §§ 99.021 and 876.05, respectively, for an indefinite period.

LOYALTY OF STATE OFFICERS AND EMPLOYEES

1. ELECTIVE AND NONELECTIVE PERSONNEL

Florida Stat. Anno. § 876.05 (Supp. 1963). *Loyalty oath required.*—All persons who now or hereafter are employed by or who now or hereafter are on the payroll of the State, or any of its departments and agencies, subdivisions, counties, cities, school boards, and districts of the free public school system of the State or counties, or institutions of higher learning, and all candidates for public office, are hereby required to take an oath before any person duly authorized to take acknowledgments of instruments for public record in the State in the following form:

I, _____, a citizen of the State of Florida and of the United States of America, and being employed by or an officer of _____ and a recipient of public funds as such employee or officer, do hereby solemnly swear or affirm that I will support the Constitution of the United States and of the State of Florida; that I am not a member of the Communist Party; that I have not and will not lend my aid, support, advice, counsel or influence to the Communist Party; that I do not believe in the overthrow of the Government of the United States or of the State of Florda by force or violence; that I am not a member of any organization or party which believes in or teaches, directly or indirectly, the overthrow of the Government of the United States or of Florida by force or violence.

And said oath shall be filed with the records of the governing official or employing governmental agency prior to the approval of any voucher for the payment of salary, expenses, or other compensation.

Id. § 876.06. *Failure to execute oath cause for discharge.*—If any person required by §§ 876.05–876.10 to take the oath herein provided for fails to execute the same, the governing authority under which such person is employed shall cause said person to be immediately discharged, and his name removed from the payroll, and such person shall not be permitted to receive any payment as an employee or as an officer where he or she was serving.

Id. § 876.07. *Engaging in activities contrary to oath cause for discharge.*—Any person having taken the oath provided for in § 876.05 and who thereafter should become a member of the Communist Party or who lends aid, support, advice, counsel or influence to the Communist Party or who expresses any belief in or advocates the overthrow of the Government of the United States or of the State by violence or force or thereafter becomes a member of an organization or party which believes in or teaches directly or indirectly the overthrow of the Government of the United States or of the State by force or violence, shall immediately be discharged from his employment by the employing authority and his name shall be removed from the payroll, and thereafter such person shall not be permitted to receive any payment as an employee or an officer where he or she then was serving. Any person seeking to qualify for public office who fails or refuses to file the oath required by this act shall be held to have failed to qualify as a candidate for public office, and the name of such person shall not be printed on the ballot as a qualified candidate.

Id. § 876.08 (Supp. 1963). *Penalty for failing to discharge employee.*—Any governing authority or person, under whom any employee is serving or by whom employed who shall knowingly or carelessly permit any such employee to continue in employment after failing to comply with the provisions of §§ 876.05–876.10, shall be guilty of a misdemeanor and shall be punished by a fine not exceeding five hundred dollars or by imprisonment not exceeding six months or by both fine and imprisonment.

Id. § 876.09 (Supp. 1963). *Scope of law.*—(1) The provisions of §§ 876.05–876.10 shall apply to all employees and elected officers of the State, including the Governor and constitutional officers and all employees and elected officers of all cities, towns, counties, and political subdivisions, including the educational system.

(2) This act shall take precedence over all laws relating to merit, and of civil service law.

Id. § 876.10 (Supp. 1963). *Penalty.*—If any person required by the provisions of §§ 876.05–876.10 to execute the oath herein required executes such oath, and it is subsequently proven that at the time of the execution of said oath said individual was guilty of making a false statement in said oath, he shall be guilty of perjury, and shall be prosecuted and punished for the crime of perjury in the event of conviction.

Id. § 876.25 (Supp. 1963). *Persons convicted of engaging in subversive activities or membership in subversive organizations barred from public office or employment.*—Any person convicted by a court of competent jurisdiction of violating any of the provisions of §§ 876.23, 876.24, in addition to all other penalties therein provided, shall from the date of such conviction be barred from:

(1) Holding any office, elective or appointive, or any other position of profit or trust in or employment by the government of the State or of any agency thereof or of any county, municipal corporation or other political subdivision of said State;

(2) Filing or offering for election to any public office in the State; or

(3) Voting in any election held in this State.

Id. § 876.29 (Supp. 1963). *Persons convicted as subversive person barred from public employment.*—No subversive person, as defined in § 876.22, shall after conviction be eligible for employment in, or appointment to any office, or any position of trust or profit in the government of, or in the administration of the business of this State, or of any county, municipality, or other political subdivision of this State.

NOTE.—For definition of subversive person, see Subversive Activities under Unlawful Advocacy, *supra*.

2. CIVIL DEFENSE PERSONNEL

Florida Stat. Anno § 252.21. *Loyalty oath required.*—No person shall be employed or associated in any capacity in any civil defense organization established under this chapter who advocates a change by force or violence in the constitutional form of the Government of the United States or in this State or the overthrow of any government in the United States by force or violence, or who has been convicted of or is under indictment or information charging any subversive act against the United States. Each person who is appointed to serve in an organization for civil defense shall, before entering upon his duties, take an oath, in writing, before a person authorized to administer oaths in this State, or, for the purposes of this law only, before a State, county, or municipal civil defense director, which oath shall be substantially as follows:

"I, _____, do solemnly swear that I will support and defend the Constitution of the United States and the constitution of the State of Florida, against all enemies, foreign and domestic; that I will bear true faith and allegiance to the same; that I take this obligation freely, without any mental reservation or purpose of evasion; and that I will well and faithfully discharge the duties upon which I am about to enter.

"And I do further swear that I do not advocate, nor am I a member of a political party or organization that advocates, the overthrow of the Government of the United States or of this State by force or violence; and that during such time as I am a member of the (name of civil defense organization) I will not advocate nor become a member of any political party or organization that advocates the overthrow of the Government of the United States or of this State by force or violence."

Id. § 252.22. *Penalty.*—Any person violating any provision of this chapter or any rule, order, or regulation made pursuant to this chapter shall, upon conviction thereof, be punishable by a fine not exceeding five hundred dollars or imprisonment in a county jail for not exceeding six months, or both.

TEACHERS' LOYALTY

Florida Stat. Anno. § 231.18. *Applicant for teaching certificate required to execute statement of loyalty to Constitution.*—Each person applying for a certificate which would make him eligible to serve in an administrative or instructional capacity in the schools of Florida in addition to meeting all other requirements, and before receiving a certificate, shall file along with his other credentials a written statement under oath that he subscribes to and will uphold the principles incorporated in the Constitution of the United States.

Florida Stat. Anno. § 876.05 (Supp. 1963). *Loyalty oath required.*— All persons who now or hereafter are employed by or who now or hereafter are on the payroll of the State, or any of its departments and agencies, subdivisions, counties, cities, school boards and districts of the free public school system of the State or counties, or institutions of higher learning and all candidates for public office, are hereby required to take an oath before any person duly authorized to take acknowledgments of instruments for public record in the State in the following form:

I, _____, a citizen of the State of Florida and of the United States of America, and being employed by or an officer of _____ and a recipient of public funds as such employee or officer, do hereby solemnly swear or affirm that I will support the Constitution of the United States and of the State of Florida; that I am not a member of the Communist Party; that I have not and will not lend my aid, support, advice, counsel or influence to the Communist Party; that I do not believe in the overthrow of the Government of the United States or of the State of Florida by force or violence; that I am not a member of any organization or party which believes in or teaches, directly or indirectly, the overthrow of the Government of the United States or of Florida by force or violence.

And said oath shall be filed with the records of the governing official or employing governmental agency prior to the approval of any voucher for the payment of salary, expenses, or other compensation.

Id. § 876.06 (Supp. 1963). *Failure to execute oath cause for discharge.*—If any person required by §§ 876.05–876.10 to take the oath herein provided for fails to execute the same, the governing authority under which such person is employed shall cause said person to be immediately discharged, and his name removed from the payroll, and such person shall not be permitted to receive any payment as an employee or as an officer where he or she was serving.

Id. § 876.07 (Supp. 1963). *Engaging in activities contrary to oath cause for discharge.*—Any person having taken the oath provided for in § 876.05 and who thereafter should become a member of the Communist Party or who lends aid, support, advice, counsel or influence to the Communist Party or who expresses any belief in or advocates the overthrow of the Government of the United States or of the State by violence or force or thereafter becomes a member of an organization or party which believes in or teaches directly or indirectly the overthrow of the Government of the United States or of the State by force or violence, shall immediately be discharged from his employment by the employing authority and his name shall be removed from the payroll, and thereafter such person shall not be permitted to receive any payment as an employee or an officer where he or she then was serving. Any person seeking to qualify for public office who fails or refuses to file the oath required by this act shall be held to have failed to qualify as a candidate for public office, and the name of such person shall not be printed on the ballot as a qualified candidate.

Id. §. 876.08 (Supp. 1963). *Penalty for failure to discharge employee.*—Any governing authority or person, under whom any employee is serving or by whom employed who shall knowingly or carelessly permit any such employee to continue in employment after failing to comply with the provisions of §§ 876.05–876.10, shall be guilty of a misdemeanor and shall be punished by a fine not exceeding five hundred dollars or by imprisonment not exceeding six months or by both fine and imprisonment.

Id. § 876.09 (Supp. 1963). *Scope of law.*—(1) The provisions of §§ 876.05–876.10 shall apply to all employees and elected officers of the State, including the Governor and constitutional officers and all employees and elected officers of all cities, towns, counties and political subdivisions, including the educational system.

(2) This act shall take precedence over all laws relating to merit, and of civil service law.

Id. § 876.10 (Supp. 1963). *Penalty.*—If any person required by the provisions of §§ 876.05–876.10 to execute the oath herein required executes such oath, and it is subsequently proven that at the time of the execution of said oath said individual was guilty of making a false statement in said oath, he shall be guilty of perjury, and shall be prosecuted and punished for the crime of perjury in the event of conviction.

Id. § 876.25 (Supp. 1963). *Persons convicted of engaging in subversive activities or membership in subversive organizations barred from employment.*—Any person convicted by a court of competent jurisdiction of violating any of the provisions of 876.23, 876.24, in addition to all other penalties therein provided, shall from the date of such conviction be barred from:

(1) Holding any office, elective or appointive, or any other position of profit or trust in or employment by the government of the State or of any agency thereof or of any county, municipal corporation or other political subdivision of said State;

(2) Filing or offering for election to any public office in the State; or

(3) Voting in any election held in this State.

Id. § 876.29 (Supp. 1963). *Persons convicted as subversive persons barred from employment.*—No subversive person, as defined in § 876.22, shall after conviction be eligible for employment in, or appointment to any office, or any position of trust or profit in the government of, or in the administration of the business of this State, or of any county, municipality, or other political subdivision of this State.

Annotations:

Cramp v. *Bd. of Public Instruction,* 368 U.S. 278, 82 S. Ct. 275, 7 L. Ed. 2d 285 (1961). In this case the Court sustained a school teacher's challenge to the Florida statute requiring all public employees on pain of dismissal to sign an affidavit stating in part "that I have not and will not lend aid, support, advice, counsel, or influence to the Communist Party." The Court held the statute was so vague and ambiguous as to deprive the plaintiff of liberty or property without due process of law. It called attention to the fact that the "provision is completely lacking in * * * terms of objective measurement," and that the vagueness was further aggravated where, as here, the statute operated to inhibit the exercise of individual freedoms affirmatively protected by the constitution.

Cramp v. *Bd. of Public Instruction,* 137 So. 2d 828 (1962). On motions for entry of judgment pursuant to the mandate of the Supreme Court, *supra,* the Supreme Court of Florida held, *inter alia,* that the United States Supreme Court held unconstitutional only that portion of the loyalty oath which related to the past and future lending of aid, support, advice, counsel, or influence to the Communist Party, and that the remainder of statute requiring the loyalty oath, with the unconstitutional portion thereof eliminated, remained in full force and effect.

1961 Op. Atty. Gen. 061–83. A Cuban citizen loyal to the Castro government of Cuba cannot be issued a certificate to teach since that government could not properly be defined as "not antagonistic to the democratic form of government."

EXCLUSION FROM THE BAR

The Rules Relating to Admission to the Florida Bar contain no specific reference to subversive activity or association with the Communist Party. Correspondence received from the Florida Board of Bar Examiners states that "subversive activity or Communist Party association is attacked under the general provisions of Article IV, section 20 of the Rules, the good moral character requirement." Since the decision of the Supreme Court in the second *Konigsberg* case, the board has designed "a form of admonition" in an attempt to satisfy the "due warning" requirment. Every applicant appearing before the board receives by certified mail a copy of the "Admonition." Included in the information contained in the "Admonition" is a comment respecting the importance of answering all questions fully. It reads as follows:

2. You are advised that your refusal to answer any questions propounded to you by the board, which is directed to an inquiry of your character, fitness, or qualifications, may, in and of itself, constitute grounds for denial of admission into the examination.

Question 32 on the application form elicits information concerning Communist Party membership, attendance at Party meetings, etc. It reads as follows:

32. (a) Are you now or have you ever been a member of the Communist Party or enrolled as a member of that party?

(b) Have you ever attended a meeting of the Communist Party or a meeting of any of its leaders? If so, state the circumstances.

(c) Are you now or have you ever been a member of an organization listed as subversive by the Attorney General of the United States? If so, list below.

The board reports that none of its denials of admission have been based on ideological holdings.

Annotation:

Sheiner v. *State*, 82 So. 2d 657 (1955). Appellant testified before a subcommittee of the United States Senate but declined to answer questions relating to his alleged membership in the Communist Party and other subversive organizations. Appellant based his refusal to answer on the protection given him against self-incrimination by the First and Fifth Amendments to the Constitution. Thereafter proceedings were brought to disbar appellant. Reversing the judgment adverse to appellant and remanding the cause for further consideration, the Supreme Court of Florida held that the disbarment of an attorney because he had invoked the protection against self-incrimination when questioned by a congressional subcommittee concerning his alleged membership in the Communist Party and other subversive organizations more than a half dozen years before the disbarment proceeding was instituted, was a denial of due process. In the course of its opinion the court stated that no lawyer trained and educated in the democratic tradition could become a member of the Communist Party or other subversive organization without forfeiting his privilege to practice law.

EXCLUSION FROM INCIDENTAL BENEFITS

Florida Stat. Anno. § 370.21 (Supp. 1963). *Salt water products license.*—(1) This act may be known and cited as the Florida territorial waters act.

(2) It is the purpose of this act to exercise and exert full sovereignty and control of the territorial waters of the State.

(3) No license shall be issued by the board of conservation § 370.06, to any vessel owned in whole or in part by any alien power, which subscribes to the doctrine of international communism, or any subject or national thereof, who subscribes to the doctrine of international communism, or any individual who subscribes to the doctrine of international communism, or who shall have signed a treaty of trade, friendship and alliance or a nonaggression pact with any Communist power. The board shall grant or withhold said licenses where other alien vessels are involved on the basis of reciprocity and retorsion, unless the nation concerned shall be designated as a friendly ally or neutral by a formal suggestion transmitted to the Governor of Florida by the Secretary of State of the United States. Upon the receipt of such suggestion licenses shall be granted under § 370.06, without regard to reciprocity and retorsion, to vessels of such nations.

(4) It is unlawful for any unlicensed alien vessel to take by any means whatsoever, attempt to take, or having so taken to possess, any natural resource of the State's territorial waters, as such waters are described by Art. I of the State constitution.

(5) It is the duty of all harbor masters of the State to prevent the use of any port facility in a manner which they reasonably suspect

may assist in the violation of this act. Harbor masters shall endeavor by all reasonable means, which may include the inspection of nautical logs, to ascertain from masters of newly arrived vessels of all types other than warships of the United States, the presence of alien commercial fishing vessels within the territorial waters of the' State, and shall transmit such information promptly to the State department of conservation and such law enforcement agencies of the State as the situation may indicate. Harbor masters shall request assistance from the United States Coast Guard in appropriate cases to prevent unauthorized departure from any port facility.

(6) All licensed harbor pilots are required to promptly transmit any knowledge coming to their attention regarding possible violations of this act to the harbor master of the port or the appropriate law enforcement officials.

(7) All law enforcement agencies of the State, including but not limited to sheriffs and agents of the department of conservation are empowered and directed to arrest the masters and crews of vessels who are reasonably believed to be in violation of this law, and to seize and detain such vessels, their equipment and catch. Such arresting officers shall take the offending crews or property before the court having jurisdiction of such offenses. All such agencies are directed to request assistance from the United States Coast Guard in the enforcement of this act when having knowledge of vessels operating in violation or probable violation of this act within their jurisdiction when such agencies are without means to effectuate arrest and restraint of vessels and their crews.

(8) The fine or imprisonment of persons and confiscation proceedings against vessels, gear and catch prescribed for violations of chapter 370, shall be imposed for violation of this act; provided that nothing herein shall authorize the repurchase of property for a nominal sum by the owner upon proof of lack of complicity in the violation or undertaking.

(9) No crew member or master seeking bona fide political asylum shall be fined or imprisoned hereunder.

(10) Harbor masters and law enforcement agencies are authorized to request asistance from the civil air patrol in the surveillance of suspect vessels. Aircraft of the State forestry department or other State or county agencies which are conveniently located and not otherwise occupied may be similarly utilized.

MISCELLANEOUS

Florida Stat. Anno. § 230.23(1) (Supp. 1963). *Course on communism.*—1. The legislature of the State hereby finds it to be a fact that:

a. The political ideology commonly known and referred to as communism is in conflict with and contrary to the principles of constitutional Government of the United States as epitomized in its national Constitution,

b. The successful exploitation and manipulation of youth and student groups throughout the world today are a major challenge which free world forces must meet and defeat, and

c. The best method of meeting this challenge is to have the youth of the State and Nation thoroughly and completely informed as to the evils, dangers, and fallacies of communism by giving them a thorough understanding of the entire Communist movement, including its history, doctrines, objectives, and techniques.

2. The public high schools shall each teach a complete course of not less than thirty hours, to all students enrolled in said public high schools entitled "Americanism versus communism."

3. The course shall provide adequate instruction in the history, doctrines, objectives and techniques of communism and shall be for the primary purpose of instilling in the minds of the students a greater appreciation of democratic processes, freedom under law, and the will to preserve that freedom.

4. The course shall be one of orientation in comparative governments and shall emphasize the free-enterprise-competitive economy of the United States as the one which produces higher wages, higher standards of living, greater personal freedom and liberty than any other system of economics on earth.

5. The course shall lay particular emphasis upon the dangers of communism, the ways to fight communism, the evils of communism, the fallacies of communism, and the false doctrines of communism.

6. The State textbook committee and the State board of education shall take such action as may be necessary and appropriate to prescribe suitable textbook and instructional material as provided by State law, using as one of its guides the official reports of the House Committee on Un-American Activities and the Senate Internal Security Subcommittee of the United States Congress.

7. No teacher or textual material assigned to this course shall present communism as preferable to the system of constitutional government and the free-enterprise-competitive economy indigenous to the United States.

8. The course of study hereinabove provided for shall be taught in all of the public high schools of the State no later than the school year commencing in September 1962.

GEORGIA

UNLAWFUL ADVOCACY

SEDITION AND SUBORDINATE SUBVERSIVE ACTIVITIES

Georgia Code Anno. § 26–902a (Supp. 1963.) *"Organization," "Subversion organization," "Foreign subversive organization," "Foreign government" and "Subversive person" defined.*—For the purposes of this chapter: "Organization" means an organization, corporation, company, partnership, association, trust, foundation, fund, club, society, committee, political party, or any group of persons, whether or not incorporated, permanently, or temporarily associated together for joint action or advancement of views on any subject or subjects.

"Subversive organization" means an organization which engages in or advocates, abets, advises, or teaches, or a purpose for which is to engage in or advocate, abet, advise, or teach activities intended to overthrow, destroy, or to assist in the overthrow or destruction of the Government of the United States, government of the State of Georgia, or of any political subdivision of either of them, by revolution, force or violence.

"Foreign subversive organizations" means any organization, directed, dominated, or controlled directly or indirectly by a foreign government which engages in or advocates, abets, advises, or teaches, or a purpose of which is to engage in or to advocate, abet, advise, or teach activities intended to overthrow, destroy, or to assist in the overthrow or destruction of the Government of the United States or of the State of Georgia, or of any political subdivision of either of them, and to establish in place thereof any form of government the direction and control of which is to be vested in, or exercised by or under, the domination or control of any foreign government, organization, or individual.

"Foreign government" means the government of any country, nation, or group of nations other than the Government of the United States of America or of one of the States thereof.

"Subversive person" means any person who commits, attempts to commit, or aids in the commission, or advocates, abets, advises, or teaches by any means any person to commit, attempt to commit, or aid in the commission of any act intended to overthrow, destroy, or to assist in the overthrow or destruction of the Government of the United States, or of the State of Georgia, or any political subdivision of either of them, by revolution, force or violence; or who is a knowing member of a subversive organization or a foreign subversive organization.

Id. § 26–903a (Supp. 1963). *Unlawful acts and penalty.*—It shall be a felony for any person knowingly and willfully to:

(a) Commit, attempt to commit, or aid, abet or advise in the commission of any act the utilmate purposes of which is to overthrow or destroy or assist in the overthrow or destruction of the Government (or to alter or destroy the constitutional form thereof) of the United States or of the State of Georgia or any political subdivision of either of them by revolution, force, or violence; or

(b) Advocate, abet, advise, or teach by any means the duty, necessity, desirability, or propriety of overthrowing and destroying or altering the Government of the United States or of the State of Georgia or any political subdivision of either of them by revolution, force and violence; or

(c) Print, publish, edit, issue, circulate, sell, distribute, or publicly display any written or printed matter advocating, advising, or teaching the duty, necessity, desirability, propriety of overthrowing or destroying or altering the Government of the United States or of the State of Georgia or any political subdivision of either of them by revolution, force or violence; or

(d) Assist in the formation, participate in the management, or contribute to the support of any subversive organization or foreign subversive organization knowing said organization to be a subversive organization or a foriegn subversive organization; or

(e) Destroy any books, records, or files, or secrete any funds in this State of a subversive organization or a foreign subversive organization, knowing said organization to be such; or

(f) Withhold information regarding any activity of subversive organization or foreign subversive organization, or its membership knowing the organization to be such; or

(g) Conspire with one or more persons to commit any of the acts or do any of the things prohibited by this section.

Any person who violates any of the provisions of this section shall be fined not more than $20,000, or imprisoned in the penitentiary for not less than one year nor more than 20 years, or both.

Id. § 26–904a. *Membership in subversive organization unlawful.*— It shall be a felony for any person after the effective date of this chapter to become, or after March 1, 1953, to remain a member of a subversive organization or a foreign subversive organization knowing said organization to be a subversive organization or foreign subversive organization. Any person convicted of violating this section shall be fined not more than $5,000, or imprisoned in the penitentiary for not less than one year nor more than five years, or both.

Id. § 26.905a. *Additional penalties.*—Any person convicted by a court of competent jurisdiction of violating any of the provisions of section 26–903a or 26–904a, in addition to all other penalties therein provided, shall from the date of such conviction be barred from:

(a) Holding any office, elective or appointive, or any other position of profit or trust in or employment by the government of the State of Georgia or of any agency thereof or of any county, municipal corporation, or other political subdivision of said State;

(b) Filling or offering for election to any public office in the State of Georgia; or

(c) Voting in any election held in this State.

Id. § 26–906a. *Subversive organizations outlawed.*—It shall be unlawful for any subversive organization or foreign subversive organization to exist or function in the State of Georgia and any organization which by a court of competent jurisdiction is found to have violated the provisions of this section shall be dissolved, and if it be a corporation organized and existing under the laws of the State of Georgia, a finding by a court of competent jurisdiction that it has violated the provisions of this section shall constitute legal cause for forfeiture of its charter and its charter shall be forfeited, and all funds, books, records and files of every kind and all other property of any organization found to have violated the provision of this section shall be seized by and for the State of Georgia, the funds to be deposited in the State treasury and the books, records, files and other property to be turned over to the attorney general of Georgia.

Id. § 26-907a (Supp. 1963). *Enforcement.*—The Governor, with the concurrence of the attorney general, is hereby authorized and directed to appoint a special assistant attorney general, for investigating and prosecuting subversive activities, whose responsibility it shall be, under the supervision of the attorney general, to assemble, arrange and deliver to the solicitor general of any county, together with a list of necessary witnesses for presentation to the next grand jury to meet in said county, all information and evidence of matters within said county which have come to his attention, relating in any manner to the acts prohibited by this chapter, and relating generally to the purpose, processes and activities of communism and any other or related subversive organizations, associations, groups or persons. Such evidence may be presented by the attorney general (or the special assistant attorney general) to the grand jury of any county directly, and he may represent the State on the trial of such a case, should he feel the ends of justice would be best served thereby, and the special assistant attorney general herein provided may testify before any grand jury as to matters referred to in this chapter as to which he may have information.

Id. § 26-908a (Supp. 1963). *Obtaining evidence.*—For the collection of any evidence and information referred to in this chapter, the Governor and the attorney general are hereby authorized and directed to call upon all prosecuting attorneys, the director of public safety, sheriffs, county and municipal police authorities to furnish to the special assistant hereinbefore provided for, such assistance as may from time to time be required. Such police authorities are directed to furnish information and assistance as may be from time to time so requested. Such police authorities shall transmit immediately to the special assistant attorney general any information coming to their notice and attention regarding the activities of any subversive persons, subversive organizations, or foreign subversive organizations. The Governor by executive order is authorized to establish within existing departments such special enforcement agencies, designate such personnel and fix such duties as may from time to time be required to perform any of the functions and duties required by this chapter.

Id. § 26-909a (Supp. 1963). *Records keeping.*—The attorney general shall require the special assistant herein provided for, to maintain complete records of all information received by him and all matters handled by him under the requirements of the chapter. Such records as may reflect on the loyalty of any resident of this State, shall not be made public or divulged to any person except with permission of the Governor or the attorney general to effectuate the purposes of this chapter. All such records shall be classified as confidential State secrets until declassified by the Governor or the attorney general.

Id. § 26–910a (Supp. 1963). *Grand jury investigations.*—The judge of any court exercising general criminal jurisdiction, when in his discretion it appears appropriate, or when informed by the attorney general or solicitor general that there is information or evidence of the character described in section 26–907a to be considered by the grand jury, shall charge the grand jury to inquire into violations of this chapter for the purpose of proper action, and further to inquire generally into the purposes, processes, and activities and any other matters affecting communism or any related or other subversive organizations, associations, groups, or persons.

Exclusion From the Elective Process

Georgia Code Anno. § 26–903a (Supp. 1963). *Seditious and subversive activities and penalty.*—It shall be a felony for any person knowingly and willfully to:

(a) Commit, attempt to commit, or aid, abet, or advise in the commission of any act the ultimate purpose of which is to overthrow or destroy or assist in the overthrow or destruction of the Government (or to alter or destroy the constitutional form thereof) of the United States or of the State of Georgia or any political subdivision of either of them by revolution, force, or violence; or

(b) Advocate, abet, advise, or teach by any means the duty, necessity, desirability, or propriety of overthrowing and destroying or altering the Government of the United States or of the State of Georgia or any political subdivision of either of them by revolution, force, and violence; or

(c) Print, publish, edit, issue, circulate, sell, distribute, or publicly display any written or printed matter advocating, advising, or teaching the duty, necessity, desirability, propriety of overthrowing or destroying or altering the Government of the United States or of the State of Georgia or any political subdivision of either of them by revolution, force or violence; or

(d) Assist in the formation, participate in the management, or contribute to the support of any subversive organization or foreign subversive organization knowing said organization to be a subversive organization or a foreign subversive organization; or

(e) Destroy any books, records, or files, or secrete any funds in this State of a subversive organization or a foreign subversive organization, knowing said organization to be such; or

(f) Withhold information regarding any activity of subversive organization or foreign subversive organization, or its membership knowing the organization to be such; or

(g) Conspire with one or more persons to commit any of the acts or do any of the things prohibited by this section.

Any person who violates any of the provisions of this section shall be fined not more than $20,000, or imprisoned in the penitentiary for not less than one year nor more than 20 years, or both.

Id. § 26–904a. *Membership in subversive organization unlawful.*—It shall be a felony for any person after the effective date of this chapter to become, or after March 1, 1953, to remain a member of a subversive organization or a foreign subversive organization knowing said organization to be a subversive organization or foreign subversive organization. ·Any person convicted of violating this sec-

tion shall be fined not more than $5,000, or imprisoned in the penitentiary for not less than one year nor more than five years, or both.
Id. § 26–905a. *Persons convicted of subversive activities disenfranchised and ineligible for public office.*—Any person convicted by a court of competent jurisdiction of violating any of the provisions of sections 26–903a or 26–904a, in addition to all other penalties therein provided, shall from the date of such conviction be barred from:

(a) Holding any office, elective or appointive, or any other position of profit or trust in or employment by the government of the State of Georgia or of any agency thereof or of any county, municipal corporation or other political subdivision of said State;

(b) Filling or offering for election to any public office in the State of Georgia; or

(c) Voting in any election held in this State.
Id. § 26–906a. *Subversive organizations outlawed.*—It shall be unlawful for any subversive organization or foreign subversive organization to exist or function in the State of Georgia and any organization which by a court of competent jurisdiction is found to have violated the provisions of this section shall be dissolved, and if it be a corporation organized and existing under the laws of the State of Georgia, a finding by a court of competent jurisdiction that it has violated the provisions of this section shall constitute legal cause for forfeiture of its charter and its charter shall be forfeited, and all funds, books, records and files of every kind and all other property of any organization found to have violated the provision of this section shall be seized by and for the State of Georgia, the funds to be deposited in the State treasury and the books, records, files and other property to be turned over to the attorney general of Georgia.
Id. § 34–1904(d) (Supp. 1963). *Candidates for electors of President and Vice President required to execute non-Communist affidavit.*

* * * * * * *

The party authorities certifying the names of candidates for electors of President and Vice President shall accompany such certification with an affidavit signed by each candidate for elector, stating that such candidate is not now and never has been a member of the Communist Party, and does not believe in or sympathize with the principles of such Communist Party.

LOYALTY OF STATE OFFICERS AND EMPLOYEES

1. ELECTIVE AND NONELECTIVE PERSONNEL

Georgia Code Anno. § 89–311. *Loyalty oath required.*—All persons who are employed by and are on the payroll of and the recipient of wages per diem and/or salary of the State of Georgia, or its departments and agencies (with the exception of pages employed by the General Assembly), all counties and cities, school districts and local educational systems throughout the entire State, are hereby required to take an oath that they will support the Constitution of the United States and the constitution of the State of Georgia.
Id. § 89–312. *Non-Communist requirement of oath.*—The oath required shall definitely state that such persons are not members of the Communist Party and that they have no sympathy with the doctrines of communism.

41–738—65——8

Id. § 89–313. *Form of oath.*—Said oath, above described, shall be in the following form:

"I, _____, a citizen of_____
                    (Name)
and being an employee of _____
and the recipient of public funds for services rendered as such employee, do hereby solemnly swear and affirm that I will support the Constitution of the United States and the constitution of the State of Georgia, and that I am not a member of the Communist Party and that I have no sympathy for the doctrines of communism and will not lend my aid, my support, my advice, my counsel nor my influence to the Communist Party or to the teachings of communism."

Id. § 89–314. *Failure to execute oath cause for dismissal.*—If any person required by this law [§§ 89–311 through 89–316] to execute a loyalty oath fails to sign said oath then the governing authority under whom such person is employed shall cause such person's name to be taken from the payroll and such person shall not be permitted to receive any payment from the State.

Id. § 89–315. *Scope of law.*—The loyalty oath required by the provisions of this law [§§ 89–311 through 89–316] shall apply to all elected officers of this State, including the Governor and constitutional officers as well as elected officials of any political subdivision of the government of Georgia, including local school board officials.

Id. § 89–316. *Penalty.*—If any person required by the provisions of this law [§§ 89–311 through 89–316] executes a loyalty oath and subsequently it is proved that said individual has violated the oath, then the governing authority shall institute proceedings in the proper court against such person for false swearing.

2. NONELECTIVE PERSONNEL

Georgia Code Anno. § 26–902a (Supp. 1963). *"Organization," "Subversive organization," "Foreign subversive organizations," "Foreign government," and "Subversive person" defined.*—For the purposes of this chapter:

"Organization" means an organization, corporation, company, partnership, association, trust, foundation, fund, club, society, committee, political party, or any group of persons, whether or not incorporated, permanently, or temporarily associated together for joint action or advancement of views on any subject or subjects.

"Subversive organization" means an organization which engages in or advocates, abets, advises, or teaches, or a purpose for which is to engage in or advocate, abet, advise, or teach activities intended to overthrow, destroy, or to assist in the overthrow or destruction of the Government of the United States, government of the State of Georgia, or of any political subdivision of either of them, by revolution, force or violence.

"Foreign subversive organizations" means any organization, directed, dominated or controlled directly or indirectly by a foreign government which engages in or advocates, abets, advises, or teaches, or a purpose of which is to engage in or to advocate, abet, advise, or teach activities intended to overthrow, destroy, or to assist in the overthrow or destruction of the Government of the United States, or of the

State of Georgia, or of any political subdivision of either of them, and to establish in place thereof any form of government the direction and control of which is to be vested in, or exercised by or under, the domination or control of any foreign government, organization or individual.

"Foreign government" means the government of any country, nation or group of nations other than the Government of the United States of America or of one of the States thereof.

"Subversive person" means any person who commits, attempts to commit, or aids in the commission, or advocates, abets, advises or teaches by any means any person to commit, attempt to commit, or aid in the commission of any act intended to overthrow, destroy, or to assist in the overthrow or destruction of the Government of the United States, or of the State of Georgia, or any political subdivision of either of them, by revolution, force or violence; or who is a knowing member of a subversive organization or a foreign subversive organization.

Id. § 26–911a (Supp. 1963). *Subversive persons ineligible for public employment.*—No subversive person, as defined in this Chapter, shall be eligible for employment in, or appointment to, any office, or any position of trust or profit in the government of, or in the administration of the business of this State, or of any county, municipality, or other political subdivision of this State.

Id. § 26–912a (Supp. 1963). *Investigation of prospective public employees.*—Every person and every board, commission, council, department, or other agency of the State of Georgia, or any political subdivision thereof, who, or which, appoints or employs or supervises in any manner the appointment, or employment, of public officials, or employees, shall establish by rules, regulations, or otherwise procedures designated to ascertain before any person, including teachers and other employees of any public educational institution in this State, is appointed or employed, that he, or she, as the case may be, is not a subversive person, and that there are no reasonable grounds to believe such persons are subversive persons. In the event such reasonable grounds exist, he or she, as the case may be, shall not be appointed or employed. In securing any facts necessary to ascertain the information herein required all applicants and employees shall be required to sign a written statement, or questionnaire, containing answers to such inquiries as may be material, which statement or questionnaire shall contain notice that it is subject to the penalties of false swearing. The form of the questionnaire, or statement, proposing such questions as may be material, shall be prescribed and prepared by the assistant attorney general named under the provisions of this chapter. Such questionnaire so prepared and prescribed shall be submitted to the Governor and the attorney general for approval, and may be changed from time to time as deemed necessary by the assistant attorney general with the approval of the Governor and the attorney general. The Governor is authorized to make appropriate orders, rules and regulations to effectuate the purposes of sections 26–911a through 26–914a.

Id. § 26–913a (Supp. 1963). *Investigation of present public employees.*—Every person who on January 1, 1954, shall be in the employ of the State of Georgia, or any agency thereof, including public educational institutions supported in whole or in part by State funds, shall execute a written questionnaire to determine facts concerning his or her personal history, qualifications, and loyalty, which shall include a statement that the same is being made under penalties of false swearing. This questionnaire shall be executed in the form prescribed by the assistant attorney general with the approval of the attorney general and the Governor. Reasonable grounds on all the evidence to believe that any person is a subversive person, as defined in this chapter, shall be cause for discharge from any appointive office or other position of profit or trust in the government of, or in the administration of the business of this State, or of any county, municipality or other political subdivision of this State, or any agency thereof.

Every person, before being discharged by reason of being a subversive person, shall be given notice of the charges against such person and afforded an opportunity to be heard upon the charges. Notice shall be given in writing at least 10 days before a hearing shall be held by the employing, appointing, or supervising authority: *Provided*, *however*, That nothing contained herein shall be construed to create any tenure rights or to in any wise limit employing, appointing, or supervising authorities in the administration of personnel matters, nor be construed to apply to section 26–912a, it being recognized by the General Assembly that the holding of public office or being a public employee is a privilege, and no person has any property or right vested in him by reason of his public employment and has only such entitlements as may be conferred upon him specifically by statute.

Id. § 26–914a (Supp. 1963). *Penalty.*—Every written statement made pursuant to this chapter by an applicant for appointment or employment, or by any employee, who shall be deemed to have been made under oath if it contains a declaration preceding the signature of the maker to the effect that it is made under the penalties of false swearing. Any person who makes a material misstatement of fact (a) in any such written statement, or (b) in any affidavit made pursuant to the provisions of this chapter, or (c) under oath in any hearing conducted by any agency of this State, or of any of its political subdivisions, pursuant to this chapter, or (d) in any written statement by an applicant for appointment or employment or by an employee in any State-aid or private institution of learning in this State, intended to determine whether or not such applicant or employee is a subversive person as defined in this chapter, which statement contains notice that it is subject to the penalties of false swearing, shall be subject to the penalties of false swearing as prescribed in section 26–4004: *Provided*, *further, however,* That nothing contained in the foregoing shall be construed to repeal in any way the laws of this State dealing with perjury and false swearing.

Id. § 26–915a (Supp. 1963). *Data concerning relatives of person supplying information not required.*—No person giving any information, whether by answering a questionnaire or otherwise, as provided in sections 26–912a and 26–913a, shall be required to give any information or answer any questions relative to the membership in any organization of any relative of such person.

Id. § 26–916a (Supp. 1963). *Records keeping.*—Any questionnaires or statements prepared as provided in sections 26–912a and 26–913a shall be filed at the place of employment rather than with a central State agency.

3. CIVIL DEFENSE PERSONNEL

Georgia Code Anno. § 86–1819. *Loyalty oath required.*—No person shall be employed or associated in any capacity in any civil defense organization established under this chapter who advocates a change by force or violence in the constitutional form of the Government of the United States or in this State or the overthrow of any Government in the United States by force or violence, or who has been convicted of or is under indictment or information charging any subversive act against the United States. Each person who is appointed to serve in an organization for civil defense shall, before entering upon his duties, take an oath, in writing, before a person authorized to administer oaths in this State, which oath shall be substantially as follows:

"I, _____, do solemnly swear (or affirm) that I will support and defend the Constitution of the United States and the constitution of the State of Georgia, against all enemies, foreign and domestic; that I will bear true faith and allegiance to the same; that I take this obligation freely, without any mental reservation or purpose of evasion; and that I will well and faithfully discharge the duties upon which I am about to enter.

"And I do further swear (or affirm) that I do not advocate, nor am I a member of any political party or organization that advocates, the overthrow of the Government of the United States or of this State by force or violence; and that during such time as I am a member of the (name of civil defense organization) I will not advocate nor become a member of any political party or organization that advocates the overthrow of the Government of the United States or of this State by force or violence."

TEACHERS' LOYALTY

Georgia Code Anno. § 89–311. *Loyalty oath required.*—All persons who are employed by and are on the payroll of and the recipient of wages per diem and/or salary of the State of Georgia, or its departments and agencies (with the exception of pages employed by the General Assembly), all counties and cities, school districts and local educational systems throughout the entire State, are hereby required to take an oath that they will support the Constitution of the United States and the constitution of the State of Georgia.

Id. § 89–312. *Non-Communist requirement of oath.*—The oath required shall definitely state that such persons are not members of the Communist Party and that they have no sympathy with the doctrines of communism.

Id. § 89–313. *Form of oath.*—Said oath, above described, shall be in the following form:

"I, _____, a citizen of _____
            (name)
and being an employee of _____
and the recipient of public funds for services rendered as such employee, do hereby solemnly swear and affirm that I will support the Constitution of the United States and the constitution of the State of Georgia, and that I am not a member of the Communist Party and that I have no sympathy for the doctrines of communism and will not lend my aid, my support, my advice, my counsel nor my influence to the Communist Party or to the teachings of communism."

Id. § 89–314.   *Failure to execute oath cause for dismissal.*—If any person required by this law [§§ 89–311 through 89–316] to execute a loyalty oath fails to sign said oath then the governing authority under whom such person is employed shall cause such person's name to be taken from the payroll and such person shall not be permitted to receive any payment from the State.

Id. § 89–315.   *Scope of law.*—The loyalty oath required by the provisions of this law [§§ 89–311 through 89–316] shall apply to all elected officers of this State, including the Governor and constitutional officers as well as elected officials of any political subdivision of the government of Georgia, including local school board officials.

Id. § 89–316.   *Penalty.*—If any person required by the provisions of this law [§§ 89–311 through 89–316] executes a loyalty oath and subsequently it is proved that said individual has violated the oath, then the governing authority shall institute proceedings in the proper court against such person for false swearing.

Georgia Code Anno. § 32–1022.   *Teachers' oath.*—Every teacher in the public schools of this State whether elementary, high school, college, or university, and all other employees, of the State or subdivision thereof drawing a weekly, monthly, or yearly salary, shall before entering upon the discharge of their duties, take and subscribe a solemn oath to uphold, support, and defend the constitution and laws of this State and of the United States, and to refrain from directly or indirectly subscribing to or teaching any theory of government or economics or of social relations which is inconsistent with the fundamental principles of patriotism and high ideals of Americanism.

Id. § 32–1023.   *Form of oath prescribed by State Superintendent.*—The form of such oath shall be prescribed by the State superintendent of schools, and the oath of each teacher shall be filed in the office of the superintendent of schools of the county or other school system in which such teacher is employed; other employees shall file their oaths with the department in which they may be employed; which oaths shall be annually renewed.

Id. § 32–1024.   *Employment conditioned upon execution of oath.*—No teacher or employee who shall fail or refuse to take and subscribe such oath shall be employed in any school, college, or university or other office or position of this State, or be paid from the public school fund or by any other public fund.

NOTE.—For provisions relating to investigation of teachers, etc., see Nonelective Personnel under Loyalty of State Officers and Employees, *supra.*

EXCLUSION FROM THE BAR

Question 20 of Part B of the Questionnaire for Applicants for Georgia Bar Examination relates specifically to the matter of whether the applicant has ever been a member of or affiliated with the Communist Party or any subversive group. The text of the question follows:

20. Are you or have you ever been a member of or affiliated with (a) the Communist Party, or (b) any political party or other organization which advocated or advocates the overthrow of our constitutional form of government by force and violence, or (c) any group, association or organization which lent or lends support to any organization or movement advocating the overthrow of our constitutional

form of government in the United States by force and violence, or (d) have you been a member of any organization classified as subversive by the Attorney General of the United States. If so, explain fully on an attached sheet all circumstances surrounding such membership or affiliation, the name of the organization, and resignation or termination of such membership or affiliation, if such is the case.

Correspondence received from the State Board of Bar Examiners of Georgia states that (1) "no application to take the bar examination has been filed in this State under * * * present procedures (which have been in effect for some thirteen years) by a person who stated in his application that he was or had been, or was found upon investigation to be or have to have been, a Communist or a member of a subversive group"; (2) "no superior court judge has [therefore] had occasion to rule on the effect or weight to be given this circumstance in determining whether the applicant was 'of good moral character' within the meaning of the statute"; (3) "there is thus no practice or general policy in this respect, nor are there any regulations or official opinions with respect thereto." It thus appears that should a person who is or who has been a Communist, subversive, etc., apply for admission, the problem "would be one for determination by the judge of the superior court with whom the application was filed."

HAWAII

UNLAWFUL ADVOCACY

1. ANARCHY

Rev. Laws 1955, § 261–1. *Publication or circulation of anarchistic literature prohibited.*—Any person who prints, publishes, sells, distributes, or circulates in the Territory, any written or printed article or matter, in any form or language which advocates or incites or is intended to advocate or incite the commission of any act of violence, such as sabotage, incendiarism, sedition, anarchy, rioting, or breach of the peace, or which directly or indirectly advocates or incites or is intended to advocate or incite the use or exercise of force, fear, intimidation, threats, ostracism, or blackmail, for the purpose of restraining or coercing or intimidating any person from freely engaging in lawful business or employment or the enjoyment of rights of liberty or property, or which by deliberate misrepresentation is designed and intended to create or have the effect of creating distrust or dissension between peoples of different races or between citizens and aliens, shall upon the first conviction be fined not more than $1,000 or imprisoned not more than one year, and shall upon a second conviction for again violating this section within five years of the first conviction, be fined not more than $5,000 or imprisoned not more than one year, or both.

2. CRIMINAL SYNDICALISM

Rev. Laws 1955, § 261–2. *Criminal syndicalism defined.*—Criminal syndicalism is defined to be the doctrine which advocates crime, sabotage, violence or other unlawful methods of terrorism as a means of accomplishing industrial or political ends.

Id. § 261–3. *Unlawful acts and penalty.*—Any person who:

(a) By word of mouth or writing, advocates or teaches the duty, necessity or propriety of crime, sabotage, violence or other unlawful methods of terrorism as a means of accomplishing industrial or political ends; or

(b) Prints, publishes, edits, issues or knowingly circulates, sells, distributes or publicly displays any book, paper, document or written matter in any form containing or advocating, advising or teaching the doctrine that industrial or political ends should be brought about by crime, sabotage, violence or other unlawful methods of terrorism; or

(c) Openly, willfully and deliberately justifies, by word of mouth or writing, the commission or the attempt to commit crime, sabotage, violence or other unlawful methods of terrorism with intent to exemplify, spread or advocate the propriety of the doctrines of criminal syndicalism; or

(d) Organizes or helps to organize, or becomes a member of or voluntarily assembles with any society, group or assemblage of persons

103

formed to teach or advocate the doctrines of criminal syndicalism; shall be fined not more than $5,000 or imprisoned not more than ten years, or both.

Id. § 261–4. *Assemblage to advocate criminal syndicalism.*—Whenever two or more persons assemble for the purpose of advocating or teaching the doctrines of criminal syndicalism as defined in this chapter, such an assemblage is unlawful and every person voluntarily participating therein by his presence, aid or instigation shall be fined not more than $5,000 or imprisoned not more than ten years, or both.

Id. § 261–5. *Permitting premises to be used to advocate criminal syndicalism.*—The owner, agent, superintendent, janitor, caretaker, or occupant of any place, building, or room, who willfully and knowingly permits therein any assemblage of persons prohibited by the provisions of section 261–4, or who, after notification by the police authorities that the premises are so used, permits the use to be continued, shall be fined not more than $500 or imprisoned not more than one year, or both.

EXCLUSION FROM THE ELECTIVE PROCESS

Rev. Laws 1955 § 11–96.5 (Supp. 1963). *Loyalty oath required.*—The name of no candidate for any office shall be printed upon any official ballot, in any primary or general election, unless the candidate shall have taken and subscribed the following written oath or affirmation, and at the time of filing his nomination papers shall have filed the same therewith.

The aforesaid written oath or affirmation shall be in the following form:

"I, _____, do solemnly swear and declare, on oath, that I do not advocate, or aid or belong to any party, organization, or association which advocates the overthrow by force or violence of the government of Hawaii or of the United States; that if elected to office I will support and defend the Constitution and laws of the United States of America, and the constitution and laws of the State of Hawaii, and will bear true faith and allegiance to the same; that if elected I will faithfully discharge my duties as ____ (name of office) ____ to the best of my ability; that I take this obligation freely, without any mental reservation or purpose of evasion; So help me God."

Upon being satisfied as to the sincerity of any person claiming that he is unwilling to take the above prescribed oath only because due to religious beliefs he is unwilling to be sworn, he may be permitted, in lieu of such oath, to make his solemn affirmation which shall be in the same form as the oath except that the words "sincerely and truly affirm" shall be substituted for the word "swear" and the phrases "on oath" and "So help me God" shall be omitted. Such affirmation shall be of the same force and effect as the prescribed oath.

The oath or affirmation shall be subscribed before the officer administering the same, who shall endorse thereon the fact that the oath was subscribed and sworn to or the affirmation was made together with the date thereof and affix the seal of his office or of the court of which he is a judge or clerk.

It shall be the duty of every notary public or other public officer by law authorized to administer oaths to administer the oath or affirmation by this section prescribed and to furnish the required endorsement and authentication. No charge shall be made for the performance of this duty.

LOYALTY OF STATE OFFICERS AND EMPLOYEES

1. ELECTIVE AND NONELECTIVE PERSONNEL

Hawaii Constitution, Art. XIV, § 3 (Supp. 1963). *Persons advo-cating subversion and members of subversive organizations ineligible for public office or employment.*—No person who advocates, or who aids or belongs to any party, organization, or association which advocates the overthrow by force or violence of the government of this State or of the United States shall be qualified to hold any public office or employment.

Rev. Laws 1955, § 5–120. *Loyalty oath required.*—All persons elected to or appointed or employed in the government of the Territory or any county, or in any political subdivision thereof, or appointed to or employed in any office or employment, any part of the compensation of which is paid out of public funds shall, before entering upon the duties of their respective offices or employments, take and subscribe to the following written oath or affirmation:

"I, _____, do solemnly swear and declare, on oath, that I will support and defend the Constitution and laws of the United States of America against all enemies, foreign and domestic; that I will bear true faith and allegiance to the same; that I do not hold membership in, pay assessments, dues, or make contributions to any organization or any political party which advocates the overthrow of the constitutional form of Government of the United States of America or any change in the Government of the United States of America, except as provided by its Constitution; that I take this obligation freely, without any mental reservation or purpose of evasion. So help me God."

Upon being satisfied as to the sincerity of any person claiming that he is unwilling to take the above prescribed oath only because due to religious beliefs he is unwilling to be sworn, he may be permitted, in lieu of such oath, to make his solemn affirmation which shall be in the same form as the oath except that the words "sincerely and truly affirm" shall be substituted for the word "swear" and the phrases "on oath" and "So help me God" shall be omitted. Such affirmation shall be of the same force and effect as the prescribed oath.

The oath or affirmation shall be subscribed in duplicate before the officer administering the same, who shall endorse thereon the fact that the oath was subscribed and sworn to or the affirmation was made together with the date thereof and affix the seal of his office or of the court of which he is a judge or clerk.

Id. § 5–121. *Administering oath.*—Every notary public or other public officer by law authorized to administer oaths shall administer the oath or affirmation prescribed by this part and shall furnish the required endorsement and authentication. No charge shall be made for the performance of this duty.

The head of any department of the government of the Territory or of any county, or the governing authority of any independent board or commission established under territorial law, may designate in writing one or more officers or employees in or under such department, board or commission, including such department head or any number of such board or commission, to administer such oaths or affirmations, and upon the filing of such written designation with the civil service commission or other authority charged with the administration of chapter 3 with respect to employees of such department, the officers or employees so designated shall have the same powers to administer such oaths or affirmations as are possessed by notaries public.

Id. § 5–122. *Permitted exclusions from scope of law.*—The Governor may waive compliance with all or any part of the provisions of this part in respect to the following classes of officers or employees of any portion therof:

(a) Officers or employees of the Territory (including kokuas and voluntary helpers) located or stationed at any hospital, settlement or place for the care and treatment of persons affected with Hansen's disease;

(b) Institutional inmate or patient employees or help in territorial or county institutions;

(c) Aliens employed by the Territory or any county, under the exceptions designated (b) and (c) of section 5–1;

(d) Referees, receivers, masters, and jurors;

(e) Casual and temporary employees, whether on a monthly salary or a per diem basis, and inspectors and clerks of elections.

Id. § 5–123. *Permitted grace period to comply with oath requirements.*—The Governor may extend the time within which any officer or employee of the Territory, or any county thereof, is required to take or make the prescribed oath or affirmation, but in no case shall such extension be for a period longer than 60 days and then only after such officer or employee has shown in writing to the satisfaction of the Governor that he failed to comply with the requirements of this part because of illness, absence from the Territory, disability or any other reason deemed to be sufficient by the Governor.

Id. § 5–124. *Repeated oath taking not required.*—No officer or employee continued in employment or appointed to or employed in another office or position or reappointed to succeed himself in any office or position, except where such new office or position involves a change of residence from one county to another, shall be required to renew such oath or affirmation if he took the oath or made the affirmation on original appointment or employment.

Id. § 5–125. *Loyalty oath constitutes additional oath.*—The oath or affirmation prescribed and required by this part shall be in addition to any other oath or affirmation prescribed or required by law of any officer or employee.

Id. § 5–126. *Filing of oath.*—(a) The oath or affirmation of each territorial officer or employee, when taken or made as in section 5–120 prescribed, shall be delivered, in duplicate, to the head of the department in which the person is an officer or employee, or, in the case of the head of a department, to the Governor. The head of the department or the Governor, as the case may be, shall file a copy with the civil service commission and in his own department or office. The civil service commission of the Territory shall immediately certify to the auditor or other officer, whose duty it is to pay or draw, sign or issue any warrant or check for the salary or compensation of each such person the name and position of each person taking or making the oath or affirmation.

(b) In the case of an officer or employee in the judicial branch of the government, the oath or affirmation by section 5–120 prescribed shall be delivered, in duplicate, in the case of a court of record, to the chief clerk thereof, and, in the case of a district court, to the district magistrate thereof. The oath or affirmation of each district magistrate, member of the tax appeal court or other such territorial court shall be delivered to the chief justice of the supreme court and of each chief clerk of a court of record to the presiding judge thereof. The oath or affirmation shall then be filed in the same manner and the name and position certified as in paragraph (a) provided.

(c) In the case of an officer or employee in the legislative branch of the government, the oath or affirmation by section 5–120 prescribed shall be delivered, in duplicate, to the clerk of the body of which the person is an officer or employee, or, in the case of the clerk, to the presiding officer thereof. The oath or affirmation shall then be filed in the same manner and the name and position certified as in paragraph (a) provided.

(d) The oath or affirmation of each county officer or employee, when taken or made as in section 5–120 prescribed, shall be delivered, in duplicate, to the head of the department in which the person is an officer or employee, or, in the case of the head of a department or a supervisor, to the mayor or chairman of the board of supervisors, as the case may be. The head of the department or the mayor or chairman of the board of supervisors, as the case may be, shall file a copy with the civil service commission of the county of which he is an officer and in his own department or office. The civil service commission shall immediately certify to the auditor or other officer whose duty it is to pay or draw, sign or issue any warrant or check for the salary or compensation of each such person the name and position of each person taking or making the oath of affirmation.

(e) In all cases not hereinbefore provided for, the oath or affirmation shall be delivered to the Governor and then filed in the same manner and the name and position certified as in paragraph (a) provided.

Upon being filed, each such oath or affirmation shall become a public record and open, at all times during business hours, to public inspection.

(f) The head of any department or any officer in the government of the Territory or any county, whose duty it is to authorize the drawing, signing, or issuing of any warrant or check for the salary or compensation of any person required to comply with this part may be required by the Governor to certify on each such authorization that such person has taken and subscribed to the prescribed oath or made the required affirmation.

Id. § 5–127 (Supp. 1963). *Failure or refusal to take oath constitutes grounds for disqualification.*—Any person who fails or refuses to take the oath or make the affirmation prescribed within the time specified shall thereupon become disqualified to continue to hold such office or employment under the State, or any county thereof, shall not be permitted to continue upon the duties of such office or employment, and shall be deemed to have released and forfeited all claim or right thereafter to any compensation payable by the State, or any county thereof. In any event, the comptroller of the State, or auditor of any county, is hereby prohibited from issuing any warrant to any such person for any services rendered after the time specified for taking and subscribing to the oath or making the affirmation. The failure or refusal of any such officer or employee to comply with the requirements of this part shall not be deemed to invalidate any act performed by him or by any court, board, commission, agency, or any body of which he was a member during the time within which he was required and failed or refused to comply with this part.

Id. § 5–128 (Supp. 1963). *Failure or refusal to take oath constitutes grounds for removal from elected county office.*—Any elected county officer who fails or refuses to take or subscribe, the oath or affirmation prescribed and in the manner and time provided in this part, shall be immediately removed from office in the manner provided in section 144–30 or 149–59, as the case may be, except that it shall not be necessary to charge any such officer failing or refusing to take or subscribe the oath or affirmation on a petition of citizens and voters or of legal voters, but that any such officer shall be so charged by the county attorney. The several county attorneys shall immediately institute removal proceedings against any such officer failing or refusing to take and subscribe the oath or affirmation prescribed by this part.

Id. § 5–129 (Supp. 1963). *Civil service applicants required to execute oath.*—The several civil service commissions shall by rule or regulation require all applicants for examination to take and subscribe the oath or affirmation prescribed in section 5–120, and no person shall be permitted to take any such examination and the name of no person shall be placed upon any registration, employment, or re-employment list who has not taken and subscribed the oath or affirmation. The several civil service commissions may require the oath or affirmation to be printed on the application blank for employment. If the person receives employment, the application shall become a part of the permanent records of the civil service office and no further oath shall be necessary, notwithstanding any other provisions of this part to the contrary.

Upon the removal or discharge of any person who fails or refuses to take the oath or affirmation prescribed and required by section 5–120, the provisions of chapter 3 shall not be applicable.

Id. § 5–130. *Scope of provisions.*—The provisions of this part shall apply to any person appointed or employed under any contract by the Territory or any county and any such person failing or refusing to take the oath or affirmation prescribed and required by section 5–120 shall be removed or discharged as by this part provided. All such contracts shall contain a provision requiring any person appointed or employed thereunder to comply with this part. The section shall also be applicable to contracts made for the exchange of personnel.

Id. § 5–131. *Removal of certain appointed officers.*—In the case of any officer who may only be removed from office by the Governor by and with the advice and consent of the senate of the Territory and who fails or refuses to take the oath or make the affirmation by this part prescribed, the advice and consent of the senate is hereby given to such removal and, in any such case, the Governor is requested to remove any such officer by and with the consent so given.

Id. § 5–132. *Claims against the Government barred.*—The provisions of chapter 245 shall not apply to any person removed or discharged under the provisions of this part nor to any claim for wages, salary, or compensation of any such person.

No court shall have jurisdiction to hear and determine any claim for wages, salary, or compensation of any person lawfully removed or discharged under the provisions of this part.

This section shall not be construed so as to prohibit any court of competent jurisdiction from entertaining or hearing any proper suit or action of which it would otherwise have jurisdiction for the removal or discharge of any officer or employee refusing or failing to comply with the provisions of this part.

NOTE.—Chapter 245, Rev. Laws 1955, deals with suits by and against the Government.

Id. § 5–133. *Compensation for services conditioned upon compliance with loyalty oath requirements.*—No officer of the Territory or any county thereof whose duty it is so to do, shall authorize the drawing, signing, or issuing of or shall draw, sign, or issue any warrant on the treasury of the Territory or any county or other disbursing agency of or for the Territory or any county or against funds available for such purpose for the payment of any salary or compensation to any person in the public service of the Territory or any county whose appointment, employment, or retention has not been in accordance with this part and any rules or regulations in force thereunder. Any salary or wage paid contrary to the provisions of this part and the rules or regulations established thereunder may be recovered from any person approving such payment or from any officer authorizing the signing or countersigning of a voucher, payroll, check, or warrant for such payment in an action maintained, in the case of the Territory, by the attorney general or, in the case of a county, by the county attorney, or, in the case of either the Territory or a county, by any taxpayer who is a citizen. All moneys recovered in any action brought under this section shall, in case of the Territory, be paid into the treasury of the Territory, or, in case of a county, be paid into the treasury of such county.

Id. § 5–134. *Penalty.*—Whoever willfully and falsely takes or subscribes the oath or affirmation by this part prescribed, when required or authorized to take the same, shall be subject to the punishment for perjury.

Section 299–2 shall apply to any indictment for the crime prescribed by this section.

Any person convicted under this part shall be forever barred from holding office or employment under the government of the Territory or any county thereof, and he shall not be eligible for suspension of imposition or execution of sentence or probation.

Id. § 5–135. *Exceptions.*—To the extent that the Territory is without authority to require, under the Constitution or laws of the United States, compliance by any territorial officer or employee herewith, this part shall not apply to any such officer or employee, but it shall apply to the extent that it or any part thereof can lawfully be made applicable. Any such officer or employee may have the privilege to comply fully and voluntarily herewith and, in such event, any oath or affirmation of any such officer or employee may be taken or made, subscribed and endorsed, delivered and filed as by this part provided.

Id. § 5–136. *Rules and regulations.*—The Governor may from time to time make such rules or regulations as he deems necessary concerning the administration of this part. Without limitation to the generality of the foregoing, such rules or regulations may prescribe standard forms; provide for the printing and distribution of such forms, for the qualifications, oath, compensation, and duties of interpreters, for the administration of the oath or affirmation through interpreters, for the administration of the oath or affirmation and the powers and duties of officers administering the same, for the subscribing of oaths and affirmations and the marking thereof by persons unable to subscribe their names, for the delivery and filing of oaths or affirmations, for the duties of the respective civil service commissions and auditors, and for the duties of all territorial and county officers, commissions, boards, and agencies under this part.

Such regulations shall apply to the Territory and the several counties thereof and shall not require a public hearing thereon or publication in order to be valid.

Id. § 5–137. *Printing and distribution of oath forms.*—Standard forms of such oath and affirmation and of rules and regulations prescribed under this part shall be printed and furnished free of charge to territorial and county officers and employees at the expense respectively of the Territory and the counties. All expenses of the administration of this part shall be paid out of the respective appropriations of the territorial offices, departments, boards, commissions, or agencies required to perform any duty under this part, and out of the funds of each county respectively, to the extent necessary to perform such duty.

Id. § 5–138. *"Head of the department" and "department head" defined.*—As used in this part the terms "head of the department" or "department head" mean the head of any department, commission, board, agency, instrumentality, or other body.

Annotation:

Atty. Gen. Op. 62–7. The oath required by § 5–120 was not affected by the decision of the Supreme Court in *Cramp v. Board of Public Instruction,* 368 U.S. 278, 82 S. Ct. 275, 7 L. Ed. 2d 285 (1961) wherein the Florida loyalty oath was held unconstitutional.

Rev. Laws 1955 § 5–90. *Loyalty board; "Board," "Commission," "Registrant" and "Public officer," and "public employee" defined.*— Whenever used in this part, unless the context otherwise requires:

(a) "Board" means the territorial loyalty board created by section 5–91;

(b) "Commission" means the commission on subversive activities of the Territory;

(c) "Registrant" means and includes every person who is required by the terms of section 5–97 to execute a personal history statement;

(d) "Public officer" and "public employee" mean and include all persons now or hereafter elected to or appointed or employed in the government of the Territory or any county, or in any political subdivision thereof, or appointed to or employed in any office or employment any part of the compensation of which is paid out of public funds.

NOTE.—Section 5–91 formerly dealt with appointment and tenure of the loyalty board. The board has been abolished and its functions and authority have been transferred to the department of personnel services. Rev. Laws §§ 14A–10, 14A–34 (Supp. 1963). All references to the abolished agency apply to the department to which the functions have been transferred. Id. § 14A–30.

Id. § 5–92. *Salaries and expenses of board members.*—The members appointed to the board shall serve without compensation but shall be reimbursed for their actual traveling and hotel expenses incurred by them while attending sessions of the board or any panel thereof at any time or times during the lawful existence of the board and in the performance of any individual duty required of them by the board. Reimbursement shall be made upon vouchers approved by the chairman or vice chairman of the board, from such funds as may be made available therefor. The salaries and expenses of any expert, technical and other assistants employed by the board and all other proper costs, charges, and expenses incurred by the board shall be paid upon vouchers approved by the chairman or vice chairman of the board from such funds.

Id. § 5–93. *Powers and duties of the board.*—The board, in exercising the powers and performing the functions vested in it by this part, shall have all powers necessary or convenient to accomplish the objects and purposes of this part, including, but not limited to, the following duties and powers:

(a) To adopt and, from time to time, amend or revise rules as may be necessary or desirable to govern its procedure (including the fixing of its own quorum and the number of votes necessary to take action on any matter);

(b) To meet at any and all places in this Territory;

(c) With the approval of the Governor, to make regulations it may deem necessary for the administration of this part, which regulations shall apply to the Territory and its political subdivisions and shall not require a public hearing thereon or publication in order to be valid;

(d) To preserve the secrecy of every loyalty proceeding and of the records and files of the board;

(e) To provide that every respondent and every witness appearing before the board or any panel thereof shall have the right to be accompanied by counsel, who shall be permitted to advise his client of his rights;

(f) To provide that every respondent be permitted to inspect a stenographic record of his own testimony.

Id. § 35–94. *Oaths and perjury in connection with board activities.*—Each member of the board and every subordinate designated by the board in its rules is authorized and empowered to administer oaths. False swearing by any respondent or by any witness before the board or any panel thereof or by any registrant in any statement required or authorized to be filed under the provisions, of this part shall constitute perjury and shall be punished as such.

Section 299–2 shall apply to any indictment for any crime prescribed by this section.

Any person convicted under this section shall be forever barred from holding office or employment under the government of the Territory or any political subdivision thereof, and he shall not be eligible for suspension of imposition or execution of sentence or probation.

Id. § 5–95. *Persons determined to be of doubtful loyalty ineligible for public office or employment.*—No person shall be allowed to become or to remain a public officer or public employee if it shall be found, in proceedings, conducted under the provisions of this part, that there is a reasonable doubt of such person's loyalty to the Government of the United States or to the government of the Territory, or if such person shall fail or refuse to comply with any of the provisions of this part. The provisions of section 5–127 shall apply with like force and effect to any person who, being required by the provisions of this part to subscribe and file a personal history statement, shall refuse or neglect to do so or who shall refuse or neglect to accomplish the same in the manner required by this part and any regulations of the board promulgated in pursuance hereof.

Id. § 5–96 (Supp. 1963). *Registrants required to execute personal history statement.*—The board shall prescribe a form of personal history statement to be executed by every registrant. Such statement may call for such information as the board shall prescribe, provided that such statement shall not require the registrant to answer any questions of the registrant's personal history beyond five years with respect to or in connection with any matters relating to Communist, Fascist, or any subversive activity or association of any kind whatsoever. Whenever the board deems it necessary or advisable, the form and content of the personal history statement may be revised. Each such form of personal history statement shall be approved by the Governor before its use shall be authorized and required. Blank copies of the form of personal history statement shall be printed and distributed free of charge to all departments, commissions, boards, agencies, officers, and employees having need for the same, the cost of such printing and distribution to be borne by the board.

Id. § 5–97. *Persons required to execute personal history statement.*—Every public officer and public employee required by part V to take, subscribe and file a loyalty oath or affirmation shall execute and subscribe under oath or affirmation the form of personal history statement prescribed by the board. The board may waive compliance with all or any part of the provisions of this part in respect to any person who has been or may be exempted by the Governor from compliance with the provisions of part V, under the authority given the Governor by section 5–122. Each registrant shall file the prescribed form of personal history statement with the person, officer, or agency with whom the registrant is required by law to file a loyalty oath or affirmation, and such person, officer, or agency receiving the statement shall forward the same to the territorial civil service commission. The civil service commission shall maintain the same as a confidential record and shall not reveal the statement or any of the contents thereof to anyone other than the registrant, the commission on subversive activities, the board, or the Governor. Except for the registrant, no person having access to the statement or to any of the contents thereof shall divulge the same to any person not authorized by law to have access thereto. The territorial civil service commission shall immediately certify to the appropriate auditor or disbursing officer the name and position of each registrant who shall execute and file such personal history statement.

Id. § 5–98. *Time for filing personal history statement.*—All persons who are public officers or public employees and who are subject to the provisions of this part shall execute and file such personal history statement before entering upon the duties of their respective offices or employments. The board may extend the time within which any registrant is required to execute and file such personal history statement, but in no case shall such extension be for a period longer than sixty days and then only after the registrant has shown in writing to the satisfaction of the board that he is or was unable to comply with the requirements of this part because of illness, absence from the Territory, disability, or any other reason deemed to be sufficient by the board.

Id. § 5–99. *Repeated execution of personal history statement not required.*—No registrant continued in office or employment or appointed to or employed in another office or position or reelected or reappointed to succeed himself in any office or position shall be required to reexecute and file the form of personal history statement required by section 5–97 if he did execute and file such a statement on his original election, appointment, or employment and his service in office or employment has been continuous.

Id. § 5–100. *Exceptions to scope of law.*—To the extent that the Territory is without authority to require, under the Constitution or laws of the United States, compliance by any public officer or public employee herewith, this part shall not apply to any such officer or employee, but it shall apply to the extent that it or any part thereof can lawfully be made applicable. Any such officer or employee may have the privilege to comply fully and voluntarily herewith and, in such event, any personal history statement of any such officer or employee may be taken or made, subscribed, delivered, and filed as by this part provided.

Id. § 5–101. *Commission investigations.*—The commission on subversive activities shall receive on a confidential basis from the civil service commission and analyze and evaluate every personal history statement submitted pursuant to this part. Where any such statement reveals derogatory information indicating that the loyalty of a registrant is possibly in doubt, or where similar information is received by the commission from any other source, the commission may initiate such investigative action as in its judgment appears warranted. After having finished its analysis and evaluation of a personal history statement, the commission on subversive activities shall return the statement to the custody of the civil service commission.

NOTE.—For provisions dealing with commission on subversive activities, see Miscellaneous, *infra.*

Id. § 5–102. *Commission referral of information to board.*—When the commission shall have reliable information indicating that there is reason to believe that there may exist a reasonable doubt of a registrant's loyalty, the commission shall refer such information to the board. The commission may refuse to disclose to the board the name of any confidential informant, provided it furnishes sufficient information about such informant to enable the board to make an adequate evaluation of the information furnished by the commission, and provided the commission advises the board in writing ,that it is essential to the protection of the informant or to the investigation of other cases that the identity of the informant be not revealed. The commission shall not use this discretion to decline to reveal sources of information where such action is not essential.

Id. § 5-103. *Action by the board.*—The board shall consider the case of each registrant whose loyalty is deemed questionable because of derogatory information brought to the attention of the board. After considering such information the board shall take one or more of the following actions, as may be deemed appropriate by it:

(a) Decline to initiate proceedings of any kind against the registrant;

(b) Request the commission to conduct further investigation of matters specified by the board in its written request;

(c) Notify the registrant in writing that the board is considering certain derogatory information concerning the registrant, and request (but not require) the registrant to answer under oath an interrogatory propounded by the board;

(d) Serve written charges on the registrant, thereby commencing a loyalty hearing proceeding.

Id. § 25-104. *Loyalty hearing procedures.*—If a loyalty hearing proceeding is instituted against any registrant, the following procedures shall be adhered to:

(a) Unless otherwise ordered by the board, all hearings shall be held by panels of the board. Such panels shall consist of not less than three members designated by the chairman. The chairman shall designate the board member who shall be the presiding member of the panel, and such presiding member shall make due report to the board of all acts and proceedings of the panel.

(b) The charge against the registrant shall be stated in writing, shall specify the information upon which the board bases the charge, and shall inform the registrant that he will be given a hearing on the charge if he so demands in writing.

(c) The registrant against whom a hearing procedure is instituted (and who shall in such case be called the "respondent") may controvert the charge by filing with the board within twenty days after service of the charge a written answer, verified upon oath or affirmation, which answer shall respond specifically to every allegation contained in the charge. The board may for good cause allow the registrant additional time in which to file such answer.

(d) If the respondent desires a hearing on the charge he shall within twenty days after service of the same upon him notify the board in writing of his demand. The respondent may make such demand with or without filing an answer to the charge. If the respondent demands a hearing, the board or its panel having cognizance of the case shall set the time and place of such hearing and in writing notify the respondent thereof.

(e) If the respondent does not make answer as provided in subparagraph (c) of this section, the board or the panel shall consider the case on the complete file (which shall include all reports of investigation or other inquiry, all charges and interrogatories, all transcripts of hearings and exhibits, all memoranda analyzing the evidence or setting forth conclusions, findings, recommendations, determinations, decisions, or other actions in the case, and all affidavits, supporting documents, correspondence, or memoranda in connection with the investigation, determination, decision, and closing of the case). Despite the respondent's failure or refusal to answer, the board or the panel shall notify him of the time and place the case will be considered, in order that the respondent and his counsel or other representative may appear if he so desires.

(f) If the respondent makes answer as provided in subparagraph (c) but does not demand a hearing, the board or the panel shall then consider the case on the complete file (including such answer). Before making a determination, however, the board or the panel may, in its discretion, if it deems a hearing necessary or desirable, request the respondent to appear for a hearing, but cannot require him to appear and cannot require him to be a witness if he does appear.

(g) No inference or presumption shall be assumed by the board or any panel because of the failure or refusal of any registrant or respondent to reply to an interrogatory, or to answer a charge, or to demand a hearing on a charge, or to appear at a hearing on a charge, or to refuse to be a witness at such a hearing which he may attend.

(h) The board may take testimony and receive other evidence or information at the time of or prior to the hearing on the charge. It may require a representative of the commission to be present before it and evaluate information furnished by the commission to the board, but it shall not be empowered at any time to require the commission or its representative to divulge any confidential source of information. Any such appearance by a representative of the commission shall be in private and before the board members only.

(i) At the hearing on a charge, testimony shall be given under oath or affirmation. Strict rules of evidence shall not be applied, but reasonable bounds shall be maintained as to competency, relevancy, and materiality.

(j) Every board or panel hearing on a loyalty charge shall be private, except that the respondent may be present in person and with one attorney or representative of his choosing.

(k) Witnesses produced by the respondent shall be subject to cross-examination by the board.

(l) The respondent may not be required to testify in the proceeding, but may testify in his own behalf if he so desires. If he so testifies, he shall be subject to cross-examination by the board.

Id. § 5–105. *Review of panel decision.*—If the decision of the panel is adverse to the respondent, the case shall then be considered by the board on the record of proceedings and exhibits had before the panel. The board shall then take one or more of the following actions, as it deems appropriate and just:

(a) Affirm the decision of the panel without further proceedings;

(b) Reverse the decision of the panel without further proceedings;

(c) Require a rehearing or a further hearing of the case before the board, and at the conclusion thereof affirm or reverse the decision of the panel. The board shall notify the respondent in writing of the decision in the case.

Id. § 5–106 (Supp. 1963). *Orders of the board.*—Where the decision of the board is unfavorable to the respondent, the board shall issue an order, directed to the appropriate appointing or employing authority and directed to the comptroller or other disbursing officer who issues warrants to pay the respondent for his services as a public officer or public employee, certifying the board's finding that there is a reasonable doubt of the respondent's loyalty to the Government of the United States or to the government of the State. Upon receipt of the board's order, (a) the appointing or employing authority shall discharge the respondent from office or employment, and (b) the appropriate auditor or other disbursing officer shall make no further payments of public funds to the respondent, except to pay the respondent the salary, wages, bonus, or other compensation to which the respondent otherwise would be entitled if he were voluntarily terminating his office or employment on the day such order is served on the appropriate auditor or other disbursing officer.

Where the respondent who is the subject of such order is a candidate for public office, the board shall direct and deliver its order to the official whose duty it would be to certify the election of the respondent were the latter to be elected, and such official shall not certify the election of such respondent.

Where the respondent who is the subject of such order is an applicant for public employment, the board shall direct and deliver its order to the appropriate appointing or employing authority who or which is considering the appointment or employment of the respondent.

In any case where the decision of the board is unfavorable to the respondent holding public office or employment, but the board shall find mitigating circumstances, the board may include in its order a provision that the respondent be permitted to resign his office of employment. If the respondent shall not resign within three days after such order is served upon him, he shall be discharged as hereinbefore provided.

Any such order of the board shall be a confidential record and shall not be made public by anyone other than the respondent.

Id. § 5-107. *Suspension before final determination in limited cases.*—No registrant shall be suspended from office or employment until after a final determination of an unfavorable nature by the board, except in cases where the circumstances are such that a retention of the registrant in an active duty status may be detrimental to the interests of the Territory or any political subdivision thereof. In such exceptional cases the registrant may be temporarily assigned to duties in which this condition would not exist, or be placed on vacation leave (provided he has sufficient vacation leave to his credit to cover the required period), be placed on leave without pay with his consent, or be suspended. Any such action against a registrant shall be taken only by the appropriate appointing or employing authority, but the board may suggest that such action be taken.

Id. § 5-108. *Standard of evidence.*—The standard for the refusal of employment or office or the removal from employment or office on grounds relating to loyalty shall be that, on all the information before the board, there exists a reasonable doubt of the respondent's loyalty to the Government of the United States or to the government of the Territory. Activities or associations of a respondent which may be considered in connection with the determination of the issue whether such reasonable doubt exists may include one or more of the following:

(a) Sabotage, espionage, or attempts or preparations therefor, or knowingly associating with spies or saboteurs;

(b) Treason or sedition or advocacy thereof;

(c) Advocacy of revolution or force or violence to alter the constitutional form of Government of the United States or of the Territory;

(d) Intentional, unauthorized disclosure to any person, under circumstances which may indicate disloyalty to the United States, of documents or information of a confidential or nonpublic character obtained by the person making the disclosure as a result of his employment by the Government of the United States or of the Territory;

(e) Performing or attempting to perform his duties, or otherwise acting, so as to serve the interests of another government in preference to the interest of the United States;

(f) Membership in, affiliation with or sympathetic association with any foreign or domestic organization, association, movement, group or combination of persons, designated by the Attorney General of the United States as totalitarian, Fascist, Communist, or subversive, or as having adopted a policy of advocating or approving the commission of acts of force or violence to deny other persons their rights under the Constitution of the United States, or as seeking to alter the form of Government of the United States by unconstitutional means.

A finding against the respondent on any of the matters specified in the above subparagraphs shall not require the board to find against the respondent in the case, it being intended that the subparagraphs are merely specifications of information or evidence which the board may consider in making its determination of the case. The board may consider any other information relevant to the issue to be determined.

Id. §5–109. *Review of board decisions in limited cases.*—Except where the board shall exceed its powers given by this part or shall deprive a respondent of his rights guaranteed herein, the proceedings and orders of the board had under the provisions of this part shall not be subject to review by any court. The provisions of chapter 3 shall not apply to any person suspended, removed or discharged under the provisions of this part.

Id. § 5–110. *Board records confidential.*—The files and records of the board shall be confidential records. Such files and records shall not be subject to subpoena in any matter or proceeding, nor shall the testimony of any member or subordinate of the board be compellable or given concerning such files and records and any contents thereof. The commission shall be permitted to examine such files and records and make copies of or extracts therefrom.

Id. § 5–111. *Effect of removal.*—No person removed from public office or public employment by virtue of proceedings had before the board under the provisions of this part shall be eligible thereafter to hold public office or public employment unless, upon new or further proceedings had before the board, it shall be determined that there no longer exists a reasonable doubt as to such person's loyalty to the Government of the United States and of the Territory.

Id. § 5–112. *Claims against the Government barred.*—The provisions of chapter 245 shall not apply to any person suspended, removed, or discharged under the provisions of this part nor to any claim for wages, salary, bonus or other compensation of any such person. No court shall have jurisdiction to hear and determine any claim for wages, salary, bonus or other compensation of any person lawfully suspended, removed, or discharged under the provisions of this part. This part shall not be construed so as to prohibit any court of competent jurisdiction from entertaining or hearing any proper suit or action of which it would otherwise have jurisdiction to effect the suspension, removal, or discharge of any officer or employee refusing or failing to comply with the provisions of this part.

Id. § 5–113. *Restrictions on disbursing officers relative to circumstances covered by the Loyalty Board provisions.*—The provisions of section 5–133 shall apply with like force and effect in the case of every person whose election, appointment, employment or retention in office or employment has not been in accordance with this part and any regulations in force hereunder.

Id. § 5–114. *Procedure in the case of certain appointive officers.*—In the case of any officer who may only be removed from office by the governor by and with the advice and consent of the senate of the Territory, (a) if any such officer shall fail or refuse to execute and file the personal history statement authorized and required by this part, or (b) if the board shall find that there is a reasonable doubt of such officer's loyalty to the Government of the United States or to the government of the Territory, then in either such case, upon the fact thereof being certified in the manner herein otherwise provided, the appropriate auditor or other disbursing officer shall make no further payments of public funds to such officer, except to pay such officer the salary, wages, bonus or other compensation to which he would otherwise be entitled if he were voluntarily vacating his office on the day a certificate of such fact is received by said appropriate auditor or other disbursing officer.

Id. § 5–115. *Cooperation with the board.*—Every department, commission, board, agency, officer and employee of the Territory and of any political subdivision thereof shall furnish the board or any panel thereof, upon request, any and all such assistance, information, records and documents as the board or panel deems proper for the accomplishment of the purposes for which the board is created. Any officer or employee of the Territory, or of any political subdivision thereof, upon written request of the board, or of any panel thereof, shall appear before the board or such panel, as the case may be, and shall give such evidence, information or testimony and produce such official records as may be required of him.

Id. § 5–116. *Clerical and legal staff assistance.*—The territorial civil service commission shall furnish to the board such clerical and administrative assistance as the board reasonably may require. The board may select as its executive secretary or administrative officer some subordinate of the civil service commission, who shall serve in such capacity without additional compensation. The attorney general shall be the legal adviser to the board.

Id. § 5–4. *Failure to appear or testify constitutes grounds for termination of employment.*—If any person subject to the provisions of sections 5–3 to 5–6, after lawful notice or process, willfully refuses or fails to appear before any court or judge, any legislative committee, or any officer, board, commission or other body authorized to conduct any hearing or inquiry, or having appeared refuses to testify or to answer any question regarding (a) the government, property or affairs of the Territory or of any political subdivision thereof, or

(b) the person's qualifications for public office or employment (including matters pertaining to loyalty or disloyalty), or (c) the qualifications of any officer or employee of the Territory or any political subdivision thereof, on the ground that his answer would tend to incriminate him, or refuses to testify or to answer any such question without right, his term or tenure of office or employment shall terminate and such office or employment shall be vacant, and he shall not be eligible to election or appointment to any office or employment under the Territory or any political subdivision thereof. To the extent that the Territory is without authority to require, under the Constitution or laws of the United States, compliance by any public officer or public employee herewith, sections 5–3 to 5–6 shall not apply to any such officer or employee, but such sections shall apply to the extent that they or any part thereof can lawfully be made applicable.

2. CIVIL DEFENSE PERSONNEL

Rev. Laws 1955, § 359–20. *Loyalty oath required.*—In order to comply with the Federal Civil Defense Act of 1950 it is hereby provided that each person appointed to serve in an organization for civil defense who is so required by the Federal Civil Defense Act of 1950, shall, before entering upon his duties, take an oath in writing before a person authorized to administer oaths, which oath shall be substantially as follows:

"I, ------------------, do solemnly swear (or affirm) that I will support and defend the Constitution of the United States against all enemies, foreign and domestic; that I will bear true faith and allegiance to the same; that I take this obligation freely, without any mental reservation or purpose of evasion; and that I will well and faithfully discharge the duties upon which I am about to enter.

"And I do further swear (or affirm) that I do not advocate, nor am I a member or an affiliate of any organization, group, or combination of persons that advocates the overthrow of the Government of the United States by force or violence; and that during such time as I am a member of the (name of civil defense organiaztion), I will not advocate nor become a member or an affiliate of any organization, group, or combination of persons that advocates the overthrow of the Government of the United States by force or violence."

Provided, that to the extent permitted by the Federal Civil Defense Act of 1950 the Governor by rule may provide for additional time for the taking of the oath, in cases where compliance with such requirement before the person so required enters upon his duties is or may be impracticable; for like reasons the Governor similarly may provide as to the oath required by part V of chapter 5.

The Governor by rule may relieve persons, or classes of persons, subject to the requirements imposed by this section, from compliance with part V of chapter 5.

TEACHERS' LOYALTY

Rev. Laws 1955, § 5–120. *Loyalty oath required.*—All persons elected to or appointed or employed in the government of the Territory or any county, or in any political subdivision thereof, or appointed to or employed in any office or employment, any part of the compensation of which is paid out of public funds shall, before entering upon the duties of their respective offices or employments, take and subscribe to the following written oath or affirmation:

"I, _____, do solemnly swear and declare, on oath, that I will support and defend the Constitution and laws of the United States of America against all enemies, foreign and domestic; that I will bear true faith and allegiance to the same; that I do not hold membership in, pay assessments, dues, or make contributions to any organization or any political party which advocates the overthrow of the constitutional form of Government of the United States of America or any change in the Government of the United States of America, except as provided by its Constitution; that I take this obligation freely, without any mental reservation or purpose of evasion. So help me God."

Upon being satisfied as to the sincerity of any person claiming that he is unwilling to take the above prescribed oath only because due to religious beliefs he is unwilling to be sworn, he may be permitted, in lieu of such oath, to make his solemn affirmation which shall be in the same form as the oath except that the words "sincerely and truly affirm" shall be substituted for the word "swear" and the phrases "on oath" and "So help me God" shall be omitted. Such affirmation shall be of the same force and effect as the prescribed oath.

The oath or affirmation shall be subscribed in duplicate before the officer administering the same, who shall endorse thereon the fact that the oath was subscribed and sworn to or the affirmation was made together with the date thereof and affix the seal of his office or of the court of which he is a judge or clerk.

NOTE.—See Loyalty of State Officers and Employees, *supra*, for comprehensive loyalty oath statutory scheme.

Id. § 5–4. *Failure to appear or testify constitutes grounds for termination of employment.*—If any person subject to the provisions of sections 5–3 to 5–6, after lawful notice or process, wilfully refuses or fails to appear before any court or judge, any legislative committee, or any officer, board, commission, or other body authorized to conduct any hearing or inquiry, or having appeared refuses to testify or to answer any question regarding (a) the government, property, or affairs of the Territory or of any political subdivision thereof, or (b) the person's qualifications for public office or employment (including matters pertaining to loyalty or disloyalty), or (c) the qualifications of any officer or employee of the Territory or any political subdivision thereof, on the ground that his answer would tend to incriminate him, or refuses to testify or to answer any such question without right, his term or tenure of office or employment shall terminate and such office or employment shall be vacant, and he shall not be eligible to election or appointment to any office or employment under the Territory or any political subdivision thereof. To the extent that the Territory is without authority to require, under the Constitution or laws of the United States, compliance by any public officer or public employee herewith, sections 5–3 to 5–6 shall not apply to any such officer or employee, but such sections shall apply to the extent that they or any part thereof can lawfully be made applicable.

Exclusion From the Bar

Rule 15 (Admission to the Bar) of the Rules of the Supreme Court of Hawaii, provides, in relevant part, that "every applicant for admission to the bar shall file with the clerk a verified typewritten application, in duplicate, setting forth * * * that he is a citizen of the United States of America, and that he bears no allegiance or fidelity to any foreign nation, state, or sovereign, * * *"

The application form for admission to the bar contains the following statement of allegiance to be subscribed to by the applicant.

I am a citizen of the United States of America, and I bear no allegiance or fidelity to any foreign nation, state, or sovereign.

An "additional questionnaire" requires the applicant to answer questions relating to membership in the Communist Party or Communist dominated or affiliated organizations. It reads as follows:

1. Are you now, or have you ever been, a member of the Communist Party of the United States of America, a member of the Communist Party of any other country, or a member of the Communist Political Association?

2. Have you ever attended any meeting of a cell, fraction, school or other unit of either the Communist Party of the United States of America or the Communist Political Association?

3. Are you now, or have you ever been, a member of any organization, association, committee, movement, group or combination of persons which you have reason to believe is or has been dominated by, affiliated with or sympathetic to the Communist Party of the United States of America or to the Communist Political Association?

4. Are you now, or have you ever been, a member of or affiliated with any foreign or domestic organization, association, committee, movement, group or combination of persons, designated by the Attorney General of the United States as totalitarian, Fascist, Communist, or subversive, or as having adopted a policy of advocating or approving the commission of acts of force or violence to deny other persons their rights under the Constitution of the United States, or as seeking to alter the form of Government of the United States by unconstitutional means?

5. Have you ever paid dues or made any donation or other financial contribution to any of the organizations or other groups named or described in paragraphs, 1, 2, 3, and 4 above?

Correspondence received from the board of examiners of the Supreme Court of Hawaii discloses that "in the event an applicant has been a Communist or a subversive or if the application, questionnaire or information received by the board indicates any question as to an applicant's loyalty," it is the practice to intensify the investigation. A hearing may also be ordered by the board of examiners in such cases. Although the mentioned correspondence does not state the manner in which these cases are finally disposed of, indications are that membership in the party or other relevant activities bars admission.

Miscellaneous

Rev. Laws 1955, § 361–1. *Commission on subversive activities authorized.*—There shall be a fact-finding commission to be known as "The Commission on subversive activities," hereinafter referred to as the "commission," for the purposes and with the powers and duties herein stated.

The commission shall be composed of seven members, three of whom shall respectively be residents of the islands of Kauai, Maui, and Hawaii, nominated and appointed for a term of four years by the Governor by and with the advice and consent of the Senate, one of whom shall be designated in the appointment as chairman, and at least three of whom, including the chairman, shall be attorneys licensed to practice in all of the courts of the Territory, and no more than four of whom shall be members of any one political party. Any vacancy occurring in the membership of the commission may be forthwith filled by the Governor and such appointment shall be effective at once.

In case of the chairman's absence, illness or incapacity, the commission shall select from its membership an acting chairman, to serve during such absence, illness or incapacity. The chairman or acting chairman, as the case may be, shall: (a) preside at all meetings of the commission; (b) certify or authenticate all actions, doings, proceedings or documents of the commission; (c) approve all vouchers for expenditure authorized by this chapter; (d) hold in his custody, for the commission, all records, papers, books, accounts and other documents of the commission; (e) subject to the directions of the commission, supervise all employees of the commission; and (f) perform all other acts authorized by the commission pursuant to the provisions of this chapter.

NOTE.—The Commission has been placed within the department of the attorney general for administrative purposes and is subject to the administrative control of the attorney general. Rev. Laws 1955 § 14A–12 (Supp. 1963). For the extent of such control, see § 14A–4; appointment, tenure and removal of members, see § 14A–3.

Id. § 361–2. *Investigations.*—The commission shall:

(a) Investigate, ascertain, collate, appraise, study and analyze all facts directly or indirectly relating to any person or persons or groups of persons, within the Territory, who (1) endanger the provision for the common defense against aggression by any foreign nation, (2) seek to destroy by force, threats or sabotage, liberties and freedom guaranteed by or provided for in the United States Constitution, (3) seek to subject the United States and the Territory to the domination of any foreign nation, (4) seek to achieve by subversion or conspiracy, the subsitution for American ideals and processes in the Territory a Communist or other program of totalitarian government subservient to a foreign nation, (5) advocate the overthrow of the Government of the United States or of the Territory by force or violence or other unlawful means, (6) seek to corrupt or subvert officers or employees of the government or for the purposes of substituting for American ideals and processes in the Territory a Communist or other program of totalitarian government for the purpose of overthrowing the Government of the United States or of the Territory by force or violence or other unlawful means, (7) unlawfully engage in espionage or fifth column activities on behalf of any foreign nation, or (8) seek to undermine the stability of American institutions or individual rights, liberties and freedoms:

(b) Investigate, ascertain, study and report on the activities of persons, groups or organizations, within the Territory, whose membership includes persons who are Communists, or any other persons, groups or organizations, within the Territory, known or suspected to be dominated or controlled by a foreign nation or to have as an objective the overthrow of the governments of the Territory or of the United States by force or violence or other unlawful means;

(c) Perform all investigative and other duties required of it by the provisions of any other law;

(d) Investigate, ascertain, collate, appraise, study and analyze subversive propaganda originated or disseminated in the Territory and make and publish such analyses thereof as in the judgment of the commission appears necessary or desirable.

Id. § 361–3. *Commission reports; records and files confidential.*— The commission may file interim reports to every special session of the legislature of the Territory, and shall file a report to the legislature not later than the tenth legislative day of every regular session. A copy of each such report shall be forwarded to the Governor. The commission may make a report to the Governor whenever, in its judgment, the circumstances so warrant.

Except for reports analyzing or exposing subversive propaganda (which report the commission may make public), no report of the commission shall be made public except by the legislature or the Governor.

The files and records of the commission shall be confidential. Such files and records shall not be subject to subpoena in any matter of proceeding, nor shall the testimony of any member or subordinate of the commission be compellable or given concerning such files and records and any contents thereof; provided, that the commission may furnish information from such files and records on a confidential basis to Federal and territorial law enforcement agencies and to the responsible heads of any territorial or county agency whom the commission deems proper to receive the same. Any officer or employee of the Territory or any political subdivision thereof who is furnished any such information by the commission shall maintain the confidential nature of such information and shall observe such conditions upon the use of such information as may be imposed by the commission when it disseminates the information.

Id. § 361–4. *Powers and duties of the Commission.*—The commission in exercising the powers and performing the functions vested in it by law shall have all powers necessary or convenient to accomplish the objects and purposes for which the commission was created, including but not limited to the following duties and powers:

(a) To employ, without regard to any residence qualifications provided for government officers and employees in other laws, and to fix the compensation of such clerical, investigative, legal, expert, and technical assistants as it may deem necessary, which assistants shall not be subject to the territorial civil service and classification laws;

(b) To create committees from its membership and to designate the chairman thereof, assigning to the committee any study, inquiry, investigation, or hearing which the commission itself has authority to undertake or hold, and the committee shall have and exercise all of the powers conferred upon the commission, limited by the express terms of the resolution or resolutions of the latter defining the powers and duties of the committees, which powers may be withdrawn or terminated at any time by the commission; provided that no report of a committee shall be made public until and unless it is adopted and released by the commission;

(c) To adopt, and from time to time, amend or revise rules as may be necessary or desirable to govern its procedure (including the fixing of its own quorum and the number of votes necessary to take action on any matter);

(d) To contract with such other agencies, public or private, within or without the Territory, as it deems necessary for the rendition and affording of such services, facilities, studies, and reports to the commission as will best assist it to carry out the purposes for which it is created, and to lease, rent or buy such supplies and facilties as may be required;

(e) To make a complete study, survey and investigation of every phase of the subject of this chapter, including but not limited to the operation, effect, administration, enforcement, needed revision and enactment of any and all laws in anywise bearing upon or relating to the subject of this chapter;

(f) To meet at any and all places in the Territory, in public or executive session;

(g) To maintain confidential files and records, to make reports, and to disseminate information as required or permitted by law;

(h) To do any and all other things necessary or convenient to enable it fully and adequately to exercise its powers, perform its duties, and accomplish the objects and purposes for which the commission was created.

Id. § 361–5. *Rules of procedure.*—The commission shall adopt proper rules to provide:

(a) That the subject of any investigation be set forth clearly in advance to witnesses called;

(b) That witnesses will have the right to be accompanied by counsel, permitted to advise the witness while on the stand of his rights;

(c) That witnesses may be permitted reasonable opportunity at the conclusion of the examination by the commission to supplement their testimony in writing on matters with regard to which they have been previously examined;

(d) That witnesses will be permitted to inspect a stenographic record of their testimony, and, if the testimony is given at a public session, witnesses may receive a copy of their testimony at their expense;

(e) That no photographs, moving pictures, television or radio broadcasting of the proceedings shall be permitted while any witness is testifying.

Id. § 361–6. *Administration of oath; penalty.*—Each member of the commission, and any person designated by the commission or by its chairman, may administer oaths. False swearing by any witness before the commission or any committee thereof shall constitute perjury and shall be punished as such.

Id. § 361–7. *Subpoena power.*—In the discharge of any duty herein imposed, the commission, or any committee thereof, may through its designated members or subordinates issue subpoenas, compel the attendance of witnesses and the production of any papers, books, accounts, documents and testimony, cause the deposition of witnesses, either residing within or without the Territory, to be taken in the manner prescribed by law for taking depositions in civil actions in the circuit courts, pay fees and traveling expenses of witnesses to insure their attendance, if necessary, and procure, from any court having jurisdiction upon complaint showing probable cause to believe that pertinent evidence is being concealed or withheld from the commission, or a committee thereof, as the case may be, a search warrant, and cause search to be made therefor. In any case of disobedience on the part of any person to comply with any subpoena issued in behalf of such commission, or any committee thereof, or on the refusal of any witness to testify to any matters regarding which he may be lawfully interrogated before the commission, or any committee thereof, the circuit court of any circuit, or the judge thereof, upon application of such commission, or committee, or any member thereof, shall compel obedience by proceedings for contempt, as in the case of disobedience of the requirements of a subpoena issued from such court or a refusal to testify therein.

Id. § 361–8. *Form of subpoena and service.*—Every such subpoena shall run in the name of "The Territory of Hawaii" and shall be sufficient if it: (a) states whether the proceeding is before the commission, or a committee; (b) is addressed to the person desired as a witness; (c) requires the attendance of the person desired as a witness at a time and place certain; and (d) is signed by the chairman of the commission, or the chairman of a committee thereof before whom attendance of the person as a witness is desired.

Every such subpoena shall be served upon the person to whom it is addressed by the high sheriff of the Territory or his deputy, or a sheriff of a county or his deputy, or any police officer, or any other person designated by the commission to serve the same.

Id. § 361–9. *Cooperation with the commission.*—Every department, commission, board, agency, officer and employee of the Territory and of any political subdivision thereof shall furnish the commission and any committee, upon request, any and all such assistance, and information, records and documents as the commission or committee deems proper for the accomplishment of the purposes for which the commission is created; and any officer or employee of the Territory, or of any political subdivision thereof, shall, upon written request of the commission, or of any committee thereof, appear before the commission or such committee, as the case may be, and shall give such evidence, information or testimony as may be required of him.

Id. § 361–10. *Witness fees and expenses.*—Every witness who appears before the commission, or any committee thereof, by its order, other than an officer or employee of the Territory or any political subdivision thereof, shall receive for his attendance the fees provided for witnesses in civil cases in the courts of record and the actual cost of his transportation (but not to exceed the mileage allowed witnesses in such civil cases) and such fees and transportation costs shall be paid from the appropriation made for the commission upon the presentation of proper vouchers sworn to by such witness and approved by the chairman of the commission; provided, that in the case of expert witnesses the commission may pay such additional amounts as it deems proper in the circumstances.

Id. § 361–11. *Duties and privileges of witnesses.*—No person shall be excused from attending and testifying or from producing books, papers or documents before the commission or any committee thereof in obedience to the subpoena of the commission or of any committee thereof; but no individual shall be prosecuted or subjected to any penalty or forfeiture on account of any transaction, matter or thing concerning which he is compelled, after having claimed his privilege against self-incrimination, to testify or to produce evidence, documentary or otherwise, except that any individual so testifying shall not be exempt from prosecution and punishment for perjury committed in so testifying.

Id. § 361–12. *Salaries and expenses of Commission members, staff, experts.*—The members of the commission shall be reimbursed for their actual traveling and hotel expenses incurred by them while attending sessions of the commission or any committee thereof at any time or times during the lawful existence of the commission and in the performance of any individual duty required of them by the commission, the same to be paid upon their individual vouchers, approved by the chairman of the commission, from such funds as may be made available therefor. The salaries and expenses of any expert, clerical, investigative, legal, technical and other assistants employed by the commission and all other proper costs, charges and expenses incurred by the commission shall be paid upon vouchers approved by the chairman of the commission from such funds.

IDAHO

Idaho Code § 18-2001. *Criminal syndicalism defined.*—Criminal syndicalism is the doctrine which willfully and maliciously advocates crime, sabotage (sabotage, for the purposes of this chapter, is defined to mean damage, injury or destruction of real or personal property; work done in an improper manner; tampering with or disabling of machinery; improper use of materials; loitering at work; slack work; slowing down work or production; scamped work; waste of property; the publication of trade secrets; or either or any of the foregoing acts) violence or unlawful methods of terrorism as a means of accomplished industrial or political reform. The advocacy of such doctrine, whether by word of mouth or writing is a felony punishable as in this chapter otherwise provided.

Id. § 18-2002. *Unlawful acts and penalty.*—Any person who:

1. By word of mouth or writing advocates or teaches the duty, necessity or propriety of crime, sabotage, violence or other unlawful methods of terrorism as a means of accomplishing industrial or political reform; or,

2. Prints, publishes, edits, issues or knowingly circulates, sells, distributes or publicly displays any book, paper, document or written matter in any form, containing or advocating, advising or teaching the doctrine that industrial or political reform should be brought about by crime, sabotage, violence, or other unlawful methods of terrorism; or

3. Openly, willfully, and deliberately justifies, by word of mouth or writing, the commission or the attempt to commit crime, sabotage, violence, or other unlawful methods of terrorism with intent to exemplify, spread, or advocate the propriety of the doctrines of criminal syndicalism; or

4. Organizes or helps to organize or attempts to organize or becomes a member of or who, being a member thereof, continues or retains such membership or voluntarily assembles with any society, group, or assemblage of persons formed to teach or advocate, or which does teach or advocate the doctrines of criminal syndicalism;

Is guilty of a felony and punishable by imprisonment in the State prison for not more than ten years or by a fine of not more than $5,000, or both.

Id. § 18-2003. *Assemblage to advocate criminal syndicalism.*—Whenever two or more persons assemble for the purpose of advocating or teaching the doctrines of criminal syndicalism as defined in this chapter, such an assemblage is unlawful, and every person voluntarily participating therein by his presence, aid or instigation is guilty of a felony and punishable by imprisonment in the State prison for not more than ten years, or by a fine of not more than $5,000, or both.

127

Id. § 18–2004. *Permitting premises to be used to advocate criminal syndicalism.*—The owner, agent, superintendent, janitor, caretaker or occupant of any place, building, or room, who willfully and knowingly permits therein any assemblage of persons prohibited by the provisions of the foregoing section, or who, after notification that the premises are so used, permits such use to be continued, is guilty of a misdemeanor and punishable by imprisonment in the county jail for not more than one year or by a fine of not more than $500.00, or both.

Annotation:

State v. *Dingman*, 37 Idaho 253, 219 Pac. 760 (1923). Appellant and others were convicted of the crime of criminal syndicalism in that they did "willfully, unlawfully, and feloniously advocate, teach, and advise the duty, necessity, and propriety of crime, sabotage, violence, and unlawful methods of terrorism as a means of accomplishing industrial and political reform, by unlawful means of a society, group, and assemblage of persons, then, and there known as the 'Industrial Workers of the World,' which * * * was formed to teach and advocate, and does teach and advocate, the doctrines of criminal syndicalism and the duty, necessity, and propriety of crime, sabotage, violence, and unlawful methods of terrorism as a means of accomplishing industrial and political reform, and they * * * did * * * organize and help to organize and become members of * * * Industrial Workers of the World * * *."

The conviction was reversed on grounds that extrajudicial statements of persons who claimed to be members of the IWW but who were in no way connected with the transaction being tried or any of the parties, were hearsay and inadmissible. "Where a conviction follows the admission of incompetent evidence, it is never possible for the court to say to what extent its admission influenced the verdict." During the course of its opinion, the court sustained the constitutionality of the criminal syndicalism statute over objections that it violated the Fifth, Sixth, and Fourteenth Amendments and that it violated the proscription against cruel and unusual punishments.

Exclusion From the Elective Process

Idaho Code § 34–807. *"Elector's Oath."*—Said registrar having posted notices shall proceed to enter in the original and all copies of such register, in alphabetical order, the names of all electors personally registering before him, at any time prior to nine (9) o'clock P.M. on the last Saturday next preceding the primary election and, in the original register and copies to be used for the general election, likewise enter the names of all electors personally registering before him subsequent to the primary election and prior to nine (9) o'clock P.M. on the last Saturday next preceding the general election, and which electors subscribe to the following oath to be known as the "Elector's Oath":

I do swear (or affirm) that I am a citizen of the United States, and an elector of _____ precinct, of the age of twenty-one years, or will be on the _____ day of _____, 19___, (naming the date of the next succeeding primary election, or if the elector offers to register subsequently to the primary election, then name the date of the next ensuing general election); that I have (or will have) actually resided in this State for six months, and in this county for thirty days next preceding the next ensuing _____ election (if registration is made prior to the primary election, insert the word "primary"; if registration is subsequent to the primary election, insert the word "general") ; that I have never been convicted of treason, felony, embezzlement of public funds, bartering or selling or offering to barter or sell my vote, or purchase or offer to purchase the vote of another, or other infamous crime, without thereafter being restored to the rights of citizenship; that I will not commit any act in violation of the provisions of this oath; that I am not now registered and entitled to vote at any other place in this State; that I do regard the Constitution of the United States and the laws thereof, and the constitution of this State and the laws thereof, as interpreted by the courts as the supreme law of the land; so help me God.

Signed _____
   Subscribed and sworn to before me this _____ day of _____,
19____.

                         _____
                         Registrar of _____ Precinct,
                         _____ County, Idaho.

* * * * * * *

LOYALTY OF STATE OFFICERS AND EMPLOYEES

1. ELECTIVE AND NONELECTIVE PERSONNEL

Laws 1963, ch. 210, pp. 599–600. *Loyalty oath required.*—
SECTION 1. That Section 59–401, Idaho Code, be, and the same is hereby amended to read as follows:
59–401. FORM OF OATH—LOYALTY OATH.—Before any public officer or employee elected or appointed to fill any office, created by the laws of the State of Idaho, enters upon the duties of his office, he must take and subscribe an oath, to be known as the official oath, which is as follows:
I do solemnly swear (or affirm) that I will support the Constitution of the United States, and the constitution and the laws of this State; that I will faithfully discharge all the duties of the office of _____ according to the best of my ability.
I, _____, do further solemnly swear (or affirm) that I will support and defend the Constitution of the United States and the constitution of the State of Idaho against all enemies, foreign or domestic; that I will bear true faith and allegiance to the Constitution of the United States and the constitution of the State of Idaho; that I take this obligation freely, without any mental reservation or purpose of evasion; and that I will well and faithfully discharge the duties upon which I am about to enter.
And I do further swear (or affirm) that I do not advocate, nor am I a member of any party or organization, political or otherwise, that now advocates the overthrow of the Government of the United States or of the State of Idaho by force or violence or other unlawful means; that within the five years immediately preceding the taking of this oath (or affirmation) I have not been a member of any party or organization, political or otherwise, that advocates the overthrow of the

Government of the United States or of the State of Idaho by force or violence or other unlawful means except as follows:

(If no affiliation, write in the words "No Exceptions") and that during such time as I hold the office of _____ I will not advocate nor become a member of any party or organization, political or otherwise, that advocates the overthrow of the Government of the United States or of the State of Idaho by force or violence or other unlawful means. So help me God.

And no other oath, declaration, or test, shall be required as a qualification for any public office or employment, except as otherwise provided by law.

A failure or refusal to take and subscribe such oath shall make such person ineligible to hold such office or to receive compensation for the same.

Public "Officer" and "employee" includes every officer and employee of the State, University of Idaho, Idaho State College, every other college and every county, city, school district, and authority, including any department, division, bureau, board, commission, agency, or instrumentality of any of the foregoing.

SECTION 2. SEPARABILITY.—If any of the provisions of this act or the application thereof to any person, or circumstance is held invalid, such invalidity shall not affect other provisions or applications which can be given effect without said invalid provisions or applications.

SECTION 3. REPEALING CONFLICTING LAWS.—All laws or parts of laws in conflict, in whole or in part, with the provisions of this act are hereby repealed.

2. CIVIL DEFENSE PERSONNEL

Idaho Code § 46–1006 (Supp. 1961). *Loyalty oath required.*— (1) No person shall be employed or associated in any capacity in any civil defense organization established under this act who advocates or has advocated a change by force or violence in the constitutional form of the Government of the United States or in this State or the overthrow of any government in the United States by force or violence, or who has been convicted of or is under indictment or information charging any subversive act against the United States. Each person who is appointed to serve in an organization for civil defense shall, before entering upon his duties, take an oath, in writing, before a person authorized to administer oaths in this State, which oath shall be substantially as follows:

"I, _____, do solemnly swear (or affirm) that I will support and defend the Constitution of the United States and the constitution of the State of Idaho, against all enemies, foreign and domestic; that I will bear true faith and allegiance to the same; that I take this obligation freely, without any mental reservation or purpose of evasion; and that I will well and faithfully discharge the duties upon which I am about to enter.

"And I do further swear (or affirm) that I do not advocate, nor am I a member of any political party or organization that advocates the overthrow of the Government of the United States or of this State by force or violence; and that during such time as I am a member of the (name of civil defense organization), I will not advocate nor become a member of any political party or organization that advocates the overthrow of the Government of the United States or of this State by force or violence."

TEACHERS' LOYALTY

Laws 1963, ch. 210, pp. 599–600. *Loyalty oath required.*—
SECTION 1. That Section 59–401, Idaho Code, be and the same is hereby amended to read as follows:

59–401. FORM OF OATH—LOYALTY OATH.—Before any public officer or employee elected or appointed to fill any office, created by the laws of the State of Idaho, enters upon the duties of his office, he must take and subscribe an oath, to be known as the official oath, which is as follows:

I do solemnly swear (or affirm) that I will support the Constitution of the United States, and the constitution and the laws of this State; that I will faithfully discharge all the duties of the office of _____ _____ according to the best of my ability.

I, _____, do further solemnly swear (or affirm) that I will support and defend the Constitution of the United States and the constitution of the State of Idaho against all enemies, foreign or domestic; that I will bear true faith and allegiance to the Constitution of the United States and the constitution of the State of Idaho; that I take this obligation freely, without any mental reservation or purpose of evasion; and that I will well and faithfully discharge the duties upon which I am about to enter.

And I do further swear (or affirm) that I do not advocate, nor am I a member of any party or organization, political or otherwise, that now advocates the overthrow of the Government of the United States or of the State of Idaho by force or violence or other unlawful means; that within the five years immediately preceding the taking of this oath (or affirmation) I have not been a member of any party or organization, political or otherwise, that advocates the overthrow of the Government of the United States or of the State of Idaho by force or violence or other unlawful means except as follows:

_____
(If no affiliation, write in the words "No Exceptions") and that during such time as I hold the office of _____ I will not advocate nor become a member of any party or organization, political or otherwise, that advocates the overthrow of the Government of the United States or of the State of Idaho by force or violence or other unlawful means. So help me God.

And no other oath, declaration, or test, shall be required as a qualification for any public office or employment, except as otherwise provided by law.

A failure or refusal to take and subscribe such oath shall make such person ineligible to hold such office or to receive compensation for the same.

Public "Officer" and "employee" includes every officer and employee of the State, University of Idaho, Idaho State College, every other college and every county, city, school district, and authority, including any department, division, bureau, board, commission, agency, or instrumentality of any of the foregoing.

SECTION 2. SEPARABILITY.—If any of the provisions of this act or the application thereof to any person or circumstance is held invalid, such invalidity shall not affect other provisions or applications which can be given effect without said invalid provisions or applications.

SECTION 3. REPEALING CONFLICTING LAWS.—All laws or parts of laws in conflict, in whole or in part, with the provisions of this act are hereby repealed.

EXCLUSION FROM THE BAR

Paragraph 19 of the Idaho Application for Examination and Admission to Practice Law specifically requests information as to membership in the Communist Party, or other subversive organizations. It reads as follows:

19(a) Are you now, or have you ever been, a member of the Communist Party or any of its affiliates? (Yes or No). If married, answer with respect to your spouse (Yes or No).

(b) Are you now, or have you ever been, a member of any organization which, to your knowledge, is or has been classified by the Attorney General of the United States as being a subversive organization? (Yes or No). If so, list all such organizations of which you have been a member.

Other questions contained in the application indirectly pertain to possible membership in a subversive organization. They include:

17. (d) Have you ever invoked the protection of the Fifth Amendment to the Constitution of the United States (or of any other provisions of the Constitution of the United States or of any State) in refusing to testify under oath in any proceeding on the ground or for the reason that your answer might tend to incriminate you? (Yes or No).

20. Do you now and will you hereafter, without any mental reservation, loyally support the Constitution of the United States and the constitution of the State of Idaho? (Yes or No).

21. Have you read the oath required of attorneys upon admission (Rule 115)? (Yes or No). If recommended for admission, will you willingly assume the obligations of such oath? (Yes or No).

The oath referred to in question 21 is contained in Rule 115, Governing Admission To Practice Law, and reads, in relevant part, as follows:

I Do SOLEMNLY SWEAR:

I will support the Constitution of the United States and the constitution of the State of Idaho.

*   *   *   *   *   *

Correspondence received from the board of commissioners indicates that no Communist or member of a subversive organization has ever applied to take the Idaho bar examination. As a consequence, the board does not have "any prior experience or established policy pertaining to this problem."

ILLINOIS

Unlawful Advocacy

ADVOCATING OVERTHROW OF GOVERNMENT

Illinois Rev. Stat. 1963, ch. 38, § 30–3. *Unlawful acts and penalty.*— A person who advocates, or with knowledge of its contents knowingly publishes, sells, or distributes any document which advocates or with knowledge of its purpose, knowingly becomes a member of any organization which advocates the overthrow or reformation of the existing form of government of this State by violence or unlawful means shall be imprisoned in the penitentiary from one to 10 years.

Exclusion From The Elective Process

S.H. Anno., ch. 46, § 7–2. *Communist groups barred from ballot.*—

*　　*　　*　　*　　*　　*　　*

Provided, that no political organization or group shall be qualified as a political party hereunder, or given a place on a ballot, which organization or group is associated, directly or indirectly, with Communist, Fascist, Nazi, or other un-American principles and engages in activities or propaganda designed to teach subservience to the political principles and ideals of foreign nations or the overthrow by violence of the established constitutional form of Government of the United States and the State of Illinois.

Id. § 7–10.1 (Supp. 1963). *Non-Communist statement to accompany nominating petition.*—Each petition or certificate of nomination shall include as a part thereof, a statement for each of the candidates filing, or in whose behalf the petition or certificate of nomination is filed, said statement shall be subscribed and sworn to by such candidate or nominee before some officer authorized to take acknowledgment of deeds in this State and may be in substantially the following form:

United States of America,
State of Illinois, ss:

I, _____, do swear that I am a citizen of the United States and the State of Illinois, that I am not affiliated directly or indirectly with any Communist organization or any Communist-front organization, or any foreign political agency, party, organization, or government which advocates the overthrow of constitutional government by force or other means not permitted under the Constitution of the United States or the constitution of the State; that I do not directly or indirectly teach or advocate the overthrow of the Government of the United States or of this State or any unlawful

133

change in the form of the governments thereof by force or any unlawful means.

_____

Subscribed and sworn to by me this ___ day of _____, 19__

_____
Notary Public

My commission expires:

_____

Id. § 8–2. *Communist groups excluded from definition of "political party" for purpose of nominations to general assembly.*—The term "political party" as used in this article shall mean a political party which, at the next preceding election for Governor, polled at least five percent of the entire vote cast in the State; Provided, that no political organization or group shall be qualified as a political party hereunder, or given a place on a ballot, which organization or group is associated, directly or indirectly, with Communist, Fascist, Nazi, or other un-American principles and engages in activities or propaganda designed to teach subservience to the political principles and ideals of foreign nations or the overthrow by violence of the established constitutional form of Government of the United States and the State of Illinois.

Id. § 10–2 (Supp. 1962). *Communist groups excluded from definition of "political party" for purpose making nominations to certain lesser officers.*—The term "political party," as hereinafter used in this Article 10, shall mean any "established political party," as hereinafter defined and shall also mean any political group which shall hereafter undertake to form an established political party in the manner provided for in this Article 10: Provided, that no political organization or group shall be qualified as a political party hereunder, or given a place on a ballot, which organization or group is associated, directly or indirectly, with Communist, Fascist, Nazi or other un-American principles and engages in activities or propaganda designed to teach subservience to the political principles and ideals of foreign nations or the overthrow by violence of the established constitutional form of Government of the United States and the State of Illinois.

_____

Annotation:

Feinglass v. *Reinecke*, 48 F. Supp. 438 (1942). Petitioner in this action sought to enjoin various State officials from barring candidates of the Communist Party from the Cook County ballot. Although no reason was given for the refusal of defendants to endorse the nominating petition, the court assumed that it was done on the belief that the Communist Party was barred by statute from having the names of its candidates placed on the ballot. The statute in question provided that "no political organization or group shall be qualified as a political party hereunder, or given a place on a ballot, which organization or group is associated, directly or indirectly, with Communist, Fascist, Nazi, or other un-American principles and engages in activities or propaganda designed to teach subservience to the political principles and ideals of foreign nations or the overthrow by violence of the established constitutional form of Government of the United States and the State of Illinois." The court denied petitioner's request for an injunction on grounds that there was insufficient time before election day to print new ballots containing the candidates of the Communist Party. The latter, it held, should have been certified, since the statute in question was void for vagueness and indefiniteness. "Such terms as 'un-American' and 'the political principles of foreign nations' lack the precision required in a statute which affects the rights of a political group to appeal to the electorate." Construing the term Communist "to mean simply a belief in a system in which goods and the instruments of production [were] held in common," the court concluded that "certainly a party may not be excluded from a place on the ballot because it advocates economic ideas which may happen to be unpopular at the time."

LOYALTY OF STATE OFFICERS AND EMPLOYEES

1. ELECTIVE AND NONELECTIVE PERSONNEL

Illinois Constitution, Art. V, § 25. *Oath.*—All civil officers, except members of the General Assembly and such inferior officers as may be by law exempted, shall, before they enter on the duties of their respective offices, take and subscribe the following oath or affirmation:

"I do solemnly swear (or affirm, as the case may be) that I will support the Constitution of the United States, and the constitution of the State of Illinois, and that I will faithfully discharge the duties of the office of _____ according to the best of my ability."

And no other oath, declaration or test shall be required as a qualification.

2. NONELECTIVE PERSONNEL

S. H. Anno., ch. 127, § 166a (Supp. 1963). *Payment of compensation or expenses to persons advocating overthrow of Government prohibited.*—No part of any appropriation which has been heretofore made, or which shall hereafter be made, shall be used to pay any part of the compensation or the expenses of any officer or employee of the government of the State of Illinois, or any political subdivision, agency or instrumentality thereof, but excluding cities, villages, incorporated towns, townships and counties, who, directly or indirectly advocates the overthrow of the Government of the United States or the State of Illinois by force, or who knowingly joins, or who knowingly remains for a period of twenty days a member of, any organization which advocates the overthrow of the Government of the United States or the State of Illinois by force, or who knowingly remains for a period of twenty days a member of any organization which is founded by or whose activities are controlled in whole or in part by any individual or any organization which advocates the overthrow of the Government of the United States or the State of Illinois by force, after he has knowledge, or has reasonable cause to believe that such organization of which he is about to become a member, or of which he is a member, either advocates the overthrow of the Government of the United States or the State of Illinois by force, or is affiliated with another organization which advocates the overthrow of the Government of the United States or the State of Illinois by force.

Id. § 166b (Supp. 1963). *Non-Communist affidavit required to be executed.*—No employee of the State of Illinois, or any political subdivision, agency or instrumentality thereof, but excluding cities, villages, incorporated towns, townships and counties, shall receive compensation or expenses from any appropriation which has been heretofore made, or which shall hereafter be made until such person has on file with his or her employing authority the following affidavit signed under oath:

United States of America,
State of Illinois, ss:

I, _____ do swear (or affirm) that I am not a member of nor affiliated with the Communist Party and that I am not knowingly a member of nor knowingly affiliated with any organization which advocates the overthrow or destruction of the constitutional form of the Government of the United States or of the State of Illinois, by force, violence or other unlawful means.

(Signed) _____

_____ (seal)
Notary Public

3. CIVIL DEFENSE PERSONNEL

S. H. Anno., ch. 121, § 286. *Loyalty oath required.*—Each person whether compensated or noncompensated, who is appointed to serve in any capacity in an organization for civil defense, shall, before entering upon his duties, take an oath, in writing, before a person authorized to administer oaths in this State, which oath shall be filed with the executive head of the civil defense organization with which he shall serve and which oath shall be substantially as follows:

"I, _____, do solemnly swear (or affirm) that I will support and defend and bear true faith and allegiance to the Constitution of the United States and the constitution of the State of Illinois, and the territory, institutions, and facilities thereof, both public and private, against all enemies, foreign and domestic; that I take this obligation freely, without any mental reservation or purpose of evasion; and that I will well and faithfully discharge the duties upon which I am about to enter. And I do further swear (or affirm) that I do not advocate, nor am I nor have I been a member of any political party or organization that advocates the overthrow of the Government of the United States or of this State by force or violence; and that during such time as I am affiliated with the (name of organization), I will not advocate nor become a member of any political party or organization that advocates the overthrow of the Government of the United States or of this State by force or violence."

TEACHERS' LOYALTY

S.H. Anno., ch. 127, §166 a (Supp. 1963). *Payment of compensation or expenses to persons advocating overthrow of Government prohibited.*—No part of any appropriation which has been heretofore made, or which shall hereafter be made, shall be used to pay any part of the compensation or the expenses of any officer or employee of the government of the State of Illinois, or any political subdivision, agency or instrumentality thereof, but excluding cities, villages, incorporated towns, townships and counties, who, directly or indirectly advocates the overthrow of the Government of the United States or the State of Illinois by force, or who knowingly joins, or who knowingly remains for a period of twenty days a member of, any organization which advocates the overthrow of the Government of the United States or the State of Illinois by force, or who knowingly remains for a period of twenty days a member of any organization which is founded by or whose activities are controlled in whole or in part by any individual or any organization which advocates the overthrow of the Government of the United States or the State of Illinois by force, after he has knowledge, or has reasonable cause to believe that such organization of which he is about to become a member, or of which he is a member, either advocates the overthrow of the Government of the United States or the State of Illinois by force, or is affiliated with another organization which advocates the overthrow of the Government of the United States or the State of Illinois by force.

Id. § 166b (Supp. 1963). *Non-Communist affidavit required to be executed.*—No employee of the State of Illinois, or any political subdivision, agency or instrumentality thereof, but excluding cities, villages, incorporated towns, townships and counties, shall receive compensation or expenses from any appropriation which has been heretofore made, or which shall hereafter be made until such person has on file with his or her employing authority the following affidavit signed under oath:
United States of America,
State of Illinois, ss:

I, _____ do swear (or affirm) that I am not a member of nor affiliated with the Communist Party and that I am not knowingly a member of nor knowingly affiliated with any organization which advocates the overthrow or destruction of the constitutional form of the Government of the United States or of the State of Illinois, by force, violence or other unlawful means.

(Signed)_____

_____ (seal)
        Notary Public

_____

Annotation:

Pinkus v. *Board of Education of City of Chicago,* 9 Ill. 2d 603, 138 N.E. 2d 532 (1956). Plaintiffs, Chicago school teachers, instituted this action to enjoin defendants from withholding their compensation for failing to execute a loyalty affidavit. A State statute authorized the withholding of compensation from State employees who refuse to sign the loyalty affidavit therein set forth. The Supreme Court of Illinois affirmed the judgment, dismissing the plaintiffs' petition. The court held petitioners, although employed by the city board, were subject to the act. It also sustained the constitutionality of the oath requirement over objections that it violated due process and other constitutionally protected rights.

S.H. Anno., ch. 24½, § 38 b 15. *Loyalty oath required of applicants for employment in University System.*—In the administration of the University System, no applicant shall be denied employment by the merit board or by any employer because of race, color, religious, or political affiliations, except that any applicant for employment may be required as a condition of employment, to sign a valid oath attesting his loyalty to the State and the United States.

Exclusion From the Bar

Question 20 on the application for admission to the Bar of Illinois inquires as to the applicant's loyalty to the Federal and State constitutions. It reads as follows:

20. Do you now without any mental reservation and will you hereafter support the Constitution of the United States and the constitution of the State of Illinois?

Correspondence received from the State Board of Law Examiners states that the examination of applicants on character and fitness is carried on by a separate character and fitness committee. There does not appear to be any general policy with respect to the admission of persons alleged to be Communists.

Annotation:

In re Anastaplo, 366 U.S. 82, 81 S. Ct. 978, 6 L. Ed. 2d 135 (1961), rehearing denied 368 U.S. 869, 82 S. Ct. 21, 7 L. Ed. 2d 69. Petitioner was denied admission to the bar for refusing to answer any questions posed by the Committee on Character and Fitness pertaining to membership in the Communist Party. He based his refusal on grounds of free speech and association. The committee's decision was sustained by the Illinois Supreme Court which expressly stated that it drew no inference of disloyalty or subversion from the applicant's refusal to answer. Rather, it held that petitioner's failure to respond obstructed the proper functions of the committee which included among other things, a determination respecting applicants adherence "to our basic institutions and form of government." The Supreme Court of the United States affirmed reiterating its ruling in *Konigsberg*—decided the same day—that it is "not constitutionally impermissible for a state legislatively, or "through court-made regulation * * * to adopt a rule that an applicant will not be admitted to the practice of law if, and so long as, by refusing to answer material questions, he obstructs a bar examining committee in its proper functions of interrogating and cross-examining him upon his qualifications." As in *Konigsberg,* it also held that the state's interest in "enforcing such a rule as applied to refusals to answer questions about membership in the Communist Party outweighed any deterrent effect upon freedom of speech and association. The court found that petitioner was given adequate warning as to the consequences of his refusal to answer the committee's question. Petitioner's exclusion from the bar, it concluded, was not arbitrary or discriminatory.

Exclusion From Incidental Benefits

1. PUBLIC HOUSING

S. H. Anno., ch. 67½, § 25. *Tenancy conditioned upon execution of loyalty oath.*—In the operation or management of housing projects an authority shall at all times observe the following duties with respect to rentals and tenant selection:

*　　*　　*　　*　　*　　*　　*

(d) It shall not accept any person as a tenant who does not take and subscribe the oath or affirmation prescribed in section 25.01.

Id. § 25.01. *Form of oath.*—Every tenant in any dwelling in a housing project shall take and subscribe an oath or affirmation in substantially the following form:

United States of America,
State of Illinois, ss:

I, ------------, do swear that I am a citizen of the United States and the State of Illinois, that I am not affiliated directly or indirectly with any Communist organization or any Communist front organization, or any foreign political agency, party, organization, or government which advocates the overthrow of constitutional government by force or other means not permitted under the Constitution of the United States or the constitution of this State; that I do not directly or indirectly teach or advocate the overthrow of the Government of the United States or of this State or any unlawful change in the form of the governments thereof by force or any unlawful means.

Subscribed and sworn to by me this -------- day of -------- 19---.

My commission expires: Notary Public

Id. § 25–02. *Failure to execute oath cause for eviction.*—Any tenant in any dwelling in a housing project who has not taken and subscribed the oath prescribed in section 25.01 on or before September 1, 1953, shall be evicted.

Annotation:

Chicago Housing Authority v. *Blackman*, 4 Ill. 2d 325, 122 N.E. 2d 523(1954). Appellants, tenants in low-rent public housing projects, were ordered evicted for failure and refusal to subscribe to the loyalty oath required of such tenants by state statute. The Supreme Court of Illinois reversed the judgment holding that it would violate due process to permit the state to exclude persons from public housing solely on the basis of organizational membership, regardless of their knowledge about the organization. The oath was unqualified in its terms. "It does not require the tenant to swear merely that he 'knowingly' or 'to the best of his knowledge' is not affiliated with organizations of the proscribed character. Instead it requires him to know as a matter of certainty whether every organization to which he belongs in fact advocates the overthrow of constitutional government by force or other unlawful means, unless he is sure that it does not he cannot conscientiously take the oath, and as a result he is excluded from the public housing accommodations. It is clear that under the authority of the *Wieman* case [*Wieman* v. *Updegraff*, 344 U.S. 183, 73 S. Ct. 215, 97 L. Ed. 216 (1952)] the present requirement violates due process of law and is void."

2. USE OF UNIVERSITY FACILITIES

S. H. Anno., ch. 144, § 48.8 (Supp. 1963). *Subversive organizations barred from using university facilities.*—No trustee, official, instructor, or other employee of the University of Illinois shall extend to any subversive, seditious, and un-American organization, or to its representatives, the use of any facilities of the University for the purpose of carrying on, advertising or publicizing the activities of such organization.

MISCELLANEOUS

S. H. Anno., ch. 38, § 850 (Supp. 1963). *Crime commission authorized to investigate subversive activities.*—The Commission has power to investigate all fields of organized or syndicate crime, including, but without limiting the generality thereof, prostitution, narcotics, liquor, gambling, subversive activities, lotteries, counterfeiting, and tax frauds.

INDIANA

1. INCITING VIOLENCE

Burns Anno. Stat. § 10–1302. *Unlawful acts.*—It shall be unlawful for any person to advocate or incite or to write or with intent to forward such purpose to print, publish, sell or distribute any document, book, circular, paper, journal or other written or printed communication in or by which there is advocated or incited the overthrow by force or violence, or by physical injury to personal property, or by the general cessation of industry, of the Government of the United States, of the State of Indiana, or all government.

Id. § 10–1303. *Penalty.*—Any person or persons convicted of violating any section of this act shall be fined not more than five thousand dollars [$5,000] or imprisoned for not more than five [5] years, or both.

Annotations:

McKee v. *State*, 219 Ind. 247, 37 N.E. 2d 940 (1941). Appellants were convicted of conspiring to incite the people of Fayette County against all forms of organized government and to disrespect the flag of the United States. The judgment was reversed and appellants' motion for a new trial granted. The court held that the flag desecration statute defined only a misdemeanor and there was no such statutory offense as conspiracy to commit a misdemeanor. It further held that since the literature distributed by appellants was limited to the advocacy of the overthrow of government without more, that is, without mention of the resort to force and violence, the evidence was insufficient to sustain a conviction of criminal syndicalism.

Butash v. *State*, 213 Ind. 492, 9 N.E. 2d (1937). In this case, the court reversed a conviction for the crime of advocating and inciting the overthrow of the Government. Defendant, at the request of others had made a speech and answered various questions during which he expressed opinions upon current economic and political questions. The court held that the expression of personal opinions upon the economic or political questions of the time and a possible solution for them did not constitute a violation of the State statute.

---

2. COMMUNISM

Burns Anno. Stat. § 10–5201. *Declaration of public policy to protect the State from Communism.*—It is hereby declared to be the public policy of the State of Indiana and of this act [§§ 10–5201—10–5209] to protect the peace, domestic tranquility, property rights and interests of the State of Indiana and the people thereof from the

141

tenets of the ideology known as communism as the same is known and presently exists in the world today.

Id. § 10–5202. *Declaration of public policy to promote the Constitution and to exterminate communism.*—It is further declared to be the public policy of the State of Indiana, and of this act [§§ 10–5201— 10–5209] to promote and to enforce the Constitution of the United States of America, the constitution of the State of Indiana, and all laws passed pursuant thereto guaranteeing and defining the rights of all free Americans and, to that end, to exterminate communism and Communists, and any or all teachings of the same.

Id. § 10–5203. *Communism, Communist, and Communist Party defined.*—For the purpose of this act [§§ 10–5201—10–5209], the term "communism" or "Commmunist" as herein defined shall include, but shall not be limited to the Communist political party as it presently exists. The Communist Party for the purpose of this act is hereby defined as an organization which engages in or advocates, abets, advises, or teaches, or has a purpose which is to engage in or advocate, abet, advise, or teach, activities intended to overthrow, destroy, or alter, or to assist in the overthrow, destruction, or alteration of, the constitutional form of the Government of the United States, or of the State of Indiana, or of any political subdivision thereof, by revolution, force, or violence.

Id. § 10–5204. *Unlawful acts.*—(A) It shall be unlawful for any person to be a member of the Communist Party or of any party, group, or organization which advocates in any manner the overthrow, destruction, or alteration of the constitutional form of the Government of the United States or of the State of Indiana, or any political subdivision thereof by revolution, force, violence, sedition, or which engages in any un-American activities.

(B) It shall be unlawful for any person by word of mouth or writing to advocate, advise, or teach the duty, necessity, or propriety of overthrowing or overturning the Government of the United States or of the State of Indiana or any political subdivision thereof by force or violence; or print, publish, edit, issue, or knowingly circulate, sell, distribute, or publicly display any book, paper, document, or written or printed matter in any form for the purpose of advocating, advising, or teaching the doctrine that the Government of the United States, or of the State of Indiana, shall be overthrown by force, violence, or any unlawful means.

Id. § 10–5205. *Assemblage to advocate overthrow of the government.*—Whenever two [2] or more persons assemble for the purpose of advocating or teaching the doctrine that the Government of the United States, or of the State of Indiana, should be overthrown by force, violence, or any unlawful means, such an assembly is unlawful, and every person voluntarily participating therein by his presence, aid, or instigation, shall be guilty of a felony.

Id. § 10–5206. *Liability of editor, etc., for contents of publication.*— Every editor or proprietor of a book, newspaper, or circular and every manager of a partnership or incorporated association by which a book, newspaper, or circular is issued, is chargeable with the publication of any matter contained in such book, newspaper, or circular. But in every prosecution therefor, the defendant may show in his defense that the matter complained of was published without his knowledge or fault and against his wishes, by another who had no authority from him to make the publication and whose act was disavowed by him as soon as known.

Annotation:

Indiana v. *Levitt*, Criminal No. 30611, Supreme Court of Indiana, Jan. 25, 1965. Appellees, three students at Indiana University, were charged with sedition following a speech made at a rally of the Young Socialist Alliance on the campus in 1963. The indictment charged that appellees "* * * did then and there assemble for the purpose of advocating and teaching the doctrine that the Government of the United States and of the State of Indiana should be overthrown by force, violence, and any unlawful means, voluntarily participating therein by their presence, aid and instigation, contrary to the * * * peace and dignity of the State of Indiana." The trial court sustained their motion to quash on the grounds that the Indiana Anti-Communism Statute had been superseded by the Federal Smith Act. The Indiana Supreme Court reversed and held the statute constitutional as applied to seditious activity directed solely against the State. The court stated all governments had an inherent right to self-preservation and the authority to pass laws against assembling to advocate violent overthrow of State government.

OUTLAWING THE COMMUNIST PARTY

Burns Anno. Stat. § 10–5201. *Declaration of public policy—to protect the State from Communism.*—It is hereby declared to be the public policy of the State of Indiana and of this act [§§ 10–5201—10–5309] to protect the peace, domestic tranquility, property rights, and interests of the State of Indiana and the people thereof from the tenets of the ideology known as communism as the same is known and presently exists in the world today.

Id. § 10–5202. *Declaration of public policy—to promote the Constitution and to exterminate communism.*—It is further declared to be the public policy of the State of Indiana, and of this act [§§ 10–5201—10–5209] to promote and to enforce the Constitution of the United States of America, the constitution of the State of Indiana, and all laws passed pursuant thereto, guaranteeing and defining the rights of all free Americans and, to that end, to exterminate communism and Communists, and any or all teachings of the same.

Id. § 10–5203. *Communism, Communist, and Communist Party defined.*—For the purpose of this act [§§ 10–5201—10–5209], the term communism or Communist as herein defined shall include, but shall not be limited to the Communist political party as it presently exists. The Communist Party for the purpose of this act is hereby defined as an organization which engages in or advocates, abets, advises, or teaches, or has a purpose which is to engage in or advocate, abet, advise, or teach, activities intended to overthrow, destroy or alter, or to assist in the overthrow, destruction, or alteration of, the consitutional form of the Government of the United States, or of the State of Indiana, or of any political subdivision thereof, by revolution, force, or violence.

41–738—65——11

Id. § 10–5204. *Membership in the Communist Party, etc., unlawful.*—(A) It shall be unlawful for any person to be a member of the Communist Party or of any party, group, or organization which advocates in any manner the overthrow, destruction, or alteration of the constitutional form of the Government of the United States or of the State of Indiana, or any political subdivision thereof by revolution, force, violence, sedition, or which engages in any un-American activities.

(B) It shall be unlawful for any person by word of mouth or writing to advocate, advise, or teach the duty, necessity, or propriety of overthrowing or overturning the Government of the United States or of the State of Indiana or any political subdivision thereof by force or violence; or print, publish, edit, issue, or knowingly circulate, sell, distribute, or publicly display any book, paper, document, or written or printed matter in any form for the purpose of advocating, advising, or teaching the doctrine that the Government of the United States, or of the State of Indiana, shall be overthrown by force, violence, or any unlawful means.

Id. § 10–5205. *Assemblage to advocate overthrow of the government.*—Whenever two [2] or more persons assemble for the purpose of advocating or teaching the doctrine that the Government of the United States, or of the State of Indiana, should be overthrown by force, violence, or any unlawful means, such an assembly is unlawful, and every person voluntarily participating therein by his presence, aid, or instigation, shall be guilty of a felony.

Exclusion From the Elective Process

Burns Anno. Stat. § 29–3812. *Political parties advocating overthrow of the government and candidates barred from ballot.*—No political party or organization shall be recognized and given a place on or have the names of its candidates printed on the ballot used at any election which advocates the overthrow, by force or violence, of the local, State or National Government, or which advocates, or carries on, a program of sedition or of treason, and which is affiliated or cooperates with or has any relation with any foreign government, or any political party or group of individuals of any foreign government. Any political party or organization which is in existence at the time of the passage of this act, or which shall have had a ticket on the ballot one [1] or more times prior to any election, and which does not advocate any of the doctrines the advocacy of which is prohibited by this act, shall insert a plank in its platform that it does not advocate any of the doctrines prohibited by this act. No existing or newly organized political party or organization shall be permitted on or to have the names of its candidates printed on the ballot used at any election until it has filed an affidavit, by its officers, under oath, that it does not advocate the overthrow of local, State or National Government by force or violence, and that it is not affiliated with and does not cooperate with nor has any relation with any foreign government, or any political party, organization or group of individuals of any foreign government. The affidavit herein provided for shall be filed with the State election board or the county election board having charge of the printing of the ballot on which such ticket is to appear. The election board with which such affidavit is filed shall make, or cause to be made such investigation as it may deem necessary to determine the character and nature of the political doctrines of such existing or proposed new party and the expense of such investigation by the State election board shall be paid out of the general funds of the State treasury not otherwise appropriated, provided the amount of such appropriation shall not exceed five hundred dollars [$500]; and the expense of the investigation by the county election board shall be paid out of the funds in the treasury, not otherwise appropriated, provided the amount of such appropriation shall not exceed three hundred dollars [$300], and if the board is of the opinion that such existing or proposed new party advocates doctrines which are in violation of the provisions of this act, or that any of the statements in said affidavit are false, the board shall not permit such ticket or candidates on the ballot.

NOTE.—See Outlawing the Communist Party, *supra.*

Burns Anno. Stat. § 10–5205. *Assemblage to advocate overthrow of the government.*—Whenever two [2] or more persons assemble for the purpose of advocating or teaching the doctrine that the Government of the United States, or the State of Indiana, should be overthrown by force, violence or any unlawful means, such an assembly is unlawful, and every person voluntarily participating therein by his presence, aid or instigation, shall be guilty of a felony.

Id. § 10–5207. *Persons convicted of unlawful assemblage disenfranchised and barred from public office.*—Any person violating any of the provisions of section 5 [§ 10–5205] of this act shall be guilty of a felony and shall, upon conviction, be disenfranchised and rendered incapable of holding any office of profit or trust and shall be imprisoned in the Indiana State prison for not less than one [1] year nor more than three [3] years.

LOYALTY OF STATE OFFICERS AND EMPLOYEES

1. ELECTIVE AND NONELECTIVE PERSONNEL

Indiana Constitution, Art. 15, § 4. *Oath.*—Every person elected or appointed to any office under this constitution, shall, before entering on the duties thereof, take an oath or affirmation, to support the constitution of this State, and of the United States, and also an oath of office.

Burns Anno. Stat. § 10–5207. *Members of the Communist Party ineligible for public office and employment.*—No person shall hold public office or be employed by any department, board, bureau, commission, institution, or agency of the State of Indiana, or any of its political subdivisions, who is a member of the Communist Party or participating in any of the activities declared unlawful by this act or has been convicted under any of the provisions of section 4 [§ 10–5204] of this act and any person now employed by any department, board, bureau, commission, institution, or agency of the State of Indiana or any political subdivisions, who is a member of the Communist Party or who is engaged in any of the activities declared unlawful by this act shall be forthwith discharged. Evidence satisfactory to the head of such department, board, institution, or agency of the State of Indiana or any of its political subdivisions shall be sufficient for refusal to employ any person or cause for discharge of any employee for the reasons set forth by this section. Any person discharged or refused employment under the provisions of this section shall have the right to judicial review provided for by chapter 365 of the Acts of 1947, being an act entitled "An Act concerning the proceedings, orders, and determinations of State officers and agencies and judicial review thereof"

Burns Anno. Stat. § 10–5207. *Assemblage to advocate overthrow of government.*—Whenever two [2] or more persons assemble for the purpose of advocating or teaching the doctrine that the Government of the United States, of the State of Indiana, should be overthrown by force, violence, or any unlawful means, such an assembly is unlawful, and every person voluntarily participating therein by his presence, aid, or instigation, shall be guilty of a felony.

Id. § 10–5208. *Persons convicted of unlawful assemblage barred from office.*—Any person violating any of the provisions of section 5 [10–5205] of this act shall be guilty of a felony and shall, upon conviction, be disenfranchised and rendered incapable of holding any office of profit or trust and shall be imprisoned in the Indiana State prison for not less than one [1] year nor more than three [3] years.

2. CIVIL DEFENSE PERSONNEL

Burns Anno. Stat. § 45–1534. *Loyalty oath required.*—(a) No person shall be employed or associated in any capacity in any civil defense organization established under this act [§§ 45–1516—45—1535] who advocates a change by force or violence in the constitutional form of the Government of the United States or the overthrow of any government in the United States by force or violence, or who has been convicted of or is under indictment or information charging any subversive act against the United States. Each person who is appointed to serve in an organization for civil defense shall, before entering upon his duties, take an oath, in writing, before a person authorized to administer oaths in this State, which oath shall be substantially as follows:

"I_____, do solemnly swear (or affirm) that I will support and defend the Constitution of the United States and the constitution of the State of Indiana, against all enemies, foreign and domestic; that I will bear true faith and allegiance to the same; that I take this obligation freely, without any mental reservation or purpose of evasion; and that I will well and faithfully discharge the duties upon which I am about to enter.

"And I do further swear (or affirm) that I do not advocate, nor am I a member of any political party or organization that advocates, the overthrow of the Government of the United States or of this State by force or violence; and that during such time as I am a member of the (name of civil defense organization) I will not advocate nor become a member of any political party or organization that advocates the overthrow of the Government of the United States or of this State by force or violence."

(b) For the purposes of this section, the State civil defense director and the county civil defense directors shall be authorized to administer the foregoing oath to civil defense personnel, and they may delegate such authority to such designated deputies and assistants as may be approved by the State civil defense director and the council.

Id. § 45–1535. *Penalty.*—Any person violating any provision of this act [§§ 45–1516—45–1535] or any rule, order, or regulation made pursuant to this act shall, upon conviction thereof, be punishable by a fine not exceeding one hundred dollars ($100.00) or imprisonment for not exceeding ninety (90) days or both.

TEACHERS' LOYALTY

Burns Anno. Stat. § 28–5112. *Oath of allegiance required to be executed by teachers employed in public schools.*—Every person who applies for a license, or any renewal thereof, to teach in any of the public schools of this State, shall subscribe to the following oath or affirmation:

I solemnly swear (or affirm) that I will support the Constitution of the United States of America, the constitution of the State of Indiana and the laws of the United States and the State of Indiana, and will, by precept and example, promote respect for the flag and the institutions of the United States and of the State of Indiana, reverence for law and order and undivided allegiance to the Government of the United States of America.

Such oath or affirmation shall be executed in duplicate and one [1] copy thereof shall be filed with the State superintendent of public instruction at the time when the application for a license is made and the other copy shall be retained by the person who subscribed to such oath or affirmation. No license shall be issued unless such oath shall have been filed.

Id. § 28–5113. *Oath of allegiance required to be executed by persons employed in institutions of higher education.*—Every professor, instructor, or teacher who shall be employed hereafter by any university or normal school in this State which is supported in whole or in part by public funds, shall, before entering upon the discharge of his or her duties, subscribe to the oath or affirmation as prescribed in section one [§ 28–5112] of this act, before some officer authorized by law to administer oaths. Such oath or affirmation shall be executed in duplicate and one [1] copy thereof shall be filed with the president of such university or normal school and one [1] copy shall be retained by the person who subscribed to such oath or affirmation.

Id. § 28–5114. *Aliens employed in institutions of higher education required to take oath to support national institutions and policies.*—Any person who is a citizen or subject of any country other than the United States, and who is employed in any capacity as a professor, instructor, or teacher in any university or normal school in this State which is supported in whole or in part by public funds, shall, before entering upon the discharge of his duties, subscribe to an oath to support the institutions and policies of the United States during the period of his sojourn within this State.

Burns Anno. Stat. § 10–5207. *Members of the Communist Party ineligible for employment.*—No person shall hold public office or be employed by any department, board, bureau, commission, institution, or agency of the State of Indiana, or any of its political subdivisions, who is a member of the Communist Party or participating in any of the activities declared unlawful by this act or has been convicted under any of the provisions of section 4 [§ 10–5204] of this act and any person now employed by any department, board, bureau, commission, institution, or agency of the State of Indiana or any political subdivisions, who is a member of the Communist Party or who is engaged in any of the activities declared unlawful by this act shall be forthwith discharged. Evidence satisfactory to the head of such department, board, institution, or agency of the State of Indiana or any of its political subdivisions shall be sufficient for refusal to employ any person or cause for discharge of any employee for the reasons set forth by this section. Any person discharged or refused employment under the provisions of this section shall have the right to judicial review provided for by chapter 365 of the Acts of 1947, being an act entitled "An Act concerning the proceedings, orders, and determinations of State officers and agencies and judicial review thereof" approved March 14, 1947 [§§ 63–3001—63–3030].

Exclusion From the Bar

Question 22 of the application for admission to the Bar inquires whether the applicant has been a member of or affiliated with a subversive organization. It provides:

22. I have never been a member of or affiliated with an organization which advocates the overthrow of the Government of the United States by force and violence, and I have never been a member of or affiliated with an organization which is on the subversive list of the Attorney General of the United States, except as follows.

The form of inquiry which the State Board of Law Examiners sends to references listed by the applicant and other persons elicits pertinent information about the applicant. Question 7 deals with the applicant's loyalty and asks:

7. There (is) (is no) reason for me to believe that he (she) would ever advocate the overthrow of the Government of the United States by use of force, because—.

Correspondence received from the board reveals that it "has never been faced with the problem of a Communist or other subversive who has applied for admission to the practice of law."

IOWA

UNLAWFUL ADVOCACY

1. SEDITION

54 Iowa Code Anno. § 689.4. *Inciting insurrection or sedition.*— If any person shall excite an insurrection or sedition amongst any portion or class of the population of this State, or shall attempt by writing, speaking, or by any other means to excite such insurrection or sedition, the person or persons so offending shall be punished by imprisonment in the State penitentiary not exceeding twenty years and shall be fined not less than one thousand nor more than ten thousand dollars.

Annotation:

State v. *Gibson,* 189 Iowa 1212, 174 N.W. 34 (1919), rehearing denied 181 N.W. 704. In this case the court sustained a conviction for inciting hostility. It held, *inter alia,* that the statute making it unlawful to incite, abet, promote or encourage hostility or opposition to the Governments of the State and the United States defined only one offense but two distinct means of its accomplishment, i.e., a violation of the statute may be committed by directing the forbidden acts against the Government of the State, that of the United States, or both. The right of free speech guaranteed by the State constitution was held not to include the right to promote sedition.

2. CRIMINAL SYNDICALISM

54 Iowa Code Anno. § 689.10. *Criminal syndicalism defined.*— Criminal sydicalism is the doctrine which advocates crime, sabotage, violence, or other unlawful methods of terrorism as a means of accomplishing industrial or political reform. The advocacy of such doctrine, whether by word of mouth or writing, is a felony punishable as provided in sections 689.11 to 689.13, inclusive.

Id. § 689.11. *Unlawful acts and penalty.*—Any person who:

1. By word of mouth or writing, advocates or teaches the duty, necessity, or propriety of crime, sabotage, violence, or other unlawful methods of terrorism as a means of accomplishing industrial or political reform; or

2. Prints, publishes, edits, issues, or knowingly circulates, sells, distributes, or publicly displays any book, paper, document, or written matter in any form, containing or advocating, advising, or teaching the doctrine that industrial or political reform should be brought about by crime, sabotage, violence, or other unlawful methods of terrorism; or

3. Openly, willfully and deliberately justifies, by word of mouth or writing, the commission or the attempt to commit crime, sabotage,

violence, or other unlawful methods of terrorism with intent to ex-emplify, spread, or advocate the propriety of the doctrines of criminal syndicalism; or

4. Organizes or helps to organize, or becomes a member of or vol-untarily assembles with any society, group, or assemblage of persons formed to teach or advocate the doctrines or criminal syndicalism—is guilty of a felony and punishable by imprisonment in the State penitentiary or reformatory for not more than ten years, or by a fine of not more than five thousand dollars, or both.

Id. § 689.12. *Assemblage to advocate criminal syndicalism.*—Whenever two or more persons assemble for the purpose of advo-cating or teaching the doctrines of criminal syndicalism as defined in sections 689.10 and 689.11, such an assemblage is unlawful and every person voluntarily participating therein by his aid or instiga-tion is guilty of a felony and punishable by imprisonment in the State penitentiary or reformatory for not more than ten years or by a fine of not more than five thousand dollars or both.

Id. § 689.13. *Permitting use of premises to advocate criminal syndicalism.*—The owner, agent, superintendent, janitor, caretaker, or occupant of any place, building, or room, who willfully and know-ingly permits therein any assemblage of persons prohibited by the provisions of section 689.12, or who, after notification by the sheriff of the county or the police authorities that the premises are so used, permits such use to be continued, is guilty of a misdemeanor and punishable by imprisonment in the county jail for not more than one year or by a fine of not more than five hundred dollars or both.

Annotation:

State v. *Sentner,* 230 Iowa 590, 298 N.W. 813 (1941). Defendant, a labor union strike leader, was convicted of the crime of criminal syndicalism because some of the workers destroyed property at the struck plant. Reversing the conviction, the court held *inter alia,* that the admission into evidence of testimony compelled by a military commission to the effect that defendant was or had been a member of the Communist Party and believed in the philosophy and policies of the party, was prejudicial error. "* * * there was nothing which the defendant said in the hearing before the military commission, nor in the contempt hearing, which could be construed as advocating the doctrines of criminal syndicalism. Neither is there any evidence in the record that the Communist Party advocates such doctrines * * *. Defendant was indicted for advocating the doctrines by word of mouth, and the fact that he may have been a member of the Communist Party in no way tended to sustain the indictment."

---

3. INCITING HOSTILITIES

54 Iowa Code Anno. § 689.8. *Unlawful acts and penalty.*—Any person who shall in public or private, by speech, writing, printing, or by any other mode or means advocate the subversion and destruction by force of the government of the State of Iowa or of the United States, or attempt by speech, writing, printing, or in any other way whatsoever to incite or abet, promote or encourage hostility or op-

position to the government of the State of Iowa or of the United States, shall be guilty of a misdemeanor and upon conviction shall be punished by imprisonment in the county jail not less than six months nor more than one year and shall be fined not less than three hundred nor more than one thousand dollars.

Id. § 689.9. *Membership in organizations formed to incite hostilities.*—Any person who shall become a member of any organization, society, or order organized or formed, or attend any meeting or council or solicit others so to do, for the purpose of inciting, abetting, promoting, or encouraging hostility or opposition to the government of the State of Iowa or to the United States, or who shall in any manner aid, abet, or encourage any such organization, society, order, or meeting in the propagation or advocacy of such a purpose, shall be guilty of a misdemeanor and upon conviction shall be imprisoned in the county jail not less than six months nor more than one year and shall be fined not less than three hundred nor more than one thousand dollars.

LOYALTY OF STATE OFFICERS AND EMPLOYEES

1. ELECTIVE AND NONELECTIVE PERSONNEL

Iowa, Const., Art. XI, § 5. *Oath.*—Every person elected or appointed to any office, shall, before entering upon the duties thereof, take an oath or affirmation to support the Constitution of the United States, and of this State, and also an oath of office.

2. CIVIL DEFENSE PERSONNEL

3 Iowa Code Anno. § 28A.12 (Supp. 1963). *Loyalty oath required.*—No person shall be employed or associated in any capacity in any civil defense organization established under this administration, who advocates or has advocated a change by force or violence in the constitutional form of Government of the United States or of this State, or who advocates the overthrow of any government in the United States by force or violence, or who has been convicted of, or is under indictment or information charging any subversive act against the United States. Each person who is appointed to serve in an organization for civil defense shall, before entering upon his duties, take an oath in writing, before a person authorized to administer oaths in this State, which oath shall be substantially as follows:

"I, ----------, do solemnly swear (or affirm) that I will support and defend the Constitution of the United States and the constitution of the State of Iowa, against all enemies, foreign or domestic; that I will bear true faith and allegiance to the same; that I take this obligation freely, without any mental reservation or purpose of evasion; and that I will well and faithfully discharge the duties upon which I am about to enter.

"And I do further swear (or affirm) that I do not advocate nor am I a member of any political party or organization that advocates the overthrow of the Government of the United States or of this State by force or violence; and that during such time as I am a member of the (name of the civil defense organization), I will not advocate nor become a member of any political party or organization that advocates the overthrow of the Government of the United States or of this State by force or violence."

EXCLUSION FROM THE BAR

Iowa does not appear to have any rule or regulation which pertains to the admission of persons who are or who have been Communists or subversives. Similarly, the various forms employed by the State do not contain any questions directly on the subject.

KANSAS

1. SEDITION

Gen. Stat. 1949, § 21–06. *Unlawful acts against the government.—* (*a*) It shall be unlawful for any person: (1) To knowingly or willfully advocate, abet, advise, or teach the duty, necessity, desirability, or propriety of overthrowing or destroying any government in the United States by force or violence, or by the assassination of any officer of any such government; (2) with the intent to cause the overthrow or destruction of any government in the United States, to print, publish, edit, issue, circulate, sell, distribute, or publicly display any written or printed matter advocating, advising, or teaching the duty, necessity, desirability, or propriety of overthrowing or destroying any government in the United States by force or violence; (3) to organize or help to organize any society, group, or assembly of persons who teach, advocate, or encourage the overthrow or destruction of any government in the United States by force or violence; or to be or become a member of, or affiliate with, any such society, group, or assembly of persons, knowing the purposes thereof. (*b*) For the purposes of this section, the term "government in the United States" means the Government of the United States, or the government of this State.

Id. § 21–307. *Unlawful attempts and conspiracies.—*It shall be unlawful for any person to attempt to commit, or to conspire to commit, any of the acts prohibited by the provisions of this act.

Id. § 21–308. *Penalty.—*Any person who violates any of the provisions of this act shall be deemed guilty of a felony and, upon conviction thereof, be fined not more than ten thousand dollars or imprisoned for not more than ten years, or both such fine and imprisonment.

Annotation:

Fiske v. *Kansas*, 274 U.S. 380, 47 S. Ct. 655, 71 L. Ed. 1108 (1927). Defendant was convicted of violating the Criminal Syndicalism Act by reason of having secured members in a branch of the I.W.W., an organization whose constitution proclaimed: "That the working class and the employing class have nothing in common, and that there can be no peace so long as hunger and want are found among millions of working people and the few who make up the employing class have all the good things of life. Between these two classes a struggle must go on until the workers of the world organize as a class, take possession of the earth and the machinery of production and abolish the wage system. Instead of the conservative motto, 'a fair day's wage for a fair day's work,' we must inscribe on our banner the revolutionary watchword, 'abolition of the wage system.' By organizing industrially we are forming the structure of the new society within the shell of the old." At the trial the State offered the above quoted information. The court reversed the conviction stating that the Syndicalism Act as applied—without any evidence that the organization in which defendant secured members advocated any crime—was an arbitrary and unreasonable exercise of the police power and an unwarrantable infringement on defendant's liberty in violation of the due process clause of the Fourteenth Amendment.

---

2. CRIMINAL SYNDICALISM

Gen. Stat. 1949, § 21–301. *Criminal syndicalism defined.*—Criminal syndicalism is hereby defined to be the doctrine which advocates crime, physical violence, arson, destruction of property, sabotage, or other unlawful acts or methods, as a means of accomplishing or effecting industrial or political ends, or as a means of effecting industrial or political revolution, or for profit.

Id. § 21–303. *Unlawful acts and penalty.*—Any person who by word of mouth, or writing, advocates, affirmatively suggests, or teaches the duty, necessity, propriety, or expediency of crime, criminal syndicalism, or sabotage, or who shall advocate, affirmatively suggest, or teach the duty, necessity, propriety, or expediency of doing any act of violence, the destruction of or damage to any property, the bodily injury to any person or persons, or the commission of any crime or unlawful act as a means of accomplishing or effecting any industrial or political ends, change or revolution, or for profit; or who prints, publishes, edits, issues, or knowingly, circulates, sells, distributes, or publicly displays any books, pamphlets, paper, handbill, poster, document or written or printed matter in any form whatsoever, containing matter advocating, advising, affirmatively suggesting or teaching crime, criminal syndicalism, sabotage, the doing of any act of physical violence, the destruction of or damage to any property, the injury to any person, or the commission of any crime or unlawful act as a means of accomplishing, effecting or bringing about any industrial or political ends or change, or as a means of accomplishing, effecting or bringing about any industrial or political revolution, or for profit, or who shall openly, or at all attempt to justify by word of mouth or writing, the commission or the attempt to commit sabotage, or any act of physical violence, or the destruction of or damage to any property, or the injury of any person or the commission of any crime, or unlawful act, with the intent to exemplify, spread, or teach, or affirmatively suggest criminal syndicalism, or organizes, or helps to organize or become a member of, or voluntarily assembles with any society or assemblage of persons which teaches, advocates or affirmatively suggests the doctrine of criminal syndicalism, sabotage, or the necessity, propriety or expediency of doing any act of physical violence or the commission of any crime or unlawful act as a means of accomplishing or effecting any industrial or political ends, change or revolution or for profit, is guilty of a felony and, upon conviction thereof, shall be punished by imprisonment in the State penitentiary for a term of not less than one year nor more than ten years, or by a fine of not more than $1,000, or by both such imprisonment and fine.

Id. § 21–304. *Permitting premises to be used to advocate criminal syndicalism.*—The owner, lessee, agent, superintendent, or person in charge or occupation of any place, building, room or rooms, or structure, who knowingly permits therein any assembly or consort of persons prohibited by the provisions of section 3 [21–303] of this act, or who after notification by authorized public or peace officer that the place or premises, or any part thereof, is or are so used, permits such use to be continued, is guilty of a misdemeanor and punishable upon conviction thereof by imprisonment in the county jail for not less than sixty days nor for not more than one year, or by a fine of not less than $100, nor more than $500, or by both such imprisonment and fine.

Exclusion From the Elective Process

Gen. Stat. 1949, § 25–116. *Communist Party affiliates and candidates barred from ballot.*—No political party (*a*) which is directly or indirectly affiliated by any means whatsoever with the Communist Party of the United States, the Communist international, or any other foreign agency, political party, organization, or government; or (*b*) which either directly or indirectly advocates, teaches, justifies, aids or abets the overthrow by force or violence, or by any unlawful means, of the Government of the United States or this State; or (*c*) which directly or indirectly carries on, advocates, teaches, justifies, aids or abets a program of sabotage, force and violence, sedition or treason against the Government of the United States or this State, shall be recognized, or qualified to participate, or permitted to have the names of its candidates printed on the ballot, in any election in this State.

Id. § 25.117. *Non-Communist affidavit required to qualify as a recognized political party.*—No newly organized political party shall be recognized or qualified to participate or permitted to have the names of its candidates printed on the ballot in any election in this State until it has filed an affidavit, by the officers of the party in the State, under oath that (*a*) it is not directly or indirectly affiliated by any means whatsoever with the Communist Party of the United States, the Communist international, or any other foreign agency, political party, organization, or government; or (*b*) that it does not either directly or indirectly advocate, teach, justify, aid or abet the overthrow by force or violence, or by any unlawful means, of the Government of the United States or this State; or (*c*) it does not directly or indirectly carry on, advocate, teach, justify, aid or abet a program of sabotage, force and violence, sedition or treason against the Government of the the United States or this State. The affidavit herein provided for shall be filed with the secretary of state and he shall make such investigation as he may deem necessary to determine the character and nature of the political doctrines of such proposed new party and, if he finds that such proposed new party advocates doctrines or has affiliations which are in violation of the provisions of this act, he shall not permit such party to participate in the election.

LOYALTY OF STATE OFFICERS AND EMPLOYEES

1. ELECTIVE AND NONELECTIVE PERSONNEL

Gen. Stat. 1949, § 21–305. *Loyalty oath required.*—Every officer and employee of the State, county, city or other municipality of the State, including members of the legislature, private and public school teachers and university and college professors and instructors shall be required to sign the following oath:

"I, _____ swear (or affirm) that I do not advocate, nor am I a member of any political party or organization that advocates the overthrow of the Government of the United States or of this State by force or violence; and that during such time as I am an officer or employee of the _____, I will not advocate nor become a member of any political party or organization that advocates the overthrow of the Government of the United States or of this State by force or violence." Any officer, member of the legislature, employee, teacher or instructor who shall refuse to sign the oath required by this section shall, in addition to any other penalties prescribed in this act, be subject to immediate dismissal from office.

Id. § 21–308. *Penalty.*—Any person who violates any of the provisions of this act shall be deemed guilty of a felony and, upon conviction thereof, be fined not more than ten thousand dollars or imprisoned for not more than ten years, or both such fine and imprisonment.

2. CIVIL DEFENSE PERSONNEL

Gen. Stat. 1949 § 48–917 (Supp. 1961). *Persons advocating overthrow of government barred from employment.*—No person shall be employed or associated in any capacity in any civil defense organization established under this act who advocates a change by force or violence in the constitutional form of the Government of the United States or in this State or the overthrow of any government in the United States by force or violence, or who has been convicted of or is under indictment or information charging any subversive act against the United States.

TEACHERS' LOYALTY

Gen. Stat. 1949, § 21–305. *Loyalty oath required.*—Every officer and employee of the State, county, city, or other municipality of the State, including members of the legislature, private and public school teachers and university and college professors and instructors shall be required to sign the following oath:

"I, _____, swear (or affirm) that I do not advocate, nor am I a member of any political party or organization that advocates the overthrow of the Government of the United States or of this State by force or violence; and that during such time as I am an officer or employee of the _____, I will not advocate nor become a member of any political party or organization that advocates the overthrow of the Government of the United States or of this State by force or violence." Any officer, member of the legislature, employee, teacher or instructor who shall refuse to sign the oath required by this section shall, in addition to any other penalties prescribed in this act, be subject to immediate dismissal from office.

Id. § 21-308. *Penalty.*—Any person who violates any of the provisions of this act shall be deemed guilty of a felony and, upon conviction thereof, be fined not more than ten thousand dollars or imprisoned for not more than ten years, or both such fine and imprisonment.

KENTUCKY

Unlawful Advocacy

CRIMINAL SYNDICALISM AND SEDITION

Baldwin's Rev. Stat. Anno. 1963, § 432.020. *Criminal syndicalism defined; penalty.*—Any person who commits, aids or counsels any crime, physical violence, destruction of property, intimidation, terrorism or other unlawful act or method to accomplish any political end or to bring about political revolution shall be confined in the penitentiary for not more than 21 years, or fined not more than ten thousand dollars, or both.

Id. § 432.030. *Advocating overthrow of government by force or violence; penalty.*—Any person who advocates or suggests by word, act, or writing any public disorder or resistance to, or the change or modification of, the Government, Constitution, or laws of the United States or of this State by force or violence or by any unlawful means shall be confined in the penitentiary for not more than twenty-one years, or fined not more than ten thousand dollars, or both.

Id. § 432.040. *Teaching, publishing, or joining organization to advocate criminal syndicalism or sedition.*—Any person who by word or writing advocates, suggests, or teaches the duty, necessity, propriety, or expediency of criminal syndicalism or sedition, or who prints, publishes, edits, issues, or knowingly circulates, sells, distributes, publicly displays, or has in his possession for the purpose of publication or circulation any written or printed matter in any form advocating, suggesting, or teaching criminal syndicalism or sedition, or who organizes or helps to organize, or becomes a member of or voluntarily assembles with any society or assemblage of persons that teaches, advocates, or suggests the doctrine of criminal syndicalism or sedition shall be confined in the penitentiary for not more than 21 years, or fined not more than ten thousand dollars, or both.

Id. § 432.050. *Permitting use of premises or printing machinery for seditious or syndicalistic activities.*—(1) Any owner, lessee, agent, superintendent, or other person in charge or occupation of any place who knowingly permits therein any assembly or consort of persons to indulge in any act prohibited by KRS 432.020 to 432.040, shall be fined not more than five hundred dollars, or confined in the county jail for not more than one year, or both.

(2) Any person who rents or furnishes any place or any printing press or other machinery to print or circulate any matter prohibited by KRS 432.020 to 432.040 shall be fined not more than one thousand dollars, or imprisoned for not more than one year, or both.

Id. § 432.060. *Conspiracy to commit sedition or criminal syndicalism.*—Any two or more persons who agree, band, or confederate themselves together to do any of the things prohibited by KRS 432.020 to 432.050 shall be confined in the penitentiary for not more

159

than twenty-one years, or fined not more than ten thousand dollars, or both. In any prosecution under this section, it shall not be necessary to prove any overt act on the part of the accused pursuant to any unlawful combination or agreement.

Id. § 432.070. *Witnesses required to testify in prosecution for sedition or criminal syndicalism.*—In any prosecution under KRS 432.020 to 432.060, no witness may claim privilege or exemption on the ground that his testimony may incriminate him, but may be required to testify for the Commonwealth. However, no testimony given by him shall be used against him in any prosecution except for perjury, and he shall be discharged from any liability for any violation of KRS 432.020 to 432.060 necessarily disclosed in his testimony. The provisions of section 241 of the Criminal Code shall not apply in any such prosecution.

Annotations:

Beeler v. *Smith*, 40 F. Supp. 139 (1941). In this case the District Court for the Eastern District of Kentucky held that the sale, circulation and distribution of printed matter published by the Watch Tower Bible & Tract Society, Inc., an organization of the Jehovah's Witnesses, was not a violation of the State sedition statute.

Gregory v. *Commonwealth*, 226 Ky. 617, 11 S.W. 2d 432 (1928). Appellants were convicted of sedition for forcefully interfering with the county sheriff in the performance of his official duties. Reversing the conviction, the court held that to intimidate an officer in the discharge of his duties, without more, fell far short of sedition. The latter comprehended the advocacy by word, act, deed or writing of public disorder or resistance to the government of the Commonwealth.

Braden v. *Commonwealth*, 291 S.W. 2d 842 (1956). Appellant was convicted of sedition in that he knowingly and feloniously advocated by word or writing the expediency of physical violence to bring about a political revolution to change or modify the Government, Constitution, and laws of the United States and the Commonwealth of Kentucky. The court reversed the judgment of the lower court, citing *Pennsylvania* v. *Nelson*, 350 U.S. 497, 76 S. Ct. 477, 100 L. Ed. 777 (1956), wherein the Supreme Court declared that Congress by the Smith Act of 1940, as amended in 1948, 18 U.S.C. § 2385, as well as other security acts passed by Congress, showed an intention to occupy the field of prosecutions for sedition. The Court stated that its opinion should not be construed as foreclosing the possibility of a prosecution by the Commonwealth of the crime of sedition directed exclusively against the Commonwealth of Kentucky.

LOYALTY OF STATE OFFICERS AND EMPLOYEES

1. ELECTIVE AND NONELECTIVE PERSONNEL

Kentucky Constitution, § 228. *Oath.*—Members of the General Assembly and all officers, before they enter upon the execution of the duties of their respective offices, and all members of the bar, before they enter upon the practice of their profession, shall take the following oath or affirmation: I do solemnly swear (or affirm, as the case

may be) that I will support the Constitution of the United States
and the constitution of this Commonwealth, and be faithful and true
to the Commonwealth of Kentucky so long as I continue a citizen
thereof, and that I will faithfully execute, to the best of my ability,
the office of _____ according to law; and I do further
solemnly swear (or affirm) that since the adoption of the present
constitution, I, being a citizen of this State, have not fought a duel
with deadly weapons within this State nor out of it, nor have I sent
or accepted a challenge to fight a duel with deadly weapons, nor have
I acted as second in carrying a challenge, nor aided or assisted any
person thus offending, so help me God.

2. CIVIL DEFENSE PERSONNEL

Baldwin's Rev. Stat. Anno. 1963, § 39.432. *Loyalty oath required.*—
No person shall be employed or associated in any capacity in any
civil defense organization established under KRS 39.400 to 39.432
and 39.990 who advocates a change by force or violence in the constitutional form of the Government of the United States or in this
State or the overthrow of any government in the United States by
force or violence, or who has been convicted of or is under indictment or information charging any subversive act against the United
States. Each person who is appointed to serve in an organization
for civil defense shall, before entering upon his duties, take an oath,
in writing, before a person authorized to administer oaths in this
State, which oath shall be substantially as follows:

"I, _____, do solemnly swear (or affirm) that I will support
and defend the Constitution of the United States and the constitution of the State of Kentucky, against all enemies, foreign and
domestic; that I will bear true faith and allegiance to the same; that
I take this obligation freely, without any mental reservation or purpose of evasion; and that I will well and faithfully discharge the
duties upon which I am about to enter.

"And I do further swear (or affirm) that I do not advocate, nor am
I a member of any political party or organization that advocates,
the overthrow of the Government of the United States or of the
State by force or violence; and that during such time as I am a
member of the (name of civil defense organization) I will not
advocate nor become a member of any political party or organization that advocates the overthrow of the Government of the United
States or of this State by force or violence."

EXCLUSION FROM THE BAR

Rule 2.010(a) of the Rules of the Court of Appeals of Kentucky relating to the Admission of Persons to Practice Law prohibits the admission of Communists and subversives. It provides:
* * * no person who is a Communist or who advocates the overthrow of government by force may become or remain a member of
the bar of the State of Kentucky.
Item 12, subpart (b) on the application form requires the applicant to subscribe to a statement that he is not a Communist. It
provides:
"I am not a Communist and do not advocate the overthrow of the
government by force."

LOUISIANA

Unlawful Advocacy

1. ANARCHY

Louisiana Stat. Anno. § 14:115. *Criminal anarchy defined.*—Criminal anarchy is:

(1) The advocating or teaching, in any manner, in public or private, of the subversion, opposition, or destruction of the Government of the United States or of the State of Louisiana by violence or other unlawful means; or

(2) The organizing or becoming a member of any organization or society which is known to the offender to advocate, teach, or practice the subversion, opposition, or destruction of the Government of the United States or of the State of Louisiana by violence or other unlawful means.

Whoever commits the crime of criminal anarchy shall be imprisoned at hard labor for not more than ten years.

Annotation:

State v. *Cade*, 244 La. 534, 153 So. 2d 382 (1963). Defendant, a leader of a religious sect known as Islam (Black Muslims), was prosecuted for the crime of criminal anarchy. He was charged with having (1) taught and advocated that the Negro under our system "gets nothing but slavery, hell, and death" and that a separate and new nation and government must be established by the Negro people and that this nation and government shall be within the United States, and that this Negro nation is entitled to the State of Louisiana and other Southern States because "we feel that 310 years of slave labor that our parents have undergone in America should be enough pay; and that the owners of such land today have no rights or interest, and that such new nation and government must be established whether by violence or any other unlawful means within the boundary of the United States, and that such teaching is being done to adults and children; (2) that the defendant was a member of an organization or society which advocates and teaches subversion of the Government of the United States and the State of Louisiana. On appeal, defendant contended, *inter alia*, that criminal anarchy was a crime against the Nation that the State statute was unenforceable, and that the State courts were without jurisdiction to punish this crime. He relied in the main upon *Commonwealth of Pennsylvania* v. *Nelson*, 350 U.S. 497, 76 S. Ct. 477, 100 L. Ed. 640 (1956). The Supreme Court of Louisiana reversed on grounds that there was no evidence in the record to establish that violence or other unlawful means had been advocated by the defendant or his organization. With respect to defendant's argument, the court held that the State

163

statute proscribing criminal anarchy had been superseded by Federal legislation only insofar as they specifically punished sedition against the United States Government.

---

2. SUBVERSIVE ACTIVITIES

Louisiana Stat. Anno. § 14:359 (Supp. 1963). *"Communist," "Communist Party," "Communist front organization," "Organization," "Subversive organization," "Foreign subversive organization," "Foreign government," and "Subversive person" defined.*—(1) A "Communist" means a person who is a member of the Communist Party or is proven to be substantially under the discipline and control of the International Communist Conspiracy.

(2) The "Communist Party" means the Communist Party, U.S.A. or any of its direct successors and shall include any other organization which is directed, dominated or controlled by the Soviet Union, by any of its satellite countries or by the government of any other Communist country; or any organization which in any manner advocates or acts to further the success of the program of world domination of the international Communist conspiracy.

(3) "Communist front organization" shall, for the purpose of this act include any Communist action organization, Communist front organization, Communist infiltrated organization, or Communist controlled organization and the fact that an organization has been officially cited or identified by the Attorney General of the United States, the Subversive Activities Control Board of the United States or any Committee or Subcommittee of the United States Congress as a Communist organization, a Communist action organization, a Communist front organization, a Communist infiltrated organization or has been in any other way officially cited or identified by any of these aforementioned authorities as a Communist controlled organization, shall be considered presumptive evidence of the factual status of any such organization.

(4) "Organization" means an organization, corporation, company, partnership association, trust, foundation, fund, club, society, committee, political party, or any group of persons, whether or not incorporated, permanently or temporarily associated together for joint action or advancement of views on any subject or subjects.

(5) "Subversive organization" means any organization which engages in or advocates, abets, advises, or teaches, or a purpose of which is to engage in or advocate, abet, advise, or teach activities intended to overthrow, destroy, or to assist in the overthrow or destruction of the constitutional form of the government of the State of Louisiana, or of any political subdivision thereof by revolution, force, violence or other unlawful means, or any other organization which seeks by unconstitutional or illegal means to overthrow or destroy the government of the State of Louisiana or any political subdivision thereof and to establish in place thereof any form of government not responsible to the people of the State of Louisiana under the constitution of the State of Louisiana.

(6) "Foreign subversive organization" means any organization, directed, dominated or controlled directly or indirectly by a foreign

government which engages in or advocates, abets, advises, or teaches, or a purpose of which is to engage in or to advocate, abet, advise, or teach, activities intended to overthrow, destroy, or to assist in the overthrow or destruction of the constitutional form of the government of the State of Louisiana, or of any political subdivision thereof to establish in place thereof any form of government the direction and control of which is to be vested in, or exercised by or under, the domination or control of any foreign government, organization, or individual.

(7) "Foreign Government" means the government of any country, nation, or group of nations other than the Government of the United States of America or one of the States thereof.

(8) "Subversive person" means any person who commits, attempts to commit, or aids in the commission, or advocates, abets, advises or teaches by any means any person to commit, attempt to commit, or aid in the commission of any act intended to overthrow, destroy, or to assist in the overthrow or destruction of the constitutional form of the government of the State of Louisiana, or any political subdivision thereof by revolution, force, violence or other unlawful means; or who is a member of a subversive organization or a foreign subversive organization.

Id. § 14:364 (Supp. 1963). *Unlawful acts.*—It shall be a felony for any person knowingly and willfully to

(1) Commit, attempt to commit, or aid in the commission of any act intended to overthrow or destroy, or to assist in the overthrow or destruction of the constitutional form of government of the State of Louisiana, or any political subdivision thereof, by revolution, force, violence, or other unlawful means, or

(2) Advocate, abet, advise, or teach by any means any person to commit, attempt to commit, or assist in the commission of any such act under such circumstances as to constitute a clear and present danger to the security of the State of Louisiana, or of any political subdivision thereof, or

(3) Conspire with one or more persons to commit any such act; or

(4) Assist in the formation or participate in the management or to contribute to the support of any subversive organization or foreign subversive organization knowing said organization to be a subversive organization or a foreign subversive organization; or

(5) Destroy any books, records, or files, or secrete any funds in this State of a subversive organization or a foreign subversive organization, knowing said organization to be such; or

(6) To become or to remain a member of a subversive organization or a foreign subversive organization knowing said organization to be a subversive organization or foreign subversive organization; or

(7) Fail to register as required in R.S. 14:360 or to make any registration which contains any material false statement or omission.

NOTE.—See Registration, *infra.*

Id. § 14:365 (Supp. 1963). *Penalty.*—Any person convicted of violating any of the provisions of R.S. 14:364 shall be fined not more than ten thousand dollars or imprisoned at hard labor for not more than ten years, or both.

Annotation:

State v. *Jenkins*, 236 La. 300, 107 So. 2d 648 (1957). Appellee was charged with violating the Subversive Activities law (§§ 14:366–380) by reason of her membership in the Communist Party. She moved to quash the bill of information on grounds that the power of the State to enact and enforce antisubversive legislation had been superseded by the enactment of the Federal Smith Act. The lower court sustained the motion and dismissed the charge on the authority of *Commonwealth of Pennsylvania* v. *Nelson*, 350 U.S. 497, 76 S. Ct. 477, 100 L. Ed. 640 (1956). The State supreme court affirmed although withholding judgment with respect to the effect of the *Nelson* ruling on cases not involving seditious acts against the Federal Government; i.e., against the State government alone.

REGISTRATION

Louisiana Stat. Anno. § 14:358 (Supp. 1963). *Declaration of public policy.*—In the interpretation and application of R.S. 14:358 through R.S. 14:374 the public policy of this State is declared to be as follows:

There exists a world Communist movement, directed by the Union of Soviet Socialist Republics and its satellites, which has as its declared objective world control. Such world control is to be brought about by agression, force, and violence, and is to be accomplished in large by infiltrating tactics involving the use of fraud, espionage, sabotage, infiltration, propaganda, terrorism, and treachery. Since the State of Louisiana is the location of many of the Nation's most vital military establishments, and since it is a producer of many of the most essential products for national defense, the State of Louisiana is a most probable target for those who seek by force and violence to overthrow constitutional government, and is in imminent danger of Communist espionage, infiltration, and sabotage. Communist control of a country is characterized by an absolute denial of the right of self-government and by the abolition of those personal liberties which are cherished and held sacred in the State of Louisiana and in the United States of America. The world Communist movement constitutes a clear and present danger to the citizens of the State of Louisiana. The public good, and the general welfare of the citizens of this State require the immediate enactment of this measure.

Id. § 14:359 (Supp. 1963). *"Communist," "Communist Party," "Communist front organization," "Organization," "Subversive organization," "Foreign subversive organization," "Foreign government," and "Subversive person" defined.*—(1) A "Communist" means a person who is a member of the Communist Party or is proven to be substantially under the discipline and control of the International Communist Conspiracy.

(2) The "Communist Party" means the Communist Party, U.S.A. or any of its direct successors and shall include any other organization which is directed, dominated or controlled by the Soviet Union, by any of its satellite countries or by the Government of any other Communist country; or any organization which in any manner advocates or acts to further the success of the program of world domination of the international Communist conspiracy.

(3) "Communist front organization" shall, for the purpose of this act include any Communist action organization, Communist front organization, Communist infiltrated organization, or Communist controlled organization and the fact that an organization has been officially cited or identified by the Attorney General of the United States, the Subversive Activities Control Board of the United States or any committee or subcommittee of the United States Congress as a Communist organization, a Communist action organization, a Communist front organization, a Communist infiltrated organization or has been in any other way officially cited or identified by any of these aforementioned authorities as a Communist controlled organization, shall be considered presumptive evidence of the factual status of any such organization.

(4) "Organization" means an organization, corporation, company, partnership association, trust, foundation, fund, club, society, committee, political party, or any group of persons, whether or not incorporated, permanently or temporarily associated together for joint action or advancement of views on any subject or subjects.

(5) "Subversive organization" means any organization which engages in or advocates, abets, advises, or teaches, or a purpose of which is to engage in or advocate, abet, advise, or teach activities intended to overthrow, destroy, or to assist in the overthrow or destruction of the constitutional form of the government of the State of Louisiana, or of any political subdivision thereof by revolution, force, violence or other unlawful means, or any other organization which seeks by unconstitutional or illegal means to overthrow or destroy the government of the State of Louisiana or any political subdivision thereof and to establish in place thereof any form of government not responsible to the people of the State of Louisiana under the constitution of the State of Louisiana.

(6) "Foreign subversive organization" means any organization, directed, dominated or controlled directly or indirectly by a foreign government which engages in or advocates, abets, advises, or teaches, or a purpose of which is to engage in or to advocate, abet, advise, or teach, activities intended to overthrow, destroy, or to assist in the overthrow or destruction of the constitutional form of government of the State of Louisiana, or of any political subdivision thereof to establish in place thereof any form of government the direction and control of which is to be vested in, or exercised by or under, the domination or control of any foreign government, organization, or individual.

(7) "Foreign government" means the government of any country, nation or group of nations other than the Government of the United States of America or one of the States thereof.

(8) "Subversive person" means any person who commits, attempts to commit, or aids in the commission, or advocates, abets, advises or teaches by any means any person to commit, attempt to commit, or aid in the commission of any act intended to overthrow, destroy, or to assist in the overthrow or destruction of the constitutional form of the government of the State of Louisiana, or any political subdivision thereof by revolution, force, violence, or other unlawful means; or who is a member of a subversive organization or a foreign subversive organization.

Id. § 14:360 (Supp. 1963). *Persons required to register.*—A. Each person remaining in this State for as many as five consecutive days after July 30, 1962, who is a Communist or is knowingly a member of a Communist front organization, shall register with the Department of Public Safety of the State of Louisiana on or before the fifth consecutive day that such person remains in this State; and, so long as he remains in this State, shall register annually with said department between the first and fifteenth day of January.

B. Registration shall be under oath and shall set forth the name (including any assumed name used or in use), address, business occupation, purpose of presence in the State of Louisiana, sources of income, place of birth, places of former residence, and features of identification, including fingerprints of the registrant; organizations of which registrant is a member; and any other information requested by the Department of Public Safety which is reasonably relevant to the purpose of R.S. 14:358 through R.S. 14:374.

C. Under order of any court of record, the registration records shall be open for inspection by any person in whose favor such order is granted; and the records shall at all times, without the need for a court order, be open for inspection by any law enforcement officer of this State, of the United States, or of any State or territory of the United States. At the discretion of the Department of Public Safety, these records may also be open for inspection by the general public or by any member thereof.

Id. § 14:363 (Supp. 1963). *Enforcement.*—The attorney general of the State of Louisiana, all district and parish attorneys, the Department of Public Safety, and all law enforcement officers of this State shall each be charged with the duty of enforcing the provisions of R.S. 14:358 through R.S. 14:374.

Id. § 14:364 (Supp. 1963). *Unlawful acts.*—It shall be a felony for any person knowingly and willfully to—

(1) Commit, attempt to commit, or aid in the commission of any act intended to overthrow or destroy, or to assist in the overthrow or destruction of the constitutional form of government of the State of Louisiana, or any political subdivision thereof, by revolution, force, violence, or other unlawful means; or

(2) Advocate, abet, advise, or teach by any means any person to commit, attempt to commit, or assist in the commission of any such act under such circumstances as to constitute a clear and present danger to the security of the State of Louisiana, or of any political subdivision thereof; or

(3) Conspire with one or more persons to commit any such act; or

(4) Assist in the formation or participate in the management or to contribute to the support of any subversive organization or foreign subversive organization knowing said organization to be a subversive organization or a foreign subversive organization; or

(5) Destroy any books, records, or files, or secrete any funds in this State of a subversive organization or a foreign subversive organization, knowing said organization to be such; or

(6) To become or to remain a member of a subversive organization or a foreign subversive organization knowing said organization to be a subversive organization or foreign subversive organization; or

(7) Fail to register as required in R.S. 14:360 or to make any registration which contains any material false statement or omission. Id. § 14:365 (Supp. 1963). *Penalty.*—Any person convicted of violating any of the provisions of R.S. 14:364 shall be fined not more than ten thousands dollars or imprisoned at hard labor for not more than ten years, or both.

Id. § 14:366 (Supp. 1963). *Additional penalties.*—Any person convicted by a court of competent jurisdiction of violating any of the provisions of R.S. 14:358 through 14:374 in addition to all other penalties therein provided shall from the date of conviction be barred from:

(1) Holding any office, elective or appointive, or any other position of profit or trust in or employment by the government of the State of Louisiana or of any agency thereof or of any parish, municipal corporation or other political subdivision of said State;

(2) Filing or offering for election to any public office in the State of Louisiana; or

(3) Voting in any election in this State.

Id. § 14:367 (Supp. 1963). *Failure to register cause for dissolution.*—It shall be unlawful for any subversive organization or foreign subversive organizations to exist or function in the State of Louisiana and any organization which by a court of competent jurisdiction is found to have violated the provisions of this section shall be dissolved, and if it be a corporation organized and existing under the laws of the State of Louisiana a finding by a court of competent jurisdiction that it has violated the provisions of this section shall constitute legal cause for forfeiture of its charter and its charter shall be forfeited, and all funds, books, records, and files of every kind and all other property of any organization found to have violated the provisions of this section shall be seized by and for the State of Louisiana, the funds to be deposited in the State treasury and the books, records, files, and other property to be turned over to the Department of Public Safety of Louisiana.

Id. § 14:368 (Supp. 1963). *Grand jury investigations.*—The judge of any court exercising general criminal jurisdiction, when in his discretion it appears appropriate, or when informed by the attorney general or district attorney that there is information or evidence of violations of the provisions of this act to be considered by the grand jury, shall charge the grand jury to inquire into violations of R.S. 14:358 through 14:374 for the purpose of proper action, and further to inquire generally into the purposes, processes, and activities and any other matters affecting communism or any related or other subversive organizations, associations, groups, or persons.

Annotation:

Dombrowski v. *Pfister*, 33 U.S.L. Week 4321 (U.S. April 26, 1965.) Appellants, a civil rights organization and its chief officer, as well as other persons active in civil rights cases, sought a declaratory judgment that the Louisiana Subversive Activities and Communist Control Law was unconstitutional and requested a permanent injunction prohibiting State officers from enforcing same. A three-judge district court dismissed the suit and held that it would not determine the constitutionality of the legislation in advance of appropriate proceedings in a State court. The Supreme Court reversed, declaring that abstention and the denial of injunctive relief cannot be justified where it results in the denial of any effective safeguards against the loss of protected freedoms of expression. Proceeding to the constitutional issues raised by appellants, the Court held that the statutory definition of "a subversive organization" denied due process because it was "unduly vague, uncertain and broad." The registration requirement was also held unconstitutional:

"We also find the registration requirement of § 364(7) invalid. That section creates an offense of failure to register as a member of a Communist-front organization, and, under § 359(3), 'the fact that an organization has been officially cited or identified by the Attorney General of the United States, the Subversive Activities Control Board of the United States or any committee or subcommittee of the United States Congress as a * * * Communist front organization * * * shall be considered presumptive evidence of the factual status of such organization.' There is no requirement that the organizations have been so cited only after compliance by the congressional committees with the procedural safeguards demanded by *Anti-Fascist Committee* v. *Mc-Grath, supra.*

"A designation resting on such safeguards is a minimum requirement to insure the rationality of the presumptions of the Louisiana statute and, in its absence, the presumptions cast an impermissible burden upon the appellants to show that the organizations are not Communist fronts. 'Where the transcendent value of speech is involved, due process certainly requires * * * that the State bear the burden of persuasion to show that the appellants engaged in criminal speech.' *Speiser* v. *Randall, supra,* at 526. It follows that § 364(7), resting on the invalid presumption, is unconstitutional on its face."

EXCLUSION FROM THE ELECTIVE PROCESS

Louisiana Stat. Anno. § 14:366 (Supp. 1963). *Persons convicted of subversive activities disenfranchised and ineligible to be candidates.*— Any person convicted by a court of competent jurisdiction of violating any of the provisions of R.S. 14:358 through 14:374 in addition to all other penalties therein provided shall from the date of conviction be barred from:

(1) Holding any office, elective or appointive, or any other position of profit or trust in or employment by the government of the State of Louisiana or of any agency thereof or of any parish, municipal corporation, or other political subdivision of said State;

(2) Filing or offering for election to any public office in the State of Louisiana; or

(3) Voting in any election in this State.

Id. § 14:373 (Supp. 1963). *Candidates required to execute nonsubversive affidavit.*—No person shall become a candidate nor shall be certified by any political party as a candidate for election to any public office created by the constitution or laws of this State unless such candidate or certification by the political party shall have attached to the qualifying papers, the nominating petition or nominating papers filed with the appropriate party committee of this State or the secretary of state, whichever the case may be, a sworn affidavit that the candidate is not and never has been a subversive person as defined in R.S. 14:359. No qualification of candidates, nominating petition, or nominating papers for such office shall be received for filing by the official aforesaid unless the same are accompanied by the affidavit, and there shall not be entered upon any ballot or voting machine at any election the name of any person who has failed or refused to make the required affidavit.

Annotation:

State ex rel. Wood v. Lassiter, 99 So. 2d 186 (1958). This case involved an action to oust a mayor for failure to comply with the provision of the Subversive Activities Act providing that no person shall become a candidate unless he shall have attached to qualifying papers, a sworn affidavit that he is not and never has been a subversive person. The suit was dismissed by the lower court. The court of appeals affirmed and held that the statute related only to candidates for public office, and therefore, the district attorney could not be compelled to commence an action for ouster of a mayor who was in fact holding office, notwithstanding his failure to file the affidavit at the time he was a candidate for the office.

LOYALTY OF STATE OFFICERS AND EMPLOYEES

1. ELECTIVE AND NONELECTIVE PERSONNEL

Louisiana constitution, Art. **XIX**, § 1. *Oath.*—All officers before entering upon the duties of their respective offices, except as otherwise provided in this constitution, shall take the following oath or affirmation:

"I, (A.B.) do solemnly swear (or affirm) that I will support the Constitution and laws of the United States and the constitution and laws of this State; and that I will faithfully and impartially discharge and perform all the duties incumbent upon me as_____ _____according to the best of my ability and understanding. So help me God."

2. NONELECTIVE PERSONNEL

Louisiana Stat. Anno. § 14:358 (Supp. 1963). *"Communist," "Communist Party," "Communist front organization," "Organization," "Subversive organization," "Foreign subversive organization," "Foreign government," and "Subversive person" defined.*—(1) A "Communist" means a person who is a member of the Communist Party or is proven to be substantially under the discipline and control of the International Communist Conspiracy.

(2) The "Communist Party" means the Communist Party, U.S.A. or any of its direct successors and shall include any other organization which is directed, dominated, or controlled by the Soviet Union, by any of its satellite countries, or by the government of any other Communist country; or any organization which in any manner advocates or acts to further the success of the program of world domination of the International Communist Conspiracy.

(3) "Communist front organization" shall, for the purpose of this act, include any Communist-action organization, Communist-front organization, Communist-infiltrated organization, or Communist-controlled organization, and the fact that an organization has been officially cited or identified by the Attorney General of the United States, the Subversive Activities Control Board of the United States, or any committee or subcommittee of the United States Congress as a Communist organization, a Communist-action organization, a Communist-front organization, a Communist-infiltrated organization, or has been in any other way officially cited or identified by any of these aforementioned authorities as a Communist-controlled organization; shall be considered presumptive evidence of the factual status of any such organization.

(4) "Organization" means an organization, corporation, company, partnership association, trust, foundation, fund, club, society, committee, political party, or any group of persons, whether or not incorporated, permanently or temporarily associated together for joint action or advancement of views on any subject or subjects.

(5) "Subversive organization" means any organization which engages in or advocates, abets, advises, or teaches, or a purpose of which is to engage in or advocate, abet, advise, or teach activities intended to overthrow, destroy, or to assist in the overthrow or destruction of the constitutional form of the government of the State of Louisiana, or of any political subdivision thereof by revolution, force, violence, or other unlawful means, or any other organization which seeks by unconstitutional or illegal means to overthrow or destroy the government of the State of Louisiana or any political subdivision thereof and to establish in place thereof any form of government not responsible to the people of the State of Louisiana under the constitution of the State of Louisiana.

(6) "Foreign subversive organization" means any organization, directed, dominated, or controlled directly or indirectly by a foreign government which engages in or advocates, abets, advises, or teaches, or a purpose of which is to engage in or to advocate, abet, advise, or teach, activities intended to overthrow, destroy, or to assist in the overthrow or destruction of the constitutional form of the government of the State of Louisiana, or of any political subdivision thereof to establish in place thereof any form of government the direction and control of which is to be vested in, or exercised by or under, the domination or control of any foreign government, organization, or individual.

(7) "Foreign government" means the government of any country, nation, or group of nations other than the Government of the United States of America or one of the States thereof.

(8) "Subversive person" means any person who commits, attempts to commit, or aids in the commission, or advocates, abets, advises, or teaches by any means any person to commit, attempt to commit, or aid in the commission of any act intended to overthrow, destroy, or to assist in the overthrow or destruction of the constitutional form of the government of the State of Louisiana, or any political subdivision thereof by revolution, force, violence or other unlawful means; or who is a member of a subversive organization or a foreign subversive organization.

Id. § 14:362 (Supp. 1963). *Communists and members of Communist front organizations ineligible for public office and employment.*—No person may hold any nonelective position, job, or office for the State of Louisiana, or any political subdivision thereof, where the remuneration of said position, job, or office is paid in whole or in part by public moneys or funds of the State of Louisiana, or of any political subdivision thereof, where the evidence shows such person to be a Communist or a knowing member of a Communist front organization.

Id. § 14:369 (Supp. 1963). *Subversive persons ineligible for public office or employment.*—No subversive person, as defined in R.S. 14: 359, shall be eligible for employment in, or appointment to any office, or any position of trust or profit in the government of, or in the administration of the business of this State, or of any parish, municipality, or other political subdivision of this State.

Id. § 14:370 (Supp. 1963). *Rules and regulations to determine loyalty of persons.*—Every person and every board, commission, council, department, court, or other agency of the State of Louisiana or any political subdivision thereof, who appoints, employs, or supervises in any manner the appointment or employment of public officials or employees shall establish by rules, regulations, or otherwise, procedures designed to ascertain, before any person, including teachers and other employees of any public educational institution in this State, is appointed or employed, that he is not a subversive person, and that there are no reasonable grounds to believe such person is a subversive person. In the event reasonable grounds exist, he shall not be appointed or employed. In securing any facts necessary to ascertain the information herein required, the applicant shall be required to sign a written affidavit containing answers to such inquiries as may be reasonably material.

Id. § 14:371 (Supp. 1963). *Exclusions from scope of law.*—The inquiries prescribed in R.S. 14:370, other than the written statement to be executed by an applicant for employment, shall not be required as a prerequisite to the employment of any persons in the classification of laborers in any case in which the employing authority shall in his or its discretion determine, and by rule or regulation specify the reason why the nature of the work to be performed is such that employment of persons as to whom there may be reasonable grounds to believe that they are subversive persons as defined in R.S. 14:359, will not be dangerous to the health or security of the citizens or the security of the government of the State of Louisiana, or any political subdivision thereof.

Id. § 14:372 (Supp. 1963). *Standard of evidence and procedures for dismissal.*—Reasonable grounds to believe that any person is a subversive person, as defined in R.S. 14:359, shall be cause for discharge from any appointive office or other position of profit or trust in the government of or in the administration of the business of this State, or of any parish, municipality, or other political subdivision of this State, or any agency thereof. The appropriate civil service commission or board shall, by appropriate rules or regulations, prescribe that persons charged with being subversive persons, as defined in R.S. 14:359, shall be accorded notice and opportunity to be heard in accordance with the procedures prescribed by law for discharges for other reasons. Every person and every board, commission, council, department, or other agency of the State of Louisiana or any political subdivision thereof having responsibility for the appointment, employment, or supervision of public employees shall establish rules or procedures similar to those required herein for classified services for a hearing for any person charged with being a subversive person, as defined in R.S. 14:359, after notice and opportunity to be heard. Every employing authority discharging any person pursuant to any provision of R.S. 14:358–14:374 shall promptly report to the department of public safety the fact of and the circumstances surrounding such discharge.

Louisiana Stat. Anno. § 42:51. *Declaration of legislative findings.*— The legislature of Louisiana does hereby take cognizance of the fact that much of the world is in a state of political unrest; that foreign agents and others who seek the overthrow or destruction of the Government of the United States are known to be working in our country, and that such a situation presents a clear and present danger; and it is hereby declared to be public policy that subversive activities by any public employee, or by any student in a public educational institution in this State, should not be permitted, and this act is enacted to prohibit such subversive activities.

Id. § 42:52 (Supp. 1963). *Oath required.*—No person owing allegiance to the United States hereafter shall be employed by any department, board, commission, or agency of the State of Louisiana, or of any political subdivision or municipal corporation of the State of Louisiana, unless and until he shall take, and file with the administrative head of such department, board, commission, or agency, the following oath or affirmation:

"I (A. B.) do solemnly swear (or affirm) that I will support the Constitution and laws of the United States and the constitution and laws of this State; and I will faithfully and impartially discharge and perform all the duties incumbent upon me as * * *, and according to the best of my ability and understanding. So help me God."

Provided, however, that such persons may be temporarily employed for fifteen days, and if the oath is not taken and filed within fifteen days, they shall be discharged.

Id. § 42:53. *Contract of employment conditioned upon execution of oath.*—Before any contract of employment between any person and a State department, board, commission, or agency of the State of Louisiana, or of any political subdivision or municipal corporation of the State of Louisiana, is made or renewed after July 26, 1950, the oath or affirmation prescribed in R.S. 42:52 hereof shall be taken and filed by the prospective employee.

Id. § 42:54. *Subversive activities prohibited.*—No public employee, and no student in a public educational institution, shall by word of mouth or writing knowingly or willfully advocate, abet, advise, or teach, the duty, necessity, desirability, or propriety, of overthrowing or destroying the Government of the United States or of any State or of any political subdivision thereof, by force, violence, or any other unlawful means, or the adherence to the government of any foreign nation in the event of war between the United States and such foreign government.

Id. § 42:55. *"Public employee" defined.*—As used in this Part: (1) "Public employee" shall mean and include every officer or employee of any department, board, commission, or agency of the State of Louisiana, or of any political subdivision or municipal corporation of the State of Louisiana.

(2) "Student in a public educational institution" shall mean and include every student enrolled in any public school of the State, or in any State-supported trade school, vocational school, college, or university.

Id. § 42:56. *Penalty; dismissal.*—Any public employee found guilty of committing any act prohibited by R.S. 42:54 hereof shall be dismissed from his public employment. Any student in a public educational institution found guilty of committing any act prohibited by R.S. 42:54 hereof shall be expelled from the public educational institution in which he is enrolled.

Id. § 42:57. *Investigation, hearing, etc.*—No person shall be dismissed or expelled under the provisions of this part unless found guilty after a hearing, and review, as provided hereinafter. No person shall be tried under the provisions of this part unless the administrative head of the public educational institution or public body concerned shall have made a complete investigation of the accusation, shall have found that probable cause exists for such a hearing, and shall prefer in writing a charge specifying the act or acts alleged to have been committed by the person accused. Every such hearing shall be had before a committee of not less than three nor more than seven citizens, some or all of whom might be employees of the public educational institution or public body, appointed by the administrative head thereof.

Not less than ten nor more than twenty days prior to such hearing, a written statement specifying the charges, and setting out the time and place of the hearing, shall be served personally or by registered mail upon the person charged. Such hearing shall be conducted by the committee appointed therefor, and shall not be public unless the person charged so requests in writing. Both the accused and the public educational institution or public body may be represented by counsel, and shall have the right to subpoena, examine, and cross-examine witnesses, all of whom shall be sworn by the chairman of the committee before testifying. A stenographic record of all proceedings at the hearing shall be provided by the administrative officer preferring the charges.

If the committee finds the charge proved, it shall transmit a copy of the proceedings at the hearing to the administrative officer preferring the charges, and shall recommend the dismissal or the expulsion, as the case may be, of the person charged. The governing authority (if any) of the department, board, commission, or agency, and if none, the administrative head thereof, shall review all proceedings at any hearing where the committee conducting it has found the charges proven. If the reviewing authority disagrees with such finding, it shall set it aside, dismiss the proceedings, and notify the person charged accordingly. If the reviewing authority agrees with such finding, it shall approve the proceedings, find the person charged guilty, and dismiss or expel, as the case may be, the person so found guilty.

Any committee conducting such a hearing shall have the same authority to subpoena witnesses, or to order the taking of testimony by deposition, as is now enjoyed by the district courts. Failure to appear at a committee hearing, or to appear to have testimony taken by deposition, or refusal to answer any proper question propounded, shall be deemed contempt of the committee, and certified as such by the committee to the district court having jurisdiction over the parish in which the offender is domiciled. If such person is found guilty thereof by such court, he may be punished in the same manner, and to the same extent, as if he had been guilty of contempt of such court. Perjury committed by persons testifying at such hearing shall be punished in the same manner, and to the same extent, as perjury committed in the district courts of the State.

The written record of all proceedings at all hearings at which the committee found the charges not proved, and in all cases where the reviewing authority sets aside the committee's finding that the charges had been proved, shall be kept confidential, and shall not be deemed public records, except at the written request of the person charged.

Id. § 42 : 58. *Judicial review.*—Any person dismissed or expelled as set forth in R.S. 42 : 57 hereof may prosecute an appeal from such dismissal or expulsion, within thirty days of notice thereof, to the district court having jurisdiction over the parish of the domicile of the public educational institution or public body concerned. On such appeal, which shall be a trial de novo, the written record of the proceedings before the committee shall be admissible in evidence for all purposes, but either party shall have the right to introduce all other competent evidence desired, whether introduced at the hearing by the committee or not.

_____

Annotation:

Op. Atty. Gen. 1958–1960, p. 329. The State statute providing that no person owing allegiance to the United States shall be employed by any agency or political subdivision of the State unless he takes the oath applies to both old and new employees.

_____

Louisiana Stat. Anno. § 2:37 (Supp. 1963). *Refusal to testify constitutes insubordination and grounds for dismissal.*—Every person in the employ of the State of Louisiana or any political subdivision thereof, or in the employ in any capacity of any parish or city school board or any public school, college, university, or other institution of higher learning which is supported in whole or in part by public funds of the State of Louisiana, whenever he may or shall be called and sworn as a witness before the Joint Legislative Committee of the Legislature of Louisiana, shall be required to answer under oath whether he has been or is a member of the Communist Party. Refusal to give such information, in which the State of Louisiana has a legitimate interest in securing, in response to questions asked by the chairman, or any member of the Joint Legislative Committee, whenever any legislative investigation is being made or undertaken by the said committee in accordance with the provisions of Article V, section 17, of the constitution of the State of Louisiana, shall constitute insubordination on the part of any such employee, and he shall, by reason of such refusal to answer any such question or questions, be subject to dismissal or discharge, in the manner provided by law, from his said employment.

3. CIVIL DEFENSE PERSONNEL

Louisiana Stat. Anno. § 29:612. *Loyalty oath required.*—A. All persons both compensated and noncompensated in any way connected with the administration or operation of the civil defense program shall take and subscribe to the following oath:

"I, _____, do solemnly swear (or affirm) that I will support and defend the Constitution of the United States and the constitution of the State of Louisiana, and the territory, institutions, and facilities thereof, both public and private, against all enemies, foreign and domestic; that I will bear true faith and allegiance to the same; and I take this obligation freely, without any mental reservation or purpose of evasion; and that I will well and faithfully discharge the duties on which I am about to enter.

"And I do further swear (or affirm) that I do not advocate, nor am I a member of any political party or organization that advocates the overthrow of the Government of the United States or of this State by force or violence; and that during such time as I am a member of the State Civil Defense Agency, I will not advocate nor become a member of any political party or organization that advocates the overthrow of the Government of the United States or of this State by force or violence."

B. State, regional, district, parish, and municipal directors of civil defense are authorized to administer the oath required by subsection A of this section.

TEACHERS' LOYALTY

Louisiana Stat. Anno. § 14:362 (Supp. 1963). *Communists and members of Communist front organizations ineligible for employment.*—No person may hold any nonelective position, job, or office for the State of Louisiana, or any political subdivision thereof, where the remuneration of said position, job, or office is paid in whole or in part by public moneys or funds of the State of Louisiana, or of any political subdivision thereof, where the evidence shows such persons to be a Communist or a knowing member of a Communist front organization.

Id. § 14:369 (Supp. 1963). *Subversive persons ineligible for employment.*—No subversive person, as defined in R.S. 14:359, shall be eligible for employment in, or appointment to any office, or any position of trust or profit in the government of, or in the administration of the business of this State, or of any parish, municipality, or other political subdivision of this State.

Id. § 14:370 (Supp. 1963). *Rules and regulations to determine loyalty.*—Every person and every board, commission, council, department, court or other agency of the State of Louisiana or any political subdivision thereof, who appoints, employs or supervises in any manner the appointment or employment of public officials or employees shall establish by rules, regulations or otherwise, procedures designed to ascertain, before any person, including teachers and other employees of any public educational institution in this State, is appointed or employed, that he is not a subversive person, and that there are no reasonable grounds to believe such person is a subversive person. In the event reasonable grounds exist, he shall not be appointed or employed. In securing any facts necessary to ascertain the information herein required, the applicant shall be required to sign a written affidavit containing answers to such inquiries as may be reasonably material.

Louisiana Stat. Anno. 42:52 (Supp. 1963). *Oath required.*—No person owing allegiance to the United States hereafter shall be employed by any department, board, commission, or agency of the State of Louisiana, or of any political subdivision or municipal corporation of the State of Louisiana, unless and until he shall take, and file with the administrative head of such department, board, commission, or agency, the following oath or affirmation:

"I (A. B.) do solemnly swear (or affirm) that I will support the Constitution and laws of the United States and the constitution and laws of this State; and I will faithfully and impartially discharge and perform all the duties incumbent upon me as _____, and according to the best of my ability and understanding. So help me God."

Provided, however, that such persons may be temporarily employed for fifteen days, and if the oath is not taken and filed within fifteen days, they shall be discharged.

Id. § 42:54. *Subversive activities prohibited.*—No public employee, and no student in a public educational institution, shall by word of mouth or writing knowingly or willfully advocate, abet, advise, or teach, the duty, necessity, desirability, or propriety, of overthrowing or destroying the Government of the United States or of any State or of any political subdivision thereof, by force, violence, or any other unlawful means, or the adherence to the government of any foreign nation in the event of war between the United States and such foreign government.

Louisiana Stat. Anno. 42:37 (Supp. 1963). *Refusal to testify constitutes insubordination and grounds for dismissal.*—Every person in the employ of the State of Louisiana or any political subdivision thereof, or in the employ in any capacity of any parish or city school board or any public school, college, university or other institution of higher learning which is supported in whole or in part by public funds of the State of Louisiana, whenever he may or shall be called and sworn as a witness before the Joint Legislative Committee of the Legislature of Louisiana, shall be required to answer under oath whether he has been or is a member of the Communist Party. Refusal to give such information, in which the State of Louisiana has a legitimate interest in securing, in response to questions asked by the chairman, or any member of the Joint Legislative Committee, whenever any legislative investigation is being made or undertaken by the said committee in accordance with the provisions of Article V, section 17, of the constitution of the State of Louisiana, shall constitute insubordination on the part of any such employee, and he shall, by reason of such refusal to answer any such question or questions, be subject to dismissal or discharge, in the manner provided by law, from his said employment.

EXCLUSION FROM THE BAR

Louisiana does not appear to have any rule or regulation which pertains to the admission of persons who are or have been Communists or subversives. Similarly, the various forms employed by the State do not contain any questions directly on the subject.

EXCLUSION FROM INCIDENTAL BENEFITS

1. PUBLIC EDUCATION

Louisiana Stat. Anno. § 42:54. *Subversive activities prohibited.*— No public employee, and no student in a public educational institution, shall by word of mouth or writing knowingly or willfully advocate, abet, advise, or teach, the duty, necessity, desirability, or propriety, of overthrowing or destroying the Government of the United States or of any State or of any political subdivision thereof, by force, violence, or any other unlawful means, or the adherence to the government of any foreign nation in the event of war between the United States and such foreign government.

Id. § 42:55. *"Student in a public educational institution" defined.*— As used in this Part: (1) "Public employee" shall mean and include every officer or employee of any department, board, commission, or agency of the State of Louisiana, or of any political subdivision or municipal corporation of the State of Louisiana.

(2) "Student in a public educational institution" shall mean and include every student enrolled in any public school of the State, or in any State-supported trade school, vocational school, college, or university.

Id. § 42:56. *Penalty; dismissal.*—Any public employee found guilty of committing any act prohibited by R.S. 42:54 hereof shall be dismissed from his public employment. Any student in a public educational institution found guilty of committing any act prohibited by R.S. 42:54 hereof shall be expelled from the public educational institution in which he is enrolled.

2. NONTRADING ASSOCIATIONS

Louisiana Stat. Anno.—§ 14:385 (Supp. 1963). *Prohibited affiliations.*—Nontrading corporations, partnerships and associations of persons operating in the State of Louisiana and engaged in social, educational or political activities are prohibited from being affiliated with any foreign or out-of-State nontrading corporations, partnerships, or associations of persons, any of the officers or members of the board of directors of which are members of Communist, Communist-front, or subversive organizations as cited by the House of Congress Un-American Activities Committee, or the United States Attorney. Reports or information from the files of the Committee on Un-American Activities of the U.S. House of Representatives shall constitute prima facie evidence of such membership in said organizations.

Id. § 14:386 (Supp. 1963). *Non-Communist affidavit.*—As a condition precedent to being authorized to operate or conduct any activities in the State of Louisiana, every nontrading corporation, partnership, or association of persons engaged in social, educational, or political activities, affiliated with any similar nontrading corporation, partnership, or association of persons, chartered, created, or operating under the laws of any other State, shall file with the secretary of state yearly, on or before December 31, an affidavit attesting to the fact that none of the officers of such out-of-State or foreign corporation, partnership, or association of persons with which it is affiliated, is a member of any such organization cited by the House of Congress Un-American Activities Committee, or the United States Attorney General, as Communist, Communist-front, or subversive.

Id. § 14:387 (Supp. 1963). *Penalty—failure to file affidavit.*— Failure to file the affidavit required by R.S. 14:386 shall constitute a misdemeanor, and the officers and members of such nontrading corporation, partnership, or association of persons operating in this State and affiliated with such out-of-State or foreign organizations, failing to file such affidavit, shall be deemed guilty of a misdemeanor and upon conviction by a court of competent jurisdiction shall be fined $100.00 and imprisoned 30 days in the parish jail.

Id. § 14:388 (Supp. 1963). *Penalty—false statements.*—Any false statement under oath contained in the affidavit required by R.S. 14:386 filed with the secretary of state shall constitute perjury and shall be punished as provided by R.S. 14:123.

Annotation:

Louisiana v. *N.A.A.C.P.*, 366 U.S. 293, 8 S. Ct. 1333, 6 L. Ed. 2d 301 (1961). The State attorney general sought to enjoin appellee from doing business in the State. The action was removed to the Federal courts. Thereafter the appellee instituted an action for a judgment declaring unconstitutional two laws of Louisiana. One of the two statutes in question prohibited any "nontrading" association from doing business in Louisiana if it is affiliated with any "foreign or out-of-State nontrading" association "any of the officers or members of the board of directors of which are members of Communist, Communist-front, or subversive organizations, as cited by the House of Representatives Un-American Activities Committee or the United States Attorney." Every nontrading association affiliated with an out-of-State association must file annually with Louisiana's secretary of state an affidavit that "none of the officers" of the affiliate is "a member of any such organization." Penalties against the officers and members are provided for failure to file the affidavit and for false filings. The second statute required the principal officer of "each fraternal, patriotic, charitable, benevolent, literary, scientific, athletic, military, or social organization, or organization created for similar purposes" and operating in Louisiana to file with the secretary of state annually "a full, complete, and true list of the names and addresses of all of the members and officers" in the State. Members of organizations whose lists have not been filed are prohibited from holding or attending any meeting of the organization. Criminal penalties are attached both to officers and to members. Noting that the "statute would require the impossible" of the comparatively few of appellee's residents or workers, the district court enjoined State officers from enforcing the act. The Supreme Court affirmed on grounds that where disclosure of membership lists result in reprisals and hostility to the members, disclosure is not required. The Court concluded by pointing out that—

"At one extreme is criminal conduct which cannot have shelter in the First Amendment. At the other extreme are regulatory measures which, no matter how sophisticated, cannot be employed in purpose or in effect to stifle, penalize, or curb the exercise of First Amendment rights. These lines mark the area in which the present controversy lies, * * *"

MISCELLANEOUS

1. COMMUNIST PROPAGANDA

Louisiana Stat. Anno. Rev. Stat. § 14:390 (Supp. 1963). *Declaration of public policy.*—In the interpretation and application of R.S. 14:390 and the subsections thereof, and as a result of certain evidence having been presented to the Joint Legislative Committee on Un-American Activities of this Legislature, the public policy of this State is declared to be as follows:

There exists a clear, present, and distinct danger to the security of the State of Louisiana and the well-being and security of the citizens of Louisiana arising from the infiltration of a significant amount of Communist propaganda into the State. In addition, this State is a stopping place or "way station" for sizable shipments of dangerous Communist propaganda to the rest of the United States and to many foreign countries.

The danger of Communist propaganda lies not in its being "different" in the philosophy it expresses from the philosophy generally held in this State and Nation, but instead in the fact that it is a specific tool or weapon used by the Communists for the express purpose of bringing about the forcible total destruction or subjugation of this State and Nation and the total eradication of the philosophy of freedom upon which this State and Nation were founded. "Words are bullets" and the Communists know it and use them so. Whatever guarantees of sovereignty and freedom are enjoyed by this State and its citizens are certain to vanish if the United States of America is destroyed or taken over by the Communists, and we, therefore, declare that any Communist effort by propaganda infiltration or otherwise against the United States is and should rightly be considered an attack upon or clear and present danger to the State of Louisiana and its citizens. Such attacks should, therefore, be the subject of concurrent jurisdiction through remedial legislation such as is now in effect on both the State and Federal level concerning such dangers as the narcotics traffic, bank robbery, kidnaping, etc. We hereby declare that the danger of Communist propaganda infiltration is even greater than the danger from narcotics, pornographic literature, switch blade knives, burglar tools, or illicit alcohol in dry jurisdictions, all of which have been the subject of valid statutory regulation by the States within the constitutional framework. The Federal legislation on this subject matter is either inadequate in its scope, or not being effectively enforced, as much communistic propaganda material unlabeled and unidentified as such, is in fact entering the State of Louisiana at this time.

We further declare that Communist propaganda, properly identified in terms similar to those used in the Foreign Agents Registration Act of the United States, is hereby identified as illicit dangerous contraband material. We further declare that certain exemptions hereinafter provided are for the purpose of allowing bona fide students of foreign languages, foreign affairs, or foreign political systems, other interested individuals, and also bona fide educational institutions, to obtain this contraband upon specifically requesting its delivery for the purpose of personal or institutional use in the due course of the educational process. We do not believe that the possession or use of such material by knowing and informed individuals for their personal use is any significant danger, and in fact it might be of some benefit in informing such individuals of the cynical and insidious nature of the Communist Party line. In view of these facts and so that any user of such materials will be adequately forewarned, we declare that all such material in any way entering the State of Louisiana should be required to be clearly labeled as Communist propaganda as hereinafter provided.

Id. § 14:390.1 (Supp. 1963). *"Communist propaganda" defined.*— (1) "Communist propaganda" means any oral, visual, graphic, written, pictorial, or other communication which is issued, prepared, printed, procured, distributed, or disseminated by the Soviet Union, any of its satellite countries, or by the government of any other Communist country or any agent of the Soviet Union, its satellite countries, or any other Communist country, wherever located, or by any Communist organization, Communist action organization, Communist front organization, Communist infiltrated organization, or Communist controlled organization, or by any agent of any such organization, which communication or material from any of the above listed sources is

(a) reasonably adopted to, or which the person disseminating the same believes will, or which he intends to, prevail upon, indoctrinate, convert, induce, or in any way influence a recipient or any section of the public with reference to the political or public interests, policies or relations of a government of a foreign country or a foreign political party, or promote in the United States or the State of Louisiana, any attitude or state of mind that tends to undermine the determination of any citizen of the United States or of any of the various States to uphold and defend the Constitution of the United States or the constitutions of the respective States, or tends to create or encourage disrespect for duly constituted legal authority, either Federal, or State, or

(b) which advocates, advises, instigates, or promotes any racial, social, political, or religious disorder, civil riot, or other conflict involving the use of force or violence in the United States, the State of Louisiana or any other American republic, or the overthrow of any government or political subdivision of the United States; the State of Louisiana or any other American republic by any means involving the use of force or violence.

(2) For the purposes of R.S. 14:390–14:390.8, the fact that an organization has been officially cited or identified by the Attorney General of the United States, the subversive activities control board of the United States, or any committee of the United States Congress as a Communist organization, a Communist action organization, a Communist front organization, or a Communist infiltrated organization or has been in any other way officially cited or identified by any of these aforementioned authorities as a Communist controlled organization, shall be considered presumptive evidence of the factual status of any such organization.

Id. § 14:390.2 (Supp. 1963). *Unlawful acts.*—It shall be a felony for any person to knowingly, willfully, and intentionally deliver, distribute, disseminate, or store Communist propaganda in the State of Louisiana except under the specific exemptions hereinafter provided.

Id. § 14:390.3 (Supp. 1963). *Exclusions from scope of law.*—Bona fide students of foreign languages, foreign affairs, or foreign political systems, other interested individuals, and also bona fide officially accredited educational institutions may obtain Communist propaganda and have the same legally delivered to them within the State of Louisiana upon specifically requesting the delivery of the same for the purpose of personal or institutional use in the due course of the educational process. All such Communist propaganda legally entering this State under this exemption shall be clearly and legibly labeled on both the front and back cover thereof, or on the front if not covered, with the words "Communist Propaganda" printed or stamped conspicuously in red ink, and failure to so label said material shall constitute a violation of R.S. 14:390–14:390.8 on the part of the sender or distributor thereof, the violation to be considered to take place at the point of actual delivery to the ultimate user who requested the material.

Id. § 14:390.4 (Supp. 1963). *Site of violation.*—Violations of R.S. 14:390–14:390.9 are considered to take place at the location where the prohibited contraband material is found, either stored in bulk or placed in the hands of the ultimate user.

Id. § 14:390.5 (Supp. 1963). *Enforcement.*—It is the duty of the sheriffs of the respective parishes, upon the finding of any bulk storage of any Communist propaganda, to enter upon the premises where the material is found, clear the premises of all human occupants, and padlock the premises until judicially ordered to reopen them. The owner of any padlocked premises may, upon application to the district court of proper jurisdiction and upon showing the court that the premises can be immediately cleared of the prohibited contraband material, obtain an order from the court to the sheriff, authorizing him to supervise the removal of the contraband by the owner of the premises and to reopen the premises thereafter.

Id. § 14:390.6 (Supp. 1963). *Seizure of prohibited matter.*—All Communist propaganda discovered in the State of Louisiana in violation of R.S. 14:390–14:390.8 shall be seized and after proper identification and upon summary order of the district court of proper jurisdiction, destroyed, unless needed for official purposes.

Id. § 14:390.7 (Supp. 1963). *Penalty.*—Any person who violates any of the provisions of R.S. 14:390–14:390.6 shall be fined not more than ten thousand dollars or imprisoned at hard labor for not more than six years, or both.

Id. § 14:390.8 (Supp. 1963). *Short title.*—R.S. 14:390 through 14:390.7 may be cited as the "Communist Propaganda Control Law."

2. "ANTICOMMUNIST DIVISION"

Louisiana Stat. Anno. 25:17 (Supp. 1963). *Creation and purpose of Division.*—A. The Louisiana State Library shall organize, maintain, and operate a special division of the library to be designated as "Anti-Communist Division" of the Louisiana State Library which will be in charge of a trained and experienced librarian.

B. The purpose of this special division will be to collect, maintain, lend, circulate, and disseminate books, pamphlets, films, tapes, slides, congressional and other reports and studies and all other available materials which explain, discuss, espouse, or disseminate information relative to the fundamental principles of the American form of government, free enterprise, capitalism, the American social and economic system, the philosophy, purposes, strategy, tactics, nature, effects, logistics, and fallacies of communism in its goal of world domination, the evils of socialism, and the contrast between liberty under law and communism and socialism.

C. The anti-Communist division shall arrange for the free loan of all such materials and distribution (including shipping costs) from this special collection to civic clubs, veterans' organizations, patriotic societies, bar associations, women's clubs, study groups, labor unions, chambers of commerce, schools, classes, libraries and other organizations and individuals in Louisiana for use in pro-American and anti-Communist programs, instruction, study or reading.

3. COMMUNIST PRODUCTS

Louisiana Stat. Anno. 33:4787 (Supp. 1963). *Authority to prohibit sale of products made in Communist countries, etc.*—A. The governing authority of the parishes and municipalities of this State are hereby authorized to adopt ordinances to prohibit the sale and offering for sale of products manufactured or produced in any Communist country, any Communist controlled country, or any country which is a satellite of a Communist country, including but not necessarily restricted to products manufactured or produced in any form or manner in the U.S.S.R., Poland, Yugoslavia, Czechoslovakia, North Vietnam, Hungary, Cuba, Bulgaria, East Germany, North Korea, and Red China.

B. Any ordinance adopted pursuant to the authority herein granted may include provisions for enforcement of the ordinance, including criminal penalties for the violation thereof which shall consist of a fine not in excess of five thousand dollars or imprisonment for not to exceed two years in the parish jail, or both a fine and imprisonment not exceeding the limits herein stated.

4. COURSE ON COMMUNISM

Louisiana Stat. Anno. § 17:2851. *Seminars on philosophy of communism authorized.*—The State department of education, in accordance with such rules and regulations therefor as shall be established by the State board of education which shall not be inconsistent with the provisions of R.S. 17:2851 and 17:2852, shall provide for and shall administer, supervise and conduct, seminars annually in each parish and city school system at a time during each school year at the discretion of the State department of education and in cooperation with the parish and city school systems, which shall have for their purpose instruction and dissemination of information designed to give high school students and teachers who attend such seminars a clear understanding of the fundamental principles of the American form of government, the evils of socialism, and the basic philosophy of communism and the strategy and tactics used by Communists in their efforts to achieve their ultimate goal of world domination. Provided the State department of education in cooperation with the parish and city school systems may hold separate seminars at a time and place to be determined by the department for training teachers in such field.

The seminars herein provided for shall be held for a minimum of two days. The State department shall determine the scope of and the methods to be used at said seminars, and shall make such preparations as are necessary to provide instructors, lecturers, and personnel for said seminars.

Id. § 17:2852. *Persons eligible to attend seminars.*—The seminars herein provided for shall be attended by certain teachers and eleventh and twelfth grade high school students selected from the high schools of the State in accordance with such rules and regulations as to eligibility as shall be established by the State board of education. The appropriation made in Act No. 73 of 1961 shall be used for the purposes of these seminars.

Id. § 17:2853. *Appropriations.*—In order to provide funds for the expenses of the seminars herein provided for and for the expenses of room and board of students attending said seminars, there is hereby appropriated, allocated, and dedicated to the State public school fund out of the general fund of the State annually the sum of $30,000.00, or so much thereof as may be necessary for said purposes.

MAINE

Maine Rev. Code 1954, c. 143, § 4. *Subversive activities defined; penalty.*—Any person who advocates, aids or takes any active part in the overthrow by force and violence of the Government of the United States or the State of Maine or any political subdivision thereof is guilty of a felony and, upon conviction thereof, shall be punished by imprisonment in the State prison for not more than 5 years or by a fine of not more than $5,000, or by both such fine and imprisonment.

LOYALTY OF STATE OFFICERS AND EMPLOYEES

1. ELECTIVE AND NONELECTIVE PERSONNEL

Maine Constitution, Art. IX, § 1. *Oath.*—Every person elected or appointed to either of the places or offices provided in this constitution, and every person elected, appointed, or commissioned to any judicial, executive, military or other office under this State, shall, before he enter on the discharge of the duties of his place or office, take and subscribe the following oath or affirmation: "I, _____, do swear, that I will support the Constitution of the United States and of this State, so long as I shall continue a citizen thereof. So help me God."

"I, _____, do swear, that I will faithfully discharge, to the best of by abilities, the duties incumbent on me as _____ according to the constitution and laws of the State. So help me God." *Provided,* that an affirmation in the above forms may be substituted, when the person shall be conscientiously scrupulous of taking and subscribing an oath.

The oaths or affirmations shall be taken and subscribed by the Governor and counsellors before the presiding officer of the senate, in the presence of both houses of the legislature, and by the senators and representatives before the Governor and council, and by the residue of said officers before such persons as shall be prescribed by the legislature; and whenever the Governor or any counsellor shall not be able to attend during the session of the legislature to take and subscribe said oaths or affirmations, such oaths or affirmations may be taken and subscribed in the recess of the legislature before any justice of the supreme judicial court.

2. CIVIL DEFENSE PERSONNEL

Maine Rev. Code, c. 12, § 15. *Loyalty oath required.*—No person shall be employed or associated in any capacity in any civil defense and public safety organization established under the provisions of this chapter who advocates or has advocated a change in the con-

187

stitutional form of the Government of the United States or in this State or the overthrow of any government in the United States by force or violence, or who has been convicted of or is under indictment or information charging any subversive act against the United States. Each person who is appointed to serve in an organization for civil defense and public safety shall, before entering upon his duties, take an oath, in writing, before a person authorized to administer oaths in this State, which oath shall be substantially as follows:

"I _____, do solemnly swear (or affirm) that I will support and defend the Constitution of the United States and the constitution of the State of Maine, against all enemies, foreign and domestic; that I will bear true faith and allegiance to the same; that I take this obligation freely, without any mental reservation or purpose of evasion; and that I will well and faithfully discharge the duties of the office on which I am about to enter.

"And I do further swear (or affirm) that I do not advocate, nor am I a member of any political party or organization that advocates the overthrow of the Government of the United States by force or violence; and that during such time as I am a member of the _____, I will not advocate nor become a member of any political party or organization that advocates the overthrow of the Government of the United States by force or violence."

EXCLUSION FROM THE BAR

Maine does not appear to have any rule or regulation which pertains to the admission of persons who are or have been Communists or subversive. Similarly, the various forms employed by the State do not contain any questions directly on the subject.

MARYLAND

Anno. Code of Maryland, art. 85A, § 1. *"Organization," "Subversive organization," "Foreign subversive organization," "Foreign government," and "Subversive person"* defined.—For the purposes of this article:

"Organization" means an organization, corporation, company, partnership, association, trust, foundation, fund, club, society, committee, association, political party, or any group of persons, whether or not incorporated, permanently or temporarily associated together for joint action or advancement of views on any subject or subjects.

"Subversive organization" means any organization which engages in or advocates, abets, advises, or teaches, or a purpose of which is to engage in or advocate, abet, advise, or teach activities intended to overthrow, destroy or alter, or to assist in the overthrow, destruction or alteration of, the constitutional form of the Government of the United States, or of the State of Maryland, or of any political subdivision of either of them, by revolution, force, or violence.

"Foreign subversive organization" means any organization directed, dominated or controlled directly or indirectly by a foreign government which engages in or advocates, abets, advises, or teaches, or a purpose of which is to engage in or to advocate, abet, advise, or teach, activities intended to overthrow, destroy or alter, or to assist in the overthrow, destruction or alteration of the constitutional form of the Government of the United States, or of the State of Maryland, or of any political subdivision of either of them, and to establish in place thereof any form of government the direction and control of which is to be vested in, or exercised by or under, the domination or control of any foreign government, organization, or individual; but does not and shall not be construed to mean an organization the bona fide purpose of which is to promote world peace by alliances or unions with other governments or world federations, unions or governments to be effected through constitutional means.

"Foreign government" means the government of any country or nation other than the Government of the United States of America or of one of the States thereof.

"Subversive person" means any person who commits, attempts to commit, or aids in the commission, or advocates, abets, advises or teaches by any means any person to commit, attempt to commit, or aid in the commission of any act intended to overthrow, destroy or alter, or to assist in the overthrow, destruction or alteration of, the constitutional form of the Government of the United States, or of the State of Maryland, or any political subdivision of either of them, by revolution, force, or violence; or who is a member of a subversive organization or a foreign subversive organization.

189

Id. § 2. *Unlawful acts and penalty.*—It shall be a felony for any person knowingly and willfully to:

(a) Commit, attempt to commit, or aid in the commission of any act intended to overthrow, destroy or alter, or to assist in the overthrow, destruction or alteration of, the constitutional form of the Government of the United States, or of the State of Maryland, or any political subdivision of either of them, by revolution, force, or violence; or

(b) Advocate, abet, advise, or teach by any means any person to commit, attempt to commit, or assist in the commission of any such act under such circumstances as to constitute a clear and present danger to the security of the United States, or of the State of Maryland or of any political subdivision of either of them; or

(c) Conspire with one or more persons to commit any such act; or

(d) Assist in the formation or participate in the management or to contribute to the support of any subversive organization or foreign subversive organization knowing said organization to be a subversive organization or a foreign subversive organization; or

(e) Destroy any books, records or files, or secrete any funds in this State of a subversive organization or a foreign subversive organization, knowing said organization to be such.

Any person who shall be convicted by a court of competent jurisdiction of violating any of the provisions of this section shall be fined not more than twenty thousand dollars ($20,000), or imprisoned for not more than twenty (20) years, or both, at the discretion of the court.

Id. § 3. *Membership in subversive organization unlawful.*—It shall be a felony for any person after June 1, 1949, to become, or after September 1, 1949, to remain a member of a subversive organization or a foreign subversive organization knowing said organization to be a subversive organization or foreign subversive organization. Any person who shall be convicted by a court of competent jurisdiction of violating this section shall be fined not more than five thousand dollars ($5,000), or imprisoned for not more than five (5) years, or both, at the discretion of the court.

Id. § 4. *Additional penalties.*—Any person who shall be convicted by a court of competent jurisdiction of violating any of the provisions of §§ 2 and 3 of this article, in addition to all other penalties therein provided, shall from the date of such conviction be barred from:

(a) Holding any office, elective or appointive, or any other position of profit or trust in or employment by the government of the State of Maryland or of any agency thereof or of any county, municipal corporation or other political subdivision of said State;

(b) Filing or standing for election to any public office in the State of Maryland; or

(c) Voting in any election held in this State.

Id. § 5. *Subversive organizations outlawed.*—It shall be unlawful for any subversive organization or foreign subversive organization to exist or function in the State of Maryland and any organization which by a court of competent jurisdiction is found to have violated the provisions of this section shall be dissolved, and if it be a corporation organized and existing under the laws of the State of Maryland a finding by a court of competent jurisdiction that it has violated the provisions of this section shall constitute legal cause for forfeiture of its charter and its charter shall be forfeited under the provisions of Article 23, §§ 104–108, inclusive, Annotated Code of Maryland [1939 Code] and all funds, books, records, and files of every kind and all other property of any organization found to have violated the provisions of this section shall be seized by and for the State of Maryland, the funds to be deposited in the State treasury and the books, records, files, and other property to be turned over to the attorney general of Maryland.

Id. § 6. *Enforcement.*—The attorney general of Maryland is hereby authorized and directed to appoint an additional assistant to perform the duties of special assistant attorney general in charge of subversive activities whose annual salary shall be provided in the budget, and whose responsibility it shall be, under the supervision of the attorney general, to assemble, arrange, and deliver to the State's attorney of any county or of Baltimore city, together with a list of necessary witnesses, for presentation to the next grand jury to meet in said county or city, all information and evidence of matters within said county or Baltimore city which have come to his attention, relating in any manner to the acts prohibited by this article, and relating generally to the purposes, processes, and acivities of communism and any other or related subversive organizations, associations, groups, or persons.

Id. § 7. *Collection of evidence.*—For the collection of any evidence and information referred to in this article, the attorney general is hereby directed to call upon the superintendent of State police, the police commissioner of Baltimore city and other county and municipal police authorities of the State to furnish to the special assistant hereinbefore provided for, such assistance as may from time to time be required. Such police authorities are directed to furnish information and assistance as may be from time to time so requested. The special assistant attorney general herein provided for may testify before any grand jury as to matters referred to in this article as to which he may have information.

Id. § 8. *Records keeping; confidential; reports.*—The attorney general shall require the special assistant herein provided for, to maintain complete records of all information received by him and all matters handled by him under the requirements of this article. Such records as may reflect on the loyalty of any resident of this State, shall not be made public or divulged to any person except with permission of the attorney general to effectuate the purposes of this article. He shall further require the publication, printing and appropriate distribution of all reports of grand juries of this State made as hereinafter provided. The attorney general shall include in his budget estimates, adequate moneys for the printing and distribution of the said reports, and for all other expenses of administering this article. To the extent that his time may not be required in his duties under this article, the special assistant attorney general shall be available for and perform such other duties as may be assigned to him by the attorney general.

Id. § 9. *Grand jury investigations.*—The judge of the criminal court of each county and of Baltimore city, when in his discretion it appears appropriate, or when informed by the state's attorney that there is information or evidence of the character described in § 6 of this article to be considered by the grand jury, shall charge the grand jury to inquire into violations of this article for the purpose of proper action, and further to inquire generally into the purposes, processes and activities and any other matters affecting communism or any related or other subversive organizations, associations, groups or persons. Any grand jury charged by the court as provided herein shall not later than the conclusion of its term of service prepare a written report, separate from all other matters considered by said grand jury, of its findings upon the subjects placed before it under the requirements of this article, provided, however, such report shall not charge any residents of this State with being disloyal unless they shall have been indicted under the provisions of this article or other provisions of the criminal law of this or some other jurisdiction.

Annotation:

Hammand v. *Lancaster*, 194 Md. 463, 71A. 2d 474 (1950). Petitioners, college professors, and teachers, a salesman, two physicians and a sculptor, sought a judgment declaring unconstitutional the Maryland Subversive Activities Act and an injunction prohibiting State officers from enforcing the act. The lower court held the act unconstitutional on grounds, *inter alia*, that it violated certain fundamental freedoms. On appeal, the court reversed the judgment and dismissed the petition, declaring that petitioners did not have standing to maintain the suit, i.e., "none of the complainants have been threatened with prosecution, nor do they allege any facts to indicate that they have violated, or are about to violate, any of the criminal provisions of the act."

EXCLUSION FROM THE ELECTIVE PROCESS

Anno. Code of Maryland, Art. 85A, § 4. *Persons convicted of engaging in subversive activities or of membership in subversive organizations barred from voting and standing for election.*—Any person who shall be convicted by a court of competent jurisdiction of violating any of the provisions of §§ 2 and 3 of this article, in addition to all other penalties therein provided, shall from the date of such conviction be barred from:

(a) Holding any office, elective or appointive, or any other position of profit or trust in or employment by the government of the State of Maryland or of any agency thereof or of any county, municipal corporation or other political subdivision of said State;

(b) Filing or standing for election to any public office in the State of Maryland; or

(c) Voting in any election held in this State.

Id. § 5. *Subversive organizations outlawed.*—It shall be unlawful for any subversive organization or foreign subversive organization to exist or function in the State of Maryland and any organization which by a court of competent jurisdiction is found to have violated the provisions of this section shall be dissolved, and if it be a corporation organized and existing under the laws of the State of Maryland a finding by a court of competent jurisdiction that it has violated the provisions of this section shall constitute legal cause for forfeiture of its charter and its charter shall be forfeited under the provisions of Article 23, §§ 104–108, inclusive, Annotated Code of Maryland [1939 Code] and all funds, books, records, and files of every kind and all other property of any organization found to have violated the provisions of this section shall be seized by and for the State of Maryland, the funds to be deposited in the State treasury and the books, records, files, and other property to be turned over to the attorney general of Maryland.

Id. § 15. *Candidates required to file nonsubversive affidavit.*—No person shall become a candidate for election under the provisions of Article 33 of the Annotated Code of Maryland to any public office whatsoever in this State, unless he or she shall file with the certificate of nomination required by the foregoing article 33, an affidavit that he or she is not a subversive person as defined in this article; provided that, in the case of certificates of nomination for President or Vice President of the United States, the affidavit may be made on behalf of such candidates by those persons who file the certificate of nomination for such candidates. No certificate of nomination shall be received for filing by any board of supervisors of elections or by the secretary of state of Maryland unless accompanied by the affidavit aforesaid, and there shall not be entered upon any ballot or voting machine at any election the name of any person who has failed or refused to make the affidavit aforesaid.

_____

Annotations:

Shub v. *Simpson*, 196 Md. 179, 76A. 2d 332 (1950), appeal dismissed 340 U.S. 881, 71 S. Ct. 198, 95. L. Ed. 635. Petitioners, candidates of the Progressive Party for various State and Federal offices, requested the courts to order the secretary of state to receive their nomination certificates. The certificates had been rejected because of the failure of all the petitioners to file the nonsubversive affidavit required by statute. On appeal, the court dismissed as moot the petitions of two candidates who had chosen to comply with the affidavit requirement. The issue before the court was the validity of the affidavit requirement as applied to a candidate for State office and to a candidate for Federal office. The court held that the statute was operative against the former but not against the latter. In the case of the candidate for Federal office, the court declared that the State cannot, in any manner, impose additional qualifications for office than those set forth in the Federal Constitution. The court sustained the applicability of the statute to State offices over objections that it constituted a superadded oath, that it violated fundamental first amendment rights, and that it violated due process by reason of vagueness and uncertainty.

Gerende v. *Election Board*, 341 U.S. 56, 71 S. Ct. 565, 95 L. Ed. 745 (1951). In this case, the Supreme Court sustained a State statute requiring that, in order for a candidate for public office to obtain a place on the ballot, he must make an oath that he has not engaged in one way or another to overthrow the Government by force or violence and that he is not knowingly a member of an organization engaged in such an attempt, on the understanding that an affidavit in those terms fully satisfied the requirement.

LOYALTY OF STATE OFFICERS AND EMPLOYEES

1. ELECTIVE AND NONELECTIVE PERSONNEL

Maryland Constitution, Art. 15, § 11. *Persons advocating overthrow of government ineligible for elective or appointive office and employment.*—No person who is a member of an organization that advocates the overthrow of the Government of the United States or of the State of Maryland through force or violence shall be eligible to hold any office, be it elective or appointive, or any other position of profit or trust in the government of or in the administration of the business of this State or of any county, municipality, or other political subdivision of this State.

Anno. Code of Maryland, Art. 85A, § 4. *Persons convicted of engaging in subversive activities or of membership in subversive organizations barred from elective or appointive office or employment.*—Any person who shall be convicted by a court of competent jurisdiction of violating any of the provisions of §§ 2 and 3 of this article, in addition to all other penalties therein provided, shall from the date of such conviction be barred from:

(a) Holding any office, elective or appointive, or any other position of profit or trust in or employment by the government of the State of Maryland or of any agency thereof or of any county, municipal corporation, or other political subdivision of said State;

(b) Filing or standing for election to any public office in the State of Maryland; or

(c) Voting in any election held in this State.

2. NONELECTIVE PERSONNEL

Anno. Code of Maryland, Art. 85A, § 10. *Subversive persons ineligible for appointive office or employment.*—No subversive person, as defined in this article, shall be eligible for employment in, or appointment to any office, or any position of trust or profit in the government of, or in the administration of the business of this State, or of any county, municipality, or other political subdivision of this State.

Id. § 11. *Rules and regulations to determine loyalty.*—Every person and every board, commission, council, department, court, or other agency of the State of Maryland or any political subdivision thereof, who or which appoints or employs or supervises in any manner the appointment or employment of public officials or employees shall establish by rules, regulations, or otherwise, procedures designed to ascertain before any person, including teachers and other employees of any public educational institution in this State, is appointed or employed, that he or she, as the case may be, is not a subversive person, and that there are no reasonable grounds to believe such persons are subversive persons. In the event such reasonable grounds exist, he or she, as the case may be, shall not be appointed or employed. In securing any facts necessary to ascertain the information herein required, the applicant shall be required to sign a written statement containing answers to such inquiries as may be material, which statement shall contain notice that it is subject to the penalties of perjury.

Id. § 12. *Exclusions from scope of law.*—The inquiries prescribed in § 11, other than the written statement to be executed by an applicant for employment, shall not be required as a prerequisite to the employment of any persons in the classification of laborers in any case in which the employing authority shall in his or its discretion determine, and by rule or regulation specify the reasons why, the nature of the work to be performed is such that employment of persons as to whom there may be reasonable grounds to believe that they are subversive persons as defined in this article will not be dangerous to the health of the citizens or the security of the governments of the United States, the State of Maryland, or any political subdivision thereof.

Id. § 13. *Nonsubversive statement required.*—Every person, who on June 1, 1949, shall be in the employ of the State of Maryland or of any political subdivision thereof, other than those now holding elective office shall be required on or before August 1, 1949, to make a written statement which shall contain notice that it is subject to the penalties of perjury, that he or she is not a subversive person as defined in this article, namely, any person who commits, attempts to commit, or aids in the commission, or advocates, abets, advises, or teaches by any means any person to commit, attempt to commit, or aid in the commission of any act intended to overthrow, destroy, or alter, or to assist in the overthrow, destruction, or alteration of, the constitutional form of the Government of the United States, or of the State of Maryland, or any political subdivision of either of them, by revolution, force, or violence; or who is a member of a subversive organization or a foreign subversive organization, as more fully defined in this article. Such statement shall be prepared and execution required by the State commissioner of personnel for all persons whose employment is subject to the provisions of Article 64A of the Annotated Code of Maryland and by the city service commission of Baltimore for all employees whose employment is subject to the provisions of §§ 142 to 156 of the Baltimore city charter and by every person and every board, commission, council, department, court, or other agency of the State of Maryland or any political subdivision thereof responsible for the supervision of other employees, for employees under its jurisdiction. Any such person failing or refusing to execute such a statement or who admits he is a subversive person as defined in this article shall immediately be discharged.

Id. § 14. *Standard of evidence.*—Reasonable grounds on all the evidence to believe that any person is a subversive person, as defined in this article, shall be cause for discharge from any appointive office or other position of profit or trust in the government of or in the administration of the business of this State, or of any county, municipality, or other political subdivision of this State, or any agency thereof. The State commissioner of personnel and the civil service commission of Baltimore shall, by appropriate rules or regulations, prescribe that persons charged with being subversive persons, as defined in this article, shall be accorded notice and opportunity to be heard, in accordance with the procedures prescribed by law for discharges for other reasons. Every person and every board, commission, council, department, or other agency of the State of Maryland or any political subdivision thereof having responsibility for the appointment, employment, or supervision of public employees not covered by the classified service in this section referred to, shall establish rules or procedures similar to those required herein for classified services for a hearing for any person charged with being a subversive person, as defined in this article, after notice and opportunity to be heard. Every employing authority discharging any person pursuant to any provision of this article shall promptly report to the special assistant attorney general in charge of subversive activities the fact of and the circumstances surrounding such discharge. A person discharged under the provisions of this section shall have the right to appeal to the circuit court of the county or to the Baltimore city court wherein such person may reside for a determination by such court (with the aid of a jury, if the appellant so elects) as to whether or not the discharge appealed from was justified under the provisions of this article. The court shall speedily hear and determine such appeals, and from the judgment of the court, there shall be a further appeal to the Court of Appeals of Maryland as in civil cases.

Id. § 17. *Penalty.*—Every written statement made pursuant to this article by an applicant for appointment or employment, or by any employee, shall be deemed to have been made under oath if it contains a declaration preceding the signature of the maker to the effect that it is made under the penalties of perjury. Any person who makes a material misstatement of fact (a) in any such written statement, or (b) in any affidavit made pursuant to the provisions of this article, or (c) under oath in any hearing conducted by any agency of the State, or of any of its political subdivisions, pursuant to this article, or (d) in any written statement by an applicant for appointment or employment or by an employee in any State aid or private institution of learning in this State, intended to determine whether or not such applicant or employee is a subversive person as defined in this article, which statement contains notice that it is subject to the penalties of perjury, shall be subject to the penalties of perjury prescribed in Article 27, § 439 of the Annotated Code.

Teachers' Loyalty

Anno. Code of Maryland, art. 85A, § 10. *Subversive persons ineligible for public employment.*—No subversive person, as defined in this article, shall be eligible for employment in, or appointment to any office, or any position of trust or profit in the government of, or in the administration of the business of this State, or of any county, municipality, or other political subdivision of this State.

Note.—Subversive person defined in § 13, *infra.*

Id. § 11. *Rules and regulations to determine loyalty.*—Every person and every board, commission, council, department, court, or other agency of the State of Maryland or any political subdivision thereof, who or which appoints or employs or supervises in any manner the appointment or employment of public officials or employees shall establish by rules, regulations, or otherwise, procedures designed to ascertain before any person, including teachers and other employees of any public educational institution in this State, is appointed or employed, that he or she as the case may be, is not a subversive person, and that there are no reasonable grounds to believe such persons are subversive persons. In the event such reasonable grounds exist, he or she as the case may be shall not be appointed or employed. In securing any facts necessary to ascertain the information herein required, the applicant shall be required to sign a written statement containing answers to such inquiries as may be material, which statement shall contain notice that it is subject to the penalties of perjury.

Id. § 13. *Nonsubversive statement required.*—Every person, who on June 1, 1949, shall be in the employ of the State of Maryland or of any political subdivision thereof, other than those now holding elective office shall be required on or before August 1, 1949, to make a written statement which shall contain notice that it is subject to the penalties of perjury, that he or she is not a subversive person as defined in this article, namely, any person who commits, attempts to commit, or aids in the commission, or advocates, abets, advises, or teaches by any means any person to commit, attempt to commit, or aid in the commission of any act intended to overthrow, destroy, or alter, or to assist in the overthrow, destruction, or alteration of, the constitutional form of the Government of the United States, or of the State of Maryland, or any political subdivision of either of them, by revolution, force, or violence; or who is a member of a subversive organization or a foreign subversive organization, as more fully defined in this article. Such statement shall be prepared and execution required by the State commissioner of personnel for all persons whose employment is subject to the provisions of Article 64A of the Annotated Code of Maryland and by the city service commission of Baltimore for all employees whose employment is subject to the provisions of §§ 142 to 156 of the Baltimore city charter and by every person and every board, commission, council, department, court, or other agency of the State of Maryland or any political subdivision thereof responsible for the supervision of other employees, for employees under its jurisdiction. Any such person failing or refusing to execute such a statement or who admits he is a subversive person as defined in this article shall immediately be discharged.

EXCLUSION FROM THE BAR

Anno. Code of Maryland, art. 10, § 3 (c). *Factors to be considered by the State Board of Law Examiners.*—The said board shall report their proceedings in the examination of applicants to the court of appeals, with any recommendations said board shall desire to make. If the court of appeals shall then find the applicant to be qualified under the provisions of this section and also under the provisions of § 4 to discharge the duties of an attorney, and to be of good moral character, worthy to be admitted, and not a subversive person as defined by the Subversive Activities Act of 1949, they shall pass an order admitting him or her to practice in all the courts of the State.

Id. § 7. *Admission on motion; nonsubversive person, etc., requirement.*—Members of the bar of any State, district, or territory of the United States, who, for five years after admission, have been engaged as practitioners, judges, or teachers of law, shall be admitted without examination on proof of good moral character, and that they are not subversive persons, as defined by the Subversive Activities Act of 1949, after becoming actual residents of this State. Members of the bar of any other State, district, or territory of the United States, who may be employed as counsel in any case pending before any of the courts of this State, may be admitted for all the purposes of the case in which they are so employed by the court before which said case is pending, without examination. Nothing herein contained shall be construed to deprive the courts of this State of the power, as at present existing, of disbarring or otherwise punishing members of the bar.

Id. § 12. *Prosecution of attorneys for subversive activities, etc.*— Whenever a judge of any of the several courts of this State shall have reasonable ground to believe that any attorney admitted to the practice of law in his court is guilty of professional misconduct, malpractice, fraud, deceit, crime involving moral turpitude, conduct prejudicial to the administration of justice, or is a subversive person, as defined by the Subversive Activities Act of 1949, he shall issue an order directed to the bar association and/or State's attorney of the city or county, as the case may be, in which his said court is located, requiring said bar association and/or state's attorney to prosecute the charges named in said order on a day specified therein, which day shall not be less than fifteen or more than sixty days from the date of said order, and shall direct that a copy of said order be forthwith served on said attorney. If it appear that said charges cannot be served on said attorney within the State, the same may be served upon him without the State by mail or otherwise, as the court shall by its order direct.

Id. § 13 (Supp. 1964). *Judicial proceedings.*—Charges of professional misconduct, malpractice, fraud, deceit, crime involving moral turpitude, or conduct prejudicial to the administration of justice, against any attorney at law may be filed in any court where such attorney is admitted to practice by any bar association acting through its appropriate committee or by any group of five or more members of the bar, but if he has not been admitted to practice by the circuit court of any county or by the Supreme Bench of Baltimore City, but has been admitted to practice by the Court of Appeals of Maryland, then such charges may be filed in the circuit court of the county or in the Supreme Bench of Baltimore City, where such attorney resides, or last resided in Maryland, or where the offense was committed, and thereupon such proceedings shall be had as if said charges had been filed by the court and specified in the order directing the prosecution thereof, referred to in § 12 of this article. In addition, any bar association of the State, acting through its appropriate committee, may file charges of being a subversive person, as defined by the Subversive Activities Act of 1949, against any attorney at law admitted to practice by the Court of Appeals of Maryland in the same court as specified above with respect to other charges, and thereupon, such proceedings shall be had as if said charges had been filed by the court and specified in the order directing the prosecution thereof, referred to in § 12 of this article.

Id. § 16. *Causes for suspension or disbarment.*—Every attorney who shall, after having an opportunity to be heard, as provided in § 15 of this article, be found guilty of professional misconduct, malpractice, fraud, deceit, crime involving moral turpitude, conduct prejudicial to the administration of justice, or of being a subversive person, as defined by the Subversive Activities Act of 1949, shall, by order of the judges finding him guilty, be suspended or disbarred from the practice of his profession in this State.

Id. § 17. *Judicial review.*—Every attorney who shall, after a hearing held as hereinbefore prescribed, be found guilty of professional misconduct, malpractice, fraud, deceit, crime involving moral turpitude, conduct prejudicial to the administration of justice, or of being a subversive person, as defined by the Subversive Activities Act of 1949, shall have the right of appeal to the Court of Appeals of Maryland.

Item 4 on the Application for Registration as a Law Student requires the applicant to indicate by signing his name that he is not a subversive person. It provides:

4. That the applicant is not a subversive person as defined by the Subversive Activities Act of 1949 of the General Assembly of Maryland.

Question 18 on the Character Questionnaire makes a similar inquiry. It provides:

*18. Are you now or have you ever been a subversive person as defined by the Subversive Activities Act of 1949 of the General Assembly of Maryland? If answer is "Yes", give full details on separate schedule.

*Question 18 in Form (A) of the questionnaire indicated by an asterisk in the left hand margin, should be answered by the applicant only after examining the provisions of the Subversive Activities Act of 1949 of the General Assembly of Maryland (Art. 85A of the Annotated Code of Maryland—1957 Edition). In connection therewith the applicant is referred to section 3(c) of Article 10 of the Annotated Code of Maryland (1957 Edition) in Volume 1 at page 262, which provides that before any applicant may be admitted to practice in the courts of this State, the court of appeals must find that he is "not a subversive person as defined by the Subversive Activities Act of 1949."

Item 4 on the Original Petition to take the Bar Examination also makes a similar inquiry. It provides:

4. That the petitioner is not a subversive person as defined by the Subversive Activities Act of 1949 of the General Assembly of Maryland.

Similar inquiries are made in the petition (7) and questionnaire (17) used in connection with admission to practice on motion. These provide:

7. That the petitioner is not a subversive person as defined by the Subversive Activities Act of 1949 of the General Assembly of Maryland.

17. Have you ever been a subversive person as defined by the Subversive Activities Act of 1949 of the General Assembly of Maryland, that is to say, a person who commits, attempts to commit, or aids in the commission, or advocates, abets, advises or teaches by any means any person to commit, attempt to commit, or aid in the commission of any act intended to overthrow, destroy or alter, or to assist in the overthrow, destruction or alteration of, the constitutional form of Government of the United States, or of the State of Maryland, or any political subdivision of either of them, by revolution, force or violence; or who is a member of a subversive organization or a foreign subversive organization?

Annotation:

Character Committee for Third Jud. Cir. v. *Mandras*, 233 Md. 287, 196A. 2d 630 (1964). This case involved an appeal from an order of the Maryland Board of Law Examiners reversing the action of the character committee of Baltimore county finding and reporting appellee did not "possess the good moral character requisite for admission to the Maryland bar." Appellee, in filling out a form, denied that he had ever been a subversive person. Thereafter, the committee discovered that he had been a member of the Communist Party.

When called to testify he acknowledged that he had been a member for less than one year and mainly because he was interested in the candidacy of Henry Wallace. He denied that he had ever been a subversive person, or that he had ever advocated the overthrow of the Government by force. On appeal the court affirmed applicant's right to admission on grounds that the evidence was insufficient to support a finding of a lack of good moral character.

MASSACHUSETTS

Unlawful Advocacy

ANARCHY

Massachusetts Gen. Laws Anno. c. 264, § 11. *Unlawful acts and penalty.*—Whoever by speech or by exhibition, distribution, or promulgation of any written or printed document, paper, or pictorial representation advocates, advises, counsels, or incites assault upon any public official, or the killing of any person, or the unlawful destruction of real or personal property, or the overthrow by force or violence or other unlawful means of the Government of the commonwealth or of the United States, shall be punished by imprisonment in the State prison for not more than three years, or in jail for not more than two and one-half years, or by a fine of not more than one thousand dollars; provided, that this section shall not be construed as reducing the penalty now imposed for the violation of any law. It shall be unlawful for any person who shall have been convicted of a violation of this section, whether or not any sentence shall have been imposed, to perform the duties of a teacher or of an officer of administration in any public or private educational institution, and the superior court, in a suit by the commonwealth, shall have jurisdiction in equity to restrain and enjoin any such person from performing such duties thereafter; provided, that any such restraining order or injunction shall be forthwith vacated if such conviction shall be set aside.

Annotations:

Commonwealth v. *Gilbert*, 334 Mass. 71, 134 N.E. 2d 13 (1956). Defendant was charged with conspiring to advocate, advise, counsel, and incite the overthrow by force and violence of the governments of Massachusetts and the United States. The State supreme judicial court sustained defendant's motion to quash the indictments on the ground that the field of sedition had been occupied by Federal legislation particularly with respect to conduct directed at overthrowing the Government of the United States. The court reserved judgment with respect to the possibility of sedition "directed so exclusively against the State as to fall outside the sweep of *Pennsylvania* v. *Nelson*, 350 U.S. 497, 76 S. Ct. 477, 100 L. Ed. 640 (1956)."

Kaplan v. *Bowker*, 333 Mass. 455, 131 N.E. 2d 372 (1963). This case involved a mandamus action to compel the State commission authorized to investigate communism and subversive activities from including in any report the name or other identifying data of any individual concerning whom the commission determined that it had received creditable evidence that he was a member of the Communist Party, a Communist, or a subversive. The action was instituted by five members of the bar on behalf of the general public. The court affirmed the judgment dismissing the petition on grounds that since the petitioners did not allege that they suffered or were in danger of suffering any legal wrong peculiar to themselves they lacked standing to maintain the petition.

Jones v. *Commonwealth*, 327 Mass. 491, 99 N.E. 2d 456 (1951).—In a prosecution for violation of a regulation prohibiting the display of signs on other advertising in reservations under the control of the metropolitan district commission, the question whether defendant was a Communist or a member of the Communist Party was held to have no bearing in establishing that fact and was not competent for the purpose of impeachment.

OUTLAWING THE COMMUNIST PARTY

Massachusetts Gen. Laws Anno. c. 264, § 16. *"Subversive organization" defined.*—The term "subversive organization" as used in sections seventeen, eighteen, nineteen, twenty-one, twenty-two and twenty-three of this chapter shall mean any form of association of three or more persons, however named or characterized, and by whatever legal or non-legal entity or non-entity it be established, and whether incorporated or otherwise for the common purpose of advocating, advising, counseling or inciting the overthrow by force or violence, or by other unlawful means, of the government of the Commonwealth or of the United States.

Id. § 16A. *Communist Party.*—The Communist Party is hereby declared to be a subversive organization.

Id. § 17. *Subversive organizations outlawed.*—A subversive organization is hereby declared to be unlawful.

Id. § 18. *Enforcement.*—The attorney general shall bring an action in the superior court by an information or petition in equity against any organization which he has reasonable cause to believe is a subversive organization. The fact that such information or petition has been or is to be filed shall not be made public until an order of notice, hereinafter referred to, is issued.

A justice of the superior court shall, upon a summary examination of the information or petition and such supporting depositions, other testimony or evidence as he may require, if he is of the opinion that there is reasonable cause to believe that such organization is subversive, issue an order of notice against such organization to show cause why there should not be an adjudication to that effect. Notice of such order of notice shall be sent by registered mail to such officers of such organization as are known to the court, and to any other persons, including members, as the court may order, at least fourteen days before the return day of said order of notice. Notice of such order shall also be given by publication once each week for two successive weeks in a daily newspaper published in the city of Boston. Any officer or member of any such organization or its attorney may appear and answer on its behalf on or before the return day or such later time as the court may allow. The respondent shall have the right to claim a trial by jury within the time allowed for filing its answer or within such further time as the court may allow within its discretion. If no person appears and answers the court may on its own motion or upon motion of the petitioner default the organization.

If an appearance is entered and answer filed the case shall be set down for a speedy hearing.

Such hearing shall be conducted in accordance with the usual course of proceedings in equity, including all rights of exception and appeal. Upon such hearing or upon default the court may make an adjudication that the organization is a subversive organization and may enjoin such organization from acting further as such, may order the dissolution of the organization and shall cause the secretary of state to be notified of the finding of the court; provided, however, that the effectiveness of any such adjudication, injunction and order shall be stayed pending determination by the supreme judicial court of any exceptions or appeals; or the court may find that the organization is not a subversive organization. Upon any final determination that the organization is subversive notice thereof shall be published by the secretary of state once each week for two successive weeks in a daily newspaper published in the city of Boston and the court shall order any funds or property of such organization turned over to the treasurer of the Commonwealth which shall then be considered escheated. The fact that proceedings have begun or findings or decision made under this section shall not be admissible in evidence in any action brought under the provisions of sections eleven, nineteen, twenty-one or twenty-three.

Id. § 19. *Membership in subversive organization unlawful.*—Any person who becomes or remains a member of any organization knowing it to be a subversive organization shall be punished by imprisonment in the State prison for not more than three years or in jail for not more than two and one half years or by a fine of not more than one thousand dollars, provided that this section shall not be construed as reducing the penalty now imposed for the violation of any law.

Id. § 20. *Additional penalties.*—No person who has been convicted of a violation of the provisions of section eleven, nineteen or twenty-three shall be eligible to election or appointment to any public office, or employment, nor as a teacher in any public or private educational institution, nor shall any person continue to hold any such office after final conviction. The superior court on petition of the attorney general shall have jurisdiction in equity to restrain and enjoin any such person from performing such duties thereafter and to prevent any such person's name being placed on any ballot for election to any office. The court may upon petition in its discretion after a lapse of five years from the date of final conviction under sections eleven, nineteen or twenty-three remove the disability if in its opinion such person can then be adjudged to be loyal to the government of the Commonwealth and the United States.

Id. § 21. *Destruction or concealment of books, records, etc.*—Whoever destroys or conceals books, records, files, membership lists or funds belonging to an organization which he knows to be a subversive organization shall be punished by imprisonment in the State prison for not more than three years or in jail for not more than two and one-half years or by a fine of not more than one thousand dollars; provided, that this section shall not be construed as reducing the penalty now imposed for the violation of any law.

Id. § 22. *Permitting use of premises by Communist Party or subversive organization.*—Whoever being in charge of an auditorium, hall, or other building shall knowingly permit it to be used by the Communist Party or by an organization which has been adjudicated a subversive organization under the provisions of section eighteen shall be punished by a fine of not more than one thousand dollars or by imprisonment for not more than one year, or both.

Id. § 23. *Financial contributions to subversive organizations unlawful.*—Whoever contributes money or any other property having a value in money to an organization which he knows to be a subversive organization shall be punished by imprisonment in the State prison for not more than three years or in jail for not more than two and one-half years or by a fine of not more than one thousand dollars.

Annotation:

Commonwealth v. *Hood*, 334 Mass. 76, 134 N. E. 2d 76 (1956). This case, a companion to the *Gilbert* case, *supra*, involved a prosecution for having contributed money and property to the Communist Party, knowing it to be a subversive organization, and becoming and remaining a member of the Communist Party, knowing it to be a subversive organization. The court dismissed the proceedings ruling that it fell within the area of prosecutions for sedition which the Supreme Court of the United States held had been exclusively preempted by statutes of the United States.

EXCLUSION FROM THE ELECTIVE PROCESS

Massachusetts Gen. Laws Anno. c. 50, § 1. *Communist Party and other subversive organizations excluded from definition of "political party."*—"Political party" shall apply to a party which at the preceding biennial State election polled for Governor at least three percent of the entire vote cast in the Commonwealth for that office; but when a candidate for Governor receives two or more nominations for that office "political party" shall apply only to a party which made a nomination at the preceding State primary and which in said primary polled at least three percent of the entire vote for nomination for Governor therein cast in the Commonwealth. With reference to municipal elections and primaries and caucuses for the nomination of city and town officers, "political party" shall include a municipal party. A political party, as used in this section, shall not include any organization which has been adjudicated subversive under section eighteen of chapter two hundred and sixty-four, nor shall it include the Communist Party.

Massachusetts Gen. Laws Anno. c. 264, § 16A. *Communist Party.*—The Communist Party is hereby declared to be a subversive organization.

Id. § 17. *Subversive organizations outlawed.*—A subversive organization is hereby declared to be unlawful.

Id. § 20. *Persons convicted of anarchy, membership in subversive organizations, or contributing to support of subversive organizations ineligible for election to any public office.*—No person who has been convicted of a violation of the provisions of section eleven, nineteen or twenty-three shall be eligible to election or appointment to any public office, or employment, nor as a teacher in any public or private educational institution, nor shall any person continue to hold any such office after final conviction. The superior court on petition of the attorney general shall have jurisdiction in equity to restrain and enjoin any such person from performing such duties thereafter and to prevent any such person's name being placed on any ballot for election to any office. The court may upon petition in its discretion after a lapse of five years from the date of final conviction under sections eleven, nineteen or twenty-three remove the disability if in its opinion such person can then be adjudged to be loyal to the government of the Commonwealth and the United States.

LOYALTY OF STATE OFFICERS AND EMPLOYEES

1. ELECTIVE AND NONELECTIVE PERSONNEL

Massachusetts Constitution, Amend. Art. VI. *Oath.*—Instead of the oath of allegiance prescribed by the constitution, the following oath shall be taken and subscribed by every person chosen or appointed to any office, civil or military under the government of this Commonwealth, before he shall enter on the duties of his office, to wit;

"I A. B. do solemnly swear that I will bear true faith and allegiance to the Commonwealth of Massachusetts, and will support the constitution thereof. So help me GOD."

Provided, that when any person shall be of the denomination called Quakers, and shall decline taking said oath, he shall make his affirmation in the foregoing form, omitting the word "swear" and inserting instead thereof the word "affirm;" and omitting the words "So help me GOD," and subjoining, instead thereof, the words "this I do under the pains and penalties of perjury."

Massachusetts Gen. Laws Ann. c. 264, § 20. *Persons convicted of anarchy, membership in subversive organizations, or contributing to support of subversive organizations ineligible for election or appointment to public office or employment.*—No person who has been convicted of a violation of the provisions of section eleven, nineteen or twenty-three shall be eligible to election or appointment to any public office, or employment, nor as a teacher in any public or private educational institution, nor shall any person continue to hold any such office after final conviction. The superior court on petition of the attorney general shall have jurisdiction in equity to restrain and enjoin any such person from performing such duties thereafter and to prevent any such person's name being placed on any ballot for election to any office. The court may upon petition in its discretion after a lapse of five years from the date of final conviction under sections eleven, nineteen or twenty-three remove the disability if in its opinion such person can then be adjudged to be loyal to the government of the Commonwealth and the United States.

2. NONELECTIVE PERSONNEL

Massachusetts Gen. Laws Anno. c. 264, § 14. *Oath required.*—Every person entering the employ of the commonwealth or any political subdivision thereof, before entering upon the discharge of his duties, shall take and subscribe to, under the pains and penalty of perjury, the following oath or affirmation—

"I do solemnly swear (or affirm) that I will uphold and defend the Constitution of the United States of America, and the constitution of the Commonwealth of Massachusetts and that I will oppose the overthrow of the Government of the United States of America or of this Commonwealth by force, violence, or by any illegal or unconstitutional method."

Such oath or affirmation shall be filed by the subscriber, if he shall be employed by the State, with the secretary of the Commonwealth, if an employee of a county, with the county commissioners, and if an employee of a city or town, with the city clerk or the town clerk, as the case may be.

Annotations:

1950 Op. Atty. Gen. 54. Student nurses in the Department of Mental Health who are affiliated with various private hospitals and who, while gaining psychiatric experience, render services as nurses at some institution for which they are allowed maintenance are "employed in any capacity by the Commonwealth" and are therefore required to take the oath of loyalty.

1949 Op. Atty. Gen. 22. Every person upon entering the employment of the Commonwealth or of any political subdivision thereof, including counties, cities, towns, and districts, is required under the express terms of the statute, before entering upon the discharge of his duties, to take the prescribed oath or affirmation in the form set out in the statute and subscribe his or her name to it on a blank form prepared for the purpose, under the penalties of perjury.

Those presently in the employ of the Commonwealth, or of any political subdivision thereof, in any capacity were not required to take the prescribed oath or affirmation when the statute became effective, as a condition precedent in the public service. But any person after the effective date of the statute who thereafter by reason of his or her acts of conduct brings himself or herself within the prohibitions of the statute would be subject to removal from the public service.

1949 Op. Otty. Gen. 33. The Department of Public Works in employing temporary laborers and chauffeurs must comply with the provisions of the law requiring the taking of a loyalty oath before a person may enter upon the discharge of his duty.

1936 Op. Atty. Gen. 31. Since the statute confines mandatory oaths to every citizen of the United States, a Canadian citizen does not come within its scope.

3. CIVIL DEFENSE PERSONNEL

Massachusetts Gen. Laws Anno. c. 33 App., § 13–18. _Loyalty oath required._—No person shall be employed or associated in any capacity in any civil defense organization established under this act who advocates, or has advocated, a change by force or violence in the constitutional form of the Government of the United States, or in this Commonwealth, or the overthrow of any government in the United States by force or violence, or who has been convicted of, or is under indictment or information charging any subversive act against the United States. Each person who is appointed to serve in an organization for civil defense shall, before entering upon his duties, take an oath, in writing, before a person authorized to administer oaths in this Commonwealth, which oath shall be substantially as follows:—

"I, ----------------------------, do solemnly swear (or affirm) that I will support and defend the Constitution of the United States and the constitution of the Commonwealth of Massachusetts against all enemies, foreign and domestic; that I will bear true faith and allegiance to the same; that I take this obligation freely, without any mental reservation or purpose of evasion; and that I will well and faithfully discharge the duties on which I am about to enter.

"And I do further swear (or affirm) that I do not advocate, nor am I a member of any political party or organization that advocates, the overthrow of the Government of the United States or of this Commonwealth by force or violence; and that during such time as I am a member of the (name of civil defense organization), I will not advocate nor become a member of any political party or organization that advocates the overthrow of the Government of the United States or of this Commonwealth by force or violence."

TEACHERS' LOYALTY

Massachusetts Gen. Laws. Anno. c. 71, § 30A. *Oath required of certain professors, instructors, and teachers.*—Every citizen of the United States entering service, on or after October first, nineteen hundred and thirty-five, as professor, instructor, or teacher at any college, university, teachers' college, or public or private school, in the Commonwealth shall, before entering upon the discharge of his duties, take and subscribe to, before an officer authorized by law to administer oaths, or, in case of a public school teacher, before the superintendent of schools or a member of the school committee of the city or town in whose schools he is appointed to serve, each of whom is hereby authorized to administer oaths and affirmations under this section, the following oath or affirmation:—"I do solemnly swear (or affirm) that I will support the Constitution of the United States and the constitution of the Commonwealth of Massachusetts, and that I will faithfully discharge the duties of the position of (insert name of position) according to the best of my ability." Such oath or affirmation shall be so taken and subscribed to by him in duplicate. One of such documents shall be filed with such superintendent of schools or principal officer of such college, university, or school in the Commonwealth and shall be transmitted by him to the commissioner of education, and the other shall be delivered by the subscriber to the board, institution, or person employing him. No professor, instructor, or teacher who is a citizen of the United States shall be permitted to enter upon his duties within the Commonwealth unless and until such oath or affirmation shall have been so subscribed and one copy thereof so filed and the other so delivered. Whoever violates such oath or affirmation so far as it relates to the support of the Constitution of the United States and the constitution of the Commonwealth, shall be punished by a fine of not more than one thousand dollars.

Massachusetts Gen. Laws Anno. c. 264, § 11. *Persons convicted of anarchy barred from employment in the school.*—Whoever by speech or by exhibition, distribution, or promulgation of any written or printed document, paper, or pictorial representation advocates, advises, counsels, or incites assault upon any public official, or the killing of any person, or the unlawful destruction of real or personal property, or the overthrow by force or violence or other unlawful means of the government of the Commonwealth or of the United States, shall be punished by imprisonment in the State prison for not more than three years, or in jail for not more than two and one-half years, or by a fine of not more than one thousand dollars; provided, that this section shall not be construed as reducing the penalty now imposed for the violation of any law. It shall be unlawful for any person who shall have been convicted of a violation of this section, whether or not any sentence shall have been imposed, to perform the duties of a teacher or of an officer of administration in any public or private educational institution, and the superior court, in a suit by the Commonwealth, shall have jurisdiction in equity to restrain and enjoin any such person from performing such duties thereafter; provided, that any such restraining order or injunction shall be forthwith vacated if such conviction shall be set aside.

Id. § 14. *Oath required.*—Every person entering the employ of the Commonwealth or any political subdivision thereof, before entering upon the discharge of his duties, shall take and subscribe to, under the pains and penalty of perjury, the following oath or affirmation:

"I do solemnly swear (or affirm) that I will uphold and defend the Constitution of the United States of America and the constitution of the Commonwealth of Massachusetts and that I will oppose the overthrow of the Government of the United States of America or of this Commonwealth by force, violence, or by any illegal or unconstitutional method."

Such oath or affirmation shall be filed by the subscriber, if he shall be employed by the State, with the secretary of the Commonwealth, if an employee of a county, with the county commissioners, and if an employee of a city or town, with the city clerk or the town clerk, as the case may be.

Id. § 20. *Persons convicted of anarchy, membership in subversive organizations, or contributing to support of subversive organizations, ineligible for employment in any public or private educational institution.*—No person who has been convicted of a violation of the provisions of section eleven, nineteen, or twenty-three shall be eligible to election or appointment to any public office, or employment, nor as a teacher in any public or private educational institution, nor shall any person continue to hold any such office after final conviction. The superior court on petition of the attorney general shall have jurisdiction in equity to restrain and enjoin any such person from performing such duties thereafter and to prevent any such person's name being placed on any ballot for election to any office. The court may upon petition in its discretion after a lapse of five years from the date of final conviction under sections eleven, nineteen, or twenty-three remove the disability if in its opinion such person can then be adjudged to be loyal to the Government of the Commonwealth and the United States.

***

Annotations:

Faxon v. School Committee of Boston, 331 Mass. 531, 120 N.E. 2d 772 (1954). Petitioner, a teacher who had been dismissed, instituted a mandamus proceeding against the school committee of Boston to compel his reinstatement. He had been employed for many years as a teacher to serve "at discretion" in the public schools of the city. Called before a subcommittee of the United States Senate, he declined on the ground of self-incrimination, to answer questions as to whether he was then a member of the Communist Party, whether while teaching in various designated Boston schools he had tried to recruit students or others into the Communist Party or into the Young Communist League, whether he had ever made an effort to recruit a fellow teacher into the Communist Party, and whether he had attended any secret meetings of the Communist Party in or out of Massachusetts. The school committee, after notice, charges, a hearing, and upon recommendation of the superintendent, unanimously voted to dismiss the petitioner for conduct unbecoming a teacher in refusing to answer these questions. The court dismissed the petition holding that the dismissal of a teacher employed "at discretion" for pleading self-incrimination before a Senate committee when asked about affiliation with the Communist Party was neither arbitrary, or irrational or unreasonable, or irrelevant. The school committee was acting well within its powers, and its actions were not in derogation of the Fifth Amendment as applied by the due process clause of the Fourteenth. The court concluded by saying that there was no question of a bill of attainder or expost facto law involved.

1936 Op. Atty. Gen. 31. A clergyman teaching in a private school must submit to the oath.

A printer who neither teaches nor instructs the students in his trade, but merely supervises the setting of type and the running of presses is an employee as distinguished from a teacher and does not come within the provisions of the statute.

1936 Op. Atty. Gen. 53. The words "public school" were intended to embrace high schools, evening and night schools, and others of diverse characters, as well as the common schools which all young children between certain ages are obliged to attend regularly. The words "private school" embrace any institution of learning not maintained at public expense which gives instruction substantially the same as that given in any public school.

EXCLUSION FROM THE BAR

Massachusetts does not appear to have any rule or regulation which pertains to the admission of persons who are or who have been Communists or subversives. Similarly, the various forms employed by the State do not contain any questions directly on the subject.

MICHIGAN

UNLAWFUL ADVOCACY

1. SEDITION

Michigan Stat. Anno. § 28.813(1). *Crime of subversion; penalty.*—Every person who shall commit the crime of subversion against this State shall be punished by imprisonment in the State prison for life, or any term of years, in the discretion of the court.

Id. § 28.813(2). *Concealing subversion.*—Any person who shall have knowledge of the commission of the crime of subversion against this State and shall conceal the same, and shall not, as soon as may be, disclose and make known such subversion to the judge of a court of record within this State, shall be guilty of a felony.

Id. § 28.813(3). *Member, organizer or officer of association guilty of subversion.*—Any person who shall knowingly be a member, organizer, or officer of any association, corporation, or organized group of persons whose purpose as known to him is to commit subversion shall be guilty of the crime of subversion.

Id. § 28.813(4). *Aid to persons or firms engaged in subversion constitutes grounds for termination of corporate charter.*—Any corporation doing business under the laws of the State of Michigan which, by corporate action, lends any aid by gifts or money or by any other payments of money, or furnishes the services of personnel or lends its name or credit to any person, association, firm or corporation engaged in acts of subversion, knowing them to be so engaged, shall forfeit its charter or certificate of authority and shall be fined not more than the total amount of the assets of the corporation.

Michigan Stat. Anno. 1962, § 28.243.1. *Declaration of legislative finding.*—It is hereby declared that the Governments of the United States and of this and other States of the United States are threatened by attempts to overthrow exising government by force and violence. In the light of the present world situation, it is deemed necessary to enact legislation preventing activity leading to such forceful overthrow. It is declared to be the purpose of this statute to maintain, preserve, and strengthen our established form of government and to prevent changes therein except by the procedures provided by our constitutions. (CL '48, § 752.311.)

Id. § 28.243(2). *Unlawful acts and penalty.*—Whoever knowingly or willfully advocates, aids, abets, advises, encourages or teaches the duty, necessity, desirability, or propriety of overthrowing or destroying the Government of the United States or of this or any other State of the United States or any political subdivision thereof, by force, violence, sabotage, or terrorism or attempts or conspires to do so; or

Whoever, with intent to cause the overthrow or destruction of the Government of the United States or of this or of any other State of the

United States or any political subdivision thereof, commits any act of force, violence, sabotage, or terrorism, or attempts or conspires to do so; or

Whoever, with intent to cause the overthrow or destruction of the Government of the United States, or this or any other State of the United States or any political subdivision thereof, prints, publishes, edits, issues, circulates, sells, distributes, or publicly displays any written or printed matter advocating, advising, encouraging, or teaching the duty, necessity, desirability or propriety of overthrowing or destroying any such government by force, violence, sabotage, or terrorism or attempts or conspires to do so; or

Whoever organizes, or helps or attempts to organize, or becomes or is a member of or affiliates with, any society, group, or assembly of persons which has as one of its purposes advocating, abetting, advising, encouraging, or teaching the duty, necessity, desirability or propriety of overthrowing or destroying the Government of the United States or of this or any other State of the United States or any political subdivision thereof, by force, violence, sabotage, or terrorism, knowing such purpose;

Shall be guilty of a felony, punishable by imprisonment in the State prison for life or for any term of years.

Id. § 28.243(3). *Enforcement.*—(a) The attorney general shall maintain complete records of all information received by him and may deliver to the prosecuting attorney of any county all information and evidence of matters which have come to his attention relating in any manner to the activities prohibited by section 2 of this act. The attorney general may cooperate with the prosecuting attorneys of the several counties or may intervene in any proceedings or may initiate proceedings in enforcing the provisions of this act. The expense incurred by any county of this State in the prosecution of any person charged with violation of this act shall, upon approval by the attorney general, be reimbursed to such county from the general fund of the State.

(b) The attorney general may cooperate with the Attorney General of the United States, the Department of Justice of the United States, the Federal Bureau of Investigation, and all other police agencies which collect and exchange information and evidence relating to activities prohibited by this act.

(c) The State police shall collect information and evidence relating in any manner to activities prohibited by this act and may cooperate and exchange information relating thereto with any police agency and shall, at the request of the attorney general, report to him any such information and evidence so collected, necessary to any prosecution for the violation of the provisions of this act.

(d) Any person who discloses any information or evidence collected under authority of this act, except as authorized hereby or except as specifically authorized by the attorney general, shall be guilty of a felony.

NOTE.—The definition of subversion was spelled out in the Constitution of 1908, Art. II, § 22, which reads as follows:

Subversion shall consist of any act, or advocacy of any act, intended to overthrow the form of Government of the United States or the form of government of this State, as established by the constitution, and as guaranteed by section 4 of Article 4 of the Constitution of the United States of America, by force or violence or by any unlawful means.

Subversion is declared to be a crime against the State, punishable by any penalty provided by law.

Subversion shall constitute an abuse of the rights secured by section 4 of this article, and the right secured thereby shall not be valid as a defense in any trial for subversion.

The recently adopted constitution of the State of Michigan, effective January 1, 1964, contains no similar provisions.

2. CRIMINAL SYNDICALISM

Michigan Stat. Anno. § 28.235. *Criminal syndicalism defined.*— Criminal syndicalism is hereby defined as the doctrine which advocates crime, sabotage, violence or other unlawful methods of terrorism as a means of accomplishing industrial or political reform. The advocacy of such doctrine, whether by word of mouth or writing, is a felony punishable as provided in this chapter.

Id. § 28.236. *Unlawful acts and penalty.*—Any person who by word of mouth or writing, advocates or teaches the duty, necessity or propriety of crime, sabotage, violence or other unlawful methods of terrorism as a means of accomplishing industrial or political reform; or prints, publishes, edits, issues or knowingly circulates, sells, distributes or publicly displays any book, paper, document, or written matter in any form, containing or advocating, advising, or teaching the doctrine that industrial or political reform should be brought about by crime, sabotage, violence or other unlawful methods of terrorism; or openly, willfully and deliberately justifies by word of mouth or writing, the commission or the attempt to commit crime, sabotage, violence or other unlawful methods of terrorism with intent to exemplify, spread or advocate the propriety of the doctrines of criminal syndicalism; or organizes or helps to organize, or becomes a member of or voluntarily assembles with any society, group or assemblage of persons formed to teach or advocate the doctrines of criminal syndicalism[, or who commits or attempts to commit crime, sabotage, violence or other unlawful methods of terrorism for the purpose of accomplishing industrial or political reform, shall be] guilty of a felony, punishable by imprisonment in the State prison not more than 10 years or by a fine of not more than $5,000.00.

Annotations:

People v. *Ruthenberg*, 229 Mich. 315 (1924). Appellant, a member of the central executive committee of the Communist Party of America, was convicted of the crime of criminal syndicalism. He was charged with having voluntarily assembled at a national delegate convention of the Communist Party, a society formed to teach and advocate the doctrines of criminal syndicalism. On appeal the Michigan Supreme Court affirmed the conviction over numerous objections, constitutional and others, of appellant. The court declared: (1) that the State criminal syndicalism statute did not contravene the right of the people to peaceably assemble; (2) that the statute did not restrain free speech but was directed as an abuse of the right to free speech; (3) that the statute did not offend due process by reasons of vagueness or as punishing as a felony the enunciation of a doctrine without regard to the intent, the occasion, the result, or the imminent result of the enunciation; (4) that felonious intent was not an element of the offense; (5) that the words "sabotage" and "violence" had a sufficiently fixed meaning and were not void for vagueness or uncertainty.

Op. Atty. Gen. 1930–1933, p. 544. The advocacy of communism is a subversive activity which is not protected by the guarantees of Federal and State Constitutions as to freedom of speech.

REGISTRATION

Michigan Stat. Anno. § 18.58(1). *Declaration of policy.*—The purpose of this act is to safeguard the security and welfare of the people of the State of Michigan.

Id. § 18.58(2). *"Foreign agency" defined.*—For the purposes of this act, the term "foreign agency" means any individual, group, club, league, society, committee, association, political party, or combination of individuals, or individuals acting in concert therewith, whether incorporated or otherwise, subsidized by a foreign government or serving directly or indirectly the purposes, aims, or objects of a foreign power or powers as follows:

(a) Any agency whose origin is directly or indirectly of foreign inspiration and whose object is the control or overthrow of the government;

(b) Any agency, political or otherwise, which acts in conjunction with a similar organization or organizations in other countries in the interest of a foreign power or powers, and which is or has been affiliated with international bodies originating with or dependent upon foreign governments or their subsidiaries, or under their jurisdiction, influence, or direction, or whose objects, aims, or activities are identical with those of said foreign government or political parties dominating said government;

(c) Any agency which, being of the origin or inspiration set forth in subsection (b), pursues the objects of a foreign power or powers and has been or may be declared subversive by the Congress of the United States of America, or the Attorney General of the United States of America, or the attorney general of the State of Michigan: Provided, That as to the attorney general of Michigan such determination shall have been made after a hearing before the attorney general of the State of Michigan, at which such agency shall have the right to testify and present evidence in defense;

(d) Any publishing enterprise, radio station, and/or similar institution for influencing public opinion, whether incorporated or unincorporated, which has originated with the organizations as defined in subsections (a), (b), (c), and (e), or who have come under the control of organizations serving the objects of a foreign power;

(e) Labor unions, societies, or corporations of all kinds who have originated and remain or come under the control of organizations or agencies serving the objects and purposes of a foreign power as described in subsections (a), (b), (c), and (d).

Id. § 18.58(3). *Agencies required to register.*—The agencies defined in subsections (a), (b), (c), and (d) of section 2 shall be individually and/or as a group required to register with the attorney general by filing with the attorney general on such forms and in such detail as the attorney general may by rules and regulations prescribe, a registered statement containing detailed information concerning their membership status, activities, income and expenditures, and other particulars as may be requested by the attorney general. Every such statement required to be filed by this section shall be subscribed to under oath by all of the individuals and/or officers of the agency.

Id. § 18.58(4). *Legend required on books and papers published by foreign agencies.*—All periodicals, books, pamphlets, or other printed matter published or distributed within the State of Michigan by persons and/or organizations declared to be foreign agents or agencies within the meaning of this act shall at its masthead bear the legend: "published in compliance with the law of the State of Michigan governing the operation of foreign agencies."

Id. § 18.58(5). *Statements and reports to be available for public inspection.*—All statements and reports filed under the provisions of this act shall be public records and open to public inspection and examination at all reasonable hours and under such rules and regulations as the attorney general may prescribe.

Id. § 18.58(6). *Rules and regulations.*—The attorney general is authorized at any time to make, amend, and rescind such rules and regulations as may be necessary to carry out the provisions of this act, including the rules and regulations governing the statements and reports required to be filed by this act and to establish such other rules and regulations as are deemed necessary or pertinent to the purposes of this act, as he may from time to time require.

Id. § 18.58(7). *Penalty.*—Any person or foreign agency, as defined in this act, who shall violate any of the provisions of this act shall be guilty of a felony, and upon conviction shall be punishable by a fine of not more than $5,000 or imprisonment in the State prison for not more than 5 years, or both such fine and imprisonment in the discretion of the court.

Annotations:

1948–50 Ops. Atty. Gen. 128. The Callahan Act (Foreign Agencies Registration Act) is unconstituttional and void.

Michigan Stat. Anno. § 28.243(11). *Declaration of legislative findings.*—The legislature hereby finds and declares that there are present in the State of Michigan subversive groups and elements, particularly of the Communist Party and certain of its affiliated organizations, which have infiltrated into both private and public employment and into the public schools of the State. This has occurred and continues despite the existence of present statutes. The consequence of any such infiltration into the public schools is that subversive propaganda can be disseminated among children of tender years by those who teach them and to whom the children look for guidance, authority, and leadership. Infiltration of these elements into the public service results in employment and retention of groups which teach and advocate that the Government of the United States or of any State or of any political subdivision thereof shall be overthrown by force or violence or by any unlawful means. The legislature finds that members of such groups frequently use their office or position to advocate and teach subversive doctrines. The legislature finds that members of such groups are frequently bound by oath, agreement, pledge, or understanding to follow, advocate, and teach a prescribed party line or group, dogma or doctrine without regard to truth or free inquiry. The legislature finds that such dissemination of propaganda may be and frequently is sufficiently subtle to escape detection in the classroom. It is difficult, therefore, to measure the menace of such infiltration in the schools by conduct in the classroom. The legislature further finds and declares that in order to protect the children and our State institutions from such subversive influence it is essential that the laws prohibiting persons who are members of subversive groups, such as the Communist Party and its affiliated organizations, from obtaining or retaining employment in the public schools or State financed positions, be vigorously enforced. The legislature deplores the failure heretofore to prevent such infiltration which threatens dangerously to become a commonplace in our schools and institutions.

Id. § 28.243(12). *"Communist" defined.*—A "Communist" is a person who:

(a) Is a member of the Communist Party, [knowing it to be such as herein defined,] notwithstanding the fact that he may not pay dues to, or hold a card in, said party; or

(b) Contributes funds or any character of property to the Communist Party[, knowing it to be such as herein defined]; or

(c) Commits or advocates the commission of any act reasonably calculated to further the overthrow of the Government of the United States of America, the government of the State of Michigan, or the government of any political subdivision of either of them, by force or violence; or

(d) Commits or advocates the commission of any act reasonably calculated to further the overthrow of the Government of the United States, the government of the State of Michigan, or the government of any political subdivision of either of them, by unlawful or unconstitutional means, and the substitution [therefor] of a Communist government.

Id. § 28.243(13). *"Communist Party" defined.*—The "Communist Party" is any organization which in any manner advocates, [participates in] or acts to further, the world Communist movement [which has as its objectives, among others, the overthrow of the Government of the United States or the government of the State of Michigan by force and violence or other unlawful means].

Id. § 28.243(14). *"Communist front organization" defined.*—A "Communist front organization" is any organization, the members of which are not all Communist, but which is substantially directed, dominated or controlled by Communists or by the Communist Party, or which in any manner advocates, or acts to further, the world Communist movement. The attorney general of the State of Michigan [shall after hearing as "in any contested case" as provided by Act No. 197 of the Public Acts of 1952, being section 24.101 et seq. of the Compiled Laws of 1948, prepare a list of Communist front organizations, as herein defined, which list shall be published at least annually. Any such organization, but not the individual members or officers thereof, shall be deemed to be a party to such proceedings and shall have those rights as such including those of an aggrieved party, which are prescribed by that act].

Id. § 28.243(15). *Communists, members of Communist front organizations, Communist Party, and Communist front organizations required to register; penalty.*—(a) Each person in this State who is a Communist or is knowingly a member of a Communist front organization, shall forthwith register with the Michigan State police; and, so long as he remains in this State, shall register annually with said Michigan State police.

(b) Such registration shall be under oath [upon a questionnaire prepared by the attorney general] and shall set forth the name, including any assumed name used or in use, business, occupation, purpose of presence in the State of Michigan, sources of income, place of birth, places of former residence, and features of identification, including fingerprints, of the registrant; organizations of which registrant is a member; names of persons known by registrant to be Communists or members of any Communist front organization; and any other information [deemed by the attorney general to be] relevant to the purposes of this act [as herein declared. Such questionnaire shall be so prepared as to afford each registrant opportunity to refuse to answer any specific question on the ground that such answer would tend to incriminate him].

(c) Each and every officer of the Communist Party and each and every officer of Communist front organizations, knowing said organizations to be Communist front organizations, shall register or cause to be registered said party or organizations with the Michigan State police, if said party or organizations have any members who reside, permanently or for a period of time more than 30 days, in the State of Michigan. Such registration shall be under oath [upon a questionnaire prepared by the attorney general] and shall include the name of the organization, the location of its principal officer and of its offices and meeting places in the State of Michigan; the names, real and assumed, of its officers; the names, real and assumed, of its members in the State of Michigan and of any person who has attended its meetings in the State of Michigan; a financial statement reflecting receipts and disbursements and by whom and to whom paid; and any other information [deemed by the attorney general to be] relevant to the purposes of this act [as herein declared]. Such registration shall be made within 30 days after the effective date of this act, and thereafter at such intervals as are directed by the Michigan State police. [Such questionnaire shall be so prepared as to afford each registrant opportunity to refuse to answer any specific question on the ground that such answer would tend to incriminate him.]

(d) Failure to register as herein required, or the making of any registration which contains any material false statement or omission, shall constitute a felony and shall be punishable by a fine of not more than $10,000.00, or by imprisonment of not more than 10 years, or by both such fine and imprisonment.

(e) Under order of any court of record, the registration records shall be open for inspection by any person in whose favor such order is granted; and the records shall at all times, without the need for a court order, be open for inspection by any law enforcement officer of this State, of the United States or of any State or Territory of the United States. At the discretion of the Michigan State police, such records may also be open for inspection by the general public or by any member thereof.

(f) The commissioner of the Michigan State police shall transmit to the attorney general of the State of Michigan the name of any person who holds a nonelective position, job or office for the State of Michigan, or any political subdivision thereof, and who from all of the evidence available to the commissioner of Michigan State police appears to be a Communist or a member of a Communist front organization. The attorney general of the State of Michigan may transmit the name of such person to his employer or superior, and may submit such evidence that such person is a Communist or a member of a Communist front organization as the attorney general of the State of Michigan and the commissioner of State police shall deem advisable.

Id. § 28.243 (19). *Enforcement.*—The attorney general of the State of Michigan, all prosecuting attorneys, the Michigan State police, and all law enforcement officers of this State shall each be charged with the duty of enforcing the provisions of this act.

Id. § 28.243 (20). *Effect of act.*—This act is cumulative of all existing laws and does not repeal any such laws.

Id. § 28.243 (21). *Short title.*—This act may be cited as the "Michigan Communist control law."

Id. § 28.243 (22). *Registration deemed an imperative public necessity.*—The need for registration and location of the conspiratorial members of the Communist movement and the need for protection against the acts and conspiracies of such persons create an emergency and an imperative public necessity.

Annotations:

Albertson v. *Millard,* 345 U.S. 242, 73 S. Ct. 600, 97 L.Ed. 983 (1953). Appellant, Executive Secretary of the Communist Party of Michigan, sought a judgment declaring unconstitutional various sections of the State Communist Control Bill, along with an injunction to prevent State officials from enforcing it. A three-judge district court found the act constitutional. On appeal appellant contended that the definitions of "Communist," "Communist Party," and "Communist front organization" as used in the act were void for vagueness. The Supreme Court of the United States reversed the conviction and remanded the cause in order to permit construction of the statute by the State courts.

Albertson v. *Attorney General,* 345 Mich. 519, 77 N.W. 2d 104 (1956). In this case, a continuation of the Michigan Communist Party's challenge to the State Communist Control Act, the Supreme Court of Michigan held the act unconstitutional. The court concluded that enactment of the Federal Smith Act had exclusively occupied the field of sedition against all government in the Nation.

EXCLUSION FROM THE ELECTIVE PROCESS

Michigan Stat. Anno. 1962, § 28.243(17). *Communist and nominees of the Communist Party barred from ballot.*—The name of any Communist or of any nominee of the Communist Party shall not be printed upon any ballot used in any primary or general election in this State or in any political subdivision thereof.

LOYALTY OF STATE OFFICERS AND EMPLOYEES

1. ELECTIVE AND NONELECTIVE PERSONNEL

Constitution, Art. XI, § 1. *Oath.*—All officers, legislative, executive and judicial, before entering upon the duties of their respective offices, shall take and subscribe the following oath or affirmation: I do solemnly swear (or affirm) that I will support the Constitution of the United States and the constitution of this State, and that I will faithfully discharge the duties of the office of _____ according to the best of my ability. No other oath, affirmation, or any religious test shall be required for any public office or trust.

2. NONELECTIVE PERSONNEL

Michigan Stat. Anno. 1962, § 28.243(12). *"Communist" defined.*— A "Communist" is a person who:

(a) Is a member of the Communist Party, [knowing it to be such as herein defined,] notwithstanding the fact that he may not pay dues to, or hold a card in, said party; or

(b) Contributes funds or any character of property to the Communist Party[, knowing it to be such as herein defined]; or

(c) Commits or advocates the commission of any act reasonably calculated to further the overthrow of the Government of the United States of America, the government of the State of Michigan, or the government of any political subdivision of either of them, by force or violence; or

(d) Commits or advocates the commission of any act reasonably calculated to further the overthrow of the Government of the United States, the government of the State of Michigan, or the government of any political subdivision of either of them, by unlawful or unconstitutional means, and the substitution [therefor] of a Communist government.

Id. § 28.243(13). *"Communist Party" defined.*—"Communist Party" is any organization which in any manner advocates, [participates in] or acts to further, the world Communist movement [which has as its objectives, among others, the overthrow of the Government of the United States or the government of the State of Michigan by force and violence or other unlawful means].

Id. § 28.243(14). *"Communist-front organization defined.*—A "Communist-front organization" is any organization, the members of which are not all Communists, but which is substantially directed, dominated, or controlled by Communists or by the Communist Party, or which in any manner advocates, or acts to further, the world Communist movement. The attorney general of the State of Michigan [shall after hearing as "in any contested case" as provided by Act

No. 197 of the Public Acts of 1952, being section 24.101 et seq. of the Compiled Laws of 1948, prepare a list of Communist-front organizations, as herein defined, which list shall be published at least annually. Any such organization, but not the individual members or officers thereof, shall be deemed to be a party to such proceedings and shall have those rights as such including those of an aggrieved party, which are prescribed by that act**].**

Id. § 28.243 (18). *Communists and members of Communist front organizations barred from public employment.*—No person may hold any nonelective position, job or office for the State of Michigan, or any political subdivision thereof, where the remuneration of said position, job or office is paid in whole or in part by public moneys or funds of the State of Michigan, or of any political subdivision thereof, where reasonable grounds exist, on all of the evidence, from which, after hearing, the employer or superior of such person can say with reasonable certainty that such person is a Communist or a knowing member of a Communist front organization. In cases involving a person within the classified service of the State of Michigan such hearing shall be held by the civil service commission: Provided, That the refusal of any person who holds a nonelective position, job or office for the State of Michigan, or any political subdivision thereof, who upon being called before a duly authorized tribunal or in an investigation under authority of law, to testify concerning his being a Communist or a member of a Communist front organization on the ground that his answers might tend to incriminate him, shall be, in the hearing provided for in this section, prima facie evidence that such person is a Communist or a knowing member of a Communist front organization.

3. CIVIL DEFENSE PERSONNEL

Michigan Stat. Anno. § 4.823 (54). *Loyalty oath required.*—No person shall be employed or associated in any capacity in any civilian defense organization established under this act who advocates a change by force or violence in the constitutional form of the Government of the United States or in this State or the overthrow of any government in the United States by force or violence, or who has been convicted of or is under indictment or information charging any subversive act against the United States. Each person who is appointed to serve in an organization for civilian defense shall, before entering upon his duties, take an oath, in writing, before a person authorized to administer oaths in this State, which oath shall be substantially as follows:

"I, _____, do solemnly swear (or affirm) that I will support and defend the Constitution of the United States and the constitution of the State of Michigan, against all enemies, foreign and domestic; that I will bear true faith and allegiance to the same; that I take this obligation freely, without any mental reservation or purpose of evasion; and that I will well and faithfully discharge the duties upon which I am about to enter.

"And I do further swear (or affirm) that I do not advocate, nor am I a member of any political party or organization that advocates the overthrow of the Government of the United States or of this State by force or violence; and that during such time as I am a member of the (name of civilian defense organization) I will not advocate nor become a member of any political party or organization that advocates the overthrow of the Government of the United States or of this State by force or violence."

TEACHERS' LOYALTY

Michigan Stat. Anno. § 15.3851. *Teachers' certificate to include oath to support constitution.*—Before any teacher's certificate shall be valid in any school district, the holder thereof shall record the same in the office of the county superintendent of schools of the county or in the office of the superintendent of schools of any school district, of the first, second, or third class or in the office of the superintendent of schools of any school district located wholly or partly within a village or city having a population of 10,000 or more where such person expects to teach. Such certificate shall not be liable to be annulled, except by the board or officer issuing such certificate, for any cause which would have justified the withholding of such certificate.

Before any teacher's certificate shall be valid in this State, the holder thereof shall make and subscribe the following oath (or affirmation) : "I do solemnly swear (or affirm) that I will support the Constitution of the United States of America and the constitution of the State of Michigan and that I will faithfully discharge the duties of the office of teacher according to the best of my ability." Any teacher's certificate issued after the effective date of this act shall have attached thereto or superimposed thereon said oath of allegiance signed by the teacher, a duplicate of which oath shall be signed and filed with the superintendent of public instruction : Provided, That said duplicate oath need not be so filed if the teacher has heretofore filed with the superintendent of public instruction an oath in the form herein prescribed. All teachers who hold certificates issued in this State prior to the effective date of this act shall file said oath with the superintendent of public instruction. The oath in all cases shall be notarized. Any oath in the form herein prescribed heretofore filed with the superintendent of public instruction shall be deemed to have been filed in compliance with this act.

Michigan Stat. Anno. 28.243(18). *Communists and members of Communist front organizations barred from employment.*—No person may hold any nonelective position, job or office for the State of Michigan, or any political subdivision thereof, where the remuneration of said position, job or office is paid in whole or in part by public moneys or funds of the State of Michigan, or of any political subdivision thereof, where reasonable grounds exist, on all of the evidence, from which, after hearing, the employer or superior of such person can say with reasonable certainty that such person is a Communist or a knowing member of a Communist front organization. In cases involving a person within the classified service of the State of Michigan such hearing shall be held by the civil service commission : *Provided,* That the refusal of any person who holds a nonelective position, job or office for the State of Michigan, or any political subdivision thereof, who upon being called before a duly authorized tribunal or in an investigation under authority of law, to testify concerning his being a Communist or a member of a Communist front organization on the ground that his answers might tend to incriminate him, shall be, in the hearing provided for in this section, prima facie evidence that such person is a Communist or a knowing member of a Communist front organization.

Annotations:

Sauder v. *School District No. 10,* 271 Mich. 414 (1935). Plaintiff, schoolteacher, sought to recover damages for breach of her teaching contract. Defendant contended that his act of terminating the contract was fully justified by plaintiff's failure to take constitutional oath of office. On appeal the court reversed the judgment in favor of plaintiff and held that all contracts which are founded on an act prohibited by a statute under a penalty are void. The purpose of the act requiring the execution of the oath, the court said, was to make certain that teachers coming in contact with youth were such as believe in the constitution and principles of government of the State and Nation.

June v. *School District No. 11,* 283 Mich. 533 (1938). Plaintiff, school teacher, sought damages from defendant school district for breach of an employment contract. Defendant claimed that plaintiff failed to comply with provisions of State law requiring a teacher's oath to be included in all contracts. While a signed oath appeared at the end of the contract, the trial court held that the contract was inadmissable for the reason that the jurat of the officer administering the oath was lacking and that the oath was not embodied in the contract. The State supreme court reversed on the ground that plaintiff had done all that was required of her. The intent of the legislature in enacting the oath requirement was "to make certain and exact a guaranty, that teachers in public school should believe in and support the government and the Constitutions of State and Nation; and that the statute aimed to prevent the inculcation of subversive, disloyal and unpatriotic principles in the minds of schoolchildren."

Op. Atty. Gen. 1933–34, p. 82. A teacher's contract which does not contain the statutory oath of allegiance is invalid.

EXCLUSION FROM THE BAR

Question 28i of the Affidavit of Personal History inquires as to past association with subversive organizations. It provides,

28. Have you ever been:

i. A member of any organization which advocates or has advocated the overthrow of the Government of the United States by force or violence.

Question 29 asks the applicant to manifest his loyalty by copying a simple statement printed in the affidavit. It provides;

29. If you are in accord with the following, write in your own handwriting: I believe in the principles underlying the Government of the United States of America, and I affirm that I am, without any mental reservation, loyal to such Government. I have read carefully the Canons of Professional and Judicial Ethics of the State Bar of Michigan and I understand that while I practice law in Michigan I will be bound thereby.

Correspondence received from the Michigan State Board of Law Examiners states that since 1948, "certain persons, being disclosed by questionnaire to have been formerly members of a Communist or subversive group, have been examined by the full board in face-to-face interview. In each case the board determined that the candidate had renounced the former affiliation and had become sincerely dedicated to the Constitution of the United States and of the State of Michigan. These men were passed for admission to the bar."

Exclusion From Incidental Benefits

Michigan Stat. Anno. § 27.3178(71a). *Testamentary bequests to associations engaged in subversion prohibited.*—No person shall, by his last will and testament or by any codicil thereto, devise or bequeath, in trust or otherwise, any part of his estate to or for any association or corporation, existing or to be created, so constituted as to use said devise or bequest for subversion as defined in section 22 of Article 2 of the constitution, and such devise or bequest shall be invalid.

NOTE.—See note following Sedition, *supra.*

Miscellaneous

SUBVERSIVE ACTIVITIES INVESTIGATION DIVISION

Michigan Stat. Anno. § 4.448(1). *Subversive activities investigation division authorized.*—The commissioner of the Michigan State police is authorized to establish within the department of the Michigan State police a division to be known as the subversive activities investigation division, the personnel of which shall be appointed by the commissioner.

Id. § 4.448(2). *Duties of division.*—The duties of the subversive activities investigation division shall be to investigate activities within the State that are subversive of State or Federal Government, to obtain and compile information concerning such activities, to cooperate with military authorities, and to cooperate with Federal, State and local law enforcing and investigating agencies in the enforcement of Federal and State laws relating thereto.

Id. § 4.448(3). *Powers of the Commissioner of State police.*—The commissioner shall have power:

(a) To maintain in the subversive activities investigation division confidential files of information on activities that are subversive of Government, and activities contrary to Federal law as aforesaid. Such files shall not be open for public inspection, nor shall information contained therein be released: Provided, That the commissioner may furnish information to Federal, State and local law enforcement agencies or to the responsible heads of any agency having charge of employment by the State whom he considers proper to receive the same when, in his opinion, it is necessary to carry out the objectives of this act.

(b) To call upon any sheriff or other police officer of any county, city, or township or village, for information on such activities and for aid and assistance, within the limits of their respective jurisdictions, in the performance of any duty imposed by this act and, upon being notified or called upon for such aid and assistance, it shall be the duty of the officer concerned to comply with such order to the extent requested. Refusal or neglect to comply therewith shall be deemed nonfeasance in office and shall subject the officer so refusing or neglecting to removal from office.

(c) To appoint, employ, assign or retain such persons outside of or within the department of the Michigan State police as he may deem necessary, in carrying out the provisions of this act regarding subversive activities, at such compensation as he may determine and at his discretion to designate 1 or more of them to have the powers of an officer of the Michigan State police.

(d) To make such rules and regulations for the administration of the subversive activities investigation division as he shall deem necessary.

Id. § 4.448(4). *Prohibition against revealing identity of personnel and expenditure of funds.*—Unless otherwise directed by the commissioner of the Michigan State police, no information concerning the identity of personnel engaged in such subversive investigation work or the specific expenditure of moneys appropriated for the purpose of carrying out such investigations shall be revealed publicly or to any unauthorized person by any State agency, official or employee. Any person violating the provisions of this section shall be deemed guilty of a felony.

Id. § 4.448(5). *Cooperation with investigations.*—To effectuate the broad objectives of this act, officials and employees of State and local governmental units and agencies thereof are hereby authorized to assist officers of the Michigan State police in the investigation of subversive activities.

Id. § 4.448(6). *"Subversive Activities" defined.*—The term "subversive activities" as used in this act shall be construed to mean and include criminal syndicalism as it relates to political reform only and as it is otherwise defined under section 46 of Act No. 328 of the Public Acts of 1931, being section 750.46 of the Compiled Laws of 1948, or as the term "subversive activities" may be defined by other laws of the State of Michigan heretofore or hereafter enacted.

MINNESOTA

Unlawful Advocacy

CRIMINAL SYNDICALISM

Minnesota Stat. Anno. § 609.405. *Criminal syndicalism defined; unlawful acts and penalty; permitting premises to be used for assemblage to advocate criminal syndicalism.*—Subdivision 1. "Criminal syndicalism" is the doctrine which advocates crime, malicious damage or injury to the property of an employer, violence, or other unlawful methods of terrorism as a means of accomplishing industrial or political ends.

Subdivision 2. Whoever does any of the following may be sentenced to imprisonment for not more than five years or to payment of a fine of not more than $5,000, or both:

(1) Orally or by means of writing advocates or promotes the doctrine of criminal syndicalism; or

(2) Intentionally organizes or becomes a member of any assembly, group, or organization which he knows is advocating or promoting the doctrine of criminal syndicalism; or

(3) For or on behalf of another person, distributes, sells, publishes, or publicly displays any writing, which is intended by that person to be used to, and which does, advocate or promote the doctrine of criminal syndicalism.

Subdivision 3. Whoever, being the owner or in possession or control of any premises intentionally permits any assemblage of persons to use such premises for the purpose of advocating or promoting the doctrine of criminal syndicalism may be sentenced to imprisonment for not more than one year, or to payment of a fine of not more than $1,000, or both.

Annotations:

State v. *Worker's Socialist Pub. Co.*, 150 Minn. 406, 185 N.W. 931 (9121). Defendants were convicted of criminal syndicalism which was defined as—

"Any person who by word of mouth or writing, advocates or teaches the duty, necessity or propriety of crime, sabotage, violence or other unlawful methods of terrorism as a means of accomplishing industrial or political ends, or prints, publishes, edits, issues or knowingly circulates, sells, distributes or publicly displays any book, paper, document or written matter in any form, containing or advocating advising or teaching the doctrine that industrial or political ends should be brought about by crime, sabotage, violence or other unlawful methods of terrorism * * * is guilty of a felony."

Affirming the conviction the court held that a printed article stating that capital would never submit without the "bloodiest battle history has ever known" and that the workers must learn to fight

225

always and unceasingly until the capitalist class was overthrown, and "until it rests bloodstained at the feet of the labor giant" was a violation of the statute. The court stated: (1) that the criminal syndicalism statute was applicable to corporations as well as natural persons; (2) that the intent of the teacher or advocate was not an element of the offense and therefore need not be proved; (3) that the managing editor of a newspaper was criminally responsible for an unlawful publication made in the paper unless the unlawful publication was made under such circumstances as to negate any presumption of privity or connivance or want of ordinary precaution on his part to prevent it.

State v. *Moilen*, 140 Minn. 112, 167 N.W. 345 (1918). Defendants were convicted of criminal syndicalism for displaying posters advocating sabotage to achieve certain political and industrial ends. The court affirmed the convictions and held that the statute did not violate any rights secured by the Fourteenth Amendment.

LOYALTY OF STATE OFFICERS AND EMPLOYEES

1. NONELECTIVE PERSONNEL

Minnesota Stat. Anno. § 43.16 (Supp. 1962). *Applicants for competitive examination required to take oath to defend Federal and State Constitutions.*—Every officer or employee of the State, and every person making application for examination under this chapter, shall take and subscribe an oath or affirmation, under the penalty of perjury and without the necessity of a notary acknowledgment or seal, in writing, to the effect that such person will honestly and faithfully protect and preserve the property and money of the State and will abide by, uphold, and defend the Constitution of the United States of America and the constitution of the State of Minnesota and, except as provided in these constitutions, he will not take part in any movement to alter or change our form of government.

Every person making application for examination under this chapter shall execute an application form in which he shall declare that the statements therein are true and complete, with the same force and effect as though given under oath.

2. CIVIL DEFENSE PERSONNEL

Minnesota Stat. Anno. § 12.43 (Supp. 1962). *Loyalty oath required.*—

No person shall be employed or associated in any capacity in any civil defense organization established under this chapter who advocates or has advocated a change by force or violence in the constitutional form of the Government of the United States or in this State or the overthrow of any government in the United States by force or violence, or who has been convicted of or is under indictment or information charging any subversive act against the United States. Each person who is appointed to serve in an organization for civil defense shall before entering upon his duties, take an oath, in writing, before a person authorized to administer oaths in this State, which oath shall be substantially as follows:

"I, _____, do solemnly swear (or affirm) that I will support and defend the Constitution of the United States and the constitution of the State of _____ against all enemies, foreign and domestic; that I will bear true faith and allegiance to the same; that I take this obligation freely, without any mental reservation or purpose of evasion; and that I will well and faithfully discharge the duties upon which I am about to enter. And I do further swear (or affirm) that I do not advocate, nor am I a member of any political party or organization that advocates the overthrow of the Government of the United States or of this State by force or violence; and that, during such time as I am a member of the (name of civil defense organization), I will not advocate nor become a member of any political party or organization that advocates the overthrow of the Government of the United States, or of this State, by force or violence."

This oath may be administered by any officer of the State Department of Civil Defense, local civil defense director, or ground observer corps supervisor.

EXCLUSION FROM THE BAR

Correspondence received from the State Board of Law Examiners disclosed the absence of any specific provision governing the admission to practice of persons having or having had Communist affiliations. The fact of such affiliation "would undoubtedly result in his [applicant's] failure to be admitted."

MISSISSIPPI

1. SUBVERSIVE ACTIVITIES

Mississippi Code Anno. 1942, § 4064–10. *Unlawful acts and penalty.*—(a) If any person shall commit, attempt to commit, or knowingly aid in the commission of any act intended to overthrow, destroy, or alter, or to assist in the overthrow, destruction, or alteration of the constitutional form of Government of the United States or the State of Mississippi, or of any political subdivision of the United States or the State of Mississippi by revolution, force, violence, or other means not provided for or sanctioned by the constitution of the State of Mississippi or the Constitution of the United States, then such person shall be guilty of a felony and upon conviction shall be punished by imprisonment in the State penitentiary for a term not exceeding ten (10) years.

(b) If any two or more persons shall enter into any agreement, combination, or conspiracy for the purpose of committing, attempting to commit, or aiding in the commission of any act intended to overthrow, destroy, or alter or to assist in the overthrow, destruction, or alteration of the constitutional form of Government of the United States or of the State of Mississippi or any political subdivision of the United States or the State of Mississippi by revolution, force, violence, or other means not provided for or sanctioned by the constitution of the State of Mississippi or the Constitution of the United States, and one or more of such persons shall do or perform any act to effect any object of the agreement, combination, or conspiracy, then each of the parties to such agreement, combination, or conspiracy shall be guilty of a felony and upon conviction thereof shall be punished by imprisonment in the State penitentiary for a term not exceeding ten (10) years.

(c) If any person shall advocate, abet, advise, or teach by any means any person to commit, attempt to commit, or assist in the commission of any act intended to overthrow, destroy, or alter the constitutional form of Government of the United States or the State of Mississippi or of any political subdivision of the United States or the State of Mississippi under such circumstances that same shall constitute a clear and present danger to the security of the United States or of the State of Mississippi or of any political subdivision of either of them, then such person shall be guilty of a felony and upon conviction shall be punished by imprisonment in the State penitentiary for a term not to exceed five (5) years.

2. ANARCHY

Mississippi Code Anno. 1942, § 2399. *Offense and penalty.*—Any person who advocates in writing or in print or verbally, or otherwise, the overthrow of the Constitution or Government of the United States or the constitution or the government of the State of Mississippi, by violence, shall be deemed guilty of a felony and on conviction be imprisoned in the State penitentiary not less than three and not more than twenty years.

REGISTRATION

Mississippi Code Anno. 1942, § 4194–01 (Supp. 1962). *Investigation of local organizations to determine connection with subversive organizations.*—In those cases in which an unincorporated or incorporated organization or association having a chapter, branch, or unit in this State, has a National or State officer or director who either in the past, or at present, is, or has been, an officer, or director, of any organization, association, or group listed, or designated, as a subversive or Communist-front group, or organization, by the United States Attorney General, or a Congressional Committee on Un-American Activities, the secretary of state is authorized and empowered to request the attorney general of the State of Mississippi, or the General Legislative Investigating Committee, or both, to investigate that organization, association, or group which has such a chapter, branch, or unit in this State. As used in this Act, the term "subversive group" shall mean any group or organization so listed or designated by the United States Attorney General or a Congressional Committee on Un-American Activities.

The attorney general of the State of Mississippi or the General Legislative Investigating Committee, or both, when requested by the secretary of state, shall make said investigation, and for such purpose the General Legislative Investigating Committee is hereby vested with all powers and authority granted to said committee by chapter 281, Laws of 1946 [§§ 3365–01 et seq.], as now or hereafter amended.

Id. § 4194–02 (Supp. 1962). *Persons required to register.*—The secretary of state shall require any officer or director or member of an organization or association described in section 1 [§ 4194–01] hereof to file with his office a full, complete, and true list of the names and addresses of all officers and members of the organization or association who are officers, directors, and members at the time of the filing of the list, or who have been officers, directors, and members at any time during the twelve (12) months preceding such date. Said lists shall be furnished by those requested to do so, or good cause shown for inability so to do, and the lists shall be certified under oath. Any person, able to furnish such list in whole or in part, who shall fail or refuse to do so, shall be deemed guilty of a misdemeanor and, upon conviction, shall be imprisoned for not less than sixty (60) days, nor more than six (6) months.

Id. § 4194–03 (Supp. 1962). *Covered organizations forbidden to hold meetings unless registered.*—No person shall hold, assist in holding, or attend any assembly, meeting, or gathering of an organization or association described in section 1 [§ 4194–01] hereof, or of a subdivision or subordinate chapter, unit, or other branch thereof unless the list of officers and members required by section 2 [§ 4194–02] has been filed with the secretary of state. If any person shall violate the provisions of this section, he shall be deemed guilty of a misdemeanor and, upon conviction thereof, shall be punished by a fine of not less than one hundred dollars ($100.00), nor more than five hundred dollars ($500.00), or imprisoned for not less than thirty (30) days, nor more than six (6) months, or both.

Id. § 4194–04 (Supp. 1962). *Enforcement.*—District attorneys, throughout this State, shall prosecute without delay any violations of this Act.

Id. § 4194–05 (Supp. 1962). *Penalty.*—The Attorney General shall proceed by injunction or otherwise to dissolve any organization or association described in section 1 [§ 4194–01] or a subdivision or subordinate chapter, unit, or other branch thereof violating the provisions of this Act and to prevent any meeting of the officers and members thereof.

Id. § 4194–06 (Supp. 1962). *Exclusions from the scope of law.*— Nothing in this Act shall apply to any regularly organized churches or National Guard organizations.

Id. § 4194–07 (Supp. 1962). *Member defined.*—Any person shall be deemed a member in contemplation of this Act, of any organization or association described in section 1 [§ 4194–01] hereof, or of any subdivision or subordinate chapter, unit, or other branch thereof, who would be considered a member in the ordinary accepted sense of the word or who has taken any oath or obligation in connection with any such organization or association, or who has received any degree or initiation from members or officers or such organization or association, or who, while living or residing in the territorial jurisdiction of any such organization or association, or any subdivision or subordinate chapter, unit, or other branch thereof, has attended and participated in meetings or assemblies thereof, or any of them, or paid dues or fees thereto.

Id. § 4194–08 (Supp. 1962). *Records keeping.*—The secretary of state shall keep the lists filed with him under the terms of this Act as part of the permanent public records of his office.

Id. § 4194–09 (Supp. 1962). *Separability.*—If any section, subsection, clause, phrase, or word of this Act is held unconstitutional or invalid for any reason, such holding, or invalidity, shall not affect the remaining portions of this Act.

Id. § 4194–10 (Supp. 1962). *Effective date.*—This Act shall take effect and be in force from and after its passage.

Exclusion From the Elective Process

Mississippi Code Anno. 1942, § 4064–07. *Candidates required to file nonsubversive affidavit.*—No person shall become a candidate for election to any State, district, or county office, or a candidate in a primary election for party nomination as a candidate for any such office, unless he or she shall file with the secretary of state or the circuit clerk at or prior to the time of becoming such a candidate an affidavit that he or she is not a subversive person as defined in this act. Candidates for county and county district offices and candidates for party nominations for such offices shall file such an affidavit with the circuit clerk of their respective counties, and candidates for all other offices or for party nominations for such offices shall file such affidavit with the secretary of state. The provisions of this section shall be applicable to candidates for electors for President and Vice President, and there shall not be entered upon any ballot at any election the name of any person who has failed or refused to file the affidavit required by this section.

It is hereby expressly provided that the affidavit required by the foregoing paragraph shall be filed with the circuit clerk or the secretary of state, as the case may be, prior to the expiration of the time for the candidate for election or party nomination to qualify with the proper executive committee or election commission, and if such affidavit be not filed within such time, then the name of such candidate shall not be placed on the ballot.

It is hereby expressly provided that each candidate for the office of State senator or representative shall file said affidavit with the circuit clerk of the county or counties which participate in the election or nomination of such candidates.

It is hereby expressly provided that the circuit clerk of each county is hereby required to file notice with the county or other proper executive committee of any political party of all persons seeking political office in any primary election as defined in paragraph one, and with the county or other proper election commission of all persons seeking political office in any special or general election as defined in paragraph one. Such notice shall contain the name of the candidate, and the date such affidavit was filed with the circuit clerk, and shall be delivered in person by the circuit clerk or his duly authorized deputy to the chairman or secretary of the proper executive committee, or election commission, as the case may be, on or before the final date on which the names of candidates are required to be submitted to the county executive committee or election commmission, as the case may be.

LOYALTY OF STATE OFFICERS AND EMPLOYEES

1. NONELECTIVE PERSONNEL

Mississippi Code Anno. 1942, § 4064–01. *"Organization,"* *"Subversive organization,"* *"Foreign subversive organization,"* *"Foreign government,"* *and "Subversive person" defined.*—For the purpose of this act—

"Organization" means an organization, corporation, company, partnership, association, trust, foundation, fund, club, society, committee, political party, or any group of persons, whether or not incorporated, permanently or temporarily associated together for joint action or advancement of views on any subject or subjects.

"Subversive organization" means any organization which engages in or advocates, abets, advises, or teaches, or a purpose of which is to engage in or advocate, abet, advise, or teach activities intended to overthrow, destroy, or alter, or to assist in the overthrow, destruction or alteration of, the constitutional form of the Government of the United States, or of the State of Mississippi, or of any political subdivision of either of them, by revolution, force, violence, or other means not provided for or sanctioned by the constitution of the State of Mississippi or the Constitution of the United States.

"Foreign subversive organization" means any organization directed, dominated or controlled directly or indirectly by a foreign government which engages in or advocates, abets, advises, or teaches, or a purpose of which is to engage in or to advocate, abet, advise, or teach activities intended to overthrow, destroy, or alter, or to assist in the overthrow, destruction or alteration of the constitutional form of the Government of the United States, or of the State of Mississippi, or of any political subdivision of either of them, and to establish in place thereof any form of government the direction and control of which is to be vested in, or exercised by or under, the domination or control of any foreign government, organization, or individual; but does not and shall not be construed to mean an organization the bona fide purpose of which is to promote world peace by alliances or unions with other governments or world federations, unions or governments to be effected through constitutional means.

"Foreign government" means the government of any country or nation other than the Government of the United States of America or of one of the States thereof.

"Subversive person" means any person who commits, attempts to commit, or aids in the commission, or advocates, abets, advises, or teaches by any means any person to commit, attempt to commit, or aid in the commission of any act intended to overthrow, destroy, or alter, or to assist in the overthrow, destruction, or alteration of, the constitutional form of the Government of the United States, or of the State of Mississippi, or any political subdivision of either of them, by revolution, force, violence, or other means not provided for or sanctioned by the constitution of the State of Mississippi or the Constitution of the United States; or who is a member of a subversive organization or a foreign subversive organization.

Id. § 4064–02. *Subversive persons ineligible for public employment.*—No subversive person, as defined in this act, shall be eligible for employment in, or appointment to any office, or any position of trust or profit in the government of, or in the administration of the business of this State, or of any county, municipality, or other political subdivision of this State.

Id. § 4064–03. *Rules and regulations to determine loyalty.*—Every person and every board, commission, council, department, court or other agency of the State of Mississippi or any political subdivision thereof, who or which appoints or employs or supervises in any manner the appointment or employment of public officials or employees shall establish by rules, regulations or otherwise, procedures designed to ascertain before any person, including teachers and other employees of any public educational institution in this State, is appointed or employed, that he or she as the case may be is not a subversive person, and that there are no reasonable grounds to believe such persons are subversive persons. In the event such reasonable grounds exist, he or she as the case may be shall not be appointed or employed. In securing any facts necessary to ascertain the information herein required, the applicant shall be required to sign a written statement containing answers to such inquiries as may be material, which statement shall contain notice that it is subject to the penalties of perjury.

Id. § 4064–04. *Exclusions from investigating procedure.*—The inquiries prescribed in section 3 [§ 4064–03], other than the written statement to be executed by an applicant for employment, shall not be required as a prerequisite to the employment of any persons in the classification of laborers in any case in which the employing authority shall in his or its discretion determine, and by rule or regulation specify the reasons why, the nature of the work to be performed is such that employment of persons as to whom there may be reasonable grounds to believe that they are subversive persons as defined in this act will not be dangerous to the health of the citizens or the security of the Governments of the United States, the State of Mississippi, or any political subdivision thereof.

Id. § 4064–05. *Nonsubversive statement required.*—Every person, who on July 1, 1950, shall be in the employ of the State of Mississippi or of any political subdivision thereof, other than those now holding elective office shall be required on or before August 1, 1950, to make a written statement which shall contain notice that it is subject to the penalties of perjury, that he or she is not a subversive person as defined in this act; namely, any person who commits, attempts to commit, or aids in the commission, or advocates, abets, advises or teaches by any means any person to commit, attempt to commit, or aid in the commission of any act intended to overthrow, destroy or alter, or to assist in the overthrow, destruction or alteration of, the constitutional form of the Government of the United States, or of the State of Mississippi, or any political subdivision of either of them, by revolution, force, violence, or other means not provided for or sanctioned by the constitution of the State of Mississippi or the Constitution of the United States, or who is a member of a subversive organization or a foreign subversive organization, as more fully defined in this act. Such statement shall be prepared and execution required by the elected or appointed head of each department or institution of the State or any of its political subdivisions. Any person failing or refusing to execute such a statement or who admits he is a subversive person as defined in this act shall immediately be discharged.

Id. § 4064–06. *Standard of evidence for discharge of alleged subversive person.*—Reasonable grounds on all the evidence to believe that any person is a subversive person, as defined in this act, shall be cause for discharge from any appointive office or other position of profit or trust in the government of or in the administration of the business of this State, or of any county, municipality, or other political subdivision of this State, or any agency thereof. Every person and every board, commission, council, department, or other agency of the State of Mississippi or any political subdivision thereof having responsibility for the appointment, employment or supervision of public employees shall establish rules or procedures for a hearing for any person charged with being a subversive person, as defined in this act, after notice and opportunity to be heard. Every employing authority discharging any person pursuant to any provisions of this act shall promptly report to the attorney general the fact of and the circumstances surrounding such discharge.

Id. § 4064–09. *Penalty.*—Every written statement made pursuant to this act by an applicant for appointment or employment, or by any employee, shall be deemed to have been made under oath if it contains a declaration preceding the signature of the maker to the effect that it is made under the penalties of perjury. Any person who makes a material misstatement of fact (a) in any such written statement, or (b) in any affidavit made pursuant to the provisions of this act, or (c) under oath in any hearing conducted by any agency of the State, or of any of its political subdivisions, pursuant to this act, or (d) in any written statement by an applicant for appointment or employment or by an employee in any State institution of learning in this State, intended to determine whether or not such applicant or employee is a subversive person as defined in this act, which statement contains notice that it is subject to the penalties of perjury, shall be subject to the penalties of perjury prescribed by law.

2. CIVIL DEFENSE PERSONNEL

Mississippi Code Anno. 1942, § 8610–18 (Supp. 1962). *Loyalty oath required.*—No person shall be employed or associated in any capacity in any civil defense organization established under this act who advocates or has advocated a change by force or violence in the constitutional form of the Government of the United States or in this State or the overthrow of any government in the United States by force or violence, or who has been convicted of or is under indictment or information charging any subversive act against the United States. Each person who is appointed to serve in any organization for civil defense shall before entering upon his duties, take an oath, in writing, before a person authorized to administer oaths in this State, which oath shall be substantially as follows:

"I, _____, do solemnly swear (or affirm) that I will support and defend the Constitution of the United States and the constitution of the State of Mississippi, against all enemies, foreign and domestic; that I will bear true faith and allegiance to the same; that I take this obligation freely, without any mental reservation or purpose of evasion; and that I will well and faithfully discharge the duties upon which I am about to enter.

"And I do further swear (or affirm) that I do not advocate, nor am I a member of any political party or organization that advocates the overthrow of the Government of the United States or of this State by force or violence; and that during such time as I am a member of the (name of civil defense organization), I will not advocate nor become a member of any political party or organization that advocates the overthrow of the Government of the United States or of this State by force or violence; that I am not a subversive person as defined in the Subversive Activities Act of 1950; that this statement is made by me subject to the penalties for perjury as provided in said Subversive Activities Act of 1950 for any material misstatement of fact herein, and that for such purpose this statement shall be deemed to have been made under oath, as provided in said act."

For the purposes of this section, any State public officer, whether elected or appointed for a fixed term, shall be authorized and empowered to administer oaths to regular personnel under the jurisdiction of such officer and to auxiliary personnel selected, organized, and trained for civil defense purposes.

TEACHERS' LOYALTY

Mississippi Code Anno. 1942, § 4064–01. *"Subversive person" defined.*—

* * * * * * *

"Subversive person" means any person who commits, attempts to commit, or aids in the commission, or advocates, abets, advises or teaches by any means any person to commit, attempt to commit, or aid in the commission of any act intended to overthrow, destroy or alter, or to assist in the overthrow, destruction or alteration of, the constitutional form of the Government of the United States, or of the State of Mississippi, or any political subdivision of either of them, by revolution, force, violence, or other means not provided for or sanctioned by the constitution of the State of Mississippi or the Constitution of the United States; or who is a member of a subversive organization or a foreign subversive organization.

Id. § 4064–03. *Rules and regulations to determine subversive persons.*—Every person and every board, commission, council, department, court or other agency of the State of Mississippi or any political subdivision thereof, who or which appoints or employs or supervises in any manner the appointment or employment of public officials or employees shall establish by rules, regulations, or otherwise, procedures designed to ascertain before any person, including teachers and other employees of any public educational institution in this State, is appointed or employed, that he or she as the case may be is not a subversive person, and that there are no reasonable grounds to believe such persons are subversive persons. In the event such reasonable grounds exist, he or she as the case may be shall not be appointed or employed. In securing any facts necessary to ascertain the information herein required, the applicant shall be required to sign a written statement containing answers to such inquiries as may be material, which statement shall contain notice that it is subject to the penalties of perjury.

Id. § 4064–05. *Nonsubversive statement required.*—Every person, who on July 1, 1950, shall be in the employ of the State of Mississippi or of any political subdivision thereof, other than those now holding elective office shall be required on or before August 1, 1950, to make a written statement which shall contain notice that it is subject to the penalties of perjury, that he or she is not a subversive person as defined in this act, namely, any person who commits, attempts to commit, or aids in the commission, or advocates, abets, advises or teaches by any means any person to commit, attempt to commit, or aid in the commission of any act intended to overthrow, destroy or alter, or to assist in the overthrow, destruction or alteration of, the constitutional form of the Government of the United States, or of the State of Mississippi, or any political subdivision of either of them, by revolution, force, violence, or other means not provided for or sanctioned by the constitution of the State of Mississippi or the Constitution of the United States, or who is a member of a subversive organization or a foreign subversive organization, as more fully defined in this act. Such statement shall be prepared and execution required by the elected or appointed head of each department or institution of the State or any of its political subdivisions. Any person failing or refusing to execute such a statement or who admits he is a subversive person as defined in this act shall immediately be discharged.

Id. § 4064–08. *State aid to institutions of higher learning conditioned upon adoption of procedures to determine subversive persons.*—Before any appropriation of public funds of any character shall be made by the State of Mississippi to any institution of higher learning, including junior colleges, there shall be filed with the Governor, the president of the senate and the speaker of the house of representatives, on behalf of said institution, a written report setting forth what procedures it has adopted to determine whether it has reasonable grounds to believe that any subversive persons are in its employ, and what steps, if any, have been or are being taken to terminate such employment. In the absence of such a report no appropriation shall be included in the State budget or approved by the legislature.

Id. § 4064–09. *Penalty.*—Every written statement made pursuant to this act by an applicant for appointment or employment, or by any employee, shall be deemed to have been made under oath if it contains a declaration preceding the signature of the maker to the effect that it is made under the penalties of perjury. Any person who makes a material misstatement of fact (a) in any such written statement, or (b) in any affidavit made pursuant to the provisions of this act, or (c) under oath in any hearing conducted by any agency of the State, or of any of its political subdivisions, pursuant to this act, or (d) in any written statement by an applicant for appointment or employment or by an employee in any State institution of learning in this State, intended to determine whether or not such applicant or employee is a subversive person as defined in this act, which statement contains notice that it is subject to the penalties of perjury, shall be subject to the penalties of perjury prescribed by law.

EXCLUSION FROM THE BAR

Question 3 on the application form for admission inquires as to the applicant's loyalty. It provides:

3. Do you believe in the form of, and are you loyal to, the Government of the United States?

MISSOURI

Vernon's Anno. Missouri Stat. § 120.140, subsec. 1 (Supp. 1963). *Political organizations advocating overthrow of Government barred from ballot.*—The term "political party" as used in sections 120.140 to 120.230 shall mean any established political party" as hereinafter defined and shall also mean any political group which shall hereafter undertake to form an established political party provided for in sections 120.140 to 120.230: provided, that no political organization or group shall be qualified as a political party, or given a place on a ballot, which organization or group advocates the overthrow by violence of the established constitutional form of Government of the United States or the State of Missouri.

* * * * * * *

Loyalty of State Officers and Employees

ELECTIVE AND NONELECTIVE PERSONNEL

Missouri Constitution, Art. VII, § 11. *Oath.*—Before taking office, all civil and military officers in this State shall take and subscribe an oath or affirmation to support the Constitution of the United States and of this State, and do demean themselves faithfully in office.

Exclusion From the Bar

Missouri does not have any rule or regulation which pertains to the admission of persons who are or have been Communists or subversives. Similarly, the various forms employed by the State do not contain any questions directly on the subject.

MONTANA

1. SEDITION

Montana Rev. Code 1947, § 94–4401. *Unlawful acts.*—Any person or persons who shall utter, print, write, or publish any disloyal, profane, violent, scurrilous, contemptuous, slurring, or abusive language about the United States, the Government of the United States, or the form of Government of the United States, or the Constitution of the United States, or the soldiers or sailors of the United States, or the flag of the United States, or the uniform of the Army or Navy of the United States, or any language calculated to bring the form of Government of the United States, or the Constitution of the United States, or the soldiers or sailors of the United States, or the flag of the United States, or the uniform of the Army or Navy of the United States, into contempt, scorn, contumely, or disrepute, or shall utter, print, write, or publish any language calculated to incite or inflame resistance to any duly constituted Federal or State authority, or who shall display the flag of any foreign enemy, or who shall, by utterance, writing, printing, publication, or language spoken, urge, incite, or advocate any curtailment of production in the United States of any thing or things, product or products, necessary or essential to the prosecution of any war in which the United States may be engaged, with intent by such curtailment to cripple or hinder the United States in the prosecution of any war; or who, in time of war in which the United States may be engaged, shall willfully make or convey false reports or statements with intent to interfere with the operation or success of the military or naval forces of the United States, or promote the success of its enemy or enemies, or shall willfully cause, or attempt to cause, disaffection in the military or naval forces of the United States, or who shall, by uttering, printing, writing, publishing, language spoken, or by any act or acts, interfere with, obstruct, or attempt to obstruct, the operation of any national selective draft law or the recruiting or the enlistment service of the United States, to the injury of the military or naval service thereof, shall be guilty of the crime of sedition.

Id. § 94–4402. *Penalty.*—Every person found guilty of the crime of sedition shall be punished for each offense by a fine of not less than two hundred dollars nor more than twenty thousand dollars, or by imprisonment in the State prison for not less than one year nor more than twenty years, or by both such fine and imprisonment. In the event of a fine imposed for violation of any of the provisions of this act and not paid, the guilty person shall be imprisoned for a period represented by a credit of two dollars per day until the amount of the fine is fully paid.

Id. § 94–4403. *Declaration of purpose.*—This act is hereby declared to be an emergency law and a law necessary for the immediate preservation of the public peace and safety.

241

Annotations:

State v. *Kahn,* 56 Mont. 108, 182 P. 107 (1919). Appellant was convicted of the crime of sedition. He was charged with making the following seditious utterance:

"This is a rich man's war, and we have no business in it. They talk about Hooverism—it's a joke. Nobody pays any attention to it. It don't amount to anything. The *Lusitania* was warned not to sail. They were carrying munitions and wheat for the Allies. The poor man has no show in this war. The soldiers are fighting the battles of the rich."

The court affirmed this judgment and held, *inter alia*: (1) that a State sedition statute was a valid exercise of legislative power and did not impinge upon the exclusive war powers of Congress; (2) that neither the Federal nor the State constitutional guarantees of free speech was intended to protect seditious utterance; (3) that for purposes of preserving the peace and safety of the people, and the good order of society, the legislature could prohibit certain acts and attach a penalty for disobedience without including any evil intent as an ingredient of the offense other than the general intent implied from violation of the statute.

State v. *Griffith,* 56 M. 214, 184 P. 219 (1919). Appellant was tried and convicted of the crime sedition. The violation consisted of a statement to the effect that "We [the Industrial Workers of the World] are going to win the case." The court reversed the conviction with directions to dismiss the information and discharge the appellant. It held that the expression of an opinion as to the probable outcome of a trial conducted 1,500 miles away, however coarsely stated, did not constitute sedition.

State v. *Wyman,* 56 M. 600, 186 P. 1 (1919). In this case the court sustained a conviction for sedition consisting of a statement by the accused that American soldiers would perpetrate atrocities similar to those committed by enemy soldiers. The court reasoned that the utterance tended to bring the former into contempt, contumely scorn or disrepute.

---

2. CRIMINAL SYNDICALISM

Montana Rev. Code 1947, § 94–4404. *Criminal syndicalism defined.*—Criminal syndicalism is hereby defined to be the doctrine which advocates crime, violence, force, arson, destruction of property, sabotage, or other unlawful acts or methods, or any such acts, as a means of accomplishing or effecting industrial or political ends, or as a means of effecting industrial or political revolution.

Id. § 94–4406. *Unlawful acts and penalty.*—Any person who, by word of mouth or writing, advocates, suggests, or teaches the duty, necessity, propriety, or expediency of crime, criminal syndicalism, or sabotage, or who shall advocate, suggest, or teach the duty, necessity, propriety, or expediency of doing any act of violence, the destruction of or damage to any property, the bodily injury to any person or persons, or the commission of any crime or unlawful act, as a means of accomplishing or effecting any industrial or political ends, change, or revolution, or who prints, publishes, edits, issues, or knowingly circulates, sells, distributes, or publicly displays any books, pamphlets, paper, handbill, poster, document, or written or printed matter in any form whatsoever, containing, advocating, advising, suggesting, or teaching crime, criminal syndicalism, sabotage, the doing of any act of violence, the destruction of or damage to any property, the injury to any person, or the commission of any crime or unlawful act, as a means of accomplishing, effecting, or bringing about any industrial or political ends, or change, or as a means of accomplishing, effecting, or bringing about any industrial or political revolution, or who shall openly, or at all, attempt to justify, by word of mouth or writing, the commission or the attempt to commit sabotage, any act of violence, the destruction of or damage to any property, the injury of any person, or the commission of any crime or unlawful act, with the intent to exemplify, spread, or teach or suggest criminal syndicalism, or organizes, or helps to organize, or become a member of, or voluntarily assembles with, any society or assemblage of persons formed to teach or advocate, or which teaches, advocates, or suggests the doctrine of criminal syndicalism, sabotage, or the necessity, propriety, or expediency of doing any act of violence, or the commission of any crime or unlawful act, as a means of accomplishing or effecting any industrial or political ends, change, or revolution, is guilty of a felony, and, upon conviction thereof, shall be punished by imprisonment in the State penitentiary for a term of not less than one year or more than five years, or by a fine of not less than two hundred dollars or not more than one thousand dollars, or by both such fine and imprisonment.

Id. § 94.4407. *Assemblage to a d v o c a t e criminal syndicalism.*— Wherever two or more persons assemble or consort for the purpose of advocating, teaching, or suggesting the doctrine of criminal syndicalism, as defined in this act, or to advocate, teach, suggest, or encourage sabotage, as defined in this act, or the duty, necessity, propriety, or expendiency of doing any act of violence, the destruction of or damage to any property, the bodily injury to any person or persons, or the commission of any crime or unlawful act, as a means of accomplishing or effecting any industrial or political ends, change, or revolution, it is hereby declared unlawful, and every person voluntarily participating therein, by his presence aids or instigates, is guilty of a felony, and, upon conviction thereof, shall be punished by imprisonment in the State prison for not less than one year or more than five years, or by a fine of not less than two hundred dollars or more than one thousand dollars, or by both such imprisonment and fine.

Id. § 94.4408. *Permitting premises to be used to advocate criminal syndicalism.*—The owner, lessee, agent, superintendent, or person in charge or occupation of any place, building, room or rooms, or structure, who knowingly permits therein any assembly or consort of persons prohibited by the provisions of the preceding section, or who, after notification that the place or premises, or any part thereof, is or are so used, permits such use to be continued, is guilty of a misdemeanor, and punishable, upon conviction thereof, by imprisonment in the county jail for not less than sixty days or for not more than one year, or by a fine of not less than one hundred dollars or more than five hundred dollars, or by both such imprisonment and fine.

REGISTRATION

Montana Rev. Code 1947, § 94–4411 (Supp. 1963). *Short title.—* This act may be cited as the "Subversive Organization Registration Law."

Id. § 94–4412 (Supp. 1963). *Declaration of purpose.*—This act is adopted in the exercise of the police power of this State for the protection of the public peace and safety by requiring the registration of subversive organizations which are conceived and exist for the purpose of undermining and eventually destroying the democratic form of government in this State and in the United States.

Id. § 94–4413 (Supp. 1963). *"Subversive organization" defined.—* As used in this title, "subversive organization" means every corporation, association, society, camp, group, political party, assembly, and everybody or organization composed of two [2] or more persons or members, which comes within all or any of the following descriptions:

(a) Which directly or indirectly advocates, advises, teaches, or practices, the duty, necessity, or propriety of controlling, conducting, seizing, or overthrowing the Government of the United States, of this State, or of any political subdivision thereof by force or violence;

(b) Which is subject to foreign control as defined in section 4 [94–4414] hereof.

Id. § 94–4414. *Organization "subject to foreign control" defined.—* An organization is "subject to foreign control" if it comes within either of the following descriptions:

(a) It solicits or accepts financial contributions, loans, or support of any kind directly or indirectly from, or is affiliated directly or indirectly with, a foreign government or a political subdivision thereof, an agent, agency, or instrumentality of a foreign government or political subdivision thereof, a political party in a foreign country, or an international political organization;

(b) Its policies, or any of them, are determined by or at the suggestion of, or in collaboration with, a foreign government or a political subdivision thereof, an agent, agency, or instrumentality of a foreign government or a political subdivision thereof, a political party in a foreign country, or an international political organization.

Id. § 94–4415 (Supp. 1963). *Exclusions from scope of phrase "subversive organization."*—"Subversive organization" does not include any labor union or religious, fraternal, or patriotic organizations, society, or association whose objectives and aims do not contemplate the overthrow of the Government of the United States, of this State, or of any political subdivision thereof by force.

Id. § 94–4416 (Supp. 1963). *Effect and scope of law.*—This act imposes additional requirements upon corporations, associations, or organizations which are subversive organizations. either the fact that such a corporation, association, or organization was organized pursuant to law nor that its affairs and activities are in any respect regulated by law exempts it from complying with this title.

Id. § 94–4417 (Supp. 1963). *Rules and regulations.*—The secretary of state may adopt and promulgate such rules and regulations as may be necessary to carry out the provisions of this title, and may alter, amend, or repeal such rules and regulations.

Id. § 94–4418 (Supp. 1963). *Subversive organization required to register.*—Every subversive organization in existence on July 1, 1951, shall within thirty (30) days after that date, and every subversive organization thereafter organized shall within ten (10) days after its organization, file with the secretary of state, on such forms and in such detail as he may prescribe, the following information and documents:

(a) A complete and detail statement subscribed, under oath, by all of its officers, showing all of the following:

(1) Its name and post office address;

(2) The names and addresses of all its branches, chapters, and affiliates;

(3) The names, nationalities, and residence addresses of its officers and members, and the qualifications required for membership in it;

(4) The nature and extent of its existing and proposed aims, purposes, and activities;

(5) The times and places of its meetings;

(6) The description and location of the real property and the kind, quantity, and quality of the personal property owned by it, its assets and liabilities, the methods for the financing of its activities, and the names and addresses of all persons, organizations, and other sources who or which have contributed money, property, literature, or other things of value to the organization or any of its branches, chapters, or affiliates for any of its purposes;

(7) Such other information as the secretary of state may from time to time require.

(b) A true copy, certified by all of its officers, of all of the following:

(1) Its charter, articles of association, or constitution, and its by-laws, rules, and regulations;

(2) Its oath, affirmation, or pledge of membership, if any;

(3) Each agreement, resolution, and other instrument or document relating to its organization, powers, and purposes, and the powers and duties of its officers and members;

(4) Each book, pamphlet, leaflet, or other printed, written, or illustrated matter directly or indirectly issued or distributed by it or in its behalf, or to or by its members with its knowledge, consent, or approval;

(5) Such other documents as the secretary of state may from time to time require.

(c) A description of the uniforms, badges, insignia, or other means of identification prescribed by it, and worn or carried by its officers or members, or any of such officers or members.

(d) In case it is subject to foreign control, a statement of the manner in which it is subject.

Id. § 94–4419 (Supp. 1963). *Changes in charter, etc., required to be reported.*—Every subversive organization shall within ten (10) days after any revision or amendment of, or other change with respect to, its charter, articles of association, constitution, bylaws, rules, regulations, oath, affirmation, or pledge of membership, or any part thereof, file with the secretary of state a true copy certified by all of its officers of the revised, amended, or changed charter, articles of association, constitution, bylaws, rules, regulations, oath, affirmation, or pledge of membership, or part thereof.

Id. § 94–4420 (Supp. 1963). *Changes in officers, aims, purposes, etc., required to be reported.*—Every subversive organization shall within ten (10) days after a change has been made in its officers, or in its aims, purposes, activities, property holdings, or methods and sources of financing its activities, file with the secretary of state a statement subscribed under oath by all of its officers showing the change.

Id. § 94–4421 (Supp. 1963). *Periodic membership reports required.*—Every subversive organization shall at least once in each period of six (6) months file with the secretary of state a statement subscribed under oath by all of its officers showing the names and residence addresses of all persons who have been admitted to membership during that period or, if no members have been admitted during that period, a statement to that effect similarly subscribed.

Id. § 94–4422 (Supp. 1963). *Report of political activities required.*—Every subversive organization shall within ten (10) days after the adoption thereof file with the secretary of state, on such form and in such detail as he may prescribe, each resolution adopted, or the minutes of any meeting held by it, authorizing or providing for concerted action by its officers, members, or a part of its membership, to promote or prevent the passage of any act of legislation by any local, State, or Federal legislative body, or to support or defeat any candidate for public office.

Id. § 94–4423 (Supp. 1963). *Reports, etc., open to public.*—All statements or documents filed with the secretary of state under this title [94–4411 to 94–4427] are public records and shall be open to public examination and inspection at all reasonable hours.

Id. § 94–4424 (Supp. 1963). *Mail privileges restricted.*—A subversive organization shall not send, deliver, mail, or transmit, or suffer or permit to be sent, delivered, mailed, or transmitted, to any person in this State who is not a member of the organization any anonymous letter, document, leaflet, or other written or printed matter. All letters, documents, leaflets, or other written or printed matter issued by a subversive organization which are intended to come to the attention of a person who is not a member of the organization shall bear the name of the organization and the name and residences of its officers.

Id. § 94–4425 (Supp. 1963). *Penalty for violation by organization.*—Any subversive organization which violates any provisions of this title [94–4411 to 94–4427] is guilty of a felony punishable by fine of not less than one thousand dollars ($1,000.00) nor more than ten thousand dollars ($10,000.00). Any such violation constitutes a separate and distinct offense for each day, or part thereof, during which it is continued.

Id. § 94–4426 (Supp. 1963). *Penalty for violations by officers, etc.*—Any officer or member of the board of directors, board of trustees, executive committee, or other similar governing body of a subversive organization who violates any provision of this title [94–4411 to 94–4427], or permits or acquiesces in the violation of any provision of this title by the organization is guilty of a felony punishable by fine of not less than five hundred dollars ($500.00) nor more than five thousand dollars ($5,000.00), or by imprisonment in a State prison for not less than six (6) months nor more than five (5) years, or by both.

Id. § 94–4427 (Supp. 1963). *Penalty for violations by members, etc.*—Any person who becomes or remains a member of any subversive organization, or attends a meeting thereof, with knowledge that the organization has failed to comply with any provision of this title [94–

4411 to 94–4427], is guilty of a misdemeanor punishable by fine of not less than ten dollars ($10.00) nor more than one thousand dollars ($1,000.00), or by imprisonment in the county jail for not less than ten (10) days nor more than one (1) year, or by both.

LOYALTY OF STATE OFFICERS AND EMPLOYEES

1. ELECTIVE AND NONELECTIVE PERSONNEL

Montana Constitution, Art. XIX, § 1.   *Oath.*—Members of the legislative assembly and all officers, executive, ministerial or judicial, shall, before they enter upon the duties of their respective offices, take and subscribe the following oath or affirmation, to wit: "I do solemnly swear (or affirm) that I will support, protect, and defend the Constitution of the United States, and the constitution of the State of Montana, and that I will discharge the duties of my office with fidelity; and that I have not paid, or contributed, or promised to pay or contribute, either directly or indirectly, any money or other valuable thing to procure my nomination or election (or appointment) except for necessary and proper expenses expressly authorized by law; that I have not knowingly violated any election law of this State, or procured it to be done by others in my behalf; that I will not knowingly receive, directly or indirectly, any money or other valuable thing for the performance or nonperformance of any act or duty pertaining to my office other than the compensation allowed by law, so help me God." And no other oath, declaration, or test shall be required as a qualification for any office or trust.

2. CIVIL DEFENSE PERSONNEL

Montana Rev. Code 1947 § 77–1313.   *Loyalty oath required.*—No person shall be employed or associated in any capacity in any civil defense organization established under this act who advocates a change by force or violence in the constitutional form of the Government of the United States or in this State or the overthrow of any government in the United States by force or violence, or who has been convicted of or is under indictment or information charging any subversive act against the United States.   Each person who is appointed to serve in an organization for civil defense shall, before entering upon his duties, take an oath, in writing, before a person authorized to administer oaths in this State, which oath shall be substantially as follows:

"I, _____, do solemnly swear (or affirm) that I will support and defend the Constitution of the United States and the constitution of the State of Montana, against all enemies, foreign and domestic; that I will bear true faith and allegiance to the same; that I take this obligation freely, without any mental reservation or purpose of evasion; and that I will well and faithfully discharge the duties upon which I am about to enter.   And I do further swear (or affirm) that I do not advocate nor am I a member of any political party or organization that advocates the overthrow of the Government of the United States or of this State by force or violence; and that during such time as I am a member of the Montana civil defense agency I will not advocate nor become a member of any political party or organization that advocates the overthrow of the Government of the United States or of this State by force or violence."

TEACHERS' LOYALTY

Montana Rev. Code 1947, § 75–4706. *Loyalty oath required.*—Every person who applies for a contract, or any renewal thereof, to teach in any of the public schools of this State, shall subscribe to the following oath or affirmation before some officer authorized by law to administer oaths:

"I solemnly swear (or affirm) that I will support the Constitution of the United States of America, the constitution of the State of Montana, and the laws of the United States and the State of Montana, and will, by precept and example, promote respect for the flag and the institutions of the United States and the State of Montana, reverence for law and order and undivided allegiance to the Government of the United States of America."

Such oath or affirmation shall be executed in duplicate and one copy thereof shall be filed with the State superintendent of public instruction at the time when the application for a license is made, and the other copy shall be retained by the person who subscribed to such oath or affirmation. No such contract shall be entered into, or be effective, unless such oath shall have been filed.

Id. § 75–4707. *Teaching personnel in institutions of higher education required to take loyalty oath.*—Every professor, instructor, or teacher who shall hereafter be employed by any university, normal school, or college in this State which is supported in whole or in part by public funds, shall, before entering upon the discharge of his or her duties, subscribe to the oath or affirmation as prescribed in section 75–4706 before some officer authorized by law to administer oaths. Such oath or affirmation shall be executed in duplicate and one copy thereof shall be filed with the president of such university, normal school, or college, and one copy shall be retained by the person who subscribed to such oath or affirmation; provided, however, the above requirement shall not apply to exchange professors or temporary employees.

EXCLUSION FROM THE BAR

Montana does not appear to have any rule or regulation which pertains to the admission of persons who are Communists or subversives. Similarly, the various forms employed by the State do not contain any questions directly on the subject.

EXCLUSION FROM INCIDENTAL BENEFITS

EMPLOYMENT

Montana Rev. Code 1947, § 77–606 *Policy against employment of members of the Communist Party.*—It is expressed policy of the legislature of the State of Montana that wherever a vacancy is caused in the employment rolls of any business or industry by reason of induction into the service of the United States of an employee pursuant to the provisions of said selective training act of 1940, or the national guard and reserve officers mobilization act such vacancy shall not be filled by any person who is a member of the Communist Party or the German-American Bund.

NEBRASKA

1. SEDITION

Rev. Stat. Nebraska § 28–748 (Supp. 1963). *Unlawful acts and penalty.*—(1) Any person who knowingly or willfully commits, or aids in the commission of any act to overthrow by force or violence the government of this State, or of any of its political subdivisions, shall be guilty of sedition against this State.

(2) Any person who knowingly or willfully advocates the overthrow by force or violence of the government of this State, or of any of its political subdivisions, shall be guilty of sedition against this State.

(3) Any person who knowingly or willfully becomes or remains a member of the Communist Party of the United States, or its successors, or any of its subordinate organizations, or any other organization having for one of its purposes the overthrow by force or violence of the government of this State, or any of its political subdivisions, and said person had knowledge of said unlawful purpose of said Communist Party of the United States or of said subordinate or other organization, shall be guilty of sedition against this State.

(4) Any person who violates any provisions of this section shall be guilty of a felony, and shall, upon conviction thereof, be punished by imprisonment in the Nebraska Penal and Correctional Complex for not less than one year nor more than twenty years.

Id. § 28–749 (Supp. 1963). *Additional penalty.*—Any person who is convicted of violating any provision of section 28–748 shall automatically be disqualified and barred from holding any office, elective or appointive, or any position of trust, profit or employment with this State, or any political subdivision of this State, or any county, city, town, municipal corporation, school district, public educational institution, or any board, commission or agency of any of the foregoing.

Id. § 27–750 (Supp. 1963). *Enforcement.*—The attorney general shall have exclusive authority to conduct investigations of and institute prosecutions for any violations of sections 28–747 to 28–749.

2. CRIMINAL SYNDICALISM

Rev. Stat. Nebraska § 28–815. *Criminal syndicalism defined.*—Criminal syndicalism is hereby defined to be the doctrine which advocates crime, physical violence, arson, destruction of property or sabotage as a means of accomplishing or effecting industrial or political ends, or for profit.

Id. § 28–816. *Unlawful acts and penalty.*—Any person who, by word of mouth or writing, advocates, affirmatively suggests, or teaches the duty, necessity, propriety, or expedience of crime, criminal syndicalism, or sabotage, or who shall advocate, affirmatively suggest, or teach the duty, necessity, propriety, or expediency of doing any act of violence, the destruction of or damage to any property, the bodily injury to any person or persons, or the commission of any crime as a means of accomplishing or effecting any industrial or political ends or for profit; or who prints, publishes, edits, issues, or knowingly circulates, sells, distributes, or publicly displays any books, pamphlets, paper, handbill, poster, document, or written or printed matter in any form whatsoever, containing matters advocating, advising, affirmatively suggesting, or teaching crime, criminal syndicalism, sabotage, the doing of any act of physical violence, the destruction of or damage to any property, the injury to any person, or the commission of any crime as a means of accomplishing, effecting, or bringing about any industrial or political ends or for profit, or who shall openly, or at all attempt to justify, by word of mouth or writing, the commission of, or the attempt to commit sabotage, any act of physical violence, the destruction of or damage to any property, the bodily injury of any person or persons, or the commission of any crime, with the intent to exemplify, spread, or teach or affirmatively suggest criminal syndicalism; or whoever organizes, or helps to organize or become a member of, or voluntarily assembles with, any society or assemblage of persons which teaches, advocates or affirmatively suggests the doctrine of criminal syndicalism, sabotage or the necessity, propriety, or expediency of doing any act of physical violence or the commission of any crime as a means of accomplishing or effecting any industrial or political ends or for profit, shall be deemed guilty of a felony, and upon conviction thereof shall be punished by imprisonment in the penitentiary for a term of not less than one year nor more than ten years, or by a fine of not more than one thousand dollars, or by both such imprisonment and fine.

Id. § 28–817. *Permitting premises to be used to advocate criminal syndicalism.*—The owner, lessee, agent, superintendent, or person in charge or occupation of any place, building, room or rooms, or structure, who knowingly permits therein any assembly or consort of persons prohibited by the provisions of section 28–816, or who after notification by an authorized public or peace officer that the place or premises, or any part thereof, is or are so used, permits such use to be continued, shall be deemed guilty of a misdemeanor, and shall upon conviction thereof be punished by imprisonment in the county jail for not less than sixty days or for not more than one year, or by a fine of not less than one hundred dollars or more than five hundred dollars, or by both such imprisonment and fine.

Outlawing the Communist Party

Rev. Stat. Nebraska § 28–747 (Supp. 1963). *Communist Party outlawed.*—The Communist Party of the United States, or any successors of such party regardless of the assumed name, the object of which is to overthrow by force or violence the Government of the United States, or the government of this State, or its political subdivisions shall not be entitled to be recognized or certified as a political party under the laws of this State and shall not be entitled to any of the privileges, rights or immunities attendant upon legal political bodies recognized under the laws of this State, or any political subdivision thereof.

Whatever rights, privileges or immunities shall have heretofore been granted to said Communist Party of the United States as defined in this section, or to any of its subsidiary organizations, by reason of the laws of this State, or of any political subdivisions thereof, are hereby terminated and shall be void.

Id. § 28–748 (Supp. 1963). *Membership in the Communist Party, etc., unlawful.*—(1) Any person who knowingly or willfully commits, or aids in the commission of any act to overthrow by force or violence the government of this State, or of any of its political subdivisions, shall be guilty of sedition against this State.

(2) Any person who knowingly or willfully advocates the overthrow by force or violence of the government of this State, or of any of its political subdivisions, shall be guilty of sedition against this State.

(3) Any person who knowingly or willfully becomes or remains a member of the Communist Party of the United States, or its successors, or any of its subordinate organizations, or any other organization having for one of its purposes the overthrow by force or violence of the government of this State, or any of its political subdivisions, and said person had knowledge of said unlawful purpose of said Communist Party of the United States or of said subordinate or other organization, shall be guilty of sedition against this State.

(4) Any person who violates any provisions of this section shall be guilty of a felony, and shall, upon conviction thereof, be punished by imprisonment in the State penitentiary for not less than one year nor more than twenty years.

Id. § 28–750 (Supp. 1963). *Enforcement.*—The attorney general shall have exclusive authority to conduct investigations of and institute prosecutions for any violation of this act.

Exclusion From the Elective Process

Rev. Stat. Nebraska § 28–747 (Supp. 1963). *Communist Party not entitled to recognition or certificated as political party.*—The Communist Party of the United States, or any successors of such party regardless of the assumed name, the object of which is to overthrow by force or violence the Government of the United States, or the government of this State, or its political subdivisions shall not be entitled to be recognized or certified as a political party under the laws of this State and shall not be entitled to any of the privileges, rights or immunities attendant upon legal political bodies recognized under the laws of this State, or any political subdivision thereof. Whatever rights, privileges, or immunities shall have heretofore been granted to said Communist Party of the United States as defined in this section, or to any of its subsidiary organizations, by reason of the laws of this State, or of any political subdivision thereof, are hereby terminated and shall be void.

Loyalty of State Officers and Employees

1. ELECTIVE AND NONELECTIVE PERSONNEL

Constitution, Art. XV, § 1. *Oath.*—Executive and judicial officers and members of the Legislature, before they enter upon their official duties shall take and subscribe the following oath, or affirmation: "I do solemnly swear (or affirm) that I will support the Constitution of the United States, and the constitution of the State of Nebraska, and will faithfully discharge the duties of _____ according to the best of my ability, and that at the election at which I was chosen to fill said office, I have not improperly influenced in any way the vote of any elector, and have not accepted, nor will I accept or receive, directly or indirectly, any money or other valuable thing from any corporation, company, or person, or any promise of office, for any official act or influence (for any vote I may give or withhold on any bill, resolution, or appropriation)." Any such officer or member of the Legislature who shall refuse to take the oath herein prescribed, shall forfeit his office, and any person who shall be convicted of having sworn falsely to, or of violating his said oath shall forfeit his office, and thereafter be disqualified from holding any office of profit or trust in this State unless he shall have been restored to civil rights.

Rev. Stat. Nebraska § 28–748 (Supp. 1963). *Unlawful acts and penalty.*—(1) Any person who knowingly or willfully commits, or aids in the commission of any act to overthrow by force or violence the government of this State, or of any of its political subdivisions, shall be guilty of sedition against this State.

(2) Any person who knowingly or willfully advocates the overthrow by force or violence of the government of this State, or of any of its political subdivisions, shall be guilty of sedition against this State.

(3) Any person who knowingly or willfully becomes or remains a member of the Communist Party of the United States, or its successors, or any of its subordinate organizations, or any other organization having for one of its purposes the overthrow by force or violence of the government of this State, or any of its political subdivisions, and said person had knowledge of said unlawful purpose of said Communist Party of the United States or of said subordinate or other organization, shall be guilty of sedition against this State.

(4) Any person who violates any provisions of this section shall be guilty of a felony, and shall, upon conviction thereof, be punished by imprisonment in the State penitentiary for not less than one year nor more than twenty years.

Id. § 28–749 (Supp. 1963). *Additional penalty—disqualification from public office and employment.*—Any person who is convicted of violating any provision of section 28–748 of this act shall automatically be disqualified and barred from holding any office, elective or appointive, or any position of trust, profit of employment with this State, or any political subdivision of this State, or any county, city, town, municipal corporation, school district, public educational institution, or any board, commission or agency of any of the foregoing.

3. NONELECTIVE PERSONNEL

Rev. Stat. Nebraska § 11-101. *Public officers required to take loyalty oath.*—All State, district, county, precinct, township, municipal, and especially appointed officers, except those mentioned in Article XV, section 1, of the constitution of the State of Nebraska, shall, before entering upon their respective duties, take and subscribe the following oath, which shall be endorsed upon their respective bonds:

I, _____, do solemnly swear that I will support the Constitution of the United States and the constitution of the State of Nebraska, against all enemies, foreign and domestic; that I will bear true faith and allegiance to the same; that I take this obligation freely and without mental reservation or for purpose of evasion; and that I will faithfully and impartially perform the duties of the office of _____, according to law, and to the best of my ability. And I do further swear that I do not advocate, nor am I a member of any political party or organization that advocates the overthrow of the Government of the United States or of this State by force or violence; and that during such time as I am in this position I will not advocate nor become a member of any political party or organization that advocates the overthrow of the Government of the United States or of this State by force or violence. So help me God.

If any such officer is not required to give bond, the oath shall be filed in the office of the secretary of state, or of the clerk of the county, city, village, or other municipal subdivision of which he shall be an officer.

Id. § 11-101.01. *Loyalty oath required to be executed by all persons paid from public funds.*—All persons in Nebraska, with the exception of executive and judicial officers and members of the legislature who are required to take the oath prescribed by Article XV, section 1, of the constitution of Nebraska, who are paid from public funds for their services, including teachers and all other employees paid from public school funds, shall be required to take and subscribe an oath in writing, before a person authorized to administer oaths in this State, and file same with the secretary of state, or the county clerk of the county where such services are performed, which oath shall be as follows:

I, _____, do solemnly swear that I will support and defend the Constitution of the United States and the constitution of the State of Nebraska, against all enemies, foreign and domestic; that I will bear true faith and allegiance to the same; that I take this obligation freely, without any mental reservation or for purpose of evasion; and that I will faithfully and impartially perform the duties of the office of _____ according to law, and to the best of my ability. And I do further swear that I do not advocate, nor am I a member of any political party or organization that advocates the overthrow of the Government of the United States or of this State by force or violence; and that during such time as I am in this position I will not advocate nor become a member of any political party or organization that advocates the overthrow of the Government of the United States or of this State by force or violence. So help me God.

Id. § 11–101.02. *Penalty.*—If any false statement is made in taking either of the oaths prescribed in sections 11–101 and 11–101.01, the person making such false statement shall be deemed guilty of perjury as defined in section 28–701, and upon conviction thereof shall be punished as provided in section 28–701. No person convicted of perjury in taking the oath as prescribed in either section 11–101 or 11–101.01, shall hold any nonelective position, job, or office for the State of Nebraska, or any political subdivision thereof, where the remuneration of such position, job, or office is paid in whole or in part by public money or funds of the State of Nebraska, or of any political subdivision thereof.

3. CIVIL DEFENSE PERSONNEL

Rev. Stat. Nebraska § 81–829.28. *Loyalty oath required.*—No person shall be employed or associated in any capacity in any civil defense organization established under the provisions of sections 81–829.05 to 81–829.30 who advocates or has advocated a change by force or violence in the constitutional form of the Government of the United States or in this State or the overthrow of any government in the United States by force or violence, or who has been convicted of or is under indictment or information charging any subversive act against the United States. Each person who is appointed to serve in an organization for civil defense shall, before entering upon his duties, take an oath, in writing, before a person authorized to administer oaths in this State: *Provided*, that the adjutant general and any subordinate civil defense officer within this State, designated by the adjutant general in writing, shall be qualified to administer any such oath within this State under such regulations as the adjutant general shall prescribe. The oath shall be substantially as follows:

"I _____, do solemnly swear (or affirm) that I will support and defend the Constitution of the United States and the constitution of the State of Nebraska, against all enemies, foreign and domestic; that I will bear true faith and allegiance to the same; that I take this obligation freely, without any mental reservation or purpose of evasion; and that I will well and faithfully discharge the duties upon which I am about to enter. And I do further swear (or affirm) that I do not advocate, nor am I a member of any political party or organization that advocates the overthrow of the Government of the United States or of this State by force or violence; and that during such time as I am a member of the (name of civil defense organization), I will not advocate nor become a member of any political party or organization that advocates the overthrow of the Government of the United States or of this State by force or violence. So help me God."

TEACHERS' LOYALTY

Rev. Stat. Nebraska § 11–101.01. *Loyalty oath required.*—All persons in Nebraska, with the exception of executive and judicial officers and members of the legislature who are required to take the oath prescribed by Article XV, section 1, of the constitution of Nebraska, who are paid from public funds for their services, including teachers and all other employees paid from public school funds, shall be required to take and subscribe an oath in writing, before a person authorized to administer oaths in this State, and file same with the secretary of state, or the county clerk of the county where such services are performed, which oath shall be as follows:

I, ----------------------------, do solemnly swear that I will support and defend the Constitution of the United States and the constitution of the State of Nebraska, against all enemies, foreign and domestic; that I will bear true faith and allegiance to the same; that I take this obligation freely, without any mental reservation or for purpose of evasion; and that I will faithfully and impartially perform the duties of the office of ---------------------------- according to law, and to the best of my ability. And I do further swear that I do not advocate, nor am I a member of any political party or organization that advocates the overthrow of the Government of the United States or of this State by force or violence; and that during such time as I am in this position I will not advocate nor become a member of any political party or organization that advocates the overthrow of the Government of the United States or of this State by force or violence. So help me God.

Id. § 11–101.02. *Penalty.*—If any false statement is made in taking either of the oaths prescribed in sections 11–101 and 11–101.01, the person making such false statement shall be deemed guilty of perjury as defined in section 28–701, and upon conviction thereof shall be punished as provided in section 28–701. No person convicted of perjury in taking the oath as prescribed in either section 11–101 or 11–101.01, shall hold any nonelective position, job, or office for the State of Nebraska, or any political subdivision thereof, where the remuneration of such position, job, or office is paid in whole or in part by public money or funds of the State of Nebraska, or of any political subdivision thereof.

Id. § 79–4, 148. *Loyalty pledge required to be executed.*—All persons engaged in teaching in the public schools of the State of Nebraska and all other employees paid from public school funds, shall sign the following pledge:

"I, ----------------------------, do believe in the United States of America as a government of the people, by the people, for the people; whose just powers are derived from the consent of the governed; a democracy in a republic; an indissoluble nation of many sovereign states; a perfect union, one and inseparable; established upon those principles of freedom, equality, justice, and humanity for which American patriots sacrificed their lives and fortunes.

"I acknowledge it to be my duty to inculcate in the hearts and minds of all pupils in my care, so far as it is in my power to do, (1) an understanding of the Constitutions of the United States and of the State of Nebraska, (2) a knowledge of the history of the Nation and of the sacrifices that have been made in order that it might achieve its present greatness, (3) a love and devotion to the policies and institutions that have made America the finest country in the world in which to live, and (4) opposition to all organizations and activities that would destroy our present form of government."

41–738—65——18

EXCLUSION FROM THE BAR

Nebraska does not appear to have any rule or regulation which pertains to the admission of persons who are or have been Communists or subversives. Similarly, the various forms employed by the State do not contain any questions directly on the subject.

MISCELLANEOUS

Rev. Stat. Nebraska § 79–213. *School boards required to promote loyalty and patriotism.*—An informed, loyal, and patriotic citizenry is necessary to a strong, stable, and prosperous America. Such a citizenry necessitates that every member thereof be fully acquainted with the Nation's history, that he be in full accord with our form of government, and fully aware of the liberties, opportunities, and advantages of which we are possessed and the sacrifices and struggles of those through whose efforts these benefits were gained. Since youth is the time most susceptible to the acceptance of principles and doctrines that will influence men throughout their lives, it is one of the first duties of our educational system to so conduct its activities, choose its textbooks, and arrange its curriculum in such a way that the love of liberty, democracy, and America will be instilled in the heart and mind of the youth of the State.

(1) Every school board shall at the beginning of each school year, appoint from its members a committee of three, to be known as the Committee on Americanism, whose duties shall be:

(a) To carefully examine, inspect, and approve all textbooks used in the teaching of American history and civil government in the school. Such textbooks shall adequately stress the services of the men who achieved our national independence, established our constitutional government, and preserved our union and shall be so written as to develop a pride and respect for our institutions and not be a mere recital of events and dates.

(b) Assure themselves as to the character of all teachers employed, and their knowledge and acceptance of the American form of Government.

(c) Take all such other steps as will assure the carrying out of the provisions of this section.

(2) All grades of all public, private, denominational, and parochial schools, below the sixth grade, shall devote at least one hour per week to exercises or teaching periods for the following purposes:

(a) The recital of stories having to do with American history, or the deeds and exploits of American heroes.

(b) The singing of patriotic songs and the insistence that every pupil shall memorize the "Star-Spangled Banner" and "America."

(c) The development of reverence for the flag and instruction as to proper conduct in its presentation.

(3) In at least two of the three grades from the fifth grade to the eighth grade in all public, private, denominational, and parochial schools at least three periods per week shall be set aside to be devoted to the teaching of American history from approved textbooks, taught in such a way as to make the course interesting and attractive, and to develop a love of country.

(4) In at least two grades of every high school, at least three periods per week shall be devoted to the teaching of civics, during which courses specific attention shall be given to the following matters:

(a) The Constitution of the United States and of the State of Nebraska.

(b) The benefits and advantages of our form of government and the dangers and fallacies of nazism, communism, and similar ideologies,

(c) The duties of citizenship.

(5) Appropriate patriotic exercises suitable to the occasion shall be held under the direction of the school superintendent in every public, private, denominational, and parochial school on Lincoln's birthday, Washington's birthday, Flag Day, Memorial Day, and Armistice Day, or on the day preceding or following such holiday, if the school is in session.

(6) Every school board, the department of education, each county superintendent of schools, and the superintendent of each individual school in the State shall be held directly responsible, in the order named, for the carrying out of the provisions of this section, and neglect thereof shall be considered a dereliction of duty and cause for dismissal.

NEVADA

Unlawful Advocacy

1. ANARCHY

Nevada Rev. Stat. § 203.120. *Criminal anarchy defined.*—Criminal anarchy is the doctrine that organized government should be overthrown by force or violence, or by assassination of the executive head or of any of the executive officials of government, or by any unlawful means. The advocating of such doctrine either by word of mouth or writing is a felony.

Id. § 203.130. *Unlawful acts and penalty.*—Every person who:

1. By word of mouth or writing shall advocate, advise or teach the duty, necessity or propriety of overthrowing or overturning organized government by force or violence, or by assassination of the executive head or of any of the executive officials of government, or by any unlawful means; or

2. Shall print, publish, edit, issue or knowingly circulate, sell, distribute or publicly display any book, paper, document, or written or printed matter in any form, containing or advocating, advising or teaching the doctrine that organized government should be overthrown by force, violence or any unlawful means; or

3. Shall openly, willfully and deliberately justify by word of mouth or writing the assassination or unlawful killing or assaulting of any executive or other officer of the United States or of any State or of any civilized nation having an organized government because of his official character, or any other crime, with intent to teach, spread or advocate the propriety of the doctrines of criminal anarchy; or

4. Shall organize or help to organize or become a member of or voluntarily assemble with any society, group or assembly of persons formed to teach or advocate such doctrine;

shall be punished by imprisonment in the State prison for not more than 10 years, or by a fine of not more than $5,000, or by both fine and imprisonment.

Id. § 203.140. *Assemblage to advocate criminal anarchy.*—Whenever two or more persons assemble for the purpose of advocating or teaching the doctrines of criminal anarchy, as defined in NRS 203.120, such an assembly is unlawful, and every person voluntarily participating therein by his presence, aid or instigation shall be punished by imprisonment in the State prison for not more than 10 years, or by a fine of not more than $5,000, or by both fine and imprisonment.

Id. § 203.150. *Permitting premises to be used to advocate criminal anarchy.*—Every owner, agent, superintendent, janitor, caretaker or occupant of any place, building or room, who shall willfully and knowingly permit therein any assemblage of persons prohibited by NRS 203.140, or who, after notification that the premises are so used, shall permit such use to be continued, shall be guilty of a gross misdemeanor.

2. CRIMINAL SYNDICALISM

Nevada Rev. Stat. § 203.160. *Criminal syndicalism defined.*—Criminal syndicalism is the doctrine which advocates or teaches crime, sabotage, violence or unlawful methods of terrorism as a means of accomplishing industrial or political reform. The advocacy or teaching of such doctrine, whether by word of mouth or writing, is a felony punishable as provided in NRS 203.170, 203.180 and 203.190.

Id. § 203.170. *Unlawful acts and penalty.*—Any person who:

1. By word of mouth or writing, advocates or teaches the duty, necessity or propriety of crime, sabotage, violence or other unlawful methods of terrorism as a means of accomplishing industrial or political reform; or

2. Prints, publishes, edits, issues or knowingly circulates, sells, distributes or publicly displays any book, paper, document or written matter in any form, containing or advocating, advising or teaching the doctrine that industrial or political reform should be brought about by crime, sabotage, violence or other unlawful methods of terrorism; or

3. Openly, willfully and deliberately justifies, by word of mouth or writing, the commission or the attempt to commit crime, sabotage, violence or other unlawful methods of terrorism with intent to exemplify, spread or advocate the propriety of the doctrine of criminal syndicalism; or

4. Organizes or helps to organize or becomes a member of, or voluntarily assembles with, any society, group or assemblage of persons formed to teach or advocate the doctrine of criminal syndicalism:

is guilty of a felony, and upon conviction shall be punished by imprisonment in the State prison for not more than 10 years, or by a fine of not more than $5,000, or by both fine and imprisonment.

Id. § 203.180. *Assemblage to advocate criminal syndicalism.*—Whenever two or more persons assemble for the purpose of advocating or teaching the doctrines of criminal syndicalism as defined in NRS 203.160, such an assemblage is unlawful, and every person voluntarily participating therein by his presence, aid or instigation is guilty of a felony, and upon conviction shall be punished by imprisonment in the State prison for not more than 10 years, or by a fine of not more than $5,000, or by both fine and imprisonment.

Id. § 203.190. *Permitting premises to be used to advocate criminal syndicalism.*—The owner, agent, superintendent, janitor, caretaker or occupant of any place, building or room, who willfully and knowingly permits therein any assemblage of persons prohibited by the provisions of NRS 203.180, or who, after the notification that the premises are so used, permits such use to be continued, is guilty of a misdemeanor, and upon conviction shall be punished by imprisonment in the county jail for not more than 1 year, or by a fine of not more than $500, or by both fine and imprisonment.

LOYALTY OF STATE OFFICERS AND EMPLOYEES

1. ELECTIVE AND NONELECTIVE PERSONNEL

Nevada Constitution, Art. 15, § 2. *Loyalty oath required.*—Members of the legislature, and all officers, executive, judicial and ministerial, shall, before they enter upon the duties of their respective offices, take and subscribe to the following oath:

"I, _____, do solemnly [solemnly] swear (or affirm) that I will support, protect and defend the Constitution and Government of the United States, and the constitution and government of the State of Nevada, against all enemies, whether domestic or foreign, and that I will bear true faith, allegiance and loyalty to the same, any ordinance, resolution or law of any State notwithstanding, and that I will well and faithfully perform all the duties of the office of _____, on which I am about to enter; (if an oath) so help me God; (if an affirmation) under the pains and penalties of perjury."

Nevada Rev. Stat. § 282.020. *Loyalty oath required.*—Members of the legislature and all officers, executive, judicial and ministerial, shall, before they enter upon the duties of their respective offices, take and subscribe to the following oath:

"I, _____, do solemnly swear (or affirm) that I will support, protect and defend the Constitution and Government of the United States, and the constitution and government of the State of Nevada, against all enemies, whether domestic or foreign, and that I will bear true faith, allegiance and loyalty to the same, any ordinance, resolution or law of any State notwithstanding, and that I will well and faithfully perform all the duties of the office of _____, on which I am about to enter; (if an oath) so help me God; (if an affirmation) under the pains and penalties of perjury."

Id. § 281.330. *Advocating overthrow of government cause for dismissal.*—It shall be sufficient cause for the dismissal of any public employee when such public employee advocates or is a member of an organization which advocates overthrow of the Government of the United States or of the State by force, violence, or other unlawful means.

2. CIVIL DEFENSE PERSONNEL

Nevada Rev. Stat. § 414.150. *Loyalty oath required.*—1. No person shall be employed or associated in any capacity in any civil defense organization established under this chapter, who advocates or has advocated a change by force or violence in the constitutional form of the Government of the United States or in this State or the overthrow of any government in the United States by force or violence, or who has been convicted of or is under indictment or information charging any subversive act against the United States.

2. Each person who is appointed to serve in an organization for civil defense shall, before entering upon his duties, take an oath, in writing, before a person authorized to administer oaths in this State, which oath shall be substantially as follows:

I, _____, do solemnly swear (or affirm) that I will support and defend the Constitution of the United States and the constitution of the State of Nevada against all enemies, foreign and domestic; that I will bear true faith and allegiance to the same; that I take this obligation freely, without any mental reservation or purpose of evasion; and that I will well and faithfully discharge the duties upon which I am about to enter.

And I do further swear (or affirm) that I do not advocate, nor am I a member of any political party or organization that advocates the overthrow of the Government of the United States or of this State by force or violence; and that, during such time as I am a member of the (name of civil defense organization), I will not advocate nor become a member of any political party or organization that advocates the overthrow of the Government of the United States or of this State by force or violence.

TEACHERS' LOYALTY

Constitution, art. 11, § 5. *Establishment of schools; oath required.*—The legislature shall have power to establis [establish] normal schools, and such different grades of schools, from the primary department to the university, as in their discretion they may deem necessary, and all professors in said university and teachers in said schools of whatever grade, shall be required to take and subscribe to the oath as prescribed in Article Fifteenth of this constitution. No professor or teacher who fails to comply with the provisions of any law framed in accordance with the provisions of this section, shall be entitled to receive any portion of the public monies set apart for school purposes.

Id. art. 15, § 2. *Loyalty oath required.*—Members of the legislature, and all officers, executive, judicial, and ministerial, shall, before they enter upon the duties of their respective offices, take and subscribe to the following oath:

I, _____, do solemly [solemnly] swear (or affirm) that I will support, protect and defend the Constitution and Government of the United States, and the constitution and government of the State of Nevada, against all enemies, whether domestic or foreign, and that I will bear true faith, allegiance, and loyalty to the same, any ordinance, resolution, or law of any State notwithstanding, and that I will well and faithfully perform all the duties of the office of _____, on which I am about to enter; (if an oath) so help me God; (if an affirmation) under the pains and penalties of perjury.

Nevada Rev. Stat. § 282.020. *Loyalty oath required.*—Members of the legislature and all officers, executive, judicial, and ministerial, shall, before they enter upon the duties of their respective offices, take and subscribe to the following oath:

I, _____, do solemnly swear (or affirm) that I will support, protect, and defend the Constitution and Government of the United States, and the constitution and government of the State of Nevada, against all enemies, whether domestic or foreign, and that I will bear true faith, allegiance, and loyalty to the same, any ordinance, resolution, or law of any State notwithstanding, and that I will well and faithfully perform all the duties of the office of _____, on which I am about to enter; (if an oath) so help me God; (if an affirmation) under the pains and penalties of perjury.

Id. § 391.310. *Advocating overthrow of government cause for dismissal.*—It shall be sufficient cause for the dismissal of any teacher in the public schools when such teacher advocates, or is a member of an organization which advocates, overthrow of the Government of the United States or of the State by force, violence, or other unlawful means.

Exclusion From the Bar

Supreme Court Rule 44 requires applicants for examination for license to practice law to give information regarding past or present membership in the Communist Party. It provides:

2. The application shall state:

(k) Whether or not the applicant is, or has ever been, a member of the Communist Party, or of any organization devoted to, or advocating support of, communism, giving full particulars.

Questions 47 and 48 of the application for admission to practice law in the State of Nevada relate to membership in the Communist Party. They read as follows:

47. Are you now or have you ever been, a member of the Communist Party, or of any organization devoted to, or advocating support of, communism?

48. If your answer to the preceding question is "Yes," give names of such organizations, dates of your membership, offices or positions held in said organizations, and the dates when you held the respective offices. Give also the addresses of the present headquarters of all such organizations in which you presently are a member, or officer, or in which you have been a member or officer, within the last five years.

Exclusion From Incidental Benefits

Nevada Rev. Stat. § 393.0715. *Restrictions in connection with use of school property.*—1. No school property, buildings or grounds may be used to further any program or movement the purpose of which is to accomplish the overthrow of the Government of the United States or of any State by force, violence, or other unlawful means.

2. No board of trustees of any school district may grant the use of any school property, building, or grounds to any person or organization for any use in violation of this section.

3. Any violation of this section is a misdemeanor.

NEW HAMPSHIRE

1. ADVOCATING THE OVERTHROW OF THE GOVERNMENT BY FORCE

Rev. Stat. Anno. § 587:32. *Advocating force.*—No persons shall congregate, assemble, organize, or associate themselves together, for the purpose of advocating or encouraging, or when assembled, organized, or associated for any purpose shall advocate or encourage, or in any public or private place advocate or encourage by any act or in any manner, or bring into this State, prepare, produce, publish, distribute, or have in possession for distribution, any printed or written matter of any kind, including pictures, which so advocates, encourages, or favors the overthrow of, or change in the form of, the Government of the United States or this State or any subdivision thereof, or the interference with any public or private right by force, unlawful means, or act of violence.

Id. § 587:33. *Equity jurisdiction.*—The superior court shall have jurisdiction in equity, upon petition filed by the attorney-general or the county solicitor, to enjoin the bringing into this State, preparing, producing, publishing, distributing, or having in possession for distribution any of said printed or written matter of any kind, including pictures, and may enjoin the owner, occupant, or lessee of any building, structure, or premises whereon or wherein any such written or printed matter is prepared, produced, published, or stored, or where persons congregate or assemble for any of the purposes aforesaid, from continuing such use thereof, and the violation of any order issued by said court shall be contempt.

Id. § 587:36. *Penalty.*—Any person violating any of the provisions of the preceding section 32 or 34 shall be fined not more than $5,000, or imprisoned not more than 10 years, or both, and in addition all printed or written matter, including pictures, prohibited in section 32, shall be seized and destroyed in accordance with the provisions of chapter 617. RSA.

2. SUBVERSIVE ACTIVITIES

Rev. Stat. Anno. § 588:1. *"Organization," "Subversive organization," "Foreign subversive organization," "Foreign government," and "Subversive person" defined.*—For the purpose of this chapter "organization" means an organization, corporation, company, partnership, association, trust, foundation, fund, club, society, committee, political party, or any group of persons, whether or not incorporated, permanently or temporarily associated together for joint action or advancement of views on any subject or subjects.

"Subversive organization" means any organization which engages in or advocates, abets, advises, or teaches, or a purpose of which is to engage in or advocate, abet, advise, or teach activities intended to over-

265

throw, destroy or alter, or to assist in the overthrow, destruction or alteration of, the constitutional form of the Government of the United States, or of the State of New Hampshire, or of any political subdivision of either of them, by force, or violence.

"Foreign subversive organization" means any organization directed, dominated, or controlled directly or indirectly by a foreign government which engages in or advocates, abets, advises, or teaches, or a purpose of which is to engage in or to advocate, abet, advise, or teach, activities intended to overthrow, destroy or alter, or to assist in the overthrow, destruction or alteration of the constitutional form of Government of the United States, or of the State of New Hampshire, or of any political subdivision of either of them, and to establish in place thereof any form of government the direction and control of which is to be vested in, or exercised by or under, the domination or control of any foreign government, organization, or individual; but does not and shall not be construed to mean an organization the *bona fide* purpose of which is to promote world peace by alliances or unions with other governments or world federations, unions, or governments to be effected through constitutional means.

"Foreign government" means the government of any country or nation other than the Government of the United States of America or of one of the States thereof.

"Subversive person" means any person who commits, attempts to commit, or aids in the commission, or advocates, abets, advises, or teaches, by any means any person to commit, attempt to commit, or aid in the commission of any act intended to overthrow, destroy or alter, or to assist in the overthrow, destruction or alteration of, the constitutional form of the Government of the United States, or of the State of New Hampshire, or any political subdivision of either of them, by force, or violence; or who is a member of a subversive organization or a foreign subversive organization.

Id. § 588:2. *Unlawful acts and penalty.*—It shall be a felony for any person knowingly and willfully to:

(a) commit, attempt to commit, or aid in the commission of any act intended to overthrow, destroy, or alter, or to assist in the overthrow, destruction, or alteration of, the constitutional form of the Government of the United States, or of the State of New Hampshire, or any political subdivision of either of them, by force or violence; or

(b) advocate, abet, advise, or teach by any means any persons to commit, attempt to commit, or assist in the commission of any such act under such circumstances as to constitute a clear and present danger to the security of the United States, or of the State of New Hampshire or of any political subdivision of either of them; or

(c) conspire with one or more persons to commit any such act; or

(d) assist in the formation or participate in the management or to contribute to the support of any subversive organization or foreign subversive organization knowing said organization to be a subversive organization or a foreign subversive organization; or

(e) destroy any books, records or files, or secrete any funds in this State of a subversive organization or a foreign subversive organization, knowing said organization to be such.

Any person who shall be convicted by a court of competent jurisdiction of violating any of the provisions of this section shall be fined not more than $20,000, or imprisoned for not more than 20 years, or both, at the discretion of the court.

Id. § 588:3. *Membership in subversive organization or foreign subversive organization unlawful.*—It shall be a felony for any person after August 1, 1951, to become, or after November 1, 1951, to remain a member of a subversive organization or a foreign subversive organization knowing said organization to be a subversive organization or foreign subversive organization. Any person who shall be convicted by a court of competent jurisdiction of violating this section shall be fined not more than $5,000 or imprisoned for not more than 5 years, or both, at the discretion of the court.

Id. § 588:3-a (Supp. 1963). *Evidence of membership or participation in a subversive organization.*—In determining membership or participation in a subversive organization or a foreign subversive organization as defined in this chapter, or knowledge of the purpose or objective of such organization, the jury, under instructions from the court, may consider evidence, if presented, as to whether the accused person to his knowledge: (1) has been listed as a member in any book or any of the lists, records, correspondence, or any other document of the organization;

(2) Has made financial contribution to the organization in dues, assessments, loans, or in any other form;

(3) Has made himself subject to the discipline of the organization in any form whatsoever;

(4) Has executed orders, plans, or directives of any kind of the organization;

(5) Has acted as an agent, courier, messenger, correspondent, organizer, or in any other capacity in behalf of the organization;

(6) Has conferred with officers or other members of the organization in behalf of any plan or enterprise of the organization;

(7) Has been accepted as an officer or member of the organization or as one to be called upon for services by other officers or members of the organization;

(8) Has written, spoken, or in any other way communicated by signal, semaphore, sign, or in any other form of communication orders, directives, or plan of the organization;

(9) Has prepared documents, pamphlets, leaflets, books, or any other type of publication in behalf of the objectives and purposes of the organization;

(10) Has mailed, shipped, circulated, distributed, delivered, or in any other way sent or delivered to others material or propaganda of any kind in behalf of the organization;

(11) Has advised, counseled or in any other way imparted information, suggestions, recommendations to officers or members of the organization or to anyone else in behalf of the objectives of the organization;

(12) Has indicated by word, action, conduct, writing or in any other way a willingness to carry out in any manner and to any degree the plans, designs, objectives, or purposes of the organization;

(13) Has in any other way participated in the activities, planning, actions, objectives, or purposes of the organization;

(14) The enumeration of the above subjects of evidence on membership or participation in a subversive organization or a foreign subversive organization as above defined, shall not limit the inquiry into

and consideration of any other subject of evidence on membership and participation as herein stated.

Id. § 588:3–b (Supp. 1963). *Construction of section.*—Nothing in the preceding section shall be construed to limit the supervisory power of the court over the admission and exclusion of evidence or over the sufficiency of the evidence as a whole.

Id. § 588:4. *Additional penalty.*—Any person who shall be convicted by a court of competent jurisdiction of violating any of the provisions of sections 2 and 3 of this chapter, in addition to all other penalties therein provided, shall from the date of such conviction be barred from

(a) Holding any office, elective or appointive, or any other position of profit or trust in or employment by the government of the State of New Hampshire or of any agency thereof or of any county, municipal corporation or other political subdivision of said State;

(b) Filing or standing for election to any public office in the State of New Hampshire.

Id. § 588:5. *Subversive organization and foreign subversive organization unlawful.*—It shall be unlawful for any subversive organization or foreign subversive organization to exist or function in the State of New Hampshire and any organization which by a court of competent jurisdiction is found to have violated the provisions of this section shall be dissolved, and if it be a corporation organized and existing under the laws of the State of New Hampshire, a finding by a court of competent jurisdiction that it has violated the provisions of this section shall constitute legal cause for forfeiture of its charter and its charter shall be forfeited, and all funds, books, records, and files of every kind and all other property of any organization found to have violated the provisions of this section shall be seized by and for the State of New Hampshire, the funds to be deposited in the State treasury and the books, records, files, and other property to be turned over to the attorney general of New Hampshire.

Id. § 588:6. *Assistance in collection of evidence.*—For the collection of any evidence and information referred to in this chapter, the attorney general is hereby directed to call upon the superintendent of State police, and county and municipal police authorities of the State to furnish him such assistance as may from time to time be required. Such police authorities are directed to furnish information and assistance as may be from time to time so requested. The attorney general may testify before any grand jury as to matters referred to in this chapter as to which he may have information.

Id. § 588:7. *Records keeping; restriction on use.*—The attorney general shall maintain complete records of all information received by him and all matters handled by him under the requirements of this chapter. Such records as may reflect on the loyalty of any resident of this State shall not be made public nor divulged to any person except with the permission of the attorney general to effectuate the purposes hereof.

Id. § 588:8 (Supp. 1963). *Grand jury investigation.*—The superior court, when in its discretion it appears appropriate, or when informed by the attorney general that there is information or evidence of the character described in section 2 of this chapter to be con-

sidered by the grand jury, shall charge the grand jury to inquire into violations of this chapter for the purpose of proper action.
Id. § 588:8–a (Supp. 1963). *Investigation by attorney general.*—
At any time when the attorney general has information which he deems reasonable or reliable relating to violations of the provisions of this chapter he shall make full and complete investigation thereof and shall report to the general court the results of this investigation, together with his recommendations, if any, for legislation. In any investigation hereunder the attorney general or any duly authorized member of his staff is authorized to require by subpena or otherwise the attendance of such witnesses and the production of such correspondence, books, papers, and documents and to administer such oaths, and to take such testimony and to make such expenditures within the funds provided as he deems advisable. The provisions of section 7 of this chapter shall be inapplicable to the investigation provided for herein and the attorney general is hereby authorized to make public such information received by him, testimony given before him, and matters handled by him as he deems fit to effectuate the purposes hereof.

Id. § 588:17 (Supp. 1963). *Privilege against self-incrimination.*—
No witness summoned by the attorney general in the course of the investigation of subversive activities as provided in chapter 307 of the Laws of 1953 as amended by chapter 197, Laws of 1955, or as provided in RSA 588, shall be excused from giving his testimony or producing documentary evidence upon the ground that such testimony or documentary evidence could tend to incriminate him provided that upon claim of privilege against self-incrimination, on relation of the attorney general, any justice of the superior court has adjudged the testimony of such witness or the production of such evidence to be necessary in the public interest confirmed by such justice in a written communication to the witness which shall be made a part of the record of the hearing, case, or proceeding in which such testimony or evidence is given. But no such witness shall be prosecuted or subjected to any penalty or forfeiture for or on account of any transaction, matter, or thing concerning which he is compelled, after having claimed his privilege against self-incrimination, to testify or produce evidence, documentary or otherwise and no testimony so given by him shall in any prosecution be used as evidence, either directly or indirectly, against him nor shall he thereafter be prosecuted for any offense so disclosed by him.

Id. § 588:18 (Supp. 1963). *Limitation.*—No witness shall be exempt under any provision hereof from prosecution for perjury or contempt committed while giving testimony or producing evidence under compulsion as provided for herein.

Id. § 588:19 (Supp. 1963). *Federal immunity.*—Should Federal law subsequently permit a grant of concurrent Federal immunity the attorney general is directed to request such concurrent Federal immunity in the case of each witness about to be compelled to testify by authority of this act.

Annotations:

Sweezy v. *New Hampshire,* 354 U.S. 234, 77 S. Ct. 1203, 1 L. Ed. 2d 1311 (1954). Appellant was convicted for contempt for refusing to answer questions during a legislative investigation. The investigation was conducted pursuant to a State statute which, in effect, made the State's attorney general a one-man legislative committee to investigate subversive activities. Petitioner appeared twice before the attorney general and was generally cooperative despite his claims that some of the questions posed were unconstitutional. He refused, however, to answer any questions about the Progressive Party or various lectures he had given at the University of New Hampshire. As prescribed by statute, the attorney general petitioned the State court which, after argument, ruled that the questions were pertinent, propounded them to appellant, and when he again refused to answer, ordered him committed to the county jail until purged of the contempt. The State supreme court affirmed. The Supreme Court reversed on the ground that there was nothing to indicate that the State legislature wanted the information the attorney general had sought, and, absent such a legislative desire, "the use of the contempt power, notwithstanding the interference with constitutional rights, was not in accordance with the due process requirements of the Fourteenth Amendment."

Uphaus v. *Wyman*, 360 U.S. 72, 79 S. Ct. 1040, 3 L. Ed. 2d 109 (1959) rehearing denied, 361 U.S. 856, 80 S. Ct. 40, L. Ed. 2d 95. Appellant, officer of an organization which operated a summer camp in New Hampshire, was judged guilty of civil contempt for refusing to answer questions in the course of a State legislative investigation of subversive activities. Although he testified about his own activities, he refused to comply with two subpoenas *duces tecum* ordering him to produce lists of the guests at the summer camp. Appellant contended that by the Smith Act Congress had so completely occupied the field of subversive activities that the States were without power to investigate in that area; that due process precluded enforcement of the subpoenas because the resolution under which the attorney general was authorized to operate was vague, and because the documents were not relevant to the inquiry; that enforcement would violate his rights of free speech and association. The judgment of the State court ordering appellant to jail until he complied with the subpoenas calling for production of the guests lists was affirmed by the Supreme Court. The Court held that *Pennsylvania* v. *Nelson*, 350 U.S. 497, 76 S. Ct. 477, 100 L. Ed. 777 (1956) had not preempted State prosecutions for sedition against itself. "All the [Nelson] opinion proscribed," the Court declared, "was a race between Federal and State prosecutions to the courthouse door." With respect to the due process arguments, the Court found that the attorney general had valid reasons for believing that the guests at the summer camp might be subversive and the subpoenas were therefore directed toward a proper legislative purpose, i.e., the security of the State.

Wyman v. *De Gregory*, 103 N.H. 214, 169 A. 2d 1 (1961). This case arose out of defendant's refusal to answer questions regarding his membership in the Communist Party during a legislative investigation conducted by the attorney general. The court overruled defendant's exceptions to the lower court's order committing him to confinement for contempt. It held, *inter alia*, that the provision authorizing the attorney general to make an investigation when he had information which he deemed reasonable or reliable relating to a violation of the statute did not require that there must be a violation before the legislative investigation could begin. The question whether defendant was a member of the Communist Party was held to be one proper and pertinent to the inquiry. Insofar as the wisdom of authorizing such investigations was concerned, the court declared this to be a matter for legislative rather than judicial determination. *Kahn* v. *Wyman*, 100 N.H. 245, 123 A. 2d 166 (1956). Plaintiff had been ordered by defendant, the State attorney general, to appear before him in his investigation of subversive activities. Plaintiff then instituted this action seeking to halt the investigation on grounds that the field of prosecution and investigation of subversive activities was now exclusively occupied by the Federal authorities. The court dismissed the petition holding that the decision of the Supreme Court in *Pennsylvania* v. *Nelson* 350 U.S. 497, 76 S. Ct. 477, 100 L. Ed. 777 (1956), precluding a State from prosecuting sedition and subversive activities against the United States, did not preclude a State legislature from investigating subversive activities within the State.

Nelson v. *Wyman*, 99 N.H. 33, 105 A. 2d 756 (1954). This case involved a petition for a judgment declaring unconstitutional the Subversive Activities Act and the joint resolution directing the State attorney general to investigate subversive activities and for an order relieving plaintiff from complying with a subpoena directing her appearance before such an investigation. The lower court dismissed plaintiff's petition and ordered her to either answer or invoke her constitutional privilege against self-incrimination. The Supreme Court of New Hampshire upheld the constitutionality of the legislation and dismissed the case. In the course of its opinion the court declared: (1) that the legislature had broad and extensive powers to investigate and to inquire particularly with respect to the preservation of the State; (2) that it was of little importance that the resolution failed to specify in explicit terms the use to which the legislature intended to put the information gained since it related to a subject matter into which the legislature had authority to inquire; (3) that the fact that the resolution required an investigation with respect to violations of law as well as a determination of whether subversive persons as defined in the act were presently located within the State did not remove the inquiry from the category of a legislative investigation; (4) that no basis existed for denying to the legislature the power to investigate the effectiveness of its enactment even though, as an incident to that general investigation, it may be necessary to inquire as to whether a particular person had violated the act; (5) that the legislature's choice of the attorney general as its investigating committee instead of its own members or a special board or commission, was proper and did not transform the inquiry into executive action; (6) that the fact that the resolution authorized the attorney general to commence criminal prosecution whenever evidence presented to him in the course of an investigation indicated a violation thereof, did not derrogate from the legislative purpose which was to seek information; (7) that inquiries concerning the commission of acts of unlawful advocacy and membership in subversive organizations were not a part of an unauthorized general inquiry into subversive activities but were pertinent to the main object of the investigation and fell within the authority granted by the resolution; (8) that in the judgment of the legislature, the interest of the State in acquiring information concerning subversion justified the intrusion upon any right of privacy which the plaintiff may have as a judicially determined incident to other rights guaranteed to her by the State and Federal Constitutions; (9) that the broad authority given by the resolution under which even persons who are suspected of violating the criminal provisions of the act may be required to appear as a witness is not improper; (10) that there was no impropriety in permitting the attorney general under powers delegated by the legislature, to question the plaintiff concerning activities violative of the act which are the subject matter of this legislative investigation simply because she is liable to prosecution by him in his executive capacity if she has violated the law; (11) that the grant of authority to publicize information or testimony previously given and deemed fit by the attorney general to effectuate the purposes of the resolution did not violate any constitutional privilege and, that plaintiff's rights were protected by invocation of her fifth amendment privilege; (12) that the enactment of the Smith Act which defines and penalizes sedition and subversive activities against the Governments of the United States, the States or any of their subdivisions, did not preclude State legislation on the same subject matter.

EXCLUSION FROM THE ELECTIVE PROCESS

Rev. Stat. Anno. § 588:2. *Unlawful acts and penalty.*—It shall be a felony for any person knowingly and willfully to—

(a) commit, attempt to commit, or aid in the commission of any act intended to overthrow, destroy, or alter, or to assist in the overthrow, destruction, or alteration of, the constitutional form of the Government of the United States, or of the State of New Hampshire, or any political subdivision of either of them, by force or violence; or

(b) advocate, abet, advise, or teach by any means any person to commit, attempt to commit, or assist in the commission of any such act under such circumstances as to constitute a clear and present danger to the security of the United States, or of the State of New Hampshire or of any political subdivision of either of them; or

(c) conspire with one or more persons to commit any such act; or

(d) assist in the formation or participate in the management or to contribute to the support of any subversive organization or foreign subversive organization knowing said organization to be a subversive organization or a foreign subversive organization; or

(e) destroy any books, records, or files, or secrete any funds in this State of a subversive organization or a foreign subversive organization, knowing said organization to be such.

Any person who shall be convicted by a court of competent jurisdiction of violating any of the provisions of this section shall be fined not more than twenty thousand dollars, or imprisoned for not more than twenty years, or both, at the discretion of the court.

Id. § 588:3. *Membership in subversive organization or foreign subversive organization unlawful.*—It shall be a felony for any person after August 1, 1951, to become, or after November 1, 1951, to remain a member of a subversive organization or a foreign subversive organization knowing said organization to be a subversive organization or foreign subversive organization. Any person who shall be convicted by a court of competent jurisdiction of violating this section shall be fined not more than five thousand dollars, or imprisoned for not more than five years, or both, at the discretion of the court.

Id. § 588:4. *Persons convicted of subversive activities barred from ballot.*—Any person who shall be convicted by a court of competent jurisdiction of violating any of the provisions of sections 2 and 3 of this chapter, in addition to all other penalties therein provided shall, from the date of such conviction, be barred from

(a) holding any office, elective or appointive, or any other position of profit or trust in or employment by the government of the State of New Hampshire or of any agency thereof or of any county, municipal corporation, or other political subdivision of said State;

(b) filing or standing for election to any public office in the State of New Hampshire.

Id. § 588:5. *Subversive organizations and foreign subversive organizations unlawful.*—It shall be unlawful for any subversive organization or foreign subversive organization to exist or function in the State of New Hampshire and any organization which by a court of competent jurisdiction is found to have violated the provisions of this section shall be dissolved, and if it be a corporation organized and existing under the laws of the State of New Hampshire, a finding by a court of competent jurisdiction that it has violated the provisions of this section shall constitute legal cause for forfeiture of its charter and its charter shall be forfeited, and all funds, books, records, and files of every kind and all other property of any organization found to have violated the provisions of this section shall be seized by and for the State of New Hampshire, the funds to be deposited in the State treasury and the books, records, files, and other property to be turned over to the attorney general of New Hampshire.

Id. § 588:14. *Candidates required to execute nonsubversive affidavit.*—No person shall become a candidate for election to, nor qualify for, any public office under the election laws of this State unless he or she shall file with the declaration of candidacy, or prior to qualifying, an affidavit that he or she is not a subversive person as defined in this chapter. No declaration of candidacy shall be received for filing by any town or city clerk or by the secretary of state unless accompanied by the affidavit aforesaid and there shall not be entered upon any ballot or voting machine at any election the name of the person who has failed or refused to make the affidavit aforesaid.

LOYALTY OF STATE OFFICERS AND EMPLOYEES

1. ELECTIVE AND NONELECTIVE PERSONNEL

New Hampshire Constitution, pt. II, Art. 84. *Oath.*—Any person chosen Governor, councilor, senator, or representative, military or civil officer (town officers excepted), accepting the trust, shall, before he proceeds to execute the duties of his office, make and subscribe the following declaration, viz—

I, A. B., do solemnly swear that I will bear faith and true allegiance to the State of New Hampshire and will support the constitution thereof. *So help me God.*

I, A. B., do solemnly and sincerely swear and affirm that I will faithfully and impartially discharge and perform all the duties incumbent on me as—, according to the best of my abilities, agreeably to the rules and regulations of this constitution and the laws of the State of New Hampshire, *So help me God.*

Any person having taken and subscribed the oath of allegiance, and the same being filed in the secretary's office, he shall not be obliged to take said oath again.

Provided always, when any person chosen or appointed as aforesaid, shall be of the denomination called Quakers, or shall be scrupulous of swearing, and shall decline taking the said oaths, such [person] shall take and subscribe them, omitting the word "*swear*," and likewise the words "*So help me God,*" subjoining instead thereof, "*This I do under the pains and penalties of perjury.*"

Rev. Stat. Anno. § 588:2. *Unlawful acts and penalty.*—It shall be a felony for any person knowingly and willfully to

(a) commit, attempt to commit, or aid in the commission of any act intended to overthrow, destroy, or alter, or to assist in the overthrow, destruction, or alteration of, the constitutional form of the Government of the United States, or of the State of New Hampshire, or any political subdivision of either of them, by force or violence; or

(b) advocate, abet, advise, or teach by any means any person to commit, attempt to commit, or assist in the commission of any such act under such circumstances as to constitute a clear and present danger to the security of the United States, or of the State of New Hampshire, or of any political subdivision of either of them; or

(c) conspire with one or more persons to commit any such act; or

(d) assist in the formation or participate in the management or to contribute to the support of any subversive organization or foreign subversive organization knowing said organization to be a subversive organization or a foreign subversive organization; or

(e) destroy any books, records, or files, or secrete any funds in this State of a subversive organization or a foreign subversive organization, knowing said organization to be such.

Any person who shall be convicted by a court of competent jurisdiction of violating any of the provisions of this section shall be fined not more than twenty thousand dollars, or imprisoned for not more than twenty years, or both, at the discretion of the court.

Id. § 588:3. *Membership in subversive organization or foreign subversive organization unlawful.*—It shall be a felony for any person after August 1, 1951, to become, or after November 1, 1951, to remain a member of a subversive organization or a foreign subversive organization knowing said organization to be a subversive organization or foreign subversive organization. Any person who shall be convicted by a court of competent jurisdiction of violating this section shall be fined not more than five thousand dollars, or imprisoned for not more than five years, or both, at the discretion of the court.

Id. § 588:4. *Persons convicted of subversive activities barred from office.*—Any person who shall be convicted by a court of competent jurisdiction of violating any of the provisions of sections 2 and 3 of this chapter, in addition to all other penalties therein provided, shall from the date of such conviction be barred from

(a) holding any office, elective or appointive, or any other position of profit or trust in or employment by the government of the State of New Hampshire or of any agency thereof or of any county, municipal corporation, or other political subdivision of said State;

(b) filing or standing for election to any public office in the State of New Hampshire.

2. NONELECTIVE PERSONNEL.

Rev. Stat. Anno. § 588 : 9. *Subversive persons ineligible for public employment.*—No subversive person, as defined in this chapter, shall be eligible for employment in, or appointment to, any office or any position of trust or profit in the government of, or in the administration of the business of, this State, or of any county, municipality, or other political subdivision of this State.

Id. § 588 :10. *Appointment procedure; nonsubversive statement required.*—Every person and every board, commission, council, department, court, or other agency of the State of New Hampshire or any political subdivision thereof, who or which appoints or employs or supervises in any manner the appointment or employment of public officials or employees shall establish by rules, regulations, or otherwise, procedures designed to ascertain before any person, including teachers and other employees of any public educational institution in this State, is appointed or employed, that he or she, as the case may be, is not a subversive person, and that there are no reasonable grounds to believe such persons are subversive persons. In the event such reasonable grounds exist, he or she, as the case may be, shall not be appointed or employed. In securing any facts necessary to ascertain the information herein required, the applicant shall be required to sign a written statement containing answers to such inquiries as may be material, which statement shall contain notice that it is subject to the penalties of perjury.

Id. § 588 :11. *Exclusions from scope of law.*—The inquiries prescribed in section 10, other than the written statement to be executed by an applicant for employment, shall not be required as a prerequisite to the employment of any persons in the classification of laborers in any case in which the employing authority shall in his or its discretion determine, and by rule or regulation specify the reasons why, the nature of the work to be performed is such that employment of persons as to whom there may be reasonable grounds to believe that they are subversive persons as defined in this chapter will not be dangerous to the health of the citizens or the security of the Government of the United States, the State of New Hampshire, or any political subdivision thereof.

Id. § 588 :12. *Present employees; nonsubversive statement required.*—Every person, who on August 1, 1951, shall be in the employ of the State of New Hampshire or of any political subdivision thereof, other than those now holding elective office shall be required on or before October 1, 1951, to make a written statement which shall contain notice that it is subject to the penalties of perjury, that he or she is not a subversive person as defined in this chapter; namely, any person who commits, attempts to commit, or aids in the commission, or advocates, abets, advises or teaches by any means any person to commit, attempt to commit, or aid in the commission of any act intended to overthrow, destroy or alter, or to assist in the overthrow, destruction or alteration of, the constitutional form of the Government of the United States, or of the State of New Hampshire, or any political subdivision of either of them, by force, or violence; or who is a member of a subversive organization or a foreign subversive organization, as more fully defined in this chapter. Such statement shall be prepared and execution required by every person and every board, commission, council, department, court, or other agency of the State of New Hampshire or any political subdivision thereof responsible for the supervision of employees under its jurisdiction. Any such person failing or refusing to execute such a statement or who admits he is a subversive person as defined in this chapter shall immediately be discharged.

Id. § 588:13. *Dismissal of subversive persons.*—Reasonable grounds on all the evidence to believe that any person is a subversive person, as defined in this chapter shall be cause for discharge from any appointive office or other position of profit or trust in the government of or in the administration of the business of this State, or of any county, municipality or other political subdivision of this State, or any agency thereof. The personnel commission shall, by appropriate rules or regulations, prescribe that persons charged with being subversive persons, as defined in this chapter, shall be accorded notice and opportunity to be heard, in accordance with the procedures prescribed by law for discharges for other reasons. Every person and every board, commission, council, department, or other agency of the State of New Hampshire or any political subdivision thereof having responsibility for the appointment, employment or supervision of public employees not covered by the State classified service shall establish rules or procedures similar to those required herein for classified services for a hearing for any person charged with being a subversive person, as defined in this chapter after notice and opportunity to be heard. Every employing authority discharging any person pursuant to any provision of this chapter shall promptly report to the attorney general the fact of and the circumstances surrounding such discharge. A person discharged under the provisions of this section shall have the right within thirty days thereafter to appeal to the superior court of the county where such person may reside for a determination by such court (with the aid of a jury if the appellant so elects) as to whether or not the discharge appealed from was justified under the provisions of this act. The court shall speedily hear and determine such appeals, and from the judgment of the court, there shall be a further appeal to the Supreme Court of New Hampshire as in civil cases.

Id. § 588:15. *Penalty.*—Every written statement made pursuant to this chapter by an applicant for appointment or employment, or by any employee shall be deemed to have been made under oath if it contains a declaration preceding the signature of the maker to the effect that it is made under the penalties of perjury. Any person who makes a material misstatement of fact (a) in any such written statement, or (b) in any affidavit made pursuant to the provisions of this chapter, or (c) under oath in any hearing conducted by any agency of the State, or of any of its political subdivisions, pursuant to this chapter, or (d) in any written statement by an applicant for appointment or employment or by an employee in any State aid institution of learning in this State, intended to determine whether or not such applicant or employee is a subversive person as defined in this chapter, which statement contains notice that it is subject to the penalties of perjury shall be subject to the penalties of perjury prescribed in chapter 587, RSA.

3. CIVIL DEFENSE PERSONNEL

Rev. Stat. Anno. § 107:17. *Loyalty oath required.*—No person shall be employed or associated in any capacity in any civil defense organization established hereunder who advocates or has advocated a change by force or violence in the constitutional form of the Government of the United States or in this State or the overthrow of any government in the United States by force and violence, or who has been convicted of or is under indictment or information charging any subversive act against the United States. Each person who is appointed to serve in an organization for civil defense shall, before entering upon his duties, take an oath, in writing, before a person authorized to administer oaths in this State, which oath shall be as follows:

"I, ___, do solemnly swear (or affirm) that I will support and defend the Constitution of the United States, and the constitution of the State of New Hampshire, against all enemies, foreign and domestic; that I will bear true faith and allegiance to the same; that I take this oath freely, without any mental reservation or purpose of evasion; and that I will well and faithfully discharge the duties upon which I am about to enter. And I do further swear (or affirm) that I do not advocate, nor am I a member of any political party or organization that advocates the overthrow of the Government of the United States or of the State of New Hampshire by force or violence; and that during such time as I am a member of the State Civil Defense Agency, I will not advocate nor become a member of any political party or organization that advocates the overthrow of the Government of the United States or of the State of New Hampshire by force or violence."

For the purposes of administering the foregoing loyalty oath, the State director of civil defense and such local and State civil defense officials as may be designated by him in writing are authorized to administer said oath in this State to persons appointed to serve in any organization for civil defense.

TEACHERS' LOYALTY

Rev. Stat. Anno. § 191:1. *Advocating subversive doctrines prohibited.*—No teacher shall advocate communism as a political doctrine or any other doctrine which includes the overthrow by force of the Government of the United States or of this State in any public or State-approved school or in any State institution.

Id. § 191:2. *Loyalty oath required.*—All persons engaged directly or indirectly in teaching in public or State approved schools or in any State institution shall take an oath in writing before a person authorized to administer oaths in this State and this oath shall be as follows:

"I _____, do solemnly swear (or affirm) that I will support and defend the Constitution of the United States and the constitution of the State of New Hampshire against all enemies, foreign and domestic; that I will bear true faith and allegiance to the same; that I take this obligation freely, without any mental reservation or purpose of evasion; and that I will well and faithfully discharge the duties upon which I am about to enter.

"And I do further swear (or affirm) that I do not advocate, nor am I a member of any political party or organization which advocates the overthrow of the Government of the United States or of this State by force or violence; and that during such time as I am a teacher in any school or institution in New Hampshire, I will not advocate nor become a member of any political party or organization which advocates the overthrow of the Government of the United States or of this State by force or violence."

Id. § 191 : 3. *Penalty.*—Any teacher as defined in section 1 who refuses to take the oath prescribed in section 2 or who violates said oath after taking the same shall forthwith be dismissed from his position as a teacher and shall no longer be eligible for any position connected with teaching in this State.

Id. § :19 :4. *Enforcement.*—It shall be the duty of the attorney general to administer the provisions of this chapter, so that the oaths required hereunder are taken and provide for the dismissal of those ineligible to teach as provided in section 3.

Id. § 191 :5. *Exclusions from scope of law.*—The provisions of sections 2 and 3 of this chapter shall not apply to *bona fide* exchange professors or teachers who are not citizens of the United States provided that they declare their citizenship and nationality.

Id. § 588 :9. *Subversive persons ineligible for public employment.*— No subversive person, as defined in this chapter, shall be eligible for employment in, or appointment to any office or any position of trust or profit in the government of, or in the administration of the business of this State, or of any county, municipality, or other political subdivision of this State.

Id. § 588 :10. *Appointment procedure; nonsubversive statement required.*—Every person and every board, commission, council, department, court, or other agency of the State of New Hampshire or any political subdivision thereof, who or which appoints or employs or supervises in any manner the appointment or employment of public officials or employees shall establish by rules, regulations, or otherwise, procedures designed to ascertain before any person, including teachers and other employees of any public educational institution in this State, is appointed or employed, that he or she as the case may be, is not a subversive person, and that there are no reasonable grounds to believe such persons are subversive persons. In the event such reasonable grounds exist, he or she as the case may be, shall not be appointed or employed. In securing any facts necessary to ascertain the information herein required, the applicant shall be required to sign a written statement containing answers to such inquiries as may be material, which statement shall contain notice that it is subject to the penalties of perjury.

Id. § 588 :15. *Penalty.*—Every written statement made pursuant to this chapter by an applicant for appointment or employment, or by any employee shall be deemed to have been made under oath if it contains a declaration preceding the signature of the maker to the effect that it is made under the penalties of perjury. Any person who makes a material misstatment of fact (a) in any such written statement, or (b) in any affidavit made pursuant to the provisions of this chapter, or (c) under oath in any hearing conducted by any agency of the State, or of any of its political subdivisions, pursuant to this chapter, or (d) in any written statement by an applicant for appointment or employment or by an employee in any State aid institution of learning in this

State, intended to determine whether or not such applicant or employee is a subversive person as defined in this chapter, which statement contains notice that it is subject to the penalties of perjury shall be subject to the penalties of perjury prescribed in chapter 587, RSA.

EXCLUSION FROM THE BAR

New Hampshire has no provision dealing with the admission of Communists and other subversive persons and the question "has never arisen or been passed upon."

NEW JERSEY

Unlawful Advocacy

1. ANARCHY

New Jersey Stat. Anno. § 2A:148-7. *Advocating anarchy.*—Any person who, in public or private, by speech, writing, printing or otherwise, advocates the subversion or destruction by force of any and all government, or attempts by speech, writing, printing or otherwise to incite or abet, promote or encourage hostility or opposition to any and all government, is guilty of a high misdemeanor and shall be punished by a fine of not more than $5,000, or by imprisonment for not more than 15 years, or both.

Id. § 2A:148-8. *Membership in anarchistic society unlawful.*—Any person who becomes a member of, or attends or counsels or solicits any other person to attend a meeting or council of, an organization, society or order organized or formed for the purpose of inciting, abetting, promoting or encouraging hostility or opposition to, or the subversion or destruction by force of any and all government, or who in any manner aids, abets or encourages any such organization, society, order, council or meeting in the propagation or advocacy or such a purpose, is guilty of a high misdemeanor, and shall be punished by a fine of not more than $5,000, or by imprisonment for not more than 15 years, or both.

Id. § 2A:148-9. *Circulating printed matter promoting anarchy.*— If any person, organization, society or order brings, introduces or circulates, or aids, assists or is instrumental in bringing, introducing or circulating within this State any printed or written paper, pamphlet, book or circular with intent to incite, promote or encourage hostility or opposition to, or the subversion or destruction of any and all government, such person or the members of such organization, society or order in any way responsible therefor, shall be guilty of a high misdemeanor and punished by a fine of not more than $5,000, or by imprisonment for not more than 15 years, or both.

Annotation:

State v. *Scott*, 86 N.J.L. 133, 90 A. 235 (1915). Defendant was tried and convicted of the crime of anarchy for publishing a newspaper article strongly condemning the action of the police in suppressing a strike. The court reversed the conviction and held that the statute denouncing as anarchy hostility or opposition to "any and all government" did not apply to criticism, however scathing, of any political division of the State. "Such a construction," the court declared, "would render the act clearly unconstitutional" since it would prevent all free discussion relating to a change of political administrations.

281

2. SEDITION

New Jersey Stat. Anno. § 2A:148–12. *Inciting sedition; penalty.*—Any person who incites an insurrection or sedition among any portion or class of the population of this State, or attempts by writing, speaking, or otherwise, to incite such insurrection or sedition, is guilty of a high misdemeanor, and shall be punished by a fine of not more than $10,000, or by imprisonment for not more than 20 years, or both.

Id. § 2A:148–13. *Advocating subversion; penalty.*—Any person who advocates, in public or private, by speech, writing, printing, or otherwise, the subversion or destruction by force of the Government of the United States or of this State, or attempts by speech, writing, printing, or otherwise, to incite or abet, promote, or encourage the subversion or destruction by force of the Government of the United States or of this State, is guilty of a high misdemeanor, and shall be punished by a fine of not more than $5,000, or by imprisonment for not more than 10 years, or both.

Id. § 8A:148–14. *Membership in or attending meetings of subversive organization unlawful.*—Any person who becomes a member of, or attends or counsels or solicits any other person to attend a meeting or council of, an organization, society, or order organized or formed for the purpose of inciting, abetting, promoting, or encouraging the subversion or destruction by force of the Government of the United States or of this State, or who in any manner aids, abets or encourages any such organization, society or order, council or meeting in the propagation or advocacy of such a purpose, is guilty of a high misdemeanor and shall be punished by a fine of not more than $5,000, or by imprisonment for not more than 10 years, or both.

Id. § 2A:148–15. *Producing subversive books, etc., unlawful.*—Any person who prints, writes, multigraphs, or otherwise makes or produces, or by any means sets out and makes legible, in any language:

a. Any book, speech, article, circular, or pamphlet which in any way, in any part thereof, incites, counsels, promotes, advocates, or encourages the subversion or destruction by force of the Government of the United States or of this State; or

b. Any constitution, bylaws, rules, or record of the proceedings of any organization, association, society, order, club, or meeting of three or more persons, which in any way incites, counsels, promotes, advocates, or encourages the subversion or destruction by force of the Government of the United States or of this State; or

c. Any picture, photograph, emblem, representation, sign, or token which in any way incites, counsels, promotes, advocates, encourages, or symbolizes the subversion or destruction by force of the Government of the United States or of this State—

Is guilty of a high misdemeanor.

Id. § 2A:148–16. *Circulating or possessing subversive books, etc., unlawful.*—Any person who utters, sells, gives away, circulates, distributes, or exhibits to the view of another, or possesses with intent to utter, sell, give away, circulate, distribute, or exhibit to the view of another:

a. Any book, speech, article, circular, or pamphlet, made or produced in any manner or by any means set out and made legible, in any language, which in any way, in any part thereof, incites, counsels, promotes, advocates, or encourages the subversion or destruction by force of the Government of the United States or of this State; or

b. Any constitution, bylaws, rules, or record of the proceedings of any organization, association, society, order, club, or meeting of three or more persons, made or produced in any manner or by any means set out and made legible, in any language, which in any way, in any part thereof, incites, counsels, promotes, advocates or encourages the subversion or destruction by force of the Government of the United States or of this State; or

c. Any picture, photograph, emblem, representation, sign, or token, made or produced in any manner or by any means set out and made legible, which in any way incites, counsels, promotes, advocates, encourages, or symbolizes the subversion or destruction by force of the Government of the United States or of this State—

Is guilty of a high misdemeanor.

Id. § 2A:148–17. *Leasing, etc., premises to advocate subversion unlawful.*—Any owner, lessee, manager, agent, or other person, who knowingly lets or hires out any building, structure, auditorium, hall, or room, whether licensed or not, or any part thereof, to or for the use of any organization, association, society, order, club, or meeting of three or more persons, the constitution, bylaws, or rules of which in any way, or in any part thereof, incite, counsel, promote, advocate, or encourage the subversion or destruction by force of the Government of the United States or of this State, is guilty of a high misdemeanor.

Id. § 2A:148–18. *Hiring premises to advocate subversion unlawful.*—Any person who hires any building, structure, auditorium, hall, or room, whether licensed or not, or any part thereof, in the name of or for the use of any organization, association, society, order, club, or meeting of three or more persons, the constitution, bylaws, or rules of which in any way, or in any part thereof, incite, counsel, promote, advocate, or encourage the subversion or destruction by force of the Government of the United States or of this State, is guilty of a high misdemeanor.

Id. § 2A: 148–19. *Permitting premises to be used to advocate subversion unlawful.*—Any owner, lessee, manager, or other person in control of any building, structure, auditorium, hall, or room, whether licensed or not, or any part thereof, who, whether with or without a letting or a hiring for a consideration, knowingly suffers or permits any organization, association, society, order, club, or meeting of three or more persons, the constitution, bylaws, or rules of which in any way, or in any part thereof, incite, counsel, promote, advocate, or encourage the subversion or destruction by force of the Government of the United States or of this State, to occupy or to hold a meeting in said building, structure, auditorium, hall, or room, or any part thereof, is guilty of a high misdemeanor.

Annotations:

State v. *Tachin*, 92 N.J.L. 269, 106 A. 145 (1919), affirmed 93 N.J.L. 485, 108 A. 813, error dismissed 254 U.S. 662, 41 S. Ct. 61, 65 L. Ed. 463. Defendants were convicted of inciting, abetting, promoting, and encouraging hostility and opposition to the Government of the United States. The evidence against the defendants consisted of statements made by them at a public gathering to the effect that the war with Germany was for the benefit of capitalists, that the President at the behest of capitalists was sending American boys abroad to be slaughtered, that the American people did not need any Government and that the persons present at the gathering should arm themselves for protection against the Government. The court affirmed and held that it was perfectly proper for the State to punish for sedition directed against the Federal Government alone. It reasoned that "under our system the Federal and State Governments are so closely interwoven that an attack on the former may imperil the existence of the latter." As to the right of free speech, the court declared that it could not properly be construed to protect seditious utterances. Defendants' objection that the State failed to prove intent was without substance since criminal intent was not an element of the offense.

Colgan v. *Sullivan,* 94 N.J.L. 201, 109 A. 568 (1920). This case involved an action for malicious prosecution based upon actions by defendant charging plaintiff with sedition. The court affirmed a directed verdict for the defendant and held, *inter alia*, that a statement characterizing the chairman of a draft board (defendant) as a person who discriminated between persons of draft age was seditious in character.

State v. *Gabriel,* 95 N.J.L. 337, 112 A. 611 (1921). Defendant was charged with violating a State statute punishing the advocacy of subversion in public in that in responding to a committing magistrate's question, he stated that he believed in the revolutionary change of government if necessary. The court reversed the conviction holding that this was not advocating in public by speech within the meaning of the statute. A second charge—that defendant was a member of an organization encouraging opposition to the Government—was also dismissed. As to the latter, the court declared that under the Constitution and Bill of Rights the legislature could not make it a crime to belong to a party organized or formed for the purpose of encouraging hostility or opposition to the Government, unless the hostility or opposition included a purpose to overthrow or subvert the Government.

3. DEFENDING FOREIGN AUTHORITY

New Jersey Stat. Anno. § 2A:148–3. *Unlawful act defined.*—Any person owing allegiance to this State who, by speech, writing, open deed or act, advisedly and wittingly maintains and defends the authority or jurisdiction of a foreign power, potentate, republic, king, state or nation, in and over this State, or the people thereof, is guilty of a high misdemeanor.

EXCLUSION FROM THE ELECTIVE PROCESS

New Jersey Stat. Anno. § 19:13–8. *Acceptance of nomination to be accompanied by oath of allegiance.*—A candidate nominated for an office in a petition shall manifest his acceptance of such nomination by a written acceptance thereof, signed by his hand, upon or annexed to such petition, to which shall be annexed the oath of allegiance prescribed in section 41:1–1 of the Revised Statutes duly taken and subscribed by him before an officer authorized to take oaths in this State, or if the same person be named for the same office in more than one petition, annexed to one of such petitions. Such acceptance shall certify that the candidate is a resident of and a legal voter in the jurisdiction of the office for which the nomination is made. No candidate so named shall sign such acceptance if he has signed an acceptance for the primary nomination or any other petition of nomination under this chapter for such office.

Id. § 19:23–7. *Certificate of intent to execute oath of allegiance to accompany nominating petition.*—Each such petition shall set forth that the signers thereof are qualified voters of the State, congressional district, county, municipality, ward or election district, as the case may be, in which they reside and for which they desire to nominate candidates; that they are members of a political party (naming the same), and that at the last general election preceding the execution of the petition they voted for a majority of the candidates of such political party, and that they intend to affiliate with that political party at the ensuing election; that they endorse the person or persons named in their petition as candidate or candidates for nomination for the office or offices therein named, and that they request that the name of the person or persons therein mentioned be printed upon the official primary ballots of their political party as the candidate or candidates for such nomination. The petition shall further state the residence and post office address of each person so indorsed, and shall certify that the person or persons so indorsed is or are legally qualified under the laws of this State to be nominated, and is or are a member or members of the political party named in the petition.

Accompanying the petition each person indorsed therein shall file a certificate, stating that he is qualified for the office mentioned in the petition, that he is a member of the political party named therein; that he consents to stand as a candidate for nomination at the ensuing primary election of such political party, and that, if nominated, he consents to accept the nomination, to which shall be annexed the oath of allegiance prescribed in section 41:1–1 of the Revised Statutes duly taken and subscribed by him before an officer authorized to take oaths in this State.

Id. § 19:23–12. *Vacancy committee; certificate of oath of allegiance to accompany petition of substitute candidate.*—The signers to petitions for "Choice for President," delegates and alternates to national conventions, for Governor, United States Senator, Member of the House of Representatives, State Senator, member of the General Assembly, and any county office may name three persons in their petition as a committee on vacancies.

This committee shall have power in case of death or resignation or otherwise of the person indorsed as a candidate in said petition to fill such vacancy by filing with the Secretary of State in the case of officers to be voted for by the voters of the entire State or a portion thereof involving more than one county thereof or any congressional district, and with the county clerk in the case of officers to be voted for by the voters of the entire county, a certificate of nomination to fill the vacancy.

Such certificate shall set forth the cause of the vacancy, the name of the person nominated, and that he is a member of the same political party as the candidate for whom he is substituted, the office for which he is nominated, the name of the person for whom the new nominee is to be substituted, the fact that the committee is authorized to fill vacancies, and such further information as is required to be given in any original petition of nomination.

The certificate so made shall be executed and sworn to by the members of such committee and shall, upon being filed at least thirty-four days before election, have the same force and effect as the original petition of nomination for the primary election for the general election and there shall be annexed thereto the oath of allegiance prescribed in section 41:1–1 of the Revised Statutes duly taken and subscribed by the person so nominated before an officer authorized to take oaths in this State. The name of the candidate submitted shall be immediately certified to the proper municipal clerks.

Id. § 19:23–13. *Vacancy caused by death; oath of allegiance of substitute nominee.*—Should any person indorsed in any petition as as a candidate to be voted for at any primary election, except for the office of "Choice for President," delegates and alternates to national conventions, Governor, United States Senator, Member of the House of Representatives, State Senator, members of the General Assembly, and any county office, die within three days after the last day for filing such petition, or in writing filed within three days after the last day for filing such petition with the county clerk or municipal clerk with whom such petition had been filed, decline to stand as a candidate, the vacancy or vacancies thus caused shall be filled by a majority of the persons signing the petition in and by which the person so dying or declining was indorsed, filing within three days after the occurrence of the vacancy with the municipal clerk, a new petition, setting forth the name of the person dying or declining the office for which he was indorsed, and the name of the person to be substituted, to which shall be annexed the oath of allegiance prescribed in section 41:1–1 of the Revised Statutes duly taken and subscribed by the person so nominated before an officer authorized to take oaths in this State.

Such petition shall be verified by three of the signers, and shall have the same force and effect as the original petition.

Id. § 19:23–15. *Acceptance by candidate to be accompanied by oath of allegiance.*—Accompanying the petition and attached thereto each person indorsed therein shall file a certificate, stating that he is qualified for the office mentioned in the petition; that he consents to stand as a candidate for nomination at the ensuing primary election and that, if nominated, he agrees to accept the nomination. Such acceptance shall certify that the candidate is a resident of and a legal voter in the jurisdiction of the office for which the nomination is to be made and there shall be annexed thereto the oath of allegiance prescribed in section 41:1–1 of the Revised Statutes duly taken and subscribed by the person so nominated before an officer authorized to take oaths in this State.

No candidate who has accepted the nomination by a direct petition of nomination for the general election shall sign an acceptance to a petition of nomination for such office for the primary election.

Id. § 19:23–16 (Supp. 1963). *Acceptance by write-in candidate to be accompanied by oath of allegiance.*—Any person nominated at the primary by having his name written or pasted upon the primary ballot shall file a certificate stating that he is qualified for the office for which he has been nominated, that he is a resident of and a legal voter in the jurisdiction of the office for which the nomination is made, and that he consents to stand as a candidate at the ensuing general election to which shall be annexed the oath of allegiance prescribed in section 41:1–1 of the Revised Statutes duly taken and subscribed by the person so nominated before an officer authorized to take oaths in this State. Such acceptance shall be filed within seven days after the holding of the primary with the county clerk in the case of county and municipal offices and with the Secretary of State for all other offices.

Id. § 41:1–1. *Form of oath of allegiance.*—Every person who is or shall be required by law to give assurance of fidelity and attachment to the Government of this State shall take the following oath of allegiance:

"I, ------------------, do solemnly swear (or affirm) that I will support the Constitution of the United States and the constitution of the State of New Jersey, and that I will bear true faith and allegiance to the same and to the Governments established in the United States and in this State, under the authority of the people; and will defend them against all enemies, foreign and domestic; that I do not believe in, advocate, or advise the use of force, or violence, or other unlawful or unconstitutional means, to overthrow or make any change in the Government established in the United States or in this State; and that I am not a member of or affiliated with any organization, association, party, group or combination of persons, which approves, advocates, advises, or practices the use of force, or violence, or other unlawful or unconstitutional means, to overthrow or make any change in either of the Governments so established; and that I am not bound by any allegiance to any foreign prince, potentate, state, or sovereignty whatever. So help me God."

Annotation:

Imbrie v. *Marsh*, 3 N.J. 578, 71 A. 2d 352 (1950). This case involved an action by nominees of the Progressive Party for an injunction restraining State officers from printing the legend "refused oath of allegiance" under their names on the the ballot. Petitioners also requested a judgment declaring unconstitutional a State statute requiring every candidate for public office to file a loyalty oath. The Supreme Court of New Jersey affirmed the ruling of the lower court holding the statute unconstitutional on the ground that it added qualifications to those prescribed by the constitution. "When the constitution prescribes the manner in which an officer shall be appointed or elected, the constitutional prescription is exclusive, and it is not competent for the legislature to provide another mode of obtaining or holding office."

LOYALTY OF STATE OFFICERS AND EMPLOYEES

ELECTIVE AND NONELECTIVE PERSONNEL

New Jersey Stat. Anno. §41:1–1 (Supp. 1963). *Form of oath of allegiance.*—Every person who is or shall be required by law to give assurance of fidelity and attachment to the Government of this State shall take the following oath of allegiance:

"I, _____, do solemnly swear (or affirm) that I will support the Constitution of the United States and the constitution of the State of New Jersey, and that I will bear true faith and allegiance to the same and to the Governments established in the United States and in this State, under the authority of the people; and will defend them against all enemies, foreign and domestic; that I do not believe in, advocate or advise the use of force, or violence, or other unlawful or unconstitutional means, to overthrow or make any change in the Government established in the United States or in this State; and that I am not a member of or affiliated with any organization, association, party, group, or combination of persons, which approves, advocates, advises, or practices the use of force, or violence, or other unlawful or unconstitutional means, to overthrow or make any change in either of the Governments so established; and that I am not bound by any allegiance to any foreign prince, potentate, State, or sovereignty whatever. So help me God."

Id. § 41: 1-2. *Persons required to execute oath of allegiance.*—The Governor for the time being of this State, and every person who shall be appointed or elected to any office, legislative, executive, or judicial, under the authority of this State, or to any office in the militia thereof, and every counselor, solicitor, and attorney at law, shall, before he enters upon the execution of his trust, office, or duty, take and subscribe the oath of allegiance prescribed by section 41: 1-1 of this title.

Id. § 41:1-3 (Supp. 1963). *Additional oath.*—In addition to any official oath that may be specially prescribed, every person who shall be elected, appointed or employed to, or in, any public office, position or employment, legislative, executive or judicial, of, or in, any county, municipality, or special district other than a municipality therein, or of, or in, any department, board, commission, agency, or instrumentality thereof shall, before he enters upon the execution of his said office, position, employment or duty take and subscribe the oath of allegiance and office as follows:

"I, _____ do solemnly swear (or affirm) that I will support the Constitution of the United States and the constitution of the State of New Jersey, and that I will faithfully discharge the duties of _____ according to the best of my ability.

"I do further solemnly swear (or affirm) that I do not believe in, advocate or advise the use of force, or violence, or other unlawful or unconstitutional means, to overthrow or make any change in the Government established in the United States or in this State; and that I am not a member of or affiliated with any organization, association, party, group or combination of persons, which so approves, advocates or advises the use of such means. So help me God."

Annotations:

Op. Atty. Gen., June 12, 1953, No. 26. The statute requiring a loyalty oath remains operative and effective with respect to positions and employments as distinguished from offices, application to the last mentioned having been invalidated by *Imbrie* v. *Marsh*, 3 N.J. 578, 71 A., 2d, 353 (1950).

Op. Atty. Gen., June 15, 1949, No. 62. The oath of allegiance and office required of persons elected or appointed to certain public offices, positions or employments does not apply to any person who, before the effective date of the act, had already entered upon his duties.

TEACHERS' LOYALTY

New Jersey Stat. Anno., § 18:3–9.1 (Supp. 1963). *Persons applying for teacher's license required to take oath of allegiance.*—Every person, whose application is pending, or who hereafter applies for a license, or any renewal thereof, to teach or supervise in any of the public schools of this State shall subscribe to the oath of allegiance and office prescribed in section 41.1–3 of the Revised Statutes.

Such oath or affirmation shall be executed in duplicate and one copy thereof shall be filed with the county superintendent and by him transmitted to the commissioner and the other copy thereof shall be retained by the person subscribing to such oath or affirmation to be by him or her delivered to the board or body, person or persons, employing him or her within this State.

No certificate shall be issued unless such oath or affirmation shall have been filed.

The oath may be subscribed before any officer authorized by law to administer oaths and any county superintendent, president, secretary, or district clerk of a board of education of this State may administer the oath referred to in this section and sections 18:13–9.2 and in 18:13–9.3 of this title.

Id. § 18:13–9.2 (Supp. 1963). *Persons employed in State-aided institutions of higher education required to execute oath of allegiance—*Every professor, instructor, teacher, or person employed in any teaching capacity who shall be employed hereafter by, or in, any college, university, teachers college, or other school in this State which is supported in whole or in part by public funds, directly or through contract or otherwise with the State board of education, shall, before entering upon the discharge of his or her duties, susbcribe to the oath of allegiance and office prescribed in section 41:1–3 of the Revised Statutes, before an officer authorized by law to administer oaths. A copy of such oath shall be filed with the board or body, person or persons employing him or her within this State.

Id. § 18:13–9.3 (Supp. 1963). *Aliens employed in State-aided institutions of higher education required to execute oath of allegiance.*—Any person who is a citizen or subject of any country other than the United States, and who is employed, in any capacity, as a professor, instructor or teacher in any college, university, normal school, teachers college, or other school in this State which is supported in whole or in part by public funds shall, before entering upon the discharge of his duties, subscribe to an oath to support the institutions of the United States during the period of his employment within the State.

Id. § 41:1–3 (Supp. 1963). *Form of oath of allegiance.*—In addition to any official oath that may be specifically prescribed, every person who shall be elected, appointed or employed to, or in, any public office, position or employment, legislative, executive or judicial, of, or in, any county, municipality or special district other than a municipality therein, or of, or in, any department, board, commission, agency or instrumentality thereof shall, before he enters upon the execution of his said office, position, employment or duty take and subscribe the oath of allegiance and office as follows:

"I, _____, do solemnly swear (or affirm) that I will support the Constitution of the United States and the constitution of the State of New Jersey, and that I will faithfully discharge the duties of _____ according to the best of my ability.

"I do further solemnly swear (or affirm) that I do not believe in, advocate or advise the use of force, or violence, or other unlawful or unconstitutional means, to overthrow or make any change in the government established in the United States or in this State; and that I am not a member of or affiliated with any organization, association, party, group or combination of persons, which so approves, advocates or advises the use of such means. So help me God."

Annotations:

Laba v. *Newark Board of Education*, 23 N.J. 364, 129 A. 2d 273 (1957). In this case three school teachers were dismissed after they had pleaded the fifth amendment during a hearing before a subcommittee of the House Un-American Activities Committee. The State commissioner of education determined that the dismissals were contrary to the ruling in the *Slochower* case and remanded the proceedings to enable a full and fair inquiry as to their continued competence and fitness to teach. The New Jersey Supreme Court held that the commissioner had acted properly by remanding the matter for a hearing before a local board rather than ordering reinstatement. The court further held that they would be subject to dismissal if they either were Communist Party members or subject to Communist ideology or if they refused to answer the superintendent's questions relating to these matters. The invocation of the fifth amendment, however, could not constitute *per se* conduct unbecoming a teacher and just cause for dismissal.

Lowenstein v. *Newark Board of Education*, 35 N.J. 94, 171 A. 2d 265 (1961). This case grew out of appellant's refusal to answer questions concerning past and present Communist membership and association propounded by a congressional investigating committee. The declination was grounded on the Fifth Amendment privilege against self incrimination and was made on the advise of counsel. He was never cited by the committee for contempt of Congress. At that time appellant had 20 years' service and was protected from dismissal "except for inefficiency, incapacity, conduct unbecoming a teacher or other just cause" after notice and hearing on written charges. The city superintendent of schools suspended appellant on the day of the committee session. Four days later he was formally charged with conduct unbecoming a teacher based solely on the invocation of the constitutional privilege and consequent refusal to testify before the committee. The board sustained the charges and ordered dismissal as of the date of suspension. The commissioner reversed the dismissal and was sustained by the court by reason of the decision of the Supreme Court in *Slochower* v. *Board of Higher Education*, 350 U.S. 551, 76 S. Ct. 637, 100 L. Ed. 692 (1956), handed down after the board's action. It was there held that violation of the constitutional safeguard of due process of law occurs where a discharge from public employment is based entirely upon the exercise of the privilege before a body whose inquiry is not directed at the witness' fitness or conduct in his employment and that no sinister meaning either of guilt or presumption of perjury can be imputed from the exercise of this constitutional right. Following the reversal, a new inquiry was made into appellant's fitness to continue teaching. The board again ordered appellant dismissed for refusing to respond to allegedy pertinent questions of the superintendent. The question related primarily to past associations and conduct as distinct from the present. The New Jersey Supreme Court again reversed on the ground that the only proper subject of the inquiry was present membership or subjection to the ideologies and disciplines of the Communist Party. There followed a second interview which formed the basis for the instant appeal. Again appellant, after thoroughly attesting to his present loyalty, declined to answer questions which related to views and events prior to 1953. Charges were preferred on the basis that the questions were pertinent and the refusal to reply thereto impeded a fair inquiry to determine if he was presently subject to Communist ideology. He was found guilty of conduct unbecoming a teacher grounded thereon and the board ordered dismissal by a 5–4 vote. The New Jersey Supreme Court again reversed on grounds that two members voting for dismissal, more than likely, did so on the uncharged substantive offense of present unfitness to teach by reason of refusal to reveal past Communist affiliation. The court also found that these two members appeared to have in their minds a vestige of guilt because of appellant's exercise of the Fifth Amendment privilege before the congressional committee in 1955. As a result, the court, concluded that fundamental unfairness had resulted when two decisive votes were based on extraneous issues. Appellant was ordered to be reinstated.

Thorp v. *Board of Trustees of Schools for Ind. Ed.*, 6 N.J. 498, 79 A. 2d 462 (1951). Appellant, a "special lecturer" in mechanical engineering at the Newark College of Engineering, had his contract terminated for refusing to subscribe to an oath disavowing allegiance to doctrines of force or violence as a mode of overthrowing the Government. The State supreme court affirmed holding the oath requirement to be constitutional over objections that it violated the First and Fourteenth Amendments.

EXCLUSION FROM THE BAR

New Jersey Stat. Anno. § 41:1–1 (Supp. 1963). *Form of oath of allegiance.*—Every person who is or shall be required by law to give assurance of fidelity and attachment to the Government of this State shall take the following oath of allegiance:

"I, ---------------------------, do solemnly swear (or affirm) that I will support the Constitution of the United States and the constitution of the State of New Jersey, and that I will bear true faith and allegiance to the same and to the Governments established in the United States and in this State, under the authority of the people; and will defend them against all enemies, foreign and domestic; that I do not believe in, advocate or advise the use of force, or violence, or other unlawful or unconstitutional means, to overthrow or make any change in the Government established in the United States or in this State; and that I am not a member of or affiliated with any organization, association, party, group or combination of persons, which approves, advocates, advises or practices the use of force, or violence, or other unlawful or unconstitutional means, to overthrow or make any change in either of the Governments so established; and that I am not bound by any allegiance to any foreign prince, potentate, state or sovereignty whatever. So help me God."

Id. § 41:1–2. *Attorneys, etc., required to execute oath of allegiance.*—The Governor for the time being of this State, and every person who shall be appointed or elected to any office, legislative, executive or judicial, under the authority of this State, or to any office in the militia thereof, and every counselor, solicitor and attorney at law, shall, before he enters upon the execution of his trust, office or duty, take and subscribe the oath of allegiance prescribed by section 41:1–1 of this title.

Question 17 of the preliminary statement required of applicants for admission to the Bar of New Jersey inquires as to loyalty to the Government of the United States. It provides:

17. Do you believe in the form of and are you loyal to the Government of the United States?

EXCLUSION FROM INCIDENTAL BENEFITS

1. LICENSE

New Jersey Stat. Anno. § 32:23–14. *Subversive persons not eligible for pier superintendent's license.*—No such license shall be granted

*   *   *   *   *   *   *

(c) If the prospective licensee knowingly or willfully advocates the desirability of overthrowing or destroying the Government of the United States by force or violence or shall be a member of a group which advocates such desirability, knowing the purposes of such group include such advocacy.

2. BIRTH CERTIFICATE

Id. § 26:8–40.5 (Supp. 1963). *Subversive person not eligible for birth certificate.*—No order shall be made under this act to any person—

(a) Who advises, advocates, or teaches, or who is a member of or affiliated with any organization, association, society, or group that advises, advocates, or teaches opposition to all organized government; or

(b) Who believes in, advises, advocates, or teaches, or who is a member of or affiliated with any organization, association, society, or group that believes in, advises, advocates, or teaches—

(1) the overthrow by force or violence of the government of this State or of the United States or of all forms of law; or

(2) the duty, necessity, or propriety of the unlawful assaulting or killing of any officer or officers (either of specific individuals or of officers generally) of the government of this State or of the United States or any other organized government, because of his or their official character; or

(3) the unlawful damage, injury, or destruction of property; or

(4) sabotage.

(c) Who writes, publishes, or causes to be written or published, or who knowingly circulates, distributes, prints, or displays, or knowingly causes to be circulated, distributed, printed, published, or displayed, or who knowingly has in his possession for the purpose of circulation, distribution, publication, or display any written or printed matter advising, advocating, or teaching opposition to all organized government, or advising, advocating, or teaching—

(1) the overthrow by force or violence of the government of this State or of the United States or of all forms of law; or

(2) the duty, necessity, or propriety of the unlawful assaulting or killing of any officer or officers (either of specific individuals or of officers generally) of the government of this State or of the United States or of any other organized government; or

(3) the unlawful damage, injury, or destruction of property; or

(4) sabotage.

(d) Who is a member of or affiliated with any organization, association, society, or group that writes, circulates, distributes, prints, publishes, or displays, or causes to be written, circulated, distributed, printed, published, or displayed, or that has in its possession for the purpose of circulation, distribution, publication, issue, or display, any written or printed matter of the character described in subdivision (c).

For the purpose of this section—

(1) the giving, loaning, or promising of money or anything of value to be used for the advising, advocacy or teaching of any doctrine above enumerated shall constitute the advising, advocacy, or teaching of such doctrine; and

(2) the giving, loaning, or promising of money or anything of value to any organization, association, society, or group of the character above described shall constitute affiliation therewith; but nothing in this paragraph shall be taken as an exclusive definition of advising, advocacy, teaching, or affiliation.

The provisions of this section shall be applicable to any applicant for an order fixing the time and place of his birth who at any time within a period of 10 years immediately preceding the filing of the petition therefor, is or has been found to be within any of the classes enumerated within this section notwithstanding that at the time petition is filed he may not be included in such classes.

NEW MEXICO

REGISTRATION

New Mexico Stat. 1953, § 4–15–1. *Declaration of public policy concerning Communist organizations.*—It is the public policy of the State of New Mexico that no Communist organization, affiliate of the Communist Party or supporter or advocate of communistic doctrine, or any person or organization which believes in, teaches or advocates the overthrow of the Government of the United States or of the State of New Mexico by force or by any illegal or unconstitutional method or means, shall remain within the State and be unknown or unrecognized.

Id. § 4–15–2. *Communist organizations and supporters required to register.*—To effectuate the public policy as set out in section 1 [4–15–1] hereinabove every Communist organization, affiliate of the Communist Party or supporter or advocate of communistic doctrine, or any person or organization which believes in, teaches or advocates the overthrow of the Government of the United States or of the State of New Mexico by force or by any illegal or unconstitutional methods or means, shall register with the secretary of state of New Mexico. Such registration shall be accomplished in such manner and on such forms as may be prescribed by the secretary of state. All organized groups or associations falling into the category required to register under this act [4–15–1 to 4–15–3], shall file a list of all of the members of such organization with the secretary of state, such list to show the names of all members, their addresses, and designation of all officials of such organization. All individuals required by this act [4–15–1 to 4–15–3] to register shall file their name[s], address[es] and the names of the organizations or associations to which they belong as members.

Registration under this act [4–15–1 to 4–15–3] shall be completed within 6 calendar months after the passage of this act, and registrants shall reregister annually thereafter, such reregistration period to begin on April 1 and ending on May 1 of each year.

Id. § 4–15–3. *Penalty.*—The officers of any organization, association, party or group which shall fail to register under the provisions of this act [4–15–1 to 4–15–3], or any person who shall knowingly fail to comply with the provisions of this act [4–15–1 to 4–15–3], shall be guilty of a felony and on conviction thereof shall be punished by a fine of not less than $500 nor more than $5,000, or by imprisonment for not less than 3 or more than 10 years, or by both such fine and imprisonment.

LOYALTY OF STATE OFFICERS AND EMPLOYEES

NONELECTIVE PERSONNEL

New Mexico Stat. 1953, § 5–1–12. *Persons advocating sedition ineligible for public employment.*—No person shall be knowingly employed by any State department, office, board, commission or bureau, county, municipality or other political subdivision, board of education or school board, who either directly or indirectly carries on, advocates, teaches, justifies, aids or abets a program of sabotage, force and violence, sedition or treason against the Government of the United States or of this State.

When it becomes reasonably apparent to his appointing power that any employee has committed any of the acts hereinabove described it shall be the duty of such employer to refer the data and information available to him to the district attorney of the judicial district wherein such employee resides, and it shall thereupon become the mandatory duty of the district attorney to institute a proceeding in the district court to determine whether the employee has violated this act [section]. If such court determines that this act has been violated, such employee shall be immediately discharged and shall not be again employed in any capacity by any State department, office, board, commission or bureau, county, municipality, or other political subdivision, board of education or school board.

No part of any money appropriated from the State treasury shall ever be expended to compensate any person whose employment is forbidden by this section.

TEACHERS' LOYALTY

New Mexico Stat. 1953, § 5–1–12. *Persons advocating sedition ineligible for employment.*—No person shall be knowingly employed by any State department, office, board, commission or bureau, county, municipality or other political subdivision, board of education or school board, who either directly or indirectly carries on, advocates, teaches, justifies, aids, or abets a program of sabotage, force and violence, sedition, or treason against the Government of the United States or of this State.

When it becomes reasonably apparent to his appointing power that any employee has committed any of the acts hereinabove described it shall be the duty of such employer to refer the data and information available to him to the district attorney of the judicial district wherein such employee resides, and it shall thereupon become the mandatory duty of the district attorney to institute a proceeding in the district court to determine whether the employee has violated this act [section]. If such court determines that this act has been violated, such employee shall be immediately discharged and shall not be again employed in any capacity by any State department, office, board, commission, or bureau, county, municipality, or other political subdivision, board of education, or school board.

No part of any money appropriated from the State treasury shall ever be expended to compensate any person whose employment is forbidden by this section.

EXCLUSION FROM THE BAR

All applicants for admission to the New Mexico bar are required to execute a non-Communist affidavit. The form of the affidavit follows:

In the Matter of the Application of _____
_____ for Admission to the State Bar of New Mexico.

AFFIDAVIT

STATE OF _____
County of _____ , *ss:*
_____ , being
first duly sworn, on oath deposes and states:
That _he is not now nor has _he ever been a member of the Communist Party.
Dated this_____day of_____, 19____.

_____
Subscribed and sworn to before me this_____day of_____
19____.

_____
Notary Public, State of_____,
County of_____:
My commission expires:
_____

Annotation:

Schware v. *Board of Bar Examiners*, 353 U.S. 232, 77 S. Ct. 752 1 L. Ed. 2d 796 (1957). Petitioner was a law student who applied for permission to take the New Mexico bar examination. His application disclosed that he had used aliases some years earlier and had been arrested on several occasions. The board of bar examiners denied him permission to take the examination, apparently relying upon confidential information that he had been a member of the Communist Party. He requested a formal hearing, during which his entire background was minutely examined. The board reaffirmed its decision and the State supreme court upheld the denial of permission to take the examination. The Supreme Court reversed and remanded the cause for proceedings not inconsistent with its opinion. In its opinion the Court noted that petitioner had employed aliases to escape anti-Semitic prejudice in obtaining employment and while working in the labor union movement. Although arrested during a maritime strike on the West Coast, he was never formally charged nor tried. Similarly, although arrested for violation of the Neutrality Act of 1917 for trying to recruit men to fight on the side of the Loyalist Government during the Spanish Civil War, the charges were dropped. The petitioner testified that he had been a member of the Communist Party but quit in 1940 following the Nazi-Soviet Non-Aggression Pact of 1939. Petitioner, on the other hand, made a "forceful" showing of good moral character. The Court held that the evidence amply supported a showing of good moral character and that the denial of his request to take the bar examination amounted to a deprivation of due process. The Court declared that nothing in the record showed any moral turpitude on the part of the applicant, since even with respect to his former membership in the Communist Party, there was no showing that he had participated in any illegal activity or done anything morally reprehensible.

Penal Law, § 160. *Criminal anarchy defined.*—Criminal anarchy is the doctrine that organized government should be overthrown by force or violence, or by assassination of the executive head or of any of the executive officials of government, or by any unlawful means. The advocacy of such doctrine either by word of mouth or writing is a felony.

Id. § 161. *Unlawful acts and penalty.*—Any person who:

1. By word of mouth or writing advocates, advises, or teaches the duty, necessity, or propriety of overthrowing or overturning organized government by force or violence, or by assassination of the executive head or of any of the executive officials of government, or by any unlawful means; or

2. Prints, publishes, edits, issues, or knowingly circulates, sells, distributes, or publicly displays any book, paper, document, or written or printed matter in any form, containing or advocating, advising or teaching the doctrine that organized government should be overthrown by force, violence, or any unlawful means; or

3. Openly, willfully, and deliberately justifies by word of mouth or writing the assassination or unlawful killing or assaulting of any executive or other officer of the United States or of any State or of any civilized nation having an organized government because of his official character, or any other crime, with intent to teach, spread, or advocate the propriety of the doctrines of criminal anarchy; or

4. Organizes or helps to organize or becomes a member of or voluntarily assembles with any society, group, or assembly of persons formed to teach or advocate such doctrine;

is guilty of a felony and punishable by imprisonment for not more than ten years, or by a fine of not more than five thousand dollars, or both.

Id. § 162. *Assemblage to advocate criminal anarchy.*—Whenever two or more persons assemble for the purpose of advocating or teaching the doctrines of criminal anarchy, as defined in section one hundred and sixty, such an assembly is unlawful, and every person voluntarily participating therein by his presence, aid or instigation, is guilty of a felony and punishable by imprisonment for not more than ten years, or by a fine of more than five thousand dollars, or both.

Id. § 163. *Permitting premises to be used to advocate criminal anarchy.*—The owner, agent, superintendent, janitor, caretaker, or occupant of any place, building or room, who willfully and knowingly permits therein any assemblage of persons prohibited by section one hundred and sixty-two, or who, after notification that the premises are so used permits such use to be continued, is guilty of a misdemeanor, and punishable by imprisonment for not more than two years, or by a fine of not more than two thousand dollars, or both.

Id. § 164. *Liability of editor, etc., for contents of publication.*— Every editor or proprietor of a book, newspaper or serial and every manager of a partnership or incorporated association by which a book, newspaper or serial is issued, is chargeable with the publication of any matter contained in such book, newspaper or serial. But in every prosecution therefor, the defendant may show in his defense that the matter complained of was published without his knowledge or fault and against his wishes, by another who had no authority from him to make the publication and whose act was disavowed by him so soon as known.

Id. § 165. *Extraterritorial application and penalty.*—A person who leaves the State, with intent to elude any provision of this article, or to commit any act without the State, which is prohibited by this article, or who, being a resident of this State, does any act without the State, which would be punishable by the provisions of this article if committed within the State, is guilty of the same offense and subject to the same punishment, as if the act had been committed within this State.

Id. § 166 (Supp. 1963). *Immunity from prosecution.*—In any criminal proceeding before any court. magistrate or grand jury for a violation of any of the provisions of this article, the court, magistrate or grand jury may confer immunity in accordance with the provisions of section two thousand four hundred forty-seven of this chapter.

Annotations:

People v. *Gitlow*, 268 U.S. 652, 45 S. Ct. 625, 69 L. Ed. 1138(1925). Defendant, a member of the left wing section of the Socialist Party, was convicted of the crime of criminal anarchy. The evidence against the defendant consisted principally, of having advocated the necessity of overturning organized government by force, violence and unlawful means in publication entitled "The Left Wing Manifesto" and a paper called "The Revolutionary Age." The conviction was affirmed by the New York Court of Appeals. On appeal to the Supreme Court of the United States, defendant contended that there was no evidence of any concrete result flowing from the publication of the mentioned writings or circumstances showing the likelihood of such result; that the statute as applied penalized the mere utterance as such, of doctrine having no quality of incitement, without regard either to the circumstances of its utterance or the likelihood of unlawful sequences; and that, as the exercise of the right of free expression with relation to government is only punishable "in circumstances involving likelihood of substantive evil," the statute contravened the due process clause of the Fourteenth Amendment. Assuming for the sake of argument that freedom of speech and press were among the rights protected by the Fourteenth Amendment, the Court nevertheless affirmed the judgment on the ground that the criminal anarchy statute as construed and applied in this case did not deprive the defendant of these rights. The Court found that defendant's writings advocated not merely the abstract doctrine of overthrowing organized government by force, violence, and unlawful means, "but action to that end [was] clear."

Although the First Amendment freedoms were "an inestimable privilege in a free government," devoid of reasonable limitations, "it might become the scourge of the republic." There was no gainsaying that a state in the exercise of its police power may punish persons who abuse this freedom "by utterances inimical to the public welfare, tending to corrupt public morals, incite to crime, or disturb the public peace." "In short this freedom does not deprive a state of the primary and essential right of self-preservation; which, so long as human governments endure, they cannot be denied."

Matter of Lithuanian Workers Literature Society, 196 App. Div. 262, 187 N.Y.S. 612 (1921). This case involved an appeal from a denial of a motion to amend a certificate of incorporation so as to extend membership in a society whose main purpose was to disseminate Socialist propaganda to persons who were not opposed to "Marxian principles." The court affirmed holding that while the publication of literature was an exercise of the right of free speech, that right did not embrace the right to advise or encourage attempts to overthrow by force existing governments. It found the phrase "Marxian principles" was sufficiently broad to include propaganda of the type punished as criminal anarchy.

REGISTRATION

Civil Rights Law, § 53. *Societies prescribing oath as a condition of membership required to register.*—Every existing membership corporation, and every existing unincorporated association having a membership of twenty or more persons, which corporation or association requires an oath as a prerequisite or condition of membership, other than a labor union, a fraternity or sorority having chapters composed only of students in or alumni of colleges and universities in this and another State or States, or a chapter of such fraternity or sorority, or a benevolent order mentioned in the benevolent orders law, within thirty days after this article takes effect, and every such corporation or association hereafter organized, within ten days after the adoption thereof, shall file with the secretary of state a sworn copy of its constitution, by-laws, rules, regulations, and oath of membership, together with a roster of its membership and a list of its officers for the current year. Every such corporation and association shall, in case its constitution, bylaws, rules, regulations, or oath of membership, or any part thereof, be revised, changed, or amended, within ten days after such revision or amendment, file with the secretary of state a sworn copy of such revised, changed, or amended constitution, bylaw, rule, regulation, or oath of membership. Every such corporation or association shall, within thirty days after a change has been made in its officers, file with the secretary of state a sworn statement showing such change. Every such corporation or association shall, at intervals of six months, file with the secretary of state a sworn statement showing the names and addresses of such additional members as have been received in such corporation or association during such interval.

Id. § 54. *Report of political activities required.*—Every such corporation or association shall, within ten days after the adoption thereof, file in the office of the secretary of state every resolution, or the minutes of any action of such corporation or association, providing for concerted action of its members or of a part thereof to promote or defeat legislation, Federal, State or municipal, or to support or to defeat any candidate for political office.

Id. § 55. *Mail privileges restricted.*—It shall be unlawful for any such corporation or association to send, deliver, mail, or transmit to any person in this State, who is not a member of such corporation or association, any anonymous letter, document, leaflet, or written or printed matter, and all such letters, documents, leaflets, or other written or printed matter, intended for a person not a member of such corporation or association, shall bear on the same the name of such corporation or association and the names of the officers thereof together with the addresses of the latter.

Id. § 56. *Penalty.*—Any corporation or association violating any provision of this article shall be guilty of a misdemeanor punishable by a fine of not less than one thousand dollars nor more than ten thousand dollars. Any officer of such corporation or association and every member of the board of directors, trustees, or other similar body, who violates any provision of this article or permits or acquiesces in the violation of any provision of this article by any such corporation, shall be guilty of a misdemeanor. Any person who becomes a member of any such corporation or association, or remains a member thereof, or attends a meeting thereof, with knowledge that such corporation or association has failed to comply with any provision of this article, shall be guilty of a misdemeanor.

Id. § 57. *Injunctions.*—In addition to the penalties provided by section fifty-six of this article, a violation of the provisions of this article may be restrained at the suit of the people by the attorney general.

Annotations:

Bryant v. *Zimmerman*, 278 U.S. 63, 49 S. Ct. 61, 73 L. Ed. 184 (1928). This case originated as a habeas corpus proceeding. Appellant, a member of an association of the Ku Klux Klan, was convicted of having failed to comply with the statutory requirement that unincorporated association requiring an oath as a condition of membership shall file with the secretary of state a sworn copy of its constitution, oath, and other particulars, including a list of officers and members. The State courts sustained the validity of the statute and refused to discharge appellant. The Supreme Court affirmed and held that the State in the exercise of its police powers may require associations having an oath-bound membership to submit to any reasonable regulation calculated to confine their purposes and activities within the rights of others and the public welfare. With respect to the due process clause, the Court declared that it had not been violated. After a review of the precedents the Court declared that the statute did not deny equal protection of the laws since the classification, "secret societies," was neither arbitrary nor unreasonable.

LOYALTY OF STATE OFFICERS AND EMPLOYEES

1. ELECTIVE AND NONELECTIVE PERSONNEL

New York Constitution, Art. XIII, § 1. *Oath.*—Members of the legislature, and all officers, executive and judicial, except such inferior officers as shall be by law exempted, shall, before they enter on the duties of their respective offices, take and subscribe the following oath or affirmation: "I do solemnly swear (or affirm) that I will support the Constitution of the United States, and the constitution of the State of New York, and that I will faithfully discharge the duties of the office of_____, according to the best of my ability;" and no other oath, declaration or test shall be required as a qualification for any· office of public trust, except that any committee of a political party may, by rule, provide for equal representation of the sexes on any such committee, and a State convention of a political party at which candidates for public office are nominated, may, by rule, provide for equal representation of the sexes on any committee of such party.

Public Officers Law § 35–a. *Seditious utterances cause for removal.*—A person holding any public office shall be removable therefrom, in the manner provided by law, for the utterance of any treasonable or seditious word or words or the doing of any treasonable or seditious act or acts during his term.

2. NONELECTIVE PERSONNEL

Civil Service Law, § 105. *Persons advocating overthrow of government ineligible for public office.*—1. Ineligibility of persons advocating overthrow of government by force or unlawful means. No person shall be appointed to any office or position in the service of the State or of any civil division thereof, nor shall any person employed in any such office or position be continued in such employment, nor shall any person be employed in the public service as superintendent, principal, or teacher in a public school or academy or in a State college or any other State educational institution who:

(a) by word of mouth or writing willfully and deliberately advocates, advises or teaches the doctrine that the Government of the United States or of any State or of any political subdivision thereof should be overthrown or overturned by force, violence, or any unlawful means; or

(b) prints, publishes, edits, issues, or sells any book, paper, document, or written or printed matter in any form containing or advocating, advising or teaching the doctrine that the Government of the United States or of any State or of any political subdivision thereof should be overthrown by force, violence or any unlawful means, and who advocates, advises, teaches, or embraces the duty, necessity, or propriety of adopting the doctrine contained therein; or

(c) organizes or helps to organize or becomes a member of any society or group of persons which teaches or advocates that the Government of the United States or of any State or of any political subdivision thereof shall be overthrown by force or violence, or by any unlawful means.

For the purposes of this section, membership in the Communist Party of the United States of America or the Communist Party of the State of New York shall constitute prima facie evidence of disqualification for appointment to or retention in any office or position in the service of the State or of any city or civil division thereof.

2. A person dismissed or declared ineligible pursuant to this section may within four months of such dismissal or declaration of ineligibility be entitled to petition for an order to show cause signed by a justice of the supreme court, why a hearing on such charges should not be had. Until the final judgment on said hearing is entered, the order to show cause shall stay the effect of any order of dismissal or ineligibility based on the provisions of this section; provided, however, that during such stay a person so dismissed shall be suspended without pay, and if the final determinaton shall be in his favor he shall be restored to his position with pay for the period of such suspension less the amount of compensation which he may have earned in any other employment or occupation and any unemployment insurance benefits he may have received during such period. The hearing shall consist of the taking of testimony in open court with opportunity for cross examination. The burden of sustaining the validity of the order of dismissal or ineligibility by a fair preponderance of the credible evidence shall be upon the person making such dismissal or order of ineligibility.

3. Removal for treasonable or seditious acts or utterances. A person in the civil service of the State or of any civil division thereof shall be removable therefrom for the utterance of any treasonable or seditious word or words or the doing of any treasonable or seditious act or acts while holding such position. For the purpose of this subdivision, a treasonable word or act shall mean "treason," as defined in the penal law; a seditious word or act shall mean "criminal anarchy" as defined in the penal law.

3. CIVIL DEFENSE PERSONNEL

Unconsol. Laws, § 9138. *Loyalty oath required.*—1. The commission and each local director shall have power by regulation or order to designate or provide for the designation of members of civil defense forces under their respective jurisdictions to administer the written oath which the Federal Civil Defense Act of 1950 requires persons in State or local organizations for civil defense to take before entering upon their duties therein.

2. Each such designation of a person serving under the jurisdiction of the commission shall be filed in the Department of State. Each such designation of a person serving under the jurisdiction of a county director shall be filed in the office of the clerk of the county and each such designation of a person serving under the jurisdiction of a city director shall be filed in the office of the city clerk.

3. Designations so made may be revoked in the same manner in which they may be made pursuant hereto, provided that notice thereof is given to each person whose designation is so revoked.

4. In addition to the requirements of any other law, the certificate of a person administering an oath pursuant to such a designation shall specify (a) county clerk's or city clerk's office in which his designation was filed and (b) that such designation has not been revoked.

TEACHERS' LOYALTY

Educ. Law, § 3002. *Oath required.*—It shall be unlawful for any citizen of the United States to serve as teacher, instructor, or professor in any school or institution in the public school systems of the State or in any schools, college, university, or other educational institution in this State, whose real property, in whole or in part, is exempt from taxation under section 4 of the tax law unless and until he or she shall have taken and subscribed the following oath or affirmation:

"I do solemnly swear (or affirm) that I will support the Constitution of the United States of America and the constitution of the State of New York, and that I will faithfully discharge, according to the best of my ability, the duties of the position of _____ (title of position and name or designation of school, college, university, or institution to be here inserted), to which I am now assigned.

Id. § 3021. *Seditious utterances cause for removal.*—A person employed as superintendent of schools, teacher, or employee in the public schools, in any city or school district of the State, shall be removed from such position for the utterance of any treasonable or seditious word or words or the doing of any treasonable or seditious act or acts while holding such position.

Id. § 3022. *Rules and regulations; disqualification.*—1. The board of regents shall adopt, promulgate, and enforce rules and regulations for the disqualification or removal of superintendents of schools, teachers, or employees in public schools in any city or school district of the State and the faculty members and all other personnel and employees of any college or other institution of higher education owned and operated by the State or any subdivision thereof who violate the provisions of section three thousand twenty-one of this article or who are ineligible for appointment to or retention in any office or position in such public schools or such institutions of higher education on any of the grounds set forth in section twelve-a of the civil service law and shall provide therein appropriate methods and procedure for the enforcement of such sections of this article and the civil service law.

2. The board of regents shall, after inquiry, and after such notice and hearing as may be appropriate, make a listing of organizations which it finds to be subversive in that they advocate, advise, teach or embrace the doctrine that the Government of the United States or of any State or of any political subdivision thereof shall be overthrown or overturned by force, violence or any unlawful means or that they advocate, advise, teach or embrace the duty, necessity or propriety of adopting any such doctrine, as set forth in section twelve-a of the civil service law. Such listings may be amended and revised from time to time. The board, in making such inquiry, may utilize any similar listings or designations promulgated by any Federal agency or authority authorized by Federal law, regulation or executive order, and for the purposes of such inquiry, the board may request and receive from such Federal agencies or authorities any supporting material or evidence that may be made available to it. The board of regents shall provide in the rules and regulations required by subdivision one hereof that membership in any such organization included in such listing made by it shall constitute prima facie evidence of disqualification for appointment to or retention in any office or position in the public schools of the State.

3. The board of regents shall annually, on or before the fifteenth day of February, by separate report, render to the legislature, a full statement of measures taken by it for the enforcement of such provisions of law and to require compliance therewith. Such reports shall contain a description of surveys made by the board of regents, from time to time, as may be appropriate, to ascertain the extent to which such provisions of law have been enforced in the city and school districts of the State.

Civil Service Law, § 105. *Persons advocating overthrow of government ineligible for employment.*—1. Ineligibility of persons advocating overthrow of government by force or unlawful means. No person shall be appointed to any office or position in the service of the State or of any civil division thereof, nor shall any person employed in any such office or position be continued in such employment, nor shall any person be employed in the public service as superintendent, principal, or teacher in a public school or academy or in a State college or any other State education institution who:

(a) by word of mouth or writing willfully and deliberately advocates, advises, or teaches the doctrine that the Government of the United States or of any State or of any political subdivision thereof should be overthrown or overturned by force, violence or any unlawful means; or

(b) prints, publishes, edits, issues, or sells any book, paper, document, or written or printed matter in any form containing or advocating, advising or teaching the doctrine that the Government of the United States or of any State or of any political subdivision thereof should be overthrown by force, violence, or any unlawful means, and who advocates, advises, teaches, or embraces the duty, necessity or propriety of adopting the doctrine contained therein; or

(c) organizes or helps to organize or becomes a member of any society or group of persons which teaches or advocates that the Government of the United States or of any State or of any political subdivision thereof shall be overthrown by force or violence, or by any unlawful means.

For the purposes of this section, membership in the Communist Party of the United States of America or the Communist Party of the State of New York shall constitute prima facie evidence of disqualification for appointment to or retention in any office or position in the service of the State or of any city or civil division thereof.

2. A person dismissed or declared ineligible pursuant to this section may within four months of such dismissal or declaration of ineligibility be entitled to petition for an order to show cause signed by a justice of the supreme court, why a hearing on such charges should not be had. Until the final judgment on said hearing is entered, the order to show cause shall stay the effect of any order of dismissal or ineligibility based on the provisions of this section; provided, however, that during such stay a person so dismissed shall be suspended without pay, and if the final determination shall be in his favor he shall be restored to his position with pay for the period of such suspension less the amount of compensation which he may have earned in any other employment or occupation and any unemployment insurance benefits he may have received during such period. The hearing shall consist of the taking of testimony in open court with

opportunity for cross examination. The burden of sustaining the validity of the order of dismissal or ineligibility by a fair preponderance of the credible evidence shall be upon the person making such dismissal or order of ineligibility.

3. Removal for treasonable or seditious acts or utterances. A person in the civil service of the State or of any civil division thereof shall be removable therefrom for the utterance of any treasonable or seditious word or words or the doing of any treasonable or seditious act or acts while holding such position. For the purpose of this subdivision, a treasonable word or act shall mean "treason," as defined in the penal law; a seditious word or act shall mean "criminal anarchy" as defined in the penal law.

Annotations:

Adler v. *Board of Education*, 342 U.S. 485, 72 S. Ct. 380, 96 L. Ed. 517 (1952). Appellant brought an action seeking a judgment declaring unconstitutional New York's Feinberg Law. The law barred employment in any public school of any member of a subversive organization. It authorized the board of regents, the State's governing educational body, to implement this legislative direction. Petitioner contended that the law and the rules promulgated pursuant thereto constituted an abridgment of freedom of speech and association and violated due process. The Supreme Court affirmed the decision of the New York Court of Appeals declaring the law to be constitutional. With respect to appellant's First Amendment contention, the Court reaffirmed its holding in *Garner* v. *Los Angeles Board*, 341 U.S. 716, 71 S. Ct. 909, 95 L. Ed. 1317 (1951), wherein it sustained the power of a public employer to inquire of its employees as to matters which relate to their continued fitness to serve as public employees including past and present membership in the Communist Party and associated organizations, and to discharge employees who fail to disclose pertinent information which the supervising employees may require. In brief, a State may dismiss public employees who, after notice and hearing, are found to advocate the overthrow of the Government by unlawful means or who are unable to explain, satisfactorily, membership in organizations found to have that aim. The Court declared that it did not agree with appellant's contention that the presumption of disqualification because of membership in a subversive organization violated due process. In other words, the member by his membership is presumed to support the thing the organization stands for, namely, the overthrow of the Government by unlawful means. "We cannot say that such a finding is contrary to fact or that 'generality of experience' points to a different conclusion."

Slochower v. *Board of Education*, 350 U.S. 551, 76 S. Ct. 637, 100 L. Ed. 692 (1956), rehearing denied 351 U.S. 944, 76 S. Ct. 843, 100 L. Ed. 1470. Appellant, an associate professor at Brooklyn College, had appeared before the Internal Security Subcommittee of the Committee on the Judiciary of the United States Senate and refused to answer questions concerning his Communist Party membership during 1940 and 1941 on the ground that his answers might tend to incriminate him. Shortly thereafter he was suspended from his position at the college and it was later declared vacant under section 903 of the New York City Charter. That section provided that if any city employee refused to answer questions on the ground that his answers may tend to incriminate him, then his employment would terminate. The New York Court of Appeals sustained the automatic dismissal and appellant appealed asserting violations of the due process and the privileges and immunities clause of the Fourteenth Amendment. The Supreme Court sustained his claim under the due process clause, and held that a State or its subdivisions may not dismiss a public employee solely because they exercise their privilege under the Fifth Amendment before a congressional investigating committee.

EXCLUSION FROM THE BAR

Civil Practice Law and Rules, § 9406. *Proof of loyalty required.*— No person shall receive said certificate from any committee and no person shall be admitted to practice as an attorney and counselor at law in the courts of this State, unless he shall furnish satisfactory proof to the effect:

1. that he believes in the form of the Government of the United States and is loyal to such Government;

＊   ＊   ＊   ＊   ＊   ＊   ＊

Annotation:

Application of Cassidy, 268 App. Div. 282, 51 N.Y., S. 2d, 202 (1944), reargument denied 270 App. Div. 1046, 63 N.Y., S. 2d 840, affirmed 296 N.Y. 926, 73NE. 2d 41. In this case, a proceeding for admission to the bar, documentary evidence before the court indicated (1) that the applicant was convinced that the constitutional processes were inadequate to effect the changes which he considered necessary or desirable in our existing form of government; (2) that he advocated and counseled the unlawful formation of armed units for use against what he considered subversive elements; and (3) that if the Government failed to act promptly to suppress such subversive elements these privately organized arm units should take the law into their own hands and act independently without regard to the Government. The court reversed the decision of the Committee on Character and Fitness holding that an application for admission to the bar could not be approved where undisputed evidence established the applicant's belief in the resort to force to overthrow the existing form of government.

EXCLUSION FROM INCIDENTAL BENEFITS

1. EDUCATIONAL TV

Educ. Law, § 236 (Supp. 1963). *Employment of subversive persons, etc., grounds for terminating charter.*—1. The board of regents may incorporate any group, institution or association for the purpose of constructing, owning, operating or maintaining a nonprofit and noncommercial educational television station or for providing educational television programs, or for any combination of such purposes. Any such corporation shall be subject to all the provisions applicable to corporations created by the board of regents and, in addition, shall be subject to the provisions of this section.

＊   ＊   ＊   ＊   ＊   ＊   ＊

7. The use of programs for partisan or political purposes or to influence the enactment of legislation, or the employment of persons found to have been members of organizations listed by the board of regents as subversive within the meaning of section three thousand twenty-two of this chapter and who continue membership in such organizations after listing by the board of regents or by any other authorized State or Federal agency, or who would be ineligible for appointment to a public position because of section twelve-a of the civil service law, shall, in the discretion of the board of regents, be basis for termination of the corporate charter.

2. TEXTBOOKS

Id. § 704. *Use of textbooks containing disloyal statements prohibited.*—No textbook in any subject used in the public schools in this State shall contain any matter or statements of any kind which are seditious in character, disloyal to the United States or favorable to the cause of any foreign country with which the United States may be at war. The commission, consisting of the commissioner of education and of two persons to be designated by the regents, whose duty it shall be on complaint to examine textbooks used in the public schools of the State, in the subjects of civics, economics, English, history, language and literature, for the purpose of determining whether such textbooks contain any matter or statements of any kind which are seditious in character, disloyal to the United States or favorable to the cause of any foreign country with which the United States may be at war, is hereby continued. Any person may present a written complaint to such commission that a textbook in any of the aforesaid subjects for use in the public schools of this State or offered for sale for use in the public schools of this State contains matter or statements in violation of this section, specifying such matter or statements in detail. If the commission determine that the textbook against which complaint is made contains any such matter or statements, it shall issue a certificate disapproving the use of such textbook in the public schools of this State, together with a statement of the reasons for its disapproval, specifying the matter found unlawful. Such certificate of disapproval of a textbook, with a detailed statement of the reasons for its disapproval, shall be duly forwarded to the boards of education or other boards or authorities having jurisdiction of the public schools of the school districts of this State, and after the receipt of such certificate the use of a textbook so disapproved shall be discontinued in such school district.

Any contract hereafter made by any such board of education or other school authorities for the purchase of a textbook in any of such subjects, which has been so disapproved, shall be void. Any school officer or teacher who permits a textbook in any of such subjects, which has been so disapproved, to be used in the public schools of the State, shall be guilty of a misdemeanor.

Id. § 705. *Penalty.*—Any person violating any of the provisions of this article shall be liable to a penalty of not less than fifty dollars nor more than one hundred dollars for every such violation, to be sued for by any taxpayer of the school district, and recovered before any justice of the peace ànd when collected, to be paid to the collector or treasurer for the benefit of said school district.

3. SUBVERSIVE SUMMER CAMPS

Exec. Law, § 167 (Supp. 1963). *Publicity by State organs prohibited.*—Notwithstanding any inconsistent provision of law, general or special, no department, bureau, board, commission, authority, agency or other instrumentality of the State shall knowingly advertise, publicize, assist support or advise, or in any manner promote in any publication or otherwise, any summer camp cited by the Attorney General of the United States, the attorney general of the State of New York, any duly authorized State agency or any legislative investigating body for teaching, advocating or embracing the doctrine that the Government of the United States or of any State or any political subdivision thereof shall be overthrown or overturned by force, violence or any unlawful means, or advocating, advising, teaching or embracing the duty, necessity or propriety of adopting any such doctrine.

4. JURY SERVICE

Judiciary Law, § 655–a (Supp. 1963). *Members of the Communist Party ineligible.*—The following persons shall be ineligible to serve as jurors: Any person who is knowingly a member of the Communist Party or any party or organization which advocates, advises or teaches the duty, necessity, desirability, or propriety of overthrowing or destroying the Government of the United States, the government of any State, Territory, district or possession thereof, or of any political subdivision therein, by force or violence, or who refuses to take the oath as provided by this law.

NORTH CAROLINA

SUBVERSIVE ACTIVITIES

Gen. Stat. § 14–11. *Subversive activities defined.*—It shall be unlawful for any person, by word of mouth or writing, willfully and deliberately to advocate, advise or teach a doctrine that the Government of the United States, the State of North Carolina or any political subdivision thereof shall be overthrown or overturned by force or violence or by any other unlawful means. It shall be unlawful for any public building in the State, owned by the State of North Carolina, any political subdivision thereof, or by any department or agency of the State or any institution supported in whole or in part by State funds, to be used by any person for the purpose of advocating, advising or teaching a doctrine that the Government of the United States, the State of North Carolina or any political subdivision thereof should be overthrown by force, violence or any other unlawful means.

Id. § 14–12. *Penalty.*—Any person or persons violating any of the provisions of this article shall, for the first offense, be guilty of a misdemeanor and be punished accordingly, and for the second offense shall be guilty of a felony and punished accordingly.

Id. § 14–12.1 (Supp. 1963). *Assemblage to advocate subversive activities.*—Whenever two or more persons assemble for the purpose of advocating or teaching the doctrine that the Government of the United States or a political subdivision of the United States should be overthrown by force, violence or any unlawful means, such an assembly is unlawful, and every person voluntarily participating therein by his presence, aid or instigation, shall be guilty of a felony and punishable by a fine or imprisonment, or both in the discretion of the court.

LOYALTY OF STATE OFFICERS AND EMPLOYEES

1. ELECTIVE AND NONELECTIVE PERSONNEL

North Carolina Constitution, Art. VI, § 7. *Oath.*—Every voter in North Carolina except as in this article disqualified, shall be eligible to office, but before entering upon the duties of the office, he shall take and subscribe the following oath:

"I_____, do solemnly swear (or affirm) that I will support and maintain the Constitution and laws of the United States, and the constitution and laws of North Carolina not inconsistent therewith, and that I will faithfully discharge the duties of my office as _____ So help me, God."

2. CIVIL DEFENSE PERSONNEL

Gen. Stat. § 166–12. *Loyalty oath required.*—(a) No person shall be employed or associated in any capacity in any civil defense organization established under this chapter who advocates or has advocated a change by force or violence in the constitutional form of the government of the United States or in this State, or the overthrow of any government in the United States by force or violence, or who has been convicted of or is under indictment or information charging any subversive act against the United States, or has ever been a member of the Communist Party. Each person who is appointed to serve in an organization for civil defense shall, before entering upon his duties, take an oath, in writing, before a person authorized to administer oaths in this State, which oath shall be substantially as follows:

"I, _____, do solemnly swear (or affirm) that I will support and defend the Constitution of the United States and the constitution of the State of North Carolina, against all enemies, foreign and domestic; and that I will bear true faith and allegiance to the same; that I take this obligation freely, without any mental reservation or purpose of evasion; and that I will well and faithfully discharge the duties upon which I am about to enter. And I do further swear (or affirm) that I do not advocate, nor am I, nor have I ever knowingly been, a member of any political party or organization that advocates the overthrow of the Government of the United States or of this State by force or violence; and that during such time as I am a member of the State Civil Defense Agency, I will not advocate nor become a member of any political party or organization that advocates the overthrow of the Government of the United States or of this State by force or violence, so help me God."

(b) No person shall be barred from holding office in any capacity under this chapter by reason of the prohibition against double office holding.

EXCLUSION FROM THE BAR

Questions 23 and 24 of the Application for Registration as a law student deal with membership in the Communist Party and other subversive organizations. They provide:

23. Are you now or have you ever been a member of the Communist Party, and if so, give the date or dates of your membership?

24. Are you now or have you ever been a member of any organization, organized or unorganized group, affiliated with, dominated by, or sympathetic with the Communist Party, or having other antisocial aims or objectives, or identified as being so affiliated?

Questions 42–45 on the application form makes inquiries into similar areas. They provide:

42. Are you now or have you ever been a member of any organization, association, movement, group or combination of persons which advocates the overthrow of our constitutional form of government, or which has adopted the policy of advocating or approving the commission of acts of force or violence to deny other persons their rights under the Constitution of the United States, or which seeks to alter the form of Government of the United States by unconstitutional means? If so, give full particulars.

43. Are you now or have you ever been a member of the Communist Party?

If so, give the date or dates of your membership.

44. Are you now or have you ever been a member of or associated with any organization, association, movement, group or combination of persons affiliated with, dominated by, or sympathetic to the Communist Party, or having other antisocial aims or objectives, or identified as being so affiliated?

If so, give full particulars.

45. Have you ever engaged in any of the following activities of any organization of the type described above (questions 41 through 44): contribution(s) to, attendance at or participation in any organizational, social, educational, or other activities of said organizations or of any projects sponsored by them; the sale, gift, or distribution of any written, printed, or other matter, prepared, reproduced, or published, by them or any of their agents or instrumentalities?

If so, give full particulars.

Correspondence received from the North Carolina State Bar indicates that Communists and other subversive persons are ineligible for admission to the bar.

MISCELLANEOUS

Gen. Stat. § 116–199 (Supp. 1963). *Communists, etc., forbidden to speak at State colleges and universities.*—No college or university, which receives any State funds in support thereof, shall permit any person to use the facilities of such college or university for speaking purposes, who:

(1) Is a known member of the Communist Party;

(2) Is known to advocate the overthrow of the Constitution of the United States or the State of North Carolina;

(3) Has pleaded the Fifth Amendment of the Constitution of the United States in refusing to answer any question, with respect to Communist or subversive connections, or activities, before any duly constituted legislative committee, any judicial tribunal, or any executive or administrative board of the United States or any State.

Id. § 116–200 (Supp. 1963). *Enforcement.*—This article shall be enforced by the board of trustees, or other governing authority, of such college or university, or by such administrative personnel as may be appointed therefor by the board of trustees or other governing authority of such college or university.

NORTH DAKOTA

Loyalty of State Officers and Employees

CIVIL DEFENSE PERSONNEL

North Dakota Cent. Code § 37–17–15 (Supp. 1963). *Persons advocating overthrow of government ineligible for employment.*—No person shall be employed or associated in any capacity in any civil defense organization established under this chapter who advocates or has advocated a change by force or violence in the constitutional form of the Government of the United States or in this State or the overthrow of any government in the United States by force or violence, or who has been convicted of or is under indictment or information charging any subversive act against the United States.

Teachers' Loyalty

North Dakota Cent. Code § 15–37–01. *Teacher's oath.*—Every person who applies for a certificate to teach in any of the public schools of the State, or for a renewal thereof, shall subscribe to the following oath or affirmation:

I do solemnly swear (or affirm) that I will support the Constitution of the United States and the constitution of the State of North Dakota, and that I will faithfully discharge the duties of my position, according to the best of my ability.

The oath or affirmation shall be executed in duplicate, and one copy thereof shall be filed with the superintendent of public instruction when the application for a certificate is made, and the other copy shall be retained by the person who subscribes to such oath or affirmation. No certificate shall be issued unless such an oath or affirmation shall have been filed.

Id. § 15–37–02. *Faculty members of State-aided institutions of higher education required to take oath.*—Every professor, instructor, or teacher employed by any university, college, or nomal school in this State which is supported in whole or in part by public funds, before entering upon the discharge of his duties, shall take the oath or affirmation prescribed in this chapter. The oath shall be executed in duplicate and one copy shall be filed with the State board of higher education, and one copy shall be retained by the person who subscribes thereto.

Id. § 15–37–03. *Aliens employed in State-aided institutions of higher education required to take oath.*—Any person who is a citizen or subject of any country other than the United States and who is employed as a professor, instructor, or teacher in any university, college, or normal school in this State which is supported in whole or in part by public funds, before entering upon the discharge of his duties, shall subscribe to an oath to support the institutions and policies of the United States during the period of his sojourn within the State.

315

Id. § 15–37–04. *Administration of oaths.*—The several township supervisors, school directors, members of the State board of higher education, and members of school boards and boards of education may administer the oath required by this chapter.

EXCLUSION FROM THE BAR

The application for admission to practice law inquires whether the applicant is now, or ever has been, a member of the Communist Party or any organization seeking the overthrow of the Government. It provides:

Are you now or have you ever been a member of the Communist Party or any organization seeking the overthrow of our Government?

OHIO

Unlawful Advocacy

1. Criminal Syndicalism

Ohio Rev. Code § 2923.12. *Criminal syndicalism defined.*—As used in sections 2923.13 to 2923.15, inclusive, of the Revised Code, "criminal syndicalism" is the doctrine which advocates crime; sabotage, which is defined as the malicious injury or destruction of the property of another; violence; or unlawful methods of terrorism as a means of accomplishing industrial or political reform.

Id. § 2923.13 (Supp. 1963). *Unlawful acts and penalty.*—No person shall by word of mouth or writing, advocate or teach the duty, necessity, or propriety of crime, sabotage, violence, or unlawful methods of terrorism as a means of accomplishing industrial or political reform; or print, publish, edit, issue, or knowingly circulate, sell, distribute, or publicly display any book, paper, document, or written matter in any form, containing or advocating, advising or teaching the doctrine that industrial or political reform should be brought about by crime, sabotage, violence, or unlawful methods of terrorism; or openly, willfully, and deliberately justify, by word of mouth or writing, the commission or the attempt to commit crime, sabotage, violence, or unlawful methods of terrorism with intent to exemplify, spread or advocate the propriety of the doctrines of criminal syndicalism; or organize or help to organize or become a member of, or voluntarily assemble with any society, group, or assemblage of persons formed to teach or advocate the doctrine of criminal syndicalism.

Whoever violates this section shall be fined not more than five thousand dollars or imprisoned not more than ten years, or both.

Id. § 2923.14. (Supp. 1963). *Participation in assembly to advocate criminal syndicalism.*—No person shall, by his presence, aid, or instigation, voluntarily participate in an assembly with one or more others for the purpose of advocating or teaching the doctrines of criminal syndicalism.

Whoever violates this section shall be fined not more than five thousand dollars, or imprisoned not less than one nor more than ten years, or both.

Id. § 2923.15. *Permitting premises to be used to advocate criminal syndicalism.*—No owner, agent, superintendent, janitor, caretaker, or occupant of any place, building, or room, shall willfully and knowingly permit therein any assemblage of persons prohibited by section 2923.14 of the Revised Code, or after notification that the premises are so used, knowingly permit such use to be continued.

Whoever violates this section shall be fined not more than five hundred dollars or imprisoned not more than one year, or both.

317

Annotations:

State v. *Kassay,* 126 O.S. 177, 184 N.E. 521 (1932). In this case the constitutionality of the State criminal syndicalism statute was called into question. The first section defined criminal syndicalism as the doctrine which "advocates crime, sabotage, which is defined as the malicious injury or destruction of the property of another, violence, or unlawful methods of terrorism as a means of accomplishing industrial or political reform." The second section declared the advocacy of criminal syndicalism to be a felony. The lower court sustained a demurrer to the indictment upon the ground that these sections were unconstitutional. The Supreme Court of Ohio upheld their constitutionality as a valid exercise of the police power. The court denied that they abridged the right of free speech declaring that "to advocate the use of violence and terrorism was an abuse of that right." "These statutes are designed to punish those of communistic habits of thought who prefer force to reason."

Burke v. *American Legion,* 18 OLR 115 affirmed 14 App. 243, 32 O.C.A. 81 (1921). This case involved an action brought by the Communist Party of Ohio against American Legion for destruction of communistic literature. The court affirmed judgment for the defendant or grounds that since the advocacy of the forceful overthrow of the Government was unlawful, defendant's destruction of the printed matter did not contravene a legal right.

---

2. SUBVERSIVE ACTIVITIES

Ohio Rev. Code § 2921.21. *"Organization," "Subversive organization," "Foreign subversive organization," and "Foreign government" defined.*—As used in sections 2921.21 to 2921.27, inclusive, of the Revised Code:

(A) "Organization" means a corporation, company, partnership, association, trust, foundation, fund, club, society, committee, political party, or any group of persons, whether or not incorporated, permanently or temporarily associated together for joint action or advancement of views on any subject or subjects.

(B) "Subversive organization" means any organization which engages in or advocates, abets, advises, or teaches, or a purpose of which is to engage in or advocate, abet, advise, or teach activities intended to overthrow, destroy or alter, or to assist in the overthrow, destruction or alteration of the constitutional form of the Government of the United States or of this State by force, violence or other unlawful means.

(C) "Foreign subversive organization" means any organization directed, dominated, or controlled directly or indirectly by a foreign government which engages in or advocates, abets, advises, or teaches or a purpose of which is to engage in, advocate, abet, advise, or teach activities intended to overthrow, destroy, or alter or assist in the overthrow, destruction or alteration of the constitutional form of the Government of the United States or of this State and to establish in place thereof any form of government, the direction and control of which, is to be vested in, or exercised by or under, the domination or control of any foreign government, organization, or individual; but does not and shall not be construed to mean an organization the bona fide purpose of which is to promote world peace by alliances or unions with other governments or world federations, unions, or governments to be effected through constitutional means.

(D) "Foreign government" means the government of any country, nation, or group of nations other than the Government of the United States of America or one of the States, Territories, or possessions thereof.

Id. § 2921.22. *Unlawful acts and penalty.*—No person shall knowingly and willfully:

(A) Commit, attempt to commit, or aid in the commission of any act intended to overthrow, destroy, or alter or to assist in the overthrow, destruction, or alteration of the constitutional form of the Government of the United States or of this State by force, violence or other unlawful means;

(B) Advocate, abet, advise, or teach by any means any person to commit, attempt to commit, or assist in the commission of any such act under such circumstances as to constitute a clear and present danger to the security of the United States or of this State;

(C) Conspire with one or more persons to commit any such act;

(D) Assist in the formation, participate in the activities or management, or contribute in any way to the support of any subversive organization or foreign subversive organization, knowing such organization to be a subversive organization or a foreign subversive organization;

(E) Destroy any books, records, or files or secrete any funds in this State of a subversive organization or foreign subversive organization, knowing such organization to be a subversive organization or a foreign subversive organization.

Whoever violates this section shall be fined not more than twenty thousand dollars or imprisoned for not more than twenty years, or both.

Id. § 2921.23. *Membership in subversive organizations and foreign subversive organizations unlawful.*—No person shall become or, being a member, shall remain a member of a subversive organization or a foreign subversive organization, knowing such organization to be a subversive organization or foreign subversive organization.

Whoever violates this section shall be fined not more than five thousand dollars or imprisoned for not more than five years or both.

Id. § 2921.24. *Subversive organizations and foreign subversive organizations barred.*—No subversive organization or foreign subversive organization shall exist or function in this State and any organization which is found by a court of competent jurisdiction to be a subversive organization or foreign subversive organization shall be deemed to have forfeited all rights and privileges to which it would otherwise be entitled under the laws of this State. If a corporation organized under the laws of this State is found by a court of competent jurisdiction to be a subversive organization or a foreign subversive organization, its articles of incorporation shall be canceled in a proceeding instituted by the attorney general. The funds, books, records, files, and all other property in this State belonging to any organization found to be a subversive organization or a foreign subversive organization by a court of competent jurisdiction shall be seized by and for the State, the funds shall be deposited in the State treasury to the credit of the general revenue fund, and the books, records, files and other property shall be turned over to the attorney general.

Id. § 2921.25. *Investigations.*—The attorney general shall appoint a special assistant attorney general to investigate subversive activities, whose annual salary shall be fixed by the attorney general and whose responsibility it shall be, under supervision of the attorney general, to assemble, arrange, and deliver to the prosecuting attorney of the proper county, together with a list of necessary witnesses, for prompt presentation to the grand jury if in session, otherwise, to the next grand jury to meet in such county or to a special session, all information and evidence of matters which have come to his attention, relating in any manner to the acts prohibited by sections 2921.21 to 2921.27, inclusive, of the Revised Code, and relating generally to the purposes, processes, and activities of any subversive organization or foreign subversive organization.

The attorney general shall employ such assistants, stenographers and clerks and engage the services of such professional investigators, technical advisers, or other personnel as he deems necessary to carry out the objects and purposes of sections 2921.21 to 2921.27, inclusive, of the Revised Code. Such employees shall be in the unclassified service of the State and shall be paid compensation as fixed by the attorney general.

For the collection of any evidence and information referred to in this section the attorney general is hereby directed to call upon the State highway patrol and county and municipal police authorities of the State to furnish to the special assistant attorney general such assistance as he may require. Such police authorities shall furnish such information and assistance as may be requested. The special assistant attorney general may testify before any grand jury as to matters referred to in this section concerning which he may have information.

The attorney general shall require the special assistant attorney general to maintain complete records of all information received by him and all matters handled by him pursuant to this section. He shall further require the publication, printing, and appropriate distribution of all reports of grand juries of this State made as hereinafter provided.

Id. § 2921.26. *Grand jury inquiry.*—The judge of the court of common pleas of each county, when in his discretion it appears appropriate, or when informed by the prosecuting attorney that there is information or evidence of the character described in section 2921.25 of the Revised Code to be considered by the grand jury, shall charge the grand jury to inquire into violations of sections 2921.21 to 2921.27, inclusive, of the Revised Code for the purpose of proper action, and further to inquire generally into the purposes, processes, activities, and any other matters affecting subversive organizations or foreign subversive organizations. Any grand jury charged by the court, as provided herein, shall, not later than the conclusion of its term of service, prepare a written report of its findings upon the subjects placed before it under the requirements of this section, separate from all other matters considered by said grand jury.

The special assistant attorney general may appear before any grand jury acting under this section to interrogate any witnesses presented and may present additional witnesses.

Id § 2921.27. *Restrictions on use of records.*—No records or information acquired pursuant to sections 2921.21 to 2921.27, inclusive, of the Revised Code, which may reflect on the loyalty of any resident of the United States shall be made public or divulged to any person except with permission of the attorney general unless such resident has been indicted under the criminal law of this or some other jurisdiction.

EXCLUSION FROM THE ELECTIVE PROCESS

Ohio Rev. Code § 3517.07. *Party advocating overthrow of government barred from ballot.*—No political party or group which advocates, either directly or indirectly, the overthrow, by force or violence, of our local, State, or National Government or which carries on a program of sedition or treason by radio, speech, or press or which has in any manner any connection with any foreign government or power or which in any manner has any connection with any group or organization so connected or so advocating the overthrow, by force or violence, of our local, State, or National Government or so carrying on a program of sedition or treason by radio, speech, or press shall be recognized or be given a place on the ballot in any primary or general election held in the State or in any political subdivision thereof.

Any party or group desiring to have a place on the ballot shall file with the secretary of state and with the board of elections in each county in which it desires to have a place on the ballot an affidavit made by not less than ten members of such party, not less than three of whom shall be executive officers thereof, under oath stating that it does not advocate, either directly or indirectly, the overthrow, by force or violence, of our local, State, or National Government; that it does not carry on any program of sedition or treason by radio, speech, or press; that it has no connection with any foreign government or power; that it has no connection with any group or organization so connected or so advocating, either directly or indirectly, the overthrow, by force or violence, of our local, State, or National Government or so carrying on a program of sedition or treason by radio, speech, or press.

Said affidavit shall be filed not less than six nor more than nine months prior to the primary or general election in which the party or group desires to have a place on the ballot. The secretary of state shall investigate the facts appearing in the affidavit and shall within sixty days after the filing thereof find and certify whether or not this party or group is entitled under this section to have a place on the ballot.

Any qualified member of such party or group or any elector of this State may appeal from the finding of the secretary of state to the supreme court of Ohio.

This section does not apply to any political party or group which has had a place on the ballot in each national and gubernatorial election since the year 1900.

Annotation:

State v. Hummel, 150 O.S. 127, 37 O.O. 435, 80 N.E. 2d 899 (1948). This case involved an action by the State on the relation of various persons for a writ of mandamus to compel the secretary of state to certify the Ohio Wallace-for-President group on the ballot. A State statute barred groups advocating the forceful overthrow of the government from the ballot. The law required that any group desiring to have a place on the ballot had to file an affidavit stating that it did not advocate the overthrow of the government. The Ohio Wallace-for-President Committee filed an affidavit in strict compliance with the statutory requirement. The secretary of state certified that the group was not entitled to have a place on the ballot. The basis of the secretary's finding was a report indicating that three persons who signed the affidavit were members of the Communist Party. In allowing the mandamus, the court held that the State provision requiring an affidavit stating that the group did not advocate the overthrow of the government did not bar a place on the ballot to a group because three of its members belonged to the Communist Party. The Wallace group consisted of at least 46,000 people who signed the nominating petitions, and the statute provided that the *group* must not advocate overthrow of the government. There was no showing in the record that any one connected with the group advocated the overthrow of the government, and the fact that some members belonged to the Communist Party or that Communists advocated the election of Wallace, was no proof that the affidavit was not filed in good faith or efficacious for the purpose for which it was filed.

LOYALTY OF STATE OFFICERS AND EMPLOYEES

1. ELECTIVE AND NONELECTIVE PERSONNEL

Ohio Constitution, Art. XV, § 7. *Oath.*—Every person chosen or appointed to any office under this State, before entering upon the discharge of its duties, shall take an oath or affirmation, to support the Constitution of the United States, and of this State, and also an oath of office.

2. NONELECTIVE PERSONNEL

Ohio Rev. Code § 143.271. *Failure to testify constitutes unfitness.*— In any hearing on the question of fitness and continued employment of any person holding a position, job, or office under the authority of this state, the fact that he, being called before a duly authorized tribunal, or in an investigation under authority of law, refuses to testify concerning his membership in an organization which advocates overthrow of the Government of the United States or of this State, by force, violence or other unlawful means on the ground that his answers might tend to incriminate him, shall constitute unfitness of such person for holding such position, job or office.

Id. § 143.272 (Supp. 1963). *Advocating overthrow of government or membership in organization having that purpose cause for removal.*—It shall be sufficient cause for the removal of any public employees including teachers in the public schools or any State-supported educational institution when such public employee or teacher advocates or willfully retains membership in an organization which advocates overthrow of the Government of the United States or of the State, by force, violence or other unlawful means.

The procedure for the termination of a contract of a teacher under the provisions of this section shall be in the manner set forth in section

3319.16 of the Revised Code. The procedure for the removal of all other public employees under the provisions of this section shall be the same as is provided in section 143.27 of the Revised Code except that the decision of the State personnel board of review or the municipal civil service commission shall be subject to appeal to the court of common pleas of the county in which such public employees are employed to determine the sufficiency of the cause of removal. Such appeal shall be taken within ten days from the finding of the board or commission.

Ohio Rev. Code § 5920.07. *Commissioned officers in the Ohio defense corps required to take oath.*—Commissioned officers of the Ohio defense corps shall take and subscribe to the following oath of office:

"I, ------------------, do solemnly swear that I will support and defend the Constitution of the United States and the constitution of the State of Ohio, against all enemies, foreign and domestic; that I will bear true faith and allegiance to the same; that I will obey the orders of the Governor of the State of Ohio, that I make this obligation freely, without any mental reservation or purpose of evasion, and that I will well and faithfully discharge the duties of the office of ------------------ in the Ohio defense corps, upon which I am about to enter; and, I do solemnly swear that I do not advocate, nor am I a member of any political party or organization that advocates the overthrow of the Government of the United States or of this State by force or violence and that during such time that I am a member of the Ohio defense corps, I will not advocate or become a member of any political party or organization that advocates the overthrow of the Government of the United States or of this State by force or violence, so help me God."

Every officer, before being commissioned shall take and subscribe to such oath within ten days after his appointment, and unless he does so he is deemed to have declined his office and the appointment shall be vacated.

Id. § 5920.08. *Enlisted persons in Ohio defense corps required to take oath.*—All persons enlisted in the Ohio defense corps shall sign an enlistment contract and take and subscribe to an oath of enlistment as follows:

"I do hereby acknowledge to have voluntarily enlisted this -------- day of ----------------, 19----, as a member of the Ohio defense corps for a period of three years, under the conditions prescribed by law, unless sooner discharged by proper authority. And I do solemnly swear that I will bear true faith and allegiance to the United States of America and to the State of Ohio; that I will serve them honestly and faithfully against all their enemies whomsoever; and that I will obey the orders of the Governor of the State of Ohio and of the officers appointed over me according to law and the rules and regulations in accordance therewith."

3. CIVIL DEFENSE PERSONNEL

Ohio Rev. Code § 5915.14 (Supp. 1963). *Loyalty oath required.*— No person shall be employed or associated in any capacity in any civil defense position, organization, or agency established under sections 5915.01 to 5915.143, inclusive, of the Revised Code, who advocates or has advocated a change by force or violence in the constitutional form of the Government of the United States or of this State, or who has been convicted of or is under indictment or information charging any subversive act against the United States or this State. Each person who is appointed to serve in any position in civil defense, or in an organization, or agency for civil defense shall, before entering upon his duties, take an oath, in writing, before a person authorized to administer oaths in this State, which oath shall be as follows:

"I, _____, do solemnly swear (or affirm) that I will support and defend the Constitution of the United States and the constitution of the State of Ohio, against all enemies, foreign and domestic; that I will bear true faith and allegiance to the same; that I will obey the orders of the Governor of the State of Ohio, that I take this obligation freely, without any mental reservation or purpose of evasion; and that I will faithfully discharge the duties upon which I am about to enter.

"And I do further swear (or affirm) that I do not advocate, nor am I a member of any political party or organization that advocates the overthrow of the Government of the United States or of this State by force or violence; and that during such time as I am engaged in civil defense employment or activities, I will not advocate nor become a member of any political party or organization that advocates the overthrow of the Government of the United States or of this State by force or violence."

Annotations:

1955 Ops. Atty. Gen. No. 4705. The loyalty oath is primarily a test of qualification for membership in a civil agency. The members of such agencies enter and serve therein as civil defense volunteers and neither such oath nor any other provision of law binds such members to serve as such for any designated period.

1956 Ops. Atty. Gen. No. 6902. There is no age limitation regarding the subscription to loyalty oaths by teenagers.

TEACHERS' LOYALTY

Ohio Rev. Code § 143.271 *Failure to testify constitutes unfitness.*— In any hearing on the question of fitness and continued employment of any person holding a position, job, or office under the authority of this State, the fact that he, being called before a duly authorized tribunal, or in an investigation under authority of law, refuses to testify concerning his membership in an organization which advocates overthrow of the Government of the United States or of this State, by force, violence or other unlawful means on the ground that his answer might tend to incriminate him, shall constitute unfitness of such person for holding such position, job, or office.

Id. § 143.272 (Supp. 1963). *Advocating overthrow of Government and membership in organization having that purpose cause for removal.*—It shall be sufficient cause for the removal of any public employees, including teachers in the public schools or any State supported educational institution when such public employee or teacher advocates or willfully retains membership in an organization which advocates overthrow of the Government of the United States or of the State by force, violence or other unlawful means.

The procedure for the termination of a contract of a teacher under the provisions of this section shall be in the manner set forth in section 3319.16 of the Revised Code.

EXCLUSION FROM THE BAR

Question 12(g) of the application for registration as a law student inquires as to membership in subversive organizations. It reads as follows:

12. State whether you have been, or presently are:

(g) a member of any organization which advocates the overthrow of the Government of the United States by force.

If your answer to any section of the above question is "yes," set forth the facts in detail, designating by letter the portion of the question to which you refer. Include names of cases and dates of all court proceedings, the disposition made thereof, and the name and address of the court in which the record may be found.

Correspondence received from the Supreme Court of Ohio discloses the absence of any rule or policy pertaining to the admission to the Ohio Bar of Communists or other subversive persons. Precedents in this area appear to be nonexistent.

EXCLUSION FROM INCIDENTAL BENEFITS

1. WORKMEN'S COMPENSATION

Ohio Rev. Code § 4123.037 (Supp. 1963). *Civil defense workers required to execute loyalty oath in order to qualify for workmen's compensation.*—(A) The provisions of sections 4123.01 to 4123.94, inclusive, of the Revised Code shall inure to the benefit of those civil defense workers who have previously complied with the minimum requirements as set forth in sections 4123.031 to 4123.036 [4123.03.1 to 4123.03.6], inclusive, of the Revised Code, including those who have executed either the State form of the loyalty oath under section 5915.14 of the Revised Code or the Federal form of oath administered under the provisions of Public Law No. 268, 82d Congress, insofar as the Federal loyalty oath is concerned.

(B) Any person who has executed the Federal oath under the provisions of Public Law No. 268, 82d Congress prior to September 29, 1955, is considered to have complied with the requirements for the execution of loyalty oath as required under the provisions of sections 5915.01 to 5915.31, inclusive, of the Revised Code.

2. UNEMPLOYMENT BENEFITS

Ohio Rev. Code § 4141.28(A) (Supp. 1963). *Nonsubversive affidavit required.*—Applications for determination of benefit rights and claims for benefits shall be filed with a deputy of the administrator of the bureau of unemployment compensation designated for the purpose. Such applications and claims may also be filed with an employee of another State or Federal agency or with an employee of the unemployment insurance commission of Canada, charged with the duty of accepting applications and claims for unemployment benefits. Every person filing an application for determination of benefit rights in accordance with this section shall attach to such application his written affidavit stating whether he advocates or does not advocate and whether he is or is not a member of a party which advocates the overthrow of our Government by force. In the absence of such affidavit no application shall be valid. Such affidavit shall be produced in court by the administrator or his deputy upon the order of a judge of any court of record.

MISCELLANEOUS

Ohio Rev. Code § 103.31. *Un-American Activities Commission created.*—There is hereby created an un-American activities commission in the legislative branch of the government, consisting of six members of the senate and six members of the house of representatives, respectively. The president pro tempore of the senate and the speaker of the house of representatives shall be members and shall appoint as members of the commission five additional members in each house, not more than three of whom shall be members of the same political party. When a vacancy of the membership of the commission occurs it shall be filled in the same manner as the original appointments.

Id. § 103.32. *Organization.*—The un-American activities commission shall organize by selecting from its membership a chairman, a vice-chairman, and a secretary. The members of the commission shall serve without compensation but shall be reimbursed for their actual and necessary expenses incurred in the discharge of their official duties.

Id. § 103.33. *Commission staffing.*—The un-American activities commission shall employ and fix the compensation of a legal director who shall employ, with the approval of the commission, such assistants, stenographers, and clerks, and engage the services of such professional investigators or technical advisers as the commission deems necessary to carry out the objects and purposes of section 103.34 of the Revised Code.

The salaries and all expenses incurred by the commission shall be paid from the State treasury upon the warrant of the auditor of State by voucher approved by its chairman.

Id. § 103.34. *Duties of the Commission.*—The un-American activities commission shall:

(A) Investigate, study, and analyze:

(1) All facts relating to the activities of persons, groups, and organizations whose membership includes persons who have as their objective or may be suspected of having as their objective the overthrow or reform of our constitutional governments by fraud, force, violence, or other unlawful means;

(2) All facts concerning persons, groups, and organizations, known to be or suspected of being dominated by or giving allegiance to a foreign power or whose activities might adversely affect the contribution of this State, to the national defense, the safety and security of this State, the functioning of any agency of the State or National Government, or the industrial potential of this State;

(3) The operation and effect of the laws of this State, of the several other States, and of the United States, which purport to outlaw and control the activities enumerated in this section and to recommend such additional legislation or revision of existing laws as may seem advisable and necessary;

(B) Maintain a liaison with any agency of the Federal, State, or local governments in devising and promoting means of disclosing those persons and groups who seek to alter or destroy the government of this State or of the United States by force, violence, intimidation, sabotage, or threats of the same.

The commission has such additional rights, duties, and powers as are necessary to enable it fully to exercise those specifically set forth in this section and to accomplish its lawful objectives and purposes.

Id. § 103.35. *Powers of the Commission.*—In the discharge of any duties imposed by sections 103.31 to 103.38, inclusive, of the Revised Code, the chairman of the un-American activities commission may, throughout the State, administer oaths, issue subpoenas compelling the attendance of witnesses and the production of any papers, books, accounts, records, documents, and testimony, and cause the deposition of witnesses either residing within or without the State. In case of disobedience on the part of any person to comply with a subpoena issued on behalf of the commission or on the refusal of any person or officer to testify to any matters regarding which he may be lawfully interrogated, or to conform to section 2705.02 of the Revised Code, the chairman may be authorized by a majority of the members sitting at the time the alleged offense is committed, to cause a proceeding for contempt to be filed and prosecuted in the court of common pleas of any county under sections 2705.03 to 2705.09, inclusive, of the Revised Code. Each witness appearing before the commission by its order, other than a State official or employee, shall receive such compensation as the commission directs and mileage in the amounts provided by section 2335.08 of the Revised Code. Fees shall be authorized and paid after a notation has been made on the proper voucher sworn to by such witness and approved by the chairman of the commission.

Id. § 103.36. *Assistance authorized.*—Each officer, board, commission, or department of the State government or of any local government shall make such studies as the un-American activities commission requires within the limitations of its budget and shall furnish the commission all such assistance, information, records, and documents as it requires for the accomplishment of its duties. Reports and recommendations resulting from such studies shall be presented to the commission at least within sixty days prior to the regular session of the 100th General Assembly.

The commission may require the services of the bureau of code revision, judicial council, legislative reference bureau, legislative research commission, the Ohio program commission, and such other departments and agencies as it deems necessary to prepare a program of legislation as provided by section 103.34 of the Revised Code.

Id. § 103.37. *Meetings and rules of procedure.*—The un-American activities commission shall meet as often as is necessary to perform its duties, provided that in any event it shall meet at least once each quarter. Five members constitute a quorum, and the majority thereof have authority to act on matters within the jurisdiction of the commission. The commission shall formulate such rules of procedure and policies to be followed in the performance of its duties and functions as it deems necessary and appropriate. The chairman may appoint subcommittees, consisting of not less than three members of the commission, which shall have all of the powers conferred upon the commission itself by sections 103.31 to 103.38, inclusive, of the Revised Code, and such specific duties as are assigned to them. A majority of each subcommittee constitutes a quorum. The chairman of any subcommittee has all of the powers conferred upon the chairman of the commission by sections 103.31 to 103.38, inclusive, of the Revised Code.

Id. § 103.38. *Commission reports.*—The un-American activities commission shall keep minutes of each meeting or hearing and a record of all testimony and evidence submitted to it. It may make such reports, findings, and recommendations, based upon its investigations and studies, as it deems advisable and necessary, to the people, the members of the One Hundredth General Assembly, individually, or in any special session thereof, and to the Governor. It shall complete its work by and render a final report of its activities and of its recommendations to the One Hundredth General Assembly, the Governor, and the attorney general on January 31, 1954, at which time all of its records, books, documents, and other property shall be committed to the attorney general. Any member of the general assembly, the Governor, or the attorney general shall have the right to attend any session of the commission, and may present his views on matters which the commission may be considering. ─────────

Annotations:

Slagle v. *Ohio*, 366 U.S. 259, 81 S. Ct. 1076, 6 L. Ed. 2d 277 (1961). Petitioner was convicted for contempt for refusing to answer any questions in an appearance before the Ohio Un-American Activities Commission. He relied upon the privilege against self-incrimination of both the Ohio and United States Constitutions. In some instances petitioner's objections were sustained or acquiesced in by the commission. In others, petitioner refused despite directions to answer and knowledge of the existence of an Ohio immunity statute. Affirming in part, and reversing in part, the court sustained the conviction based upon refusals to answer questions which the commission directed to be answered. Reversing the conviction where there was no such direction, the court declared that to hold him guilty of contempt in these circumstances would deeply offend traditional notions of fair play and deprive him of due process.

State v. *Arnold,* 69 O.L.A. 148, 124 N.E. 2d 473 (1954). In this case the court sustained a conviction for criminal contempt for refusal to answer questions before the Ohio Un-American Activities Commission. The court held that where the witness is granted State immunity, automatically, as in Ohio, the fact that the answer may possibly result in Federal prosecution did not justify the witness in refusing to answer.

OKLAHOMA

1. CRIMINAL SYNDICALISM

21 Oklahoma Stat. Anno. § 1261. *Criminal syndicalism defined.*— Criminal syndicalism is hereby defined to be the doctrine which advocates crime, physical violence, arson, destruction of property, sabotage, or other unlawful acts or methods, as a means of accomplishing or effecting industrial or political ends, or as a means of effecting industrial or political revolution, or for profit.

Id. § 1263. *Unlawful acts and penalty.*—Any person who, by word of mouth, or writings, advocates, affirmatively suggests or teaches the duty, necessity, propriety or expediency of crime, criminal syndicalism, or sabotage, or who shall advocate, affirmatively suggest or teach the duty, necessity, propriety or expediency of doing any act of violence, the destruction of or damage to any property, the bodily injury to any person or persons, or the commission of any crime or unlawful act as a means of accomplishing or effecting any industrial or political ends, change, or revolution, or for profit; or who prints, publishes, edits, issues, or knowingly circulates, sells, distributes, or publicly displays any books, pamphlets, paper, handbill, poster, document, or written or printed matter in any form whatsover, containing matter advocating, advising, affirmatively suggesting, or teaching crime, criminal syndicalism, sabotage, the doing of any act of physical violence, the destruction of or damage to any property, the injury to any person, or the commission of any crime or unlawful act as a means of accomplishing, effecting or bringing about any industrial or political ends, or change, or as a means of accomplishing, effecting or bringing about any industrial or political revolution, or for profit; or who shall openly, or at all attempt to justify by word of mouth or writing, the commission or the attempt to commit sabotage, any act of physical violence, the destruction of or damage to any property, the injury to any person or the commission of any crime or unlawful act, with the intent to exemplify, spread or teach or affirmatively suggest criminal syndicalism; or who organizes, or helps to organize or becomes a member of or voluntarily assembles with any society or assemblage of persons which teaches, advocates, or affirmatively suggests the doctrine of criminal syndicalism, sabotage, or the necessity, propriety or expediency of doing any act of physical violence or the commission of any crime or unlawful act as a means of accomplishing or effecting any industrial or political ends, change or revolution, or for profit, is guilty of a felony, and upon conviction thereof shall be punished by imprisonment in the State penitentiary for a term not to exceed ten years, or by a fine of not more than five thousand dollars, or by both such fine and imprisonment. Provided, that none of the provisions of this act shall be construed to modify or affect section 3764, chapter 42, of the Revised Laws of Oklahoma, 1910.

329

Id. § 1264. *Permitting use of premises to advocate criminal syndicalism.*—The owner, lessee, agent, superintendent, or person in charge or occupation of any place, building, room or rooms, or structure, who knowingly permits therein any assembly or consort of persons prohibited by the provisions of section 3 of this Act, or who after notification by authorized public or peace officers that the place or premises, or any part thereof, is or are so used, permits such use to be continued, is guilty of a misdemeanor and punishable upon conviction thereof by imprisonment in the county jail for not less than sixty days or for not more than one year, or by a fine of not less than one hundred dollars or more than five hundred dollars, or by both such fine and imprisonment. Laws 1919, ch. 70, p. 111, § 4.

Annotations:

Berg v. *State,* 29 Okl. Cr. 112, 223 P. 497 (1925). Appellant was convicted of violating the criminal syndicalism act which outlawed the circulation or display of books or printed matter advocating, teaching, or affirmatively suggesting syndicalism or sabotage. The court reversed and remanded on grounds, in part, of insufficient proof. It held, however, the statute constitutional over appellant's objections that the legislature was without power to proscribe criminal syndicalism since treason was defined in the constitution and that it violated the right of free speech.

Jaffee v. *State,* 76 Okl. Cr. 95, 134 P. 2d 1027 (1943) ; *Wood* v. *State,* 76 Okl. Cr. 89, 134 P. 2d 1021 (1943) ; *Shaw* v. *State,* 76 Okl. Cr. 271, 134 P. 2d 999 (1943). Defendants were convicted of criminal syndicalism because of their membership in the Communist Party, an organization advocating forcible revolution and violent overthrow of the government. The court reversed the conviction and remanded the cause for a finding as to whether the advocacy was reasonably likely to result within the immediate future in the commission of serious violence or unlawful acts for the purpose of bringing about political or industrial change or revolution by such means. The court stated : (1) that each State when not restrained by its own fundamental law or by the supreme law of the land possessed all legislative power consistent with a republican form of government, and had the power and authority to provide by legislation, not only for the protection of the health, morals, and safety of the people, but for the common good, as involved in the well-being, peace, and prosperity of its people; (2) that the criminal syndicalism act which defined criminal syndicalism as the doctrine which advocates crime, physical violence, arson, destruction of property, sabotage, or other unlawful acts or methods, as a means of accomplishing or effecting industrial or political ends and declared guilty of a felony any person who becomes a member of or voluntarily assembled with any society or assemblage of persons which teaches or advocates the doctrine of criminal syndicalism, was sufficiently clear and explicit to satisfy the requirements of due process of law; (3) that the criminal syndicalism statute did not violate the equal protection clause of the Fourteenth Amendment in penalizing those who advocate a resort to violent and unlawful methods as a means of changing industrial and political conditions while not penalizing those who may advocate a resort to such methods for maintaining such conditions, since the distinction is not arbitrary but within the discretionary power of the State to direct its legislation against what it deems an evil without covering the whole field of abuses; (4) that it was error to admit in evidence, over the objection of defendant, books, pamphlets, and other writings of which defendant was not the author for the purpose of showing the principles of the Communist Party, allegedly advocated by the defendant, where the books or other writings are not properly authenticated and there is no evidence from which the jury might find that defendant sanctioned the principles set forth in such writing; (5) that a general commentary or dissertation upon the principles or doctrines of the Communist Party, unless defendant himself is the author or unless shown to have been published or adopted by said organization, would not be admissible over objection of the defendant; (6) that to justify suppression of free speech, there must be reasonable ground to fear that serious evil will result if free speech is practiced, and there must be reasonable ground to believe that the danger apprehended is imminent; (7) that the likelihood, however great, that a substantive evil will result cannot alone justify a restriction on freedom of speech or the press, but the evil itself must be substantial and must be serious, and even the expression of legislative preference or beliefs cannot transform minor matters of public inconvenience or annoyance into substantive evils of sufficient weight to warrant the curtailment of liberty of expression; (8) that the First Amendment, which prohibits any law abridging the freedom of speech or of press, must be taken as a command of the broadest scope that explicit language, read in the context of a liberty-loving society will allow, and before utterances can be punished the substantive evil will likely result must be extremely serious and the degree of imminence must be extremely high; (9) that neither the "inherent tendency" nor "reasonable tendency" to cause a substantive evil is enough to justify a restriction of free expression; (10) that before an individual may be condemned for membership in an organization there must be proof of conscious guilt by individual action showing that the individual adopts and approves the principles advanced by such organization.

---

2. ADVOCATING OVERTHROW OF THE GOVERNMENT

21 Oklahoma Stat. Anno. § 1266. *Unlawful act and penalty.*— Any person above the age of eighteen (18) years who advocates revolution, teaches or justifies a program of sabotage, force and violation, sedition or treason against the Government of the United States or of this State, or who directly or indirectly advocates or teaches by any means the overthrow of the Government of the United States or of this State by force or any unlawful means shall be guilty of a felony, and upon conviction shall be punished by imprisonment in the State penitentiary from five (5) years to life.

Id. § 1267.1 (Supp. 1963). *Penalty for organizing or assisting in organizing subversive group.*—Any person organizing or assisting to organize any group, company, assembly of persons, or association with the intent of advocating or encouraging the overthrow of the United States or State governments, or of acting to overthrow such governments, by force or violence, or who is or becomes a member or affiliate of any such organization knowing its purposes shall, upon conviction thereof, be guilty of a felony and punished accordingly.

3. COMMUNISM

21 Oklahoma Stat. Anno. § 1266.4. *Unlawful acts.*—It shall be unlawful for any person knowingly or willfully to:

(1) Commit, attempt to commit, or aid in the commission of any act intended to overthrow, destroy, or alter, or to assist in the overthrow, destruction, or alteration of, the constitutional form of the Government of the United States, or of the State of Oklahoma, or of any political subdivision of either of them by force or violence; or

(2) Advocate, abet, advise, or teach by any means any person to commit, attempt to commit, or aid in the commission of any such act, under such circumstances as to constitute a clear and present danger to the security of the United States, or of the State of Oklahoma, or of any political subdivision of either of them; or

(3) Conspire with one or more persons to commit any of the above acts; or

(4) Assist in the formation of, or participate in the management of, or contribute to the support of, or become or remain a member of, or destroy any books or records or files of, or secrete any funds in this State of the Communist Party of the United States or any component or related part or organization thereof, or any organization which engages in or advocates, abets, advises, or teaches, or a purpose of which is to engage in or advocate, abet, advise or teach, any activities intended to overthrow, destroy, or alter, or to assist in the overthrow, destruction, or alteration of, the constitutional form of the Government of the United States, or of the State of Oklahoma, or of any political subdivision of either of them, by force or violence, knowing the nature of such organization.

Id. § 1266.5. *Penalty.*—Any person who shall violate any of the provisions of section 4 of this Act shall be guilty of a felony, and upon conviction thereof shall be fined not more than twenty thousand dollars ($20,000.00), or imprisoned not less than one (1) year nor more than twenty (20) years in the State penitentiary, or may be both so fined and imprisoned. No person convicted of any violation of this Act shall ever be entitled to suspension or probation of sentence by the trial court.

REGISTRATION

21 Oklahoma Stat. Anno. § 1267.1 (Supp. 1963). *Penalty for organizing or assisting to organize a subversive group.*—Any person organizing or assisting to organize any group, company, assembly of persons, or association with the intent of advocating or encouraging the overthrow of the United States or State Governments, or of acting to overthrow such governments, by force or violence, or who is or becomes a member or affiliate of any such organization knowing its purposes shall, upon conviction thereof, be guilty of a felony and punished accordingly.

Id. § 1267.2 (Supp. 1963). *Officers of subversive groups required to register.*—(a) The officers of each group, company, assembly of persons, or association with the intent designated in section 1 of this joint resolution [§ 1267.1] shall, within thirty days of the effective date hereof, register with the attorney general, on forms prescribed by him by regulations, as such an organization, and shall thereafter register annually on or before July 1.

(b) The registration statements shall include the following information:

(1) The name of the organization and address of its principal office;

(2) The name and present address of each person who is currently an officer of the organization or who has been an officer of the organization any time in the course of the twelve months preceding the filing of each registration statement;

(3) An accounting of all money received and expended by the organization, including the sources of receipt and purposes of expenditures, in the course of the twelve months preceding the filing of each registration statement;

(4) The name and present address of each person who is or was a member of the organization at any time in the course of the twelve months preceding the filing of each registration statement.

(5) If any officer or member of the organization uses or has used more than one name, all such names shall be included in the registration statements.

(c) All such organizations shall maintain, in the form and manner as the attorney general shall by regulations provide, an accurate and complete record of all information required by the registration statement forms.

(d) If the officers of any such organization violate any provision of section 2 of this joint resolution [this section] they shall, upon conviction, be guilty of a felony and punished accordingly.

OUTLAWING THE COMMUNIST PARTY

21 Oklahoma Stat. Anno. § 1266.1. *Declaration of legislative findings.*—Upon evidence and proof already presented before this legislature, Congress, the courts of this State, and the courts of the United States, it is here now found and declared to be a fact that there exists an International Communist conspiracy which is committed to the overthrow of the Government of the United States and of the several States, including that of the State of Oklahoma, by force or violence, such conspiracy including the Communist Party of the United States, its component or related parts and members, and that such conspiracy constitutes a clear and present danger to the Government of the United States and of this State.

Id. § 1266.2. *Communist Party and component organizations outlawed.*—The Communist Party of the United States, together with its component or related parts and organizations, no matter under what name known, and all other organizations, incorporated or unincorporated, which engage in or advocate, abet, advise, or teach, or a purpose of which is to engage in or advocate, abet, advise, or teach, any activities intended to overthrow, destroy, or alter, or to assist in the overthrow, destruction, or alteration of, the constitutional form of the Government of the United States, or of the State of Oklahoma, or of any political subdivision of either of them, by force or violence, are hereby declared to be illegal and not entitled to any rights, privileges, or immunities attendant upon bodies under the jurisdiction of the

State of Oklahoma or any political subdivision thereof. It shall be unlawful for such party or any of its component or related parts or organizations, or any such other organization, to exist, function, or operate in the State of Oklahoma. Any organization which is found by a court of competent jurisdiction to have violated any provisions of this section, in a proceeding brought for that purpose by the county attorney, shall be dissolved, and if it be a corporation organized and existing under the laws of this State or having a permit to do business in this State, its charter or permit shall be forfeited and, whether incorporated or unincorporated, all funds, records, and other property belonging to such party or any component or related part or organization thereof, or to any such other organization, shall be seized by and forfeited to the State of Oklahoma to escheat to the State as in the case of a person dying without heirs. All books, records, and files of any such organizations shall be turned over to the attorney general.

Id. § 1266.3. *Proof of affiliation deemed to be prima facie evidence of guilt.*—As to any particular organization, proof of its affiliation with a parent or superior organization, inside or outside of this State, which engages in or advocates, abets, advises, or teaches, or a purpose of which is to engage in or advocate, abet, advise, or teach, any activities intended to overthrow, destroy, or alter, or to assist in the overthrow, destruction, or alteration of, the constitutional form of the Government of the United States, or of the State of Oklahoma, or of any political subdivision of either of them, by force or violence, shall constitute prima facie evidence that such particular organization engages in or advocates, abets, advises, or teaches, or has as a purpose the engaging in or advocating, abetting, advising, or teaching of, the same activities with the same intent.

Id. § 1266.4. *Unlawful acts.*—It shall be unlawful for any person knowingly or willfully to:

(1) Commit, attempt to commit, or aid in the commission of any act intended to overthrow, destroy, or alter, or to assist in the overthrow, destruction, or alteration of, the constitutional form of the Government of the United States, or of the State of Oklahoma, or of any political subdivision of either of them, by force or violence; or

(2) Advocate, abet, advise, or teach by any means any person to commit, attempt to commit, or aid in the commission of any such act, under such circumstances as to constitute a clear and present danger to the security of the United States, or of the State of Oklahoma, or of any political subdivision of either of them; or

(3) Conspire with one or more persons to commit any of the above acts; or

(4) Assist in the formation of, or participate in the management of, or contribute to the support of, or become or remain a member of, or destroy any books or records or files of, or secrete any funds in this State of the Communist Party of the United States or any component or related part or organization thereof, or any organization which engages in or advocates, abets, advises, or teaches, or a purpose of which is to engage in or advocate, abet, advise or teach, any activities intended to overthrow, destroy, or alter, or to assist in the overthrow, destruction, or alteration of, the constitutional form of the Government of the United States, or of the State of Oklahoma, or any political subdivision of either of them, by force or violence, knowing the nature of such organization.

Id. § 1266.5. *Penalty.*—Any person who shall violate any of the provisions of section 4 of this Act shall be guilty of a felony, and upon conviction thereof shall be fined not more than twenty thousand dollars ($20,000.00), or imprisoned not less than one (1) year nor more than twenty (20) years in the State penitentiary, or may be both so fined and imprisoned. No person convicted of any violation of this Act shall ever be entitled to suspension or probation of sentence by the trial court.

Id. § 1266.6. *Additional penalty—barred from holding public office.*—Any person who shall be convicted finally by a court of competent jurisdiction of violating any of the provisions of this Act shall from the date of such final conviction automatically be disqualified and barred from holding any office, elective or appointive, or any other position of profit, trust, or employment with the Government of the State of Oklahoma or any agency thereof, or of any county, municipal corporation, or other political subdivision of the State.

Id. § 1266.7. *Powers of district courts.*—The district courts of this State and the judges thereof shall have full power, authority, and jurisdiction, upon the application of the State of Oklahoma, acting through the county attorney, to issue any and all proper restraining orders, temporary and permanent injunctions, and any other writs and processes appropriate to carry out and enforce the provisions of this Act; no injunction or other writ shall be granted, used or relied upon under the provisions of this Act in any labor dispute or disputes. Such proceedings shall be instituted, prosecuted, tried, and heard as other civil proceedings of like nature in such courts, provided that such proceedings shall have priority over other cases in settings for hearing.

Nothing in this Act shall be construed to alter in any way the powers now held by the courts of this State or of this Nation under the laws of this State in labor disputes.

Id. § 1266.8. *Search warrant.*—A search warrant may issue for the purpose of searching for and seizing any books, records, pamphlets, cards, receipts, lists, memoranda, pictures, recordings, or any written instruments showing that a person or organization is violating or has violated any provision of this Act. Search warrants may be issued by any judge of a court of record in this State upon the written application of the county attorney, within their respective jurisdictions, accompanied by the affidavit of a credible person setting forth the name or description of the owner or person in charge of the premises to be searched, or stating that his name and description are unknown, the address or description of the premises, and showing that the described premises is a place where some specified phase or phases of this Act are violated or are being violated, or where are kept any books, records, pamphlets, cards, receipts, lists, memoranda, pictures, recordings, or written instruments of any kind showing a violation of some phase or phases of this Act; provided that if the premises to be searched constitute a private residence, such application for a search warrant shall be accompanied by the affidavits of two (2) credible citizens. Except as herein provided, the application, issuance, and execution of any such warrant and all proceedings relative thereto shall conform to the applicable provisions of the Code of Criminal Procedure; provided that any evidence obtained by virtue of a search warrant issued under the provisions of this Act shall not be admissible in evidence in the trial of any proceeding, administrative or judicial, save and except those arising under this Act.

Id. § 1266.9. *Utilization of personnel by Governor to enforce act.*— The Governor is authorized to utilize any personnel of the department of public safety and any other State agency to conduct such investigations and to render such assistance to local law enforcement officers as the governor may deem necessary in carrying out the provisions of this Act.

Id. § 1266.10. *Separability.*—If any section or any part whatever of this Act, or the application thereof to any person or circumstances, should be held for any reason to be invalid, such invalidity shall not affect or invalidate any portion of the remainder of this Act, and it is hereby declared that such remaining portions would have been enacted in any event.

Id. § 1266.11. *Effect on other laws.*—The provisions of this Act are expressly declared to be cumulative to existing laws.

EXCLUSION FROM THE ELECTIVE PROCESS

26 Oklahoma Stat. Anno. § 6.1. *Parties affiliated with Communist Party ineligible to participate in elections.*—No political party shall be recognized or qualified to participate in any primary, special or general election in this State, which is directly or indirectly affiliated, by any means whatsoever, with the Communist Party, the Third Communist International, or with any foreign political agency, party, organization or government; or which either directly or indirectly carries on or advocates revolution, teaches or justifies a program of sabotage, force and violation, sedition or treason against the Government of the United States of America or of this State, or which directly or indirectly carries on, advocates revolution, teaches or justifies, by any means whatsoever, the overthrow of the Government of the United States or of this State, or change in the form of government thereof by force or violence.

Id. § 6.2. *Political parties required to file nonsubversive statement.*— From and after the effective date of this Act all political parties now organized in this State and any newly organized political party, shall file with the secretary of state a statement by its officers, under oath, upon the following form:

United States of America \
State of Oklahoma } SS.

I, _____, after being first duly sworn, upon oath say: I am the chairman or executive head of the duly constituted governing body of the _____ political party in the State of Oklahoma, and am authorized to make this statement. I swear that said political party advocates and teaches its members to support and defend the Constitution of the United States and the Constitution of Oklahoma; that said party is not affiliated with the Communist Party, the Third Communist International, or any foreign political agency, party, organization or government, nor does said party, either directly or indirectly, advocate or teach a program of sabotage, force or violence, sedition or treason against the Government of the United States of America or of this State, nor does it directly or indirectly advocate or teach by any means the overthrow of

the Government of the United States of America or of this State, or change in the form of government thereof.
Attest:

(Secretary)
[Seal]
Subscribed and sworn to before me this_____day of____ 19___.

(Notary Public)
My commission expires:
The above provisions shall be cumulative to other requirements made by law in this State.

Id. § 162b. *Persons affiliated with Communist Party ineligible to be candidates.*—No person shall be eligible to file as a candidate for nomination of any political party, or as an independent or nonpartisan candidate, who is directly or indirectly affiliated with the Communist Party, the Third Communist International or any foreign political agency, party, organization or government, or who advocates revolutions, teaches or justifies a program of sabotage, force or violence, sedition or treason against the Government of the United States or of this State, or who directly or indirectly advocates or teaches by any means whatsoever the overthrow of the Government of the United States or of this State, or change in the form of government thereof by force or any unlawful means.

LOYALTY OF STATE OFFICERS AND EMPLOYEES

1. ELECTIVE AND NONELECTIVE PERSONNEL

51 Oklahoma Stat. Anno. § 36.1. *Loyalty oath required.*—Every officer and employee of the State of Oklahoma, or of a county, school district, municipality, public agency, public authority, or public district thereof, who, on or after July 1, 1953, is appointed or elected to office, or who after said date is employed, for a continuous period of thirty (30) days or more, in order to qualify and enter upon the duties of his office or employment and/or receive compensation, if any, therefor, shall first take and subscribe to the loyalty oath or affirmation required by this Act and file the same as hereinafter set forth. Provided, that a public employee who is employed or whose employment is extended on a fiscal year basis and who has duly taken and filed the oath required by this Act in order to qualify for and enter upon, or continue in, the duties of his employment, need not again take and file such an oath so long as his said employment, or re-employment is continuous or consecutive.

Id. § 36.2. *Form of oath.*—The oath or affirmation required by this Act, same being cumulative to the oath of office required by 51 O.S. 1951, § 2, shall be as follows:

I, _____, do solemnly swear (or affirm) that, consistent with my citizenship, I will support, obey and defend the Constitution of the United States and the constitution of the State of Oklahoma, will not violate any of the provisions thereof, and will discharge the duties of my office or employment with fidelity.

I do further swear (or affirm) that I do not advocate by the medium of teaching, or justify, directly or indirectly, and am not a member of or affiliated with the Communist Party or the Cominform or with any party or organization, political or otherwise, known to me to advocate by the medium of teaching, or justify, directly or indirectly, revolution, sedition, treason or a program of sabotage, or the overthrow of the Government of the United States or of the State of Oklahoma or a change in the form of government thereof by force, violence or other unlawful means.

I do further swear (or affirm) that I will take up arms or render noncombatant service in the defense of the United States in time of war or national emergency, that is, if by valid law required.

I do further swear (or affirm) that during such time as I am _____

_____

_____

(Here put name of office, or, if an employee, insert "An Employee Of"—followed by the complete designation of the employing officer. agency, authority, commission, department or institution.)

I will not advocate by the medium of teaching, or justify, directly or indirectly, and will not become a member of or affiliated with the Communist Party or the Cominform, or with any party or organization, political or otherwise, known to me to advocate through the medium of teaching, or justify, directly or indirectly, revolution, sedition, treason or a program of sabotage, or the overthrow of the Government of the United States or of the State of Oklahoma or a change in the form of government thereof by force, violence or other unlawful means.

Subscribed and sworn to before me this _____ day of _____, 19_____.

_____

Notary Public, or other officer authorized to administer oaths or affirmations.

Id. § 36.3. *Filing of oath.*—The above oath or affirmation of State officers and employees shall be filed thereby with the secretary of state of Oklahoma, and of all other officers and employees shall be filed thereby, if an officer—in the office of the county clerk of the county of his official residence, and if an employee, in the office of the county clerk of the county in which the officer or agency employing him is located. No fee shall be charged for such filings or for the administration of such oaths or affirmation. Blank oath forms will be furnished, without charge, by the secretary of state to such officers and employees upon request.

Id. § 36.4. *Compensation for services conditioned upon execution of oath.*—No compensation or reimbursement for expenses earned or incurred on or after July 1, 1953, shall be paid to any public officer or employee by any public agency unless and until he has taken and filed the oath or affirmation required by this Act. Said public officer or employee, if his name is to appear on a public payroll claim, and who is not the certifying officer thereof, shall immediately, after he takes and files his oath or affirmation notify, in writing, said certifying officer that he has taken and filed his said oath or affirmation and the date of such filing. It shall be the duty of the person certifying to said payroll to certify thereon that he has taken and filed said oath or affirmation and that every other officer or employee whose name appears on the payroll has notified him in writing that he has taken and filed the same.

Id. § 36.5. *Penalty.*—Every public officer or employee who, in tak- and subscribing to the oath or affirmation required by this Act, states as true any material matter which he knows to be false, shall be guilty of perjury, and upon conviction be punished by imprisonment in the State prison for not less than one (1) year nor more than fourteen (14) years; and in addition thereto, shall forfeit any public office or employment held thereby.

Id. § 36.6. *Penalty for violating oath.*—Every public officer or em- ployee having taken and subscribed to the oath or affirmation required by this Act and having entered upon the duties of his office or em- ployment, who, while holding his office or while being so employed, advocates by the medium of teaching, or justifies, directly or indi- rectly, or becomes a member of or affiliated with the Communist Party or the Cominform, or with any party or organization, political or otherwise, known by him to advocate by the medium of teaching, or justify, directly or indirectly, revolution, sedition, treason or a pro- gram of sabotage, or the overthrow of the Government of the United States or of the State of Oklahoma or a change in the form of govern- ment thereof by force, violence, or other unlawful means, shall be guilty of a felony and upon conviction, be punished by imprisonment in the State prison for not less than one (1) year nor more than four- teen (14) years; and in addition thereto, shall forfeit his office or employment.

21 Oklahoma Stat. Anno. § 1266.4. *Unlawful acts.*—It shall be unlawful for any person knowingly or willfully to:

(1) Commit, attempt to commit, or aid in the commission of any act intended to overthrow, destroy, or alter, or to assist in the over- throw, destruction, or alteration of, the constitutional form of the Government of the United States, or of the State of Oklahoma, or of any political subdivision of either of them, by force or violence, or

(2) Advocate, abet, advise, or teach by any means any person to commit, attempt to commit, or aid in the commission of any such act, under such circumstances as to constitute a clear and present danger to the security of the United States, or of the State of Oklahoma, or of any political subdivision of either of them; or

(3) Conspire with one or more persons to commit any of the above acts; or

(4) Assist in the formation of, or participate in the management of, or contribute to the support of, or become or remain a member of, or destroy any books or records or files of, or secrete any funds in this State of the Communist Party of the United States or any component or related party or organization thereof, or any organization which engages in or advocates, abets, advises, or teaches, or a purpose of which is to engage in or advocate, abet, advise or teach, any activities intended to overthrow, destroy, or alter, or to assist in the overthrow, destruction, or alteration of, the constitutional form of the Govern- ment of the United States, or of the State of Oklahoma, or of any political subdivision of either of them, by force or violence, knowing the nature of such organization.

Id. § 1266.6. *Penalty—bar to public office.*—Any person who shall be convicted finally by a court of competent jurisdiction of violating any of the provisions of this Act shall from the date of such final conviction automatically be disqualified and barred from holding any office, elective or appointive, or any other position of profit, trust, or employment with the government of the State of Oklahoma or any agency thereof, or of any county, municipal corporation, or other political subdivision of the State.

2. CIVIL DEFENSE PERSONNEL

63 Oklahoma Stat. Anno. § 679. *Loyalty oath required.*—No person shall be permanently employed in any capacity in any civil defense organization established under this Act who advocates or has advocated a change by force or violence in the constitutional form of the Government of the United States or in this State or the overthrow of any government in the United States by force or violence, or who has been convicted of or is under indictment or information charging any subversive act against the United States. Each person who is appointed to serve in an organization of civil defense shall, before entering upon his duties, take the Oklahoma Loyalty Oath, in writing, before a person authorized to administer oaths in this State.

TEACHERS' LOYALTY

51 Oklahoma Stat. Anno. § 36.1. *Loyalty oath required.*—Every officer and employee of the State of Oklahoma, or of a county, school district, municipality, public agency, public authority, or public district thereof, who, on or after July 1, 1953, is appointed or elected to office, or who after said date is employed, for a continuous period of thirty (30) days or more, in order to qualify and enter upon the duties of his office or employment and/or receive compensation, if any, therefor, shall first take and subscribe to the loyalty oath or affirmation required by this Act and file the same as hereinafter set forth. Provided, that a public employee who is employed or whose employment is extended on a fiscal year basis and who has duly taken and filed the oath required by this Act in order to qualify for and enter upon, or continue in, the duties of his employment, need not again take and file such an oath so long as his said employment, or reemployment is continuous or consecutive.

Id. § 36.2. *Form of oath.*—The oath or affirmation required by this Act, same being cumulative to the oath of office required by 51 O.S.1951, § 2, shall be as follows:

I, _____, do solemnly swear (or affirm) that, consistent with my citizenship, I will support, obey and defend the Constitution of the United States and the constitution of the State of Oklahoma, will not violate any of the provisions thereof, and will discharge the duties of my office or employment with fidelity.

I do further swear (or affirm) that I do not advocate by the medium of teaching, or justify, directly or indirectly, and am not a member of or affiliated with the Communist Party or the Cominform or with any party or organization, political or otherwise, known to me to advocate by the medium of teaching, or justify, directly or indirectly, revolution, sedition, treason or a program of sabotage, or the overthrow of the Government of the United States or of the State of Oklahoma or a change in the form of government thereof by force, violence or other unlawful means.

I do further swear (or affirm) that I will take up arms or render noncombatant service in the defense of the United States in time of war or national emergency, that is, if by valid law required.

I do further swear (or affirm) that during such time as I am

(Here put name of office, or, if an employee, insert "An Employee Of"—followed by the complete designation of the employing officer, agency, authority, commission, department, or institution.)

I will not advocate by the medium of teaching, or justify, directly or indirectly, and will not become a member of or affiliated with the Communist Party or the Cominform, or with any party or organization, political or otherwise, known to me to advocate through the medium of teaching, or justify, directly or indirectly, revolution, sedition, treason or a program of sabotage, or the overthrow of the Government of the United States or of the State of Oklahoma or a change in the form of government thereof by force, violence or other unlawful means.

Subscribed and sworn to before me this _____ day of _____, 19_____.

Notary Public, or other officer authorized
to administer oaths or affirmations.

Id. § 36.3. *Filing of oath.*—The above oath or affirmation of State officers and employees shall be filed thereby with the secretary of state of Oklahoma, and of all other officers and employees shall be filed thereby, if an officer—in the office of the county clerk of the county of his official residence, and if an employee, in the office of the county clerk of the county in which the officer or agency employing him is located. No fee shall be charged for such filings or for the administration of such oaths or affimations. Blank oath forms will be furnished, without charge, by the secretary of state to such officers and employees upon request.

Id. § 36.4. *Compensation for services conditioned upon execution of oath.*—No compensation or reimbursement for expenses earned or incurred on or after July 1, 1953, shall be paid to any public officer or employee by any public agency unless and until he has taken and filed the oath or affirmation required by this Act. Said public officer or employee, if his name is to appear on a public payroll claim, and who is not the certifying officer thereof, shall immediately, after he takes and files his oath or affirmation, notify, in writing, said certifying officer that he has taken and filed his said oath or affirmation and the date of such filing. It shall be the duty of the person certifying to said payroll to certify thereon that he has taken and filed said oath or affirmation and that every other officer or employee whose name appears on the payroll has notified him in writing that he has taken and filed the same.

Id. § 36.5. *Penalty.*—Every public officer or employee who, in taking and subscribing to the oath or affirmation required by this Act, states as true any material matter which he knows to be false, shall be guilty of perjury, and upon conviction be punished by imprisonment in the State prison for not less than one (1) year nor more than fourteen (14) years; and in addition thereto, shall forfeit any public office or employment held thereby.

Id. § 36.6. *Penalty for violating oath.*—Every public officer or employee having taken and subscribed to the oath or affirmation required by this Act and having entered upon the duties of his office or employment, who, while holding his office or while being so employed, advocates by the medium of teaching, or justifies, directly or indirectly, or becomes a member of or affiliated with the Communist Party or the Cominform, or with any party or organization, political or otherwise, known by him to advocate by the medium of teaching, or justify, directly or indirectly, revolution, sedition, treason or a program of sabotage, or the overthrow of the Government of the United States or of the State of Oklahoma or a change in the form of government thereof by force, violence, or other unlawful means, shall be guilty of a felony and upon conviction, be punished by imprisonment in the State prison for not less than one (1) year nor more than fourteen (14) years; and in addition thereto, shall forfeit his office or employment.

Annotation:

Wieman v. *Updegraff,* 344 U.S. 183, 73 S. Ct. 215, 97 L. Ed. 216 (1952). Appellants, members of the faculty and staff of Oklahoma A. and M., failed to take the loyalty oath within the prescribed thirty day period. The oath was required of each officer and employee as a condition of employment and provided that he forswear membership in any party or organization "that now advocates the overthrow of the Government of the United States or of the State of Oklahoma by force or violence or other unlawful means" and further to disavow any connection with "the Communist Party, the Third International, with any foreign political agency, party, organization or Government, or with any agency, party, organization, association, or group whatever which has been officially determined by the United States Attorney General or other authorized agency of the United States to be a Communist front or subversive organization." The trial court upheld the act over objections that it was a bill of attainder, an *ex post facto* law, impaired the obligation of contracts and violated the due process clause of the Fourteenth Amendment. It enjoined State officers from making further salary payments to appellants, and its decision was sustained by the State supreme court. The Supreme Court reversed and held the statute to be unconstitutional. The Court pointed out that in earlier cases involving loyalty oaths, the statute expressly or impliedly limited the oath so as to require a forswearing only in connection with an organization known by affiant to be subversive. The State supreme court had refused to extend to appellants an opportunity to take the oath with that construction placed upon it and had denied a petition for rehearing in which it was urged that failure to permit appellants to take the oath as so interpreted deprived them of due process. The Supreme Court held this to be a determination by the State court that knowledge was not a factor under the Oklahoma statute, despite the fact that membership in a proclaimed organizaion might be innocent or that the group itself might be innocent at the time affiant joined. The Court concluded, saying, "Indiscriminate classification of innocent with knowing activity must fall as an assertion of arbitrary power. The oath offends due process."

70 Oklahoma Stat. Anno. § 6.2. *Teaching disloyalty cause for dismissal.*—Upon hearing as hereinafter provided any teacher may be dismissed at any time for immorality, willful neglect of duty, cruelty, incompetency, teaching disloyalty to the American constitutional system of government, or any reason involving moral turpitude. Before any teacher may be dismissed, written notice of the proposed dismissal shall be given him by the board of education in independent school districts, and by the county superintendent of schools in dependent school districts. Said notice shall contain a statement of the charges upon which a hearing is sought and by whom brought. The teacher complained of shall be notified of the date of the hearing, which shall be not less than ten (10) days from the date of said notice. The teacher shall be entitled to be present and to be represented by counsel. In the case of a teacher in a dependent school district the hearing shall be before the county superintendent of schools and the board of education of the district in which the teacher is employed. In independent school districts it shall be before the board of education of such school district. In all cases a majority vote of those constituting the board, before which said hearing is held, shall be required in order to convict the teacher charged and in dependent school districts the county superintendent of schools must concur. Provided in cases involving incompetency or neglect of duty, the decision arrived at said hearing shall be final and in those involving moral turpitude an appeal may be taken to the district court of the county.

No school district nor any member of a board of education shall be liable for the payment of any teacher for the unexpired term of any contract if the school building is destroyed by accident, storm, fire, or otherwise and it becomes necessary to close the school because of inability to secure a suitable building or buildings for continuation of school. Teachers shall be entitled to pay for any time lost when school is closed on account of epidemics or otherwise when an order for such closing has been issued by a health officer authorized by law to issue the order.

EXCLUSION FROM THE BAR

Questions 22 and 23 of the Applicant's Questionnaire and Affidavit relate to membership in the Communist Party and loyalty. They provide as follows:

22. a. Are you now, or have you ever been a member or affiliated with the Communist Party, U.S.A., or any Communist organization?

b. Are you now or have you ever been a member of any foreign or domestic organization, association, movement, group, or combination, of persons which is totalitarian, Fascist, Communist, or subversive, or which has adopted, or shows a policy of advocating or approving the commission of acts of force or violence to deny other persons their rights under the Constitution of the United States, or which seeks to alter the form of Government of the United States by unconstitutional means?

If answer to either a or b is Yes, identify and explain fully.

23. Do you believe in the form of and are you loyal to the Government of the United States of America?

If your answer is No, explain your beliefs and the reason therefor fully.

OREGON

Unlawful Advocacy

Although the State of Oregon does not appear to have any existing criminal statute in this area, an earlier criminal syndicalism act was the subject of a Supreme Court decision.

De Jonge v. *Oregon*, 299 U.S. 353, 57 S. Ct. 255, 81 L. Ed. 278 (1937). Appellant was convicted of violating the Criminal Syndicalism Law. The act defined criminal syndicalism as "the doctrine which advocates crime, physical violence, sabotage, or any unlawful acts or methods as a means of accomplishing or affecting industrial or political change or revolution." The act then described a number of offenses, embracing the teaching of criminal syndicalism, the printing or distribution of books, pamphlets, etc., advocating that doctrine, the organization of a society or assemblage which advocated it, and presiding at or assisting in conducting a meeting of such an organization, society, or group. The prohibited acts were made felonies, punishable by imprisonment for not less than one year nor more than ten years, or by a fine of not more than $1,000, or by both. Appellant was charged with having assisted in the conduct of a meeting which was called under the auspices of the Communist Party. During the course of the meeting appellant, a member of the Communist Party, addressed the group in its name. The parties stipulated that in his talk he protested against conditions in the county jail, the action of city police in relation to the maritime strike then in progress in Portland and numerous other matters; that he discussed the reason for the raids on the Communist headquarters and the workers' halls and offices; that he told the workers that these attacks were due to efforts on the part of the steamship companies and stevedoring companies to break the maritime longshoremen's and seamen's strike; that they hoped to break the strike by pitting the longshoremen and seamen against the Communist movement; that there was also testimony to the effect that defendant asked those present to do more work in obtaining members for the Communist Party and requested all to be at the meeting of the party to be held in Portland on the following evening and to bring their friends to show their defiance to local police authority and to assist them in their revolutionary tactics; that there was also testimony that defendant urged the purchase of certain Communist literature which was sold at the meeting; that while the meeting was still in progress it was raided by the police; that the meeting was conducted in an orderly manner; that defendant and several others who were actively conducting the meeting were arrested by the police and that on searching the hall the police found a quantity of Communist literature. Appellant contended that the meeting was public and orderly and was held for a lawful purpose; that while it was held under the auspices of the Communist Party, neither criminal syndicalism nor any unlawful conduct was taught

345

or advocated at the meeting either by appellant or others. Appellant moved for a directed verdict of acquittal, arguing that the statute as applied to him for merely assisting at a meeting called by the Communist Party at which nothing unlawful was done or advocated, violated due process. The State supreme court denied appellant's motion, stating that the indictment referred not to the meeting in question, or to anything then and there said or done, but to the advocacy of criminal syndicalism and sabotage by the Communist Party. In brief, appellant was convicted of having assisted in the conduct of a meeting, otherwise lawful, which was held under the auspices of the Communist Party. The Supreme Court reversed the conviction and remanded the cause, holding that the Oregon statute as applied to the particular charge as defined by the State court was repugnant to the due process clause of the Fourteenth Amendment. The Court declared:

"* * * that, consistently with the Federal Constitution, peaceable assembly for lawful discussion cannot be made a crime. The holding of meetings for peaceable political action cannot be proscribed. Those who assist in the conduct of such meetings cannot be branded as criminals on that score. The question, if the rights of free speech and peaceable assembly are to be preserved, is not as to the auspices under which the meeting is held but as to its purpose; not as to the relations of the speakers, but whether their utterances transcend the bounds of freedom of speech which the Constitution protects. If the persons assembling have committed crimes elsewhere, if they have formed or are engaged in a conspiracy against the public peace and order, they may be prosecuted for their conspiracy or other violation of valid laws. But it is a different matter when the State, instead of prosecuting them for such offenses, seizes upon mere participation in a peaceable assembly and a lawful public discussion as the basis for a criminal charge."

EXCLUSION FROM THE ELECTIVE PROCESS

Oregon Rev. Stat. § 236.030. *Persons advocating overthrow of the government ineligible to be candidates: barred from ballot.*—(1) No person who is a member of, or affiliated with, any organization which teaches the doctrine of, or advocates, the overthrow of the Government of the United States by force or violence shall be a candidate for public office or eligible for appointment to a public office.

(2) The name of a person defined in subsection (1) of this section shall not be placed upon any ballot in connection with any election.

LOYALTY OF STATE OFFICERS AND EMPLOYEES

1. ELECTIVE AND NONELECTIVE PERSONNEL

Oregon Constitution, Art. XV, § 3. *Oath.*—Every person elected or appointed to any office under this constitution, shall, before entering on the duties thereof, take an oath or affirmation to support the Constitution of the United States, and of this State, and also an oath of office.

Oregon Rev. Stat. § 236.030. *Persons advocating overthrow of government ineligible for elective or appointive office.*—(1) No person who is a member of, or affiliated with, any organization which teaches the doctrine of, or advocates, the overthrow of the Government of the United States by force or violence shall be a candidate for public office or eligible for appointment to a public office.

(2) The name of a person defined in subsection (1) of this section shall not be placed upon any ballot in connection with any election.

2. NONELECTIVE PERSONNEL

Oregon Rev. Stat. § 240.340 (Supp. 1963–1964). *Civil service questionnaire may elicit information concerning beliefs inimical to the government.*—(1) No question in any form of application or in any test shall be so framed as to elicit any information concerning the political or religious opinions or affiliations of any applicant, nor shall any inquiry be made concerning such opinions or affiliations and all disclosures thereof shall be discountenanced. No discrimination shall be exercised, threatened or promised by any person in the employ of any division or the commission against or in favor of any applicant, eligible or employe because of his race or religious or political opinions or affiliations.

(2) However, the limitations of subsection (1) of this section shall not prevent any inquiry as to whether the applicant, employe or eligible has any beliefs inimicable to the government or who advocates or is a member of an organization which advocates the overthrow or resistance by force of our form of government.

Id. § 182.030. *Persons advocating sedition ineligible for public employment; cause for dismissal.*—(1) No State department, board or commission shall knowingly employ any person who either directly or indirectly carries on, advocates, teaches, justifies, aids or abets a program of sabotage, force and violence, sedition, or treason against the Government of the United States or of the State of Oregon.

(2) Any person employed by any State department, board or commission shall immediately be discharged from employment when it becomes known to the appointing employer that such person has, during the period of his employment, committed any offense set forth in subsection (1) of this section.

(3) Any person denied employment or discharged pursuant to this section shall have a right of appeal in accordance with the provisions of the State civil service law.

3. CIVIL DEFENSE PERSONNEL

Oregon Rev. Stat. § 401.160 (Supp. 1963–1964). *Loyalty oath required.*—(1) No person shall be employed or associated in any capacity in any civil defense organization established under ORS 401.010 to 401.190 who personally advocates or has advocated, or who is a member of any political party or organization which advocates a change by force or violence in the constitutional form of the government in the United States or of this State or the overthrow of any government in the United States by force or violence, or who has been convicted of, or is under indictment or information charging any subversive act against the United States.

(2) Each person who is employed or associated in any organization for civil defense shall, before entering upon his duties, take an oath or affirmation, in writing, before a person authorized to administer

oaths in this State, or before a civil defense director or a person designated by such civil defense director in writing, which oath shall be
as follows:

I, _____, do solemnly swear (or affirm) that I will
support and defend the Constitution of the United States and the
constitution of the State of Oregon against all enemies, foreign and
domestic; that I will bear true faith and allegiance thereto; that I
take this obligation freely, without any mental reservation or purpose
of evasion; and that I will well and faithfully discharge the duties
on which I am about to enter.

And I do further swear (or affirm) that I have never advocated,
that I do not now advocate and that during such time as I am a
member of (name of civil defense organization) I will not advocate
the change or overthrow of the Government of the United States or
of this State by force or violence.

And I do further swear (or affirm) that I have never been a member
of any political party or organization that I knew to advocate the
change or overthrow of the Government of the United States or of
this State by force or violence and that I am not now a member and
that during such time as I am a member of (name of civil defense
organization) I will not become a member of any political party or
organization that I know advocates the change or overthrow of the
Government of the United States or of this State by force or violence.

Annotation:

52–54 A.G. 251. The loyalty oath or affirmation prescribed by
Oregon Rev. Stat. § 401.160 is required to be subscribed in writing by
every member of a civil defense organization, whether employed or appointed to serve therein or otherwise associated with the organization.

The validity of a law requiring the taking of a loyalty oath has been
upheld by the courts of the United States, including the Supreme
Court.

The oath is almost identical with that prescribed by the Federal
Civil Defense Act.

TEACHERS' LOYALTY

Oregon Rev. Stat. § 342.615. *Oath required.*—Any person entering
into a contract to teach in the public schools of the State shall, as a
part of the contract, subscribe to the following oath or affirmation:

"I solemnly swear, or affirm, that I will support the constitution
of the State of Oregon * * * and the laws enacted thereunder, and
that I will teach, by precept and example, respect for the flags of the
United States and of the State of Oregon; * * * reverence for law
and order and undivided allegiance to the Government of our country,
the United States of America."

The oath or affirmation, duly signed, shall be filed in the office of the
examiner issuing the certificate and a copy shall be given to the
applicant.

Id. § 342.620. *Teachers employed in private and parochial schools
required to take oath.*—With the exception of exchange professors or
teachers whose term of service is temporary and who do not become

permanent residents of the United States, every teacher employed in a private or parochial school or in any academy, college, university or other institution of learning shall, before entering upon the discharge of his duties, take the same oath or affirmation of allegiance as that prescribed for public school teachers in ORS 342.615. The oath or affirmation shall be taken and subscribed to before some officer authorized by the State to administer oaths. A copy of the oath or affirmation shall be filed with the officer or board in charge of such school or other institution of learning.

Id. § 342.625. *Oath required to be taken before entering upon performance of duties.*—No person in charge of any public, private or parochial school, or any academy, college, university or other institution of learning shall allow or permit any teacher to enter upon the discharge of his duties, or to give instruction therein unless such teacher has taken and subscribed to the oath or affirmation of allegiance required by ORS 342.615 or 342.620.

Id. § 182.030. *Persons advocating sedition ineligible for employment; cause for dismissal.*—(1) No State department, board, or commission shall knowingly employ any person who either directly or indirectly carries on, advocates, teaches, justifies, aids or abets a program of sabotage, force and violence, sedition or treason against the Government of the United States or of the State of Oregon.

(2) Any person employed by any State department, board or commission shall immediately be discharged from employment when it becomes known to the appointing employers that such person has, during the period of his employment, committed any offense set forth in subsection (1) of this section.

(3) Any person denied employment or discharged pursuant to this section shall have a right of appeal in accordance with the provisions of the State Civil Service Law.

EXCLUSION FROM THE BAR

The application form currently employed by the State of Oregon contains three questions designed to elicit information concerning the applicant's possible membership in the Communist Party and engagement in subversive activities. They are as follows:

18. (d) Have you ever invoked the protection of the Fifth Amendment to the Constitution of the United States (or of any other provision of the Constitution of the United States, or of any State) in refusing to testify under oath in any proceeding on the ground or for the reason that your answer might tend to incriminate you?

20. Are you now, or have you ever been, a member of the Communist Party?

21. Do you now, and will you hereafter, without any mental reservation, loyally support the Constitution of the United States and the constitution of the State of Oregon?

Annotations:

Application of Patterson, 210 Or. 495, 302 P. 2d 227 (1956) reversed and remanded 353 U.S. 952, 77 S. Ct., 869, 1 L. Ed. 2d 906, reaffirmed 213 Or. 398, 318 P. 2d 907 (1957) certiorari denied 356 U.S. 957, 78 S. Ct. 795, 2 L. Ed. 2d 822. Upon its initial consideration, the Supreme Court of Oregon denied petitioner's application for admission to the bar on grounds that he failed to meet the good moral character requirement. The court found that petitioner, expelled from the Communist Party for disloyalty, gave false testimony to the board of bar examiners by declaring under oath that the party did not teach and advocate the overthrow of the government by force and violence, and that he, as a member of the party, did not believe in that doctrine. The Supreme Court vacated the judgment and remanded the case for reconsideration in light of its decisions in *Konigsberg* v. *State Bar of California*, 353 U.S. 252, 77 S. Ct. 722, 1 L. Ed. 2d 810 and *Schware* v. *Board of Bar Examiners of New Mexico*, 353 U.S. 232, 77 S. Ct. 752, 1 L. Ed. 2d 796. The court adhered to its former opinion stating that the basis for denial of petitioner's admission was not the fact of his past membership in the party, but rather the fact that he had falsely testified under oath before the board of bar examiners.

In re Application of Jolles, 235 Or. 262, 383 P. 2d 388 (1963). Petitioner, having passed the bar examination made application for admission to the State bar. The board of bar examiners recommended that his application be denied on the ground that Jolles failed to establish that he was a person of good moral character. Although petitioner was forthright regarding his past Communist activities with the board, a majority of the examiners found that the evidence of his rehabilitation unconvincing. The State supreme court, two judges dissenting, found petitioner eligible for admission to the Oregon State Bar. It held that despite the evidence of past conduct, there was sufficient evidence of present good moral character to qualify him for membership in the bar.

PENNSYLVANIA

Unlawful Advocacy

SEDITION

18 Pennsylvania Stat. § 4207. *Unlawful acts and penalty.*—The word "sedition," as used in this section, shall mean:

Any writing, publication, printing, cut, cartoon, utterance, or conduct, either individually or in connection or combination with any other person, the intent of which is:

(a) To make or cause to be made any outbreak or demonstration of violence against this State or against the United States.

(b) To encourage any person to take any measures or engage in any conduct with a view of overthrowing or destroying or attempting to overthrow or destroy, by any force or show or threat of force, the Government of this State or of the United States.

(c) To incite or encourage any person to commit any overt act with a view of bringing the Government of this State or of the United States into hatred or contempt.

(d) To incite any person or persons to do or attempt to do personal injury or harm to any officer of this State or of the United States, or to damage or destroy any public property or the property of any public official because of his official position.

The word "sedition" shall also include:

(e) The actual damage to, or destruction of, any public property or the property of any public official, perpetrated because the owner or occupant is in official position.

(f) Any writing, publication, printing, cut, cartoon, or utterance which advocates or teaches the duty, necessity, or propriety of engaging in crime, violence, or any form of terrorism, as a means of accomplishing political reform or change in government.

(g) The sale, gift, or distribution of any prints, publications, books, papers, documents, or written matter in any form, which advocates, furthers or teaches sedition as hereinbefore defined.

(h) Organizing or helping to organize or becoming a member of any assembly, society, or group, where any of the policies or purposes thereof are seditious as hereinbefore defined.

Sedition shall be a felony. Whoever is guilty of sedition shall, upon conviction thereof, be sentenced to pay a fine not exceeding ten thousand dollars ($10,000), or to undergo imprisonment not exceeding twenty (20) years, or both.

Annotation:

Pennsylvania v. *Nelson,* 350 U.S. 497, 76 S. Ct. 477, 100 L. Ed. 777 (1956), rehearing denied 351 U.S. 934, 76 S. Ct. 785, 100 L. Ed. 1462. Respondent, an acknowledged member of the Communist Party, was convicted of violating the Pennsylvania Sedition Act. The State

351

supreme court reversed the conviction on grounds that the Federal Smith Act preempted the area of sedition against the United States. The Supreme Court affirmed and declared that supersession or preemption was indicated by three factors, namely: (1) that the scheme of Federal regulations was so pervasive as to make reasonable the inference that Congress left no room for the States to supplement it; (2) that the Federal legislation touched a field in which the Federal interest is so dominant that the Federal system must be assumed to preclude enforcement of State statutes on the same subject; and (3) that the enforcement of the act presented a serious danger of conflict with the administration of the Federal program.

OUTLAWING THE COMMUNIST PARTY

18 Pennsylvania Stat. § 3811. *Communist Party outlawed.*—Upon evidence which has been presented and proof which has already been established before the Congress of the United States, the Federal courts of the United States, the courts of the Commonwealth of Pennsylvania, and the General Assembly of the Commonwealth of Pennsylvania, there exists an international revolutionary Communist conspiracy which is committed to the overthrow by force and violence of the Government of the United States and of the several States, including that of the Commonwealth of Pennsylvania, such conspiracy including the Communist Party of the United States, its local components in Pennsylvania, and the members thereof.

The Communist Party of the United States in Pennsylvania and all other organizations, no matter under what name, whose object or purpose is to overthrow the Federal or State Government by force and violence, are hereby declared illegal and not entitled to any of the rights, privileges, and immunities attendant upon legal bodies created under the jurisdiction of the Commonwealth of Pennsylvania, or any political subdivision thereof; and whatever rights, privileges, and immunities heretofore granted to said party and other organizations with the same revolutionary purpose by the Commonwealth of Pennsylvania, the same are hereby terminated.

Whoever, therefore, being a member of the Communist Party of the United States or any other organization, no matter how named, whose object or purpose is to overthrow the Federal or State Government by force and violence, knowing the revolutionary object or purpose thereof, or, whoever participates in the revolutionary activities of the Communist Party or any other organization with the same revolutionary purpose, knowing the revolutionary object or purpose thereof, is guilty of a felony, and, upon conviction thereof, shall be sentenced to imprisonment for not exceeding twenty (20) years, or fined not exceeding ten thousand dollars ($10,000), or both.

Annotation:

Panzino v. *Unemployment Compensation Board of Review,* 188 Pa. Super. 275, 146 A. 2d 736 (1958). Claimants were identified as members of the Communist Party at a hearing before the Senate Internal Security Subcommittee and although given an opportunity to refute the allegations refused to do so. Thereafter, they were discharged by their employer, a defense contractor. The court reversed and returned the case to the board for clarification of whether claimants had the opportunity of answering their employer concerning the accusations made against them. In the course of its opinion the court stated that active membership in the Communist Party was sufficient grounds for termination of employment and for a finding of nonentitlement for unemployment compensation. Sworn testimoney before a court or legally constituted governmental body that an employee in a plant engaged in defense contracts is an active member of the Communist Party gave not only the right, but imposed a duty on the employer to question the employee, and if the latter refused to discuss the matter and make satisfactory explanation to discharge him. In view of its designation by the State legislature as a conspiracy to overthrow the government by force, continued activity in the Communist Party by an employee in a defense industry amounted to willful misconduct.

Exclusion From the Elective Process

18 Pennsylvania Stat. § 3811. *Communist Party outlawed.*—Upon evidence which has been presented and proof which has already been established before the Congress of the United States, the Federal courts of the United States, the courts of the Commonwealth of Pennsylvania, and the General Assembly of the Commonwealth of Pennsylvania, there exists an international revolutionary Communist conspiracy which is committed to the overthrow by force and violence of the Government of the United States and of the several States, including that of the Commonwealth of Pennsylvania, such conspiracy including the Communist Party of the United States, its local components in Pennsylvania, and the members thereof.

The Communist Party of the United States in Pennsylvania and all other organizations, no matter under what name, whose object or purpose is to overthrow the Federal or State Government by force and violence, are hereby declared illegal and not entitled to any of the rights, privileges and immunities attendant upon legal bodies created under the jurisdiction of the Commonwealth of Pennsylvania, or any political subdivision thereof; and whatever rights, privileges and immunities heretofore granted to said party and other organizations with the same revolutionary purpose by the Commonwealth of Pennsylvania, the same are hereby terminated.

Whoever, therefore, being a member of the Communist Party of the United States or any other organization, no matter how named, whose object or purpose is to overthrow the Federal or State Government by force and violence, knowing the revolutionary object or purpose thereof, or, whoever participates in the revolutionary activities of the Communist Party or any other organization with the same revolutionary purpose, knowing the revolutionary object or purpose thereof, is guilty of a felony, and, upon conviction thereof, shall be sentenced to imprisonment for not exceeding twenty (20) years, or fined not exceeding ten thousand dollars ($10,000), or both.

25 Pennsylvania Stat. § 2831(d). *"Political party" defined to exclude groups seeking to overthrow the government.*—Provided, how-

ever, That the words "political party" and the words "political body", as hereinabove defined, shall not include any political party, political organization, or political body composed of a group of electors, whose purposes or aims, or one of whose purposes or aims, is the establishment, control, conduct, seizure or overthrow of the Government of the Commonwealth of Pennsylvania or the United States of America by the use of force, violence, military measures, or threats of one or more of the foregoing.

65 Pennsylvania Stat. § 224 (Supp. 1963). *Candidates required to execute loyalty oath.*—No person shall become a candidate for election under the provisions of the act, approved the third day of June, one thousand nine hundred thirty-seven (Pamphlet Laws 1333), known as the "Pennsylvania Election Code," and its amendments, to any State, district, county, or local public office whatsoever in this Commonwealth, unless he shall file with his nomination petition, nomination paper or nomination certificate a statement, under oath or affirmation, that he is not a subversive person, as defined in this act, which statement shall contain notice that it is subject to the penalties of perjury. No nomination petition, nomination paper or nomination certificate shall be received for filing by any county board of elections or by the Secretary of the Commonwealth unless accompanied by the statement required hereby, nor shall the name of any person who has failed or refused to make the statement be printed on any ballot or ballot label to be used at any general, municipal, primary, or special election.

The statement required by this section shall be filed by any person nominated at a primary election as a write-in candidate within sixty (60) days after the primary election in which he is nominated, and shall be filed by any person not previously nominated, who is elected as a write-in candidate at a general, municipal or special election, prior to being sworn into the office to which he is elected.

Annotation:

In re: Election Returns for Justice of the Peace for Hamilton Township, Monroe County, Pennsylvania, 22 Monroe L.R. 39, 52 Mun. 18(1962). This case involved an election contest arising out of the failure of the winning candidate to file a loyalty oath subsequent to receiving the nomination and before the election as required by statute. The court held the loyalty oath requirement was mandatory and since the candidate had not qualified as a candidate under the law, his name was on the ballot illegally. As a result the votes cast for him were necessarily void.

LOYALTY OF STATE OFFICERS AND EMPLOYEES

1. ELECTIVE AND NON-ELECTIVE PERSONNEL

Pennsylvania Constitution, Art. VII, § 1. *Oath*—Senators and Representatives and all judicial, State and county officers shall, before entering on the duties of their respective offices, take and subscribe the following oath or affirmation: "I do solemnly swear (or affirm) that I will support, obey and defend the Constitution of the United States, and the constitution of this Commonwealth, and that I will discharge the duties of my office with fidelity; that I have not paid or contributed, or promised to pay or contribute, either directly or indirectly, any money or other valuable thing, to procure my nomination or election (or appointment), except for necessary and proper expenses expressly authorized by law; that I have not knowingly violated any election law of this Commonwealth, or procured it to be done by others in my behalf; that I will not knowingly receive, directly or indirectly, any money or other valuable thing for the performance or nonperformance of any act or duty pertaining to my office, other than the compensation allowed by law."

The foregoing oath shall be administered by some person authorized to administer oaths, and in the case of State officers and judges of the supreme court, shall be filed in the office of the secretary of the Commonwealth, and in the case of other judicial and county officers, in the office of the prothonotary of the county in which the same is taken; any person refusing to take said oath or affirmation shall forfeit his office; and any person who shall be convicted of having sworn or affirmed falsely, or of having violated said oath or affirmation, shall be guilty of perjury, and be forever disqualified from holding any office of trust or profit within this Commonwealth. The oath to the members of the Senate and House of Representatives shall be administered by one of the judges of the supreme court or a court of common pleas, learned in the law, in the hall of the House to which the members shall be elected.

2. NONELECTIVE PERSONNEL

65 Pennsylvania Stat. § 211. *Short title.*—This act shall be known and may be cited as the "Pennsylvania Loyalty Act."

Id. § 212. *"Organization," "Subversive organization," "Subversive person," and "Appointing authority" defined.*—For the purposes of this act:

"Organization" means an organization, corporation, company, partnership, association, trust, foundation, fund, club, society, committee, political party, or any group of persons, whether or not incorporated, permanently or temporarily associated together for joint action or advancement of views on any subject or subjects.

"Subversive organization" means any organization which engages in or advocates, abets, advises or teaches, or a purpose of which is to engage in or advocate, abet, advise or teach, activities intended to overthrow, destroy or alter, or to assist in the overthrow, destruction or alteration of, the constitutional form of the Government of the United States or of the Commonwealth of Pennsylvania, or of any political subdivision of either of them, by force or violence.

"Subversive person" means any person who commits, attempts to commit, or aids in the commission, or advocates, abets, advises or teaches, by any means, any person to commit, attempt to commit, or aid in the commission of, any act intended to overthrow, destroy, alter, or to assist in the overthrow, destruction or alteration of the constitutional form of Government of the United States or of the Commonwealth of Pennsylvania, or any political subdivision of either of them, by force or violence, or who is knowingly a member of a subversive organization or a foreign subversive organization as defined in this act.

"Appointing authority" means any person, department, board, commission, or other agency of the Commonwealth, or of any political subdivision thereof, who appoints or employs officers or employees. Id. § 213. *Subversive persons and persons of doubtful loyalty ineligible for public employment.*—No subversive person, as defined in this act, nor any person as to whom on all the evidence there is reasonable doubt concerning his loyalty to the Government of the United States or the Commonwealth of Pennsylvania, shall be eligible for employment in or appointment to any office or any position of trust or profit in the government of or in the administration of the business of this Commonwealth, or of any school district, county, municipality or other political subdivision of this Commonwealth.

Id. § 214. *Appointment procedure; statement of loyalty required.*—Every appointing authority shall establish, by rules, regulations, or otherwise, procedures designed to ascertain, before any person, including teachers and other employees of the public school system, is appointed or employed, that he is not a subversive person and that there is no reasonable doubt on all the evidence as to the loyalty of the person involved to the Government of the United States or the Commonwealth of Pennsylvania. In the event the applicant is deemed to be a subversive person, or in the event reasonable doubt as to loyalty exists, he shall not be appointed or employed. In addition, each applicant shall be required to make a written statement, under oath or affirmation, which statement shall contain notice that it is subject to the penalties of perjury, and shall be in the following form:

"I, _____, do solemnly swear (or affirm) that I will support, obey and defend the Constitution of the United States and the constitution of this Commonwealth, and that I will discharge the duties of _____ with fidelity.

"And I do further swear (or affirm) that I do not advocate, nor am I knowingly a member of any organization that advocates, the overthrow of the Government of the United States or of this Commonwealth by force or violence or other unconstitutional means, or seeking by force or violence to deny other persons their rights under the Constitution of the United States or of this Commonwealth.

"And I do further swear (or affirm) that I will not so advocate nor will I knowingly become a member of such organization during the period that I am an employee of the Commonwealth of Pennsylvania (or political subdivision thereof)."

Id. § 215. *Present employees; statement of loyalty required.*—The appointing authority of each person, including teachers and other employes of the public school system who, on the first day of March, one thousand nine hundred fifty-two, shall be in the employ of the Commonwealth of Pennsylvania or of any of its political subdivisions, other than those holding State or local elective offices of any kind, shall require such person to, and every such person shall, on or before the first day of April, one thousand nine hundred fifty-two, make a written statement, under oath or affirmation, which statement shall contain notice that it is subject to the penalties of perjury, and shall be in the following form:

"I, _____, do solemnly swear (or affirm) that I will support, obey and defend the Constitution of the United States and the constitution of this Commonwealth, and that I will discharge the duties of _____ with fidelity.

"And I do further swear (or affirm) that I do not advocate, nor am I knowingly a member of any organization that advocates, the overthrow of the Government of the United States or of this Commonwealth by force or violence or other unconstitutional means, or seeking by force or violence to deny other persons their rights under the Constitution of the United States or of this Commonwealth.

"And I do further swear (or affirm) that I will not so advocate nor will I knowingly become a member of such organization during the period that I am an employee of the Commonwealth of Pennsylvania (or political subdivision thereof)."

Any person failing or refusing to execute either statement required hereby shall be discharged immediately by the proper appointing authority.

Id. § 216. *Investigations.*—Any appointing authority may at any time, upon written complaint, investigate any person, including teachers and other employees of the public school system, appointed or employed by him, to determine whether he is a subversive person. If, upon any investigation, it appears that such person is a subversive person, the person shall immediately be privately and confidentially notified of the recommendation by the appointing authority. No public announcement, release, statement or comment concerning the investigation, recommendation or notification shall be made by the appointing authority in any way whatsoever, unless and until the person so notified is discharged under section seven of this act.

Id. § 217. *Hearing.*—Any person, including teachers and other employes of the public school system, who has been so notified under this act, shall have a right to a hearing before the proper appointing authority within thirty (30) days after receiving said notification. If no hearing is requested within thirty (30) days after said notification is received, the person shall immediately be discharged by the appointing authority. He may appear before such appointing authority personally, accompanied by counsel or representative of his own choosing, and present evidence on his own behalf through witnesses. The person who has been so notified shall at the same time be further informed in writing of such hearing, at least ten days before the day set for the hearing, and shall be informed therein of the nature of the charges against him; and the person who has been so notified shall be informed in the notice (1) of his right to reply to such charges in writing within ten days after the date of service, (2) of his right to a hearing on such charges before the appointing authority, which hearing may be private and confidential or may be public, at the option of the person so notified, and (3) of his right to appear before such appointing authority personally, to be accompanied by counsel or representative of his own choosing, and to present evidence on his own behalf through witnesses. If, after due hearing, it is determined by the appointing authority by a fair preponderance of the evidence that the person who has been so notified is a subversive person, as defined in this act, the person who has been so notified shall be discharged; otherwise, the recommendation shall be ignored. Said determination shall be made within sixty (60) days after the hearing. If the appointing authority shall be comprised of three or more members, a vote of two-thirds of the members shall be necessary in order to discharge a person.

Id. § 218. *Standard of evidence.*—(a) The standard for the refusal of employment on grounds relating to loyalty shall be, that on all the evidence there is a reasonable doubt as to the loyalty of the person involved to the Government of the United States or the Commonwealth of Pennsylvania.

(b) Activities and associations of an applicant which may be considered in connection with the determination of ineligibility may include, but shall not be limited to, one or more of the following:

(1) Sabotage, espionage, or attempts or preparations therefor, or knowingly associating with spies or saboteurs.

(2) Treason or sedition or advocacy thereof.

(3) Advocacy of revolution or force or violence to alter the constitutional form of Government of the United States or the Commonwealth of Pennsylvania.

(4) Intentional unauthorized disclosure to any person, under circumstances which may indicate disloyalty to the United States or the Commonwealth of Pennsylvania, of documents or information of a confidential or nonpublic character, obtained by the person making the disclosure as a result of his employment by the Commonwealth of Pennsylvania or any political subdivision.

Id. § 219. *Appeal to the Civil Service Commission.*—After a final determination of discharge under this act by an appointing authority, any person, other than teachers and other employes of the public school system, in the employ of the Commonwealth or of any political subdivision who believes himself aggrieved by the determination may appeal from the determination by an application in writing to the Civil Service Commission of the Commonwealth within twenty days after receiving written notice of the determination. The commission shall set a time and place for hearing the appeal on the record, which hearing shall not be more than thirty (30) days after receipt thereof, and give due notice of said hearing to the appellant and to the appointing authority whose determination is under review. The hearing shall be held by the commission or by a person or persons, not exceeding three, designated by the commission in writing to hear the appeal in its behalf. The commission, in its discretion, may designate such person or persons to hear the appeal and to report to the commission. The report shall be acted upon by the entire commission. The persons so designated by the commission may be officers or employees of the civil service of the Commonwealth. The person or persons holding the hearing may make such inquiry as may be deemed advisable. Within sixty (60) days after the hearing on appeal, the commission shall affirm or reverse the findings and determination under review, and, in the case of reversal, shall order the reinstatement of the appellant, who shall be entitled to back pay from the date of his discharge. For the purposes of this section, officers and employees of the Department of Public Instruction or of any of its departmental administrative boards or commissions shall not be construed to be employes of the public school system. They shall be entitled to appeal to the Civil Service Commission as provided herein.

Id. § 221. *Applicability of the rules of evidence.*—Evidence shall be restricted by the rules of evidence and procedure prevailing in the courts. All testimony shall be given under oath or affirmation, and the right of subpoena shall be accorded to either the appointing authority or the person so notified. Any judge of a court of record, either in term time or in vacation, shall, upon proper application of the appointing authority or person so notified, compel the attendance of witnesses, the production of books and papers, and the giving of testimony before the appointing authority, by attachment for contempt or otherwise, in the same manner as the production of evidence may be compelled before such court. Reasonable examination and cross-examination shall be permitted.

Id. § 222. *Judicial review.*—(a) The decision of the Civil Service Commission or the superintendent of public instruction shall be final unless, within thirty (30) days after receipt by registered mail of written notice of the decision or order of the Civil Service Commission or the superintendent of public instruction, an appeal which may be taken by either party is taken therefrom to the court of common pleas of the county in which the proper appointing authority is located. A copy of such appeal shall be filed in writing in the office of the prothonotary and a copy shall be served on the Civil Service Commission or the superintendent of public instruction, either by filing it in the office of the Civil Service Commission or the superintendent of public instruction, or by delivering the same to the Civil Service Commission or the superintendent of public instruction.

(b) When appeal is taken from the decision of the Civil Service Commission or the superintendent of public instruction to the court of common pleas, the judge of the court of common pleas to whom such petition is presented shall fix a date for hearing by the court, which shall be not sooner than ten (10) days nor more than twenty (20) days after the presentation of such petition. If the employee aggrieved shall so request in his petition, such hearing shall be de novo. Upon the hearing of said petition, the court shall make whatever order it considers just, either affirming or reversing the action of the Civil Service Commission or the superintendent of public instruction, and stating plainly whether the employee is to be discharged.

Id. § 225. *Effect and application of act.*—(a) The provisions of this act shall not affect the right to discharge any person for any cause other than those provided for by this act or without cause under existing law. No procedure provided by any existing tenure or civil service law shall be applicable in any proceeding under this act.

(b) The provisions of this act shall not apply to exchange teachers who are citizens or subjects of a foreign government and whose appointments to teach in the public school system of the Commonwealth of Pennsylvania have been approved by the superintendent of public instruction.

* * * * * * *

Annotations:

Powell v. *Unemployment Compensation Board of Review,* 146 Pa. Super. 147, 22 A. 2d 43 (1941). Appellants were discharged from public employment because they were representatives of the Communist Party and because they were dishonest in attempting to conceal the fact. The court affirmed the dismissal on the latter ground. In the course of the opinion it stated that the mandate of the act against discrimination because of "political affiliation" referred to politics in its narrow application to groups with legitimate aims and not to movements which advocate destruction of government by violence.

Fitzgerald v. *City of Philadelphia,* 376 Pa. 379, 102 A. 2d 887 (1954). Appellant, a staff nurse in the operating room of the city hospital, was dismissed for refusing to take the oath required of public employees by the State loyalty act. Affirming the dismissal of appellant's suit, the court stated that the legislature, as a condition of public employment, may prescribe qualifications with respect to not only general attainments, but also to moral character and loyalty to the State and Federal Governments, and, to that end may deny any persons public employment if they are knowingly members of a disloyal and seditious organization. The prescribed oath was justified for the purpose of informing the appointing authority as to whether the employee is in fact a member of an organization which he knows is subversive in character and therefore is not a fit person to be entrusted with the duty of supporting and advancing the interests of the very government whose destruction he is seeking to accomplish. The court found little merit in appellant's contention that the oath was unduly vague in terminology and set up a dubious standard for guidance. Since the oath proscribed membership in an organization which the employee knows is subversive, he cannot suffer the danger of incurring a criminal penalty if innocent of any criminal intent. As for appellant's First Amendment contentions, the court held that the oath did not constitute an infringement of the rights of free speech and peaceable assembly, free communication of thoughts and opinions and freedom from interference with the right of conscience.

3. CIVIL DEFENSE PERSONNEL

71 Pennsylvania Stat. § 1689.12. *Loyalty oath required.*—No person shall be employed or associated in any capacity in any civil defense organization established under this act who advocates or has advocated a change by force or violence in the constitutional form of Government of the United States or in this State, or the overthrow of any government in the United States by force or violence, or who has been convicted of or is under indictment or information charging any subversive act against the United States. Each person who is appointed to serve in an organization for civil defense shall, before entering upon his duties, take an oath in writing before a person authorized to administer oaths in this State, which oath shall be substantially as follows:

"I, _____, do solemnly swear (or affirm) that I will support and defend the Constitution of the United States and the constitution of the State of Pennsylvania against all enemies, foreign and domestic; that I will bear true faith and allegiance to the same; that I take this obligation freely without any mental reservation or purpose of evasion and that I will well and faithfully discharge the duties upon which I am about to enter;

"And I do further swear (or affirm) that I do not advocate nor am I a member or an affiliate of any organization, group or combination of persons that advocates the overthrow of the Government of the United States or of this State by force or violence, and that during such time as I am a member of the (name of civil defense organization) I will not advocate nor become a member nor an affiliate of any organization, group or combination of persons that advocates the overthrow of the Government of the United States or of this State by force or violence."

65 Pennsylvania Stat. § 211. *Short title.*—This act shall be known and may be cited as the "Pennsylvania Loyalty Act."

Id. § 212. *"Organization," "Subversive organization," "Subversive person," and "Appointing authority" defined.*—For the purposes of this act:

"Organization" means an organization, corporation, company partnership, association, trust, foundation, fund, club, society, committee, political party, or any group of persons, whether or not incorporated, permanently or temporarily associated together for joint action or advancement of views on any subject or subjects.

"Subversive organization" means any organization which engages in or advocates, abets, advises or teaches, or a purpose of which is to engage in or advocate, abet, advise or teach, activities intended to overthrow, destroy or alter, or to assist in the overthrow, destruction or alteration of, the constitutional form of the Government of the United States or of the Commonwealth of Pennsylvania, or of any political subdivision of either of them, by force or violence.

"Subversive person" means any person who commits, attempts to commit, or aids in the commission, or advocates, abets, advises or teaches, by any means, any person to commit, attempt to commit, or aid in the commission of, any act intended to overthrow, destroy, alter, or to assist in the overthrow, destruction or alteration of the constitutional form of Government of the United States or of the Commonwealth of Pennsylvania, or any political subdivision of either of them, by force or violence, or who is knowingly a member of a subversive organization or a foreign subversive organization as defined in this act.

"Appointing authority" means any person, department, board, commission, or other agency of the Commonwealth, or of any political subdivision thereof, who appoints or employs officers or employes.

Id. § 213. *Subversive persons and persons of doubtful loyalty ineligible for employment in or appointment to any school district.*—No subversive person, as defined in this act, nor any person as to whom on all the evidence there is reasonable doubt concerning his loyalty to the Government of the United States or the Commonwealth of Pennsylvania, shall be eligible for employment in or appointment to any office or any position of trust or profit in the government of or in the administration of the business of this Commonwealth, or of any school district, county, municipality or other political subdivision of this Commonwealth.

Id. § 214. *Appointment procedure; statement of loyalty required.*—Every appointing authority shall establish, by rules, regulations, or otherwise, procedures designed to ascertain, before any person, including teachers and other employes of the public school system, is appointed or employed, that he is not a subversive person and that there is no reasonable doubt on all the evidence as to the loyalty of the person involved to the Government of the United States or the Commonwealth of Pennsylvania. In the event the applicant is deemed to be a subversive person, or in the event reasonable doubt as to loyalty exists, he shall not be appointed or employed. In addition, each applicant shall be required to make a written statement, under oath or affirmation, which statement shall contain notice that it is subject to the penalties of perjury, and shall be in the following form:

"I, _____, do solemnly swear (or affirm) that I will support, obey and defend the Constitution of the United States and the constitution of this Commonwealth, and that I will discharge the duties of _____ with fidelity.

"And I do further swear (or affirm) that I do not advocate, nor am I knowingly a member of any organization that advocates, the overthrow the Government of the United States or of this Commonwealth by force or violence or other unconstitutional means, or seeking by force or violence to deny other persons their rights under the Constitution of the United States or of this Commonwealth.

"And I do further swear (or affirm) that I will not so advocate nor will I knowingly become a member of such organization during the period that I am an employee of the Commonwealth of Pennsylvania (or political subdivision thereof)."

Id. § 215. *Present employees; statement of loyalty required.*—The appointing authority of each person, including teachers and other employees of the public school system who, on the first day of March, one thousand nine hundred fifty-two, shall be in the employ of the Commonwealth of Pennsylvania or of any of its political subdivisions, other than those holding State or local elective offices of any kind, shall require such persons to, and every such person shall, on or before the first day of April, one thousand nine hundred fifty-two, make a written statement, under oath or affirmation, which statement shall contain notice that it is subject to the penalties of perjury, and shall be in the following form:

"I, _____, do solemnly swear (or affirm) that I will support, obey and defend the Constitution of the United States and the constitution of this Commonwealth, and that I will discharge the duties of _____ with fidelity.

"And I do further swear (or affirm) that I do not advocate, nor am I knowingly a member of any organization that advocates, the overthrow of the Government of the United States or of this Commonwealth by force or violence or other unconstitutional means, or seeking by force or violence to deny other persons their rights under the Constitution of the United States or of this Commonwealth.

"And I do further swear (or affirm) that I will not so advocate nor will I knowingly become a member of such organization during the period that I am an employe of the Commonwealth of Pennsylvania (or political subdivision thereof)."

Any person failing or refusing to execute either statement required hereby shall be discharged immediately by the proper appointing authority.

NOTE.—For provisions dealing with investigations, etc., see Nonelective Personnel, Loyalty of State Officers and Employees, *supra.*

Annotations:

Beilan v. *Board of Education,* 357 U.S. 399, 78 S. Ct. 1317, 2 L. Ed. 2d 1414 (1958). Petitioner, a public school teacher, was discharged by the board of education on the ground of "incompetency." The charge was predicated on his refusal to confirm or refute information as to his loyalty and his activities in certain allegedly subversive organizations. The Supreme Court affirmed the decision of the board and held that the Federal Constitution was not violated by petitioner's discharge for statutory "incompetency" based on his refusal to answer the superintendent's questions relating to communistic affiliation and activities. Although petitioner did not surrender his freedoms of belief, speech, or association by engaging in teaching, he did undertake obligations of frankness, candor, and cooperation in answering inquiries made of him by his employing board examining into his fitness to serve it as a public school teacher. Nothing in the Constitution, the Court declared, required that a teacher's classroom conduct be the sole basis for determining his fitness.

Board of Public Education, School District of Philadelphia v. Intille, 401 Pa. 1, 163 A. 2d 420 (1960), certiorari denied 364 U.S. 910, 81 S. Ct. 273, 5 L. Ed. 2d 225. Appellants, teachers in the public schools of Philadelphia, were dismissed by the board of public education on the ground of "incompetency" based solely on their refusal to answer certain questions propounded by a congressional subcommittee. In refusing to testify, each appellant invoked the privilege against self-incrimination. Reversing the dismissal, the court ruled that the action of the board in dismissing teachers upon the ground of incompetency was a penalty inflicted upon them by State action for having invoked, in a strictly Federal proceeding, the privilege against self-incrimination under the Fifth Amendment. The discharge of an employee in these circumstances constituted a denial of due process.

Board of Public Education, School District of Philadelphia v. Soler, 406 Pa. 168, 176 A. 2d 653 (1963). This case dealt with the discharge of a teacher on grounds of incompetency. The charge grew out of appellant's refusal to answer questions relating to his loyalty unless a copy of each question was submitted in advance. The court sustained the dismissal on the ground that the refusal by a teacher to answer relevant questions concerning his loyalty propounded by his administrative superior constitutes grounds for a finding of incompetency under the tenure provisions of the Public School Code. The court characterized appellant's insistence on advance copies of the questions to be asked as unreasonable and at odds with the teacher-superior relationship.

Board of Public Education, School District of Philadelphia v. August, 406 Pa. 229. 177 A. 2d 809 (1962). In this case, a schoolteacher was dismissed for incompetency for refusing to cooperate with the school superintendent in an inquiry on the matter of loyalty to the United States. The court sustained the dismissal on the ground that appellant's refusal to cooperate in a matter peculiarly within his own knowledge—his loyalty—amounted to insubordination, as well as a lack of frankness, candor, and intellectual honesty, all of which added up to incompetence.

Board of School Directors of School District of Borough of Wilmerding, Allegheny County v. Gillies, 343 Pa. 382, 23 A. 2d 447 (1942). In this case the court reversed the dismissal of a schoolteacher on grounds of immorality and incompetency because he signed an election nominating paper for a candidate of the Communist Party.

Board of Public Education School District of Philadelphia v. Watson, 401 Pa. 62, 163 A. 2d 60 (1960). Appeilant, a public school teacher, was dismissed for incompetency for refusing to answer questions about alleged associations with the Communists propounded by a congressional subcommittee. She relied upon the constitutional guarantees of the First Amendment in justification of her refusal to testify. The court reversed the dismissal on the ground that the State could not draw unfavorable inferences as to truthfulness, candor, or moral character in general if appellant's refusal to answer was based on a belief that the Constitution prohibited the type of inquiry the committee was making.

24 Pennsylvania Stat. § 11.1122. *Advocating un-American or subversive doctrines cause for terminating contract of employment.*—The only valid causes for termination of a contract heretofore or hereafter entered into with a professional employee shall be immorality, incompetency, intemperance, cruelty, persistent negligence, mental derangement, advocation of or participating in un-American or subversive doctrines, persistent and willful violation of the school laws of this Commonwealth on the part of the professional employee: Provided, That boards of school directors may terminate the service of any professional employee who has attained to the age of sixty-two except a professional employee who is a member of the old age and survivors insurance system pursuant to the provisions of the act, approved the first day of June, one thousand nine hundred fifty-six (Pamphlet Laws 1973). In such case the board may terminate the service of any such professional employee at the age of sixty-five or at the age at which the employee becomes eligible to receive full benefits under the Federal Social Security Act.

Nothing within the foregoing enumeration of causes, shall be interpreted to conflict with the retirement of professional employees upon proper evidence of disability, or the election by professional employees to retire during the period of voluntary retirement, or the authority of the board of school directors to require professional employees to retire during said period of voluntary retirement, or the compulsion on the part of professional employees to retire at the attainment of age seventy.

Annotation:

Appeal of Albert, 372 Pa. 13, 92 A. 2d 663 (1953). This case involved the discharge of a teacher pursuant to a State statute which authorized termination of a contract with a professional employee for "advocation or participation in un-American or subversive doctrines." The court sustained the dismissal holding that the legislature can prescribe qualifications for teachers in the public schools with respect not only to their academic attainments but also to their moral characters and their loyalty to the State and Federal Governments.

Exclusion From the Bar

Pennsylvania has neither a rule of the Supreme Court nor a Regulation of the State board of law examiners which pertains to the admission of persons who are or have been Communists or subversives. Similarly, the various forms employed by the State do not contain any questions directly on the subject.

Exclusion From Incidental Benefits

PUBLIC ASSISTANCE

65 Pennsylvania Stat. § 2509 (Supp. 1963). *Persons advocating overthrow of the government ineligible for public assistance.*—Any person residing within this Commonwealth shall hereafter be entitled to receive public assistance, as provided by law, without regard to the period of time he or she has resided therein, and the department of public welfare shall grant assistance without regard to the period of time any person seeking public assistance and otherwise entitled thereto shall have resided within this State: Provided, however, That if the applicant for public assistance has resided in Pennsylvania for less than one year immediately preceding the date of making application for assistance, such person shall only be entitled to receive public assistance if he or she was last a resident of a State which by law, regulation or reciprocal agreement with Pennsylvania grants public assistance to a person who has resided therein for less than one year. A child less than one year of age is considered as deriving residence from either (1) a parent, or (2) other relative with whom he is living, as provided in this section. Except as hereinafter specifically otherwise provided in the case of pensions for the blind, all persons of the following classes, except those who hereafter advocate and actively participate by an overt act or acts in a movement proposing a change in the form of Government of the United States by means not provided for in the Constitution of the United States, shall be eligible to receive assistance, in accordance with rules, regulations and standards established by the department of public welfare, as to eligibility for assistance, and as to its nature and extent. Absence in the service of the Commonwealth or of the United States shall not be deemed to interrupt residence in the Commonwealth if a domicile has not been acquired outside the Commonwealth.

*　　　*　　　*　　　*　　　*　　　*　　　*

RHODE ISLAND

Unlawful Advocacy

1. ANARCHY

Gen. Laws § 11–43–12. *Advocating anarchy.*—Any person who shall wilfully teach or advocate anarchy or the overthrow by force or violence of the Government of the State of Rhode Island or of the United States, or of all forms of law, or opposition to organized government, or any person who shall willfully become a member of or affiliated with any organization teaching and advocating disbelief in or opposition to organized government, or advocating or teaching the duty, necessity or propriety of the unlawful assaulting or killing of any officer or officers, either of specific individuals or of officers generally of the government of the State of Rhode Island or of the United States, or of any organized government because of his or their official character, or advocating or teaching the unlawful destruction of property, shall be guilty of a felony and upon conviction shall be punished by a fine of not more than ten thousand dollars ($10,000) or imprisonment not exceeding ten (10) years or both.

Id. § 11–43–13. *Conspiring to advocate anarchy.*—If two (2) or more persons conspire to violate any of the provisions of §§ 11–43–11 and 11–43–12 and one or more of such persons does any act to effect the object of the conspiracy, each of the parties to said conspiracy shall be guilty of a felony and upon conviction, shall be punished by a fine of not more than ten thousand dollars ($10,000) or imprisonment not exceeding ten (10) years or both.

Id.§ 11–43–14. *Unlawful assembly.*—Any meeting at which any of the things forbidden in §§ 11–43–11 and 11–43–12 are advocated, taught or discussed, or any meeting called for the purpose of advocating, teaching or discussing any of the things forbidden by §§ 11–43–11 and 11–43–12, is hereby declared to be an unlawful assembly, and may be dispersed in the manner provided for dispersing of riotous, tumultuous and treasonable assemblies in § 11–43–5.

Id. § 11–43–5. *Dispersal of unlawful assembly.*—Such meetings as are described in § 11–43–4 and also all meetings of persons other than those authorized by law, calling themselves when collected or claiming to be the general assembly of this State or either house thereof, are hereby declared to be riotous, tumultuous and treasonable assemblies, and the commander-in-chief, the sheriff of any county or any deputy sheriff, any justice of the supreme or superior court, the mayors of the several cities or in their absence the city councils of said cities, are hereby authorized and required to command such assemblies or any of them to disperse, and if they do not forthwith obey said command, then, by the civil posse, or, if they deem it necessary, by calling out and using for that purpose the whole or any portion of the military force of this State within their respective jurisdictions that they or either of them may deem sufficient therefor, to disperse such assemblies or any of them within their jurisdictions, and all such officers, civil and military, and persons under their command, are hereby directed to govern themselves accordingly.

2. ADVOCATING FORCIBLE OVERTHROW OF GOVERNMENT

Gen. Laws § 11–43–11. *Unlawful acts and penalty.*—Any person who shall willfully speak, utter, print, write or publish any language intended to incite, provoke or encourage forceful resistance to the State of Rhode Island or to the United States of America, or a defiance or disregard of the constitution or laws of the State of Rhode Island or of the United States, or shall advocate any change, alteration or modification in the form of government of the State of Rhode Island or of the United States except in the manner provided by the constitution or the laws of the State of Rhode Island or by the Constitution or the laws of the United States, or shall advocate any change in the form of government of the State of Rhode Island or of the United States by means of revolution or violence, or shall advocate the assassination of persons occupying public positions or offices created by the constitution and laws of the State of Rhode Island or of the United States, or shall advocate, incite, provoke or encourage the destruction, burning, blowing up, or damaging of any public or private property as a part or incident of a program of force, violence or revolution, having for its purpose the overthrow of the form of government of the State of Rhode Island or of the United States, or shall willfully display publicly any flag or emblem, except the flag of the United States, as symbolic or emblematic of the Government of the United States or of a form of government proposed by its adherents or supporters as superior or preferable to the form of Government of the United States as prescribed by the Constitution of the United States, shall be guilty of a felony and upon conviction be punished by a fine of not more than ten thousand dollars ($10,000) or imprisonment not exceeding ten (10) years or both.

Id. § 11–43–14. *Unlawful assembly.*—Any meeting at which any of the things forbidden in §§ 11–43–11 and 11–43–12 are advocated, taught or discussed, or any meeting called for the purpose of advocating, teaching or discussing any of the things forbidden by §§ 11–43–11 and 11–43–12, is hereby declared to be an unlawful assembly, and may be dispersed in the manner provided for dispersing of riotous, tumultuous and treasonable assemblies in § 11–43–5.

Id. § 11–43–5. *Dispersal of unlawful assembly.*—Such meetings as are described in § 11–43–4 and also all meetings of persons other than those authorized by law, calling themselves when collected or claiming to be the general assembly of this State or either house thereof, are hereby declared to be riotous, tumultuous and treasonable assemblies, and the commander-in-chief, the sheriff of any county or any deputy sheriff, any justice of the supreme or superior court, the mayors of the several cities or in their absence the city councils of said cities, are hereby authorized and required to command such assemblies or any of them to disperse, and if they do not forthwith obey said command, then, by the civil posse, or, if they deem it necessary, by calling out and using for that purpose the whole or any portion of the military force of this State within their respective jurisdictions that they or either of them may deem sufficient therefor, to disperse such assemblies or any of them within their jurisdictions, and all such officers, civil and military, and persons under their command, are hereby directed to govern themselves accordingly.

LOYALTY OF STATE OFFICERS AND EMPLOYEES

ELECTIVE AND NONELECTIVE PERSONNEL

Rhode Island Constitution, Art. IX, § 3. *Oath.*—All general officers shall take the following engagement before they act in their respective offices, to wit: You, _____, being by the free vote of the electors of this State of Rhode Island and Providence Plantations, elected unto the place of _____ do solemnly swear (*or*, affirm) to be true and faithful unto this State, and to support the constitution of this State and of the United States, that you will faithfully and impartially discharge all the duties of your aforesaid office to the best of your abilities, according to law: So help you God. [*Or:* This affirmation you make and give upon the peril of the penalty of perjury.]

SOUTH CAROLINA

REGISTRATION

Code of Laws, 1962, § 16–581. *Short title.*—This chapter may be cited as the "Subversive Activities Registration Act."

Id. § 582. *"Subversive organization," "Organization subject to foreign control," "Foreign agent," and "Business" defined.*—For the purposes of this chapter the following words, phrases, and terms are defined as follows:

(1) *"Subversive organization"* means every corporation, society, association, camp, group, bund, political party, assembly, body, or organization, composed of two or more persons, which directly or indirectly advocates, advises, teaches, or practices the duty, necessity, or propriety of controlling, conducting, seizing, or overthrowing the Government of the United States, of this State, or of any political subdivision thereof by force or violence or other unlawful means;

(2) *"Organization subject to foreign control"* means every corporation, society, association, camp, group, bund, political party, assembly, body, or other organization, composed of two or more persons, which comes within either of the following:

(a) it solicits or accepts financial contributions, loans, or support of any kind directly or indirectly from, or is affiliated directly or indirectly with, a foreign government or a political subdivision thereof, an agent, agency, or instrumentality of a foreign government or political subdivision thereof, a political party in a foreign country, or an international political organization; or

(b) its policies, or any of them, are determined by or at the suggestion of, or in collaboration with, a foreign government or political subdivision thereof, an agent, agency, or instrumentality of a foreign government or a political subdivision thereof, a political party in a foreign country or an international political organization;

(3) *"Foreign agent"* means any person whose actions, or any of them, are determined by or at the suggestion of, or in collaboration with, a foreign government or political subdivision thereof, an instrumentality or agency of a foreign government or political subdivision thereof, a political party in a foreign country or an international political organization; and

(4) *"Business"* includes, but is not limited to, speaking engagements.

Id. § 16–583. *Abridgment of constitutional rights disclaimed.*—Nothing in this chapter shall be construed to authorize, require or establish censorship or to limit in any way or infringe upon freedom of the press or of speech as guaranteed by the Constitution of the United States and no regulation shall be promulgated hereunder having that effect.

Id. § 16–584. *Exclusions from scope of law.*—The terms of this chapter do not apply to any labor union or religious, fraternal or

371

patriotic organization, society or association, or their members, whose objectives and aims do not contemplate the overthrow of the Government of the United States, of this State or of any political subdivision thereof by force or violence or other unlawful means.

Id. § 16–585. *Subversive organizations, etc., required to register.*— Every subversive organization and organization subject to foreign control shall register with the secretary of state on forms prescribed by him within thirty days after coming into existence in this State.

Id. § 16–586. *Members of subversive organizations, organizations subject to foreign control, foreign agents and persons advocating subversion required to register.*—Every member of a subversive organization, or an organization subject to foreign control, every foreign agent and every person who advocates, teaches, advises or practices the duty, necessity or propriety of controlling, conducting, seizing or overthrowing the Government of the United States, of this State or of any political subdivision thereof by force or violence or other unlawful means, who resides, transacts any business or attempts to influence political action in this State, shall register with the secretary of state on the forms and at the times prescribed by him.

Id. § 16–587. *Filing of required information and forms.*—Every organization or person coming within the provisions of this chapter shall file with the secretary of state all information which he may request, on the forms and at the times he may prescribe.

Id. § 16–588. *Rules and regulations.*—The secretary of state may adopt and promulgate any rules and regulations, not inconsistent with the terms of this chapter, which may be necessary to carry out the provisions of this chapter and may alter or repeal such rules and regulations.

Id. § 16–589. *Penalty.*—Any organization or person who violates any of the provisions of this chapter shall, upon conviction thereof, be punished by a fine of not more than twenty-five thousand dollars or imprisonment for not more than ten years, or by both fine and imprisonment.

LOYALTY OF STATE OFFICERS AND EMPLOYEES

ELECTIVE AND NONELECTIVE PERSONNEL

South Carolina Constitution, Art. 111, § 26. *Oath.*—Members of the General Assembly, and all officers, before they enter upon the duties of their respective offices, and all members of the bar, before they enter upon the practice of their profession, shall take and subscribe the following oath: "I do solemnly swear (or affirm) that I am duly qualified, according to the constitution of this State, to exercise the duties of the office to which I have been elected (or appointed), and that I will, to the best of my ability, discharge the duties thereof, and preserve, protect and defend the constitution of this State and of the United States. So help me God."

TEACHERS' LOYALTY

Code of Laws, 1962, § 21–372. *Applicants for teacher's certificate required to demonstrate loyalty.*—All persons applying for certificates authorizing them to become teachers in the public schools of this State shall, in addition to other requirements and before receiving such certificate, be required to pass a satisfactory examination upon the provisions and principles of the Constitution of the United States and shall also satisfy the examining power of their loyalty thereto.

EXCLUSIONS FROM THE BAR

Paragraph 20, Application for Examination and Admission to Practice Law, requires applicant to state whether he is a member of the Communist Party or any of its affiliates. It reads as follows:

20. (a) Are you now, or have you ever been, a member of the Communist Party or any of its affiliates?

(b) Are you now, or have you ever been, a member of any organization which is or has been classified by the Attorney General of the United States as being a subversive organization. If so, list all such organizations of which you have been a member.

Other probative though less direct questions appear on the application form. These include:

18. (d) Have you ever invoked the protection of the Fifth Amendment to the Constitution of the United States, or of any other provision of the Constitution of the United States or of any States, in refusing to testify under oath in any proceeding on the ground or for the reason that your answer might tend to incriminate you?

22. So you now and will you hereafter, without any reservations, loyally support the Constitution of the United States and the constitution of the State of South Carolina?

Identical paragraphs appear on the application form for admission of attorneys from other States (Nos. 16(d), 18, 20).

EXCLUSION FROM INCIDENTAL BENEFITS

GRADUATION CERTIFICATE

Code of Laws, 1962, § 21–420. *Graduation certificate conditioned upon demonstration of loyalty.*—All high schools, colleges and universities in this State that are sustained or in any manner supported by public funds shall give instruction in the essentials of the United States Constitution, including the study of and devotion to American institutions and ideals, and no student in any such school, college or university shall receive a certificate of graduation without previously passing a satisfactory examination upon the provisions and principles of the United States Constitution, and, if a citizen of the United States, satisfying the examining power of his loyalty thereto.

MISCELLANEOUS

Code of Laws, 1962, § 30–141. *Committee to investigate Communist activities.*—In order to supply information as the basis for legislation to preserve the government of this State, there is hereby created a committee to investigate Communist activities within this State to be composed of six members, three of whom shall be appointed by the Speaker of the House of Representatives from the membership of that body, and three of whom shall be appointed by the President of the Senate from the membership of that body. The terms of the members shall be coterminous with their terms as members of the General Assembly and until their successors are appointed and qualify. Vacancies shall be filled in the manner of the original appointment for the unexpired term. Members shall receive such per diem and mileage as is authorized by law for members of boards and commissions.

Id. § 30–142 (Supp. 1963). *Duties of committee.*—It shall be the duty of the committee to investigate Communist activities in this State. The committee shall make a report of its activities to the General Assembly at each session and shall offer such advice as it deems appropriate. It shall also recommend such legislation as it may determine to be advisable, as a result of its investigation, to preserve the government of the State. The committee shall develop and execute an educational program to inform the people of the State of South Carolina of the threat of communism to the national security.

Id. § 30–143. *Powers of committee.*—(1) The committee, or any subcommittee thereof, shall have power to hold hearings, to sit and act at such times and places within the State as the chairman shall designate, and require, by subpoena or otherwise, the attendance of such witnesses and the production of such books, papers and documents, as it deems necessary to effect the functions of the committee.

(2) Any subpoena shall be issued under the signature of the chairman of the committee and shall be served by any lawful peace officer designated by him.

(3) Any person whom the committee may subpoena to appear in person shall be required to answer under oath any and all questions that the committee determines relevant and may propound to him. Upon the failure or refusal of such person to obey such summons or notice, or to answer such question or questions, such person may be cited by the committee to the attorney general who shall bring an appropriate action to have such person adjudged in contempt of the committee, and upon conviction, shall be punished with fine or imprisonment, or both, in the discretion of the court. All testimony given before the committee shall be privileged, and no testimony given by any witness before the committee shall be used as evidence in any criminal proceeding against him in any court, except in a prosecution for perjury committed in giving such testimony, but an official paper or record produced by him is not within such privilege. No witness shall be privileged to refuse to testify to any fact or to produce any paper, or document, upon the ground that his testimony to such fact or production of such paper or document may tend to disgrace him or otherwise render him infamous.

(4) The committee may require the production of any and all books, papers or other documents or writings which may be deemed relevant to an investigation, and may require the person in custody or possession of such papers to produce them before the committee. The committee may also designate its attorney or agent to examine such papers prior to their production before the committee in order that orderly hearings may be held. Any person who fails or refuses to permit such examinations, or to act on the order or notice of the committee to produce such books, papers, documents or other writings shall be deemed guilty of contempt of the committee and shall be punished therefor, upon conviction in a court of competent jurisdiction in an action brought in the name of the State by the attorney general after citation of such person by the committee to the attorney general.

(5) The committeee may administer all necessary oaths; and any person who, after being sworn before the committee or its members, shall swear falsely, shall be guilty of perjury, and, upon conviction, shall be punished therefor as provided by law.

Id. § 30–144. *Professional and clerical staff.*—The committee may employ an executive secretary or general counsel and such stenographic and clerical help as is necessary to carry out the provisions of this chapter and shall fix the compensation of such employees.

Id. § 30–145. *Appropriations.*—Such funds as are necessary to defray the expenses of the committee shall be appropriated in the annual general appropriation act.

SOUTH DAKOTA

Unlawful Advocacy

CRIMINAL SYNDICALISM

South Dakota Code 1939, § 13.0801. *Criminal syndicalism defined; unlawful acts and penalty.*—Criminal syndicalism is hereby defined as any doctrine or practice which teaches, advocates, or practices crime, sabotage, violence, or other methods of terrorism, or the destruction of life or property, for the accomplishment of social, economic, industrial, or political ends.

The advocacy, teaching, support, practice, or furtherance of any such doctrine or practice, whether by act, speech, or writing, or by any means or in any manner, is hereby declared to be a felony and punishable as in this chapter provided.

Any person who shall, by act, or speech, or in writing, or by symbol, precept, suggestion, example or illustration, advocate, suggest or teach the duty, necessity or propriety of crime, sabotage, violence or other methods of terrorism, or the destruction of life or property for the accomplishment of social, economic, industrial or political ends, or who shall print, publish, utter, sell, circulate, distribute, display or have in his or her possession any book, paper, document, writing or article in any form which shall contain any doctrine, or advocate, advise, teach, or suggest that social, economic, industrial or political ends should be brought about by crime, sabotage, violence or other means of terrorism with intent to suggest, exemplify, illustrate, spread or advocate any of the doctrines of criminal syndicalism, or who shall organize or assist in the organization, or become a member of, or assemble with any persons, societies, associations, groups or assemblages of persons formed for or engaging in the teaching or advocacy of any of the doctrines of criminal syndicalism, or who shall, directly or indirectly, in any manner destroy, or attempt to destroy, contribute to, or cause the destruction of life or property of any description, or who shall have in his possession or control anything with intent to destroy life or property, in the pursuance or furtherance of any of the doctrines of criminal syndicalism as defined in this chapter, shall upon conviction be guilty of a felony and be punished by imprisonment in the State penitentiary for not less than one nor more than twenty-five years, or by a fine of not less than one thousand dollars nor more than ten thousand dollars, or by both such fine and imprisonment, in the discretion of the court.

Id. § 13.0803. *Assemblage to advocate criminal syndicalism.*— Whenever two or more persons assemble for the purpose of advocating, teaching, suggesting, or illustrating, in any manner, any doctrine or practice of criminal syndicalism, or of any of the acts in this chapter hereinbefore defined or referred to, such assemblage shall be unlawful, and every person participating therein by his presence, or who shall aid or in any manner instigate the holding of such an assemblage, shall upon conviction be guilty of a felony and shall be punished by imprisonment in the State penitentiary for not less than one year nor more than twenty-five years, or by a fine of not less than one thousand dollars nor more than ten thousand dollars, or by both such fine and imprisonment, in the discretion of the court.

Id. § 13.0804. *Permitting use of premises to advocate criminal syndicalism.*—Any owner, agent, custodian, occupant, or superintendent of any place who shall permit therein any assemblage of persons for any of the purposes prohibited by the provisions of this chapter, or who, after notification that the said place is so used, shall permit such use to continue, shall be guilty of a felony and shall be punished by imprisonment in the State penitentiary for not less than one year nor more than twenty-five years, or by a fine of not less than one thousand dollars nor more than ten thousand dollars, or by both fine and imprisonment in the discretion of the court.

LOYALTY OF STATE OFFICERS AND EMPLOYEES

1. ELECTIVE AND NONELECTIVE PERSONNEL

South Dakota Constitution, Art. III, § 8. *Oath.*—Members of the legislature and officers thereof, before they enter upon their official duties, shall take and subscribe the following oath or affirmation: I do solemnly swear (or affirm) that I will support the Constitution of the United States and the constitution of the State of South Dakota, and will faithfully discharge the duties of (senator, representative, or officer) according to the best of my abilities, and that I have not knowingly or intentionally paid or contributed anything, or made any promise in the nature of a bribe, to directly or indirectly influence any vote at the election at which I was chosen to fill said office, and have not accepted, nor will I accept or receive directly or indirectly, any money, pass, or any other valuable thing, from any corporation, company or person, for any vote or influence I may give or withhold on any bill or resolution, or appropriation, or for any other official act.

This oath shall be administered by a judge of the supreme or circuit court, or the presiding officer of either house, in the hall of the house to which the member or officer is elected, and the secretary of state shall record and file the oath subscribed by each member and officer.

Any member or officer of the legislature who shall refuse to take the oath herein prescribed shall forfeit his office.

Any member or officer of the legislature who shall be convicted of having sworn falsely to, or violated his said oath, shall forfeit his office and be disqualified thereafter from holding the office of senator or member of the house of representatives or any office within the gift of the legislature.

South Dakota Constitution, Art. 21, § 3. *Oath to support constitution required.*—Every person elected or appointed to any office in this State, except such inferior offices as may be by law exempted, shall, before entering upon the duties thereof, take an oath or affirmation to support the Constitution of the United States and of this State, and faithfully to discharge the duties of his office.

2. NONELECTIVE PERSONNEL

South Dakota Code 1939, § 17.0315 (Supp. 1960). *Loyalty oath required.*—All persons in South Dakota, with the exception of executive and judicial officers and members of the legislature who are required to take the oath prescribed by Article III, section 8 of the constitution of South Dakota, who are paid from public funds for their services, including teachers and all other employees paid from public school funds shall be required to take and subscribe an oath in writing, before a person authorized to administer oaths in this State, and file same without charge therefor with the secretary of state or with the clerk of courts of the county where such services are performed, prior to the approval of any voucher for the payment of salary, expenses, or other compensation, which oath shall be as follows:

"I, --------------------- do solemnly swear or affirm that I will support and defend the Constitution of the United States and the constitution of the State of South Dakota, against all enemies, foreign and domestic; that I will bear true faith and allegiance to the same; that I take this obligation freely, without any mental reservation or for the purpose of evasion; and that I will faithfully and impartially perform the duties of the office of ------------------- according to law, and to the best of my ability. And I do further swear or affirm that I do not advocate, nor am I a member, nor have I been within a period of a year a member, of any political party or organization that advocates, the overthrow of the Government of the United States or of this State by force or violence; and that during such time as I am in this position I will not advocate nor become a member of any political party or organization that advocates the overthrow of the Government of the United States or of this State by force or violence. So help me God."

Id. § 17.9917 (Supp. 1960). *Penalty.*—Any person taking and subscribing the oath prescribed by SDC 1960 Supp. 17.0315, knowing the same to be false, shall be guilty of a felony, and upon conviction thereof shall be punished by a fine not exceeding one thousand dollars, or imprisonment in the State penitentiary not exceeding five years, or by both such fine and imprisonment.

No person convicted under the provisions of this act shall hold any position, job or office for the State of South Dakota, political subdivision thereof, or school therein, either elective or appointive, where the remuneration of such position, job or office is paid in whole or in part by public money or funds from the State of South Dakota, any political subdivision thereof, or school district.

3. CIVIL DEFENSE PERSONNEL

South Dakota Code 1939, § 41.01C13 (Supp. 1960). *Loyalty oath required.*—No person shall be employed or associated in any capacity in any civil defense organization established under this chapter who advocates or has advocated a change by force or violence in the constitutional form of the Government of the United States or in this State or the overthrow of any government in the United States by force or violence, or who has been convicted of or is under indictment or information charging any subversive act against the United States. Each person who is appointed to serve in an organization for civil defense shall, before entering upon his duties, take an oath, in writing, before a person authorized to administer oaths in this State, which oath shall be substantially as follows:

State of South Dakota,

County of _____

I, _____,
do solemnly swear (or affirm) that I will support and defend the Constitution of the United States and the constitution of the State of South Dakota against all enemies, foreign and domestic; that I will bear true faith and allegiance to the same; that I take this obligation freely, without any mental reservation or purpose of evasion; and that I will well and faithfully discharge the duties on which I am about to enter. And I do further swear (or affirm) that I do not advocate nor am I a member of any political party or organization that advocates the overthrow of the Government of the United States or of this State by force or violence; and that during such time as I am a member of the (name of civil defense organization), I will not advocate nor become a member of any political party or organization that advocates the overthrow of the Government of the United States or of this State by force or violence.

Id. 41.9911 (Supp. 1960). *Penalty.*—Any person who shall be found guilty of having falsely taken such oath shall be guilty of a misdemeanor.

TEACHERS' LOYALTY

South Dakota Code 1939, § 17.0315 (Supp. 1960). *Loyalty oath required.*—All persons in South Dakota, with the exception of executive and judicial officers and members of the legislature who are required to take the oath prescribed by Article III, section 8 of the constitution of South Dakota, who are paid from public funds for their services, including teachers and all other employees paid from public school funds shall be required to take and subscribe an oath in writing, before a person authorized to administer oaths in this State, and file same without charge therefor with the secretary of state or with the clerk of courts of the county where such services are performed, prior to the approval of any voucher for the payment of salary, expenses, or other compensation, which oath shall be as follows:

"I, _____, do solemnly swear or affirm that I will support and defend the Constitution of the United States and the constitution of the State of South Dakota, against all enemies, foreign and domestic; that I will bear true faith and allegiance to the same; that I take this obligation freely, without any mental reservation or for the purpose of evasion; and that I will faithfully and impartially perform the duties of the office of _____ according to law, and to the best of my ability. And I do further swear or affirm that I do not advocate, nor am I a member, nor have I been within a period of a year a member, of any political party or organization that advocates, the overthrow of the Government of the United States or of this State by force or violence; and that during such time as I am in this position I will not advocate nor become a member of any political party or organization that advocates the overthrow of the Government of the United States or of this State by force or violence. So help me God."

Id. § 17.9917 (Supp. 1960). *Penalty.*—Any person taking and subscribing the oath prescribed by SDC 1960 Supp. 17.0315, knowing the same to be false, shall be guilty of a felony, and upon conviction thereof shall be punished by a fine not exceeding one thousand dollars, or imprisonment in the State penitentiary not exceeding five years, or by both such fine and imprisonment.

No person convicted under the provisions of this act shall hold any position, job or office for the State of South Dakota, political subdivision thereof, or school therein, either elective or appointive, where the remuneration of such position, job or office is paid in whole or in part by public money or funds from the State of South Dakota, any political subdivision thereof, or school district.

Id. § 15.3803 (Supp. 1960). *Issuance of teacher's certificate conditioned upon execution of loyalty oath.*—No teacher's certificate of any grade shall hereafter be issued unless the applicant shall first take and subscribe to an oath to support the Constitution of the United States and of the State of South Dakota, which shall be kept on file in the office of the superintendent of public instruction. The superintendent of public instruction or his deputy and the county superintendent or his deputy are hereby authorized to administer the oath required under this chapter; said oath of allegiance may also be administered by any other officer authorized by law to administer oaths.

Any teacher who shall have publicly reviled, ridiculed, or otherwise spoken or acted with disrespect and contumacy toward the flag of the United States or its official uniforms or insignia, or toward the system of Government of the United States and its Constitution, or shall refuse to take and subscribe the oath of allegiance hereinbefore required shall upon satisfactory proof of the commission of such offense have his certificate revoked by the superintendent of public instruction.

Exclusion From The Bar

South Dakota does not appear to have any rule or regulation which pertains, to the admission of persons who are or who have been Communists or subversives. Similarly, the various forms employed by the State do not contain any questions directly on the subject.

TENNESSEE

Unlawful Advocacy

1. ADVOCATING FORCIBLE OVERTHROW OF GOVERNMENT

Tennessee Code § 39–4405 (Supp. 1964). *Unlawful acts and penalty.*—Whoever knowingly or willfully advocates, abets, advises, or teaches the duty, necessity, desirability, or propriety of overthrowing or destroying the government of the State of Tennessee or of the United States by force or violence, or by the assassination of any officer of either government, or whoever, with intent to cause the overthrow or destruction of the government of Tennessee or of the United States, prints, publishes, edits, issues, circulates, sells, distributes, or publicly displays any written or printed matter advocating, advising, or teaching the duty, necessity, desirability, or propriety of overthrowing or destroying the government of Tennessee or the United States by force or violence, or attempts to do so, or whoever organizes or helps or attempts to organize any society, group, or assembly of persons, who teach, advocate, or encourage the overthrow or destruction of the government of Tennessee or of the United States by force or violence, or becomes or is a member of, or affiliates with, any such society, group, or assembly of persons, knowing the purpose thereof, shall be fined not more than ten thousand dollars ($10,000) or imprisoned not more than ten (10) years in the State penitentiary, or both, and shall be ineligible for employment by the State of Tennessee or any department or agency thereof, for the five (5) years next following his conviction.

2. COMMUNISM

Tennessee Code § 39–4420 (Supp. 1964). *"Communist Party" defined.*—For the purpose of this act, "Communist Party" shall mean:
    (a) The Communist Party of the United States.
    (b) The Communist political association.
    (c) The Communist Party of any State of the United States, of any foreign state, or of any political or geographical subdivision of any foreign state.
    (d) Any section, subsidiary, branch, affiliate, or subdivision of any such association or party.
    (e) Any organization which advocates or teaches the overthrowal by force or violence or other unconstitutional means of the Government of the United States or the State of Tennessee.

Id. § 39–4421 (Supp. 1964). *Declaration of legislative findings.*—The general assembly of the State of Tennessee hereby finds and determines that the Communist Party advocates, teaches, and encourages the overthrowal of the Government of the United States and of the State of Tennessee by force and violence, the same being contrary to the Constitution of the United States and of the State of Tennessee, and, that the existence of the Communist Party, and membership in such party, is an immediate and constant threat to the peace, safety, and security of the State of Tennessee and of the people thereof.

Id. § 39–4422 (Supp. 1964). *Communist Party and membership in party unlawful.*—It shall be unlawful for the Communist Party to operate in the State of Tennessee, and it shall be unlawful for any person in the State of Tennessee to knowingly be a member of, or belong to, the Communist Party. Membership in the Communist Party shall be prima facie evidence that a person advocates, teaches, and encourages the forceful and violent overthrowal of the government of the State of Tennessee.

Id. § 39–4423 (Supp. 1964). *Penalty.*—Any person violating the provisions of §§ 39–4420—39–4422 shall, upon conviction thereof, be imprisoned for a period of not less than one (1) year nor more than twenty-one (21) years, or shall be fined in an amount of not less than one thousand dollars ($1,000) nor more than five thousand dollars ($5,000), or be both so fined and imprisoned.

OUTLAWING THE COMMUNIST PARTY

Tennessee Code § 39–4420 (Supp. 1964). *"Communist Party" defined.*—For the purpose of this act. "Communist Party" shall mean:

    (a) The Communist Party of the United States.

    (b) The Communist political association.

    (c) The Communist Party of any State of the United States, of any foreign state, or of any political or geographical subdivision of any foreign state.

    (d) Any section, subsidiary, branch, affiliate, or subdivision of any such association or party.

    (e) Any organization which advocates or teaches the overthrowal by force or violence or other unconstitutional means of of the Government of the United States or the State of Tennessee.

Id. § 39–4421 (Supp. 1964). *Declaration of legislative findings.*—The general assembly of the State of Tennessee hereby finds and determines that the Communist Party advocates, teaches, and encourages the overthrowal of the Government of the United States and of the State of Tennessee by force and violence, the same being contrary to the Constitution of the United States and of the State of Tennessee, and that the existence of the Communist Party, and membership in such party, is an immediate and constant threat to the peace, safety, and security of the State of Tennessee and of the people thereof.

Id. § 39–4422 (Supp. 1964). *Communist Party and membership in party unlawful.*—It shall be unlawful for the Communist Party to operate in the State of Tennessee, and it shall be unlawful for any person in the State of Tennessee to knowingly be a member of, or belong to, the Communist Party. Membership in the Communist Party shall be prima facie evidence that a person advocates, teaches and encourages the forceful and violent overthrowal of the government of the State of Tennessee.

Id. § 39–4423 (Supp. 1964). *Penalty.*—Any person violating the provisions of §§ 39–4420—39–4422 shall, upon conviction thereof, be imprisoned for a period of not less than one (1) year nor more than twenty-one (21) years, or shall be fined in an amount of not less than one thousand dollars ($1,000) nor more than five thousand dollars ($5,000), or be both so fined and imprisoned.

EXCLUSION FROM THE ELECTIVE PROCESS

Tennessee Code § 2–1203. *Party or person advocating forceful overthrow of government barred from ballot.*—No political party, individual or candidate of any group shall be recognized and given a place on the ballot which or who advocates the overthrow, by force or violence, or advocates or carries on a program of sedition or of treason by radio, speech, or press of or against any local or State government or the National Government. No newly organized political party shall be represented on the ballot until it has filed an affidavit by its officers, under oath, that it does not advocate the overthrow of local, State or National Government by force or violence, and that it is not affiliated in any way with any political party or organization, or subdivisions of organizations, which do advocate such a policy by radio, speech, or press.

Id. § 2–1204. *Penalty.*—Any person or persons who cause a name to be placed upon the ballot in violation of § 2–1203 shall be guilty of misdemeanor. 72, § 2; C. Supp. 1950, § 2045.2.

Tennessee Code § 39–4422 (Supp. 1964). *Communist Party outlawed.*—It shall be unlawful for the Communist Party to operate in the State of Tennessee, and it shall be unlawful for any person in the State of Tennessee to knowingly be a member of, or belong to, the Communist Party. Membership in the Communist Party shall be prima facie evidence that a person advocates, teaches, and encourages the forceful and violent overthrowal of the government of the State of Tennessee.

LOYALTY OF STATE OFFICERS AND EMPLOYEES

1. ELECTIVE AND NONELECTIVE PERSONNEL

Tennessee Constitution, Art. X, § 1. *Oath.*—Every person who shall be chosen or appointed to any office of trust or profit under this constitution, or any law made in pursuance thereof, shall before entering on the duties thereof, take an oath to support the constitution of this State, and of the United States, and an oath of office.

2. CIVIL DEFENSE PERSONNEL

Tennessee Code § 7–627. *Loyalty oath required.*—All persons, both compensated and noncompensated, in any way connected with the administration or operation of the civil defense program, shall take and subscribe to the following oath:

"I, _____, do solemnly swear (or affirm) that I will support and defend the Constitution of the United States, and the constitution of the State of Tennessee, and the territory, institutions and facilities thereof, both public and private, against all enemies, foreign and domestic; that I will bear true faith and allegiance to the same; and I take this obligation freely, without any mental reservation or purpose of evasion; and that I will well and faithfully discharge the duties on which I am about to enter.

"And I do further swear (or affirm) that I do not advocate, nor am I a member of any political party or organization that advocates the overthrow of the Government of the United States or of this State by force or violence; and that during such time as I am a member of the State civil defense agency, I will not advocate nor become a member of any political party or organization that advocates the overthrow of the Government of the United States or of this State by force or violence."

TEACHERS' LOYALTY

Tennessee Code § 49–1303. *Persons advocating overthrow of government ineligible for employment.*—It shall be unlawful for the trustees of the University of Tennesse, the State board of education or any county or city board of education, or any other person to employ any superintendent, principal, teacher, tutor, supervisor, or other person to have in any way the custody and care of students of the public educational institutions of this State who is not a citizen of the United States of America; provided that nothing in this section shall be construed to prohibit arrangements whereby professors and teachers who are citizens of other nations may be employed on a temporary basis on the faculties of colleges, universities or public schools in Tennessee; provided, further, that no person who advocates the overthrow of the American form of Government or who is a member of a political party subscribing to a political faith which advocates the overthrow of the American form of Government shall be employed on either a temporary or permanent basis in any school in this State financed in whole or in part with public funds. Any person who shall violate any of the provisions of this section shall be guilty of a misdemeanor, punishable by a fine of not less than fifty dollars ($50.00) nor more than one hundred dollars ($100), and shall forfeit his office.

Id. § 49–1304. *Oath.*—All persons now teaching or who may hereafter be employed as teachers in any school supported in whole or in part by public funds of the State, county, or municipality, shall be required to take and subscribe to an oath to support the constitution of the State of Tennessee and of the United States of America. Any person who is an applicant for a position as a teacher in the schools above referred to who refuses to take such oath shall not be employed, and those who are now employed and who refuse to take the oath above referred to shall be immediately dismissed from the service.

EXCLUSION FROM THE BAR

Tennessee Supreme Court Rule 37, section 17, gives the Board of Law Examiners discretionary authority to deny admission to persons of doubtful loyalty. It provides:

The board may, in its discretion, refuse to issue a license if it has reasonable grounds to believe that the applicant has conducted himself in a manner as to raise questions concerning his intentions or ability to support the constitution of the State of Tennessee and of the United States and to truly and honestly demean himself in the practice of the legal profession to the best of his skill and abilities.

Correspondence received from the Board of Law Examiners states that during the past five or so years, "there has been one applicant disclosed by investigations to be an associate of the Communists and a participant in organizations listed as subversive. This applicant was denied a Tennessee license to practice law." It would appear that Rule 37, section 17 "would be applied in such a manner as to lead to refusal of a license by the board to any person known to be a Communist."

TEXAS

Vernon's Anno. Civ. Stat., Art. 6889–3A, § 5. *Unlawful acts.*— It shall be unlawful for any person knowingly or willfully to:

(1) Commit, attempt to commit, or aid in the commission of any act intended to overthrow, destroy, or alter, or to assist in the overthrow, destruction, or alteration of, the constitutional form of the Government of the United States, or of the State of Texas, or of any political subdivision of either of them, by force or violence; or

(2) Advocate, abet, advise, or teach by any means any person to commit, attempt to commit, or aid in the commission of any such act, under such circumstances as to constitute a clear and present danger to the security of the United States, or of the State of Texas, or of any political subdivision of either of them; or

(3) Conspire with one or more persons to commit any of the above acts; or

(4) Assist in the formation of, or participate in the management of, or contribute to the support of, or become or remain a member of, or destroy any books or records or files of, or secrete any funds in this State of the Communist Party of the United States or any component or related part or organization thereof, or any organization which engages in or advocates, abets, advises, or teaches, or a purpose of which is to engage in or advocate, abet, advise, or teach, any activities intended to overthrow, destroy, or alter, or to assist in the overthrow, destruction, or alteration of, the constitutional form of the Government of the United States, or of the State of Texas, or of any political subdivision of either of them, by force or violence, knowing the nature of such organization.

Id. § 6. *Penalty.*—Any person who shall violate any of the provisions of section 5 of this Act shall be guilty of a felony, and upon conviction thereof shall be fined not more than twenty thousand ($20,000.00) dollars, or imprisoned not less than one (1) year nor more than twenty (20) years in the State penitentiary, or may be both so fined and imprisoned. Provided that nothing in this act shall be construed to repeal any part of Articles 83, 84, and 85 of the Penal Code of the State of Texas, relating to treason, nor any part of Articles 153 and 155 of the Penal Code of the State of Texas, relating to seditious writings and language; and provided further, that no person convicted of any violation of this act shall ever be entitled to suspension or probation of sentence by the trial court.

REGISTRATION

Vernon's Anno. Civ. Stat., Art. 6889-3, § 1. *"Communist" defined.*—
A "Communist" is a person who:

(A) Is a member of the Communist Party, notwithstanding the
fact that he may not pay dues to, or hold a card in, said party; or

(B) Knowingly contributes funds or any character of property to
the Communist Party; or

(C) Commits or advocates the commission of any act reasonably
calculated to further the overthrow of the Government of the United
States of America, the government of the State of Texas, or the government of any political subdivision of either of them, by force or
violence; or

(D) Commits or advocates the commission of any act reasonably
calculated to further the overthrow of the Government of the United
States, the government of the State of Texas, or the government of
any political subdivision of either of them, by unlawful or unconstitutional means, and the substitution of a Communist government
or a government intended to be substantially directed, dominated or
controlled by the Union of Soviet Socialist Republics or its satellites.

Id. § 2. *"Communist Party" defined.*—The "Communist Party"
is any organization which is substantially directed, dominated or
controlled by the Union of Soviet Socialist Republics or its satellites,
or which in any manner advocates, or acts to further, the world
Communist movement.

Id. § 3. *"Communist front organization" defined.*—A "Communist front organization" is any organization the members of which
are not all Communists, but which is substantially directed, dominated
or controlled by Communists or by the Communist Party, or which
in any manner advocates, or acts to further, the world Communist
movement.

Id. § 4. *Communists, members of Communist front organizations
and officers of the Communist Party and Communist front organizations required to register.*—(A) Each person remaining in this
State for as many as five (5) consecutive days after the effective date
of this statute, who is a Communist or is knowingly a member of a
Communist front organization, shall register with the department
of public safety of the State of Texas on or before the fifth consecutive day that such person remains in this State; and, so long as he
remains in this State, shall reregister annually with said department
between the first and fifteenth days of January.

(B) Such registration shall be under oath and shall set forth the
name (including any assumed name used or in use), address, business
occupation, purpose of presence in the State of Texas, sources of income, place of birth, places of former residence, and features of identification, including fingerprints, of the registrant; organizations of
which registrant is a member; names of persons known by registrant
to be Communists or members of any Communist front organization;
and any other information requested by the department of public
safety which is relevant to the purposes of this statute.

(C) Each and every officer of the Communist Party and each and
every officer of Communist front organizations, knowing said organizations to be Communist front organizations, shall register or
cause to be registered said party or organizations with the depart-

ment of public safety, if said party or organizations have any members who reside, permanently or for a period of time more than thirty (30) days, in the State of Texas. Such registration shall be under oath and shall include the name of the organization, the location of its principal office and of its offices and meeting places in the State of Texas; the names, real and assumed, of its officers; the names, real and assumed, of its members in the State of Texas and of any person who has attended its meetings in the State of Texas; a financial statement reflecting receipts and disbursements and by whom and to whom paid; and any other information requested by the department of public safety which is relevant to the purposes of this statute. Such registration shall be made within thirty (30) days after the effective date of this statute, and thereafter at such intervals as are directed by the department of public safety.

(D) Failure to register as herein required, or the making of any registration which contains any material false statement or omission, shall constitute a felony and shall be punishable by a fine of not less than one thousand dollars ($1,000) or more than ten thousand dollars ($10,000), or by imprisonment of not less than two (2) or more than ten (10) years, or by both.

(E) Under order of any court of record, the registration records shall be open for inspection by any person in whose favor such order is granted; and the records shall at all times, without the need for a court order, be open for inspection by any law enforcement officer of this State, of the United States or of any State or Territory of the United States. At the discretion of the department of public safety, such records may also be open for inspection by the general public or by any member thereof.

Id. § 8. *Enforcement.*—The attorney general of the State of Texas, all district and county attorneys, the department of public safety, and all law enforcement officers of this State shall each be charged with the duty of enforcing the provisions of this statute.

Id. § 9. *Separability.*—If any section, subparagraph, sentence, phrase, part or application of this statute shall be held unconstitutional, such unconstitutionality shall not affect the validity of the remaining portions hereof, and the legislature here declares that it would have enacted such remaining portions notwithstanding any holding of unconstitutionality with respect to any other portions of this statute.

Id. § 10. *Effect on other laws.*—This statute is cumulative of all existing laws and does not repeal any such laws.

Id. § 11. *Short title.*—This Act may be cited as the "Texas Communist Control Law."

OUTLAWING THE COMMUNIST PARTY

Vernon's Anno. Civ. Stat., Art. 6889–3A, § 1. *Declaration of legislative findings.*—Upon evidence and proof already presented before this legislature, Congress, the courts of this State, and the courts of the United States, it is here now found and declared to be a fact that there exists an international Communist conspiracy which is committed to the overthrow of the Government of the United States and of the several States, including that of the State of Texas, by force or violence, such conspiracy including the Communist Party of the United States, its component or related parts and members, and that such conspiracy constitutes a clear and present danger to the Government of the United States and of this State.

Id. § 2. *Communist Party and component or related organizations outlawed.*—The Communist Party of the United States, together with its component or related parts and organizations, no matter under what name known, and all other organizations, incorporated or unincorporated, which engage in or advocate, abet, advise, or teach or a purpose of which is to engage in or advocate, abet, advise, or teach, any activities intended to overthrow, destroy, or alter, or to assist in the overthrow, destruction, or alteration of, the constitutional form of the Government of the United States, or of the State of Texas, or of any political subdivision of either of them, by force or violence, are hereby declared to be illegal and not entitled to any rights, privileges, or immunities attendant upon bodies under the jurisdiction of the State of Texas or any political subdivision thereof. It shall be unlawful for such party or any of its component or related parts or organizations, or any such other organization, to exist, function, or operate in the State of Texas. Any organization which is found by a court of competent jurisdiction to have violated any provisions of this section, in a proceeding brought for that purpose by the district attorney, criminal district attorney, or county attorney, shall be dissolved, and if it be a corporation organized and existing under the laws of this State or having a permit to do business in this State, its charter or permit shall be forfeited, and, whether incorporated or unincorporated, all funds, records, and other property belonging to such party or any component or related part or organization thereof, or to any such other organization, shall be seized by and forfeited to the State of Texas, to escheat to the State as in the case of a person dying without heirs. All books, records, and files of any such organization shall be turned over to the attorney general.

Id. § 3. *Fact of registration inadmissible in evidence.*—The fact of the registration of any person under the provisions of Article 6889—3 of the Revised Civil Statutes of Texas as an officer or member of any Communist organization shall not be received in evidence against such person in any proceeding for any alleged violation of this Act.

Id. § 3. *Proof of affiliation with subversive organization prima facie evidence of similar aims.*—As to any particular organization, proof of its affiliation with a parent or superior organization, inside or outside of this State, which engages in or advocates, abets, advises, or teaches, or a purpose of which is to engage in or advocate, abet, advise, or teach, any activities intended to overthrow, destroy, or alter, or to assist in the overthrow, destruction, or alteration of, the constitutional form of the Government of the United States, or of the State of Texas, or of any political subdivision of either of them, by force or violence, shall constitute prima facie evidence that such particular organization engages in or advocates, abets, advises, or teaches, or has as a purpose the engaging in or advocating, abetting, advising, or teaching of, the same activities with the same intent.

Id. § 5. *Unlawful acts.*—It shall be unlawful for any person knowingly or willfully to:

(1) Commit, attempt to commit, or aid in the commission of any act intended to overthrow, destroy, or alter, or to assist in the overthrow, destruction, or alteration of, the constitutional form of the Government of the United States, or of the State of Texas, or of any political subdivision of either of them, by force or violence; or

(2) Advocate, abet, advise, or teach by any means any person to commit, attempt to commit, or aid in the commission of any such act, under such circumstances as to constitute a clear and present danger to the security of the United States, or of the State of Texas, or of any political subdivision of either of them; or

(3) Conspire with one or more persons to commit any of the above acts; or

(4)· Assist in the formation of, or participate in the management of, or contribute to the support of, or become or remain a member of, or destroy any books or records or files of, or secrete any funds in this State of the Communist Party of the United States or any component or related part or organization thereof, or any organization which engages in or advocates, abets, advises, or teaches, or a purpose of which is to engage in or advocate, abet, advise, or teach, any activities intended to overthrow, destroy, or alter, or to assist in the overthrow, destruction, or alteration of, the constitutional form of the Government of the United States, or of the State of Texas, or of any political subdivision of either of them, by force or violence, knowing the nature of such organization.

Id. § 6. *Penalty.*—Any person who shall violate any of the provisions of section 5 of this Act shall be guilty of a felony, and upon conviction thereof shall be fined not more than twenty thousand ($20,-000.00) dollars, or imprisoned not less than one (1) year nor more than twenty (20) years in the State penitentiary, or may be both so fined and imprisoned. Provided that nothing in this Act shall be construed to repeal any part of Articles 83, 84, and 85 of the Penal Code of the State of Texas, relating to treason, nor any part of Articles 153 and 155 of the Penal Code of the State of Texas, relating to seditious writings and language; and provided further, that no person convicted of any violation of this Act shall ever be entitled to suspension or probation of sentence by the trial court.

Id. § 8. *Injunctions.*—The District Courts of this State and the judges thereof shall have full power, authority, and jurisdiction, upon the application of the State of Texas, acting through the district attorney, criminal district attorney, or county attorney, to issue any and all proper restraining orders, temporary and permanent injunctions, and any other writs and processes appropriate to carry out and enforce the provisions of this Act; no injunction or other writ shall be granted, used or relied upon under the provisions of this Act in any labor dispute or disputes. Such proceedings shall be instituted, prosecuted, tried, and heard as other civil proceedings of like nature in such courts, provided that such proceedings shall have priority over other cases in settings for hearing; provided further, that no such proceeding shall be instituted unless and until the Director of the Texas State department of public safety or his assistant in charge has been notified by telephone, telegraph, or in person of the intention to institute such proceeding, and an affidavit of such notice filed with the application for such injunction proceedings shall be sufficient for the filing of the same.

Nothing in this Act shall be construed to alter in any way the powers now held by the courts of this State or of this Nation under the laws of this State in labor disputes.

Id. § 9. *Search warrant.*—A search warrant may issue under Title 6 of the Code of Criminal Procedure for the purpose of searching for and seizing any books, records, pamphlets, cards, receipts, lists, memoranda, pictures, recordings, or any written instruments showing that a person or organization is violating or has violated any provision of this Act. Search warrants may be issued by any judge of a court of record in this State upon the written application of the district attorney, criminal district attorney, or county attorney, within their respective jurisdictions, accompanied by the affidavit of a credible person setting forth the name or description of the owner or person in charge of the premises to be searched, or stating that his name and description are unknown, the address or description of the premises, and showing that the described premises is a place where some specified phase or phases of this Act are violated or are being violated, or where are kept any books, records, pamphlets, cards, receipts, lists, memoranda, pictures, recordings, or written instruments of any kind showing a violation of some phase or phases of this Act; provided that if the premises to be searched constitute a private residence, such application for a search warrant shall be accompanied by the affidavits of two credible citizens. Except as herein provided, the application, issuance, and execution of any such warrant and all proceedings relative thereto shall conform to the applicable provisions of Title 6 of the Code of Criminal Procedure; provided that any evidence obtained by virtue of a search warrant issued under the provisions of this Act shall not be admissible in evidence in the trial of any proceeding, administrative or judicial, save and except those arising under this Act.

Id. § 9a. *Enforcement.*—The internal security section of the Texas department of public safety shall assist in the enforcement of the provisions of this Act, and for such purpose said department may employ and pay the salaries and wages of such personnel and make such capital outlay purchases as it may deem necessary and pay necessary expenses, including but not limited to travel expenses (including automobile maintenance), all necessary operating expenses (including seasonal help), wages and salaries of employees, and make any and all other expenditures whatsoever necessary for the proper enforcement of the provisions of this Act; and for such purposes there is hereby appropriated out of the operators and chauffeurs license fund such money as may be necessary, not to exceed the sum of seventy-five thousand $75,000.00) dollars for the biennium ending August 31, 1955.

Exclusion From the Elective Process

Vernon's Anno. Civ. Stat., Election Code, Art. 1.05, § 5 (Supp. 1963). *Persons advocating overthrow of government barred from ballot.*— No person shall be eligible to be a candidate for, or to be elected or appointed to, any public office in this State unless he shall be eligible to hold such office under the constitution and laws of this State, and unless he is a citizen of the United States and shall have resided in this State for a period of twelve months next preceding the date of any primary, general or special election at which he offers himself as a candidate or next preceding the date of his appointment, as the case may be, and for any office which is less than State-wide, shall have resided for six months next preceding such election in the district, county, precinct, municipality or other political subdivision for which the office is to be filled; provided, however, that the foregoing residence requirements shall not apply to any office for which the Constitution or statutes of the United States or of this State prescribe residence qualifications in conflict herewith, and in case of conflict the provisions of such other laws shall control. No ineligible candidate shall ever have his name placed upon the ballot at any primary, general or special election; and no ineligible candidate shall ever be voted upon nor have votes counted for him at any such primary, general or special election. No person who advocates the overthrow by force or violence or change by unconstitutional means of the present constitutional form of Government of the United States or of this State, shall be eligible to have his name printed on any official ballot in any general, special or primary election in this State.

Id. Art. 602 (Supp. 1963). *Appearance on ballot conditioned upon execution of loyalty oath.*—(a) No person shall be permitted to have his name appear upon the official ballot as a candidate or nominee for any public office, as hereinafter stated, at any general, special, or primary election in this State, unless and until he shall have filed a loyalty affidavit as required by this section. The provisions of this section shall apply to candidates for all elective State, district, county, and precinct offices, including the offices of United States Senator and United States Representative, and to all elective offices of cities, school districts, conservation districts, and other political subdivisions of the State, except candidates for President or Vice President of the United States and presidential elector candidates.

(b) A candidate whose name is to appear on the ballot in any general primary (first primary) election shall file the affidavit with the chairman of the executive committee with whom the request to have his name placed on the ballot is filed, or if filed with more than one, with each chairman. The affidavit must be filed before the deadline for filing applications for that election. Before the name of a write-in candidate in a first primary election is ordered placed on the ballot for a second or runoff primary election or is certified to be placed on the ballot for a general or special election as the party nominee, he shall file the affidavit with the chairman of the State executive committee in the case of a district or State-wide office and with the chairman of the county executive committee in the case of a county or precinct office. A candidate nominated by a party convention or a party executive committee shall file the affidavit with the committee chairman who certifies his nomination, and the affidavit must be filed before his name is certified. An independent or nonpartisan candidate shall file the affidavit with the officer with whom his petition or application for a place on the ballot is filed, and the affidavit must be filed before the deadline for filing applications for a place on the ballot at that election.

(c) The affidavit shall be in the following form:

I _____, of the County of _____, State of Texas, being a candidate for the office of _____ do solemnly swear that I believe in and approve of our present representative form of government, and, if elected, I will support and defend our present representative form of government and will resist any effort or movement from any source which seeks to subvert or destroy the same or any part thereof, and I will support and defend the Constitution and laws of the United States and of the State of Texas.

(Signature of candidate)

Sworn to and subscribed before me at _____, this _____ day of _____, A.D. _____.

(Signature of officer administering oath)

(Title of officer administering oath)

(d) The name of no candidate or nominee of any political party whose principles include any thought or purpose of setting aside representative form of government and substituting therefor any other form of government shall be permitted on the official ballot. It is specifically provided that no candidate or nominee of the Communist Party or the Fascist Party or the Nazi Party shall ever be allowed a place on the official ballot at any election in this State.

(e) The certification of a candidate as the nominee of a political party shall be sufficient evidence of the filing of the affidavit with the proper party chairman to permit the officer to whom the certification is made to place the candidate's name on the general or special election ballot, and it shall not be necessary for the candidate to file an affidavit with any other officer in connection with his candidacy, nor shall it be necessary for the certificate to state that the affidavit has been filed.

(f) If any officer with whom the loyalty affidavit as prescribed herein is required to be filed, fails or refuses to require the affidavit before ordering or certifying the candidate's name for a place on the ballot, he shall be deemed guilty of a misdemeanor and upon conviction shall be fined in a sum of not less than fifty dollars nor more than two hundred dollars.

Vernon's Anno. Civ. Stat., Art. 6889–3, § 6. *Communists and nominees of the Communist Party barred from ballot.*—The name of any Communist or of any nominee of the Communist Party shall not be printed upon any ballot used in any primary or general election in this State or in any political subdivision thereof.

LOYALTY OF STATE OFFICERS AND EMPLOYEES

I. ELECTIVE AND NONELECTIVE PERSONNEL

Texas Constiution, Art. XVI, § 1. *Oath.*—Members of the legislature, and all officers, before they enter upon the duties of their offices, shall take the following oath or affirmation:

"I, _____, do solemnly swear (or affirm), that I will faithfully execute the duties of the office of _____ of the State of Texas, and will to the best of my ability preserve, protect, and defend the Constitution and laws of the United States and of this State; and I furthermore solemnly swear (or affirm), that I have not directly nor indirectly paid, offered, or promised to pay, contributed, nor promised to contribute any money, or valuable thing, or promised any public office or employment, as a reward for the giving or withholding a vote at the election at which I was elected. So help me God."

Vernon's Anno. Civ. Stat., Art. 6889–3A, § 5. *Communist control law offenses.*—It shall be unlawful for any person knowingly or willfully to:

(1) Commit, attempt to commit, or aid in the commission of any act intended to overthrow, destroy, or alter, or to assist in the overthrow, destruction, or alteration of, the constitutional form of the Government of the United States, or of the State of Texas, or of any political subdivision of either of them, by force or violence; or

(2) Advocate, abet, advise, or teach by any means any person to commit, attempt to commit, or aid in the commission of any such act, under such circumstances as to constitute a clear and present danger to the security of the United States, or of the State of Texas, or of any political subdivision of either of them; or

(3) Conspire with one or more persons to commit any of the above acts; or

(4) Assist in the formation of, or participate in the management of, or contribute to the support of, or become or remain a member of, or destroy any books or records or files of, or secrete any funds in this State of the Communist Party of the United States or any component or related part or organization thereof, or any organization which engages in or advocates, abets, advises, or teaches, or a purpose of which is to engage in or advocate, abet, advise, or teach, any activities intended to overthrow, destroy, or alter, or to assist in the overthrow, destruction, or alteration of, the constitutional form of the Government of the United States, or of the State of Texas, or of any political subdivision of either of them, by force or violence, knowing the nature of such organization.

Id. § 7. *Conviction for violating Communist control law cause for disqualification.*—Any person who shall be convicted finally by a court of competent jurisdiction of violating any of the provisions of this Act shall from the date of such final conviction automatically be disqualified and barred from holding any office, elective or appointive, or any other position of profit, trust, or employment with the government of the State of Texas or any agency thereof, or of any county, municipal corporation, or other political subdivision of the State.

2. NONELECTIVE PERSONNEL

Vernon's Anno. Civ. Stat., Art. 6252–7, § 1. *Compensation for services dependent upon execution of loyalty oaths.*—No funds of the State of Texas shall be paid to any person as salary or as other compensation for personal services unless and until such person has filed with the payroll clerk, or other officer by whom such salary or compensation is certified for payment, an oath or affirmation stating:

"1. That the affiant is not, and has never been, a member of the Communist Party. (The term 'Communist Party' as used herein means any organization which (a) is substantially directed, dominated or controlled by the Union of Soviet Socialistic Republics, or its satellites, or which (b) seeks to overthrow the Government of the United States, or of any State, by force, violence or any other unlawful means) ; and

"2. That the affiant is not, and, during the preceding five year period, has not been, a member of any organization, association, movement, group or combination which the Attorney General of the United States, acting pursuant to Executive Order No. 9835, March 21, 1947, 12 Federal Register 1935, has designated as totalitarian, Fascist, Communist or subversive, or as having adopted a policy of advocating or approving the commission of acts of force or violence to deny others their rights under the Constitution of the United States, or as seeking to alter the form of Government of the United States by unconstitutional means; or, in the event that the affiant has during such five year period been a member of any such organization, association, movement, group or combination, he shall state its name, shall state in detail the circumstances which led him to join it, and shall state that, at the time when he joined and throughout the period during which he was a member, he did not know that its purposes were the purposes which the Attorney General of the United States has designated; and

"3. That the affiant is not, and during the preceding five year period, has not been, a member of any 'Communist political organization' or 'Communist front organization' registered under the Federal Internal Security Act of 1950 (50 U.S.C.A., sec. 781, et seq.) or required to so register under said Act by final order of the Federal Subversive Activities Control Board; or, in the event that the affiant has during such five year period been a member of any such organization, he shall state its name, shall state in detail the circumstances which led him to join it, and shall state that, at the time when he joined it and throughout the period during which he was a member, he did not know that its purpose was to further the goals of the Communist Party or that it was controlled by the Communist Party."

Id. 7 § 2. *List of subversive organizations.*—The department of public safety shall obtain a list of the organizations, associations, movements, groups and combinations comprehended by subdivisions 2 and 3 of section 1 hereof, and shall furnish a copy of such list to the various agencies which expend funds of this State. Such agencies shall make copies of such list and shall furnish them to their employees in order that the employees can readily perceive whether they can lawfully and truthfully file the oath or affirmation required herein.

Id. § 4. *Effect on other laws.*—It is specifically provided, however, that the oath required herein shall supersede all other loyalty oaths now required by law or that may be required in appropriation Acts by the legislature.

Id. § 5. *Separability.*—If any portion of this Act should be held to be unconstitutional, the unconstitutionality of such portion shall not affect the validity or application of the remainder of the Act.

Annotation:

Op. Atty. Gen. 1956. S–32.—The nonsubversive oath does not apply to receipt of statutory witness fees in criminal cases, compensation paid by the State to expert witnesses, constitutionally fixed salaries of State officers nor to legislators.

The nonsubversive oath required by this article applies to State funds paid for services by doctors, lawyers, engineers, architects, skilled craftsmen, and laborers, and for special and undercover services of law enforcement, if such services are rendered in the capacity of an employee and not as an independent contractor.

Id. § 7. *Communists and members of Communist front organization barred from any nonelective position.*—No person may hold any nonelective position, job or office for the State of Texas, or any political subdivision thereof, where the remuneration of said position, job or office is paid in whole or in part by public moneys or funds of the State of Texas, or of any political subdivision thereof, where reasonable grounds exist, on all of the evidence, for the employer or other superior of such person to believe that such person is a Communist or a knowing member of a Communist front organization.

TEACHERS' LOYALTY

Vernon's Anno. Civ. Stat., Art. 2908a. *Oath to support constitution required; alien instructors required to execute non-Communist affidavit; advocating overthrow of government cause for dismissal.*— Section 1. That on and after the date this Act becomes effective, no public funds may be paid to any person as a teacher, instructor, visiting instructor, or other employee in, for or connected with any tax-supported school, college, university or other tax-supported institution of learning in this State, unless and until such person shall have taken the oath of office required to be taken by members of the legislature and all other officers, as provided in Article XVI, section 1, as amended by amendment adopted November 8, 1939.

Sec. 2. Exempting foreign visiting instructors, refugees and political refugees from conquered countries from the provisions set out in section 1 of this Act, and providing that such foreign visiting instructors, refugees and political refugees from conquered countries shall file an affidavit, on form to be prescribed by the attorney general of the State of Texas, stating, among other things, that they are not members of the Communist, Fascist or Nazi Parties, nor members of any Bund, or any affiliated organization, and further stating that they will not engage in any un-American activities, nor teach any doctrines contrary to the Constitution and laws of the United States of America or of the State of Texas.

Sec. 3. That any teacher or instructor of any tax-supported school, college, university or other institution of learning in this State who shall have been found guilty of openly advocating doctrines which seek to undermine or overthrow by force or violence the republican and democratic forms of Government in the United States, or which in any way seek to establish a government that does not rest upon the fundamental principle of the consent of the governed, upon and after a full hearing by the employing or appointing authority of such teacher or instructor, shall be dismissed from such service.

Texas Constitution, Art. XVI, § 1. *Form of oath.*—I, _____, do solemnly swear (or affirm), that I will faithfully execute the duties of the office of _____ of the State of Texas, and will to the best of my ability preserve, protect, and defend the Constitution and laws of the United States and of this State; and I furthermore solemnly swear (or affirm), that I have not directly nor indirectly paid, offered, or promised to pay, contributed, or promised to contribute any money, or valuable thing, or promised any public office or employment, as a reward for the giving or withholding a vote at the election at which I was elected. So help me God.

Vernon's Anno. Civ., Stat., Art. 2908b, § 1. *Higher education—employment is conditioned upon execution of loyalty oath.*—No person owing allegiance to the United States hereafter shall be permitted to register for attendance in or be employed by any State-supported college or university unless and until he shall file with the registrar or president thereof his oath or affirmation reciting the following:

"I swear or affirm that I believe in and approve the Constitution of the United States and the principles of government therein contained, and will not in any manner aid or assist in any effort or movement to subvert or destroy the Government of the United States or of any State or of any political subdivision thereof by force, violence, or any other unlawful means. In the event of war with any foreign nation, I will not support or adhere to the government of such foreign nation.

"I swear or affirm that I am not and have not during the past two (2) years been a member of or affiliated with any society or group of persons which teaches or advocates that the Government of the United States or of any State or of any political subdivision thereof should be overthrown or destroyed by force, violence, or any other unlawful means, or the adherence to the government of any foreign nation in the event of war between the United States and such foreign nation."

Id. § 3 (Supp. 1963). *Oath required to be executed before contract.*—The foregoing affidavit or affirmation shall also be executed by every person before any contract of employment between such person and a State-supported college or university is signed or renewed after the date this Act becomes effective. All such oaths, affidavits or affirmations signed by any such person shall be retained and preserved by such college or university until the person filing the same shall cease to be employed in such college or university, at which time the same may be destroyed.

Id. § 4. *Persons ineligible for employment.*—No person hereafter shall be enrolled or reenrolled in or be employed or reemployed by any State-supported college or university, nor shall any person presently employed by such college or university be continued in such employment, who:

(a) By word of mouth or writing knowingly or willfully advocates, abets, advises, or teaches the duty, necessity, desirability, or propriety of overthrowing or destroying the Government of the United States or of any State or of any political subdivision thereof, by force, violence, or any other unlawful means, or the adherence to the government of any foreign nation in the event of war between the United States and such foreign government; or

(b) Prints, publishes, edits, issues, circulates, sells, distributes, or publicly displays any written or printed matter advocating, advising, or teaching the duty, necessity, desirability, or propriety of overthrowing or destroying any government in the United States by force, violence, or any other unlawful means, or the adherence to the government of any foreign nation in the event of war between the United States and such foreign government; or

(c) Organizes or helps or attempts to organize, or becomes a member of, or affiliates with any society, group, or assembly of persons who teach, advocate, or encourage the overthrow or destruction of any such government by force, violence, or any other unlawful means, or the adherence to the government of any foreign nation in the event of war between the United States and such foreign government.

Id. § 6. *Violation cause for dismissal.*—Any employee found guilty of committing any act described in section 4 upon and after a full hearing, pursuant to due notice hereinafter provided, by the governing board of the college or university, or by a committee of the governing board designated and authorized by said board to hold such a hearing and a review of the record by said board, shall be dismissed from such employment.

Id. § 7. *Dismissal procedure.*—No person shall be expelled or dismissed unless he is served in person or by registered mail with a written statement specifying the charges and naming a date and place at which such person may appear and answer such charges. The notice may be served, except when registered mail is used, by any person designated by the president of the institution. The date for the hearing shall not be less than ten (10) nor more than twenty (20) days after service.

The issues shall be heard at the time and place set, and the hearing shall be public. All parties may be represented by counsel and shall have the right to call, examine, and cross-examine witnesses, and it shall be the duty of the party or a member of the body conducting such hearing to swear any and all witnesses called to testify. A stenographic recorder shall be provided for by the party or body calling the hearing.

Id. § 8. *Judicial review.*—Any student or employee expelled or dismissed under the authority of this Act shall be entitled to appeal within thirty (30) days of such expulsion, or dismissal to a district court in Travis County, Texas. In any such appeal the written transcript of evidence adduced before the president or person designated by him or the governing board or committee thereof shall be admissible in evidence for all purposes.

EXCLUSION FROM THE BAR

Question 8 on the Application for Admission to the Bar of Texas specifically inquires into possible Communist affiliations. It provides:

8. Are you a Communist or a member of a Communist front organization as such terms are defined by Article 6889–3, Vernon's Annotated Revised Civil Statutes of Texas?

NOTE.—For definitions of "Communist" and "Communist front organization," see Registration, *supra*.

EXCLUSION FROM INCIDENTAL BENEFITS

1. HIGHER EDUCATION

Vernon's Anno. Civ. Stat., Art. 2908b, § 1.—*Higher education—admission to conditioned upon execution of loyalty oath.*—No person owing allegiance to the United States hereafter shall be permitted to register for attendance in or be employed by any State-supported college or university unless and until he shall file with the registrar or president thereof his oath or affirmation reciting the following:

"I swear or affirm that I believe in and approve the Constitution of the United States and the principles of government therein contained, and will not in any manner aid or assist in any effort or movement to subvert or destroy the Government of the United States or of any State or of any political subdivision thereof by force, violence, or any other unlawful means. In the event of war with any foreign nation, I will not support or adhere to the government of such foreign nation.

"I swear or affirm that I am not and have not during the past two (2) years been a member of or affiliated with any society or group of persons which teaches or advocates that the Government of the United States or of any State or of any political subdivision thereof should be overthrown or destroyed by force, violence, or any other unlawful means, or the adherence to the government of any foreign nation in the event of war between the United States and such foreign nation."

Id. § 2. (Supp. 1963).—*Reexecution upon registration.*—The foregoing affidavit or affirmation shall be executed by every person each time such person seeks to register for attendance in any State-supported college or university after the date this Act becomes effective. All such oaths, affidavits or affirmations signed by any such person shall be retained and preserved by such college or university until the person filing the same shall have graduated, or withdrawn, from the college or university, at which time the same may be destroyed.

Id. § 4. *Persons ineligible for enrollment.*—No person hereafter shall be enrolled or reenrolled in or be employed or reemployed by any State-supported college or university, nor shall any person presently employed by such college or university be continued in such employment, who:

(a) By word of mouth or writing knowingly or willfully advocates, abets, advises, or teaches the duty, necessity, desirability, or propriety of overthrowing or destroying the Government of the United States or of any State or of any political subdivision thereof, by force, violence, or any other unlawful means, or the adherence to the government of any foreign nation in the event of war between the United States and such foreign government; or

(b) Prints, publishes, edits, issues, circulates, sells, distributes, or publicly displays any written or printed matter advocating, advising, or teaching the duty, necessity, desirability, or propriety of overthrowing or destroying any government in the United States by force, violence, or any other unlawful means, or the adherence to the government of any foreign nation in the event of war between the United States and such foreign government; or

(c) Organizes or helps or attempts to organize, or becomes a member of, or affiliates with any society, group, or assembly of persons who teach, advocate, or encourage the overthrow or destruction of any such government by force, violence, or any other unlawful means, or the adherence to the government of any foreign nation in the event of war between the United States and such foreign government.

Id. § 5. *Violation cause for expulsion.*—Any student found guilty of committing any act described in section 4, after having signed the affidavit or affirmation set forth in section 1, upon and after a full hearing, pursuant to due notice hereinafter provided, by the president of the college or university, or by any other college or university official designated and authorized by said president to hold such a hearing and a review of the record by the president, shall be expelled from said college or university.

Id. § 7. *Expulsion procedure.*—No person shall be expelled or dismissed unless he is served in person or by registered mail with a written statement specifying the charges and naming a date and place at which such person may appear and answer such charges. The notice may be served, except when registered mail is used, by any person designated by the president of the institution. The date for the hearing shall not be less than ten (10) nor more than twenty (20) days after service.

The issues shall be heard at the time and place set, and the hearing shall be public. All parties may be represented by counsel and shall have the right to call, examine, and cross-examine witnesses, and it shall be the duty of the party or a member of the body conducting such hearing to swear any and all witnesses called to testify. A stenographic recorder shall be provided for by the party or body calling the hearing.

Id. § 8. *Expulsion procedure.*—Any student or employee expelled or dismissed under the authority of this Act shall be entitled to appeal within thirty (30) days of such expulsion or dismissal to a district court in Travis County, Texas. In any such appeal the written transcript of evidence adduced before the president or person designated by him or the governing board or committee thereof shall be admissible in evidence for all purposes.

2. PROFESSIONAL LICENSE

Vernon's Anno. Civ. Stat., Art. 4542a, § 9. *Members of Communist Party, etc., barred from practice of pharmacy.*

* * * * * * *

No person who is a member of the Communist Party, or who is affiliated with such party, or who believes in, supports, or is a member of any group or organization that believes in, furthers, or teaches the overthrow of the United States Government by force or by any illegal or unconstitutional methods, shall be authorized to practice pharmacy in the State of Texas, or to receive a license to practice pharmacy in the State of Texas.

* * * * * * *

3. TEXTBOOKS

Vernon's Anno. Civ. Stat., Art. 6252-7, § 1. *Form of loyalty oath.*—No funds of the State of Texas shall be paid to any person as salary or as other compensation for personal services unless and until such person has filed with the payroll clerk, or other officer by whom such salary or compensation is certified for payment, an oath or affirmation stating:

"1. That the affiant is not, and has never been, a member of the Communist Party. (The term 'Communist Party' as used herein means any organization which (a) is substantially directed, dominated or controlled by the Union of Soviet Socialistic Republics, or its satellites, or which (b) seeks to overthrow the Government of the United States, or of any State, by force, violence or any other unlawful means) ; and

"2. That the affiant is not, and, during the preceding five year period, has not been, a member of any organization, association, movement, group or combination which the Attorney General of the United States, acting pursuant to Executive Order No. 9835, March 21, 1947, 12 Federal Register 1935, has designated as totalitarian, Fascist, Communist or subversive, or as having adopted a policy of advocating or approving the commission of acts of force or violence to deny others their rights under the Constitution of the United States, or as seeking to alter the form of Government of the United States by unconstitutional means; or, in the event that the affiant has during such five year period been a member of any such organization, association, movement, group or combination, he shall state its name, shall state in detail the circumstances which led him to join it, and shall state that, at the time when he joined and throughout the period during which he was a member, he did not know that its purposes were the purposes which the Attorney General of the United States has designated; and

"3. That the affiant is not, and, during the preceding five year period, has not been, a member of any 'Communist political organization' or 'Communist front organization' registered under the Federal Internal Security Act of 1950 (50 U.S.C.A., sec. 781, et seq.) or required to so register under said Act by final order of the Federal Subversive Activities Control Board; or, in the event that the affiant has during such five year period been a member of any such organization, he shall state its name, shall state in detail the circumstances which led him to join it, and shall state that, at the time when he joined it and throughout the period during which he was a member, he did not know that its purpose was to further the goals of the Communist Party or that it was controlled by the Communist Party."

Id. art. 6252–7 § 3. *Authors of textbooks required to execute loyalty oath.*—The State Board of Education shall neither adopt nor purchase any textbook for use in the schools of this State unless and until the author of such textbook files with the Board an oath or affirmation reciting the matters set forth in subdivisions 1, 2 and 3 of section 1 hereof; provided, however, that if the publisher of any such textbook shall represent to the Board under oath that the author of any text-book is dead or cannot be located, the board may adopt and purchase such textbook if the publisher thereof executes an oath or affirmation stating that, to the best of his knowledge and belief, the author of the textbook, if he were alive or available, could truthfully execute the oath or affirmation required by the first clause of this section 3.   If the board is not satisfied with respect to the truthfulness of any oath or affirmation submitted to it by either an author or publisher of a textbook, it may require that evidence of the truthfulness of such oath or affirmation be furnished it, and it may decline to adopt or purchase such textbook if it is not satisfied from the proof that the oath or affirmation is truthful.

4. TAX EXEMPTIONS

Vernon's Anno. Civ. Stat., Art. 7150, § 20. *Subversive organizations ineligible for property tax exemption.*—The following property shall be exempt from taxation, to wit:

* * * * * * *

Provided, however, that no organization listed by the Attorney General of the United States or the secretary of state of this State as subversive shall be entitled to exemption from taxation under the laws of this State.

UTAH

CRIMINAL SYNDICALISM

Utah Code 1953, § 76–57–1. *Criminal syndicalism defined.*—Criminal syndicalism is hereby defined to be the doctrine which advocates crime, violence, force, arson, destruction of property, sabotage or other unlawful acts or methods, as a means of accomplishing or effecting industrial or political ends, or as a means of effecting industrial or political revolution.

Id. § 76–57–3. *Unlawful acts and penalty.*—Any person who by word of mouth or writing, advocates, suggests or teaches the duty, necessity, propriety or expediency of crime, criminal syndicalism or sabotage, or who advocates, suggests or teaches the duty, necessity, propriety or expediency or doing any act of violence, the destruction of or damage to any property, the bodily injury to any person, or the commission of any crime or unlawful act, as a means of accomplishing or effecting any industrial or political ends, change or revolution, or who prints, publishes, edits or issues, or knowingly circulates, sells or distributes, or publicly displays, any books, pamphlets, paper, handbill, poster, document, or written or printed matter in any form whatsoever, containing, advocating, advising, suggesting or teaching crime, criminal syndicalism, sabotage, the doing of any act of violence, the destruction of or damage to any property, the injury to any person, or the commission of any crime or unlawful act, as a means of accomplishing, effecting or bringing about any industrial or political ends or change, or as a means of accomplishing, effecting or bringing about any industrial or political revolution, or who openly or at all attempts to justify by word of mouth or writing the commission or the attempt to commit sabotage, any act of violence, the destruction of or damage to any property, the injury of any person or the commission of any crime or unlawful act, with the intent to exemplify, spread or teach or suggest criminal syndicalism, or organizes, or helps to organize, or becomes a member of, or voluntarily assembles with, any society or assemblage of persons formed to teach or advocate, or which teaches, advocates or suggests the doctrine of criminal syndicalism or sabotage, or the necessity, propriety or expediency of doing any act of violence or the commission of any crime or unlawful act as a means of accomplishing or effecting any industrial or political ends, change or revolution, is guilty of a felony, and shall be punished by a fine of not less than $200 nor more than $1,000 or by imprisonment in the State prison for a term of not less than one year nor more than five years, or by both such fine and imprisonment.

Id. § 76–57–4. *Assemblage to advocate criminal syndicalism.*— The assembly or consorting of two or more persons for the purpose of advocating, teaching or suggesting the doctrine of criminal syndicalism, or to advocate, teach, suggest or encourage sabotage, or the duty, necessity, propriety or expediency of doing any act of violence, the destruction of or damage to any property, the bodily injury to any person, or the commission of any crime or unlawful act as a means of accomplishing or effecting any industrial or political ends, change or revolution, is hereby declared unlawful, and every person voluntarily participating therein, or by his presence aiding and instigating the same, is guilty of a felony, and shall be punished by imprisonment in the State prison for not less than one year nor more than five years, or by a fine of not less than $200, nor more than $1,000, or by both such imprisonment and fine.

Id. § 76–57–5. *Permitting premises to be used to advocate criminal syndicalism.*—The owner, lessee, agent, superintendent or person in charge or occupation of any place, building, room or structure, who knowingly permits therein any assembly or consort of persons prohibited by the provisions of section 76–57–4, or who after notification that the place or premises, or any part thereof, is so used, permits such use to be continued, is guilty of a misdemeanor and punishable by imprisonment in the county jail for not less than sixty days, nor more than one year, or by a fine of not less than $100, nor more than $500, or by both such imprisonment and fine.

LOYALTY OF STATE OFFICERS AND EMPLOYEES

1. ELECTIVE AND NONELECTIVE PERSONNEL

Utah Constitution, Art. 4, § 10. *Oath.*—All officers made elective or appointive by this constitution or by the laws made in pursuance thereof, before entering upon the duties of their respective offices, shall take and subscribe the following oath or affirmation: "I do solemnly swear (or affirm) that I will support, obey and defend the Constitution of the United States and the constitution of this State, and that I will discharge the duties of my office with fidelity.["]

2. NONELECTIVE PERSONNEL

Utah Code 1953, § 27–11–11. *Persons connected with subversive organizations ineligible to take civil service examination.*—The civil service commission shall provide for examination and qualification of applicants for appointment under the civil service of this State. Its examiners shall acquaint themselves with the qualification requirements of each class of service under the civil service law, and shall design and arrange such examinations as shall best test the qualifications of the applicant for the service to which he seeks appointment. They shall hold all examinations as ordered by the civil service commission and shall certify to the commission the names and ratings of all applicants taking the examinations as ordered by the commission. Only persons shall be permitted to take examinations for the eligible list of the civil service who are citizens of the United States, are actually, and in good faith, domiciled within the State of Utah, who have not been convicted of any high crime or misdemeanor involving moral turpitude, who have not been guilty of offensive or opprobrious conduct, and who are not connected, in any way, with any organization, group, or association whose purpose, interest, or activity is subversive of the best and most democratic interest of the United States or of the State of Utah, or who has not therefore been dismissed from the service as in this act provided. Announcements of examinations shall be printed and given publicity for at least fifteen days prior to the closing date for receiving applications. The commission shall prepare all applications for examination which shall provide space for the name, age, address or residence, occupation, education, service in the armed forces of the United States, previous employment record, marital status, and citizenship of the applicant for statement of qualifications as first above set forth, and such other further factual material as the commission shall deem best calculated to fully and truly state the personal qualifications of the applicant for the position for which he seeks to be examined. Such applications for examination shall be supplied without charge to any person desiring to apply for such examination.

Id. § 27–11–15(b). *Un-American activity cause for removal, suspension or reprimand of employees.*—The appointing authority may remove, suspend, or reprimand any civil service employee within his department or service for violation of any law or any rule of the civil service commission or for conduct subversive of the best interest of the service or of the State of Utah as follows:

*   *   *   *   *   *   *

(b) If any civil service employee shall be convicted of any crime involving moral turpitude, intoxication, or immorality, or if he shall absent himself from his duties without reasonable excuse for three working days, or if he shall be guilty of un-American activity or of conduct not becoming to his position, or of continued intoxication, drug addiction, immoral conduct, or of any act or course of conduct calculated to bring disrepute upon the service, the State of Utah or its inhabitants, he may be dismissed from service by the commission upon the filing with the commission in triplicate of accusations in writing by the appointing authority, or by any person within or without the civil service of the State, setting forth in detail the facts concerning such act, failure, or neglect. Upon the filing of such charges, the commission shall cause a copy thereof to be forthwith served upon the accused together with notice that he may file answer or explanation as he desires within the time set forth in such notice. If answer or explanation thereof is not so filed, the commission shall take the accusations therein as true and shall enter in the cause and serve upon the accused and the appointing authority notice thereof. If answer or explanation is filed, the commission shall set a date for public hearing of the charges and shall give notice thereof by registered mail to the accused and to his counsel, if any. For such hearing, the commission shall subpoena such witnesses for and against the accused as shall be necessary to fully examine into the charges, provided, that any witness subpoenaed for the accused shall be upon his or his counsel's nomination and request in writing and after payment of the costs of service thereof to the commission. Hearing upon such charges may be informal and conducted in such a manner as to establish the truth or falsity of the charges presented. Upon being fully advised, the commission shall prepare findings of fact upon which it shall base its order removing the accused from the service or confirming him in the service as the facts shall warrant. Either party to the controversy may request and be granted a rehearing where it is made to appear from the record that the findings of fact of the commission are materially incomplete or defective, not supported by the evidence, or that they do not support the order entered. Upon rehearing, the cause, in the discretion of the commission, may be heard de novo or may be reviewed on the record of facts and findings theretofore entered. Any finding, act, or determination of the commission made and entered in excess of its authority as prescribed by this act, or arbitrarily, or without support of fact as shown by the record may be reviewed by the Supreme Court of the State of Utah upon certiorari when such facts are made to appear to such court in the manner and form as provided by title 104, chapter 67, Utah Code Annotated 1943.

(c) Any appointing authority may administer reprimand to any employee for misconduct of such employee which is improper and for which no punishment is prescribed as set forth in subparagraphs "a" and "b" above.

3. CIVIL DEFENSE PERSONNEL

Utah Code 1953, § 63–5–15. *Loyalty oath required.*—No person shall be employed or associated in any capacity in any civil defense organization established under this act who advocates or has advocated a change by force or violence in the constitutional form of the Government of the United States or of this State or the overthrow of any government in the United States by force or violence, or who has been convicted of, or is under indictment or information charging any subversive act against the United States. Each person who is appointed to serve in an organization for civil defense shall, before entering upon his duties, take an oath in writing before a person authorized to administer oaths in this State, which oath shall be substantially as follows:

"I, _____ _____, do solemnly swear (or affirm) that I will support and defend the Constitution of the United States and the constitution of the State of Utah, against all enemies, foreign and domestic; that I will bear true faith and allegiance to the same; I take this obligation freely, without any mental reservation or purpose of evasion; and that I will well and faithfully discharge the duties upon which I am about to enter.

"And I do further swear (or affirm) that I do not advocate, nor have I ever advocated, nor am I a member nor have I ever been a member of any political party or organization that advocates the overthrow of the Government of the United States or of this State by force or violence; and that during such time as I am a member of the (name of civil defense organization), I will not advocate nor become a member of any political party or organization that advocates the overthrow of the Government of the United States or of this State by force or violence."

VERMONT

Unlawful Advocacy

ANARCHY

13. Vermont Stat. Anno. § 3405. *Unlawful acts and penalty.*—
A person who by speech or directly or indirectly by exhibition, distribution or promulgation of any written or printed document or paper or pictorial representation, shall advocate, advise, counsel or incite unlawful assault upon, or the killing of a public official, or the unlawful destruction of property, or the overthrow by force or violence of the government of the State, or who, at any meeting or in the presence of more than three persons in any place or in any manner, shall advise, advocate or counsel the violation of or unlawful refusal to obey a law of the State respecting the preservation of the peace and the protection of life or property shall be imprisoned not more than three years or fined not more than $1,000.00, or both.

Exclusion From the Elective Process

QUALIFICATIONS OF FREEMEN

Vermont Constitution, ch. 2, 34. *Freemen's oath.*—Every person of the full age of twenty-one years, who is a natural born citizen of this or some one of the United States or who has been naturalized agreeably to the Acts of Congress, having resided in this State for the space of one whole year next before the election of representatives, and who is of a quiet and peaceable behavior, and will take the following oath or affirmation, shall be entitled to all the privileges of a freeman of this State:

You solemnly swear (or affirm) *that whenever you give your vote or suffrage, touching any matter that concerns the State of Vermont, you will do it so as in your conscience you shall judge will most conduce to the best good of the same, as established by the constitution, without fear or favor of any person.*

Loyalty of State Officers and Employees

1. ELECTIVE AND NONELECTIVE PERSONNEL

Vermont Constitution, ch. 2, § 52. *Oath of allegiance required.*—
Every officer, whether judicial, executive, or military, in authority under this State, before he enters upon the execution of his office, shall take and subscribe the following oath or affirmation of allegiance to this State (unless he shall produce evidence that he has before taken the same), and also the following oath or affirmation of office, except military officers, and such as shall be exempted by the legislature.

THE OATH OR AFFIRMATION OF ALLEGIANCE

You do solemnly swear (or affirm) that you will be true and faithful to the State of Vermont, and that you will not, directly or indirectly, do any act or thing injurious to the constitution or government thereof. (If an oath) So help you God. (If an affirmation) Under the pains and penalties of perjury.

THE OATH OR AFFIRMATION OF OFFICE

You, _____, do solmenly swear (or affirm) that you will faithfully execute the office of _____ for the _____ of _____ and will therein do equal right and justice to all men, to the best of your judgment and ability, according to law. (If an oath) So help you God. (If an affirmation) Under the pains and penalties of perjury.

2. CIVIL DEFENSE PERSONNEL

20 Vermont Stat. Anno. § 18. *Loyalty oath required.*—No person shall be employed or associated in any capacity in any civil defense organization established under this chapter who advocates a change by force or violence in the constitutional form of the Government of the United States or in this State or the overthrow of any government in the United States by force or violence, or who has been convicted of or is under indictment or information charging any subversive act against the United States. Each person who is appointed shall take an oath of allegiance to the United States and the State of Vermont substantially as prescribed by Federal law. This oath shall be taken in writing before a person authorized by law to administer oaths in this State and a copy shall be filed in the office of the director.

TEACHERS' LOYALTY

16 Vermon Stat. Anno. § 4. *Loyalty oath required.*—(a) A superintendent, principal or teacher in a public school of the State, or a professor, instructor or teacher who shall be employed hereafter by a university, college or normal school in the State, which is supported in whole or in part by public funds, or in a private school or other educational institution accepted by the State department of education as furnishing equivalent education, before entering upon the discharge of his or her duties, shall subscribe to an oath or affirmation to support the Constitution of the United States of America, the constitution of the State of Vermont, and the laws of the United States and the State of Vermont; provided, however, that such oath shall not be required of any person so employed who is a citizen of a foreign country.

(b) A person so employed shall not indulge in, give or permit, either directly or indirectly, any instruction, propaganda or activity in connection with such school, university, college or normal school, contrary to or subversive of the Constitution and laws of the United States or of the State of Vermont, but shall so organize, administer and conduct such school, university, college or normal school as most effectively will promote ethical character, good citizenship and patriotic loyalty to the United States and to its Constitution and laws.

Exclusion From the Bar

Vermont does not appear to have any rule or regulation which pertains to the admission of persons who are or who have been Communists or subversives. Similarly, the various forms employed by the State do not contain any questions directly on the subject.

VIRGINIA

ADVOCATING OVERTHROW OF THE GOVERNMENT

Code of Virginia 1950, § 18.1–421 (Supp. 1962). *Unlawful acts and penalty.*—It shall be unlawful for any person, group, or organization to advocate any change, by force, violence, or other unlawful means in the government of the Commonwealth of Virginia or any of its subdivisions or in the Government of the United States of America.

It shall be unlawful for any person to join, assist or otherwise contribute to any group or organization which, to the knowledge of such person, advocates or has as its purpose, aim or objective, any change, by force, violence, or other unlawful means in the government of the Commonwealth of Virginia or any of its subdivisions or in the Government of the United States of America.

Violation of this section is hereby declared to be a felony, punishable, upon conviction, by a fine of not less than one thousand nor more than five thousand dollars or by confinement in the penitentiary for not less than two years nor more than five years, or by both such fine and imprisonment.

Nothing herein shall be construed to limit or prohibt the advocacy, orally or otherwise, of any change, by peaceful means, in the government of the Commonwealth or any of its subdivisions or in the Government of the United States.

LOYALTY OF STATE OFFICERS AND EMPLOYEES

1. ELECTIVE AND NONELECTIVE PERSONNEL

Virginia Constitution, Art. II, § 34. *Oath.*—Sec. 34. Oath to be prescribed. Members of the General Assembly, and all officers, executive and judicial, elected or appointed after this constitution goes into effect shall, before they enter on the performance of their public duties, severally take and subscribe the following oath or affirmation:

"I do solemnly swear (or affirm) that I will support the Constitution of the United States, and the constitution of the State of Virginia, and that I will faithfully and impartially discharge and perform all of the duties incumbent on me as _____, according to the best of my ability, so help me God."

2. CIVIL DEFENSE PERSONNEL

Code of Virginia 1950, § 44–145.5. *Loyalty oath required.*—No person shall be employed or associated in any capacity in any civil defense organization established under this chapter who advocates or has advocated a change by force or violence in the constitutional form of the Government of the United States or in this State or the overthrow

415

of any government in the United States by force or violence, or who has been convicted of or is under indictment or information charging any subversive act against the United States. Each person who is appointed to serve in an organization for civil defense shall, before entering upon his duties, take an oath, in writing, before a person authorized to administer oaths in this State, which oath shall be substantially as follows:

"I, _____, do solemnly swear (or affirm) that I will support and defend the Constitution of the United States and the constitution of the Commonwealth of Virginia, against all enemies foreign and domestic; that I will bear true faith and allegiance to the same; that I take this obligation freely, without any mental reservation or purpose of evasion; and that I will well and faithfully discharge the duties upon which I am about to enter.

"And I do further swear (or affirm) that I do not advocate, nor am I a member of any political party or organization that advocates the overthrow of the Government of the United States or of this State by force or violence; and that during such time as I am a member of the (name of civil defense organization), I will not advocate nor become a member of any political party or organization that advocates the overthrow of the Government of the United States or of this State by force or violence."

Exclusion From the Bar

Virginia does not appear to have any rule or regulation which pertains to the admission of persons who are or who have been Communists or subversives. Similarly the various forms employed by the State do not contain any questions directly on the subject.

WASHINGTON

1. ANARCHY

Rev. Code Washington Anno. § 9.05.010. *Criminal anarchy defined.*—Criminal anarchy is the doctrine that organized government should be overthrown by force or violence, or by assassination of the executive head or of any of the executive officials of government, or by any unlawful means. The advocating of such doctrine either by word of mouth, by writing, by radio, or by printing is a felony.

Id. § 9.05.020. *Unlawful acts and penalty.*—Every person who

(1) By word of mouth, by writing, by radio, or by printing shall advocate, advise or teach the duty, necessity or propriety of overthrowing or overturning organized government by force or violence, or by assassination of the executive head or of any of the executive officials of government, or by any unlawful means; or,

(2) Shall print, publish, edit, issue or knowingly circulate, sell, distribute or publicly display any book, paper, document, or written or printed matter in any form, containing or advocating, advising or teaching the doctrine that organized government should be overthrown by force, violence or any unlawful means; or,

(3) Shall openly, willfully and deliberately justify by word of mouth, by writing, by radio or by printing the assassination or unlawful killing or assaulting of any executive or other officer of the United States or of any State or of any civilized nation having an organized government because of his official character, or any other crime, with intent to teach, spread or advocate the propriety of the doctrines of criminal anarchy; or,

(4) Shall organize or help to organize or become a member of or voluntarily assemble with any society, group, or assembly of persons formed to teach or advocate such doctrine,

Shall be punished by imprisonment in the State penitentiary for not more than ten years, or by a fine of not more than five thousand dollars, or by both.

No person convicted of violating any of the provisions of RCW 9.05.010 or 9.05.020 shall be an employee of the State, or any department, agency, or subdivision thereof during the five years next following his conviction.

Id. § 9.05.030. *Assemblage to advocate criminal anarchy.*—Whenever two or more persons assemble for the purpose of advocating or teaching the doctrines of criminal anarchy, as defined in RCW 9.05.010, such an assembly is unlawful, and every person voluntarily participating therein by his presence, aid or instigation, shall be punished by imprisonment in the State penitentiary for not more than ten years, or by a fine of not more than five thousand dollars, or both.

417

Id. § 9.05.040. *Permitting premises to be used to advocate criminal anarchy.*—Every owner, agent, superintendent, janitor, caretaker or occupant of any place, building or room, who shall willfully and knowingly permit therein any assemblage of persons prohibited by RCW 9.05.030, or who, after notification that the premises are so used, shall permit such use to be continued, shall be guilty of a gross misdemeanor.

Id. § 9.05.050. *Evidence.*—No person shall be excused from giving evidence upon an investigation or prosecution for any of the offenses specified in RCW 9.05.020 or 9.05.030, upon the ground that the evidence might tend to criminate himself.

Annotation:

State v. *Lowery*, 104 Washington 520, 177 P. 335 (1918). Defendant was convicted of the crime of criminal anarchy which was defined as (1) advocating, advising or teaching, orally or in writing, the necessity or propriety of overthrowing or overturning organized government by force or violence or by assassination of the executive head, or of any of the executive officials of government, or by any unlawful means, or (2) organizing or helping to organize or becoming a member of or voluntarily assembling with any society, group or assembly of persons formed to teach or advocate such doctrine. The evidence against the defendant consisted of written propaganda issued by the Industrial Workers of the World found on his person at the time of arrest. The court upheld the conviction over objections that the information was insufficient and that the defendant did not receive an impartial and fair hearing. To defendant's claim that he was not responsible for the statements contained in the circulars, the court held that he had made these doctrines—overthrow of the Government of the United States—his own by accepting membership in the organization whose principles they represented.

---

2. INCITING VIOLENCE

Rev. Code Washington Anno., § 9.05.150. *Publishing or circulating printed matter to incite violence.*—Every person who shall willfully print, publish, edit, issue, or knowingly circulate, sell, distribute, or display any book, paper, document, or written or printed matter, in any form, advocating, encouraging or inciting, or having a tendency to encourage or incite the commission of any crime, breach of the peace or act of violence, or which shall tend to encourage or advocate disrespect for law or for any court or courts of justice, shall be guilty of a gross misdemeanor.

Id. § 9.05.160. *Editors, etc., liable for contents of publication.*— Every editor or proprietor of a book, newspaper or serial and every manager of a partnership or incorporated association by which a book, newspaper or serial is issued, is chargeable with the publication of any matter contained in such book, newspaper or serial. But in every prosecution therefor, the defendant may show in his defense that the matter complained of was published without his knowledge or fault and against his wishes by another who had no authority from him to make the publication, and was retracted by him as soon as known.

Annotation:

Fox v. *Washington,* 236 U.S. 273, 35 S. Ct. 383, 59 L. Ed. 573 (1915). Defendant was convicted for editing printed matter tending to encourage and advocate disrespect for law contrary to a State statute against indecent exposure. The statute provided that "every person who shall willfully print, publish, edit, issue, or knowingly circulate, sell, distribute or display any book, paper, document, or written or printed matter in any form advocating, encouraging or inciting, or having a tendency to encourage or incite the commission of any crime, breach of the peace or act of violence, or which shall tend to encourage or advocate disrespect for law or for any court or courts of justice, shall be guilty of a misdemeanor. The court affirmed the conviction and held that the statute did not infringe upon the liberties guaranteed by the fourteenth. In view of the fact that the statute was confined to encouraging an actual breach of law, there was no merit in petitioner's arguments that it restricted liberty and was void for vagueness.

---

3. SUBVERSIVE ACTIVITIES

Rev. Code Washington Anno. § 9.81.010. *"Organization," "Subversive organization," "Foreign subversive organization," "Foreign government," and "Subversive person" defined.*—(1) "Organization" means an organization, corporation, company, partnership, association, trust, foundation, fund, club. society, committee, political party, or any group of persons, whether or not incorporated, permanently or temporarily associated together for joint action or advancement of views on any subject or subjects.

(2) "Subversive organization" means any organization which engages in or advocates, abets, advises, or teaches, or a purpose of which is to engage in or advocate, abet, advise, or teach activities intended to overthrow, destroy or alter, or to assist in the overthrow, destruction or alteration of, the constitutional form of the Government of the United States, or of the State of Washington, or of any political subdivision of either of them, by revolution, force, or violence.

(3) "Foreign subversive organization" means any organization directed, dominated, or controlled directly or indirectly by a foreign government which engages in or advocates, abets, advises, or teaches, or a purpose of which is to engage in or to advocate, abet, advise, or teach, activities intended to overthrow, destroy or alter, or to assist in the overthrow, destruction or alteration of the constitutional form of the Government of the United States, or of the State of Washington, or of any political subdivision of either of them, and to establish in place thereof any form of government the direction and control of which is to be vested in, or exercised by or under, the domination or control of any foreign government, organization, or individual.

(4) "Foreign government" means the government of any country or nation other than the Government of the United States of America or of one of the States thereof.

(5) "Subversive person" means any person who commits, attempts to commit, or aids in the commission, or advocates, abets, advises, or teaches by any means any person to commit, attempt to commit, or aid

in the commission of any act intended to overthrow, destroy or alter, or to assist in the overthrow, destruction or alteration of, the constitutional form of the Government of the United States, or of the State of Washington, or any political subdivision of either of them by revolution, force, or violence; or who with knowledge that the organization is an organization as described in subsection (2) and (3) hereof, becomes or remains a member of a subversive organization or a foreign subversive organization.

Id. § 9.81.020. *Unlawful acts and penalty.*—It shall be a felony for any person knowingly and willfully to:

(1) Commit, attempt to commit, or aid in the commission of any act intended to overthrow, destroy or alter, or to assist in the overthrow, destruction or alteration of, the constitutional form of the Government of the United States, or of the State of Washington or any political subdivision of either of them, by revolution, force, or violence; or

(2) Advocate, abet, advise, or teach by any means any person to commit, attempt to commit, or assist in the commission of any such act under such circumstances as to constitute a clear and present danger to the security of the United States, or of the State of Washington or of any political subdivision of either of them; or

(3) Conspire with one or more persons to commit any such act; or

(4) Assist in the formation or participate in the management or to contribute to the support of any subversive organization or foreign subversive organization knowing said organization to be a subversive organization or a foreign subversive organization; or

(5) Destroy any books, records or files, or secrete any funds in this State of a subversive organization or a foreign subversive organization, knowing said organization to be such.

Any person upon a plea of guilty or upon conviction of violating any of the provisions of this section shall be fined not more than ten thousand dollars, or imprisoned for not more than ten years, or both, at the discretion of the court.

Id. § 9.81.030. *Membership in subversive organization or foreign subversive organization unlawful.*—It shall be a felony for any person after June 1, 1951, to become, or after September 1, 1951, to remain a member of a subversive organization or a foreign subversive organization knowing said organization to be a subversive organization or foreign subversive organization. Any person upon a plea of guilty or upon conviction of violating any of the provisions of this section shall be fined not more than five thousand dollars, or imprisoned for not more than five years, or both, at the discretion of the court.

Id. § 9.81.050. *Subversive organizations and foreign subversive organizations outlawed.*—It shall be unlawful for any subversive organization or foreign subversive organization to exist or function in the State of Washington and any organization which by a court of competent jurisdiction is found to have violated the provisions of this section shall be dissolved. and if it be a corporation organized and existing under the laws of the State of Washington a finding by a court of competent jurisdiction that it has violated the provisions of this section shall constitute legal cause for forfeiture of its charter and its charter shall be forfeited and all funds, books, records and files of every kind and all other property of any organization found to have violated the provisions of this section shall be seized by and for the State of Washington, the funds to be deposited in the State treasury and the books, records, files and other property to be turned over to the attorney general of Washington.

Id. § 9.81.082. *Membership in subversive organization defined.*— For the purpose of this act, membership in a subversive organization shall be membership in any organization after it has been placed on the list of organizations designated by the Attorney General of the United States as being subversive pursuant to Executive Order No. 9835.

Id. § 9.81.083. *Communist Party declared to be a subversive organization.*—The Communist Party is a subversive organization within the purview of chapter 9.81 and membership in the Communist Party is a subversive activity thereunder.

OUTLAWING THE COMMUNIST PARTY

Rev. Code Washington Anno. § 9.81.050. *Subversion organizations outlawed.*—It shall be unlawful for any subversive organization or foreign subversive organization to exist or function in the State of Washington and any organization which by a court of competent jurisdiction is found to have violated the provisions of this section shall be dissolved, and if it be a corporation organized and existing under the laws of the State of Washington a finding by a court of competent jurisdiction that it has violated the provisions of this section shall constitute legal cause for forfeiture of its charter and its charter shall be forfeited and all funds, books, records and files of every kind and all other property of any organization found to have violated the provisions of this section shall be seized by and for the State of Washington, the funds to be deposited in the State treasury and the books, records, files and other property to be turned over to the attorney general of Washington.

Id. § 9.81.083. *Communist Party declared to be a subversive organization.*—The Communist Party is a subversive organization within the purview of chapter 9.81 and membership in the Communist Party is a subversive activity thereunder.

EXCLUSION FROM THE ELECTIVE PROCESS

Washington Rev. Code Anno. § 9.81.020. *Subversive activities and penalty.*—It shall be a felony for any person knowingly and willfully to:

(1) Commit, attempt to commit, or aid in the commission of any act intended to overthrow, destroy or alter, or to assist in the overthrow, destruction or alteration of, the constitutional form of the Government of the United States, or of the State of Washington or any political subdivision of either of them, by revolution, force or violence; or

(2) Advocate, abet, advise, or teach by any means any person to commit, attempt to commit, or assist in the commission of any such act under such circumstances as to constitute a clear and present danger to the security of the United States, or of the State of Washington or of any political subdivision of either of them; or

(3) Conspire with one or more persons to commit any such act; or

(4) Assist in the formation or participate in the management or to contribute to the support of any subversive organization or foreign subversive organization knowing said organization to be a subversive organization or a foreign subversive organization; or

(5) Destroy any books, records or files, or secrete any funds in this State of a subversive organization or a foreign subversive organization, knowing said organization to be such.

Any person upon a plea of guilty or upon conviction of violating any of the provisions of this section shall be fined not more than ten thousand dollars, or imprisoned for not more than ten years, or both, at the discretion of the court.

Id. § 981.030. *Membership in subversive organization and foreign subversive organization unlawful.*—It shall be a felony for any person after June 1, 1951, to become, or after September 1, 1951, to remain a member of a subversive organization or a foreign subversive organization knowing said organization to be a subversive organization or foreign subversive organization. Any person upon a plea of guilty or upon conviction of violating any of the provisions of this section shall be fined not more than five thousand dollars, or imprisoned for not more than five years, or both, at the discretion of the court.

Id. § 9.81.040. *Penalty—barred from ballot and voting.*—Any person who shall be convicted or shall plead guilty of violating any of the provisions of RCW 9.81.020 and 9.81.303, in addition to all other penalties therein provided, shall from the date of such conviction be barred from

(1) Holding any office, elective or appointive, or any other position of profit or trust in, or employment by the government of the State of Washington or of any agency thereof or of any county, municipal corporation or other political subdivision of said State;

(2) Filing or standing for election to any public office in the State of Washington; or

(3) Voting in any election held in this State.

Id. § 9.81.050. *Subversive organizations outlawed.*—It shall be unlawful for any subversive organization or foreign subversive organization to exist or function in the State of Washington and any organization which by a court of competent jurisdiction is found to have violated the provisions of this secton shall be dissolved, and if it be a corporation organized and existing under the laws of the State of Washington a finding by a court of competent jurisdiction that it has violated the provisions of this section shall constitute legal cause for forfeiture of its charter and its charter shall be forfeited and all funds, books, records and files of every kind and all other property of any organization found to have violated the provisions of this section shall be seized by and for the State of Washington, the funds to be deposited in the State treasury and the books, records, files and other property to be turned over to the attorney general of Washington.

Id. § 9.81.083. *Communist Party declared to be a subversive organization.*—The Communist Party is a subversive organization within the purview of chapter 9.81 and membership in the Communist Party is a subversive activity thereunder.

Id. § 9.81.100. *Candidates required to file nonsubversive affidavit.*—
No person shall become a candidate for election under the laws of the
State of Washington to any public office whatsoever in this State,
unless he or she shall file an affidavit that he or she is not a subversive
person as defined in this act. No declaration of candidacy shall be
received for filing by any election official of any county or subdivision
in the State of Washington or by the secretary of state of the State
of Washington unless accompanied by the affidavit aforesaid, and
there shall not be entered upon any ballot or voting machine at any
election the name of any person who has failed or refused to make
the affidavit as set forth herein.

Annotation:

State v. *Reeves,* 5 Wn. 2d 637, 106 P. 2d 729 (1940). This action was
brought on behalf of various registered voters and electors who participated in a convention of the Communist Party, U.S.A., to compel
the secretary of state to certify the names of party candidates for certain offices. The State election laws provide, *inter alia,* that the certificate of nomination "shall designate, in not more than five words, the
party or principle which such convention represents." The secretary
of state refused to accept the certificate on various grounds, including,
(1) that it was defective in that it contained a designation in more
than the required number of words, the party or principle which
"such convention represents"; (2) that the certificate contained a declaration of principles which were at variance with the avowed principles of the Communist Party; (3) that in view of these principles it
would be contrary to public policy to accept the certification; (4) that
it would be a useless action since no party candidate could take the
oath of office except by fraud. The court ordered the issuance of the
mandamus on grounds that the secretary had exceeded her statutory
power to refuse to file a certificate of nomination.

Loyalty of State Officers and Employees

1. ELECTIVE AND NONELECTIVE PERSONNEL

Rev. Code Washington Anno. § 9.81.020. *Subversive activities and
penalty.*—It shall be a felony for any person knowingly and willfully
to:
(1) Commit, attempt to commit, or aid in the commission of any
act intended to overthrow, destroy or alter, or to assist in the overthrow, destruction or alteration of, the constitutional form of the
Government of the United States, or of the State of Washington or
any political subdivision of either of them, by revolution, force or
violence; or
(2) Advocate, abet, advise, or teach by any means any person to
commit, attempt to commit, or assist in the commission of any such
act under such circumstances as to constitute a clear and present danger to the security of the United States, or of the State of Washington or of any political subdivision of either of them; or
(3) Conspire with one or more persons to commit any such act; or
(4) Assist in the formation or participate in the management or

to contribute to the support of any subversive organization or foreign subversive organization knowing said organization to be a subversive organization or a foreign subversive organization; or

(5) Destroy any books, records or files, or secrete any funds in this State of a subversive organization or a foreign subversive organization, knowing said organization to be such.

Any person upon a plea of guilty or upon conviction of violating any of the provisions of this section shall be fined not more than ten thousand dollars, or imprisoned for not more than ten years, or both, at the discretion of the court.

Id. § 9.81.040. *Penalty—barred from office.*—Any person who shall be convicted or shall plead guilty of violating any of the provisions of RCW 9.81.020 and 9.81.030, in addition to all other penalties therein provided, shall from the date of such conviction be barred from—

(1) Holding any office, elective or appointive, or any other position of profit or trust in, or employment by the government of the State of Washington or of any agency thereof or of any county, municipal corporation or other political subdivision of said State;

(2) Filing or standing for election to any public office in the State of Washington; or

(3) Voting in any election held in this State.

2. NONELECTIVE PERSONNEL

Rev. Code Washington Anno. § 9.05.010. *Criminal anarchy defined.*—Criminal anarchy is the doctrine that organized government should be overthrown by force or violence, or by assassination of the executive head or of any of the executive officials of government, or by any unlawful means. The advocating of such doctrine either by word of mouth, by writing, by radio, or by printing is a felony.

Id. § 9.05.020. *Unlawful acts and penalty—temporary bar from public employment.*—Every person who

(1) By word of mouth, by writing, by radio, or by printing shall advocate, advise or teach the duty, necessity or propriety of overthrowing or overturning organized government by force or violence, or by assassination of the executive head or of any of the executive officials of government, or by any unlawful means; or,

(2) Shall print, publish, edit, issue or knowingly circulate, sell, distribute or publicly display any book, paper, document, or written or printed matter in any form, containing or advocating, advising or teaching the doctrine that organized government should be overthrown by force, violence or any unlawful means; or,

(3) Shall openly, willfully and deliberately justify by word of mouth, by writing, by radio or by printing the assassination or unlawful killing or assaulting of any executive or other officer of the United States or of any State or of any civilized nation having an organized government because of his official character, or any other crime, with intent to teach, spread or advocate the propriety of the doctrines of criminal anarchy; or,

(4) Shall organize or help to organize or become a member of or voluntarily assemble with any society, group or assembly of persons formed to teach or advocate such doctrine,

Shall be punished by imprisonment in the State penitentiary for not more than ten years, or by a fine of not more than five thousand dollars, or by both.

No person convicted of violating any of the provisions of RCW 9.05.010 or 9.05.020 shall be an employee of the State, or any department, agency, or subdivision thereof during the five years next following his conviction.

Id. § 9.81.060. *Subversive persons ineligible for public employment.*—No subversive person, as defined in this act, shall be eligible for employment in, or appointment to any office, or any position of trust or profit in the government, or in the administration of the business, of this State, or of any county, municipality, or other political subdivision of this State.

Note.—For definition of subversive person, see Subversive Activities under Unlawful Advocacy, *supra.*

Id. § 9.81.070. *Investigations.*—Every person and every board, commission, council, department, court or other agency of the State of Washington or any political subdivision thereof, who or which appoints or employs or supervises in any manner the appointment or employment of public officials or employees shall establish by rules, regulations or otherwise, procedures designed to ascertain whether any person is a subversive person. In securing any facts necessary to ascertain the information herein required, the applicant shall be required to sign a written statement containing answers to such inquiries as may be material, which statement shall contain notice that it is subject to the penalties of perjury. Every such person, board, commission, council, department, court, or other agency shall require every employee or applicant for employment to state under oath whether or not he or she is a member of the Communist Party or other subversive organization, and refusal to answer on any grounds shall be cause for immediate termination of such employee's employment or for refusal to accept his or her application for employment.

Id. § 9.81.080. *Exclusions from scope of law.*—The inquiries prescribed in preceding sections, other than the written statement to be executed by an applicant for employment and the requirement set forth in RCW 9.81.070, relative to membership in the Communist Party or other subversive organization, shall not be required as a prerequisite to the employment of any persons in any case in which the employing authority may determine, and by rule or regulation specify the reasons why, the nature of the work to be performed is such that employment of such persons will not be dangerous to the health of the citizens or the security of the Governments of the United States, the State of Washington, or any political subdivision thereof.

Id. § 9.81.090. *Standard of evidence for discharge.*—Reasonable grounds on all the evidence to believe that any person is a subversive person, as defined in this act, shall be cause for discharge from any appointive office or other position of profit or trust in the government of or in the administration of the business of this State, or of any county, municipality or other political subdivision of this State, or any agency thereof. The attorney general and the personnel director, and the civil service commission of any county, city or other political subdivision of this State, shall, by appropriate rules or regulations, prescribe that persons charged with being subversive persons, as defined in this act, shall have the right of reasonable notice, date, time and place of hearing, opportunity to be heard by himself and witnesses on his behalf, to be represented by counsel, to be confronted by witnesses against him, the right to cross-examination, and such other rights which are in accordance with the procedures prescribed by law for the discharge of such person for other reasons. Every person and every board, commission, council, department, or other agency of the State of Washington or any political subdivision thereof having responsibility for the appointment, employment or supervision of public employees not covered by the classified service in this section referred to, shall establish rules or procedures similar to those required herein for classified services for a hearing for any person charged with being a subversive person, as defined in this act, after notice and opportunity to be heard. Every employing authority discharging any person pursuant to any provision of this act, shall promptly report to the special assistant attorney general in charge of subversive activities the fact of and the circumstances surrounding such discharge. Any person discharged under the provisions of this act shall have the right within thirty days thereafter to appeal to the superior court of the county wherein said person may reside or wherein he may have been employed for determination by said court as to whether or not the discharge appealed from was justified under the provisions of this act. The court shall regularly hear and determine such appeals and the decision of the superior court may be appealed to the supreme court of the State of Washington as in civil cases. Any person appealing to the superior court may be entitled to trial by jury if he or she so elects.

Id. § 9.81.110. *Penalty.*—Every written statement made pursuant to this act by an applicant for appointment or employment, or by any employee, shall be deemed to have been made under oath if it contains a declaration preceding the signature of the maker to the effect that it is made under the penalties of perjury. Any person who willfully makes a material misstatement of fact (1) in any such written statement, or (2) in any affidavit made pursuant to the provisions of this act, or (3) under oath in any hearing conducted by any agency of the State, or of any of its political subdivisions pursuant to this act, or (4) in any written statement by an applicant for appointment or employment or by an employee in any State aid or private institution of learning in this State, intended to determine whether or not such applicant or employee is a subversive person as defined in this act, which statement contains notice that it is subject to the penalties of perjury, shall be subject to the penalties of perjury, as prescribed in chapter 9.41.

3. CIVIL DEFENSE PERSONNEL

Rev. Code Washington Anno. § 38.52.130. *Loyalty oath required.*— (1) No person shall be employed or associated in any capacity in any civil defense organization established under this chapter who advocates or has advocated a change by force or violence in the constitutional form of the Government of the United States or in this State or the overthrow of any government in the United States by force or violence, or who has been convicted of or is under indictment or information charging any subversive act against the United States. Each person who is appointed to serve in an organization for civil defense shall, before entering upon his duties, take an oath, in writing, before a person authorized to administer oaths in this State, which oath shall be substantially as follows:

"I, ------------------, do solemnly swear (or affirm) that I will support and defend the Constitution of the United States and the constitution of the State of Washington, against all enemies, foreign and domestic; that I will bear true faith and allegiance to the same; that I take this obligation freely, without any mental reservation or purpose of evasion; and that I will well and faithfully discharge the duties upon which I am about to enter.

"And I do further swear (or affirm) that I do not advocate, nor am I a member of any political party or organization that advocates the overthrow of the Government of the United States or of this State by force or violence; and that during such time as I am a member of the (name of civil defense organization), I will not advocate nor become a member of any political party or organization that advocates the overthrow of the Government of the United States or of this State by force or violence."

(2) The director of civil defense or any civil defense official designated by him is authorized to administer the loyalty oath as required by this chapter.

Annotation:

Ops. Atty. Gen. 57–58 No. 65. Foreign nationals are not prohibited from serving in local civil defense organizations but they must take the oath of allegiance to the United States.

Seventh Day Adventists may attach any statement to their personnel records which does not limit or qualify their oath of allegiance.

TEACHERS' LOYALTY

Rev. Code Washington Anno. § 28.67.020. *Alien teachers employed in public schools required to take non-Communist oath.*—No person, who is not a citizen of the United States of America, shall teach or be permitted or qualified to teach in the public schools in this State: *Provided, however,* That the superintendent of public instruction may grant to an alien a permit to teach in the public schools of this State; providing such teacher has all the other qualifications required by law, has declared his or her intention of becoming a citizen of the United States of America, and that five years and six months have not expired since such declaration was made: *Provided, further,* That the superintendent of public instruction may grant to an alien teacher whose qualifications have been approved by the State board of education a temporary permit to teach as an exchange teacher in the public schools of this State, irrespective of requirements respecting citizenship and oath of allegiance. Before such alien shall be granted a temporary permit he or she shall be required to subscribe to an oath or affirmation in writing that such alien applicant is not a member of or affiliated with a Communist or Communist-sponsored organization or a Fascist or Fascist-sponsored organization. The form of such oath or affirmation shall be prepared by the State superintendent of public instruction. All oaths or affirmations subscribed as herein provided shall be filed in the office of the superintendent of public instruction and shall be there retained for a period of five years. Such permits shall at all times be subject to revocation by and at the discretion of the superintendent of public instruction.

Id. § 28.67.030. *Disqualification for lack of patriotism.*—No person, whose certificate or diploma authorizing him or her to teach in the public schools of this State shall have been revoked on account of his or her failure to endeavor to impress on the minds of his or her pupils the principles of patriotism, or to train them up to the true comprehension of the rights, duty and dignity of American citizenship, shall teach or be permitted or qualified to teach in any public school in this State, and no certificate or diploma shall be issued to such person.

Id. § 28.67.035. *Penalty.*—Any person teaching in any school in violation of RCW 28.67.020 or 28.67.030, and any school director knowingly permitting any person to teach in any school in violation of RCW 28.67.020 or 28.67.030, shall be guilty of a misdemeanor.

Id. § 28.70.150. *Oath of allegiance required.*—Every person applying for a license to teach or renewing an existing contract, in the State of Washington, shall take and subscribe to the following oath or affirmation:

"I solemnly swear (or affirm) that I will support the Constitution and laws of the United States of American and the State of Washington, and will by precept and example promote respect for the flag and the institutions of the United States of America and the State of Washington, reverence for law and order and undivided allegiance to the Government of the United States."

No license to teach in the State of Washington shall be issued, or contract, or renewal thereof, signed by any school board, unless it shall affirmatively appear on said license or in said contract, or renewal thereof that such teacher has taken, subscribed and filed therewith the foregoing oath or affirmation.

Id. § 9.81.060. *Subversive person ineligible for employment.*—No subversive person, as defined in this act, shall be eligible for employment in, or appointment to any office, or any position of trust or profit in the government, or in the administration of the business, of this State, or of any county, municipality, or other political subdivision of this State.

Id. § 9.81.070. *Investigations.*—Every person and every board, commission, council, department, court or other agency of the State of Washington or any political subdivision thereof, who or which appoints or employs or supervises in any manner the appointment or employment of public officials or employees shall establish by rules, regulations or otherwise, procedures designed to ascertain whether any person is a subversive person. In securing any facts necessary to ascertain the information herein required, the applicant shall be required to sign a written statement containing answers to such inquiries as may be material, which statement shall contain notice that it is subject to the penalties of perjury. Every such person, board, commission, council, department, court, or other agency shall require every employee or applicant for employment to state under oath whether or not he or she is a member of the Communist Party or other subversive organization, and refusal to answer on any grounds shall be cause for immediate termination of such employee's employment or for refusal to accept his or her application for employment.

Annotations:

Nostrand v. *Little*, 362 U.S. 474, 80 S. Ct. 840, 4 L. Ed. 2d 892 (1960). This case involved an action for a judgment declaring unconstitutional a statute requiring each State employee under pain of immediate dismissal, to swear that he was not a "subversive person," defined as one actually seeking to overthrow, destroy or alter the government by revolution, violence or force. The State supreme court sustained the validity of the statute without passing upon the claims that the dismissal of an employee without an opportunity to explain his refusal to take the oath violated due process. The Supreme Court vacated the judgment and remanded the case for consideration of the point by the State court.

Nostrand v. *Little*, 368 U.S. 436, 82 S. Ct. 49, 4 L. Ed. 2d 426 (1962). After the Court's remand of the case, supra, the State supreme court held that the appellants, university professors, were entitled to a hearing before they could be discharged for refusing to swear that they were not members of the Communist Party or any other subversive organization as required by statute. Appellants again appealed from the judgment of the court sustaining the constitutionality of the statute against their claims that it violated the First and Fourteenth Amendments. In a *per curiam* opinion the Court dismissed the appeal for want of a substantial Federal question.

Baggett v. *Bullitt*, 377 U.S. 360, 84 S. Ct. 1316, 12 L. Ed. 2d 377 (1964). Appellants, sixty-four members of the faculty, staff and student body of the University of Washington, brought an action for a judgment declaring unconstitutional several Washington statutes requiring the execution of two different oaths by employees. One oath adopted in 1931 applied only to teachers when applying for a license to teach or renewing an existing contract (§ 28.70.150). It required teachers to swear by precept and example to promote respect for the flag and the institutions of the United States and the State of Washington, reverence for law and order, and undivided allegiance to the Government of the United States. The other oath, adopted in 1955, incorporated provisions of the State Subversive Activities Act, and required the affiant to swear that he was not a subversive person; that he did not commit, or advise, teach, abet or advocate another to commit or aid in the commission of any act intended to overthrow, alter, or assist in the overthrow or alteration, of the constitutional form of government by revolution, force, or violence (§ 9.81.060). A three-judge district court held that the 1955 statute and the oath were not unduly vague and did not violate the constitution, and abstained from ruling on the 1931 oath until it was considered by the State courts. The Supreme Court held that the 1955 statute and the 1931 act violated due process by reason of vagueness and uncertainty. The Court stated: (1) that the 1955 oath was lacking in terms susceptible of objective measurement and failed to inform as to what the State commanded or forbade; (2) that the 1955 oath extended beyond overthrow or alteration by force and violence and included all change by revolution, i.e., any rapid or fundamental change; (3) that the range of activities which were or might be deemed inconsistent with the promise exacted by the 1931 act were very wide; (4) that it was difficult to ascertain what might be done without transgressing the promise to promote undivided allegiance to the Government of the United States; (5) that indulging in every presumption of a narrow construction of the provisions of the 1931 oath, it could not be said that it provided an ascertainable standard of conduct or that it did not require more than a State may command under the guarantees of the First and Fourteenth Amendments.

Exclusion From the Bar

Questions 11 and 12 of the application for admission by examination inquire as to membership in the Communist Party or other subversive organization. They provide as follows:

11. Are you now or have you ever been a member of the Communist Party or any of its affiliates?

12. Have you ever been a member of any organization or party having for its purpose and object the overthrow of the United States Government by force or violence? If so, give details.

Question 23 contained in the application for admission by motion makes a similar inquiry:

23. Are you now or have you ever been a member of any organization or party having for its purpose and object the overthrow of the United States Government by force or violence?

WEST VIRGINIA

UNLAWFUL ADVOCACY

SEDITION

West Virginia Code 1961, § 5912. *Unlawful speeches, publications and communications.*—It shall be unlawful for any person to speak, print, publish or communicate, by language, sign, picture or otherwise, any teachings, doctrines or counsels in sympathy with or in favor of ideals, institutions or forms of government hostile, inimical or antagonistic to those now or hereafter existing under the constitution and laws of this State or of the United States, or in sympathy with or in favor of the propriety, duty and necessity of crime, violence or other unlawful methods of terrorism, as a means of accomplishing economic or political reform, or in sympathy with or in favor of the overthrow of organized society, the unlawful destruction of property or the violation of law.

Id. § 5914. *Penalty.*—Any person violating any of the provisions of sections five and six (§§ 5912, 5913) of this article, shall, for the first offense, be guilty of a misdemeanor, and, upon conviction, shall be fined not less than one hundred nor more than five hundred dollars, or in the discretion of the court, be imprisoned in the county jail not exceeding twelve months, or both; and, for the second offense, shall be guilty of a felony, and, upon conviction shall be confined in the penitentiary not less than one nor more than five years.

LOYALTY OF STATE OFFICERS AND EMPLOYEES

1. ELECTIVE AND NONELECTIVE PERSONNEL

West Virginia Constitution, Art. IV, § 5. *Oath.*—Every person elected or appointed to any office, before proceeding to exercise the authority, or discharge the duties thereof, shall make oath or affirmation that he will support the Constitution of the United States and the constitution of this State, and that he will faithfully discharge the duties of his said office to the best of his skill and judgment; and no other oath, declaration or test shall be required as a qualification, unless herein otherwise provided.

2. CIVIL DEFENSE PERSONNEL

West Virginia Code 1961, § 1264 (38). *Loyalty oath required.*— No person shall be employed or associated in any capacity in any civil defense organization established under this article who advocates or has advocated a change by force or violence in the constitutional form of the Government of the United States or in this State or the overthrow of any government in the United States by force or violence, or

431

who has been convicted of or is under indictment or information charging any subversive act against the United States. Each person who is appointed to serve in an organization for civil defense shall, before entering upon his duties, take an oath, in writing, before a person authorized to administer oaths in this State, which oath shall be substantially as follows:

"I, _____, do solemnly swear, or affirm, that I will support and defend the Constitution of the United States and the constitution of the State of West Virginia, against all enemies, foreign and domestic; that I will bear true faith and allegiance to the same; that I take this obligation freely, without any mental reservation or purpose of evasion, and that I will well and faithfully discharge the duties upon which I am about to enter.

"And I do further swear, or affirm, that I do not advocate, nor am I a member of any political party or organization that advocates the overthrow of the Government of the United States or of this State by force or violence; and that during such time as I am a member of the (name of organization), I will not advocate nor become a member of any political party or organization that advocates the overthrow of the Government of the United States or of this State by force or violence."

TEACHERS' LOYALTY

West Virginia Code 1961, § 1807. *Loyalty oath required.*—Every teacher shall, at the time of signing the yearly contract to teach, take an oath to support the Constitution of the United States and the constitution of the State of West Virginia, and to honestly demean himself in the teaching profession, and to the best of his ability execute his position of teacher. Such oath shall be taken before a notary authorized to take oaths, or before a school trustee or member of the board of education of the district in which such contract is made; but no trustee or member of the board of education shall charge for administering such oath. If any such teacher enter upon the discharge of the duties pertaining to his employment without having taken the prescribed oath, he shall be guilty of a misdemeanor, and, upon conviction thereof, shall be fined not less than five nor more than twenty dollars, each month to be classed as a separate offense. If the secretary of the board of education shall issue and deliver an order or draft to any teacher in payment of his compensation, without such oath having been filed beforehand in his office, he shall be guilty of a misdemeanor, and, upon conviction thereof, shall be fined not less than ten nor more than twenty dollars; and the order so issued and delivered to said teacher shall be illegal, invalid and of no effect.

EXCLUSION FROM THE BAR

West Virginia does not appear to have any rule or regulation which pertains to the admission of persons who are or who have been Communists or subversives. Similarly, the various forms employed by the State do not contain any question directly on the subject.

WISCONSIN

Unlawful Advocacy

SEDITION

Wisconsin Stat. Anno. § 946.03. *Unlawful acts and penalty.*—(1) Whoever does any of the following may be fined not more than $5,000 or imprisoned not more than 10 years or both:

(a) Attempts the overthrow of the Government of the United States or this State by the use or threat of physical violence; or

(b) Is a party to a conspiracy with or a solicitation of another to overthrow the Government of the United States or this State by the use or threat of physical violence; or

(c) Advocates or teaches the duty, necessity, desirability or propriety of overthrowing the Government of the United States or this State by the use or threat of physical violence with intent that such government be overthrown; or

(d) Organizes or assists in the organization of an assembly with knowledge that the purpose of the assembly is to advocate or teach the duty, necessity, desirability or propriety of overthrowing the Government of the United States or this State by the use or threat of physical violence with intent that such government be overthrown.

(2) Whoever permits any premises under his care, control or supervision to be used by an assembly with knowledge that the purpose of the assembly is to advocate or teach the duty, necessity, desirability or propriety of overthrowing the Government of the United States or this State by the use or threat of physical violence with intent that such government be overthrown or, after learning that the premises are being so used, permits such use to be continued may be fined not more than $1,000 or imprisoned not more than one year in county jail or both.

Exclusion From the Elective Process

Wisconsin Stat. Anno. § 6.85. *Communist and affiliated parties barred from participation in elections.*—(1) Notwithstanding any other provisions of this chapter, no party shall be recognized or qualified to participate in any election which is directly or indirectly affiliated, by any means whatsoever, with the Communist Party of the United States, the Third Communist International, or any other foreign agency, political party, organization or government which either directly or indirectly carries on, advocates, teaches, justifies, aids or abets the overthrow by any unlawful means of, or which directly or indirectly carries on, advocates, teaches, justifies, aids or abets a program of sabotage, force and violence, sedition or treason against the Government of the United States or of this State.

(2) The secretary of state shall, with the advice and consent of the attorney general, determine which parties are qualified to participate in any election. Such determination shall be subject to review as provided in ch. 227.

(3) This section is declared to be enacted in the exercise of the police power of this State for the protection of the public peace, safety and general welfare of the residents of this State.

LOYALTY OF STATE OFFICERS AND EMPLOYEES

1. ELECTIVE AND NONELECTIVE PERSONNEL

Wisconsin Constitution, Art. V, § 28. *Oath.*—Members of the legislature, and all officers, executive and judicial, except such inferior officers as may be by law exempted, shall before they enter upon the duties of their respective offices, take and subscribe an oath or affirmation to support the Constitution of the United States and the constitution of the State of Wisconsin, and faithfully to discharge the duties of their respective offices to the best of their ability.

2. CIVIL DEFENSE PERSONNEL

Wisconsin Stat. Anno. § 22.01(11)(c) (Supp. 1964). *Persons advocating overthrow of government ineligible for employment.*—No person shall be employed or associated in any capacity in any civil defense organization under this section who advocates a change by force or violence in the constitutional form of Government of the United States or this State or who has been convicted of or is under indictment or information charging any subversive act against the United States.

EXCLUSION FROM THE BAR

Paragraph 9 on the Application for Permission to Take Wisconsin Bar Examination refers to membership in the Communist Party. It provides:

9. I am not and never have been a member of, or affiliated with, the Communist Party or any party or organization which advocates or advocated the overthrow of our constitutional form of government in the United States by force and violence except as follows (If none, state "No exceptions." If there are any exceptions state fully all facts and circumstances relating to such membership or affiliation):

Question 11 on the questionnaire on applicants makes a similar inquiry. It provides:

11. Has applicant ever been a member of or affiliated with the Communist Party?—or any party or organization which advocates or advocated the overthrow of our constitutional form of government in the United States by force and violence?—(Unless your answer is "No," please explain fully on an attached sheet the basis of your knowledge and whether such membership or affiliation continues to date.)

WYOMING

INCITEMENT TO CRIME

Wyoming Stat. 1957, § 6–111. *Offense and penalty.*—Whoever in any manner or by any means incites, advises, advocates, suggests or encourages crime as a means of coercion or for the accomplishment of any political or industrial reform, change or purpose in this State or in any foreign state or country, whether action may follow such incitement or not, shall be deemed guilty of incitement to crime and shall be punished by a fine not exceeding five thousand dollars, or by imprisonment in the penitentiary not exceeding five years, or by both such fine and imprisonment. Any person who shall be guilty of conduct described in this section shall be subject to peace proceedings for the prevention of crime and may be proceeded against upon complaint in writing by any persons having knowledge of the facts, and required to give security for good behavior or be committed in default of such recognizance.

REGISTRATION

Wyoming Stat. 1957, § 9–963. *Short title.*—This act [§§ 9–963 to 9–699] may be cited as the "Wyoming Communist Control Act of 1955."

Id. 39–694. *"Communist" defined.*—As used in the act [§ 9–693 to 9–699]: (a) A "Communist" is a person who is a member of the Communist Party, notwithstanding the fact that he may not pay dues to, or hold a card in said party; or who knowingly contributes funds or any character of property to the Communist Party.

Id. § 9–695. *Declaration of legislative policy.*—(a) By reason of the existence of a worldwide Communist movement, directed by foreign nations and individual coconspirators, which has as its declared objective, the seizure of world control to be brought about by conspiracy, aggression, force and violence, and is to be accomplished in large part by infiltrating tactics involving the use, [of] fraud, espionage, terrorism and treachery, it is found and declared to be necessary: (1) To require the registration of Communists and their members and adherents in order to protect the people of the State of Wyoming, their cites, towns, homes, industries and public works from the unlawful acts enumerated herein; (2) to assure cooperation with the Government of the United States in its efforts to stamp out Communist activities throughout the Nation.

(b) It is further declared to be the policy of this act [§§ 9–693 to 9–699] to protect individual liberties of the citizens of the State of Wyoming in all of their lawful pursuits and to protect them from the known insidious infiltration and propaganda tactics of Communists.

Id. § 9–696. *Communists and officers of the Communist Party required to register.*—(a) *Individual Communists.*—Each person, who is a Communist and who is a resident of, or shall remain in this State for as many as five (5) consecutive days after the effective date of this act [§§ 9–693 to 9–699], shall register with the secretary of state on or before the fifth consecutive day that such person remains in this State.

(b) *Party or organizations.*—Each and every officer of the Communist Party shall register or cause to be registered, said party or organizations, with the secretary of state, if said party or organizations have any members who reside, permanently or for a period of more than thirty (30) days, within the State of Wyoming.

Id. § 9–697. *Penalty.*—Failure of any person to register as required by this act [§§ 9–693 to 9–699], or the making of any registration which contains any false statement or any omission, shall constitute a felony, and upon conviction shall be punishable by a fine of not less than one thousand dollars ($1,000.00) or more than ten thousand dollars ($10,000.00), or by imprisonment of not less than two (2) or more than ten (10) years, or by both.

EXCLUSION FROM THE ELECTIVE PROCESS

Wyoming Stat. 1957, § 9–698. *Communists and nominees of the Communist Party barred from ballot.*—The name of any Communist or of any nominees of the Communist Party shall not be printed upon any ballot used in any primary or general election in this State or in any political subdivision thereof.

Id. § 22–118.79 (Supp. 1963). *Communist Party and affiliated groups ineligible to participate in any election.*—Every general election ballot shall contain the name of every candidate whose nomination for any office specified in the ballot has been certified to or has been properly filed in the office of the county clerk, according to law, and no other name. The name of a candidate shall be printed upon the ballot once and no more. All nominations made by any political party shall be placed in a separate column under the name of such party. If a nomination has been made by petition, and the persons nominated is running under the auspices of any group or organization, his name shall be placed in a separate column under the name of such group or organization. Only one word preceding the word "party" shall be used on a ballot to designate the name of any political party, group, or organization. To the right of the party columns shall be one or more columns for those nominated by petition, but who are not running under the auspices of any political group or organization, and any such column or columns shall be headed by the designation "Independent."

Notwithstanding any other provisions of this law, no party, group or organization shall be recognized or qualified to participate in or appear on the ballot in any primary or general election which is affiliated, by any means whatsoever, with the Communist Party of the United States, the Third Communist International, or any other foreign agency which carries on, advocates, teaches, justifies, aids, or abets the overthrow by any unlawful means of the Government of the United States or of this State, or which directly or indirectly carries on, advocates, teaches, justifies, aids, or abets a program of sabotage, force and violence, sedition or treason against the Government of the United States or of this State.

LOYALTY OF STATE OFFICERS AND EMPLOYEES

1. NONELECTIVE PERSONNEL

Wyoming Stat. 1957, § 9–699. *Communists ineligible for employment compensated by public funds.*—No Communist may hold any nonelective position, job or office for the State of Wyoming, or any political subdivision thereof; or be appointed to fill a vacancy in any elective office of the State of Wyoming, or any political subdivision thereof; where the remuneration of said position, job or office is paid in whole or in part by public moneys or funds of the State of Wyoming, or any political subdivision thereof.

2. CIVIL DEFENSE PERSONNEL

Wyoming Stat. 1957, § 19–113. *Loyalty oath required.*—No person shall be employed or associated in any capacity in any civil defense organization established under this act [§§ 19–99 to 19–115] who advocates or who has advocated a change by force or violence in the constitutional form of the Government of the United States or of this State or the overthrow of any government in the United States by force or violence, or who has been convicted of or is under indictment of information charging any subversive act against the United States. Each person who is appointed to serve in an organization for civil defense shall, before entering upon his duties, take an oath, in writing, before a person authorized to administer oaths in this State, which oath shall be substantially as follows:

"I _____ do solemnly swear (or affirm that I will support and defend the Constitution of the United States and the constitution of the State of Wyoming, against all enemies, foreign and domestic; that I will bear true faith and allegiance to the same; that I take this obligation freely, without any mental reservation or purpose of evasion; and that I will well and faithfully discharge the duties on which I am about to enter.

"And I do further swear (or affirm) that I do not advocate, nor am I a member or an affiliate of any organization, group, or combination of persons that advocates the overthrow of the Government of the United States or of this State by force or violence; and that during such time as I am a member of the (name of civil defense organization), I will not advocate nor become a member of any political party or organization that advocates the overthrow of the Government of the United States or of this State by force or violence."

TEACHERS' LOYALTY

Wyoming Stat. 1957, § 9–699. *Communists ineligible for employment compensated by State funds.*—No Communist may hold any nonelective position, job or office for the State of Wyoming, or any political subdivision thereof; or be appointed to fill a vacancy in any elective office of the State of Wyoming, or any political subdivision thereof;

where the remuneration of said position, job or office is paid in whole or in part by public moneys or funds of the State of Wyoming, or any political subdivision thereof.

EXCLUSION FROM THE BAR

Wyoming does not appear to have any rule or regulation which pertains to the admission of persons who are or who have been Communists or subversives. Similarly, the various forms employed by the State do not contain any questions directly on the subject.

APPENDIXES

Appendix A—Tables

Table 1.—*Unlawful advocacy: States which make it a crime to advocate the overthrow of the Government by force or violence or other unlawful means*

Alabama	Title 14, § 19, § 22(1).
Alaska	§ 11.50.010.
Arizona	§ 13–707 (Supp. 1963).
Arkansas	§ 41–4111.
California	Penal Code, § 14000
Colorado	§ 40–23.7.
Delaware	Title 11, § 862.
Florida	§§ 876.01, 876.23 (Supp. 1963).
Georgia	§ 26–903a (Supp. 1963).
Hawaii	§ 261–2.
Idaho	§ 18–2001.
Illinois	Ch. 38, § 30–3.
Indiana	§§ 10–1302, 10–5204.
Iowa	Title 54, §§ 689.8, 689.10.
Kansas	§§ 21–301, 21–306.
Kentucky	§ 432.030.
Louisiana	§§ 14:115, 14:364 (Supp. 1963).
Maine	C. 143, § 4.
Maryland	Art. 85A, § 2.
Massachusetts	C. 264, § 11.
Michigan	Constitution (1908), Art. II, § 22; §§ 28.813(1), 28:235, 28.243(2).
Minnesota	§ 609.405.
Mississippi	§ 4064–10; § 2399.
Montana	§ 94–4404.
Nebraska	§ 28–748 (Supp. 1963); § 28–816.
Nevada	§ 203.120; § 203.160.
New Hampshire	§ 587:32; § 588:2.
New Jersey	§2A:148–7; § 2A:148–13.
New York	Penal Law § 160.
North Carolina	§ 14–11.
Ohio	§ 2923.12; § 2921.22.
Oklahoma	Title 21, §§ 1261, 1266, 1266.4.
Pennsylvania	Title 18, § 4207.
Rhode Island	§§ 11–43–11, 11–43–12.
South Dakota	§ 13.0801.
Tennessee	§ 39–4405 (Supp. 1964).
Texas	Art. 6889–3A, § 5.
Utah	§ 76–57–1.
Vermont	Title 3, § 3405.
Virginia	§ 18.1–421 (Supp. 1962).
Washington	§ 9.05.010; § 9.81.020.
West Virginia	§ 5912.
Wisconsin	§ 946.03.
Wyoming	§ 6–111.

TABLE 2.—*Unlawful advocacy: States which make it a crime to be a member of an organization advocating the overthrow of the Government by force or violence or other unlawful means*

Alabama_____ Title 14, § 20.
Alaska_____ § 11.50.020.
Arizona_____ § 13–707 (Supp. 1963).
Arkansas_____ § 41–4111.
California_____ Penal Code, § 11401.
Delaware_____ Title 11, § 862.
Florida_____ §§ 876.02, 876.24 (Supp. 1963).
Georgia_____ § 26–904a.
Hawaii_____ § 261–3.
Idaho_____ § 18–2002.
Iowa_____ Title 54, §§ 689.9, 689.11.
Kansas_____ §§ 21–303, 21–306.
Kentucky_____ § 432.040.
Louisiana_____ §§ 14 :115, 14 :364 (Supp. 1963).
Maryland_____ Art. 85A, § 3.
Massachusetts_____ C. 264, § 19.
Michigan_____ §§ 28.813(3), 28.236, 28.243(2).
Minnesota_____ § 609.405.
Montana_____ § 94–4406.
Nebraska_____ § 28–748 (Supp. 1963) ; § 28–816.
Nevada_____ § 203.130 ; § 203.170.
New Hampshire_____ § 588 :3.
New Jersey_____ § 2A :148–8 ; § 2A :148–14.
New York_____ Penal Law § 160.
Ohio_____ § 2923.13 (Supp. 1963) ; § 2921.23.
Oklahoma_____ Title 21, §§ 1263, 1267.1 (Supp. 1963).
Pennsylvania_____ Title 18, § 4207.
Rhode Island_____ § 11–43–12.
South Dakota_____ § 13.0801.
Tennessee_____ § 39–4405 (Supp. 1964) ; §§ 39–4420 (Supp. 1964), 39–4422 (Supp. 1964).
Texas_____ Art. 6889–3A, § 5.
Utah_____ § 76–57–3.
Virginia_____ § 18.1–421 (Supp. 1962).
Washington_____ § 9.05.020 ; § 9.81.030.

TABLE 3.—*Unlawful advocacy: States which outlaw organizations advocating the overthrow of the Government by force or violence or other unlawful means*

Alabama_____ Title 14, § 22(2).
Arkansas_____ §§ 41–4128, 41–4130 (Supp. 1963).
Colorado_____ § 40–23–9.
Florida_____ § 876.26 (Supp. 1963).
Georgia_____ § 26–906a.
Maryland_____ Art. 85A, § 5.
Massachusetts_____ C. 264, § 17.
New Hampshire_____ § 588 :5.
Ohio_____ § 2921.24.
Oklahoma_____ Title 21, § 1266.2.
Pennsylvania_____ Title 18, § 3811.
Tennessee_____ §§ 39–4420 (Supp. 1964), 39–4421 (Supp. 1964).
Texas_____ Art. 6889–3A, § 2.
Washington_____ § 9.81.050.

TABLE 4.—*Registration: States which require registration of Communists, Communist Party, members and officers of the Communist Party, Communist front organizations, etc.*

Alabama	Title 14, § 97(4a) (Supp. 1963). Communists, members and officers of Communist Party, and Communist front organizations.
Arkansas	§ 41–4125 (Supp. 1963). Members of Communist Party, subsidiary, branch, affiliate, or subdivision of the party.
Delaware	Title 20, § 3501 (Supp. 1962). Communists, members of Communist front organizations, and officers of Communist Party.
Louisiana	§ 14:360 (Supp. 1963). Communists and members of Communist front organizations.
Michigan	§ 28.243(15). Communists, members of Communist front organizations, Communist Party, and Communist front organizations.
Mississippi	§ 4194–02 (Supp. 1962). Officer, director, or member.
New Mexico	§ 4–15–2. Communist organizations, affiliates, supporters, and advocates of doctrine and related organizations.
Texas	Art. 6889–3, § 4. Communists, members of Communist front organizations, and officers of Communist Party and Communist front organizations.
Wyoming	§ 9–696. Communists and officers of Communist Party.

TABLE 5.—*Registration: States which require registration of organizations advocating overthrow of the Government by force or violence or other unlawful means*

Arkansas	§ 41–4125 (Supp. 1963).
California	Corp. Code §§ 3500–35302.
Michigan	§ 18.58(3).
Montana	§ 94–4412 (Supp. 1963).
New Mexico	§ 4–15–2.
Oklahoma	Title 21, § 1267.2 (Supp. 1963).
South Carolina	§ 16–585.

TABLE 6.—*Outlawing the Communist Party (by name)*

Arizona	§ 16–206 (Supp. 1963).
Arkansas	§ 41–4130 (Supp. 1963).
Indiana	§§ 10–5201—10–5205.
Massachusetts	C. 264 § 16A, 17.
Nebraska	§ 28–747 (Supp. 1963).
Oklahoma	Title 21, § 1266.2.
Pennsylvania	Title 18, § 3811.
Tennessee	§ 39–4422 (Supp. 1964).
Texas	Art. 6889–3A, § 2.
Washington	§§9.81.050, 9.81.083.

TABLE 7.—*States which make it a crime to be a member of the Communist Party (by name)*

Arkansas	§ 13–707 (Supp. 1963).
Indiana	§ 10–5204.
Massachusetts	C. 264, §§ 16A, 17, 19.
Nebraska	§ 28–748 (Supp. 1963).
Oklahoma	Title 21, § 1266.4.
Pennsylvania	Title 18, § 3811.
Tennessee	§ 39–4422 (Supp. 1964).
Texas	Art. 6889–3A, § 5.
Virginia	§§ 9.81.082, 9.81.083.

Table 8.—*Exclusion from the elective process: States which bar the Communist Party (nominees or candidates) from the ballot*

Alabama_____ Title 14, § 97 (6).
Arizona_____ § 16–206 (Supp. 1963). Not entitled to recognition or certification as political party.
Arkansas_____ § 3–1604.
Illinois_____ Ch. 46 §§ 7–2, 8–2, 10–2 (Supp. 1963).
Indiana_____ §§ 10–5201—10–5205. Outlaws Communist Party.
Kansas_____ § 25–116.
Louisiana_____ § 14 :361 (Supp. 1963).
Massachusetts_____ C. 50 § 1; C. 264 §§ 16A, 17.
Michigan_____ § 28.243 (17).
Nebraska_____ § 28–747 (Supp. 1936). Not entitled to recognition or certification as political party.
Oklahoma_____ Title 26, § 6.1.
Pennsylvania_____ Title 18, § 3811. Outlaws Communist Party.
Tennessee_____ § 39–4422 (Supp. 1964). Outlaws Communist Party.
Texas_____ Art. 6889–3 § 6.
Washington_____ §§ 9.81.050, 99.81.083. Outlaws the Communist Party.
Wisconsin_____ § 6.85.
Wyoming_____ § 9–698; § 22–118.79 (Supp. 1963).

Table 9.—*Exclusion from the elective process: States which bar organizations or persons advocating the overthrow of the Government by force or violence or other unlawful means from the ballot*

Alabama_____ Title 14, § 22(2). Denied all rights as political party.
Arkansas_____ § 13–1604.
California_____ Elec. Code, § 6431.
Delaware_____ Title 15, § 4104.
Illinois_____ Ch. 46, § 7–2.
Indiana_____ § 29–3812.
Kansas_____ § 25–116.
Maryland_____ Art. 85A, § 15.
Massachusetts_____ C. 50, § 1; C. 264, §§ 16A, 17.
Mississippi_____ § 4064.07.
Missouri_____ § 120.140.
Ohio_____ § 3517.07.
Oklahoma_____ Title 26, § 6.1.
Oregon_____ § 236.030.
Pennsylvania_____ Title 25, § 2831(d).
Tennessee_____ § 2–1203.
Texas_____ Elec. Code., Art. 1.05, § 5 (Supp. 1963).
Wisconsin_____ § 6.85.
Wyoming_____ § 22–118.79 (Supp. 1963).

Table 10.—*Exclusion from the elective process: Persons convicted of advocating the overthrow of the Government by force or violence or other unlawful means or of membership in organizations having that purpose ineligible to be candidates*

Florida___ _____ §§ 876.25 (Supp. 1963), 876.30 (Supp. 1963).
Georgia_____ § 26–905a.
Indiana_____ § 10–5205.
Louisiana_____ § 14 : 366 (Supp. 1963).
Maryland_____ Art. 85A, § 4.
Massachusetts_____ C. 264, § 20.
New Hampshire_____ § 588 :4.
Oklahoma_____ Title 26, § 162b.
Washington_____ § 9.81.040.

TABLE 11.—*Exclusion from the elective process: Oath to refrain from membership in the Communist Party or organizations which advocate the overthrow of the Government by force or violence or other unlawful means*

Florida_____ §§ 99.021(1)(i), 876.05. Candidates.
Georgia_____ § 34–1904(d) (Supp. 1963). Candidates for presidential electors.
Hawaii_____ § 11–96.5 (Supp. 1963). Candidates.
Illinois_____ Ch. 46 § 7–10.1 (Supp. 1963).
Kansas_____ § 25–117. Candidates.
Louisiana_____ §14:373 (Supp. 1963). Candidates.
Maryland_____ Art. 85A, § 15. Candidates.
Mississippi_____ § 4064–07. Candidates.
New Hampshire_____ § 588 :14.
New Jersey_____ § 41 :1–1 (Supp. 1963). Candidates. § 19 :23–7 (Supp. 1963) et seq.
Pennsylvania_____ Title 65, § 224 (Supp. 1963). Candidates.
Texas_____ Elec. Code, Art. 6.02 (Supp. 1963). Candidates.
Washington_____ § 9.81.100. Candidates.

TABLE 12.—*Loyalty of State officers and employees: Elective personnel— Communists (by name) ineligible for public office*

Arizona_____ §§ 13–707, 13–707.01 (Supp. 1963). Upon conviction.
Indiana_____ § 10–5207.
Massachusetts_____ C. 264, § 20. Upon conviction.
Nebraska_____ § 228–749 (Supp. 1963). Upon conviction.
Oklahoma_____ Title 21, §§ 1266.4, 1266.6. Upon conviction.
Texas_____ Art. 6889–3A, §§ 5, 7. Upon conviction.

TABLE 13.—*Loyalty of State officers and employees: Nonelective personnel— Communists (by name) ineligible for public office or employment*

Alabama_____ Title 14, § 97(7). Communists and members of Communist front organization.
Arizona_____ §§ 13–707, 13–707.01 (Supp. 1963). Upon conviction.
Arkansas_____ § 41–4113(c).
California_____ Government Code 1028.
Indiana_____ § 10–5207.
Louisiana_____ § 14 :362 (Supp. 1963).
Massachusetts_____ C. 264, § 20. Upon conviction.
Michigan_____ § 28.243(18).
Nebraska_____ § 28–749 (Supp. 1963). Upon conviction.
Oklahoma_____ Title 21, §§ 1266.4, 1266.6. Upon conviction.
Texas_____ Art. 6889–3A, §§ 5, 7. Upon conviction; Art. 6889–3, § 7.
Wyoming_____ § 9–699.

TABLE 14.—*Loyalty of State officers and employees: Elective personnel—Persons advocating overthrow of the Government by force or violence or other unlawful means or members of organization having that purpose ineligible for public office*

Alaska_____ Constitution, Art. XII, § 4.
Arizona_____ §§ 13–707, 13–707.01 (Supp. 1963). Upon conviction.
California_____ Constitution, Art. 20, § 19.
Florida_____ §§ 876.25 (Supp. 1963), 876.29 (Supp. 1963). Upon conviction.
Hawaii_____ Constitution, Art. XIV, § 3 (Supp. 1963).
Indiana_____ § 10–5207.
Maryland_____ Constitution, Art. 15, § 11; Code, Art. 85A, § 4. Upon conviction.
Massachusetts_____ C. 264, § 20. Upon conviction.
Nebraska_____ § 28–749 (Supp. 1963). Upon conviction.
New Hampshire_____ § 588 :4. Upon conviction.
Oklahoma_____ Title 21, §§ 1266.4, 1266.6. Upon conviction.
Oregon_____ § 236.030.
Texas_____ Art. 6889–3A, §§ 5, 7. Upon conviction.
Washington_____ § 9.81.040. Upon conviction.

TABLE 15.—*Loyalty of State officers and employees: Nonelective personnel—Persons advocating the overthrow of the Government by force or violence or other unlawful means or members of organizations having that purpose ineligible for public office*

Alabama	Title 14, §§ 97(1), 97(7).
Alaska	Constitution, Art. XII, § 4.
Arizona	§§ 13–707, 13–707.01 (Supp. 1963). Upon conviction.
Arkansas	§§ 41–4111, 41–4112; §§ 3–1404, 3–1405. Upon conviction.
California	Constitution, Art. 20, § 19; Government Code, § 1028.
Florida	§§ 876.25 (Supp. 1963), 876.29 (Supp. 1963). Upon conviction.
Georgia	§ 26–911a (Supp. 1963).
Hawaii	Constitution, Art. XIV, § 3 (Supp. 1963).
Illinois	Ch. 127, § 166a (Supp. 1963). Payment of compensation to, prohibited.
Indiana	§ 10–5207.
Louisiana	§ 14:369 (Supp. 1963).
Maryland	Constitution, Art. 15, § 11; Code, Art. 85A, § 10.
Massachusetts	C. 264 § 20. Upon conviction.
Michigan	§§ 28.243(12), 28.243(18).
Mississippi	§ 4064–02.
Nebraska	§ 28–749 (Supp. 1963). Upon conviction
New Hampshire	§ 588:9.
New Mexico	§ 5–1–12.
New York	Civil service law, § 105.
Oklahoma	Title 21 §§ 1266.4, 1266.6. Upon conviction.
Oregon	§ 236.030; § 182.030.
Pennsylvania	Title 65, § 213.
Texas	Art. 6889–3A §§ 5, 7. Upon conviction.
Utah	§ 27–11–11. Applicants for civil service examination.
Washington	§ 9.81.060, §§ 9.81.040, 9.05.020. Upon conviction.

TABLE 16.—*Loyalty of State officers and employees: Nonelective personnel—Required to testify before authorized investigating committee*

California	Government Code, § 1028.1 (Supp. 1963).
Hawaii	§ 5–4.
Louisiana	§ 42:37 (Supp. 1963).
Michigan	§ 28.243(18).
Ohio	§ 143.271.

TABLE 17.—*Loyalty of public officers and employees: Elective personnel—Oath to support and defend the Constitution*

Alabama	Constitution, Art. XV, § 279. Support only.
Alaska	Constitution, Art. XII, § 5.
Arizona	§ 38–231 (Supp. 1963).
Arkansas	Constitution, Art. XIX, § 20. Support only.
California	Constitution, Art. 20, § 3.
Colorado	Constitution, Art. XII, § 8. Support only.
Connecticut	Constitution, Art. X, § 1. Support only.
Delaware	Constitution, Art. XIV. Support only.
Florida	§ 876.05 (Supp. 1963). Support only.
Georgia	§ 89–313. Support only.
Hawaii	§ 5–120.
Idaho	Laws, 1963, ch. 210, pp. 599–600.
Illinois	Constitution, Art. V. § 25.
Indiana	Constitution, Art. 15, § 4. Support only.
Iowa	Constitution, Art. XI, § 5. Support only.
Kentucky	Constitution, § 228. Support only.
Louisiana	Constitution, Art. XIX § 1. Support only.
Maine	Constitution, Art. IX, § 1. Support only.
Michigan	Constitution, Art XI, § 1. Support only.
Missouri	Constitution, Art. VII, § 11. Support only.
Montana	Constitution, Art. XIX, § 1.
Nebraska	Constitution, Art. XV, § 1. Support only.
Nevada	Constitution, Art 15, § 2; § 282.020.

TABLE 17.—*Loyalty of public officers and employees: Elective personnel—Oaths to support and defend the Constitution—Continued*

New Jersey	§ 41 :1–1 (Supp. 1963). Support only.
New York	Constitution, Art. XIII, § 1. Support only.
North Carolina	Constitution, Art. VI, § 7. Support only.
Ohio	Constitution, Art. XV, § 7. Support only.
Oklahoma	Title 51, § 36.2.
Oregon	Constitution, Art. XV, § 3. Support only.
Pennsylvania	Constitution, Art. VII, § 1.
Rhode Island	Constitution, Art. IX, § 3. Support only.
South Carolina	Constitution, Art. III, § 26.
South Dakota	Constitution, Art. III, § 8. Support only. Art. XXI, § 3. Support only.
Tennessee	Constitution, Art. X, § 1. Support only.
Texas	Constitution, Art. XVI, § 1.
Utah	Constitution, Art. 4, § 10.
Virginia	Art. II, § 34. Support only.
West Virginia	Constitution, Art. IV, § 5. Support only.
Wisconsin	Constitution, Art. V, § 78. Support only.

TABLE 18.—*Loyalty of public officers and employees: Nonelective personnel— Oath to support and defend the Constitution*

Alabama	Constitution, Art. XV, § 279. Support only.
Alaska	Constitution, Art. XII, § 5; § 39.05.130.
Arizona	§ 38–231 (Supp. 1963).
Arkansas	Constitution, Art. XIX, § 20.
California	Constitution, Art. 20, § 3.
Colorado	Constitution, Art. XII, § 8. Support only.
Connecticut	Constitution, Art. X, § 1. Support only.
Delaware	Title 29, § 5102; Constitution, Art. XIV. Support only.
Florida	§ 876.05 (Supp. 1963). Support only.
Georgia	§ 89–313. Support only.
Hawaii	§ 5–120.
Idaho	Laws, 1963, ch. 210, pp. 599–600.
Illinois	Constitution, Art. V, § 25.
Indiana	Constitution, Art. 15, § 4. Support only.
Iowa	Constitution, Art. XI, § 5. Support only.
Kentucky	Constitution, § 228. Support only.
Louisiana	§ 42 :52 (Supp. 1963). Support only. Constitution, Art. XIX, § 1. Support only.
Maine	Constitution, Art. IX, § 1.
Massachusetts	C. 264, § 14.
Michigan	Constitution, Art. XI, § 1. Support only.
Minnesota	§ 43.16 (Supp. 1962). Abide, uphold, defend; applies to applicants for competitive examinations.
Missouri	Constitution, Art. VII, § 11. Support only.
Montana	Constitution, Art. XIX, § 1.
Nebraska	§ 11–101. Support only; § 11–101.01; Constitution, Art. XV, § 1. Support only.
Nevada	Constitution, Art. 15, 82; § 282.020.
New Jersey	§ 41 :1–1 (Supp. 1963). Support only.
New York	Constitution, Art. XIII, § 1.
North Carolina	Constitution, Art. VI, § 7. Support only.
Ohio	Constitution, Art. XV, § 7. Support only.
Oklahoma	Title 51, § 2.
Oregon	Constitution, Art. XV, § 3. Support only.
Pennsylvania	Title 65, § 214; Constitution, Art. VII, § 1.
Rhode Island	Constitution, Art. IX, § 3. Support only.
South Carolina	Constitution, Art. III, § 26.
South Dakota	Constitution, Art. XXI, § 3. Support only. § 17.0315 (Supp. 1960) ; § 17.0315 (Supp. 1960).
Tennessee	Constitution, Art. X, § 1.
Texas	Constitution, Art. XVI, § 1.
Utah	Constitution, Art. 4, § 10.
Virginia	Constitution, Art. II, § 34. Support only.
West Virginia	Constitution, Art. IV, § 5. Support only.
Wisconsin	Constitution, Art. V, § 28. Support only.

TABLE 19.—*Loyalty of State officers and employees: Elective personnel—Oath to faithfully perform all duties*

Alabama	Constitution, Art. XV, § 279.
Alaska	Constitution, Art. XII, § 5.
Arizona	§ 38–231 (Supp. 1963).
Arkansas	Constitution, Art. XIX, § 20.
California	Constitution, Art. 20, § 3.
Colorado	Constitution, Art. XII, § 8.
Connecticut	Constitution, Art. X, § 1.
Delaware	Constitution, Art. XIV.
Idaho	Laws, 1963, ch. 210, pp. 599–600.
Illinois	Constitution, Art. V, § 25.
Kentucky	Constitution, § 228.
Louisiana	Constitution, Art. XIX, § 1.
Maine	Constitution, Art. IX, § 1.
Michigan	Constitution, Art. XI, § 1.
Missouri	Constitution, Art. VII, § 11.
Montana	Constitution, Art. XIX, § 1.
Nebraska	Constitution, Art. XV, § 1.
Nevada	Constitution, Art. 15, § 2 ; § 282.020.
New Hampshire	Constitution, Pt. II, Art. 84.
New Jersey	§ 41 :1–3 (Supp. 1963).
New York	Constitution, Art. XIII, § 1.
North Carolina	Constitution, Art. VI, § 7.
Oklahoma	Title 51, § 36.2.
Pennsylvania	Constitution, Art. VII, § 1.
Rhode Island	Constitution, Art. IX, § 23.
South Carolina	Constitution, Art. III, § 26.
South Dakota	Constitution, Art. III, § 8.
Texas	Constitution, Art. XVI, § 1.
Utah	Constitution, Art. 4, § 10.
Vermont	Constitution, Ch. 2, § 52.
Virginia	Constitution, Art. II, § 34.
West Virginia	Constitution, Art. IV, § 5.
Wisconsin	Constitution, Art. V, § 28.

TABLE 20.—*Loyalty of State officers and employees: Nonelective personnel—Oath to faithfully perform all duties*

Alabama	Constitution, Art. XV, § 279.
Alaska	Constitution, Art. XII, § 5 ; § 39.05.130.
Arizona	§ 38–231 (Supp. 1963).
Arkansas	Constitution, Art. XIX, § 20.
California	Constitution, Art. 20, § 3.
Colorado	Constitution, Art. XII, § 8.
Connecticut	Constitution, Art. X, §1.
Delaware	Constitution, Art. XIV.
Idaho	Laws, 1963, ch. 210, pp. 599–600.
Illinois	Constitution, Art. V, § 25.
Kentucky	Constitution, § 228.
Louisiana	§ 42 :52 (Supp. 1963) ; Constitution, Art. XIX, § 1.
Maine	Constitution, Art. IX, § 1.
Michigan	Constitution, Art. XI, §1.
Missouri	Constitution, Art. VII, § 11.
Montana	Constitution, Art. XIX, § 1.
Nebraska	§§ 11–101, 11–101.01 ; Constitution, Art. XV, § 1.
Nevada	Constitution, Art. 15, § 2 ; § 282.020.
New Hampshire	Constitution, Pt. II, Art. 84.
New Jersey	§ 41 :1–1 (1963).
New York	Constitution, Art. XIII, § 1.
North Carolina	Constitution, Art. VI, § 7.
Oklahoma	Title 51, § 36.2.
Pennsylvania	Title 65, § 214 ; Constitution, Art. VII, § 1.
Rhode Island	Constitution, Art. IX, § 3.
South Carolina	Constitution, Art. III, § 26.
South Dakota	§ 17.0315 (Supp. 1960).

TABLE 20.—*Loyalty of State officers and employees: Nonelection personnel—Oath to faithfully perform all duties*—Continued

Texas	Constitution, Art. XVI, §1.
Utah	Constitution, Art. 4, § 10.
Vermont	Constitution, ch. 2, § 52.
Virginia	Constitution, Art. II, § 34.
West Virginia	Constitution, Art. IV, § 5.
Wisconsin	Constitution, Art. V, § 28.

TABLE 21.—*Loyalty of State officers and employees: Elective personnel—Oath to refrain from advocating the overthrow of the Government by force or violence or other unlawful means*

California	Constitution, Art 20, § 3.
Hawaii	§ 5–120.
Idaho	Laws 1963, ch. 210, pp. 599–600.
Kansas	§ 21–305.
New Jersey	§ 41 :1–1 (Supp. 1963) ; § 41 :1–3 (Supp. 1963). Support only.
Oklahoma	Title 51, § 36.2.

TABLE 22.—*Loyalty of State officers and employees: Nonelective personnel— Oath to refrain from advocating the overthrow of the Government by force or violence or other unlawful means*

California	Constitution, Art. 20, § 3.
Hawaii	§ 5–120.
Idaho	Laws 1963, ch. 210, pp. 599–600.
Kansas	§ 21–305.
Massachusetts	§ C.264, § 14. Oath to oppose overthrow.
Mississippi	§ 4064–05.
Nebraska	§§ 11–101, 11–101.01.
New Hampshire	§ 588 :12.
New Jersey	§ 41 :1–1 (Supp. 1963) ; § 41 :1–3 (Supp. 1963). Support only.
Oklahoma	Title 51, § 36.2.
Pennsylvania	Title 65, § 214.
South Dakota	§ 17.0315 (Supp. 1960).

TABLE 23.—*Loyalty of State officers and employees: Elective personnel—Oath to refrain from membership in the Communist Party or other organizations advocating the overthrow of the Government by force or violence or other unlawful means*

California	Constitution, Art. 20, § 3.
Florida	§ 876.05 (Supp. 1963).
Georgia	§ 89–313.
Hawaii	§ 5–120.
Idaho	Laws 1963, ch. 210, pp. 599–600.
Illinois	ch. 127, § 166b (Supp. 1963).
Kansas	§ 21–305.
New Jersey	§ 41 :1–1 (Supp. 1963) ; § 41 :1–3 (Supp. 1963).
Oklahoma	Title 51, § 36.2.

TABLE 24.—*Loyalty of State officers and employees: Nonelective personnel—Oath to refrain from membership in the Communist Party or other organization advocating the overthrow of the Government by force or violence or other unlawful means*

California_____ Constitution, Art. 20, § 3.
Florida_____ § 876.05 (Supp. 1963).
Georgia_____ § 89–313.
Hawaii_____ § 5–120.
Idaho_____ Laws 1963, ch. 210, pp. 599–600.
Illinois_____ Ch. 127, § 166b (Supp. 1963).
Kansas_____ § 21–305.
Nebraska_____ §§ 11–101, 11–101.01.
New Jersey_____ § 41 :1–1 (Supp. 1963) ; § 41 :1–3 (Supp. 1963).
Oklahoma_____ Title 51, § 36.2.
Pennsylvania_____ Title 65, § 214.
South Dakota_____ § 17.0315 (Supp. 1960).

TABLE 25.—*Loyalty of State officers and employees: Civil defense personnel—Loyalty oath required*

Alabama_____ Title 37A, § 19(85).
Alaska_____ § 26.20.160.
Arizona_____ § 26–356.
Arkansas_____ § 11–1931.
California_____ Government Code, §§ 3102, 3103.
Colorado_____ § 24–1–15.
Connecticut_____ § 28–12.
Delaware_____ Title 20, § 3118.
Florida_____ § 252.21.
Georgia_____ § 86–1819.
Hawaii_____ § 359–20.
Idaho_____ § 46–1006 (Supp. 1961).
Illinois_____ Ch. 121, § 286.
Indiana_____ § 45–1534.
Iowa_____ Title 3, § 28A.12 (Supp. 1963).
Kentucky_____ § 39.432.
Louisiana_____ § 29–612.
Maine_____ C. 12, § 15.
Massachusetts_____ C. 33, App., § 13–18.
Michigan_____ § 4.823 (54).
Minnesota_____ § 12.43 (Supp. 1962).
Mississippi_____ § 8610–18 (Supp. 1962).
Montana_____ § 77–1313.
Nebraska_____ § 81–829.28.
Nevada_____ § 414.150.
New Hampshire_____ § 107 :17.
New York_____ Unconsol. Laws, § 9138.
North Carolina_____ § 166–12.
Ohio_____ § 5915.14 (Supp. 1963).
Oklahoma_____ Title 63, § 679.
Oregon_____ § 401 :160 (Supp. 1963–1964).
Pennsylvania_____ Title 71, § 1689.12.
South Dakota_____ § 41.01C13 (Supp. 1960).
Tennessee_____ § 7–627.
Utah_____ § 63–5–15.
Vermont_____ Title 20, § 18.
Virginia_____ § 44–145.5.
Washington_____ § 38.52.130.
West Virginia_____ § 1264(38).
Wyoming_____ § 19–113.

TABLE 26.—*Loyalty of State officers and employees: Civil defense personnel—Bars employment of persons advocating overthrow of the Government by force or violence or other unlawful means*

Alabama	Title 37A, § 19(85).
Alaska	§ 26.20.160.
Arizona	§ 26–356.
Arkansas	§ 11–1931.
Colorado	§ 24–1–15.
Connecticut	§ 28–12.
Delaware	Title 20, § 3118.
Florida	§ 252.21.
Georgia	§ 86–1819.
Idaho	§ 46–1006 (Supp. 1961).
Indiana	§ 45–1534.
Iowa	§ 28A.12 (Supp. 1963).
Kansas	§ 48–917 (Supp. 1963).
Kentucky	§ 39.432
Maine	C. 12, § 15.
Massachusetts	C. 33 App., § 13–18.
Michigan	§ 4.823 (54).
Minnesota	§ 12.43 (Supp. 1962).
Mississippi	§ 8610–18 (Supp. 1962).
Montana	§ 77–1313.
Nebraska	§ 81–829.28.
Nevada	§ 414.150.
New Hampshire	§ 107 :17.
North Carolina	§ 166–2.
North Dakota	§ 37–17–15 (Supp. 1963).
Ohio	§ 5915.14 (Supp. 1963).
Oklahoma	Title 63, § 679.
Oregon	§ 401.160 (Supp. 1963).
Pennsylvania	Title 71, § 1689.12.
South Dakota	§ 41.01C13 (Supp. 1960).
Utah	§ 63–5–15.
Vermont	Title 20, § 18.
Virginia	§ 44–145.5
Washington	§ 38.52.130.
West Virginia	§ 1264(38).
Wisconsin	§ 22.01(11) (c), Supp. 1964.
Wyoming	§ 19–113.

TABLE 27.—*Teachers' loyalty: Members of the Communist Party or other organization advocating the overthrow of the Government by force or violence or other unlawful means ineligible for employment*

Alabama	Title 14, § 97(7).
Arkansas	§ 3–1404.
California	Educ. Code, § 12952.
Florida	§ 876.29 (Supp. 1963).
Illinois	Ch. 127, § 166a (Supp. 1963). Payment of compensation to barred.
Indiana	§ 10–5207.
Louisiana	§§ 14 :362 (Supp. 1963), 14 :369 (Supp. 1964).
Maryland	Art. 85A, § 10.
Massachusetts	C. 264, § 20.
Michigan	§ 28.243(18).
New Hampshire	§ 588 :9.
New York	Civil Service Law, § 105.
Tennessee	§ 49–1303.
Washington	§§ 9.81.060, 9.81.083.
Wyoming	§ 9–699.

TABLE 28.—*Teachers' loyalty: Required to testify before authorized investigating committee*

California_____ Educ. Code, §§ 12955, 12956.
Hawaii_____ § 5–4.
Louisiana_____ § 42 :37 (Supp. 1963).
Michigan_____ § 28.243(18).
Ohio_____ § 143.271.

TABLE 29.—*Teachers' loyalty: Required to refrain from teaching or advocating communism or the overthrow of the Government by force or violence or other unlawful means*

California_____ Educ. Code, § 8455.
Louisiana_____ § 42 : 54.
New Hampshire_____ § 191.1.
Vermont_____ Title 16, § 4.

TABLE 30.—*Teachers' loyalty: Oath to refrain from teaching theories inconsistent with American principles*

Georgia_____ § 32–1022.
Oklahoma_____ Title 51, § 36.2.

TABLE 31.—*Teachers' loyalty: Oath to support and defend the Constitution*

Arizona_____ § 38–231 (Supp. 1963).
California_____ Educ. Code, § 1312. Support only.
Colorado_____ § 123–17–14 (Supp. 1961). Support only.
Delaware_____ Title 29, § 5102.
Florida_____ § 876.05 (Supp. 1963). Support only. § 231.18. Subscribe and uphold.
Georgia_____ § 89–313. Support only. § 32–1022. Support and defend.
Hawaii_____ § 5–120.
Idaho_____ Laws, 1963, ch. 210, pp. 599–600.
Indiana_____ § 28–5112. Support only.
Louisiana_____ § 42–52 (Supp. 1963). Support only.
Massachusetts_____ C. 71, § 30a. Support only ; C. 264, § 14.
Michigan_____ § 15.3851. Support only.
Montana_____ § 75–4706. Support only.
Nebraska_____ § 11–101.01.
Nevada_____ Constitution, Art. 15, § 2 ; § 282.020.
New Hampshire_____ § 191 :2.
New Jersey_____ § 41 :1–3 (Supp. 1963). Support only.
New York_____ Educ. Law, § 3002. Support only.
North Dakota_____ § 15–37–01. Support only.
Oklahoma_____ Title 51, § 36.2.
Oregon_____ § 342.615. Support only.
Pennsylvania_____ Title 65, § 214.
South Dakota_____ § 17.0315 (Supp. 1960).
Tennessee_____ § 49–1304. Support only.
Texas_____ Constitution, Art. XVI, § 1.
Vermont_____ Title 16, § 4. Support only.
Washington_____ § 28.70.150. Support only.
West Virginia_____ § 1807. Support only.

TABLE 32.—*Teachers' loyalty: Oath to faithfully perform all duties*

Arizona_____ § 38–231 (Supp. 1963).
Idaho_____ Laws, 1963, ch. 210, pp. 599–600.
Louisiana_____ § 42–52 (Supp. 1963). Support only.
Massachusetts_____ C. 71, § 30A.
Michigan_____ § 15.3851.
Nebraska_____ § 11–101.01.
Nevada_____ Constitution, Art. 15, § 2 ; § 282.020.
New Hampshire_____ § 191 :2.

New Jersey_____ § 41:1–3 (Supp. 1963).
New York_____ Educ. Law, § 3002.
North Dakota_____ § 15–37–01.
Oklahoma_____ Title 51, § 36.2.
Pennsylvania_____ Title 65, § 214.
South Dakota_____ § 17.0315 (Supp. 1960).
Texas_____ Constitution, Art. XVI, § 1.
West Virginia_____ § 1807.

TABLE 33.—*Teachers' loyalty: Oath to promote patriotism or allegiance*

California_____ Educ. Code, § 13121.
Colorado_____ § 123–17–14 (Supp. 1961).
Indiana_____ § 28–5112.
Montana_____ § 75–4706.
Nebraska_____ § 79–4, 148.
Oregon_____ § 342.615.
Washington_____ § 28.70.150.

TABLE 34.—*Teachers' loyalty: Oath to refrain from membership in the Communist Party or other organizations advocating the overthrow of the Government
by force or violence or other unlawful means*

California_____ Educ. Code, § 12951.
Florida_____ § 876.05 (Supp. 1963).
Georgia_____ § 89–313.
Hawaii_____ § 5–120.
Idaho_____ Laws 1963, ch. 210, pp. 599–600.
Illinois_____ Ch. 127, § 166b (Supp. 1963). Affidavit.
Kansas_____ § 21–305.
Mississippi_____ § 4064–05.
Nebraska_____ § 11–101.01.
New Hampshire_____ § 191:2.
New Jersey_____ § 41:1–3 (Supp. 1963).
Oklahoma_____ Title 51, § 36.2.
Pennsylvania_____ Title 65, § 214.
South Dakota_____ § 17.0315 (Supp. 1960).

TABLE 35.—*Teachers' loyalty: Oath to refrain from advocating the overthrow
of the Government by force or violence or other unlawful means*

Idaho_____ Laws 1963, ch. 210, pp. 599–600.
Kansas_____ § 21–305.
Maryland_____ Art. 85A, § 13. Statement.
Massachusetts_____ Section C. 264, § 14. Oath to oppose overthrowing.
Mississippi_____ § 4064–05.
Nebraska_____ § 11–101.01.
New Hampshire_____ § 191:2.
New Jersey_____ § 41:1–3 (Supp. 1963).
Oklahoma_____ Title 51, § 36.2.
Pennsylvania_____ Title 65, § 214.
South Dakota_____ § 17.0315 (Supp. 1960).
Texas_____ Art. 2908b, § 1.

TABLE 36.—*Exclusion from the bar: States which prohibit by statute the admission to the practice of law of persons advocating the overthrow of the Government by force or violence or other unlawful means or membership in organizations having that purpose*

California_____ Bus. and Prof. Code, § 6064.1.
Maryland_____ Art. 10, §§ 3(c), 7.
New York_____ Civ. Pract. Law and Rules, § 9406. Must prove loyalty
to United States.

ANARCHY

GITLOW v. PEOPLE OF NEW YORK.

ERROR TO THE SUPREME COURT OF THE STATE OF NEW YORK.

No. 19. Argued April 12, 1923; reargued November 23, 1923.—Decided June 8,
1925.

1. *Assumed*, for the purposes of the case, that freedom of speech and of the press
   are among the personal rights and liberties protected by the due process
   clause of the Fourteenth Amendment from impairment by the States. P. 666.
2. Freedom of speech and of the press, as secured by the Constitution, is not an
   absolute right to speak or publish without responsibility whatever one may
   choose or an immunity for every possible use of language. P. 666.
3. That a State, in the exercise of its police power, may punish those who abuse
   this freedom by utterances inimical to the public welfare, tending to corrupt
   public morals, incite to crime or disturb the public peace, is not open to
   question. P. 667.
4. For yet more imperative reasons, a State may punish utterances endangering
   the foundations of organized government and threatening its overthrow by
   unlawful means. P. 667.
5. A statute punishing utterances advocating the overthrow of organized government by force, violence and unlawful means, imports a legislative determination that such utterances are so inimical to the general welfare and involve
   such danger of substantive evil that they may be penalized under the police
   power; and this determination must be given great weight, and every presumption be indulged in favor of the validity of the statute. P. 668.
6. Such utterances present sufficient danger to the public peace and security of
   the State to bring their punishment clearly within the range of legislative
   discretion, even if the effect of a given utterance cannot accurately be
   foreseen. P. 669.
7. A State can not reasonably be required to defer taking measures against these
   revolutionary utterances until they lead to actual disturbances of the peace
   or imminent danger of the State's destruction. P. 669.
8. The New York statute punishing those who advocate, advise or teach the duty,
   necessity or propriety of overthrowing or overturning organized government
   by force, violence, or any unlawful means, or who print, publish, or knowingly circulate any book, paper, etc., advocating, advising or teaching the
   doctrine that organized government should be so overthrown, does not penalize the utterance or publication of abstract doctrine or academic discussion
   having no quality of incitement to any concrete action, but denounces the
   advocacy of action for accomplishing the overthrow of organized government by unlawful means, and is constitutional as applied to a printed
   "Manifesto" advocating and urging mass action which shall progressively
   foment industrial disturbances and, through political mass strikes and
   revolutionary mass action overthrow and destroy organized parliamentary
   government; even though the advocacy was in general terms and not addressed to particular immediate acts or to particular persons. Pp. 654, 672.
9. The statute being constitutional, it may constitutionally be applied to every
   utterance—not too trivial to be beneath the notice of the law—which is of
   such a character and used with such intent and purpose as to bring it
   within the prohibition of the statute; and the question whether the specific
   utterance in question was likely to bring about the substantive evil aimed
   at by the statute, is not open to consideration. *Schenck* v. *United States,*
   249 U.S. 47, explained. P. 670.

195 App. Div. 773; 234 N.Y., 132, 539, affirmed.

ERROR to a judgment of the Supreme Court of New York, affirmed by the Appellate Division thereof and by the Court of Appeals, sentencing the plaintiff in error for the crime of criminal anarchy (New York Laws, 1909, c. 88), of which he had been convicted by a jury.

Messrs. Walter Nelles and *Walter H. Pollak*, with whom *Messrs. Albert De Silver* and *Charles S. Ascher* were on the brief, for plaintiff in error.

Messrs. W. J. Weatherbee, Deputy Attorney General of New York, and *John Caldwell Myers*, Assistant District Attorney of New York County, with whom *Messrs. Carl Sherman*, Attorney General of New York, *Claude T. Dawes*, Deputy Attorney General of New York, *Joab H. Banton*, District Attorney of New York County, and *John F. O'Neil*, Assistant District Attorney of New York County, were on the briefs, for defendant in error.

MR. JUSTICE SANFORD delivered the opinion of the Court.

Benjamin Gitlow was indicted in the Supreme Court of New York, with three others, for the statutory crime of criminal anarchy. New York Penal Laws, §§ 160, 161.[1] He was separately tried, convicted, and sentenced to imprisonment. The judgment was affirmed by the Appellate Division and by the Court of Appeals. 195 App. Div. 773; 234 N.Y. 132 and 539. The case is here on writ of error to the Supreme Court, to which the record was remitted. 260 U.S. 703.

The contention here is that the statute, by its terms and as applied in this case, is repugnant to the due process clause of the Fourteenth Amendment. Its material provisions are:

"§ 160. *Criminal anarchy defined.* Criminal anarchy is the doctrine that organized government should be overthrown by force or violence, or by assassination of the executive head or of any of the executive officials of government, or by any unlawful means. The advocacy of such doctrine either by word of mouth or writing is a felony.

"§ 161. *Advocacy of criminal anarchy.* Any person who:

"1. By word of mouth or writing advocates, advises or teaches the duty, necessity or propriety of overthrowing or overturning organized government by force or violence, or by assassination of the executive head or of any of the executive officials of government, or by any unlawful means; or,

"2. Prints, publishes, edits, issues or knowingly circulates, sells, distributes or publicly displays any book, paper, document, or written or printed matter in any form, containing or advocating, advising or teaching the doctrine that organized government should be overthrown by force, violence or any unlawful means . . . ,

"Is guilty of a felony and punishable" by imprisonment or fine, or both.

The indictment was in two counts. The first charged that the defendant had advocated, advised and taught the duty, necessity and propriety of overthrowing and overturning organized government by force, violence and unlawful means, by certain writings therein set forth entitled "The Left Wing Manifesto"; the second that he had printed, published and knowingly circulated and distributed a certain paper called "The Revolutionary Age," containing the writings set forth in the first count advocating, advising and teaching the doctrine

---

[1] Laws of 1909, ch. 88; Consol. Laws, 1909, ch. 40. This statute was originally enacted in 1902. Laws of 1902, ch. 371.

that organized government should be overthrown by force, violence and unlawful means.

The following facts were established on the trial by undisputed evidence and admissions: The defendant is a member of the Left Wing Section of the Socialist Party, a dissenting branch or faction of that party formed in opposition to its dominant policy of "moderate Socialism." Membership in both is open to aliens as well as citizens. The Left Wing Section was organized nationally at a conference in New York City in June, 1919, attended by ninety delegates from twenty different States. The conference elected a National Council, of which the defendant was a member, and left to it the adoption of a "Manifesto." This was published in The Revolutionary Age, the official organ of the Left Wing. The defendant was on the board of managers of the paper and was its business manager. He arranged for the printing of the paper and took to the printer the manuscript of the first issue which contained the Left Wing Manifesto, and also a Communist Program and a Program of the Left Wing that had been adopted by the conference. Sixteen thousand copies were printed, which were delivered at the premises in New York City used as the office of the Revolutionary Age and the headquarters of the Left Wing, and occupied by the defendant and other officials. These copies were paid for by the defendant, as business manager of the paper. Employees at this office wrapped and mailed out copies of the paper under the defendant's direction; and copies were sold from this office. It was admitted that the defendant signed a card subscribing to the Manifesto and Program of the Left Wing, which all applicants were required to sign before being admitted to membership; that he went to different parts of the State to speak to branches of the Socialist Party about the principles of the Left Wing and advocated their adoption; and that he was responsible for the Manifesto as it appeared, that "he knew of the publication, in a general way and he knew of its publication afterwards, and is responsible for its circulation."

There was no evidence of any effect resulting from the publication and circulation of the Manifesto.

No witnesses were offered in behalf of the defendant.

Extracts from the Manifesto are set forth in the margin.[2] Coupled with a review of the rise of Socialism, it condemned the dominant

---

[2] Italics are given as in the original, but the paragraphing is omitted.

"The Left Wing Manifesto"

"*Issued on Authority of the Conference by the National Council of the Left Wing.*

"The world is in crisis. Capitalism, the prevailing system of society, is in process of disintegration and collapse. . . . Humanity can be saved from its last excesses only by the Communist Revolution. There can now be only the Socialism which is one in temper and purpose with the proletarian revolutionary struggle. . . . The class struggle is the heart of Socialism. Without strict conformity to the class struggle, in its revolutionary implications, Socialism becomes either sheer Utopianism, or a method of reaction. . . . The dominant Socialism united with the capitalist governments to prevent a revolution. The Russian Revolution was the first act of the proletariat against the war and Imperialism. . . . [The] proletariat, urging on the poorer peasantry, conquered power. It accomplished a proletarian revolution by means of the Bolshevik policy of 'all power to the Soviets,'—organizing the new transitional state of proletarian dictatorship. . . . Moderate Socialism affirms that the bourgeois, democratic parliamentary state is the necessary basis for the introduction of Socialism. . . . Revolutionary Socialism, on the contrary, insists that the democratic parliamentary state can never be the basis for the introduction of Socialism; that it is necessary to destroy the parliamentary state, and construct a new state of the organized producers, which will deprive the bourgeoisie of political power, and function as a revolutionary dictatorship of the proletariat. . . . Revolutionary Socialism alone is capable of mobilizing the proletariat for Socialism, for the conquest of the power of the state, by means of revolutionary mass action and proletarian dictatorship. . . . Imperialism is dominant in the United States, which is now a world power. . . . The war has aggrandized American "moderate Socialism" for its recognition of the necessity of the democratic parliamentary state; repudiated its policy of introducing Socialism by legislative measures; and advocated, in plain and unequivocal language, the necessity of accomplishing the "Communist Revolution" by a militant and "revolutionary Socialism", based on "the class struggle" and mobilizing the "power of the proletariat in action," through mass industrial revolts developing into mass political strikes and "revo-

Capitalism, instead of weakening it as in Europe. . . . These conditions modify our immediate task, but do not alter its general character; this is not the moment of revolution, but it is the moment of revolutionary struggle. . . . Strikes are developing which verge on revolutionary action, and in which the suggestion of proletarian dictatorship is apparent, the striker-workers trying to usurp functions of municipal government, as in Seattle and Winnipeg. The mass struggle of the proletariat is coming into being. . . . These strikes will constitute the determining feature of proletarian action in the days to come. Revolutionary Socialism must use these mass industrial revolts to broaden the strike, to make it general and militant; use the strike for political objectives, and, finally, develop the mass political strike against Capitalism and the state. Revolutionary Socialism must base itself on the mass struggles of the proletariat, engage directly in these struggles while emphasizing the revolutionary purposes of Socialism and the proletarian movement. The mass strikes of the American proletariat provide the material basis out of which to develop the concepts and action of revolutionary Socialism. . . . Our task . . . is to articulate and organize the mass of the unorganized industrial proletariat, which constitutes the basis for a militant Socialism. The struggle for the revolutionary industrial unionism of the proletariat becomes an indispensable phase of revolutionary Socialism, on the basis of which to broaden and deepen the action of the militant proletariat, developing reserves for the ultimate conquest of power. . . . Revolutionary Socialism adheres to the class struggle because through the class struggle alone—the mass struggle—can the industrial proletariat secure immediate concessions and finally conquer power by organizing the industrial government of the working class. The class struggle is a political struggle . . . in the sense that its objective is political—the overthrow of the political organization upon which capitalistic exploitation depends, and the introduction of a new social system. The direct objective is the conquest by the proletariat of the power of the state. Revolutionary Socialism does not propose to 'capture' the bourgeois parliamentary state, but to conquer and destroy it. Revolutionary Socialism, accordingly, repudiates the policy of introducing Socialism by means of legislative measures on the basis of the bourgeois state. . . . It proposes to conquer by means of political action . . . in the revolutionary Marxian sense, which does not simply mean parliamentarism, but the class action of the proletariat in any form having as its objective the conquest of the power of the state. . . . Parliamentary action which emphasizes the implacable character of the class struggle is an indispensable means of agitation. . . . But parliamentarism cannot conquer the power of the state for the proletariat. . . . It is accomplished, not by the legislative representatives of the proletariat, but by the mass power of the proletariat in action. The supreme power of the proletariat inheres in the political mass strike, in using the industrial mass power of the proletariat for political objectives. Revolutionary Socialism, accordingly, recognizes that the supreme form of proletarian political action is the political mass strike. . . . The power of the proletariat lies fundamentally in its control of the industrial process. The mobilization of this control in action against the bourgeois state and Capitalism means the end of Capitalism, the initial form of the revolutionary mass action that will conquer the power of the state. . . . The revolution starts with strikes of protest, developing into mass political strikes and then into revolutionary mass action for the conquest of the power of the state. Mass action becomes political in purpose while extra-parliamentary in form: it is equally a process of revolution and the revolution itself in operation. The final objective of mass action is the conquest of the power of the state, the annihilation of the bourgeois parliamentary state and the introduction of the transition proletarian state, functioning as a revolutionary dictatorship of the proletariat. . . . The bourgeois parliamentary state is the organ of the bourgeoisie for the coercion of the proletariat. The revolutionary proletariat must, accordingly, destroy this state. . . . It is therefore necessary that the proletariat organize its own state for the coercion and suppression of the bourgeoisie. . . . Proletarian dictatorship is a recognition of the necessity for a revolutionary state to coerce and suppress the bourgeoisie; it is equally a recognition of the fact that, in the Communist reconstruction of society, the proletariat as a class alone counts. . . . The old machinery of the state cannot be used by the revolutionary proletariat. It must be destroyed. The proletariat creates a new state, based directly upon the industrially organized producers, upon the industrial unions or Soviets, or a combination of both. It is this state alone, functioning as a dictatorship of the proletariat, that can realize Socialism. . . . While the dictatorship of the proletariat performs its negative task of crushing the old order, it performs the positive task of constructing the new. Together with the government of the proletarian dictatorship, there is developed a new 'government,' which is no longer government in the old sense, since it concerns itself with the management of production and not with the government of persons. Out of workers' control of industry, introduced by the proletarian dictatorship, there develops the complete structure of Communist Socialism,—industrial self-government of the communistically organized producers. When this structure is completed, which implies the complete expropriation of the bourgeoisie economically and politically, the dictatorship of the proletariat ends, in its place coming the full and free social and individual autonomy of the Communist order. . . . It is not a problem of immediate revolution. It is a problem of the immediate revolutionary struggle. The revolutionary epoch of the final struggle against Capitalism may last for years and tens of years; but the Communist International offers a policy and program immediate and ultimate in scope, that provides for the immediate class struggle against Capitalism, in its revolutionary implications, and for the final act of the conquest of power. The old order is in decay. Civilization is in collapse. The proletarian revolution and the Communist reconstruction of society—the struggle for these—is now indispensable. This is the message of the Communist International to the workers of the world. The Communist International calls the proletariat of the world to the final struggle!"

lutionary mass action," for the purpose of conquering and destroying the parliamentary state and establishing in its place, through a "revolutionary dictatorship of the proletariat," the system of Communist Socialism. The then recent strikes in Seattle and Winnepeg [3] were cited as instances of a development already verging on revolutionary action and suggestive of proletarian dictatorship, in which the strike-workers were "trying to usurp the functions of municipal government"; and revolutionary Socialism, it was urged, must use these mass industrial revolts to broaden the strike, make it general and militant, and develop it into mass political strikes and revolutionary mass action for the annihilation of the parliamentary state.

At the outset of the trial the defendant's counsel objected to the introduction of any evidence under the indictment on the grounds that, as a matter of law, the Manifesto "is not in contravention of the statute," and that "the statute is in contravention of" the due process clause of the Fourteenth Amendment. This objection was denied. They also moved, at the close of the evidence, to dismiss the indictment and direct an acquittal "on the grounds stated in the first objection to evidence", and again on the grounds that "the indictment does not charge an offense" and the evidence "does not show an offense." These motions were also denied.

The court, among other things, charged the jury, in substance, that they must determine what was the intent, purpose and fair meaning of the Manifesto; that its words must be taken in their ordinary meaning, as they would be understood by people whom it might reach; that a mere statement or analysis of social and economic facts and historical incidents, in the nature of an essay, accompanied by prophecy as to the future course of events, but with no teaching, advice or advocacy of action, would not constitute the advocacy, advice or teaching of a doctrine for the overthrow of government within the meaning of the statute; that a mere statement that unlawful acts might accomplish such a purpose would be insufficient, unless there was a teaching, advising and advocacy of employing such unlawful acts for the purpose of overthrowing government; and that if the jury had a reasonable doubt that the Manifesto did teach, advocate or advise the duty, necessity or propriety of using unlawful means for the overthrowing of organized government, the defendant was entitled to an acquittal.

The defendant's counsel submitted two requests to charge which embodied in substance the statement that to constitute criminal anarchy within the meaning of the statute it was necessary that the language used or published should advocate, teach or advise the duty, necessity or propriety of doing "some definite or immediate act or acts" of force, violence or unlawfulness directed toward the overthrowing of organized government. These were denied further than had been charged. Two other requests to charge embodied in substance the statement that to constitute guilt the language used or published must be "reasonably and ordinarily calculated to incite certain persons" to acts of force, violence or unlawfulness, with the

---

[3] There was testimony at the trial that "there was an extended strike at Winnipeg commencing May 15, 1919, during which the production and supply of necessities, transportation, postal and telegraphic communication and fire and sanitary protection were suspended or seriously curtailed."

object of overthrowing organized government. These were also denied.

The Appellate Division, after setting forth extracts from the Manifesto and referring to the Left Wing and Communist Programs published in the same issue of the Revolutionary Age, said:[4] "It is perfectly plain that the plan and purpose advocated . . . contemplate the overthrow and destruction of the Governments of the United States and of all the States, not by the free action of the majority of the people through the ballot box in electing representatives to authorize a change of government by amending or changing the Constitution, . . . but by immediately organizing the industrial proletariat into militant Socialist unions and at the earliest opportunity through mass strike and force and violence, if necessary, compelling the government to cease to function, and then through a proletarian dictatorship, taking charge of and appropriating all property and administering it and governing through such dictatorship until such time as the proletariat is permitted to administer and govern it. . . . The articles in question are not a discussion of ideas and theories. They advocate a doctrine deliberately determined upon and planned for militantly disseminating a propaganda advocating that it is the duty and necessity of the proletariat engaged in industrial pursuits to organize to such an extent that, by massed strike, the wheels of government may ultimately be stopped and the government overthrown . . ."

The Court of Appeals held that the Manifesto "advocated the overthrow of this government by violence, or by unlawful means."[5] In one of the opinions representing the views of a majority of the court,[6] it was said: "It will be seen . . . that this defendant through the manifesto . . . advocated the destruction of the state and the establishment of the dictatorship of the proletariat. . . . To advocate . . . the commission of this conspiracy or action by mass strike whereby government is crippled, the administration of justice paralyzed, and the health, morals and welfare of a community endangered, and this for the purpose of bringing about a revolution in the state, is to advocate the overthrow of organized government by unlawful means." In the other[7] it was said: "As we read this manifesto . . . we feel entirely clear that the jury were justified in rejecting the view that it was a mere academic and harmless discussion of the advantages of communism and advanced socialism" and "in regarding it as a justification and advocacy of action by one class which would destroy the rights of all other classes and overthrow the state itself by use of revolutionary mass strikes. It is true that there is no advocacy in specific terms of the use of . . . force or violence. There was no need to be. Some things are so commonly incident to others that they do not need to be mentioned when the underlying purpose is described."

[4] 195 App. Div. 773, 782, 790.
[5] Five judges, constituting the majority of the court, agreed in this view.   234 N.Y. 132, 138.   And the two judges, constituting the minority—who dissented solely on a question as to the construction of the statute which is not here involved—said in reference to the Manifesto: "Revolution for the purpose of overthrowing the present form and the established political system of the United States government by direct means rather than by constitutional means is therein clearly advocated and defended . . ." p. 154.
[6] Pages 141, 142.
[7] Pages 149, 150.

And both the Appellate Division and the Court of Appeals held the statute constitutional.

The specification of the errors relied on relates solely to the specific rulings of the trial court in the matters hereinbefore set out.[8] The correctness of the verdict is not questioned, as the case was submitted to the jury. The sole contention here is, essentially, that as there was no evidence of any concrete result flowing from the publication of the Manifesto or of circumstances showing the likelihood of such result, the statute as construed and applied by the trial court penalizes the mere utterance, as such, of "doctrine," having no quality of incitement, without regard either to the circumstances of its utterance or to the likelihood of unlawful sequences; and that, as the exercise of the right of free expression with relation to government is only punishable "in circumstances involving likelihood of substantive evil," the statute contravenes the due process clause of the Fourteenth Amendment. The argument in support of this contention rests primarily upon the following propositions: 1st, That the "liberty" protected by the Fourteenth Amendment includes the liberty of speech and of the press; and 2nd, That while liberty of expression "is not absolute," it may be restrained "only in circumstances where its exercise bears a casual relation with some substantive evil, consummated, attempted or likely," and as the statute "takes no account of circumstances," it unduly restrains this liberty and is therefore unconstitutional.

The precise question presented, and the only question which we can consider under this writ of error, then is, whether the statute, as construed and applied in this case by the state courts, deprived the defendant of his liberty of expression in violation of the due process clause of the Fourteenth Amendment.

The statute does not penalize the utterance or publication of abstract "doctrine" or academic discussion having no quality of incitement to any concrete action. It is not aimed against mere historical or philosophical essays. It does not restrain the advocacy of changes in the form of government by constitutional and lawful means. What it prohibits is language advocating, advising or teaching the overthrow of organized government by unlawful means. These words imply urging to action. Advocacy is defined in the Century Dictionary as: "1. The act of pleading for, supporting, or recommending; active espousal." It is not the abstract "doctrine" of overthrowing organized government by unlawful means which is denounced by the statute, but the advocacy of action for the accomplishment of that purpose. It was so construed and applied by the trial judge, who specifically charged the jury that: "A mere grouping of historical events and a prophetic deduction from them would neither constitute advocacy, advice or teaching of a doctrine for the overthrow of government by force, violence or unlawful means. [And] if it were a mere essay on the subject, as suggested by counsel, based upon deductions from alleged historical events, with no teaching, advice or advocacy of action, it would not constitute a violation of the statute. . . ."

The Manifesto, plainly, is neither the statement of abstract doctrine nor, as suggested by counsel, mere prediction that industrial disturb-

---

[8] Exceptions to all of these rulings had been duly taken.

ances and revolutionary mass strikes will result spontaneously in an inevitable process of evolution in the economic system. It advocates and urges in fervent language mass action which shall progressively foment industrial disturbances and through political mass strikes and revolutionary mass action overthrow and destroy organized parliamentary government. It concludes with a call to action in these words: "The proletariat revolution and the Communist reconstruction of society—*the struggle for these*—is now indispensable. . . . The Communist International calls the proletariat of the world to the final struggle!" This is not the expression of philosophical abstraction, the mere prediction of future events; it is the language of direct incitement.

The means advocated for bringing about the destruction of organized parliamentary government, namely, mass industrial revolts usurping the functions of municipal government, political mass strikes directed against the parliamentary state, and revolutionary mass action for its final destruction, necessarily imply the use of force and violence, and in their essential nature are inherently unlawful in a constitutional government of law and order. That the jury were warranted in finding that the Manifesto advocated not merely the abstract doctrine of overthrowing organized government by force, violence and unlawful means, but action to that end, is clear.

For present purposes we may and do assume that freedom of speech and of the press—which are protected by the First Amendment from abridgment by Congress—are among the fundamental personal rights and "liberties" protected by the due process clause of the Fourteenth Amendment from impairment by the States. We do not regard the incidental statement in *Prudential Ins. Co.* v. *Cheek*, 259 U.S. 530, 543, that the Fourteenth Amendment imposes no restrictions on the States concerning freedom of speech, as determinative of this question.[9]

It is a fundamental principle, long established, that the freedom of speech and of the press which is secured by the Constitution, does not confer an absolute right to speak or publish, without responsibility; whatever one may choose, or an unrestricted and unbridled license that gives immunity for every possible use of language and prevents the punishment of those who abuse this freedom. 2 Story on the Constitution, 5th ed., § 1580, p. 634; *Robertson* v. *Baldwin*, 165 U.S. 275, 281; *Patterson* v. *Colorado*, 205 U.S. 454, 462; *Fox* v. *Washington*, 236 U.S. 273, 276; *Schenck* v. *United States*, 249 U.S. 47, 52; *Frohwerk* v. *United States*, 249 U.S. 204, 206; *Debs* v. *United States*, 249 U.S. 211, 213; *Schaefer* v. *United States*, 251 U.S. 466, 474; *Gilbert* v. *Minnesota*, 254 U.S. 325, 332; *Warren* v. *United States* (C.C.A.) 183 Fed. 718, 721. Reasonably limited, it was said by Story in the passage cited, this freedom is an inestimable privilege in a free government; without such limitation, it might become the scourge of the republic.

That a State in the exercise of its police power may punish those who abuse this freedom by utterances inimical to the public welfare, tending to corrupt public morals, incite to crime, or disturb the public peace, is not open to question. *Robertson* v. *Baldwin, supra*, p. 281;

---

[9] Compare *Patterson* v. *Colorado*, 205 U.S. 454, 462; *Twining* v. *New Jersey*, 211 U.S. 78, 108; *Coppage* v. *Kansas*, 236 U.S. 1, 17; *Fox* v. *Washington*, 236 U.S. 273, 276; *Schaefer* v. *United States*, 251 U.S. 466, 474; *Gilbert* v. *Minnesota*, 254 U.S. 325, 338; *Meyer* v. *Nebraska*, 262 U.S. 390, 399; 2 Story On the Constitution, 5th Ed., § 1950, p. 698.

Patterson v. *Colorado, supra,* p. 462; *Fox* v. *Washington, supra,* p. 277; *Gilbert* v. *Minnesota, supra,* p. 339; *People* v. *Most,* 171 N.Y. 423, 431; *State* v. *Holm,* 139 Minn. 267, 275; *State* v. *Hennessy,* 114 Wash. 351, 359; *State* v. *Boyd,* 86 N.J.L. 75, 79; *State* v. *McKee,* 73 Conn. 18, 27. Thus it was held by this Court in the *Fox Case,* that a State may punish publications advocating and encouraging a breach of its criminal laws; and, in the *Gilbert Case,* that a State may punish utterances teaching or advocating that its citizens should not assist the United States in prosecuting or carrying on war with its public enemies.

And, for yet more imperative reasons, a State may punish utterances endangering the foundations of organized government and threatening its overthrow by unlawful means. These imperil its own existence as a constitutional State. Freedom of speech and press, said Story (*supra*) does not protect disturbances to the public peace or the attempt to subvert the government. It does not protect publications or teachings which tend to subvert or imperil the government or to impede or hinder it in the performance of its governmental duties. *State* v. *Holm, supra,* p. 275. It does not protect publications prompting the overthrow of government by force; the punishment of those who publish articles which tend to destroy organized society being essential to the security of freedom and the stability of the State. *People* v. *Most, supra,* pp. 431, 432. And a State may penalize utterances which openly advocate the overthrow of the representative and constitutional form of government of the United States and the several States, by violence or other unlawful means. *People* v. *Lloyd,* 304 Ill. 23, 24. See also, *State* v. *Tachin,* 92 N. J. L. 269, 274; and *People* v. *Steelik,* 187 Cal. 361, 375. In short this freedom does not deprive a State of the primary and essential right of self preservation; which, so long as human governments endure, they cannot be denied. *Turner* v. *Williams,* 194 U.S. 279, 294. In *Toledo Newspaper Co.* v. *United States,* 247 U.S. 402, 419, it was said: "The safeguarding and fructification of free and constitutional institutions is the very basis and mainstay upon which the freedom of the press rests, and that freedom, therefore, does not and cannot be held to include the right virtually to destroy such institutions."

By enacting the present statute the State has determined, through its legislative body, that utterances advocating the overthrow of organized government by force, violence and unlawful means, are so inimical to the general welfare and involve such danger of substantive evil that they may be penalized in the exercise of its police power. That determination must be given great weight. Every presumption is to be indulged in favor of the validity of the statute. *Mugler* v. *Kansas,* 123 U.S. 623, 661. And the case is to be considered "in the light of the principle that the State is primarily the judge of regulations required in the interest of public safety and welfare;" and that its police "statutes may only be declared unconstitutional where they are arbitrary or unreasonable attempts to exercise authority vested in the State in the public interest." *Great Northern Ry.* v. *Clara City,* 246 U.S. 434, 439. That utterances inciting to the overthrow of organized government by unlawful means, present a sufficient danger of substantive evil to bring their punishment within the range of legislative discretion, is clear. Such utterances, by their very nature, involve danger to the public peace and to the security of the State. They threaten breaches of the peace and ultimate revolution. And the immediate danger is none the less real and substantial, because the effect of a given utterance cannot be accurately foreseen. The State cannot reasonably be required to measure the danger from every such utterance in the nice balance of a jeweler's scale. A single revolutionary spark may kindle a fire that, smouldering for a time, may burst into a sweeping and destructive conflagration. It cannot be said that the State is acting arbitrarily or unreasonably when in the exercise of its judgment as to the measures necessary to protect the public peace and safety, it seeks to extinguish the spark without waiting until it has enkindled the flame or blazed into the conflagration. It cannot reasonably be required to defer the adoption of measures for its own peace and safety until the revolutionary utterances lead to actual disturbances of the public peace or imminent and immediate danger of its own destruction; but it may, in the exercise of its judgment, suppress the threatened danger in its incipiency. In *People* v. *Lloyd, supra,* p. 35, it was aptly said: "Manifestly, the legislature has authority to forbid the advocacy of a doctrine designed and intended to overthrow the government without waiting until there is a present and imminent danger of the success of the plan advocated. If the State were compelled to wait until the apprehended danger became certain, then its right to protect itself would come into being simultaneously with the overthrow of the government, when there would be neither prosecuting officers nor courts for the enforcement of the law."

We cannot hold that the present statute is an arbitrary or unreasonable exercise of the police power of the State unwarrantably infringing the freedom of speech or press; and we must and do sustain its constitutionality.

This being so it may be applied to every utterance—not too trivial to be beneath the notice of the law—which is of such a character and used with such intent and purpose as to bring it within the prohibition of the statute. This principle is illustrated in *Fox* v. *Washington, supra,* p. 277; *Abrams* v. *United States,* 250 U. S. 616, 624; *Schaefer* v. *United States, supra,* pp. 479, 480; *Pierce* v. *United States,* 252 U.S. 239, 250, 251;[10] and *Gilbert* v. *Minnesota, supra,* p. 333. In other words, when the legislative body has determined generally, in the constitutional exercise of its discretion, that utterances of a certain kind involve such danger of substantive evil that they may be punished, the question whether any specific utterance coming within the prohibited class is likely, in and of itself, to bring about the substantive evil, is not open to consideration. It is sufficient that the statute itself be constitutional and that the use of the language comes within its prohibition.

It is clear that the question in such cases is entirely different from that involved in those cases where the statute merely prohibits certain acts involving the danger of substantive evil, without any reference to language itself, and it is sought to apply its provisions to language used by the defendant for the purpose of bringing about the prohibited

---

[10] This reference is to so much of the decision as relates to the conviction under the third count. In considering the effect of the decisions under the Espionage Act of 1917 and the amendment of 1918, the distinction must be kept in mind between indictments under those provisions which specifically punish certain utterances, and those which merely punish specified acts in general terms, without specific reference to the use of language.

results. There, if it be contended that the statute cannot be applied to the language used by the defendant because of its protection by the freedom of speech or press, it must necessarily be found, as an original question, without any previous determination by the legislative body, whether the specific language used involved such likelihood of bringing about the substantive evil as to deprive it of the constitutional protection. In such cases it has been held that the general provisions of the statute may be constitutionally applied to the specific utterance of the defendant if its natural tendency and probable effect was to bring about the substantive evil which the legislative body might prevent. *Schenck* v. *United States, supra,* p. 51; *Debs* v. *United States, supra,* pp. 215, 216. And the general statement in the *Schenck Case* (p. 52) that the "question in every case is whether the words are used in such circumstances and are of such a nature as to create a clear and present danger that they will bring about the substantive evils,"— upon which great reliance is placed in the defendant's argument—was manifestly intended, as shown by the context, to apply only in cases of this class, and has no application to those like the present, where the legislative body itself has previously determined the danger of substantive evil arising from utterances of a specified character.

The defendant's brief does not separately discuss any of the rulings of the trial court. It is only necessary to say that, applying the general rules already stated, we find that none of them involved any invasion of the constitutional rights of the defendant. It was not necessary, within the meaning of the statute, that the defendant should have advocated "some definite or immediate act or acts" of force, violence or unlawfulness. It was sufficient if such acts were advocated in general terms; and it was not essential that their immediate execution should have been advocated. Nor was it necessary that the language should have been "reasonably and ordinarily calculated to incite certain persons" to acts of force, violence or unlawfulness. The advocacy need not be addressed to specific persons. Thus, the publication and circulation of a newspaper article may be an encouragement or endeavor to persuade to murder, although not addressed to any person in particular. *Queen* v. *Most,* L. R., 7 Q. B. D. 244.

We need not enter upon a consideration of the English common law rule of seditious libel or the Federal Sedition Act of 1798, to which reference is made in the defendant's brief. These are so unlike the present statute, that we think the decisions under them cast no helpful light upon the questions here.

And finding, for the reasons stated, that the statute is not in itself unconstitutional, and that it has not been applied in the present case in derogation of any constitutional right, the judgment of the Court of Appeals is

Affirmed.

MR. JUSTICE HOLMES, dissenting.

MR. JUSTICE BRANDEIS and I are of opinion that this judgment should be reversed. The general principle of free speech, it seems to me, must be taken to be included in the Fourteenth Amendment, in view of the scope that has been given to the word 'liberty' as there used, although perhaps it may be accepted with a somewhat larger latitude of interpretation than is allowed to Congress by the sweeping language that governs or ought to govern the laws of the United States.

If I am right, then I think that the criterion sanctioned by the full Court in *Schenck* v. *United States*, 249 U.S. 47, 52, applies. "The question in every case is whether the words used are used in such circumstances and are of such a nature as to create a clear and present danger that they will bring about the substantive evils that [the State] has a right to prevent." It is true that in my opinion this criterion was departed from in *Abrams* v. *United States*, 250 U.S. 616, but the convictions that I expressed in that case are too deep for it to be possible for me as yet to believe that it and *Schaefer* v. *United States*, 251 U.S. 466, have settled the law. If what I think the correct test is applied, it is manifest that there was no present danger of an attempt to overthrow the government by force on the part of the admittedly small minority who shared the defendant's views. It is said that this manifesto was more than a theory, that it was an incitement. Every idea is an incitement. It offers itself for belief and if believed it is acted on unless some other belief outweighs it or some failure of energy stifles the movement at its birth. The only difference between the expression of an opinion and an incitement in the narrower sense is the speaker's enthusiasm for the result. Eloquence may set fire to reason. But whatever may be thought of the redundant discourse before us it had no chance of starting a present conflagration. If in the long run the beliefs expressed in proletarian dictatorship are destined to be accepted by the dominant forces of the community, the only meaning of free speech is that they should be given their chance and have their way.

If the publication of this document had been laid as an attempt to induce an uprising against government at once and not at some indefinite time in the future it would have presented a different question. The object would have been one with which the law might deal, subject to the doubt whether there was any danger that the publication could produce any result, or in other words, whether it was not futile and too remote from possible consequences. But the indictment alleges the publication and nothing more.

SEDITION

PENNSYLVANIA *v.* NELSON.

CERTIORARI TO THE SUPREME COURT OF PENNSYLVANIA, WESTERN DISTRICT.

No. 10.   Argued November 15–16, 1955.—Decided April 2, 1956.

The Smith Act, as amended, 18 U.S.C. § 2385, which prohibits the knowing advocacy of the overthrow of the Government of the United States by force and violence, supersedes the enforceability of the Pennsylvania Sedition Act, which proscribes the same conduct. Pp. 498–510.

1. The scheme of Federal regulation is so pervasive as to make reasonable the inference that the Congress left no room for the States to supplement it. Pp. 502–504.

2. The Federal statutes touch a field in which the Federal interest is so dominant that the Federal system must be assumed to preclude enforcement of state laws on the same subject. Pp. 504–505.

3. Enforcement of State sedition acts presents a serious danger of conflict with the administration of the Federal program. Pp. 505–510.

377 Pa. 58, 104 A. 2d 133, affirmed.

Frank F. Truscott, Special Deputy Attorney General of Pennsylvania, and *Harry F. Stambaugh* argued the cause for petitioner. With them on the brief were *Frank P. Lawley, Jr.*, Deputy Attorney General, and *Albert A. Fiok.*

Herbert S. Thatcher argued the cause for respondent. With him on the brief was *Victor Rabinowitz.*

By special leave of Court, *Charles F. Barber* argued the cause for the United States, and *Louis C. Wyman*, Attorney General, for the State of New Hampshire, as *amici curiae*, urging reversal. On the brief with *Mr. Barber* were *Solicitor General Sobeloff, Assistant Attorney General Tompkins, Harold D. Koffsky* and *Philip R. Monahan. Mr. Wyman* also filed a brief.

Briefs of *amici curiae* urging reversal were filed by *George Fingold*, Attorney General, and *Lowell S. Nicholson, Samuel H. Cohen* and *Fred L. True, Jr.*, Assistant Attorneys General, for the State of Massachusetts, and *Ralph B. Gregg* for the American Legion.

Briefs of *amici curiae* urging affirmance were filed by *Osmond K. Fraenkel* and *Herbert Monte Levy* for the American Civil Liberties Union, *Walter C. Longstreth, Allen S. Olmsted, 2d* and *William Allen Rahil* for the Civil Liberties Committee of the Philadelphia Yearly Meeting of the Religious Society of Friends, and *Frank J. Donner, Royal W. France, Arthur Kinoy* and *Marshall Perlin* for Feldman et al.

MR. CHIEF JUSTICE WARREN delivered the opinion of the Court.

The respondent Steve Nelson, an acknowledged member of the Communist Party, was convicted in the Court of Quarter Sessions of Allegheny County, Pennsylvania, of a violation of the Pennsylvania Sedition Act [1] and sentenced to imprisonment for twenty years and to a fine of $10,000 and to costs of prosecution in the sum of $13,000. The Superior Court affirmed the conviction. 172 Pa. Super. 125, 92 A. 2d 431. The Supreme Court of Pennsylvania, recognizing but not reaching many alleged serious trial errors and conduct of the trial court infringing upon respondent's right to due process of law, [2] decided the case on the narrow issue of supersession of State law by the Federal Smith Act. [3] In its opinion, the court stated:

"And, while the Pennsylvania statute proscribes sedition against either the Government of the United States or the government of Pennsylvania, it is only alleged sedition against the United States with which the instant case is concerned. Out of all the voluminous testimony, we have not found, nor has anyone pointed to, a single word indicating a seditious act or even utterance directed against the Government of Pennsylvania." [4]

---

[1] Pa. Penal Code § 207, 18 Purdon's Pa. Stat. Ann. § 4207. The text of the statute is set out in an Appendix to this opinion, *post*, p. 510.

[2] The Supreme Court also did not have to reach the question of the constitutionality of subdivision (c) of the Pennsylvania Act, the basis of four counts of the twelve-count indictment, which punishes utterances "or conduct [intended to] incite or encourage any person to commit any overt act with a view to bringing the Government of this State or of the United States into hatred or contempt." Cf. *Winters* v. *New York*, 333 U.S. 507. This provision is strangely reminiscent of the Sedition Act of 1798, 1 Stat. 596, which punished utterances made "with intent to defame the . . . government, or either house of the . . . Congress, or the . . . President, or to bring them . . . into contempt or disrepute; or to excite against them . . . the hatred of the good people of the United States . . ."

[3] 377 Pa. 58, 104 A. 2d 133.

[4] 377 Pa., at 69, 104 A. 2d, at 139.

The precise holding of the court, and all that is before us for review, is that the Smith Act of 1940,[5] as amended in 1948,[6] which prohibits the knowing advocacy of the overthrow of the Government of the United States by force and violence, supersedes the enforceability of the Pennsylvania Sedition Act which proscribes the same conduct.

Many State attorneys general and the Solicitor General of the United States appeared as *amici curiae* for petitioner, and several briefs were filed on behalf of the respondent. Because of the important question of Federal-State relationship involved, we granted certiorari. 348 U.S. 814.

It should be said at the outset that the decision in this case does not affect the right of States to enforce their sedition laws at times when the Federal Government has not occupied the field and is not protecting the entire country from seditious conduct. The distinction between the two situations was clearly recognized by the court below.[7] Nor does it limit the jurisdiction of the States where the Constitution and Congress have specifically given them concurrent jurisdiction, as was done under the Eighteenth Amendment and the Volstead Act. *United States* v. *Lanza*, 260 U.S. 377. Neither does it limit the right of the State to protect itself at any time against sabotage or attempted violence of all kinds.[8] Nor does it prevent the State from prosecuting where the same act constitutes both a Federal offense and a State offense under the police power, as was done in *Fox* v. *Ohio*, 5 How. 410, and *Gilbert* v. *Minnesota*, 254 U.S. 325, relied upon by petitioner as authority herein. In neither of those cases did the State statute impinge on Federal jurisdiction. In the *Fox* case, the Federal offense was counterfeiting. The State offense was defrauding the person to whom the spurious money was passed. In the *Gilbert* case this Court, in upholding the enforcement of a State statute, proscribing conduct which would "interfere with or discourage the enlistment of men in the military or naval forces of the United States or of the State of Minnesota," treated it not as an act relating to "the raising of armies for the national defense, nor to rules and regulations for the government of those under arms [a constitutionally exclusive Federal power]. It [was] simply a local police measure . . . ."[9]

---

[5] 54 Stat. 670.
[6] 18 U.S.C. § 2385. The text of the statute is set out in an Appendix to this opinion, *post*, p. 511. (Another part of the Smith Act, punishing the advocacy of mutiny, is now 18 U.S.C. § 2387.)
[7] "No question of Federal supersession of a State statute was in issue . . . when the Supreme Court upheld the validity of the State statutes in *Gitlow* v. *New York*, 268 U.S. 652 (1925), and *Whitney* v. *California*, 274 U.S. 357 (1927)." 377 Pa., at 73–74, 104 A. 2d, at 141.
Although the judgments of conviction in both *Gitlow* and *Whitney* were rendered in 1920, before repeal of the Federal wartime sedition statute of 1918, 41 Stat. 1359, the question of supersession was not raised in either case and, of course, not considered in this Court's opinions.
[8] "Nor is a State stripped of its means of self-defense by the suspension of its sedition statute through the entry of the Federal Government upon the field. There are many valid laws on Pennsylvania's statute books adequate for coping effectively with actual or threatened internal civil disturbances. As to the nationwide threat to all citizens, imbedded in the type of conduct interdicted by a sedition act, we are—all of us—protected by the Smith Act and in a manner more efficient and more consistent with the service of our national welfare in all respects." 377 Pa., at 70, 104 A. 2d, at 139.
[9] 254 U.S., at 331. The Court went on to observe : ". . . the State knew the conditions which existed and could have a solicitude for the public peace, and this record justifies it. Gilbert's remarks were made in a public meeting. They were resented by his auditors. There were protesting interruptions, also accusations and threats against him, disorder and intimations of violence. And such is not an uncommon experience. On such occasions feeling usually runs high and is impetuous ; there is a prompting to violence and when violence is once yielded to, before it can be quelled, tragedies may be enacted. To preclude such result or a danger of it is a proper exercise of the power of the State." *Id.*, at 331–332.

Where, as in the instant case, Congress has not stated specifically whether a Federal statute has occupied a field in which the States are otherwise free to legislate,[10] different criteria have furnished touchstones for decision. Thus,

"[t]his Court, in considering the validity of State laws in the light of . . . Federal laws touching the same subject, has made use of the following expressions: conflicting; contrary to; occupying the field; repugnance; difference; irreconcilability; inconsistency; violation; curtailment; and interference. But none of these expressions provides an infallible constitutional test or an exclusive constitutional yardstick. In the final analysis, there can be no one crystal clear distinctly marked formula." *Hines* v. *Davidowitz*, 312 U.S. 52, 67.

And see *Rice* v. *Santa Fe Elevator Corp.*, 331 U.S. 218, 230–231. In this case, we think that each of several tests of supersession is met.

First, "[t]he scheme of Federal regulation [is] so pervasive as to make reasonable the inference that Congress left no room for the States to supplement it." *Rice* v. *Santa Fe Elevator Corp.*, 331 U.S., at 230. The Congress determined in 1940 that it was necessary for it to re-enter the field of antisubversive legislation, which had been abandoned by it in 1921. In that year, it enacted the Smith Act which proscribes advocacy of the overthrow of any government— Federal, State or local—by force and violence and organization of and knowing membership in a group which so advocates.[11] Conspiracy to commit any of these acts is punishable under the general criminal conspiracy provisions in 18 U.S.C. § 371. The Internal Security Act of 1950 is aimed more directly at Communist organizations.[12] It distinguishes between "Communist-action organizations" and "Communist-front organizations," [13] requiring such organizations to register and to file annual reports with the Attorney General giving complete details as to their officers and funds.[14] Members of Communist-action organizations who have not been registered by their organization must register as individuals.[15] Failure to register in accordance with the requirements of sections 786–787 is punishable by a fine of not more than $10,000 for an offending organization and by a fine of not more than $10,000 or imprisonment for not more than five years or both for an individual offender—each day of failure to register constituting a separate offense.[16] And the Act imposes certain sanctions upon both "action" and "front" organizations and their members.[17] The Communist Control Act of 1954 declares "that the Com-

---

[10] Petitioner makes the subsidiary argument that 18 U.S.C. § 3231 shows a congressional intention not to supersede State criminal statutes by any provision of Title 18. Section 3231 provides:
"The district courts of the United States shall have original jurisdiction, exclusive of the courts of the States, of all offenses against the laws of the United States.
"Nothing in this title shall be held to take away or impair the jurisdiction of the courts of the several States under the laws thereof."
The office of the second sentence is merely to limit the effect of the jurisdictional grant of the first sentence. There was no intention to resolve particular supersession questions by the Section.
[11] See Appendix, *post*, p. 511. See also the Voorhis Act passed in 1940, now codified as 18 U.S.C. § 2386, and the Foreign Agents Registration Act passed in 1938, 22 U.S.C. § 611 *et seq.*
[12] 50 U.S.C. § 781 *et seq.*
[13] *Id.,* § 782 (3), (4).
[14] *Id.,* § 786.
[15] *Id.,* § 787.
[16] *Id.,* § 794(a).
[17] *Id.,* §§ 784, 785, 789, 790.

munist Party of the United States, although purportedly a political party, is in fact an instrumentality of a conspiracy to overthrow the Government of the United States" and that "its role as the agency of a hostile foreign power renders its existence a clear present and continuing danger to the security of the United States." [18]   It also contains a legislative finding that the Communist Party is a "Communist-action organization" within the meaning of the Internal Security Act of 1950 and provides that "knowing" members of the Communist Party are "subject to all the provisions and penalties" of that Act.[19] It furthermore sets up a new classification of "Communist-infiltrated organizations" [20] and provides for the imposition of sanctions against them.

We examine these Acts only to determine the congressional plan. Looking to all of them in the aggregate, the conclusion is inescapable that Congress has intended to occupy the field of sedition. Taken as a whole, they evince a congressional plan which makes it reasonable to determine that no room has been left for the States to supplement it.   Therefore, a State sedition statute is superseded regardless of whether it purports to supplement the Federal law.   As was said by Mr. Justice Holmes in *Charleston & Western Carolina R. Co.* v. *Varnville Furniture Co.*, 237 U.S. 597, 604:

> "When Congress has taken the particular subject-matter in hand coincidence is as ineffective as opposition, and a State law is not to be declared a help because it attempts to go farther than Congress has seen fit to go."

Second, the Federal statutes "touch a field in which the Federal interest is so dominant that the Federal system [must] be assumed to preclude enforcement of State laws on the same subject." *Rice* v. *Santa Fe Elevator Corp.*, 331 U. S., at 230, citing *Hines* v. *Davidowitz, supra.*[21]   Congress has devised an all-embracing program for resistance to the various forms of totalitarian aggression.   Our external defenses have been strengthened, and a plan to protect against internal subversion has been made by it.   It has appropriated vast sums, not only for our own protection, but also to strengthen freedom throughout the world.   It has charged the Federal Bureau of Investigation and the Central Intelligence Agency with responsibility for intelligence concerning Communist seditious activities against our Government, and has denominated such activities as part of a world conspiracy.   It accordingly proscribed sedition against all government in the Nation—National, State and local.   Congress declared that these steps were taken "to provide for the common defense, to preserve the sovereignty of the United States as an independent Nation, and to guarantee to each State a republican form of government. . . ." [22]   Congress having thus treated seditious conduct as a matter of vital national concern, it is in no sense a local enforcement problem.   As was said in the court below:

---

[18] 50 U.S.C. (1955 Supp.) § 841.
[19] *Id.*, § 843.
[20] *Id.*, § 782(4A).
[21] It is worth observing that in *Hines* this Court held a Pennsylvania statute providing for alien registration was superseded by Title III of the same Act of which the commonly called Smith Act was Title I.   Title II amended certain statutes dealing with the exclusion and deportation of aliens.   The provisions of Title I involve a field of no less dominant Federal interest than Titles II and III, in which Congress manifestly did not desire concurrent State action.
[22] 50 U.S.C. § 781(15).

"Sedition against the United States is not a *local* offense. It is a crime against the *Nation*. As such, it should be prosecuted and punished in the Federal courts where this defendant has in fact been prosecuted and convicted and is now under sentence.[23] It is not only important but vital that such prosecutions should be exclusively within the control of the Federal Government. . . ." [24]

Third, enforcement of State sedition acts presents a serious danger of conflict with the administration of the Federal program. Since 1939, in order to avoid a hampering of uniform enforcement of its program by sporadic local prosecutions, the Federal Government has urged local authorities not to intervene in such matters, but to turn over to the Federal authorities immediately and unevaluated all information concerning subversive activities. The President made such a request on September 6, 1939, when he placed the Federal Bureau of Investigation in charge of investigation in this field:

"The Attorney General has been requested by me to instruct the Federal Bureau of Investigation of the Department of Justice to take charge of investigative work in matters relating to espionage, sabotage, and violations of the neutrality regulations.

"This task must be conducted in a comprehensive and effective manner on a national basis, and all information must be carefully sifted out and correlated in order to avoid confusion and irresponsibility.

"To this end I request all police officers, sheriffs, and all other law enforcement officers in the United States promptly to turn over to the nearest representative of the Federal Bureau of Investigation any information obtained by them relating to espionage, counterespionage, sabotage, subversive activities and violations of the neutrality laws." [25]

And in addressing the Federal-State Conference on Law Enforcement Problems of National Defense, held on August 5 and 6, 1940, only a few weeks after the passage of the Smith Act, the Director of the Federal Bureau of Investigation said:

"The fact must not be overlooked that meeting the spy, the saboteur and the subverter is a problem that must be handled on a nation-wide basis. An isolated incident in the middle west may be of little significance, but when fitted into a national pattern of similar incidents, it may lead to an important revelation of subversive activity. It is for this reason that the President requested all of our citizens and law enforcing agencies to report directly to the Federal Bureau of Investigation any complaints or information dealing with espionage, sabotage or subversive activities. In such matters, time is of the essence. It is unfortunate that in a few States efforts have been made by individuals not fully acquainted with the far-flung ramifications of this problem to interject superstructures of agencies between local law enforcement and the FBI to sift what might be vital

[23] *United States* v. *Mesarosh* [Nelson], 116 F. Supp. 345, aff'd, 223 F. 2d 449, cert. granted, 350 U.S. 922.
[24] 377 Pa., at 76, 104 A. 2d, at 142.
[25] The Public Papers and Addresses of Franklin D. Roosevelt, 1939 Volume, pp. 478–479 (1941).

information, thus delaying its immediate reference to the FBI. This cannot be, if our internal security is to be best served. This is no time for red tape or amateur handling of such vital matters. There must be a direct and free flow of contact between the local law enforcement agencies and the FBI. The job of meeting the spy or saboteur is one for experienced men of law enforcement." [26]

Moreover, the Pennsylvania Statute presents a peculiar danger of interference with the Federal program. For, as the court below observed:

"Unlike the Smith Act, which can be administered only by Federal officers acting in their official capacities, indictment for sedition under the Pennsylvania statute can be initiated upon an information made by a private individual. The opportunity thus present for the indulgence of personal spite and hatred or for furthering some selfish advantage or ambition need only be mentioned to be appreciated. Defense of the Nation by law, no less than by arms, should be a public and not a private undertaking. It is important that punitive sanctions for sedition *against the United States* be such as have been promulgated by the central governmental authority and administered under the supervision and review of that authority's judiciary. If that be done, sedition will be detected and punished, no less, wherever it may be found, and the right of the individual to speak freely and without fear, even in criticism of the government, will at the same time be protected." [27]

In his brief, the Solicitor General states that forty-two States plus Alaska and Hawaii have statutes which in some form prohibit advocacy of the violent overthrow of established government. These statutes are entitled anti-sedition statutes, criminal anarchy laws, criminal syndicalist laws, etc. Although all of them are primarily directed against the overthrow of the United States Government, they are in no sense uniform. And our attention has not been called to any case where the prosecution has been successfully directed against an attempt to destroy State or local government. Some of these Acts are studiously drawn and purport to protect fundamental rights by appropriate definitions, standards of proof and orderly procedures in keeping with the avowed congressional purpose "to protect freedom from those who would destroy it, without infringing upon the freedom of all our people." Others are vague and are almost wholly without such safeguards. Some even purport to punish mere membership in subversive organizations which the Federal statutes do not punish where Federal registration requirements have been fulfilled. [28]

---

[26] Proceedings, p. 23.
[27] 377 Pa., at 74–75, 104 A. 2d, at 141.
[28] *E.g.*, compare Fla. Stat. 1953, § 876.02: "Any person who— . . . (5) Becomes a member of, associated with or promotes the interest of any criminal anarchistic, communistic, nazi-istic or fascistic organization, . . . [s]hall be guilty of a felony . . . ," with 50 U.S.C. § 783(f): "Neither the holding of office nor membership in any Communist organization by any person shall constitute per se a violation of subsection (a) or subsection (c) of this section or of any other criminal statute. The fact of the registration of any person under section 787 or section 788 of this title as an officer or member of any Communist organization shall not be received in evidence against such person in any prosecution for any alleged violation of subsection (a) or subsection (c) of this section or for any alleged violation of any other criminal statute."

When we were confronted with a like situation in the field of labor-management relations, Mr. Justice Jackson wrote:

"A multiplicity of tribunals and a diversity of procedures are quite as apt to produce incompatible or conflicting adjudications as are different rules of substantive law." [29]

Should the States be permitted to exercise a concurrent jurisdiction in this area, Federal enforcement would encounter not only the difficulties mentioned by Mr. Justice Jackson, but the added conflict engendered by different criteria of substantive offenses.

Since we find that Congress has occupied the field to the exclusion of parallel State legislation, that the dominant interest of the Federal Government precludes State intervention, and that administration of State Acts would conflict with the operation of the Federal plan, we are convinced that the decision of the Supreme Court of Pennsylvania is unassailable.

We are not unmindful of the risk of compounding punishments which would be created by finding concurrent state power. In our view of the case, we do not reach the question whether double or multiple punishment for the same overt acts directed against the United States has constitutional sanction.[30] Without compelling indication to the contrary, we will not assume that Congress intended to permit the possibility of double punishment. Cf. *Houston* v. *Moore*, 5 Wheat. 1, 31, 75; *Jerome* v. *United States*, 318 U.S. 101, 105.

The judgment of the Supreme Court of Pennsylvania is

Affirmed.

[For dissenting opinion of MR. JUSTICE REED, joined by MR. JUSTICE BURTON and MR. JUSTICE MINTON, see *post*, p. 512.]

Pennsylvania Penal Code § 207.

The word "sedition," as used in this section, shall mean:

Any writing, publication, printing, cut, cartoon, utterance, or conduct, either individually or in connection or combination with any other person, the intent of which is:

(a) To make or cause to be made any outbreak or demonstration of violence against this State or against the United States.

(b) To encourage any person to take any measures or engage in any conduct with a view of overthrowing or destroying or attempting to overthrow or destroy, by any force or show or threat of force, the Government of this State or of the United States.

(c) To incite or encourage any person to commit any overt act with a view to bringing the Government of this State or of the United States into hatred or contempt.

(d) To incite any person or persons to do or attempt to do personal injury or harm to any officer of this State or of the United States, or to damage or destroy any public property or the property of any public official because of his official position.

The word "sedition" shall also include:

(e) The actual damage to, or destruction of, any public property or the property of any public official, perpetrated because the owner or occupant is in official position.

---

[29] *Garner* v. *Teamsters Union*, 346 U.S. 485, 490–491.
[30] But see Grant, The *Lanza* Rule of Successive Prosecutions, 32 Col. L. Rev. 1309.

(f) Any writing, publication, printing, cut, cartoon, or utterance which advocates or teaches the duty, necessity, or propriety of engaging in crime, violence, or any form of terrorism, as a means of accomplishing political reform or change in government.

(g) The sale, gift or distribution of any prints, publications, books, papers, documents, or written matter in any form, which advocates, furthers or teaches sedition as hereinbefore defined.

(h) Organizing or helping to organize or becoming a member of any assembly, society, or group, where any of the policies or purposes thereof are seditious as hereinbefore defined.

Sedition shall be a felony. Whoever is guilty of sedition shall, upon conviction thereof, be sentenced to pay a fine not exceeding ten thousand dollars ($10,000), or to undergo imprisonment not exceeding twenty (20) years, or both.

18 U.S.C. § 2385.

Whoever knowingly or willfully advocates, abets, advises, or teaches the duty, necessity, desirability, or propriety of overthrowing or destroying the Government of the United States or the government of any State, Territory, District or Possession thereof, or the government of any political subdivision therein, by force or violence, or by the assassination of any officer of any such government; or

Whoever, with intent to cause the overthrow or destruction of any such government, prints, publishes, edits, issues, circulates, sells, distributes, or publicly displays any written or printed matter advocating, advising, or teaching the duty, necessity, desirability, or propriety of overthrowing or destroying any government in the United States by force or violence, or attempts to do so; or

Whoever organizes or helps or attempts to organize any society, group, or assembly of persons who teach, advocate, or encourage the overthrow or destruction of any such government by force or violence; or becomes or is a member of, or affiliates with, any such society, group, or assembly of persons, knowing the purposes thereof—

Shall be fined not more than $10,000 or imprisoned not more than ten years, or both, and shall be ineligible for employment by the United States or any department or agency thereof, for the five years next following his conviction.

MR. JUSTICE REED, with whom MR. JUSTICE BURTON and MR. JUSTICE MINTON join, dissenting.

The problems of governmental power may be approached in this case free from the varied viewpoints that focus on the problems of national security. This is a jurisdictional problem of general importance because it involves an asserted limitation on the police power of the States when it is applied to a crime that is punishable also by the Federal Government. As this is a recurring problem, it is appropriate to explain our dissent.

Congress has not, in any of its statutes relating to sedition, specifically barred the exercise of State power to punish the same Acts under State law. And, we read the majority opinion to assume for this case that, absent Federal legislation, there is no constitutional bar to punishment of sedition against the United States by both a

State and the Nation.[1] The majority limits to the Federal courts the power to try charges of sedition against the Federal Government.

First, the Court relies upon the pervasiveness of the antisubversive legislation embodied in the Smith Act of 1940, 18 U.S.C. § 2385, the Internal Security Act of 1950, 64 Stat. 987, and the Communist Control Act of 1954, 68 Stat. 775. It asserts that these Acts in the aggregate mean that Congress has occupied the "field of sedition" to the exclusion of the States. The "occupation of the field" argument has been developed by this Court for the Commerce Clause and legislation thereunder to prevent partitioning of this country by locally erected trade barriers. In those cases this Court has ruled that State legislation is superseded when it conflicts with the comprehensive regulatory scheme and purpose of a Federal plan. *Cloverleaf Butter Co.* v. *Patterson*, 315 U. S. 148. The two cases cited by the Court to support its argument that the broad treatment of any subject within the Federal power bars supplemental action by States are of this nature. In our view neither case is apposite to the Smith Act. The *Varnville* case dealt with general regulation of interstate commerce making the originating carrier liable to the holder of its interstate bill of lading for damage caused by a common carrier of property. This Court held that the section through the Federal commerce power superseded a State right of action against a nonoriginating carrier for damages and a penalty for injury occurring on another line. The pertinent section, 34 Stat. 595, § 7, expressed a controlling Federal policy for this commerce. The *Rice* case dealt with regulations of warehouses. We barred State action in that area because the Act declared that the authority it conferred "shall be exclusive with respect to all persons securing a license" under the Act. 331 U.S., at 224 and 233.

But the Federal sedition laws are distinct criminal statutes and punish willful advocacy of the use of force against "the Government of the United States or the government of any State." These criminal laws proscribe certain local activity without creating any statutory or administrative regulation. There is, consequently, no question as to whether some general congressional regulatory scheme might be upset by a coinciding State plan.[2] In these circumstances the conflict should be clear and direct before this Court reads a congressional intent to void State legislation into the Federal sedition acts.[3] Chief Justice Marshall wrote:

"To interfere with the penal laws of a State, where they . . . have for their sole object the internal government of the country, is a very serious measure, which Congress cannot be supposed to adopt lightly, or inconsiderately. . . . It would be taken deliberately, and the intention would be clearly and unequivocally expressed." *Cohens* v. *Virginia*, 6 Wheat. 264, 443.

Moreover, it is quite apparent that since 1940 Congress has been keenly aware of the magnitude of existing State legislation proscribing sedition. It may be validly assumed that in these circumstances this

---

[1] No problem of double punishment exists in this case. See the Court's opinion. p. 499, and its last paragraph, p. 509. See *United States* v. *Lanza*, 260 U.S. 377, 382; The Federalist, No. 32. Cf. *Houston* v. *Moore*, 5 Wheat. 1, statement at p. 22 with that at pp. 44–45.

[2] Hunt, Federal Supremacy and State Anti-Subversive Legislation, 53 Mich. L. Rev. 407, 427–428; Note, 55 Col. L. Rev. 83, 90.

[3] *Gilbert* v. *Minnesota*, 254 U.S. 325, 328–333; *Reid* v. *Colorado*, 187 U.S. 137, 148; *Sinnot* v. *Davenport*, 22 How. 227, 243; *Fox* v. *Ohio*, 5 How. 410, 432–435.

Court should not void State legislation without a clear mandate from Congress.[4]

We cannot agree that the Federal criminal sanctions against sedition directed at the United States are of such a pervasive character as to indicate an intention to void State action.

Secondly, the Court states that the Federal sedition statutes touch a field "in which the Federal interest is so dominant" they must preclude State laws on the same subject. This concept is suggested in a comment on *Hines* v. *Davidowitz*, 312 U.S. 52, in the *Rice* case, at 230. The Court in *Davidowitz* ruled that Federal statutes compelling alien registration preclude enforcement of State statutes requiring alien registration. We read *Davidowitz* to teach nothing more than that, when the Congress provided a single nation-wide integrated system of regulation so complete as that for aliens' registration (with fingerprinting, a scheduling of activities, and continuous information as to their residence), the Act bore so directly on our foreign relations as to make it evident that Congress intended only one uniform national alien registration system.[5]

We look upon the Smith Act as a provision for controlling incitements to overthrow by force and violence the Nation, or any State, or any political subdivision of either.[6] Such an exercise of Federal police power carries, we think, no such dominancy over similar State powers as might be attributed to continuing Federal regulations concerning foreign affairs or coinage, for example.[7] In the responsibility of national and local governments to protect themselves against sedition, there is no "dominant interest."

---

[4] Forty-two States, along with Alaska and Hawaii, now have laws which penalize the advocacy of violent overthrow of the federal or state governments. Digest of the Public Record of Communism in the United States (Fund for the Republic, 1955) 266–306. In hearings before the House Judiciary Committee on the proposed Smith Act, both witnesses and members of the Committee made references to existing State sedition laws. Hearings before Subcommittee No. 3, Committee on the Judiciary, House of Representatives, on H.R. 5138, 76th Cong., 1st Sess., pp. 7, 69, 83–85. Similar comment was heard in the congressional debates. 84 Cong. Rec. 10452. In fact, the Smith Act was patterned on the New York Criminal Anarchy Statute. *Commonwealth* v. *Nelson*, 377 Pa. 58, 86, 104 A. 2d 133, 147. The original text of the Smith Act is set out in the hearings before Subcommittee No. 3, *supra*, p. 1, and the New York Act may be read in *Gitlow* v. *New York*, 268 U.S. 652, 654–655. Further evidence of congressional notice of State legislation may be found since the passage of the Smith Act. S. Rep. No. 1358, 81st Cong., 2d Sess., p. 9; H.R. Rep. No. 2980, 81st Cong., 2d Sess., p. 2; H.R. Rep. No 1950, 81st Cong., 2d Sess., pp. 25–46 (Un-American Activities Committee). See 67 Harv. L. Rev. 1419, 1420; 40 Cornell L. Rev. 130, 133.

[5] In *Allen-Bradley Local* v. *Board*, 315 U.S. 740, 749, we said: "In the *Hines* case, a Federal system of alien registration was held to supersede a State system of registration. But there we were dealing with a problem which had an impact on the general field of foreign relations. The delicacy of the issues which were posed alone raised grave questions as to the propriety of allowing a State system of regulation to function alongside of a Federal system. In that field, any 'concurrent State power that may exist is restricted to the narrowest of limits.' p. 68. Therefore, we were more ready to conclude that a Federal Act in a field that touched international relations superseded State regulation than we were in those cases where a State was exercising its historic powers over such traditionally local matters as public safety and order and the use of streets and highways."

The *Davidowitz* case is distinguishable on other grounds. Alien registration is not directly related to control of undesirable conduct; consequently there is no imperative problem of local law enforcement. 102 Pa. L. Rev., at 1091. There is also considerable legislative history behind the Alien Registration Act which suggests that Congress was trying to avoid overburdening of aliens; some features of the conflicting State law had been expressly rejected by Congress. 312 U.S., at 71–73. See 39 Minn. L. Rev. 213. It should be noted also that the coincidence between the State and Federal laws in the *Davidowitz* case was so great that no real purpose was served by the State law. 34 Boston U. L. Rev. 514, 517–518.

States are barred by the Constitution from entering into treaties and by 18 U.S.C. § 953 from correspondence or intercourse with foreign governments with relation to their disputes or controversies with this Nation.

[6] Such efforts may be punishable crimes. *Dennis* v. *United States*, 341 U.S. 494, 508–510.

[7] It seems quite reasonable to believe "that the exclusion principle is to be more strictly applied when the Congress acts in a field wherein the constitutional grant of power to the Federal Government is exclusive, as in its right to protect interstate commerce and to control international relations." *Albertson* v. *Millard*, 106 F. Supp. 635, 641.

We are citizens of the United States and of the State wherein we reside and are dependent upon the strength of both to preserve our rights and liberties. Both may enact criminal statutes for mutual protection unless Congress has otherwise provided. It was so held in *Gilbert* v. *Minnesota*, 254 U.S. 325. In *Gilbert* the Federal interest in raising armies did not keep this Court from permitting Minnesota to punish persons who interfered with enlistments (*id.*, at 326), even though a comprehensive Federal criminal law proscribed identical activity. 40 Stat. 553. We do not understand that case as does the majority. In our view this Court treated the Minnesota statute only alternatively as a police measure, p. 331. Minnesota made it unlawful to advocate "that men should not enlist in the military or naval forces of the United States." It was contended, pp. 327–328, that the power to punish such advocacy was "conferred upon Congress and withheld from the States." This Court ruled against the contention, saying:

"An army, of course, can only be raised and directed by Congress, in neither has the State power, but it has power to regulate the conduct of its citizens and to restrain the exertion of baleful influences against the promptings of patriotic duty to the detriment of the welfare of the Nation and State. To do so is not to usurp a National power, it is only to render a service to its people, ..." *Id.*, at 330–331.[8]

Thirdly, the Court finds ground for abrogating Pennsylvania's antisedition statute because, in the Court's view, the State's administration of the Act may hamper the enforcement of the Federal law. Quotations are inserted from statements of President Roosevelt and Mr. Hoover, the Director of the Federal Bureau of Investigation, to support the Court's position. But a reading of the quotations leads us to conclude that their purpose was to gain prompt knowledge of evidence of subversive activities so that the Federal agency could be fully advised. We find no suggestion from any official source that State officials should be less alert to ferret out or punish subversion. The Court's attitude as to interference seems to us quite contrary to that of the Legislative and Executive Departments. Congress was advised of the existing State sedition legislation when the Smith Act was enacted and has been kept current with its spread.[9] No declaration of exclusiveness followed. In this very case the Executive appears by brief of the Department of Justice, *amicus curiae*. The brief summarizes this point:

"The administration of the various State laws has not, in the course of the fifteen years that the Federal and State sedition laws have existed side by side, in fact interfered with, embarrassed, or impeded the enforcement of the Smith Act. The significance of this absence of conflict in administration or enforcement of the

---

[8] Mr. Justice Brandeis, dissenting, emphasized the ruling here applicable thus :
"Congress has the exclusive power to legislate concerning the Army and the Navy of the United States, and to determine, among other things, the conditions of enlistment. . . .
". . . The States act only under the express direction of Congress. . . .
". . . As exclusive power over enlistments in the Army and the Navy of the United States and the responsibility for the conduct of war is vested by the Federal Constitution in Congress. legislation by a State on this subject is necessarily void unless authorized by Congress. . . . Here Congress not only had exclusive power to act on the subject; it had exercised that power directly that the Espionage Law before Gilbert spoke the words for which he was sentenced. . . . The States may not punish treason against the United States . . . although indirectly acts of treason may affect them vitally. No more may they arrogate to themselves authority to punish the teaching of pacifism which the legislature of Minnesota appears to have put into that category." *Id.*, at 336–343.
[9] See note 4, *supra*.

Federal and State sedition laws will be appreciated when it is realized that this period has included the stress of wartime security requirements and the Federal investigation and prosecution under the Smith Act of the principal national and regional Communist leaders." [10]   *Id.*, at 30–31.

Mere fear by courts of possible difficulties does not seem to us in these circumstances a valid reason for ousting a State from exercise of its police power.   Those are matters for legislative determination.

Finally, and this one point seems in and of itself decisive, there is an independent reason for reversing the Pennsylvania Supreme Court.   The Smith Act appears in Title 18 of the United States Code, which Title codifies the Federal criminal laws.   Section 3231 of that Title provides:

"Nothing in this title shall be held to take away or impair the jurisdiction of the courts of the several States under the laws thereof."

That declaration springs from the Federal character of our Nation. It recognizes the fact that maintenance of order and fairness rests primarily with the States.   The section was first enacted in 1825 and has appeared successively in the Federal criminal laws since that time. [11]   This Court has interpreted the section to mean that States may provide concurrent legislation in the absence of explicit congressional intent to the contrary.   *Sexton* v. *California*, 189 U.S. 319, 324–325.   The majority's position in this case cannot be reconciled with that clear authorization of Congress.

The law stands against any advocacy of violence to change established governments.   Freedom of speech allows full play to the processes of reason.   The State and National legislative bodies have legislated within constitutional limits so as to allow the widest participation by the law enforcement officers of the respective governments.   The individual States were not told that they are powerless to punish local acts of sedition, nominally directed against the United States.   Courts should not interfere.   We would reverse the judgment of the Supreme Court of Pennsylvania.

CRIMINAL SYNDICALISM

WHITNEY *v.* CALIFORNIA.

ERROR TO THE DISTRICT COURT OF APPEAL, FIRST APPELLATE DISTRICT, DIVISION ONE, OF THE STATE OF CALIFORNIA.

No. 3.   Argued October 6, 1925; reargued March 18, 1926.—Decided May 16, 1927.

1. This Court acquires no jurisdiction to review the judgment of a State court of last resort on a writ of error, unless it affirmatively appears on the face of the record that a Federal question constituting an appropriate ground for such review was presented in and expressly or necessarily decided by such State court.   P. 360.

---

[10] The brief added, p. 31: ". . . the Attorney General of the United States recently informed that attorneys general of the several States . . . that a full measure of Federal-State cooperation would be in the public interest.   See *New York Times*, Sept. 15, 1955, p. 19."

[11] 4 Stat. 115, 122–123; 18 U.S.C.A. § 3231 (Historical and Revision Notes).

2. Where the fact that a Federal question was considered and passed upon by the State court does not appear by the record, it may be shown by a certified copy of an order of that court made after the return of the writ of error and brought here as an addition to the record. P. 361.

3. In reviewing the judgment of a State court this Court will consider only such Federal questions as are shown to have been presented to the State court and expressly or necessarily decided by it. P. 362.

4. The question whether the petitioner, who joined and assisted in the organization of a Communist Labor Party contravening the California Criminal Syndicalism Act, did so with knowledge of its unlawful character and purpose, was a mere question of the weight of the evidence, foreclosed by the verdict of guilty approved by the State court, and not a question of the constitutionality of the Act, reviewable by this Court. P. 366.

5. The California Criminal Syndicalism Act, which defines "criminal syndicalism" as "any doctrine or precept advocating, teaching or aiding and abetting the commission of crime, sabotage (which word is hereby defined as meaning willful and malicious physical damage or injury to physical property), or unlawful acts of force and violence or unlawful methods of terrorism as a means of accomplishing a change in industrial ownership or control, or effecting any political change," and declares guilty of a felony any person who "organizes or assists in organizing, or is or knowingly becomes a member of, any organization, society, group or assemblage of persons organized or assembled to advocate, teach or aid and abet criminal syndicalism," is sufficiently clear and explicit to satisfy the requirement of due process of law. P. 368.

6. The statute does not violate the Equal Protection Clause of the Fourteenth Amendment in penalizing those who advocate a resort to violent and unlawful methods as a means of changing industrial and political conditions while not penalizing those who may advocate a resort to such methods for maintaining such conditions, since the distinction is not arbitrary but within the discretionary power of the State to direct its legislation against what it deems an evil without covering the whole field of possible abuses. P. 369.

7. Such a statute is not open to objection unless the classification on which it is based is so lacking in any adequate or reasonable basis as to preclude the assumption that it was made in the exercise of the legislative judgment and discretion. P. 369.

8. This Act is not class legislation; it affects all alike, no matter what their business associations or callings, who come within its terms and do the things prohibited. P. 370.

9. Nor is it repugnant to the Due Process Clause as a restraint of the rights of free speech, assembly, and association. P. 371.

10. The determination of the legislature that the acts defined involve such danger to the public peace and security of the State that they should be penalized in the exercise of the police power must be given great weight and every presumption be indulged in favor of the validity of the statute, which could be declared unconstitutional only if an attempt to exercise arbitrarily and unreasonably the authority vested in the State in the public interest. P. 371.

57 Cal. App. 449; *ib.* 453, affirmed.

ERROR to a judgment of the District Court of Appeal of California which affirmed a conviction of the petitioner under the State act against criminal syndicalism. The Supreme Court of California denied a petition for appeal. On the first hearing in this Court the writ of error was dismissed for want of jurisdiction, but later a petition for rehearing was granted. 269 U.S. 530, 538.

Mr. Walter H. Pollak, with whom *Messrs. John F. Neylan, Thomas L. Lennon, Walter Nelles,* and *Ruth I. Wilson* were on the brief, for plaintiff in error.

Mr. John H. Riordan, Deputy Attorney General of California, with whom *Mr. U. S. Webb,* Attorney General, was on the brief, for the State of California.

MR. JUSTICE SANFORD delivered the opinion of the Court.

By a criminal information filed in the Superior Court of Alameda County, California, the plaintiff in error was charged, in five counts, with violations of the Criminal Syndicalism Act of that State. Statutes, 1919, c. 188, p. 281. She was tried, convicted on the first count, and sentenced to imprisonment. The judgment was affirmed by the District Court of Appeal. 57 Cal. App. 449. Her petition to have the case heard by the Supreme Court [1] was denied. *Ib.* 453. And the case was brought here on a writ of error which was allowed by the Presiding Justice of the Court of Appeal, the highest court of the State in which a decision could be had. Jud. Code, § 237.

On the first hearing in this Court, the writ of error was dismissed for want of jurisdiction. 269 U.S. 530. Thereafter, a petition for rehearing was granted, *Ib.* 538; and the case was again heard and reargued both as to the jurisdiction and the merits.

The pertinent provisions of the Criminal Syndicalism Act are:

"Section 1. The term 'criminal syndicalism' as used in this act is hereby defined as any doctrine or precept advocating, teaching or aiding and abetting the commission of crime, sabotage (which word is hereby defined as meaning willful and malicious physical damage or injury to physical property), or unlawful acts of force and violence or unlawful methods of terrorism as a means of accomplishing a change in industrial ownership or control, or effecting any political change.

"Sec. 2. Any person who: . . . 4. Organizes or assists in organizing, or is or knowingly becomes a member of, any organization, society, group or assemblage of persons organized or assembled to advocate, teach or aid and abet criminal syndicalism . . .

"Is guilty of a felony and punishable by imprisonment."

The first count of the information, on which the conviction was had, charged that on or about November 28, 1919, in Alameda County, the defendant, in violation of the Criminal Syndicalism Act, "did then and there unlawfully, willfully, wrongfully, deliberately and feloniously organize and assist in organizing and was, is, and knowingly became a member of an organization, society, group and assemblage of persons organized and assembled to advocate, teach, aid and abet criminal syndicalism."

It has long been settled that this Court acquires no jurisdiction to review the judgment of a State court of last resort on a writ of error, unless it affirmatively appears on the fact of the record that a Federal question constituting an appropriate ground for such review was presented in and expressly or necessarily decided by such State court. *Crowell* v. *Randell*, 10 Pet. 368, 392; *Railroad Co.* v. *Rock*, 4 Wall, 177, 180; *California Powder Works* v. *Davis*, 151 U.S. 389, 393; *Cincinnati, etc. Railway* v. *Slade*, 216 U.S. 78, 83; *Hiawassee Power Co.* v. *Carolina-Tenn. Co.*, 252 U.S. 341, 343; *New York* v. *Kleinert*, 268 U.S. 646, 650.

Here the record does not show that the defendant raised or that the State courts considered or decided any Federal question whatever, excepting as appears in an order made and entered by the Court of Appeal after it had decided the case and the writ of error had issued and been returned to this Court. A certified copy of that order, brought here as an addition to the record, shows that it was made and

---

[1] Statutes, 1919, c. 58, p. 88.

entered pursuant to a stipulation of the parties, approved by the court, and that it contains the following statement:

"The question whether the California Criminal Syndicalism Act . . . and its application in this case is repugnant to the provisions of the Fourteenth Amendment to the Constitution of the United States, providing that no State shall deprive any person of life, liberty, or property, without due process of law, and that all persons shall be accorded the equal protection of the laws, was considered and passed upon by this Court."

In *Cincinnati Packet Co.* v. *Bay*, 200 U.S. 179, 182, where it appeared that a Federal question had been presented in a petition in error to the State supreme court in a case in which the judgment was affirmed without opinion, it was held that the certificate of that court, to the effect that it had considered and necessarily decided this question, was sufficient to show its existence. And see *Marvin* v. *Trout*, 199 U.S. 212, 217, *et seq.; Consolidated Turnpike* v. *Norfolk, etc. Railway*, 228 U.S. 596, 599.

So—while the unusual course here taken to show that Federal questions were raised and decided below is not to be commended—we shall give effect to the order of the Court of Appeal as would be done if the statement had been made in the opinion of that court when delivered. See *Gross* v. *United States Mortgage Co.*, 108 U.S. 477, 484–486; *Philadelphia Fire Association* v. *New York*, 119 U.S. 110, 116; *Home for Incurables* v. *City of New York*, 187 U.S. 155, 157; *Land & Water Co.* v. *San Jose Ranch Co.*, 189 U.S. 177, 179–180; *Rector* v. *City Deposit Bank*, 200 U.S. 405, 412; *Haire* v. *Rice*, 204 U.S. 291, 299; *Chambers* v. *Baltimore, etc. Railroad*, 207 U.S. 142, 148; *Atchison, etc. Railway* v. *Sowers*, 213 U.S. 55, 62; *Consolidated Turnpike Co.* v. *Norfolk, etc. Railway*, 228 U.S. 596, 599; *Miedreich* v. *Lauenstein*, 232 U.S. 236, 242; *North Carolina Railroad* v. *Zachary*, 232 U.S. 248, 257; *Chicago, etc. Railway* v. *Perry*, 259 U.S. 548, 551.

And here, since it appears from the statement in the order of the Court of Appeal that the question whether the Syndicalism Act and its application in this case was repugnant to the due process and equal protection clauses of the Fourteenth Amendment, was considered and passed upon by that court—this being a Federal question constituting an appropriate ground for a review of the judgment—we conclude that this Court has acquired jurisdiction under the writ of error. The order dismissing the writ for want of jurisdiction will accordingly be set aside.

We proceed to the determination, upon the merits, of the constitutional question considered and passed upon by the Court of Appeal. Of course our review is to be confined to that question, since it does not appear, either from the order of the Court of Appeal or from the record otherwise, that any other Federal question was presented in and either expressly or necessarily decided by that court. *National Bank* v. *Commonwealth*, 9 Wall. 353, 363; *Edwards* v. *Elliott*, 21 Wall. 532, 557; *Dewey* v. *Des Moines*, 173 U.S. 193, 200; *Keokuk & Hamilton Bridge Co.* v. *Illinois*, 175 U.S. 626, 633; *Capital City Dairy Co.* v. *Ohio*, 183 U.S. 238, 248; *Haire* v. *Rice*, 204 U.S. 291, 301; *Selover, Bates & Co.* v. *Walsh*, 226 U.S. 112, 126; *Missouri Pacific Railway* v. *Coal Co.*, 256 U.S. 134, 135. It is not enough that there may be somewhere hidden in the record a question which, if it had been raised, would have been of a Federal nature. *Dewey v. Des Moines, supra,* 199; *Keokuk & Hamilton Bridge Co. v. Illinois, supra,* 634. And this necessarily excludes from our consideration a question sought to be raised for the first time by the assignments of error here—not presented in or passed upon by the Court of Appeal—whether apart from the constitutionality of the Syndicalism Act, the judgment of the Superior Court, by reason of the rulings of that court on questions of pleading, evidence and the like, operated as a denial to the defendant of due process of law. *See Oxley Stave Co. v. Butler County,* 166 U.S. 648, 660; *Capital City Dairy Co. v. Ohio, supra,* 248; *Manhattan Life Ins. Co. v. Cohen,* 234 U.S. 123, 134; *Bass, etc. Ltd. v. Tax Commission,* 266 U.S. 271, 283.

The following facts, among many others, were established on the trial by undisputed evidence: The defendant, a resident of Oakland, in Alameda County, California, had been a member of the Local Oakland branch of the Socialist Party. This Local sent delegates to the national convention of the Socialist Party held in Chicago in 1919, which resulted in a split between the "radical" group and the old-wing Socialists. The "radicals"—to whom the Oakland delegates adhered—being ejected, went to another hall, and formed the Communist Labor Party of America. Its constitution provided for the membership of persons subscribing to the principles of the party and pledging themselves to be guided by its platform, and for the formation of State organizations conforming to its platform as the supreme declaration of the party. In its "Platform and Program" the party declared that it was in full harmony with "the revolutionary working class parties of all countries" and adhered to the principles of communism laid down in the manifesto of the Third International at Moscow, and that its purpose was "to create a unified revolutionary working class movement in America," organizing the workers as a class in a revolutionary class struggle to conquer the capitalist state, for the overthrow of capitalist rule, the conquest of political power and the establishment of a working class government, the dictatorship of the proletariat, in place of the State machinery of the capitalists, which should make and enforce the laws, reorganize society on the basis of communism and bring about the Communist Commonwealth—advocated, as the most important means of capturing State power, the action of the masses, proceeding from the shops and factories, the use of the political machinery of the capitalist state being only secondary; the organization of the workers into "revolutionary industrial unions"; propaganda pointing out their revolutionary nature and possibilities; and great industrial battles showing the value of the strike as a political weapon—commended the propaganda and example of the Industrial Workers of the World and their struggles and sacrifices in the class war—pledged support and cooperation to "the revolutionary industrial proletariat of America" in their struggles against the capitalist class—cited the Seattle and Winnipeg strikes and the numerous strikes all over the country "proceeding without the authority of the old reactionary Trade Union officials," as manifestations of the new tendency—and recommended that strikes of national importance be supported and given a political character, and that propagandists and organizers be mobilized "who can not only teach, but actually help to put in practice the principles of revolutionary industrial unionism and communism."

Shortly thereafter the local Oakland withdrew from the Socialist Party, and sent accredited delegates, including the defendant, to a convention held in Oakland in November, 1919, for the purpose of organizing a California branch of the Communist Labor Party. The defendant, after taking out a temporary membership in the Communist Labor Party, attended this convention as a delegate and took an active part in its proceedings. She was elected a member of the Credentials Committee, and, as its chairman, made a report to the convention upon which the delegates were seated. She was also appointed a member of the Resolutions Committee, and as such signed the following resolution in reference to political action, among others proposed by the committee: "The C.L.P. of California fully recognizes the value of political action as a means of spreading Communist propaganda; it insists that in proportion to the development of the economic strength of the working class, it, the working class, must also develop its political power. The C.L.P. of California proclaims and insists that the capture of political power, locally or nationally by the revolutionary working class can be of tremendous assistance to the workers in their struggle of emancipation. Therefore, we again urge the workers who are possessed of the right of franchise to cast their votes for the party which represents their immediate and final interest—the C.L.P.—at all elections, being fully convinced of the utter futility of obtaining any real measure of justice or freedom under officials elected by parties owned and controlled by the capitalist class." The minutes show that this resolution, with the others proposed by the committee, was read by its chairman to the convention before the Committee on the Constitution had submitted its report. According to the recollection of the defendant, however, she herself read this resolution. Thereafter, before the report of the Committee on the Constitution had been acted upon, the defendant was elected an alternate member of the State Executive Committee. The constitution, as finally read, was then adopted. This provided that the organization should be named the Communist Labor Party of California; that it should be "affiliated with" the Communist Labor Party of America, and subscribe to its program, platform and constitution, and "through this affiliation" be "joined with the Communist International of Moscow;" and that the qualifications for membership should be those prescribed in the national constitution. The proposed resolutions were later taken up and all adopted, except that on political action, which caused a lengthy debate, resulting in its defeat and the acceptance of the national program in its place. After this action, the defendant, without, so far as appears, making any protest, remained in the convention until it adjourned. She later attended as an alternate member one or two meetings of the State Executive Committee in San Jose and San Francisco, and stated, on the trial, that she was then a member of the Communist Labor Party. She also testified that it was not her intention that the Communist Labor Party of California should be an instrument of terrorism or violence, and that it was not her purpose or that of the convention to violate any known law.

In the light of this preliminary statement, we now take up, in so far as they require specific consideration, the various grounds upon which it is here contended that the Syndicalism Act and its application in this case is repugnant to the due process and equal protection clauses of the Fourteenth Amendment.

1. While it is not denied that the evidence warranted the jury in finding that the defendant became a member of and assisted in organizing the Communist Labor Party of California, and that this was organized to advocate, teach, aid or abet criminal syndicalism as defined by the Act, it is urged that the Act, as here construed and applied, deprived the defendant of her liberty without due process of law in that it has made her action in attending the Oakland convention unlawful by reason of "a subsequent event brought about against her will, by the agency of others," with no showing of a specific intent on her part to join in the forbidden purpose of the association, and merely because, by reason of a lack of "prophetic" understanding she failed to foresee the quality that others would give to the convention. The argument is, in effect, that the character of the State organization could not be forecast when she attended the convention; that she had no purpose of helping to create an instrument of terrorism and violence; that she "took part in formulating and presenting to the convention a resolution which, if adopted, would have committed the new organization to a legitimate policy of political reform by the use of the ballot"; that it was not until after the majority of the convention turned out to be "contrary-minded, and other less temperate policies prevailed" that the convention could have taken on the character of criminal syndicalism; and that as this was done over her protest, her mere presence in the convention, however violent the opinions expressed therein, could not thereby become a crime. This contention, while advanced in the form of a constitutional objection to the Act, is in effect nothing more than an effort to review the weight of the evidence for the purpose of showing that the defendant did not join and assist in organizing the Communist Labor Party of California with a knowledge of its unlawful character and purpose. This question, which is foreclosed by the verdict of the jury—sustained by the Court of Appeal over the specific objection that it was not supported by the evidence—is one of fact merely which is not open to review in this Court, involving as it does no constitutional question whatever. And we may add that the argument entirely disregards the facts: that the defendant had previously taken out a membership card in the national party, that the resolution which she supported did not advocate the use of the ballot to the exclusion of violent and unlawful means of bringing about the desired changes in industrial and political conditions; and that, after the constitution of the California party had been adopted, and this resolution had been voted down and the national program accepted, she not only remained in the convention, without protest, until its close, but subsequently manifested her acquiescence by attending as an alternate member of the State Executive Committee and continuing as a member of the Communist Labor Party.

2. It is clear that the Syndicalism Act is not repugnant to the due process clause by reason of vagueness and uncertainty of definition. It has no substantial resemblance to the statutes held void for uncertainty under the Fourteenth and Fifth Amendments in *International Harvester Co.* v. *Kentucky*, 234 U.S. 216, 221; and *United States* v. *Cohen Grocery*, 255 U.S. 81, 89, because not fixing an ascer-

tainable standard of guilt. The language of § 2, subd. 4, of the Act, under which the plaintiff in error was convicted, is clear; the definition of "criminal syndicalism" specific.

The Act, plainly, meets the essential requirement of due process that a penal statute be "sufficiently explicit to inform those who are subject to it, what conduct on their part will render them liable to its penalties," and be couched in terms that are not "so vague that men of common intelligence must necessarily guess at its meaning and differ as to its application." *Connally* v. *General Construction Co.*, 269 U.S. 385, 391. And see *United States* v. *Brewer*, 139 U.S. 278, 288; *Chicago, etc., Railway* v. *Dey* (C.C.) 35 Fed. 866, 876; *Tozer* v. *United States* (C.C.) 52 Fed. 917, 919. In *Omaechevarria* v. *Idaho*, 246 U.S. 343, 348, in which it was held that a criminal statute prohibiting the grazing of sheep on any "range" previously occupied by cattle "in the usual and customary use" thereof, was not void for indefiniteness because it failed to provide for the ascertainment of the boundaries of a "range" or to determine the length of time necessary to constitute a prior occupation a "usual" one, this Court said: "Men familiar with range conditions and desirous of observing the law will have little difficulty in determining what is prohibited by it. Similar expressions are common in the criminal statutes of other States. The statute presents no greater uncertainty or difficulty, in application to necessarily varying facts, than has been repeatedly sanctioned by this court. *Nash* v. *United States*, 229 U.S. 373, 377; *Miller* v. *Strahl*, 239 U.S. 426, 434." So, as applied here, the Syndicalism Act required of the defendant no "prophetic" understanding of its meaning.

And similar Criminal Syndicalism statutes of other States, some less specific in their definitions, have been held by the State courts not to be void for indefiniteness. *State* v. *Hennessy*, 114 Wash. 351, 364; *State* v. *Laundy*, 103 Ore. 443, 460; *People* v. *Ruthenberg*, 229 Mich. 315, 325. And see *Fox* v. *Washington*, 236 U.S. 273, 277; *People* v. *Steelik*, 187 Cal. 361, 372; *People* v. *Lloyd*, 304 Ill. 23, 34.

3. Neither is the Syndicalism Act repugnant to the equal protection clause, on the ground that, as its penalties are confined to those who advocate a resort to violent and unlawful methods as a means of changing industrial and political conditions, it arbitrarily discriminates between such persons and those who may advocate a resort to these methods as a means of maintaining such conditions.

It is settled by repeated decisions of this Court that the equal protection clause does not take from a State the power to classify in the adoption of police laws, but admits the exercise of a wide scope of discretion, and avoids what is done only when it is without any reasonable basis and therefore is purely arbitrary; and that one who assails the classification must carry the burden of showing that it does not rest upon any reasonable basis, but is essentially arbitrary. *Lindsley* v. *National Carbonic Gas Co.*, 220 U.S. 61, 78, and cases cited.

A statute does not violate the equal protection clause merely because it is not all-embracing. *Zucht* v. *King*, 260 U.S. 174, 177; *James-Dickinson Farm Mortgage Co.* v. *Harry*, 273 U.S. 119. A State may properly direct its legislation against what it deems an existing evil without covering the whole field of possible abuses. *Patsone* v.

Pennsylvania, 232 U.S. 138, 144; *Farmers Bank* v. *Federal Reserve Bank*, 262 U.S. 649, 661; *James-Dickinson Mortgage Co.* v. *Harry, supra.* The statute must be presumed to be aimed at an evil where experience shows it to be most felt, and to be deemed by the legislature coextensive with the practical need; and is not to be overthrown merely because other instances may be suggested to which also it might have been applied; that being a matter for the legislature to determine unless the case is very clear. *Keokee Coke Co.* v. *Taylor*, 234 U.S. 224, 227. And it is not open to objection unless the classification is so lacking in any adequate or reasonable basis as to preclude the assumption that it was made in the exercise of the legislative judgment and discretion. *Stebbins* v. *Riley*, 268 U.S. 137, 143; *Graves* v. *Minnesota*, 272 U.S. 425; *Swiss Oil Corporation* v. *Shanks*, 273 U.S. 407.

The Syndicalism Act is not class legislation; it affects all alike, no matter what their business associations or callings, who come within its terms and do the things prohibited. See *State v. Hennessy, supra,* 361; *State* v. *Laundy, supra,* 460. And there is no substantial basis for the contention that the legislature has arbitrarily or unreasonably limited its application to those advocating the use of violent and unlawful methods to effect changes in industrial and political conditions; there being nothing indicating any ground to apprehend that those desiring to maintain existing industrial and political conditions did or would advocate such methods. That there is a widespread conviction of the necessity for legislation of this character is indicated by the adoption of similar statutes in several other States.

4. Nor is the Syndicalism Act as applied in this case repugnant to the due process clause as a restraint of the rights of free speech, assembly, and association.

That the freedom of speech which is secured by the Constitution does not confer an absolute right to speak, without responsibility, whatever one may choose, or an unrestricted and unbridled license giving immunity for every possible use of language and preventing the punishment of those who abuse this freedom; and that a State in the exercise of its police power may punish those who abuse this freedom by utterances inimical to the public welfare, tending to incite to crime, disturb the public peace, or endanger the foundations of organized government and threaten its overthrow by unlawful means, is not open to question. *Gitlow* v. *New York*, 268 U.S. 652, 666–668, and cases cited.

By enacting the provisions of the Syndicalism Act the State has declared, through its legislative body, that to knowingly be or become a member of or assist in organizing an association to advocate, teach or aid and abet the commission of crimes or unlawful acts of force, violence or terrorism as a means of accomplishing industrial or political changes; involves such danger to the public peace and the security of the State, that these acts should be penalized in the exercise of its police power. That determination must be given great weight. Every presumption is to be indulged in favor of the validity of the statute, *Mugler* v. *Kansas*, 123 U.S. 623, 661; and it may not be declared unconstitutional unless it is an arbitrary or unreasonable attempt to exercise the authority vested in the State in the public interest. *Great Northern Railway* v. *Clara City*, 246 U.S. 434, 439.

The essence of the offense denounced by the Act is the combining with others in an association for the accomplishment of the desired ends through the advocacy and use of criminal and unlawful methods. It partakes of the nature of a criminal conspiracy. See *People* v. *Steelik, supra,* 376. That such united and joint action involves even greater danger to the public peace and security than the isolated utterances and acts of individuals, is clear. We cannot hold that, as here applied, the Act is an unreasonable or arbitrary exercise of the police power of the State, unwarrantably infringing any right of free speech, assembly or association, or that those persons are protected from punishment by the due process clause who abuse such rights by joining and furthering an organization thus menacing the peace and welfare of the State.

We find no repugnancy in the Syndicalism Act as applied in this case to either the due process or equal protection clauses of the Fourteenth Amendment on any of the grounds upon which its validity has been here challenged.

The order dismissing the writ of error will be vacated and set aside, and the judgment of the Court of Appeal

Affirmed.

MR. JUSTICE BRANDEIS, concurring.

Miss Whitney was convicted of the felony of assisting in organizing, in the year 1919, the Communist Labor Party of California, of being a member of it, and of assembling with it. These acts are held to constitute a crime, because the party was formed to teach criminal syndicalism. The statute which made these acts a crime restricted the right of free speech and of assembly theretofore existing. The claim is that the statute, as applied, denied to Miss Whitney the liberty guaranteed by the Fourteenth Amendment.

The felony which the statute created is a crime very unlike the old felony of conspiracy or the old misdemeanor of unlawful assembly. The mere act of assisting in forming a society for teaching syndicalism, of becoming a member of it, or of assembling with others for that purpose is given the dynamic quality of crime. There is guilt although the society may not contemplate immediate promulgation of the doctrine. Thus the accused is to be punished, not for contempt, incitement or conspiracy, but for a step in preparation, which, if it threatens the public order at all, does so only remotely. The novelty in the prohibition introduced is that the statute aims, not at the practice of criminal syndicalism, nor even directly at the preaching of it, but at association with those who propose to preach it.

Despite arguments to the contrary which had seemed to me persuasive, it is settled that the due process clause of the Fourteenth Amendment applies to matters of substantive law as well as to matters of procedure. Thus all fundamental rights comprised within the term liberty are protected by the Federal Constitution from invasion by the States. The right of free speech, the right to teach and the right of assembly are, of course, fundamental rights. See *Meyer* v. *Nebraska,* 262 U.S. 390; *Pierce* v. *Society of Sisters,* 268 U.S. 510; *Gitlow* v. *New York,* 268 U.S. 652, 666; *Farrington* v. *Tokushige,* 273 U.S. 284. These may not be denied or abridged. But, although the rights of free speech and assembly are fundamental, they are not in their nature absolute. Their exercise is subject to restriction, if the particular restriction proposed is required in order to protect the State from destruction or from serious injury, political, economic or moral. That the necessity which is essential to a valid restriction does not exist unless speech would produce, or is intended to produce, a clear and imminent danger of some substantive evil which the State constitutionally may seek to prevent has been settled. See *Schenck* v. *United States*, 249 U.S. 47, 52.

It is said to be the function of the legislature to determine whether at a particular time and under the particular circumstances the formation of, or assembly with, a society organized to advocate criminal syndicalism constitutes a clear and present danger of substantive evil; and that by enacting the law here in question the legislature of California determined that question in the affirmative. Compare *Gitlow* v. *New York*, 268 U.S. 652, 668–671. The legislature must obviously decide, in the first instance, whether a danger exists which calls for a particular protective measure. But where a statute is valid only in case certain conditions exist, the enactment of the statute cannot alone establish the facts which are essential to its validity. Prohibitory legislation has repeatedly been held invalid, because unnecessary, where the denial of liberty involved was that of engaging in a particular business.[1] The power of the courts to strike down an offending law is no less when the interests involved are not property rights, but the fundamental personal rights of free speech and assembly.

This Court has not yet fixed the standard by which to determine when a danger shall be deemed clear; how remote the danger may be and yet be deemed present; and what degree of evil shall be deemed sufficiently substantial to justify resort to abridgement of free speech and assembly as the means of protection. To reach sound conclusions on these matters, we must bear in mind why a State is, ordinarily, denied the power to prohibit dissemination of social, economic and political doctrine which a vast majority of its citizens believes to be false and fraught with evil consequence.

Those who won our independence believed that the final end of the State was to make men free to develop their faculties; and that in its government the deliberative forces should prevail over the arbitrary. They valued liberty both as an end and as a means. They believed liberty to be the secret of happiness and courage to be the secret of liberty. They believed that freedom to think as you will and to speak as you think are means indispensable to the discovery and spread of political truth; that without free speech and assembly discussion would be futile; that with them, discussion affords ordinarily adequate protection against the dissemination of noxious doctrine; that the greatest menace to freedom is an inert people; that public discussion is a political duty; and that this should be a fundamental principle of the American government.[2] They recognized the risks to which all human institutions are subject. But they knew that order cannot be secured merely through fear of punishment for its infraction; that

---

[1] Compare *Frost* v. *R.R. Comm. of California*, 271 U.S. 583 ; *Weaver* v. *Palmer Bros. Co.*, 270 U.S. 402 ; *Jay Burns Baking Co.* v. *Bryan*, 264 U.S. 504 ; *Pennsylvania Coal Co.* v. *Mahon*, 260 U.S. 393 ; *Adams* v. *Tanner*, 244 U.S. 590.

[2] Compare Thomas Jefferson : "We have nothing to fear from the demoralizing reasonings of some, if others are left free to demonstrate their errors and especially when the law stands ready to punish the first criminal act produced by the false reasonings ; these are safer corrections than the conscience of the judge." Quoted by Charles A. Beard, The Nation, July 7, 1926, vol. 123, p. 8. Also in first Inaugural Address : "If there be any amoung us who would wish to dissolve this union or change its republican form, let them stand undisturbed as monuments of the safety with which error of opinion may be tolerated where reason is left free to combat it."

it is hazardous to discourage thought, hope and imagination; that fear breeds repression; that repression breeds hate; that hate menaces stable government; that the path of safety lies in the opportunity to discuss freely supposed grievances and proposed remedies; and that the fitting remedy for evil counsels is good ones. Believing in the power of reason as applied through public discussion, they eschewed silence coerced by law—the argument of force in its worst form. Recognizing the occasional tyrannies of governing majorities, they amended the Constitution so that free speech and assembly should be guaranteed.

Fear of serious injury cannot alone justify suppression of free speech and assembly. Men feared witches and burnt women. It is the function of speech to free men from the bondage of irrational fears. To justify suppression of free speech there must be reasonable ground to fear that serious evil will result if free speech is practiced. There must be reasonable ground to believe that the danger apprehended is imminent. There must be reasonable ground to believe that the evil to be prevented is a serious one. Every denunciation of existing law tends in some measure to increase the probability that there will be violation of it.[3] Condonation of a breach enhances the probability. Expressions of approval add to the probability. Propagation of the criminal state of mind by teaching syndicalism increases it. Advocacy of law-breaking heightens it still further. But even advocacy of violation, however reprehensible morally, is not a justification for denying free speech where the advocacy falls short of incitement and there is nothing to indicate that the advocacy would be immediately acted on. The wide difference between advocacy and incitement, between preparation and attempt, between assembling and conspiracy, must be borne in mind. In order to support a finding of clear and present danger it must be shown either that immediate serious violence was to be expected or was advocated, or that the past conduct furnished reason to believe that such advocacy was then contemplated.

Those who won our independence by revolution were not cowards. They did not fear political change. They did not exalt order at the cost of liberty. To courageous, self-reliant men, with confidence in the power of free and fearless reasoning applied through the processes of popular government, no danger flowing from speech can be deemed clear and present, unless the incidence of the evil apprehended is so imminent that it may befall before there is opportunity for full discussion. If there be time to expose through discussion the falsehood and fallacies, to avert the evil by the processes of education, the remedy to be applied is more speech, not enforced silence. Only an emergency can justify repression. Such must be the rule if authority is to be reconciled with freedom.[4] Such, in my opinion, is the command of the Constitution. It is therefore always open to Americans to challenge a law abridging free speech and assembly by showing that there was no emergency justifying it.

---

[3] Compare Judge Learned Hand in *Masses Publishing Co.* v. *Patten,* 244 Fed. 535. 540; Judge Amidon in *United States* v. *Fontana,* Bull. Dept. of Justice No. 148, pp. 4–5; Chafee, "Freedom of Speech," pp. 46–56, 174.

[4] Compare Z. Chafee, Jr., "Freedom of Speech", pp. 24–39, 207–221, 228, 262–265; H. J. Laski, "Grammar of Politics", pp. 120, 121; Lord Justice Scrutton in *Rex* v. *Secretary of Home Affairs, Ex parte O'Brien,* [1923] 2 K.B. 361, 382: "You really believe in freedom of speech, if you are willing to allow it to men whose opinions seem to you wrong and even dangerous; . . ." Compare Warren, "The New Liberty Under the Fourteenth Amendment," 39 Harvard Law Review, 431, 461.

Moreover, even imminent danger cannot justify resort to prohibition of these functions essential to effective democracy, unless the evil apprehended is relatively serious. Prohibition of free speech and assembly is a measure so stringent that it would be inappropriate as the means for averting a relatively trivial harm to society. A police measure may be unconstitutional merely because the remedy, although effective as means of protection, is unduly harsh or oppressive. Thus, a State might, in the exercise of its police power, make any trespass upon the land of another a crime, regardless of the results or of the intent or purpose of the trespasser. It might, also, punish an attempt, a conspiracy, or an incitement to commit the trespass. But it is hardly conceivable that this Court would hold constitutional a statute which punished as a felony the mere voluntary assembly with a society formed to teach that pedestrians had the moral right to cross unenclosed, unposted, waste lands and to advocate their doing so, even if there was imminent danger that advocacy would lead to a trespass. The fact that speech is likely to result in some violence or in destruction of property is not enough to justify its suppression. There must be the probability of serious injury to the State. Among free men, the deterrents ordinarily to be applied to prevent crime are education and punishment for violations of the law, not abridgment of the rights of free speech and assembly.

The California Syndicalism Act recites in § 4:

"Inasmuch as this act concerns and is necessary to the immediate preservation of the public peace and safety, for the reason that at the present time large numbers of persons are going from place to place in this State advocating, teaching and practicing criminal syndicalism, this act shall take effect upon approval by the Governor."

This legislative declaration satisfies the requirement of the constitution of the State concerning emergency legislation. *In re McDermott*, 180 Cal. 783. But it does not preclude enquiry into the question whether, at the time and under the circumstances, the conditions existed which are essential to validity under the Federal Constitution. As a statute, even if not void on its face, may be challenged because invalid as applied, *Dahnke-Walker Milling Co.* v. *Bondurant*, 257 U.S. 282, the result of such an enquiry may depend upon the specific facts of the particular case. Whenever the fundamenal rights of free speech and assembly are alleged to have been invaded, it must remain open to a defendant to present the issue whether there actually did exist at the time a clear danger; whether the danger, if any, was imminent; and whether the evil apprehended was one so substantial as to justify the stringent restriction interposed by the legislature. The legislative declaration, like the fact that the statute was passed and was sustained by the highest court of the State, creates merely a rebuttable presumption that these conditions have been satisfied.

Whether in 1919, when Miss Whitney did the things complained of, there was in California such clear and present danger of serious evil, might have been made the important issue in the case. She might have required that the issue be determined either by the court or the jury. She claimed below that the statute as applied to her violated the Federal Constitution; but she did not claim that it was void because there was no clear and present danger of serious evil, nor

did she request that the existence of these conditions of a valid measure
thus restricting the rights of free speech and assembly be passed upon
by the court or a jury. On the other hand, there was evidence on
which the court or jury might have found that such danger existed.
I am unable to assent to the suggestion in the opinion of the Court
that assembling with a political party, formed to advocate the desirability of a proletarian revolution by mass action at some date
necessarily far in the future, is not a right within the protection of
the Fourteenth Amendment. In the present case, however, there
was other testimony which tended to establish the existence of a
conspiracy, on the part of members of the International Workers of
the World, to commit present serious crimes; and likewise to show that
such a conspiracy would be furthered by the activity of the society
of which Miss Whitney was a member. Under these circumstances
the judgment of the State court cannot be disturbed.

Our power of review in this case is limited not only to the question
whether a right guaranteed by the Federal Constitution was denied,
Murdock v. *City of Memphis*, 20 Wall. 590; *Haire* v. *Rice*, 204 U.S.
291, 301; but to the particular claims duly made below, and denied.
Seaboard Air Line Ry. v. *Duvall*, 225 U.S. 477, 485–488. We lack
here the power occasionally exercised on review of judgments of
lower Federal courts to correct in criminal cases vital errors, although
the objection was not taken in the trial court. *Wiborg* v. *United
States*, 163 U.S. 632, 658–660; *Clyatt* v. *United States*, 197 U.S. 207,
221–222. This is a writ of error to a State court. Because we may
not enquire into the errors now alleged, I concur in affirming the
judgment of the State court.

Mr. Justice Holmes joins in this opinion.

DE JONGE *v.* OREGON.

APPEAL FROM THE SUPREME COURT OF OREGON.

No. 123. Argued December 9, 1936.—Decided January 4, 1937.

1. The practice of substituting for the evidence a stipulation of facts not shown
   to have received the approval of the court below, is disapproved. P. 358.
2. Upon appeal from a judgment of a State supreme court sustaining a conviction,
   this Court in this case takes the indictment as construed by the court below.
   P. 360.
3. Criminal punishment under a State statute for participation in the conduct of a
   public meeting, otherwise lawful, merely because the meeting was held
   under the auspices of an organization which teaches or advocates the use
   of violence, or other unlawful acts or methods to effect industrial or political
   change or revolution, though no such teaching or advocacy attended the
   meeting in question, violates the constitutional principles of free speech and
   assembly. P. 362.
   The Criminal Syndicalism Law of Oregon, as applied in this case, is invalid.
4. The rights of free speech and peaceable assembly are fundamental rights
   which are safeguarded against State interference by the due process clause
   of the Fourteenth Amendment. P. 364.
5. The fact that these rights are guaranteed specifically by the First Amendment
   against abridgement by Congress, does not argue their exclusion from the
   due process clause of the Fourteenth Amendment. *Id.*
6. The legislature may protect against abuses of the rights of free speech and
   assembly by dealing with the abuses; the rights themselves must not be
   curtailed. *Id.*

152 Ore. 315; 51 P. (2d) 674, reversed.

APPEAL from the affirmance of a conviction under the Criminal Syndicalism Law of Oregon.

Mr. Osmond K. Fraenkel, with whom *Mr. Gus J. Solomon* was on the brief, for appellant.

Mr. Maurice E. Tarshis, Deputy District Attorney, Multnomah County, with whom *Mr. James R. Bain,* District Attorney, and *Mr. Willis S. Moore,* Assistant Attorney General of Oregon, were on the brief, for appellee.

The Act as applied to this case is definite and certain and is constitutional. *Whitney* v. *California,* 274 U.S. 357, 368; *Connally* v. *General Construction* Co., 269 U.S. 385, 391; *Miller* v. *Strahl,* 239 U.S. 426, 434; *Nash* v. *United States,* 229 U.S. 373, 377; *Waters-Pierce Oil Co.* v. *Texas,* 212 U.S. 86, 108; *State* v. *Hennessy,* 114 Wash. 351; *State* v. *Laundy,* 103 Ore. 443, 463; *People* v. *Ruthenberg,* 229 Mich. 315; *People* v. *Steelik,* 187 Cal. 361, 373; *People* v. *Lloyd,* 304 Ill. 23, 35; *State* v. *Dingman,* 37 Idaho 253, 265; *Berg* v. *State,* 29 Okla. Cr. Rep. 112, 121; *State* v. *Worker's Socialist Publishing Co.,* 150 Min. 406, 407.

The statute explicitly informs every person subject to the jurisdiction of the courts of Oregon that he commits the crime of criminal syndicalism if he presides at, conducts, or assists in conducting a meeting of an organization or group which teaches or advocates criminal syndicalism or sabotage.

The statute does not prohibit peaceful and orderly opposition to government, but only such conduct as may tend to incite to crime, disturb the public peace, or endanger the foundation of organized government and threaten its overthrow by unlawful means.

The right of free speech and assembly is not absolute. A State, in the exercise of its police power, may punish those who abuse this freedom by utterances of the kind aimed at by this statute.

The case is ruled by *Gitlow* v. *New York,* 268 U.S. 652; and *Whitney* v. *California,* 274 U.S. 357.

See *Herndon* v. *Georgia,* 295 U.S. 441; *Carr* v. *Georgia,* 176 Ga. 747.

The State has determined, through its legislative body, that to preside at, conduct, or assist in conducting a meeting of an organization which has as its objective the advocacy, teaching or affirmative suggestion of crime, sabotage or violence as a means of affecting a change or revolution in industry or government, involves such dangers to the public peace and the security of the State, that these acts should be penalized in the exercise of its police power. That determination must be given great weight. Every presumption is to be indulged in favor of validity. *Whitney* v. *California, supra; Mugler* v. *Kansas,* 123 U.S. 623, 661. To be unconstitutional, the Act must be arbitrary or unreasonable. *Whitney* v. *California, supra; Great Northern Ry. Co.* v. *Clara City,* 246 U.S. 434, 439. Its wisdom is not for the courts. *Fox* v. *Washington,* 236 U.S. 273, 278; *State* v. *Boloff,* 138 Ore. 568, 611.

The sole purpose of the Act is to prevent the advocacy or use of violence by forbidding anyone to preside at, conduct or assist in conducting a meeting of an organization which teaches it. Laws of this type are founded upon the principle that morons, especially those who are class conscious, and who believe that men in high places got there through imposition upon the toilers, are likely to translate into action the words of their voluble leaders. The will of the schemer is often carried out by the acts of the unthinking. *State* v. *Boloff, supra,* p. 622.

MR. CHIEF JUSTICE HUGHES delivered the opinion of the Court.

Appellant, Dirk De Jonge, was indicted in Multnomah County, Oregon, for violation of the Criminal Syndicalism Law of that State.[1] The Act, which we set forth in the margin, defines "criminal syndicalism" as "the doctrine which advocates crime, physical violence, sabotage or any unlawful acts or methods as a means of accomplishing or effecting industrial or political change or revolution." With this preliminary definition the Act proceeds to describe a number of offenses, embracing the teaching of criminal syndicalism, the printing or distribution of books, pamphlets, etc., advocating that doctrine, the organization of a society or assemblage which advocates it, and presiding at or assisting in conducting a meeting of such an organization, society or group. The prohibited acts are made felonies, punishable by imprisonment for not less than one year nor more than ten years, or by a fine of not more than $1,000, or by both.

We are concerned with but one of the described offenses and with the validity of the statute in this particular application. The charge is that appellant assisted in the conduct of a meeting which was called under the auspices of the Communist Party, an organization advocating criminal syndicalism. The defense was that the meeting was public and orderly and was held for a lawful purpose; that while it was held under the auspices of the Communist Party, neither criminal syndicalism nor any unlawful conduct was taught or advocated at the meeting either by appellant or by others. Appellant moved for a direction of acquittal, contending that the statute as applied to him, for merely assisting at a meeting called by the Communist Party at which nothing unlawful was done or advocated, violated the due process clause of the Fourteenth Amendment of the Constitution of the United States.

This contention was overruled. Appellant was found guilty as charged and was sentenced to imprisonment for seven years. The judgment was affirmed by the supreme court of the State, which considered the constitutional question and sustained the statute as thus applied. 152 Ore. 315; 51 P. (2d) 674. The case comes here on appeal.

The record does not present the evidence adduced at the trial. The parties have substituted a stipulation of facts, which was made and

---

[1] Oregon Code, 1930, § § 14–3110–3112—as amended by chapter 459, Oregon Laws, 1933:
"Section 14–3110. Criminal syndicalism hereby is defined to be the doctrine which advocates crime, physical violence, sabotage, or any unlawful acts or methods as a means of accomplishing or effecting industrial or political change or revolution.
"Section 14–3111. Sabotage hereby is defined to be intentional and unlawful damage, injury or destruction of real or personal property.
"Section 14–3112. Any person who, by word of mouth or writing, advocates or teaches the doctrine of criminal syndicalism, or sabotage, or who prints, publishes, edits, issues or knowingly circulates, sells, distributes or publicly displays any books, pamphlets, paper, hand-bill, poster, document or written or printed matter in any form whatsoever, containing matter advocating criminal syndicalism, or sabotage, or who shall organize or help to organize, or solicit or accept any person to become a member of any society or assemblage of persons which teaches or advocates the doctrine of criminal syndicalism, or sabotage, or any person who shall orally or by writing or by printed matter call together or who shall distribute or circulate written or printed matter calling together or who shall preside at or conduct or assist in conducting any assemblage of persons, or any organization, or any society, or any group which teaches or advocates the doctrine of criminal syndicalism or sabotage is guilty of a felony and, upon conviction thereof, shall be punished by imprisonment in the State penitentiary for a term of not less than one year nor more than ten years, or by a fine of not more than $1,000, or by both such imprisonment and fine."

filed after the decision of the supreme court of the State and after the Chief Justice of that court had allowed the appeal and had directed transmission here of a certified transcript of the record. We do not approve of that practice, where it does not appear that the stipulation has received the approval of the court, as we think that adherence to our rule as to the preparation of records is important for the protection of the court whose decision is under review as well as of this Court. See Rule 10. But as the question presented in this instance does not turn upon an appreciation of the facts on any disputed point, we turn to the merits.

The stipulation, after setting forth the charging part of the indictment, recites in substance the following: That on July 27, 1934, there was held in Portland, a meeting which had been advertised by handbills issued by the Portland section of the Communist Party; that the number of persons in attendance was variously estimated at from 150 to 300; that some of those present, who were members of the Communist Party, estimated that not to exceed ten to fifteen per cent of those in attendance were such members; that the meeting was open to the public without charge and no questions were asked of those entering, with respect to their relation to the Communist Party; that the notice of the meeting advertised it as a protest against illegal raids on workers' halls and homes and against the shooting of striking longshoremen by Portland police; that the chairman stated that it was a meeting held by the Communist Party; that the first speaker dwelt on the activities of the Young Communist League; that the defendant De Jonge, the second speaker, was a member of the Communist Party and went to the meeting to speak in its name; that in his talk he protested against conditions in the county jail, the action of city police in relation to the maritime strike then in progress in Portland and numerous other matters; that he discussed the reason for the raids on the Communist headquarters and workers' halls and offices; that he told the workers that these attacks were due to efforts on the part of the steamship companies and stevedoring companies to break the maritime longshoremen's and seamen's strike; that they hoped to break the strike by pitting the longshoremen and seamen against the Communist movement; that there was also testimony to the effect that defendant asked those present to do more work in obtaining members for the Communist Party and requested all to be at the meeting of the party to be held in Portland on the following evening and to bring their friends to show their defiance to local police authority and to assist them in their revolutionary tactics; that there was also testimony that defendant urged the purchase of certain Communist literature which was sold at the meeting; that while the meeting was still in progress it was raided by the police; that the meeting was conducted in an orderly manner; that defendant and several others who were actively conducting the meeting were arrested by the police and that on searching the hall the police found a quantity of Communist literature.

The stipulation then set forth various extracts from the literature of the Communist Party to show its advocacy of criminal syndicalism. The stipulation does not disclose any activity by the defendant as a basis for his prosecution other than his participation in the meeting in question. Nor does the stipulation show that the Communist literature distributed at the meeting contained any advocacy of criminal syndicalism or of any unlawful conduct. It was admitted by the attorney general of the State in his argument at the bar of this Court that the literature distributed in the meeting was not of that sort and that the extracts contained in the stipulation were taken from Communist literature found elsewhere. Its introduction in evidence was for the purpose of showing that the Communist Party as such did advocate the doctrine of criminal syndicalism, a fact which is not disputed on this appeal.

While the stipulation of facts is but a condensed statement, still much of it is irrelevant in the light of the particular charge of the indictment as construed by the Supreme Court. The indictment charged as follows:

"The said Dirk De Jonge, Don Cluster, Edward R. Denny and Earl Stewart on the 27th day of July, A. D., 1934, in the county of Multnomah and State of Oregon, then and there being, did then and there unlawfully and feloniously preside at, conduct and assist in conducting an assemblage of persons, organization, society and group, to-wit: The Communist Party, a more particular description of which said assemblage of persons, organization, society and group is to this grand jury unknown, which said assemblage of persons, organization, society and group did then and there unlawfully and feloniously teach and advocate the doctrine of criminal syndicalism and sabotage, contrary to the statutes in such cases made and provided, and against the peace and dignity of the State of Oregon."

On the theory that this was a charge that criminal syndicalism and sabotage were advocated at the meeting in question, defendant moved for acquittal insisting that the evidence was insufficient to warrant his conviction. The trial court denied his motion and error in this respect was assigned on appeal. The supreme court of the State put aside that contention by ruling that the indictment did not charge that criminal syndicalism or sabotage was advocated at the meeting described in the evidence, either by defendant or by anyone else. The words of the indictment that "said assemblage of persons, organization, society and group did then and there unlawfully and feloniously teach and advocate the doctrine of criminal syndicalism and sabotage," referred not to the meeting in question, or to anything then and there said or done by defendant or others, but to the advocacy of criminal syndicalism and sabotage by the Communist Party in Multnomah County. The ruling of the State court upon this point was precise. The court said (152 Ore. p. 330):

"Turning now to the grounds for a directed verdict set forth in defendant's motion therefor, we note that he asserts and argues that the indictment charges the assemblage at which he spoke with unlawfully and feloniously teaching and advocating the doctrine of criminal syndicalism and sabotage, and elsewhere in the same motion he contends that the indictment charges the defendant with unlawfully and feloniously teaching and advocating said doctrine at said meeting. The indictment does not, however, charge the defendant, nor the assemblage at which he spoke, with teaching or advocating at said meeting at 68 Southwest Alder Street, in the city of Portland, the doctrine of criminal syndicalism or sabotage. What the indictment does charge, in plain and concise language, is that the defendant presided at, conducted and assisted in conducting an assemblage of persons, organizations, society and group, to wit, the Communist Party, which said assemblage of persons, organization, society and group was unlawfully teaching and advocating in Multnomah County the doctrine of criminal syndicalism and sabotage."

In this view, lack of sufficient evidence as to illegal advocacy or action at the meeting became immaterial. Having limited the charge to defendant's participation in a meeting called by the Communist Party, the State court sustained the conviction upon that basis regardless of what was said or done at the meeting.

We must take the indictment as thus construed. Conviction upon a charge not made would be sheer denial of due process. It thus appears that, while defendant was a member of the Communist Party, he was not indicted for participating in its organization, or for joining, it or for soliciting members or distributing its literature. He was not charged with teaching or advocating criminal syndicalism or sabotage or any unlawful acts, either at the meeting or elsewhere. He was accordingly deprived of the benefit of evidence as to the orderly and lawful conduct of the meeting and that it was not called or used for the advocacy of criminal syndicalism or sabotage or any unlawful action. His sole offense as charged, and for which he was convicted and sentenced to imprisonment for seven years, was that he had assisted in the conduct of a public meeting, albeit otherwise lawful, which was held under the auspices of the Communist Party.

The broad reach of the statute as thus applied is plain. While defendant was a member of the Communist Party, that membership was not necessary to conviction on such a charge. A like fate might have attended any speaker, although not a member, who "assisted in the conduct" of the meeting. However innocuous the object of the meeting, however lawful the subjects and tenor of the addresses, however reasonable and timely the discussion, all those assisting in the conduct of the meeting would be subject to imprisonment as felons if the meeting were held by the Communist Party. This manifest result was brought out sharply at this bar by the concessions which the attorney general made, and could not avoid, in the light of the decision of the State court. Thus if the Communist Party had called a public meeting in Portland to discuss the tariff, or the foreign policy of the Government, or taxation, or relief, or candidacies for the offices of President, members of Congress, Governor, or State legislators, every speaker who assisted in the conduct of the meeting would be equally guilty with the defendant in this case, upon the charge as here defined and sustained. The list of illustrations might be indefinitely extended to every variety of meetings under the auspices of the Communist Party although held for the discussion of political issues or to adopt protests and pass resolutions of an entirely innocent and proper character.

While the States are entitled to protect themselves from the abuse of the privileges of our institutions through an attempted substitution of force and violence in the place of peaceful political action in order to effect revolutionary changes in government, none of our decisions go to the length of sustaining such a curtailment of the right of free speech and assembly as the Oregon statute demands in its present application. In *Gitlow* v. *New York*, 268 U.S. 652, under the New

York statute defining criminal anarchy, the defendant was found to be responsible for a "manifesto" advocating the overthrow of the government by violence and unlawful means. *Id.*, pp. 656, 662, 663. In *Whitney* v. *California*, 274 U.S. 357, under the California statute relating to criminal syndicalism, the defendant was found guilty of willfully and deliberately assisting in the forming of an organization for the purpose of carrying on a revolutionary class struggle by criminal methods. The defendant was convicted of participation in what amounted to a conspiracy to commit serious crimes. *Id.*, pp. 363, 364, 367, 379. The case of *Burns* v. *United States*, 274 U.S. 328, involved a similar ruling under the California statute as extended to the Yosemite National Park. *Id.*, pp. 330, 331. On the other hand, in *Fiske* v. *Kansas*, 274 U.S. 380, the criminal syndicalism act of that State was held to have been applied unconstitutionally and the judgment of conviction was reversed, where it was not shown that unlawful methods had been advocated. *Id.*, p. 387. See also, *Stromberg* v. *California*, 283 U.S. 359.

Freedom of speech and of the press are fundamental rights which are safeguarded by the due process clause of the Fourteenth Amendment of the Federal Constitution. *Gitlow* v. *New York, supra*, p. 666; *Stromberg* v. *California, supra*, p. 368; *Near* v. *Minnesota*, 283 U.S. 697, 707; *Grosjean* v. *American Press Co.*, 297 U.S. 233, 243, 244. The right of peaceable assembly is a right cognate to those of free speech and free press and is equally fundamental. As this Court said in *United States* v. *Cruikshank*, 92 U.S. 542, 552: "The very idea of a government, republican in form, implies a right on the part of its citizens to meet peaceably for consultation in respect to public affairs and to petition for a redress of grievances." The First Amendment of the Federal Constitution expressly guarantees that right against abridgment by Congress. But explicit mention there does not argue exclusion elsewhere. For the right is one that cannot be denied without violating those fundamental principles of liberty and justice which lie at the base of all civil and political institutions—principles which the Fourteenth Amendment embodies in the general terms of its due process clause. *Hebert* v. *Louisiana*, 272 U.S. 312, 316; *Powell* v. *Alabama*, 287 U.S. 45, 67; *Grosjean* v. *American Press Co., supra*.

These rights may be abused by using speech or press or assembly in order to incite to violence and crime. The people through their legislatures may protect themselves against that abuse. But the legislative intervention can find constitutional justification only by dealing with the abuse. The rights themselves must not be curtailed. The greater the importance of safeguarding the community from incitements to the overthrow of our institutions by force and violence, the more imperative is the need to preserve inviolate the constitutional rights of free speech, free press and free assembly in order to maintain the opportunity for free political discussion, to the end that government may be responsive to the will of the people and that changes, if desired, may be obtained by peaceful means. Therein lies the security of the Republic, the very foundation of constitutional government.

It follows from these considerations that, consistently with the Federal Constitution, peaceable assembly for lawful discussion cannot be made a crime. The holding of meetings for peaceable political action cannot be proscribed. Those who assist in the conduct of such meetings cannot be branded as criminals on that score. The question, if the rights of free speech and peaceable assembly are to be preserved, is not as to the auspices under which the meeting is held but as to its purpose; not as to the relations of the speakers, but whether their utterances transcend the bounds of the freedom of speech which the Constitution protects. If the persons assembling have committed crimes elsewhere, if they have formed or are engaged in a conspiracy against the public peace and order, they may be prosecuted for their conspiracy or other violation of valid laws. But it is a different matter when the State, instead of prosecuting them for such offenses, seizes upon mere participation in a peaceable assembly and a lawful public discussion as the basis for a criminal charge.

We are not called upon to review the findings of the State court as to the objectives of the Communist Party. Notwithstanding those objectives, the defendant still enjoyed his personal right of free speech and to take part in a peaceable assembly having a lawful purpose, although called by that Party. The defendant was none the less entitled to discuss the public issues of the day and thus in a lawful manner, without incitement to violence or crime, to seek redress of alleged grievances. That was of the essence of his guaranteed personal liberty.

We hold that the Oregon statute as applied to the particular charge as defined by the State court is repugnant to the due process clause of the Fourteenth Amendment. The judgment of conviction is reversed and the cause is remanded for further proceedings not inconsistent with this opinion.

Reversed.

MR. JUSTICE STONE took no part in the consideration or decision of this case.

STATE INVESTIGATIONS

SWEEZY v. NEW HAMPSHIRE,
BY WYMAN, ATTORNEY GENERAL

APPEAL FROM THE SUPREME COURT OF NEW HAMPSHIRE

No. 175.   Argued March 5, 1957.—Decided June 17, 1957.

1. This case was brought here on appeal under 28 U.S.C. § 1257 (2) ; but the
   appellant has failed to meet his burden of showing that jurisdiction by
   appeal was properly invoked. *Held:* The appeal is dismissed. Treating
   the papers as a petition for certiorari under 28 U.S.C. § 2103, certiorari is
   granted. Pp. 235–236.

2. In an investigation conducted by a State Attorney General acting on behalf
   of the State Legislature under a broad resolution directing him to determine
   whether there were "subversive persons" in the State and to recommend
   further legislation on that subject, appellant answered most questions asked
   him, including whether he was a Communist ; but he refused to answer questions related to (1) the contents of a lecture he had delivered at the
   State University, and (2) his knowledge of the Progressive Party of the
   State and its members. He did not plead his privilege against self-incrimination, but based his refusal to answer such questions on the grounds that
   they were not pertinent to the inquiry and violated his rights under the
   First Amendment. Persisting in his refusal when hailed into a State Court
   and directed to answer, he was adjudged guilty of contempt. This judgment was affirmed by the State Supreme Court, which construed the term
   "subversive persons" broadly enough to include persons engaged in conduct
   only remotely related to actual subversion and done completely apart from
   any conscious intent to be a part of such activity. It also held that the
   need of the Legislature to be informed on the subject of self-preservation of
   government outweighed the deprivation of constitutional rights that occurred in the process. *Held:* On the record in this case, appellant's rights
   under the Due Process Clause of the Fourteenth Amendment were violated,
   and the judgment is reversed. Pp. 235–267.

100 N. H. 103, 121 A. 2d 783, reversed.

For the opinions of the Justices' constituting the majority of the Court, see :
Opinion of THE CHIEF JUSTICE, joined by MR. JUSTICE BLACK, MR. JUSTICE
DOUGLAS, and MR. JUSTICE BRENNAN, p. 235.
Opinion of MR. JUSTICE FRANKFURTER, joined by MR. JUSTICE HARLAN, con-
curring in the result, *post*, p. 255.

For dissenting opinion of MR. JUSTICE CLARK, joined by MR. JUSTICE BURTON,
see *post*, p. 267.

Thomas I. Emerson argued the cause for appellant.   With him on
the brief was *William L. Phinney*.

Louis C. Wyman, Attorney General of New Hampshire, argued
the cause for appellee.   With him on the brief were *Joseph F. Gall*,
Special Assistant to the Attorney General, and *Elmer T. Bourque*,
Assistant Attorney General.

MR. CHIEF JUSTICE WARREN announced the judgment of the Court
and delivered an opinion, in which MR. JUSTICE BLACK, MR. JUSTICE
DOUGLAS, and MR. JUSTICE BRENNAN join.

This case, like *Watkins* v. *United States, ante,* p. 178, brings before
us a question concerning the constitutional limits of legislative inquiry.
The investigation here was conducted under the aegis of a State legislature, rather than a House of Congress.   This places the controversy
in a slightly different setting from that in *Watkins*.   The ultimate
question here is whether the investigation deprived Sweezy of due
process of law under the Fourteenth Amendment.   For the reasons to
be set out in this opinion, we conclude that the record in this case

does not sustain the power of the State to compel the disclosures that the witness refused to make.

This case was brought here as an appeal under 28 U.S.C. § 1257 (2). Jurisdiction was alleged to rest upon contentions, rejected by the State courts, that a statute of New Hampshire is repugnant to the Constitution of the United States. We postponed a decision on the question of jurisdiction until consideration of the merits. 352 U.S. 812. The parties neither briefed nor argued the jurisdictional question. The appellant has thus failed to meet his burden of showing that jurisdiction by appeal was properly invoked. The appeal is therefore dismissed. Treating the appeal papers as a petition for writ of certiorari, under 28 U.S.C. § 2103, the petition is granted. Cf. *Union National Bank* v. *Lamb*, 337 U.S. 38, 39–40.

The investigation in which petitioner was summoned to testify had its origins in a statute passed by the New Hampshire legislature.[1] It was a comprehensive scheme of regulation of subversive activities. There was a section defining criminal conduct in the nature of sedition. "Subversive organizations" were declared unlawful and ordered dissolved. "Subversive persons" were made ineligible for employment by the State government. Included in the disability were those employed as teachers or in other capacities by any public educational institution. A loyalty program was instituted to eliminate "subversive persons" among government personnel. All present employees, as well as candidates for elective office in the future, were required to make sworn statements that they were not "subversive persons."

In 1953, the legislature adopted a "Joint Resolution Relating to the Investigation of Subversive Activities."[2] It was resolved:

"That the attorney general is hereby authorized and directed to make full and complete investigation with respect to violations of the Subversive Activities Act of 1951 and to determine whether subversive persons as defined in said Act are presently located within this State. The attorney general is authorized to act upon his own motion and upon such information as in his judgment may be reasonable or reliable. . . .

.   .   .   .   .

"The attorney general is directed to proceed with criminal prosecutions under the Subversive Activities Act whenever evidence presented to him in the course of the investigation indicates violations thereof, and he shall report to the 1955 session on the first day of its regular session the results of this investigation, together with his recommendations, if any, for necessary legislation."[3]

Under State law, this was construed to constitute the attorney general as a one-man legislative committee.[4] He was given the authority

---

[1] N.H. Laws 1951, c. 193; now N.H. Rev. Stat. Ann., 1955, c. 588, §§ 1–6.
[2] N.H. Laws 1953, c. 307.
[3] The authority of the attorney general was continued for another two-year period by N.H. Laws 1955, cc. 197, 340.
[4] "Having determined that an investigation should be conducted concerning a proper subject of action by it, the legislature's choice of the attorney general as its investigating committee, instead of a committee of its own members or a special board or commission, was not in and of itself determinative of the nature of the investigation. His position as the chief law enforcement officer of the State did not transform the inquiry which was otherwise legislative into executive action." *Nelson* v. *Wyman*, 99 N.H. 33, 38, 105 A. 2d 756, 762–763.

The Attorney General of New Hampshire is appointed to office by the Governor and the State Council, a group of five persons who share some of the executive responsibilities in to delegate any part of the investigation to any member of his staff. The legislature conferred upon the attorney general the further authority to subpoena witnesses or documents. He did not have power to hold witnesses in contempt, however. In the event that coercive or punitive sanctions were needed, the attorney general could invoke the aid of a State Superior Court which could find recalcitrant witnesses in contempt of court.[5]

Petitioner was summoned to appear before the attorney general on two separate occasions. On January 5, 1954, petitioner testified at length upon his past conduct and associations. He denied that he had ever been a member of the Communist Party or that he had ever been part of any program to overthrow the government by force or violence. The interrogation ranged over many matters, from petitioner's World War II military service with the Office of Strategic Services to his sponsorship, in 1949, of the Scientific and Cultural Conference for World Peace, at which he spoke.

During the course of the inquiry, petitioner declined to answer several questions. His reasons for doing so were given in a statement he read to the Committee at the outset of the hearing.[6] He declared

---

the State Government. The principal duties of the attorney general are set forth in N.H. Rev. Stat. Ann., 1955, c. 7, §§ 6–11. He represents the State in all cases before the State Supreme Court. He prosecutes all criminal cases in which the accused is charged with an offense punishable by twenty-five years in prison or more. All other criminal cases are under his general supervision. He gives opinions on questions of law to the legislature, or to state boards, departments, commissions, officers, etc., on questions relating to their official duties.

[5] "Whenever any official or board is given the power to summon witnesses and take testimony, but has not the power to punish for contempt, and any witness refuses to obey such summons, either as to his appearance or as to the production of things specified in the summons, or refuses to testify or to answer any question, a petition for an order to compel him to testify or his compliance with the summons may be filed in the superior court, or with some justice thereof." N.H. Rev. Stat. Ann., 1955, c. 491, § 19. "Upon such petition the court or justice shall have authority to proceed in the matter as though the original proceeding had been in the court, and may make orders and impose penalties accordingly." Id., § 20. See State v. Uphaus, 100 N.H. 1, 116 A. 2d 887.

[6] "Those called to testify before this and other similar investigations can be classified in three categories.

"First there are Communists and those who have reason to believe that even if they are not Communists they have been accused of being and are in danger of harassment and prosecution.

"Second, there are those who approve of the purposes and methods of these investigations.

"Third, there are those who are not Communists and do not believe they are in danger of being prosecuted, but who yet deeply disapprove of the purposes and methods of these investigations.

"The first group will naturally, and I think wholly justifiably, plead the constitutional privilege of not being witnesses against themselves.

"The second group will equally naturally be cooperative witnesses.

"The third group is faced with an extremely difficult dilemma. I know because I belong to this third group, and I have been struggling with its problems for many weeks now. I would like to explain what the nature of that dilemma is. I think it is important that both those conducting these inquiries and the public should understand.

"It is often said: If a person is not a Communist and has nothing to fear, why should he not answer whatever questions are put to him and be done with it? The answer, of course, is that some of us believe these investigations are evil and dangerous, and we do not want to give our approval to them, either tacitly or otherwise. On the contrary, we want to oppose them to the best of our ability and persuade others to do likewise, with the hope of eventually abolishing them altogether.

"Our reasons for opposing these investigations are not captious or trivial. They have deep roots in principle and conscience. Let me explain with reference to the present New Hampshire investigation. The official purpose of the inquiry is to uncover and lay the basis for the prosecution of persons who in one way or another promote the forcible overthrow of constitutional forms of government. Leaving aside the question of the constitutionality of the investigation, which is now before the courts, I think it must be plain to any reasonable person who is at all well informed about conditions in New Hampshire today that strict adherence to this purpose would leave little room for investigation. It is obvious enough that there are few radicals or dissenters of any kind in New Hampshire; and if there are any who advocate use of force and violence, they must be isolated crackpots who are no danger to anyone, least of all to the constitutional form of government of State and Nation. The attorney general should be able to check these facts quickly and issue a report satisfying the mandate laid upon him by the legislature.

"But this is not what he has done. We do not know the whole story, but enough has come out to show that the attorney general has issued a considerable number of subpoenas and has held hearings in various parts of the state. And so far as the available information allows us to judge, most of those subpoenaed have fallen into one or both of two groups :

he would not answer those questions which were not pertinent to the subject under inquiry as well as those which transgress the limitations of the First Amendment. In keeping with this stand, he refused to disclose his knowledge of the Progressive Party in New Hampshire or of persons with whom he was acquainted in that organization.[7] No action was taken by the attorney general to compel answers to these questions.

The attorney general again summoned petitioner to testify on June 3, 1954. There was more interrogation about the witness' prior contacts with Communists. The attorney general lays great stress

---

first professors at Dartmouth and the University of New Hampshire who have gained a reputation for liberal or otherwise unorthodox views, and, second, people who have been active in the Progressive Party. It should be specially noted that whatever may be thought of the Progressive Party in any other respect, it was certainly not devoted to violent overthrow of constitutional forms of government but on the contrary to effecting reforms through the very democratic procedures which are the essence of constitutional forms of government.

"The pattern I have described is no accident. Whatever their official purpose, these investigations always end up by inquiring into the politics, ideas, and beliefs of people who hold what are, for the time being, unpopular views. The federal House Committee on Un-American Activities, for example, is supposed to investigate various kinds of propaganda and has no other mandate whatever. Over the years, however, it has spent almost no time investigating propaganda and has devoted almost all of its energies to 'exposing' people and their ideas, their affiliations, their associations. Similarly, this New Hampshire investigation is supposed to be concerned with violent overthrow of government, but it is actually turning out to be concerned with what few manifestations of political dissent have made themselves felt in the state in recent years.

"If all this is so, and if the very first principle of the American constitutional form of government is political freedom—which I take to include freedoms of speech, press, assembly, and association—then I do not see how it can be denied that these investigations are a grave danger to all that Americans have always claimed to cherish. No rights are genuine if a person, for exercising them, can be hauled up before some tribunal and forced under penalties of perjury and contempt to account for his ideas and conduct.

"Let us now return to the problem of the witness who would have nothing to fear from being what is nowadays styled a 'friendly' witness, but who feels deeply that to follow such a course would be a betrayal of his principles and repugnant to his conscience. What other courses are open to him?

"He can claim the privilege not to be a witness against himself and thus avoid a hateful inquisition. I respect the decision of those who elect to take this course. My own reason for rejecting it is that, with public opinion in its present state, the exercise of the privilege is almost certain to be widely misinterpreted. One of the noblest and most precious guarantees of freedom, won in the course of bitter struggles and terrible suffering, has been distorted in our own day to mean a confession of guilt, the more sinister because undefined and indeed undefinable. It is unfortunate, but true, that the public at large has accepted this distortion and will scarcely listen to those who have invoked the privilege.

"Alternatively, the witness can seek to uphold his principles and maintain his integrity, not by claiming the protection of the Fifth Amendment (or the Fifteenth Article of the New Hampshire Bill of Rights), but by contesting the legitimacy of offensive questions on other constitutional and legal grounds.

"Just how far the First Amendment limits the right of legislative inquiry has not been settled. The Supreme Court of the United States is at this very moment considering a case (the *Emspak* case) which may do much to settle the question. But even before the Court has handed down its decision in the *Emspak* case, it is quite certain that the First Amendment does place *some* limitations on the power of investigation, and it is always open to a witness to challenge a question on the ground that it transgresses these limitations and, if necessary, to take the issue to the courts for decision.

"Moreover, a witness may not be required to answer questions unless they are 'pertinent to the matter under inquiry" (the words are those of the United States Supreme Court).

"What is the 'matter under inquiry' in the present investigation? According to the Act of the New Hampshire legislature directing the investigation, its purpose is twofold: (1) 'to make full and complete investigation with respect to violations of the subversive activities act of 1951,' and (2) 'to determine whether subversive persons as defined in said act are presently located within this State.'

"I have studied the subversive activities act of 1951 with care, and I am glad to volunteer the information that I have absolutely no knowledge of any violations of any of its provisions; further, that I have no knowledge of subversive persons presently located within the State.

"That these statements may carry full conviction, I am prepared to answer certain questions about myself, though in doing so I do not mean to concede the right to ask them. I am also prepared to discuss my views relating to the use of force and violence to overthrow constitutional forms of government.

"But I shall respectfully decline to answer questions concerning ideas, beliefs, and associations which could not possibly be pertinent to the matter here under inquiry and/ or which seem to me to invade the freedoms guaranteed by the First Amendment to the United States Constitution (which, of course, applies equally to the several states)."

[7] The Progressive Party offered a slate of candidates for national office in the 1948 presidential election. Henry A. Wallace, former Vice President of the United States, was the party's selection for the presidency. Glen Taylor, former United States Senator, was the vice-presidential nominee of the party. Nationwide, the party received a popular vote of 1,156,103. Of this total, 1,970 votes for Progressive Party candidates were cast in New Hampshire. Statistics of the Presidential and Congressional Election of November 2, 1948, pp. 24, 48–49.

upon an article which petitioner had co-authored. It deplored the use of violence by the United States and other capitalist countries in attempting to preserve a social order which the writers thought must inevitably fall. This resistance, the article continued, will be met by violence from the oncoming socialism, violence which is to be less condemned morally than that of capitalism since its purpose is to create a "truly human society." Petitioner affirmed that he styled himself a "classical Marxist" and a "Socialist" and that the article expressed his continuing opinion.

Again, at the second hearing, the attorney general asked, and petitioner refused to answer, questions concerning the Progressive Party, and its predecessor, the Progressive Citizens of America. Those were:

"Was she, Nancy Sweezy, your wife, active in the formation of the Progressive Citizens of America?"

"Was Nancy Sweezy then working with individuals who were then members of the Communist Party?"

"Was Charles Beebe active in forming the Progressive Citizens of America?"

"Was Charles Beebe active in the Progressive Party in New Hampshire?"

"Did he work with your present wife—Did Charles Beebe work with your present wife in 1947?"

"Did it [a meeting at the home of Abraham Walenko in Weare during 1948] have anything to do with the Progressive Party?"

The attorney general also turned to a subject which had not yet occurred at the time of the first hearing. On March 22, 1954, petitioner had delivered a lecture to a class of 100 students in the humanities course at the University of New Hampshire. This talk was given at the invitation of the faculty teaching that course. Petitioner had addressed the class upon such invitations in the two preceding years as well. He declined to answer the following questions:

"What was the subject of your lecture?"

"Didn't you tell the class at the University of New Hampshire on Monday, March 22, 1954, that socialism was inevitable in this country?"

"Did you advocate Marxism at that time?

"Did you express the opinion, or did you make the statement at that time that socialism was inevitable in America?"

"Did you in this last lecture on March 22 or in any of the former lectures espouse the theory of dialectical materialism?"

Distinct from the categories of questions about the Progressive Party and the lectures was one question about petitioner's opinions. He was asked: "Do you believe in communism?" He had already testified that he had never been a member of the Communist Party, but he refused to answer this or any other question concerning opinion or belief.

Petitioner adhered in this second proceeding to the same reasons for not answering he had given in his statement at the first hearing. He maintained that the questions were not pertinent to the matter under inquiry and that they infringed upon an area protected under the First Amendment.

Following the hearings, the attorney general petitioned the Superior Court of Merrimack County, New Hampshire, setting forth the circumstances of petitioner's appearance before the Committee and his refusal to answer certain questions.[8] The petition prayed that the court propound the questions to the witness. After hearing argument, the court ruled that the questions set out above were pertinent.[9] Petitioner was called as a witness by the court and persisted in his refusal to answer for constitutional reasons. The court adjudged him in contempt and ordered him committed to the county jail and purged of the contempt.

The New Hampshire Supreme Court affirmed. 100 N.H. 103, 121 A. 2d 783. Its opinion discusses only two classes of questions addressed to the witness: those dealing with the lectures and those about the Progressive Party and the Progressive Citizens of America. No mention is made of the single question concerning petitioner's belief in communism. In view of what we hold to be the controlling issue of the case, however, it is unnecessary to resolve affirmatively that that particular question was or was not included in the decision by the State supreme court.

There is no doubt that legislative investigations, whether on a Federal or State level, are capable of encroaching upon the constitutional liberties of individuals. It is particularly important that the exercise of the power of compulsory process be carefully circumscribed when the investigative process tends to impinge upon such highly sensitive areas as freedom of speech or press, freedom of political association, and freedom of communication of ideas, particularly in the academic community. Responsibility for the proper conduct of investigations rests, of course, upon the legislature itself. If that assembly chooses to authorize inquiries on its behalf by a legislatively created committee, that basic responsibility carries forward to include the duty of adequate supervision of the actions of the committee. This safeguard can be nullified when a committee is invested with a broad and ill-defined jurisdiction. The authorizing resolution thus becomes especially significant in that it reveals the amount of discretion that has been conferred upon the committee.

In this case, the investigation is governed by provisions in the New Hampshire Subversive Activities Act of 1951.[10] The attorney general was instructed by the legislature to look into violations of that Act. In addition, he was given the far more sweeping mandate to find out if there were subversive persons, as defined in that Act, present in New Hampshire. That statute, therefore, measures the breadth and scope of the investigation before us.

"Subversive persons" are defined in many gradations of conduct. Our interest is in the minimal requirements of that definition since they will outline its reach. According to the statute, a person is a "subversive person" if he, by any means, aids in the commission of any

---

[8] See note 5, *supra.*
[9] The court made a general ruling that questions concerning the opinions or beliefs of the witness were not pertinent. Nevertheless, it did propound to the witness the one question about his belief in communism.
[10] See note 1, *supra.*

act intended to assist in the alteration of the constitutional form of government by force or violence.[11] The possible remoteness from armed insurrection of conduct that could satisfy these criteria is obvious from the language. The statute goes well beyond those who are engaged in efforts designed to alter the form of government by force or violence. The statute declares, in effect, that the assistant of an assistant is caught up in the definition. This chain of conduct attains increased significance in light of the lack of a necessary element of guilty knowledge in either stage of assistants. The State supreme court has held that the definition encompasses persons engaged in the specified conduct ". . . whether or not done 'knowingly and willfully . . . .'" *Nelson* v. *Wyman*, 99 N.H. 33, 39, 105, A. 2d 756, 763. The potential sweep of this definition extends to conduct which is only remotely related to actual subversion and which is done completely free of any conscious intent to be a part of such activity.

The statute's definition of "subversive organizations" is also broad. An association is said to be any group of persons, whether temporarily or permanently associated together, for joint action or advancement of views on any subject.[12] An organization is deemed subversive if it has a purpose to abet, advise or teach activities intended to assist in the alteration of the constitutional form of government by force or violence.

The situation before us is in many respects analogous to that in *Wieman* v. *Updegraff*, 344 U.S. 183. The Court held there that a loyalty oath prescribed by the State of Oklahoma for all its officers and employees violated the requirements of the Due Process Clause because it entailed sanctions for membership in subversive organizations without scienter. A State cannot, in attempting to bar disloyal individuals from its employ, exclude persons solely on the basis of organizational membership, regardless of their knowledge concerning the organizations to which they belonged. The Court said:

"There can be no dispute about the consequences visited upon a person excluded from public employment on disloyalty grounds. In the view of the community, the stain is a deep one; indeed, it has become a badge of infamy. Especially is this so in time of cold war and hot emotions when 'each man begins to eye his neighbor as a possible enemy.' Yet under the Oklahoma Act, the fact of association alone determines disloyalty and disqualification; it matters not whether association existed innocently or knowingly. To thus inhibit individual freedom of movement is

---

[11] " 'Subversive person' means any person who commits, attempts to commit, or aids in the commission, or advocates, abets, advises or teaches, by any means any person to commit, attempt to commit, or aid in the commission of any act intended to overthrow, destroy or alter, or to assist in the overthrow, destruction or alteration of, the constitutional form of the Government of the United States, or the State of New Hampshire, or any political subdivision of either of them, by force, or violence ; or who is a member of a subversive organization or a foreign subversive organization." N.H. Rev. Stat. Ann., 1955, c. 588, § 1.

[12] "For the purpose of this chapter 'organization' means an organization, corporation, company, partnership, association, trust, foundation, fund, club, society, committee, political party, or any group of persons, whether or not incorporated, permanently or temporarily associated together for joint action or advancement of views on any subject or subjects.

" 'Subversive organization' means any organization which engages in or advocates, abets, advises, or teaches, or a purpose of which is to engage in or advocate, abet, advise, or teach activities intended to overthrow, destroy or alter, or to assist in the overthrow, destruction or alteration of, the constitutional form of the Government of the United States, or of the State of New Hampshire, or of any political subdivision of either of them, by force, or violence." *Ibid.*

to stifle the flow of democratic expression and controversy at one of its chief sources." 344 U.S., at 190–191.

The sanction emanating from legislative investigations is of a different kind than loss of employment. But the stain of the stamp of disloyalty is just as deep. The inhibiting effect in the flow of democratic expression and controversy upon those directly affected and those touched more subtly is equally grave. Yet here, as in *Wieman*, the program for the rooting out of subversion is drawn without regard to the presence or absence of guilty knowledge in those affected.

The nature of the investigation which the attorney general was authorized to conduct is revealed by this case. He delved minutely into the past conduct of petitioner, thereby making his private life a matter of public record. The questioning indicates that the investigators had thoroughly prepared for the interview and were not acquiring new information as much as corroborating data already in their possession. On the great majority of questions, the witness was cooperative, even though he made clear his opinion that the interrogation was unjustified and unconstitutional. Two subjects arose upon which petitioner refused to answer: his lectures at the University of New Hampshire, and his knowledge of the Progressive Party and its adherents.

The State courts upheld the attempt to investigate the academic subject on the ground that it might indicate whether petitioner was a "subversive person." What he taught the class at a State university was found relevant to the character of the teacher. The State supreme court carefully excluded the possibility that the inquiry was sustainable because of the State interest in the State university. There was no warrant in the authorizing resolution for that. 100 N.H., at 110, 121 A. 2d, at 789–790. The sole basis for the inquiry was to scrutinize the teacher as a person, and the inquiry must stand or fall on that basis.

The interrogation on the subject of the Progressive Party was deemed to come within the attorney general's mandate because that party might have been shown to be a "subversive organization." The State supreme court held that the " . . . questions called for answers concerning the membership or participation of named persons in the Progressive Party which, if given, would aid the attorney general in determining whether that party and its predecessor are or were subversive organizations." 100 N.H., at 112, 121 A. 2d, at 791.

The New Hampshire court concluded that the ". . . right to lecture and the right to associate with others for a common purpose, be it political or otherwise, are individual liberties guaranteed to every citizens by the State and Federal Constitutions but are not absolute rights. . . . The inquiries authorized by the legislature in connection with this investigation concerning the contents of the lecture and the membership, purposes and activities of the Progressive Party undoubtedly interfered with the defendant's free exercise of those liberties." 100 N.H., at 113, 121 A. 2d, at 791–792.

The State supreme court thus conceded without extended discussion that petitioner's right to lecture and his right to associate with others were constitutionaly protected freedoms which had been abridged through this investigation. These conclusions could not be seriously debated. Merely to summon a witness and compel him, against his will, to disclose the nature of his past expressions and associations is a measure of governmental interference in these matters. These are rights which are safeguarded by the Bill of Rights and the Fourteenth Amendment. We believe that there unquestionably was an invasion of petitioner's liberties in the areas of academic freedom and political expression—areas in which government should be extremely reticent to tread.

The essentiality of freedom in the community of American universities is almost self-evident. No one should underestimate the vital role in a democracy that is played by those who guide and train our youth. To impose any straitjacket upon the intellectual leaders in our colleges and universities would imperil the future of our Nation. No field of education is so thoroughly comprehended by man that new discoveries cannot yet be made. Particularly is that true in the social sciences, where few, if any, principles are accepted as absolutes. Scholarship cannot flourish in an atmosphere of suspicion and distrust. Teachers and students must always remain free to inquire, to study and to evaluate, to gain new maturity and understanding; otherwise our civilization will stagnate and die.

Equally manifest as a fundamental principle of a democratic society is political freedom of the individual. Our form of government is built on the premise that every citizen shall have the right to engage in political ideas cannot and should not be channeled into the programs First Amendment of the Bill of Rights. Exercise of these basic freedoms in America has traditionally been through the media of political associations. Any interference with the freedom of a party is simultaneously an interference with the freedom of its adherents. All political ideas cannot and should not be channeled into the programs of our two major parties. History has amply proved the virtue of political activity by minority, dissident groups, who innumerable times have been in the vanguard of democratic thought and whose programs were ultimately accepted. Mere unorthodoxy or dissent from the prevailing mores is not to be condemned. The absence of such voices would be a symptom of grave illness in our society.

Notwithstanding the undeniable importance of freedom in the areas, the Supreme Court of New Hampshire did not consider that the abridgment of petitioner's rights under the Constitution vitiated the investigation. In the view of that court, "the answer lies in a determination of whether the object of the legislative investigation under consideration is such as to justify the restriction thereby imposed upon the defendant's liberties." 100 N.H., at 113–114, 121 A. 2d, at 791–792. It found such justification in the legislature's judgment, expressed by its authorizing resolution, that there exists a potential menace from those who would overthrow the government by force and violence. That court concluded that the need for the legislature to be informed on so elemental a subject as the self-preservation of government outweighed the deprivation of constitutional rights that occurred in the process.

We do not now conceive of any circumstance wherein a State interest would justify infringement of rights in these fields. But we do not need to reach such fundamental questions of State power to decide this case. The State supreme court itself recognized that there was a weakness in its conclusion that the menace of forcible overthrow of the government justified sacrificing constitutional rights. There was a missing link in the chain of reasoning. The syllogism was not complete. There was nothing to connect the questioning of petitioner with this fundamental interest of the State. Petitioner had been interrogated by a one-man legislative committee, not by the legislature itself. The relationship of the committee to the full assembly is vital, therefore, as revealing the relationship of the questioning to the State interest.

In light of this, the State court emphasized a factor in the authorizing resolution which confined the inquiries which the attorney general might undertake to the object of the investigation. That limitation was thought to stem from the authorizing resolution's condition precedent to the institution of any inquiry. The New Hampshire legislation specified that the attorney general should act only when he had information which ". . . in his judgment may be reasonable or reliable." The State court construed this to mean that the attorney general must have something like probable cause for conducting a particular investigation. It is not likely that this device would prove an adequate safeguard against unwarranted inquiries. The legislature has specified that the determination of the necessity for inquiry shall be left in the judgment of the investigator. In this case, the record does not reveal what reasonable or reliable information led the attorney general to question petitioner. The State court relied upon the attorney general's description of prior information that had come into his possession.[13]

The respective roles of the legislature and the investigator thus revealed are of considerable significance to the issue before us. It is eminently clear that the basic discretion of determining the direction of the legislative inquiry has been turned over to the investigative agency. The attorney general has been given such a sweeping and uncertain mandate that it is his decision which picks out the subjects that will be pursued, what witnesses will be summoned and what questions will be asked. In this circumstance, it cannot be stated authoritatively that the legislature asked the attorney general to gather the kind of facts comprised in the subjects upon which petitioner was interrogated.

Instead of making known the nature of the data it desired, the legislature has insulated itself from those witnesses whose rights may be vitally affected by the investigation. Incorporating by reference provisions from its subversive activities act, it has told the attorney general, in effect to screen the citizenry of New Hampshire to bring to light anyone who fits into the expansive definitions.

---

[13] The State supreme court illustrated the "reasonable or reliable" information underlying the inquiries on the Progressive Party by quoting from a remark made by the attorney general at the hearing in answer to petitioner's objection to a line of questions. The attorney general had declared that he had ". . . considerable sworn testimony . . . to the effect that the Progressive Party in New Hampshire has been heavily infiltrated by members of the Communist Party and that the policies and purposes of the Progressive Party have been directly influenced by members of the Communist Party." 100 N.H., at 111, 121 A. 2d, at 790–791. None of this testimony is a part of the record in this case. Its existence and weight were not independently reviewed by the State courts.

The court did not point to anything that supported the questioning on the subject of the lecture. It stated that the attorney general could inquire about lectures only if he ". . . possesses reasonable or reliable information indicating that the violent overthrow of existing government may have been advocated or taught, either 'knowingly and willfully' or not." 100 N.H., at 110, 121 A. 2d, at 789–790. What, if anything, indicated that petitioner knowingly or innocently advocated or taught violent overthrow of existing government does not appear. At one point in the hearing, the attorney general said to petitioner: "I have in the file here a statement from a person who attended your class, and I will read it in part because I don't want you to think I am just fishing. 'His talk this time was on the inevitability of the Socialist program. It was a glossed-over interpretation of the materialist dialectic.'" R. 107. The court did not cite this statement.

Within the very broad area thus committed to the discretion of the attorney general there may be many facts which the legislature might find useful. There would also be a great deal of data which that assembly would not want or need. In the classes of information that the legislature might deem it desirable to have, there will be some which it could not validly acquire because of the effect upon the constitutional rights of individual citizens. Separating the wheat from the chaff, from the standpoint of the legislature's object, is the legislature's responsibility because it alone can make that judgment. In this case, the New Hampshire legislature has delegated that task to the attorney general.

As a result, neither we nor the state courts have any assurance that the questions peitioner refused to answer fall into a category of matters upon which the legislature wanted to be informed when it initiated this inquiry. The judiciary are thus placed in an untenable position. Lacking even the elementary fact that the legislature wants certain questions answered and recognizing that petitioner's constitutional rights are in jeopardy, we are asked to approve or disapprove his incarceration for contempt.

In our view, the answer is clear. No one would deny that the infringement of constitutional rights of individuals would violate the guarantee of due process where no State interest underlies the State action. Thus, if the attorney general's interrogation of petitioner were in fact wholly unrelated to the object of the legislature in authorizing the inquiry, the Due Process Clause would preclude the endangering of constitutional liberties. We believe that an equivalent situation is presented in this case. The lack of any indications that the legislature wanted the information the attorney general attempted to elicit from petitioner must be treated as the absence of authority. It follows that the use of the contempt power, notwithstanding the interference with constitutional rights, was not in accordance with the due process requirements of the Fourteenth Amendment.

The conclusion that we have reached in this case is not grounded upon the doctrine of separation of powers. In the Federal Government, it is clear that the Constitution has conferred the powers of government upon three major branches: the Executive, the Legislative and the Judicial. No contention has been made by petitioner that the New Hampshire legislature, by this investigation, arrogated to itself executive or judicial powers. We accept the finding of the State supreme court that the employment of the attorney general as the investigating committee does not alter the legislative nature of the proceedings. Moreover, this Court has held that the concept of separation of powers embodied in the United States Constitution is not mandatory in State governments. *Dreyer* v. *Illinois*, 187 U.S. 71; but cf. *Tenney* v. *Brandhove*, 341 U.S. 367, 378. Our conclusion does rest upon a separation of the power of a State legislature to conduct investigations from the responsibility to direct the use of that power insofar as that separation causes a deprivation of the constitutional rights of individuals and a denial of due process of law.

The judgment of the Supreme Court of New Hampshire is

Reversed.

MR. JUSTICE WHITTAKER took no part in the consideration or decision of this case.

Mr. Justice Frankfurter, whom Mr. Justice Harlan joins, concurring in the result.

For me this is a very different case from *Watkins* v. *United States*, *ante*, p. 178. This case comes to us solely through the limited power to review the action of the States conferred upon the Court by the Fourteenth Amendment. Petitioner claims that respect for liberties guaranteed by the Due Process Clause of that Amendment precludes the State of New Hampshire from compelling him to answer certain questions put to him by the investigating arm of its legislature. Ours is the narrowly circumscribed but exceedingly difficult task of making the final judicial accommodation between the competing weighty claims that underlie all such questions of due process.

In assessing the claim of the State of New Hampshire to the information denied it by petitioner, we cannot concern ourselves with the fact that New Hampshire chose to make its attorney general in effect a standing committee of its legislature for the purpose of investigating the extent of "subversive" activities within its bounds. The case must be judged as though the whole body of the legislature had demanded the information of petitioner. It would make the deepest inroads upon our Federal system for this Court now to hold that it can determine the appropriate distribution of powers and their delegation within the forty-eight States. As the earlier Mr. Justice Harlan said for a unanimous Court in *Dreyer* v. *Illinois*, 187 U.S. 71, 84:

> "Whether the legislative, executive and judicial powers of a State shall be kept altogether distinct and separate, or whether persons or collections of persons belonging to one department may, in respect to some matters, exert powers which, strictly speaking, pertain to another department of government, is for the determination of the State. And its determination one way or the other cannot be an element in the inquiry whether the due process of law prescribed by the Fourteenth Amendment has been respected by the State or its representatives when dealing with matters involving life or liberty."

Whether the State legislature should operate largely by committees, as does the Congress, or whether committees should be the exception, as is true of the House of Commons, whether the legislature should have two chambers or only one, as in Nebraska, whether the State's chief executive should have the pardoning power, whether the State's judicial branch must provide trial by jury, are all matters beyond the reviewing powers of this Court. Similarly, whether the attorney general of New Hampshire acted within the scope of the authority given him by the State legislature is a matter for the decision of the courts of that State, as it is for the Federal courts to determine whether an agency to which Congress has delegated power has acted within the confines of its mandate. See *United States* v. *Rumely*, 345 U.S. 41. Sanction of the delegation rests with the New Hampshire Supreme Court, and its validation in *Nelson* v. *Wyman*, 99 N.H. 33, 105A. 2d 756, is binding here.

Pursuant to an investigation of subversive activities authorized by a joint resolution of both houses of the New Hampshire Legislature, the State attorney general subpoenaed petitioner before him on January 8, 1954, for extensive questioning. Among the matters about which petitioner was questioned were: details of his career and personal life, whether he was then or ever had been a member of the Communist Party, whether he had ever attended its meetings, whether he had ever attended meetings that he knew were also attended by Party members, whether he knew any Communists in or out of the State, whether he knew named persons with alleged connections with organizations either on the United States attorney general's list or cited by the Un-American Activities Committee of the United States House of Representatives or had ever attended meetings with them, whether he had ever taught or supported the overthrow of the State by force or violence or had ever known or assisted any persons or groups that had done so, whether he had ever been connected with organizations on the attorney general's list, whether he had supported or written in behalf of a variety of allegedly subversive, named causes, conferences, periodicals, petitions, and attempts to raise funds for the legal defense of certain person, whether he knew about the Progressive Party, what positions he had held in it, whether he had been a candidate for presidential elector for that party, whether certain persons were in that party, whether Communists had influenced or been members of the Progressive Party, whether he had sponsored activities in behalf of the candidacy of Henry A. Wallace, whether he advocated replacing the capitalist system with another economic system, whether his conception of socialism involved force and violence, whether by his writings and actions he had ever attempted to advance the Soviet Union's "propaganda line," whether he had ever attended meetings of the Liberal Club at the University of New Hampshire, whether the magazine of which he was co-editor was "a Communist-line publication," and whether he knew named persons.

Petitioner answered most of these questions, making it very plain that he had never been a Communist, never taught violent overthrow of the Government, never knowingly associated with Communists in the State, but was a Socialist believer in peaceful change who had at one time belonged to certain organizations on the list of the United States Attorney General (which did not include the Progressive Party) or cited by the House Un-American Activities Committee. He declined to answer as irrelevant or violative of free speech guarantees certain questions about the Progressive Party and whether he knew particular persons. He stated repeatedly, however, that he had no knowledge of Communists or of Communist influence in the Progressive Party, and he testified that he had been a candidate for that party, signing the required loyalty oath, and that he did not know whether an alleged Communist leader was active in the Progressive Party.

Despite the exhaustive scope of this inquiry, the attorney general again subpoenaed petitioner to testify on June 3, 1954, and the interrogation was similarly sweeping. Petitioner again answered virtually all questions, including those concerning the relationship of named persons to the Communist Party or other causes deemed subversive under State laws, alleged Communist influence on all organizations with which he had been connected including the Progressive Party, and his own participation in organizations other than the Progressive Party and its antecedent, the Progressive Citizens of America. He refused, however, to answer certain questions regarding (1) a lecture given by him at the University of New Hampshire, (2) activities of himself and others in the Progressive political organizations, and (3) "opinions and beliefs," invoking the constitutional guarantees of free speech.

The attorney general then petitioned the superior court to order petitioner to answer questions in these categories. The court ruled that petitioner had to answer those questions pertaining to the lectures and to the Progressive Party and its predecessor but not those otherwise pertaining to "opinions and beliefs." Upon petitioner's refusal to answer the questions sanctioned by the court, he was found in contempt of court and ordered committed to the county jail until purged of contempt.

The Supreme Court of New Hampshire affirmed the order of the superior court. It held that the questions at issue were relevant and that no consitutional provision permitted petitioner to frustrate the State's demands. 100 N. H. 103, 121 A. 2d 783.

The questions that petitioner refused to answer regarding the university lecture, the third given by him in three years at the invitation of the faculty for humanities, were :

"What was the subject of your lecture ?"

"Didn't you tell the class at the University of New Hampshire on Monday, March 22, 1954, that socialism was inevitable in this country ?"

"Did you advocate Marxism at that time ?"

"Did you express the opinion, or did you make the statement at that time that socialism was inevitable in America ?"

"Did you in this last lecture on March 22 or in any of the former lectures espouse the theory of dialectical materialism ?"

"I have in the file here a statement from a person who attended your class, and I will read it in part because I don't want you to think I am just fishing. 'His talk this time was on the inevitability of the Socialist program. It was a glossed-over interpretation of the materialist dialetic.' Now, again I ask you the original question."

In response to the first question of this series, petitioner had said at the hearing :

"I would like to say one thing in this connection, Mr. Wyman. I stated under oath at my last appearance that, and I now repeat it, that I do not advocate or in any way further the aim of overthrowing constitutional government by force and violence. I did not so advocate in the lecture I gave at the University of New Hampshire. In fact I have never at any time so advocated in a lecture anywhere. Aside from that I have nothing I want to say about the lecture in question."

The New Hampshire Supreme Court, although recognizing that such inquiries "undoubtedly interfered with the defendant's free exercise" of his constitutionally guaranteed right to lecture, justified the interference on the ground that it would occur "in the limited area in which the legislative committee may reasonably believe that the overthrow of existing government by force and violence is being or has been taught, advocated or planned, an area in which the interest of the State justifies this intrusion upon civil liberties." 100 N. H., at 113, 114, 121 A. 2d, at 792. According to the court, the facts that made reasonable the Committee's belief that petitioner had taught violent overthrow in his lecture were that he was a Socialist with a record of affiliation with groups cited by the Attorney General of the

United States or the House Un-American Activities Committee and that he was co-editor of an article stating that, although the authors hated violence, it was less to be deplored when used by the Soviet Union than by capitalist countries.

When weighed against the grave harm resulting from governmental intrusion into the intellectual life of a university, such justification for compelling a witness to discuss the contents of his lecture appears grossly inadequate. Particularly is this so where the witness has sworn that neither in the lecture nor at any other time did he ever advocate overthrowing the Government by force and violence.

Progress in the natural sciences is not remotely confined to findings made in the laboratory. Insights into the mysteries of nature are born of hypothesis and speculation. The more so is this true in the pursuit of understanding in the grouping endeavors of what are called the social sciences, the concern of which is man and society. The problems that are the respective preoccupations of anthropology, economics, law, psychology, sociology and related areas of scholarship are merely departmentalized dealing, by way of manageable division of analysis, with interpenetrating aspects of holistic perplexities. For society's good—if understanding be an essential need of society—inquiries into these problems, speculations about them, stimulation in others of reflection upon them, must be left as unfettered as possible. Political power must abstain from intrusion into this activity of freedom, pursued in the interests of wise government and the people's well-being, except for reasons that are exigent and obviously compelling.

These pages need not be burdened with proof, based on the testimony of a cloud of impressive witnesses, of the dependence of a free society on free universities. This means the exclusion of governmental intervention in the intellectual life of a university. It matters little whether such intervention occurs avowedly or through action that inevitably tends to check the ardor and fearlessness of scholars, qualities at once so fragile and so indispensable for fruitful academic labor. One need only refer to the address of T. H. Huxley at the opening of Johns Hopkins University, the Annual Reports of President A. Lawrence Lowell of Harvard, the Reports of the University Grants Committee in Great Britain, as illustrative items in a vast body of literature. Suffice it to quote the latest expression on this subject. It is also perhaps the most poignant because its plea on behalf of continuing the free spirit of the open universities of South Africa has gone unheeded.

"In a university knowledge is its own end, not merely a means to an end. A university ceases to be true to its own nature if it becomes the tool of Church or State or any sectional interest. A university is characterized by the spirit of free inquiry, its ideal being the ideal of Socrates—'to follow the argument where it leads.' This implies the right to examine, question, modify or reject traditional ideas and beliefs. Dogma and hypothesis are incompatible, and the concept of an immutable doctrine is repugnant to the spirit of a university. The concern of its scholars is not merely to add and revise facts in relation to an accepted framework, but to be ever examining and modifying the framework itself.

"Freedom to reason and freedom for disputation on the basis of observation and experiment are the necessary conditions for the advancement of scientific knowledge. A sense of freedom is also necessary for creative work in the arts which, equally with scientific research, is the concern of the university.

. . . . .

". . . It is the business of a university to provide that atmosphere which is most conducive to speculation, experiment and creation. It is an atmosphere in which there prevail the 'four essential freedoms' of a university—to determine for itself on academic grounds who may teach, what may be taught, how it shall be taught, and who may be admitted to study." The Open Universities in South Africa 10–12. (A statement of a conference of senior scholars from the University of Cape Town and the University of the Witwatersrand, including A. v. d. S. Centlivres and Richard Feetham, as Chancellors of the respective universities.[1])

I do not suggest that what New Hampshire has here sanctioned bears any resemblance to the policy against which this South African remonstrance was directed. I do say that in these matters of the spirit inroads on legitimacy must be resisted at their incipiency. This kind of evil grows by what it is allowed to feed on. The admonition of this Court in another context is applicable here. "It may be that it is the obnoxious thing in its mildest and least repulsive form; but illegitimate and unconstitutional practices get their first footing in that way, namely, by silent approaches and slight deviations from legal modes of procedure." *Boyd* v. *United States*, 116 U.S. 616, 635.

Petitioner stated, in response to questions at the hearing, that he did not know of any Communist interest in, connection with, influence over, activity in, or manipulation of the Progressive Party. He refused to answer, despite court order, the following questions on the ground that, by inquiring into the activities of a lawful political organization, they infringed upon the inviolability of the right to privacy in his political thoughts, actions and associations.

"Was she, Nancy Sweezy, your wife, active in the formation of the Progressive Citizens of America?"

"Was Nancy Sweezy then working with individuals who were then members of the Communist Party?" [2]

"Was Charles Beebe active in forming the Progressive Citizens of America?"

"Did he work with your present wife—Did Charles Beebe work with your present wife in 1947?"

"Did it [a meeting at the home of one Abraham Walenko] have anything to do with the Progressive Party?"

The Supreme Court of New Hampshire justified this intrusion upon his freedom on the same basis that it upheld questioning about the university lecture, namely, that the restriction was limited to situa-

---

[1] The Hon. A. v. d. S. Centlivres only recently retired as Chief Justice of South Africa, and the Hon. Richard Feetham is also an eminent, retired South African judge.

[2] Inclusion of this question among the unanswered questions appears to have been an oversight in view of the fact that petitioner attempted to answer it at the hearing by stating that he had never to his knowledge known members of the Communist Party in New Hampshire. In any event, petitioner's brief states that he is willing to repeat the answer to this question if the attorney general so desires. This is consistent with his demonstrated willingness to answer all inquiries regarding the Communist Party, including its relation to the Progressive Party.

tions where the Committee had reason to believe that violent overthrow of the Government was being advocated or planned. It ruled:

". . . That he [the attorney general] did possess information which was sufficient to reasonably warrant inquiry concerning the Progressive Party is evident from his statement made during the hearings held before him that 'considerable sworn testimony has been given in this investigation to the effect that the Progressive Party in New Hampshire has been heavily infiltrated by members of the Communist Party and that the policies and purposes of the Progressive Party have been directly influenced by members of the Communist Party.'" 100 N. H., at 111, 121 A. 2d, at 790.

For a citizen to be made to forego even a part of so basic a liberty as his political autonomy, the subordinating interest of the State must be compelling. Inquiry pursued in safeguarding a State's security against threatened force and violence cannot be shut off by mere disclaimer, though of course a relevant claim may be made to the privilege against self-incrimination. (The New Hampshire Constitution guarantees this privilege.) But the inviolability of privacy belonging to a citizen's political loyalties has so overwhelming an importance to the well-being of our kind of society that it cannot be constitutionally encroached upon on the basis of so meagre a countervailing interest of the State as may be argumentatively found in the remote, shadowy threat to the security of New Hampshire allegedly presented in the origins and contributing elements of the Progressive Party and in petitioner's relations to these.

In the political realm, as in the academic, thought and action are presumptively immune from inquisition by political authority. It cannot require argument that inquiry would be barred to ascertain whether a citizen had voted for one or the other of the two major parties either in a State or National election. Until recently, no difference would have been entertained in regard to inquiries about a voter's affiliations with one of the various so-called third parties that have had their day, or longer, in our political history. This is so, even though adequate protection of secrecy by way of the Australian ballot did not come into use till 1888. The implications of the United States Constitution for national elections and "the concept of ordered liberty" implicit in the Due Process Clause of the Fourteenth Amendment as against the States, *Palko* v. *Connecticut*, 302 U.S. 319, 325, were not frozen as of 1789 or 1868, respectively. While the language of the Constitution does not change, the changing circumstances of a progressive society for which it was designed yield new and fuller import to its meaning. See *Hurtado* v. *California*, 110 U.S. 516, 528–529; *McCulloch* v. *Maryland*, 4 Wheat. 316. Whatever, on the basis of massive proof and in the light of history, of which this Court may well take judicial notice, be the justification for not regarding the Communist Party as a conventional political party, no such justification has been afforded in regard to the Progressive Party. A foundation in fact and reason would have to be established far weightier than the intimations that appear in the record to warrant such a view of the Progressive Party.[3] This precludes the questioning that petitioner resisted in regard to that Party.

---

[3] The Progressive Party was on the ballot in forty-four States, including New Hampshire, in 1948, and in twenty-six States in 1952.

To be sure, this is a conclusion based on a judicial judgment in balancing two contending principles—the right of a citizen to political privacy, as protected by the Fourteenth Amendment, and the right of the State to self-protection. And striking the balance implies the exercise of judgment. This is the inescapable judicial task in giving substantive content, legally enforced, to the Due Process Clause, and it is a task ultimately committed to this Court. It must not be an exercise of whim or will. It must be an overriding judgment founded on something much deeper and more justifiable than personal preference. As far as it lies within human limitations, it must be an impersonal judgment. It must rest on fundamental presuppositions rooted in history to which widespread acceptance may fairly be attributed. Such a judgment must be arrived at in a spirit of humility when it counters the judgment of the State's highest court. But, in the end, judgment cannot be escaped—the judgment of this Court. See concurring opinions in *Haley* v. *Ohio*, 332 U.S. 596, 601; *Louisiana ex rel. Francis* v. *Resweber*, 329 U.S. 459, 466, 470–471; *Malinski* v. *New York*, 324 U.S. 401, 412, 414–417.

And so I am compelled to conclude that the judgment of the New Hampshire court must be reversed.

MR. JUSTICE CLARK, with whom MR. JUSTICE BURTON joins, dissenting.

The Court today has denied the State of New Hampshire the right to investigate the extent of "subversive activities" within its boundaries in the manner chosen by its legislature. Unfortunately there is no opinion for the Court, for those who reverse are divided and they do so on entirely different grounds. Four of my Brothers join in what I shall call the principal opinion. They hold that the appointment of the attorney general to act as a committee for the legislature results in a separation of its power to investigate from its "responsibility to direct the use of that power" and thereby "causes a deprivation of the constitutional rights of individuals and a denial of due process . . . ." This theory was not raised by the parties and is, indeed, a novel one.

My Brothers FRANKFURTER and HARLAN do not agree with this opinion because they conclude, as do I, that the internal affairs of the New Hampshire State Government are of no concern to us. See *Dreyer* v. *Illinois*, 187 U.S. 71, 84 (1902). They do join in the reversal, however, on the ground that Sweezy's rights under the First Amendment have been violated. I agree with neither opinion.

The principal opinion finds that "The attorney general has been given such a sweeping and uncertain mandate that it is his decision which picks out the subjects that will be pursued, what witnesses will be summoned and what questions will be asked." The New Hampshire Act clearly indicates that it was the legislature that determined the general subject matter of the investigation, subversive activities; the legislature's committee, the attorney general, properly decided what witnesses should be called and what questions should be asked. My Brothers surely would not have the legislature as a whole make these decisions. But they conclude, nevertheless, that it cannot be said that the legislature "asked the attorney general to gather the kind of facts comprised in the subjects upon which petitioner was interrogated." It follows, says this opinion, that there is no "assurance that the questions petitioner refused to answer fall into a category of matters upon which the legislature wanted to be informed . . . ." But New Hampshire's Supreme Court has construed the State statute. It has declared the purpose to be to investigate "subversive" activities within the State; it has approved the use of the "one-man" technique; it has said the questions were all relevant to the legislative purpose. In effect the State court says the attorney general was "directed" to inquire as he did. Furthermore, the legislature renewed the Act in the same language twice in the year following Sweezy's interrogation. N.H. Laws 1955, c. 197. In ratifying the attorney general's action it used these words: "The investigation . . . provided for by chapter 307 of the Laws of 1953, as continued by a resolution approved January 13, 1955, is hereby continued in full force and effect, in form, *manner* and authority as therein provided . . . ." (Emphasis added.) We are bound by the State court findings. We have no right to strike down the State action unless we find not only that there has been a deprivation of Sweezy's constitutional rights, but that the interest in protecting those rights is greater than the State's interest in uncovering subversive activities within its confines. The majority has made no such findings.

The short of it is that the Court blocks New Hampshire's effort to enforce its law. I had thought that in *Pennsylvania* v. *Nelson*, 350 U.S. 497 (1956), we had left open for legitimate State control any subversive activity leveled against the interest of the State. I for one intended to suspend State action only in the field of subversion against the Nation and thus avoid a race to the courthouse door between Federal and State prosecutors. Cases concerning subversive activities against the National Government have such interstate ramifications that individual State action might effectively destroy a prosecution on the national level. I thought we had left open a wide field for State action, but implicit in the opinions today is a contrary conclusion. They destroy the fact-finding power of the State in this field and I dissent from this wide sweep of their coverage.

The principal opinion discusses, by way of dictum, due process under the Fourteenth Amendment. Since the basis of the opinion is not placed on this ground, I would not think it necessary to raise it here. However, my Brothers say that the definition of "subversive person" lacks "a necessary element of guilty knowledge . . . ." *Wieman* v. *Updegraff*, 344 U.S. 183 (1952), is heavily depended upon as authority for the view expressed. I do not so regard it. I authored that opinion. It was a loyalty oath case in which Oklahoma had declared *ipso facto* disqualified any employee of the State who failed to take a prescribed oath that, *inter alia*, he belonged to no subversive organizations. We struck down the Act for lack of a requirement of *scienter*. We said there that "constitutional protection . . . extend[s] to the public servant whose *exclusion pursuant to a statute* is patently arbitrary or discriminatory." *Id.*, at 192. But Sweezy is not charged as a "subversive person" and the committee has made no finding that he is. In fact, had he been found to be such a person, there is no sanction under the Act. New Hampshire is invoking no statute like Oklahoma's. Its Act excludes no one from anything. *Updegraff* stands for no such broad abstraction as the principal opinion suggests.

Since the conclusion of a majority of those reversing is not predicated on the First Amendment questions presented, I see no necessity for discussing them. But since the principal opinion devotes itself largely to these issues I believe it fair to ask why they have been given such an elaborate treatment when the case is decided on an entirely different ground. It is of no avail to quarrel with a straw man. My view on First Amendment problems in this type of case is expressed in my dissent in *Watkins*, decided today, *ante*, p. 217. Since a majority of the Court has not passed on these problems here, and since I am not convinced that the State's interest in investigating subversive activities for the protection of its citizens is outweighed by any necessity for the protection of Sweezy I would affirm the judgment of the New Hampshire Supreme Court.

UPHAUS *v.* WYMAN, ATTORNEY GENERAL OF NEW HAMPSHIRE

APPEAL FROM THE SUPREME COURT OF NEW HAMPSHIRE

No. 34.   Argued November 17–18, 1958.—Decided June 8, 1959.

In an investigation conducted by the attorney general of New Hampshire on behalf of the State legislature under a resolution directing him to investigate violations of the State Subversive Activities Act and to determine whether "subversive persons" were then in the State, appellant, who is executive director of a corporation organized under the laws of the State and operating a summer camp in the State, testified concerning his own activities but refused to comply with subpoenas *duces tecum* calling for the production of the names of all persons who attended the camp during 1954 and 1955. Pursuant to State procedure, he was brought before a State court. There he did not plead the privilege against self-incrimination but claimed that the investigation was beyond the power of the State, that the resolution was too vague, that the documents sought were not relevant to the inquiry, and that to compel him to produce them would violate his rights of free speech and association. These claims were decided against him and, persisting in his refusal, he was adjudged guilty of civil contempt and ordered committed to jail until he complied with the order. *Held:* The judgment and sentence are sustained. Pp. 73–82.

(a) The New Hampshire Subversive Activities Act of 1951 and the resolution authorizing and directing the State Attorney General to investigate violations thereof have not been superseded by the Smith Act, as amended. *Pennsylvania* v. *Nelson*, 350 U.S. 497, distinguished. Pp. 76–77.

(b) The right of the State to require the production of corporate papers of a State-chartered corporation to determine whether corporate activities violate State policy stands unimpaired either by the Smith Act or by *Pennsylvania* v. *Nelson, supra.* P. 77.

(c) On the record in this case, the nexus between the corporation, its summer camp and subversive activities which might threaten the security of the State justifies the investigation; the State's interests in self-preservation outweigh individual rights in associational privacy; and the Due Process Clause of the Fourteenth Amendment does not preclude the State from compelling production of the names of the guests. *Sweezy* v. *New Hampshire*, 354 U.S. 234, and *National Association for the Advancement of Colored People* v. *Alabama*, 357 U.S. 449, distinguished. Pp. 77–81.

(d) Since the demand for the documents was a legitimate one, the judgment of contempt for refusal to produce them is valid; and the sentence of imprisonment until appellant produces them does not constitute such cruel and unusual punishment as to be a denial of due process. Pp. 81–82.

101 N.H. 139, 136 A. 2d 221, affirmed.

Royal W. France and *Leonard B. Boudin* argued the cause for appellant. With them on the brief were *Hugh H. Bownes* and *Victor Rabinowitz.*

Louis C. Wyman, Attorney General of New Hampshire, argued the cause for appellee. With him on the brief was *Dort S. Bigg.*

Nathan Witt and *John M. Coe* filed a brief for the National Lawyers Guild, as *amicus curiae*, urging reversal.

Mr. Justice Clark delivered the opinion of the Court.

This case is here again on appeal from a judgment of civil contempt entered against appellant by the Merrimack County Court and affirmed by the Supreme Court of New Hampshire. It arises out of appellant's refusal to produce certain documents before a New Hampshire legislative investigating committee which was authorized and directed to determine, *inter alia*, whether there were subversive persons or organizations present in the State of New Hampshire. Upon the first appeal from the New Hampshire court, 100 N.H. 436, 130 A. 2d 278, we vacated the judgment and remanded the case to it, 355 U.S. 16, for consideration in the light of *Sweezy* v. *New Hampshire*, 354 U.S. 234 (1957). That court reaffirmed its former decision, 101 N.H. 139, 136 A. 2d 221, deeming *Sweezy* not to control the issues in the instant case. For reasons which will appear, we agree with the Supreme Court of New Hampshire.

As in *Sweezy*, the attorney general of New Hampshire, who had been constituted a one-man legislative investigating committee by joint resolution of the legislature,[1] was conducting a probe of subversive activities in the State. In the course of his investigation the attorney general called appellant, Executive Director of World Fellowship, Inc., a voluntary corporation organized under the laws of New Hampshire and maintaining a summer camp in the State. Appellant testified concerning his own activities, but refused to comply with two subpoenas *duces tecum* which called for the production of certain corporate records for the years 1954 and 1955. The information sought consisted of: (1) a list of the names of all the camp's nonprofessional employees for those two summer seasons; (2) the correspondence which appellant had carried on with and concerning those persons who came to the camp as speakers; and (3) the names of all persons who attended the camp during the same periods of time. Met with appellant's refusal, the attorney general, in accordance with State procedure, N.H. Rev. Stat. Ann., c. 491, §§ 19, 20, petitioned the Merrimack County Court to call appellant before it and require compliance with the subpoenas.

In court, appellant again refused to produce the information. He claimed that by the Smith Act,[2] as construed by this Court in *Pennsylvania* v. *Nelson*, 350 U.S. 497 (1956), Congress had so completely occupied the field of subversive activities that the States were without power to investigate in that area. Additionally, he contended that the Due Process Clause precuded enforcement of the subpoenas, first, because the resolution under which the attorney general was authorized to operate was vague and, second, because the documents sought were not relevant to the inquiry. Finally, appellant argued that enforcement would violate his rights of free speech and association.

---

[1] *"Resolved by the Senate and House of Representatives in General Court convened:* "That the attorney general is hereby authorized and directed to make full and complete investigation with respect to violations of the subversive activities act of 1951 and to determine whether subversive persons as defined in said act are presently located within this State. . . ." N.H. Laws, 1953 c. 307.
The investigation authorized by this resolution was continued by N.H. Laws, 1955, c. 197.

[2] U.S.C. § 2385 (1956).

The Merrimack County Court sustained appellant's objection to the production of the names of the nonprofessional employees. The attorney general took no appeal from that ruling, and it is not before us. Appellant's objections to the production of the names of the camp's guests were overruled, and he was ordered to produce them. Upon his refusal, he was adjudged in contempt of court and ordered committed to jail until he should have complied with the court order. On the demand for the correspondence and the objection thereto, the trial court made no ruling but transferred the question to the Supreme Court of New Hampshire. That court affirmed the trial court's action in regard to the guest list. Concerning the requested production of the correspondence, the supreme court entered no order, but directed that on remand the trial court "may exercise its discretion with respect to the entry of an order to enforce the command of the subpoena for the production of correspondence." 100 N. H., at 448, 130 A. 2d, at 287. No remand having yet been effected, the trial court has not acted upon this phase of the case, and there is no final judgment requiring the appellant to produce the letters. We therefore do not treat with that question. 28 U.S.C. § 1257. See *Radio Station WOW* v. *Johnson*, 326 U.S. 120, 123–124 (1945). We now pass to a consideration of the sole question before us, namely, the validity of the order of contempt for refusal to produce the list of guests at World Fellowship, Inc., during the summer seasons of 1954 and 1955. In addition to the arguments appellant made to the trial court, he urges here that the "indefinite sentence" imposed upon him constitutes such cruel and unusual punishment as to be a denial of due process.

Appellant vigorously contends that the New Hampshire Subversive Activities Act of 1951 [3] and the resolution creating the committee have been superseded by the Smith Act, as amended.[4] In support of this position appellant cites *Pennsylvania* v. *Nelson, supra*. The argument is that *Nelson*, which involved a prosecution under a State sedition law, held that "Congress has intended to occupy the field of sedition." This rule of decision, it is contended, should embrace legislative investigations made pursuant to an effort by the legislature to inform itself of the presence of subversives within the State and possibly to enact laws in the subversive field. The appellant's argument sweeps too broad. In *Nelson* itself we said that the "precise holding of the court * * * is that the Smith Act * * * which prohibits the knowing advocacy of the overthrow of the Government of the United States by force and violence, supersedes the enforceability of the Pennsylvania Sedition Act which proscribed the *same conduct*." (Italics supplied.) 350 U.S., at 499. The basis of *Nelson* thus rejects the notion that it stripped the States of the right to protect themselves. All the opinion proscribed was a race between Federal and State prosecutors to the courthouse door. The opinion made clear that a State could proceed with prosecutions for sedition against the State itself; that it can legitimately investigate in this are follows *a fortiori*. In *Sweezy* v. *New Hampshire, supra*, where the same contention was made as to the identical State Act, it was denied *sub silentio*. Nor did our opinion in *Nelson* hold that the Smith Act had proscribed State activity in protection of itself either from actual or threatened "sabotage or attempted violence of all kinds." In footnote 8 of the opinion it is

---

[3] N. H. Rev. Stat. Ann., 1955, c. 588, §§ 1–16.
[4] Note 2, *supra*.

pointed out that the State had full power to deal with internal civil disturbances. Thus registration statutes, *quo warranto* proceedings as to subversive corporations, the subversive instigation of riots and a host of other subjects directly affecting State security furnish grist for the State's legislative mill. Moreover, the right of the State to require the production of corporate papers of a State-chartered corporation in an inquiry to determine whether corporate activity is violative of State policy is, of course, not touched upon in *Nelson* and today stands unimpaired, either by the Smith Act or the *Nelson* opinion.

Appellant's other objections can be capsuled into the single question of whether New Hampshire, under the facts here, is precluded from compelling the production of the documents by the Due Process Clause of the Fourteenth Amendment. Let us first clear away some of the underbrush necessarily surrounding the case because of its setting.

First, the academic and political freedoms discussed in *Sweezy* v. *New Hampshire, supra,* are not present here in the same degree, since World Fellowship is neither a university nor a political party. Next, since questions concerning the authority of the committee to act as it did are questions of State law, *Dreyer* v. *Illinois,* 187 U.S. 71, 84 (1902), we accept as controlling the New Hampshire Supreme Court's conclusion that "[t]he legislative history makes it clear beyond a reasonable doubt that it [the legislature] did and does desire an answer to these questions." 101 N.H., at 140, 136 A. 2d, at 221–222. Finally, we assume, without deciding, that Uphaus had sufficient standing to assert any rights of the guests whose identity the committee seeks to determine. See *National Association for the Advancement of Colored People* v. *Alabama,* 357 U.S. 449 (1958). The interest of the guests at World Fellowship in their associational privacy having been asserted, we have for decision the Federal question of whether the public interests overbalance these conflicting private ones. Whether there was "justification" for the production order turns on the "substantiality" of New Hampshire's interests in obtaining the identity of the guests when weighed against the individual interests which the appellant asserts. *National Association for the Advancement of Colored People* v. *Alabama, supra.*

What was the interest of the State? The attorney general was commissioned [5] to determine if there were any subversive persons [6] within New Hampshire. The obvious starting point of such an inquiry was to learn what persons were within the State. It is therefore clear that the requests relate directly to the legislature's area of interest, *i.e.,* the presence of subversives in the State, as announced in its resolution. Nor was the demand of the subpoena burdensome; as to time, only a few months of each of the two years were involved; as to place, only the camp conducted by the corporation; nor as to the lists of names, which included about 300 each year.

---

[5] Note 1, *supra.*

[6] Section 1 of the Subversive Activities Act, N. H. Rev. Stat. Ann., 1955, c. 588, §§ 1–16, defines "subversive person":

" 'Subversive person' means any person who commits, attempts to commit, or aids in the commission, or advocates, abets, advises or teaches, by any means any person to commit, attempt to commit, or aid in the commission of any act intended to overthrow, destroy or alter, or to assist in the overthrow, destruction or alteration of, the constitutional form of the Government of the United States, or of the State of New Hampshire, or any political subdivision of either of them, by force, or violence; or who is a member of a subversive organization or a foreign subversive organization."

Moreover, the attorney general had valid reason to believe that the speakers and guests at World Fellowship might be subversive persons within the meaning of the New Hampshire Act. The Supreme Court of New Hampshire found Uphaus' contrary position "unrelated to reality." Although the evidence as to the nexus between World Fellowship and subversive activities may not be conclusive, we believe it sufficiently relevant to support the attorney general's action. The New Hampshire definition of subversive persons was born of the legislative determination that the Communist movement posed a serious threat to the security of the State. The record reveals that appellant had participated in "Communist front" activities and that "[n]ot less than nineteen speakers invited by Uphaus to talk at World Fellowship had either been members of the Communist Party or had connections or affiliations with it or with one or more of the organizations cited as subversive or Communist controlled in the United States Attorney General's list." 100 N.H., at 442, 130 A. 2d, at 283. While the Attorney General's list is designed for the limited purpose of determining fitness for Federal employment, *Wieman* v. *Updegraff*, 344 U.S. 183 (1952), and guilt by association remains a thoroughly discredited doctrine, it is with a legislative investigation—not a criminal prosecution—that we deal here. Certainly the investigatory power of the State need not be constricted until sufficient evidence of subversion is gathered to justify the institution of criminal proceedings.

The nexus between World Fellowship and subversive activities disclosed by the record furnished adequate justification for the investigation we here review. The attorney general sought to learn if subversive persons were in the State because of the legislative determination that such persons, statutorily defined with a view toward the Communist Party, posed a serious threat to the security of the State. The investigation was, therefore, undertaken in the interest of self-preservation, "the ultimate value of any society," *Dennis* v. *United States*, 341 U.S. 494, 509 (1951). This governmental interest outweighs individual rights in an associational privacy which, however real in other circumstances, cf. *National Association for the Advancement of Colored People* v. *Alabama, supra*, were here tenuous at best. The camp was operating as a public one, furnishing both board and lodging to persons applying therefor. As to them, New Hampshire law requires that World Fellowship, Inc., maintain a register, open to inspection of sheriffs and police officers.[7] It is contended that the list might "be circulated throughout the State and the attorneys general throughout the States have cross-indexed files, so that any guest whose name is mentioned in that kind of proceeding immediately becomes suspect, even in his own place of residence." Record, p. 7. The record before us, however, only reveals a report to the legislature of New Hampshire made by the attorney general in accordance with the requirements of the resolution. We recognize, of course, that compliance with the subpoena will result in exposing the fact that the

---

[7] Since 1927, there has been in effect the following statute in New Hampshire:
"All hotel keepers and all persons keeping public lodging houses, tourist camps, or cabins shall keep a book or card system and cause each guest to sign therein his own legal name or name by which he is commonly known. Said book or card system shall at all times be open to the inspection of the sheriff or his deputies and to any police officer. . . ." N. H. Rev. Stat. Ann., 1955, c. 353, § 3.
The attorney general represents that the public camp of World Fellowship, Inc., is clearly within the purview of this statute. Although the lists sought were more extensive than those required by the statute, it appears that most of the names were recorded pursuant to it.

persons therein named were guests at World Fellowship. But so long as a committee must report to its legislative parent, exposure—in the sense of disclosure—is an inescapable incident of an investigation into the presence of subversive persons within a State. And the governmental interest in self-preservation is sufficiently compelling to subordinate the interest in associational privacy of persons who, at least to the extent of the guest registration statute, made public at the inception the association they now wish to keep private. In the light of such a record we conclude that the State's interest has not been "pressed, in this instance, to a point where it has come into fatal collision with the overriding" constitutionally protected rights of appellant and those he may represent. *Cantwell* v. *Connecticut*, 310 U.S. 296, 307 (1940).

We now reach the question of the validity of the sentence. The judgment of contempt orders the appellant confined until he produces the documents called for in the subpoenas. He himself admitted to the court that although they were at hand, not only had he failed to bring them with him to court, but that, further, he had no intention of producing them. In view of appellant's unjustified refusal we think the order a proper one. As was said in *Green* v. *United States*, 356 U.S. 165, 197 (1958) (dissenting opinion):

"Before going any further, perhaps it should be emphasized that we are not at all concerned with the power of courts to impose conditional imprisonment for the purpose of compelling a person to obey a valid order. Such coercion, where the defendant carries the keys to freedom in his willingness to comply with the court's directive, is essentially a civil remedy designed for the benefit of other parties and has quite properly been exercised for centuries to secure compliance with judicial decrees."

We have concluded that the committee's demand for the documents was a legitimate one; it follows that the judgment of contempt for refusal to produce them is valid. We do not impugn appellant's good faith in the assertion of what he believed to be his rights. But three courts have disagreed with him in interpreting those rights. If appellant chooses to abide by the result of the adjudication and obey the order of New Hampshire's courts, he need not face jail. If however, he continues to disobey, we find on this record no constitutional objection to the exercise of the traditional remedy of contempt to secure compliance.

Affirmed.

Mr. JUSTICE BRENNAN, with whom THE CHIEF JUSTICE, MR. JUSTICE BLACK and MR. JUSTICE DOUGLAS join, dissenting.

The Court holds today that the constitutionally protected rights of speech and assembly of appellant and those whom he may represent are to be subordinated to New Hampshire's legislative investigation because, as applied in the demands made on him, the investigation is rationally connected with a discernible legislative purpose. With due respect for my Brothers' views, I do not agree that a showing of any requisite legislative purpose or other State interest that constitutionally can subordinate appellant's rights is to be found in this record. Exposure purely for the sake of exposure is not such a valid subordinating purpose. *Watkins* v. *United States*, 354 U.S. 178, 187, 200; *Sweezy* v. *New Hampshire*, 354 U.S. 234; *NAACP* v. *Alabama*, 357

U.S. 449. This record, I think, not only fails to reveal any interest of the State sufficient to subordinate appellant's constitutionally protected rights, but affirmatively shows that the investigatory objective was the impermissible one of exposure for exposure's sake. I therefore dissent from the judgment of the Court.

I fully appreciate the delicacy of the judicial task of questioning the workings of a legislative investigation. A proper regard for the primacy of the legislative function in its own field, and for the broad scope of the investigatory power to achieve legislative ends, necessarily should constrain the judiciary to indulge every reasonable intendment in favor of the validity of legislative inquiry. However, our frame of government also imposes another inescapable duty upon the judiciary, that of protecting the constitutional rights of freedom of speech and assembly from improper invasion, whether by the National or the State legislatures. See *Watkins* v. *United States, supra; Sweezy* v. *New Hampshire, supra; NAACP* v. *Alabama, supra.* Where that invasion is as clear as I think this record discloses, the appellant is entitled to our judgment of reversal.

Judicial consideration of the collision of the investigatory function with constitutionally protected rights of speech and assembly is a recent development in our constitutional law. The Court has often examined the validity under the Federal Constitution of Federal and State statutes and executive action imposing criminal and other traditional sanctions on conduct alleged to be protected by the guarantees of freedom of speech and of assembly. The role of the State-imposed sanctions of imprisonment, fines and prohibitory injunctions directed against association or speech and their limitations under the First and Fourteenth Amendments has been canvassed quite fully, beginning as early as *Gitlow* v. *New York,* 268 U.S. 652, and *Near* v. *Minnesota,* 283 U.S. 697. And other State action, such as deprivation of public employment and the denial of admission to a profession, has also been recognized as being subject to the restraints of the Constitution. See, *e.g., Wieman* v. *Updegraff,* 344 U.S. 183; cf. *Schware* v. *Board of Bar Examiners,* 353 U.S. 232.

But only recently has the Court been required to begin a full exploration of the impact of the governmental investigatory function on these freedoms.[1] Here is introduced the weighty consideration that the power of investigation, whether exercised in aid of the governmental legislative power, see *Watkins* v. *United States, supra,* or in aid of the governmental power to adjudicate disputes, see *NAACP* v. *Alabama, supra,* is vital to the functioning of free governments and is therefore necessarily broad. But where the exercise of the investigatory power collides with constitutionally guaranteed freedoms, that power too has inevitable limitations, and the delicate and always difficult accommodation of the two with minimum sacrifice of either is the hard task of the judiciary and ultimately of this Court.

It was logical that the adverse effects of unwanted publicity—of exposure—as concomitants of the exercise of the investigatory power, should come to be recognized, in certain circumstances, as invading

---

[1] The two leading earlier cases relate generally to the congressional power to investigate, and were not required to explore it in the contexts of freedom of speech and of assembly. *Kilbourn* v. *Thompson,* 103 U.S. 168; *McGrain* v. *Daugherty,* 273 U.S. 135. See the opinion in the latter case, *ibid.,* at 175–176.

protected freedoms and offending constitutional inhibitions upon governmental actions. For in an era of mass communications and mass opinion, and of international tensions and domestic anxiety, exposure and group identification by the State of those holding unpopular and dissident views are fraught with such serious consequences for the individual as inevitably to inhibit seriously the expression of views which the Constitution intended to make free. Cf. *Speiser* v. *Randall*, 357 U.S. 513, 526. We gave expression to this truism in *NAACP* v. *Alabama:* "This Court has recognized the vital relationship between freedom to associate and privacy in one's associations. . . . Inviolability of privacy in group association may in many circumstances be indispensable to preservation of freedom of association, particularly where a group espouses dissident beliefs." 357 U.S., at 462.

Of course, the considerations entering into the weighing of the interests concerned are different where the problem is one of State exposure in the area of assembly and expression from where the problem is that of evaluating a State criminal or regulatory statute in these areas. Government must have freedom to make an appropriate investigation where there appears a rational connection with the lawmaking process, the processes of adjudication, or other essential governmental functions. In the investigatory stage of the legislative process, for example, the specific interest of the State and the final legislative means to be chosen to implement it are almost by definition not precisely defined at the start of the inquiry, and due allowance must accordingly be made. Also, when exposure is evaluated judicially as a governmental sanction, there should be taken into account the differences between it and the more traditional State-inflicted pains and penalties. True it is, therefore, that any line other than a universal subordination of free expression and association to the asserted interests of the State in investigation and exposure will be difficult of definition; but this Court has rightly turned its back on the alternative of universal subordination of protected interests, and we must define rights in this area the best we can. The problem is one in its nature calling for traditional case-by-case development of principles in the various permutations of circumstances where the conflict may appear. But guide lines must be marked out by the courts. "This is the inescapable judicial task in giving substantive content, legally enforced, to the Due Process Clause, and it is a task ultimately committed to this Court." *Sweezy* v. *New Hampshire*, 354 U.S. 234, 267 (concurring opinion). On the facts of this case I think that New Hampshire's investigation, as applied to the appellant, was demonstrably and clearly outside the wide limits of the power which must be conceded to the State even though it be attended by some exposure. In demonstration of this I turn to the detailed examination of the facts which this case requires.

The appellant, Uphaus, is Executive Director of a group called World Fellowship which runs a discussion program at a summer camp in New Hampshire, at which the public is invited to stay. Various speakers come to the camp primarily for discussion of political, economic and social matters. The appellee reports that Uphaus and some of the speakers have been said by third persons to have a history of association with "Communist front" movements, to have followed the "Communist line," signed amnesty petitions and *amicus curiae* briefs, and carried on similar activities of a sort which have recently been viewed hostilely and suspiciously by many Americans. A strain of pacifism runs through the appellant's thinking, and the appellee apparently would seek to determine whether there should be drawn therefrom an inference of harm for our institutions; he conjectures, officially, whether "the advocacy of this so-called peace crusade is for the purpose of achieving a quicker and a cheaper occupation by the Soviet Union and Communism." There is no evidence that any activity of a sort that violates the law of New Hampshire or could in fact be constitutionally punished went on at the camp. What is clear is that there was some sort of assemblage at the camp that was oriented toward the discussion of political and other public matters. The activities going on were those of private citizens. The views expounded obviously were minority views. But the assemblage was, on its face, for purposes to which the First and Fourteenth Amendments give constitutional protection against incursion by the powers of government. Cf. *Sweezy* v. *New Hampshire, supra,* at 249–251.

The investigation with which this case is concerned was undertaken under authority of a 1953 resolution of the New Hampshire General Court, N.H. Laws 1953, c. 307, and extended by an enactment in 1955, N.H. laws, 1955, c. 197. The resolution directed the attorney general of the State (appellee here) to make a "full and complete investigation" of "violations of the subversive activities act of 1951" [2] and to determine whether "subversive persons as defined in said act are presently located within the State." Under New Hampshire law, this constituted the attorney general (who is ordinarily the chief law-enforcement official of the State) a one-man legislative committee. The sanctions of prosecution of individuals and dissolution of organizations for violation of the 1951 law seem to have been discarded, with the passage of the resolution, in favor of the sanction of exposure. A provision of the 1951 Act providing for confidential treatment of material reflecting on individuals' loyalty was made inapplicable to the investigation the attorney general was directed to conduct, and the attorney general was authorized in sweeping terms to give publicity to the details of his investigation. A report to

---

[2] The Act was c. 193 of the Laws of New Hampshire, 1951. After an extensive preamble, § 1 provided various definitions, including definitions of "subversive organization" and "foreign subversive organization"; the definition of "subversive person," also provided, was: "any person who commits, attempts to commit, or aids in the commission, or advocates, abets, advises or teaches, by any means any person to commit, attempt to commit, or aid in the commission of any act intended to overthrow, destroy or alter, or to assist in the overthrow, destruction or alteration of the constitutional form of Government of the United States, or of the State of New Hampshire, or any political subdivision of either of them, by force, or violence; or who is a member of a subversive organization or a foreign subversive organization." For a discussion of the breadth of this definition, see *Sweezy* v. *New Hampshire, supra,* at 246–247.

Section 2 of the Act defines the crime of sedition. The definition is based on the quoted definition of "subversive person," except that the final "membership clause" is omitted and a "clear and present danger" test is introduced in regard to advocacy, abetting, advising and teaching. Assisting in the formation of a subversive organization or foreign subversive organization, managing one, contributing to its support, destroying its papers, or hiding its funds, "knowing said organization to be a subversive organization or a foreign subversive organization" also constitutes the offense, which is punishable by twenty years' imprisonment or a fine of $20,000, or both. Those who become or remain members of a subversive organization or a foreign subversive organization, after certain dates, "knowing said organization to be a subversive organization or a foreign subversive organization," under § 3, are liable to five years' imprisonment or a $5,000 fine, or both. Section 4 disqualifies those convicted under § 2 or § 3 from public office or employment, and § 9 erects a similar disqualification in the case of all "subversive persons." Section 5 provides for the dissolution of subversive organizations and foreign subversive organizations functioning in New Hampshire.

the legislature of the fruits of the investigation was to be made on the first day of the 1955 legislative session; the 1955 extension called for a similar report to the 1957 session.[3] Efforts to obtain from the appellant the disclosures relative to World Fellowship in controversy here began during the period covered by the 1953 resolution, but his final refusal and the proceeding for contempt under review here occured during the extension.

The fruits of the first two years of the investigation were delivered to the legislature in a comprehensive volume on January 5, 1955. The attorney general urges this report on our consideration as extremely relevant to a consideration of the investigation as it relates to appellant. I think that this is quite the case; the report is an official indication of the nature of the investigation and is, in fact, the stated objective of the duty assigned by the resolution to the attorney general. It was with this report before it that the legislature renewed the investigation, and it must be taken as characterizing the nature of the investigation before us. The report proper is divided into numerous sections. First is a series of general and introductory essays by various authors entitled "Pertinent Aspects of World Communism Today." Essays discuss "The Nature of the Russian Threat"; "The Role of the Communist Front Organizations"; "Some Important Aspects of Marxism and Marxism-Leninism"; "The Test of a Front Organization"; and "Communism vs. Religion." General descriptive matter on the Communist Party in New Hampshire follows. It hardly needs to be said that this introductory material would focus attention on the whole report in terms of "communism" regardless of what was said about the individuals later named. Next comes a general section titled "Communist Influence in a Field of Education" which is replete with names and biographical material of individuals; a similar section on "Communist Influence in the Field of Labor"; and one more generically captioned "Organizations," in which various details as to the appellant, his organization, and others associated in it are presented. Last comes a section entitled "Individuals" in which biographical sketches of 23 persons are presented.

The introductory matter in the volume, to put the matter mildly, showed consciousness of the practical effect of the change of policy from judicial prosecution to exposure by the attorney general of persons reported to be connected with groups charged to be "subversive" or "substantially Communist-influenced." Virtually the entire "Letter of Transmittal" of the attorney general addressed itself to discussing the policy used in the report in disclosing the names of individuals. The attorney general drew a significant distinction as to the names he would disclose: "Persons with past membership or affiliation with the Communist Party or substantially Communist-influenced groups have not been disclosed in this report where those persons have provided assistance to the investigation. It is felt that no good reasons exist requiring a listing of names of cooperative witnesses in these categories." A "Foreword" declared that "[t]his report deals with a controversial subject," and, concentrating on the fact that the report contained an extensive list of persons, their addresses, and miscellaneous activities and associations attributed to them, made several

---

[3] None appears to have been made.

disclaimers. The report was not to be considered an indictment of any individual, the attorney general suitably pointing out that a grand jury was the only authority in New Hampshire having the formal power of indictment. Nor was it "the result of an inquisition. No witness in this investigation has ever, at any time, been treated other than courteously." Finally, the attorney general stressed that "[t]he reporting of facts herein does NOT (nor should it be taken to by any reader) constitute a charge against any witness." He observed that "facts are facts . . . . Conclusions of opprobrium relative to any individual, while within the privilege of personal opinion, are neither recomemnded nor intended to be encouraged by any phraseology of this report." In fact, the listing of names might well contain the names of many innocent people, implied the attorney general. This was permissible, he believed, because, as interpreted in the courts of New Hampshire, "the scope of relevant questioning in the investigation goes far beyond the requirements of individual felonious intention. In fact, the General Court has directed that inquiry be made to determine the extent of innocent or ignorant membership, affiliation or support of subversive organizations . . . ."

The report certainly is one that would be suggested by the quoted parts of the foreword. No opinion was, as a matter of course, expressed by the attorney general as to whether any person named therein was in fact a "subversive person" within the meaning of the statute. The report did not disclose whether any indictments under the 1951 Act would be sought against any person. Its sole recommendations for legislation were for a broad evidentiary statute to be applied in trials of persons under the State Act as "subversive," which cannot really be said to have been the fruit of the investigation, being copied from a then recent Act of Congress,[4] and which made apparently no change in the 1951 law's standard of guilt, and for an immunity measure calculated to facilitate future investigations. The report, once the introductory material on Communism is done with, contains primarily an assorted list of names with descriptions of what had been said about the named persons. In most cases, the caveat of the attorney general that the information should not be understood as indicating a violation of the New Hampshire Subversive Activities Act was, to say the least, well-taken, in the light of the conduct ascribed to them. Many of the biographical summaries would strike a discerning analyst as very mild stuff indeed. In many cases, a positive diligence was demonstrated in efforts to add the names of individuals to a list and then render a Scotch verdict of "not proven" in regard to them. The most vivid example of this is the material relating to the appellant's group, World Fellowship. After some introductory pages, there comes extensive biographical material relating to the reported memberships, associations, advocacies, and signings of open letters on the part of certain speakers at the World Fellowship camp. A very few had admitted membership in the Communist Party, or had been "identified" as being members by third persons generally not named. Others were said to be or to have been members of "Communist influenced," "front," or "officially cited" groups. Some were said to have signed open letters and petitions against deporta-

---

4 The Communist Control Act of 1954, § 5, c. 886, 68 Stat. 776, 50 U.S.C. § 844.

tions, to have criticized the Federal Bureau of Investigation, to have given free medical treatment to Communist Party officials, and the like. Finally the report addresses itself to the remainder of the speakers: "Information easily available to this office does *not* indicate records of affiliation with or support of Communist causes on the part of these people. However, due to the burden of work imposed on the staff of the House Committee on Un-American Activities by thousands of such requests received from all over the country, it has not been possible to check each of these persons thoroughly. Inasmuch as no committee or public agency can hope to have all the information in its files concerning all subversive activity all over this country, it is not possible for this office to guarantee that the following individuals do not have such activity in their backgrounds. Therefore, it is necessary to report their identities to the General Court, with the explanation that based upon what information we have been able to assemble, the following individuals would appear at this time to be the usual contingent of 'dupes' and unsuspecting persons that surround almost every venture that is instigated or propelled by the 'perennials' and articulate apologists for Communists and Soviet chicanery, but of this fact we are not certain. This list does *not* include the many persons who were merely guests . . . ." The names of 36 persons with their addresses then followed.[5]

The emphasis of the entire report is on individual guilt, individual near-guilt, and individual questionable behavior. Its flavor and tone, regardless of its introductory disclaimers, cannot help but stimulate readers to attach a "badge of infamy," *Wieman* v. *Updegraff*, 344 U.S.

---

[5] Although the nature of the investigation of individuals is difficult to convey without reproduction of the full report, two individual write-ups from other sections of the book (the names are used in the report but not here) are illustrative.

A two-page item is entitled "The Matter of . . . [X]." It begins: "In recent years there has been opposition to legislative investigations in some academic circles. Charges have been made, usually without an accompanying scintilla of evidence, that 'hysteria' rules the country and that teachers are afraid to teach 'the truth' because of the 'witch hunters.' This line is repeated ad infinitum in the Communist 'Daily Worker.'

"In New Hampshire, during the course of this investigation, a case did arise where rumors were circulated concerning a teacher. . . ."

The report proceeds: "The teacher concerning whom the rumors were circulated was [X], a teacher in the [Y city] public school system. When the rumors concerning Mr. [X] came to the attention of this office, he was invited to testify. . . ."

The report related that X appeared "voluntarily" and testified "fully" that he was not a member of any organization on the Attorney General's list, and never had been. "This office was prepared to make full investigation of the facts and to make public the results of such an investigation if it would effectuate the purposes of the current probe. [X] resigned and secured employment outside the State. Had [X] not decided to submit his resignation, such a course of action would have been taken, but facilities were not available for inquiring into moot problems. . . ."

The report, after noting that none of its available usual informants had anything damaging to say about X, concludes its discussion of this "matter": "It should be clear to factions who oppose per se any legislative investigation into subversion that such investigations can serve the purpose of insuring legitimate academic interests against unfounded rumor or gossip." We are left to conjecture whether Mr. X would subscribe to the Attorney General's conclusion.

An 11-page write-up is the story of Y, a Chief of Police in a New Hampshire municipality. Y admitted having been a Communist from 1936 till 1944, but said that he withdrew then, and currently regarded the Communist Party as something on a par with Hitler. A witness said that Y's name was on a secret Communist Party list after then. Pages of the details of inclusive statements and counterstatements in this regard follow, including a "confrontation" of Chief Y and a witness in the attorney general's office, at which were present the Board of Selectmen of the town for which he was Police Chief. The report then lists various "situations in which Chief [Y] was not able to be of assistance to this investigation" and finally comes to the "Conclusion": "Due to the conspiratorial, clandestine, and currently underground nature of the Communist Party, as well as the inability to force witnesses to testify concerning subversive activities, the above conflicts in testimony here have not been resolved and are presented as they exist on the record, without further comment. . . ."

The usual individual biography is shorter and less detailed than this; many just state the individual's name and street address, set forth a reference to him in the Daily Worker or an "identification" with the Communist Party at some date or with a "front" group, and state that the subject invoked or took refuge in the privilege against self-incrimination when questioned before the attorney general.

183, 190–191, to the persons named in it. The authorizing resolution requested that the attorney general address himself to ascertaining whether there were "subversive persons" in New Hampshire, and the report indicates that this was interpreted as the making of lists of persons who were either classifiable in this amorphous category, or almost so, and the presenting of the result, as a public, official document, to the legislature, and to the public generally. The main thrust of the resolution itself was in terms of individual behavior—violation of the 1951 Act and the presence, in the State, of "subversive persons," were the objects of investigation. The collection of such data, and of data having some peripheral reference to it, with explicit detail as to names and places, was what the attorney general set himself to doing in response to it. As the report itself stated, "A very considerable amount of questioning is absolutely essential to separate the wheat from the chaff in applying the legislative formula to individual conduct which involves that part of the spectrum very close to the line of subversive conduct. Only through such questioning is it possible to be able to report to the legislature whether the activity of a given individual has been subversive or not subversive; whether or not intentionally so or knowingly so on his part." One must feel, on reading the report, that the first sentence—"A very considerable amount of questioning is absolutely essential . . . in applying the legislative formula to individual conduct which involves that part of the spectrum very close to the line of subversive conduct"—is a serious overstatement, because in the usual citation of a person in the report no expression of his innocence or guilt, or his precise coloration in the attorney general's spectrum was given. But still the report was made in terms of the activity of named individuals. Of course, if the attorney general had information relating to guilt under the statute, he was empowered to seek indictment and conviction of the offenders in criminal proceedings, in which of course the normal rights afforded criminal defendants and the normal limitations on State prosecution for conduct related to political association and expression, under the Constitution, would apply. The citation of names in the book does not appear to have any relation to the possibility of an orthodox or traditional criminal prosecution, and the attorney general seems to acknowledge this. The investigation in question here was not one ancillary to a prosecution—to grand jury or trial procedure. If it had been, if a definite prosecution were undertaken, we would have that narrowed context in which to relate the State's demand for exposure. Cf. *NAACP* v. *Alabama, supra,* at 464–465. This process of relation is part and parcel of examining the "substantiality" of the State's interest in the concrete context in which it is alleged. But here we are without the aid of such a precise issue and our task requires that we look further to ascertain whether this legislative investigation, as applied in the demands made upon the appellant, is connected rationally with a discernible general legislative end to which the rights of the appellant and those whom he may represent can constitutionally be subordinated.

The legislature, upon receiving the report, extended the investigation for a further two years. It was during this period that the refusals of the appellant to furnish information with which we are now concerned took place. The attorney general had already published the names of speakers at the World Fellowship camp. Now he wanted the correspondence between Uphaus and the speakers. The attorney general admitted that it was unlikely that the correspondence between Uphaus and the speakers was going to contain a damning admission of a purpose to advocate the overthrow of the government (presumably of New Hampshire) by force and violence. He said that it might indicate a sinister purpose behind the advocacy of pacifism—"the purpose of achieving a quicker and a cheaper occupation by the Soviet Union and communism." The guest list, the nonavailability of which to the attorney general was commented on in the passage from the 1955 report quoted above,[6] was also desired. Appellant's counsel, at the hearing in court giving rise to the contempt finding under review, protested that appellant did not want to allow the attorney general to have the names to expose them. The attorney general also wished the names of the nonprofessional help at the camp—the cooks and dishwashers and the like. It was objected that the cooks and dishwashers were hired from the local labor pool and that if such employment were attended by a trip to the attorney general's office and the possibility of public exposure, help might become hard to find at the camp. This last objection was sustained in the trial court, but the other two inquiries were allowed and appellant's failure to respond to the one relating to the guest list was found contemptuous.

First. The Court seems to experience difficulty in discerning that appellant has any standing to plead the rights of free speech and association he does because the material he seeks to withhold may technically belong to World Fellowship, Inc., a corporation, and may relate to the protected activities of other persons, rather than those of himself. In *NAACP* v. *Alabama, supra,* a corporation was permitted to represent its membership in pleading their rights to freedom of association for public purposes. Here appellant, as a corporate officer if one will, seeks to protect a list of those who have assembled together for public discussion on the corporation's premises. Of course this is not technically a membership list, but to distinguish *NAACP* v. *Alabama* on this ground is to miss its point. The point is that if the members of the assemblage could only plead their assembly rights themselves, the very interest being safeguarded by the Constitution here could never be protected meaningfully, since to require that the guests claim this right themselves would "result in nullification of the right at the very moment of its assertion." *Id.,* at 459. I do not think it likely that anyone would deny the right of a bookseller (including a corporate bookseller) to decline to produce the names of those who had purchased his books. Cf. *United States* v. *Rumely,* 345 U.S. 41, 57 (concurring opinion), and the opinion below in that case, 90 U.S. App. D.C. 382, 197 F. 2d 166, 172.[7]

Second. In examining the right of the State to obtain this information from the appellant by compulsory process, we must recollect what we so recently said in *NAACP* v. *Alabama:*

---

[6] See p. 92, *supra.*
[7] The Court, apparently, draws some support from the New Hampshire lodging house registration statute for its conclusions about the lack of substantiality of the guests' interest in nondisclosure. Since the statute admittedly would not cover what the attorney general desired to obtain and since the New Hampshire courts themselves did not rest on it, it is difficult to find any basis for this reliance. It would be time enough to deal with a production order based on that statute when it arose.

"Effective advocacy of both public and private points of view, particularly controversial ones, is undeniably enhanced by group association, as this Court has more than once recognized by remarking upon the close nexus between the freedoms of speech and assembly. *De Jonge* v. *Oregon*, 299 U.S. 353, 364; *Thomas* v. *Collins*, 323 U.S. 516, 530. It is beyond debate that freedom to engage in association for the advancement of beliefs and ideas is an inseparable aspect of the 'liberty' assured by the Due Process Clause of the Fourteenth Amendment, which embraces freedom of speech. See *Gitlow* v. *New York*, 268 U.S. 652, 666; *Palko* v. *Connecticut*, 302 U.S. 319, 324; *Cantwell* v. *Connecticut*, 310 U.S. 296, 303; *Staub* v. *City of Baxley*, 355 U.S. 313, 321. Of course, it is immaterial whether the beliefs sought to be advanced by association pertain to political, economic, religious or cultural matters, and State action which may have the effect of curtailing the freedom to associate is subject to the closest scrutiny." 357 U.S., at 460–461.

And in examining the State's interest in carrying out a legislative investigation, as was said in a similar context in *United States* v. *Rumely, supra*, at 44, we must strive not to be "that 'blind' Court, against which Mr. Chief Justice Taft admonished in a famous passage, . . . that does not see what '[a]ll others can see and understand.' " The problem of protecting the citizen's constitutional rights from legislative investigation and exposure is a practical one, and we must take a practical, realistic approach to it.

Most legislative investigations unavoidably involve exposure of some sort or another. But it is quite clear that exposure was the very core, and deliberately and purposefully so, of the legislative investigation we are concerned with here. The legislature had passed a broad and comprehensive statute, which included criminal sanctions. That statute was, to say the least, readily susceptible of many applications in which it might enter a constitutional danger zone. See *Yates* v. *United States*, 354 U.S. 298, 319. And it could not be applied at all insofar as it amounted to a sanction for behavior directed against the United States. *Pennsylvania* v. *Nelson*, 350 U.S. 497. Therefore, indictment would be fraught with constitutional and evidentiary problems of an obvious and hardly subtle nature. This may suggest the reason why the pattern of application of the Subversive Activities statute in New Hampshire was not through the processes of indictment. The Resolution was cast in terms of an investigation of conduct restricted by this existing statute. The resolution and the attorney general's implementation of it reveal the making of a choice. The choice was to reach the end of exposure through the process of investigation, backed with the contempt power and the making of reports to the legislature, of persons and groups thought to be somehow related to offenses under the statute or, further, to an uncertain penumbra of conduct about the proscribed area of the statute. And, as was said of the same investigation in *Sweezy* v. *New Hampshire, supra*, at 248: "[T]he program for the rooting out of subversion . . . [was] drawn without regard to the presence or absence of guilty knowledge in those affected." The sanction of exposure was applied much more widely than anyone could remotely suggest that even traditional judicial sanctions might be applied in this area.

One may accept the Court's truism that preservation of the State's existence is undoubtedly a proper purpose for legislation. But, in descending from this peak of abstraction to the facts of this case, one must ask the question: What relation did this investigation of individual conduct have to legislative ends here? If bills of attainder were still a legitimate legislative end, it is clear that the investigations and reports might naturally have furnished the starting point (though only that) for a legislative adjudication of guilt under the 1951 Act. But what other legislative purpose was actually being fulfilled by the course taken by this investigation, with its overwhelming emphasis on individual associations and conduct?

The investigation, as revealed by the report, was overwhelmingly and predominantly a roving, self-contained investigation of individual and group behavior, and behavior in a constitutionally protected area. Its whole approach was to name names, disclose information about those named, and observe that "facts are facts." The New Hampshire Supreme Court has upheld the investigation as being a proper legislative inquiry, it is true. In *Nelson* v. *Wyman*, 99 N.H. 33, 38, 105 A. 2d 756, 763, it said: "No sound basis can exist for denying to the legislature the power to so investigate the effectiveness of its 1951 act even though, as an incident to that general investigation, it may be necessary to inquire as to whether a particular person has violated the act. . . . When the investigation provided for is a general one, the discovery of a specific, individual violation of law is collateral and subordinate to the main object of the inquiry." In evaluating this, it must be admitted that maintenance of the separation of powers in the States is not, in and of itself, a concern of the Federal Constitution. *Sweezy* v. *New Hampshire, supra,* at 255; *Crowell* v. *Benson,* 285 U.S. 22, 57. But for an investigation in the field of the constitutionally protected freedoms of speech and assemblage to be upheld by the broad standards of relevance permissible in a legislative inquiry, some relevance to a valid legislative purpose must be shown, and certainly the ruling made below, that under the State law the legislature has authorized the inquiry, *Wyman* v. *Uphaus,* 100 N.H. 436, 445, 130 A. 2d 278, 285, does not conclude the issue here. The bare fact that the legislature has authorized the inquiry does not mean that the inquiry is for a valid legislative end when viewed in the light of the Federal constitutional test we must apply. Nor, while it is entitled to weight, is the determination by a State court that the inquiry relates to a valid legislative end conclusive. It is the task of this Court, as the Court recognizes in theory today, to evaluate the facts to determine if there actually has been demonstrated a valid legislative end to which the inquiry is related. With all due respect, the quoted observations of the New Hampshire Supreme Court in the case of *Nelson* v. *Wyman* bear little relationship to the course of the inquiry, as revealed by the report published after that decision. The report discloses an investigation in which the processes of law-making and law-evaluating were submerged entirely in exposure of individual behavior—in adjudication, of a sort, however much disclaimed, through the exposure process.[8] If an investigation or trial,

---

[8] While as a general matter it is true that a State can distribute its governmental powers as it sees fit, as far as the Federal Constitution is concerned, it is also true that (regardless of what organ exercises the functions) different constitutional tests apply in examining State legislative and State adjudicatory powers. See *Bi-Metallic Investment Co.* v. *State Board of Equalization,* 239 U.S. 441.

conducted by any organ of the State, which is aimed at the application of sanctions to individual behavior is to be upheld, it must meet the traditional standards that the common law in this country has established for the application of sanctions to the individual, or a constitutionally permissible modification of them. Cf. *Kilbourn* v. *Thompson*, 103 U.S. 168, 195. As a bare minimum there must be general standards of conduct, substantively constitutionally proper, applied to the individual in a fair proceeding with defined issues resulting in a binding, final determination. I had not supposed that a legislative investigation of the sort practiced here provided such a framework under the Constitution.

It is not enough to say, as the Court's position I fear may amount to, that what was taking place was an investigation and until the attorney general and the legislature had in all the data, the precise shape of the legislative action to be taken was necessarily unknown. Investigation and exposure, in the area which we are here concerned with, are not recognized as self-contained legislative powers in themselves. See *Watkins* v. *United States, supra,* at 200. Cf. *NAACP* v. *Alabama, supra.* Since this is so, it hardly fulfills the responsibility with which this Court is charged, of protecting the constitutional rights of freedom of speech and assembly, to admit that an investigation going on indefinitely in time, roving in subject matter, and cumulative in detail in this area can be in aid of a valid legislative end, on the theory that some day it may come to some point. Even the most abusive investigation, the one most totally committed to the constitutionally impermissible end of individual adjudication through publication, could pass such a test. At the stage of this investigation that we are concerned with, it continued to be a cumulative, broad inquiry into the specific details of past individual and associational behavior in the political area. It appears to have been a classic example of "a fruitless investigation into the personal affairs of individuals." *Kilbourn* v. *Thompson, supra,* at 195. Investigation appears to have been a satisfactory end product for the State, but it cannot be so for us in this case as we evaluate the demands of the Constitution. Nor can we accept the legislative renewal of the investigation, or the taking of other legislative measures to facilitate the investigation, as being themselves the legislative justification of the inquiry. The report indicates that it so viewed them; in requesting legislation renewing the investigation and an investigation immunity statute, the attorney general significantly stated that if the renewal legislation or some investigatory substitute were not passed, it "would mean, no further investigation, no continuing check upon Communist activities . . . ." This is just to admit the continuing existence of the investigation as a self-contained justification for the inquiry. However much the State may be content to rely on the investigation as its own sanction, I think it perfectly plain that it cannot be regarded as a justification here. Nor can the faint possibility that an already questionably broad criminal statute might be further broadened, if constitutionally permissible, be considered the subordinating legislative purpose here, particularly in the light of what the investigation was in fact as revealed by its report. Of course, after further investigation and further reports, legislation of some sort might eventuate, or at least be considered. Perhaps it might be rejected because of serious doubts as to its constitutionality—which would, I think, underline the point I am making. But on such airy speculation, I do not see how we can say that the State has made any showing that this investigation, which on its surface has an overwhelming appearance of a simple, wide-ranging exposure campaign, presents an implementation of a subordinating lawmaking interest that, as the Court concedes, the State must be shown to have.

This Court's approach to a very similar problem in *NAACP* v. *Alabama, supra*, should furnish a guide to the proper course of decision here. There the State demonstrated a definite purpose which was admittedly within its competence. That purpose was the ascertainment whether a foreign corporation was unlawfully carrying on local activities within Alabama's borders, because not qualified to do business in the manner required by State law. In a judicial proceeding having this as its express stated purpose, the State sought to obtain the membership list of the corporation. This Court carefully recognized the curbing of associational freedom that the disclosure called for by this inquiry would entail. It then analyzed the relationship between the inquiry and this purpose, and, concluding that there was no rational connection, it held the inquiry constitutionally impermissible. Here the situation is even more extreme; there is no demonstration at all of what the legislative purpose is, outside of the investigation of violations, suspicions of violations, and conduct raising some question of violation, of an existing statute.[9] It is anomalous to say, as I fear the Court says today, that the vaguer the State's interest is, the more laxly will the Court view the matter and indulge a presumption of the existence of a valid subordinating State interest. In effect, a roving investigation and exposure of past associations and expressions in the political field is upheld because it might lead to some sort of legislation which might be sustained as constitutional, and the entire process is said to become the more defensible rather than the less because of the vagueness of the issues. The Court says that the appellant cannot argue against the exposure because this is an investigation and the exposure may make the investigation lead somewhere, possibly to legislative action. But this is just to say that an investigation, once under State law it is classified as "legislative," needs no showing of purpose beyond its own existence. A start must be made somewhere, and if the principles this Court has announced, and to which the Court today makes some deference, are to have any meaning, it must be up to the State to make some at least plausible disclosure of its lawmaking interest so that the relevance of its inquiries to it may be tested. Then the courts could begin to evaluate the justification for the impact on the individual's rights of freedom of speech and assembly. But here not only has the State failed to begin to elucidate such an interest; it has positively demonstrated, it appears to me, through its resolution,

---

[9] Cf. the address of Mr. William T. Gossett, Vice-President and General Counsel of Ford Motor Company at the Annual Brotherhood Dinner, Detroit, Michigan, November 20, 1958, in which he said : "We must urge upon our law-makers a scrupulous exactness, particularly in the exercise of their investigative powers. When we are frustrated by the feeling that certain people—suspected subversives, gangsters or labor racketeers, for example—have flaunted society with impunity, it is tempting to pillory them through prolonged public exposure to hearsay testimony, intemperate invective and other forms of abuse. But to try by such means to destroy those whom we are unable to convict by due process of law may destroy instead the very safeguards that protect us all against tyranny and arbitrary power."

the attorney general's and the State courts' interpretation of it, and the resolution's re-enactment, that what it is interested in is exposure, in lieu of prosecution, and nothing definable else. The precise details of the inquiry we are concerned with here underlines this. The attorney general had World Fellowship's speaker list and had already made publication of it in the fashion to which I have alluded. He had considerable other data about World Fellowship, Inc., which he had already published. What reason has been demonstrated, in terms of a legislative inquiry, for going into the matter in further depth? Outside of the fact that it might afford some further evidence as to the existence of "subversive persons" within the State, which I have endeavored to show was not in itself a matter related to any legislative function except self-contained investigation and exposure themselves, the relevance of further detail is not demonstrated. But its damaging effect on the persons to be named in the guest list is obvious. And since the only discernible purpose of the investigation on this record is revealed to be investigation and exposure *per se*, and the relevance of the names to that purpose alone is quite apparent, this discloses the constitutional infirmity in the inquiry which requires us to strike down the adjudication of contempt in question here.

The Court describes the inquiry we must make in this matter as a balancing of interests. I think I have indicated that there has been no valid legislative interest of the State actually defined and shown in the investigation as it operated, so that there is really nothing against which the appellant's rights of association and expression can be balanced. But if some proper legislative end of the inquiry can be surmised, through what must be a process of speculation, I think it is patent that there is really no subordinating interest in it demonstrated on the part of the State. The evidence inquired about was simply an effort to get further details about an activity as to which there already were considerable details in the hands of the attorney general. I can see no serious and substantial relationship between the furnishing of these further minutiae about what was going on at the World Fellowship camp and the process of legislation, and it is the process of legislation, the consideration of the enactment of laws, with which ultimately we are concerned. We have a detailed inquiry into an assemblage the general contours of which were already known on the one hand, and on the other the remote and speculative possibility of some sort of legislation—albeit legislation in a field where there are serious constitutional limitations. We have this in the context of an inquiry which was in practice being conducted in its overwhelming thrust as a vehicle of exposure, and where the practice had been followed of publishing names on the basis of a "not proven" verdict. We are not asked to hold that the State cannot carry on such fact-finding at all, with or without compulsory process. Nor are we asked to hold that as a general matter compulsory process cannot be used to amass facts whose initial relevance to an ultimate legislative interest may be remote. Cf. *McGrain*

v. *Daugherty*, 273 U.S. 135, 176–180.[10] We deal with a narrow and more subtle problem. We deal here with inquiries into the areas of free speech and assemblage where the process of compulsory disclosure itself tends to have a repressive effect. Cf. *Speiser* v. *Randall*, *supra*. We deal only with the power of the State to *compel* such a disclosure. We are asked, in this narrow context, only to give meaning to our statement in *Watkins* v. *United States, supra*, at 198, "that the mere semblance of a legislative purpose would not justify an inquiry in the face of the Bill of Rights." Here we must demand some initial showing by the State sufficient to counterbalance the interest in privacy as it relates to freedom of speech and assembly. On any basis that has practical meaning, New Hampshire has not made such a showing here. I would reverse the judgment of the New Hampshire Supreme Court.

MR. JUSTICE BLACK and MR. JUSTICE DOUGLAS would decide this case on the ground that appellant is being deprived of rights under the First and Fourteenth Amendments, for the reasons developed in *Adler* v. *Board of Education*, 342 U.S. 485, 508 (dissenting opinion); *Beauharnais* v. *Illinois*, 343 U.S. 250, 267, 284 (dissenting opinions). But they join MR. JUSTICE BRENNAN's dissent because he makes clear to them that New Hampshire's legislative program resulting in the incarceration of appellant for contempt violates Art. I, § 10 of the Constitution which provides that "No State shall . . . pass any Bill of Attainder." See *United States* v. *Lovett*, 328 U.S. 303, 315–318, and cases cited; *Joint Anti-Fascist Refugee Committee* v. *McGrath*, 341 U.S. 123, 142–149 (concurring opinion).

---

[10] *McGrain* v. *Daugherty* found legislative justification in a congressional inquiry which presented a rather strong element of exposure of past wrongdoing, to be sure. But the possibility of legislation was much more real than is the case here, and the legislative subject matter—control and regulation of the structure and workings of an executive department—was one not fraught with the constitutional problems presented by legislation in the field of political advocacy and assembly. And the inquiry itself, most significantly, was not directed at private assembly and discussion, but at the conduct of a public official in office; it did not have the inhibitory effect on basic political freedoms that the inquiry we are here concerned with presents. Cf. *Watkins* v. *United States, supra*, at 200, n. 33. The *Daugherty* case is basically, then, one relating to the distribution of powers among branches of the Federal Government.

LOYALTY OF PUBLIC OFFICERS AND EMPLOYEES

GARNER et al. v. BOARD OF PUBLIC WORKS OF LOS ANGELES et al.

CERTIORARI TO THE DISTRICT COURT OF APPEAL OF CALIFORNIA, SECOND APPELLATE DISTRICT.

No. 453.   Argued April 25, 1951.—Decided June 4, 1951.

1. The Federal Constitution does not forbid a municipality to require its employees to execute affidavits disclosing whether or not they are or ever have been members of the Communist Party or the Communist Political Association. P. 720.

2. In 1941, the California Legislature amended the Charter of the City of Los Angeles so as to provide, in substance, that no person shall hold or retain or be eligible for any public office or employment in the service of the city (1) who advises, advocates or teaches the overthrow by force or violence of the State or Federal Government or belongs to an organization which does so, or (2) who, within the five years prior to the effective date, had so advised, advocated or taught or had belonged to an organization which did so. In 1948, the city passed an ordinance requiring each of its officers and employees to take an oath that he has not within the five years preceding the effective date of the ordinance, does not now, and will not while in the service of the city, advise, advocate or teach the overthrow by force, violence or other unlawful means, of the State or Federal Government or belong to an organization which does so or has done so within such five-year period. Held: The ordinance is not a bill of attainder or ex post facto law, nor, as here construed, does it violate the Due Process Clause of the Fourteenth Amendment. Pp. 720–724.

   (a) The Charter amendment is valid under the Federal Constitution to the extent that it bars from the city's public service persons who, since its adoption in 1941, advise, advocate or teach the violent overthrow of the Government or who are or become affiliated with any group doing so, since the provisions thus operating prospectively are a reasonable regulation to protect the municipal service. The question of its validity insofar as it purported to apply retrospectively for a five-year period prior to its effective date is not here involved. Pp. 720–721.

   (b) The ordinance clearly is not ex post facto, since the activity covered by the oath had been proscribed by the Charter in the same terms, for the same purpose, and to the same effect over seven years before, and two years prior to the period covered by the oath. P. 721.

   (c) The ordinance is not a bill of attainder, since no punishment is imposed by a general regulation which merely provides standards of qualification and eligibility for public employment. Lovett v. United States, 328 U.S. 303, distinguished. Pp. 722–723.

   (d) It is assumed here that the oath will not be construed as affecting adversely persons who during their affiliation with a proscribed organization were innocent of its purpose, or those who severed their relations with any such organization when its character became apparent, or those who were affiliated with organizations which were not engaged in proscribed activities at the time of their affiliation; and that, if this interpretaton of the oath is correct, the city will give those petitioners who heretofore refused to take the oath an opportunity to take it as interpreted and resume their employment. As thus construed, the requirement of the oath does not violate the Due Process Clause of the Fourteenth Amendment. Pp. 723–724.

98 Cal. App. 2d 493, 220 P. 2d 958, affirmed.

In a suit by discharged employees of a city for reinstatement and unpaid salaries, the State court denied relief. 98 Cal. App. 2d 493, 220 P. 2d 958. This Court granted certiorari. 340 U.S. 941. *Affirmed*, p. 724.

Charles J. Katz and *Samuel Rosenwein* argued the cause for petitioners. With them on the brief was *John T. McTernan*.

Alan G. Campbell argued the cause for respondents. With him on the brief were *Ray L. Chesebro, Bourke Jones* and *A. L. Lawson.*
A. L. Wirin, Fred Okrand, Loren Miller and *Clore Warne* filed a brief for the American Civil Liberties Union, as *amicus curiae*, urging reversal.

MR. JUSTICE CLARK delivered the opinion of the Court.

In 1941 the California Legislature amended the Charter of the city of Los Angeles to provide in part as follows:

". . . no person shall hold or retain or be eligible for any public office or employment in the service of the city of Los Angeles, in any office or department thereof, either elective or appointive, who has within five (5) years prior to the effective date of this section advised, advocated or taught, or who may, after this section becomes effective [April 28, 1941], advise, advocate or teach, or who is now or has been within five (5) years prior to the effective date of this section, or who may, after this section becomes effective, become a member of or affiliated with any group, society, association, organization or party which advises, advocates or teaches, or has, within said period of five (5) years, advised, advocated or taught the overthrow by force or violence of the Government of the United States of America or of the State of California.

"In so far as this section may be held by any court of competent jurisdiction not to be self-executing, the city council is hereby given power and authority to adopt appropriate legislation for the purpose of effectuating the objects hereof." Cal. Stat. 1941, c. 67.

Pursuant to the authority thus conferred, the city of Los Angeles in 1948 passed Ordinance No. 94,004, requiring every person who held an office or position in the service of the city to take an oath prior to January 6, 1949. In relevant part the oath was as follows:

"I further swear (or affirm) that I do not advise, advocate or teach, and have not within the period beginning five (5) years prior to the effective date of the ordinance requiring the making of this oath or affirmation, advised, advocated or taught, the overthrow by force, violence or other unlawful means, of the Government of the United States of America or of the State of California and that I am not now and have not, within said period, been or become a member of or affiliated with any group, society, association, organization or party which advises, advocates or teaches, or has, within said period, advised, advocated or taught, the overthrow by force, violence or other unlawful means of the Government of the United States of America, or of the State of California. I further swear (or affirm) that I will not, while I am in the service of the city of Los Angeles, advise, advocate or teach, or be or become a member of or affiliated with any group, association, society, organization or party which advises, advocates or teaches, or has within said period, advised, advocated or taught, the overthrow by force, violence or other unlawful means, of the Government of the United States of America or of the State of California . . . ."

The ordinance also required every employee to execute an affidavit "stating whether or not he is or ever was a member of the Communist Party of the United States of America or of the Communist Political

Association, and if he is or was such a member, stating the dates when he became, and the periods during which he was, such a member . . . ."
On the final date for filing of the oath and affidavit petitioners were civil service employees of the city of Los Angeles. Petitioners Pacifico and Schwartz took the oath but refused to execute the affidavit. The remaining fifteen petitioners refused to do either. All were discharged for such cause, after administrative hearing, as of January 6, 1949. In this action they sue for reinstatement and unpaid salaries. The District Court of Appeal denied relief. 98 Cal. App. 2d 493, 220 P. 2d 958 (1950). We granted certiorari, 340 U.S. 941 (1951).

Petitioners attack the ordinance as violative of the provision of Art. I, § 10 of the Federal Constitution that "No State shall . . . pass any Bill of Attainder, [or] ex post facto Law . . . ." They also contend that the ordinance deprives them of freedom of speech and assembly and of the right to petition for redress of grievances.

Petitioners have assumed that the oath and affidavit provisions of the ordinance present similar constitutional considerations and stand or fall together. We think, however, that separate disposition is indicated.

1. The affidavit raises the issue whether the city of Los Angeles is constitutionally forbidden to require that its employees disclose their past or present membership in the Communist Party or the Communist Political Association. Not before us is the question whether the city may determine that an employee's disclosure of such political affiliation justifies his discharge.

We think that a municipal employer is not disabled because it is an agency of the State from inquiring of its employees as to matters that may prove relevant to their fitness and suitability for the public service. Past conduct may well relate to present fitness; past loyalty may have a reasonable relationship to present and future trust. Both are commonly inquired into in determining fitness for both high and low positions in private industry and are not less relevant in public employment. The affidavit requirement is valid.

2. In our view the validity of the oath turns upon the nature of the Charter amendment (1941) and the relation of the ordinance (1948) to this amendment. Immaterial here is any opinion we might have as to the Charter provision insofar as it purported to apply retrospectively for a five-year period prior to its effective date. We assume that under the Federal Constitution the Charter amendment is valid to the extent that it bars from the city's public service persons who, subsequent to its adoption in 1941, advise, advocate, or teach the violent overthrow of the Government or who are or become affiliated with any group doing so. The provisions operating thus prospectively were a reasonable regulation to protect the municipal service by establishing an employment qualification of loyalty to the State and the United States. Cf. *Gerende* v. *Board of Supervisors of Elections,* 341 U.S. 56 (1951). Likewise, as a regulation of political activity of municipal employees, the amendment was reasonably designed to protect the integrity and competency of the service. This Court has held that Congress may reasonably restrict the political activity of Federal civil services employees for such a purpose, *United Public Workers* v. *Mitchell,* 330 U.S. 75, 102–103 (1947), and a State is not without power to do as much.

The Charter amendment defined standards of eligibility for employees and specifically denied city employment to those persons who thereafter should not comply with these standards. While the amendment deprived no one of employment with or without trial, yet from its effective date it terminated any privilege to work for the city in the case of persons who thereafter engaged in the activity proscribed. The ordinance provided for administrative implementation of the provisions of the Charter amendment. The oath imposed by the ordinance proscribed to employees activity which had been denied them in identical terms and with identical sanctions in the Charter provision effective in 1941. The five-year period provided by the oath extended back only to 1943.

The ordinance would be *ex post facto* if it imposed punishment for past conduct lawful at the time it was engaged in. Passing for the moment the question whether separation of petitioners from their employment must be considered as punishment, the ordinance clearly is not *ex post facto*. The activity covered by the oath had been proscribed by the Charter in the same terms, for the same purpose, and to the same effect over seven years before, and two years prior to the period embraced in the oath. Not the law but the fact was posterior.

Bills of attainder are "legislative acts . . . that apply either to named individuals or to easily ascertainable members of a group in such a way as to inflict punishment on them without a judicial trial. . . ." *United States* v. *Lovett*, 328 U.S. 303, 315 (1946). Punishment is a prerequisite. See concurring opinion in *Lovett*, *supra*, at 318, 324. Whether legislative action curtailing a privilege previously enjoyed amounts to punishment depends upon "the circumstances attending and the causes of the deprivation." *Cummings* v. *Missouri*, 4 Wall. 277, 320 (1867). We are unable to conclude that punishment is imposed by a general regulation which merely provides standards of qualification and eligibility for employment.

Cummings v. *Missouri*, 4 Wall. 277 (1867), and *Ex parte Garland*, 4 Wall. 333 (1867), the leading cases in this Court applying the Federal constitutional prohibitions against bills of attainder, recognized that the guarantees against such legislation were not intended to preclude legislative definition of standards of qualification for public or professional employment. Carefully distinguishing an instance of legislative "infliction of punishment" from the exercise of "the power of Congress to prescribe qualifications," the Court said in *Garland's* case: "The legislature may undoubtedly prescribe qualifications for the office, to which he must conform, as it may, where it has exclusive jurisdiction, prescribe qualifications for the pursuit of any of the ordinary avocations of life." 4 Wall. at 379–380. See also, *Cummings* v. *Missouri*, *supra*, at 318–319. This doctrine was reaffirmed in *Dent* v. *West Virginia*, 129 U.S. 114 (1889), in which Mr. Justice Field, who had written the *Cummings* and *Garland* opinions, wrote for a unanimous Court upholding a statute elevating standards of qualification to practice medicine. And in *Hawker* v. *New York*, 170 U.S. 189 (1898), the Court upheld a statute forbidding the practice of medicine by any person who had been convicted of a felony. Both *Dent* and *Hawker* distinguished the *Cummings* and *Garland* cases as inapplicable when the legislature establishes reasonable qualifications for a vocational pursuit with the necessary effect of disqualifying some persons presently engaged in it.

Petitioners rely heavily upon *United States* v. *Lovett*, 328 U.S. 303 (1946), in which a legislative act effectively separating certain public servants from their positions was held to be a bill of attainder. Unlike the provisions of the Charter and ordinance under which petitioners were removed, the statute in the *Lovett* case did not declare general and prospectively operative standards of qualification and eligibility for public employment. Rather, by its terms it prohibited any further payment of compensation to named individual employees. Under these circumstances, viewed against the legislative background, the statute was held to have imposed penalties without judicial trial.

Nor are we impressed by the contention that the oath denies due process because its negation is not limited to affiliations with organizations known to the employee to be in the proscribed class. We have no reason to suppose that the oath is or will be construed by the city of Los Angeles or by California courts as affecting adversely those persons who during their affiliation with a proscribed organization were innocent of its purpose, or those who severed their relations with any such organization when its character became apparent, or those who were affiliated with organizations which at one time or another during the period covered by the ordinance were engaged in proscribed activity but not at the time of affiant's affiliation.* We assume that scienter is implicit in each clause of the oath. As the city has done nothing to negative this interpretation, we take for granted that the ordinance will be so read to avoid raising difficult constitutional problems which any other application would present. *Fox* v. *Washington*, 236 U.S. 273, 277 (1915). It appears from correspondence of record between the city and petitioners that although the city welcomed inquiry as to its construction of the oath, the interpretation upon which we have proceeded may not have been explicitly called to the attention of petitioners before their refusal. We assume that, if our interpretation of the oath is correct, the city of Los Angeles will give those petitioners who heretofore refused to take the oath an opportunity to take it as interpreted and resume their employment.

The judgment as to Pacifico and Schwartz is affirmed. The judgment as to the remaining petitioners is affirmed on the basis of the interpretation of the ordinance which we have felt justified in assuming.

Affirmed.

MR. JUSTICE FRANKFURTER, concurring in part and dissenting in part.

The Constitution does not guarantee public employment. City, State and Nation are not confined to making provisions appropriate for securing competent professional discharge of the functions pertaining to diverse governmental jobs. They may also assure themselves of fidelity to the very presuppositions of our scheme of government on the part of those who seek to serve it. No unit of government can be

---

*In interpreting local legislation proscribing affiliation with defective organizations, the Supreme Court of California has gone beyond the literal text of a statute so as to require knowledge of the character of the organization, as of the time of affiliation, by the person whose affiliation is in question. In *People* v. *Steelik*, 187 Cal. 361, 203 P. 78 (1921), the Court upheld a conviction under the Criminal Syndicalism Act of 1919 which made one guilty of a felony who "is" a member of any one of a certain class of proscribed organizations. The indictment in relevant part alleged that defendants "are and each of them is" a member of a proscribed organization. The court interpreted the statute as defining and the indictment as charging "the offense of criminal syndicalism in that he *knowingly* belonged" to a proscribed organization. (Emphasis added.) 187 Cal. at 376, 203 P. at 84.

denied the right to keep out of its employ those who seek to overthrow the government by force or violence, or are knowingly members of an organization engaged in such endeavor. See *Gerende* v. *Board of Supervisors of Elections*, 341 U.S. 56.

But it does not at all follow that because the Constitution does not guarantee a right to public employment, a city or a State may resort to any scheme for keeping people out of such employment. Law cannot reach every discrimination in practice. But doubtless unreasonable discriminations, if avowed in formal law, would not survive constitutional challenge. Surely, a government could not exclude from public employment members of a minority group merely because they are odious to the majority, nor restrict such employment, say, to native-born citizens. To describe public employment as a privilege does not meet the problem.

This line of reasoning gives the direction, I believe, for dealing with the issues before us. A municipality like Los Angeles ought to be allowed adequate scope in seeking to elicit information about its employees and from them. It would give to the Due Process Clause an unwarranted power of intrusion into local affairs to hold that a city may not require its employees to disclose whether they have been members of the Communist Party or the Communist Political Association. In the context of our time, such membership is sufficiently relevant to effective and dependable government, and to the confidence of the electorate in its government. I think the precise Madison would have been surprised even to hear it suggested that the requirement of this affidavit was an "Attainder" under Art. I, § 10, of the Constitution. For reasons outlined in the concurring opinion in *United States* v. *Lovett*, 328 U.S. 303, 318, I cannot so regard it. This kind of inquiry into political affiliation may in the long run do more harm than good. But the two employees who were dismissed solely because they refused to file an affidavit stating whether or when they had been members of the Communist Party or the Communist Political Association cannot successfully appeal to the Constitution of the United States.

A very different issue is presented by the fifteen employees who were discharged because they refused to take this oath:

"I ... do solemnly swear (or affirm) ... that I ... have not, within said period [from December 6, 1943], been or become a member of or affiliated with any group, society, association, organization or party which advises, advocates or teaches, or has within said period, advised, advocated or taught, the overthrow by force, violence or other unlawful means of the Government of the United States of America, or of the State of California."

The validity of an oath must be judged on the assumption that it will be taken conscientiously. This ordinance does not ask the employee to swear that he "knowingly" or "to the best of his knowledge" had no proscribed affiliation. Certainty is implied in the disavowal exacted. The oath thus excludes from city employment all persons who are not certain that every organization to which they belonged or with which they were affiliated (with all the uncertainties of the meaning of "affiliated") at any time since 1943 has not since that date advocated the overthrow by "unlawful means" of the Government of the United States or of the State of California.

The vice in this oath is that it is not limited to affiliation with organizations known at the time to have advocated overthrow of government. We have here a very different situation from that recently before us in *Gerende* v. *Board of Supervisors*, 341 U.S. 56. There the attorney general of Maryland assured this Court that he would advise the appropriate authorities to accept as the oath required by State law from a candidate for office, an affirmation that he is not engaged in the attempt to overthrow the Government by force or violence and that he is not knowingly a member of an organization engaged in such an attempt. The attorney general did not give this assurance as a matter of personal relaxation of a legal requirement. He was able to give it on the basis of the interpretation that the Court of Appeals of Maryland, the highest court of that State, had placed upon the legislation. No such assurance was remotely suggested on behalf of Los Angeles. Naturally not. Nothing in the decisions under review would warrant such restricted interpretation of the assailed ordinance.* To find *scienter* implied in a criminal statute is the obvious way of reading such a statute, for guilty knowledge is the normal ingredient of criminal responsibility. The ordinance before us exacts an oath as a condition of employment; it does not define a crime. It is certainly not open to this Court to rewrite the oath required by Los Angeles of its employees, after the oath as written has been sustained by the California courts.

If this ordinance is sustained, sanction is given to like oaths for every governmental unit in the United States. Not only does the oath make an irrational demand. It is bound to operate as a real deterrent to people contemplating even innocent associations. How can anyone be sure that an organization with which he affiliates will not at some time in the future be found by a State or National official to advocate overthrow of government by "unlawful means"? All but the hardiest may well hesitate to join organizations if they know that by such a proscription they will be permanently disqualified from public employment. These are considerations that cut deep into the traditions of our people. Gregariousness and friendliness are among the most characteristic of American attitudes. Throughout our history they have been manifested in "joining." See Arthur M. Schlesinger, Sr., Biography of a Nation of Joiners, published in 50 American Historical Review 1, reprinted in Schlesinger, Paths to the Present, 23.

Giving full scope to the selective processes open to our municipalities and States in securing competent and reliable functionaries free from allegiance to any alien political authority, I do not think that it is consonant with the Due Process Clause for men to be asked, on pain of giving up public employment, to swear to something they cannot be expected to know. Such a demand is at war with individual integrity; it can no more be justified than the inquiry into belief which Mr. Justice Black, Mr. Justice Jackson and I deemed invalid in *American Communications Assn.* v. *Douds*, 339 U.S. 382.

The needs of security do not require such curbs on what may well be innocuous feelings and associations. Such curbs are indeed self-

---

*Nothing in the decision or opinion of the Supreme Court of California in *People* v. *Steelik*, 187 Cal. 361, 203 P. 78, indicates that the courts of California would at their own instance read into the Los Angeles oath a limitation which is not there expressed. In the *Steelik* case the court was considering a statute which provided that "Any person who . . . [o]rganizes or assists in organizing, or is or knowingly becomes a member of, any organization" teaching criminal syndicalism is guilty of a felony. Cal. Stat. 1919, c. 188, § 2. The court held only that the word "knowingly" qualified the word "is" in addition to the word "becomes."

defeating. They are not merely unjustifiable restraints on individuals. They are not merely productive of an atmosphere of repression uncongenial to the spiritual vitality of a democratic society. The inhibitions which they engender are hostile to the best conditions for securing a high-minded and high-spirited public service.

It is not for us to write the oath that Los Angeles may exact. And so as to the fifteen employees I think the case should go back to the State court, with instructions that these petitioners be reinstated unless they refuse to take an oath or affirmation within the scope indicated in this opinion.

MR. JUSTICE BURTON, dissenting in part and concurring in part.

I.

I cannot agree that under our decisions the oath is valid. *United States* v. *Lovett*, 328 U.S. 303; *Ex parte Garland*, 4 Wall. 333; *Cummings* v. *Missouri*, 4 Wall. 277. The oath is so framed as to operate retrospectively as a perpetual bar to those employees who held certain views at any time since a date five years preceding *the effective date of the ordinance*. It leaves no room for a change of heart. It calls for more than a profession of present loyalty or promise of future attachment. It is not limited in retrospect to any period measured by reasonable relation to the present. In time this ordinance will amount to the requirement of an oath that the affiant has *never* done any of the proscribed acts. Cf. *Gerende* v. *Board of Supervisors*, 341 U.S. 56; *American Communications Assn.* v. *Douds*, 339 U.S. 382, 413–414.

The oath is not saved by the fact that it reaches back only to December 6, 1943, and that city employees have been forbidden since April 28, 1941, under § 432 of the Los Angeles Charter, to advise, teach or advocate the violent overthrow of the Government. See the *Lovett*, *Garland* and *Cummings* cases, *supra*.

II.

I agree with the Court that the judgment should be affirmed as to petitioners Pacifico and Schwartz. They executed the oath but refused to sign an affidavit calling for information as to their past or present membership in the Communist Party or the Communist Political Association. Such refusal does not now present the question of whether the Constitution permits the city to discharge them from municipal employment on the basis of information in their affidavits. We have before us only the question of whether municipal employees may be required to give to their employer factual information which is relevant to a determination of their present loyalty and suitability for public service. Such loyalty and suitability is no less material in candidates for appointment as municipal employees than in candidates for elective office, *Gerende* v. *Board of Supervisors*, *supra*, or union officers, *American Communications Assn.* v. *Douds*, *supra*.

MR. JUSTICE BLACK, dissenting.

I agree with the dissenting opinion of MR. JUSTICE DOUGLAS but wish to emphasize two objections to the opinion of the Court:

1. Our *per curiam* opinion in *Gerende* v. *Board of Supervisors*, 341 U.S. 56, in no way stands for the principle for which the Court cites

it today. In *Gerende*, we upheld a Maryland law that had been interpreted by the highest court of that state to require only an oath that a candidate "is not a person who is engaged 'in one way or another in the attempt to overthrow the government *by force or violence*,' and that he is not knowingly a member of an organization engaged in such an attempt." The oath and affidavit in the present case are obviously not so limited.

2. The opinion of the Court creates considerable doubt as to the continued vitality of three of our past decisions: *Cummings* v. *Missouri*, 4 Wall. 277; *Ex parte Garland*, 4 Wall. 333; *United States* v. *Lovett*, 328 U.S. 303. To this extent it weakens one more of the Constitution's great guarantees of individual liberty. See, *e.g.*, *Dennis* v. *United States, ante*, p. 494, and *Breard* v. *Alexandria, ante*, p. 622, decided this day.

MR. JUSTICE DOUGLAS, with whom MR. JUSTICE BLACK joins, dissenting.

Petitioners are citizens of the United States and civil service employees of the city of Los Angeles. In 1948 the city of Los Angeles passed Ordinance No. 94,004 which requires each of its employees to subscribe to an oath of loyalty which included, *inter alia*, an affirmation that he does not advise, advocate, or teach, and has not within the five years prior to the effective date of the ordinance "advised, advocated or taught, the overthrow by force, violence or other unlawful means, of the Government of the United States of America or of the State of California," and that he is not and has not within that period been "a member of or affiliated with any group, society, association, organization or party which advises, advocates or teaches, or has, within said period, advised, advocated or taught, the overthrow by force, violence or other unlawful means of the Government of the United States of America, or of the State of California."

The ordinance also requires each employee to execute an affidavit stating "whether or not he is or ever was a member of the Communist Party of the United States of America or of the Communist Political Association, and if he is or was such a member, stating the dates when he became, and the periods during which he was, such a member."

The ordinance was passed to effectuate the provisions of § 432 of the Charter of Los Angeles (Cal. Stat. 1941, c. 67, p. 3409) which provides, *inter alia*, that no person who has within five years prior to the adoption of § 432 advised, advocated or taught the overthrow by force or violence of the government of the United States or of California, or who during that time has been a member of or affiliated with any group or party which has advised, advocated, or taught that doctrine, shall hold or retain or be eligible for any employment in the service of the city. Thus the ordinance and § 432 of the Charter read together make plain that prior advocacy or membership is without more a disqualification for employment. Both the oath and the affidavit are methods for enforcement of that policy.

Fifteen of the petitioners refused to sign either the oath or the affidavit. Two took the oath but refused to sign the affidavit. All seventeen were discharged—the sole ground being their refusal to sign the affidavit or to sign and to take the oath, as the case may be. They had an administrative review, which afforded them no relief. This suit was thereupon instituted in the California court, claiming reinstatement and unpaid salaries. Relief was denied by the District Court of Appeal, 98 Cal. App. 2d 493, 220 P. 2d 958; and a hearing was denied by the Supreme Court, three justices dissenting. The case is here on certiorari.

The case is governed by *Cummings* v. *Missouri*, 4 Wall. 277, and *Ex parte Garland*, 4 Wall. 333, which struck down test oaths adopted at the close of the Civil War. The *Cummings* case involved provisions of the Missouri Constitution requiring public officials and certain classes of professional people, including clergymen, to take an oath that, *inter alia*, they had never been "in armed hostility" to the United States; that they had never "by act or word" manifested their "adherence to the cause" of enemies of the country or their "desire" for the triumph of its enemies; that they had never "knowingly and willingly harbored, aided, or countenanced" an enemy; that they had never been a "member of, or connected with, any order, society, or organization inimical to the Government of the United States" or engaged "in guerrilla warfare" against its inhabitants; that they had never left Missouri "for the purpose of avoiding enrollment for or draft into the military service of the United States" or become enrolled as a southern sympathizer.

The *Garland* case involved certain Acts of Congress requiring public officials and attorneys practicing before the Federal courts to take an oath that they had "voluntarily given no aid, countenance, counsel, or encouragement to persons engaged in armed hostility" against the United States and that they had "neither sought nor accepted, nor attempted to exercise the functions of any office whatever, under any authority or pretended authority in hostility to the United States." The Court amended its rules of admission to require this oath.

Cummings, a Catholic priest, was indicted and convicted for teaching and preaching without having first taken the oath.

Garland, a member of the Bar of the Court, had served in the Confederate Government, for which he had received a pardon from the President conditioned on his taking the customary oath of loyalty. He applied for permission to practice before the Court without taking the new oath.

Article I, § 10 of the Constitution forbids any State to "pass any Bill of Attainder" or any "ex post facto Law." Article I, § 9 curtails the power of Congress by providing that "No Bill of Attainder or ex post facto Law shall be passed." The Court ruled that the test oaths in the *Cummings* and *Garland* cases were bills of attainder and ex post facto laws within the meaning of the Constitution. "A bill of attainder," wrote Mr. Justice Field for the Court, "is a legislative act which inflicts punishment without a judicial trial."[1] *Cummings* v. *Mis-*

---

[1] Mr. Justice Field continued: "If the punishment be less than death, the act is termed a bill of pains and penalties. Within the meaning of the Constitution, bills of attainder include bills of pains and penalties. In these cases the legislative body, in addition to its legitimate functions, exercises the powers and office of judge; it assumes, in the language of the text-books, judicial magistracy; it pronounces upon the guilt of the party, without any of the forms or safeguards of trial; it determines the sufficiency of the proofs produced, whether conformable to the rules of evidence or otherwise; and it fixes the degree of punishment in accordance with its own notions of the enormity of the offense." 4 Wall. p. 323.

In addition to the history of bills of attainder in England, the draftsmen of the Constitution had before them recent examples of such legislation by the Revolutionary governments of the states. Legislative action against persons of known or suspected Loyalist sympathies included outright attaint of treason or subversion (*e. g.*, Georgia, Act of March 1, 1778; Pennsylvania Laws 1778, c. 49; New York Laws 1779, Third Session, c. 25); proscription and banishment (*e. g.*, Massachusetts, Act of Sept. 1778, Charters and Gen.

souri, supra, p. 323; and see *United States* v. *Lovett*, 328 U.S. 303, 317, 318. The Court held that deprivation of the right to follow one's profession is punishment. A bill of attainder, though generally directed against named individuals, may be directed against a whole class. Bills of attainder usually declared the guilt; here they assumed the guilt and adjudged the punishment conditionally, *i. e.*, they deprived the parties of their right to preach and to practice law unless the presumption were removed by the expurgatory oath. That was held to be as much a bill of attainder as if the guilt had been irrevocably pronounced. The laws were also held to be *ex post facto* since they imposed a penalty for an act not so punishable at the time it was committed.

There are, of course, differences between the present case and the *Cummings* and *Garland* cases. Those condemned by the Los Angeles ordinance are municipal employees; those condemned in the others were professional people. Here the past conduct for which punishment is exacted is single—advocacy within the past five years of the overthrow of the Government by force and violence. In the other cases the acts for which Cummings and Garland stood condemned covered a wider range and involved some conduct which might be vague and uncertain. But those differences, seized on here in hostility to the constitutional provisions, are wholly irrelevant. Deprivation of a man's means of livelihood by reason of past conduct, not subject to this penalty when committed, is punishment whether he is a professional man, a day laborer who works for private industry, or a government employee. The deprivation is nonetheless unconstitutional whether it be for one single past act or a series of past acts. The degree of particularity with which the past act is defined is not the criterion. We are not dealing here with the problem of vagueness in criminal statutes. No amount of certainty would have cured the laws in the *Cummings* and *Garland* cases. They were stricken down because of the mode in which punishment was inflicted.

Petitioners were disqualified from office not for what they are today, not because of any program they currently espouse (cf. *Gerende* v. *Board of Supervisors*, 341 U. S. 56), not because of standards related to fitness for the office (cf. *Dent* v. *West Virginia*, 129 U. S. 114; *Hawker* v. *New York*, 170 U. S. 189), but for what they once advocated. They are deprived of their livelihood by legislative act, not by judicial processes. We put the case in the aspect most invidious to petitioners. Whether they actually advocated the violent overthrow of Government does not appear. But here, as in the *Cummings* case, the vice is in the presumption of guilt which can only be removed by the expurgatory oath. That punishment, albeit conditional, violates here as it did in the *Cummings* case the constitutional prohibition against bills of attainder. Whether the ordinance also amounts to an *ex post facto* law is a question we do not reach.

Laws, c. 48; New Hampshire Laws 1778, Fourth Sessioon, c. 9) ; confiscation (*e. g.,* Delaware Laws 1778, c. 29b; New Jersey, Act of Dec. 11, 1778, Laws, p. 40) ; as well as numerous test oaths involving, among other penalties, disqualification from holding office or practicing certain professions. See laws collected in Van Tyne, The Loyalists in the American Revolution, App. B, C; and generally, Thompson, Anti-Loyalist Legislation During the American Revolution, 3 Ill. L. Rev. 81, 147.

CASES ADJUDGED IN THE SUPREME COURT OF THE UNITED STATES AT
OCTOBER TERM, 1959.

NELSON ET AL. *v.* COUNTY OF LOS ANGELES ET AL.

CERTIORARI TO THE DISTRICT COURT OF APPEAL OF CALIFORNIA,
SECOND APPELLATE DISTRICT.

No. 152. Argued January 13, 1960.—Decided February 29, 1960.

Petitioners, when employees of a California County, were subpoenaed by and
appeared before a Subcommittee of the House Un-American Activities Committee; but, in violation of specific orders of the County Board of Supervisors
and the requirements of § 1028.1 of the Government Code of California, refused to answer certain questions concerning subversion. The County discharged them on grounds of insubordination and violation of § 1028.1. Nelson,
a permanent employee, was given a Civil Service Commission hearing, which
resulted in confirmation of his discharge. Globe, a temporary employee, was
denied a hearing, since he was not entitled to it under the applicable rules.
Both sued for reinstatement, contending that § 1028.1 and their discharges
violated the Due Process Clause of the Fourteenth Amendment; but their
discharges were affirmed by a California State Court. *Held:*
1. In Nelson's case, the judgment is affirmed by an equally divided Court.
P. 4.
2. Globe's discharge did not violate the Due Process Clause of the Fourteenth Amendment, and the judgment in his case is affirmed. Pp. 4–9.
(a) Globe's discharge was not based on his invocation before the Subcommittee of his rights under the First and Fifth Amendments; it was based
solely on insubordination and violation of § 1028.1. P. 6.
(b) Under California law, Globe had no vested right to county employment and was subject to summary discharge. P. 6.
(c) Globe's discharge was not arbitrary and unreasonable. *Slochower*
v. *Board of Education,* 350 U.S. 551, distinguished. *Beilan* v. *Board of Education,* 357 U.S. 399, and *Lerner* v. *Casey,* 357 U.S. 468, followed. Pp. 6–8.
(d) The remand on procedural grounds required in *Vitarelli* v. *Seaton,*
359 U.S. 535, has no bearing on this case. Pp. 8–9.

163 Cal. App. 2d 607, 329 P. 2d 978, affirmed by an equally divided Court.
163 Cal. App. 2d 595, 329 P. 2d 971, affirmed.

A. L. Wirin and *Fred Okrand* argued the cause for petitioners.
With them on the brief was *Nanette Dembitz.*

Wm. E. Lamoreaux argued the cause for respondents. With him
on the brief was *Harold W. Kennedy.*

Murray A. Gordon filed a brief for the National Association of
Social Workers, as *amicus curiae,* urging reversal.

MR. JUSTICE CLARK delivered the opinion of the Court.

Petitioners, when employees of the County of Los Angeles, California, were subpoenaed by and appeared before a Subcommittee of
the House Un-American Activities Committee, but refused to answer
certain questions concerning subversion. Previously, each petitioner
had been ordered by the County Board of Supervisors to answer any
questions asked by the Subcommittee relating to his subversive activity, and § 1028.1 of the Government Code of the State of California [1]
made it the duty of any public employee to give testimony relating
to such activity on pain of discharge "in the manner provided by
law." Thereafter the County discharged petitioners on the ground

---

[1] California Government Code, § 1028.1:
"It shall be the duty of any public employee who may be subpenaed or ordered by the
governing body of the State or local agency by which such employee is employed, to appear
before such governing body, or a committee or subcommittee thereof, or by a duly
authorized committee of the Congress of the United States or of the Legislature of this
State, or any subcommittee of any such committee, to appear before such committee or

of insubordination and violation of § 1028.1 of the Code. Nelson, a permanent social worker employed by the County's Department of Charities, was, upon his request, given a Civil Service Commission hearing which resulted in a confirmation of his discharge. Globe was a temporary employee of the same department and was denied a hearing on his discharge on the ground that, as such, he was not entitled to a hearing under the Civil Service Rules adopted pursuant to the County Charter. Petitioners then filed these petitions for mandates seeking reinstatement, contending that the California statute and their discharges violated the Due Process Clause of the Fourteenth Amendment. Nelson's discharge was affirmed by the District Court of Appeal, 163 Cal. App. 2d 607, 329 P. 2d 978, and Globe's summary dismissal was likewise affirmed, 163 Cal. App. 2d 595, 329 P. 2d 971. A petition for review in each of the cases was denied without opinion by the Supreme Court of California, three judges dissenting.   163 Cal. App. 2d 614, 329 P. 2d 983; 163 Cal. App. 2d 606, 329 P. 2d 978.   We granted certiorari.   360 U.S. 928.   The judgment in Nelson's case is affirmed by an equally divided Court and will not be discussed. We conclude that Globe's dismissal was valid.

On April 6, 1956, Globe was served with a subpoena to appear before the Subcommittee at Los Angeles. On the same date, he was served with a copy of an order of the County Board of Supervisors, originally issued February 19, 1952, concerning appearances before the Subcommittee. This order provided, among other things, that it was the duty of any employee to appear before the Subcommittee when so ordered or subpoenaed, and to answer questions concerning subversion. The order specifically stated that any "employee who disobeys the declaration of this duty and order will be considered to have been insubordinate . . . and that such insubordination shall constitute grounds for discharge . . . ." [2] At the appointed time, Globe appeared before the Subcommittee and was interrogated by its counsel concerning his familiarity with the John Reid Club. He claimed that this was a matter which was entirely his "own business," and, upon being pressed for an answer, he stated that the question was "completely out of line as far as my rights as a citizen are concerned, [and] I refuse to answer this question under the First and Fifth Amendments of the Constitution of the United States." On the same grounds he refused to answer further questions concerning the club, including one relating to his own membership. Upon being

---

subcommittee, and to answer under oath a question or questions propounded by such governing body, committee or subcommittee, or a member or counsel thereof, relating to:
   "(a) Present personal advocacy by the employee of the forceful or violent overthrow of the Government of the United States or of any State.
   "(b) Present knowing membership in any organization now advocating the forceful or violent overthrow of the Government of the United States or of any State.
   "(c) Past knowing membership at any time since October 3, 1945, in any organization which, to the knowledge of such employee, during the time of the employee's membership advocated the forceful or violent overthrow of the Government of the United States or of any State.
   "(d) Questions as to present knowing membership of such employee in the Communist Party or as to past knowing membership in the Communist Party at any time since October 3, 1945.
   "(e) Present personal advocacy by the employee of the support of a foreign government against the United States in the event of hostilities between said foreign government and the United States.
   "Any employee who fails or refuses to appear or to answer under oath on any ground whatsoever any such questions so propounded shall be guilty of insubordination and guilty of violating this section and shall be suspended and dismissed from his employment in the manner provided by law."
   [2] This original order was the forerunner of § 1028.1 of the California Government Code, enacted in 1953, which with certain refinements embodied the requirements of the order into State law. It is against this section that petitioner levels his claims of unconstitutionality. See note 1, supra.

asked if he had observed any Communist activities on the part of members of the club, Globe refused to answer, and suggested to committee counsel "that you get one of your trained seals up here and ask them." He refused to testify whether he was "a member of the Communist Party now" "on the same grounds" and "as previously stated for previous reasons." On May 2, by letter, Globe was discharged, "without further notice," on "the grounds that [he had] been guilty of insubordination and of violation of section 1028.1 of the Government Code of the State of California . . . ." The letter recited the fact that Globe had been served with a copy of the board order relating to his "duty to testify as a county employee . . . before said committee" and that, although appearing as directed, he had refused to answer the question, "Are you a member of the Communist Party now?" Thereafter Globe requested a hearing before the Los Angeles County Civil Service Commission, but it found that, as a temporary employee, he was not entitled to a hearing under the Civil Service Rules.[3] This the petitioner does not dispute.

However, Globe contends that, despite his temporary status, his summary discharge was arbitrary and unreasonable and, therefore, violative of due process. He reasons that his discharge was based on his invocation before the Subcommittee of his rights under the First and Fifth Amendments. But the record does not support even an inference in this regard, and both the order and the statute upon which the discharge was based avoided it. In fact, California's court held to the contrary, saying, "At no time has the cause of petitioner's discharge been alleged to be anything but insubordination and a violation of section 1028.1, nor indeed under the record before us could it be." 163 Cal. App. 2d, at 599, 329 P. 2d, at 974. Moreover, this finding is buttressed by the language of the order and of California's statute. Both require the employee to answer any interrogation in the field outlined. Failure to answer "on any ground whatsoever any such questions" renders the employee "guilty of insubordination" and requires that he "be suspended and dismissed from his employment in the manner provided by law." California law in this regard, as declared by its court, is that Globe "has no vested right to county employment and may therefore be discharged summarily." We take this interpretation of California law as binding upon us.

We, therefore, reach Globe's contention that his summary discharge was nevertheless arbitrary and unreasonable. In this regard he places his reliance on *Slochower* v. *Board of Education*, 350 U.S. 551 (1956). However, the New York statute under which Slochower was discharged specifically operated "to discharge every city employee who invokes the Fifth Amendment. In practical effect the questions asked are taken as confessed and made the basis of the discharge." *Id.*, at 558. This "built-in" inference of guilt, derived solely from a Fifth

---

[3] "19.07. *Probationary Period Following First Appointment.*

"An employee who has not yet completed his first probationary period may be discharged or reduced in accordance with Rule 19.09 by the appointing power by written notice, served on the employee and copy filed with the Commission, specifying the grounds and the particular facts on which the discharge or reduction is based. Such an employee shall be entitled to answer, explain, or deny the charges in writing within ten business days but shall not be entitled to a hearing, except in case of fraud or of discrimination because of political or religious opinions, racial extraction, or organized labor membership."
"19.09. *Consent of Commission.*

"No consent need be secured to the discharge or reduction of a temporary or recurrent employee."

Amendment claim, we held to be arbitrary and unreasonable. But the test here, rather than being the invocation of any constitutional privilege, is the failure of the employee to answer. California has not predicated discharge on any "built-in" inference of guilt in its statute, but solely on employee insubordination for failure to give information which we have held that the State has a legitimate interest in securing. See *Garner* v. *Board of Public Works of Los Angeles*, 341 U.S. 716 (1951); *Adler* v. *Board of Education*, 342 U.S. 485 (1952). Moreover it must be remembered that here—unlike *Slochower*—the Board had specifically ordered its employees to appear and answer.

We conclude that the case is controlled by *Beilan* v. *Board of Education of Philadelphia*, 357 U.S. 399 (1958), and *Lerner* v. *Casey*, 357 U.S. 468 (1958). It is not determinative that the interrogation here was by a Federal body rather than a State one, as it was in those cases. Globe had been ordered by his employer as well as by California's law to appear and answer questions before the Federal subcommittee. These mandates made no reference to Fifth Amendment privileges. If Globe had simply refused, without more, to answer the subcommittee's questions, we think that under the principles of *Beilan* and *Lerner* California could certainly have discharged him. The fact that he chose to place his refusal on a Fifth Amendment claim puts the matter in no different posture, for as in *Lerner, supra*, at 477, California did not employ that claim as the basis for drawing an inference of guilt. Nor do we think that this discharge is vitiated by any deterrent effect that California's law might have been on Globe's exercise of his Federal claim of privilege. The State may nevertheless legitimately predicate discharge on refusal to give information touching on the field of security. See *Garner* and *Adler, supra*. Likewise, we cannot say as a matter of due process that the State's choice of securing such information by means of testimony before a Federal body [4] can be denied. Finally, we do not believe that California's grounds for discharge constituted an arbitrary classification. See *Lerner, id.*, at 478. We conclude that the order of the county board was not invalid under the Due Process Clause of the Fourteenth Amendment.

Nor do we believe that the remand on procedural grounds required in *Vitarelli* v. *Seaton*, 359 U.S. 535 (1959), has any bearing here. First, we did not reach the constitutional issues raised in that case. Next, Vitarelli was a Federal Department of Interior employee who "could have been summarily discharged by the Secretary at any time without the giving of a reason." *Id.* at 539. The Court held, however, that, since Vitarelli was dismissed on the grounds of national security rather than by summary discharge, and his dismissal "fell substantially short of the requirements of the applicable departmental regulations," it was "illegal and of no effect." *Id.*, at 545. But petitioner here raises no such point, and clearly asserts that "whether or not petitioner Globe was accorded a hearing is not the issue here." [5] He bases his whole case on the claim "that due process affords petitioner Globe protection against the State's depriving him of employ-

---

[4] It is noteworthy that the California statute requires such information to be given before both State and Federal bodies.

[5] Nor does petitioner make any attack on the failure of California's statute to afford temporary employees such as he an opportunity to explain his failure to answer questions. It will be noted that permanent employees are granted such a privilege.

ment on this arbitrary ground" of his refusal on Federal constitutional grounds to answer questions of the subcommittee. Having found that on the record here the discharge for "insubordination" was not arbitrary, we need go no further.

We do not pass upon petitioner's contention as to the Privileges and Immunities Clause of the Fourteenth Amendment, since it was neither raised in nor considered by the California courts. The judgments are   *Affirmed.*

MR. CHIEF JUSTICE WARREN took no part in the consideration or decision of this case.

MR. JUSTICE BLACK, whom MR. JUSTICE DOUGLAS joins, dissenting.

Section 1028.1 of the California Code, as here applied, provides that any California public employee who refuses to incriminate himself when asked to do so by a Congressional Committee "shall be suspended and dismissed from his employment in the manner provided by law." The Fifth Amendment, which is a part of the Bill of Rights, provides that no person shall be compelled to incriminate ("to be a witness against") himself. The petitioner, Globe, an employee of the State of California, appeared before the House Un-American Activities Committee of the United States Congress and claimed this Federal constitutional privilege. California promptly discharged him, as the Court's opinion says, for "insubordination and violation of § 1028.1 of the Code." The "insubordination and violation" consisted exclusively of Globe's refusal to testify before the Congressional Committee; a ground for his refusal was that his answers might incriminate him. It is beyond doubt that the State took Globe's job away from him only because he claimed his privilege under the Federal Constitution.

Here, then, is a plain conflict between the Federal Constitution and § 1028.1 of the California Code. The Federal Constitution told Globe he could, without penalty, refuse to incriminate himself before any arm of the Federal Government; California, however, has deprived him of his job solely because he exercised this Federal constitutional privilege. In giving supremacy to the California law, I think the Court approves a plain violation of Article VI of the Constitution of the United States which makes that Constitution "the supreme Law of the Land . . . any thing in the constitution or laws of any State to the contrary notwithstanding." I also think that this discharge under State law is a violation of the Due Process Clause of the Fourteenth Amendment in its authentic historical sense: that a State may not encroach upon the individual rights of people except for violation of a law that is valid under the "law of the land." "Law of the land" of necessity includes the supreme law, the Constitution itself.

The basic purpose of the Bill of Rights was to protect individual liberty against governmental procedures that the Framers thought should not be used. That great purpose can be completely frustrated by holdings like this. I would hold that no State can put any kind of penalty on any person for claiming a privilege authorized by the Federal Constitution. The Court's holding to the contrary here does not bode well for individual liberty in America.

MR. JUSTICE BRENNAN, with whom MR. JUSTICE DOUGLAS joins, dissenting.

This is another in the series of cases involving discharge of State and local employees from their positions after they claim their constitutional privilege against self-incrimination before investigating committees. See *Slochower* v. *Board of Higher Education*, 350 U.S. 551; *Beilan* v. *Board of Public Education*, 357 U.S. 399; *Lerner* v. *Casey*, 357 U.S. 468. While I adhere on this matter of constitutional law to the views I expressed in dissent in the latter two cases, 357 U.S., at 417, it is enough to say here that I believe this case to be governed squarely by *Slochower*, and on that basis I put my dissent. Of course this opinion is limited solely to Globe's discharge.

California has commanded that its employees answer certain broad categories of questions when propounded to them by investigating bodies, including Federal bodies such as the Subcommittee of the Un-American Activities Committee involved here. Cal. Government Code § 1028.1. Invocation of the privilege against self-incrimination before such a body, in response to questions of those sorts, is made a basis for discharge.[1] In the case of a permanent employee, it is held that discharge may come only after a hearing at which the employee is given, at least, an opportunity to explain his exercise of the privilege. *Board of Education* v. *Mass*, 47 Cal. 2d 494, 304 P. 2d 1015. But for a temporary or probationary employee like Globe the State law, as interpreted authoritatively by the California courts below requires a discharge of the employee upon his claim of the privilege, without further ado. 163 Cal. App. 2d, at 605–606, 329 P. 2d, at 978. Opportunity for an explanation by the employee or for administrative consideration of the circumstances of the claim of privilege is foreclosed under the State law.

In *Slochower*, this Court had a substantially identical situation before it. There a local law which made a claim of the constitutional privilege "equivalent to a resignation" was struck down as violative of the Due Process Clause of the Fourteenth Amendment. Only one word is necessary to add here to the Court's statement there of its reason for voiding the provision: "As interpreted and applied by the State courts, it operates to discharge every [temporary] . . . employee who invokes the Fifth Amendment. In practical effect the questions asked are taken as confessed and made the basis of the discharge. No consideration is given to such factors as the subject matter of the questions, remoteness of the period to which they are directed, or justification for exercise of the privilege. It matters not whether the plea resulted from mistake, inadvertence or legal advice conscientiously given, whether wisely or unwisely. The heavy hand of the

---

[1] The Court appears to treat the fact that the California statute is not in terms directed at the exercise of the privilege against self-incrimination, but rather covers all refusals to answer, as a factor militating in favor of its validity. The Court seems to view the privilege against self-incrimination as a somewhat strange and singular basis on which to decline to answer questions put in an investigation; or at most as an individual private soldier in a large army of reasons that might commonly be given for declining to respond. I am afraid I must view the matter more realistically. But even if the statute were taken as wholeheartedly at face value as the Court does, the consequence would not be that it was more reasonable, but rather that it was more arbitrary. It hardly avoids the rationale of this Court's decision in the *Slochower* case if the State adds other constitutional privileges to the list, exercise of which results *per se* in discharge. Such a statute would be even the more undifferentiating and arbitrary in its basis for discharge than the one involved in *Slochower*. And of course the crowning extent of arbitrariness is exposed by the contention that the fact that discharge would have followed a refusal to answer predicated on no reason at all justifies discharge upon claim of a constitutional privilege. It would appear of the essence of arbitrariness for the State to lump together refusals to answer based on good reasons and those on no reason at all, and make discharge automatically ensue on all. What was struck down in *Slochower* as unconstitutionally arbitrary—undifferentiating treatment merely among those pleading the self-incrimination privilege—seems almost reasonable by comparison.

statute falls alike on all who exercise their constitutional privilege, the full enjoyment of which every person is entitled to receive." 350 U.S., at 558. The Court distinguished instances in which the employing government itself might be conducting an investigation into the "fitness" of the employee.

As applied, then, to temporary or probationary employees, the California statute contains the identical vice of automatic discharge for a Fifth Amendment plea made before another body, not concerned with investigating the "fitness" of the employee involved. It is sought here to equate Globe's case with those of Beilan and Lerner. But in the latter cases the Court took the view that the State discharges were sustainable because the employees' pleas of self-incrimination before local administrative agency investigations of their competence and reliability prevented those employing bodies from having an adequate record on which to reach an affirmative conclusion as to their competence and reliability. This failure to cooperate fully (styled lack of candor) within the framework of the employer's own proceeding to determine fitness, was said to be a constitutional basis for discharge. 357 U.S., at 405–408; 357 U.S., at 475–479; and see 357 U.S., at 410 (concurring opinion). But here there was not the vaguest semblance of any local administrative procedure designed to determine the fitness of Globe for further employment.[2] It has not been hitherto suggested that the authorizing resolutions of the Un-American Activities Committee extend to enabling it to perform these functions on a grant-in-aid basis to the States. Accordingly there is presented here the very same arbitrary action—the drawing of an inference of unfitness for employment from exercise of the privilege before another body, without opportunity to explain on the part of the employee, or duty on the part of the employing body to attempt to relate the employee's conduct specifically to his fitness for employment—as was involved in *Slochower*. There is the same announced abdication of the local administrative body's own function of determining the fitness of its employees, in favor of an arbitrary and *per se* rule dependent on the behavior of the employee before another body not charged with determining his fitness.

It is said that this case differs from *Slochower* because that case involved a determination, based on his invocation of the privilege, that the employee was guilty of substantive misconduct, while this one simply involves a case of "insubordination" in the employees' failure to answer questions asked by the Congressional Committee which the employing agency has ordered be answered. In the first place, *Slochower* did not involve any finding by the New York authorities that the employee was guilty of the matters as to which he claimed the privilege. The claim of the privilege was treated by the State as equivalent to a resignation, 350 U.S., at 554, and it was only "in practical effect," *id.*, at 558, that the questions asked were taken as confessed;[3] that is, the State claimed the power to take the same action,

---

[2] In *Slochower* it was said, "It is one thing for the city authorities themselves to inquire into Slochower's fitness, but quite another for his discharge to be based entirely on events occurring before a Federal committee whose inquiry was announced as not directed at 'the property, affairs, or government of the city, or . . . official conduct of city employees.'" 350 U.S., at 558. This distinction was asserted in *Beilan* and *Lerner*. 357 U.S., at 408; 357 U.S., at 477.

[3] The opinion in the New York Court of Appeals also makes it quite clear that Slochower was not being discharged as guilty of the matters inquired about. *Daniman* v. *Board of Education*, 306 N.Y. 532, 538, 119 N.E. 2d 373, 377.

discharge of the employee from employment, upon a plea of the privilege, as it could have taken upon a confession of the matters charged. The case involved an inference of unfitness for office, then, drawn arbitrarily and without opportunity to explain, from the assertion of the privilege. The same is involved here, and the thin patina of "insubordination" that the statute encrusts on the exercise of the privilege does not change the matter. If the State labeled as "insubordination" and the mandatory ground for discharge every failure by an employee to respond to questions asked him by strangers on the street, its action would be as pointless as it was arbitrary. The point of the direction given to all employees here to answer the sort of questions covered by the statute must have been that the State though that the matters involved in the questions bore some generic relationship to the "fitness" of the employee to hold his position. But on this basis the case is again indistinguishable from *Slochower*. If it is unconstitutionally arbitrary for the State to treat every invocation of the privilege as conclusive on his fitness and in effect as an automatic discharge, then the command of the State that no temporary employee shall claim the privilege under pain of automatic discharge must be an unconstitutionally arbitrary command. A State could not I suppose, discharge an employee for attending religious services on Sunday, see *Wieman* v. *Upegraff*, 344 U.S. 183, 192; and equally so it could not enforce, by discharges for "insubordination," a general command to its employees not to attend such services.

The State court distinguished this case from *Slochower* on the grounds that Slochower was a State employee with tenure, but Globe was a temporary or probationary employee not entitled to a hearing on discharge. On this basis, it concluded that the requirement outlined by this Court in *Slochower*—that he could not be discharged *ipso facto* on his claim of the privilege, but only after a more particularized inquiry administered by his employer—did not apply. 163 Cal. App. 2d, at 601–603, 329 P. 2d, at 975–976. But this Court has nothing to do with the civil service systems of the States, as such. And Globe does not here contend that he could not have been discharged without a hearing; but he does attack the specified basis of his discharge. Doubtless a probationary employee can constitutionally be discharged without specification of reasons at all; and this Court has not held that it would offend the Due Process Clause, without more, for a State to put its entire civil service on such a basis, if as a matter of internal polity it could stand to do so. But if a State discharged even a probationary employee because he was a Negro or a Jew, giving that explicit reason, its action could not be squared with the Constitution. So with Slochower's case; this Court did not reverse the judgment of New York's highest court because it had disrespected Slochower's State tenure rights, but because it had sanctioned administrative action taken expressly on an unconstitutionally arbitrary basis. So here California could have summarily discharged Globe, and that would have been an end to the matter; without more appearing, its action would be taken to rest on a permissible judgment by his superiors as to his fitness. But if it chooses expressly to bottom his discharge on a basis—like that of an automatic, unparticularized reaction to a plea of self-incrimination—which cannot by itself be sustained constitutionally, it cannot escape its constitutional obligations on the ground that as a general matter it could have effected his discharge with a minimum of formality. Cf. *Vitarelli* v. *Seaton*, 359 U.S. 535, 539.

For these reasons the judgment as to Globe should be reversed.

TEACHERS' LOYALTY

ADLER ET AL. *v.* BOARD OF EDUCATION OF THE CITY OF NEW YORK.

APPEAL FROM THE COURT OF APPEALS OF NEW YORK.

No. 8.   Argued January 3, 1952.—Decided March 3, 1952.

The Civil Service Law of New York, § 12–a, makes ineligible for employment in any public school any member of any organization advocating the overthrow of the Government by force, violence or any unlawful means. Section 3022 of the Education Law, added by the Feinberg Law, requires the Board of Regents (1) to adopt and enforce rules for the removal of any employee who violates, or is ineligible under, § 12–a, (2) to promulgate a list of organizations described in § 12–a, and (3) to provide in its rules that membership in any organization so listed is prima facie evidence of disqualification for employment in the public schools.   No organization may be so listed, and no person severed from or denied employment, except after a hearing and subject to judicial review.   *Held:* This Court finds no constitutional infirmity in § 12–a of the Civil Service Law of New York or in § 3022 of the Education Law.   Pp. 486–496.

   1. Section 3022 and the rules promulgated thereunder do not constitute an abridgment of the freedom of speech and assembly of persons employed or seeking employment in the public schools of New York.   *Garner* v. *Los Angeles Board*, 341, U.S. 716.   Pp. 491–493.

   2. The provision of § 3022 directing the Board of Regents to provide in rules thereunder that membership in any organization so listed by the board shall constitute prima facie evidence of disqualification for employment in the public schools does not deny members of such organizations due process of law.   Pp. 494–496.

   3. The use of the word "subversive" in § 1 of the Feinberg Law, which is a preamble and not a definitive part of the Act, does not render the statute void for vagueness under the Due Process Clause, in view of the fact that in subdivision 2 of § 3022 it is given a very definite meaning—*i.e.*, an organization that advocates the overthrow of government by force or violence. P. 496.

   4. The constitutionality of § 3021 of the Education Law not having been questioned in the proceedings in the lower courts and being raised here for the first time, it will not be passed upon by this Court before the State courts have had an opportunity to pass upon it.   P. 496.

301 N.Y. 476, 95 N.E. 2d 806, affirmed.

   In a declaratory judgment action, the Supreme Court of New York, Kings County, held that subdivision (c) of § 12–a of the New York Civil Service Law, § 3022 of the New York Education Law, and the rules of the State Board of Regents promulgated thereunder violated the Due Process Clause of the Fourteenth Amendment, and enjoined action thereunder by the Board of Education of New York City.   196 Misc. 873, 95 N.Y.S. 2d 114.   The Appellate Division reversed.   276 App. Div. 527, 96 N.Y.S. 2d 466.   The Court of Appeals of New York affirmed the decision of the Appellate Division.   301 N.Y. 476, 95 N.E. 2d 806.   On appeal to this Court, *affirmed*, p. 496.

   Osmond K. Fraenkel argued the cause for appellants.   With him on the brief was *Arthur Garfield Hays*.

Michael A. Castaldi argued the cause for appellee. With him on
the brief were *Denis M. Hurley, Seymour B. Quel, Daniel T. Scannell* and *Bernard Friedlander.*

By special leave of Court, *Wendell P. Brown,* Solicitor General,
argued the cause for the State of New York, as *amicus curiae,* urging
affirmance. With him on the brief were *Nathaniel L. Goldstein,*
Attorney General, and *Ruth Kessler Toch,* Assistant Attorney General.

Dorothy Kenyon, Raymond L. Wise and *Herbert Monte Levy*
filed a brief for the American Civil Liberties Union, as *amicus
curiae,* supporting appellants.

Mr. Justice Minton delivered the opinion of the Court.

Appellants brought a declaratory judgment action in the Supreme
Court of New York, Kings County, praying that § 12–a of the Civil
Service Law,[1] as implemented by the so-called Feinberg Law,[2] be
declared unconstitutional, and that action by the Board of Education of the City of New York thereunder be enjoined. On motion for
judgment on the pleadings, the court held that subdivision (c)
of § 12–a, the Feinberg Law, and the Rules of the State Board of
Regents promulgated thereunder violated the Due Process Clause of
the Fourteenth Amendment, and issued an injunction. 196 Misc.
873, 95 N.Y.S. 2d 114. The Appellate Division of the Supreme
Court reversed, 276 App. Div. 527, 96 N.Y.S. 2d 466, and the Court
of Appeals affirmed the judgment of the Appellate Division, 301
N.Y. 476, 95 N.E. 2d 806. The appellants come here by appeal
under 28 U.S.C. § 1257.

Section 12–a of the Civil Service Law, hereafter referred to as
§ 12–a, is set forth in the margin.[3] To implement this law, the
Feinberg Law was passed, adding a new section, § 3022, to the
Education Law of the State of New York, which section so far as

---

[1] N.Y. Laws 1939, c. 547, as amended N.Y. Laws 1940, c. 564.
[2] N.Y. Laws 1949, c. 360.
[3] " § 12–a. *Ineligibility*
"No person shall be appointed to any office or position in the service of the State or of
any civil division or city thereof, nor shall any person presently employed in any such
office or position be continued in such employment, nor shall any person be employed in the
public service as superintendents, principals or teachers in a public school or academy or
in a State normal school or college, or any other State educational institution who:
(a) By word of mouth or writing willfully and deliberately advocates, advises or teaches
the doctrine that the Government of the United States or of any State or of any political
subdivision thereof should be overthrown or overturned by force, violence or any unlawful
means ; or
"(b) Prints, publishes, edits, issues or sells, any book, paper, document or written or
printed matter in any form containing or advocating, advising or teaching the doctrine
that the Government of the United States or of any State or of any political subdivision
thereof should be overthrown by force, violence or any unlawful means, and who advocates,
advises, teaches, or embraces the duty, necessity or propriety of adopting the doctrine
contained therein ;
"(c) Organizes or helps to organize or becomes a member of any society or group of
persons who teaches or advocates that the Government of the United States or of any
State or of any political subdivision thereof shall be overthrown by force or violence, or
by any unlawful means ;
"(d) A person dismissed or declared ineligible may within four months of such dismissal
or declaration of ineligibility be entitled to petition for an order to show cause signed by
a justice of the supreme court, why a hearing on such charges should not be had. Until
the final judgment on said hearing is entered, the order to show cause shall stay the effect
of any order of dismissal or ineligibility based on the provisions of this section. The
hearing shall consist of the taking of testimony in open court with opportunity for cross-
examination. The burden of sustaining the validity of the order of dismissal or ineligibility
by a fair preponderance of the credible evidence shall be upon the person making such
dismissal or order of ineligibility."

here pertinent is set forth in the margin.[4] The Feinberg Law was also to implement § 3021 of the Education Law of New York.[5] The constitutionality of this section was not attacked in the proceedings below.

The preamble of the Feinberg Law, § 1, makes elaborate findings that members of subversive groups, particularly of the Communist Party and its affiliated organizations, have been infiltrating into public employment in the public schools of the State; that this has occurred and continues notwithstanding the existence of protective statutes designed to prevent the appointment to or retention in employment in public office, and particularly in the public schools, of members of any organizations which teach or advocate that the Government of the United States or of any State or political subdivision thereof shall be overthrown by force or violence or by any other unlawful means. As a result, propaganda can be disseminated among the children by those who teach them and to whom they look for guidance, authority, and leadership. The legislature further found that the members of such groups use their positions to advocate and teach their doctrines, and are frequently bound by oath, agreement, pledge, or understanding to follow, advocate and teach a prescribed party line or group dogma or doctrine without regard to truth or free inquiry. This propaganda, the legislature declared, is sufficiently subtle to escape detection in the classroom; thus, the menace of such infiltration into the classroom is difficult to measure. Finally, to protect the children from such influence, it was thought essential that the laws prohibiting members of such groups, such as the Communist Party or its affiliated organizations, from obtaining or retaining employment in the public schools be rigorously enforced. It is the purpose of the Feinberg Law to provide for the disqualification and removal of superintendents of schools, teachers, and employees in the public schools in any city or school district of the State who advocate the overthrow of the Government by unlawful means or who are members of organizations which have a like purpose.

---

[4] § 3022. *Elimination of subversive persons from the public school system*

"1. The board of regents shall adopt, promulgate, and enforce rules and regulations for the disqualification or removal of superintendents of schools, teachers or employees in the public schools in any city or school district of the State who violate the provisions of section three thousand twenty-one of this article or who are ineligible for appointment to or retention in any office or position in such public schools on any of the grounds set forth in section twelve-a of the civil service law and shall provide therein appropriate methods and procedure for the enforcement of such sections of this article and the civil service law.

"2. The board of regents shall, after inquiry, and after such notice and hearing as may be appropriate, make a listing of organizations which it finds to be subversive in that they advocate, advise, teach or embrace the doctrine that the Government of the United States or of any State or of any political subdivision thereof shall be overthrown or overturned by force, violence or any unlawful means, or that they advocate, advise, teach or embrace the duty, necessity, or propriety of adopting any such doctrine, as set forth in section twelve-a of the civil service law. Such listings may be amended and revised from time to time. The board, in making such inquiry, may utilize any similar listings or designations promulgated by any Federal agency or authority authorized by Federal law, regulation or executive order, and for the purposes of such inquiry, the board may request and receive from such Federal agencies or authorities any supporting material or evidence that may be made available to it. The board of regents shall provide in the rules and regulations required by subdivision one hereof that membership in any such organization included in such listing made by it shall constitute prima facie evidence of disqualification for appointment to or retention in any office or position in the public schools of the State."

[5] § 3021. *Removal of superintendents, teachers and employees for treasonable or seditious acts or utterances*

"A person employed as superintendent of schools, teacher or employee in the public schools, in any city or school district of the state, shall be removed from such position for the utterance of any treasonable or seditious word or words or the doing of any treasonable or seditious act or acts while holding such position."

Section 3022 of the Education Law, added by the Feinberg Law, provides that the Board of Regents, which has charge of the public school system in the State of New York, shall, after full notice and hearing, make a listing of organizations which it finds advocate, advise, teach, or embrace the doctrine that the government should be overthrown by force or violence or any other unlawful means, and that such listing may be amended and revised from time to time.

It will be observed that the listings are made only after full notice and hearing. In addition, the Court of Appeals construed the statute in conjunction with Article 78 of the New York Civil Practice Act, Gilbert-Bliss' N.Y. Civ. Prac., Vol. 6B, so as to provide listed organizations a right of review.

The Board of Regents is further authorized to provide in rules and regulations, and has so provided, that membership in any listed organization, after notice and hearing, "shall constitute prima facie evidence for disqualification for appointment to or retention in any office or position in the school system"; [6] but before one who is an employee or seeks employment is severed from or denied employment, he likewise must be given a full hearing with the privilege of being represented by counsel and the right to judicial review.[7] It is § 12–a of the Civil Service Law, as implemented by the Feinberg Law as above indicated, that is under attack here.

It is first argued that the Feinberg Law and the rules promulgated thereunder constitute an abridgment of the freedom of speech and assembly of persons employed or seeking employment in the public schools of the State of New York.

It is clear that such persons have the right under our law to assemble, speak, think and believe as they will. *Communications Assn.* v. *Douds,* 339 U.S. 382. It is equally clear that they have no right to work for the State in the school system on their own terms. *United Public Workers* v. *Mitchell,* 330 U.S. 75. They may work for the school system upon the reasonable terms laid down by the proper authorities of New York. If they do not choose to work on such terms, they are at liberty to retain their beliefs and associations and go elsewhere. Has the State thus deprived them of any right to free speech or assembly? We think not. Such persons are or may be denied, under the statutes in question, the privilege of working for the school system of the State of New York because, first, of their advocacy of the overthrow of the government by force or violence, or, secondly, by unexplained membership in an organization found by the school

---

6 "§ 254. *Disqualification or removal of superintendents, teachers and other employes.*

"2. *List of subversive organizations to be issued.* Pursuant to chapter 360 of the Laws of 1949, the Board of Regents will issue a list, which may be amended and revised from time to time, of organizations which the board finds to be subversive in that they advocate, advise, teach or embrace the doctrine that the Government of the United States, or of any State or of any political subdivision thereof, shall be overthrown or overturned by force, violence or any unlawful means, or that they advocate, advise, teach or embrace the duty, necessity or propriety of adopting any such doctrine, as set forth in section 12–a of the Civil Service Law. Evidence of membership in any organization so listed on or after the tenth day subsequent to the date of official promulgation of such list shall constitute *prima facie* evidence of disqualification for appointment to or retention of any office or position in the school system. Evidence of membership in such an organization prior to said day shall be presumptive evidence that membership has continued, in the absence of a showing that such membership has been terminated in good faith." Official Compilation of Codes, Rules and Regulations of the State of New York (Fifth Supp.), Vol. 1, pp. 205–206.

7 The Court of Appeals construed the statute in conjunction with § 12–a subd. [d], *supra,* n. 3. The Rules of the Board of Regents provided: "In all cases all rights to a fair trial, representation by counsel and appeal or court review as provided by statute or the Constitution shall be scrupulously observed." Section 254, 1(e), Official Compilation of Codes, Rules and Regulations of the State of New York (Fifth Supp.), Vol. 1, p. 206.

authorities, after notice and hearing, to teach and advocate the overthrow of the government by force or violence, and known by such persons to have such purpose. The constitutionality of the first proposition is not questioned here. *Gitlow* v. *New York*, 268 U.S. 652, 667–672, construing § 161 of the New York Penal Law.

As to the second, it is rather subtly suggested that we should not follow our recent decision in *Garner* v. *Los Angeles Board*, 341 U.S. 716. We there said:

"We think that a municipal employer is not disabled because it is an agency of the State from inquiring of its employees as to matters that may prove relevant to their fitness and suitability for the public service. Past conduct may well relate to present fitness; past loyalty may have a reasonable relationship to present and future trust. Both are commonly inquired into in determining fitness for both high and low positions in private industry and are not less relevant in public employment." 341 U.S. at p. 720.

We adhere to that case. A teacher works in a sensitive area in a schoolroom. There he shapes the attitude of young minds towards the society in which they live. In this, the State has a vital concern. It must preserve the integrity of the schools. That the school authorities have the right and the duty to screen the officials, teachers, and employees as to their fitness to maintain the integrity of the schools as a part of ordered society, cannot be doubted. One's associates, past and present, as well as one's conduct, may properly be considered in determining fitness and loyalty. From time immemorial, one's reputation has been determined in part by the company he keeps. In the employment of officials and teachers of the school system, the State may very properly inquire into the company they keep, and we know of no rule, constitutional or otherwise, that prevents the State, when determining the fitness and loyalty of such persons, from considering the organizations and persons with whom they associate.

If, under the procedure set up in the New York law, a person is found to be unfit and is disqualified from employment in the public school system because of membership in a listed organization, he is not thereby denied the right of free speech and assembly. His freedom of choice between membership in the organization and employment in the school system might be limited, but not his freedom of speech or assembly, except in the remote sense that limitation is inherent in every choice. Certainly such limitation is not one the State may not make in the exercise of its police power to protect the schools from pollution and thereby to defend its own existence.

It is next argued by appellants that the provision in § 3022 directing the Board of Regents to provide in rules and regulations that membership in any organization listed by the board after notice and hearing, with provision for review in accordance with the statute, shall constitute prima facie evidence of disqualification, denies due process, because the fact found bears no relation to the fact presumed. In other words, from the fact found that the organization was one that advocated the overthrow of government by unlawful means and that the person employed or to be employed was a member of the organization and knew of its purpose,[8] to presume that such member is disqualified for employment is so unreasonable as to be a denial of due process of law. We do not agree.

"The law of evidence is full of presumptions either of fact or law. The former are, of course, disputable, and the strength of any inference of one fact from proof of another depends upon the generality of the experience upon which it is founded. . . .

"Legislation providing that proof of one fact shall constitute *prima facie* evidence of the main fact in issue is but to enact a rule of evidence, and quite within the general power of government. Statutes, National and State, dealing with such methods of proof in both civil and criminal cases abound, and the decisions upholding them are numerous." *Mobile, J. & K. C. R. Co.* v. *Turnipseed,* 219 U.S. 35, at p. 42.

Membership in a listed organization found to be within the statute and known by the member to be within the statute is a legislative finding that the member by his membership supports the thing the organization stands for, namely, the overthrow of government by unlawful means. We cannot say that such a finding is contrary to fact or that "generality of experience" points to a different conclusion. Disqualification follows therefore as a reasonable presumption from such membership and support. Nor is there here a problem of procedural due process. The presumption is not conclusive but arises only in a hearing where the person against whom it may arise has full opportunity to rebut it. The holding of the Court of Appeals below is significant in this regard:

"The statute also makes it clear that . . . proof of such membership 'shall constitute prima facie evidence of disqualification' for such employment. But, as was said in *Potts* v. *Pardee* (220 N.Y. 431, 433): 'The presumption growing out of a *prima facie* case . . . remains only so long as there is no substantial evidence to the contrary. When that is offered the presumption disappears, and unless met by further proof there is nothing to justify a finding based solely upon it.' Thus the phrase '*prima facie* evidence of disqualification,' as used in the statute, imports a hearing at which one who seeks appointment to or retention in a public school position shall be afforded an opportunity to present substantial evidence contrary to the presumption sanctioned by the *prima facie* evidence for which subdivision 2 of section 3022 makes provision. Once such contrary evidence has been received, however, the official who made the order of ineligibility has thereafter the burden of sustaining the validity of that order by a fair preponderance of the evidence. (Civil Service Law, § 12–a, subd. [d].) Should an order of ineligibility then issue, the party aggrieved thereby may avail himself of the provisions for review prescribed by the section of the statute last cited above. In that view there here arises no question of procedural due process." 301 N.Y. 476, at p. 494, 95 N. E. 2d 806, at 814–815.

---

[8] In the proceedings below, both the Appellate Division of the Supreme Court and the Court of Appeals construed the statute to require such knowledge. 276 App. Div. 527, 530, 96 N.Y. S. 2d 466, 470–471 ; 301 N.Y. 476, 494, 95 N.E. 2d 806, 814–815.

Where, as here, the relation between the fact found and the presumption is clear and direct and is not conclusive, the requirements of due process are satisfied.

Without raising in the complaint or in the proceedings in the lower courts the question of the constitutionality of § 3021 of the Education Law of New York, appellants urge here for the first time that this section is unconstitutionally vague. The question is not before us. We will not pass upon the constitutionality of a State statute before the State courts have had an opportunity to do so. *Asbury Hospital* v. *Cass County*, 326 U.S. 207, 213–216; *Alabama State Federation of Labor* v. *McAdory*, 325 U.S. 450, 460–462; *Plymouth Coal Co.* v. *Pennsylvania*, 232 U.S. 531, 546.

It is also suggested that the use of the word "subversive" is vague and indefinite. But the word is first used in § 1 of the Feinberg Law, which is the preamble to the Act, and not in a definitive part thereof. When used in subdivision 2 of § 3022, the word has a very definite meaning, namely, an organization that teaches and advocates the overthrow of the government by force or violence.

We find no constitutional infirmity in § 12–a of the Civil Service Law of New York or in the Feinberg Law which implemented it, and the judgment is

Affirmed.

Mr. Justice Black, dissenting.

While I fully agree with the dissent of Mr. Justice Douglas, the importance of this holding prompts me to add these thoughts.

This is another of those rapidly multiplying legislative enactments which make it dangerous—this time for school teachers—to think or say anything except what a transient majority happen to approve at the moment. Basically these laws rest on the belief that government should supervise and limit the flow of ideas into the minds of men. The tendency of such governmental policy is to mould people into a common intellectual pattern. Quite a different governmental policy rests on the belief that government should leave the mind and spirit of man absolutely free. Such a governmental policy encourages varied intellectual outlooks in the belief that the best views will prevail. This policy of freedom is in my judgment embodied in the First Amendment and made applicable to the States by the Fourteenth. Because of this policy public officials cannot be constitutionally vested with powers to select the ideas people can think about, censor the public views they can express, or choose the persons or groups people can associate with. Public officials with such powers are not public servants; they are public masters.

I dissent from the Court's judgment sustaining this law which effectively penalizes school teachers for their thoughts and their associates.

Mr. Justice Frankfurter, dissenting.

We are asked to pass on a scheme to counteract what are currently called "subversive" influences in the public school system of New York. The scheme is formulated partly in statutes and partly in administrative regulations, but all of it is still an unfinished blueprint. We are asked to adjudicate claims against its constitutionality before the scheme has been put into operation, before the limits that it imposes upon free inquiry and association, the scope of scrutiny that it sanctions, and the procedural safeguards that will be found to be implied for its enforcement have been authoritatively defined. I think we should adhere to the teaching of this Court's history to avoid constitutional adjudications on merely abstract or speculative issues and to base them on the concreteness afforded by an actual, present, defined controversy, appropriate for judicial judgment, between adversaries immediately affected by it. In accordance with the settled limits upon our jurisdiction I would dismiss this appeal.

An understanding of the statutory scheme and the action thus far taken under it is necessary to a proper consideration of the issues which for me control disposition of the case, namely, standing of the parties and ripeness of the constitutional question.

A New York enactment of 1949 precipitated this litigation. But that legislation is tied to prior statutes. By a law of 1917 "treasonable or seditious" utterances or acts barred employment in the public schools. New York Education Law, § 3021. In 1939 a further enactment disqualified from the civil service and the educational system anyone who advocates the overthrow of government by force, violence or any unlawful means, or publishes material advocating such overthrow or organizes or joins any society advocating such doctrine. New York Civil Service Law, § 12–a. This states with sufficient accuracy the provisions of this law, which also included detailed provisions for the hearing and review of charges.

During the thirty-two years and ten years, respectively, that these laws have stood on the books, no proceedings, so far as appears, have been taken under them. In 1949 the legislature passed a new act, familiarly known as the Feinberg Law, designed to reinforce the prior legislation. The law begins with a legislative finding, based on "common report" of widespread infiltration by "members of subversive groups, and particularly of the Communist Party and certain of its affiliated organizations," into the educational system of the State and the evils attendant upon that infiltration. It takes note of existing laws and exhorts the authorities to greater endeavor of enforcement. The State Board of Regents, in which are lodged extensive powers over New York's educational system, was charged by the Feinberg Law with these duties:

(1) to promulgate rules and regulations for the more stringent enforcement of existing law;

(2) to list "after inquiry, and after such notice and hearing as may be appropriate" those organizations membership in which is proscribed by subsection (c) of § 12–a of the civil service law;

(3) to provide in its rules and regulations that membership in a listed organization shall be *prima facie* evidence of disqualification under § 12–a;

(4) to report specially and in detail to the legislature each year on measures taken for the enforcement of these laws.

Accordingly, the Board of Regents adopted rules for ferreting out violations of § 3021 or § 12–a. An elaborate machinery was designed for annual reports on each employee with a view to discovering evidence of violations of these sections and to assuring appropriate action on such discovery. The board also announced its intention to publish the required list of proscribed organizations and defined the significance of an employee's membership therein in proceedings for his dismissal. These rules by the Board of Regents were published with an accompanying memorandum by the commissioner of education. He is the administrative head of New York's school system and his memorandum was for the guidance of school officials throughout the State. It warned of the danger of indiscriminate or careless action under the Feinberg Law and the Regents' Rules, and laid down this duty:

"The statutes and the Regents' Rules make it clear that it is a primary duty of the school authorities in each school district to take positive action to eliminate from the school system any teacher in whose case there is evidence that he is guilty of subversive activity. School authorities are under obligation to proceed immediately and conclusively in every such case."

The rules and memorandum appear in the record; we shall have occasion to refer later to their relevance to what was decided below. Our attention has also been called to an order of the board of education of the city of New York, the present appellee. This order further elaborates the part of the Regents' Rules dealing with reports on teachers. It is not clear whether this order has gone into effect. In any event it was not before the lower courts and is not in the record here.

It thus appears that we are asked to review a complicated statutory scheme prohibiting those who engage in the kind of speech or conduct that is proscribed from holding positions in the public school system. The scheme is aligned with a complex system of enforcement by administrative investigation, reporting and listing of proscribed organizations. All this must further be related to the general procedures under the New York law for hearing and reviewing charges of misconduct against educational employees, modified as those procedures may be by the Feinberg Law and the Regents' Rules.

This intricate machinery has not yet been set in motion. Enforcement has been in abeyance since the present suit, among others, was brought to enjoin the board of education from taking steps or spending funds under the statutes and rules on the theory that these transgressed various limitations which the United States Constitution places on the power of the States. The case comes here on the bare bones of the Feinberg Law only partly given flesh by the Regents' Rules. It was decided wholly on pleadings: a complaint, identifying the plaintiffs and their interests, setting out the offending statutes and rules, and concluding in a more or less argumentative fashion that these provisions violate numerous constitutional rights of the various plaintiffs; an answer, denying that the impact of the statute is unconstitutional and that the plaintiffs have any interest to support the suit. On these pleadings summary judgment in favor of some of the plaintiffs was granted by the Supreme Court in Kings County, 196 Misc. 873, 95 N.Y.S. 2d 114; this was reversed by the Appellate Division for the Second Department with direction that the complaint be dismissed, 276 App. Div. 527, 96 N.Y.S. 2d 466, and the Court of Appeals affirmed the Appellate Division. 301 N.Y. 476, 95 N.E. 2d 806. These pleadings and the opinions below are the basis on which we are asked to decide this case.

About forty plaintiffs brought the action initially; the trial court dismissed as to all but eight. 196 Misc., at 877, 95 N.Y.S. 2d, at

117–118. The others were found without standing to sue under New York law. The eight who are here as appellants alleged that they were municipal taxpayers and were empowered, by virtue of N.Y. Gen. Municipal Law § 51, to bring suit against municipal agencies to enjoin waste of funds. New York is free to determine how the views of its courts on matters of constitutionality are to be invoked. But its action cannot of course confer jurisdiction on this Court, limited as that is by the settled construction of Article III of the Constitution. We cannot entertain, as we again recognize this very day, a constitutional claim at the instance of one whose interest has no material significance and is undifferentiated from the mass of his fellow citizens. *Doremus* v. *Board of Education*, 342 U.S. 429. This is not a "pocketbook action." As taxpayers these plaintiffs cannot possibly be affected one way or the other by any disposition of this case, and they make no such claim. It may well be that the authorities will, if left free, divert funds and effort from other purposes for the enforcement of the provisions under review, though how much leads to the merest conjecture. But the total expenditure, certainly the new expenditure, necessary to implement the Act and Rules may well be *de minimis*. The plaintiffs at any rate have not attempted to show that any such expenditure would come from funds to which their taxes contribute. In short, they have neither alleged nor shown that our decision on the issues they tender would have the slightest effect on their tax bills or even on the aggregate bill of all the city's taxpayers whom they claim to represent. The high improbability of being able to make such a demonstration, in the circumstances of this case, does not dispense with the requirements for our jurisdiction. If the incidence of taxation in a city like New York bears no relation to the factors here under consideration, that is precisely why these taxpayers have no claim on our jurisdiction.

This ends the matter for plaintiffs Krieger and Newman. But six of the plaintiffs advanced grounds other than that of being taxpayers in bringing this action. Two are parents of children in New York City schools. Four are teachers in these schools. On the basis of the record before us these claims, too, are insufficient, in view of our controlling adjudications, to support the jurisdiction of this Court.

The trial court found the interests of the plaintiffs as parents inconsequential. 196 Misc., at 875, 95 N.Y.S. 2d, at 816. I agree. Parents may dislike to have children educated in a school system where teachers feel restrained by unconstitutional limitations on their freedom. But it is like catching butterflies without a net to try to find a legal interest, indispensable for our jurisdiction, in a parent's desire to have his child educated in schools free from such restrictions. The hurt to parents' sensibilities is too tenuous or the inroad upon rightful claims to public education too argumentative to serve as the earthly stuff required for a legal right judicially enforceable. The claim does not approach in immediacy or directness or solidity that which our whole process of constitutional adjudication has deemed a necessary condition to the Court's settlement of constitutional issues.

An apt contrast is provided by *McCollum* v. *Board of Education*, 333 U.S. 203, where a parent did present an individualized claim of his own that was direct and palpable. There the parent alleged that Illinois imposed restrictions on the child's free exercise of faith and thereby on the parent's. The basis of jurisdiction in the *McCollum* case was not at all a parental right to challenge in the courts—or at least in this Court—educational provisions in general. The closely defined encroachment of the particular arrangement on a constitutionally protected right of the child, and of the parent's right in the child, furnished the basis for our review. The Feinberg Law puts no limits on any definable legal interest of the child or of its parents.

This leaves only the teachers, Adler, Spencer, and George and Mark Friedlander. The question whether their interest as teachers was sufficient to give them standing to sue was thought by the trial court to be conclusively settled by our decision in *United Public Workers* v. *Mitchell*, 330 U.S. 75. I see no escape from the controlling relevance of the *Mitchell* case. There individual government employees sought to enjoin enforcement of the provisions of the Hatch Act forbidding government employees to take active part in politics. The complaint contained detailed recitals of the desire, intent and specific steps short of violation on the part of plaintiffs to engage in the prohibited activities. See *id.*, at 87–88, n. 18. There as here the law was attacked as violating constitutional guaranties of freedom of speech. We found jurisdiction wanting to decide the issue except as to one plaintiff whose conduct had already violated the applicable standards.

The allegations in the present action fall short of those found insufficient in the *Mitchell* case. These teachers do not allege that they have engaged in proscribed conduct or that they have any intention to do so. They do not suggest that they have been, or are, deterred from supporting causes or from joining organizations for fear of the Feinberg Law's interdict, except to say generally that the system complained of will have this effect on teachers as a group. They do not assert that they are threatened with action under the law, or that steps are imminent whereby they would incur the hazard of punishment for conduct innocent at the time, or under standards too vague to satisfy due process of law. They merely allege that the statutes and rules permit such action against some teachers. Since we rightly refused in the *Mitchell* case to hear government employees whose conduct was much more intimately affected by the law there attacked than are the claims of plaintiffs here, this suit is wanting in the necessary basis for our review.

This case proves anew the wisdom of rigorous adherence to the prerequisites for pronouncement by this Court on matters of constitutional law. The absence in these plantiffs of the immediacy and solidity of interest necessary to support jurisdiction is reflected in the atmosphere of abstraction and ambiguity in which the constitutional issues are presented. The broad, generalized claims urged at the bar touch the deepest interests of a democratic society: its right to self-preservation and ample scope for the individual's freedom, especially the teacher's freedom of thought, inquiry and expression. No problem of a free society is probably more difficult than the reconciliation or accommodation of these too often conflicting interests. The judicial role in this process of accommodation is necessarily very limited and must be carefully circumscribed. To that end the Court, in its long history, has developed "a series of rules" carefully formulated by Mr. Justice

Brandeis, "under which it has avoided passing upon a large part of all the constitutional questions pressed upon it for decision." *Ashwander* v. *Tennessee Valley Authority*, 297 U.S. 288, 346.

We have emphasized that, as to the kind of constitutional questions raised by the Feinberg Law, "the distinction is one of degree, and it is for this reason that the effect of the statute in proscribing beliefs—like its effect in restraining speech or freedom of association—must be carefully weighed by the courts in determining whether the balance struck by [the State] comports with the dictates of the Constitution." *American Communications Assn.* v. *Douds*, 339 U.S. 382, 409. But as the case comes to us we can have no guide other than our own notions—however uncritically extra-judicial—of the real bearing of the New York arrangement on the freedom of thought and activity, and especially on the feeling of such freedom, which are, as I suppose no one would deny, part of the necessary professional equipment of teachers in a free society. The scheme for protecting the school system from being made the instrument of purposes other than a school system should serve in a free society—certainly a concern within the constitutional powers of a State—bristles with ambiguities which must enter into any constitutional decision we may make. Of these only a few have been considered by the courts below. We are told that an organization cannot be listed by the Regents except after hearing. 301 N.Y., at 488, 493, 494, 95 N.E. 2d, at 810–811, 814–815. From this it may be assumed that the hearing contemplated is that found wanting by some members of this Court in *Joint Anti-Fascist Refugee Committee* v. *McGrath*, 341 U.S. 123. The effect of the requirement that membership in a listed organization be prima facie evidence of disqualification in a dismissal proceeding is enlarged upon. 301 N.Y., at 494, 95 N.E. 2d, at 814–815. And the Court of Appeals indicates that only one who "knowingly holds membership in an organization named upon any listing" is subjected to the operation of that rebuttable presumption. *Id.*, at 494, 95 N.E. 2d, at 814.

These are the only islands of clarity. Otherwise we are at sea. We are not told the meaning to be attributed to the words "treasonable or seditious" in § 3021 of the education law, though that is one of the two sections of preexisting law which the elaborate apparatus of the Feinberg Law is designed to enforce. In light of the experience under the Sedition Act of 1798, 1 Stat. 596, "seditious" can hardly be deemed a self-defining term or a word of art. See Miller, Crisis in Freedom, 136–137. Nor can we turn to practical application or judicial construction for sufficient particularity of the meaning to be attributed to the range of activity proscribed by § 12–a. Concern over the latitude afforded by such phrases as "the overthrow of government by . . . any unlawful means" when positions of trust or public employment are conditioned upon disbelief in such an objective cannot be deemed without warrant. See *American Communications Assn.* v. *Douds*, 339 U.S. 382, 415, 435; *Garner* v. *Board of Public Works of Los Angeles*, 341 U.S. 716, 724. In those cases the Court had ground for limiting the reach of a dubious formula. No such alternative is available here.

These gaps in our understanding of the precise scope of the statutory provisions are deepened by equal uncertainties in the implementing rules. Indeed, according to the Appellate Division these rules are not in the case. 276 App. Div., at 531, 96 N.Y.S. 2d, at 471. And the

Court of Appeals was silent on the point. Therefore we are without enlightenment, for example, on the nature of the reporting system described by the rules. This may be a vital matter, affecting not the special circumstances of a particular case but coloring the whole scheme. For it may well be of constitutional significance whether the reporting system contemplates merely the notation as to each teacher that no evidence of disqualification has turned up, if such be the case, or whether it demands systematic and continuous surveillance and investigation of evidence. The difference cannot be meaningless, it may even be decisive, if our function is to balance the restrictions on freedom of utterance and of association against the evil to be suppressed. Again, the rules seem to indicate that past activities of the proscribed organizations or past membership in listed organizations may be enough to bar new applicants for employment. But we do not know, nor can we determine it. This, too, may make a difference. See *Garner* v. *Board of Public Works of Los Angeles, supra,* at 729 (MR. JUSTICE BURTON dissenting in part). We do not know, nor can we ascertain, the effect of the presumption of continuing membership in proscribed organizations that is drawn from evidence of past membership "in the absence of a showing that such membership has been terminated in good faith." We are uninformed of the effect in law of the Commissioner's memorandum, and there is no basis on which to appraise its effect in practice. As for the order of the Board of Education of the city of New York, it is not even formally in the case. In the face of such uncertainties this Court has in the past found jurisdiction wanting, howsoever much the litigants were eager for constitutional pronouncements. *Alabama State Federation of Labor* v. *McAdory*, 325 U.S. 450; *Congress of Industrial Organizations* v. *McAdory*, 325 U.S. 472; *Rescue Army* v. *Municipal Court*, 331 U.S. 549; *Parker* v. *County of Los Angeles*, 338 U.S. 327.

This statement of reasons for declining jurisdiction sounds technical, perhaps, but the principles concerned are not so. Rare departures from them are regrettable chapters in the Court's history, and in well-known instances they caused great public misfortune.

MR. JUSTICE DOUGLAS, with whom MR. JUSTICE BLACK concurs, dissenting.

I have not been able to accept the recent doctrine that a citizen who enters the public service can be forced to sacrifice his civil rights.* I cannot for example find in our constitutional scheme the power of a State to place its employees in the category of second-class citizens by denying them freedom of thought and expression. The Constitution guarantees freedom of thought and expression to everyone in our society. All are entitled to it; and none needs it more than the teacher. The public school is in most respects the cradle of our democracy. The increasing role of the public school is seized upon by proponents of the type of legislation represented by New York's Feinberg law as proof of the importance and need for keeping the school free of "subversive influences." But that is to misconceive the effect of this type of legislation. Indeed the impact of this kind of censorship on

---

United Public Workers v. *Mitchell*, 330 U.S. 75; *Garner* v. *Board of Public Works of Los Angeles*, 341 U.S. 716.

the public school system illustrates the high purpose of the First Amendment in freeing speech and thought from censorship.

The present law proceeds on a principle repugnant to our society—guilt by association. A teacher is disqualified because of her membership in an organization found to be "subversive." The finding as to the "subversive" character of the organization is made in a proceeding to which the teacher is not a party and in which it is not clear that she may even be heard. To be sure, she may have a hearing when charges of disloyalty are leveled against her. But in that hearing the finding as to the "subversive" character of the organization apparently may not be reopened in order to allow her to show the truth of the matter. The irrebuttable charge that the organization is "subversive" therefore hangs as an ominous cloud over her own hearing. The mere fact of membership in the organization raises a prima facie case of her own guilt. She may, it is said, show her innocence. But innocence in this case turns on knowledge; and when the witch hunt is on, one who must rely on ignorance leans on a feeble reed.

The very threat of such a procedure is certain to raise havoc with academic freedom. Youthful indiscretions, mistaken causes, misguided enthusiasms—all long forgotten—become the ghosts of a harrowing present. Any organization committed to a liberal cause, any group organized to revolt against an hysterical trend, any committee launched to sponsor an unpopular program becomes suspect. These are the organizations into which Communists often infiltrate. Their presence infects the whole, even though the project was not conceived in sin. A teacher caught in that mesh is almost certain to stand condemned. Fearing condemnation, she will tend to shrink from any association that stirs controversy. In that manner freedom of expression will be stifled.

But that is only part of it. Once a teacher's connection with a listed organization is shown, her views become subject to scrutiny to determine whether her membership in the organization is innocent or, if she was formerly a member, whether she has *bona fide* abandoned her membership.

The law inevitably turns the school system into a spying project. Regular loyalty reports on the teachers must be made out. The principals become detectives; the students, the parents, the community become informers. Ears are cocked for tell-tale signs of disloyalty. The prejudices of the community come into play in searching out the disloyal. This is not the usual type of supervision which checks a teacher's competency; it is a system which searches for hidden meanings in a teacher's utterances.

What was the significance of the reference of the art teacher to socialism? Why was the history teacher so openly hostile to Franco Spain? Who heard overtones of revolution in the English teacher's discussion of the Grapes of Wrath? What was behind the praise of Soviet progress in metallurgy in the chemistry class? Was it not "subversive" for the teacher to cast doubt on the wisdom of the venture in Korea?

What happens under this law is typical of what happens in a police state. Teachers are under constant surveillance; their pasts are combed for signs of disloyalty; their utterances are watched for clues to dangerous thoughts. A pall is cast over the classrooms. There can be no real academic freedom in that environment. Where suspicion fills the air and holds scholars in line for fear of their jobs, there can be no exercise of the free intellect. Supineness and dogmatism take the place of inquiry. A "party line"—as dangerous as the "party line" of the Communists—lays hold. It is the "party line" of the orthodox view, of the conventional thought, of the accepted approach. A problem can no longer be pursued with impunity to its edges. Fear stalks the classroom. The teacher is no longer a stimulant to adventurous thinking; she becomes instead a pipe line for safe and sound information. A deadening dogma takes the place of free inquiry. Instruction tends to become sterile; pursuit of knowledge is discouraged; discussion often leaves off where it should begin.

This, I think, is what happens when a censor looks over a teacher's shoulder. This system of spying and surveillance with its accompanying reports and trials cannot go hand in hand with academic freedom. It produces standardized thought, not the pursuit of truth. Yet it was the pursuit of truth which the First Amendment was designed to protect. A system which directly or inevitably has that effect is alien to our system and should be struck down. Its survival is a real threat to our way of life. We need be bold and adventuresome in our thinking to survive. A school system producing students trained as robots threatens to rob a generation of the versatility that has been perhaps our greatest distinction. The framers knew the danger of dogmatism; they also knew the strength that comes when the mind is free, when ideas may be pursued wherever they lead. We forget these teachings of the First Amendment when we sustain this law.

Of course the school systems of the country need not become cells for Communist activities; and the classrooms need not become forums for propagandizing the Marxist creed. But the guilt of the teacher should turn on overt acts. So long as she is a law-abiding citizen, so long as her performance within the public school system meets professional standards, her private life, her political philosophy, her social creed should not be the cause of reprisals against her.

SLOCHOWER v. BOARD OF HIGHER EDUCATION OF NEW YORK CITY.

APPEAL FROM THE COURT OF APPEALS OF NEW YORK.

No. 23. Argued October 18–19, 1955.—Decided April 9, 1956.

Section 903 of the New York City Charter provides that, whenever a city employee utilizes the privilege against self-incrimination to avoid answering before a legislative committee a question relating to his official conduct, his employment shall terminate. A teacher in a college operated by the city was summarily discharged under this section, without notice or hearing, because, while testifying before a Federal legislative committee, he refused to answer questions concerning his membership in the Communist Party in 1940 and 1941, on the ground that his answers might tend to incriminate him. Under the New York Education Law, he was entitled to tenure and could be discharged only for cause and after notice, hearing and appeal. *Held:* In the circumstances of this case, his summary dismissal violated the Due Process Clause of the Fourteenth Amendment. Pp. 552–559.

(a) The privilege against self-incrimination would be reduced to a hollow mockery if its exercise could be taken as equivalent either to a confession of guilt or a conclusive presumption of perjury. Pp. 556–558.

(b) On the record in this case, it cannot be claimed that the Board's action in dismissing the teacher was part of a bona fide attempt to gain needed and relevant information regarding his qualifications for his position. Pp. 558–559.

(c) Since no inference of guilt was possible from the claim of the privilege against self-incrimination before the Federal committee, the discharge falls of its own weight as wholly without support. P. 559.

(d) *Adler* v. *Board of Education*, 342 U.S. 485, and *Garner* v. *Los Angeles Board*, 341 U.S. 716, distinguished. Pp. 555–556.

(e) *Wieman* v. *Updegraff*, 344 U.S. 183, followed. Pp. 556–558.

306 N.Y. 532, 119 N.E. 2d 373, 307 N.Y. 806, 121 N.E. 2d 629, reversed and remanded.

Ephraim London argued the cause and filed a brief for appellant.

Daniel T. Scannell argued the cause for appellee. With him on the brief were *Peter Campbell Brown, Seymour B. Quel* and *Helen R. Cassidy.*

Osmond K. Fraenkel and *Emanuel Redfield* filed a brief for the New York Civil Liberties Union, as *amicus curiae*, urging reversal.

MR. JUSTICE CLARK delivered the opinion of the Court.

This appeal brings into question the constitutionality of § 903 of the Charter of the City of New York. That section provides that whenever an employee of the ctiy utilizes the privilege against self-incrimination to avoid answering a question relating to his official conduct, "his term or tenure of office or employment shall terminate and such office or employment shall be vacant, and he shall not be eligible to election or appointment to any office or employment under the city or any agency." [1] Appellant Slochower invoked the privilege against self-incrimination under the Fifth Amendment before an investigating committee of the United States Senate, and was summarily discharged from his position as associate professor at Brooklyn College, an institution maintained by the city of New York. He now claims that the charter provision, as applied to him, violates both the Due Process and Privileges and Immunities Clauses of the Fourteenth Amendment.

On September 24, 1952, the Internal Security Subcommittee of the Committee on the Judiciary of the United States Senate held open hearings in New York City. The investigation, conducted on a national scale, related to subversive influences in the American educational system. At the beginning of the hearings the chairman stated that education was primarily a State and local function, and therefore the inquiry would be limited to "considerations affecting national security, which are directly within the purview and authority of the subcommittee." Hearing before the Subcommittee To Investigate the Administration of the Internal Security Act and Other Internal Security Laws of Senate Committee on the Judiciary, 82d Cong., 2d sess. 1. Professor Slochower, when called to testify, stated that he was not a member of the Communist Party, and indicated complete willing-

---

[1] The full text of § 903 provides:

"If any councilman or other officer or employee of the city shall, after lawful notice or process, willfully refuse or fail to appear before any court or judge, any legislative committee, or any officer, board or body authorized to conduct any hearing or inquiry, or having appeared shall refuse to testify or to answer any question regarding the property, government or affairs of the city or of any county included within its territorial limits, or regarding the nomination, election, appointment or official conduct of any officer or employee of the city or of any such county, on the ground that his answer would tend to incriminate him, or shall refuse to waive immunity from prosecution on account of any such matter in relation to which he may be asked to testify upon any such hearing or inquiry, his term or tenure of office or employment shall terminate and such office or employment shall be vacant, and he shall not be eligible to election or appointment to any office or employment under the city or any agency."

ness to answer all questions about his associations or political beliefs since 1941. But he refused to answer questions concerning his membership during 1940 and 1941 on the ground that his answers might tend to incriminate him. The chairman of the Senate Subcommittee accepted Slochower's claim as a valid assertion of an admitted constitutional right.

It had been alleged that Slochower was a Communist in 1941 in the testimony of one Bernard Grebanier before the Rapp-Coudert Committee of the New York Legislature. See *Report of the Subcommittee of the Joint Legislative Committee to Investigate Procedures and Methods of Allocating State Moneys for Public School Purposes and Subversive Activities*, Legislative Document (1942), No. 49, State of New York, at 318. Slochower testified that he had appeared twice before the Rapp-Coudert Committee, and had subsequently testified before the board of faculty relating to his charge. He also testified that he had answered questions at these hearings relating to his Communist affiliations in 1940 and 1941.

Shortly after testifying before the Internal Security Subcommittee, Slochower was notified that he was suspended from his position at the college; three days later his position was declared vacant "pursuant to the provisions of section 903 of the New York City Charter." [*]

Slochower had 27 years' experience as a college teacher and was entitled to tenure under State law. McKinney's New York Laws, Education Law, § 6206 (2). Under this statute, appellant may be discharged only for cause, and after notice, hearing, and appeal. § 6206 (10). The Court of Appeals of New York, however, has authoritatively interpreted § 903 to mean that "the assertion of the privilege against self incrimination is equivalent to a resignation." *Daniman* v. *Board of Education*, 306 N. Y. 532, 538, 119 N. E. 2d 373, 377. Dismissal under this provision is therefore automatic and there is no right to charges, notice, hearing, or opportunity to explain.

The Supreme Court of New York, County of Kings, concluded that appellant's behavior fell within the scope of § 903, and upheld its application here. 202 Misc. 915, 118 N. Y. S. 2d 487. The Appellate Division, 282 App. Div. 718, 122 N. Y. S. 2d 286, reported *sub nom. Shlakman* v. *Board*, and the Court of Appeals, reported *sub nom. Daniman* v. *Board, supra*, each by a divided court, affirmed. We noted probable jurisdiction, 348 U. S. 935, because of the importance of the question presented.[2]

Slochower argues that § 903 abridges a privilege or immunity of a citizen of the United States since it in effect imposes a penalty on the exercise of a federally guaranteed right in a Federal proceeding. It also violates due process, he argues, because the mere claim of privilege under the Fifth Amendment does not provide a reasonable basis for the State to terminate his employment. Appellee insists that no question of "privileges or immunities" was raised or passed on below,

---

* [Reporter's Note: A sentence which was reported in the Preliminary Print at p. 554, lines 13–18, was deleted by an order of the Court entered May 28, 1956, 351 U.S. 944.]
[2] Thirteen other individuals brought suit for reinstatement after their dismissal for pleading the privilege against self-incrimination in the same Federal investigation. We dismissed the appeal of these individuals "for want of a properly presented Federal question." *Daniman* v. *Board*, 348 U. S. 933. See *Daniman* v. *Board*, 307 N. Y. 806, 121 N. E. 2d 629, where the New York Court of Appeals declined to amend its remittitur to state that a Federal question had been presented and passed on as to these appellants, but did so amend its remittitur as to Slochower.

and therefore directs its argument solely to the proposition that § 903 does not operate in an arbitrary or capricious manner. We do not decide whether a claim under the "privileges or immunities" clause was considered below, since we conclude the summary dismissal of appellant in the circumstances of this case violates due process of law.

The problem of balancing the State's interest in the loyalty of those in its service with the traditional safeguards of individual rights is a continuing one. To state that a person does not have a constitutional right to government employment is only to say that he must comply with reasonable, lawful, and nondiscriminatory terms laid down by the proper authorities. *Adler* v. *Board of Education*, 342 U. S. 485, upheld the New York Feinberg Law which authorized the public school authorities to dismiss employees who, after notice and hearing, were found to advocate the overthrow of the government by unlawful means, or who were unable to explain satisfactorily membership in certain organizations found to have that aim.[3] Likewise *Garner* v. *Los Angeles Board*, 341 U. S. 716, 720, upheld the right of the city to inquire of its employees as to "matters that may prove relevant to their fitness and suitability for the public service," including their membership, past and present, in the Communist Party or the Communist Political Association. There it was held that the city had power to discharge employees who refused to file an affidavit disclosing such information to the school authorities.[4]

But in each of these cases it was emphasized that the State must conform to the requirements of due process. In *Wieman* v. *Updegraff*, 344 U. S. 183, we struck down a so-called "loyalty oath" because it based employability solely on the fact of membership in certain organizations. We pointed out that membership itself may be innocent and held that the classification of innocent and guilty together was arbitrary.[5] This case rests squarely on the proposition that "constitutional protection does extend to the public servant whose exclusion pursuant to a statute is patently arbitrary or discriminatory." 344 U. S., at 192.

Here the board, in support of its position, contends that only two possible inferences flow from appellant's claim of self-incrimination: (1) that the answering of the question would tend to prove him guilty of a crime in some way connected with his official conduct; or (2) that in order to avoid answering the question he falsely invoked the privilege by stating that the answer would tend to incriminate him, and thus committed perjury. Either inference, it insists, is sufficient to justify the termination of his employment. The Court of Appeals, however, accepted the committee's determination that the privilege had been properly invoked and it further held that no inference of Communist Party membership could be drawn from such a refusal to testify. It found the statute to impose merely a condition on public employment and affirmed the summary action taken in the case. With this conclusion we cannot agree.

---

[3] MR. JUSTICE BLACK and MR. JUSTICE DOUGLAS *dissented*. MR. JUSTICE FRANKFURTER dissented on grounds of standing and ripeness.

[4] MR. JUSTICE BLACK and MR. JUSTICE DOUGLAS dissented. MR. JUSTICE FRANKFURTER and MR. JUSTICE BURTON concurred in this aspect of the case, but dissented from other portions of the decision in separate opinions.

[5] MR. JUSTICE BLACK and MR. JUSTICE FRANKFURTER concurred in separate opinions in which MR. JUSTICE DOUGLAS joined. MR. JUSTICE BURTON concurred in the result.

At the outset we must condemn the practice of imputing a sinister meaning to the exercise of a person's constitutional right under the Fifth Amendment. The right of an accused person to refuse to testify, which had been in England merely a rule of evidence, was so important to our forefathers that they raised it to the dignity of a constitutional enactment, and it has been recognized as "one of the most valuable prerogatives of the citizen." *Brown* v. *Walker*, 161 U.S. 591, 610. We have reaffirmed our faith in this principle recently in *Quinn* v. *United States*, 349 U.S. 155. In *Ullmann* v. *United States*, 350 U.S. 422, decided last month, we scored the assumption that those who claim this privilege are either criminals or perjurers. The privilege against self-incrimination would be reduced to a hollow mockery if its exercise could be taken as equivalent either to a confession of guilt or a conclusive presumption of perjury. As we pointed out in *Ullmann*, a witness may have a reasonable fear of prosecution and yet be innocent of any wrongdoing. The privilege serves to protect the innocent who otherwise might be ensnared by ambiguous circumstances. See Griswold, The Fifth Amendment Today (1955).

With this in mind, we consider the application of § 903. As interpreted and applied by the State courts, it operates to discharge every city employee who invokes the Fifth Amendment. In practical effect the questions asked are taken as confessed and made the basis of the discharge. No consideration is given to such factors as the subject matter of the questions, remoteness of the period to which they are directed, or justification for exercise of the privilege. It matters not whether the plea resulted from mistake, inadvertence or legal advice conscientiously given, whether wisely or unwisely. The heavy hand of the statute falls alike on all who exercise their constitutional privilege, the full enjoyment of which every person is entitled to receive. Such action falls squarely within the prohibition of *Wieman* v. *Updegraff, supra.*

It is one thing for the city authorities themselves to inquire into Slochower's fitness, but quite another for his discharge to be based entirely on events occurring before a Federal committee whose inquiry was announced as not directed at "the property, affairs, or government of the city, or . . . official conduct of city employees." In this respect the present case differs materially from *Garner*, where the city was attempting to elicit information necessary to determine the qualifications of its employees. Here, the board had possessed the pertinent information for 12 years, and the questions which Professor Slochower refused to answer were admittedly asked for a purpose wholly unrelated to his college functions. On such a record, the board cannot claim that its action was part of a bona fide attempt to gain needed and relevant information.

Without attacking Professor Slochower's qualification for his position in any manner, and apparently with full knowledge of the testimony he had given some 12 years before at the State committee hearing, the board seized upon his claim of privilege before the Federal committee and converted it through the use of § 903 into a conclusive presumption of guilt. Since no inference of guilt was possible from the claim before the Federal committee, the discharge falls of its own weight as wholly without support. There has not been the "protection of the individual against arbitrary action" which Mr.

Justice Cardozo characterized as the very essence of due process. *Ohio Bell Telephone Co.* v. *Commission*, 301 U.S. 292, 302.

This is not to say that Slochower has a constitutional right to be an associate professor of German at Brooklyn College. The State has broad powers in the selection and discharge of its employees, and it may be that proper inquiry would show Slochower's continued employment to be inconsistent with a real interest of the State. But there has been no such inquiry here. We hold that the summary dismissal of appellant violates due process of law.

The judgment is reversed and the cause is remanded for further proceedings not inconsistent with this opinion.

Reversed and remanded.

MR. JUSTICE BLACK and MR. JUSTICE DOUGLAS join the Court's judgment and opinion, but also adhere to the views expressed in their dissents in *Adler* v. *Board of Education*, and *Garner* v. *Los Angeles Board*, *supra*, and to their concurrences in *Wieman* v. *Updegraff*, *supra*.

MR. JUSTICE REED with whom MR. JUSTICE BURTON and MR. JUSTICE MINTON join, dissenting.

In reliance upon the Due Process Clause of our Constitution, the Court strikes deep into the authority of New York to protect its local governmental institutions from influences of officials whose conduct does not meet the declared State standards for employment. This New York City Charter, § 903, adopted in 1936, to take effect in 1938, was designed to eliminate from public employment individuals who refused to answer legally authorized inquiries as to the "official conduct of any officer or employee of the city . . . on the ground that his answer would tend to incriminate him." Its provisions, as applicable to Professor Slochower and others, have been upheld by the Court of Appeals of New York under multipronged State grounds of attack in the instances where he and other city teachers of New York have sought to bar their removal from their positions.[1]

The sole reliance of the Court for reversal of the New York Court of Appeals is that § 903, as here applied, violates the Due Process Clause of the Fourteenth Amendment to the Federal Constitution. The Court of Appeals amended its remittitur to show that it held Federal due process was not violated. 307 N.Y. 806, 121 N.E. 2d 629. In view of the conclusions of the Court of Appeals we need deal only with that problem. The Court of Appeals has exclusive power to determine the reach of its own statute.

The Court finds it a denial of due process to discharge an employee merely because he relied upon the Fifth Amendment plea of self-incrimination to avoid answering questions which he would be otherwise required to answer. We assert the contrary—the city does have reasonable grounds to require its employees either to give evidence

---

[1] *Matter of Daniman* v. *Board of Education*, *Matter of Shlakman* v. *Board of Higher Education*, 306 N. Y. 532, 119 N. E. 2d 373.
"In this court we are all agreed that the Communist Party is a continuing conspiracy against our Government. . . . We are also all in agreement that an inquiry into past or present membership in the Communist Party is an inquiry regarding the official conduct of an officer or employee of the city of New York. Loyalty to our Government goes to the very heart of official conduct in service rendered in all branches of Government. . . . Communism is opposed to such loyalty. . . . Internal security affects local as well as National Governments." *Id.*, at 540–541, 119 N. E. 2d, at 379. The majority decided § 903 was applicable to a "hearing before a Federal legislative committee" and that this appellant was an employee of the city. *Id.*, at 541, 119 N. E. 2d, at 379.

regarding facts of official conduct within their knowledge or to give up the positions they hold. Petitioners never contended that error or inadvertence led them to refuse to answer. Their contention is set out in the margin below.[2] Discharges under § 903 do not depend upon any conclusion as to the guilt of the employee of some crime that might be disclosed by his testimony or as to his guilt of perjury, if really there was no prosecution to fear. We disagree with the Court's assumption that § 903 as a practical matter takes the questions asked as confessed. Cities, like other employers, may reasonably conclude that a refusal to furnish appropriate information is enough to justify discharge. Legally authorized bodies have a right to demand that citizens furnish facts pertinent to official inquiries. The duty to respond may be refused for personal protection against prosecution only, but such avoidance of public duty to furnish information can properly be considered to stamp the employee as a person unfit to hold certain official positions. Such a conclusion is reinforced when the claimant for protection has the role of instructor to youth. The fact that the witness has a right to plead the privilege against self-incrimination protects him against prosecution but not against the loss of his job.[3]

The Court may intend merely to hold that since the facts of Slochower's alleged Communist affiliations prior to 1941 were known to the board before the Federal claim, and since the inquiries of the committee were asked for a purpose unrelated to his college functions, therefore it was a denial of due process to vacate his office. If so, its conclusion is likewise, we think erroneous. We agree that this case is not like *Garner* v. *Los Angeles Board*, 341 U.S. 716, an attempt to elicit information about professional qualifications. But § 903 is directed at the propriety of employing a man who refuses to give needed information to appropriate public bodies.

Consideration of the meaning of "due process" under the Fourteenth Amendment supports our position that § 903 of the City Charter does not violate that concept. For this Court to hold that State action in the field of its unchallenged powers violates the due process of the Federal Constitution requires far more than mere disagreement with the legal conclusions of State courts. To require, as the Court does, that New York stay its hand in discharging a teacher whom the city deems unworthy to occupy a chair in its Brooklyn College, demands that this Court say, if it follows our prior cases, that the action of the board in declaring Professor Slochower's position vacant was inconsistent with the fundamental principles of liberty and justice which lie at the base of all our civil and political institutions.[4] A denial of

---

[2] Appellant's petition to the Supreme Court of the State of New York stated in pertinent part as follows:
"9. Petitioners answered some and refused to answer others of the questions referred to in paragraph 8 on various and numerous grounds, including the ground that the Subcommittee had not jurisdiction to inquire into such matters, the ground that the First Amendment to the Constitution of the United States forbade such inquiry, the ground that the procedures of the Subcommittee violated their rights under the Fifth Amendment to the Constitution of the United States and that they could not be required under the Fifth Amendment to answer such questions, and on other grounds. The Subcommittee acquiesced in the refusal of petitioners to answer such questions."
[3] Cf. *Ullmann* v. *United States*, 350 U.S. 422, at 438–439: "For the history of the privilege establishes not only that it is not to be interpreted literally, but also that its sole concern is, as its name indicates, with the danger to a witness forced to give testimony leading to the infliction of 'penalties affixed to the criminal acts. . . .'"
[4] *Hebert* v. *Louisiana*, 272 U.S. 312, 316. Cf. *Twining* v. *New Jersey*, 211 U.S. 78, 100.

due process is "a practice repugnant to the conscience of mankind."[5] Surely no such situation exists here.

Those charged with educational duties in a State bear heavy responsibilities. Only a few years ago, in *Adler* v. *Board of Education*, 342 U.S. 485, we upheld against three dissents the Feinberg Law of New York making ineligible for employment as a teacher in any public school a member of any subversive organization, if he knew its purpose. The argument that the "fact found bears no relation to the fact presumed," *i.e.*, "disqualification for employment," was rejected. There also the contention was denial of due process. We said:

"A teacher works in a sensitive area in a schoolroom. There he shapes the attitude of young minds towards the society in which they live. In this, the State has a vital concern. It must preserve the integrity of the schools. That the school authorities have the right and the duty to screen the officials, teachers, and employees as to their fitness to maintain the integrity of the schools as a part of ordered society, cannot be be doubted. One's associates, past and present, as well as one's conduct, may properly be considered in determining fitness and loyalty." *Id.*, at 493.

A great American university has declared that members of its faculty who invoked the Fifth Amendment before committees of Congress were guilty of "misconduct" though not grave enough to justify dismissal.[6] Numerous other colleges and universities have treated the plea of the Fifth Amendment as a justification for dismissal of faculty members.[7] When educational institutions themselves feel the impropriety of reserving full disclosure of facts from duly authorized official investigations, can we properly say a city cannot protect itself against such conduct by its teachers?

The New York rule is not the patently arbitrary and discriminatory statute of *Wieman* v. *Updegraff*, 344 U.S. 183. There "[a] State servant may have joined a proscribed organization unaware of its activities and purposes." P. 190. This Court unanimously condemned as arbitrary the requirement of an oath that covered both innocent and knowing membership without distinction. A different situation exists here. Section 903 was included in the Seabury Report to help in the elimination of graft and corruption.[8] Numerous employees had refused to testify as to criminal acts on the ground of self-incrimination. New York decided it did not want that kind of public employees.

---

[5] *Palko* v. *Connecticut*, 302 U.S. 319, 323, 325, 326. Cf. *Francis* v. *Resweber*, 329 U.S. 459, 463; *Adamson* v. *California*, 332 U.S. 46, 53.

[6] 42 American Association of University Professors Bulletin 96. Compare The Rights and Responsibilities of Universities and their Faculties, Association of American Universities, March 24, 1953, III:

"As in all acts of association, the professor accepts conventions which become morally binding. Above all, he owes his colleagues in the university complete candor and perfect integrity, precluding any kind of clandestine or conspiratorial activities. He owes equal candor to the public. If he is called upon to answer for his convictions it is his duty as a citizen to speak out. It is even more definitely his duty as a professor. Refusal to do so, on whatever legal grounds, cannot fail to reflect upon a profession that claims for itself the fullest freedom to speak and the maximum protection of that freedom available in our society. In this respect, invocation of the Fifth Amendment places upon a professor a heavy burden of proof of his fitness to hold a teaching position and lays upon his university an obligation to reexamine his qualifications for membership in its society.

". . . When the powers of legislative inquiry are abused, the remedy does not lie in noncooperation or defiance; it is to be sought through the normal channels of informed public opinion."

[7] 42 American Assn. of University Professors Bulletin 61–94.

[8] In the Matter of the Investigation of the Departments of the Government of the City of New York, Final Report by Samuel Seabury, December 27, 1932, pp. 9–10.

We think New York had that right. We would affirm the judgment of the Court of Appeals.

MR. JUSTICE HARLAN, dissenting.

I dissent because I think the Court has misconceived the nature of § 903 as construed and applied by the New York Court of Appeals, and has unduly circumscribed the power of the State to ensure the qualifications of its teachers.

As I understand MR. JUSTICE CLARK's opinion, the Court regards § 903 as raising some sort of presumption of guilt from Dr. Slochower's claim of privilege. That is not the way the Court of Appeals construed the statute. On the contrary, that Court said: "we do not presume, of course, that these petitioners [one of whom was Dr. Slochower] by their action have shown cause to be discharged under the Feinberg Law (L. 1949, ch. 360) since no inference of membership in the Communist Party may be drawn from the assertion of one's privilege against self incrimination." [1] Since § 903 is inoperative if even incriminating answers are given, it is apparent that it is the exercise of the privilege itself which is the basis for the discharge, quite apart from any inference of guilt. Thus the Court of Appeals could say that "The assertion of the privilege against self incrimination is equivalent to a resignation." [2] It is also clear that the Board of Education's discharge of Dr. Slochower was on this same premise. The question this case presents, therefore, is not whether any inferences can constitutionally be drawn from a claim of privilege, but whether a State violates due process when it makes a claim of privilege grounds for discharge.

In effect, what New York has done is to say that it will not employ teachers who refuse to cooperate with public authorities when asked questions relating to official conduct. Does such a statute bear a reasonable relation to New York's interest in ensuring the qualifications of its teachers? The majority seems to decide that it does not. This Court has already held, however, that a State may properly make knowing membership in an organization dedicated to the overthrow of the Government by force a ground for disqualification from public school teaching. *Adler* v. *Board of Education*, 342 U.S. 485. A requirement that public school teachers shall furnish information as to their past or present membership in the Communist Party is a relevant step in the implementation of such a State policy, and a teacher may be discharged for refusing to comply with that requirement. *Garner* v. *Los Angeles Board*, 341 U.S. 716. Moreover, I think that a State may justifiably consider that teachers who refuse to answer questions concerning their official conduct are no longer qualifed for public school teaching, on the ground that their refusal to answer jeopardizes the confidence that the public should have in its school system. On either view of the statute, I think Dr. Slochower's discharge did not violate due process.

It makes no difference that the question which Dr. Slochower refused to answer was put to him by a Federal rather than a State body. The authority of the subcommittee to ask the question is not controverted. While as an original matter I would be doubtful whether § 903 was intended to apply to Federal investigations, the Court of

---

1 306 N.Y. 532, 538. 119 N.E. 2d 373, 377.
2 *Ibid.*

Appeals has ruled otherwise, and its interpretation is binding on us. Dr. Slochower cannot discriminate between forums in deciding whether or not to answer a proper and relevant question, if the State requires him to answer before every lawfully constituted body. Here, the information sought to be elicited from Dr. Slochower could have been considered by State authorities in reviewing Dr. Slochower's qualifications, and the effect of his claim of privilege on the public confidence in its school system was at least as great as it would have been had his refusal to answer been before a State legislative committee.

There is some evidence that Dr. Slochower had already answered, before a State committee, the same question which he refused to answer before the congressional subcommittee.[3] Even assuming that New York already had the information, I cannot see how that would prevent New York from constitutionally applying § 903 to this claim of privilege. Apart from other considerations, who call tell whether Dr. Slochower would have answered the question the same way as he had before?

On this record I would affirm the decision of the Court of Appeals. A different question would be presented under the Privileges and Immunities Clause of the Fouteenth Amendment. But that question was not raised below, and is therefore not open here. *Dewey* v. *Des Moines*, 173 U.S. 193.

BEILAN *v.* BOARD OF PUBLIC EDUCATION, SCHOOL DISTRICT OF PHILADELPHIA.

CERTIORARI TO THE SUPREME COURT OF PENNSYLVANIA, EASTERN DISTRICT.

No. 63. Argued March 4, 1958. Decided June 30, 1958.

Petitioner, a teacher in the public schools of Philadelphia, refused to answer questions relating to communistic affiliations and activities asked by his superintendent, after being warned that the inquiry related to his fitness to be a teacher and that refusal to answer might lead to his dismissal. After administrative proceedings in which his loyalty and his political beliefs and associations were not in issue, the Board of Education found that his refusal to answer his superintendent's questions constituted "incompetency," a ground for discharge under the State tenure statute, and discharged him. The State supreme court sustained this action. *Held:* His discharge did not violate the Due Process Clause of the Fourteenth Amendment. Pp. 400–409.

(a) By engaging in teaching in public schools petitioner did not give up his right to freedom of belief, speech or association; but he did undertake obligations of frankness, candor and cooperation in answering inquiries made by his superior examining into his fitness to serve as a public school teacher. P. 405.

(b) A municipal employer is not disabled because it is an agency of the State from inquiry of its employees as to matters that may prove relevant to their fitness and suitability for the public service. *Garner* v. *Board of Public Works*, 341 U.S. 716. P. 405.

(c) The questions petitioner refused to answer were relevant to his fitness and suitability as a teacher, and his discharge was based upon his insubordination and lack of frankness and candor in refusing to answer such questions— not upon disloyalty or any of the activities inquired about. Pp. 405–406.

---

[3] At the Senate subcommittee hearing, in response to Senator Ferguson's inquiry whether or not Dr. Slochower had "ever" answered a question concerning Communist Party membership in 1940 or 1941, Dr. Slochower replied: "Yes, I did answer it."

(d) The Federal Constitution does not require that a teacher's classroom conduct be the sole basis for determining his fitness. P. 406.

(e) The State supreme court held that "incompetency," within the meaning of the relevant State statute, includes petitioner's "deliberate and insubordinate refusal to answer the questions of his administrative superior in a vitally important matter pertaining to his fitness," and this interpretation is not inconsistent with the Federal Constitution. Pp. 406–408.

(f) Petitioner's claim that he was denied due process because he was not sufficiently warned of the consequences of his refusal to answer his superintendent's questions is not supported by the record. P. 408.

(g) *Slochower* v. *Board of Education*, 350 U.S. 551, and *Konigsberg* v. *State Bar of California*, 353 U.S. 252, distinguished. Pp. 408–409.

386 Pa. 82, 125 A. 2d 327, affirmed.

John Rogers Carroll argued the cause for petitioner. With him on the brief was *A. Harry Levitan*.

C. Brewster Rhoads argued the cause for respondent. With him on the brief was *Edward B. Soken*.

MR. JUSTICE BURTON delivered the opinion of the Court.

The question before us is whether the Board of Public Education for the School District of Philadelphia, Pennsylvania, violated the Due Process Clause of the Fourteenth Amendment to the Constitution of the United States when the board, purporting to act under the Pennsylvania Public School Code, discharged a public school teacher on the ground of "incompetency," evidenced by the teacher's refusal of his superintendent's request to confirm or refute information as to the teacher's loyalty and his activities in certain allegedly subversive organizations. For the reasons hereafter stated, we hold that it did not.

On June 25, 1952, Herman A. Beilan, the petitioner, who had been a teacher for about 22 years in the Philadelphia Public School System, presented himself at his superintendent's office in response to the latter's request. The superintendent said he had information which reflected adversely on petitioner's loyalty and he wanted to determine its truth or falsity. In response to petitioner's suggestion that the superintendent do the questioning, the latter said he would ask one question and petitioner could then determine whether he would answer it and others of that type. The superintendent, accordingly, asked petitioner whether or not he had been the Press Director of the Professional Section of the Communist Political Association in 1944.[1] Petitioner asked permission to consult counsel before answering and the superintendent granted his request.

On October 14, 1952, in response to a similar request, petitioner again presented himself at the superintendent's office. Petitioner stated that he had consulted counsel and that he declined to answer the question as to his activities in 1944. He announced he would also decline to answer any other "questions similar to it," "questions of this type," or "questions about political and religious beliefs . . . ." The superintendent warned petitioner that this "was a very serious and a very important matter and that failure to answer the questions might lead to his dismissal." The superintendent made it clear that he was investigating "a real question of fitness for [petitioner] to be a teacher or to continue in the teaching work." These interviews were given

---

[1] The Communist Political Association was the predecessor organization of the Communist Party of the United States. See *Yates* v. *United States*, 354 U.S. 298, 304, n. 5.

no publicity and were attended only by petitioner, his superintendent and the assistant solicitor of the board.

On November 25, 1953, the board instituted dismissal proceedings against petitioner under § 1127 of the Pennsylvania Public School Code of 1949.[2] The only specification which we need consider[3] charged that petitioner's refusal to answer his superintendent's questions constituted "incompetency" under § 1122 of that Code.[4] The board conducted a formal hearing on the charge. Petitioner was present with counsel but did not testify. Counsel for each side agreed that petitioner's loyalty was not in issue, and that evidence as to his disloyalty would be irrelevant.[5] On January 7, 1954, the board found that the charge of incompetency had been sustained and, by a vote of fourteen to one, discharged petitioner from his employment as a teacher.

On an administrative appeal, the Superintendent of Public Instruction of Pennsylvania sustained the local board. However, on petitioner's appeal to the County Court of Common Pleas, that court set aside petitioner's discharge and held that the board should have fol-

---

[2] Pa. Laws 1949, No. 14, Purdon's Pa. Stat. Ann., 1950, Tit. 24, § 11–1127.

[3] Petitioner's refusal to answer his superintendent was also charged as persistent and willful violation of the school laws, another statutory ground for dismissal. See note 4, infra.

On November 18, 1953, petitioner had been called to testify as a witness in a Philadelphia hearing of a Subcommittee of the United States House Committee on Un-American Activities. There he was asked to confirm or refute several reports as to his alleged subversive activities in 1949 and earlier years. He declined to answer, relying upon the Fifth Amendment to the Federal Constitution. That invocation of the Fifth Amendment was specified by the board as a further ground of "incompetency." All charges were sustained on the administrative level.

The Pennsylvania supreme court found that petitioner's refusal to answer his superintendent evidenced a statutory "incompetency" sufficient to support his dismissal and, therefore, found it unnecessary to pass on the other grounds for dismissal. 386 Pa. 82, 94, 125 A. 2d 327, 333. It is suggested that petitioner has a right to the initial judgment of the administrative authorities on whether refusal to answer the superintendent, independent of the other charges, would support the dismissal. Under the Pennsylvania Public School Code, Common Pleas Courts exercise *de novo* review of dismissals. Purdon's Pa. Stat. Ann., 1950 (Cum. Ann. Pocket Pt., 1957), Tit. 24, § 11–1132(b). A dismissal can be sustained if the court finds support for any one of the multiple grounds relied upon by the dismissing school board. Cf. *Brown Case*, 347 Pa. 418, affirming 151 Pa. Super. 522, 30 A. 2d 726, reported *sub nom. Appeal of School District of City of Bethlehem*, 32 A. 2d 565. This allocation of functions between the Pennsylvania courts and administrative agencies does not violate due process. Accordingly, it is necessary for us to consider only the one ground relied upon by the Pennsylvania supreme court. As a matter of jurisdiction, or only jurisdiction is over the Pennsylvania supreme court, as the highest court of the State.

[4] Section 1122 of that Code, in 1952 and 1953, provided that "The only valid causes for termination of a contract heretofore or hereafter entered into with a professional employe shall be immorality, *incompetency*, intemperance, cruelty, persistent negligence, mental derangement, persistent and willful violation of the school laws of this Commonwealth on the part of the professional employee." (Emphasis supplied.) Pa. Laws 1949, No. 14, as amended, Pa. Laws 1951. No. 463, § 16; Purdon's Pa. Stat. Ann., 1950 (Cum. Ann. Pocket Pt., 1957), Tit. 24, § 11–1122.

As enacted in 1949, § 1122 had contained, after the words "mental derangement," the clause, "advocation of or participating in un-American or subversive doctrines." Pa. Laws 1949, No. 14. That clause, however, was deleted by § 16 of the Pennsylvania Loyalty Act, approved December 22, 1951, effective March 1, 1952. Pa. Laws 1951, No. 463.

[5] Counsel for the board, at the outset of the hearing, stated:

"It is my contention, and it has been the thought of your counsel since these proceedings were initiated, that these are not proceedings brought against these respondents charging them with disloyalty. If that were the situation we would have a completely different record, a completely different set of facts, a completely different section under which the charges would be made, if made at all.

.   .   .   .

"Now, so far as I am concerned, sir, and so far as my presentation of testimony is concerned, I don't think whether this man is loyal or disloyal has anything to do with this case. And if your counsel's advice were being asked in the matter, I should say that any testimony directed toward present loyalty or disloyalty is completely out of this case.

.   .   .   .

"So far as this case is concerned, we are not delving into present or past loyalty."

Counsel for petitioner stated: "Mr. President, if you please, I have no intention of seeing this proceeding become a loyalty hearing. Mr. Rhoads [counsel for the Board] has stated that it is not. I agree with him completely."

lowed the procedure specified by the Pennsylvania Loyalty Act, rather than the Public School Code. Finally, on the board's appeal, the Supreme Court of Pennsylvania, with two justices dissenting, reversed the Court of Common Pleas and reinstated petitioner's discharge. 386 Pa. 82, 98, 110, 125 A. 2d 327, 334, 340. We granted certiorari. 353 U. S. 964.

In addition to the Public School Code Pennsylvania has a comprehensive Loyalty Act which provides for the discharge of public employees on grounds of disloyalty or subversive conduct. Purdon's Pa. Stat. Ann., 1941 (Cum. Ann. Pocket Pt., 1957), Tit. 65, §§ 211–225. Petitioner stresses the fact that the question asked of him by his superintendent related to his loyalty. He contends that he was discharged for suspected disloyalty and that his discharge is invalid because of failure to follow the Loyalty Act procedure. However, the Pennsylvania Supreme Court held that the board was not limited to proceeding under the Loyalty Act, even though the questions asked of petitioner related to his loyalty. We are bound by the interpretation thus given to the Pennsylvania statutes by the Supreme Court of Pennsylvania. *Barsky* v. *Board of Regents,* 347 U.S. 442, 448; *Chicago, M., St. P. & P. R. Co.* v. *Risty,* 276 U.S. 567, 570. The only question before us is whether the Federal Constitution prohibits petitioner's discharge for statutory "incompetency" based on his refusal to answer the superintendent's questions.[6]

By engaging in teaching in the public schools, petitioner did not give up his right to freedom of belief, speech or association. He did, however, undertake obligations of frankness, candor and cooperation in answering inquiries made of him by his employing board examining into his fitness to serve it as a public school teacher.

"A teacher works in a sensitive area in a schoolroom. There he shapes the attitude of young minds towards the society in which they live. In this, the State has a vital concern. It must preserve the integrity of the schools. That the school authorities have the right and the duty to screen the officials, teachers, and employees as to their fitness to maintain the integrity of the schools as a part of ordered society, cannot be doubted." *Adler* v. *Board of Education,* 342 U. S. 485, 493.

As this Court stated in *Garner* v. *Board of Public Works,* 341 U. S. 716, 720, "We think that a municipal employer is not disabled because it is an agency of the State from inquiring of its employees as to matters that may prove relevant to their fitness and suitability for the public service."

The question asked of petitioner by his superintendent was relevant to the issue of petitioner's fitness and suitability to serve as a teacher. Petitioner is not in a position to challenge his dismissal merely because of the remoteness in time of the 1944 activities. It was apparent from the circumstances of the two interviews that the superintendent had other questions to ask. Petitioner's refusal to answer was not based on the remoteness of his 1944 activities. He made it clear that he would not answer any question of the same type as the one asked. Petitioner blocked from the beginning any inquiry into his Communist activities, however relevant to his present loyalty. The board

---

[6] There is no showing that the statute was discriminatorily applied. Cf. *Yick Wo* v. *Hopkins,* 118 U.S. 356 ; *Lane* v. *Wilson,* 307 U.S. 268.

based its dismissal upon petitioner's refusal to answer any inquiry about his relevant activities—not upon those activities themselves. It took care to charge petitioner with incompetency, and not with disloyalty. It found him insubordinate and lacking in frankness and candor—it made no finding as to his loyalty.

We find no requirement in the Federal Constitution that a teacher's classroom conduct be the sole basis for determining his fitness. Fitness for teaching depends on a broad range of factors. The Pennsylvania tenure provision [7] specifies several disqualifying grounds, including immorality, intemperance, cruelty, mental derangement and persistent and willful violation of the school laws as well as "incompetency." However, the Pennsylvania statute, unlike those of many other States, contains no catch-all phrase, such as "conduct unbecoming a teacher," [8] to cover disqualifying conduct not included within the more specific provisions. Consequently, the Pennsylvania courts have given "incompetency" a broad interpretation. This was made clear in *Horosko* v. *Mt. Pleasant School District*, 335 Pa. 369, 371, 374–375, 6 A. 2d 866, 868, 869–870:

> "If the fact be that she 'now commands neither the respect nor the good will of the community' and if the record shows that effect to be the result of her conduct within the clause quoted, it will be conclusive evidence of incompetency. It has always been the recognized duty of the teacher to conduct himself in such way as to command the respect and good will of the community, though one result of the choice of a teacher's vocation may be to deprive him of the same freedom of action enjoyed by persons in other vocations. Educators have always regarded the example set by the teacher as of great importance. * * *

> .   .   .   .   .   .

> "The term 'incompetency' has a 'common and approved usage'. The context does not limit the meaning of the word to lack of substantive knowledge of the subjects to be taught. Common and approved usage give a much wider meaning. For example, in 31 C.J., with reference to a number of supporting decisions, it is defined: 'A relative term without technical meaning. It may be employed as meaning disqualification; inability; incapacity; lack of ability, legal qualifications, or fitness to discharge the required duty.' In Black's Law Dictionary (3rd edition) page 945, and in Bouvier's Law Dictionary, (3rd revision) p. 1528, it is defined as 'Lack of ability or fitness to discharge the required duty.' Cases construing the word to the same effect are found in Words and Phrases, 1st series, page 3510, and 2nd series, page 1013. Webster's New International Dictionary defines it as 'want of physical, intellectual, or moral ability; insufficiency; inadequacy; specif., want of legal qualifications or fitness.' Funk &

---

[7] See note 4, *supra*.

[8] *E.g.*, Baldwin's Ky. Rev. Stat. Ann., 1955, § 161.790(1), "conduct unbecoming a teacher," "during good behavior."

Mass. Ann. Laws, 1953 (Cum. Supp., 1957), c. 71, § 42, "conduct unbecoming a teacher," "or other good cause."

West's Ann. Cal. Code, Education, § 13521 (a), (e), "unprofessional conduct," "Evident unfitness for service."

Smith-Hurd's Ill. Ann. Stat., 1946 (Cum. Ann. Pocket Pt., 1957), c. 122, § 6–36, "other sufficient cause."

Burns' Ann. Ind. Stat., 1948 Replacement Vol., § 28–4308, "other good and just cause."

Wagnalls Standard Dictionary defines it as 'General lack of capacity of fitness, or lack of the special qualities required for a particular purpose'." In the *Horosko* case, a teacher was discharged for "incompetency" because of her afterhours activity in her husband's beer garden, serving as a bartender and waitress, occasionally drinking beer, shaking dice with the customers for drinks and playing the pinball machine. Cf. *Schwer's Appeal*, 36 Pa. D. & C. 531, 536.

In the instant case, the Pennsylvania supreme court has held that "incompetency" includes petitioner's "deliberate and insubordinate refusal to answer the questions of his administrative superior in a vitally important matter pertaining to his fitness." 386 Pa., at 91, 125 A. 2d, at 331. This interpretation is not inconsistent with the Federal Constitution.

Petitioner complains that he was denied due process because he was not sufficiently warned of the consequences of his refusal to answer his superintendent. The record, however, shows that the superintendent, in his second interview, specifically warned petitioner that his refusal to answer "was a very serious and a very important matter and that failure to answer the questions might lead to his dismissal." That was sufficient warning to petitioner that his refusal to answer might jeopardize his employment. Furthermore, at petitioner's request, his superintendent gave him ample opportunity to consult counsel. There was no element of surprise.

Our recent decisions in *Slochower* v. *Board of Education*, 350 U.S. 551, and *Konigsberg* v. *State Bar of California*, 353 U.S. 252, are distinguishable. In each we envisioned and distinguished the situation now before us. In the *Slochower* case, at 558, the Court said:

"It is one thing for the city authorities themselves to inquire into Slochower's fitness, but quite another for his discharge to be based entirely on events occurring before a Federal committee whose inquiry was announced as not directed at 'the property, affairs, or government of the city, or . . . official conduct of city employees.' In this respect the present case differs materially from *Garner* [341 U.S. 716], where the city was attempting to elicit information necessary to determine the qualifications of its employees. Here, the board had possessed the pertinent information for 12 years, and the questions which Professor Slochower refused to answer were admittedly asked for a purpose wholly unrelated to his college functions. On such a record the board cannot claim that its action was part of a bona fide attempt to gain needed and relevant information."

In the *Konigsberg* case, *supra*, at 259–261, this Court stressed the fact that the action of the State was not based on the mere refusal to answer relevant questions—rather, it was based on inferences impermissibly drawn from the refusal. In the instant case, no inferences at all were drawn from petitioner's refusal to answer. The Pennsylvania supreme court merely equated refusal to answer the employing board's relevant questions with statutory "incompetency."

Inasmuch as petitioner's dismissal did not violate the Federal Constitution, the judgment of the Supreme Court of Pennsylvania is

Affirmed.

Mr. Justice Frankfurter, concurring.*

---

*[Note: This opinion applies also to No. 165, *Lerner* v. *Casey*, *post*, p. 468.]

Although I join the opinion of the Court in both these cases, a word of emphasis is appropriate against finding that New York and Pennsylvania—for the highest courts of those States are for our purposes the States—have violated the United States Constitution by attributing to them determinations that they have not made and have carefully avoided making. Such a finding would rest, as I understand it, on the theory that although the States, with a due sense of responsibility, have not made these determinations, they may be attributed to them because persons who do not make distinctions that are important in law and the conduct of government may loosely infer them.

The services of two public employees have been terminated because of their refusals to answer questions relevant, or not obviously irrelevant, to an inquiry by their supervisors into their dependability. When these two employees were discharged, they were not labeled "disloyal." They were discharged because governmental authorities, like other employers, sought to satisfy themselves of the dependability of employees in relation to their duties. Accordingly, they made inquiries that, it is not contradicted, could in and of themselves be made. These inquiries were balked. The services of the employees were therefore terminated.

Because the specific questions put to these employees were part of a general inquiry relating to what is compendiously called subversion and to conduct that on due proof may amount to disloyalty, every part of the process of inquiry is given the attribute of an inquiry into disloyalty and every resulting severance from service is deemed a finding of disloyalty. The argument runs, in essence, that because such an inquiry may in certain instances lead to a determination of disloyalty, the refusal to answer any questions in this process and dismissal therefor themselves establish disloyalty. To make such an attribution to a State, to draw such an inference from a carefully limited exercise of State power, to disallow State action because there are those who may draw inferences that the State itself has not drawn and has avoided drawing, is a curbing of the States through the Fourteenth Amendment that makes of that amendment an instrument of general censorship by this Court of State action. In refusing to put the Fourteenth Amendment to such a use, I am of course wholly unconcerned with what I may think of the wisdom or folly of the State authorities. I am not charged with administering the transportation system of New York or the school system of Pennsylvania. The Fourteenth Amendment does not check foolishness or unwisdom in such administration. The good sense and right standards of public administration in those States must be relied upon for that, and ultimately the electorate.

Mr. Chief Justice Warren, dissenting.*

I believe the facts of record in No. 63 compel the conclusion that Beilan's plea of the Fifth Amendment before a subcommittee of the House Committee on Un-American Activities was so inextricably involved in the board's decision to discharge him that the validity of the board's action cannot be sustained without consideration of this ground. The clearest indication of this is the fact that for 13 months following petitioner's refusal to answer the superintendent's questions, he was retained as a school teacher and continually rated "sat-

---

*[NOTE: This opinion applies also to No. 165, *Lerner* v. *Casey, post*, p. 468.]

isfactory," yet five days after his appearance before the House sub-committee petitioner was suspended. Since a plea of the Fifth Amendment before a congressional committee is an invalid basis for discharge from public employment, *Slochower* v. *Board of Higher Education*, 350 U.S. 551, I would reverse the judgment approving petitioner's dismissal.

I cannot agree that the invalidity of the board's action is cured by the Pennsylvania Supreme Court's conclusion that the dismissal was "justified" if any charge against petitioner was sustained. Whether the first refusal alone would "justify" the discharge we need not decide. This Court has previously held that where a conclusion of guilt may rest on a constitutionally impermissible basis, the adjudication must be set aside, notwithstanding a State court's conclusion that permissible bases existed on which the decision might have rested. *Stromberg* v. *California*, 283 U.S. 359, 368; see also *Williams* v. *North Carolina*, 317 U.S. 287, 292. There may be exceptions to the application of this principle to the full range of State administrative action. Neverthe-less, on the particular facts of this case, the invalid basis of the State's action is too critical to be ignored.

For these reasons MR. JUSTICE BLACK, MR. JUSTICE DOUGLAS and I dissent in No. 63. I also dissent in No. 165 for the reasons stated in the dissenting opinion of MR. JUSTICE BRENNAN.

MR. JUSTICE DOUGLAS, with whom MR. JUSTICE BLACK concurs, dissenting.*

The holding of the Court that the teacher in the *Beilan* case and the subway conductor in the *Lerner* case could be discharged from their respective jobs because they stood silent when asked about their Communist affiliations cannot, with due deference, be squared with our constitutional principles.

Among the liberties of the citizens that are guaranteed by the Four-teenth Amendment are those contained in the First Amendment. *Stromberg* v. *California*, 283 U.S. 359; *De Jorge* v. *Oregon*, 299 U.S. 353; *Murdock* v. *Pennsylvania*, 319 U.S. 105; *E. erson* v. *Board of Education*, 330 U.S. 1; *Staub* v. *City of Baxley*, 355 U.S. 313, 321. These include the right to believe what one chooses, the right to differ from his neighbor, the right to pick and choose the political philosophy that he likes best, the right to associate with whomever he chooses, the right to join the groups he prefers, the privilege of selecting his own path to salvation. The Court put the matter succinctly in *Board of Education* v. *Barnette*, 319 U.S. 624, 641–642:

"We can have intellectual individualism and the rich cultural di-versities that we owe to exceptional minds only at the price of occasional eccentricity and abnormal attitudes. When they are so harmless to others or to the State as those we deal with here, the price is not too great. But freedom to differ is not limited to things that do not matter much. That would be a mere shadow of free-dom. The test of its substance is the right to differ as to things that touch the heart of the existing order.

"If there is any fixed star in our constitutional constellation, it is that no official, high or petty, can prescribe what shall be orthodox in politics, nationalism, religion, or other matters of

---

*[NOTE: This opinion applies also to No. 165, *Lerner* v. *Casey*, *post*, p. 468.]

opinion or force citizens to confess by word or act their faith
therein."
We deal here only with a matter of belief. We have no evidence in
either case that the employee in question ever committed a crime, ever
moved in treasonable opposition against this country. The only
mark against them—if it can be called such—is a refusal to answer
questions concerning Communist Party membership. This is said to
give rise to doubts concerning the competence of the teacher in the
Beilan case and doubts as to the trustworthiness and reliability of the
subway conductor in the *Lerner* case.

Our legal system is premised on the theory that every person is innocent until he is proved guilty. In this country we have, however,
been moving away from that concept. We have been generating the
belief that anyone who remains silent when interrogated about his
unpopular beliefs or affiliations is guilty. I would allow no inference
of wrongdoing to flow from the invocation of any constitutional right.
I would not let that principle bow to popular passions. For all we
know we are dealing here with citizens who are wholly innocent of any
wrongful action. That must indeed be our premise. When we make
the contrary assumption, we part radically with our tradition.

If it be said that we deal not with guilt or innocence but with
frankness, the answer is the same. There are areas where government
may not probe. Private citizens, private clubs, private groups may
make such deductions and reach such conclusions as they choose from
the failure of a citizen to disclose his beliefs, his philosophy, his associates. But government has no business penalizing a citizen merely
for his beliefs or associations. It is government action that we have
here. It is government action that the Fourteenth and First Amendments protect against. We emphasized in *N.A.A.C.P.* v. *Alabama*,
decided this day, *post*, p. 449, that freedom to associate is one of
those liberties protected against governmental action and that freedom from "compelled disclosure of affiliation with groups engaged
in advocacy" is vital to that constitutional right. We gave protection in the *N.A.A.C.P.* case against governmental probing into
political activities and associations of one dissident group of people.
We should do the same here.

If we break with tradition and let the government penalize these
citizens for their beliefs and associations, the most we can assume
from their failure to answer is that they were Communists. Yet,
as we said in *Wieman* v. *Updegraff*, 344 U.S. 183, 190, membership
in the Communist Party "may be innocent." The member may have
thought that the Communist movement would develop in the parliamentary tradition here, or he may not have been aware of any unlawful aim, or knowing it, may have embraced only the Socialist
philosophy of the group, not any political tactics of violence and
terror. Many join associations, societies, and fraternities with less
than full endorsement of all their aims.

We compound error in these decisions. We not only impute wrongdoing to those who invoke their constitutional rights. We go further
and impute the worst possible motives to them.

As Judge Fuld said in dissent in the *Lerner* case, "It is a delusion
to think that the Nation's security is advanced by the sacrifice of
the individual's basic liberties. The fears and doubts of the moment

may loom large, but we lose more than we gain if we counter with a resort to alien procedures or with a denial of essential constitutional guarantees." 2 N.Y. 2d 355, 378, 141 N.E. 2d 533, 546.

Our initial error in all this business (see *Dennis* v. *United States*, 341 U.S. 494) was our disregard of the basic principle that government can concern itself only with the actions of men, not with their opinions or beliefs. As Thomas Jefferson said in 1779:

> ". . . the opinions of men are not the object of civil government, nor under its jurisdiction; . . . it is time enough for the rightful purposes of civil government for its officers to interfere when principles break out into overt acts against peace and good order." [1]

The fitness of a subway conductor for his job depends on his health, his promptness, his record for reliability, not on his politics or philosophy of life. The fitness of a teacher for her job turns on her devotion to that priesthood, her education, and her performance in the library, in the laboratory, and the classroom, not on her political beliefs. Anyone who plots against the government and moves in treasonable opposition to it can be punished. Government rightly can concern itself with the actions of people. But it's time we called a halt to government's penalizing people for their beliefs. To repeat, individuals and private groups can make any judgments they want. But the realm of belief—as opposed to action—is one which the First Amendment places beyond the long arm of government.

A teacher who is organizing a Communist cell in a schoolhouse or a subway conductor who is preparing the transportation system for sabotage would plainly be unfit for his job. But we have no such evidence in the records before us. As my Brother BRENNAN points out, to jump to those conclusions on these records is to short-cut procedural due process.

In sum, we have here only a bare refusal to testify; and the Court holds that sufficient to show that these employees are unfit to hold their public posts. That makes qualification for public office turn solely on a matter of belief—a notion very much at war with the Bill of Rights.

When we make the belief of the citizen the basis of government action, we move toward the concept of *total security*. Yet *total security* is possible only in a totalitarian regime [2]—the kind of system we profess to combat.

---

[1] 2 Papers of Thomas Jefferson (Boyd ed. 1950) 546.

[2] In an analogous situation, Judge Pope stated the problem for the Court of Appeals in *Parker* v. *Lester*, 227 F. 2d 708, 721:

"It cannot be said that in view of the large problem of protecting the national security against sabotage and other acts of subversion we can sacrifice and disregard the individual interest of these merchant seamen because they are comparatively few in number. It is not a simple case of sacrificing the interests of a few to the welfare of the many. In weighing the considerations of which we are mindful here, we must recognize that if these regulations may be sustained, similar regulations may be made effective in respect to other groups as to whom Congress may next choose to express its legislative fears. No doubt merchant seamen are in a sensitive position in that the opportunities for serious sabotage are numerous. If it can be said that a merchant seaman notwithstanding his being on board might sink the ship loaded with munitions for Korea, it is plain that many persons other than seamen would be just as susceptible to security doubts. The enginemen and trainmen hauling the cargo to the docks, railroad track and bridge inspectors, switchmen and dispatchers, have a multitude of opportunities for destruction. Dangerous persons might infiltrate the shipping rooms of factories where the munitions are being packed for shipment to Korea with opportunities for inserting bombs appropriately timed for explosion on board ship. All persons who are in factories making munitions and material for the armed forces have opportunities for sabotage, and the same may be said of all operators of transportation facilities, not to mention workers upon the docks.

"It may be possible that we have reached an age when our system of constitutional

Mr. Justice Brennan, dissenting.*

It is instructive on occasion to ask why particular cases are brought before this Court for review. The Court has said again and again that the incorrectness of a decision of a court below—and especially of a State court—is not sufficient reason for us to exercise our discretionary power to bring the case here. There must be "special and important reasons therefor." Rule 19(1) of this Court. We must, therefore, ask ourselves the question: What special character and importance of the right asserted justified our taking these cases for review?

The Court treats the cases as though the only right involved were the right of an unreliable subway conductor and an incompetent schoolteacher to hold their jobs. But if that were really all that was involved in these cases, I fail to see why it should take some nine pages in each case to justify the State's action. I can scarcely believe that such concern would be displayed if the question were whether there was evidence to show that Lerner was unreliable about getting the subway doors opened promptly at each station, or that Beilan was incompetent as an algebra teacher. It is obvious that more is at stake here than the loss of positions of public employment for unreliability or incompetence. Rather, it is the simultaneous public labeling of the employees as disloyal that gives rise to our concern.

New York and Pennsylvania have publicly announced that the subway conductor and teacher are disloyal Americans. This consequence of the States' actions is devastating beside the loss of employment. In each case a man's honor and reputation are indelibly stained. "There can be no dispute about the consequences visited upon a person excluded from public employment on disloyalty grounds. In the view of the community, the stain is a deep one; indeed, it has become a badge of infamy." *Wieman* v. *Updegraff*, 344 U.S. 183, 190–191. The petitioners thus not only lose their present jobs, but their standing in the community is so undermined as doubtless to cost them most opportunities for future jobs.

Moreover, the States' actions touch upon important political rights which have ever warranted the special attention of the courts. It may be stated as a generality that government is never at liberty to be arbitrary in its relations with its citizens, and close judicial scrutiny is essential when State action infringes on the right of a man to be accepted in his community, to express his ideas in an atmosphere of calm decency, and to be free of the dark stain of suspicion and distrust of his loyalty on account of his political beliefs and associations. *N.A.A.C.P.* v. *Alabama, post,* p. 449, decided this day. It is these rights which stand before the bar today, and it is in the awareness of their implications that these cases must be decided.

The people of New York and Pennsylvania have voiced through their legislatures their determination that the stain of disloyalty shall

freedom and individual rights cannot hold its own against those who, under totalitarian discipline are prepared to infiltrate not only our public services, but our civilian employments as well. In the event of war we may have to anticipate Black Tom explosions on every waterfront, poison in our water systems, and sand in all important industrial machines. But the time has not come when we have to abandon a system of liberty for one modeled on that of the Communists. Such a system was not that ordained by the framers of our Constitution. It is the latter we are sworn to uphold."

*[Note: This dissenting opinion of Mr. Justice Brennan applies also to No. 165, *Lerner* v. *Casey, post,* p. 468.]

not be impressed upon a State employee without fair procdures in which the State carries the burden of proving specific charges by a fair preponderance of evidence. Cf. *Adler* v. *Board of Education*, 342 U.S. 485. In the New York Security Risk Law and the Pennsylvania Loyalty Act the States have endeavored to provide the traditional Anglo-American standards of procedural due process for the ascertainment of guilt. Yet this Court today finds no denial of due process in the palpable evasion of these standards of fair play by administrative officials. This Court refuses to pierce the transparent denials that each of these employees was publicly branded disloyal. The Court holds that we are bound by the definition of State law pronounced by the States' high courts that the dismissals were for unreliability and incompetency. Of course, we accept State law as the high court of a State pronounces it, but certainly our duty to secure to the individual the safeguards, embodied in due process, against a State's arbitrary exercise of power is no less when the State courts refuse to recognize what has in fact occurred. Cf. *Payne* v. *Arkansas*, 356 U.S. 560; *Moore* v. *Michigan*, 355 U.S. 155. See also *Broad River Power Co.* v. *South Carolina ex rel. Daniel*, 281 U.S. 537, 540. In my view the judgments in both cases must be reversed because each petitioner has been branded a disloyal American without the due process of law required of the States by the Fourteenth Amendment. "Strict adherence to required legal procedures, especially where one's loyalty is being impugned, affords the greatest and, in last analysis, the ultimate assurance of the inviolability of our freedoms as we have heretofore known them in this Country. Least of all, should they be impaired or trenched upon by procedural shortcuts." *Board of Public Education* v. *Beilan*, 386 Pa. 82, 99, 125 A. 2d 327, 335 (Jones, J., dissenting).

Lerner v. Casey.

In response to the outbreak of hostilities in Korea in 1950 the New York Legislature, early in its next session, enacted its Security Risk Law, Laws 1951, c. 233. Section 1 of the Act is a declaration of legislative finding that the Korean hostilities had brought about the existence "of a serious public emergency in this State" and that "the employment of members of subversive groups and organizations by government presents a grave peril to the national security." Section 5 of the Act provides that the appointing officer may transfer or suspend a person occupying a position within a "security agency" of the State after a finding based "upon all the evidence" that, "because of doubtful trust and reliability, the employment of such person in such position would endanger the security or defense of the Nation and the State." Pursuant to § 3 of the Act the State Civil Service Commission determined in 1953 that the New York Transit Authority is a "security agency" for purposes of the Act. In 1954, appellant Lerner, a subway conductor, was directed to appear before the Department of Investigation of the City of New York. On this and a subsequent appearance he refused to answer the question whether he was then a member of the Communist Party on the grounds that his answer might tend to incriminate him.

When this information was brought to the attention of the Transit Authority they sent a notice to appellant advising him that he was suspended under § 5 of the Security Risk Law because "reasonable grounds exist for belief that, because of doubtful trust and reliability your employment in the position of conductor will endanger the security or defense of the Nation and State." The Transit Authority specified the grounds for this belief: "[Y]ou refused to answer questions as to whether you were then a member of the Communist Party and invoked the Fifth Amendment to the Constitution of the United States." Appellant brought this action in the New York State courts alleging, *inter alia*, that the finding that he was a security risk within the meaning of the New York statute is wholly without evidence and therefore violative of the Due Process Clause of the Fourteenth Amendment. The New York courts dismissed this contention by the following reasoning: (1) appellant's refusal to answer whether he was then a member of the Communits Party proves a lack of candor; (2) the lack of candor proves that he was of doubtful trust and reliability; and (3) doubtful trust and reliability proves further that appellant was a security risk within the meaning of the Act. This Court, without discussion, follows this chain of reasoning. But careful analysis, I believe, shows that it is fallacious and leads to an arbitrary result.

The proper consideration of this case requires, I repeat, that the true issue be stated with clarity. We are concerned with far more than, in the Court's phrase, "the validity of appellant's dismissal from his position as a subway conductor in the New York City Transit System." The issue is, rather, the validity of his dismissal *as a security risk*. The difference is profound, as I have suggested, for the label "security risk" inevitably invites in the public mind the deep suspicion of disloyalty, namely, that he is, in the words of the statute, a threat to "the security or defense of the Nation and the State."

Of course, the term "security risk" is not synonymous with "disloyal." In certain positions—such as those involving access to secret information, for instance—an employee who is an alcoholic or merely too talkative may well be considered a risk to security. But this is not such a case. Lerner handled no secrets. Common sense tells us that if a subway conductor is a security risk at all while at work he is such because he may engage in sabotage. Indeed, the record makes clear that it was just this danger that motivated the New York authorities in extending the Security Risk Law to the Transit System.

The only evidence relied upon to show that Lerner is a disloyal person is his refusal to answer the question whether he was a member of the Communist Party. It might be conceded that the question was relevant to his qualifications for his job and therefore properly asked. But once the propriety of the question was established, the New York Court of Appeals approved treating the nature of the question as though it were irrelevant to the determination of the ultimate fact of disloyalty. And this Court too says that the finding that Lerner is a security risk could be based on a refusal to "give any other information about himself which might be relevant to his employment." But can we suppose that a subway conductor would be branded a security risk if he refused to answer a question about his health? Of course the answer is no, although the question is plainly relevant to his qualifications for employment. It may well be that in such a case the State would be fully justified in discharging the employee as "untrustworthy and unreliable." But one would hardly stretch reason so far as further to label him a "security risk." To do so would be arbitrary in the extreme. It is equally arbitrary here, for New York and this Court expressly disavow the drawing of any inferences from the nature of the question asked or from Lerner's refusal to answer it. Nonetheless, by invoking the formalized procedures of its Security Risk Law, New York has publicly announced that it possesses the evidence required by the terms of that statute to justify the conclusion that Lerner is in fact a disloyal American. Yet the record is wholly devoid of the essential requisite of evidence to support the ultimate finding of disloyalty. Cf. *Tot* v. *United States*, 319 U.S. 463. In this plainly arbitrary manner, Lerner is gratuitously defamed, his honor and reputation indelibly stained. And the wound is far deeper than the occasion demands, for certainly New York cannot lack procedures under which he could have been discharged without blemishing his name.

BEILAN *v.* BOARD OF PUBLIC EDUCATION.

Here also, the Court has not, in my opinion, stated or decided the true issue of due process tendered by this case. I doubt that a meritorious question for our review would be presented if the issue was, as the Court says, the constitutional validity of a dismissal solely for refusal of the teacher to answer the relevant questions asked by the school superintendent in private interviews. I might agree that the Due Process Clause imposes no restraint against dismissal of a teacher who refuses to answer his superior's questions asked in the privacy of his office and related to the teacher's fitness to continue in his position.

But in reality Beilan was not dismissed by the Pennsylvania school authorities upon that ground. The question whether he had been an officer in the Communist Party in 1944 was first asked of Beilan by the superintendent at a private interview on June 25, 1952. Beilan did not refuse at that time to answer but asked permission to consult counsel. The superintendent summoned him again on October 14, 1952, and it was on that date that Beilan advised the superintendent that he declined to answer that or similar questions. The superintendent had told Beilan at the first interview that the question was asked because the superintendent had information which reflected on Beilan's loyalty. Almost fourteen months elapsed before Beilan was suspended and the charges preferred which led to his dismissal. In that interval Beilan's superiors had twice rated him in the high satisfactory range of competency. Had the authorities seriously regarded Beilan as incompetent because of his refusal to answer the superintendent's question they would hardly have waited so long before suspending him. The record is clear that proceedings were actually initiated not because of that refusal to answer but because on November 18, 1953, Beilan asserted the privilege against self-incrimination under the Fifth Amendment when interrogated at a publicly televised hearing held in Philadelphia by a Subcommittee of the Committee on Un-American Activities of the House of Representatives. Beilan testified at that hearing that he was not then a member of the Communist Party and had never advocated the overthrow of the Government by force or violence but pleaded the protection of the Fifth Amendment when asked questions directed to past party membership and activities. Five days later, on November 23, 1953, the superintendent notified

Beilan that he had been rated "unsatisfactory" because he had refused to answer the superintendent's questions and also because "[y]ou invoked the Fifth Amendment of the Federal Constitution" when questioned as to "past associations with organizations of doubtful loyalty" by the subcommittee. The opinion on Beilan's administrative appeal which sustained his dismissal by the Board of Education makes it clear that the authorities viewed Beilan's invocation of the Fifth Amendment before the subcommittee as an admission of disloyalty. The opinion states: "[B]y all the concepts of logic and reason the teacher admits that he has done something for which he might be prosecuted criminally." It is this administrative record which Beilan must present to his next employer. Cf. *Harmon* v. *Brucker*, 355 U.S. 579.

The Court of Common Pleas found that the administrative proceedings were actually concerned solely with the question of Beilan's suspected disloyalty and reversed upon the ground that "the legislature intended to deal with the matter of loyalty solely by the method of procedure provided in the [Pennsylvania] Loyalty Act."

The Pennsylvania Supreme Court, however, did not pass upon the question of propriety of the inference of disloyalty drawn by the administrative authorities from Beilan's invocation of the Fifth Amendment before the subcommittee. That question is, therefore, not before us. The Pennsylvania Supreme Court held that the action of the authorities might be sustained solely because Beilan had refused to answer the superintendent's question. But this is to sustain a finding of Beilan's disloyalty without competent evidence of the fact. As in *Lerner* the inference of disloyalty is arbitrary in the extreme. Yet Pennsylvania, like New York in the *Lerner* case, publicly announces contrary to the fact that it possesses competent evidence justifying the conclusion that Beilan is in fact a disloyal American. In my view Beilan also is, in that arbitrary manner, denied due process of law in violation of the Fourteenth Amendment.

I would reverse both judgments.

LOYALTY OATHS

WIEMAN ET AL. *v.* UPDEGRAFF ET AL.

APPEAL FROM THE SUPREME COURT OF OKLAHOMA.

No. 14.   Argued October 16, 1952.—Decided December 15, 1952.

Oklahoma Stat. Ann., 1950 Tit. 51, §§ 37.1–37.8 (1952 Supp.), requiring each State officer and employee, as a condition of his employment, to take a "loyalty oath," stating, *inter alia*, that he is not, and has not been for the preceding five years, a member of any organization listed by the Attorney General of the United States as "Communist front" or "subversive." As construed by the Supreme Court of Oklahoma, it excludes persons from State employment solely on the basis of membership in such organizations, regardless of their knowledge concerning the activities and purposes of the organizations to which they had belonged. *Held:* As thus construed, the Act violates the Due Process Clause of the Fourteenth Amendment. Pp. 184–192.

(a) The Due Process Clause does not permit a State, in attempting to bar disloyal persons from its employment on the basis of organizational membership, to classify innocent with knowing association. *Adler* v. *Board of Education*, 342 U.S. 485; *Gerende* v. *Board of Supervisors*, 341 U.S. 56; and *Garner* v. *Board of Public Works*, 341 U.S. 716, distinguished. Pp. 188–191.

(b) The protection of the Due Process Clause extends to a public servant whose exclusion pursuant to a statute is patently arbitrary or discriminatory. *Adler* v. *Board of Education,* 342 U.S. 485, and *United Public Workers* v. *Mitchell,* 330 U.S. 75, distinguished. Pp. 191–192.

205 Okla. 301, 237 P. 2d 131, reversed.

The Supreme Court of Oklahoma affirmed the judgment of a trial court sustaining the constitutionality of Okla. Stat. Ann., 1950, Tit. 51, §§ 37.1–37.8 (1952 Supp.), and enjoining payment of salaries to State employees who had refused to subscribe to the "loyalty oath" required by that Act. 205 Okla. 301, 237 P. 2d 131. On appeal to this Court, *reversed,* p. 192.

H. D. Emery argued the cause for appellants. With him on the brief was *Robert J. Emery.*

Fred Hansen, First Assistant Attorney General of Oklahoma, argued the cause for the Board of Regents of the Oklahoma Agricultural Colleges et al., appellees. With him on the brief was *Mac Q. Williamson,* Attorney General.

Paul W. Updegraff argued the cause and filed a brief *pro se.*

Osmond K. Fraenkel, filed a brief for the American Civil Liberties Union, as *amicus curiae,* urging reversal.

MR. JUSTICE CLARK delivered the opinion of the Court.

This is an appeal from a decision of the Supreme Court of Oklahoma upholding the validity of a loyalty oath [1] prescribed by Oklahoma statute for all State officers and employees. Okla. Stat. Ann. 1950, Tit. 51, §§ 37–1–37.8 (1952 Supp.). Appellants, employed by the State as members of the faculty and staff of Oklahoma Agricultural and Mechanical College, failed, within the thirty days permitted, to take the oath required by the Act. Appellee Updegraff, as a citizen and taxpayer, thereupon brought this suit in the District Court of Oklahoma County to enjoin the necessary State officials from

---

[1] "I, _____, do solemnly swear (or affirm) that I will support and defend the Constitution of the United States and the constitution of the State of Oklahoma against all enemies, foreign and domestic; that I will bear true faith and allegiance to the Constitution of the United States and the constitution of the State of Oklahoma; that I take this obligation freely, without any mental reservation or purpose of evasion; and that I will well and faithfully discharge the duties upon which I am about to enter.

"And I do further swear (or affirm) that I do not advocate, nor am I a member of any party or organization, political or otherwise, that now advocates the overthrow of the Government of the United States or of the State of Oklahoma by force or violence or other unlawful means; That I am not affiliated directly or indirectly with the Communist Party, the Third Communist International, with any foreign political agency, party, organization or government, or with any agency, party, organization, association, or group whatever which has been officially determined by the United States Attorney General or other authorized agency of the United States to be a Communist front or subversive organization; nor do I advocate revolution, teach or justify a program of sabotage, force or violence, sedition or treason, against the Government of the United States or of this State; nor do I advocate directly or indirectly, teach or justify by any means whatsoever, the overthrow of the Government of the United States or of this State, or change in the form of Government thereof, by force or any unlawful means; that I will take up arms in the defense of the United States in time of War, or National Emergency, if necessary; that within the five (5) years immediately preceding the taking of this oath (or affirmation) I have not been a member of the Communist Party, the Third Communist International, or of any agency, party, organization, association, or group whatever which has been officially determined by the United States Attorney General or other authorized public agency of the United States to be a Communist front or subversive organization, or of any party or organization, political or otherwise, that advocated the overthrow of the Government of the United States or of the State of Oklahoma by force or violence or other unlawful means;

"And I do further swear (or affirm) that during such time as I am_____

(Here put name of office, or, if an employee, insert 'An employee of' followed by the

complete designation of the employing officer, office, agency, authority, commission, depart-

ment or institution.)

"I will not advocate and that I will not become a member of any party or organization, political or otherwise, that advocates the overthrow of the Government of the United States or of the State of Oklahoma by force or violence or other unlawful means."

paying further compensation to employees who had not subscribed to the oath. The appellants, who were permitted to intervene, attacked the validity of the Act on the grounds, among others, that it was a bill of attainder; an *ex post facto* law; impaired the obligation of their contracts with the State and violated the Due Process Clause of the Fourteenth Amendment. They also sought a mandatory injunction directing the State officers to pay their salaries regardless of their failure to take the oath. Their objections centered largely on the following clauses of the oath:

". . . That I am not affiliated directly or indirectly . . . with any foreign political agency, party, organization or Government, or with any agency, party, organization, association, or group whatever which has been officially determined by the United States Attorney General or other authorized agency of the United States to be a Communist front or subversive organization; . . . that I will take up arms in the defense of the United States in time of War, or National Emergency, if necessary and that within the five (5) years immediately preceding the taking of this oath (or affirmation) I have not been a member of . . . any agency, party, organization, association, or group whatever which has been officially determined by the United States Attorney General or other authorized public agency of the United States to be a Communist front or subversive organization . . . ."

The court upheld the Act and enjoined the State officers from making further salary payments to appellants. The Supreme Court of Oklahoma affirmed, *sub nom. Board of Regents* v. *Updegraff*, 205 Okla. 301, 237 P. 2d 131 (1951).[2] We noted probable jurisdiction because of the public importance of this type of legislation and the recurring serious constitutional questions which it presents.

The District Court of Oklahoma County in holding the Act valid concluded that the appellants were compelled to take the oath as written; that the appellants "and each of them, did not take and subscribe to the oath as provided in section 2 of the Act and willfully refused to take that oath and by reason thereof the Board of Regents is enjoined from paying them, and their employment is terminated." In affirming, the Supreme Court of Oklahoma held that the phrase of the oath "any foreign political agency, party, organization or Government, or with any agency, party, organization, association, or group whatever which has been officially determined by the United States Attorney General or other authorized agency of the United States to be a Communist front or subversive organization" actually "refers to a list or lists of such organizations in existence at the time of the passage of the act which had been prepared by the Attorney General [of the United States] under governmental directive. Such list or lists are in effect made a part of the oath by reference." On this point the opinion continues: "There is no requirement in the act that an oath be taken of nonmembership in organizations not on the list of the Attorney General of the United States at the time of the passage of this act."

We read this part of the highest State court's decision as limiting the organizations proscribed by the Act to those designated on the list

---

2 The State officials named as defendants in Updegraff's suit took the position in the State courts that the statute was unconstitutional. Following a policy of the Oklahoma attorney general not to appeal from adverse decisions of the State supreme court, these defendants are here only because they were made appellees by the appellant-intervenors. They have chosen in their brief merely to restate, without argument, their position in the court below.

or lists of the Attorney General which had been issued prior to the effective date of the Act. Although this interpretation discarded clear language of the oath as surplusage, the court denied the appellants' petition for rehearing which included a plea that refusal of the court to permit appellants to take the oath as so interpreted was violative of due process.

The purpose of the Act, we are told, "was to make loyalty a qualification to hold public office or be employed by the State." 205 Okla., at 305, 237 P. 2d, at 136. During periods of international stress, the extent of legislation with such objectives accentuates our traditional concern about the relation of government to the individual in a free society. The perennial problem of defining that relationship becomes acute when disloyalty is screened by ideological patterns and techniques of disguise that make it difficult to identify. Democratic government is not powerless to meet this threat, but it must do so without infringing the freedoms that are the ultimate values of all democratic living. In the adoption of such means as it believes effective, the legislature is therefore confronted with the problem of balancing its interest in national security with the often conflicting constitutional rights of the individual.

In a series of cases coming here in recent years, we have had occasion to consider legislation aimed at safeguarding the public service from disloyalty. *Garner* v. *Board of Public Works*, 341 U.S. 716 (1951); *Adler* v. *Board of Education*, 342 U.S. 485 (1952); *Gerende* v. *Board of Supervisors*, 341 U.S. 56 (1951). It is in the context of these decisions that we determine the validity of the oath before us.

Garner involved a Los Angeles ordinance requiring all city employees to swear that they did not advocate the overthrow of the government by unlawful means or belong to organizations with such objectives. The ordinance implemented an earlier charter amendment which disqualified from municipal employment all persons unable to take such an oath truthfully. One of the attacks made on the oath in that case was that it violated due process because its negation was not limited to organizations known by the employee to be within the proscribed class. This argument was rejected because we felt justified in assuming that *scienter* was implicit in each clause of the oath.

Adler also indicated the importance of determining whether a rule of exclusion based on association applies to innocent as well as knowing activity. New York had sought to bar from employment in the public schools persons who advocate, or belong to organizations which advocate, the overthrow of the government by unlawful means. The Feinberg Law directed the New York Board of Regents to make a listing, after notice and hearing, of organizations of the type described. Under § 3022 of the statute, the Regents provided by regulation that membership in a listed organization should be *prima facie* evidence of disqualification for office in the New York public schools. In upholding this legislation, we expressly noted that the New York courts had construed the statute to require knowledge of organizational purpose before the regulation could apply. 342 U.S., at 494. Cf. *American Communications Assn.* v. *Douds*, 339 U.S. 382, 413 (1950).

The oath in *Gerende* was required of candidates for public office who sought places on a Maryland ballot. On oral argument in that case, the Maryland attorney general assured us that he would advise the proper State authorities to accept, as complying with the statute, an affidavit stating that the affiant was not engaged in an attempt to overthrow the government by force or violence or knowingly a member of an organization engaged in such an attempt. Because we read an earlier Maryland Court of Appeals' decision as interpreting the statute so that such an affidavit would satisfy its requirements, we affirmed on the basis of this assurance.

We assumed in *Garner*, that if our interpretation of the oath as containing an implicit *scienter* requirement was correct, Los Angeles would give the petitioners who had refused to sign the oath an opportunity to take it as interpreted and resume their employment. But here, with our decision in *Garner* before it, the Oklahoma supreme court refused to extend to appellants an opportunity to take the oath. In addition, a petition for rehearing which urged that failure to permit appellants to take the oath as interpreted deprived them of due process was denied. This must be viewed as a holding that knowledge is not a factor under the Oklahoma statute. We are thus brought to the question touched on in *Garner*, *Adler*, and *Gerende:* whether the Due Process Clause permits a State, in attempting to bar disloyal individuals from its employ, to exclude persons solely on the basis of organizational membership, regardless of their knowledge concerning the organizations to which they had belonged. For, under the statute before us, the fact of membership alone disqualifies. If the rule be expressed as a presumption of disloyalty, it is a conclusive one.

But membership may be innocent. A State servant my have joined a proscribed organization unaware of its activities and purposes. In recent years, many completely loyal persons have severed organizational ties after learning for the first time of the character of groups to which they had belonged. "They had joined, [but] did not know what it was, they were good, fine young men and women, loyal Americans, but they had been trapped into it—because one of the great weaknesses of all Americans, whether adult or youth, is to join something." [3] At the time of affiliation, a group itself may be innocent, only later coming under the influence of those who would turn it toward illegitimate ends. Conversely, an organization formerly subversive and therefore designated as such may have subsequently freed itself from the influences which originally led to its listing.

There can be no dispute about the consequences visited upon a person excluded from public employment on disloyalty grounds. In the view of the community, the stain is a deep one; indeed, it has become a badge of infamy. Especially is this so in time of cold war and hot emotions when "each man begins to eye his neighbor as a possible enemy." [4] Yet under the Oklahoma Act, the fact of association alone determines disloyalty and disqualification; it matters not whether association existed innocently or knowingly. To thus inhibit individual freedom of movement is to stifle the flow of democratic expression and controversy at one of its chief sources. We hold that the distinction observed between the case at bar and *Garner, Adler* and *Gerende* is decisive. Indiscriminate classification of innocent with

---

³ Testimony of J. Edgar Hoover, Hearings before House Committee on Un-American Activities on H.R. 1884 and H.R. 2122, 80th Cong., 1st Sess. 46.
⁴ Address by Judge Learned Hand at the 86th Convocation of the University of the State of New York, delivered October 24, 1952, at Albany, New York.

knowing activity must fall as an assertion of arbitrary power. The oath offends due process.

But appellee insists that *Adler* and *United Public Workers* v. *Mitchell*, 330 U.S. 75 (1947), are contra. We are referred to our statement in *Adler* that persons seeking employment in the New York public schools have "no right to work for the State in the school system on their own terms. *United Public Workers* v. *Mitchell* . . . . They may work for the school system upon the reasonable terms laid down by the proper authorities of New York." 342 U.S., at 492. To draw from this language the facile generalization that there is no constitutionally protected right to public employment is to obscure the issue. For, in *United Public Workers*, though we held that the Federal Government through the Hatch Act could properly bar its employees from certain types of political activity thought inimical to the interests of the Civil Service, we cast this holding into perspective by emphasizing that Congress could not "enact a regulation providing that no Republican, Jew or Negro shall be appointed to Federal office, or that no Federal employee shall attend mass or take any active part in missionary work." 330 U.S., at 100. See also *In re Summers*, 325 U.S. 561, 571 (1945). We need not pause to consider whether an abstract right to public employment exists. It is sufficient to say that constitutional protection does extend to the public servant whose exclusion pursuant to a statute is patently arbitrary or discriminatory.

Because of this disposition, we do not pass on the serious questions raised as to whether the Act, in proscribing those "Communist front or subversive organizations" designated as such on lists of the Attorney General of the United States, gave fair notice to those affected, in view of the fact that those listings have never included a designation of "Communist fronts," and have in some cases designated organizations without classifying them. Nor need we consider the significance of the differing standards employed in the preparation of those lists and their limited evidentiary use under the Federal Loyalty Program.

Reversed.

Mr. Justice Jackson, not having heard the argument, took no part in the consideration or decision of this case.

Mr. Justice Burton concurs in the result.

Mr. Justice Black, concurring.

I concur in all the Court says in condemnation of Oklahoma's test oath. I agree that the State Act prescribing that test oath is fatally offensive to the due process guarantee of the United States Constitution.

History indicates that individual liberty is intermittently subjected to extraordinary perils. Even countries dedicated to government by the people are not free from such cyclical dangers. The first years of our Republic marked such a period. Enforcement of the Alien and Sedition Laws by zealous patriots who feared ideas made it highly dangerous for people to think, speak, or write critically about government, its agents, or its policies, either foreign or domestic. Our constitutional liberties survived the ordeal of this regrettable period because there were influential men and powerful organized groups bold enough to champion the undiluted right of individuals to publish and argue for their beliefs however unorthodox or loathsome. Today however, few individuals and organizations of power and influence argue that unpopular advocacy has this same wholly unqualified immunity from governmental interference. For this and other reasons the present period of fear seems more ominously dangerous to speech and press than was that of the Alien and Sedition Laws. Suppressive laws and practices are the fashion. The Oklahoma oath statute is but one manifestation of a national network of laws aimed at coercing and controlling the minds of men. Test oaths are notorious tools of tyranny. When used to shackle the mind they are, or at least they should be, unspeakably odious to a free people. Test oaths are made still more dangerous when combined with bills of attainder which like this Oklahoma statute impose pains and penalties for past lawful associations and utterances.

Governments need and have ample power to punish treasonable acts. But it does not follow that they must have a further power to punish thought and speech as distinguished from acts. Our own free society should never forget that laws which stigmatize and penalize thought and speech of the unorthodox have a way of reaching, ensnaring and silencing many more people than at first intended. We must have freedom of speech for all or we will in the long run have it for none but the cringing and the craven. And I cannot too often repeat my belief that the right to speak on matters of public concern must be wholly free or eventually be wholly lost.

It seems self-evident that all speech criticizing government rulers and challenging current beliefs may be dangerous to the status quo. With full knowledge of this danger the framers rested our First Amendment on the premise that the slightest suppression of thought, speech, press, or public assembly is still more dangerous. This means that individuals are guaranteed an undiluted and unequivocal right to express themselves on questions of current public interest. It means that Americans discuss such questions as of right and not on sufferance of legislatures, courts or any other governmental agencies. It means that courts are without power to appraise and penalize utterances upon their notion that these utterances are dangerous. In my view this uncompromising interpretation of the Bill of Rights is the one that must prevail if its freedoms are to be saved. Tyrannical totalitarian governments cannot safely allow their people to speak with complete freedom. I believe with the framers that our free Government can.

MR. JUSTICE DOUGLAS concurs in this opinion.

MR. JUSTICE FRANKFURTER, whom MR. JUSTICE DOUGLAS joins, concurring.

The times being what they are, it is appropriate to add a word by way of emphasis to the Court's opinion, which I join.

The case concerns the power of a State to exact from teachers in one of its colleges an oath that they are not, and for the five years immediately preceding the taking of the oath have not been, members of any organization listed by the Attorney General of the United States, prior to the passage of the statute, as "subversive" or "Communist-front." Since the affiliation which must thus be forsworn may well have been for reasons or for purposes as innocent as membership in a club of one of the established political parties, to require such an oath, on pain of a teacher's loss of his position in case of refusal to take the oath, penalizes a teacher for exercising a right of association peculiarly characteristic of our people. See Arthur M.

Schlesinger, Sr., Biography of a Nation of Joiners, 50 Am. Hist. Rev. 1 (1944), reprinted in Schlesinger, Paths To The Present, 23. Such joining is an exercise of the rights of free speech and free inquiry. By limiting the power of the States to interfere with freedom of speech and freedom of inquiry and freedom of association, the Fourteenth Amendment protects all persons, no matter what their calling. But, in view of the nature of the teacher's relation to the effective exercise of the rights which are safeguarded by the Bill of Rights and by the Fourteenth Amendment, inhibition of freedom of thought, and of action upon thought, in the case of teachers brings the safeguards of those amendments vividly into operation. Such unwarranted inhibition upon the free spirit of teachers affects not only those who, like the appellants, are immediately before the Court. It has an unmistakable tendency to chill that free play of the spirit which all teachers ought especially to cultivate and practice; it makes for caution and timidity in their associations by potential teachers.

The Constitution of the United States does not render the United States or the States impotent to guard their governments against destruction by enemies from within. It does not preclude measures of self-protection against anticipated overt acts of violence. Solid threats to our kind of government—manifestations of purposes that reject argument and the free ballot as the means for bringing about charges and promoting progress—may be met by preventive measures before such threats reach fruition. However, in considering the constitutionality of legislation like the statute before us it is necessary to keep steadfastly in mind what it is that is to be secured. Only thus will it be evident why the Court has found that the Oklahoma law violates those fundamental principles of liberty "which lie at the base of all our civil and political institutions" and as such are imbedded in the due process of law which no State may offend. *Hebert* v. *Louisiana*, 272 U.S. 312, 316.

That our democracy ultimately rests on public opinion is a platitude of speech but not a commonplace in action. Public opinion is the ultimate reliance of our society only if it be disciplined and responsible. It can be disciplined and responsible only if habits of open-mindedness and of critical inquiry are acquired in the formative years of our citizens. The process of education has naturally enough been the basis of hope for the perdurance of our democracy on the part of all our great leaders, from Thomas Jefferson onwards.

To regard teachers—in our entire educational system, from the primary grades to the university—as the priests of our democracy is therefore not to indulge in hyperbole. It is the special task of teachers to foster those habits of open-mindedness and critical inquiry which alone make for responsible citizens, who, in turn, make possible an enlightened and effective public opinion. Teachers must fulfill their function by precept and practice, by the very atmosphere which they generate; they must be exemplars of open-mindedness and free inquiry. They cannot carry out their noble task if the conditions for the practice of a responsible and critical mind are denied to them. They must have the freedom of responsible inquiry, by thought and action, into the meaning of social and economic ideas, into the checkered history of social and economic dogma. They must be free to sift evanescent doctrine, qualified by time and circumstance, from that restless, enduring process of extending the bounds of understanding and wisdom, to assure which the freedoms of thought, of speech, of inquiry, of worship are guaranteed by the Constitution of the United States against infraction by National or State Government.

The functions of educational institutions in our national life and the conditions under which alone they can adequately perform them are at the basis of these limitations upon State and National power. These functions and the essential conditions for their effective discharge have been well described by a leading educator:

"Now, a university is a place that is established and will function for the benefit of society, provided it is a center of independent thought. It is a center of independent thought and criticism that is created in the interest of the progress of society, and the one reason that we know that every totalitarian government must fail is that no totalitarian government is prepared to face the consequences of creating free universities.

"It is important for this purpose to attract into the institution men of the greatest capacity, and to encourage them to exercise their independent judgment.

"Education is a kind of continuing dialogue, and a dialogue assumes, in the nature of the case, different points of view.

"The civilization which I work and which I am sure, every American is working toward, could be called a civilization of the dialogue, where instead of shooting one another when you differ. you reason things out together.

"In this dialogue, then, you cannot assume that you are going to have everybody thinking the same way or feeling the same way. It would be unprogressive if that happened. The hope of eventual development would be gone. More than that, of course, it would be very boring.

"A university, then, is a kind of continuing Socratic conversation on the highest level for the very best people you can think of, you can bring together, about the most important questions, and the thing that you must do to the uttermost possible limits is to guarantee those men the freedom to think and to express themselves.

"Now, the limits on this freedom—the limits on this freedom, cannot be merely prejudice, because although our prejudices might be perfectly satisfactory, the prejudices of our successors or of those who are in a position to bring pressure to bear on the institution, might be subversive in the real sense, subverting the American doctrine of free thought and free speech." Testimony of Robert M. Hutchins, Associate Director of the Ford Foundation, November 25, 1952, in Hearings before the House Select Committee To Investigate Tax-Exempt Foundations and Comparable Organizations, pursuant to H. Res. 561, 82d Cong., 2d Sess.

CRAMP v. BOARD OF PUBLIC INSTRUCTION OF ORANGE COUNTY.

APPEAL FROM THE SUPREME COURT OF FLORIDA.

No. 72. Argued October 16, 1961.—Decided December 11, 1961.

A Florida statute requires every employee of the State and its subdivisions to swear in writing that, *inter alia*, he has never lent his "aid, support, advice, counsel or influence to the Communist Party." It requires immediate discharge of any employee failing to subscribe to such an oath. Appellant, a teacher in a public school of the State, refused to file such an oath and sued in a State court for a judgment declaring the statute unconstitutional and enjoining its enforcement. He alleged, in effect, that he had not done any of the things mentioned in the statute, but that, as he understood it, its meaning was so vague as to deprive him of liberty or property without due process of law. The State supreme court held the statute constitutional and denied relief. *Held:*

1. Notwithstanding his allegation that he had not done any of the things mentioned in the required oath, appellant was not without standing to attack the statute on the ground that it was so vague as to deprive him of liberty or property without due process of law. Pp. 280–285.

2. The meaning of the required oath is so vague and uncertain that the State cannot, consistently with the Due Process Clause of the Fourteenth Amendment, force an employee either to take such an oath, at the risk of subsequent prosecution for perjury, or face immediate dismissal from public service. Pp. 285–288.

125 So. 2d 554, reversed.

Tobias Simon argued the cause and filed briefs for appellant.

J. R. Wells argued the cause and filed briefs for appellee.

Richard W. Ervin, Attorney General of Florida, *Ralph E. Odum,* Assistant Attorney General, and *William J. Roberts,* Special Assistant Attorney General, filed a brief for the State of Florida, as *amicus curiae,* urging affirmance.

MR. JUSTICE STEWART delivered the opinion of the Court.

A Florida statute requires each employee of the State or its subdivision to execute a written oath in which he must swear that, among other things, he has never lent his "aid, support, advice, counsel or influence to the Communist Party." [1] Failure to subscribe to this oath results under the law in the employee's immediate discharge. [2]

---

[1] The statute in its entirety provides as follows :

"All persons who now or hereafter are employed by or who now or hereafter are on the payroll of the State, or any of its departments and agencies, subdivisions, counties, cities, school boards and districts of the free public school system of the State or counties, or institutions of higher learning and all candidates for public office, are hereby required to take an oath before any person duly authorized to take acknowledgments of instruments for public record in the State in the following form :

"I, _____, a citizen of the State of Florida and of the United States of America, and being employed by or an officer of _____ and a recipient of public funds as such employee or officer, do hereby solemnly swear or affirm that I will support the Constitution of the United States and of the State of Florida ; that I am not a member of the Communist Party; *that I have not and will not lend my aid, support, advice, counsel or influence to the Communist Party;* that I do not believe in the overthrow of the Government of the United States or of the State of Florida by force or violence ; that I am not a member of any organization or party which believes in or teaches, directly or indirectly, the overthrow of the Government of the United States or of Florida by force or violence.

"And said oath shall be filed with the records of the governing official or employing governmental agency prior to the approval of any voucher for the payment of salary, expenses, or other compensation." Fla. Stat. § 876.05. (Italics added.)

The Supreme Court of Florida has construed the portion of the statutory oath printed in italics as follows : "We think the pertinent clause, despite its ungrammatical construction, was meant to apply retrospectively and that it should be read as if it had been written 'I have not lent and will not lend' . . . ." *State* v. *Diez,* 97 So. 2d 105, 109.

[2] "If any person required by §§ 876.05–876.10 to take the oath herein provided for fails to execute the same, the governing authority under which such person is employed shall cause said person to be immediately discharged, and his name removed from the payroll, and such person shall not be permitted to receive any payment as an employee or as an officer where he or she was serving." Fla. Stat. § 876.06. See also Fla. Stat. § 876.08, which provides that: "[a]ny governing authority or person, under whom any employee is serving or by whom employed who shall knowingly or carelessly permit any such employee to continue in employment after failing to comply with the provisions of §§ 876.05–876.10" shall be subject to fine, imprisonment, or both.

After the appellant had been employed for more than nine years as a public school teacher in Orange County, Florida, it was discovered in 1959 that he had never been required to execute this statutory oath.[3] When requested to do so he refused. He then brought an action in the State circuit court asking for a judgment declaring the oath requirement unconstitutional, and for an injunction forbidding the appellee, the Orange County Board of Public Instruction, from requiring him to execute the oath and from discharging him for his failure to do so. The circuit court held the statute valid and denied the prayer for an injunction. The Supreme Court of Florida affirmed, 125 So. 2d 554, and this is an appeal from the judgment of affirmance. Having doubt as to the jurisdiction of this Court, we postponed decision of that preliminary question until the hearing of the appeal on the merits. 366 U.S. 934.

I.

In his complaint in the State circuit court Cramp alleged that "he has, does and will support the Constitution of the United States and of the State of Florida; he is not a member of the Communist Party; that he has not, does not and will not lend aid, support, advice, counsel or influence to the Communist Party; he does not believe in the overthrow of the Government of the United States or of the State of Florida by force or violence; he is not a member of any organization or party which believes in or teaches directly or indirectly the overthrow of the Government of the United States or of Florida by force or violence." He further alleged that he "is a loyal American and does not decline to execute or subscribe to the aforesaid oath for fear of the penalties provided by law for a false oath."

It is these sworn statements in the complaint which raise two related but separate questions as to our jurisdiction of this appeal. First, did the Florida Supreme Court rest its decision, at least alternatively, upon the ground that the appellant, because of these statements, lacked standing to attack the statutory oath? If so, we should have to consider the applicability of "the settled rule that where the judgment of a State court rests upon two grounds, one of which is Federal and the other non-Federal in character, our jurisdiction fails if the non-Federal ground is independent of the Federal ground and adequate to support the judgment." *Fox Film Corp.* v. *Muller*, 296 U.S. 207, 210. Secondly, do these sworn statements of the appellant deprive him of standing to attack the State statute in this Court, irrespective of what the Florida court may have decided?

The Supreme Court of Florida ruled that "because of the allegations of his own complaint the appellant teacher has unequivocally demonstrated that he has no standing to assault the subject statute on the grounds that it is a bill of attainder, or an ex post facto law." 125 So. 2d, at 560. We may assume that this ruling by the State court would operate to foreclose our consideration of this appeal if the appellant had confined his attack upon the statute to the two grounds mentioned. But, in addition to asserting that the Florida statute constitutes an *ex post facto* law and a bill of attainder, the appellant has from the beginning also claimed that the statute is constitutionally invalid for two further and quite different reasons—that it im-

---

[3] The statute requiring execution of the oath was enacted in 1949. Laws of Florida, 1949, c. 25046.

pinges upon his constitutionally protected right of free speech and association, and that the language of the required oath is so vague and uncertain as to deny him due process of law. As we read the opinion of the Florida Supreme Court, both of these Federal constitutional issues were decided upon their merits, without even implicit reliance upon any doctrine of State law.[4]

Whether the appellant has standing to attack the State statute in this Court is, however, a separate issue, to which we must bring our independent judgment. *Tileston* v. *Ullman*, 318 U.S. 44; *Doremus* v. *Board of Education*, 342 U.S. 429. The controlling question is whether the appellant "has sustained or is immediately in danger of sustaining some direct injury as the result of [the statute's] enforcement * * *." *Massachusetts* v. *Mellon*, 262 U.S. 447, 488.

In the absence of the specific allegations in the complaint to which allusion has been made, there can be no doubt that enforcement of the State law would inflict a direct and serious injury upon the appellant. The statute unequivocally requires the appellant to execute the oath or suffer immediate discharge from public employment. See *United Public Workers* v. *Mitchell*, 330 U.S. 75, 91–92; *Adler* v. *Board of Education*, 342 U.S. 485. The argument is made, however, that the self-exonerating sworn statements in the complaint conclusively show that this appellant could not possibly sustain injury by executing the oath, and that he consequently has undercut his standing to question the constitutional validity of the State law.

Whatever the merits of this argument, it has, we think, no application to the appellant's claim that the statutory oath is unconstitutionally vague. The vices inherent in an unconstitutionally vague statute— the risk of unfair prosecution and the potential deterrence of constitutionally protected conduct—have been repeatedly pointed out in our decisions. See *Connally* v. *General Construction Co.*, 269 U.S. 385, 391; *Cline* v. *Frink Dairy Co.*, 274 U.S. 445, 465; *Stromberg* v. *California*, 283 U.S. 359, 369; *Herndon* v. *Lowry*, 301 U.S. 242, 258–259; *Lanzetta* v. *New Jersey*, 306 U.S. 451; *Winters* v. *New York*, 333 U.S. 507. See also *Smith* v. *California*, 361 U.S. 147, 151. These are dangers to which all who are compelled to execute an unconstitutionally vague and indefinite oath may be exposed. Cf. *Thornhill* v. *Alabama*, 310 U.S. 88, 96–98.

---

[4] The Florida Supreme Court disposed of the claimed violation of the right of free speech and association in the following language:

"It has long been recognized that the First Amendment freedoms are not absolutes in and of themselves. When they are asserted as a barrier to government action we are confronted by the necessity of balancing the asserted private right against the alleged public interest. The private right will certainly not be lightly regarded. However, an indirect adverse effect on the asserted right of the individual will not preclude the exercise of governmental power when the power is shown to exist and its assertion is necessitated by the exigencies of the public wellbeing. Barenblatt v. United States, 360 U. S. 109. . . .

"As we have pointed out in other parts of this opinion, the failure to take the required oath does not work an adjudication of guilt nor does it burden the employee with the responsibilty of proving innocence against an assertion of guilt. Statutes of this type have been consistently sustained on the theory that they, constitute merely a stipulation of qualifications or disqualifications for public employment. The statute contains no prohibition against the right of a citizen to speak out or to assemble peaceably. It merely provides that when one speaks out to advocate the violent overthrow of the Government of the United States, or assembles for that purpose, he cannot simultaneously work for and draw compensation from the government he seeks to overthrow." 125 So. 2d, at 558–559.

The court disposed of the claim that the oath requirement was unconstitutionally vague as follows:

"Certainly the instant statute is perfectly clear in its requirements. There could be no doubt in the minds of anyone who can read English as to the requirements of the statute and the effect of a failure to comply. Adler v. Board of Education, supra." 125 So. 2d, at 558.

There is nothing in the allegations of the complaint to indicate that the appellant will not be subjected to these hazards to the same degree as other public employees required to take the oath. The most that can be said of his having subscribed to the allegations in question is that he believes he could truthfully execute the oath, as he understands its language. But the very vice of which he complains is that the language of the oath is so vague and indefinite that others could with reason interpret it differently. He argues, in other words, that he could unconstitutionally be subjected to all the risks of a criminal prosecution *despite* the sworn allegations as to his past conduct which are contained in the complaint.[5] We cannot say that the appellant lacks standing to attack this statutory oath as unconstitutionally vague simply because he now personally believes he could eventually prevail in the event he were prosecuted for perjury. Cf. *Staub* v. *City of Baxley*, 355 U.S. 313, 319; *Jones* v. *Opelika*, 316 U.S. 584, 602, dissenting opinion, adopted *per curiam* on rehearing, 319 U.S. 103, 104; *Smith* v. *Cahoon*, 283 U.S. 553, 562.

We conclude that the appellant is not without standing to attack the Florida statute upon the ground that it is so vague as to deprive him of liberty or property without due process of law, and we turn, therefore, to the merits of that claim.

II.

The Florida Supreme Court first considered the provisions of this legislative oath in *State* v. *Diez*, 97 So. 2d 105, a case involving the validity of an indictment for perjury. There the court upheld the constitutionality of the legislation only upon finding it ". . . inherent in the law that when one takes the oath that he has not lent aid, advice, counsel and the like to the Communist Party, he is representing under oath that he has not done so knowingly." 97 So. 2d, at 110. In the present case the Florida court adhered to this construction of the statute, characterizing what had been said in *Diez* as a ruling that "the element of scienter was implicit in each of the requirements of the statute." 125 So. 2d, at 557. We accept without question this view of the statute's meaning, as of course we must. This authoritative interpretation by the Florida Supreme Court "puts these words in the statute as definitely as if it had been so amended by the legislature." *Winters* v. *New York*, 333 U.S. 507, 514. See *Kingsley Pictures Corp.* v. *Regents*, 360 U.S. 684, at 688; *Albertson* v. *Millard*, 345 U.S. 242; *United States* v. *Burnison*, 339, U.S. 87; *Aero Transit Co.* v. *Commissioners*, 332 U.S. 495.

The issue to be decided, then, is whether a State can constitutionally compel those in its service to swear that they have never "knowingly lent their aid, support, advice, counsel, or influence to the Communist Party." More precisely, can Florida consistently with the Due Process Clause of the Fourteenth Amendment force an employee either to take such an oath, at the risk of subsequent prosecution for perjury, or face immediate dismissal from public service?

---

[5] "If any person required by the provisions of §§ 876.05–876.10 to execute the oath herein required executes such oath, and it is subsequently proven that at the time of the execution of said oath said individual was guilty of making a false statement in said oath, he shall be guilty of perjury, and shall be prosecuted and punished for the crime of perjury in the event of conviction." Fla. Stat. § 876.10.

The provision of the oath here in question, it is to be noted, says nothing of advocacy of violent overthrow of State or Federal Government. It says nothing of membership or affiliation with the Communist Party, past or present. The provision is completely lacking in these or any other terms susceptible of objective measurement. Those who take this oath must swear, rather, that they have not in the unending past ever knowingly lent their "aid," or "support," or "advice," or "counsel" or "influence" to the Communist Party. What do these phrases mean? In the not too distant past Communist Party candidates appeared regularly and legally on the ballot in many state and local elections. Elsewhere the Communist Party has on occasion endorsed or supported candidates nominated by others. Could one who had ever cast his vote for such a candidate safely subscribe to this legislative oath? Could a lawyer who had ever represented the Communist Party or its members swear with either confidence or honesty that he had never knowingly lent his "counsel" to the Party? Could a journalist who had ever defended the constitutional rights of the Communist Party conscientiously take an oath that he had never lent the party his "support"? Indeed, could anyone honestly subscribe to this oath who had ever supported any cause with contemporaneous knowledge that the Communist Party also supported it?

The very absurdity of these possibilities brings into focus the extraordinary ambiguity of the statutory language. With such vagaries in mind, it is not unrealistic to suggest that the compulsion of this oath provision might weigh most heavily upon those whose conscientious scruples were the most sensitive. While it is perhaps fanciful to suppose that a perjury prosecution would ever be instituted for past conduct of the kind suggested, it requires no strain of the imagination to envision the possibility of prosecution for other types of equally guiltless knowing behaviour. It would be blinking reality not to acknowledge that there are some among us always ready to affix a Communist label upon those whose ideas they violently oppose. And experience teaches that prosecutors too are human.

We think this case demonstrably falls within the compass of those decisions of the Court which hold that ". . . a statute which either forbids or requires the doing of an act in terms so vague that men of common intelligence must necessarily guess at its meaning and differ as to its application, violates the first essential of due process of law.' *Connally* v. *General Construction Co.*, 269 U.S. 385, 391. "No one may be required at peril of life, liberty or property to speculate as to the meaning of penal statutes. All are entitled to be informed as to what the State commands or forbids." *Lanzetta* v. *New Jersey*, 306 U.S. 451, 453. "Words which are vague and fluid . . . may be as much of a trap for the innocent as the ancient laws of Caligula." *United States* v. *Cardiff*, 344 U.S. 174, 176. "In the light of our decisions, it appears upon a mere inspection that these general words and phrases are so vague and indefinite that any penalty prescribed for their violation constitutes a denial of due process of law. It is not the penalty itself that is invalid but the exaction of obedience to a rule or standard that is so vague and indefinite as to be really no rule or standard at all." *Champlin Refining Co.* v. *Corporation Commission of Oklahoma*, 286 U.S. 210, 243.

The vice of unconstitutional vagueness is further aggravated where, as here, the statute in question operates to inhibit the exercise of individual freedoms affirmatively protected by the Constitution. As we said in *Smith* v. *California*, ". . . stricter standards of permissible statutory vagueness may be applied to a statute having a potentially inhibiting effect on speech; a man may the less be required to act at his peril here, because the free dissemination of ideas may be the loser." 361 U.S. 147, at 151. "The maintenance of the opportunity for free political discussion to the end that government may be responsive to the will of the people and that changes may be obtained by lawful means, an opportunity essential to the security of the Republic, is a fundamental principle of our constitutional system. A statute which upon its face, and as authoritatively construed, is so vague and indefinite as to permit the punishment of the fair use of this opportunity is repugnant to the guaranty of liberty contained in the Fourteenth Amendment." *Stromberg* v. *California*, 283 U.S. 359, 369. See also *Herndon* v. *Lowry*, 301 U.S. 242; *Thornhill* v. *Alabama*, 310 U.S. 88; *Winters* v. *New York*, 333 U.S. 507.

As in *Wieman* v. *Updegraff*, we are not concerned here with the question "whether an abstract right to public employment exists." 344 U.S. 183, at 192. Nor do we question the power of a State to safeguard the public service from disloyalty. Cf. *Slochower* v. *Board of Education*, 350 U.S. 551; *Adler* v. *Board of Education*, 342 U.S. 485. It is enough for the present case to reaffirm "that constitutional protection does extend to the public servant whose exclusion pursuant to a statute is patently arbitrary or discriminatory." *Wieman* v. *Updegraff*, *supra*, at 192. "The fact . . . that a person is not compelled to hold public office cannot possibly be an excuse for barring him from office by State-imposed criteria forbidden by the Constitution." *Torcaso* v. *Watkins*, 367 U.S. 488, at 495–496.

Reversed.

MR. JUSTICE BLACK and MR. JUSTICE DOUGLAS join the Court's judgment and opinion, but also adhere to the view expressed in their dissents in *Adler* v. *Board of Education*, 342 U.S. 485, 496, 508; *Garner* v. *Los Angeles Board*, 341 U.S. 716, 730, 731; *Barenblatt* v. *United States*, 360 U.S. 109, 134; and to their concurrences in *Wieman* v. *Updegraff*, 344 U.S. 183, 192.

BAGGETT ET AL. *v.* BULLITT ET AL.

APPEAL FROM THE UNITED STATES DISTRICT COURT FOR THE WESTERN DISTRICT OF WASHINGTON.

No. 220.   Argued March 24, 1964.—Decided June 1, 1964.

This class action was brought by members of the faculty, staff, and students or the University of Washington for a judgment declaring unconstitutional 1931 and 1955 State statutes requiring the taking of oaths, one for teachers and the other for all State employees, including teachers, as a condition of employment. The 1931 oath requires teachers to swear, by precept and example, to promote respect for the flag and the institutions of the United States and the State of Washington, reverence for law and order and undivided allegiance to the Government of the United States. The 1955 oath for State employees, which incorporates provisions of the State Subversive Activities Act, requires the affiant to swear that he is not a "subversive person": that he does not commit, or advise, teach, abet or advocate another to commit or aid in the commission of any act intended to overthrow or alter, or assist in the overthrow or alteration, of the constitutional form of government by revolution, force or violence. "Subversive organization" and "foreign subversive organization" are defined in similar terms and the Communist Party is declared a subversive organization. A three-judge District Court held that the 1955 statute and oath were not unduly vague and did not violate the First and Fourteenth Amendments, and it abstained from ruling on the 1931 oath until it was considered by the State courts. *Held:*

1. The provisions of the 1955 statute and the 1931 Act violate due process since they, as well as the oaths based thereon, are unduly vague, uncertain and broad. *Cramp v. Board of Public Instruction,* 368 U.S. 278, followed. Pp. 361–372.

2. A State cannot require an employee to take an unduly vague oath containing a promise of future conduct at the risk of prosecution for perjury or loss of employment, particularly where the exercise of First Amendment freedoms may thereby be deterred. Pp. 373–374.

3. Federal courts do not automatically abstain when faced with a doubtful issue of State law, since abstention involves a discretionary exercise of equity power. Pp. 375–379.

(a) There are no special circumstances warranting application of the doctrine here. P. 375.

(b) Construction of the 1931 oath cannot eliminate the vagueness from its terms, and would probably raise other constitutional issues. P. 378.

(c) Abstention leads to piecemeal adjudication and protracted delays, a costly result where First Amendment freedoms may be inhibited. Pp. 378–379.

215 F. Supp. 439, reversed.

Arval A. Morris and *Kenneth A. MacDonald* argued the cause and filed a brief for appellants.

Herbert H. Fuller, Deputy Attorney General of Washington, argued the cause for appellees. With him on the brief were *John J. O'Connell,* Attorney General of Washington, and *Dean A. Floyd,* Assistant Attorney General.

MR. JUSTICE WHITE delivered the opinion of the Court.

Appellants, approximately 64 in number, are members of the faculty, staff and student body of the University of Washington who brought this class action asking for a judgment declaring unconstitutional two Washington statutes requiring the execution of two different oaths by State employees and for an injunction against the enforcement of these statutes by appellees, the president of the university, members of the Washington State Board of Regents and the State attorney general.

The statutes under attack are chapter 377, Laws of 1955, and chapter 103, Laws of 1931, both of which require employees of the

State of Washington to take the oaths prescribed in the statutes as a condition of their employment. The 1931 legislation applies only to teachers, who, upon applying for a license to teach or renewing an existing contract, are required to subscribe to the following:

"I solemnly swear (or affirm) that I will support the Constitution and laws of the United States of America and of the State of Washington, and will by precept and example promote respect for the flag and the institutions of the United States of America and the State of Washington, reverence for law and order and undivided allegiance to the Government of the United States." Wash. Laws 1931, c. 103.

The oath requirements of the 1955 Act, Wash. Laws 1955, c. 377, applicable to all State employees, incorporate various provisions of the Washington Subversive Activities Act of 1951, which provides generally that "[n]o subversive person, as defined in this act, shall be eligible for employment in, or appointment to any office, or any position of trust or profit in the government, or in the administration of the business, of this State, or of any county, municipality, or other political subdivision of this State." Wash. Rev. Code § 9.81.060. The term "subversive person" is defined as follows:

" 'Subversive person' means any person who commits, attempts to commit, or aids in the commission, or advocates, abets, advises or teaches by any means any person to commit, attempt to commit, or aid in the commission of any act intended to overthrow, destroy or alter, or to assist in the overthrow, destruction or alteration of, the constitutional form of the Government of the United States, or of the State of Washington, or any political subdivision of either of them by revolution, force, or violence; or who with knowledge that the organization is an organization as described in subsections (2) and (3) hereof, becomes or remains a member of a subversive organization or a foreign subversive organization." Wash. Rev. Code § 9.81.010(5).

The Act goes on to define at similar length and in similar terms "subversive organization" and "foreign subversive organization" and to declare the Communist Party a subversive organization and membership therein a subversive activity.[1]

On May 28, 1962, some four months after this Court's dismissal of the appeal in *Nostrand* v. *Little*, 368 U.S. 436, also a challenge to the

---

[1] " 'Subversive organization' means any organization which engages in or advocates, abets, advises, or teaches, or a purpose of which is to engage in or advocate, abet, advise, or teach activities intended to overthrow, destroy or alter, or to assist in the overthrow, destruction or alteration of, the constitutional form of the Government of the United States, or of the State of Washington, or of any political subdivision of either of them, by revolution, force or violence." Wash. Rev. Code § 9.81.010(2).

" 'Foreign subversive organization' means any organization directed, dominated or controlled directly or indirectly by a foreign government which engages in or advocates, abets, advises, or teaches, or a purpose of which is to engage in or to advocate, abet, advise, or teach, activities intended to overthrow, destroy or alter, or to assist in the overthrow, destruction or alteration of the constitutional form of the Government of the United States, or of the State of Washington, or of any political subdivision of either of them, and to establish in place thereof any form of government the direction and control of which is to be vested in, or exercised by or under, the domination or control of any foreign government, organization, or individual." Wash. Rev. Code § 9.81.010(3).

"COMMUNIST PARTY DECLARED A SUBVERSIVE ORGANIZATION.

"The Communist Party is a subversive organization within the purview of chapter 9.81 and membership in the Communist Party is a subversive activity thereunder." Wash. Rev. Code § 9.81.083.

1955 oath,[2] the university president, acting pursuant to directions of the Board of Regents, issued a memorandum to all university employees notifying them that they would be required to take an oath. Oath Form A [3] requires all teaching personnel to swear to the oath of allegiance set out above, to aver that they have read, are familiar with and understand the provisions defining "subversive person" in the Subversive Activities Act of 1951 and to disclaim being a subversive person and membership in the Communist Party or any other subversive or foreign subversive organization. Oath Form B [4] requires

---

[2] Although the 1931 Act has not been the subject of previous challenge, an attack upon the 1955 loyalty statute was instituted by two of the appellants in the present case, Professors Howard Nostrand and Max Savelle, who brought a declaratory judgment action in the Superior Court of the State of Washington asking that Chapter 377, Laws of 1955, be declared unconstitutional and that its enforcement be enjoined. The Washington Supreme Court held that one section was unconstitutional but severable from the rest of the Act, whose validity was upheld. *Nostrand* v. *Balmer*, 53 Wash. 2d 460, 335 P. 2d 10. On appeal to this Court the decision of the Washington court was vacated and the case remanded for a determination of whether employees who refused to sign the oath would be afforded a hearing at which they could explain or defend the reasons for their refusal. *Nostrand* v. *Little*, 362 U.S. 474. The Washington Supreme Court held upon remand that since Professors Nostrand and Savelle were tenured professors the terms of their contracts and rules promulgated by the Board of Regents entitled them to a hearing. *Nostrand* v. *Little*, 58 Wash. 2d 111, 361 P. 2d 551. This Court dismissed a further appeal, *Nostrand* v. *Little*, 368 U.S. 436. The issue we find dispositive of the case at bar was not presented to this Court in the above proceedings.

[3] "Oath Form A
"STATE OF WASHINGTON
"Statement and Oath for Teaching Faculty of the University of Washington

"I, the undersigned, do solemnly swear (or affirm) that I will support the Constitution and laws of the United States of America and the State of Washington, and will by precept and example promote respect for the flag and the institutions of the United States of America and the State of Washington; reverence for law and order, and undivided allegiance to the Government of the United States;
"I further certify that I have read the provisions of RCW 9.81.010 (2), (3), and (5); RCW 9.81.060; RCW 9.81.070; and RCW 9.81.083, which are printed on the reverse hereof; that I understand and am familiar with the contents thereof; that I am not a subversive person as therein defined; and
"I do solemnly swear (or affirm) that I am not a member of the Communist Party or knowingly of any other subversive organization.
"I understand that this statement and oath are made subject to the penalties of perjury.

(SIGNATURE)

(TITLE AND DEPARTMENT)

"Subscribed and sworn (or affirmed) to before me this _____
day of _____, 19___.

NOTARY PUBLIC IN AND FOR THE STATE OF WASHINGTON, RESIDING AT_____

"(To be executed in duplicate, one copy to be retained by individual.)
"NOTE: Those desiring to affirm may strike the words 'swear' and 'sworn to' and substitute 'affirm' and 'affirmed,' respectively."

[4] "Oath Form B
"STATE OF WASHINGTON
"Statement and Oath for Staff of the University of Washington Other Than Teaching Faculty

"I certify that I have read the provisions of RCW 9.81.010 (2), (3), and (5); RCW 9.81.060; RCW 9.81.070; and RCW 9.81.083 which are printed on the reverse hereof; that I understand and am familiar with the contents thereof; that I am not a subversive person as therein defined; and
"I do solemnly swear (or affirm) that I am not a member of the Communist Party or knowingly of any other subversive organization.
"I understand that this statement and oath are made subject to the penalties of perjury.

(SIGNATURE)

(TITLE AND DEPARTMENT OR OFFICE)

"Subscribed and sworn (or affirmed) to before me this _____
day of _____, 19___.

NOTARY PUBLIC IN AND FOR THE STATE OF WASHINGTON RESIDING AT_____

"To be executed in duplicate, one copy to be retained by individual.)
"NOTE: Those desiring to affirm may strike the words 'swear' and 'sworn to' and substitute 'affirm' and 'affirmed,' respectively."

other State employees to subscribe to all of the above provisions except the 1931 oath. Both forms provide that the oath and statements pertinent thereto are made subject to the penalties of perjury.

Pursuant to 28 U.S.C. §§ 2281, 2284, a three-judge District Court was convened and a trial was had. That court determined that the 1955 oath and underlying statutory provisions did not infringe upon any First and Fourteenth Amendment freedoms and were not unduly vague. In respect to the claim that the 1931 oath was unconstitutionally vague on its face, the court held that although the challenge raised a substantial constitutional issue, adjudication was not proper in the absence of proceedings in the State courts which might resolve or avoid the constitutional issue. The action was dismissed. 215 F. Supp. 439. We noted probable jurisdiction because of the public importance of this type of legislation and the recurring serious constitutional questions which it presents. 375 U.S. 808. We reverse.

I.

Appellants contend in this Court that the oath requirements and the statutory provisions on which they are based are invalid on their face because their language is unduly vague, uncertain and broad. We agree with this contention and therefore, without reaching the numerous other contentions pressed upon us, confine our considerations to that particular question.[5]

In *Cramp* v. *Board of Public Instruction*, 368 U.S. 278, the Court invalidated an oath requiring teachers and other employees of the State to swear that they had never lent their "aid, support, advice, counsel or influence to the Communist Party" because the oath was lacking in "terms susceptible of objective measurement" and failed to inform as to what the State commanded or forbade. The statute therefore fell within the compass of those decisions of the Court holding that a law forbidding or requiring conduct in terms so vague that men of common intelligence must necessarily guess at its meaning and differ as to its application violates due process of law. *Connally* v. *General Construction Co.*, 269 U.S. 385; *Lanzetta* v. *New Jersey*, 306 U.S. 451; *Joseph Burstyn, Inc.*, v. *Wilson*, 343 U.S. 495; *United States* v. *Cardiff*, 344 U.S. 174; *Champlin Refining Co.* v. *Corporation Comm'n of Oklahoma*, 286 U.S. 210.

The oath required by the 1955 statute suffers from similar infirmities. A teacher must swear that he is not a subversive person: that he is not one who commits an act or who advises, teaches, abets or advocates by any means another person to commit or aid in the commission of any act intended to overthrow or alter, or to assist the overthrow or alteration, of the constitutional form of government by revolution, force or violence. A subversive organization is defined as one which engages in or assists activities intended to alter or overthrow the Government by force or violence or which has as a purpose the commission of such acts. The Communist Party is declared in the statute to be a subversive organization, that is, it is presumed that the party does

---

[5] Since the ground we find dispositive immediately affects the professors and other State employees required to take the oath, and the interests of the students at the University in academic freedom are fully protected by a judgment in favor of the teaching personnel, we have no occasion to pass on the standing of the students to bring this suit.

and will engage in activities intended to overthrow the Government.[6] Persons required to swear they understand this oath may quite reasonably conclude that any person who aids the Communist Party or teaches or advises known members of the party is a subversive person because such teaching or advice may now or at some future date aid the activities of the party. Teaching and advising are clearly acts, and one cannot confidently assert that his counsel, aid, influence or support which adds to the resources, rights and knowledge of the Communist Party or its members does not aid the party in its activities, activities which the statute tells us are all in furtherance of the stated purpose of overthrowing the Government by revolution, force, or violence. The questions put by the Court in *Cramp* may with equal force be asked here. Does the statute reach endorsement or support for Communist candidates for office? Does it reach a lawyer who represents the Communist Party or its members or a journalist who defends constitutional rights of the Communist Party or its members or anyone who supports any cause which is likewise supported by Communists or the Communist Party? The susceptibility of the statutory language to require forswearing of an undefined variety of "guiltless knowing behavior" is what the Court condemned in *Cramp*. This statute, like the one at issue in *Cramp*, is unconstitutionally vague.[7]

The Washington statute suffers from additional difficulties on vagueness grounds. A person is subversive not only if he himself commits the specified acts but if he abets or advises another in aiding a third person to commit an act which will assist yet a fourth person in the overthrow or alteration of constitutional government. The Washington Supreme Court has said that knowledge is to be read into every provision and we accept this construction. *Nostrand* v. *Balmer*, 53 Wash. 2d 460, 483–484, 335 P. 2d 10, 24; *Nostrand* v. *Little*, 58 Wash. 2d 111, 123–124, 361 P. 2d 551, 559. But what is it that the Washington professor must "know"? Must he know that his aid or teaching will be used by another and that the person aided has the requisite guilty intent or is it sufficient that he know that his aid or teaching would or might be useful to others in the commission of acts intended to overthrow the Government? Is it subversive activity, for example, to attend and participate in international conventions of mathematicians and exchange views with scholars from Communist

---

[6] The drafters of the 1951 Subversive Activities Act stated to the Washington Legislature that "[t]he [Communist Party] dovetailed, nation-wide program is designed to . . . create unrest and civil strife, and impede the normal processes of state and national government, all to the end of weakening and ultimately destroying the United States as a constitutional republic and thereby facilitating the avowed Soviet purpose of substituting here a totalitarian dictatorship." First Report of the Joint Legislative Fact-Finding Committee on Un-American Activities in Washington State, 1948, p. IV.

[7] The contention that the Court found no constitutional difficulties with identical definitions of subversive person and subversive organizations in *Gerende* v. *Board of Supervisors*, 341 U.S. 56, is without merit. It was forcefully argued in *Gerende* that candidates for State office in Maryland were required to take an oath incorporating a section of the Maryland statutes defining subversive person and organization in the identical terms challenged herein. But the Court rejected this interpretation of Maryland law and did not pass upon or approve the definitions of subversive person and organization contained in the Maryland statutes. Instead it made very clear that the judgment below was affirmed solely on the basis that the actual oath to be imposed under Maryland law requires one to swear that he is not a person who is engaged " in the attempt to overthrow the government *by force or violence*,' and that he is not knowingly a member of an organization engaged in such an attempt." *Id.*, at 56–57 (emphasis in original). The Court said: "At the bar of this Court the Attorney General of the State of Maryland declared that he would advise the proper authorities to accept an affidavit in these terms as satisfying in full the statutory requirement. Under these circumstances and with this understanding, the judgment of the Maryland Court of Appeals is *Affirmed*." *Id.*, at 57.

countries? What about the editor of a scholarly journal who analyzes and criticizes the manuscripts of Communist scholars submitted for publication? Is selecting outstanding scholars from Communist countries as visiting professors and advising, teaching, or consulting with them at the University of Washington a subversive activity if such scholars are known to be Communists, or regardless of their affiliations, regularly teach students who are members of the Communist Party, which by statutory definition is subversive and dedicated to the overthrow of the Government?

The Washington oath goes beyond overthrow or alteration by force or violence. It extends to alteration by "revolution" which, unless wholly redundant and its ordinary meaning distorted, includes any rapid or fundamental change. Would, therefore, any organization or any person supporting, advocating or teaching peaceful but far-reaching constitutional amendments be engaged in subversive activity? Could one support the repeal of the Twenty-second Amendment or participation by this country in a world government? [8]

II.

We also conclude that the 1931 oath offends due process because of vagueness. The oath exacts a promise that the affiant will, by precept and example, promote respect for the flag and the institutions of the United States and the State of Washington. The range of activities which are or might be deemed inconsistent with the required promise is very wide indeed. The teacher who refused to salute the flag or advocated refusal because of religious beliefs might well be accused of breaching his promise. Cf. *West Virginia State Board of Education* v. *Barnette*, 319 U.S. 624. Even criticism of the design or color scheme of the State flag or unfavorable comparison of it with that of a sister State or foreign country could be deemed disrespectful and therefore violative of the oath. And what are "institutions" for the purposes of this oath? Is it every "practice, law, custom, etc., which is a material and persistent element in the life or culture of an organized social group" or every "established society or corporation," every "establishment, esp[ecially] one of a public character"? [9] The oath may prevent a professor from criticizing his State judicial system or the supreme court or the institution of judicial review. Or it might be deemed to proscribe advocating the abolition, for example, of the Civil

---

[8] It is also argued that § 2 of the Smith Act, 18 U.S.C. § 2385, upheld over a vagueness challenge in *Dennis* v .*United States*, 341 U.S. 494, proscribes the same activity in the same language as the Washington statute. This argument is founded on a misreading of § 2 and *Dennis* v. *United States, supra.*

That section provides:
"Whoever knowingly or willfully advocates, abets, advises, or teaches the duty, necessity, desirability, or propriety of overthrowing or destroying the Government of the United States or the government of any State . . . by force or violence . . .."
The convictions under this provision were sustained in *Dennis, supra*, on the construction that the statute means "teaching and advocacy of action for the accomplishment of [overthrowing or destroying organized government] by language reasonably and ordinarily calculated to incite persons to such action . . . as speedily as circumstances would permit." *Id.*, at 511–512. In connection with the vagueness attack, it was noted that "[t]his is a Federal statute which we must interpret as well as judge. Herein lies the fallacy of reliance upon the manner in which this Court has treated judgments of State courts. . . ." *Id.*, at 502.
In reversing convictions under this section in *Yates* v. *United States*, 354 U.S. 298, the Court made quite clear exactly what all the above terms do and do not proscribe: "[T]he Smith Act reaches only advocacy of action for the overthrow of government by force and violence." *Id.*, at 324.

[9] Webster's New Int. Dictionary (2d ed.), at 1288.

Rights Commission, the House Committee on Un-American Activities, or foreign aid.

It is likewise difficult to ascertain what might be done without transgressing the promise to "promote . . . undivided allegiance to the government of the United States." It would not be unreasonable for the serious-minded oathtaker to conclude that he should dispense with lectures voicing far-reaching criticism of any old or new policy followed by the Government of the United States. He could find it questionable under this language to ally himself with any interest group dedicated to opposing any current public policy or law of the Federal Government, for if he did, he might well be accused of placing loyalty to the group above allegiance to the United States.

Indulging every presumption of a narrow construction of the provisions of the 1931 oath, consistent, however, with a proper respect for the English language, we cannot say that this oath provides an ascertainable standard of conduct or that it does not require more than a State may command under the guarantees of the First and Fourteenth Amendments.

As in *Cramp* v. *Board of Public Instruction*, "[t]he vice of unconstitutional vagueness is further aggravated where, as here, the statute in question operates to inhibit the exercise of individual freedoms affirmatively protected by the Constitution." 368 U.S. 278, 287. We are dealing with indefinite statutes whose terms, even narrowly construed, abut upon sensitive areas of basic First Amendment Freedoms. The uncertain meanings of the oaths require the oath-taker—teachers and public servants—to "steer far wider of the unlawful zone," *Speiser* v. *Randall*, 357 U.S. 513, 526, than if the boundaries of the forbidden areas were clearly marked. Those with a conscientious regard for what they solemnly swear or affirm, sensitive to the perils posed by the oath's indefinite language, avoid the risk of loss of employment, and perhaps profession, only by restricting their conduct to that which is unquestionably safe. Free speech may not be so inhibited.[10] *Smith* v. *California*, 361 U.S. 147; *Stromberg* v. *California*, 283 U.S. 359, 369. See also *Herndon* v. *Lowry*, 301 U.S. 242; *Thornhill* v. *Alabama*, 310 U.S. 88; and *Winters* v. *New York*, 333 U.S. 507.

III.

The State labels as wholly fanciful the suggested possible coverage of the two oaths. It may well be correct, but the contention only emphasizes the difficulties with the two statutes; for if the oaths do not reach some or any of the behavior suggested, what specific conduct to the oaths cover? Where does fanciful possibility end and intended coverage begin?

It will not do to say that a prosecutor's sense of fairness and the Constitution would prevent a successful perjury prosecution for some

---

[10] "The maintenance of the opportunity for free political discussion to the end that government may be responsive to the will of the people and that changes may be obtained by lawful means, an opportunity essential to the security of the Republic, is a fundamental principle of our constitutional system. A statute which upon its face . . . is so vague and indefinite as to permit the punishment of the fair use of this opportunity is repugnant to the guaranty of liberty contained in the Fourteenth Amendment." *Stromberg* v. *California*, 283 U.S. 359, 369. "[S]tatutes restrictive of or purporting to place limits to those [First Amendment] freedoms must be narrowly drawn to meet the precise evil the legislature seeks to curb . . . and . . . the conduct proscribed must be defined specifically so that the person or persons affected remain secure and unrestrained in their rights to engage in activities not encompassed by the legislation." *United States* v. *Congress of Industrial Organizations*, 335 U.S. 106, 141–142 (Rutledge, J., concurring).

of the activities seemingly embraced within the sweeping statutory definitions. The hazard of being prosecuted for knowing but guiltless behavior nevertheless remains. "It would be blinking reality not to acknowledge that there are some among us always ready to affix a Communist label upon those whose ideas they violently oppose. And experience teaches us that prosecutors too are human." *Cramp, supra,* at 286–287. Well-intentioned prosecutors and judicial safeguards do not neutralize the vice of a vague law. Nor should we encourage the casual taking of oaths by upholding the discharge or exclusion from public employment of those with a conscientious and scrupulous regard for such undertakings.

It is further argued, however, that, notwithstanding the uncertainties of the 1931 oath and the statute on which it is based, the oath does not offend due process because the vagaries are contained in a promise of future conduct, the breach of which would not support a conviction for perjury. Without the criminal sanctions, it is said, one need not fear taking this oath, regardless of whether he understands it and can comply with its mandate, however understood. This contention ignores not only the effect of the oath on those who will not solemnly swear unless they can do so honestly and without prevarication and reservation, but also its effect on those who believe the written law means what it says. Oath Form A contains both oaths, and expressly requires that the signer "understand that this statement and oath are made subject to the penalties of perjury." Moreover, Wash. Rev. Code § 9.72.030 provides that "[e]very person who, whether orally or in writing . . . shall knowingly swear falsely concerning any matter whatsoever" commits perjury in the second degree. Even if it can be said that a conviction for falsely taking this oath would not be sustained, the possibility of a prosecution cannot be gainsaid. The State may not require one to choose between subscribing to an unduly vague and broad oath, thereby incurring the likelihood of prosecution, and conscientiously refusing to take the oath with the consequent loss of employment, and perhaps profession, particularly where "the free dissemination of ideas may be the loser." *Smith* v. *California,* 361 U. S. 147, 151. "It is not the penalty itself that is invalid but the exaction of obedience to a rule or standard that is so vague and indefinite as to be really no rule or standard at all." *Champlin Refg. Co.* v. *Corporation Comm'n of Oklahoma,* 286 U.S. 210, 243; cf. *Small Co.* v. *American Refg. Co.,* 267 U.S. 233.

IV.

We are asked not to examine the 1931 oath statute because, although on the books for over three decades, it has never been interpreted by the Washington courts. The argument is that ever since *Railroad Comm'n* v. *Pullman Co.,* 312 U.S. 496, the Court on many occasions has ordered abstention where State tribunals were thought to be more appropriate for resolution of complex or unsettled questions of local law. *A. F. L.* v. *Watson,* 327 U.S. 582; *Spector Motor Service* v. *McLaughlin,* 323 U.S. 101; *Harrison* v. *NAACP,* 360 U.S. 167. Because this Court ordinarily accepts the construction given a State statute in the local courts and also presumes that the statute will be construed in such a way as to avoid the constitutional question presented, *Fox* v. *Washington,* 236 U.S. 273; *Poulos* v. *New Hampshire,* 345 U.S. 395, an interpretation of the 1931 oath in the Washington courts in light of the vagueness attack may eliminate the necessity of deciding this issue. We are not persuaded. The abstention doctrine is not an automatic rule applied whenever a Federal court is faced with a doubtful issue of State law; it rather involves a discretionary exercise of a court's equity powers. Ascertainment of whether there exist the "special circumstances," *Propper* v. *Clark*, 337 U.S. 472, prerequisite to its application must be made on a case-by-case basis. *Railroad Comm'n* v. *Pullman Co.*, 312 U.S. 496, 500; *NAACP* v. *Bennett*, 360 U.S. 471.[11] Those special circumstances are not present here. We doubt, in the first place, that a construction of the oath provisions, in light of the vagueness challenge, would avoid or fundamentally alter the constitutional issue raised in this litigation. See *Chicago* v. *Atchison, T. & S.F.R. Co.*, 357 U.S. 77. In the bulk of abstention cases in this Court,[12] including those few cases where vagueness was at issue,[13] the unsettled issue of State law principally concerned the applicability of the challenged statute to a certain person or a defined course of conduct, whose resolution in a particular manner would eliminate the constitutional

[11] "When the validity of a state statute, challenged under the United States Constitution, is properly for adjudication before a United States District Court, reference to the state courts for construction of the statute should not automatically be made." *NAACP* v. *Bennett*, 360 U.S. 471. See also *United States* v. *Livingston*, 179 F. Supp. 9, 12–13 (D.C.E.D. S.C.), aff'd *Livingston* v. *United States*, 364 U.S. 281: "Though never interpreted by a State court, if a State statute is not fairly subject to an interpretation which will avoid or modify the Federal constitutional question, it is the duty of a Federal court to decide the Federal question when presented to it." *Shelton* v. *McKinley*, 174 F. Supp. 351 (D.C.E.D. Ark.) (abstention inappropriate where there are no substantial problems of statutory construction and delay would prejudice constitutional rights); *All American Airways* v. *Village of Cedarhurst*, 201 F. 2d 273 (C.A. 2d Cir.); *Sterling Drug* v. *Anderson*, 127 F. Supp. 511, 513 (D.C.E.D. Tenn.).

[12] See, *e.g.*, *Railroad Comm'n of Texas* v. *Pullman Co.*, 312 U.S. 496; *Chicago* v. *Fieldcrest Dairies, Inc.*, 316 U.S. 168; *Spector Motor Service, Inc.*, v. *McLaughlin*, 323 U.S. 101; *Alabama State Federation of Labor* v. *McAdory*, 325 U.S. 450; *American Federation of Labor* v. *Watson*, 327 U.S. 582; *Stainback* v. *Mo Hock Ke Lok Po*, 336 U.S. 368; *Shipman* v. *DuPre*, 339 U.S. 321; *Albertson* v. *Millard*, 345 U.S. 242; *Leiter Minerals, Inc.*, v. *United States*, 352 U.S. 220; *Government & Civic Employees Organizing Committee, C.I.O.*, v. *Windsor*, 353 U.S. 364; *City of Meridian* v. *Southern Bell Tel. & Tel. Co.*, 358 U.S. 639.

[13] In *Musser* v. *Utah*, 333 U.S. 95, the appellants were convicted of committing "acts injurious to public morals." The vagueness objection to the statute, either as applied or on its face, was raised for the first time in oral argument before this Court, and the Court vacated the conviction and remanded for a determination of whether the conviction for urging persons to commit polygamy rested solely on this broad-challenged provision. In *Albertson* v. *Millard*, 345 U.S. 242, the Communist Party of the State of Michigan and its secretary sought to enjoin on several constitutional grounds the application to them of a state statute, five days after its passage, requiring registration, under pain of criminal penalties, of "any organization which is substantially directed, dominated or controlled by the Union of Soviet Socialist Republics or its satellites, or which . . . acts to further, the world communist movement" and of members of such an organization. They argued that the definitions were vague and failed to inform them if a local Communist organization and its members were required to register. The lower court took judicial notice of the fact that the Communist Party of the United States, with whom the local party was associated, was a part of the world Communist movement dominated by the Soviet Union, and held the statute constitutional in all other respects. This Court vacated the judgment and declined to pass on the appellants' constitutional claims until the Michigan courts, in a suit already pending, construed the statutory terms and determined if they required the local party and its secretary, without more, to register. The approach was that the constitutional claims, including the one founded on vagueness, would be wholly eliminated if the statute, as construed by the state court, did not require all local Communist organizations without substantial ties to a foreign country and their members to register. Stated differently, the question was whether this statute applied to these plaintiffs, a question to be authoritatively answered in the state courts.

In *Harrison* v. *NAACP*, 360 U.S. 167, the NAACP and the NAACP Legal Defense and Education Fund sought a declaratory judgment and injunction on several constitutional grounds in respect to numerous recently enacted state statutes. The lower court enjoined the implementation of three statutes, including one provision on vagueness grounds, and ordered abstention as to two others, finding them ambiguous. This Court ordered abstention as to all the statutes, finding that they were all susceptible of constructions that would limit or eliminate their effect on the litigative and legal activities of the NAACP and construction might thereby eliminate the necessity for passing on the many constitutional questions raised. The vagueness issue, for example, would not require adjudication if the State courts found that the challenged provisions did not restrict the activities of the NAACP or require the NAACP to register. Unlike the instant case, the necessity for deciding the Federal constitutional issues in the above and other abstention cases turned on whether the restrictions or requirements of an uncertain or unclear State statute were imposed on the persons bringing the action or on their activities as defined in the complaint.

issue and terminate the litigation. Here the uncertain issue of state law does not turn upon a choice between one or several alternative meanings of a State statute. The challenged oath is not open to one or a few interpretations, but to an indefinite number. There is no uncertainty that the oath applies to the appellants and the issue they raise is not whether the oath permits them to engage in certain definable activities. Rather their complaint is that they, about 64 in number, cannot understand the required promise, cannot define the range of activities in which they might engage in the future, and do not want to forswear doing all that is literally or arguably within the purview of the vague terms. In these circumstances it is difficult to see how an abstract construction of the challenged terms, such as precept, example, allegiance, institutions, and the like, in a declaratory judgment action could eliminate the vagueness from these terms. It is fictional to believe that anything less than extensive adjudications, under the impact of a variety of factual situations, would bring the oath within the bounds of permissible constitutional certainty. Abstention does not require this.

Other considerations also militate against abstention here. Construction of this oath in the State court, abstractly and without reference to concrete, particularized situations so necessary to bring into focus the impact of the terms on constitutionally protected rights of speech and association, *Ashwander* v. *Tennessee Valley Authority*, 297 U.S. 288, 341 (Brandeis, J., concurring), would not only hold little hope of eliminating the issue of vagueness but also would very likely pose other constitutional issues for decision, a result not serving the abstention-justifying end of avoiding constitutional adjudication.

We also cannot ignore that abstention operates to require piecemeal adjudication in many courts, *England* v. *Louisiana State Board of Medical Examiners*, 375 U.S. 411, thereby delaying ultimate adjudication on the merits for an undue length of time, *England, supra; Spector, supra; Government & Civic Employees Organizing Committee* v. *Windsor*, 353 U.S. 364,[14] a result quite costly where the vagueness of a State statute may inhibit the exercise of First Amendment Freedoms, Indeed the 1955 subversive person oath has been under continuous constitutional attack since at least 1957, *Nostrand* v. *Balmer*, 53 Wash. 2d 460, 463, 335 P. 2d 10, 12, and is now before this Court for the third time. Remitting these litigants to the State courts for a construction of the 1931 oath would further protract these proceedings, already pending for almost two years, with only the likelihood that the case, perhaps years later, will return to the three-judge District Court and perhaps this Court for a decision on the identical issue herein decided. See *Chicago* v. *Atchison, T. & S. F. R. Co.*, 357 U.S. 77, 84; *Public Utilities Comm'n of Ohio* v. *United Fuel Co.*, 317 U.S. 456.[15] Meanwhile, where the vagueness of the statute deters constitutionally protected conduct, "the free dissemination of ideas may be the loser." *Smith* v. *California*, 361 U.S. 147, 151.

---

[14] See Clark, Federal Procedural Reform and States' Rights, 40 Tex. L. Rev. 211 (1961); Note, 73 Harv. L. Rev. 1358, 1363 (1960).

[15] "Where the disposition of a doubtful question of local law might terminate the entire controversy and thus make it unnecessary to decide a substantial constitutional question, consideration of equity justify a rule of abstention. But where, as here, no State court ruling on local law could settle the Federal questions that necessarily remain, and where, as here, the litigation has already been in the Federal courts an inordinately long time, considerations of equity require that the litigation be brought to an end as quickly as possible." 317 U.S. 456, at 463.

V.

As in *Cramp* v. *Board of Public Instruction, supra,* we do not question the power of a State to take proper measures safeguarding the public service from disloyal conduct. But measures which purport to define disloyalty must allow public servants to know what is and is not disloyal. "The fact . . . that a person is not compelled to hold public office cannot possibly be an excuse for barring him from office by State-imposed criteria forbidden by the Constitution." *Torcaso* v. *Watkins,* 367 U.S. 488, 495–496.

Reversed.

MR. JUSTICE CLARK, whom MR. JUSTICE HARLAN joins, dissenting. The Court strikes down, as unconstitutionally vague, two Acts of the State of Washington. The first, the Act of 1955, requires every State employee to swear or affirm that he is not a "subversive person" as therein defined. The second, the Act of 1931, which requires that another oath be taken by teachers, is declared void without the benefit of an opinion of either a State or Federal court. I dissent as to both, the first on the merits, and the latter, because the Court refuses to afford the State an opportunity to interpret its own law.

I.

The Court says that the Act of 1955 is void on its face because it is "unduly vague, uncertain and broad." The Court points out that the oath requires a teacher to "swear that he is not a subversive person: that he is not one who commits an act or who advises, teaches, abets or advocates by any means another person to commit or aid in the commission of any act intended to overthrow or alter, or to assist the overthrow or alteration, of the constitutional form of government by revolution, force or violence." The Court further finds that the Act declares the Communist Party to be a subversive organization. From these premises, the Court then reasons that under the 1955 Act "any person who aids the Communist Party or teaches or advises known members of the party is a subversive person" because "at some future date" such teaching may aid the activities of the party. This reasoning continues with the assertion that "one cannot confidently assert that his counsel, aid, influence or support which adds to the resources, rights and knowledge of the Communist Party or its members does not aid the party . . . in furtherance of the stated purpose of overthrowing the Government by revolution, force, or violence." The Court then interrogates itself: Does the statute reach "endorsement or support for Communist candidates for office? . . . a lawyer who represents the Communist Party or its members? . . . [defense of the] constitutional rights of the Communist Party or its members . . . [or support of] any cause which is likewise supported by Communists or the Communist Party?" Apparently concluding that the answers to these questions are unclear, the Court then declares the Act void, citing *Cramp* v. *Board of Public Instruction,* 368 U.S. 278 (1961). Let us take up this reasoning in reverse order.

First, *Cramp* is not apposite. The majority has failed to recognize that the statute in *Cramp* required an oath of much broader scope than the one in the instant case: *Cramp* involved an oath "that I have

618 INTERNAL SECURITY AND SUBVERSION

not and will not lend my aid, support, advice, counsel or influence to
the Communist Party. . . ." That oath was replete with defects
not present in the Washington oath. As MR. JUSTICE STEWART pointed
out in *Cramp*:

> "The provision of the oath here in question, it is to be noted,
> says nothing of advocacy of violent overthrow of State or Fed-
> eral Government. It says nothing of membership or affiliation
> with the Communist Party, past or present. The provision is
> completely lacking in these or any other terms susceptible of ob-
> jective measurement." At 286.

These factors which caused the Court to find the *Cramp* oath unconstitutionally vague are clearly not present in the Washington oath.
Washington's oath proscribes only the commission of an *act* of overthrow or alteration of the constitutional form of government by revolution, force or violence; or advising, teaching, abetting or advocating by any means another person to commit or aid in the commission of any act intended to overthrow or alter or to assist the overthrow or alteration of the constitutional form of government by revolution, force or violence. The defects noted by the Court when it
passed on the *Cramp* oath have been cured in the Washington statute.

It is strange that the Court should find the language of this statute
so profoundly vague when in 1951 it had no such trouble with the
identical language presented by another oath in *Gerende* v. *Board of
Supervisors of Elections*, 341 U.S. 56. There, the constitutionality
of Maryland's Ober Law, written in language identical to Washington's 1955 Act, was affirmed by a unanimous Court against the same
attack of vagueness. It is unfortunate that *Gerende* is overruled so
quickly.* Other State laws have been copied from the Maryland
Act—just as Washington's 1955 Act was—primarily because of our
approval of it, and now this Court would declare them void. Such
action cannot command the dignity and respect due to the judicial
process. It is, of course, absurd to say that, under the words of the
Washington Act, a professor risks violation when he teaches German, English, history or any other subject included in the curriculum
for a college degree, to a class in which a Communist Party member
might sit. To so interpret the language of the Act is to extract more
sunbeams from cucumbers than did Gulliver's mad scientist. And to
conjure up such ridiculous questions, the answers to which we all know
or should know are in the negative, is to build up a whimsical and
farcical straw man which is not only grim but Grimm.

In addition to the Ober Law the Court has also found that other
statutes using similar language were not vague. An unavoidable
example is the Smith Act which we upheld against an attack based
on vagueness in the landmark case of *Denis* v. *United States*, 341 U.S.
494 (1951). The critical language of the Smith Act is again in
the same words as the 1955 Washington Act.

> "Whoever knowingly or willfully *advocates, abets, advises,* or
> *teaches* the duty, necessity, desirability, or propriety of over-

---

*It has been contended that the crucial section of Maryland's Ober Act, that which is
identical to the Washington Act, was not before the Court in *Gerende*, but a review of the
record in that case conclusively demonstrates to the contrary. Further, while the *Gerende*
opinion was stated with a qualification, the fact remains that the Court approved the
judgment of the Maryland court and rejected the argument that the Act was unconstitu-
tutionally vague.

throwing or destroying the Government of the United States . . ."
18 U.S.C. § 2385.   (Emphasis supplied.)
The opinion of the Court in *Dennis* uses this language in discussing
the vagueness claim:

"We agree that the standard as defined is not a neat, math-
matical formulary. Like all verbalizations it is subject to criticism on the score of indefiniteness. . . . We think [the statute]
well serves to indicate to those who would advocate constitutionally prohibited conduct that there is a line beyond which they
may not go—a line which they, in full knowledge of what they
intend and the circumstances in which their activity takes place,
will well appreciate and understand." At 515–516.
It appears to me from the statutory language that Washington's 1955
Act is much more clear than the Smith Act. Still the Court strikes
it down. Where does this leave the constitutionality of the Smith
Act?

II.

Appellants make other claims. They say that the 1955 Act violates
their rights of association and free speech as guaranteed by the First
and Fourteenth Amendments. But in light of *Konigsberg* v. *State
Bar of California*, 366 U.S. 36 (1961); *In re Anastaplo*, 366 U.S. 82
(1961); *Adler* v. *Board of Education*, 342 U.S. 485 (1952); *Garner*
v. *Board of Public Works*, 341 U.S. 716 (1951); and *American Communications Assn.* v. *Douds*, 339 U.S. 382 (1950), this
claim is frivolous. Likewise in view of the decision of Washington's
highest court that tenured employees would be entitled to a hearing,
Nostrand v. *Little*, 58 Wash. 2d 111, 131, 361 P. 2d 551, 563, the due
process claim is without foundation. This conclusion would also apply to those employees without tenure, since they would be entitled
to a hearing under Washington's Civil Service Act, Rev. Code Wash.
§ 41.04 *et seq.* and its Administrative Procedure Act, Rev. Code Wash.
§ 34.04.010 *et seq.*

III.

The Supreme Court of Washington has never construed the oath
of allegiance required by the 1931 Act. I agree with the District
Court that Washington's highest court should be afforded an opportunity to do so. As the District Court said:

"The granting or withholding of equitable or declaratory relief in Federal court suits which seek to limit or control State action is committed to the sound discretion of the court. Accordingly, in the absence of a concrete factual showing that any plaintiff or any member of the classes of State employees here represented has suffered actual injury by reason of the application of
the oath of allegiance statute (Chapter 103, Laws of 1931) this
court will decline to render a declaratory judgment as to the
constitutionality of that statute in advance of an authoritative
construction by the Washington Supreme Court." 215 F. Supp.
439, 455.
For these reasons, I dissent.

EXCLUSION FROM THE BAR

SCHWARE v. BOARD OF BAR EXAMINERS OF NEW MEXICO.

CERTIORARI TO THE SUPREME COURT OF NEW MEXICO.

No. 92.   Argued January 14–15, 1957.—Decided May 6, 1957.

In 1953 the Board of Bar Examiners of New Mexico refused to permit petitioner to take the bar examination, on the ground that he had not shown "good moral character," and thereby precluded his admission to the bar of that State. It was conceded that petitioner was qualified in all other respects. Petitioner made a strong showing of good moral character, except that it appeared that from 1933 to 1937 he had used certain aliases, that he had been arrested (but never tried or convicted) on several occasions prior to 1940, and that from 1932 to 1940 he was a member of the Communist Party. The State Supreme Court sustained the Board. *Held:* On the record in this case, the State of New Mexico deprived petitioner of due process in denying him the opportunity to qualify for the practice of law. Pp. 233–247.

(a) A State cannot exclude a person from the practice of law or from any other occupation in a manner or for reasons that contravene the Due Process Clause of the Fourteenth Amendment. Pp. 238–239.

(b) A State can require high standards of qualifications, such as good moral character or proficiency in its law, before it admits an applicant to the bar; but any qualification must have a rational connection with the applicant's fitness or capacity to practice law. P. 239.

(c) Even in applying permissible standards, officers of the State cannot exclude an applicant when there is no basis for their finding that he fails to meet these standards, or when their action is invidiously discriminatory. P. 239.

(d) Whether the practice of law is a "right" or a "privilege" need not here be determined; it is not a matter of the State's grace, and a person cannot be barred except for valid reasons. P. 239, n. 5.

(e) Petitioner's use from 1934 to 1937 of certain aliases, for purposes which were not wrong and not to cheat or defraud, does not support an inference of bad moral character more than 20 years later. Pp. 240–241.

(f) The arrests of petitioner are insufficient to support a finding that he had bad moral character at the time he applied to take the bar examination. Pp. 241–243.

(g) Petitioner's membership in the Communist Party from 1932 to 1940 does not justify an inference that he presently has bad moral character. Pp. 243–246.

(h) The use of aliases, the arrests, and former membership in the Communist Party do not in combination warrant exclusion of petitioner from the practice of law. P. 246.

(i) In the light of petitioner's forceful showing of good moral character, the evidence upon which the State relies cannot be said to raise substantial doubts as to his present good moral character. P. 246.

60 N.M. 304, 291 P. 2d 607, reversed and remanded.

Herbert Monte Levy argued the cause and filed a brief for petitioner.

William A. Sloan and *Fred M. Standley*, Attorney General of New Mexico, argued the cause and filed a brief for respondent.

MR. JUSTICE BLACK delivered the opinion of the Court.

The question presented is whether petitioner, Rudolph Schware, has been denied a license to practice law in New Mexico in violation of the Due Process Clause of the Fourteenth Amendment to the United States Constitution.

New Mexico has a system for the licensing of persons to practice law similar to that in effect in most States.[1] A Board of Bar Exami-

---

[1] Generally, see N.M. Stat. Ann., 1953, § 18–1–8 and the Rules Governing Admission to the Bar appended thereto.

ners determines if candidates for admission to the bar have the necessary qualifications. When the Board concludes that an applicant qualifies it recommends to the State Supreme Court that he be admitted. If the court accepts the recommendation, the applicant is entitled to practice law upon taking an oath to support the constitutions and laws of the United States and New Mexico. An applicant must pass a bar examination before the Board will give him its recommendation. The Board can refuse to permit him to take this examination unless he demonstrates that he has "good moral character."

In December 1953, on the eve of his graduation from the University of New Mexico School of Law, Schware filed an application with the Board of Bar Examiners requesting that he be permitted to take the bar examination scheduled for February 1954. His application was submitted on a form·prescribed by the Board that required answers to a large number of questions. From the record, it appears that he answered these questions in detail. Among other things, he disclosed that he had used certain aliases between 1933 and 1937 and that he had been arrested on several occasions prior to 1940. When he appeared to take the examination, the Board informed him that he could not do so. He later requested a formal hearing on the denial of his application. The Board granted his request. At the hearing the Board told him for the first time why it had refused to permit him to take the bar examination. It gave him a copy of the minutes of the meeting at which it had voted to deny his application. These minutes read:

"No. 1309, Rudolph Schware. It is moved by Board Member Frank Andrews that the application of Rudolph Schware to take the bar examination be denied for the reason that, taking into consideration the use of aliases by the applicant, his former connection with subversive organizations, and his record of arrests, he has failed to satisfy the Board as to the requisite moral character for admission to the Bar of New Mexico. Whereupon said motion is duly seconded by Board Member Ross L. Malone, and unanimously passed." [2]

At the hearing petitioner called his wife, the rabbi of his synagogue, a local attorney and the secretary to the dean of the law school to testify about his character.[3] He took the stand himself and was thoroughly examined under oath by the Board. His counsel introduced a series of letters that petitioner had written his wife from 1944 through 1946 while he was on duty in the Army. Letters were also introduced from every member of petitioner's law school graduating class except one who did not comment. And all of his law school professors who were then available wrote in regard to his moral character. The Board called no witnesses and introduced no evidence.

---

[2] Apparently the Board had received confidential information that Schware had once been a member of the Board's Communist Party. The Board's application form did not request disclosure of such information and so Schware did not mention it in his application. At the hearing he testified at length about his membership. The Board refused to let petitioner see the confidential information against him, although it appears that its initial denial of his application was partially based on this information. While this secret evidence was not made a part of the record of the hearing, counsel for petitioner contends that the Board was influenced by it in adhering to its view that petitioner was not qualified. In the New Mexico Supreme Court the members of the majority did not look at the confidential information. And while that court passed on petitioner's qualifications in the exercise of its original jurisdiction, the majority placed considerable reliance on the Board's recommendations. Therefore, petitioner contends, the Board's use of confidential information deprived him of procedural due process. Cf. *Goldsmith* v. *United States Bd. of Tax Appeals*, 270 U.S. 117; *Bratton* v. *Chandler*, 260 U.S. 110; *Minkoff* v. *Payne*, 93 U.S. App. D.C. 123, 210 F. 2d 689, 691; *In re Carter*, 89 U.S. App. D.C. 310, 192 F. 2d 15, cert. denied, 342 U.S. 862. We find it unnecessary to consider this contention.

[3] The dean was on sabbatical leave and not available.

The record of the formal hearing shows the following facts relevant to Schware's moral character. He was born in a poor section of New York City in 1914 and grew up in a neighborhood inhabited primarily by recent immigrants. His father was an immigrant and like many of his neighbors had a difficult time providing for his family. Schware took a job when he was nine years old and throughout the remainder of school worked to help provide necessary income for his family. After 1929, the economic condition of the Schware family and their neighbors, as well as millions of others, was greatly worsened. Schware was then at a formative stage in high school. He was interested in and enthusiastic for socialism and trade-unionism as was his father. In 1932, despairing at what he considered lack of vigor in the Socialist movement at a time when the country was in the depths of the great depression, he joined the Young Communist League.[4] At this time he was 18 years old and in the final year of high school.

From the time he left school until 1940 Schware, like many others, was periodically unemployed. He worked at a great variety of temporary and ill-paying jobs. In 1933, he found work in a glove factory and there he participated in a successful effort to unionize the employees. Since these workers were principally Italian, Schware assumed the name Rudolph Di Caprio to forestall the effects of anti-Jewish prejudice against him, not only in securing and retaining a job but in assisting in the organization of his fellow employees. In 1934 he went to California where he secured work on the docks. He testified that he continued to use the name Rudolph Di Caprio because Jews were discriminated against in employment for this work. Wherever Schware was employed he was an active advocate of labor organization. In 1934 he took part in the great maritime strikes on the west coast which were bitterly fought on both sides. While on strike in San Pedro, Caifornia, he was arrested twice on "suspicion of criminal syndicalism." He was never formally charged nor tried and was released in each instance after being held for a brief period. He testified that the San Pedro police in a series of mass arrests jailed large numbers of the strikers.

At the time of his father's death in 1937 Schware left the Communist Party but later he rejoined. In 1940 he was arrested and indicted for violating the Neutrality Act of 1917. He was charged with attempting to induce men to volunteer for duty on the side of the Loyalist Government in the Spanish Civil War. Before his case came to trial the charges were dismissed and he was released. Later in 1940 he quit the Communist Party. The Nazi-Soviet Non-Aggression Pact of 1939 had greatly disillusioned him and this disillusionment was made complete as he came to believe that certain leaders in the Party were acting to advance their own selfish interests rather than the interests of the working class which they purported to represent.

In 1944 Schware entered the armed forces of the United States. While in the service he volunteered for duty as a paratrooper and was sent to New Guinea. While serving in the Army here and abroad he wrote a number of letters to his wife. These letters show a desire to serve his country and demonstrate faith in a free democratic society. They reveal serious thoughts about religion which later led him and

---

[4] At times during 1932 more than 12,060,000 of the nation's 51,000,000 working persons were unemployed. Statistical Abstract of the United States (1956) 197.

his wife to associate themselves with a synagogue when he returned to civilian life. He was honorably discharged from the Army in 1946.

After finishing college, he entered the University of New Mexico law school in 1950. At the beginning he went to the dean and told him of his past activities and his association with the Communist Party during the depression and asked for advice. The dean told him to remain in school and put behind him what had happened years before. While studying law Schware operated a business in order to support his wife and two children and to pay the expenses of a professional education. During his three years at the law school his conduct was exemplary.

At the conclusion of the hearing the Board reaffirmed its decision denying Schware the right to take the bar examination. He appealed to the New Mexico Supreme Court. That court upheld the denial with one justice dissenting. 60 N.M. 304, 291 P. 2d 607. In denying a motion for rehearing the court stated that:

"[Schware's membership in the Communist Party], together with his other former actions in the use of aliases and record of arrests, and his present attitude toward those matters, were the considerations upon which [we approved the denial of his application]."

Schware then petitioned this Court to review his case alleging that he had been denied an opportunity to qualify for the practice of law contrary to the Due Process Clause of the Fourteenth Amendment. We granted certiorari. 352 U.S. 821. Cf. *In re Summers*, 325 U.S. 561, 562, 564–569. And see *Konigsberg* v. *State Bar of California*, *post*, p. 252. decided this day.

A State cannot exclude a person from the practice of law or from any other occupation in a manner or for reasons that contravene the Due Process or Equal Protection Clause of the Fourteenth Amendment.[5] *Dent* v. *West Virginia*, 129 U.S. 114. Cf. *Slochower* v. *Board of Education*, 350 U.S. 551; *Wieman* v. *Updegraff*, 344 U.S. 183. And see *Ex parte Secombe*, 19 How. 9, 13. A State can require high standards of qualification, such as good moral character or proficiency in its law, before it admits an applicant to the bar, but any qualification must have a rational connection with the applicant's fitness or capacity to practice law. *Douglas* v. *Noble*, 261 U.S. 165; *Cummings* v. *Missouri*, 4 Wall. 277, 319–320. Cf. *Nebbia* v. *New York*, 291 U.S. 502. Obviously an applicant could not be excluded merely because he was a Republican or a Negro or a member of a particular church. Even in applying permissible standards, officers of a State cannot exclude an applicant when there is no basis for their finding that he fails to meet these standards, or when their action is invidiously discriminatory. Cf. *Yick Wo* v. *Hopkins*, 118 U.S. 356.

Here the State concedes that Schware is fully qualified to take the examination in all respects other than good moral character. Therefore the question is whether the Supreme Court of New Mexico on the record before us could reasonably find that he had not shown good moral character.

---

[5] We need not enter into a discussion whether the practice of law is a "right" or 'privilege." Regardless of how the State's grant of permission to engage in this occupation is characterized, it is sufficient to say that a person cannot be prevented from practicing except for valid reasons. Certainly the practice of law is not a matter of the State's grace. *Ex parte Garland*, 4 Wall. 333, 379.

There is nothing in the record which suggests that Schware has engaged in any conduct during the past 15 years which reflects adversely on his character. The New Mexico Supreme Court recognized that he "presently enjoys good repute among his teachers, his fellow students and associates and in his synagogue." Schware's professors, his fellow students, his business associates and the rabbi of the synagogue of which he and his family are members, all gave testimony that he is a good man, a man who is imbued with a sense of deep responsibility for his family, who is trustworthy, who respects the rights and beliefs of others. From the record it appears he is a man of religious conviction and is training his children in the beliefs and practices of his faith. A solicitude for others is demonstrated by the fact that he regularly read the Bible to an illiterate soldier while in the Army and law to a blind student while at the University of New Mexico law school. His industry is depicted by the fact that he supported his wife and two children and paid for a costly professional education by operating a business separately while studying law. He demonstrated candor by informing the Board of his personal history and by going to the dean of the law school and disclosing his past. The undisputed evidence in the record shows Schware to be a man of high ideals with a deep sense of social justice. Not a single witness testified that he was not a man of good character.

Despite Schware's showing of good character, the Board and court below thought there were certain facts in the record which raised substantial doubts about his moral fitness to practice law.

(1) *Aliases.*—From 1934 to 1937 Schware used certain aliases. He testified that these aliases were adopted so he could secure a job in businesses which discriminted against Jews in their employment practices and so that he could more effectively organize non-Jewish employees at plants where he worked. Of course it is wrong to use an alias when it is done to cheat or defraud another but it can hardly be said that Schware's attempt to forestall anti-Semitism in securing employment or organizing his fellow workers was wrong. He did give an assumed name to police in 1934 when he was picked up in a mass arrest during a labor dispute. He said he did this so he would not be fired as a striker. This is certainly not enough evidence to support an inference that petitioner has bad moral character more than 20 years later.

(2) *Arrests.*—In response to the questions on the Board's application form Schware stated that he had been arrested on several occasions:

1. In 1934, while he was participating in a bitter labor dispute in the California shipyards, petitioner was arrested at least two times on "suspicion of criminal syndicalism." After being held for a brief period he was released without formal charges being filed against him. He was never indicted nor convicted for any offense in connection with these arrests.

The mere fact that a man has been arrested has very little, if any, probative value in showing that he has engaged in any misconduct.[6] An arrest shows nothing more than that someone probably suspected the person apprehended of an offense. When formal charges are not

---

[6] Arrest, by itself, is not considered competent evidence at either a criminal or civil trial to prove that a person did certain prohibited acts. Cf. Wigmore, Evidence, § 980a.

filed against the arrested person and he is released without trial, whatever probative force the arrest may have had is normally dissipated. Moreover here, the special facts surrounding the 1934 arrests are relevant in shedding light on their present significance. Apparently great numbers of strikers were picked up by police in a series of arrests during the strike at San Pedro and many of these were charged with "criminal syndicalism." [7] The California syndicalism statutes in effect in 1934 were very broad and vague.[8] There is nothing in the record which indicates why Schware was arrested on "suspicion" that he had violated this statute. There is no suggestion that he was using force or violence in an attempt to overthrow the State or National Government. Again it should be emphasized that these arrests were made more than 20 years ago and petitioner was never formally charged nor tried for any offense related to them.

2. In 1940 Schware was arrested for violating the Neutrality Act of 1917 which makes it unlawful for a person within the United States to join or to hire or retain another to join the army of any foreign state.[9] He was indicted but before the case came to trial the prosecution dropped the charges. He had been charged with recruiting persons to go overseas to aid the Loyalists in the Spanish Civil War. Schware testified that he was unaware of this old law at the time. From the facts in the record it is not clear that he was guilty of its violation.[10] But even if it be assumed that the law was violated, it does not seem that such an offense indicated moral turpitude—even in 1940. Many persons in this country actively supported the Spanish Loyalist Government. During the prelude to World War II many idealistic young men volunteered to help causes they believed right. It is commonly known that a number of Americans joined air squadrons and helped defend China and Great Britain prior to this country's entry into the war. There is no record that any of these volunteers were prosecuted under the Neutrality Act. Few Americans would have regarded their conduct as evidence of moral turpitude. In determining whether a person's character is good the nature of the offense which he has committed must be taken into account.[11]

In summary, these arrests are wholly insufficient to support a finding that Schware had bad moral character at the time he applied to take the bar examination.[12] They all occurred many years ago and in

---

[7] Petitioner testified that during a two-month period about 2,000 persons were arrested in connection with the strike. Generally, for criticism of these arrests and the conduct of the police during these and related strikes see S. Rept. No. 1150, 77th Cong., 2d Sess. 35, 131, 133–141.

[8] "The term 'criminal syndicalism' as used in this act is hereby defined as any doctrine or precept advocating, teaching or aiding and abetting the commission of crime, sabotage (which word is hereby defined as meaning willful and malicious physical damage or injury to physical property), or unlawful acts of force and violence or unlawful methods of terrorism as a means of accomplishing a change in industrial ownership or control, or effecting any political change." Cal. Stat. 1919, c. 188, § 1. See also *De Jonge* v. *Oregon,* 299 U.S. 353, where application of a similar statute was held unconstitutional.

[9] 40 Stat. 39, now 18 U. S. C. § 959(a).

[10] See Kiker, J. (dissenting), 60 N.M. 304, 321, 291 P. 2d 607, 618.

[11] For example, New Mexico makes conviction of a felony or a misdemeanor grounds for disbarment only if it involves moral turpitude. N.M. Stat. Ann., 1953, § 18–1–17 (1). Compare *In re Burch,* 73 Ohio App. 97, 54 N.E. 2d 803, where, in a disbarment proceeding, conviction for violation of a Federal statute for failing to register as an agent of the German Government in 1941 was held not to evidence moral turpitude.

[12] In 1941 Schware was arrested by police in Texas while driving a friend's car to the west coast. Apparently the police suspected the car was stolen. After a brief delay they became convinced that the car was rightfully in petitioner's possession and he was allowed to go on his way. This detention offers no proof of bad moral character and the State does not rely on it here.

no case was he ever tried or convicted for the offense for which he was arrested.

(3) *Membership in the Communist Party.*—Schware admitted that he was a member of the Communist Party from 1932 to 1940. Apparently the Supreme Court of New Mexico placed heavy emphasis on this past membership in denying his application.[13] It stated:

"We believe one who has knowingly given his loyalties to [the Communist Party] for six to seven years during a period of responsible adulthood is a person of questionable character." 60 N.M., at 319, 291 P. 2d, at 617.

The court assumed that in the 1930's when petitioner was a member of the Communist Party it was dominated by a foreign power and was dedicated to the violent overthrow of the Government and that every member was aware of this. It based this assumption primarily on a view of the nature and purposes of the Communist Party as of 1950 expressed in a concurring opinion in *American Communications Assn.* v. *Douds*, 339 U.S. 382, 422. However that view did not purport to be a factual finding in that case and obviously it cannot be used as a substitute for evidence in this case to show that petitioner participated in any illegal activity or did anything morally reprehensible as a member of that Party. During the period when Schware was a member, the Communist Party was a lawful political party with candidates on the ballot in most States.[14] There is nothing in the record that gives any indication that his association with that Party was anything more than a political faith in a political party. That faith may have been unorthodox. But as counsel for New Mexico said in his brief, "Mere unorthodoxy [in the field of political and social ideas] does not as a matter of fair and logical inference, negative 'good moral character.' "[15]

Schware joined the Communist Party when he was a young man during the midst of this country's greatest depression. Apparently many thousands of other Americans joined him in this step.[16] During the depression when millions were unemployed and our economic system was paralyzed many turned to the Communist Party out of desperation or hope. It proposed a radical solution to the grave economic crisis. Later the rise of fascism as a menace to democracy spurred others who feared this form of tyranny to align with the Communist Party.[17] After 1935, that party advocated a "Popular Front" of "all democratic parties against fascism." Its

---

[13] Petitioner argues that a State constitutionally cannot consider his membership in a lawful political party in determining whether he is qualified for admission to the bar. He contends that a denial based on such membership abridges the right of free political association guaranteed by the Fourteenth Amendment. Because of our disposition of this case, we find it unnecessary to pass on this contention.

[14] For example in 1936 its presidential nominee was on the ballot in 35 States, including New Mexico. Statistical Abstract of the United States (1937) 159.

[15] In *West Virginia State Board* v. *Barnette*, 319 U.S. 624, 642, this Court declared:
"If there is any fixed star in our constitutional constellation, it is that no official, high or petty, can prescribe what shall be orthodox in politics, nationalism, religion, or other matters of opinion or force citizens to confess by word or act their faith therein."

[16] According to figures of the Communist Party it had 14,000 members in 1932, 26,000 in 1934, 41,000 in 1936. W. Z. Foster, From Bryan to Stalin (1937), 303. It has been estimated that more than 700,000 persons in this country have been members of the Communist Party at one time or another between 1919 and 1951. Ernst and Loth, Report on The American Communist (1952), 14.

[17] For the numerous and varied reasons why individuals have joined the Communist Party, see Taylor, Grand Inquest (1955), 155–159 ; Ernst and Loth, Report on The American Communist (1952) ; Almond, The Appeals of Communism (1954) ; Crossman, The God That Failed (1949) ; Department of Defense, Know Your Communist Enemy : Who Are Communists and Why?, DOD PAM 4–6, Dec. 8, 1955. Many of these reasons are not indicative of bad moral character.

platform and slogans stressed full employment, racial equality and various other political and economic changes.[18]

During the depression Schware was led to believe that drastic changes needed to be made in the existing economic system. There is nothing in the record, however, which indicates that he ever engaged in any actions to overthrow the Government of the United States or of any State by force or violence, or that he even advocated such actions. Assuming that some members of the Communist Party during the period from 1932 to 1940 had illegal aims and engaged in illegal activities, it cannot automatically be inferred that all members shared their evil purposes or participated in their illegal conduct. As this Court declared in *Wieman* v. *Updegraff*, 344 U.S. 183, 191: "Indiscriminate classification of innocent with knowing activity must fall as an assertion of arbitrary power." Cf. *Joint Anti-Fascist Refugee Committee* v. *McGrath*, 341 U.S. 123, 136.[19] And finally, there is no suggestion that Schware was affiliated with the Communist Party after 1940—more than 15 years ago. We conclude that his past membership in the Communist Party does not justify an inference that he presently has bad moral character.

The State contends that even though the use of aliases, the arrests, and the membership in the Communist Party would not justify exclusion of petitioner from the New Mexico bar if each stood alone, when all three are combined his exclusion was not unwarranted. We cannot accept this contention. In the light of petitioner's forceful showing of good moral character, the evidence upon which the State relies—the arrests for offenses for which petitioner was neither tried nor convicted, the use of an assumed name many years ago, and membership in the Communist Party during the 1930's—cannot be said to raise substantial doubts about his present good moral character. There is no evidence in the record which rationally justifies a finding that Schware was morally unfit to practice law.[20]

On the record before us we hold that the State of New Mexico deprived petitioner of due process in denying him the opportunity to qualify for the practice of law. The judgment below is reversed and the case remanded for proceedings not inconsistent with this opinion.

It is so ordered.

MR. JUSTICE WHITTAKER took no part in the consideration or decision of this case.

MR. JUSTICE FRANKFURTER, whom MR. JUSTICE CLARK and MR. JUSTICE HARLAN join, concurring.

Certainly since the time of Edward I, through all the vicissitudes of seven centuries of Anglo-American history, the legal profession has played a role all its own. The bar has not enjoyed prerogatives; it has been entrusted with anxious responsibilities. One does not have to inhale the self-adulatory bombast of after-dinner speeches to affirm

---

[18] See Moore, The Communist Party of the U.S.A.; An Analysis of a Social Movement, 39 Am. Pol. Sci. Rev. 31, 32–33.

[19] And see *Schneiderman* v. *United States,* 320 U.S. 118, 136, where this Court stated: ". . . under our traditions beliefs are personal and not a matter of mere association, and that men in adhering to a political party or other organization notoriously do not subscribe unqualifiedly to all of its platforms or asserted principles."

[20] It must be borne in mind that if petitioner otherwise qualifies for the practice of law and is admitted to the bar, the State has ample means to discipline him for any future misconduct. N.M. Stat. Ann., 1953, §§ 18–1–15 to 18–1–18.

that all the interests of man that are comprised under the constitutional guarantees given to "life, liberty and property" are in the professional keeping of lawyers. It is a fair characterization of the lawyer's responsibility in our society that he stand "as a shield," to quote Devlin, J., in defense of right and to ward off wrong. From a profession charged with such responsibilities there must be exacted those qualities of truth-speaking, of a high sense of honor, of granite discretion, of the strictest observance of fiduciary responsibility, that have, throughout the centuries, been compendiously described as "moral character."

From the thirteenth century to this day, in England the profession itself has determined who should enter it. In the United States the courts exercise ultimate control. But while we have nothing comparable to the Inns of Court, with us too the profession itself, through appropriate committees, has long had a vital interest, as a sifting agency, in determining the fitness, and above all the moral fitness, of those who are certified to be entrusted with the fate of clients. With us too the requisite "moral character" has been the historic unquestioned prerequisite of fitness. Admission to practice in a State and before its courts necessarily belongs to that State. Of course, legislation laying down general conditions of an arbitrary or discriminatory character may, like other legislation, fall afoul of the Fourteenth Amendment. See *Cummings* v. *Missouri*, 4 Wall. 277. A very different question is presented when this Court is asked to review the exercise of judgment in refusing admission to the bar in an individual case, such as we have here.

It is beyond this Court's function to act as overseer of a particular result of the procedure established by a particular State for admission to its bar. No doubt satisfaction of the requirement of moral character involves an exercise of delicate judgment on the part of those who reach a conclusion, having heard and seen the applicant for admission, a judgment of which it may be said as it was of "many honest and sensible judgments" in a different context that it expresses "an intuition of experience which outruns analysis and sums up many unnamed and tangled impressions; impressions which may lie beneath consciousness without losing their worth." *Chicago, B. & Q. R. Co.* v. *Babcock*, 204 U.S. 585, 598. Especially in this realm it is not our business to substitute our judgment for the State's judgment—for it is the State in all the panoply of its powers that is under review when the action of its Supreme Court is under review.

Nor is the division of power between this Court and that of the States in such matters altered by the fact that the judgment here challenged involves the application of a conception like that of "moral character," which has shadowy rather than precise bounds. It cannot be that that conception—moral character—has now been found to be so indefinite, because necessarily implicating what are called subjective factors, that the States may no longer exact it from those who are to carry on "the public profession of the law." (See Elihu Root, in 2 A. B. A. J. 736.) To a wide and deep extent, the law depends upon the disciplined standards of the profession and belief in the integrity of the courts. We cannot fail to accord such confidence to the State process, and we must attribute to its courts the exercise of a fair and not a biased judgment in passing upon the applications of those seeking entry into the profession.

But judicial action, even in an individual case, may have been based on avowed considerations that are inadmissible in that they violate the requirements of due process. Refusal to allow a man to qualify himself for the profession on a wholly arbitrary standard or on a consideration that offends the dictates of reason offends the Due Process Clause. Such is the case here.

Living under hard circumstances, the petitioner, while still in his teens, encountered the confusions and dislocations of the great depression. By one of those chance occurrences that not infrequently determine the action of youth, petitioner joined the Young Communist League toward the end of his high-school days. That association led to membership in the Communist Party, which he retained until the Hitler-Stalin Pact began a disaffection that was completed by his break with the party in 1940. After 1940, the record of his life, including three years of honorable service in the army, establishes that these early associations, and the outlook they reflected, had been entirely left behind.* After his war service, three years as a small businessman, and one year at Western Michigan College, petitioner resolved on becoming a lawyer. And so in 1950, at the age of 36, he enrolled in the University of New Mexico Law School and made full disclosure of his early Communist career to its Dean. These are the facts that, taken together with the use of aliases and arrests without conviction or even prosecution, both in his early years, led the Supreme Court of New Mexico, in an original proceeding before it after adverse action by the Board of Bar Examiners, to deny petitioner's application to take the bar examination.

For me, the controlling element in determining whether such denial offended the Due Process Clause is the significance that the New Mexico Supreme Court accorded the early Communist affiliations. In its original opinion and in its opinion on rehearing, the court thus reiterated its legal position:

"We believe one who has knowingly given his loyalties to such a program and belief for six to seven years during a period of responsible adulthood is a person of questionable character." 60 N. M. 304, 319, 339, 291 P. 2d 607, 617, 630.

Since the New Mexico Supreme Court unequivocally held this to be a factor without which, on a fair reading of its opinion, it would not have denied the application, the conclusion that it drew from all the factors in necessary combination must fall if it drew an unwarranted legal conclusion from petitioner's early Communist affiliation. Not unnaturally the New Mexico Supreme Court evidently assumed that use of aliases in the pre-1940 period, several unprosecuted arrests, and what it deemed "his present attitude toward those matters," 60 N. M., at 339, 291 P. 2d, at 630 (as drawn from the printed record and not on the basis of having given the petitioner a hearing before the court) precluded denial of his application on these factors alone.

This brings me to the inference that the court drew from petitioner's early, pre-1940 affiliations. To hold, as the court did, that Communist affiliation for six to seven years up to 1940, fifteen years prior to the court's assessment of it, in and of itself made the petitioner "a per-

---

*The only bit of evidence that may be adduced to the contrary is a single phrase in a letter to his wife in 1944. To give it an unfavorable and disqualifying significance in the entire context of the letter is to draw so strained a meaning as to be inadmissibly unreasonable.

son of questionable character" is so dogmatic an inference as to be wholly unwarranted. History overwhelmingly establishes that many youths like the petitioner were drawn by the mirage of communism during the depression era, only to have their eyes later opened to reality. Such experiences no doubt may disclose a woolly mind or naive notions regarding the problems of society. But facts of history that we would be arbitrary in rejecting bar the presumption, let alone an irrebuttable presumption, that response to foolish, baseless hopes regarding the betterment of society made those who had entertained them but who later undoubtedly came to their senses and their sense of responsibility "questionable characters." Since the Supreme Court of New Mexico as a matter of law took a contrary view of such a situation in denying petitioner's application, it denied him due process of law.

I therefore concur in the judgment.

KONIGSBERG *v.* STATE BAR OF CALIFORNIA ET AL.

CERTIORARI TO THE SUPREME COURT OF CALIFORNIA

No. 5.   Argued January 14, 1957.—Decided May 6, 1957.

In 1954 the Committee of Bar Examiners of California refused to certify petitioner to practice law in that State, though he had satisfactorily passed the bar examination, on the grounds that he had failed to prove (1) that he was of good moral character, and (2) that he did not advocate forcible overthrow of the Government. He sought review by the State Supreme Court, contending that the Committee's action deprived him of rights secured by the Fourteenth Amendment. The State Supreme Court denied his petition without opinion. *Held:*

1. This Court has jurisdiction to review the case, and the constitutional issues are properly here. Pp. 254–258.

2. The evidence in the record does not rationally support the only two grounds upon which the Committee relied in rejecting petitioner's application, and therefore the State's refusal to admit him to the bar was a denial of due process and equal protection of the laws, in violation of the Fourteenth Amendment. Pp. 258–274.

(a) That petitioner was a member of the Communist Party in 1941, if true, does not support an inference that he did not have good moral character, absent any evidence that he ever engaged in or abetted or supported any unlawful or immoral activities. Pp. 266–268.

(b) An inference of bad moral character cannot rationally be drawn from editorials in which petitioner severely criticized, *inter alia,* this country's participation in the Korean War, the actions and policies of the leaders of the major political parties, the influence of "big business" in American life, racial discrimination, and this Courts decisions in *Dennis* v. *United States,* 341 U.S. 494, and other cases. Pp. 268–269.

(c) On the record in this case, inferences of bad moral character from petitioner's refusal to answer questions about his political affiliations and opinions are unwarranted. Pp. 269–271.

(d) There is no evidence in the record which rationally justifies a finding that petitioner failed to show that he did not advocate forcible overthrow of the Government. Pp. 271–274.

Reversed and remanded.

Edward Mosk argued the cause for petitioner. With him on the brief was *Samuel Rosenwein.*

Frank B. Belcher argued the cause for respondents. With him on the brief was *Ralph E. Lewis.*

Briefs of *amici curiae* in support of petitioner were filed by *A. L. Wirin* for the American Civil Liberties Union, Southern California Branch, and *Osmond K. Fraenkel* for the National Lawyers Guild.

MR. JUSTICE BLACK delivered the opinion of the Court.

The petitioner, Raphael Konigsberg, graduated from the Law School of the University of Southern California in 1953 and four months later satisfactorily passed the California bar examination. Nevertheless, the State Committee of Bar Examiners, after several hearings, refused to certify him to practice law on the grounds he had failed to prove (1) that he was of good moral character and (2) that he did not advocate overthrow of the Government of the United States or California by unconstitutional means.[1] As permitted by State law, Konigsberg asked the California Supreme Court to review the Committee's refusal to give him its certification. He contended that he had satisfactorily proved that he met all the requirements for admission to the bar, and that the Committee's action deprived him of rights secured by the Fourteenth Amendment to the United States Constitution. The State supreme court, without opinion, and with three of its seven justices dissenting, denied his petition for review. We granted certiorari because the constitutional questions presented were substantial. 351 U. S. 936.

I.

Before reaching the merits, we must first consider the State's contention that this Court does not have jurisdiction to review the case. The State argues (1) that petitioner did not present his constitutional claims to the California Supreme Court in the manner prescribed by that court's rules, and (2) that the State court's decision not to grant him relief can be attributed to his failure to conform to its procedural rules rather than to a rejection of his constitutional claims.

In considering actions of the Committee of Bar Examiners the California Supreme Court exercises original jurisdiction and is not restricted to the limited review made by an appellate court. For example, that court declared in *In re Lacey*, 11 Cal. 2d 699, at 701, 81 P. 2d 935, at 936:

"That this court has the inherent power and authority to admit an applicant to practice law in this State or to reinstate an applicant previously disbarred despite an unfavorable report upon such application by the Board of Bar Governors of the State Bar, we think is now well settled in this State. . . . The recommendation of the Board of Bar Governors is advisory only. . . . [T]he final determination in all these matters rests with this court, and its powers in that regard are plenary and its judgment conclusive." [2]

The California Supreme Court has a special rule, Rule 59(b), which governs review of actions of the Bar Examiners.[3] Rule 59(b) re-

---

[1] Under California procedure the State Supreme Court may admit a person to the bar upon certification by the Committee of Bar Examiners that he meets the necessary requirements. California Business and Professional Code, 1937, § 6064. Section 6060(c) requires that an applicant must have "good moral character" before he can be certified. Section 6064.1 provides that no person "who advocates the overthrow of the Government of the United States or of this State by force, violence, or other unconstitutional means, shall be certified to the Supreme Court for admission and a license to practice law."

[2] See also *Preston* v. *State Bar of California*, 28 Cal. 2d 643, 171 P. 2d 435; *Brydonjack* v. *State Bar of California*, 208 Cal. 439, 281 P. 1018.

[3] Rule 59(b) is set out at 36 Cal. 2d 43. Generally, the California Supreme Court divides its rules into two main parts: (1) "Rules on Appeal," which govern appeals in civil and criminal cases; and (2) "Rules on Original Proceedings in Reviewing Courts."

quires that a petition for review "shall specify the grounds relied on and shall be accompanied by petitioner's brief." Konigsberg complied with this rule. In his petition for review he specifically charged that the findings of the Committee were not supported by any lawful evidence.[4] The petition then went on to assert that the Committee's action, which was based on findings that the petition had previously alleged were not supported by evidence, was an attempt by the State of California in violation of the Fourteenth Amendment to deprive him "of liberty or property without due process of law" and to deny him "the equal protection of the laws."

Throughout the hearings before the Bar Examiners Konigsberg repeatedly objected to questions about his beliefs and associations asserting that such inquiries infringed rights guaranteed him by the First and Fourteenth Amendments. He urged that the Committee would abridge freedom of speech, press and assembly, violate due process, and deny equal protection of the laws if it denied his application because of his political opinions, writings, and affiliations. He asserted that he had affirmatively proved his good moral character and that there was no legal basis for finding that he was morally unfit to practice law. He insisted that in determining whether he was qualified the Committee had to comply with due process of law and cited as supporting his position *Wieman* v. *Updegraff*, 344 U.S. 183, and *Joint Anti-Fascist Committee* v. *McGrath*, 341 U.S. 123, where this Court condemned arbitrary findings as offensive to due process.[5] Since Konigsberg challenged the sufficiency of the evidence in his petition for review, it seems clear that the State supreme court examined the entire record of the hearings before the Bar Examiners [6] and must have been aware of the constitutional arguments made by Konigsberg during the hearings and the authorities relied on to support these arguments.

The State contends, however, that it was not enough for Konigsberg to raise his constitutional objections in his petition, in the manner prescribed by Rule 59(b), and at the hearings. It claims that under California practice the State supreme court will not consider a contention unless it is supported by an argument and citation of authorities in a brief submitted by the person seeking review. Because Konigsberg's brief did not repeat, precisely and in detail, the constitutional objections set forth in his petition,[7] the argument continues, this Court is compelled to hold that the State supreme court could have refused relief to petitioner on a narrow procedural ground. But the California cases cited by the State do not require such a conclusion. It is true that the State supreme court has insisted that on appeal in ordinary civil cases alleged errors should be pointed out clearly and concisely, with reasons why they are erroneous, and with

---

[4] The petition asserted:
"1. That the petitioner sustained his burden of proof of establishing his good moral character and all other requirements established by law in the State of California for applicants for admission to the bar.
"2. That the committee erred in asserting that the petitioner had failed to meet his burden of proof of establishing his good moral character.
"3. That no lawful evidence was received or exists supporting the denial of the application of the petitioner."

[5] He also referred to *Near* v. *Minnesota*, 283 U.S. 697, and *Frost & Frost Trucking Co.* v. *Railroad Commission of California*, 271 U.S. 583.

[6] Cf. *In re Admission to Practice Law*, 1 Cal. 2d 61, 33 P. 2d 829.

[7] The brief did refer to pages of the record where constitutional arguments were made and cases cited to support them.

reference to supporting authorities.[8] However this case was not reviewed under the rules of appeal which apply to the ordinary civil case but rather under a special rule applying to original proceedings. We are pointed to nothing which indicates that the State supreme court has adopted any rule in this type of case which requires that contentions raised in the petition for review must also be set out in the brief. The one case cited, *Johnson* v. *State Bar of California*, 4 Cal. 2d 744, 52 P. 2d 928, indicates the contrary. In challenging the recommendation of the Board of Governors of the State Bar that he be suspended from the practice of law, Johnson alleged, apparently in an offhand way, that the entire State Bar Act was "unconstitutional." He made no argument and cited no authority to support this bare, sweeping assertion. While the court said that this was an insufficient presentation of the issue it nevertheless went ahead to consider and reject Johnson's argument and to hold the Act constitutional.

Counsel for California concedes that the State courts in criminal cases often pass on issues ineptly argued in a defendant's brief or sometimes not raised there at all.[9] As counsel states, the reasons for relaxing this standard in criminal cases are obvious—such cases may involve forfeiture of the accused's property, liberty, or life. While this is not a criminal case, its consequences for Konigsberg take it out of the ordinary run of civil cases. The Committee's action prevents him from earning a living by practicing law. This deprivation has grave consequences for a man who has spent years of study and a great deal of money in preparing to be a lawyer.

In view of the grounds relied on in Konigsberg's petition for review, his repeated assertions throughout the hearings of various Federal constitutional rights, and practices of the California Supreme Court, we cannot conclude that that court, with three of its seven justices dissenting, intended to uphold petitioner's exclusion from the practice of law because his lawyer failed to elaborate in his brief the constitutional claims set forth in his petition for review and in the record of the hearings. Our conclusion is that the constitutional issues are before us and we must consider them.[10]

II.

We now turn to the merits. In passing on Konigsberg's application, the Committee of Bar Examiners conducted a series of hearings. At these hearings Konigsberg was questioned at great length about his political affiliations and beliefs. Practically all of these questions were directed at finding out whether he was or ever had been a member of the Communist Party. Konigsberg declined to respond to this line of questioning, insisting that it was an intrusion into areas protected by the Federal Constitution. He also objected on the ground that California law did not require him to divulge his political as-

---

[8] *People* v. *McLean*, 135 Cal. 306, 67 P. 770 ; *Title G. & T. Co.* v. *Fraternal Finance Co.*, 220 Cal. 362, 30 P. 2d 515.
[9] See, *e. g.*, *People* v. *Hadley*, 175 Cal. 118, 119, 165 P. 442, 443 ; *People* v. *Yaroslawsky*, 110 Cal. App. 175, 176, 293 P. 815, 816 ; *People* v. *Buck*, 72 Cal. App. 322, 237 P. 63.
[10] Cf. *Bryant* v. *Zimmerman*, 278 U.S. 63, 67 ; *Rogers* v. *Alabama*, 192 U.S. 226 ; *Bridge Proprietors* v. *Hoboken Co.*, 1 Wall. 116.

sociations or opinions in order to qualify for the bar and that questions about these matters were not relevant.[11]

The Committee of Bar Examiners rejected Konigsberg's application on the ground that the evidence in the record raised substantial doubts about his character and his loyalty which he had failed to dispel. At the conclusion of the hearings, the Committee sent a formal written notice—which later served as the basis for his petition to the California Supreme Court—stating that his application was denied because:

1. He failed to demonstrate that he was a person of good moral character and
2. He failed to show that he did not advocate the overthrow of the Government of the United States or of the State by force, violence or other unconstitutional means.

He was not denied admission to the California Bar simply because he refused to answer questions.[12]

In Konigsberg's petition for review to the State supreme court there is no suggestion that the Committee had excluded him merely for failing to respond to its inquiries. Nor did the Committee in its answer indicate that this was the basis for its action. After responding to Konigsberg's allegations, the Bar Committee set forth a defense of its action which in substance repeated the reasons it had given Konigsberg in the formal notice of denial for rejecting his application.[13]

There is nothing in the California statutes, the California decisions, or even in the Rules of the Bar Committee, which has been called to our attention, that suggests that failure to answer a Bar Examiner's inquiry is, *ipso facto*, a basis for excluding an applicant from the Bar, irrespective of how overwhelming is his showing of good character

---

[11] The record, when read as a whole, shows that Konigsberg took the position that he would answer all questions about his character or loyalty except those directed to his political views and beliefs and to questions about membership in the Communist Party. The record also shows that the Committee made no effort to pursue any other course of interrogation.

[12] Neither the Committee as a whole nor any of its members ever intimated that Konigsberg would be barred just because he refused to answer relevant inquiries or because he was obstructing the Committee. Some members informed him that they did not necessarily accept his position that they were not entitled to inquire into his political associations and opinions and said that his failure to answer would have some bearing on their determination of whether he was qualified. But they never suggested that his failure to answer their questions was, by itself, a sufficient independent ground for denial of his application.

[13] The answer, in pertinent part, read as follows :

"[P]etitioner was invited to appear at a hearing before the Southern Subcommittee of the Committee of Bar Examiners on the 25th day of September, 1953, at which time he was informed of evidence raising doubt as to his fitness to practice law, and was questioned concerning such evidence and other matters relevant to his qualifications to become a member of the State Bar of California.

. . .

"On or before the 8th day of February, 1954 the Southern Subcommittee of the Committee of Bar Examiners *considered all of the evidence which had been presented, and determined that petitioner had failed to show his good moral character* so that his application must be denied. On or about the 8th day of February, 1954 said Subcommittee informed the petitioner in writing of the denial of his application and the reasons therefor.

. . .

"On or prior to the 17th day of May, 1954 [the Full Committee] *considered all of the evidence which had been introduced and determined that petitioner had not sustained the burden of proof* that he was possessor of the good moral character required by California Business and Professions Code, Section 6060(c) and that he had not complied with Section 6064.1 of said Code, so that his application must be denied. Petitioner was notified of this decision and the reasons therefor by letter dated May 17, 1954.

"Petitioner has not complied with the requirements of California Business and Professions Code, Sections 6060(c) and 6064.1 and so is not entitled to be and should not be admitted to practice law in the State of California." (Emphasis supplied.)

As pointed out in note 1, *supra*, § 6064.1 excludes applicants who advocate the overthrow of the Government of California or the United States by "unconstitutional means," while § 6060(c) requires that an applicant must have good moral character.

or loyalty or how flimsy are the suspicions of the Bar Examiners. Serious questions of elemental fairness would be raised if the Committee had excluded Konigsberg simply because he failed to answer questions without first explicitly warning him that he could be barred for this reason alone, even though his moral character and loyalty were unimpeachable, and then giving him a chance to comply.[14] In our opinion, there is nothing in the record which indicates that the Committee, in a matter of such grave importance to Konigsberg, applied a brand new exclusionary rule to his application—all without telling him that it was doing so.[15]

If it were possible for us to say that the Board had barred Konigsberg solely because of his refusal to respond to its inquiries into his political associations and his opinions about matters of public interest, then we would be compelled to decide far-reaching and complex questions relating to freedom of speech, press and assembly. There is no justification for our straining to reach these difficult problems when the Board itself has not seen fit, at any time, to base its exclusion of Konigsberg on his failure to answer. If and when a State makes failure to answer a question an independent ground for exclusion from the Bar, then this Court, as the cases arise, will have to determine whether the exclusion is constitutionally permissible. We do not mean to intimate any view on that problem here nor do we mean to approve or disapprove Konigsberg's refusal to answer the particular questions asked him.

We now pass to the issue which we believe is presented in this case: Does the evidence in the record support any reasonable doubts about Konigsberg's good character or his loyalty to the Governments of State and Nation? In considering this issue, we must, of course, take into account the Committee's contention that Konigsberg's failure to respond to questions was evidence from which some inference of doubtful character and loyalty can be drawn.

Konigsberg claims that he established his good moral character by overwhelming evidence and carried the burden of proving that he does not advocate overthrow of the Government. He contends here, as he did in the California court, that there is no evidence in the record which rationally supports a finding of doubt about his character or loyalty. If this contention is correct, he has been denied the right to practice law although there was no basis for the finding that he failed to meet the qualifications which the State demands of a person seeking to become a lawyer. If this is true, California's refusal to admit him is a denial of due process and of equal protection of the laws because both are arbitrary and discriminatory.[16] After examination of the record,[17] we are compelled to agree with Konigsberg that the evidence does not rationally support the only two grounds upon which the Committee relied in rejecting his application for admission to the California Bar.

---

[14] Cf. *Cole* v. *Arkansas*, 333 U. S. 196, 201.

[15] In presenting its version of the questions before this Court, the Bar Committee did not suggest that the denial of Konigsberg's application could be upheld merely because he had failed to answer questions. Nor was such a position taken on oral argument. Counsel, instead, reiterated what the Bar Committee had contended throughout, namely, that Konigsberg was rejected because he failed to dispel substantial doubts raised by the evidence in the record about his character and loyalty.

[16] *Schware* v. *Board of Bar Examiners, ante*, p. 232; cf. *Wieman* v. *Updegraff*, 344 U. S. 183.

[17] Cf. *Local Union No. 10* v. *Graham*, 345 U. S. 192, 197.

A. *Good Moral Character.*—The term "good moral character" has long been used as a qualification for membership in the Bar and has served a useful purpose in this respect. However the term, by itself, is unusually ambiguous. It can be defined in an almost unlimited number of ways for any definition will necessarily reflect the attitudes, experiences, and prejudices of the definer.[18] Such a vague qualification, which is easily adapted to fit personal views and predilections, can be a dangerous instrument for arbitrary and discriminatory denial of the right to practice law.

While we do not have the benefit of a definition of "good moral character" by the California Supreme Court in this case, counsel for the State tells us that the definition of that term adopted in California "stresses elements of honesty, fairness and respect for the rights of others and for the laws of the State and Nation." The decisions of California courts cited here do not support so broad a definition as claimed by counsel. These cases instead appear to define "good moral character" in terms of an absence of proven conduct or acts which have been historically considered as manifestations of "moral turpitude." To illustrate, California has held that an applicant did not have good character who had been convicted of forgery and had practiced law without a license,[19] or who had obtained money by false representations and had committed fraud upon a court,[20] or who had submitted false affidavits to the Committee along with his application for admission.[21] It should be emphasized that neither the definition proposed by counsel nor those appearing in the California cases equates unorthodox political beliefs or membership in lawful political parties with bad moral character. Assuming for purposes of this case that counsel's broad definition of "good moral character" is the one adopted in California, the question is whether on the whole record a reasonable man could fairly find that there were substantial doubts about Konigsberg's "honesty, fairness and respect for the rights of others and for the laws of the State and Nation."

A person called on to prove his character is compelled to turn to the people who know him. Here, forty-two individuals who had known Konigsberg at different times during the past twenty years attested to his excellent character.[22] These testimonials came from persons in every walk of life. Included among them were a Catholic priest, a Jewish rabbi, lawyers, doctors, professors, businessmen and social workers. The following are typical of the statements made about Konigsberg:

> An instructor at the University of Southern California Law School:
> "He seems to hold the Constitution in high esteem and is a vigorous supporter of civil rights.. . . . He indicated to me an open-mindedness seemingly inconsistent with any calculated disregard of his duty as a loyal and conscientious citizen."

---

[18] See *Jordan* v. *De George,* 341 U. S. 223, 232 (dissenting opinion) ; *United States ex rel. Iorio* v. *Day,* 34 F. 2d 920, 921 ; Cahn, Authority and Responsibility, 51 Col. L. Rev. 838.
[19] *In re Garland,* 219 Cal. 661, 28 P. 2d 354.
[20] *In re Wells,* 174 Cal. 467, 163 P. 657.
[21] *Spears* v. *State Bar of California,* 211 Cal. 183, 294 P. 697.
[22] This testimony was in the form of written statements. Konigsberg offered to produce witnesses to testify in person but the Board preferred to have their statements in writing.

A rabbi:
   "I unreservedly recommend Mr. Konigsberg as a person who is morally and ethically qualified to serve as a member of [the bar]."
A lawyer:
   "I recommend Mr. Konigsberg unreservedly as a person of high moral principle and character. . . . He is a much more profound person than the average bar applicant and exhibits a social consciousness which, in my opinion, is unfortunately too rare among applicants."
A Catholic Monsignor:
   "I do not hesitate to recommend him to you. I am satisfied that he will measure up to the high requirements established for members of the legal profession."

Other witnesses testified to Konigsberg's belief in democracy and devotion to democratic ideas, his principled convictions, his honesty and integrity, his conscientiousness and competence in his work, his concern and affection for his wife and children and his loyalty to the country. These, of course, have traditionally been the kind of qualities that make up good moral character. The significance of the statements made by these witnesses about Konigsberg is enhanced by the fact that they had known him as an adult while he was employed in responsible professional positions. Even more significant, not a single person has testified that Konigsberg's moral character was bad or questionable in any way.

Konigsberg's background, which was also before the Committee, furnished strong proof that his life had always been honest and upright. Born in Austria in 1911, he was brought to this country when eight years old. After graduating from Ohio State University in 1931, he taught American history and literature for a time in a Cleveland high school. In 1934 he was given a scholarship to Ohio State University and there received his Master of Arts degree in Social Administration. He was then employed by the District of Columbia as a supervisor in its Department of Health. In 1936 he went to California where he worked as an executive for several social agencies and at one time served as District Supervisor for the California State Relief Administration. With our entry into the Second World War, he volunteered for the Army and was commissioned a second lieutenant. He was selected for training as an orientation officer in the Army's information and education program and in that capacity served in North Africa, Italy, France, and Germany. He was promoted to captain and while in Germany was made orientation officer for the entire Seventh Army. As an orientation officer one of his principal functions was to explain to soldiers the advantages of democracy as compared with totalitarianism. After his honorable discharge in 1946 he resumed his career in social work. In 1950, at the age of thirty-nine, Konigsberg entered the Law School of the University of Southern California and was graduated in 1953. There is no criticism in the record of his professional work, his military service, or his performance at the law school.

Despite Konigsberg's forceful showing of good moral character and the fact that there is no evidence that he has ever been convicted of any crime or has ever done anything base or depraved, the State nevertheless argues that substantial doubts were raised about his character by: (1) the testimony of an ex-Communist that Konigsberg had attended meetings of a Communist Party unit in 1941; (2) his criticism of certain public officials and their policies; and (3) his refusal to answer certain questions about his political associations and beliefs. When these items are analyzed, we believe that it cannot rationally be said that they support substantial doubts about Konigsberg's moral fitness to practice law.

(1) *Testimony of the Ex-Communist.*—The suspicion that Konigsberg was or had been a Communist was based chiefly on the testimony of a single ex-Communist that Konigsberg had attended meetings of a Communist Party unit in 1941. From the witness's testimony it appears that this unit was some kind of discussion group. On cross-examination she conceded that her sole basis for believing that Konigsberg was a member of that party was his attendance at these meetings. Her testimony concerned events that occurred many years before and her identification of Konigsberg was not very convincing.[23] She admitted that she had not known him personally and never had any contact with him except at these meetings in 1941. Konigsberg denied that he had ever seen her or known her. And in response to a Bar Examiner's question as to whether he was a Communist, in the philosophical sense, as distinguished from a member of the Communist Party, Konigsberg replied: "If you want a categorical answer to 'Are you a Communist?' the answer is no."[24]

Even if it be assumed that Konigsberg was a member of the Communist Party in 1941, the mere fact of membership would not support an inference that he did not have good moral character.[25]   There was no evidence that he ever engaged in or abetted any unlawful or immoral activities—or even that he knew of or supported any actions of this nature. It may be, although there is no evidence in the record before us to that effect, that some members of that party were involved in illegal or disloyal activities, but petitioner cannot be swept into this group solely on the basis of his alleged membership in that party. In 1941 the Communist Party was a recognized political party in the State of California. Citizens of that State were free to belong to that party if they wanted to do so. The State had not attempted to attach penalties of any kind to membership in the Communist Party. Its candidates' names were on the ballots California submitted to its voters. Those who accepted the State at its word and joined that party had a right to expect that the State would not penalize them, directly or indirectly, for doing so thereafter.[26]

(2) *Criticism of Certain Public Officials and Their Policies.*—In 1950 Konigsberg wrote a series of editorials for a local newspaper. In these editorials he severely criticized, among other things, this country's participation in the Korean War, the actions and policies of

---

[23] Counsel for the Bar Committee acknowledged this in oral argument. He stated: "Now Mrs. Bennett's testimony left much to be desired, that I concede. Her identification of this man is not all that you might wish."
[24] Konigsberg gave this answer during the first hearing held by the Committee. He was not represented by counsel at the time. At a subsequent hearing he stated that his earlier willingness to answer this question was inconsistent with his general position that the Committee had no right to inquire into his political associations and beliefs. He said he would not answer if the same question were then presented to him.
[25] *Schware* v. *Board of Bar Examiners, ante,* p. 232; *Wieman* v. *Updegraff,* 344 U.S. 183. See *Schneiderman* v. *United States,* 320 U.S. 118, 136.
[26] Cf. *Ex parte Garland,* 4 Wall. 333, where this Court struck down an attempt to exclude from the practice of law individuals who had taken up arms against the United States in the War Between the States. See also *Cummings* v. *Missouri,* 4 Wall. 277; Brown and Fassett, Loyalty Tests for Admission to the Bar, 20 U. of Chi. L. Rev. 480 (1953).

the leaders of the major political parties, the influence of "big business" in American life, racial discrimination, and this Court's dcisions in *Dennis* and other cases.[27]   When read in the light of the ordinary give-and-take of political controversy the editorials Konigsberg wrote are not unusually extreme and fairly interpreted only say that certain officials were performing their duties in a manner that, in the opinion of the writer, was injurious to the public.   We do not believe that an inference of bad moral character can rationally be drawn from these editorials.[28]   Because of the very nature of our democracy such expressions of political views must be permitted.   Citizens have a right under our constitutional system to criticize government officials and agencies.   Courts are not, and should not be, immune to such criticism.[29]   Government censorship can no more be reconciled with our national constitutional standard of freedom of speech and press when done in the guise of determining "moral character," than if it should be attempted directly.

(3) *Refusal to Answer Questions.*—During the prolonged hearings before the Committee of Bar Examiners, Konigsberg was not asked directly about his honesty, trustworthiness, or other traits which are generally thought of as related to good character.   Almost all of the Bar Examiners' questions concerned his political affiliations, editorials and beliefs.   Konigsberg repeatedly declined to answer such questions, explaining that his refusal was based on his understanding that under the First and Fourteenth Amendments to the United States Constitution a State could not inquire into a person's political opinions or associations and that he had a duty not to answer.   Essentially, this is the same stand he had taken several years before when called upon to answer similar questions before the Tenney Committee.

The State argues that Konigsberg's refusal to tell the Examiners whether he was a member of the Communist Party or whether he had associated with persons who were members of that party or groups which were allegedly Communist dominated tends to support an inference that he is a member of the Communist Party and therefore a person of bad moral character.   We find it unnecessary to decide if Konigsberg's constitutional objections to the Committee's questions were well founded.   Prior decisions by this Court indicate that his claim that the questions were improper was not frivolous [30] and we find nothing in the record which indicates that his position was not taken in good faith.   Obviously the State could not draw unfavorable infer-

---

[27] For example, petitioner wrote :
"When the Supreme Court of these benighted states can refuse to review the case of the Hollywood Ten thus making that high tribunal an integral part of the cold war machine directed against the American people—then the enemies of democracy have indeed won a major victory.   When the commanders of the last legal bulwark of our liberties sell out to the enemy, then the Fascists have gone far, much farther than most people think.   He who cannot see the dangerous damnable parallel to what happened in Germany is willfully blind."

[28] In 1948 Konigsberg appeared before the Un-American Activities Committee of the California senate, commonly known as the Tenney Committee.   At that time he sharply criticized this committee, accusing it of subverting the liberties of Americans, and declared : "I pledge my work to use every democratic means to defeat you."
The State points to petitioner's criticism of this committee as casting doubt on his moral character.   What is said in the text disposes of this contention.

[29] Cf. *Bridges* v. *California,* 314 U.S. 252.

[30] See, *e.g., United States* v. *Rumely,* 345 U.S. 41, 48 (concurring opinion) ; *Thomas* v. *Collins,* 323 U.S. 516, 531 ; *West Virginia Board of Education* v. *Barnette,* 319 U.S. 624, 642 : *Cantwell* v. *Connecticut,* 310 U.S. 296, 303–304 ; *De Jonge* v. *Oregon,* 299 U.S. 353, 365–366.   A dissenting opinion in *Jones* v. *Opelika,* 316 U.S. 584, 611, 618, which was adopted on rehearing, 319 U.S. 103, declared : "Freedom to think is absolute of its own nature ; the most tyrannical government is powerless to control the inward workings of the mind."

ences as to his truthfulness, candor or his moral character in general if his refusal to answer was based on a belief that the United States Constitution prohibited the type of inquiries which the Committee was making.[31] On the record before us, it is our judgment that the inferences of bad moral character which the Committee attempted to draw from Konigsberg's refusal to answer questions about his political affiliations and opinions are unwarranted.

B. *Advocating the Overthrow of Government by Force.*—The Committee also found that Konigsberg had failed to prove that he did not advocate the overthrow of the Government of the United States or California by force and violence. Konigsberg repeatedly testified under oath before the Committee that he did not believe in nor advocate the overthrow of any government in this country by any unconstitutional means. For example, in response to one question as to whether he advocated overthrowing the Government, he emphatically declared: "I answer specifically I do not, I never did or never will." No witness testified to the contrary. As a matter of fact, many of the witnesses gave testimony which was utterly inconsistent with the premmise that he was disloyal.[32] And Konigsberg told the Committee that he was ready at any time to take an oath to uphold the Constitution of the United States and the constitution of California.[33]

Even if it be assumed that Konigsberg belonged to the Communist Party in 1941, this does not provide a reasonable basis for a belief that he presently advocates overthrowing the Government by force.[34] The ex-Communist, who testified that Konigsberg attended meetings of a Communist unit in 1941, could not remember any statements by him or anyone else at those meetings advocating the violent overthrow of the Government. And certainly there is nothing in the newspaper editorials that Konigsberg wrote that tends to support a finding that he champions violent overthrow. Instead, the editorials expressed hostility to such a doctrine. For example, Konigsberg wrote:

"It is vehemently asserted that advocacy of force and violence is a danger to the American Government and that its proponents should be punished. With this I agree. Such advocacy is unAmerican and does undermine our democratic processes. Those who preach it must be punished."

Counsel for California offers the following editorial as evidence that Konigsberg advocates overthrow of the Government by force and violence:

"Loyalty to America, in my opinion, has always meant adherence to the basic principles of our Constitution and Declaration of Independence—not loyalty to any man or group of men. Loyalty to America means belief in and militant support of her noble ideals and the faith of her people. Loyalty to America today, therefore, must mean opposition to those who are betray-

---

[31] Cf. *Slochower* v. *Board of Education,* 350 U.S. 551, 557; *Sheiner* v. *Florida,* 82 So. 2d 657; *Ex parte Marshall,* 165 Miss. 523, 147 So. 791. And see *Ullmann* v. *United States,* 350 U.S. 422, 426–428; *Opinion of the Justices,* 332 Mass. 763, 767–768, 126 N.E. 2d 100, 102–103; *In re Holland,* 377 Iu. 346, 36 N.E. 2d 543; *Matter of Grae,* 282 N.Y. 428, 26 N.E. 2d 963.

[32] See, for example, text at pp. 264–265.

[33] California Business and Professions Code, 1937, § 6067, requires:
"Every person on his admission shall take an oath to support the Constitution of the United States and the Constitution of the State of California, and faithfully to discharge the duties of any attorney at law to the best of his knowledge and ability."

[34] Compare the discussion in the text at footnote 25, *supra,* and see cases cited in that footnote.

ing our country's traditions, who are squandering her manpower, her honor and her riches."

On its surface this editorial does not appear to be a call for armed revolution. To the contrary, it manifests a strongly held conviction for our constitutional system of government. However, the State attempts to draw an inference adverse to Konigsberg from his use of the word "militant" which it points out in one sense means "warlike." To us it seems far-fetched to say that exhortation to "militant" support of America's "noble ideals" demonstrates a willingness to overthrow our democratic institutions.[35]

We recognize the importance of leaving States free to select their own bars, but it is equally important that the State not exercise this power in an arbitrary or discriminatory manner nor in such way as to impinge on the freedom of political expression or association. A bar composed of lawyers of good character is a worthy objective but it is unnecessary to sacrifice vital freedoms in order to obtain that goal. It is also important both to society and the bar itself that lawyers be unintimidated—free to think, speak, and act as members of an Independent Bar.[36] In this case we are compelled to conclude that there is no evidence in the record which rationally justifies a finding that Konigsberg failed to establish his good moral character or failed to show that he did not advocate forceful overthrow of the Government. Without some authentic reliable evidence of unlawful or immoral actions reflecting adversely upon him, it is difficult to comprehend why the State Bar Committee rejected a man of Konigsberg's background and character as morally unfit to practice law. As we said before, the mere fact of Konigsberg's past membership in the Communist Party, if true, without anything more, is not an adequate basis for concluding that he is disloyal or a person of bad character. A lifetime of good citizenship is worth very little if it is so frail that it cannot withstand the suspicions which apparently were the basis for the Committee's action.

The judgment of the court below is reversed and the case remanded for further proceedings not inconsistent with this opinion.

Reversed and remanded.

Mr. JUSTICE WHITTAKER took no part in the consideration or decision of this case.

MR. JUSTICE FRANKFURTER, dissenting.

Insistence on establishment of the Court's jurisdiction is too often treated, with slighting intent, as a "technicality." In truth, due regard for the requirements of the conditions that alone give this Court power to review the judgment of the highest court of a State is a matter of deep importance to the working of our federalism. The admonition uttered a hundred years ago by Benjamin R. Curtis, one of the ablest Justices who ever sat on this Court, cannot be too often repeated: "Let it be remembered, also,—for just now we may

---

[35] Petitioner also contends that it violates due process to make advocacy of overthrow of the Government of the United States or of a State by force, violence, or other unconstitutional means an automatic ground for denying the right to practice law regardless of the reasons for or the nature of such advocacy. Because of our disposition of the case, it is unnecessary to consider this argument.

[36] See *Cammer* v. *United States*, 350 U.S. 399, 406–407. Compare Chafee, the Harvard Law School Record, Nov. 1, 1950, and Nov. 8, 1950.

be in some danger of forgetting it,—that questions of jurisdiction were questions of power as between the United States and the several States." 2 Memoir of Curtis 340–341. The importance of keeping within the limits of Federal jurisdiction was emphasized in the opinion of Mr. Justice Stone, for a unanimous Court, in *Healy* v. *Ratta*, 292 U.S. 263, 270: "Due regard for the rightful independence of State governments, which should actuate Federal courts, requires that they scrupulously confine their own jurisdiction to the precise limits which the statute ['the action of Congress in conformity to the judiciary sections of the Constitution'] has defined."

Prerequisites to the power of this Court to review a judgment of a State court are that a Federal claim was properly before the State court and that the State court based its decision on that claim. If a State court judgment is rested on a non-Federal ground, *i.e.*, on relevant State law, this Court is constitutionally barred from reviewing it. While a State may not, under the guise of regulating its local procedure, strangle a Federal claim so as to prevent it from coming before a State court, it has the undoubted power to prescribe appropriate procedure for bringing all questions for determination before its courts. Squeezing out of the record in this case all that can be squeezed, the most that the five pages of the Court's opinion dealing with this threshold question can be said to demonstrate is that there is doubt whether or not the claim under the United States Constitution was properly presented to the California Supreme Court, according to its requirements.

Before this Court can find that a State—and the judgment of the Supreme Court of California expresses "the power of the State as a whole," *Rippey* v. *Texas*, 193 U.S. 504, 509; *Skiriotes* v. *Florida*, 313 U.S. 69, 79—has violated the Constitution, it must be clear from the record that the State court has in fact passed on a Federal question. As a safeguard against intrusion upon State power, it has been our practice when a fair doubt is raised whether a State court has in fact adjudicated a properly presented Federal claim not to assume or presume that it has done so. The Court has not based its power to review on guess-work. It has remanded the case to the State court to enable it to make clear by appropriate certification that it has in fact rested its decision on rejection of a Federal claim and has not reached its decision on an adequate State ground. Strict adherence to the jurisdictional requirement was insisted upon in *Whitney* v. *California*, the well-known civil liberties case, by a Court that included Justices Holmes and Brandeis, as mindful as any in protecting the liberties guaranteed by the Due Process Clause. *Whitney* v. *California*, 269 U.S. 530, 538; 274 U.S. 357. See also *Honeyman* v. *Hanan*, 300 U.S. 14; cf. *Minnesota* v. *National Tea Co.*, 309 U.S. 551.

The procedure of making sure, through appropriate certification by a State court, that the Federal question was in fact adjudicated, is a safeguard against infringement of powers that belong to the States and at the same time duly protects this Court's jurisdiction to review denial of a Federal claim by a State court, if in fact it becomes clear that there was such a denial. This may involve some delay in the final determination of a Federal question. The price of such delay is small enough cost in the proper functioning of our Federal system in one of its important aspects. This Court has a special responsibility to be particularly mindful of the respective boundaries between State and Federal authority.

I would remand the case to the Supreme Court of California for its certification whether or not it did in fact pass on a claim properly before it under the Due Process Clause of the Fourteenth Amendment.

MR. JUSTICE HARLAN, whom MR. JUSTICE CLARK joins, dissenting.

I share the jurisdictional views of my brother FRANKFURTER. Even so, since the Court decides the case on the merits, I feel it appropriate to deal with it on that basis, since the case is important and my views about it differ widely from those of the Court. I feel impelled to do so, more particularly, for two reasons: (1) The record, in my opinion, reveals something quite different from that which the Court draws from it; (2) this case involves an area of Federal-State relations—the right of States to establish and administer standards for admission to their bars—into which this Court should be especially reluctant and slow to enter. Granting that this area of State action is not exempt from Federal constitutional limitations, see *Schware* v. *Board of Examiners*, *ante*, p. 232, decided today, I think that in doing what it does here the Court steps outside its proper role as the final arbiter of such limitations, and acts instead as if it were a super State court of appeals.

The following is what I believe to be an accurate statement of the issue to be decided. California makes it one of its requirements concerning admission to its Bar that no one be certified to the Supreme Court who advocates the overthrow of the Government of the United States or of California by force or violence. It also requires that an applicant be of good moral character. The applicant has the burden of proof in showing that these requirements have been met. Petitioner, under examination by the designated State agency, made unequivocal disavowal of advocacy of the overthrow of the Government by force or violence. With a view to testing the reliability of this disavowal, and the moral character of petitioner, the Bar Examiners questioned him about organizations to which he belonged, especially current or past membership in the Communist Party. Petitioner persisted in refusing to answer these questions despite the entirely reasoned and repeated efforts of members of the Committee to secure answers. His refusals were not based on a claim that the questions were irrelevant to an examination of his fitness under California law. The refusals were based solely on the ground that constitutionally the Committee was limited to asking him whether he advocated the overthrow of the Government by force and violence, and having asked that question, it could ask him no related question.

On the basis of the foregoing circumstances, the Supreme Court of California refused to overrule the finding of the Bar Committee that he had not qualified for admission to the Bar.

The question for this Court is whether in so refusing petitioner admission to the Bar, California through its supreme court deprived petitioner of liberty and property without due process.

At the outset there should be laid aside certain things which are *not* involved in this case. The Court does not find wanting in any respect California's requirements for admission to the Bar—that an applicant (a) must be "a person of good moral character,"[1] and (b) must not be an advocate of the overthrow of the Federal or State Government "by force, violence, or other unconstitutional means."[2] Nor does the Court question the State rule of practice placing the burden of proof on the applicant in both respects.[3] The Court does not hold that the First or Fourteenth Amendment entitled Konigsberg to refuse to answer any of the questions put to him by the Bar Committee,[4] or that any of such questions were irrelevant or improper. The fairness of the four hearings accorded Konigsberg is not attacked in any respect.[5] The Court's decision rests wholly on the alleged insufficiency of the record to support the Committee's conclusion that Konigsberg had failed to meet the burden of establishing that he was a person of good moral character and not an advocate of violent overthrow of the Government. The Court says:

"... we are compelled to conclude that there is no evidence in the record which rationally justifies a finding that Konigsberg failed to establish his good moral character or failed to show that he did not advocate forceful overthrow of the Government. Without some authentic reliable evidence of unlawful or immoral actions reflecting adversely upon him, it is difficult to comprehend why the State Bar Committee rejected a man of Konigsberg's background and character as morally unfit to practice law."

This makes the record important. Before turning to it, however, it will be well to revert to the true character of the issue before us. The Court decides the case as if the issue were whether the record contains evidence demonstrating as a factual matter that Konigsberg had a bad moral character. I do not think that is the issue. The question before us, it seems to me, is whether it violates the Fourteenth Amendment for a State bar committee to decline to certify for admission to the bar an applicant who obstructs a proper investigation into his qualifications by deliberately, and without constitutional justification, refusing to answer questions relevant to his fitness under valid standards, and who is therefore deemed by the State, under its law, to have failed to carry his burden of proof to establish that he is qualified.[6]

---

[1] Section 6060, Cal. Bus. and Prof. Code (1937). The Court does suggest that this standard is "unusually ambiguous" and that it "can be defined in an almost unlimited number of ways for any definition will necessarily reflect the attitudes, experiences, and prejudices of the definer." I respectfully suggest that maintenance of high professional standards requires that a State be allowed to give that term its broadest scope.

[2] *Id.*, § 6064.1.

[3] *Spears* v. *State Bar*, 211 Cal. 183, 294 P. 697; *In re Wells*, 174 Cal. 467, 163 P. 657. All but 2 of the 48 States have this practice requirement. See Farley, Admission of Attorneys from Other Jurisdictions, in Survey of the Legal Profession, Bar Examinations and Requirements for Admission to the Bar, 151, 159.

[4] The Court does say: "Prior decisions by this Court indicate that his [Konigsberg's] claim that the questions were improper was not frivolous and we find nothing in the record which indicates that his position was not taken in good faith." The record at least gives one pause as to the correctness of the latter conclusion. See pp. 292, 298–299, *infra.*

[5] The record contains the following exchange between Mr. O'Donnell, a member of the full State Bar Committee, and Mr. Mosk, the petitioner's counsel: "Mr. O'Donnell: There was some suggestion that the Subcommittee was not fair at the previous hearings. Mr. Mosk: May I interrupt immediately. There was no inference in any comments made by Mr. Konigsberg or myself. They were solely directed to the decision of the Subcommittee and our disagreement with the ultimate results. The Committee was absolutely fair and treated Mr. Konigsberg and myself with the utmost degree of fairness and impartiality. We have no complaints about the Subcommittee."

[6] Perhaps the most precise possible formulation of the question before us is whether a State may adopt a rule of administration to the effect that, in circumstances such as are disclosed here, an applicant who refuses to supply information relevant to his fitness may be deemed to have failed to sustain the burden of establishing his qualifications. I have no doubt that such a rule is constitutional. Cf. *Hammond Packing Co.* v. *Arkansas,* 212 U.S. 322, 349–351; Fed. Rules Civ. Proc., 37(b).

I do not understand the process of reasoning by which the Court attempts to make a separate issue out of petitioner's refusal to answer questions, and then, in effect, reads it out of the case because California has not constituted such refusal an "independent" ground for denying admission. What the State has done, and what the Bar Committee repeatedly warned the petitioner it would do,[7] is to say that the petitioner's refusal to answer questions made it impossible to proceed to an affirmative certification that he was qualified—*i.e.*, that his refusal placed him in a position where he must be deemed to have failed to sustain his burden of proof. Whether the State was justified in doing this under the Fourteenth Amendment is the sole issue before us, and that issue is not susceptible of the fragmentation to which the Court seeks to subject it. I am unable to follow the Court when it says, on the one hand, that on the issue of petitioner's qualifications "we must, of course, take into account the Committee's contention that Konigsberg's failure to respond to questions was evidence from which some inference of doubtful character and loyalty can be drawn,"[8] and, on the other hand, that the Committee was not entitled to treat petitioner's refusal to answer as a failure on his part to meet the burden of proof as to his qualifications.

Of course California has not laid down an abstract rule that refusal to answer any question under any circumstances *ipso facto* calls for denial of admission to the Bar. But just because the State has no such abstract statutory rule does not mean that a Bar Committee cannot in a particular case conclude that failure to answer particular questions so blocks the inquiry that it is unable to certify the applicant as qualified. In other words, what California has done here is to say that the Committee was justified in concluding that refusal to answer *these* questions under *these* circumstances means that the applicant has failed to meet the requirement that he set forth his qualifications affirmatively. Thus I think the Court is quite mistaken in stating that "the Board itself has not seen fit, at any time, to base its exclusion of Konigsberg on his failure to answer." I turn now to the State's brief and the record, which show, it seems to me, that failure to answer was the reason for exclusion.

I.

I had not supposed that it could be seriously contended that California's requirements for admission to the bar do not authorize the rejection of a candidate for constitutionally unprotected obstruction of a valid investigation into his qualifications under such requirements. Cf. *Schware* v. *Board of Examiners, supra* (concurring opinion). And it is unmistakable from the State's brief in this Court that Cali-

---

[7] See the italicized portions of pp. 286, 287, 288, 289, 290, 295, 299, 300, 301, 303, 306, 307, 308, 309, *infra*.

[8] Even on this basis I consider today's action of the Court unjustified upon this record. Whether considered as the adoption and application of a reasonable rule of administration, or as the drawing of an adverse inference of fact, the Committee's action in this case was proper. As the *Hammond* case shows, a State may treat a refusal to supply relevant information as establishing facts against the refusing party even though he does not have the burden of proof. *A fortiori*, a State need not give affirmative relief to one who refuses to supply evidence needed to support his own claim. Cf. Moore's Federal Rules and Official Forms (1956) 163–165, taking the position that judgment should be entered against a party to civil litigation who refuses to answer relevant questions, even where the refusal is justified by a valid privilege. In this case the Court takes the position, apparently, that refusal to supply relevant information cannot justify State action in a civil proceeding even where the refusal is unprivileged, and where the refusing party is a claimant upon whom rests the burden of proof.

fornia *does* claim the right, in the circumstances of this case, to reject the petitioner for his refusal to answer the questions that were relevant to his qualifications under the State's requirements for admission to the Bar.[9] The following appears on pp. 56–59 of that brief:

"Even where no serious doubt arises with respect to an applicant's qualifications, it is standard practice to inquire into many personal matters which a person is normally privileged to keep to himself. Thus, the standard application form required of all applicants asks the applicant for details of his past employment, education, whether he was ever suspended, reprimanded or censured as a member of any profession or organization, whether he has ever been arrested, whether he has ever been a party to a lawsuit and for the details of any incidents of a derogatory nature bearing on his fitness to practice law. If the answers to such questions embarrass an applicant, he is privileged to refuse to answer just as he is privileged to refuse to answer any question on the Bar examination. *However, in either case he runs the risk that failure to answer such questions will prevent his admission to the Bar.*

"Respondents submit that it is in no sense unreasonable or improper to *require an applicant to cooperate in supplying all requested information that is relevant to his statutory qualifications.* . . .

"(a) *Good Moral Character:*—Reasonable doubts that petitioner was a person of good moral character arose from many sources:

.   .   .   .   .

"(5) *Petitioner's refusal to answer questions in such broad areas of inquiry as to effectively prevent inquiry into broad areas of doubt.*

.   .   .   .   .

"Petitioner stated that he did not advocate the violent overthrow of the government. He thereafter took the position that any further inquiry by the Committee with respect to this requirement was foreclosed. This is equivalent to his appearing before the Committee and stating that he is a person of good moral character and the Committee must accept his statement and not inquire further. Even were there no adverse evidence in the record, respondents could properly refuse to certify an applicant as not having established his compliance with . . . Section 6064.1, where, as here, he took the position that his bare answer that he complied with the requirement foreclosed further inquiry. . . ."
(Italic, except as to subheading "(a)," added.)

I now turn to the record which also shows in unmistakable terms that the Committee's primary concern related to the petitioner's persistent blocking of its efforts to test the veracity of his statement that he did not advocate forcible overthrow of government.[10]

---

[9] There is no question here of drawing an unfavorable inference from a claim of the Fifth Amendment privilege. Petitioner repeatedly disclaimed any assertion of that privilege.
[10] In quoting from the record I have italicized some parts to give emphasis to this point.

II.

The story is best told in the language of the record itself. I shall interpolate only to the extent necessary to put what is quoted in context.

The first hearing before the Subcommittee took place on September 25, 1953. At that time Konigsberg appeared without counsel. After some preliminary inquiries as to Konigsberg's history, and questioning as to his connections with allegedly "subversive" organizations, the following ensued:

"Q. I assume that you are acquainted with the State statute that we now have on our books where among other things we are obliged to inquire into this type of a thing, and where we find that any people appear to have the views of endeavoring to change our government and so forth by force or violence, or in other words the popular conception of communism that we are expressly prohibited from certifying that person. You are familiar with the statute?

"A. Yes, I am.

"Q. Mr. Konigsberg, are you a Communist?

"A. Mr. Chairman, I would be very glad to answer that question.

"Q. If you will answer the question, I would be very happy to have it.

"A. I would be very glad to answer it if the circumstances were different. That is when I am faced with a question of this kind or when anyone else is faced with a question of this kind today what he is faced with is the fact that various nameless accusers or informers, or call them what you will, whom he has never had a chance to confront and cross-examine, he is put in a position of answering these statements or accusations or suspicions, and without any of the protections that ordinarily exist in such a situation, and I don't think that I can place myself in that position of having to answer something out in the void, some statement. I know these statements have been made obviously. I am not pretending to be shocked or naive about this. I can say very definitely I did not, I don't, I never would advocate the overthrow of the government by force or violence clearly and unequivocably, but to answer a specific question of that kind, whether I am a member of this party, that party or the Communist Party, that puts me in the position, whatever the truth is, whether I was or wasn't you would get a dozen informers who would say the opposite, and as indicated by an editorial just two or three days ago in the Daily News questioning seriously why the word of these informers, these turn-coats is accepted unquestionably as against the word of other responsible citizens. Therefore, Mr. Preston, I do not think that under these circumstances, first, yes, I understand that under the law as it is today you may ask me specifically do I advocate the overthrow of the government by force or violence. I answer specifically I do not, I never did or never will. When you get into the other question of specific views in a political party, it seems to me only the fact, the right of political opinion is protected under the First Amendment and is binding on the States. Certainly attorneys ought to be in the leadership of those who defend the right of diverse political views. I think the First Amendment is important. . . . I answer again on the specific question of force and violence, I did not, I don't and never would advocate the overthrow of the government by force or violence.

"Q. When answering it you don't intend to give us a specific, categorical responsive answer?

"A. As I said I would be very happy to if we met out in the hall. I would be glad to answer you, but you see under these circumstances, that is I am speaking now under oath and I am speaking for the record, I am speaking against in a sense whatever evidence that may be in the files—I shouldn't dignify it by calling it evidence; I should say whatever statements may be there from various informers. I have told you about my record both in the Army and in the community. I have been active politically, I admit it. I am proud of it. I would be happy to discuss it. This is the record that I think should be the basis for judgment, not the record of some hysterical characters that appeared before the Tenney Committee or any such group.

"Q. I am not asking anyone else. *I am trying to ask you because you are the one who is seeking admission, the privilege of practicing law in this State.* That is the reason I am asking you the question. I made the question very broad, and what I would like you to tell us, if you will answer the question; now of course as you well know and you have told me in your answer up to this point, you don't have to answer the question, of course you don't have to answer the question, but we feel that on a matter of this kind, this kind of information, we have a job to inquire about your character. The statute says character, it doesn't say reputation. *The only way I can find out and aid this Committee in finding out about your character is to ask you these questions, not what someone else thinks about you, your reputation. That is the reason I have asked the question.* Could you give us a categorical answer?

"A. I can only give you the answer I have given you, and I would be very happy to answer that under other circumstances."

At this point Konigsberg stated that his refusals to answer rested on rights of "free opinion, free speech," and that the legal profession should be the champion of "the right to diverse political opinion." He was then asked whether he had "ever knowingly participated in an organization which [he] then believed was sympathetic to the communistic cause," to which he replied that "I can't say I knowingly did that, because I don't think it would have made a great deal of difference to me if I had known one way or the other" if the organization's objectives were what he believed in, "say a better School Board or whatever the issue might have been." Then followed this:

"Q. Mr. Konigsberg, I assume that you know that your name has been listed in the public press by witnesses before the Congressional Un-American Activities Committee.

"A. Yes.

"Q. And have been identified by persons who said that you were a member of the Communist Party at the same time they were.

"A. I saw that report. That is the sort of thing I was referring to a moment ago when I referred to the various accusations."

Next there was discussion as to the attitude of the Association of American Universities with reference to teachers claiming the Fifth Amendment privilege against self-incrimination:

"Mr. Sterling: Let me try to clarify it as I understand it. This Association of Universities takes the position that complete candor on the part of the teacher with respect to his political beliefs, and in particular whether or not he subscribes to the beliefs of the Communist Party is a prerequisite to continuing in the teaching job. He doesn't have to disclose whether or not he is a Communist or is sympathetic to the Communist beliefs, but that if he doesn't answer those questions with complete candor he has lost his right to a position in the teaching community. Translating that into terms of an Association of lawyers such as our State Bar or any bar association, *you are seeking admission to the profession and that we as your prospective colleagues have a right to expect complete candor from you on this particular question, and that if you don't wish to be completely candid with us then we are justified in saying you don't belong in our profession.* That I think is the stand that the American Universities took.

"A. I understand that. I can only say what I said several times already. Under those circumstances the constitutional guarantee of free speech means nothing, if it doesn't mean you can keep your views to yourself, and certainly lawyers recognize that and should be among the first to defend that right. I think the legal profession, particularly the leaders of the legal profession, should be the first to insist on it. Put another way, of what meaning is any constitutional guarantee if it becomes a crime to invoke that guarantee?"

This answer was then elaborated by the petitioner at some length, after which the record continues as follows:

"Mr. Sterling: If you accept as true the premise that the Communist Party, as it is embodied in the present Soviet Union government, has for its objective the overthrow of not only the government of the United States but any other non-Communist government, and that that overthrow may be accomplished either from within by a bloodless revolution or if necessary by force, if you accept that premise then I think that your argument about constitutional rights of free speech and right to have your own political views and so on go by the board because then it seems to me that we are asking you no more than whether or not you belong to or believe in the principles of such an organization as Mafia, which is pretty generally, I think, regarded as one which has objectives that can be accomplished according to their tenets by what we regard as criminal acts. Now if I asked you whether or not you believed in the right to murder you would answer me no, I think, but as I say this whole business seems to be a turn on whether you accept the premise that the Communist Party—I am paraphrasing for the purpose of illustration—if you accept the premise that the Communist Party believes in murder and has that as its objective then *I don't think you have a right or justification to refuse to answer the question of whether you belong to the Communist Party or whether you believe in its principles, you see.*

"A. Well I can't argue with you.

"Mr. Sterling: Well, you can say that you think my premise is wrong. You can say the Communist Party as constituted does not believe in the overthrow, is not trying to and does not have as its objective the overthrow of the United States by one means or the other. Then I simply have to disagree with you because it seems to me that is their objective.

"A. Well, are you suggesting, Mr. Chairman, that since of course this is a critical period in our country's history that in the face of such threats as you are basing your premise on that we have to forego then the use of the constitutional privileges or the protection of the Constitution, is that what your proposal is? I would like to understand your argument.

"Mr. Sterling: No, as I say you don't feel there is any question of constitutional privilege when in a proceeding such as this where we are charged with determining the moral qualifications of an applicant in the profession, you don't feel that the constitutional privilege is hurt if I ask you if you believed in murder?

"A. No.

"Mr. Sterling: You will answer that unhesitatingly, 'No, I don't believe in murder.' So I say that most of us now accept as true the premise that the Communist Party as we know it and as embodied in the Russian Government, the present Soviet Union Government, does have as its objective world domination by the Communist Party. So we accept that premise. *Therefore it seems to us that we have the right to ask the question of applicants for admission to the Bar, because our statute as we pointed out says that you are not qualified if you do believe in overthrowing or advocate the overthrow of the United States by force or violence.*

"A. I am answering specifically in terms of that statute too that I do not. That is the question you are asking me specifically. I am answering I never did, I do not and I never would advocate the overthrow of the government by force or violence. I do believe like leaders like Jefferson people should have the right through discussion, ballot, the minority view becomes the majority view, that changes like that are sought through the ballot box but never through force and violence. That I do not believe. I think my whole experience has shown that. I don't know how more direct that can be, and the only reason as I said before that I don't specifically answer the question, 'Are you a member of this political party?' is because of the situation anyone is in who is faced with accusations as indicated by the newspaper report, accusations by people who I think are gradually being discredited by many sources, when you don't know who it is who is accusing you, you don't know on what evidence, anonymous faces, you never have a chance to cross examine them, how can anyone be put in that position? What can you fight except wind-mills and air in such a situation. The direct question, 'Do you believe in force and violence?' I answered that.

"Mr. Black: It still puzzles me a little to see why it is that you think you are prejudicing your own position by taking a position on that irrespective of whether there is any other evidence in the file or not.

"A. Because very practically this as you know has happened before. In the theory of today it is the words of these informers that is accepted above the words of anyone else.

"Mr. Black: How do you know?

"A. The newspaper report says so. Isn't that the report you were referring to where I was named before the Un-American Activities Committee?

"Mr. Preston: Yes, but that doesn't answer the question.

"Mr. Black: How do you assume this Committee accepts the hearsay report against your direct testimony?

"A. I am not assuming that. I didn't mean to give that implication. What I am saying is that where on one side we have these hearsay reports and nameless informers, and I don't need to go into a discussion of how willing they are to sell their evidence, if it is evidence, when there is the possibility of their word being placed against my word or anyone in my position, and because in view of the hysteria today their word is accepted. All it has to do is appear in the paper and you are discredited. Wasn't it two or three weeks ago in San Francisco a woman won an amount in a suit for being called a 'Red,' a teacher, when it is prima facie—libel, whatever the case was. Then it becomes not only a basic matter of principle on the First Amendment but a matter of protecting yourself in a legal situation, because this is an official body. I am not talking to a group of people like I would be talking to on the street.

"Mr. Sterling: *You are afraid if you answer the question as to membership in the Communist Party in the negative and say, 'No, I am not a member and I never have been,' assuming you made that answer, you are afraid that we could find half a dozen people who would say that you were and had been, and therefore if you were on a perjury trial and the jury believed them and not you, you committed perjury.*

"A. *I am saying no matter what answer I gave whether I was or wasn't, undoubtedly there would be several whom you could get to say the opposite, and as I said before——*

"Mr. Sterling: *Subjecting you to a perjury charge?*

"A. *Yes.* As I said before if you want to ask me outside in the hall I will tell you, but in view of these circumstances where you just have no right, you have no opportunity rather, to defend yourself against these people, I don't think that is fair play. I don't think that is justice. I don't think it is what the American democratic system teaches."

At this point Konigsberg testified that he did not recall knowing a Mrs. Bennett (formerly Mrs. Judson), the Subcommittee's next witness, the following occurring just before she testified:

"Mr. Preston: Is there any further statement you wish to make, Mr. Konigsberg?

"A. By the Witness: I can't think of anything I could add to what I said unless there is some specific point you want me to enlarge on.

"Mr. Preston: I assume, of course, if I ask you the question as to if you were ever a member of the Communist Party you would give me substantially the same answer.

"A. Yes, I think I would.

"Mr. Preston: You observed, I assumed, Mr. Konigsberg, I didn't ask you in the first instance if you were a member of the Communist Party. I asked you if you were a Communist. I recognize there is a philosophical Communist. I made my first question very broad to include that.

"A. I understood you to say a member of the Communist Party.

"Mr. Preston: Would your answer be any different?

"A. I thought you said a member of the Communist Party.

"Mr. Preston: I deliberately did not. The first question we discussed at length is, 'Are you a Communist?'

"A. I will say no, definitely no. The only thing I would describe myself very simply as one who has read a lot, studied a lot, because as a teacher of history and political education in the Army I believe strongly in the fundamental concepts of our democratic system.

"Mr. Preston: Your answer that you gave was directed to the question, 'Are you a member of the Communist Party?'

"A. Yes, and solely to that. If you want a categorical answer to 'Are you a Communist?' the answer is no.

"Mr. Preston: You gave us that.

"Mr. Sterling: That is your answer.

"A. By the Witness: No.

"Mr. Black: Would you care to state whether you have ever been a Communist?

"A. Do you mean by that as he is making the distinction philosophically or a member of the Communist Party?

"Mr. Black: I mean in the same sense you have just answered that you are not now a Communist.

"A. I would say my thinking has only been what I described a moment ago as being based on the elementary concepts of the American democracy, assuming that you mean do I think like a Communist; that is assuming we have some common understanding what you mean by that term.

"Mr. Sterling: We are not talking now about a membership in any party.

"A. Yes, philosophical views."

Mrs. Bennett, an ex-Communist Party member, then testified, in the presence of Konigsberg, that Konigsberg had attended in 1941 meetings of the party unit of which she had been a member.

The next hearing was on December 9, 1953, which was attended by Konigsberg's counsel, a Mr. Mosk. This hearing was devoted in part to the cross-examination of Mrs. Bennett by Mr. Mosk, the net of which was that Mrs. Bennett admitted that she recognized Konigsberg when she first came to the earlier hearing only after not seeing anyone else in the room with whom she was familiar. After general colloquy as to some of the petitioner's writings, the questioning returned to Konigsberg's refusal to answer questions concerning his alleged membership in the Communist Party, this time with particular reference as to how petitioner reconciled his First Amendment claim with his willingness to answer ideological questions, but not questions as to whether he had ever been a member of the Communist Party. The record continues:

"Mr. Preston: May I ask a question of counsel?

"Mr. Sterling: Yes.

"Mr. Preston: One of the things that was bothering me, Mr. Mosk, is the general answer we have received to the question concerning present and past Communist affiliation, and I recognize the objection that counsel raises under the First Amendment.

"Mr. Mosk: The witness.

"Mr. Preston: The witness has raised. *The thing that troubles me is we have an affirmative duty under the statute to certify as to this applicant's good moral character. We have endeavored to point out to him that the burden of showing that character is upon him. It appeared to me that he wasn't being quite forthright with us in not giving us an answer to those questions.* He stated in effect his reason, at least as I understood it, that he did not want to answer the questions because he might sometime be accused of or prosecuted for perjury. Now, that is the rationale as I remember it, and frankly I am left in a rather confused state. *As a member of this Committee I have to take an affirmative act of certification as to a good moral character.* I wonder if you could perhaps enlighten me or help clarify the situation so perhaps maybe I might understand it better.

"Mr. Black: May I interpose another question directed to the same point, and you can answer them at one and the same time. Just to make sure that I understand the witness' position, at the last hearing—Mr. Konigsberg's position—as I understood he was perfectly willing to deny categorically he is a Communist and took that position, am I right on that?

"The Witness: I said philosophical Communist.

"Mr. Black: It seems to me that question we wouldn't have a right to ask you under your argument, but that we would very definitely have a right to ask you whether you are now a member of the Communist Party as it is commonly understood. Now, am I right on that that you still take the position that there is no objection to your answering us categorically that you are not now a Communist, namely that you don't believe in the philosophical doctrines of communism, generally speaking, that is a matter of belief?

"The Witness: I think I understand your question.

"Mr. Black: But you do take the position that we do not have the right or you have no obligation to answer the question, 'Are you now a member of the Communist Party?' and that you refuse to answer. I am not trying to argue. I just want to be sure I understand your position. Am I correct in that?

"Mr. Mosk: Either way. The first question was addressed to me. . . . [W]e are endeavoring to address ourselves to that issue which we feel most pertinent that is 'What has Mr. Konigsberg done as an individual with relation to the people with whom he has dealt, the occupations and professions that he has followed, what has he done to show affirmitively that he is of good moral character and would be a good member of the Bar?'

"Now, as I understand Mr. Konigsberg's position it is his feeling that one of the matters of principle on which he has always stood is the principle that one may not inquire as to a person's belief, religious, political or otherwise, and that by answering such questions as they are being asked throughout the country in these days, and in all sorts of places and under all sorts of circumstances, as I understand Mr. Konigsberg's position that by answering such a question he is in effect giving way to and giving ground on the principle that one may not be asked these things, and that by his failure to answer he is neither affirming nor denying.

"Now as to the second question, which I think is most pertinent and certainly struck me at the moment when I read through the transcript for the first time, I was struck by exactly that same question, and I asked Mr. Konigsberg about it, and I think that perhaps he should answer this himself, but we did discuss this very matter, and I know that his position is now that if you were to ask the same question today he feels that it is a question he should not have answered, and that by way of principle in coming unprepared he did not think through the principle to that extent. I think I am answering correctly.

"The Witness: That is exactly what I told counsel. As you are aware I came in without counsel, without any preparation, without knowing exactly what I might be asked. I did have an indication since I had informed the Committee, I appeared before the Tenney Committee, that I might be asked about that. I came prepared with nothing. In the heat or in the tension of a meeting of this kind, as you are aware, very often one will say things that one regrets later or would have said later. If I were asked that today I think my answer would be the same as to the other question as to whether I am or am not a member of the Communist Party, or whether I ever was.

"Mr. Black: I might say without expressing my own view on the thing that I think it must be obvious to you at least under popular conception there is a distinction between what a man believes in a doctrinaire's sense, which I think everybody agrees who at least tries to follow American principles is sacred ground as to his individual concepts. The belief of the doctrines on the one side, and at least in popular view, affiliation with a party that has its policies dominated by the Soviet Union is quite a different conception, and that the argument at least is that inquiry goes to the very essence of a man's loyalty to the country and has nothing to do with his individual beliefs in the matter of religion or political philosophy or a code of ethics, and that is the distinction that we are trying to get at here.

"The Witness: I think you are quite right, and the position you take is quite correct, and I confess that I was in error at the time again due to the tension of the moment, and as I was going to say I don't think Mr. Freston's recollection is correct. I did not say that I was giving the kind of answer, was giving or refusing to answer because I was afraid of a perjury charge, as I recall. That is not the basis of refusal or the type of answer I have given. The reason that perjury discussion came up, as I recall now—I

haven't been thinking about it—was in connection with the nature
of the hearing where a person does not have the opportunity to
cross examine and confront witnesses or see documents or things
of that nature, and it so happens in the case of Owen Lattimore,
who faced a perjury charge, even though he denied a half dozen
ways any association with subversive elements—I am recalling
from memory—it had to do with whether he expressed a certain
opinion. How is a man to remember what opinions he expressed.
His appeal is pending at the moment for his conviction of perjury.
It is only with reference to that situation that I mentioned or commented upon the element of perjury, because that has nothing
to do with the basis for my giving the kind of answer I am giving
to the question as to my political affiliation, none whatsoever.
You correct me on the record if I am wrong. That is my recollection of that discussion. At least I would like to say for the
record that has nothing to do with the type of answer I have
given.

"Mr. Wright: I would like to ask a question that perhaps in
some stage of this proceeding you might enlighten at least this
member of the Committee on, *whether you consider inquiry into
present membership in the Communist Party as at all relevant in
the inquiries of this Committee as to moral character? In other
words, is it a relevant factor? Does it have any bearing? Is it
a proper scope of inquiry?*

"Mr. Mosk: I think you have to draw this distinction. It
may be under some circumstances the Committee would feel that
it would be a type of information that it would like to have to
reach its conclusion, and to that extent perhaps it may be considered relevant, but many relevant matters are not inquired into
in legal proceedings because for other reasons those matters are
not competent testimony. And it is the position of Mr. Konigsberg here that inquiries into the realm of his political, religious or
other beliefs are matters that are protected under the First
Amendment to the Constitution, and therefore while it may be
information which the Committee would feel it would like to have
it is a field in which the Committee may not inquire by Mr. Konigsberg's position, and I think therefore perhaps I am answering
your position yes and no, but I think I make my point clear as to
what position Mr. Konigsberg takes.

"Mr. Wright: *Having felt that we would like the information
and being denied, now I won't argue with you that being denied
that we have no way of compelling it, but are we therefore faced
with going forward?*

"Mr. Mosk: I think that also is a fair question, and that is why
we are approaching the hearing in the manner in which we
do. . . .

". . . I could, I know, bring responsible social workers, other
lawyers, persons at the universities with whom he has dealt, all of
whom are prepared to come and say that they have known him
in these various capacities, and that on the basis of the things
that he has done himself, not what someone else has done, but
what he, Raphael Konigsberg, has done that he is of good moral
character to become a member of the legal profession, and these

are things that as I say we will submit affirmatively, and it seems to me that this is the affirmative answer to what I can well understand the Committee feels is a void which Mr. Konigsberg, for reasons of principles he does not feel he wants to fill, but I think that even there one must always have respect for people who at recognizing the danger to him in standing on his principle is still prepared to do that in order to carry out things that he believes in so firmly.

"Mr. Wright: I commend his moral principle, let me say, but perhaps have a little doubt for his judgment.

"Mr. Mosk: If I may comment on that also I think that certainly—

"Mr. Wright: *He is making it extremely hard for the Committee.*"

The third, and last, hearing before the Subcommittee occurred on January 27, 1954. At this time the letters from character witnesses were presented, and there ensued general colloquy as to the scope of a memorandum to be filed by Mr. Mosk. The record shows the following as to the Subcommittee's concern over Konigsberg's refusal to answer:

"Mr. Wright: Thank you, Mr. Mosk. I was wondering *whether or not you in the course of your memorandum you had addressed yourself at all to the problem of the disinclination of the applicant to respond to questions proposed by the Committee.*

"Mr. Mosk: I have addressed myself to that. The memorandum, however, is not lengthy and if you wish I would like to say just a brief word in addition then on that point.

"Mr. Wright: *That is one thing that frankly bothers me that we discussed in our previous hearing.*

"Mr. Mosk: I can understand why that is a matter that does bother you. I think that I indicated at the previous hearing by analogy one of the answers that I feel is pertinent to this. I indicated and I feel that in every judicial proceeding and every legal proceeding there are many matters that the tribunal would like well to know to assist it in reaching its conclusion.

.   .   .   .   .

"Now, it is implicit in what I have said up until now that matters of the political, economic and social nature, matters of the mind, cannot become the standards upon which the decision as to whether an applicant is of good moral character can be predicated. There are basic principles as to whether the Committee or any other tribunal may inquire into matters of the mind and thinking.

"Now, Mr. Konigsberg is obviously, as indicated by many of these letters, and has always been a man of great principle, and I feel that the Committee, since it is our position that it may not inquire into these fields must not make its decision based on Mr. Konigsberg's principal refusal to answer questions in a field in which the Committee may not inquire. And this fundamentally is our answer that these are matters which can have no bearing on his moral fitness to practice law, and since they cannot I think it then becomes even a greater indication of the extreme principles upon which this man stands, and an even greater indication that as a lawyer he will be a credit to the legal profession."

The Subcommittee having reported unfavorably, a hearing to review its recommendation was held before the full State Bar Committee on March 13, 1954, at which Konigsberg read a prepared statement, following which the record shows the following:

"Mr. Fuller: What organizations do you presently belong to?

"Mr. Mosk: To which I object on the grounds that this is a violation of the witness's rights under the First Amendment of the Constitution.

"Mr. Fuller: You mean to say that he shouldn't tell us whether he belongs to the Elks or the Masons or things of that sort?

"Mr. Mosk: That would be my position.

"Mr. Fuller: We can't determine any organization he belongs to? He doesn't have to answer at all?

"Mr. Mosk: That would be my position that his beliefs and associations are not within the scope of this hearing.

"Mr. Fuller: It does not necessarily relate to beliefs. We all know many organizations are not based on beliefs. I think we are entitled to know who he associates with.

"Mr. Konigsberg: I respectfully say that you are not entitled to know my associations and any person may refuse to answer on the basis of the rights of a citizen under the First Amendment which I have previously referred to in my testimony.

．　　　．　　　．　　　．　　　．

"Mr. Konigsberg: May I ask this question, Mr. Chairman: Is it the Committee's position (and I would sincerely like to know) that it has the power to ask such a question and that questions relating to opinions do have a bearing on the applicant's moral character?

"Mr. Fuller: I don't want to put it on that basis. It is my position, not necessarily the entire Committee's position, that *we have a rather general scope of inquiry to determine whether an applicant tells the truth, for one thing. I think that is a factor in determining whether or not he is morally qualified. He may state that he is not now a Communist, if he has been a Communist in the past, and if we believe he is telling the truth, that will have a bearing on our determination. I think we have the right to test the veracity of the applicant to the extent that if he denies that, I am influenced in the final conclusion I will come to, that I haven't determined yet. I do think that the applicant who wishes to afford us the facilities for determining his moral character to the utmost, should permit us to test his veracity.*

"Mr. Konigsberg: Mr. Chairman, in all sincerity I have attempted to show in my initial analysis that under Section 6064.1, that I think sets the limit to any inquiry that any body of Examiners has. Once you ask 'Do you now?,' does that person advocate the overthrow by force, violence, or other unconstitutional means, and he answers, as I have answered, that he does not, you cannot ask any questions about his opinions. You are not empowered to ask any questions. There is some question as I pointed out in my statement whether this is constitutional even to allow it to this extent.

"Mr. Fuller: Do I understand that it is your position, and I think I understand your position, that we should not go ahead and find out whatever information we can obtain in order to make the best decision?

"Mr. Konigsberg: I make this point which I did not make before that I don't think constitutional such action, to draw inferences of the truth or falsity of any statements based on the position (whether of the First or any other Amendment) which the applicant takes. For the Bar to maintain the position, as the Chairman is doing, that it does have the right to ask about my opinions (at least as he is doing this afternoon), as I pointed out these opinions and beliefs which have been expressed coincide with those of prominent leaders of the Bar, which they are expressing today. . . . I am wondering if that is the position the Committee wishes to take.

"Mr. Fuller: There is no position of the Committee. I am only one member. We are conducting an impartial examination.

*   *   *   *   *

"A lady by the name of Bennett testified here. You heard her testimony. Is there any part of that testimony you wish to deny?

"Mr. Konigsberg: Well, again, Mr. Chairman, that is the same question. That is a question relating to opinions, beliefs, political affiliations.

"Mr. Fuller: It has nothing to do with beliefs.

"Mr. Konigsberg: It certainly is related to political organizations, political activity, however you choose to describe it.

"Mr. Fuller: Do you want to read it again?

"Mr. Konigsberg: I recall it.

"Mr. Fuller: Do you wish to deny any part?

"Mr. Konigsberg: I wish to say that any questions relating to such political affiliation, which the testimony dealt with . . .

"Mr. Fuller: You refuse to affirm or deny her testimony?

"Mr. Konigsberg: The Committee is not empowered to ask with regard to political affiliations or that type . . .

"Mr. Fuller: I am calling your attention to the fact part of it is not connected with political beliefs or associations.

"Mr. Konigsberg: Which part?

"Mr. Fuller: You are free to read it.

"Mr. Konigsberg: If you wish, I shall be glad to.

"Mr. Fuller: If you want you may either affirm or deny anything if you need to do that. We want to afford you the privilege. (Witness read the testimony referred to)

"Mr. Konigsberg: Mr. Chairman, I think I would recall all the questions relating to me. She answered a number of questions not relating to me. All relating to me are based on a matter of political affiliation or opinion and political association and I think that is amply covered under the protection of the First Amendment as I referred to a moment ago. The Committee's rights to inquire about this matter are limited to one, the present personal advocacy of the overthrow by force or violence or other means as set forth in 6064.1.

*   *   *   *   *

"Mr. O'Donnell: Are you a member of the Communist Party now?

"Mr. Konigsberg: How does that differ from the questions asked before?

"Mr. O'Donnell: I would just like you to answer it.

"Mr. Konigsberg: The answer is the same I would give. The Committee is not empowered to inquire any more than they may inquire whether I am an Elk, a Freemason, a Democrat or a Republican. It might become incriminating to be a member of the Democratic party today, like saying all Democrats are traitors.

"Mr. O'Donnell: Have you ever been a member?

"Mr. Konigsberg: I would give the same answer.

"Mr. O'Donnell: You refuse to say whether you now are?

"Mr. Konigsberg: I refuse on the ground that the Committee is not empowered to question anyone about political opinions or affiliations, whether past affiliations or present ones. I say this can have no bearing on moral qualifications to practice law, unless the Committee is prepared, as I said in my statement, to take the position that it is now a crime in California to have opinions different than general popular opinions or conforming opinions.

"Mr. Fuller: *Of course, the Committee takes the position it is doing so affirmatively, when it goes before the Supreme Court and states you have the proper moral character and we feel we have the right to inquire very deeply into that because it is an affirmative obligation on our part.*

"Mr. Konigsberg: I think, Mr. Chairman, on that point the court has said—

"Mr. Fuller: We may be wrong. The Supreme Court may tell us otherwise but that is the way it appears at the moment."

Finally, the Committee put to Konigsberg these questions:

"Mr. Whitmore: *It is not your contention, is it, Mr. Konigsberg, that the only basis which the Committee may rely on in determining whether or not it can certify you under the provisions of 6064.1 is by asking you the questions and getting a yes or no answer. It is not your position that that is the extent of the right of this body in making its determination under 6064.1?*

"Mr. Konigsberg: *In essence, that is it.* My interpretation of that code section is simply that it sets the limit as to whatever questions relating to opinion—because that is obviously a political issue—there may be asked by the Bar Examiners. It sets the limit as I interpret it. I may be wrong, as I think the Subcommittee is wrong; because of the history of this act as I have related it the Committee can only ask 'Do you now personally advocate the overthrow of the Government of the United States or of this State by force or violence or other unconstitutional means' and if I say 'No,' 'Yes' or whatever it may be, that is as far as you can go; that is without raising the question on this point (which I don't think is pertinent) as to whether that is even constitutional under the First Amendment.

"Mr. Whitmore: You are saying that the Committee is precluded under Section 6064.1 from considering acts or omissions of yours in the past with respect to that problem?

"Mr. Konigsberg: Yes, I think so. I am saying they can only ask do I advocate the overthrow by force or violence or other means.

"Mr. Whitmore: *You are contending that we are bound by your answer of yes or no which you give.*

"Mr. Konigsberg: You can decide for yourselves whether I am telling the truth. You can use any means of determining the truth. You don't have to accept any individual's yes or no answer as the truth. I think that is understood.

"Mr. Maxfield: *Doesn't your answer right there defeat the only purpose if we can cross examine as to the truth or falseness of that statement? Why can't—*

"Mr. Konigsberg: *I didn't say you could cross examine me as to the truthfulness.* The question as I understand it was whether the Committee couldn't consider other things, records, past acts.

"Mr. Whitmore: Acts or omissions.

"Mr. Konigsberg: Anything in my record to evaluate whether I am telling the truth, certainly.

"Mr. Maxfield: *The general principles of cross examination testing the veracity of a statement, those you know under the rules of evidence are pretty broad. Do you deny us the right to ask these questions for that purpose?*

"Mr. Konigsberg: Again under the rules of evidence there might be many items of hearsay, fact or whatever it might be, which the court would like to know but the court prevents the prosecution or the other side from introducing because of a deep-seated public policy or other evidentiary rule or the First Amendment. The rule of search and seizure is something else of that nature. The information might be pertinent but the courts says that the results of such act, as established over the years, may not be asked or introduced.

"It is my contention as I tried to make clear—(it might be unconstitutional, I am not questioning that now)—it may only go as far as this law permits you to go. The history of that act shows that the Legislature tried to do other things but failed to because it failed of passage. And a person can be asked (such people as myself) 'Do you?' than [*sic*] the Committee must determine and evaluate as to the truth by what is in the individual's record.

"Mr. Maxfield: *We are not entitled to an evaluation of that truth or in an effort to evaluate it to cross examine you with respect to present or past associations?*

"Mr. Konigsberg: *That is right. That is my interpretation.*"

On February 8, 1954, the State Bar Committee refused to certify Konigsberg for admission, and the California Supreme Court denied review on April 20, 1955.

III.

So ends the story. Whatever might be the conclusions to be drawn were we sitting as State judges, I am unable to understand how on this record it can be said that California violated the Federal Constitution by refusing to admit petitioner to the bar.

The members of the Committee before whom the petitioner appeared were under a statutory duty to inquire into his qualifications for admission. Among the matters into which they were obligated to inquire were moral character and the applicant's advocacy of forcible overthrow of the Government. Petitioner stated readily enough that he did not advocate overthrow of government by force, violence, or other unconstitutional means. But once that basic question was answered he took the position that the Committee's authority was exhausted; that it had no power to ask him about the facts underlying his conclusory denial or to test his response by cross-examination. The Court holds that the State's conclusion—that an applicant who so obstructs the Committee has not met his burden of proof in establishing his qualifications of good moral character and nonadvocacy of forcible overthrow—violates the Fourteenth Amendment.

I think this position is untenable. There is no conceivable reason why the Committee should not attempt by cross-examination to ascertain whether the facts squared with petitioner's bare assertion that he was qualified for admission. It can scarcely be contended that the questions were irrelevant to the matter under inquiry namely, whether petitioner advocated forcible overthrow of the Government. At least it seems apparent to me that Communist Party membership is relevant to the question of forcible overthrow. In fact petitioner himself admitted that the questions were relevant, relying entirely on his First Amendment privilege.[11] Yet the Court assumes, for the purposes of this case, that the questions did not invade an area privileged under the First Amendment. In other words, we have here a refusal to answer relevant and unprivileged questions.

We are not dealing with a case where the State excludes an applicant from the bar because of bare membership, past or present, in the Communist Party. The *Schware* case attests that that is a wholly different question. Nor are we dealing with a case where an applicant is denied admission because of his political views. We have here a case where a State bar committee was prevented by an applicant from discharging its statutory responsibilities in further investigating the applicant's qualifications. The petitioner's refusal to answer questions in order to dispel doubts conscientiously entertained by the Committee as to his qualifications under a valid statutory test can, it seems to me, derive no support from the Fourteenth Amendment.

The principle here involved is so self-evident that I should have thought it would be accepted without discussion. Can it really be said that a bar-admissions committee could not reject an applicant because he refused to reveal his past addresses, or the names of his former employers, or his criminal record? An applicant might state with the utmost sincerity that he believed that such information was none of the committee's business; yet it must be clear that his application could be rejected. And in such a case the committee would not have to point to "evidence" establishing either that the applicant had bad moral character or that he was asserting the constitutional privilege in bad faith. For the applicant is the moving party, and his failure to go forward is itself sufficient to support denial of admission.

For me it would at least be more understandable if the Court were to hold that the Committee's questions called for matter privileged under the First and Fourteenth Amendments. But the Court carefully avoids doing so. It seems to hold that the question of privilege is irrelevant, as long as the applicant is "in good faith" and as long as

---

[11] Cf. *Garner* v. *Board of Public Works,* 341 U.S. 716, 720; and see pp. 299 300, 301, *supra.*

there is other material in the record which the Court interprets as affirmatively attesting to his good moral character. I cannot agree. It is not only that we, on the basis of a bare printed record and with no opportunity to hear and observe the applicant, are in no such position as the State bar committee was to determine whether *in fact* the applicant was sincere and has a good moral character. Even were we not so disadvantaged, to make such a determination is not our function in reviewing State judgments under the Constitution. Moreover, resolution of this factual question is wholly irrelevant to the case before us, since it seems to me altogether beyond question that a State may refuse admission to its Bar to an applicant, no matter how sincere, who refuses to answer questions which are reasonably relevant to his qualifications and which do not invade a constitutionally privileged area. The opinion of the Court does not really question this; it solves the problem by denying that it exists. But what the Court has really done, I think, is simply to impose on California its own notions of public policy and judgment. For me, today's decision represents an unacceptable intrusion into a matter of State concern.

For these reasons I dissent.

KONIGSBERG *v.* STATE BAR OF CALIFORNIA ET AL.

CERTIORARI TO THE SUPREME COURT OF CALIFORNIA.

No. 28.   Argued December 14, 1960.—Decided April 24, 1961.

Under California law, the State supreme court may admit to the practice of law any applicant whose qualifications have been certified to it by the California Committee of Bar Examiners. In hearings by that Committee on his application for admission to the Bar, petitioner refused to answer any questions pertaining to his membership in the Communist Party, not on the ground of possible self-incrimination, but on the ground that such inquiries were beyond the purview of the Committee's authority and infringed rights of free thought, association and expression assured him under the State and Federal Constitutions. The Committee declined to certify him as qualified for admission to the Bar on the ground that his refusals to answer had obstructed a full investigation into his qualifications. The State supreme court denied him admission to practice. *Held:* Denial of petitioner's application for admission to the Bar on this ground did not violate his rights under the Fourteenth Amendment. Pp. 37–56.

(a) The State's refusal to admit petitioner to practice on the ground that his refusal to answer the Committee's questions had thwarted a full investigation into his qualifications was not inconsistent with this Court's decision in *Konigsberg* v. *State Bar*, 353 U. S. 252. Pp. 40–44.

(b) The Fourteenth Amendment's protection against arbitrary State action does not forbid a State from denying admission to a bar applicant so long as he refuses to anwer questions having a substantial relevance to his qualifications; and California's application of such a rule in this instance cannot be said to have been arbitrary or discriminatory. Pp. 44–49.

(c) Petitioner was not privileged to refuse to answer questions concerning membership in the Communist Party on the ground that they impinged upon rights of free speech and association protected by the Fourteenth Amendment. *Speiser* v. *Randall*, 357 U. S. 513, distinguished. Pp. 49–56.

52 Cal. 2d 769, 344 P. 2d 777, affirmed.

Edward Mosk argued the cause for petitioner. With him on the brief was *Sam Rosenwein.*

Frank B. Belcher argued the cause for respondents. With him on the brief was *Ralph E. Lewis.*

Briefs of *amici curiae*, urging reversal, were filed by *David Scribner, Leonard B. Boudin, Ben Margolis, William B. Murrish* and *Charles Stewart* for the National Lawyers Guild; *A. L. Wirin, Fred Okrand* and *Hugh R. Manes* for the American Civil Liberties Union of Southern California; and *Robert L. Brock, Pauline Epstein, Robert W. Kenny, Hugh R. Manes, Ben Margolis, Daniel G. Marshall, William B. Murrish, John McTernan, Maynard Omerberg, Alexander Schullman* and *David Sokol* on behalf of themselves and certain other members of the California Bar.

MR. JUSTICE HARLAN delivered the opinion of the Court.

This case, involving California's second rejection of petitioner's application for admission to the State bar, is a sequel of *Konigsberg* v. *State Bar*, 353 U.S. 252, in which this Court reversed the State's initial refusal of his application.

Under California law the State supreme court may admit to the practice of law any applicant whose qualifications have been certified to it by the California Committee of Bar Examiners. Cal. Bus. & Prof. Code § 6064. To qualify for certificaton an applicant must, among other things, be of "good moral character," *id.*, § 6060(c), and no person may be certified "who advocates the overthrow of the Government of the United States or of this State by force, violence, or other unconstitutional means . . . ." *Id.*, § 6064.1. The Committee is empowered and required to ascertain the qualifications of all candidates. *Id.*, § 6064. Under rules prescribed by the Board of Governors of the State Bar, an applicant before the Committee has "the burden of proving that he is possessed of good moral character, of removing any and all reasonable suspicion of moral unfitness, and that he is entitled to the high regard and confidence of the public." *Id.*, Div. 3, c. 4, Rule X, § 101. Any applicant denied certification may have the Committee's action reviewed by the State supreme court. *Id.*, § 6066.

In 1953 petitioner, having successfully passed the California bar examinations, applied for certification for bar membership. The Committee, after interrogating Konigsberg and receiving considerable evidence as to his qualifications, declined to certify him on the ground that he had failed to meet the burden of proving his eligibility under the two statutory requirements relating to good moral character and nonadvocacy of violent overthrow. That determination centered largely around Konigsberg's repeated refusals to answer Committee questions as to his present or past membership in the Communist Party.[1] The California Supreme Court denied review without opinion. See 52 Cal. 2d 769, 770, 344 P. 2d 777, 778.

On certiorari this Court, after reviewing the record, held the state determination to have been without rational support in the evidence and therefore offensive to the Due Process Clause of the Fourteenth Amendment. *Konigsberg* v. *State Bar, supra.* At the same time the

---

[1] Konigsberg rested his refusals, not on any claim of privilege against self-incrimination, but on the ground that such inquiries were beyond the purview of the Committee's authority, and infringed rights of free thought, association, and expression assured him under the State and Federal Constitutions. He affirmatively asserted, however, his disbelief in violent overthrow of government.

Court declined to decide whether Konigsberg's refusals to answer could constitutionally afford "an independent ground for exclusion from the Bar," considering that such an issue was not before it. *Id.*, 259–262. The case was remanded to the State supreme court "for further proceedings not inconsistent with this opinion." *Id.*, 274.

On remand petitioner moved the California Supreme Court for immediate admission to the bar. The court vacated its previous order denying review and referred the matter to the Bar Committee for further consideration. At the ensuing Committee hearings Konigsberg introduced further evidence as to his good moral character (none of which was rebutted), reiterated unequivocally his disbelief in violent overthrow, and stated that he had never knowingly been a member of any organization which advocated such action. He persisted, however, in his refusals to answer any questions relating to his membership in the Communist Party. The Committee again declined to certify him, this time on the ground that his refusals to answer had obstructed a full investigation into his qualifications.[2] The California Supreme Court, by a divided vote, refused review, and also denied Konigsberg's motion for direct admission to practice.[3] 52 Cal. 2d 769, 344 P. 2d. 777. We again brought the case here. 362 U.S. 910.

Petitioner's contentions in this Court in support of reversal of the California Supreme Court's order are reducible to three propositions: (1) the State's action was inconsistent with this Court's decision in the earlier *Konigsberg* case; (2) assuming the Committee's inquiries into Konigsberg's possible Communist Party membership were permissible, it was unconstitutionally arbitrary for the State to deny him admission because of his refusals to answer; and (3) in any event, Konigsberg was constitutionally justified in refusing to answer these questions.

I.

Consideration of petitioner's contentions as to the effect of this Court's decision in the former *Konigsberg* case requires that there be kept clearly in mind what is entailed in California's rule, comparable to that in many States, that an applicant for admission to the bar

---

[2] The Committee made the following findings relevant to the issues now before us:

"(1) That the questions put to the applicant by the Committee concerning past or present membership in or affiliation with the Communist Party are material to a proper and complete investigation of his qualifications for admission to practice law in the State of California.

"(2) That the refusal of applicant to answer said questions has obstructed a proper and complete investigation of applicant's qualifications for admission to practice law in the State of California."

[3] The essence of the State court's decision appears in the following extracts from its opinion:

". . . The committee action now before us contains no findings or conclusion that petitioner had failed to establish either his good moral character or his abstention from advocacy of overthrow of the government.

"Here it is the refusal to answer material questions which is the basis for denial of certification. . . .

". . . [T]o admit applicants who refuse to answer the committee's questions upon these subjects would nullify the concededly valid legislative direction to the committee. Such a rule would effectively stifle committee inquiry upon issues legislatively declared to be relevant to that issue." *Id.*, at 772, 774, 344 P. 2d, at 779, 780.

Justice Traynor dissented on the ground that the California Supreme Court, not being required by statute to exclude bar applicants on the sole ground of their refusal to answer questions concerning possible advocacy of the overthrow of government, should not adopt such an exclusionary rule, at least where the Committee on Bar Examiners has not come forward with some evidence of advocacy. He declined to reach constitutional issues. Justice Peters dissented on Federal constitutional grounds and in the belief that this Court's decision in the first *Konigsberg* case required immediate admission of the applicant. Chief Justice Gibson did not participate in the decision.

bears the burden of proof of "good moral character" [4]—a requirement whose validity is not, nor could well be, drawn in question here.[5]

Under such a rule an applicant must initially furnish enough evidence of good character to make a prima facie case. The examining Committee then has the opportunity to rebut that showing with evidence of bad character. Such evidence may result from the Committee's own independent investigation, from an applicant's responses to questions on his application form, or from Committee interrogation of the applicant himself. This interrogation may well be of decisive importance for, as all familiar with bar admission proceedings know, exclusion of unworthy candidates frequently depends upon the thoroughness of the Committee's questioning, revealing as it may infirmities in an otherwise satisfactory showing on his part. This is especially so where a bar committee, as is not infrequently the case, has no means of conducting an independent investigation of its own into an applicant's qualifications. If at the conclusion of the proceedings the evidence of good character and that of bad character are found in even balance, the State may refuse admission to the applicant, just as in an ordinary suit a plaintiff may fail in his case because he has not met his burden of proof.

In the first *Konigsberg* case this Court was concerned solely with the question whether the balance between the favorable and unfavorable evidence as to Konigsberg's qualifications had been struck in accordance with the requirements of due process. It was there held, first, that Konigsberg had made out a prima facie case of good character and of nonadvocacy of violent overthrow, and, second, that the other evidence in the record could not, even with the aid of all reasonable inferences flowing therefrom, cast such doubts upon petitioner's prima facie case as to justify any finding other than that these two California qualification requirements had been satisfied.[6] In assessing the significance of Konigsberg's refusal to answer questions as to Communist Party membership, the Court dealt only with the fact that this refusal could not provide any reasonable indication of a character not meeting these two standards for admission. The Court did not con-

---

[4] All of the 50 States, as well as Puerto Rico and the District of Columbia, prescribe qualifications of moral character as preconditions for admission to the practice of law. See West Publishing Co., Rules for Admission to the Bar (35th ed. 1957); Survey of the Legal Profession, Bar Examinations and Requirements for Admission to the Bar (1952); Jackson, Character Requirements for Admission to the Bar, 20 Fordham L. Rev. 305 (1951); Annot., 64 A.L.R. 2d 301 (1959).

The burden of demonstrating good moral character is regularly placed upon the bar applicant. *Ex parte Montgomery*, 249 Ala. 378, 31 So. 2d 85; *In re Stephenson*, 243 Ala. 342, 10 So. 2d 1; *Application of Courtney*, 83 Ariz. 231, 319 P. 2d 991; Ark. Stat. Ann., 1947, §§ 25–101, 25–103; *Spears* v. *State Bar*, 211 Cal. 183, 294 P. 697; *O'Brien's Petition*, 79 Conn. 46, 63 A, 777; *In re Durant*, 80 Conn. 140, 147, 67 A. 497; Del. Sup. Ct. Rule 31 (1)(A)(a), (2)(A)(a); *Coleman* v. *Watts*, 81 So. 2d 650 (Fla.) (burden of proof on applicant; prima facie showing shifts burden of going forward to Examiners); *Gordon* v. *Clinkscales*, 215 Ga. 843, 114 S.E. 2d 15; *In re Latimer*, 11 Ill. 2d 327, 143 N.E. 2d 20 (semble): *Rosencranz* v. *Tidrington*, 193 Ind. 472, 141 N.E. 58; *In re Meredith*, 272 S.W. 2d 456 (Ky.); *In re Meyerson*, 190 Md. 671, 59 A. 2d 489 (semble); *Matter of Keenan*, 313 Mass. 186, 47 N.E. 2d 12; *Application of Smith*, 220 Minn. 197. 19 N.W. 2d 324 (semble); *On Application for Attorney's License*, 21 N.J. L. 345; *Application of Cassidy*, 268 App. Div. 282, 51 N.Y.S. 2d 202, Aff'd, 296 N.Y. 926, 73 N.E. 2d 41; *Application of Farmer*, 191 N.C. 235, 131 S.E. 661; *In re Weinstein*, 150 Ore. 1, 42 P. 2d 744; *State ex rel. Board* v. *Poyntz*, 152 Ore. 592, 52 P. 2d 1141 (burden of proof on applicant; prima facie showing shifts burden of going forward to Examiners); *In the Matter of Eary*, 134 W. Va. 204, 58 S.E. 2d 647 (semble).

[5] For reasons given later (pp. 55–56, *infra*), we need not decide whether California's burden-of-proof rule could constitutionally be applied, as it was by the Committee after the first Konigsberg proceedings, to the requirement of nonadvocacy of violent overthrow.

[6] The Court assumed, but did not discuss, the constitutionality of California's burden-of-proof rule as applied to the nonadvocacy-of-forcible-overthrow requirement of the California statute.

sider, but reserved for later decision, all questions as to the permissibility of the State treating Konigsberg's refusal to answer as a ground for exclusion, not because it was evidence from which substantive conclusions might be drawn, but because the refusal had thwarted a full investigation into his qualifications. See 353 U.S., at 259–262. The State now asserts that ground for exclusion, an issue that is not foreclosed by anything in this Court's earlier opinion which decided a quite different question.

It is equally clear that the State's ordering of the rehearing which led to petitioner's exclusion manifested no disrespect of the effect of the mandate in that case, which expressly left the matter open for further State proceedings "not inconsistent with" the Court's opinion. There is no basis for any suggestion that the State in so proceeding has adopted unusual or discriminatory procedures to avoid the normal consequences of this Court's earlier determination. In its earlier proceeding, the California Bar Committee may have found further investigation and questioning of petitioner unnecessary when, in its view, the applicant's prima facie case of qualifications had been sufficiently rebuted by evidence already in the record. While in its former opinion this Court held that the State could not constitutionally so conclude, it did not undertake to preclude the State agency from asking any questions or from conducting any investigation that it might have thought necessary had it known that the basis of its then decision would be overturned. In recalling Konigsberg for further testimony, the Committee did only what this Court has consistently held that Federal administrative tribunals may do on remand after a reviewing court has set aside agency orders as unsupported by requisite findings of fact. *Federal Communications Comm'n* v. *Pottsville Broadcasting Co.*, 309 U.S. 134; *Fly* v. *Heitmeyer*, 309 U.S. 146.

In the absence of the slightest indication of any purpose on the part of the State to evade the Court's prior decision, principles of finality protecting the parties of this State litigation are, within broad limits of fundamental fairness, solely the concern of California law. Such limits are broad even in a criminal case, see *Bryan* v. *United States*, 338 U.S. 552; *Hoag* v. *New Jersey*, 356 U.S. 464; cf. *Palko* v. *Connecticut*, 302 U.S. 319, 328. In this instance they certainly have not been transgressed by the State's merely taking further action in this essentially administrative type of proceeding.[7]

II.

We think it clear that the Fourteenth Amendment's protection against arbitrary State action does not forbid a State from denying admission to a bar applicant so long as he refuses to provide unprivileged answers to questions having a substantial relevance to his qualifications. An investigation of this character, like a civil suit, requires procedural as well as substantive rules. It is surely not doubtful that a State could validly adopt an administrative rule analogous

---

[7] Moreover, even if there could be debate as to whether this Court's prior decision prevented new hearings on matters that had already transpired at the time of the first state hearings, there can be no doubt that such decision did not prevent California from investigating petitioner's actions during the period subsequent to the first hearing. Therefore we would in any case be presented with the question of the constitutionality of the State's refusing to admit petitioner to the practice of law because of his declining to answer whether he has been a member of the Communist Party since the termination of the first set of hearings.

to Rule 37 (b) of the Federal Rules of Civil Procedure which provides that that refusal, after due warning, to answer relevant questions may result in "the matters regarding which the questions were asked" being considered for the purposes of the proceeding to be answered in a way unfavorable to the refusing party, or even that such refusal may result in "dismissing the action or proceeding" of the party asking affirmative relief.

The State procedural rule involved here is a less broad one, for all that California has in effect said is that in cases where, on matters material to an applicant's qualifications, there are gaps in the evidence presented by him which the agency charged with certification considers should be filled in the appropriate exercise of its responsibilities, an applicant will not be admitted to practice unless and until he cooperates with the agency's efforts to fill those gaps. The fact that this rule finds its source in the supervisory powers of the California Supreme Court over admissions to the bar, rather than in legislation, is not constitutionally significant. *Nashville, C. & St. L. R. Co.* v. *Browning,* 310 U.S. 362. Nor in the absence of a showing of arbitrary or discriminatory application in a particular case, is it a matter of federal concern whether such a rule requires the rejection of all applicants refusing to answer material questions, or only in instances where the examining committee deems that a refusal has materially obstructed its investigation. Compare *Beilan* v. *Board of Education,* 357 U.S. 399, with *Nelson* v. *County of Los Angeles,* 362 U.S. 1.

In the context of the entire record of these proceedings,[8] the application of the California rule in this instance cannot be said to be arbitrary or discriminatory. In the first *Konigsberg* case this Court held that neither the somewhat weak but uncontradicted testimony, that petitioner had been a Communist Party member in 1941, nor his refusal to answer questions relating to Party membership, could rationally support any substantive adverse inferences as to petitioner's character qualifications, 353 U.S., at 266–274. That was not to say, however, that these factors, singly or together, could not be regarded as leaving the investigatory record in sufficient uncertainty as constitutionally to permit application of the procedural rule which the State has now invoked, provided that Konigsberg had been first given due warning of the consequences of his continuing refusal to respond to the Committee's questions. Cf. 353 U.S., at 261.

It is no answer to say that petitioner has made out a prima facie case of qualifications, for this is precisely the posture of a proceeding in which the Committee's right to examine and cross-examine becomes significant. Assuming, as we do for the moment, that there is no privilege here to refuse to answer, petitioner could no more insist that his prima facie case makes improper further questioning of him than he could insist that such circumstance made improper the introduction of other forms of rebutting evidence.

We likewise regard as untenable petitioner's contentions that the questions as to Communist Party membership were made irrelevant either by the fact that bare, innocent membership is not a ground of disqualification or by petitioner's willingness to answer such ultimate questions as whether he himself believed in violent overthrow or know-

---

[8] The transcript of the original hearings before the Committee has been made part of the record before us in the present case.

ingly belonged to an organization advocating violent overthrow. The Committee Chairman's answer to the former contention was entirely correct:

> "If you answered the question, for example, that you had been a member of the Communist Party during some period since 1951 or that you were presently a member of the Communist Party, the Committee would then be in a position to ask you what acts you engaged in to carry out the functions and purposes of that party, what the aims and purposes of the party were, to your knowledge, and questions of that type. You see by failing to answer the initial question there certainly is no basis and no opportunity for us to investigate with respect to the other matters to which the initial question might very well be considered preliminary."

And the explanation given to petitioner's counsel by another Committee member as to why Konigsberg's testimony about ultimate facts was not dispositive was also sound:

> "Mr. Mosk, you realize that if Mr. Konigsberg had answered the question that he refused to answer, an entirely new area of investigation might be opened up, and this Committee might be able to ascertain from Mr. Konigsberg that perhaps he is now and for many years past has been an active member of the Communist Party, and from finding out who his associates were in that enterprise we might discover that he does advocate the overthrow of this government by force and violence. I am not saying that he would do that, but it is a possibility, and we don't have to take any witness' testimony as precluding us from trying to discover if he is telling the truth. That is the point."

Petitioner's further miscellaneous contentions that the State's exclusion of him was capricious are all also insubstantial.[9]

There remains the question as to whether Konigsberg was adequately warned of the consequences of his refusal to answer. At the outset of the renewed hearings the Chairman of the Committee stated:

> "As a result of our two-fold purpose [to investigate and reach determinations], particularly our function of investigation, we believe it will be necessary for you, Mr. Konigsberg, to answer our material questions or our investigation will be obstructed. We would not then as a result be able to certify you for admission."

After petitioner had refused to answer questions on Communist Party membership, the Chairman asked:

> "Mr. Konigsberg, I think you will recall that I initially advised you a failure to answer our material questions would obstruct our investigation and result in our failure to certify you. With this in mind do you wish to answer any of the questions which you heretofore up to now have refused to answer?"

---

[9] There is no basis for any intimation that the California Supreme Court fashioned a special procedural rule for the purposes of this particular case. The California Bar Committee has in the past declined to certify applicants who refused to answer pertinent questions. See Farley (Secretary, Committee of Bar Examiners), Character Investigation of Applicants for Admission, 29 Cal. State Bar Journal, 454, 457, 466 (1954). No more does the State's action bear any of the hallmarks of a bill of attainder or of an *ex post facto* regulation, see *Cummings* v. *Missouri*, 4 Wall. 277; cf. *United States* v. *Lovett*, 328 U.S. 303, especially in light of the fact that petitioner was explicitly warned in advance of the consequences of his refusal to answer. Likewise, there is no room for attributing to the Committee a surreptitious purpose to exclude Konigsberg by the device of putting to him questions which it was known in advance he would not answer, and then justifying exclusion on the premise of his refusal to respond. So far as this record shows Konigsberg was excluded only because his refusal to answer had impeded the investigation of the Committee, a ground of rejection which it is still within his power to remove.

At the conclusion of the proceeding another Committee member stated:
"I would like to make this statement so that there will be no misunderstanding on the part of any court that may review this record in the future, that I feel that as a member of the Committee that the failure of Mr. Konigsberg to answer the question as to whether or not he is now a member of the Communist Party is an obstruction of the function of this Committee, not a frustration if that word has been used. I think it would be an obstruction. There are phases of his moral character that we haven't been able to investigate simply because we have been stopped at this point, and I for one could not certify to the Supreme Court that he was a proper person to be admitted to practice law in this State until he answers the question about his Communist affiliation."
The record thus leaves no room for doubt on the score of "warning," and petitioner does not indeed contend to the contrary.

III.

Finally, petitioner argues that, in any event, he was privileged not to respond to questions dealing with Communist Party membership because they unconstitutionally impinged upon rights of free speech and association protected by the Fourteenth Amendment.

At the outset we reject the view that freedom of speech and association (*N.A.A.C.P.* v. *Alabama*, 357 U.S. 449, 460), as protected by the First and Fourteenth Amendments, are "absolutes," not only in the undoubted sense that where the constitutional protection exists it must prevail, but also in the sense that the scope of that protection must be gathered solely from a literal reading of the First Amendment.[10]   Throughout its history this Court has consistently recognized at least two ways in which constitutionally protected freedom of speech is narrower than an unlimited license to talk.   On the one hand, certain forms of speech, or speech in certain contexts, has been considered outside the scope of constitutional protection.[11]   See, *e.g.*, *Schenck* v. *United States*, 249 U.S. 47; *Chaplinsky* v. *New Hampshire*, 315 U.S. 568; *Dennis* v. *United States*, 341 U.S. 494; *Beauharnais* v. *Illinois*, 343 U.S. 250; *Yates* v. *United States*, 354 U.S. 298; *Roth* v. *United States*, 354 U.S. 476.   On the other hand, general regulatory statutes,

---

[10] That view, which of course cannot be reconciled with the law relating to libel, slander, misrepresentation, obscenity, perjury, false advertising, solicitation of crime, complicity by encouragement, conspiracy, and the like, is said to be compelled by the fact that the commands of the First Amendment are stated in unqualified terms: "Congress shall make no law . . . abridging the freedom of speech, or of the press; or the right of the people peaceably to assemble . . . ." But as Mr. Justice Holmes once said: "[T]he provisions of the Constitution are not mathematical formulas having their essence in their form; they are organic living institutions transplanted from English soil. [T]heir significance is vital not formal; it is to be gathered not simply by taking the words and a dictionary, but by considering their origin and the line of their growth." *Gompers* v. *United States*, 233 U.S. 604, 610.   In this connection also compare the equally unqualified command of the Second Amendment: "the right of the people to keep and bear arms shall not be infringed." And see *United States* v. *Miller*, 307 U.S. 174.

[11] That the First Amendment immunity for speech, press and assembly has to be reconciled with valid but conflicting governmental interests was clear to Holmes, J. ("I do not doubt for a moment that by the same reasoning that would justify punishing persuasion to murder, the United States constitutionally may punish speech that produces or is intended to produce a clear and imminent danger that it will bring about forthwith certain substantive evils that the United States constitutionally may seek to prevent." *Abrams* v. *United States*, 250 U.S. 616, 627); to Brandeis, J. ("But, although the rights of free speech and assembly are fundamental, they are not in their nature absolute." *Whitney* v. *California*, 274 U.S. 357, 373); and to Hughes, C.J. ("[T]he protection [of free speech] even as to previous restraint is not absolutely unlimited." *Near* v. *Minnesota*, 283 U.S. 697, 716.)

not intended to control the content of speech but incidentally limiting its unfettered exercise, have not been regarded as the type of law the First or Fourteenth Amendment forbade Congress or the States to pass, when they have been found justified by subordinating valid governmental interests, a prerequisite to constitutionality which has necessarily involved a weighing of the governmental interest involved. See, *e.g.*, *Schneider* v. *State*, 308 U.S. 147, 161; *Cox* v. *New Hampshire*, 312 U.S. 569; *Prince* v. *Massachusetts*, 321 U.S. 158; *Kovacs* v. *Cooper*, 336 U.S. 77; *American Communications Assn.* v. *Douds*, 339 U.S. 382; *Breard* v. *Alexandria*, 341 U.S. 622. It is in the latter class of cases that this Court has always placed rules compelling disclosure of prior association as an incident of the informed exercise of a valid governmental function. *Bates* v. *Little Rock*, 361 U.S. 516, 524. Whenever, in such a context, these constitutional protections are asserted against the exercise of valid governmental powers a reconciliation must be effected, and that perforce requires an appropriate weighing of the respective interests involved. *Watkins* v. *United States*, 354 U.S. 178, 198; *N.A.A.C.P.* v. *Alabama, supra; Barenblatt* v. *United States*, 360 U.S. 109, 126–127; *Bates* v. *Little Rock, supra; Wilkinson* v. *United States*, 365 U.S. 399; *Braden* v. *United States*, 365 U.S. 431. With more particular reference to the present context of a state decision as to character qualifications, it is difficult, indeed, to imagine a view of the constitutional protections of speech and association which would automatically and without consideration of the extent of the deterrence of speech and association and of the importance of the State function, exclude all reference to prior speech or association on such issues as character, purpose, credibility, or intent. On the basis of these considerations we now judge petitioner's contentions in the present case.

Petitioner does not challenge the constitutionality of § 6064.1 of the California Business and Professions Code forbidding certification for admission to practice of those advocating the violent overthrow of government. It would indeed be difficult to argue that a belief, firm enough to be carried over into advocacy, in the use of illegal means to change the form of the State or Federal Government is an unimportant consideration in determining the fitness of applicants for membership in a profession in whose hands so largely lies the safekeeping of this country's legal and political institutions. Cf. *Garner* v. *Board of Public Works*, 341 U.S. 716. Nor is the State interest in this respect insubstantially related to the right which California claims to inquire about Communist Party membership. This Court has long since recognized the legitimacy of a statutory finding that membership in the Communist Party is not unrelated to the danger of use for such illegal ends of powers given for limited purposes. See *American Communications Assn.* v. *Douds*, 339 U.S. 382; see also *Barenblatt* v. *United States*, 360 U.S. 109, 128–129; cf. *Wilkinson* v. *United States*, 365 U.S. 399; *Braden* v. *United States*, 365 U.S. 431.

As regards the questioning of public employees relative to Communist Party membership it has already been held that the interest in not subjecting speech and association to the deterrence of subsequent disclosure is outweighed by the State's interest in ascertaining the fitness of the employee for the post he holds, and hence that such questioning does not infringe constitutional protections. *Beilan* v.

Board of Public Education, 357 U.S. 399; *Garner* v. *Board of Public Works*, 341 U.S. 716. With respect to this same question of Communist Party membership, we regard the State's interest in having lawyers who are devoted to the law in its broadest sense, including not only its substantive provisions, but also its procedures for orderly change, as clearly sufficient to outweigh the minimal effect upon free association occasioned by compulsory disclosure in the circumstances here presented.

There is here no likelihood that deterrence of association may result from foreseeable private action, see *N.A.A.C.P.* v. *Alabama, supra,* at 462, for bar committee interrogations such as this are conducted in private. See Rule 58, Section X, Rules of Practice and Procedure of the Supreme Court of Illinois; cf. Cal. Bus. & Prof. Code, Rules of Procedure of the State Bar of California, Rule 8; *Anonymous* v. *Baker*, 360 U.S. 287, 291–292. Nor is there the possibility that the State may be afforded the opportunity for imposing undetectable arbitrary consequences upon protected association, see *Shelton* v. *Tucker*, 364 U.S. 479, 486, for a bar applicant's exclusion by reason of Communist Party membership is subject to judicial review, including ultimate review by this Court, should it appear that such exclusion has rested on substantive or procedural factors that do not comport with the Federal Constitution. See *Konigsberg* v. *State Bar*, 353 U.S. 252; *Schware* v. *Board of Examiners of New Mexico*, 353 U.S. 232; cf. *Wieman* v. *Updegraff*, 344 U.S. 183. In these circumstances it is difficult indeed to perceive any solid basis for a claim of unconstitutional intrusion into rights assured by the Fourteenth Amendment.

If this were all there was to petitioner's claim of a privilege to refuse to answer, we would regard the *Beilan* case as controlling. There is, however, a further aspect of the matter. In *Speiser* v. *Randall*, 357 U.S. 513, we held unconstitutional a State procedural rule that in order to obtain an exemption a taxpayer must bear the burden of proof, including both the burdens of establishing a prima facie case and of ultimate persuasion, that he did not advocate the violent overthrow of government. We said (p. 526):

"The vice of the present procedure is that, where particular speech falls close to the line separating the lawful and the unlawful, the possibility of mistaken factfinding—inherent in all litigation—will create the danger that the legitimate utterance will be penalized. The man who knows that he must bring forth proof and persuade another of the lawfulness of his conduct necessarily must steer far wider of the unlawful zone than if the State must bear these burdens. This is especially to be feared when the complexity of the proofs and the generality of the standards applied, cf. *Dennis* v. *United States, supra,* provide but shifting sands on which the litigant must maintain his position. How can a claimant whose declaration is rejected possibly sustain the burden of proving the negative of these complex factual elements? In practical operation, therefore, this procedural device must necessarily produce a result which the State could not command directly. It can only result in a deterrence of speech which the Constitution makes free."

It would be a sufficient answer to any suggestion of the applicability of that holding to the present proceeding to observe that *Speiser* was explicitly limited so as not to reach cases where, as here, there is no

showing of an intent to penalize political beliefs. Distinguishing
Garner v. *Board of Public Works*, 341 U.S. 716; *Gerende* v. *Board
of Supervisors*, 341 U.S. 56, and *American Communications Assn.* v.
Douds, 339 U.S. 382, the Court said (p. 527):

> "In these cases . . . there was no attempt directly to control
> speech but rather to protect, from an evil shown to be grave, some
> interest clearly within the sphere of governmental concern . . .
> Each case concerned a limited class of persons in or aspiring to
> public positions by virtue of which they could, if evilly motivated,
> create serious danger to the public safety. The principal aim of
> those statutes was not to penalize political beliefs but to deny
> positions to persons supposed to be dangerous because the position
> might be misused to the detriment of the public."

But there are also additional factors making the rationale of *Speiser*
inapplicable to the case before us. There is no unequivocal indication
that California in this proceeding has placed upon petitioner the
burden of proof of nonadvocacy of violent overthrow, as distinguished
from its other requirement of "good moral character." [12] All it has
presently required is an applicant's cooperation with the Committee's
search for evidence of forbidden advocacy. Petitioner has been
denied admission to the California bar for obstructing the Committee in the performance of its necessary functions of examination and
cross-examination, a ruling which indeed presupposes that the burden
of producing substantial evidence on the issue of advocacy was not
upon petitioner but upon the Committee. Requiring a defendant in
a civil proceeding to testify or to submit to discovery has never been
thought to shift the burden of proof to him. Moreover, when this
Court has allowed a State to comment upon a criminal defendant's
failure to testify it has been careful to note that this does not result
in placing upon him the burden of proving his innocence. *Adamson*
v. *California*, 332 U.S. 46, 58.

In contrast to our knowledge with respect to the burden of establishing a prima facie case, we do not now know where, under California law, would rest the ultimate burden of persuasion on the issue
of advocacy of violent overthrow. But it is for the Supreme Court of
California first to decide this question. Only if and when that burden
is placed by the State upon a bar applicant can there be drawn in
question the distinction made in the *Speiser* case between penalizing
statutes and those merely denying access to positions where unfitness
may lead to the abuse of State-given powers or privileges. The issue
is not now before us.

Thus as matters now stand, there is nothing involved here which
is contrary to the reasoning of *Speiser*, for despite compelled testimony
the prospective bar applicant need not "steer far wider of the unlawful
zone" (357 U.S., at 526) for fear of mistaken judgment or fact finding
declaring unlawful speech which is in fact protected by the Constitution. This is so as to the ultimate burden of persuasion, notwithstanding his duty to testify, the loss resulting from a failure of
proof may, for all we now know, still fall upon the State. It is
likewise so as to the initial burden of production, for there is no

---

[12] Indeed, we cannot tell whether California did so even in the earlier proceeding, since
the California Supreme Court's denial of review of the Committee's original rejection of
Konigsberg was without opinion, and for all we know may have rested alone on petitioner's
failure to meet his State burden of proof as to "good moral character."

indication in the proceeding on rehearing of petitioner's application that the Bar Committee expected petitioner to "sustain the burden of proving the negative" (357 U.S., at 526) of those complex factual elements which amount to forbidden advocacy of violent overthrow. To the contrary it is clear that the Committee had assumed the burden of proving the affirmative of those elements, but was prevented from attempting to discharge that burden by petitioner's refusal to answer relevant questions.

The judgment of the Supreme Court of California is

Affirmed.

MR. JUSTICE BLACK, with whom THE CHIEF JUSTICE and MR. JUSTICE DOUGLAS concur, dissenting.

When this case was here before, we reversed a judgment of the California Supreme Court barring the petitioner Konigsberg from the practice of law in that State on the ground that he had failed to carry the burden of proving his good moral character and that he did not advocate forcible overthrow of the Government. In doing so, we held that there was "no evidence in the record" which could rationally justify such a conclusion.[1] Upon remand, the Supreme Court of California referred the matter back to the Committee of State Bar Examiners for further hearings, at which time Konigsberg presented even more evidence of his good character. The Committee produced no evidence whatever which tended in the slightest degree to reflect upon the good character and patriotism which we had already held Konigsberg to have established. The case is therefore now before us with the prior adjudication that Konigsberg possesses the requisite good character and patriotism for admission to the Bar unimpaired.

What the Committee did do upon remand was to repeat the identical questions with regard to Konigsberg's suspected association with Communists twenty years ago that it had asked and he had refused to answer at the first series of hearings. Konigsberg again refused to answer these questions and the Committee again refused to certify him as fit for admission to the Bar, this time on the ground that his refusal to answer had obstructed the required investigation into his qualifications, a ground subsequently adopted by a majority of the supreme court of that State.[2]

Thus, California purports to be denying Konigsberg admission to its Bar solely on the ground that he has refused to answer questions put to him by the Committee of Bar Examiners. But when the case was here before, we observed: "There is nothing in the California statutes, the California decisions, or even the Rules of the Bar Committee, which has been called to our attention, that suggests that failure to answer a Bar Examiner's inquiry is, *ipso facto*, a basis for excluding an applicant from the Bar, irrespective of how overwhelming in his showing of good character or loyalty or how flimsy are the suspicions of the Bar Examiners."[3] And we have been pointed to no subsequent

---

[1] *Konigsberg* v. *State Bar of California,* 353 U.S. 252, 273. That decision was reached on the basis of a record containing a large quantity of evidence favorable to Konigsberg and some scanty evidence arguably adverse to him.
[2] *Konigsberg* v. *State Bar of California,* 52 Cal. 2d 769, 344 P. 2d 777. Mr. Justice Traynor and Mr. Justice Peters dissented in separate opinions.
[3] 353 U.S., at 260–261.

California statutes, rules, regulations or court decisions which require or even permit rejection of a lawyer's application for admission solely because he refuses to answer questions.[4]   In this situation, it seems to me that Konigsberg has been rejected on a ground that is not supported by any authoritatively declared rule of law for the State of California.[5]   This alone would be enough for me to vote to reverse the judgment.   There are other reasons, however.

Konigsberg's objection to answering questions as to whether he is or was a member of the Communist Party has, from the very beginning, been based upon the contention that the guarantees of free speech and association of the First Amendment as made controlling upon the States by the Fourteenth Amendment preclude California from denying him admission to its Bar for refusing to answer such questions. In this I think Konigsberg has been correct.   California has apparently not even attempted to make actual present membership in the Communist Party a bar to the practice of law, and even if it had, I assume it would not be contended that such a law could be applied to conduct that took place before the law was passed.   For such an application would, I think, not only be a clear violation of the *ex post facto* provision of the Federal Constitution, but would also constitute a bill of attainder squarely within this Court's holdings in *Cummings* v. *Missouri* [6] and *Ex parte Garland*.[7]   And yet it seems to me that this record shows, beyond any shadow of a doubt, that the reason Konigsberg has been rejected is because the Committee suspects that he was at one time a member of the Communist Party.[8]   I agree with the implication of the majority opinion that this is not an adequate ground to reject Konigsberg and that it could not be constitutionally defended.[9]

The majority avoids the otherwise unavoidable necessity of reversing the judgment below on that ground by simply refusing to look beyond

---

[4] The total absence of any authoritative source for this rule is, in my judgment, merely accentuated by the reference in the majority opinion to the article written for the California State Bar Journal by the Secretary of the Committee of Bar Examiners.   So far as the cases relied upon in that article are even available for study, they do not in any way support the action of the Bar Committee here.

[5] Thus, it seems to me that California's rejection of Konigsberg is not supported by any "law of the land," as required by the Due Process and Equal Protection Clauses of the Fourteenth Amendment.   See *Cohen* v. *Hurley*, decided today, post, p. 117, at 135–150 (dissenting opinion).   As Daniel Webster argued in the *Dartmouth College* case: "Are then these acts of the legislature, which affect only particular persons and their particular privileges, laws of the land?   Let this question be answered by the text of Blackstone: 'And first, it (i.e. law) is a *rule:* not a transient sudden order from a superior, to, or concerning, a particular person : but something permanent, uniform, and universal.   Therefore, a particular act of the legislature to confiscate the goods of Titius, or to attaint him of high treason, does not enter into the idea of a municipal law : for the operation of this act is spent upon Titius only, and has no relation to the community in general ; it is rather a sentence than a law.'   Lord Coke is equally decisive and emphatic.   Citing and commenting on the celebrated 29th chap. of *Magna Charta*, he says, 'no man shall be disseized, &c. unless it be by the lawful judgment, that is, verdict of equals, or by the *law of the land*, that is, (to speak it once for all,) *by the due course and process of law.*' "   (Emphasis as in source.)   *Dartmouth College* v. *Woodward*, 4 Wheat. 518, 580–581.

[6] 4 Wall. 277.

[7] 4 Wall. 333.

[8] The suspicions of the Committee doubtless relate to the period around 1941 for the Committee had heard testimony from an ex-Communist that Konigsberg had attended meetings of a Communist Party unit during that period.   The unreliability of that testimony was discussed in the Court's opinion when the case was here before.   See 353 U.S., at 266–268.

[9] Under the circumstances of this case, it seems clear to me that the action of the State of California in rejecting Konigsberg is also contrary to our decision in *Schware* v. *Board of Bar Examiners of New Mexico*, 353 U.S. 232.   In that case, every member of this Court who participated in the decision expressed serious doubts with regard to the probative value of evidence as to a Bar applicant's membership in the Communist Party 15 years previous to our consideration of the case.   *Id.*, at 246 (concurring opinion) 251. I cannot believe that such evidence becomes more probative when, as here, it would, if obtained, have been five years older.

the reason given by the Committee to justify Konigsberg's rejection. In this way, the majority reaches the question as to whether the Committee can constitutionally reject Konigsberg for refusing to answer questions growing out of his conjectured past membership in the Communist Party even though it could not constitutionally reject him if he did answer those questions and his answers happened to be affirmative. The majority then goes on to hold that the Committee, by virtue of its power to reject applicants who advocate the violent overthrow of the Government, can reject applicants who refuse to answer questions in any way related to that fact, even though the applicant has sworn under oath that he does not advocate violent overthrow of the Government and even though, as the majority concedes, questions as to the political associations of an applicant subject "speech and association to the deterrence of subsequent disclosure." I cannot agree with that holding.

The recognition that California has subjected "speech and association to the deterrence of subsequent disclosure" is, under the First Amendment, sufficient in itself to render the action of the State unconstitutional unless one subscribes to the doctrine that permits constitutionally protected rights to be "balanced" away whenever a majority of this Court thinks that a State might have interest sufficient to justify abridgment of those freedoms. As I have indicated many times before,[10] I do not subscribe to that doctrine for I believe that the First Amendment's unequivocal command that there shall be no abridgment of the rights of free speech and assembly shows that the men who drafted our Bill of Rights did all the "balancing" that was to be done in this field. The history of the First Amendment is too well known to require repeating here except to say that it certainly cannot be denied that the very object of adopting the First Amendment, as well as the other provisions of the Bill of Rights, was to put the freedoms protected there completely out of the area of any congressional control that may be attempted through the exercise of precisely those powers that are now being used to "balance" the Bill of Rights out of existence.[11] Of course, the First Amendment originally applied only to the Federal Government and did not apply to the States. But what was originally true only of Congress is now no less true with respect to the governments of the States, unless a majority of this Court wants to overrule a large number of cases in which it has been held unequivocally that the Fourteenth Amendment made the First Amendment's provisions controlling upon the States.[12]

The Court attempts to justify its refusal to apply the plain mandate of the First Amendment in part by reference to the so-called "clear and present danger test" forcefully used by Mr. Justice Holmes and

---

[10] See, e.g., my dissenting opinions in *Braden* v. *United States*, 365 U.S. 431, 441–446; *Wilkinson* v. *United States*, 365 U.S. 399, 422–423; *Uphaus* v. *Wyman*, 364 U.S. 388, 392–393; *Barenblatt* v. *United States*, 360 U.S. 109, 140–144; *American Communications Assn.* v. *Douds*, 339 U.S. 382, 445–453.

[11] James Madison, for example, indicated clearly that he did not understand the Bill of Rights to permit *any* encroachments upon the freedoms it was designed to protect. "If they [the first ten Amendments] are incorporated into the Constitution, independent tribunals of justice will consider themselves in a peculiar manner the guardians of those rights; they will be an *impenetrable bulwark* against *every* assumption of power in the Legislative or Executive; they will be naturally led to resist *every* encroachment upon rights expressly stipulated for in the Constitution by the declaration of rights." 1 Annals of Congress 439 (1789). (Emphasis supplied.)

[12] See, e.g., *Minersville District* v. *Gobitis*, 310 U.S. 586, 593; *Murdock* v. *Pennsylvania*, 319 U.S. 105, 108; *Board of Education* v. *Barnette*, 319 U.S. 624, 639; *Staub* v. *City of Baxley*, 355 U.S. 313, 321.

Mr. Justice Brandeis, not to narrow but to broaden the then prevailing interpretation of First Amendment freedoms.[13] I think very little can be found in anything they ever said that would provide support for the "balancing test" presently in use. Indeed, the idea of "balancing" away First Amendment freedoms appears to me to be wholly inconsistent with the view, strongly espoused by Justices Holmes and Brandeis, that the best test of truth is the power of the thought to get itself accepted in the competition of the market.[14] The "clear and present danger test" was urged as consistent with this view in that it protected speech in all cases except those in which danger was so imminent that there was no time for rational discussion.[15] The "balancing test," on the other hand, rests upon the notion that some ideas are so dangerous that Government need not restrict itself to contrary arguments as a mean of opposing them even where there is ample time to do so. Thus here, where there is not a semblance of a "clear and present danger," and where there is more than ample time in which to combat by discussion any idea which may be involved, the majority permits the State of California to adopt measures calculated to suppress the advocacy of views about governmental affairs.

I recognize, of course, that the "clear and present danger test," though itself a great advance toward individual liberty over some previous notions of the protections afforded by the First Amendment,[16] does not go as far as my own views as to the protection that should be accorded these freedoms. I agree with Justices Holmes and Brandeis, however, that a primary purpose of the First Amendment was to insure that all ideas would be allowed to enter the "competition of the market." But I fear that the creation of "tests" by which speech is left unprotected under certain circumstances is a standing invitation to abridge it. This is nowhere more clearly indicated than by the sudden transformation of the "clear and present danger test" in *Dennis* v. *United States*. In that case, this Court accepted Judge Learned Hand's "restatement" of the "clear and present danger test": "In each case [courts] must ask whether the gravity of the 'evil,' discounted by its improbability, justifies such invasion of free speech as is necessary to avoid the danger."[17] After the "clear and present danger test" was diluted and weakened by being recast in terms of this "balancing" formula, there seems to me to be much room to doubt that Justices Holmes and Brandeis would even have recognized their test. And the reliance upon that weakened "test" by the majority here, without even so much as an attempt to find either a "clear" or a "present" danger, is only another persuasive reason for rejecting all such "tests" and enforcing the First Amendment according to its terms.

---

[13] See *Schenck* v. *United States*, 249 U.S. 47, 52, where Mr. Justice Holmes, writing for the Court said: "The question in every case is whether the words used are used in such circumstances and are of such a nature as to create a clear and present danger that they will bring about the substantive evils that Congress has a right to prevent."

[14] *Abrams* v. *United States*, 250 U.S. 616, 630 (Holmes, J., dissenting). See also *Gitlow* v. *New York*, 268 U.S. 652, 673: "If in the long run the beliefs expressed in proletarian dictatorship are destined to be accepted by the dominant forces of the community, the only meaning of free speech is that they should be given their chance and have their way." (Holmes, J., dissenting.) And see *Whitney* v. *California*, 274 U.S. 357, 378: "Among free men, the deterrents ordinarily to be applied to prevent crime are education and punishment for violations of the law, not abridgment of the rights of free speech and assembly." (Brandeis, J., concurring.)

[15] See *Abrams* v. *United States*, 250 U.S. 616, 630–631 (dissenting opinion); *Gitlow* v. *New York*, 268 U.S. 652, 672–673 (dissenting opinion); *Whitney* v. *California*, 274 U.S. 357, 378–379 (concurring opinion).

[16] See *Bridges* v. *California*, 314 U.S. 252, 260–263.

[17] 183 F. 2d 201, 212; 341 U.S. 494, 510.

The Court suggests that a "literal reading of the First Amendment" would be totally unreasonable because it would invalidate many widely accepted laws. I do not know to what extent this is true. I do not believe, for example, that it would invalidate laws resting upon the premise that where speech is an integral part of unlawful conduct that is going on at the time, the speech can be used to illustrate, emphasize and establish the unlawful conduct.[18] On the other hand, it certainly would invalidate all laws that abridge the right of the people to discuss matters of religious or public interest, in the broadest meaning of those terms, for it is clear that a desire to protect this right was the primary purpose of the First Amendment. Some people have argued, with much force, that the freedoms guaranteed by the First Amendment are limited to somewhat broad areas like those.[19] But I believe this Nation's security and tranquility can best be served by giving the First Amendment the same broad construction that all Bill of Rights guarantees deserve.[20]

The danger of failing to construe the First Amendment in this manner, is, I think, dramatically illustrated by the decision of this Court in *Beauharnais* v. *Illinois*,[21] one of the cases relied upon for this holding today. In that case, a majority of this Court upheld the conviction of a man whose only "crime" was the circulation of a petition to be presented to the City Council of Chicago urging that body to follow a policy of racial segregation in language that the State of Illinois chose to regard as "libelous" against Negroes. Holding that "libelous utterances" were not included in the "speech" protected against State invasion by the Due Process Clause of the Fourteenth Amendment,[22] this Court there concluded that the petition which had been circulated fell within that exception and therefore outside the area of constitutionally protected speech because it made charges against the entire Negro population of this country. Thus, Beauharnais was held to have simultaneously "libelled" some fifteen million people. And by this tremendous expansion of the concept of "libel," what some people might regard as a relatively minor exception to the full protection of freedom of speech had suddenly become a vehicle which could be used to justify a return to the vicious era of the laws of seditious libel, in which the political party in power, both in England and in this country, used such laws to put its opponents in jail.[23]

---

[18] *Roth* v. *United States*, 354 U.S. 476, 514 (dissenting opinion). See also *Labor Board* v. *Virginia Electric & Power Co.*, 314 U.S. 469; *Giboney* v. *Empire Storage Co.*, 336 U.S. 490.
[19] See, *e.g.*, *Meiklejohn, What Does the First Amendment Mean?* 20 U. of Chi. L. Rev. 461, 464.
[20] Cf. *Boyd* v. *United States*, 116 U.S. 616, 635: "[C]onstitutional provisions for the security of person and property should be liberally construed. A close and literal construction deprives them of half their efficacy, and leads to gradual depreciation of the right, as if it consisted more in sound than in substance. It is the duty of courts to be watchful for the constitutional rights of the citizen, and against any stealthy encroachments thereon."
[21] 343 U.S. 250.
[22] The Court opinion here apparently treats the *Beauharnais* case as having decided that the *Federal* Government has power, despite the First Amendment, to pass so-called "group libel" laws. This, I think, is wholly unjustified. The *Beauhanais* opinion was written on the assumption that the protection afforded the freedoms of speech and petition against state action by the Fourteenth Amendment amounted to something less than the protection afforded these freedoms against congressional action by the First Amendment. Thus, as pointed out in my dissent in that case, the majority in *Beauharnais* never even mentioned the First Amendment but upheld the state "group libel" law on the ground that it did not violate "civilized 'canons of decency,' reasonableness, etc." See 343 U.S., at 268–269. See also the dissent of Mr. Justice Jackson, at 287–305.
[23] The story of the use by the Federalists of the Alien and Sedition Acts of 1798 as a weapon to suppress the political opposition of the Jeffersonians has been graphically told in Bowers, Jefferson and Hamilton, at 362–411.

Whatever may be the wisdom, however, of an approach that would reject exceptions to the plain language of the First Amendment based upon such things as "libel," "obscenity" [24] or "fighting words," [25] such is not the issue in this case. For the majority does not, and surely would not, contend that the kind of speech involved in this case— wholly related as it is to conflicting ideas about governmental affairs and policies—falls outside the protection of the First Amendment, however narrowly that amendment may be interpreted. So the only issue presently before us is whether speech that must be well within the protection of the Amendment should be given complete protection or whether it is entitled only to such protection as is consistent in the minds of a majority of this Court with whatever interest the Government may be asserting to justify its abridgment. The Court, by stating unequivocally that there are no "absolutes" under the First Amendment, necessarily takes the position that even speech that is admittedly protected by the First Amendment is subject to the "balancing test" and that therefore no kind of speech is to be protected if the Government can assert an interest of sufficient weight to induce this Court to uphold its abridgment. In my judgment, such a sweeping denial of the existence of any inalienable right to speak undermines the very foundation upon which the First Amendment, the Bill of Rights, and, indeed, our entire structure of government rest.[26] The Founders of this Nation attempted to set up a limited government which left certain rights in the people—rights that could not be taken away without amendment of the basic charter of government. The majority's "balancing test" tells us that this is not so. It tells us that no right to think, speak or publish exists in the people that cannot be taken away if the Government finds it sufficiently imperative or expedient to do so. Thus, the "balancing test" turns our "Government of the people, by the people and for the people" into a goverment over the people.

I cannot believe that this Court would adhere to the "balancing test" to the limit of its logic. Since that "test" denies that any speech, publication or petition has an "absolute" right to protection under the First Amendment, strict adherence to it would necessarily mean that there would be only a conditional right, not a complete right, for any American to express his views to his neighbors—or for his neighbors to hear those views. In other words, not even a candidate for public office, high or low, would have an "absolute" right to speak in behalf of his candidacy, no newspaper would have an "absolute" right to print its opinion on public governmental affairs, and the American people would

---

[24] See, *e.g.*, *Roth* v. *United States*, 354 U.S. 476.
[25] See, *e.g.*, *Chaplinsky* v. *New Hampshire*, 315 U.S. 568.
[26] "The founders of our federal government were too close to oppressions and persecutions of the unorthodox, the unpopular, and the less influential to trust even elected representatives with unlimited powers of control over the individual. From their distrust were derived the first ten amendments, designed as a whole to 'limit and qualify the powers of Government,' to define 'cases in which the Government ought not to act, or to act only in a particular mode,' and to protect unpopular minorities from oppressive majorities. 1 Annals 437. The first of the ten amendments erected a Constitutional shelter for the people's liberties of religion, speech, press, and assembly. This amendment reflects the faith that a good society is not static but advancing, and that the fullest possible interchange of ideas and beliefs is essential to attainment of this goal. The proponents of the First Amendment, committed to this faith, were determined that every American should possess an unrestrained freedom to express his views, however odious they might be to vested interests whose power they might challenge." *Feldman* v. *United States*, 322 U.S. 487, 501 (dissenting opinion).

have no "absolute" right to hear such discussions. All of these rights would be dependent upon the accuracy of the scales upon which this Court weighs the respective interests of the Government and the people. It therefore seems to me that the Court's "absolute" statement that there are no "absolutes" under the First Amendment must be an exaggeration of its own views.

These examples also serve to illustrate the difference between the sort of "balancing" that the majority has been doing and the sort of "balancing" that was intended when that concept was first accepted as a method for insuring the complete protection of First Amendment freedoms even against purely incidental or inadvertent consequences. The term came into use chiefly as a result of cases in which the power of municipalities to keep their streets open for normal traffic was attacked by groups wishing to use those streets for religious or political purposes.[27] When those cases came before this Court, we did not treat the issue posed by them as one primarily involving First Amendment rights. Recognizing instead that public streets are avenues of travel which must be kept open for that purpose, we upheld various city ordinances designed to prevent unnecessary noises and congestions that disrupt the normal and necessary flow of traffic. In doing so, however, we recognized that the enforcement of even these ordinances, which attempted no regulation at all of the content of speech and which were neither openly nor surreptitiously aimed at speech, could bring about an "incidental" abridgment of speech. So we went on to point out that even ordinances directed at and regulating only conduct might be invalidated if, after "weighing" the reasons for regulating the particular conduct, we found them insufficient to justify diminishing "the exercise of rights so vital to the maintenance of democratic institutions" as those of the First Amendment.[28]

But those cases never intimated that we would uphold as constitutional an ordinance which purported to rest upon the power of a city to regulate traffic but which was aimed at speech or attempted to regulate the content of speech. None of them held, nor could they constitutionally have held, that a person rightfully walking or riding along the streets, and talking in a normal way could have his views controlled, licensed or penalized in any way by the city—for that would be a direct abridgment of speech itself. Those cases have only begun to take on that meaning by being relied upon, again and again as they are here, to justify the application of the "balancing test" to governmental action that is aimed at speech and depends for its application upon the content of speech. Thus, those cases have been used to support decisions upholding such obviously antispeech actions on the part of government as those involved in *American Communications Assn.* v. *Douds*[29] and *Dennis* v. *United States.*[30] And the use being made of those cases here must be considered as falling squarely within that class.[31]

---

[27] Typical of such cases are those referred to by the majority in its opinion here: *Schneider* v. *State*, 308 U.S. 147; *Cox* v. *New Hampshire*, 312 U.S. 569; *Prince* v. *Massachusetts*, 321 U.S. 158; *Kovacs* v. *Cooper*, 336 U.S. 77.
[28] *Schneider* v. *State*, 308 U.S. 147, 161.
[29] 339 U.S. 382, especially at 398–400.
[30] 341 U.S. 494, especially at 508–509.
[31] See also the discussion of these street-regulation cases in my dissenting opinion in *Barenblatt* v. *United States*, 360 U.S. 109, 141–142.

The Court seeks to bring this case under the authority of the street-regulation cases and to defend its use of the "balancing test" on the ground that California is attempting only to exercise its permissible power to regulate its Bar and that any effect its action may have upon speech is purely "incidental." But I cannot agree that the questions asked Konigsberg with regard to his suspected membership in the Communist Party had nothing more than an "incidental" effect upon his freedom of speech and association. Why does the Committee of Bar Examiners ask a bar applicant whether he is or has been a member of the Communist Party? The avowed purpose of such questioning is to permit the Committee to deny applicants admission to the Bar if they "advocate" forcible overthrow of the Government. Indeed, that is precisely the ground upon which the majority is here upholding the Committee's right to ask Konigsberg these questions. I realize that there has been considerable talk, even in the opinions of this Court, to the effect that "advocacy" is not "speech." But with the highest respect for those who believe that there is such a distinction, I cannot agree with it. For this reason, I think the conclusion is inescapable that this case presents the question of the constitutionality of action by the State of California designed to control the content of speech. As such, it is a "direct," and not an "incidental" abridgment of speech. Indeed if the characterization "incidental" were appropriate here, it would be difficult to imagine what would constitute a "direct" abridgment of speech. The use of the "balancing test" under these circumstances thus permits California directly to abridge speech in explicit contradiction to the plain mandate of the First Amendment.

But even if I thought the majority was correct in its view that "balancing" is proper in this case, I could not agree with its decision. In the first place, I think that the decision here is unduly restrictive upon individual liberty even under the penurious "balancing test." The majority describes the State's interest which is here to be "balanced" against the interest in protecting the freedoms of speech and association as an interest in "having lawyers who are devoted to the law in its broadest sense, including not only its substantive provisions, but also its procedures for orderly change." But is that an accurate statement of the interest of the State that is really at stake here? Konigsberg has stated unequivocally that he never has, does not now, and never will advocate the overthrow of the Government of this country by unconstitutional means, and we held when the case was here before that his evidence was sufficient to establish that fact. Since the Committee has introduced no evidence at any subsequent hearing that would lead to a contrary conclusion, the fact remains established.[32] So the issue in this case is not, as the majority's statement of the State's interest would seem to indicate, whether a person who advocates the overthrow of existing government by force must be admitted to the practice of law. All we really have on the State's side of the scales is its desire to know whether Konigsberg was ever a member of the Communist Party.

---

[32] The majority places some stress upon the fact that the Committee did not have independent investigatory resources with which to seek further evidence. In view of the complete reliance upon this decision to justify the use of an identical procedure in *In re Anastaplo*, decided today, *post*, p. 82, where the bar admission committee not only had investigatory resources but also utilized them to the fullest, this fact must be of little "weight" in the constitutional "balance."

The real lack of value of that information to the State is, to my mind, clearly shown by the fact that the State has not even attempted to make membership in the Communist Party a ground for disqualification from the Bar. Indeed, if the State's only real interest was, as the majority maintains, in having good men for its Bar, how could it have rejected Konigsberg, who, undeniably and as this Court has already held, has provided overwhelming evidence of his good character? Our former decision, which I still regard as resting on what is basically just good common sense, was that a man does not have to tell all about his previous beliefs and associations in order to establish his good character and loyalty.

When the majority turns to the interest on the other side of the scale, it admits that its decision is likely to have adverse effects upon free association caused by compulsory disclosures, but then goes on to say that those adverse effects will be "minimal" here, first, because Bar admission interrogations are private and, secondly, because the decisions of Bar admission committees are subject to judicial review. As to the first ground, the Court simply ignores the fact that California law does not require its Committee to treat information given it as confidential.[33] And besides, it taxes credulity to suppose that questions asked an applicant and answers given by him in the highly emotional area of communism would not rapidly leak out to the great injury of an applicant—regardless of what the facts of his particular case may happen to be. As to the second ground given, the Court fails to take into account the fact that judicial review widens the publicity of the questions and answers and thus tends further to undercut its first ground. At the same time, such review, as is demonstrated by this and the companion case decided today,[34] provides small hope that an applicant will be afforded relief against stubborn efforts to destroy him arbitrarily by innuendoes that will subject him to lasting suspicions. But even if I thought the Court was correct in its beliefs that the interrogation of a Bar applicant would be kept confidential and that judicial review is adequate to prevent arbitrary exclusions from the Bar, I could not accept its conclusion that the First Amendment rights involved in this case are "minimal."

The interest in free association at stake here is not merely the personal interest of petitioner in being free from burdens that may be imposed upon him for his past beliefs and associations. It is the interest of all the people in having a society in which no one is intimidated with respect to his beliefs or associations. It seems plain to me that the inevitable effect of the majority's decision is to condone a practice that will have a substantial deterrent effect upon the associations entered into by anyone who may want to become a lawyer in California. If every person who wants to be a lawyer is to be required to account for his associations as a prerequisite to admission into the practice of law, the only safe course for those desiring admission would seem to be scrupulously to avoid association with any organization that advocates anything at all somebody might possibly be against, including

---

[33] In this regard, the situation is identical to that invalidated as unconstitutional by our decision in *Shelton* v. *Tucker*, 364 U.S. 479. Indeed, the absence of such a requirement was there stressed as an important part of the ground upon which that decision rested. *Id.*, at 486.

[34] *In re Anastaplo, supra.* See also the discussion in my dissenting opinion in that case, especially at pp. 108–112.

groups whose activities are constitutionally protected under even the most restricted notion of the First Amendment.[35]   And, in the currently prevailing atmosphere in this country, I can think of few organizations active in favor of civil liberties that are not highly controversial.[36]   In addition, it seems equally clear that anyone who had already associated himself with an organization active in favor of civil liberties before he developed an interest in the law, would, after this case, be discouraged from spending the large amounts of time and money necessary to obtain a legal education in the hope that he could practice law in California.

Thus, in my view, the majority has reached its decision here against the freedoms of the First Amendment by a fundamental misapplication of its own currently, but I hope only temporarily, prevailing "balancing" test.   The interest of the Committee in satisfying its curiosity with respect to Konigsberg's "possible" membership in the Communist Party two decades ago has been inflated out of all proportion to its real value—the vast interest of the public in maintaining unabridged the basic freedoms of speech, press and assembly has been paid little if anything more than lipservice—and important constitutional rights have once again been "balanced" away.   This, of course, is an ever-present danger of the "balancing test" for the application of such a test is necessarily tied to the emphasis particular judges give to competing societal values.   Judges, like everyone else, vary tremendously in their choice of values.   This is perfectly natural and, indeed, unavoidable.   But it is neither natural nor unavoidable in this country for the fundamental rights of the people to be dependent upon the different emphasis different judges put upon different values at different times.   For those rights, particularly the First Amendment rights involved here, were unequivocally set out by the Founders in our Bill of Rights in the very plainest of language, and they should not be diluted by "tests" that obliterate them whenever particular judges think values they most highly cherish outweigh the values most highly cherished by the Founders.

Moreover, it seems to me that the "balancing test" is here being applied to cut the heart out of one of the very few liberty-protecting decisions that this Court has rendered in the last decade.   *Speiser* v. *Randall* [37] struck down, as a violation of the Federal Constitution, a State law which denied tax exemptions to veterans who refused to sign an oath that they did not advocate "the overthrow of the Government of the United States or of the State of California by force or violence or other unlawful means . . . ." [38]   The case arose when certain veterans insisted upon their right to the exemptions without signing the oath.   The California Supreme Court rejected the veterans' constitutional contention that the State law violated due process by placing the burden of proof upon the taxpayer to prove that he did not advocate violent overthrow of the Government.   This Court

---

[35] The situation here is thus identical to that in *Speiser* v. *Randall*, where the Court expressly recognized the danger to protected associations.   See 357 U.S. 513, 526.

[36] Cf. *Shelton* v. *Tucker, supra,* at 486, n. 7, where we took note of testimony that efforts were being made to remove from a school system all teachers who supported such organizations as the American Civil Liberties Union, the Urban League, the American Association of University Professors, and the Women's Emergency Committee to Open Our Schools.

[37] 357 U.S. 513.

[38] Section 32 of the California Revenue and Taxation Code.   This section was set out in full in the majority opinion in *Speiser.* 357 U.S., at 516–517, n. 2.

reversed, with only one Justice dissenting, on the ground that the necessary effect of such an imposition of the burden of proof "can only result in a deterrence of speech which the Constitution makes free." [39] Indeed, the majority opinion in the *Speiser* case distinguished the very cases upon which the majority here is relying on the ground that "the oaths required in those cases performed a very different function from the declaration in issue here. In the earlier cases it appears that the loyalty oath, once signed, became conclusive evidence of the facts attested so far as the right to office was concerned. If the person took the oath he retained his position. The oath was not part of a device to shift to the officeholder the burden of proving his right to retain his position." [40] But that is precisely what is happening here. For, even though Konigsberg has taken an oath that he does not advocate the violent overthrow of the Government, the Committee has persisted in the view that he has not as yet demonstrated his right to admission to the Bar. If that does not amount to the sort of shifting of the burden of proof that is proscribed by *Speiser*, I do not know what would.

The situation in the present case is closely analogous to that condemned in the *Speiser* case and, indeed, the major factual difference between the two cases tends to make this case an even stronger one. Here, as in *Speiser*, the State requires an oath that the person involved does not advocate violent overthrow of the Government. Here as there, the taking of the oath is not conclusive of the rights of the person involved. And here, as there, contrary to the implications in the majority opinion, I think it clear that the State places upon each applicant for admission to the Bar the burden of proving that he does not advocate the violent overthrow of the Government. There is one difference between the two cases, for here Konigsberg agreed to take the oath required and he refused to answer only when the State insisted upon more. Surely he cannot be penalized for his greater willingness to cooperate with the State.

The majority also suggests that the *Speiser* case may be distinguishable because it involved merely the power of the State to impose a penalty, by way of a heavier tax burden, upon a person who refused to take an oath, while this case involves the power of the State to determine the qualifications a person must have to be admitted to the Bar—a position of importance to the public. This distinction seems to me to be little more than a play on words. Speiser had the burden of proving that he did not advocate the overthrow of the Government and, upon his refusal to satisfy this burden, he was forced to pay additional taxes as a penalty. Konigsberg has the burden of proving that he does not advocate the violent overthrow of the Government and, upon his supposed failure to meet this burden, he is being denied an opportunity to practice the profession for which he has expended much time and money to prepare himself. So far as I am concerned the consequences to Konigsberg, whether considered from a financial standpoint, a social standpoint, or any other standpoint I can think of, constitute a more serious "penalty" than that imposed upon Speiser.

---

[39] 357 U.S., at 526.
[40] *Id.*, at 528. The cases so distinguished were *Garner* v. *Board of Public Works*, 341 U.S. 716; *Gerende* v. *Board of Supervisors*, 341 U.S. 56, and *American Communications Assn.* v. *Douds*, 339 U.S. 382.

In my judgment this case must take its place in the ever-lengthening line of cases in which individual liberty to think, speak, write, associate and petition is being abridged in a manner precisely contrary to the explicit commands of the First Amendment.[41] And I believe the abridgment of liberty here, as in most of the other cases in that line, is based upon nothing more than a fear that the American people can be alienated from their allegiance of our form of government by the talk of zealots for a form of government that is hostile to everything for which this country now stands or ever has stood. I think this fear is groundless for I believe that the loyalty and patriotism of the American people toward our own free way of life are too deeply rooted to be shaken by mere talk or argument from people who are wedded to totalitarian forms of government. It was this kind of faith in the American people that brought about the adoption of the First Amendment, which was expressly designed to let people say what they wanted to about government—even against government if they were so inclined. The idea underlying this then revolutionary idea of freedom was that the Constitution had set up a government so favorable to individual liberty that arguments against that government would fall harmless at the feet of a satisfied and happy citizenship. Thomas Jefferson voiced this idea with simple eloquence on the occasion of his first inauguration as President of the United States: "If there be any among us who would wish to dissolve this Union or to change its republican form, let them stand undisturbed as monuments of the safety with which error of opinion may be tolerated where reason is left free to combat it." [42]

In the main, this is the philosophy under which this country has lived and prospered since its creation. There have, however, been two notable exceptions, the first being the period of the short-lived and unlamented alien and sedition laws of the late 1700's, and the other being the period since the beginning of the "cold war" shortly after the close of World War II, in which there has been a widespread fear of an imagined overwhelming persuasiveness in Communist arguments. The most commonly offered justification for the liberty-stifling measures that have characterized this latter period is that the Communists do not themselves believe in the freedoms of speech, press and assembly so they should not be allowed to take advantage of the freedoms our Constitution provides. But, as illustrated by this and many other cases, the effect of repressive laws and inquisitions of this kind cannot be and is not limited to Communists.[43] Moreover, the fact that Communists practice repression of these freedoms is, in my judgment, the last reason in the world that we should do so. We do not have to imitate the Communists in order to survive. Our Bill of Rights placed our survival upon a firmer ground—that of freedom, not repression.

---

[41] This line has already been considerably lengthened during this very Term of Court. See, e.g., *Uphaus* v. *Wyman*, 364 U.S. 388 ; *Times Film Corp.* v. *City of Chicago*, 365 U.S. 43 ; *Wilkinson* v. *United States*, 365 U.S. 399 ; *Braden* v. *United States*, 365 U.S. 431.
[42] Thomas Jefferson, First Inaugural Address, March 4, 1801. This address is reprinted in Jones, Primer of Intellectual Freedom 142, 143 (Harvard University Press, 1949).
[43] "Centuries of experience testify that laws aimed at one political or religious group, however rational these laws may be in their beginnings, generate hatreds and prejudices which rapidly spread beyond control. Too often it is fear which inspires such passions, and nothing is more reckless or contagious. In the resulting hysteria, popular indignation tars with the same brush all those who have ever been associated with any member of the group under attack or who hold a view which, though supported by revered Americans as essential to democracy, has been adopted by that group for its own purposes." *American Communications Assn.* v. *Douds*, 339 U.S. 382, 448–449 (dissenting opinion).

Nothing in this record shows that Konigsberg has ever been guilty of any conduct that threatens our safety. Quite the contrary, the record indicates that we are fortunate to have men like him in this country for it shows that Konigsberg is a man of firm convictions who has stood up and supported this country's freedom in peace and in war. The writings that the record shows he has published constitute vehement protests against the idea of overthrowing this Government by force. No witness could be found throughout the long years of this inquisition who could say, or even who would say, that Konigsberg has ever raised his voice or his hand against his country. He is, therefore, but another victim of the prevailing fashion of destroying men for the views it is suspected they might entertain.

Mr. Justice Brennan, with whom The Chief Justice joins, dissenting.

This judgment must be reversed even if we assume with Mr. Justice Traynor in his dissent in the California Supreme Court, 52 Cal. 2d 769, 774, at 776, 344 P. 2d 777, 780, at 781–782, that "a question as to present or past membership in [the Communist Party] is relevant to the issue of possible criminal advocacy and hence to [Konigsberg's] qualifications." The Committee did not come forward, in the proceeding we passed upon in 353 U.S. 252, nor in the subsequent proceeding, with evidence to show that Konigsberg unlawfully advocated the overthrow of the Government. Under our decision in *Speiser* v. *Randall,* 357 U.S. 513, the Fourteenth Amendment therefore protects Konigsberg from being denied admission to the Bar for his refusal to answer the questions. In *Speiser* we held that ". . . when the constitutional right to speak is sought to be deterred by a State's general taxing program due process demands that the speech be unencumbered until the State comes forward with sufficient proof to justify its inhibition." 357 U.S., pp. 528–529. "There may be differences of degree," Mr. Justice Traynor said, "in the public interest in the fitness of the applicants for tax exemption and for admission to the Bar"; yet, as to the latter also, "Such a procedure is logically dictated by *Speiser. . . .*" 52 Cal. 2d, p. 776, 344 P. 2d, p. 782. And unless mere whimsy governs this Court's decisions in situations impossible rationally to distinguish, such a procedure is indeed constitutionally required here. The same reasons apply. For Mr. Justice Traynor was entirely right in saying: "Whatever its relevancy [the question as to past or present Party membership] in a particular context, . . . it is an extraordinary variant of the usual inquiry into crime, for the attendant burden of proof upon any one under question poses the immediate threat of prior restraint upon the free speech of all applicants. The possibility of inquiry into their speech, the heavy burden upon them to establish its innocence, and the evil repercussions of inquiry despite innocence, would constrain them to speak their minds so noncommittally that no one could ever mistake their innocuous words for advocacy. This grave danger to freedom of speech could be averted without loss to legitimate investigation by shifting the burden to the examiners. Confronted with a prima facie case, an applicant would then be obliged to rebut it." *Id.*, p. 776, 344 P. 2d, p. 782.

The Court admits the complete absence of any such predicate by the Committee for its questions. The Court attempts to distinguish the situations in order to escape the controlling authority of *Speiser*. The speciousness of its reasoning is exposed in MR. JUSTICE BLACK's dissent. I would reverse.

EXCLUSION FROM INCIDENTAL BENEFITS

SPEISER v. RANDALL, ASSESSOR OF CONTRA COSTA COUNTY, CALIFORNIA

APPEAL FROM THE SUPREME COURT OF CALIFORNIA

No. 483. Argued April 8–9, 1958.—Decided June 30, 1958.*

Solely because they refuse to subscribe oaths that tney do not advocate the overthrow of the Federal or State Government by force, violence or other unlawful means, or advocate the support of a foreign government against the United States in event of hostilities, appellants were denied tax exemptions provided for veterans by the California Constitution. The filing of such an oath was required by a California statute as a prerequisite to qualification for the tax exemption, in order to effectuate a provision of the State Constitution denying any tax exemption to any person who advocates such actions, which was construed by the State supreme court as denying tax exemptions only to claimants who engage in speech which may be criminally punished consistently with the free-speech guarantees of the Federal Constitution. *Held:* Enforcement of this provision through procedures which place the burdens of proof and persuasion on the taxpayers denied them freedom of speech without the procedural safeguards required by the Due Process Clause of the Fourteenth Amendment. Pp. 514–529.

1. A discriminatory denial of a tax exemption for engaging in speech is a limitation on free speech. Pp. 518–520.

2. The method chosen by California for determining whether a claimant is a member of the class to which its Supreme Court has said that the tax exemption is denied does not provide the procedural safeguards required by the Due Process Clause of the Fourteenth Amendment before free speech may be denied, since it places on the taxpayer the burden of proving that he is not a member of that class. Pp. 520–529.

(a) When a State undertakes to restrain unlawful advocacy, it must provide procedures which are adequate to safeguard against infringement of constitutionally protected rights. Pp. 520–521.

(b) The California procedure places upon the taxpayer the burden of proving that he does not criminally advocate the overthrow of the Federal or State Government by force, violence or other unlawful means or advocate the support of a foreign government against the United States in the event of hostilities. Pp. 521–523.

(c) It does not follow that because only a tax liability is here involved, the ordinary tax assessment procedures are adequate when applied to penalize speech. Pp. 523–525.

(d) Since free speech is involved, due process requires in the circumstances of this case that the State bear the burden of showing that appellants engaged in criminal speech. Pp. 525–526.

(e) *Garner* v. *Board of Public Works,* 341 U.S. 716; *Gerende* v. *Board of Supervisors,* 341 U.S. 56, and *American Communications Assn.* v. *Douds,* 339 U. S. 382, distinguished. Pp. 527–528.

(f) When the constitutional right to speak is sought to be deterred by a State's general taxing program, due process demands that the speech be unencumbered until the State comes forward with sufficient proof to justify its inhibition. Pp. 528–529.

(g) Since the entire statutory procedure violated the requirements of due process by placing the burdens of proof and persuasion on them, appellants were not obliged to take even the first step in such procedure as a condition for obtaining the tax exemption. P. 529.

48 Cal. 2d 472, 903, 311 P. 2d 544, 546, reversed and causes remanded.

*Together with No. 484, *Prince* v. *City and County of San Francisco,* also on appeal from the same Court.

Lawrence Speiser argued the cause for appellants. With him on the brief was *Franklin H. Williams*.

George W. McClure argued the cause for appellee in No. 483, and *Robert M. Desky* argued the cause for appellee in No. 484. With them on the brief was *Dion R. Holm*.

Shad Polier, Will Maslow and *Leo Pfeffer* filed a brief for the American Jewish Congress, as *amicus curiae*.

Mr. Justice Brennan delivered the opinion of the Court.

The appellants are honorably discharged veterans of World War II who claimed the veterans' property-tax exemption provided by Art. XIII, § 1¼, of the California constitution. Under California law applicants for such exemption must annually complete a standard form of application and file it with the local assessor. The form was revised in 1954 to add an oath by the applicant: "I do not advocate the overthrow of the Government of the United States or of the State of California by force or violence or other unlawful means, nor advocate the support of a foreign government against the United States in event of hostilities." Each refused to subscribe the oath and struck it from the form which he executed and filed for the tax year 1954–1955. Each contended that the exaction of the oath as a condition of obtaining a tax exemption was forbidden by the Federal Constitution. The respective assessors denied the exemption solely for the refusal to execute the oath. The Supreme Court of California sustained the assessors' actions against the appellants' claims of constitutional invalidity.[1] We noted probable jurisdiction of the appeals, 355 U.S. 880.

Article XX, § 19, of the California constitution, adopted at the general election of November 4, 1952, provides as follows:

> "Notwithstanding any other provision of this constitution, no person or organization which advocates the overthrow of the Government of the United States or the State by force or violence or other unlawful means or who advocates the support of a foreign government against the United States in the event of hostilities shall:

> .   .   .   .   .

> "(b) Receive any exemption from any tax imposed by this State or any county, city or county, city, district, political subdivision, authority, board, bureau, commission or other public agency of this State.

> "The Legislature shall enact such laws as may be necessary to enforce the provisions of this section."

To effectuate this constitutional amendment the California Legislature enacted § 32 of the Revenue and Taxation Code which requires the claimant, as a prerequisite to qualification for any property-tax exemption, to sign a statement on his tax return declaring that he

---

[1] Appellant in No. 483 sued for declaratory relief in the Superior Court of Contra Costa County. Five judges sitting *en banc* held that both § 19 of Art. XX and § 32 of the Revenue and Taxation Code were invalid under the Fourteenth Amendment as restrictions on freedom of speech. The California Supreme Court reversed. 48 Cal. 2d 903, 311 P. 2d 546.

Appellant in No. 484 sued in the Superior Court for the City and County of San Francisco to recover taxes paid under protest and for declaratory relief. The court upheld the validity of both the constitutional provision and § 32 of the Code. The Supreme Court affirmed. 48 Cal. 2d 472, 311 P. 2d 544.

In both cases the Supreme Court adopted the reasoning of its opinion in *First Unitarian Church* v. *County of Los Angeles*, 48 Cal. 2d 419, 311 P. 2d 508, in which identical issues are discussed at length. Hereinafter we will refer to that opinion as expressing the views of the California Supreme Court in the present cases.

does not engage in the activities described in the constitutional amendment.[2]   The California Supreme Court held that this declaration, like other statements required of those filing tax returns, was designed to relieve the tax assessor of "the burden . . . of ascertaining the facts with reference to tax exemption claimants." 48 Cal. 2d 419, 432, 311 P. 2d 508, 515. The declaration, while intended to provide a means of determining whether a claimant qualifies for the exemption under the constitutional amendment, is not conclusive evidence of eligibility. The assessor has the duty of investigating the facts underlying all tax liabilities and is empowered by § 454 of the Code to subpoena taxpayers for the purpose of questioning them about statements they have furnished.   If the assessor believes that the claimant is not qualified in any respect, he may deny the exemption and require the claimant, on judicial review, to prove the incorrectness of the determination.   In other words, the factual determination whether the taxpayer is eligible for the exemption under the constitutional amendment is made in precisely the same manner as the determination of any other fact bearing on tax liability.

The appellants attack these provisions, *inter alia*, as denying them freedom of speech without the procedural safeguards required by the Due Process Clause of the Fourteenth Amendment.[3]

I.

It cannot be gainsaid that a discriminatory denial of a tax exemption for engaging in speech is a limitation on free speech.   The Supreme Court of California recognized that these provisions were limitations on speech but concluded that "by no standard can the infringement upon freedom of speech imposed by section 19 of article XX be deemed a substantial one." 48 Cal. 2d 419, 440, 311 P. 2d 508, 521. It is settled that speech can be effectively limited by the exercise of the taxing power. *Grosjean* v. *American Press Co.*, 297 U.S. 233. To deny an exemption to claimants who engage in certain forms of speech is in effect to penalize them for such speech. Its deterrent effect is the same as if the State were to fine them for this speech. The appellees are plainly mistaken in their argument that, because a tax exemption is a "privilege" or "bounty," its denial may not

---

[2] Section 32 provides:
"Any statement, return, or other document in which is claimed any exemption, other than the householder's exemption, from any property tax imposed by this State or any county, city or county, city, district, political subdivision, authority, board, bureau, commission or other public agency of this State shall contain a declaration that the person or organization making the statement, return, or other document does not advocate the overthrow of the Government of the United States or of the State of California by force or violence or other unlawful means nor advocate the support of a foreign government against the United States in event of hostilities.   If any such statement, return, or other document does not contain such declaration, the person or organization making such statement, return, or other document shall not receive any exemption from the tax to which the statement, return, or other document pertains.   Any person or organization who makes such declaration knowing it to be false is guilty of a felony.   This section shall be construed so as to effectuate the purpose of Section 19 of Article XX of the Constitution."

[3] This contention was raised in the complaint and is argued in the brief in this Court. The California Supreme Court rejected the contention as without merit. 48 Cal. 2d 472, 475, 311 P. 2d 544, 545–546.
Appellants also argue that these provisions are invalid (1) as invading liberty of speech protected by the Due Process Clause of the Fourteenth Amendment; (2) as denying equal protection because the oath is required only as to property-tax and corporation-income-tax exemptions, but not as to the householder's personal-income-tax, gift-tax, inheritance-tax, or sales-tax exemptions; and (3) as violating the Supremacy Clause because this legislation intrudes in a field of exclusive Federal control. *Pennsylvania* v. *Nelson*, 350 U.S. 497. Our disposition of the cases makes considerations of these questions unnecessary.

infringe speech. This contention did not prevail before the California courts, which recognized that conditions imposed upon the granting of privileges or gratuities must be "reasonable." It has been said the Congress may not by withdrawal of mailing privileges place limitations upon the freedom of speech which if directly attempted would be unconstitutional. See *Hannegan* v. *Esquire, Inc.*, 327 U.S. 146, 156; cf. *Milwaukee Publishing Co.* v. *Burleson*, 255 U.S. 407, 430–431 (Brandeis, J., dissenting). This Court has similarly rejected the contention that speech was not abridged when the sole restraint on its exercise was withdrawal of the opportunity to invoke the facilities of the National Labor Relations Board, *American Communications Assn.* v. *Douds*, 339 U.S. 382, 402, or the opportunity for public employment, *Wieman* v. *Updegraff*, 344 U.S. 183. So here, the denial of a tax exemption for engaging in certain speech necessarily will have the effect of coercing the claimants to refrain from the proscribed speech. The denial is "frankly aimed at the suppression of dangerous ideas." *American Communications Assn.* v. *Douds, supra*, at 402.

The Supreme Court of California construed the constitutional amendment as denying the tax exemptions only to claimants who engage in speech which may be criminally punished consistently with the free-speech guarantees of the Federal Constitution. The court defined advocacy of "the overthrow of the Government . . . by force or violence or other unlawful means" and advocacy of "support of a foreign government against the United States in event of hostilities" as reaching only conduct which may constitutionally be punished under either the California Criminal Syndicalism Act, Cal. Stat. 1919, c. 188, see *Whitney* v. *California*, 274 U.S. 357, or the Federal Smith Act, 18 U.S.C. § 2385. 48 Cal. 2d, at 428, 311 p. 2d, at 513. It also said that it would apply the standards set down by this Court in *Dennis* v. *United States*, 341 U.S. 494, in ascertaining the circumstances which would justify punishing speech as a crime.[4] Of course the constitutional and statutory provisions here involved must be read in light of the restrictive construction that the California court, in the exercise of its function of interpreting State law, has placed upon them. For the purposes of this case we assume without deciding that California may deny tax exemptions to persons who engage in the proscribed speech for which they might be fined or imprisoned.[5]

II.

But the question remains whether California has chosen a fair method for determining when a claimant is a member of that class to which the California court has said the constitutional and statutory provisions extend. When we deal with the complex of strands in the web of freedoms which make up free speech, the operation and effect of the method by which speech is sought to be restrained must be subjected to close analysis and critical judgment in the light of the particular circumstances to which it is applied. *Kingsley Books*,

[4] The California Supreme Court construed these provisions as inapplicable to mere belief. On oral argument counsel for the taxing authorities further conceded that the provisions would not apply in the case of advocacy of mere "abstract doctrine." See *Yates* v. *United States*, 354 U.S. 298, 312–327.

[5] Appellants contend that under this Court's decision in *Pennsylvania* v. *Nelson*, 350 U.S. 497, the State can no longer enforce its criminal statutes aimed at subversion. We need not decide whether this contention is sound; nor need we consider whether, if it is, it follows that California cannot deny tax exemptions to those who in fact are in violation of the Federal and State sedition laws.

Inc., v. *Brown,* 354 U.S. 436, 441–442; *Near* v. *Minnesota,* 283 U.S. 697; cf. *Cantwell* v. *Connecticut,* 310 U.S. 296, 305; *Joseph Burstyn, Inc.,* v. *Wilson,* 343 U.S. 495; *Winters* v. *New York,* 333 U.S. 507; *Niemotko* v. *Maryland,* 340 U.S. 268; *Staub* v. *City of Baxley,* 355 U.S. 313.

To experienced lawyers it is commonplace that the outcome of a lawsuit—and hence the vindication of legal rights—depends more often on how the factfinder appraises the facts than on a disputed construction of a statute or interpretation of a line of precedents. Thus the procedures by which the facts of the case are determined assume an importance fully as great as the validity of the substantive rule of law to be applied. And the more important the rights at stake the more important must be the procedural safeguards surrounding those rights. Cf. *Powell* v. *Alabama,* 287 U.S. 45, 71. When the State undertakes to restrain unlawful advocacy it must provide procedures which are adequate to safeguard against infringement of constitutionally protected rights—rights which we value most highly and which are essential to the workings of a free society. Moreover, since only considerations of the greatest urgency can justify restrictions on speech, and since the validity of a restraint on speech in each case depends on careful analysis of the particular circumstances, cf. *Dennis* v. *United States, supra; Whitney* v. *California, supra,* the procedures by which the facts of the case are adjudicated are of special importance and the validity of the restraint may turn on the safeguards which they afford. Compare *Kunz v. New York,* 340 U.S. 290, with *Feiner* v. *New York,* 340 U.S. 315. It becomes essential, therefore, to scrutinize the procedures by which California has sought to restrain speech.

The principal feature of the California procedure, as the appellees themselves point out, is that the appellants, "as taxpayers under State law, have the affirmative burden of proof, in Court as well as before the assessor. . . . [I]t is their burden to show that they are proper persons to qualify under the self-executing constitutional provision for the tax exemption in question—i.e., that they are not persons who advocate the overthrow of the Government of the United States or the State by force or violence or other unlawful means or who advocate the support of a foreign government against the United States in the event of hostilities. . . . [T]he burden is on *them* to produce evidence justifying their claim of exemption." [6] Not only does the initial bur-

---

[6] The California Supreme Court held that § 19 of Art. XX of the State constitution was in effect self-executing. "[U]nder the tax laws of the state wholly apart from section 32 it is the duty of the assessor to ascertain the facts with reference to the taxability or exemption from taxation of property within his jurisdiction. And it is also the duty of the property owner to cooperate with the assessor and assist him in the ascertainment of these facts by declarations under oath." 48 Cal. 2d, at 430, 311 P. 2d, at 514–515.

In all events, if the assessor "is satisfied from his investigations that the exemption should not be allowed he may assess the property as not exempt and if contested compel a determination of the facts in a suit to recover the tax paid under protest. In such a case it would be necessary for the claimant to allege and prove facts with reference to the nature, extent and character of the property which would justify the exemption and compliance with all valid regulations in the presentation and prosecution of the claim. In any event it is the duty of the assessor to ascertain the facts from any legal source available. In performing this task he is engaged in the assembly of facts which are to serve as a guide in arriving at his conclusion whether an exemption should or should not be allowed. That conclusion is in no wise a final determination that the claimant belongs to a class proscribed by section 19 of article XX or is guilty of any activity there denounced. The presumption of innocence available to all in criminal prosecutions does not in a case such as this relieve or prevent the assessor from making the investigation enjoined upon him by law to see that exemptions are not improperly allowed. His administrative determination is not binding on the tax exemption claimant but it is sufficient to authorize him to tax the property as nonexempt and to place the burden on the claimant to test the validity of his administrative determination in an action at law." 48 Cal. 2d, at 431–432, 311 P. 2d, at 515.

den of bringing forth proof of nonadvocacy rest on the taxpayer, but throughout the judicial and administrative proceedings the burden lies on the taxpayer of persuading the assessor, or the court, that he falls outside the class denied the tax exemption. The declaration required by § 32 is but a part of the probative process by which the State seeks to determine which taxpayers fall into the proscribed category.[7] Thus the declaration cannot be regarded as having such independent significance that failure to sign it precludes review of the validity of the procedure of which it is a part. Cf. *Staub* v. *City of Baxley, supra*, at 318–319. The question for decision, therefore, is whether this allocation of the burden of proof, on an issue concerning freedom of speech, falls short of the requirements of due process.

It is of course within the power of the State to regulate procedures under which its laws are carried out, including the burden of producing evidence and the burden of persuasion, "unless in so doing it offends some principle of justice so rooted in the traditions and conscience of our people as to be ranked as fundamental." *Snyder* v. *Masschusetts*, 291 U.S. 97, 105. "[O]f course the legislature may go a good way in raising . . . [presumptions] or in changing the burden of proof, but there are limits. . . . [I]t is not within the province of a legislature to declare an individual guilty or presumptively guilty of a crime." *McFarland* v. *American Sugar Refining Co.*, 241 U.S. 79, 86. The legislature cannot "place upon all defendants in criminal cases the burden of going forward with the evidence. . . . [It cannot] validly command that the finding of an indictment, or mere proof of the identity of the accused, should create a presumption of the existence of all the facts essential to guilt. This is not permissible." *Tot* v. *United States*, 319 U.S. 463, 469. Of course, the burden of going forward with the evidence at some stages of a criminal trial may be placed on the defendant, but only after the State has "proved enough to make it just for the defendant to be required to repel what has been proved with excuse or explanation, or at least that upon a balancing of convenience or of the opportunities for knowledge the shifting of the burden will be found to be an aid to the accuser without subjecting the accused to hardship or oppression." *Morrison* v. *California*, 291 U.S. 82, 88–89. In civil cases too this Court has struck down State statutes unfairly shifting the burden of proof. *Western & A. R. Co.* v. *Henderson*, 279 U.S. 639; cf. *Mobile, J. & K. C. R. Co.* v. *Turnipseed*, 219 U.S. 35, 43.

---

[7] It is suggested that the opinion of the California Supreme Court be read as holding that "the filing, whether the oath be true or false, would conclusively establish the taxpayer's eligibility for an exemption." But the California court expressly stated that "it is the duty of the assessor to see that exemptions are not allowed contrary to law and this of course includes those which are contrary to the prohibitions provided for in section 19 of article XX," 48 Cal. 2d 419, 431, 311 P. 2d 508, 515, and that the "mandatory and prohibitory" provision of § 19 of Art. XX "applies to all tax exemption claimants." 48 Cal. 2d. at 428, 311 P. 2d, at 513. Indeed, the tax authorities of California themselves point out that the signing of the declaration is not conclusive of the right to the tax exemption. The brief of the taxing authorities in the companion case, *First Unitarian Church* v. *County of Los Angeles, post*, p. 545, states, "Section 32 is an evidentiary provision. Its purpose and effect are to afford to the Assessor information *to guide his compliance* with and his enforcement of the Constitution's prohibition . . . ." (Emphasis supplied.)
It is also suggested that this Court construe the California legislation contrary to the clearly expressed construction of the California Supreme Court and thus avoid decision of the question of procedural due process. But this construction would not avoid decision of constitutional questions but rather would create the necessity for decision of the broader constitutional question of the validity of § 19 of Art. XX. A more fundamental objection to the suggestion, of course, is that it does violence to the basic constitutional principle that the construction of State laws is the exclusive responsibility of the State courts.

It is true that due process may not always compel the full formalities of a criminal prosecution before criminal advocacy can be suppressed or deterred, but it is clear that the State which attempts to do so must provide procedures amply adequate to safeguard against invasion speech which the Constitution protects. *Kingsley Books, Inc.,* v. *Brown, supra.* It is, of course, familiar practice in the administration of a tax program for the taxpayer to carry the burden of introducing evidence to rebut the determination of the collector. *Phillips* v. *Dime Trust Co.,* 284 U.S. 160, 167; *Brown* v. *Helvering,* 291 U.S. 193, 199. But while the fairness of placing the burden of proof on the taxpayer in most circumstances is recognized, this Court has not hesitated to declare a summary tax-collection procedure a violation of due process when the purported tax was shown to be in reality a penalty for a crime. *Lipke* v. *Lederer,* 259 U.S. 557; cf. *Helwig* v. *United States,* 188 U.S. 605. The underlying rationale of these cases is that where a person is to suffer a penalty for a crime he is entitled to greater procedural safeguards than when only the amount of his tax liability is in issue. Similarly it does not follow that because only a tax liability is here involved, the ordinary tax assessment procedures are adequate when applied to penalize speech.

It is true that in the present case the appellees purport to do no more than compute the amount of the taxpayer's liability in accordance with the usual procedures, but in fact they have undertaken to determine whether certain speech falls within a class which constitutionally may be curtailed. As cases decided in this Court have abundantly demonstrated, the line between speech unconditionally guaranteed and speech which may legitimately be regulated, suppressed, or punished is finely drawn. *Thomas* v. *Collins,* 323 U. S. 516; cf. *Yates* v. *United States,* 354 U. S. 298. The separation of legitimate from illegitimate speech calls for more sensitive tools than California has supplied. In all kinds of litigation it is plain that where the burden of proof lies may be decisive of the outcome. *Cities Service Oil Co.* v. *Dunlap,* 308 U. S. 208; *United States* v. *New York, N. H. & H. R. Co.,* 355 U. S. 253; *Sampson* v. *Channell,* 110 F. 2d 754, 758. There is always in litigation a margin of error, representing error in factfinding, which both parties must take into account. Where one party has at stake an interest of transcending value—as a criminal defendant his liberty—this margin of error is reduced as to him by the process of placing on the other party the burden of producing a sufficiency of proof in the first instance, and of persuading the factfinder at the conclusion of the trial of his guilt beyond a reasonable doubt. Due process commands that no man shall lose his liberty unless the Government has borne the burden of producing the evidence and convincing the factfinder of his guilt. *Tot* v. *United States, supra.* Where the transcendent value of speech is involved, due process certainly requires in the circumstances of this case that the State bear the burden of persuasion to show that the appellants engaged in criminal speech. Cf. *Kingsley Books, Inc.,* v. *Brown, supra.*

The vice of the present procedures is that, where particular speech falls close to the line separating the lawful and the unlawful, the possibility of mistaken factfinding—inherent in all litigation—will create the danger that the legitimate utterance will be penalized. The man who knows that he must bring forth proof and persuade another of the lawfulness of his conduct necessarily must steer far wider of the unlawful zone than if the State must bear these burdens. This is especially to be feared when the complexity of the proofs and the generality of the standards applied, cf. *Dennis* v. *United States, supra,* provide but shifting sands on which the litigant must maintain his position. How can a claimant whose declaration is rejected possibly sustain the burden of proving the negative of these complex factual elements? In practical operation, therefore, this procedural device must necessarily produce a result which the State could not command directly. It can only result in a deterrence of speech which the Constitution makes free. "It is apparent that a constitutional prohibition cannot be transgressed indirectly by the creation of a statutory presumption any more than it can be violated by direct enactment. The power to create presumptions is not a means of escape from constitutional restrictions." *Bailey* v. *Alabama,* 219 U. S. 219, 239.

The appellees, in controverting this position, rely on cases in which this Court has sustained the validity of loyalty oaths required of public employees, *Garner* v. *Board of Public Works,* 341 U.S. 716, candidates for public office, *Gerende* v. *Board of Supervisors,* 341 U.S. 56, and officers of labor unions, *American Communications Assn.* v. *Douds, supra.* In these cases, however, there was no attempt directly to control speech but rather to protect, from an evil shown to be grave, some interest clearly within the sphere of governmental concern. The purpose of the legislation sustained in the *Douds* case, the Court found, was to minimize the danger of political strikes disruptive of interstate commerce by discouraging labor unions from electing Communist Party members to union office. While the Court recognized that the necessary effect of the legislation was to discourage the exercise of rights protected by the First Amendment, this consequence was said to be only indirect. The congressional purpose was to achieve an objective other than restraint on speech. Only the method of achieving this end touched on protected rights and that only tangentially. The evil at which Congress had attempted to strike in that case was thought sufficiently grave to justify limited infringement of political rights. Similar considerations governed the other cases. Each case concerned a limited class of persons in or aspiring to public positions by virtue of which they could, if evilly motivated, create serious danger to the public safety. The principal aim of those statutes was not to penalize political beliefs but to deny positions to persons supposed to be dangerous because the postion might be misused to the detriment of the public. The present legislation, however, can have no such justification. It purports to deal directly with speech and the expression of political ideas. "Encouragement to loyalty to our institutions . . . [is a doctrine] which the state has plainly promulgated and intends to foster." 48 Cal. 2d, at 439, 311 P. 2d, at 520. The State argues that veterans as a class occupy a position of special trust and influence in the community, and therefore any veteran who engages in the proscribed advocacy constitutes a special danger to the State. But while a union official or public employee may be deprived of his position and thereby removed from the place of special danger, the State is powerless to erase the service which the veteran has rendered his country; though he be denied a tax exemption, he remains a veteran. The State, consequently, can act against the veteran only as it can act against any other citizen, by imposing penalties to deter the unlawful conduct.

Moreover, the oaths required in those cases performed a very different function from the declaration in issue here. In the earlier cases it appears that the loyalty oath, once signed, became conclusive evidence of the facts attested so far as the right to office was concerned. If the person took the oath he retained his position. The oath was not part of a device to shift to the officeholder the burden of proving his right to retain his position.[8] The signer, of course, could be prosecuted for perjury, but only in accordance with the strict procedural safeguards surrounding such criminal prosecutions. In the present case, however, it is clear that the declaration may be accepted or rejected on the basis of incompetent information or no information at all. It is only a step in a process throughout which the taxpayer must bear the burden of proof.

Believing that the principles of those cases have no application here, we hold that when the constitutional right to speak is sought to be deterred by a State's general taxing program due process demands that the speech be unencumbered until the State comes forward with sufficient proof to justify its inhibition. The State clearly has no such compelling interest at stake as to justify a short-cut procedure which must inevitably result in suppressing protected speech. Accordingly, though the validity of § 19 of Art. XX of the State Constitution be conceded *arguendo*, its enforcement through procedures which place the burdens of proof and persuasion on the taxpayer is a violation of due process. It follows from this that appellants could not be required to execute the declaration as a condition for obtaining a tax exemption or as a condition for the assessor proceeding further in determining whether they were entitled to such an exemption. Since the entire statutory procedure, by placing the burden of proof on the claimants, violated the requirements of due process, appellants were not obliged to take the first step in such a procedure.

The judgments are reversed and the causes are remanded for further proceedings not inconsistent with this opinion.

Reversed and remanded.

MR. JUSTICE BURTON concurs in the result.

THE CHIEF JUSTICE took no part in the consideration or decision of this case.

MR. JUSTICE BLACK, whom MR. JUSTICE DOUGLAS joins, concurring.*

California, in effect, has imposed a tax on belief and expression. In my view, a levy of this nature is wholly out of place in this country; so far as I know such a thing has never even been attempted before. I believe that it constitutes a palpable violation of the First Amendment, which of course is applicable in all its particulars to the States. See, *e.g., Staub* v. *City of Baxley*, 355 U.S. 313; *Poulos* v. *New Hampshire*, 345 U.S. 395, 396–397; *Everson* v. *Board of Education*, 330 U.S. 1, 8; *Thomas* v. *Collins*, 323 U.S. 516; *Board of Education* v. *Barnette*,

---

[8] Significantly, the New York statute which this Court upheld in *Adler* v. *Board of Education*, 342 U.S. 485, provided that public school teachers could be dismissed on security grounds only after a hearing at which the official pressing the charges sustained his burden of proof by a fair preponderance of the evidence.

*[NOTE: This opinion applies also to No. 382, *First Unitarian Church* v. *County of Los Angeles*, and No. 385, *Valley Unitarian-Universalist Church* v. *County of Los Angeles, post,* p. 545.]

319 U.S. 624, 639; *Douglas* v. *Jeannette*, 319 U.S. 157, 162; *Martin* v. *Struthers*, 319 U.S. 141; *Murdock* v. *Pennsylvania*, 319 U.S. 105, 109; *Chaplinsky* v. *New Hampshire*, 315 U.S. 568, 571; *Bridges* v. *California*, 314 U.S. 252, 263; *Cantwell* v. *Connecticut*, 310 U.S. 296, 303; *Schneider* v. *State*, 308 U.S. 147, 160; *Lovell* v. *Griffin*, 303 U.S. 444, 450; *De Jonge* v. *Oregon*, 299 U.S. 353, 364; *Gitlow* v. *New York*, 268 U.S. 652, 666. The mere fact that California attempts to exact this ill-concealed penalty from individuals and churches and that its validity has to be considered in this Court only emphasizes how dangerously far we have departed from the fundamental principles of freedom declared in the First Amendment. We should never forget that the freedoms secured by that Amendment—Speech, Press, Religion, Petition and Assembly—are absolutely indispensable for the preservation of a free society in which government is based upon the consent of an informed citizenry and is dedicated to the protection of the rights of all, even the most despised minorities. See *American Communications Assn.* v. *Douds*, 339 U.S. 382, 445 (dissenting opinion); *Dennis* v. *United States*, 341 U.S. 494, 580 (dissenting opinion).

This case offers just another example of a wide-scale effort by government in this country to impose penalties and disabilities on everyone who is or is suspected of being a "Communist" or who is not ready at all times and all places to swear his loyalty to State and Nation. Compare *Adler* v. *Board of Education*, 342 U.S. 485, 496 (dissenting opinion); *Wieman* v. *Updegraff*, 344 U.S. 183, 193 (concurring opinion); *Barsky* v. *Board of Regents*, 347 U.S. 442, 456, 472 (dissenting opinions). Government employees, lawyers, doctors, teachers, pharmacists, veterinarians, subway conductors, industrial workers and a multitude of others have been denied an opportunity to work at their trade or profession for these reasons. Here a tax is levied unless the taxpayer makes an oath that he does not and will not in the future advocate certain things; in Ohio those without jobs have been denied unemployment insurance unless they are willing to swear that they do not hold specific views; and Congress has even attempted to deny public housing to needy families unless they first demonstrate their loyalty. These are merely random samples; I will not take time here to refer to innumerable others, such as oaths for hunters and fishermen, wrestlers and boxers and junk dealers.

I am convinced that this whole business of penalizing people because of their views and expressions concerning government is hopelessly repugnant to the principles of freedom upon which this Nation was founded and which have helped to make it the greatest in the world. As stated in prior cases, I believe "that the First Amendment grants an absolute right to believe in any governmental system, [to] discuss all governmental affairs, and [to] argue for desired changes in the existing order. This freedom is too dangerous for bad, tyrannical governments to permit. But those who wrote and adopted our First Amendment weighed those dangers against the dangers of censorship and deliberately chose the First Amendment's unequivocal command that freedom of assembly, petition, speech and press shall not be abridged. I happen to believe this was a wise choice and that our free way of life enlists such respect and love that our Nation cannot be imperiled by mere talk." *Carlson* v. *Landon*, 342 U.S. 524, 555–556 (dissenting opinion).

Loyalty oaths, as well as other contemporary "security measures," tend to stifle all forms of unorthodox or unpopular thinking or expression—the kind of thought and expression which has played such a vital and beneficial role in the history of this Nation. The result is a stultifying conformity which in the end may well turn out to be more destructive to our free society than foreign agents could ever hope to be. The course which we have been following the last decade is not the course of a strong, free, secure people, but that of the frightened, the insecure, the intolerant. I am certain that loyalty to the United States can never be secured by the endless proliferation of "loyalty" oaths; loyalty must arise spontaneously from the hearts of people who love their country and respect their government. I also adhere to the proposition that the "First Amendment provides the only kind of security system that can preserve a free government— one that leaves the way wide open for people to favor, discuss, advocate, or incite causes and doctrines however obnoxious and antagonistic such views may be to the rest of us." *Yates* v. *United States*, 354 U.S. 298, 344 (separate opinion).

If it be assumed however, as MR. JUSTICE BRENNAN does for purposes of this case, that California may tax the expression of certain views, I am in full agreement with him that the procedures it has provided to determine whether petitioners are engaged in "taxable" advocacy violate the requirements of due process.

MR. JUSTICE DOUGLAS, with whom MR. JUSTICE BLACK agrees, concurring.

While I substantially agree with the opinion of the Court, I will state my reasons more fully and more explicitly.

I. The State by the device of the loyalty oath places the burden of proving loyalty on the citizen. That procedural device goes against the grain of our constitutional system, for every man is presumed innocent until guilt is established. This technique is an ancient one that was denounced in an early period of our history.

Alexander Hamilton, writing in 1784 under the name Phocion, said:

". . . let it be supposed that instead of the mode of indictment and trial by jury, the Legislature was to declare, that every citizen who did not swear he had never adhered to the King of Great Britain, should incur all the penalties which our treason laws prescribe. Would this not be . . . a direct infringement of the Constitution? . . . it is substituting a new and arbitrary mode of prosecution to that ancient and highly esteemed one, recognized by the laws and the Constitution of the State,—I mean the trial by jury." 4 The Works of Alexander Hamilton (Fed. ed. 1904) 269–270.

Hamilton compared that hypothetical law to an actual one passed by New York on March 27, 1778, whereby a person who had served the King of England in enumerated ways was declared "to be utterly disabled disqualified and incapacitated to vote either by ballot or *viva voce* at any election" in New York. N.Y. Laws 1777–1784, 35. An oath was required [1] in enforcement of that law.[2]

Hamilton called this "a subversion of one great principle of social security: to wit, that every man shall be presumed innocent until he is proved guilty." 4 The Works of Alexander Hamilton (Fed. ed. 1904) 269. He went on to say "This was to invert the order of things; and, instead of obliging the State to prove the guilt in order to inflict the penalty, it was to oblige the citizen to establish his own innocence to avoid the penalty. It was to excite scruples in the honest and conscientious, and to hold out a bribe to perjury." *Ibid.*

If the aim is to apprehend those who have lifted a hand against the Government, the procedure is unconstitutional.

If one conspires to overthrow the Government, he commits a crime. To make him swear he is innocent to avoid the consequences of a law is to put on him the burden of proving his innocence. That method does not square with our standards of procedural due process, as the opinion of the Court points out.

The Court in *Cummings* v. *Missouri*, 4 Wall. 277, 328, denounced another expurgatory oath that had some of the vices of the present one.

> "The clauses in question subvert the presumptions of innocence, and alter the rules of evidence, which heretofore, under the universally recognized principles of the common law, have been supposed to be fundamental and unchangeable. They assume that the parties are guilty; they call upon the parties to establish their innocence; and they declare that such innocence can be shown only in one way—by an inquisition, in the form of an expurgatory oath, into the consciences of the parties."

II. If the aim of the law is not to apprehend criminals but to penalize advocacy, it likewise must fall. Since the time that Alexander Hamilton wrote concerning these oaths, the Bill of Rights was adopted; and then much later came the Fourteenth Amendment. As a result of the latter a rather broad range of liberties was newly guaranteed to the citizen against State action. Included were those

---

[1] The oath was prescribed by the Council in charge of the Southern District of New York. The Council, authorized by the Act of October 23, 1779, was composed of the Governor, President of the Senate, Chancellor, Supreme Court judges, Senators, Assemblymen, Secretary of State, Attorney General, and County Court judges. The Council was to assume authority "whenever the enemy shall abandon or be dispossessed of the same, and until the legislature can be convened," N.Y. Laws 1777–1784, 192. The Council governed from November 25, 1783, to February 5, 1784. See Barck, New York City 1776–1783 (1931), 220–221. Among the powers of the Council was control of elections.
The election oath prescribed by the Council read as follows:
"I _____ do solemnly, without any mental Reservation or Equivocation whatsoever, swear and declare, and call God to witness (or if of the People called Quakers, affirm) that I renounce and abjure all Allegiance to the King of Great-Britain; and that I will bear true Faith and Allegiance to the State of New York, as a Free and Independent State, and that I will in all Things, to the best of my Knowledge and Ability, do my Duty as a good and faithful Subject of the said State ought to do. So help me God." Independent Gazette, Dec. 13, 1783.
The Council further provided:
"That if any Person presenting himself to give his Vote, shall be suspected of, or charged with having committed any of the Offences above specified, it shall be Lawful for the Inspectors, or Superintendents (as the Case may be) to inquire into and determine the Fact whereof such Person shall be suspected, or wherewith he shall be charged, as the Cause of Disqualification, on the Oath of one or more Witnesses, or on the Oath of the Party so suspected or charged, at their Discretion; and if such Fact shall, in the Judgement of the Inspectors or Superintendents, be established, it shall be lawful for them, and they are hereby required, to reject the Vote of such Person at such Election." Independent Gazette, Dec. 13, 1783.
[2] Other loyalty oaths appeared during this early period. Suspected persons were required to take a loyalty oath. N.Y. Laws 1777–1784, 87. The same was required of lawyers. *Id.*, at 155, 420. And see Flick, Loyalism in New York During the American Revolution, 14 Studies in History, Economics and Public Law (Columbia Univ. 1901) 9 (*passim*).

contained in the First Amendment—the right to speak freely, the right to believe what one chooses, the right of conscience. *Stromberg* v. *California*, 283 U.S. 359; *Murdock* v. *Pennsylvania*, 319 U.S. 105; *Staub* v. *City of Baxley*, 355 U.S. 313. Today what one thinks or believes, what one utters and says have the full protection of the First Amendment. It is only his actions that government may examine and penalize. When we allow government to probe his beliefs and withhold from him some of the privileges of citizenship because of what he thinks, we do indeed "invert the order of things," to use Hamilton's phrase. All public officials—State and Federal—must take an oath to support the Constitution by the express command of Article VI of the Constitution. And see *Gerende* v. *Election Board*, 341 U.S. 56. But otherwise the domains of conscience and belief have been set aside and protected from government intrusion. *Board of Education* v. *Barnett*, 319 U.S. 624. What a man thinks is of no concern to government. "The First Amendment gives freedom of mind the same security as freedom of conscience." *Thomas* v. *Collins*, 323 U.S. 516, 531. Advocacy and belief go hand in hand. For there can be no true freedom of mind if thoughts are secure only when they are pent up.

In *Murdock* v. *Pennsylvania, supra,* we stated, "Plainly a community may not suppress, or the State tax, the dissemination of views because they are unpopular, annoying or distasteful." 319 U.S., at 116. If the Government may not impose a tax upon the expression of ideas in order to discourage them, it may not achieve the same end by reducing the individual who expresses his views to second-class citizenship by withholding tax benefits granted others. When government denies a tax exemption because of the citizen's belief, it penalizes that belief. That is different only in form, not substance, from the "taxes on knowledge" which have had a notorious history in the English-speaking world. See *Grosjean* v. *American Press Co.*, 297 U.S. 233, 246–247.

We deal here with a type of advocacy which, to say the least, lies close to the "constitutional danger zone." *Yates* v. *United States*, 354 U.S. 298, 319. Advocacy which is in no way brigaded with action should always be protected by the First Amendment. That protection should extend even to the ideas we despise. As Mr. Justice Holmes wrote in dissent in *Gitlow* v. *New York*, 268 U.S. 652, 673, "If in the long run the beliefs expressed in proletarian dictatorship are destined to be accepted by the dominant forces of the community, the only meaning of free speech is that they should be given their chance and have their way." It is time for Government—State or Federal—to become concerned with the citizen's advocacy when his ideas and beliefs move into the realm of action.

The California oath is not related to unlawful action. To get the tax exemption the taxpayer must swear he "does not advocate the overthrow of the Government of the United States or of the State of California by force or violence or other unlawful means nor advocate the support of a foreign government against the United States in event of hostilities"[3] The Court construes the opinion of the California Supreme Court as applying the same test of illegal advocacy as was sustained against constitutional challenge in *Dennis* v. *United States*, 341 U.S. 494. That case held that advocacy of the overthrow

---

[3] Calif. Rev. & Tax Code, § 32 ; and see Calif. Const., Art. XX, §·19.

of government by force and violence was not enough, that incitement to action, as well as clear and present danger, were also essential ingredients. *Id.*, at 512, 509–510. As *Yates* v. *United States, supra,* makes clear, there is still a clear constitutional line between advocacy of abstract doctrine and advocacy of action. The California Supreme Court said, to be sure, that the oath in question "is concerned" with that kind of advocacy.[4] But it nowhere says that oath is limited to that kind of advocacy. It seemed to think that advocacy was itself action for it said, "What one may merely believe is not prohibited. It is only advocates of the subversive doctrines who are affected. Advocacy constitutes action and the instigation of action, not mere belief of opinion." [5]

However the California opinion may be read, these judgments should fall. If the construction of the oath is the one I prefer, then the Supreme Court of California has obliterated the line between advocacy of abstract doctrine and advocacy of action. If the California oath has been limited by judicial construction to the type of advocacy condemned in *Dennis*, it still should fall. My disagreement with that decision has not abated. No conspiracy to overthrow the Government was involved. Speech and speech alone was the offense. I repeat that thought and speech go hand in hand. There is no real freedom of thought if ideas must be suppressed. There can be no freedom of the mind unless ideas can be uttered.

I know of no power that enables any government under our Constitution to become the monitor of thought, as this statute would have it become.

MR. JUSTICE CLARK, dissenting.

The decision of the Court turns on a construction of California law which regards the filing of the California tax oath as introductory, not conclusive, in nature. Hence, once the oath is filed, it may be "accepted or rejected on the basis of incompetent information or no information at all." And the filing is "only a step in a process throughout which the taxpayer must bear the burden of proof."

No California case, least of all the present one, compels such an understanding of § 32 of the California Revenue and Taxation Code. Neither appellant here filed the required oath, so the procedural skeleton of this case is not enlightening. If anything, the opinion of the State court indicates that the filing, whether the oath be true or false, would conclusively establish the taxpayer's eligibility for an exemption. Thus, in explaining the effect of § 32, the California court stated:

> "For the obvious purpose, among others, of avoiding litigation, the Legislature, throughout the years has sought to relieve the assessor of the burden, on his own initiative and at the public expense, of ascertaining the facts with reference to tax exemption claimants. In addition to the means heretofore and otherwise provided by law the Legislature, with special reference to the implementation of section 19 of article XX, has enacted section 32. That section provides a direct, time saving and relatively inexpensive method of *ascertaining the facts.*" (Emphasis added.) 48 Cal. 2d 419, 432, 311 P. 508, 515–516.

---

[4] 48 Cal. 2d 419, 440, 311 P. 2d 508, 520.
[5] 48 Cal. 2d, at 434, 311 P. 2d, at 517.

Moreover, the recourse of the State in the event a false oath is filed is expressly provided by § 32: "Any person or organization who makes such declaration knowing it to be false is guilty of a felony." The majority relies heavily on the duty of the assessor to "[investigate] the facts underlying all tax liabilities," as well as his subpoena power incident thereto under § 454 of the California Tax Code. But the California court adverts to those matters only under a hypothetical state of facts, namely, in the absence of the aid provided by § 32. 48 Cal. 2d, at 430–432, 311 P. 2d, at 515. The essential point is that, whatever the assessor's duty, § 32 provides for its discharge on the basis of the declarations alone.

On the other hand, if it be thought that the Supreme Court of California is ambiguous on this matter, then it is well established that our duty is to so construe the State oath as to avoid conflict with constitutional guarantees of due process. *Garner* v. *Board of Public Works*, 341 U.S. 716, 723–724 (1951); *Gerende* v. *Board of Supervisors of Elections*, 341 U.S. 56 (1951). Two years ago we construed filling of the non-Communist affidavit required by § 9(h) of the National Labor Relations Act as being conclusive in character, holding that the criminal sanction provided in that section was the exclusive remedy for the filing of a false affidavit. *Leedom* v. *International Union of Mine, Mill & Smelter Workers*, 352 U.S. 145 (1956). That Act bars issuance of a complaint or conducting an investigation upon the application of a union unless the prescribed non-Communist affidavit is filed by each officer of the union. Article XX, § 19, of the California Constitution expressly prohibits a tax exemption to any person or organization that advocates violent overthrow of either the California or the United States Governments, or advocates the support of a foreign government against the United States in the event of hostilities, and provides for legislative implementation thereof. By § 32 the California Legislature has required only the filing of the affidavit. The terms of § 9(h) of the National Labor Relations Act and § 32 of the California Tax Code, therefore, established identical procedures. That identity points up the inappropriateness of the Court's construction of § 32.

Even if the Court's interpretation of California law is correct, I cannot agree that due process requires California to bear the burden of proof under the circumstances of this case. This is not a criminal proceeding. Neither fine nor imprisonment is involved. So far as Art. XX, § 19, of the California Constitution and § 32 of the California Tax Code are concerned, appellants are free to speak as they wish, to advocate what they will. If they advocate the violent and forceful overthrow of the California Government, California will take no action against them under the tax provisions here in question. But it will refuse to take any action *for them*, in the sense of extending to them the legislative largesse that is inherent in the granting of any tax exemption or deduction. In the view of the California court, "An exemption from taxation is the exception and the unusual. . . . It is a bounty or gratuity on the part of the sovereign and when once granted may be withdrawn." 48 Cal. 2d, at 426, 311 P. 2d, at 512. The power of the sovereign to attach conditions to its bounty is firmly established under the Due Process Clause. Cf. *Ivanhoe Irrigation District* v. *McCracken*, 357 U.S. 275, 295 (1958). Traditionally, the burden of qualifying rests upon the one seeking the grace of the State.

The majority suggests that traditional procedures are inadequate when a "person is to suffer a penalty for a crime." But California's action here, declining to extend the grace of the State to appellants, can in no proper sense be regarded as a "penalty." The case cited by the majority, *Lipke* v. *Lederer*, 259 U.S. 557 (1922), involves an altogether different matter, imposition of a special tax upon one who engaged in certain illegal conduct, by a statute that described the levy as a "tax *or penalty*." (Emphasis added.)   259 U.S. at 561.

The majority, however, would require that California bear the burden of proof under the circumstances of this case because "the transcendent value of speech is involved." This is a wholly novel doctrine, unsupported by any precedent, and so far as I can see, inapposite to several other decisions of this Court upholding the application of similar oaths to municipal employees, *Garner* v. *Board of Public Works*, 341 U.S. 716 (1951); public school teachers, *Adler* v. *Board of Education*, 342 U.S. 485 (1952); candidates for public office, *Gerende* v. *Board of Supervisors*, 341 U.S. 56 (1951); and labor union officials, *American Communications Assn.* v. *Douds*, 339 U.S. 382 (1950). See also *Davis* v. *Beason*, 133 U.S. 333 (1890), as to voters in territorial elections. All of those decisions, by virtue of the oath involved, put the burden on the individual to come forward and disavow activity involving "the transcendent value of speech." The majority attempts to distinguish them on the basis of their involving a greater State interest in justification of restricting speech, and also on the ground that the oaths there involved were conclusive in nature. The first distinction, however, seems pertinent only to the validity of an oath requirement in the first place, not to burden of proof under such a requirement. The second distinction, which *arguendo* I accept as true at this point, seems exceedingly flimsy, since even an oath that is conclusive in nature forces the applicant to the burden of coming forward and making the requisite declaration. So far as impact on freedom of speech is concerned, the further burden of proving the declarations true appears close to being *de minimis*.

The majority assumes, without deciding, that California may deny a tax exemption to those in the proscribed class. I think it perfectly clear that the State may do so, since only that speech is affected which is criminally punishable under the Federal Smith Act, 18 U.S.C. § 2385, or the California Criminal Syndicalism Act, Cal. Stat., 1919, c. 188. And California has agreed that its interpretation of criminal speech under those Acts shall be in conformity with the decisions of this Court, *e.g.*, *Yates* v. *United States*, 354 U.S. 298 (1957); *Dennis* v. *United States*, 341 U.S. 494 (1951); *Whitney* v. *California*, 274 U.S. 357 (1927). The interest of the State that justifies restriction of speech by imposition of criminal sanctions surely justifies the far less severe measure of denying a tax exemption, provided the lesser sanction bears reasonable relation to the evil at which the State aims. Cf. *American Communications Assn.* v. *Douds*, *supra*. The general aim of the constitutional and legislative provisions in question is to restrict advocacy of violent or forceful overthrow of State or National Government; the particular aim is to avoid State subsidization of such advocacy by refusing the State's bounty to those who are so engaged. The latter has been denominated the "primary purpose" by the California Supreme Court. 48 Cal. 2d, at 428, 311 P. 2d, at 513. In view of that, reasonable relation is evident on the face of the matter.

Refusal of the taxing sovereign's grace in order to avoid subsidizing or encouraging activity contrary to the sovereign's policy is an accepted practice. We have here a parallel situation to Federal refusal to regard as "necessary and ordinary," and hence deductible under the Federal income tax, those expenses deduction of which would frustrate sharply defined State policies. See *Tank Truck Rentals, Inc.* v. *Commissioner*, 356 U.S. 30 (1958).

If the State's requirement of an oath in implementing denial of this exemption be thought to make an inroad upon speech over and above that caused by denial of the exemption, or even by criminal punishment of the proscribed speech, I find California's interest still sufficient to justify the State's action. The restriction must be considered in the context in which the oath is set—appeal to the largesse of the State. The interest of the State, as before pointed out, is dual in nature, but its primary thrust is summed up in an understandable desire to insure that those who benefit by tax exemption do not bite the hand that gives it.

Appellants raise other issues—pre-emption of security legislation under *Pennsylvania* v. *Nelson*, 350 U.S. 497 (1956), and denial of equal protection because the oath is not required for all types of tax exemptions—which the majority does not pass upon. I treat of them only so far as to say that I think neither has merit, substantially for the reasons stated in the opinion of the Supreme Court of California.

If my interpretation of § 32 is correct, I assume that California will afford appellants another opportunity to take the oath, this time knowing that its filing will have conclusive effect. For the reasons stated above, I would affirm the judgment.

O